M|P|W

Mander Portman Woodward

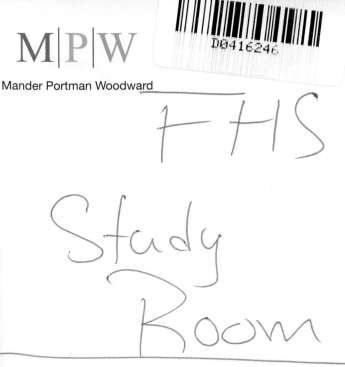

FHS

Study

Room

Do Not Remove

UNIVERSITY DEGREE COURSE OFFERS

The essential guide to winning
your place at university

Mr Bosser

Brian Heap

HEAP 2021

51st edition

HEAP 2021: UNIVERSITY DEGREE COURSE OFFERS

In order to ensure that *Heap 2021: University Degree Course Offers* retains its reputation as the definitive guide for students wishing to study at UK universities and other higher education institutions, hundreds of questionnaires are distributed, months of research and analysis are undertaken, and painstaking data checking and proofing are carried out.

Every effort has been made to maintain absolute accuracy in providing course information and to ensure that the entire book is as up to date as possible. However, changes are constantly taking place in higher education so it is important for readers to check carefully with prospectuses and websites before submitting their applications. The author, compilers and publishers cannot be held responsible for any inaccuracies in information supplied to them by third parties or contained in resources and websites listed in the book.

We hope you find this 51st edition useful, and would welcome your feedback as to how we can ensure the 52nd edition is even better.

Author Brian Heap
Advertising Sales email info@trotman.co.uk

This 51st edition published in 2020 by Trotman Education an imprint of Crimson Publishing Ltd, 21d Charles Street, Bath BA1 1HX
www.trotman.co.uk

A CIP record for this book is available from the British Library

ISBN 978 1 912943 28 9

Printed by Gutenberg Press Ltd, Malta

MIX
Paper from
responsible sources
FSC® C022612
FSC
www.fsc.org

QUOTES

'No one is better informed or more experienced than Brian Heap in mediating this range of information to university and college applicants.'
Careers Education and Guidance

'A fantastic and invaluable resource for UCAS advisers, university applicants and their parents.'
Mark Collins, Head of Economics/Business & Careers, St Teresa's School

'I've been a UCAS adviser for most of the past 25 years and I've come to rely on HEAP for clear guidance and up to date info.'
Gabe Crisp, Aspire Co-ordinator, Worthing College

'This guide contains useful, practical information for all university applicants and those advising them. I heartily recommend it.'
Dr John Dunford, General Secretary, Association of School and College Leaders

'Our first stop for students sourcing university information and the courses they are interested in.'
Lorraine Durrands, Careers Co-ordinator, Kesteven & Grantham Girls' School

'Degree Course Offers is probably the UK's longest running and best known reference work on the subject.'
Education Advisers Limited

'If I only had the budget to buy one careers book, it would be HEAP. Doing my job would be much harder without it!'
Celia Golding, Careers Guidance Manager, Langley Grammar School

'An invaluable guide to UK degree entry requirements. My "go to" handbook when kick-starting the UCAS process.'
Susan Gower, Head of Year 9 and Careers, Croydon High School

'The course-listings bible.'
The Guardian

'For those of you going through Clearing, an absolute must is the Degree Course Offers book. This guide operates subject by subject and gives you each university's requirements, standard offers and, most importantly, "course features".'
The Independent

'Invaluable – HEAP is my "go to" resource.'
Wendy Kerley, Freelance Careers Adviser

'HEAP University Degree Course Offers is simply "The Bible" for careers advisors and students alike.'
Stephen King, MA (Lib), School Librarian and Careers Coordinator, The Duke of York's Royal Military School

'We buy this book every year and use it all the time, it offers essential careers and higher education advice.'
Dr Beth Linklater, Director of Student Support, Queen Mary's College

'Degree Course Offers by Brian Heap – not to be missed. Invaluable.'
Maidstone Grammar School

'A very useful starting point for exploration of degree courses. Supplements our UCAS programme and careers advice very effectively.'
Paul Meadway, Head of Careers, Hymers College

'Degree Course Offers *remains an essential component of our careers library, providing a quick reference to entry requirements and course specific tips for university applications.'*
Mid Kent College

'The students find it an invaluable resource.'
Rebecca Mockridge, Sixth Form Administrator, Queen's College Taunton

'Up-to-date information, easy to use and accurate.'
Kenneth Nolan, Careers Adviser, Xaverian College

'An excellent one-stop shop for finding out information on different universities and courses.'
Oswestry School

'It's a really quick way of getting an overview of the standard offer for a particular course or course type ... and is helpful in terms of advising both on offer conditions, but also when choosing A-level subjects for particular interests.'
Etta Searle, Careers Co-ordinator, Wyke 6th Form College

'Degree Course Offers *is my bible and I couldn't be without it ... it gives students focus and saves them time.'*
South Thames College

'HEAP helps you make informed choices about university course offers.'
Angie Stone, Librarian, Pate's Grammar School

'Degree Course Offers ... a really good resource.'
www.sueatkinsparentingcoach.com

'An excellent, inclusive and thorough guide which ALL careers libraries should include, not just schools with sixth forms and colleges. If I were forced to narrow down my choices of higher education materials to one resource, it would be this one.'
Ray Le Tarouilly, Careers Adviser, The Midlands Academies Trust

'The definitive guide to university degree course offers ... clearly laid out and remarkably easy to navigate ... should be stocked in every sixth form library.'
Teach Secondary, October

'Degree Course Offers ... will keep aspirations realistic.'
www.tes.com/new-teachers

'The guru of university choice.'
The Times

'I would like to take this opportunity to congratulate you in maintaining the quality and currency of the information in your guide. We are aware of its wide range and its reputation for impartiality.'
University Senior Assistant Registrar

'An extremely useful guide ....'
Woodhouse Grove School

'An invaluable guide to helping students and their advisers find their way through the maze of degree courses currently on offer.'
Kath Wright, President, Association for Careers Education and Guidance

CONTENTS

Author's acknowledgements   *vii*
About this book   *ix*

1 YOUR FIRST DECISIONS   1
Section A: Choosing your course by school subjects   1
Section B: Choosing your course by career interests   4
Course Types and Differences   9
Sandwich Courses and Professional Placements   9
Degree Apprenticeship Courses   11
Mature Applicants   11
Modular Courses and Credit Accumulation and Transfer Schemes (CATS)   12
Foundation Degrees and Foundation Courses   12
Next Steps   12
Taking a Gap Year   13

2 UNIVERSITY CHOICE AND FINANCE   14
Choosing Your University or College   14
Action Points   14
Finance: What Will It Cost and What Help Is There?   15
Information Sources   16

3 UNIVERSITY AND COLLEGE PROFILES   17
Universities, Colleges and their Courses   17
Admissions Policies   17
Course and Admissions Profiles   18

4 APPLICATIONS   48
Entry Requirements   48
Applications for University and College Courses through UCAS   48
Applications for Music Courses at Conservatoires   50
Applications for Teacher Training Courses   50
Applications for Degree Apprenticeship Courses   51
The UCAS Application   51
Applications to the University of Cambridge   53
Applications to the University of Oxford   54
Applications to the Russell Group   54
Applications to Irish Universities   55
Applications to Commonwealth Universities   55
Applications to American Universities   55
The Erasmus+ Programme   55
And Finally ... Before You Send in Your Application   56
What to Do on Results Day ... and After   56

5 ADMISSIONS TESTS, SELECTION OF APPLICANTS AND INTERVIEWS   58

Admissions Tests   58
Degree Subject Examples of Universities and Colleges using Tests and Assessments   60
Selection of Applicants   72
Interviews   73
Multiple Mini Interviews (MMIs)   74

6 HOW TO USE THE SUBJECT TABLES   75

Course Offers Information   76
Degree Apprenticeships   79
Examples of Colleges Offering Courses in this Subject Field   80
Choosing Your Course   80
Admissions Information   80
After-results Advice   81
Graduate Destinations and Employment (2016/17 HESA)   81
Other Degree Subjects for Consideration   81
Institution Abbreviations   82
Course Abbreviations   83

7 SUBJECT TABLES   95

8 INFORMATION FOR INTERNATIONAL STUDENTS   471

Applications and the Points-based Immigration System   471
Selection, Admission and Finance   471
University Information and Fees for Undergraduate International Students   472
British Overseas Territories Students   484

9 DIRECTORY OF UNIVERSITIES AND OTHER INSTITUTIONS OFFERING HIGHER EDUCATION COURSES   485

Section 1: Universities and University Colleges   485
Section 2: Specialist Colleges of Agriculture and Horticulture, Art, Dance, Drama, Fashion, Music, Osteopathy and Speech   488
Section 3: Further Education and Other Colleges Offering Higher Education Courses   490

APPENDICES

Appendix 1: UCAS 2021 Entry Tariff Points Tables   496
Appendix 2: International Qualifications   500
Appendix 3: Professional Associations   504
Appendix 4: Booklist and Useful Websites   511

Course Index   512
Index of Advertisers   514
Notes   515

AUTHOR'S ACKNOWLEDGEMENTS

This book and the website https://indigo.careers/universities are a team effort, in which I, my daughter Jane, my editor Kate Michell, with Laura Davies and Emma Davies and a supporting team at Trotman Publishing, make every effort each year to check the contents for accuracy, including all offers from official sources, up to the publication deadline in March. My team's effort throughout the months of preparation therefore deserves my gratitude and praise. In respect of the offers, which are checked annually, the reader should recognise that offers are constantly changing depending on the range and abilities of candidates and therefore are shown as 'typical' or target offers.

In the ever-changing world of higher education, research must be on-going and each year many individuals are involved in providing additional up-to-date information. These include Trudi Woodhouse at UCAS, the Cambridge Admissions Office and the University of Oxford Undergraduate Admissions Office. In addition, my appreciation goes to HESA for information on graduate destinations, the many universities and colleges which annually update information, and individual admissions staff who return our requests for information, along with the many teachers and students who furnish me with information on their experiences. To all, I add my grateful thanks.

Brian Heap BA, DA (Manc), ATD
May 2020

ABOUT THIS BOOK

For 51 years **University Degree Course Offers (Heap 2021)** has been a first-stop reference for university and college applicants choosing their courses in higher education by providing information from official sources about how to choose courses and how admissions tutors select students.

For 2021/22 higher education applicants, this edition of **University Degree Course Offers** again aims to provide the latest possible information from universities to help equip applicants to obtain a degree course place in a fiercely competitive applications process. This level of competition will make it essential for every applicant to research carefully courses and institutions.

Schools, colleges and students quite rightly focus on getting through examinations, particularly when employers and, more so, universities, require specific exam grades in a variety of subjects. But once out of the exam room, where to next? There are many students who restrict their applications to a small number of well-known universities. They must realise that in doing so they are very likely to receive rejections from all of them. Applicants must spread their choices across a wide range of institutions. There are also many students who limit their choice to their best subject, but in doing so miss out on some good alternatives.

How do applicants decide on a strategy to find a place on a degree course? There are more than 1,200 separate degree subjects and over 50,000 Joint and Combined Honours courses so how can applicants choose a course that is right for their futures? What can applicants do to find a course place and a university or college that is right for them, when there are over 150 of them? For the past 51 years, for hundreds of students, the answers have been in the next 520 pages of this book.

Heap 2021: University Degree Course Offers is again intended to help applicants find their way through these problems by providing the latest possible information about university course offers from official sources, and by giving guidance and information about:

- **Degree courses** – what Honours level courses involve, the range and differences between them, and what applicants need to consider when choosing and deciding on subjects and courses
- **Degree apprenticeships** – what courses are available in different subject areas
- **Universities and higher education colleges** – the range and differences between universities and colleges, and the questions applicants might ask when deciding where to study
- **Admissions information** for every university (listed in **Chapter 3**)
- **Target A-level grades/UCAS points offers** (listed in points order in the subject tables in **Chapter 7**) for 2021 entry to Honours degree courses in universities and colleges, with additional Appendix data for applicants with Scottish Highers/Advanced Highers, the Advanced Welsh Baccalaureate – Skills Challenge Certificate, the International Baccalaureate Diploma, BTEC Level 3 National Extended Diploma, the Extended Project, Music examinations and Art and Design Foundation Studies qualifications
- **The UCAS application process** – what to do, when to do it and how to prepare the personal statement in the UCAS application
- **Your course** – how to choose by school subjects or career interests
- **Universities' and colleges' admissions policies** – how admissions tutors select students
- **Which universities, colleges and courses use admissions tests for entry**
- **Finance, fees and sources of help**

- **Graduate destinations data for each subject area**
- **Action after results day** – and what to do if your grades don't match your offer
- **Entry to UK universities and higher education colleges for international students**

Heap 2021: University Degree Course Offers provides essential information for all students preparing to go into higher education in 2021, covering all stages of researching, planning, deciding and applying to courses and universities. To provide the latest possible information the book is compiled each year between October and March for publication in May and includes important data from the many universities and colleges responding to questionnaires each year.

Every effort is made to ensure the book is as up to date as possible. Nevertheless, the increased demand for places is expected to lead to offers changes during the 2020/21 application cycle, and after prospectuses have been published some institutions may also discontinue courses as a result of government cuts and the changes in tuition fees. It will be essential for applicants to check institutions' websites **frequently** to find out any changes in offers, course availability and requirements. If you have any queries, contact admissions staff without delay to find out the latest information as institutions, for many courses, will be looking for a very close, if not precise, match between their requirements and what you offer in your application, qualifications and grades.

Heap 2021: University Degree Course Offers is your starting point for moving on into higher education and planning ahead. Used in conjunction with *Choosing Your Degree Course & University* and Indigo (see **Appendix 4**) it will take you through all the stages in choosing the course and place of study that is right for you. Now go for it!

Brian Heap
May 2020

Every effort has been made to maintain absolute accuracy in providing course information and to ensure that the entire book is as up to date as possible. However, changes are constantly taking place in higher education so it is important for readers to check carefully with prospectuses and websites before submitting their applications.

The problem You and over 500,000 students (including 100,000 from the EU and overseas) are applying for some 50,000 degree courses in the UK this year. You have a choice of about 150 main subject areas (most of which are listed in **Chapter 7**), as well as single, joint or combined courses, from over 300 universities and colleges.

The Choice It depends what you want. There are three types of degrees. 1. Academic courses, eg History, Anthropology, Geography and Philosophy. Don't worry about graduate employment yet; many occupations are open to you when you graduate and commence specialist training, eg law, accountancy, business. 2. Vocational courses, eg medical careers, engineering and hospitality management. Some courses have opportunities to spend part of your degree course in full-time employment with pay as part of the course. 3. Practical courses, eg Art and Design, Drama, Music and Sports Studies.

There are two possible options for choosing your degree course:

Many students want to follow a degree course by way of their favourite and best subject. **See Section A**. School subjects are listed along with other degree courses which have some similarities.

Section B lists careers that may appeal to you and the degree courses that are linked to them.

SECTION A
Choosing your course by school subjects
Accounting Accountancy, Accounting, Actuarial Mathematics, Banking and Finance, Business Studies (Finance), Economics, Finance Investment and Risk, Financial Mathematics, Financial Software Engineering, Management Sciences, Mathematics. See also **Section B**.

Ancient History Archaeology, Biblical Studies, Classical Greek, Classics and Classical Civilisation, Latin, Middle and Near Eastern Studies.

Arabic Arabic. See also **Languages** below.

Art and Design Art, Fine Art, Furniture Design, Graphic Design, Photography, Textile Design, Theatre Design, Three-Dimensional Design, Typography and Graphic Communication. See also **Section B**.

Bengali Bengali. See also **Languages** below.

Biblical Hebrew Hebrew, Religious Studies, Theology.

Biology Agricultural Sciences, Animal Behaviour, Audiology, Bioinformatics, Biological Sciences, Biology, Biomedical Sciences, Biotechnology, Dental Hygiene, Ecology and Conservation, Environmental Sciences, Genetics, Human Embryology, Infection and Immunity, Life Sciences, Medicine, Microbiology, Molecular Sciences, Natural Sciences, Physiology, Plant Biology, Plant Science, Veterinary Science, Zoology. See also **Section B**.

Business Accounting, Banking, Business Management, Business Statistics, Computing, Economics, Entrepreneurship, Finance, Hospitality Management, Human Resource Management, Information Systems, Logistics, Management Sciences, Marketing, Mathematics, Publishing, Retail Management, Transport Management, Web Design and Development. See also **Section B**.

Chemistry Biochemistry, Cancer Biology, Chemical Engineering, Chemical Physics, Chemistry, Dentistry, Environmental Sciences, Fire Engineering, Forensic Sciences, Medicinal Chemistry, Medicine, Microbiology, Natural Sciences, Nutritional Biochemistry, Pharmacology, Pharmacy, Veterinary Science, Virology and Immunology. See also **Section B**.

Chinese Chinese. See also **Languages** below.

Classics and Classical Civilisation Ancient History, Archaeology, Classical Studies, Classics, Greek (Classical), Latin.

Computer Science Artificial Intelligence, Business Information Systems, Computer Engineering, Computer Science, Computing, Cybernetics, E-Commerce, Electronic Engineering, Games Technology, Intelligent Product Design, Multimedia Systems Engineering, Network Management and Security, Robotics, Software Engineering. See also **Section B**.

Dance Arts Management, Ballet Education, Choreography, Dance, Drama, Education, Music, Musical Theatre, Performance Management, Performing Arts, Sport and Exercise, Street Arts, Theatre and Performance, Theatre Arts, Writing Directing and Performance. See also **Section B**.

Design Technology Food Technology, Manufacturing Engineering, Product Design, Sport Equipment Design, Systems and Control. See also **Section B**.

Drama and Theatre Studies Acting, Community Drama, Costume Production, Creative Writing, Dance, Drama, Education Studies, English Comedy: Writing and Performance, International Theatre, Music, Performing Arts, Scenic Arts, Scriptwriting, Set Design, Stage Management, Theatre Arts, Theatre Practice. See also **Section B**.

Economics Accountancy, Banking, Business Administration, Business Economics, Business Studies, Development Studies, Economics, Estate Management, Finance, Management Science, Mathematics, Political Economy, Politics, Quantity Surveying, Sociology, Statistics.

Electronics Computing, Electronics, Engineering (Aeronautical, Aerospace, Communication, Computer, Software, Systems), Mechatronics, Medical Electronics, Multimedia Technology, Technology. See also **Section B**.

English Language and Literature Communication Studies, Comparative Literature, Creative Writing, Drama, Education, English Language, English Literature, Information and Library Studies/Management, Journalism, Linguistics, Media Writing, Philosophy, Publishing, Scottish Literature, Scriptwriting, Theatre Studies.

Environmental Sciences Biological Sciences, Biology, Earth Sciences, Ecology, Environment and Planning, Environmental Management, Environmental Sciences, Forestry, Geography, Geology, Land Management, Marine Biology, Meteorology, Oceanography, Outdoor Education, Plant Sciences, Sustainable Development, Wastes Management, Water Science, Wildlife Biology, Wildlife Conservation, Zoology.

French French, International Business Studies, International Hospitality Management, Law with French Law. See also **Languages** below.

Geography Development Studies, Earth Sciences, Environmental Policy, Environmental Sciences, Estate Management, Forestry, Geographical Information Science, Geography, Geology, Land Economy, Meteorology, Oceanography, Surveying, Town and Country Planning, Urban Studies, Water Science.

Geology Earth Sciences, Geography, Geology, Geophysical Sciences, Geosciences, Meteorology, Mining Engineering, Natural Sciences, Oceanography, Palaeontology and Evolution, Planetary Sciences, Water and Environmental Management. See also **Section B**.

German German, International Business Studies, International Hospitality Management, Law with German Law. See also **Languages** below.

Government/Politics Development Studies, Economics, Global Politics, Government, History, Human Rights, Industrial Relations, International Politics, Law, Peace Studies, Politics, Public Administration, Social and Political Science, Social Policy, Sociology, Strategic Studies, War Studies.

Gujarati Gujarati. See also **Languages** below.

History African Studies, American Studies, Ancient History, Archaeology, Art History, Classical Civilisations, Classical Studies, Education, Egyptology, Fashion and Dress History, History, International Relations, Law, Literature, Medieval Studies, Museum and Heritage Studies, Philosophy, Politics, Russian Studies,

Scandinavian Studies, Scottish History, Social and Economic History, Theology and Religious Studies, Victorian Studies.

Italian Italian. See also **Languages** below.

Japanese Japanese. See also **Languages** below.

Languages Languages, Modern Languages, Translating and Interpreting. **NB** Apart from French and German – and Spanish for some universities – it is not usually necessary to have completed an A-level language course before studying the many languages (over 60) offered at degree level. Many universities provide opportunities to study a language in a wide range of degree courses. See also **The Erasmus+ Programme** details in **Chapter 4**.

Law Criminal Justice, Criminology, European Business Law, Human Rights, International Business, International Relations, Law, Legal Studies, Police Sciences, Social Sciences, Sociology, Youth Justice. See also **Section B**.

Mathematics Accountancy, Actuarial Mathematics, Aeronautical Engineering, Astrophysics, Business Management, Chemical Engineering, Civil Engineering, Computational Science, Computer Systems Engineering, Control Systems Engineering, Cybernetics, Economics, Engineering Science, Ergonomics, Financial Mathematics, Further and Additional Mathematics, Geophysics, Management Science, Materials Science and Technology, Mechanical Engineering, Meteorology, Naval Architecture, Physics, Quantity Surveying, Statistics, Systems Analysis, Telecommunications.

Media Studies Advertising, Animation, Broadcasting, Communication Studies, Creative Writing, English, Film and Television Studies, Journalism, Mass Communication, Media courses, Media Culture and Society, Media Production, Media Technology, Multimedia, Photography, Publishing, Radio Production and Communication, Society Culture and Media, Translation Media and French/Spanish, Web and Broadcasting. See also **Section B**.

Modern Greek Greek. See also **Languages** above.

Modern Hebrew Hebrew. See also **Languages** above.

Music Audio and Music Production, Creative Music Technology, Education, Music, Music Broadcasting, Music Informatics, Music Management, Music Systems Engineering, Musical Theatre, Musician, Performance Arts, Popular and World Musics, Sonic Arts. See also **Section B**.

Persian Persian. See also **Languages** above.

Philosophy Classical Studies, Cultural Studies, Divinity, Educational Studies, Ethics, History of Ideas, History of Science, Law, Mathematics, Natural Sciences, Philosophy, Politics Philosophy and Economics, Psychology, Religious Studies, Social Sciences, Theology.

Physics Aeronautical Engineering, Architecture, Astronomy, Astrophysics, Automotive Engineering, Biomedical Engineering, Biophysics, Chemical Physics, Civil Engineering, Communications Engineering, Computer Science, Cybernetics, Education, Electrical/Electronic Engineering, Engineering Science, Ergonomics, Geophysics, Materials Science and Technology, Mechanical Engineering, Medical Physics, Meteorology, Nanotechnology, Naval Architecture, Oceanography, Optometry, Photonics, Planetary Science, Quantum Informatics, Radiography, Renewable Energy, Telecommunications Engineering.

Polish Polish. See also **Languages** above.

Portuguese Portuguese. See also **Languages** above.

Psychology Advertising, Animal Behaviour, Anthropology, Artificial Intelligence, Behavioural Science, Childhood Studies, Cognitive Science, Counselling Studies, Criminology, Education, Human Resource Management, Marketing, Neuroscience, Nursing, Politics, Psychology, Social Sciences, Sociology, Speech and Language Therapy. See also **Section B**.

Punjabi Punjabi. See also **Languages** above.

Religious Studies Abrahamic Religions (Christianity, Islam and Judaism), Anthropology, Archaeology, Biblical Studies, Christian Youth Work, Comparative Religion, Divinity, Education, Ethics, History of Art,

International Relations, Islamic Studies, Jewish Studies, Philosophy, Psychology, Religious Studies, Social Policy, Theology.

Russian Russian. See also **Languages** above.

Sport and Physical Education Chiropractic, Coaching Science, Community Sport Development, Dance Studies, Exercise and Health, Exercise Science, Fitness Science, Football Studies, Golf Studies, Osteopathy, Outdoor Pursuits, Physical Education, Physiotherapy, Sport and Exercise Science, Sport and Health, Sport Coaching, Sport Equipment Design, Sport Management, Sport Marketing, Teaching (Primary) (Secondary).

Statistics Actuarial Studies, Business Analysis, Business Studies, Informatics, Management Sciences, Statistics. See also **Mathematics** above and **Section B** Mathematics-related careers.

Turkish Turkish. See also **Languages** above.

Urdu Urdu. See also **Languages** above.

SECTION B
Choosing your course by career interests

Accountancy Accountancy, Accounting, Actuarial Science, Banking, Business Studies, Economics, Finance and Business, Finance and Investment, Financial Services, Management Science, Real Estate Management, Risk Management.

Actuarial work Actuarial Mathematics, Actuarial Science, Actuarial Studies, Financial Mathematics, Risk Analysis and Insurance.

Agriculture Agri-Business, Agricultural Engineering, Agriculture, Animal Sciences, Aquaculture and Fishery Sciences, Conservation and Habitat Management, Countryside Management, Crop Science, Ecology, Environmental Science, Estate Management, Forestry, Horticulture, Landscape Management, Plant Sciences, Rural Resource Management, Soil Science, Wildlife Management.

Animal careers Agricultural Sciences, Animal Behaviour and Welfare, Biological Sciences, Bioveterinary Science, Equine Management/Science/Studies, Veterinary Nursing, Veterinary Practice Management, Veterinary Science, Zoology.

Archaeology Ancient History, Anthropology, Archaeology, Bioarchaeology, Classical Civilisation and Classics, Egyptology, Geography, History, History of Art and Architecture, Viking Studies.

Architecture Architectural Design, Architectural Technology, Architecture, Building, Building Conservation, City and Regional Planning, Civil Engineering, Conservation and Restoration, Construction Engineering and Management, Interior Architecture, Stained Glass Restoration and Conservation, Structural Engineering.

Art and Design careers Advertising, Animation, Architecture, Art, Design, Digital Media Design, Education (Art), Fashion and Textiles, Fine Art, Games Art and Design, Glassware, Graphic Design, Illustration, Industrial Design, Jewellery, Landscape Architecture, Photography, Stained Glass, Three-Dimensional Design.

Astronomy Astronomy, Astrophysics, Mathematics, Natural Sciences, Planetary Geology, Physics, Quantum and Cosmological Physics, Space Science, Space Technology and Planetary Exploration.

Audiology Audiology, Education of the Deaf, Human Communication, Nursing, Speech and Language Therapy.

Banking/Insurance Accountancy, Actuarial Sciences, Banking, Business Studies, Economics, Financial Services, Insurance, Real Estate Management, Risk Management.

Biology-related careers Agricultural Sciences, Animal Sciences, Biochemistry, Biological Sciences, Biology, Biomedical Sciences, Biotechnology, Cell Biology, Ecology, Education, Environmental Biology, Environmental Sciences, Freshwater Science, Genetics, Immunology, Life Sciences, Marine Biology, Medical Biochemistry, Medicine, Microbiology, Molecular Biology, Natural Sciences, Oceanography, Pharmacy, Plant Science, Physiology, Wildlife Conservation, Zoology.

Book Publishing Advertising, Business Studies, Communications, Creative Writing, English Literature, Illustration, Journalism, Media Communication, Photography, Printing, Publishing, Science Communication, Web and Multimedia.

Brewing and Distilling Biochemistry, Brewing and Distilling, Chemistry, Food Science and Technology, Viticulture and Oenology.

Broadcasting Audio Video and Digital Broadcast Engineering, Broadcast Documentary, Broadcast Media, Broadcast Technology and Production, Digital Media, Electronic Engineering (Broadcast Systems), Film and TV Broadcasting, Media and Communications Studies, Media Production, Multimedia, Music Broadcasting, Outside Broadcast Technology, Radio Journalism, Television Studio Production, TV Production, Video and Broadcasting.

Building Architecture, Building Conservation, Building Services Engineering, Building Studies, Building Surveying, Civil Engineering, Estate Management, General Practice Surveying, Land Surveying, Quantity Surveying.

Business Accountancy, Advertising, Banking, Business Administration, Business Analysis, Business Studies, Business Systems, E-Commerce, Economics, Estate Management, European Business, Hospitality Management, Housing Management, Human Resource Management, Industrial Relations, Insurance, Logistics, Management Sciences, Marketing, Property Development, Public Relations, Publishing, Supply Chain Management, Transport Management, Tourism.

Cartography Geographic Information Systems, Geographical Information Science, Geography, Land Surveying.

Catering Consumer Studies, Culinary Arts Management, Dietetics, Food Science, Hospitality Management, International and Hospitality Business Management, Nutrition.

Chemistry-related careers Agricultural Science, Biochemistry, Botany, Ceramics, Chemical Engineering, Chemistry, Colour Chemistry, Education, Environmental Sciences, Geochemistry, Materials Science and Technology, Medical Chemistry, Nanotechnology, Natural Sciences, Pharmacology, Pharmacy, Physiology, Technologies (for example Food, Plastics).

Computing Artificial Intelligence, Bioinformatics, Business Computing, Business Studies, Computer Engineering, Computer Games Development, Computer Science, Computers, Electronics and Communications, Digital Forensics and System Security, Electronic Engineering, Games Design, Information and Communication Technology, Internet Computing, Mathematics, Multimedia Computing, Physics, Software Systems, Telecommunications, Virtual Reality Design.

Construction Architectural Technology, Architecture, Building, Building Services Engineering, Civil Engineering, Construction Management, Fire Risk Engineering, Landscape Architecture, Quantity Surveying, Surveying, Town and Country Planning.

Dance Ballet Education, Choreography, Dance, Drama, Movement Studies, Performance/Performing Arts, Physical Education, Theatre Studies.

Dentistry Biochemistry, Dental Materials, Dental Technician, Dentistry, Equine Dentistry, Medicine, Nursing, Oral Health Sciences, Pharmacy.

Drama Dance, Drama, Education, Movement Studies, Musical Theatre, Scenic Arts, Teaching, Theatre Management.

Education Ballet Education, British Sign Language, Childhood Studies, Coach Education, Deaf Studies, Early Years Education, Education Studies, Education with QTS, Education without QTS, Music Education, Physical Education, Primary Education, Psychology, Secondary Education, Social Work, Special Educational Needs, Speech and Language Therapy, Sport and Exercise, Teaching, Technology for Teaching and Learning, Youth Studies.

Electronics Automotive Electronics, Avionics, Computer Systems, Computer Technology, Computing, Digital Electronics, Digital Media Technology, Electronic Design, Electronic Engineering, Electronics,

Information Systems, Internet Engineering, Mechatronics, Medical Electronics, Motorsport Electronic Systems, Multimedia Computing, Software Development, Sound Engineering.

Engineering Engineering (including Aeronautical, Aerospace, Chemical, Civil, Computing, Control, Electrical, Electronic, Energy, Environmental, Food Process, Manufacturing, Mechanical, Motorsport, Nuclear, Product Design, Software, Telecommunications), Geology and Geotechnics, Horology, Mathematics, Physics.

Estate Management Architecture, Building, Civil Engineering, Economics, Estate Management, Forestry, Housing Studies, Landscape Architecture, Property Development, Real Estate Management, Town and Country Planning.

Food Science and Technology Biochemistry, Brewing and Distilling, Chemistry, Culinary Arts, Dietetics, Food and Consumer Studies, Food Safety Management, Food Science and Technology, Food Supply Chain Management, Fresh Produce Management, Hospitality and Food Management, Nutrition, Public Health Nutrition, Viticulture and Oenology.

Forestry Arboriculture, Biological Sciences, Countryside Management, Ecology, Environmental Science, Forestry, Horticulture, Plant Sciences, Rural Resource Management, Tropical Forestry, Urban Forestry.

Furniture Design Furniture Design, Furniture Production, History of Art and Design, Three-Dimensional Design, Timber Technology.

Geology-related careers Chemistry, Earth Sciences, Engineering (Civil, Minerals), Environmental Sciences, Geochemistry, Geography, Geology, Land Surveying, Oceanography, Soil Science.

Graphic Design Advertising, Graphic Design, Photography, Printing, Web Design.

Health and Safety careers Biomedical Informatics, Biomedical Sciences, Community and Health Studies, Environmental Health, Exercise and Health Science, Fire Science Engineering, Health and Social Care, Health Management, Health Promotion, Health Psychology, Health Sciences, Holistic Therapy, Nursing, Occupational Safety and Health, Paramedic Science, Public Health, Public Services Management. (See also **Medical careers**.)

Horticulture Agriculture, Crop Science, Horticulture, Landscape Architecture, Plant Science, Soil Science.

Hospitality Management Business and Management, Culinary Arts Management, Events and Facilities Management, Food Science, Food Technology, Heritage Management, Hospitality Management, Human Resource Management, International Hospitality Management, Leisure Services Management, Licensed Retail Management, Spa Management, Travel and Tourism Management.

Housing Architecture, Estate Management, General Practice Surveying, Housing, Social Administration, Town and Country Planning.

Law Business Law, Commercial Law, Consumer Law, Criminal Justice, Criminology, European Law, Government and Politics, International History, Land Management, Law, Legal Studies, Politics, Sociology.

Leisure and Recreation Adventure Tourism, Airline and Airport Management, Business Travel and Tourism, Community Arts, Countryside Management, Dance, Drama, Event Management, Fitness Science, Hospitality Management, International Tourism Management, Leisure Management, Movement Studies, Music, Physical Education, Sport and Leisure Management, Sport Development, Sports Management, Theatre Studies, Travel and Tourism.

Library and Information Management Administration, Business Information Systems, Digital Media, Education Studies, Information and Communication Studies, Information and Library Studies, Information Management, Information Sciences and Technology, Management and Marketing, Media and Cultural Studies, Media Communications, Museum and Galleries Studies, Publishing.

Marketing Advertising, Business Studies, Consumer Science, E-Marketing, Health Promotion, International Business, Marketing, Psychology, Public Relations, Retail Management, Sports Development, Travel and Tourism.

Materials Science/Metallurgy Automotive Materials, Chemistry, Engineering, Glass Science and Technology, Materials Science and Technology, Mineral Surveying, Physics, Polymer Science, Sports Materials, Textile Science.

Mathematics-related careers Accountancy, Actuarial Science, Astronomy, Banking, Business Decision Mathematics, Business Studies, Computer Studies, Economics, Education, Engineering, Financial Mathematics, Mathematical Physics, Mathematics, Physics, Quantity Surveying, Statistics.

Media careers Advertising, Broadcasting, Communications, Computer Graphics, Creative Writing, Film/Video Production, Journalism, Media, Multimedia, Photography, Public Relations, Psychology, Visual Communication.

Medical careers Anatomy, Biochemistry, Biological Sciences, Biomedical Sciences, Chiropractic, Dentistry, Genetics, Human Physiology, Immunology, Medical Engineering, Medical Sciences/Medicine, Nursing, Occupational Therapy, Orthoptics, Osteopathy, Pathology and Microbiology, Pharmacology, Pharmacy, Physiotherapy, Psychology, Radiography, Speech and Language Therapy, Sports Biomedicine, Virology.

Music Commercial Music, Creative Music Technology, Digital Music, Drama, Folk and Traditional Music, Music, Music Composition, Music Education, Music Industry Management, Music Performance, Music Production, Music Studies, Musical Theatre, Performance/Performing Arts, Popular Music, Sonic Arts, Sound and Multimedia Technology, Theatre Studies.

Nautical careers Marine Engineering, Marine Studies, Nautical Studies, Naval Architecture, Oceanography, Offshore Engineering, Ship Science.

Naval Architecture Boat Design, Marine Engineering, Marine Studies, Naval Architecture, Offshore Engineering, Ship Science, Yacht and Powercraft Design, Yacht Production.

Nursing Anatomy, Applied Biology, Biochemistry, Biological Sciences, Biology, Dentistry, Education, Environmental Health and Community Studies, Health Studies, Human Biology, Medicine, Midwifery, Nursing, Occupational Therapy, Orthoptics, Physiotherapy, Podiatry, Psychology, Radiography, Social Administration, Speech and Language Therapy, Veterinary Nursing. (See also **Medical careers**.)

Nutrition Dietetics, Food Science and Technology, Health Promotion, Human Nutrition, Nursing, Nutrition, Sport and Fitness.

Occupational Therapy Art, General and Mental Nursing, Occupational Therapy, Orthoptics, Physiotherapy, Psychology, Social Sciences, Speech and Language Therapy.

Optometry Applied Physics, Optometry, Orthoptics, Physics.

Photography/Film/TV Animation, Communication Studies (some courses), Digital Video Design, Documentary Communications, Film and Media, Graphic Art, Media Studies, Moving Image, Multimedia, Photography.

Physics-related careers Applied Physics, Astronomy, Astrophysics, Avionics and Space Systems, Education, Electronics, Engineering (Civil, Electrical, Mechanical), Laser Physics, Mathematical Physics, Medical Instrumentation, Molecular Physics, Nanotechnology, Natural Sciences, Optometry, Physics, Planetary and Space Physics, Quantum and Cosmological Physics, Theoretical Physics.

Physiotherapy Chiropractic, Exercise Science, Nursing, Orthoptics, Osteopathy, Physical Education, Physiotherapy, Sport and Exercise, Sports Rehabilitation.

Production Technology Engineering (Manufacturing, Mechanical), Materials Science.

Property and Valuation Management Architecture, Building Surveying, Estate Agency, Property Investment and Finance, Property Management and Valuation, Quantity Surveying, Real Estate Management, Residential Property, Urban Land Economics.

Psychology Advertising, Animal Sciences, Anthropology, Applied Social Studies, Behavioural Science, Business, Cognitive Science, Criminology, Early Childhood Studies, Education, Human Resource Management, Human Sciences, Linguistics, Marketing, Neuroscience, Occupational Therapy, Psychology

(Clinical, Developmental, Educational, Experimental, Forensic, Health, Occupational, Social, Sports), Psychosocial Sciences, Public Relations, Social Sciences, Sociology.

Public Administration Applied Social Studies, Business Studies, Public Administration, Public Policy Investment and Management, Public Services, Social Administration, Social Policy, Youth Studies.

Quantity Surveying Architecture, Building, Civil Engineering, Construction and Commercial Management, Environmental Construction Surveying, Surveying (Building, Land and Valuation), Surveying Technology.

Radiography Anatomy, Audiology, Biological Sciences, Clinical Photography, Diagnostic Imaging, Diagnostic Radiography, Digital Imaging, Imaging Science and Technology, Medical Imaging, Moving Image, Nursing, Orthoptics, Photography, Physics, Physiology, Physiotherapy, Radiography, Radiotherapy, Therapeutic Radiography.

Silversmithing/Jewellery Design Silversmithing and Jewellery, Silversmithing Goldsmithing and Jewellery, Silversmithing Metalwork and Jewellery, Three-Dimensional Design.

Social Work Abuse Studies, Applied Social Science, Community Work, Counselling Studies, Early Childhood Studies, Education, Health and Social Care, Human Rights, Journalism, Law, Nursing, Playwork, Politics and Government, Psychology, Public Administration, Religious Studies, Social Administration, Social Policy, Social Work, Sociology, Town and Country Planning, Youth Studies.

Speech and Language Therapy Audiology, Education (Special Education), Linguistics, Nursing, Occupational Therapy, Psychology, Radiography, Speech and Language Therapy.

Sport and Physical Education Coaching Sciences, Exercise Sciences, Fitness Science, Health and Fitness Management, Leisure and Recreation Management, Physical Education, Sport and Recreational Studies, Sport Journalism, Sports Psychology, Sports Science, Sports Studies.

Statistics Business Studies, Economics, Informatics, Mathematics, Operational Research, Population Sciences, Statistics.

Surveying Building Surveying, General Practice Surveying, Property Development, Quantity Surveying, Real Estate Management.

Technology Audio Technology, Dental Technology, Design Technology, Food Science and Technology, Football Technology, Logistics Technology, Medical Technology, Music Studio Technology, Paper Science, Polymer Science, Product Design Technology, Sports Technology, Technology for Teaching and Learning, Timber Technology.

Textile Design Applied Art and Design, Art, Clothing Studies, Fashion Design, Interior Design, Textile Design (Embroidery, Constructive Textiles, Printed Textiles), Textile Management.

Theatre Design Drama, Interior Design, Leisure and Recreational Studies, Theatre Design, Theatre Management, Theatre Studies.

Three-Dimensional Design Architecture, Industrial Design, Interior Design, Theatre Design, Three-Dimensional Design.

Town and Regional Planning Architecture, Architecture and Planning, City and Regional Planning, Environmental Planning, Estate Management, Geography, Housing, Land Economy, Planning and Development, Population Sciences, Property Planning and Development, Spatial Planning, Statistics, Sustainable Development, Town and Regional Planning, Transport Management, Urban and Regional Planning.

Transport Air Transport Engineering, Air Transport Operations, Air Transport with Pilot Training, Business Studies, Civil and Transportation Engineering, Cruise Operations Management, Industrial Design (Transport), Logistics, Planning with Transport, Supply Chain Management, Sustainable Transport Design, Town and Regional Planning, Urban Planning Design and Management.

Typography and Graphic Communication Design (Graphic and Typographic Design), Digital Graphics, Fine Art (Print and Digital Media), Graphic Communication and Typography, Graphic Design, Illustration, Illustration and Print, Printmaking, Publication Design, Publishing, Visual Communication.

Veterinary careers Agricultural Sciences, Agriculture, Anatomical Science, Animal Behaviour and Welfare, Animal Sciences, Bioveterinary Sciences, Equine Dentistry, Equine Science, Medicine, Pharmacology, Pharmacy, Veterinary Medicine, Veterinary Nursing, Veterinary Practice Management, Zoology.

COURSE TYPES AND DIFFERENCES
The options
You will then need to decide on the type of course you want to follow. The way in which Honours degree courses are arranged differs between institutions. For example, a subject might be offered as a single subject course (a Single Honours degree), or as a two-subject course (a Joint Honours degree), or as one of two, three or four subjects (a Combined Honours degree) or a Major/Minor degree (75% and 25% of each subject respectively).

A Bachelor of Arts (BA) does not necessarily indicate an arts or humanities course, likewise a Bachelor of Science degree (BSc) does not necessarily have a solely scientific or technical focus. Instead, there is much variation; for example, some Management or Marketing courses are BScs, and some Architecture courses are BAs while others are BScs.

Entry requirements
Courses in the same subject at different universities and colleges can have different subject requirements so it is important to check the acceptability of your GCE A-levels and GCSE subjects (or equivalent) for all your preferred courses. Specific GCE A-levels, and in some cases, GCSE subjects, may be stipulated. (See also **Chapter 6** and **Appendix 1** for information on Scottish Highers/Advanced Highers, the Advanced Welsh Baccalaureate – Skills Challenge Certificate, the International Baccalaureate Diploma, BTEC Level 3 National Extended Diploma, the Extended Project, Music examinations and Art and Design Foundation Studies, and **Appendix 2** for international qualifications.)

SANDWICH COURSES AND PROFESSIONAL PLACEMENTS
The benefits
Media coverage on student debt and tuition fees highlights the importance of sandwich courses. Many vocational courses offer sandwich periods and placements of 6 or 12 months in which students spend time away from their university or college in industry, commerce or in the public sector as part of a four-year degree course. The advantages of these courses can be quite considerable. Not only may students receive an income from the company, but contacts made can lead to permanent employment on graduation.

Work-based learning (WBL) programmes
Some colleges also offer work-based learning programmes in which placements last a few weeks when students can gain experience of different careers.

Students report ...
'I was able to earn £15,000 during my year out and £4,000 during my three-month vacation with the same firm.' (**Bath** Engineering)

'There's really no other better way to find out what you want to do for your future career than having tried it for a year.' (**Aston** Human Resources Management)

'It was a welcome break in formal university education: I met some great people including students from other universities.' (**Kingston** Biochemistry)

'Having experienced a year in a working environment, I am more confident and more employable than students without this experience.' (**Aston** Business Studies)

'At Sanolfi in Toulouse, I learned to think on my feet – no two days were the same.' (**Aston** European Studies)

'I have seen how an organisation works at first-hand, learned how academic skills may be applied in a working environment, become proficient in the use of various software, acquired new skills in interpersonal relationships and communications and used my period away to realign my career perspectives.' (**Aston** European Studies)

'I was working alongside graduate employees and the firm offered me a job when I graduated.' (**Bath** Mathematics)

Employers, too, gain from having students ...
'We meet a lot of enthusiastic potential recruits who bring new ideas into the firm, and we can offer them commercially sponsored help for their final year project.'

'The quality of this student has remained high throughout the year. He will do well for his next employer, whoever that may be. However, I sincerely hope that it will be with us.'

University staff advise ...
'We refer to sandwich courses as professional placements, not "work experience" which is a phrase we reserve for short non-professional experiences, for example summer or pre-university jobs. The opportunity is available to all students but their success in gaining a good placement depends on academic ability.' (**Bath**)

'Where a placement year is optional, those who opt for it are more likely to be awarded a First or an Upper Second compared to those who don't, not because they are given more marks for doing it, but because they always seem to have added context and motivation for their final year.' (**Aston**)

When choosing your sandwich course, check with the university (a) that the institution will guarantee a list of employers, (b) whether placement experience counts towards the final degree result, (c) that placements are paid and (d) that placements are validated by professional bodies. Finally, once you start on the course, remember that your first-year academic performance will be taken into account by potential employers. Now read on!

What do employers require when considering students?
Aston (Biol) Successful second-year undergraduates; (Bus) Number of UCAS points, degree programme, any prior experience; (Eng) UCAS points scores and expected degree classification; (Mech Eng) Students interviewed and selected by the company according to student ability, what they are studying and specific needs of the job. **Bath** (Chem) 'Good students': Upper Second or above and non-international students (those without work visas). Students with strong vivisection views rejected; (Mech Elec Eng) Subject-based, eg electronics, aerospace, computing and electrical engineering; (Mech Eng) Good communication, IT and social skills; (Maths) Interest in positions of responsibility, teamwork, integrity, self-motivation, analytical ability, communication, recent work experience, knowledge of the company, desire to work for the company, predicted 2.1; (Phys) Many organisations have cut-offs regarding students' first-year performance (eg must be heading for a 2.1 although some require better than this), some need students to be particularly good in some areas (eg lab work, computer programming), many require UK nationality with minimum residency condition. **Brunel** Requirements not usually specified except for IT jobs since they need technical skills. **Cardiff Met** (Clsrm Asst) Disclosure and Barring Service (DBS) checks. **Kingston** (Bus Law) Theoretical knowledge and a stated interest in certain areas (eg finance, human resources, marketing, sales, IT), excellent communication skills, teamwork, ability to prioritise, time management and a professional attitude; (Sci) Grades are rarely mentioned: it's usually a specific module or course requirement undertaken by the students that they are looking for, as well as a good attitude, motivation, initiative: a good all-rounder. **Loughborough** (Civ Eng) Target specific courses.

What are the advantages of placements to the students?
Aston (Biol) Many take jobs with their placement employers (eg NHS), gaining valuable research and clinical experience; (Bus) Graduate job offers, sponsorship through the final year of the course, gym membership, staff discounts; (Eng) Some students are fast-tracked into full-time employment and, in some cases, have been given higher starting salaries as a result of the placement with the company; (Mech Eng) Offers of full-time employment on graduation, bursaries for their final year of study, final year projects following placements, better class of degree. **Bath** (Chem) Sponsorships for final year

project work, offers of full-time employment, PhD offers and work-to-study courses, industrial references, establishment of prizes; (Maths) Sponsorship in the second year, graduate employment, bonuses during placement, travel abroad during placement, sponsorship during final year; (Phys) Job offers on graduation, sponsored final year, improved study skills for final year, job market awareness, career decisions. **Bournemouth** All undergraduate full-time degrees offer students the opportunity to undertake work placements. The majority are paid and, in some cases, students may be eligible for financial support during their placement year. **Brunel** Higher percentage of students get Firsts, many students get a job offer from the placement provider, higher salaries often paid to sandwich course students, some students get exemptions from professional exams, eg ACCA, ACA and IMechE. **Cardiff Met** (Clsrm Asst) Good experience in team work, classroom experience, coaching, mentoring: decisions made whether or not to follow a teaching career. **Kingston** (Bus Law) Sponsorships fewer these days but students return with more confidence and maturity and better able to complete their final year; 70% receive job offers on completion of a successful placement; (Sci) Full-time employment on graduation and occasionally part-time work in the final year; many students are encouraged to write their final year dissertation while on placement and benefit from the company's support, subject matter and validation. **Liverpool** A year in industry can bring a number of benefits and positive impacts for students. There is strong evidence that placements are valuable in terms of enhancing academic skills, improving employment prospects and increasing an understanding of the world of work. It can also increase their social mobility and potential salary throughout their careers. **Loughborough** (Civ Eng) Most students are sponsored by their firms and perform better in their final examinations; (Prod Des) Final year bursary for some students, offer of employment by the sponsor and a final year design project for the sponsor.

DEGREE APPRENTICESHIP COURSES

An alternative route to studying for a degree is by way of a degree apprenticeship course. These courses are particularly suitable for those who have completed lower-level apprenticeships and wish to study further in order to advance their career; however, the qualifications are suitable for anyone. Degree apprenticeship courses combine a full degree with practical work. They are designed in partnership with employers – apprentices will be employed throughout and earning a wage, with part-time study taking place at a university. They can be completed to bachelor's or master's degree level and take between three and six years to complete, depending on the level of the course. Currently, the scheme operates across England and Wales only, although applications may be made from all parts of the UK. Degree apprenticeships are only available in vocational subjects, with established subject requirements set for entry. Opportunities are currently available in sectors such as engineering, business management, financial services and within the construction and digital industries. For further information see www.prospects.ac.uk/jobs-and-work-experience/apprenticeships/degree-apprenticeships.

MATURE APPLICANTS

There are a great many mature students following first degree courses in UK universities and colleges. The following is a list of key points a group of mature students found useful in exploring and deciding on a university course.

- Check with your nearest university or college to find out about the courses they can offer, for example degrees, diplomas, full-time, part-time.
- Some institutions will require examination passes in some subjects, others may not.
- An age limit may apply for some vocational courses, for example Medicine, Dentistry and Teaching.
- If entry requirements are an obstacle, prospective students should approach their local colleges for information on Access or distance-learning courses such as those offered by the National Extension College. These courses are fast-growing in number and popularity, offering adults an alternative route into higher education other than A-levels. They are usually developed jointly by colleges of further education and the local higher education institution.
- Demands of the course – how much time will be required for study? What are the assignments and the deadlines to be met? How is your work assessed – unseen examinations, continuous assessment, practicals?

- The demands on finance – cost of the course – loan needed – loss of earnings – drop in income if changing to another career – travel requirements – accommodation – need to work part-time for income?
- The availability and suitability of the course – geographical location – competition for places – where it will lead – student support services, for example childcare, library.
- What benefits will you derive? Fulfilment, transferable skills, social contacts, sense of achievement, enjoyment, self-esteem, career enhancement?
- Why would employers want to recruit you? Ability to adapt to the work scene, realistic and balanced approach, mature attitude to work?
- Why would employers not want to recruit you? Salary expectations, inability to fit in with younger colleagues, limited mobility? However, some employers particularly welcome older graduates: civil service, local authorities, health service, religious, charitable and voluntary organisations, teaching, social/probation work, careers work, housing.

MODULAR COURSES AND CREDIT ACCUMULATION AND TRANSFER SCHEMES (CATS)

Courses can also differ considerably not only in their content but in how they are organised. Many universities and colleges of higher education have modularised their courses which means you can choose modules of different subjects, and 'build' your course within specified 'pathways' with the help and approval of your course tutor. It also means that you are likely to be assessed after completing each module, rather than in your last year for all your previous years' learning. In almost every course the options and modules offered include some that reflect the research interests of individual members of staff. In some courses subsidiary subjects are available as minor courses alongside a Single Honours course. In an increasing number of courses these additional subjects include a foreign language, and the importance of this cannot be over-emphasised, as language skills are increasingly in demand by employers, and studying a language may also open up opportunities for further study abroad. A popular option has been the Erasmus+ programme (see **Chapter 4**) which enables university students to apply for courses in Europe for periods of up to a year, with some of the courses being taught in English. Please note that following the UK's departure from the EU on 31 January 2020, the UK's continued access to the Erasmus+ scheme has yet to be determined. At present, the UK will continue to access the scheme until the end of 2020. Many institutions have introduced Credit Accumulation and Transfer Schemes (CATS). These allow students to be awarded credits for modules or units of study they have successfully completed which are accumulated towards a certificate, diploma or degree. They can also put their completed modules towards higher education study in other universities or colleges. Students wanting to transfer their credits should talk to the admissions office of the university they want to enter as there may be additional special subjects or module requirements for the degree they want to study.

FOUNDATION DEGREES AND FOUNDATION COURSES

Foundation courses, not be confused with Foundation degrees, normally require two years' full-time study, or longer for part-time study. They are also often taught in local colleges and may be taken part-time to allow students to continue to work. In comparison a Foundation degree can lead into the second or final year of related Honours degree courses when offered by the university validating the Foundation degree. Two-year Higher National Diplomas will also qualify for entry into the second or final year of degree courses. These, too, are often offered at universities as well as colleges of further education and partnership colleges linked to universities.

Part-time degrees and lifelong learning or distance learning courses are also often available and details of these can be found on university websites and in prospectuses. Some universities publish separate prospectuses for part-time courses.

NEXT STEPS

When choosing your course remember that one course is not better than another – it is just different. The best course for you is the one which best suits you. To give some indication of the differences between courses, see **Chapter 3** and also *Choosing Your Degree Course & University*, the companion book to *Heap 2021: University Degree Course Offers* (see **Appendix 4**). After provisionally choosing your courses, read the prospectuses again carefully to be sure that you understand what is included in the three, four or more years of study. Each institution differs in its course content even though the course titles may be the same and courses differ in other ways, for example:

- methods of assessment (eg unseen examinations, continuous assessment, project work, dissertations)
- contact time with tutors
- how they are taught (for example, frequency and size of lectures, seminars)
- practicals; field work requirements
- library, computing, laboratory and studio facilities
- amount of free study time available.

These are useful points of comparison between courses in different institutions when you are on an Open Day visit or making final course choices. Other important factors to consider when comparing courses include the availability of opportunities for studying and working abroad during your course, professional body accreditation of courses leading to certain professional careers (see **Appendix 3**), and the career destinations of previous graduates.

Once you have chosen your course subject(s) and the type of course you want to follow, the next step is to find out about the universities and colleges offering courses in your subject area, how much a higher education course will cost you and what financial help is available. The next chapter, **University Choice and Finance** provides information to help you do this.

TAKING A GAP YEAR

Choosing your course is the first decision you need to make, the second is choosing your university and then, for an increasing number, the third is deciding whether or not to take a Gap Year. But there lies the problem. Because of the very large number of things to do and places to go, you'll find that you almost need a Gap Year to choose the right one!

Planning ahead is important but, in the end, bear in mind that you might be overtaken by events, not least in failing to get the grades you need for a place on the course or at the university you were counting on. This could mean repeating A-levels and re-applying, which in turn could mean waiting for interviews and offers and deferring the start of your 'gap'.

Once you have decided to go, however, it's a question of whether you will go under your own steam or through a Gap Year agency. Unless you are streetwise, or preferably 'world wise', then an agency offers several advantages. Some agencies may cover a broad field of opportunities while others will focus on a specific region and activity, such as the African Conservation Experience, offering animal and plant conservation work in game and nature reserves in southern Africa.

When making the choice, some students will always prefer a 'do-it-yourself' arrangement. However, there are many advantages to going through specialist agencies. Not only can they offer a choice of destinations and opportunities but also they can provide a lot of essential and helpful advice before your departure on issues such as health precautions and insurance. Support is also available in the case of accidents or illnesses when a link can be established between the agency and parents.

Finally, in order to enhance your next university or college application, applying for a job for the year could be an even better option than spending a year travelling. Not only will it provide you with some financial security but it will also introduce you to the world of work, which could be more challenging than the Inca Trail!

CHOOSING YOUR UNIVERSITY OR COLLEGE

The choice

You choose a holiday because of its location (noisy or quiet), the accommodation and the facilities. It's the same with universities or colleges, some are in or near a city; others are in quiet rural locations. Some have good accommodation for students. Some not. Some are easy to reach, others are at a distance. You already know where some of the very popular universities are located, others you have no idea! Don't let that put you off. Find out where they are.

So once you have chosen your degree find out as much as you can about the universities or colleges offering it and go and pay a visit and **talk to the students, particularly those taking your choice of degree** – they will tell you the good and not so good points about the university and the course. Institutions always arrange open days, although you can walk on to the campuses at any time without prior arrangement.

ACTION POINTS

Before deciding on your preferred universities and courses, check out the following points.

Teaching staff

How do the students react to their tutors? Do staff have a flair and enthusiasm for their subject? Are they approachable? Do they mark your work regularly and is the feedback helpful, or are you left to get on with your own work with very little direction? What are the research interests of the staff?

Teaching styles

How will you be taught, for example, lectures, seminars, tutorials? Are lectures popular? If not, why not? How much online learning will you have? How much time will you be expected to work on your own? If there are field courses, how often are they arranged and are they compulsory? How much will they cost?

Facilities

Are the facilities of a high standard and easily available? Is the laboratory equipment 'state of the art' or just adequate? Are the libraries well-stocked with software packages, books and journals? What are the computing facilities? Is there plenty of space to study or do rooms and workspaces become overcrowded? Do students have to pay for any materials?

New students

Are there induction courses for new students? What student services and facilities are available? Is it possible to buy second-hand copies of set books?

Work placements

Are work placements an optional or compulsory part of the course? Who arranges them? Are the placements popular? Do they count towards your degree? Are work placements paid? How long are they?

Transferable skills

Transferable skills are now regarded as important by all future employers. Does the department provide training in communication skills, teamwork, time-management and information technology as part of the degree course?

Accommodation
How easy is it to find accommodation? Where are the halls of residence? Are they conveniently located for libraries and lecture theatres? Are they self-catering? Alternatively, what is the cost of meals in the university refectory? Which types of student accommodation are the most popular? What is the annual cost of accommodation? If there is more than one campus, is a shuttle-bus service provided?

Costs
Find out the costs of materials, accommodation and travel in addition to tuition fees (see below) and your own personal needs. What are the opportunities for earning money, on or off campus? Does the department or faculty have any rules about part-time employment?

FINANCE: WHAT WILL IT COST AND WHAT HELP IS THERE?
Tuition fees and other costs
Tuition fees are charged for degree courses in England, Wales and Northern Ireland. Precise details of the level of the tuition fee to be charged will appear on each university and college website since levels may vary. The maximum fee currently set for English institutions is £9,250 per year, in Wales it is £9,000, and in Northern Ireland £4,395 for their home students, but the full fee for students from elsewhere in the UK. (For accelerated degrees universities in England can charge annual fees of £11,000.) Eligible students in Scotland pay £1,820 which is covered by the Student Awards Agency for Scotland (SAAS); other UK students pay the full fee of £9,250 in Scottish universities. Tuition fee loans are available and are repaid once the student has graduated and is earning above a certain threshold; for students in England and Wales this is when they are earning more than £26,575 (£18,935 for students in Scotland and Northern Ireland).

Students also face additional charges covering university accommodation (usually, the highest single cost in a typically weekly budget and may vary between universities), on top of which there are personal living costs, and possibly travel expenses. Certain courses will also require students to pay for special equipment, particularly for courses of a practical nature such as Art, Architecture, and Music.

Maintenance loans are available for students to help with living costs, which are means-tested. Details are available from local authorities and university websites. Disabled Students' Allowances (DSAs) (non-repayable) are also available to those who live in England, to cover some of the extra costs because of mental health problems, physical disabilities, long-term illness or learning difficulties, for example dyslexia or dyspraxia. These allowances come on top of any other student finance and do not depend on household income. (See www.gov.uk/disabled-students–allowances-dsas and www.thestudentroom.co.uk/student-finance.)

University scholarships These are usually merit-based and are often competitive although some universities offer valuable scholarships to any new entrant who has achieved top grades at A-level. Scholarships vary considerably and are often subject-specific, offered through faculties or departments, so check the availability of any awards with the subject departmental head. Additionally, there are often music, choral and organ awards, and scholarships and bursaries for sporting achievement. Entry scholarships are offered by several universities which normally stipulate that the applicant must place the university as their first choice and achieve the specified high grades. Changes in bursaries and scholarships take place every year so it is important to check university and college websites. See also www.thecompleteuniversityguide.co.uk.

University bursaries These are usually paid in cases of financial need: all universities charging course fees are obliged to offer some bursaries to students from lower-income families. The term 'bursary' is usually used to denote an award to students requiring financial assistance or who are disadvantaged in various ways. Universities are committed to fair access to all students from lower income backgrounds and individual universities and colleges have bursaries, trust funds and sponsorships for those students, although reports suggest that many such students fail to claim the money due to them. These non-repayable awards are linked to the student's family income and vary between universities. See also www.thecompleteuniversityguide.co.uk.

Useful websites   Students from England www.gov.uk/student-finance
Students from Scotland www.saas.gov.uk
Students from Wales www.studentfinancewales.co.uk
Students from Northern Ireland www.studentfinanceni.co.uk

For comprehensive finance information see the useful websites above and other sources listed in **Appendix 4**.

INFORMATION SOURCES

Prospectuses, websites and Open Days are key sources of the information you need to decide where to study and at the back of this book a directory of institutions is provided, with full contact details, for you to use in your research. Other sources of information include the books and websites listed in **Appendix 4**, the professional associations listed in **Appendix 3**, and the websites given in the subject tables in **Chapter 7**. It is important to take time to find out as much as you can about your preferred universities, colleges and courses, and to explore their similarities and differences. The following chapter **University and College Profiles** gives you information about the types of courses offered by each university and how they are organised. This is important information that you need to know when choosing your university or college because those factors affect, for example, the amount of choice you have in what you study, and the opportunities you have for sandwich placements (see **Chapter 1**). You therefore need to read **Chapter 3** to give you an insight into universities so that you can find the one that is right for you.

UNIVERSITY AND COLLEGE PROFILES

UNIVERSITIES, COLLEGES AND THEIR COURSES

Choosing a degree subject is one step of the way to higher education (see **Chapter 1**), choosing a university or college is the next stage (see **Chapters 2** and **9**). However, in addition to such features as location, entry requirements, accommodation, students' facilities and the subjects offered, many universities differ in the way they organise and teach their courses. The course profiles which follow aim to identify the main course features of each of the institutions and to provide some brief notes about the types of courses they offer and how they differ.

Although universities and colleges have their own distinct identities and course characteristics, they have many similarities. Apart from full-time and sandwich courses, one-year Foundation courses are also offered in many subjects which can help the student to either convert or build on existing qualifications to enable them to start an Honours degree programme. All universities and colleges also offer one-year international Foundation courses for overseas students to provide a preliminary introduction to courses and often to provide English language tuition.

ADMISSIONS POLICIES

Although the UCAS application process is standard for all undergraduate Honours degree courses (see **Chapter 4**) the admissions policies adopted by individual departments in universities and colleges often differ, and will depend on the popularity of the course and the quality of applicants.

Mature students (defined as those aged over 21 on entry) are often interviewed. Normal published offers may not apply to mature students. In all institutions certain courses require Disclosure and Barring Service (DBS) checks or medical examinations; students should check these requirements before applying for courses.

The acceptance of deferred entry varies, depending on the chosen course, and many admissions tutors ask that the intention to take a Gap Year be included on the application if firm arrangements have been made.

Several universities and colleges advise that if a student fails to achieve the grades required for an offer, they may still be awarded a place; however, they may receive a changed offer for an alternative course. Applicants are strongly advised to be wary of such offers, unless the course is similar to the original course choice.

Applicants for places at popular universities or for popular courses cannot assume that they will receive an offer even if their predicted grades are the same or higher than a stated standard offer. Even though the government has now removed the cap on the number of places that universities in England are able to offer, meaning that they can admit an unlimited number of home and EU undergraduates for most courses, not every institution has adopted these reforms.

All institutions have a number of schemes in place to enable admissions tutors to identify and make offers to applicants who, for example, may have had their education affected by circumstances outside their control. A major initiative is Widening Participation in which various schemes can assist school and college students in getting into university. These programmes focus on specific groups of students and communities including:

- students from low participation areas
- low-performing schools and colleges or those without a strong history of progression to higher education
- students with disabilities

- people living in deprived geographical areas, including deprived rural areas
- students from black or ethnic minority backgrounds
- students from the lower socio-economic groups 4–8 including mature learners
- students requiring financial assistance or who are disadvantaged in various ways
- families with little or no experience of higher education
- students from homes with low household incomes
- students returning to study after a period of time spent away.

Applicants are strongly advised to check prospectuses and websites for up-to-date information on admissions and, in particular, on alternative qualifications to A-levels as well as any entrance test to be taken (see also **Chapter 5**). Applicants whose first language is not English should refer to **Chapter 8** for details of the English Language entry requirements.

The following information provides a selection of relevant aspects of admissions policies and practice for the institutions listed.

COURSE AND ADMISSIONS PROFILES

Aberdeen One of the oldest universities in the UK, based on two campuses. Students applying for the MA degree in Arts and Social Sciences are admitted to a degree rather than a subject, selecting from a range of courses in the first year, leading up to the final choice of subject and Honours course in the fourth year. The BSc degree is also flexible but within the Science framework. Engineering students follow a common core course in Years 1 and 2, specialising in Year 3. There is less flexibility, however, in some vocational courses such as Accountancy, Law, Medicine and Dentistry. For some degree programmes, highly qualified applicants may be admitted to the second year of the course. Courses include Divinity and Theology, Music, Life Sciences, Medical Sciences and Business.

In personal statements and the referees' reports, selectors look for evidence of subject knowledge and understanding, commitment, motivation and responsibility, and the ability to cope with a university education. All degrees make unconditional offers, which, in the Scottish university tradition, admit students to study their specific subject within its broader subject area, for example Engineering. The university also makes contextual offers; information on these can be found at www.abdn.ac.uk/study/undergraduate/widening-access-criteria--2848.php

Abertay A city centre university in Dundee. Courses have a strong vocational bias and are offered in the Schools of Science, Engineering and Technology, Business, Social and Health Sciences, Arts, Media, and Computer Games which is a centre of excellence.

Only applicants for the Mental Health Nursing degree are interviewed. Applicants for the Computer Arts degree are required to provide a portfolio of artworks. The University can make contextual offers to disadvantaged applicants. Most courses offer built-in placements to try out different jobs. Ethical Hacking, Computer Games Design, and Psychology did not go into Clearing in 2019. Make sure to check the website for the most up-to-date information before applying.

Aberystwyth The University offers Single, Joint and major/minor Honours courses on a modular basis. In Year 1 core topics related to the chosen subject are studied alongside optional subjects. This arrangement allows some flexibility for change when choosing final degree subjects in Years 2 and 3 provided appropriate pathways and module prerequisites are followed. Some students take a year in industry or commerce between Years 2 and 3.

All offers are made on the basis of academic criteria, and personal statements and references are important. Offers will be made predominantly on the basis of the application form but interviews are required for some subjects. Candidates will not normally be interviewed unless there are special reasons for doing so, eg the candidate has been away from study for a long time. Decisions are normally made within four weeks of receiving the application and all those receiving an offer will be invited to visit the University and their chosen academic department.

AECC (UC) AECC University College specialises in chiropractic and other healthcare disciplines.

For information on admissions procedures see their website: www.aecc.ac.uk.

Anglia Ruskin The University has campuses in Cambridge, Chelmsford, London and Peterborough. Courses are modular which enables students to choose from a range of topics in addition to the compulsory subject core modules. Courses are delivered by five faculties: the Lord Ashcroft International Business School, Faculty of Arts, Law & Social Sciences, Faculty of Science & Technology, Faculty of Health, Social Care & Education and Faculty of Medical Science. Many programmes have a strong vocational focus, with a focus on employability, and opportunities for placements and/or study abroad.

The University interviews all shortlisted applicants for Art and Design, Paramedic Science, Nursing, Social Work, Midwifery, English, Media, Law, Humanities and Social Sciences courses. Maths and English testing is also used for Nursing, Midwifery, Paramedic Science and Social Work courses. For details of entry to the School of Medicine, see the university website.

Arden This private university offers career-focused online distance learning courses worldwide, as well as blended learning study at their following UK study centres: Ealing, Tower Hill, Holborn, Birmingham and Manchester.

Arts London University of the Arts London (UAL) is Europe's largest specialist art and design university, comprising six colleges: Camberwell College of Arts, Central Saint Martins, Chelsea College of Arts, London College of Communication, London College of Fashion and Wimbledon College of Arts. Together, the colleges offer a wealth of courses at pre-degree, undergraduate and postgraduate level in Art, Design, Fashion, Media, Communication and Performing Arts.

In addition to formally qualified applicants, UAL welcomes applications from candidates who can demonstrate equivalent skills and knowledge gained from work or life experience. The application process varies depending on the chosen course and whether the applicant is from the UK, EU or from a country outside the EU. Many courses require candidates to submit a portfolio of work and attend an interview as part of the selection process.

Aston A campus university in Birmingham city centre. The University offers modular courses in Single Honours degrees and Joint Honours (usually in related areas). Most degrees allow students to spend the third year on a one-year sandwich placement. Courses are taught in the Schools of Engineering and Applied Science, Languages and Social Sciences, Life and Health Sciences, Aston Medical School and in the Aston Business School.

Offers are not normally made simply on the basis of UCAS points. Interviews are only used in special cases, for example, mature students, or those with non-standard entry qualifications. BTEC awards are acceptable and a mix of BTEC and A-levels welcomed. High-achieving Level 3 Diploma students in relevant subjects will be considered. Key Skills will be taken into account but will not be included in offers; Access programmes are accepted.

Bangor Bangor University is situated in scenic North Wales, between the mountains and the sea. There is a wide range of subjects to choose from including Ocean Sciences, Psychology, Medical Sciences, Linguistics, Chemistry, Engineering and Law. Students can study a Single Honours course or choose to combine the study of two subjects from a range of Joint Honours courses. Some courses offer a four-year undergraduate degree eg MEnvSci, MSci, MArts, MEng, MChem. New courses being introduced for 2021 include Adventure Sport Science, Computer Science and Games Design, Law, Marketing, Music Psychology with Forensic Psychology and Zoology.

The University considers each application on its merit – assessing your potential to succeed on and benefit from the course. It uses the UCAS Tariff when making offers in addition to programme-specific requirements. For a degree course, the points total should include at least two GCE A-levels or equivalent Level 3 qualifications (eg BTECs, Access, Irish Highers, International Baccalaureate, Welsh Baccalaureate, Scottish Advanced Highers and others). The University also welcomes applications from mature applicants, individuals with European qualifications and international applicants (subject to minimum English language requirements). Merit and Entrance Scholarships are offered in most subjects.

Bath The University is situated on a large campus on a hill above the city. It is well-known for its Sports Training Village (STV), which is equipped with Olympic standard training facilities for swimming, athletics, shooting and bobsleigh. The academic year is divided into two semesters with Single and Combined

Honours degrees composed of core units and optional units, allowing students some flexibility in shaping their courses with 10–12 units taken each year. A central feature of all programmes is the opportunity to take a professional placement as part of the degree: this is usually taken as either one 12-month placement or two periods of six months.

Some departments interview promising applicants; those not receiving an offer can obtain feedback on the reasons for their rejection. Students are encouraged to take the Extended Project and to provide details on their personal statement.

Bath Spa Bath Spa is largely located on a green campus outside the city of Bath. It offers a full complement of creative, cultural and humanities-based courses, alongside social sciences and sciences. Most courses – Single Honours awards, specialised awards and Combined Honours awards – are part of a flexible modular scheme with students taking up to six modules per year.

All eligible candidates for Art & Design and Music & Performing Arts courses are invited to attend an interview or audition. Applicants with offers for subjects which do not require an audition or interview, and are not taught at a partner college, will be invited to an Applicant Visit Day. Gap years are acceptable for most courses.

Bedfordshire The campuses of Bedfordshire University are situated in Luton, Bedford, Milton Keynes, Aylesbury and Putteridge Bury. Its courses place a strong focus on entrepreneurship, not just employability. Many courses receive professional accreditation. A current Student Internship Scheme (SIS) operates, providing students with the opportunity to gain paid-for work experience, with flexible hours to fit around their studies. A Go Global programme gives students the opportunity to participate in two-week language and cultural programmes with one of Bedfordshire's partner universities. There is also a Get Into Sport programme offering students free membership throughout the year.

The University offers advice and guidance to enquirers and applicants throughout the admissions process via its website, www.beds.ac.uk/howtoapply/admissions or via its live chat function. The University considers applicants with a wide range of Level 3 qualifications and will hold interviews and auditions for a number of courses.

Birmingham The University is situated on a large campus on the edge of the city centre. Single subject and Joint Honours courses are offered. In Joint Honours courses the two chosen subjects may have common ground or can be disparate, for example Mathematics and a modern language. Some major/minor combinations are also possible. The modular system provides opportunities for students to study a subject outside their main degree. An International Foundation Year (Birmingham Foundation Academy) is available for overseas students from 12-year secondary education systems.

An Unconditional Offers Scheme applies (see website). Courses are academic and 75% of the personal statement should relate to why the applicant wants to study the subject for which they have applied. The Extended Project Qualification (EPQ) is accepted in addition to three A-levels with applicants being made an alternative offer of one grade lower plus the EPQ in addition to the standard offer. The University now has a standard overall IB points requirement for every course and makes offers relating to the higher level subject scores. Gap years are acceptable and should be mentioned on the UCAS application or as soon as arrangements have been made.

Birmingham City Courses are offered on three main campuses and additional sites throughout the city. Many courses have a vocational focus and include sandwich placements. Music and Acting is offered through the Birmingham Conservatoire. There is also an extensive International Exchange Programme, with many courses abroad being taught in English.

Admissions are administered centrally through the Admissions Unit in the Academic Registry. Some applicants will be called to interview and others invited to the department before an offer is made. If the required grades of an offer are not achieved it may still be possible to be accepted on to a course. Deferred entry can be arranged.

Birmingham (UC) The University College offers degrees within the hospitality and tourism sectors, which are awarded by the University of Birmingham. It is Europe's leading specialist in management courses for the culinary arts, hospitality and tourism management, and is also situated in the heart of

Birmingham. Teaching benefits from its central location too: it's based in the conference and hotel quarter, which means opportunities for practical experience are on its doorstep. Its vocational degree courses, experienced tutors and strong links with business give students the skills they need to tackle a career in a range of rapidly expanding industries. There are international study-exchange opportunities including industrial placement opportunities throughout Europe, the USA and the UK.

Applications must be made through UCAS. Students can apply online at www.ucas.com. Students wishing to apply for part-time courses should apply direct to the University College. Please contact the Admissions Office for further information.

Bishop Grosseteste A single-site university campus close to Lincoln city centre. It has a strong reputation in Primary Education courses but also offers a varied selection of subjects at Foundation and Single Honours degree as well as a very large number of joint degrees in subject areas such as psychology, sport and the creative arts. Employability is central to all courses with most incorporating work placements and live projects.

Candidates are advised to attend an Open Day prior to applying. Applicant days are held for students who have applied for a non-teaching course or a course that does not require an interview.

Bolton A small, tight-knit university community in Bolton, with an excellent reputation for student support. A range of courses are offered, designed with the workplace in mind, with many offering vocational or professional content and work experience elements. The University offers a number of two-year Foundation courses, including fashion, media production and cloud computing.

Academic offers are based on UCAS points from at least two A-levels (or equivalent) for most courses. The University is committed to giving equal consideration to factors other than formal academic qualifications such as work experience and vocational qualifications – any relevant information should be listed in the application.

Bournemouth The University has a strong focus on employability and offers a range of undergraduate degrees leading to BA, BSc and LLB. Courses are designed with direct input from employers, there's a work placement opportunity for every student (including opportunities to work and study abroad), and courses are accredited by the biggest names in industry. Most placements are paid. Mandatory placements are part of courses in Marketing Communications, Sport Management, Events Management, International Hospitality and Tourism Management. The University offers subjects in all aspects of Management, Media & Communication, Science & Technology and Health & Social Sciences.

Academic qualifications are an important part of the application, but this is not the only factor Bournemouth take into account when assessing applications. They look at each application on an individual basis and can make contextual offers, particularly in Social Work, Nursing and Finance. Offer making will typically be based on A-level equivalent qualifications, including any required subjects. Additional study may be valuable for breadth of study, and the University will look at a range of qualifications and subjects, including the AS and Extended Project Qualification. Lower offers were made in 2019 for Accounting, Finance and Economics, Midwifery, Nursing and Social Work. Unconditional offers were made in Business and Management, Film, Games Design and Psychology.

Bournemouth Arts Arts University Bournemouth specialises in arts, performance, design and media courses. The majority of courses offer industry placements and live briefs within the course. AUB courses are designed to prepare students for the creative industries.

The University interviews the majority of applicants who meet or potentially will meet entry requirements or invites them to a post-offer Applicant Day. There is a selection process which is based on each applicant's UCAS application, qualifications and an electronic portfolio. Film, Dance, Acting, Animation, Make-up, Fine Art, and Illustration did not go into Clearing in 2019.

BPP A private university with study centres throughout England. Courses focus on business and the professions covering Business, Law, Accountancy, Psychology and Health subjects.

A range of qualifications will be considered.

Bradford A city centre university. Honours degree courses are offered, many of which are vocational, leading to professional accreditation, and include sandwich placements in industry and commerce. Subjects are taught in the Faculty of Engineering and Informatics, the Faculty of Health Studies, the Faculty of Life Sciences, the Faculty of Management and Law and the Faculty of Social Sciences.

Offers will be based on UCAS points. Many courses require specific subjects to A-level standard or the equivalent, with particular grades. The University's typical offers are a guide; other factors other than academic achievement will be taken into account, such as evidence of relevant experience, skills or ability. GCSE English at grade 4 or C and above – or the equivalent – is a standard requirement for all courses and GCSE Maths at grade 4 or C is required for many more. Some courses require an interview as part of the selection criteria. Full details are online at: www.bradford.ac.uk/undergraduate. All students whose first language is not English need to demonstrate a minimum standard in English language such as IELTS 6.0 or the equivalent, with no subtest less than 5.5. In 2019 most vacancies existed in Business and Management and Clinical Sciences. Popular subjects in which lower offers were made were in Accounting, Business, Chemistry, Engineering, Law, Computer Science and Film and Media. Subjects that did not go into Clearing included Optometry, Diagnostic Radiography, Midwifery and Child Nursing.

Brighton BA, BSc and BEng courses are offered, many with salaried industrial placements including some in Europe, the USA and Canada. Over 500 courses are on offer at this popular university on the south coast.

Brighton welcomes applications from students with qualifications and experience other than traditional A-levels. Access courses and BTEC are acceptable alternative qualifications. The University has a Widening Participation initiative across all its courses including Medicine and makes contextual offers in consideration of applicants' backgrounds.

Brighton and Sussex (MS) Students have the opportunity to use facilities on the University of Brighton and the University of Sussex campuses, and in Year 1 can choose on which campus they would like to live. However, as the BSMS term dates currently fall outside of the term dates advertised by the University of Sussex and the University of Brighton, applicants have the choice of living at Lewes Court Halls of Residence at Sussex or Paddock Fields Halls of Residence at University of Brighton. All Year 1 Medical School students are guaranteed accommodation as long as they apply by the deadline (some students who live in the immediate local area may not be able to apply for accommodation due to more applicants requiring housing than rooms available). Students spend their first two years on the Falmer campus and then move on to associated teaching hospitals and community settings. Teaching is 'systems integrated' so students are exposed to the clinical environment from Year 1. Cadaver dissection is also part of the course from Year 1, so students get a real understanding of human anatomy, enhancing their learning experience. As the Medical School is small, so are class sizes, meaning that students have a strong relationship with academic and support staff.

Standard offers usually include three A grades at A-level with a minimum of an A grade in biology and chemistry. All applicants, to include graduates and Access applicants, are required to have a grade B or above or grade 6 or above in GCSE Maths and English Language or English Literature.

Bristol A leading research university offering Single or Joint Honours degrees. A number of courses include a year of industrial experience or the opportunity to study or work abroad. Most courses take three or four years to complete and are modular in structure. Dentistry, Medicine and Veterinary Science are longer in duration and take five or six years to complete. Most Science and Engineering courses offer a choice of four-year integrated master's (MEng, MSci) as well as the three-year bachelor's (BEng, BSc) courses.

Bristol is a popular university with a high level of competition for places on all courses. A* grades may be included in the offers for some applicants depending on the application and the course applied for; where it may be included, this is shown in the typical offers published in the online course finder. Students choosing to take the Extended Project may receive two offers, one of which includes the Extended Project, for example, AAA or AAB plus the Extended Project. The University does not generally use unit grade information when making a decision, but it may be used if applicants do not meet the terms of their offer. Most subjects will consider an application to defer entry, but you should indicate your intention to defer in your personal statement, giving information about your plans. In fairness to applicants applying in the next admissions cycle, the number of deferred places may be limited. Applicants for Law will be required to sit the LNAT (see Chapter 5). The acceptability of resitting qualifications varies depending on the course, and is outlined in each course's admissions statement. The following courses always hold interviews before making an offer: Dentistry, Medicine, Veterinary Nursing and Bioveterinary Science and Veterinary Science. Further information is available on the applicants' web pages: http://bristol.ac.uk/applicants. Information on how to apply can be found in the online course finder: www.bristol.ac.uk/study/undergraduate/apply.

Brunel A campus-based university in West London (Uxbridge). All courses are made up of self-contained modules enabling students, within their scheme of studies, to choose a broad range of topics or greater specialisation as they prefer. Some modern language modules may be taken, depending on the timetable of the chosen subjects. Almost all degree courses are available in a three-year full-time mode or in four-year thick or thin sandwich courses which combine academic work with industrial experience organised through a very successful on-campus placement centre. Some exchange schemes also operate in Europe, USA and other worldwide locations. Degree programmes are offered across three Colleges: College of Engineering, Design and Physical Science (including Computing and Maths), College of Business, Arts and Social Sciences (including Theatre, Education, Journalism, English and Law) and the College of Health and Life Science (including Biomedical Science, Psychology, Physiotherapy, Occupational Therapy and Sport Science). Many courses are accredited by professional institutions recognised by employers. Please follow this link to view available courses: www.brunel.ac.uk/courses/course-finder.

All applicants are interviewed for Design, Electrical Engineering, Physiotherapy, Occupational Therapy, Journalism, Theatre and Education courses. The required grades for your course must normally come from at least three full A-level passes, although candidates offering a combination of AS and A-levels or BTEC and A-level courses may be considered. All applicants usually need a minimum of five GCSEs at grade C or grade 4 or above, including English and Maths. Some courses may require a higher grade at GCSE in English and/or Maths, and some courses specify additional subjects – all GCSE requirements are listed on the website. Popular courses that did not go into Clearing in 2019 included Physiotherapy, Computer Science and Business Computing. Courses that did go into Clearing included Economics, Accounting and Finance, Flood and Coastal Engineering and Law.

Buckingham The private University of Buckingham has around 2,000 students and all facilities are within 10 minutes' walking distance. It specialises in subjects where employment prospects are good. Its law school puts a heavy emphasis on international and commercial subjects, while its Business school has developed a strong service management specialism, and is the first to establish an undergraduate Venture Creation Programme (Business Enterprise). The University's Computing courses offer career development opportunities with flexible modes of study. It is the first university to launch an independent medical school. The University offers a range of undergraduate programmes, with entry points in January, July and September and students can complete a traditional three year Honours degree in just two years.

Candidates apply through UCAS or directly online via the University's website. Following the reforms of A-levels and GCSEs, and the changes to the UCAS Tariff, the University makes grade offers based on the best three A-levels taken.

Bucks New Students choose from a wide range of subjects in two faculties – Design, Media and Management (Art, Design, Music, Policing, Media, Business, Travel & Tourism, Computing, Law and Sport) and Society and Health (Nursing, Social Work, Operating Department Practitioner, Health and Social Care, Psychology, Social Sciences). The Uxbridge campus is just a short walk from a London Underground tube station and the High Wycombe campus is 40 minutes to Central London.

The University is happy to consider applicants on a case by case basis and mature students (aged 21+) with relevant experience/interest are encouraged to apply. It accepts a range of equivalent qualifications at Level 3 and requires Level 2 maths and English for the majority of its courses. Admissions tests will be used for entry to Nursing and Social Work courses. The university offers an unconditional offer scheme for certain courses.

Cambridge The University has 29 undergraduate colleges located throughout the city: Christ's, Churchill, Clare, Corpus Christi, Downing, Emmanuel, Fitzwilliam, Girton, Gonville and Caius, Homerton, Hughes Hall (mature students only), Jesus, King's, Lucy Cavendish (mature, female students only), Magdalene, Murray Edwards (female students only), Newnham (female students only), Pembroke, Peterhouse, Queens', Robinson, St Catharine's, St Edmund's (mature students only), St John's, Selwyn, Sidney Sussex, Trinity, Trinity Hall, and Wolfson (mature students only). Undergraduate courses are offered in Arts and Sciences. Three-year degree courses (Triposes) provide a broad introduction to the subject followed by options at a later stage, and are divided into Part 1 (one or two years) and Part 2. In some Science and Engineering courses there is a fourth year (Part 3). Students studying courses in Modern and Medieval Languages and Asian and Middle Eastern Studies participate in a year abroad. In college-based teaching sessions (supervisions), essays are set for discussion to support university lectures, seminars and practicals.

The typical A-level offer for arts subjects (excluding Economics) and for Psychological and Behavioural Sciences is A*AA. For science subjects (excluding Psychological and Behavioural Sciences) and Economics it is A*A*A. Colleges modify offers to take account of individual circumstances. Self-discipline, motivation and commitment are required together with the ability to think critically and independently, plus passion or, at the very least, real enthusiasm for the chosen course. If examination predictions are good then the chance of admission may be better than one in five. Applicants are encouraged to take the Extended Project although it will not be a requirement of any offer. Critical Thinking is not considered acceptable as a third A-level subject for any course at Cambridge. The colleges at the University of Cambridge use common-format written assessments, to be taken by applicants for all subjects except Mathematics and Music. Applicants will take the written assessments either pre-interview or at interview, depending on the course for which they apply. Please see www.undergraduate.study.cam.ac.uk/applying/admissions-assessments and www.admissionstestingservice.org for further information on these assessments, and Chapter 5 for information you need to know before completing and submitting your application. Natural Sciences receives the most applications, Classics (four years) receives the fewest. Cambridge is strongly in favour of and will continue to use UMS scores at the end of Year 12 as long as they are available. Students are strongly encouraged to take at least three and possibly four subjects, reformed or not, at the end of Year 12. Information should appear in the UCAS reference in cases where school policy limits the student's opportunity to take AS subjects. See www.undergraduate.study.cam.ac.uk.

Canterbury Christ Church The University offers a wide range of BA, BSc, LLB and BMus programmes as well as an extensive Combined Honours scheme. The University has a main campus at Canterbury as well as a campus at Medway where a number of Health and Education programmes are taught. The University offers undergraduate initial teacher training (primary and secondary), a wide range of degrees that lead to professions within the National Health Service as well as subjects in Arts and Humanities, Social and Applied Sciences, Childhood and Education Sciences, and Health Studies. Canterbury Christ Church University and the University of Kent have been awarded funding to establish a new medical school, with places due to become available for 2020 entry.

Applications are considered individually and the university takes into account academic qualifications in addition to paying great attention to the personal statement and the reference(s) provided. All offers are tailored to individual applications. Currently the university asks for between 88–120 UCAS points for entry onto Year 1 of an undergraduate degree. Some courses require you to achieve specific grades and for some you need to have studied a particular subject. They offer a range of extended degrees where students can study a foundation year (Year 0) and then progress onto Year 1 (Level 4) of the degree programme. For details about the new forthcoming Kent and Medway Medical school, see the relevant entry in this book and the School's website. The University makes contextual offers to Medicine and Surgery applicants from disadvantaged backgrounds.

Cardiff A city centre university. All students taking the very flexible BA degree study three subjects in the first year and then follow a Single or Joint Honours course in their chosen subject(s). Similarly, BSc Economics courses offer the option to transfer to an alternative degree course at the end of Year 1, depending on the subjects originally chosen. Many degree schemes have a vocational and professional content with a period of attachment in industry, and there are well-established links with universities abroad.

Applicants are required to take only three A-levels for degree courses. Deferred entry is acceptable. The 14–19 Diploma is an acceptable qualification for entry. Key Skills should be mentioned in an application but will not form part of an offer.

Cardiff Met Campuses are located at Llandaff, Cyncoed and in the city centre Howard Gardens. Cardiff Metropolitan University specialises in courses that are career-orientated and have been designed in conjunction with business and industry. All of the courses are created with the working world in mind and include work placements, visiting lecturers, and options for sandwich courses.

Students from Foundation degree courses or with HNC/HND qualifications should contact the course director before applying.

Central Lancashire The University is based on a single site campus in Preston city centre, with a smaller campus at Burnley. It has 20 academic schools covering a wide range of subjects. Many subjects offer optional modules which gives extra choice within programmes. Foundation entry route is available for most Honours degree programmes. A number of integrated master's courses are offered, in addition to sandwich courses.

For entry to Honours degree programmes, the University looks for a minimum of 104–120 points at A-level or equivalent, or 72 points at A-level or equivalent for Foundation entry. Some courses also require an interview, audition or portfolio.

Chester The University of Chester offers an extensive range of Single and Combined Honours courses across its six sites: from Arts and Media, Science and Engineering, Social Sciences, Humanities, Business and Management, and specialist vocational pathways to nursing and education. Courses in Media, Business, Public Services, and Sport are based at the Warrington Campus. The University also accredits entrepreneurial degree courses at the University Centre Shrewsbury and the new Faculty of Agriculture and Veterinary Science is located at University Centre Reaseheath in Nantwich. Students can apply for paid sandwich placements in consultation with their faculty during their second year of study.

For entry requirements and to see what qualifications the University accepts, refer to the specific course page on the University of Chester's website (www1.chester.ac.uk/study/undergraduate). Interviews, workshops and portfolios are required for some courses to support applications. Any questions should be directed to the admissions team using the details above.

Chichester Degree courses are offered in a range of subjects covering Acting, Dance, English & Creative Writing, Fine Art, History, Music, Musical Theatre, PE, Philosophy, Politics, Psychology, Sport & Exercise Sciences and Theology at Chichester, and Business & Management, Creative & Digital Technologies, Education, Engineering & Design and Maths at the Bognor Regis campus. The Business School and Outdoor Adventure Education offer paid work experience placements.

Applicants will be interviewed for professional programmes (eg Early Childhood; Teacher Training). Applicants for programmes in the creative arts (eg Dance) will be auditioned. Most other decisions are made on the basis of the application form. The University of Chichester does not make unconditional offers to applicants still awaiting their exam results.

City The University, based in central London, offers a wide range of three-year and four-year programmes leading to degrees in Business, Management, Finance and Accounting, Computing, Engineering and Mathematical Sciences, English, Health Sciences including Nursing, Radiography and Speech Therapy, History, Law, Music and Social Sciences. Some schools and departments provide a common first year, allowing students to make a final decision on their degree course at the end of the first year. Students in some subject areas may apply to study abroad.

Most typical offers are made on the basis of three A-levels or alternative equivalent qualifications. There will also be flexible offers whereby an applicant's offer may be reduced in return for putting City as the firm choice through UCAS. In some instances an applicant may be made an unconditional offer in return for putting City as the firm choice. This only occurs after a strict triage of the application and including a review of all past achievements and the personal statement.

Coventry Coventry University courses are designed with employability in mind. Most courses offer the chance to spend a year working in industry or working or studying abroad. Most courses also include a mandatory Add+vantage module that allows students to study their choice of a wide range of career-related subjects as part of their degree. Individual programmes of study are usually made up of compulsory modules, core options from a prescribed list and free choice modules.

The University is committed to excellence in admissions and aims to provide a professional, fair, equal and transparent service to all applicants. The University operates a centralised admissions service for full-time undergraduate applications. Applications from UK students are managed by the Recruitment and Admissions Office. Applications from the EU and overseas are managed by the International Office. The University also welcomes applications from those who have significant work or life experience and who may not necessarily meet the published academic requirements for their chosen course. Coventry University makes offers for full degree courses based on three A-levels (or equivalent). AS are not usually included in these offers, and there are no plans at present to make any changes to this approach. Those applicants whose school or college chooses to purely offer the new linear A-levels will therefore not be disadvantaged in any way if applying without additional qualifications.

Cranfield A postgraduate university, specialising in technology and management. Cranfield offers courses in aerospace, defence and security, energy and power, environment and agrifood, manufacturing, transport systems, water, and management. See the website for more details: www.cranfield.ac.uk.

Creative Arts Foundation and Honours degree courses are offered covering Art and Design, Architecture, Media and Communications at this specialist university with campuses at Canterbury, Epsom, Farnham and Rochester. Interviews and portfolios are not required for all courses. There is no minimum age requirement for entry to undergraduate courses.

Cumbria The University of Cumbria offers a wide range of courses, both taught and research-based, spanning arts, business, education, health, humanities, law, policing, social science, sport, STEM and the outdoors. The University has an extensive portfolio at both undergraduate level and postgraduate level and many courses have the option to undertake placements which gives students the much needed practical experience.

The University accepts a wide range of qualifications for course entry. Required Tariff points vary across all disciplines and some courses have specific GCSE requirements. All entry requirements and course codes can be found on its website, in its prospectus or on the UCAS website. Its institutional code is C99. The University also offers undergraduate courses with Foundation entry. A new addition to the wide range of opportunities it already offers, Foundation entry is an alternative route to accessing higher education and all the experiences you'd expect as a full-time student.

De Montfort De Montfort University Leicester (DMU) offers a wide range of undergraduate and postgraduate courses, both full-time and part-time, tailored to meet the needs of today's employers.

DMU welcomes applications from UK, European and international students with a wide range of qualifications and experience. Current entry and admissions requirements are published on its website. These may differ from criteria in the printed undergraduate prospectus or course brochures – the online information is always the most up-to-date.

Derby Courses at the Derby campus are offered across three subject areas: Arts, Design and Technology, Business and Education, and Health and Sciences, while at the Buxton campus Foundation degrees are offered as well as some BA and BSc degrees. There is also a comprehensive Joint Honours programme offering two subjects and Combined Honours courses with a choice of up to three subjects. Major/minor courses are also available. Courses are offered at three campuses, Derby, Buxton and Chesterfield. Check website.

The Level 2 Diploma is regarded as equivalent to GCSEs and the Level 3 Diploma to A-levels. Students without formal qualifications can take an Access course or the Modular Foundation course to gain entry to degree programmes.

Dundee The University of Dundee offers a wide range of undergraduate degrees. Many of its courses are vocational and offer professional accreditation. Its academic schools cover Art and Design; Science and Engineering; Education and Social Work; Humanities; Social Sciences; Life Sciences; Dentistry; Nursing and Health Sciences; and Medicine.

All applicants will be invited to visit the University after receiving an offer. Some courses interview as part of the admissions process. Advanced entry is available for most courses. For most subjects the entry requirements are shown as 'minimum' and 'typical'. Please note that the University offers a wide range of degree programmes and some have a higher level of competition for places than others. For programmes with a higher level of demand, it will make offers around the 'typical' rather than the 'minimum' level. Offers to applicants who are repeating their examinations will remain the same as any previous offer.

Durham A competitive collegiate university consisting of 16 colleges. Degree options include Single and Joint Honours courses to which subsidiary subjects can be added. There are named routes in Natural Sciences and courses in Liberal Arts and Combined Honours in Social Sciences in which students may design their own degree course by choosing two to three subjects from a wide range.

The Durham admissions policy (www.durham.ac.uk/undergraduate/study/apply/policy) states that the following factors are considered when an application is reviewed: A-level or equivalent grades; GCSE performance; the personal statement; the school/college reference; motivation for the chosen degree programme; independence of thought and working; skills derived from non-academic activities, eg sport, the arts, and voluntary and community work; and contextual evidence of merit and potential. Students applying for more than one type of course or institution may submit a substitute personal statement: please see www.durham.ac.uk/undergraduate/apply/ucas/personalstatement/substitute for further details. Admission decisions are made by admissions selectors. Successful applicants will be informed of the decision on their application before a college is allocated. Durham does not use interviews as a means of selection except in specific circumstances. These include applications to courses where external bodies determine that interviewing is compulsory (for example, applicants to Primary Education), applications to the Foundation Centre, applications where the candidate is without recent and/or relevant qualifications and applications where applicants have had a break in their study prior to application. The need for an interview will be determined by academic departments on an individual basis having considered all the information provided in the application.

Dyson The Dyson Institute of Engineering and Technology in Wiltshire offers a unique four-year BEng in General Engineering, which is accredited by the University of Warwick. The course is integrated with real life engineering practice at the Dyson company site, has no tuition fees and provides a salary from the outset.

There are five stages of assessment on application. See the website for more details: www.dysoninstitute.com/apply/.

East Anglia A campus university on the outskirts of Norwich that has four faculties (Arts and Humanities, Medicine and Health Sciences, Science and Social Sciences). The University maintains an extensive network of international exchanges in which students studying certain degree programmes are able to spend up to a year. During these placements, our students are fully integrated into the culture of the host university.

Offers are normally made in terms of three A-levels. Critical Thinking and General Studies A-levels are not accepted for most courses. Interviews are necessary for some courses. Deferred entry is acceptable. Lower offers are made to disadvantaged students for Humanities and Foundation years.

East London The University, based on the Stratford, Docklands and University Square Stratford campuses in East London, offers Single Honours and Combined Honours programmes. Courses provide a flexibility of choice and are based on a modular structure with compulsory and optional course units. A very large number of extended degrees are also available for applicants who do not have the normal university entrance requirements.

Candidates are advised to apply as soon as possible and results are normally announced within seven days. Some students may be called for interview and in some cases an essay or a portfolio may be required. The interviewers will be looking for evidence of a real interest in the chosen subject. Rejected applicants may receive an offer of a place on an extended degree or on another course.

Edge Hill The University in Ormskirk, Lancashire has three-year programmes including Business, English, Film, Geographical Sciences, History, Law, Media, Midwifery, Nursing, Performance Studies, Social and Psychological Sciences, Sport and Teacher Training. The university will train doctors from 2020.

With the exception of courses in Journalism, Animation, Media (Film and TV), TV Production, Performing Arts, Teacher Training, Nursing and Midwifery, most decisions are made without an interview. Those applicants who receive offers are invited to visit the University. For details of entry to the new medicine course, see the university website.

Edinburgh The ancient University of Edinburgh's degree programmes are designed to include four years of study giving a broad and flexible education. Most programmes in the arts, humanities, engineering, sciences or social sciences allow students to study a range of subjects in Years 1 and 2, before specialising in the next two. There is a considerable choice of subjects although there may be restrictions in the case of high-demand subjects such as English, Economics and Psychology. General or Ordinary degrees take three years and Honours degrees take four years. Joint Honours degrees are also offered.

Entry to Edinburgh is competitive, with the University receiving the second highest volume of applications in the UK. Admission decisions are made by the admissions offices of the University's three colleges: the College of Arts, Humanities and Social Science, the College of Science and Engineering and the College of Medicine and Veterinary Medicine. Decisions on the majority of applications will be made after the UCAS deadline, once all applications have been received. All offers will be expressed in grades, not Tariff points. Make sure to check the website for the latest up-to-date information before applying.

Edinburgh Napier Edinburgh Napier is located across three campuses. Students choose between Single and Joint Honours degrees from a wide range of subjects.

Entry requirements for all courses can be found at www.napier.ac.uk/courses. Where the admissions selection process involves an interview, audition or portfolio review, the application will be sent to the academic department for consideration. This applies to the following programmes: Nursing, Vet Nursing, Journalism, Design programmes, Music, Acting, Film, Photography and Television. Contextual data will be considered when making admissions decisions on all programmes.

Essex The main University campus is located near Colchester. Undergraduate departments are grouped in schools of study covering Humanities, Social Sciences, Law and Sciences, Health and Engineering. Degree schemes in Health and Business are also offered at the Southend campus and degree schemes in Performing Arts are offered at both Southend and Loughton campuses.

The wide range of qualifications the University considers include the following: A-levels, BTEC qualifications, International Baccalaureate Diploma and Diploma Programmes, QAA Approved Access to HE Diplomas, Open University courses and practising professional qualifications. The typical offer for most courses requires applicants to achieve specific grades in three A-levels (or equivalent), although the University considers additional qualifications. Selected UK based applicants are usually called for interview.

Exeter The University has six Academic Colleges: the Business School; the College of Engineering, Maths and Physical Sciences; the College of Humanities; the College of Life and Environmental Sciences; the College of Social Sciences and International Studies; and the University of Exeter Medical School. Most courses include an optional study abroad opportunity. Courses are taught across three main campuses, two in Exeter and one in Cornwall at Penryn near Falmouth. Subjects taught in Cornwall include Biosciences, English, History, Geology and Mining Engineering. New courses are being introduced in 2021 in Accounting, Business, Communications, Economics, English and Creative Writing, Marine Science, Neuroscience, Nutrition, and Politics.

The University welcomes applications from students from all backgrounds. Key indicators include predicted and achieved academic performance in Level 2 and 3 qualifications; candidates would normally be expected to take three A-levels (or the equivalent). Deferred applications are welcome. In 2019 there were vacancies in Clearing in Law, Politics and Mathematics.

Falmouth Falmouth University is located in the towns of Falmouth and Penryn, on Cornwall's south coast. The courses focus on Art and Design, Music and Theatre Arts, Film and TV, Photography and Journalism.

For most courses, samples of work and/or interviews will be required.

Glasgow Applicants choose a degree from the Colleges of Arts; Medical, Veterinary & Life Sciences; Science & Engineering; Social Sciences. The flexible degree structure in Arts, Sciences and Social Sciences allows students to build their own degree programme from the courses on offer. Honours degrees normally take four years, with the decision for Honours taken at the end of Year 2. Primary Education, Health & Social Policy, and Environmental Science & Sustainability can be studied at the Dumfries Campus. New Gaelic and Materials Chemistry courses are being introduced in 2021.

The University does not accept applications after the 15 January deadline. Offers are made until late March. The University does not interview applicants except for entry to Dentistry, Education, Medicine, Music and Veterinary Medicine. Deferred entry is not guaranteed for all subjects so check with the University. See the University website for up-to-date information.

Glasgow Caledonian The University offers a wide range of career-focussed programmes offered by its Academic Schools: Glasgow School for Business and Society, School of Engineering and Built Environment, and School of Health and Life Sciences.

The University accepts a wide range of qualifications for entry, depending upon the chosen programme. Please check the website for programme-specific entry requirements.

Gloucestershire The University is located in Cheltenham and Gloucester with courses made up of individual study units (modules). Some are compulsory for the chosen course but other modules can be chosen from other subjects. All courses have strong employability focus with many opportunities to undertake placements and internships.

Students failing to meet the UCAS Tariff requirements may be eligible for entry based on life or work experience following an interview. Entry with BTEC, NVQ Level 3, International Baccalaureate Diplomas and Access to Higher Education qualifications is acceptable.

Glyndŵr Glyndŵr University is based in Wrexham, North East Wales. The University offers a wide range of courses covering areas such as Art and Design, Business, Computing, Creative Media Technology, Education, Engineering, Health, Social Science and Sport. It also has a dedicated rural campus in nearby Northop for Animal and Environment based courses. The University places a big emphasis on developing employability and linking courses with industry requirements. As well as traditional degree pathways, it has a range of four-year degree options that allow students to incorporate either a Foundation year or integrated master's year into their degree.

Offers for all courses are made through the Admissions and Enquiries team, and are usually based on UCAS Tariff point requirements. General entry requirements for three-year bachelor's degrees are 112 UCAS Tariff points, with 120 Tariff points for four-year integrated master's courses and 48 Tariff points for courses including a Foundation year. UCAS points may be counted from a wide variety of qualifications but offers are usually made based on points from GCE A-levels or equivalent. An interview is always required for Occupational Therapy and Social Work, and usually required for all Art and Design courses, Theatre, Television and Performance, Complementary Therapies, Health and Social Care, and Youth and Community. Other subject areas do not interview as standard, but may decide to interview applicants if deemed appropriate. Deferred applications for Occupational Therapy and Social Work are not accepted. Applications are welcomed from candidates who do not possess the standard qualifications but who can demonstrate their capacity to pursue the course successfully. Entrance can be based on past experience, skills, organisational capabilities and the potential to succeed, particularly for entry onto a programme including a Foundation year.

Greenwich Many courses are on offer and there is also a flexible and comprehensive Combined Honours degree programme offering two Joint subjects of equal weight or, alternatively, major/minor combinations.

For information on admissions procedures see the University website: www.gre.ac.uk/study/apply.

Harper Adams Based in Newport, Shropshire, the University focuses on agricultural, food chain and rural subjects.

Paid placements are available for all courses.

Applicants for Agriculture, Engineering, Veterinary Nursing, Veterinary Physiotherapy and the Extended Foundation Degree Programme will be required to attend an interview.

Heriot-Watt This campus university near Edinburgh has five schools offering courses in Energy, Geoscience, Infrastructure and Society, Engineering and Physical Sciences, Social Sciences, Mathematical and Computer Sciences, and Textiles and Design which is based at our second campus in Galashiels.

Admissions decisions are made through the Faculty 'Hubs'. The personal statement is regarded as highly important and students are advised to include all relevant interests and work experience. The University welcomes a wide range of entry qualifications.

Hertfordshire Full-time and sandwich courses are offered as well as Joint courses. All Hertfordshire students have a work exposure strand in their degrees and the close links with employers contribute to a consistently good work placement and graduate employment record. All students have the opportunity to develop self-employment skills through tailor-made packages in addition to their subject expertise and proficiency.

Applicants wanting to take a gap year should finalise their arrangements before asking for deferment and accepting a place. Once a place has been accepted for the following year it will not be possible to change their application for entry to the current year. They would need to withdraw their application and apply again through Clearing. Offers to applicants who are repeating examinations are the same.

Huddersfield The modular approach to study provides a flexible structure to all courses, which are offered as full-time or sandwich options. All students also have the opportunity to study a modern language either as a minor option or by studying part-time through the Modern Languages Centre. Most courses are vocational.

1,000 scholarships worth £1,000 are awarded and applied to the first year of study only. Up to 80 scholarships are available to students on Science and Engineering Foundation Years, with preference to those with the lowest family incomes. Scholarships are also available to students achieving 120 points or more whose family income is less than £25,000 per annum. For information on admissions procedures see the University website: www.hud.ac.uk.

Hull All full-time courses are made up of core and optional modules and are taught on the Hull campus. The opportunity to learn a language is available for all students irrespective of their degree course subject.

All criteria for selection are set by the academic faculty. A mandatory interview process operates for shortlisted applicants for Nursing, Operating Department Practice, Midwifery, Teaching (QTS), Legislative Studies and Social Work.

Applications are also welcomed from those who can demonstrate Level 3 work-based learning such as Advanced Apprenticeships and NVQ 3. Bridging study may be recommended by way of a Foundation year. Most courses welcome applications for deferred entry although this should be stated on the application. The University makes contextual (lower) offers to applicants on schemes including Pathways to STEM, Next Steps York and Realising Opportunities.

Hull York (MS) The Medical School is a partnership between the Universities of Hull and York with teaching and learning facilities on both campuses.

Hull York Medical School offers a Medicine with a Gateway Year programme, allowing locally based UK applicants who meet Widening Participation requirements to apply for Medicine with lower expected grades. See Medicine in Chapter 7.

Imperial London The central site is in South Kensington. Medicine is mainly based at St Mary's Hospital, Royal Brompton Hospital, Chelsea and Westminster Hospital, Charing Cross Hospital and Hammersmith Hospital. The College offers world-class programmes in Science, Medicine, Engineering and Management. Joint Honours courses and degree courses with a year abroad are also available. Science courses are offered primarily in one principal subject, but flexibility is provided by the possibility to transfer at the end of the first year and by the choice of optional subjects in the later years of the course. A Humanities programme is also open to all students with a wide range of options, while the Imperial College Business School offers Management courses which form an integral part of undergraduate degrees. Work experience and placements are a feature of all courses.

Applicants are normally required to have three A-levels, but applicants with other qualifications of equivalent standard and students with other competencies are also welcome. The College considers candidates with the Advanced Engineering Diploma if they also have A-levels in specified subjects which meet the College's entry requirements. Applicants for entry to Year 2 of some courses can also be considered if they have completed the first year of a comparable degree at another institution with a high level of achievement, but they need to contact the relevant department before applying. A College Admissions and Appeals and Complaints procedure is available to applicants dissatisfied with the way their application has been considered. Applicants should note the College's policy on dress, health and safety published on its website. An offer for an alternative course may be made to rejected applicants.

Keele Keele University's leafy campus in Staffordshire, which is the largest in the UK, is readily accessible from Birmingham, Manchester and London. Flexibility is provided through either interdisciplinary Single Honours degrees, bringing together a number of topics in an integrated form, or Dual Honours degrees in which two principal subjects are studied to degree level to the same depth as a Single Honours course. Business School courses with sandwich placements are available.

Keele's conditional offers to candidates are usually made in terms of specified grades from the qualifications they are studying. Some of its degree courses require a specific subject background. It welcomes applications from candidates with non-traditional qualifications and will take into consideration prior learning, experience and alternative qualifications. Applicants are normally required to have completed studies in the last three years. Contextual offers for applicants from a disadvantaged background are made for all subjects apart from the clinical vocations (eg Pharmacy, Medicine, Nursing) and Social Work. Further information about its approach and entry requirements can be found on the following webpage: www.keele.ac.uk/study/undergraduate/apply/admissionsfaqs.

Kent The University's main campuses are in Canterbury and Medway in the South East of England, with specialist centres in Europe where study and research are underpinned by the exceptional facilities and resources of locations in Brussels, Paris, Athens and Rome. Many courses have a year in industry, giving valuable practical experience ahead of your final year of study. The majority of programmes offer the opportunity to study or work abroad. Single Honours courses can include the option of taking up to 25% of the degree in another subject, or to change the focus of a degree at the end of the first year. Many social sciences and humanities subjects are available as Joint Honours programmes on a 50/50 basis or as major/minor Honours degrees. The University of Kent and Canterbury Christ Church University have been awarded funding to establish a new medical school (Kent and Medway), with places available for 2020 entry.

The University accepts a wide range of qualifications. Applicants returning to study after a long break are advised to contact the admissions staff before making a UCAS application. The University offers integrated Foundation year study in a number of degree subjects and an international Foundation year programme is available to non-UK students. Deferred entry is acceptable but should be mentioned on the UCAS application. The University will make contextual offers to applicants from disadvantaged backgrounds across all subjects. The University does not use the UCAS Tariff when making offers.

Kingston Kingston University is based in Kingston upon Thames, a busy riverside town in Surrey which is only 25 minutes away from central London. It has five campuses, each with its own character, but all of which combine state-of-the-art facilities with a friendly study environment. Its courses have a modular structure, and several of them are available to study as Joint Honours which allows students to combine two different subjects. The two subjects can be studied equally (half-field), or one subject can be focused on more than the other (major-minor fields). All students have the opportunity to study abroad during their degree and can choose from 36 countries spanning five continents. They can also learn one of 10 languages through the Kingston Language Scheme for free during their time at the University.

Once the University has received an application from UCAS, it looks carefully at each applicant's academic record, references and personal statement. Some courses at Kingston University have an interview as part of the selection process where one or two people will interview you to find out if you have the intellectual capability, knowledge and passion to benefit from your chosen course. If you don't have an interview, you'll be invited to an applicant day instead where you will get to experience taster sessions of the course you have applied for.

Lancaster The University is situated on a large campus some distance from the city and consists of several colleges. Each college has its own social activities and events. The degree programme is split into Part 1 (Year 1) and Part 2 (Years 2 and 3). Students study up to three subjects in Year 1 and then choose to major in one or a combination of subjects in Years 2 and 3. Single and Joint courses are offered in a wide range of subjects. There are study opportunities abroad in the USA and Canada, the Far East and Australasia. Many courses are offered with a placement year.

The University accepts a wide range of qualifications and offers are based on the best three A-level (or equivalent) results. Some departments interview applicants prior to making an offer. All applicants are invited to an informal post-offer Applicant Visit Day which encourages discussions with admissions tutors and current students.

Leeds One of the largest city-based single-site campuses in the UK and a member of the Russell Group, the University of Leeds offers excellence in learning and teaching in a wide range of courses in most subject areas, including an extensive offering of Joint Honours degrees. The size and breadth of the University allows Leeds to offer a complete student experience; studying abroad and/or industrial placements are offered as part of most courses. The research-based curriculum, combined with an unparalleled range of opportunities to complement their degree, allows students to develop skills needed for the future.

The University welcomes students with a variety of qualifications. Some courses do not accept A-levels in General Studies or Critical Thinking. Check the University's course finder for details of accepted qualifications: https://courses.leeds.ac.uk.

Leeds Arts BA courses in Art and Design, Fashion and Textiles, Fine Art and Graphics and Photography.

The University accepts a wide range of qualifications and experience.

Leeds Beckett Many of the degrees are vocational with links to industry and commerce. Courses are modular with core studies and optional modules. Degree programmes are offered in 13 different schools including the School of Clinical and Applied Sciences, Carnegie School of Education and the Leeds Business School.

Most offers are made in UCAS Tariff points, and interviews are held before an offer is made for some courses. Deferred entry is acceptable although applicants should be aware that some courses may change slightly each year.

Leeds Trinity An employer-focused, campus university located a few miles from Leeds city centre. The University offers Foundation and undergraduate degrees in a wide range of subject areas, including Business, Management and Marketing; Childhood and Education; Criminology; English; History; Journalism; Media, Film and Culture; Psychology; Secondary Education; Sociology; Sport, Health and Nutrition; and Theology and Religious Studies. Professional work placements are embedded into every undergraduate degree, and most courses include the opportunity to study abroad. Leeds Trinity is one of three UK universities with a Catholic foundation but is committed to providing maximum support to all students irrespective of their faith.

All applicants receiving an offer for non-interviewing courses will be invited to an Applicant Day. This gives them (and their families and friends) the opportunity to visit the campus, get a taste of student life and receive specific details about their chosen course. Some courses do require an interview – these courses are specified in the UCAS entry requirements. The University makes Tariff-based offers for most courses, with only a few offers based on grades. All entry requirements, whether Tariff or grade-based, are listed in the course-specific entry requirements on the University's website and through UCAS. Personal statements and references are always taken into account, alongside students' academic profiles.

All information is correct at the time of going to print, but please check the University website for the most up-to-date information.

Leicester Single Honours courses are offered in all the main disciplines and are taken by 75% of students. The main subject of study may be supported by one or two optional modules. Joint Honours courses, which are split equally between the subjects, and major/minor courses are also offered. For major/minor courses, a core area is studied in depth (75%) while an additional area (25%) is also explored. Apart from Medicine, all programmes have a common modular structure with compulsory modules and a wide choice of optional modules.

Most courses do not interview applicants although invitations to visit the University will follow any offers made. Most typical offers are made on the basis of three A-levels. For some courses we will give an offer if an EPQ is being taken with three A-levels. Other qualifications are considered, including the Access to HE Diploma, BTEC Nationals. Applications from suitably qualified students are also considered for second year entry. The university makes contextual offers in all subject areas, apart from Medicine. Contact the subject department for further information.

Lincoln A city centre university made up of the College of Arts, College of Science, College of Social Science and the Lincoln International Business School. Single and Joint subject degrees are offered on a modular basis, with some subjects offering the chance to study abroad. The degree at the new University of Nottingham Lincoln Medical School is delivered by the University of Nottingham, with placements based in Lincoln.

On some courses, notably Art and Design and Architecture, an interview with a portfolio is sometimes required before an offer can be made. The University accepts a wide range of qualifications but students without the standard entry requirements may still be offered a place on the basis of prior experience and qualifications. For details of entry to the Medical School, see the university website.

Liverpool The University offers degrees in the Faculties of Humanities and Social Sciences, Science and Engineering and Health and Life Sciences. Apart from courses with a clinical component, programmes are modular. The University offers over 20 degrees with an industrial placement year and there is the opportunity for students studying many subjects to spend a year of their degree in China. The Faculty of Humanities and Social Sciences offers the 'Honours Select' programme allowing students to combine subjects from across the Faculty as Joint (50:50) or major/minor (75:25) degrees. Paid work placements are the norm in Computer Science, Engineering, Accounting, Business, Communications and Media, Marketing, and Chemistry.

Decisions on offers for most schools/departments are made centrally. The exceptions are in the Schools of Medicine, Dentistry, Health Sciences and Veterinary Science. Most departments will invite applicants to visit the University before or after an offer is made. Some departments require interviews. Offers are normally based on three A-levels or equivalent (a wide range of qualifications are accepted). Entry requirements are reviewed annually. In 2019 the subjects with the most vacancies in Clearing were Politics, the Management School and Geography. The university makes discounted offers of one grade lower on their Scholars Scheme.

Liverpool Hope Liverpool Hope offers a wide range of Single and Combined Honours undergraduate degrees. The University offers small group teaching, which means students are taught by research-active lecturers and benefit from insights into their research.

Each application is assessed on its own merits. The policy is to select those candidates who demonstrate they have an academic ability and personal motivation to succeed in their chosen programme of study. The admissions decision will rest primarily on the qualifications and also on the aspirations of the applicant in relation to their chosen programme of study. Selectors will take into account the evidence provided on the application form against the criteria for that particular course.

Liverpool John Moores Courses are offered in the Faculties of Arts, Professional & Social Studies, Business, Education, Health and Community, Science and Engineering & Technology. The majority of courses provide the opportunity for work-based learning or for a year-long industrial placement. The majority of programmes in the Faculty of Science and Faculty of Engineering & Technology also offer a Foundation pathway.

Admissions decisions are made through the Faculty 'Hubs'. The personal statement is regarded as highly important and students are advised to include all relevant interests and work experience. The University welcomes a wide range of entry qualifications. If an applicant fails to receive an offer for their chosen course then an offer for an alternative course may be made. The University will make adjusted offers to Care Leavers and students estranged from their families.

London (Birk) Part-time and full-time evening courses are offered for mature students wishing to read for first and higher degrees. Courses are offered in the schools of Arts; Business, Economics and Informatics; Law; Science; and Social Sciences, History and Philosophy.

All applications are made online. Part-time undergraduate, all certificate and short course and all postgraduate applications are made directly through its website. Full-time undergraduate applications are made through UCAS.

London (Court) The Courtauld offers one undergraduate degree programme, the BA (Hons) History of Art. This seeks to attract students of the highest calibre, who are driven by an insatiable curiosity to learn about the visual arts and their histories.

The University welcomes applicants who can demonstrate interest in art history and enthusiasm for it. Entry is competitive, but the Courtauld is committed to admitting students with the best ability and potential regardless of their educational background or financial resources. You will not be required to have studied history of art previously, however, advanced study in the humanities is a significant advantage.

London (Gold) Goldsmiths is situated in New Cross, south-east London. The University takes an innovative and interdisciplinary approach to its degree courses, which include Art, Design, Drama, Computing, Media, the Arts, Education and Social Sciences. An undergraduate degree is made up of 360 credits from core and optional modules – 120 at each level. A standard module is worth 60 credits, although some degrees also contain 15-credit modules or can be made up of higher-value parts, such as a dissertation or a Major Project.

Goldsmiths welcomes applications from students with A-levels or equivalent qualifications. While entry requirements are stipulated, candidates are assessed individually and may receive an offer that differs from the published grades. Some applicants are interviewed, in particular those for Art and Design degrees for which examples of current art and design work are required before interview. Applicants requiring deferred entry (which may or may not be acceptable depending on the course) should contact the admissions tutor before applying.

London (Institute of Banking and Finance) A private university college. Courses focus on financial services and related professions. Both of the Institute's undergraduate degree programmes are offered as four year courses with a year in industry.

Applications are submitted through UCAS. All applications made before the closing date will be considered equally against the stated selection criteria and in the context of the number of available places. The Institute will consider late applications only for courses where places are still available. The university does make contextual offers on an individual basis.

London (Institute of Cancer Research) A postgraduate college of the University of London, the Institute of Cancer Research offers a MSc in Oncology as well as PhD studentships. For further information see the website: www.icr.ac.uk/studying-and-training.

London (Inst Paris) The Institute was established as part of London University in 1969 and offers three year courses in French Studies leading to a London University BA. Courses are taught in French. The University's website provides up to date advice regarding the possible impact of Brexit on studying in France.

Interviews are held in French. The University does consider contextual information from the UCAS form when applicants' predicted grades do not meet requirements. For information on admissions procedures see Institute website: https://ulip.london.ac.uk.

London (Interdisciplinary School) The School opens in September 2020. It is reported to be a school for polymaths and will offer one degree, a bachelor in arts and science (BASc), incorporating design, technology, and the humanities with ten weeks of work experience. Applications are made through UCAS.

London (King's) The College on the Strand offers more than 200 degree programmes in the Faculty of Arts and Humanities, Faculty of Life Sciences and Medicine, The Dickson Poon School of Law, Florence Nightingale Faculty of Nursing and Midwifery, Faculty of Natural and Mathematical Sciences, Institute of Psychiatry, Psychology and Neuroscience and the Faculty of Social Science and Public Policy and King's Business School at the Guy's, Strand, Waterloo, Denmark Hill and St Thomas's campuses. The degree course structure varies with the subject chosen and consists of Single Honours, Joint Honours, Combined Honours (a choice of over 60 programmes) and major/minor courses.

The majority of courses require three A-levels. Applicants to the Department of Mathematics are required to take Further Mathematics to at least AS. Currently, Medicine and Dentistry require students to present either an additional AS subject at grade B, or the EPQ. Where students are unable to take an AS, King's College will waive the requirement, but a statement about their school or college's AS policy must be included in the first few lines of the UCAS reference. A-level General Studies and Critical Thinking are not included in offers, though their contribution to a student's overall development is valued. Deferred entry is acceptable.

London (LSHTM) A postgraduate university, specialising in public and global health. The School offers master's and research degrees as well as distance learning programmes, short courses and free online courses. Further information can be found on their website: www.lshtm.ac.uk/study/courses

London (QM) Queen Mary University of London (QMUL), based in the heart of east London, is a member of the Russell Group of leading UK universities and in the top 200 universities in the world. Its flexible approach enables students to choose from a wide range of compulsory and optional modules to develop a degree programme to suit their interests. In addition, many of its degrees are accredited by professional bodies, which can give graduates a head-start in their chosen career. Many of its students also take advantage of study abroad and industrial experience opportunities, ranging from internships to a year in industry. Most courses in Engineering, Materials Science and Mathematics have a mandatory placement year.

For all full-time programmes, students should apply online at ucas.com. The institution code for QMUL is Q50. It may be possible for students to join undergraduate degree programmes at the beginning of the second and sometimes the third year. Those wishing to transfer their degree studies from another UK higher education institution may be considered but should contact the subject department before applying. In 2019 Clearing vacancies existed in Drama, Economics, Engineering, English, Geography, History, Materials Science, Mathematics and Physics.

London (RH) The University is situated in Egham, Surrey. It offers Single, Joint and major/minor undergraduate Honours degrees in a wide range of subjects across three faculties: Arts and Social Sciences, Management, Economics and Law, and Science. All students have the opportunity to undertake a placement year either abroad or in the UK.

Royal Holloway is committed to operating a fair, transparent and professional admissions process. Applicants likely to meet the entry requirements will either be made an offer or contacted for further information. The University may make contextual offers based on an applicant's socio-economic background.

London (RVC) Campuses in London and in Hertfordshire. Courses are offered in Veterinary Medicine, Biological Sciences and Bioveterinary Sciences (the latter two do not qualify graduates to practise as veterinary surgeons). There is also a Veterinary Gateway course and Veterinary Nursing programme.

Applications for deferred entry are considered but the offer conditions must be met in the same academic year as the application. Applicants holding offers from RVC who fall slightly below the grades required are always reconsidered and may be offered entry if places are available.

London (SOAS) Single-subject degrees focusing on Asia, Africa and the Near East include compulsory and optional units, with two-thirds of the total units studied in the chosen subject and the remaining units or 'floaters' from a complementary course offered at SOAS or another college of the University of London. In addition, two-subject degrees give great flexibility in the choice of units, enabling students to personalise their degrees to match their interests.

Particular attention is paid to past and predicted academic performance and offers may be made without an interview. SOAS is happy to consider deferred entry, which should be stated on the UCAS application.

London (St George's) Courses are offered in Biomedical Science, Medicine, Occupational Therapy, Paramedic Science, Healthcare Science, Physiotherapy and Diagnostic and Therapeutic Radiography.

Interviews are required for most courses and admissions tests are required for some courses. Candidates will be interviewed for all courses in Medicine, Physiotherapy, Occupational Therapy, Paramedic Science, Healthcare Science and Therapeutic and Diagnostic Radiography. Once admitted students are not allowed to change courses.

London (UCL) Subjects are organised in Faculties: Arts and Humanities, Brain Sciences, Built Environment (the Bartlett), Engineering Sciences, Laws, Life Sciences, Mathematical and Physical Sciences, Medical Sciences (including the UCL Medical School), Population Health Sciences, Social and Historical Sciences. In addition, there is the School of Slavonic and East European Studies and the UCL Institute of Education. UCL also offers a cross-disciplinary degree in Arts and Sciences, based on the US Liberal Arts model.

UCL welcomes applications from students proposing to spend a pre-university year engaged in constructive activity in the UK or abroad. About 9% of UCL's undergraduates take a gap year. Those wanting to enter the second year of a degree programme should make early contact with the relevant subject department to obtain approval. Applications are assessed on the basis of the personal statement, reference and the predicted academic performance, as well as additional assessment methods such as essays, questionnaires, aptitude tests and interviews. Decisions on admission are final and there is normally no right of appeal.

London LSE The London School of Economics offers 38 degrees across a wide range of social science subjects, taught in 19 departments. Degrees are three years long, except Philosophy, Politics and Economics (PPE), which is a four-year programme. All undergraduates study a compulsory course called 'LSE 100: Understanding the causes of things' which actively challenges them to analyse questions of current public concern and develops their critical skills.

A wide range of international qualifications are accepted for direct entry to the School. The standard entry requirements for the majority of the School's undergraduate programmes are based on three A-levels (or equivalent). The School does not make contextual offers but gives candidates from disadvantaged backgrounds particular consideration. The School continues to use AS grades in its admissions assessments and recommends that students, wherever possible, sit AS exams at the end of year 12. Students will not be disadvantaged if they have not been able to take AS examinations at their school or college, but the School asks that referees advise on such circumstances. In these circumstances, the School will use the information presented on the application form to make its decision (possibly in conjunction with some form of additional assessment). Applicants normally offer A-levels in LSE's preferred subjects, which do not include AS/A-level Accounting, Art and Design, Business Studies, Citizenship Studies, Communication and Culture, Creative Writing, Design and Technology, Drama and Theatre Studies, Film Studies, Health and Social Care, Home Economics, ICT, Law, Leisure Studies, Media Studies, Music Technology, Sports Studies, Travel and Tourism. Standard offers range from AAB to A*AA – applicants should check individual degree requirements. Intense competition for places means that high predicted grades on the application will not guarantee an offer. Great weight is placed on the personal statement and advice on writing this can be found on the School's website. Applications are considered on a rolling basis, but they are often held in a 'gathered field' and decisions made only when all on-time applications have been received. It is unlikely there will be any vacancies when A-level results are published. Law, Mathematics, and History are subjects in which some lower offers are made. LSE does not participate in Clearing.

London Met Single and Joint Honours courses are made up of compulsory and optional modules allowing students some flexibility to follow their particular interests.

Applicants may be required to sit a test or to submit a portfolio of work.

London Regent's Regent's private university offers undergraduate and postgraduate programmes delivered in an international learning environment. Programmes range from US-style Liberal Studies degrees to industry-led UK degree programmes in Business, Psychology, Acting, Film, Media and Fashion.

Please visit the University website for specific admissions criteria.

London South Bank All courses have flexible modes of study and many vocational courses offer sandwich placements.

Applicants not achieving the grades required for their chosen course should contact the University, which may still be able to make an offer of a place. All applicants are interviewed for Midwifery, Nursing, Allied Health Professions and Architecture courses.

Loughborough Loughborough is a single-site campus university that offers a range of courses across 19 different academic schools and departments. Degrees are structured using a combination of compulsory and optional modules so that study can be tailored to individual interest. All undergraduates have the option to incorporate a year of paid industry experience into study, where students can practise skills learned in a professional environment. As a result, Loughborough students have high graduate employment prospects and are often sought after by top national and international recruiters.

The University's admissions policy and supporting information for applicants can be found at www.lboro. ac.uk/study/apply/support.

Manchester A research-driven university offering Single and Joint Honours courses which are divided into course units, some of which are compulsory, some optional, and some are taken from a choice of subjects offered by other schools and faculties. A comprehensive Combined Studies degree enables students to choose course units from Arts, Humanities, Social Sciences and Sciences, and this provides the flexibility for students to alter the emphasis of their studies from year to year.

Strong examination results are the main factor in the admission of students to courses and the University accepts a wide range of qualifications. All decisions are made by the academic departments according to their individual requirements. For example, some programmes may require the applicant to have GCSE Maths at grade C or 4 or above for entry, others may require a compulsory subject at A-level. Other factors that are considered are prior and predicted grades, evidence of knowledge and commitment in the personal statement, and teacher references. Some courses may also take into account performance at interview, aptitude tests and portfolios. Where places are limited, they are offered to those eligible applicants who best meet the selection criteria and who, according to the admissions team, are most likely to benefit from their chosen course and to contribute to both their academic school and the wider university.

Manchester Met A large number of courses involve industrial and commercial placements. It is also possible to take Combined Honours degrees selecting a combination of two or three subjects. Many programmes have a modular structure with compulsory and optional core modules.

Admissions staff look for personal statements showing evidence of the applicants' motivation and commitment to their chosen courses, work or voluntary experience relevant to any chosen career, and extra-curricular activities, achievements and interests which are relevant to the chosen courses.

Marjon The University is based in Plymouth on the edge of the city and runs 100-plus programmes which place a high emphasis on being relevant to the labour market. Students will be provided with the relevant transferable skills in demand from employers and businesses – key skills that can help put students a step ahead of the competition. The University specialises in sport, education, languages and linguistics, journalism and creative arts.

The University welcomes applications from students with disabilities, who are well catered for on campus.

Medway Sch Pharm The School is part of a collaboration between the Universities of Greenwich and Kent. Offers undergraduate and master's degrees in pharmaceutical courses, accredited by The General Pharmaceutical Council.

See Medicine in Chapter 7.

Middlesex Single and Joint Honours courses are offered on a modular basis, most programmes having an optional work placement.

Some courses start in January (see www.mdx.ac.uk/study-with-us).

NCH London The New College of the Humanities is located in Bloomsbury and is a private university-level college. It offers liberal arts-inspired undergraduate programmes featuring majors and minors in subjects including Economics, English, History, Philosophy, and Politics & International Relations, and a Single Honours Law LLB. In addition to studying towards their degree, all students study eight core courses in subjects including Applied Ethics, Critical Reasoning, Science Literacy, and a unique professional development programme. To reflect this further study, students are awarded the NCH Diploma. Students typically experience lectures of fewer than 50 students, small group seminars and weekly one-to-one tutorials from eminent academics. Scholarships and bursaries are offered.

Students may apply direct to the College at any time or through UCAS. The application form is similar to the traditional UCAS form. NCH will consider applications individually and on their merits. Decisions are quick – usually within four to six weeks. As well as personal details and academic records, applicants are required to supply a reference and a piece of written work. An application to NCH can be made in addition to any application made to other universities through UCAS. All shortlisted students are interviewed. NCH accepts deferred entries for those wishing to take a gap year.

Newcastle Single, Joint and Combined Honours programmes are offered. Some programmes provide students with the opportunity to defer their choice of final degree to the end of the first or second year. In Accountancy and Finance there is a 'Flying Start Degree' sandwich course which offers paid work experience. Several courses are offered with optional placements.

The University accepts a wide range of qualifications and combinations of qualifications for entry to its degree programmes. Offers are made in terms of grades to be achieved (UCAS Tariff points are not used).

The University makes contextual offers to applicants from disadvantaged backgrounds, particularly in Psychology, Law and Computing Courses. Generous scholarships are offered to new undergraduate students. The following courses did not go into clearing in 2019: Medicine, Dentistry, Business, Combined Honours, Fine Art, Psychology and Architecture. Most clearing vacancies occurred in Engineering and Mathematics.

Newman A full range of full-time and part-time degree courses can be chosen with a focus on Initial Teacher Training qualifications.

Applicants are advised to submit an accurate and well-presented application. Personal statements are applicants' chance to shine, show their qualities and convince admission tutors why they should offer them a place.

Northampton The University of Northampton offers Single Honours, Joint Honours, Foundation degrees, HNDs and top-up courses. The University also offers a Year 0 in some courses for those who do not meet its entry requirements. There are also placement opportunities in the third year for certain courses, particularly within the business school. A range of courses and learning options are available including full- and part-time, distance learning and two-year fast track degrees.

Entry requirements usually range from BCC to ABB for BA/BSc degrees depending on the course.

Northumbria The University is located in Newcastle and offers a wide range of courses with an emphasis on vocational studies. Single and Joint Honours courses are offered, and a Combined Honours course allows a choice of up to three subjects.

Interviews are compulsory for most courses in Art and Design and courses in Health and Teaching. There are no admissions tests.

Norwich Arts Courses focus on Art, Design and Media Studies.

For information on admissions procedures see the University website: www.nua.ac.uk.

Nottingham Single and Joint Honours courses are available, with some industrial placements. Programmes are modular with compulsory and optional modules, the latter giving some flexibility in the selection of topics from outside the chosen subject field. Degree programmes are offered in the Faculties of Arts, Engineering, Medicine and Health Sciences, Science and Social Sciences. In addition, study-abroad opportunities are currently offered at over 320 institutions worldwide, through schemes such as Universitas 21 and Erasmus+; almost all students can apply to spend a period of time abroad. Please check the university's website for further details about this. The University of Nottingham is delivering a new Medicine degree in collaboration with the University of Lincoln. The new University of Nottingham Lincoln Medical School offers 80 places.

Although grade predictions may match the offers published for the course there is no guarantee that an offer can be made. For details of entry to the Medical School, see the university website.

Nottingham Trent Degree programmes are offered in a range of subjects. Many courses are vocational with industrial and commercial placements and some students are also able to spend periods of time studying at a partner university around the world.

The UCAS personal statement is seen as a key part of the application process; the University website provides a guide on its possible content and preparation.

Open University Distance learning and part-time higher education courses. Degree and diploma courses are offered in the following subject areas: Arts and Humanities, Business and Management, Childhood and Youth, Computing and ICT, Education, Engineering and Technology, Environmental Development and International Studies, Health and Social Care, Languages, Law, Mathematics and Statistics, Psychology, Science and Social Sciences. Students study at home and are sent learning materials by the OU, maintaining contact with their tutors by email, post and telephone. See also Chapter 1.

There are no formal entry qualifications for admission to courses.

Oxford The University has 30 colleges and five private halls admitting undergraduates. Colleges: Balliol, Brasenose, Christ Church, Corpus Christi, Exeter, Harris Manchester (mature students only), Hertford, Jesus, Keble, Lady Margaret Hall, Lincoln, Magdalen, Mansfield, Merton, New, Oriel, Pembroke, St Anne's, St Catherine's, St Edmund Hall, St Hilda's, St Hugh's, St John's, St Peter's, Somerville, Queen's, Trinity, University, Wadham, Worcester. Permanent Private Halls: Blackfriars, Regent's Park College, St Benet's Hall, St Stephen's House, Wycliffe. Candidates apply to a college and for a Single or Joint Honours programme. Courses are offered with a core element plus a variety of options. Weekly contact with a college tutor assists students to tailor their courses to suit personal interests. Arts students are examined twice, once in the first year (Preliminary or Honour Moderations examinations) and at the end of the course (Final Honours School). Science students are similarly examined although in some subjects examinations also take place in the second year.

Entrance requirements range from A*A*A to AAA depending on the course. There are specific subject requirements for some courses, particularly in the sciences. Once any subject requirements are met, any other subjects at A-level are acceptable for admission purposes with the exception of General Studies (and both General Studies and Critical Thinking for Medicine). It is generally recommended that students take those subjects which they enjoy the most and those in which they are most likely to achieve top grades. However, as the selection criteria for the University of Oxford are entirely academic, it is also a good idea for students to consider how best they can demonstrate their academic abilities in their choice of subjects. Admissions tests and written work are often part of the application process. Other equivalent qualifications such as Scottish Advanced Highers, American APs/SAT/ACT and the International Baccalaureate are also very welcome. Oxford does not participate in UCAS Clearing, Extra or Adjustment. Please see www.ox.ac.uk/enreqs for further details. There are full details on admissions tests at www.ox.ac.uk/tests.

Oxford Brookes Single Honours courses are offered with modules chosen from a field of study or, alternatively, Combined Honours courses in which two subjects are chosen. These subjects may be in related or unrelated subjects. Mandatory placement years are involved in courses in Applied Languages, Building Surveying, Construction Project Management and Japanese Studies. Optional placement years are offered in Accounting, Biological Sciences, Business, Economics, Marketing, Motor Sport Engineering and Robotics.

Conditional offers are now expressed in terms of UCAS Tariff points rather than in grades. Oxford Brookes welcomes applicants with a mixture of qualifications (eg 1 A-level plus BTEC National Diploma, or 2 A-levels plus 1 Cambridge Pre-U Certificate).

Plymouth A broad portfolio of degree courses is available. Single Honours courses are offered, with many vocational programmes offering work placements.

The University looks for evidence in the UCAS personal statement of your understanding of the course, good numeracy and literacy skills, motivation and commitment, work experience or placement or voluntary work, especially if it is relevant to your course, any sponsorships or placements you have applied for, and your possible plans for a gap year.

Portsmouth Around half of the students at Portsmouth are on courses that lead to professional accreditation, and many more study on courses that offer real-life learning. Simulated learning environments include a mock courtroom, a newsroom, a health simulation suite, a £1m model pharmacy and a forensic house, where criminologists work on staged crime scenes. Most courses include work placements and there is also the opportunity for all students to learn a foreign language.

Applications are considered using a variety of methods and a range of the following are taken into account depending on the course applied for: actual and predicted grades, references, personal statements, interviews and tests. Different courses use different criteria and selection methods to reflect the nature and demands of the course. For all courses, academic achievement through prior learning or experience is important, as is the potential to succeed, as demonstrated through commitment to the subject. The University can make contextual offers to students from disadvantaged backgrounds.

Queen Margaret QMU offers a wide range of professionally relevant courses in the areas of Healthcare; Social Sciences; Performing Arts; Film, Media and PR; and Business, Tourism and Hospitality Management.

The University does make contextual offers to eligible candidates. For information on admissions procedures see QMU's website: www.qmu.ac.uk/about-the-university/quality/committees-regulations-policies-and-procedures.

Queen's Belfast The academic year is divided into two semesters of 15 weeks each (12 teaching weeks and three examination weeks), with degree courses (pathways) normally taken over three years of full-time study. Six modules are taken each year (three in each semester) and, in theory, a degree can involve any combination of six Level 1 modules. Single, Joint and Combined Honours courses are offered and, in addition, major/minor combinations; some courses include sandwich placements.

Applications for admission to full-time undergraduate courses are made through UCAS. Interviews are essential for Medicine and Dentistry.

Ravensbourne Univ A small, industry-centred university in central London, Ravensbourne University hosts more than 100 creative businesses which its students can get involved in. The University has a strong focus on the vocational and the creative, offering a range of courses which include fashion, product design, architecture, music production, and broadcasting.

Applicants for architecture will be interviewed and also must submit a portfolio. Other courses require portfolios displaying relevant examples of creative work.

Reading The University of Reading offers more than 220 undergraduate courses in arts, humanities, business, social science and science. The modular structure of its courses means you can specialise in the areas that interest you most, while still developing core subject knowledge. If you are interested in studying two related subjects, it also has a wide range of combined degrees to choose from. Because it recognises that it is training students for 21st-century career paths which are constantly evolving, all its courses are designed to equip you with the thinking, problem-solving and creative skills to allow you to thrive in any sector. Every undergraduate student has the opportunity to take on a work placement which may be paid or unpaid. Placements may range from a few weeks to a whole year. Many courses include a mandatory placement year.

Approximately 80% of decisions on applications to undergraduate study are made by the central Admissions Office and 20% of decisions are recommended to the Admissions Office by academic departments/schools. Typical offers are presented in terms of A-level grades (with the exception of Single Honours Art degrees which use UCAS Tariff points), but applications are welcomed from those presenting a wide range of qualifications. The University of Reading makes contextual offers across all subject areas, which are typically two grades lower than the top end of the published grade. In recognition of the preparation that the Extended Project Qualification provides to students, the University also makes offers of one grade lower provided the applicant obtains a B in the EPQ. Accounting and Business did not go into Clearing in 2019.

Richmond (Am Int Univ) This private University offers British and American courses. American courses are accredited by the Middle States Commission on Higher Education, an agency recognised by the US Department of Education. Courses are also approved by the Open University and can lead to Open University Validated Awards.

Candidates can apply through UCAS, directly to the institution, or through the Common Application. Students are encouraged to visit before applying.

Robert Gordon The University offers a wide range of vocational courses. Many courses offer work placements. Several Accounting and Computing courses are offered over two years.

The University makes contextual offers to applicants from disadvantaged backgrounds. The following courses did not go into clearing in 2019: Communication Design, Painting, Children and Young People Nursing, Social Work, Physiotherapy, Occupational Therapy, Midwifery and Diagnostic Radiography.

Roehampton Roehampton has a 54-acre parkland campus in south-west London with historic buildings alongside modern, cutting edge facilities. The campus provides a close-knit community feel for students and is made up of four historic colleges and 10 academic departments. There are over 50 programmes offered at undergraduate level and Roehampton is also one of the largest providers of initial teacher training in the UK.

Tariffs for entry to undergraduate programmes vary depending on the programme; please check the website for full details. There may be additional requirements so please check before applying.

Royal Agricultural Univ The University is based in Cirencester, Gloucestershire. It offers undergraduate degree courses in subjects as varied as Real Estate, Rural Land Management, International Business Management, British Wildlife Conservation, Bloodstock and Performance Horse Management, and of course Agriculture, amongst others. The RAU is ranked third in the UK for graduate employability.

For information on admissions procedures see the University website: www.rau.ac.uk/study/undergraduate-study.

Salford The University offers BA, BSc and BEng degrees with teaching methods depending on the degree. The University is equally likely to accept students with BTECs and Access qualifications as well as those with A-levels. There is a wide range of professionally accredited programmes, many involving work placements. All undergraduates may study a foreign language.

The University is committed to widening participation but it does not make lower offers on the basis of educational or social disadvantage.

Sheffield The teaching year consists of two semesters (two periods of 15 weeks). Courses are fully modular, with the exceptions of Dentistry and Medicine. Students register for a named degree course which has a number of core modules, some optional modules chosen from a prescribed range of topics, and some unrestricted modules chosen from across the University.

The University considers qualifications already achieved (including GCSEs), predicted grades and personal statements as the most important parts of an application. Interviews are not a prerequisite of admission, however some departments do interview to further assess the motivation and personal qualities of applicants. Departments that interview include Medicine, Dentistry, Orthoptics and Human Communication Science (for Speech Science). The Applicant Information Desk can help with any questions applicants have about the process of applying to Sheffield and the current status of their application.

Sheffield Hallam A large number of vocational courses are offered in addition to those in Arts, Humanities and Social Sciences. The University is the largest provider of sandwich courses in the UK with most courses offering work placements, usually between the second and third years. Most students are able to study an additional language from French, German, Italian, Spanish and Japanese.

For information on admissions procedures see the University website: www.shu.ac.uk.

Solent Courses are offered in many vocational subjects. There are opportunities for students to gain work experience in the form of industrial placements alongside academic study.

Admissions staff look for applicants' reasons for their course choice, and for evidence of their abilities and ambitions. UK and EU applicants who have demonstrated outstanding academic ability are able to apply for the Undergraduate Academic Merit Scholarship. Students who are eligible for this scholarship may also qualify for the unconditional offer scheme.

An International Academic Merit Scheme is also in place. More information can be located on the University's website.

South Wales The University has five campuses in Cardiff, Glyntaff, Treforest, Caerleon and in Newport City. Many of the courses are vocational and can be studied as Single or Joint Honours courses or major/minor degrees.

Applicants for courses in Art and Design, Teacher Training and Social Work are interviewed.

Southampton A wide range of courses is offered in the Faculties of Business, Law and Art, Engineering and the Environment, Health Sciences, Humanities, Medicine, Natural and Environmental Sciences, Physical Sciences and Engineering and Social, Human and Mathematical Sciences. Programmes are generally for three years. All students have the chance to study a language as part of their degree and there are many opportunities for students to study abroad or on an Erasmus+ exchange programme whether or not they are studying modern languages.

The University looks for a well-considered personal statement, focusing on your reasons for choosing a particular course, the skills you would bring to it, information about any relevant work experience, your career ideas, your personal interests related to the course, and your thoughts about 'what makes you stand out in a crowd'.

St Andrews A very wide range of subjects is offered across the Faculties of Arts, Divinity, Medicine and Science. A flexible programme is offered in the first two years when students take several subjects. The decision of Honours degree subject is made at the end of the second year when students choose between Single or Joint Honours degrees for the next two years. A broadly based General degree programme is also offered lasting three years. After two years of a General degree programme students may transfer onto a named Honours degree programme if they meet the requirements of the department(s).

The University highlights the importance of the personal statement and the quality of this is likely to decide which applicants receive offers. Admissions tutors prefer candidates to achieve their grades at the first sitting. Apart from Medicine, Gateway to Physics and Gateway to Computer Science, no candidates are interviewed. St Andrews does not enter Clearing due to the competitive nature of its courses. All places are filled during the main applications cycle. The university has introduced a tiered approach to its entry requirements with 'Standard' and 'Minimum' entry requirements for each subject (check www.standrews.ac.uk/subjects/entry/indicator). All subjects can have offers made based on these new requirements. Unconditional offers can only be made to applicants who have existing qualifications achieved in previous years.

St Mary's Flexible, modular degree options allow a great deal of choice to both Joint and Single Honours students. Practical and theoretical studies are followed in the Acting course. Based in Twickenham, London.

Offers are made through UCAS. Students for over-subscribed courses or programmes of a practical or professional nature may be called for interview and may be required to take tests.

St Mary's (UC) St Mary's University College Belfast is a Catholic higher education institution in Northern Ireland, affiliated to Queen's University Belfast. St Mary's delivers degree programmes in teacher education as well as a BA (Hons) degree in Liberal Arts.

Applications are treated in accordance with the College's Admissions Policy, which is the same as that of Queen's University, with whom St Mary's enjoys a cooperative partnership of academic provision.

Staffordshire The main campus at Stoke-on-Trent offers a diverse range of courses in Art and Design, Business, Computing, Engineering, Film, Sound & Vision, Humanities, Law, Psychology, Social Sciences, Science and Sports Science. The Centres of Excellence in Stafford and Shrewsbury offer courses in Health Professions including Nursing, Midwifery, Paramedic Science and Operating Department Practice. Courses can be taught full time or part time, while a selection of courses can be taught on a 'Fast Track' two-year basis.

The University provides various ways to support prospective students with their applications and personal statements. This includes advice over the phone, workshops on campus or at schools and colleges, online information and tailored advice at Open Days.

Stirling A flexible system operates in which students can delay their final degree choice until midway through the course. The University year is divided into two 15-week semesters, from September to December and January to May with a reading/study block and exams at the end of each semester. Innovative January entry is possible to some degree programmes. There are 200 degree combinations with the opportunity to study a range of disciplines in the first two years. In addition to Single and Combined Honours degrees, there is a General degree which allows for greater breadth of choice. Subjects range across the Arts, Social Sciences and Sciences.

Admissions are administered through a central office. It is essential to include in the personal statement your reasons for choosing your specified course. The University also looks for evidence of your transferable skills, for example communication skills and teamwork, and how you acquired these, for example through work experience, voluntary work, academic studies, hobbies and general life experience. The University makes contextual offers across all disciplines.

Stranmillis (UC) This is a college of Queen's University Belfast, focusing on teacher training courses with European and international exchanges as part of the degrees.

Candidates for teacher training courses will be called for interview.

Strathclyde A credit-based modular system operates with a good degree of flexibility in course choices. The University offers many vocational courses in the Faculties of Engineering, Humanities and Social Sciences, Science and in the Strathclyde Business School. There are also degree programmes in arts subjects, Education and Law.

Formal interviews are required for some vocational courses; informal interviews are held by some science and engineering courses.

Suffolk The University of Suffolk is situated in central Ipswich and is based on the waterfront. It caters mainly for local and mature students. Several degree courses are offered.

For information on course admissions see: www.uos.ac.uk/content/applications.

Sunderland The University of Sunderland provides a range of courses across four faculties: Arts, Design and Media, Business and Law, Education and Society and Applied Science. All courses are geared towards employability, with work placements and visiting lecturers from some of the biggest companies in the UK. Several courses can include an option to study abroad in various locations including Australia, USA, Germany, France and more. The University of Sunderland recently opened a new School of Medicine, with a first intake of 50 students in 2019, and 100 in 2020.

The University holds informal interviews for certain courses, when applicants will be asked to present their portfolio, to give an audition, or to talk about themselves and why they want to study for that particular course. For details of entry to the School of Medicine, see the university website. The University's admissions team are able to guide applicants through the process, via telephone 0191 515 3154, or email: admissions@sunderland.ac.uk.

Surrey Based in Guildford, just 34 minutes from central London, the University of Surrey offers a wide variety of undergraduate degree programmes designed to reflect students' needs, and those of society and industry, while retaining academic rigour. The University works with over 2,300 partner organisations in the UK and overseas as it feels very strongly that professional training is an integral part of university life. A professional training year allows students to put their skills into practice and to experience a real professional environment.

The University is willing to consider deferring an application for one year, providing it considers that this will benefit the applicant's studies. Contact the admissions staff if you are considering deferred entry.

Sussex Teaching is structured around 12 schools of study and the Brighton and Sussex Medical School. Courses cover a wide range of subjects in Humanities, Life Sciences, Science and Technology, Social Sciences and Cultural Studies. Students are registered in a school depending on the degree taken. The flexible structure allows students to interrupt their degree programme to take a year out. In addition, students can customise their degree through a range of pathways, placements and study abroad programmes.

If you are applying to do an undergraduate course in Social Work, Pharmacy, Primary and Early Years Education (with Qualified Teacher Status) BA or Medicine, you will need to attend an interview. If you do not have formal academic qualifications, you may be asked to attend an interview. There are workshops within the admissions process for Drama Studies and portfolio reviews for Product Design. Interviews and workshops normally take place between January and April and the University tries to give you at least two weeks' notice.

Swansea Courses are offered in Arts and Social Sciences, Business, Economics and Law, Engineering, Languages, Medicine and Health Sciences and Science. Degree courses are modular with the opportunity to take some subjects outside the chosen degree course. Part-time degrees are available and study abroad arrangements are possible in several subject areas.

All applicants applying for undergraduate degrees (with the exception of 'professional' programmes where an interview is an integral part of the selection process) who apply offering the requisite subjects (and grades at GCSE) can expect to receive a conditional offer of a place.

Teesside The Middlesbrough campus offers courses at undergraduate and postgraduate level, emphasising professionalism through work placements, volunteering, live projects, accredited courses and graduate internships. Students obtaining a placement as part of their course receive a full fee waiver for their placement year.

Interviews are held for a wide range of courses, and successful applicants are given an individualised offer. Conditional offers are made in UCAS Tariff points. For some courses you may need to include points from certain subjects in your Tariff points score. In 2019 the following subjects did not go into Clearing: Dental Hygiene, Midwifery, Nursing Studies (Child) (Pre-Reg) and Paramedic Practice. All new students are provided with an iPad to access university resources and to use throughout their studies. Optional placement years are available on courses in Business, Art and Design, Computing and Engineering Sciences.

Trinity Saint David The University's main campuses are situated in various locations in and around Swansea's city centre as well as in the rural towns of Lampeter and Carmarthen in South West Wales. Study at the Lampeter campus comprises Single and Joint Honours degrees in a wide range of Humanities and Carmarthen has a strong Art and Design focus.

The University guarantees to give equal consideration to all applicants irrespective of when their applications are received. Applicants who successfully complete the residential Wales Summer School at Lampeter, Aberystwyth or Carmarthen are offered a place on an appropriate course of study on completion of their current school or college course. All other candidates will be invited to an interview to discuss their course choice. Entry is based on individual merit.

UCO This is the largest and oldest osteopathic school in the UK (based in London), offering undergraduate and postgraduate qualifications.

Shortlisted applicants will be invited to attend an interview and evaluation day at the UCO.

UHI The University of the Highlands and Islands offers a range of courses at centres throughout Scotland including Argyll, Inverness, Perth, Orkney and Shetland.

Contact the institution regarding its requirements and procedures.

Ulster The University of Ulster is based on three sites spread across Northern Ireland: Jordanstown (Belfast), Coleraine and Magee (Derry). The Faculties of Computing, Engineering and the Built Environment, Life and Health Sciences, Arts, Humanities and Social Sciences and Ulster University Business School offer a wide range of courses. There are various styles of learning supported by formal lectures and many courses include periods of work placement.

Information is available via www.ulster.ac.uk/study.

Univ Law The private University of Law offers undergraduate Law degrees with a variety of full-time, part-time and online study options, all based on a traditional three-year full-time Qualifying Law Degree. There is a choice of where to study across the country, with centres in Birmingham, Bristol, Chester, Guildford, Leeds, London and Manchester. The courses combine academic rigour and practical skills, taught by qualified lawyers, often in small group workshops, with a strong emphasis on individual tutor contact and feedback. Employability is built into the course, through learning materials and teaching. If you're looking for a career in law, it is also possible to continue postgraduate study with their Legal Practice Course (LPC) to practise as a solicitor or their Bar Professional Training Course (BPTC) to prepare you for life as a barrister. De Broc is the business school of the University of Law. It offers undergraduate business degrees with a focus on providing the training employers are looking for so that you're ready to do business from day one. If you're interested in a particular business specialism, the school offers pathways in finance, marketing and human resource management. The flexible course structure also allows you to switch to an alternative route should your aspirations change. You can choose to study on campus at the London Bloomsbury centre in the heart of London's West End or entirely online for those seeking greater flexibility.

Apply through UCAS for full-time courses, and for part-time courses apply direct to the University of Law.

UWE Bristol The University consists of several campuses in Bristol including Frenchay (the largest), Bower Ashton (Creative Industries), Glenside (Health and Applied Sciences) and Gloucester (Nursing). The University offers Single and Combined Honours courses organised on a modular basis which gives much flexibility in the choice of options. Many courses include optional sandwich placements and, in addition, students on many programmes have the opportunity to undertake a period of study in another European country.

Offers may vary between applicants since selection is based on individual merit. Students applying for courses 'subject to approval' or 'subject to validation' will be kept informed of the latest developments. Most offers will be made in terms of UCAS Tariff points with specific subjects required for some programmes.

Warwick Courses are offered by departments in the Faculties of Arts, Science and Social Studies and the Warwick Medical School, which only accepts graduate applications. The University's undergraduate students can either choose single-subject degrees or combine two or more subjects in a Joint Honours degree. Options offered in each course provide some flexibility for you to tailor your course to your own areas of academic interest. Whatever course you choose, you can apply to study abroad, and many of its courses have inbuilt overseas experiences. Some of its degrees offer work placements and/or professional accreditation.

Before you decide to apply, you should check the entry requirements for your course. You will find the typical offer levels at https://warwick.ac.uk/study/undergraduate/apply/entry. Advice on the completion of your application is available at https://warwick.ac.uk/study. Feedback can be provided if requested for candidates whose application has been unsuccessful. The University welcomes applications for deferred entry.

West London UWL provides a high quality experience connected to the world of work. Subjects offered cover Business and Accounting, Law and Criminology, Tourism, Aviation, Hospitality and Leisure, Computing and Engineering, Music and Performing Arts, Film, Media and Design, Nursing, Midwifery and Healthcare, Education, Forensic Science and Psychology. Credit-rated Honours courses are offered, many with year-long work placements between Years 2 and 3. There are some study-abroad arrangements in Europe and there is a large mature student intake.

The University accepts a wide range of qualifications for entry to all of its undergraduate courses. It is also possible to transfer credits achieved at another university to a course at this university.

West Scotland UWS has campuses in Ayr, Dumfries, Lanarkshire, London and Paisley and provides a range of vocationally related courses, with a combination of links with employers, practical opportunities and professional recognition.

Applications are considered by the Admissions Office against previously agreed academic entry qualifications provided by the following Schools: Business and Enterprise; Engineering and Computing; Media, Culture and Society; Health, Nursing and Midwifery; Education; and Science and Sport. Within the Schools of Education; Media, Culture and Society; Health, Nursing and Midwifery; Engineering and Computing; and Science and Sport, applicants may be invited to attend an audition or interview prior to an offer being made.

Westminster Based in the heart of London with over a million businesses within a 20-mile radius, the University of Westminster offers a wide range of practice-based and career-focused courses that help students gain the skills and experience required to succeed in professional life. The University has one of the country's largest university scholarship schemes available, awarding over £2.9 million per year in scholarships.

Interviews are usually required for Media, Art and Design courses and Complementary Therapy courses. Applicants for creative courses should bring a portfolio of practical work to interviews. The University accepts transfers into Years 1, 2 and 3 of a full-time degree programme if students have studied similar units to the chosen Westminster course, and have passed Year 1 and Year 2, each with 120 credits, excluding all Westminster Business School degrees, Fashion Design and Film.

Winchester The University offers undergraduate and postgraduate study on a range of subjects within the arts, humanities, social sciences, business, law, sport, education, and health and social care. Single Honours courses generally encompass core modules, complemented by a range of optional modules which enable students to tailor their degree towards their own interests.

Interviews are required for a number of courses, including Choreography & Dance, Comedy (Performance and Production), Social Work and Theology, Religion & Ethics. Scholarships are offered to applicants for Anthropology, Mathematics, Music and Sound Production and Physiotherapy. Please make sure to check the website for the most up-to-date information before applying.

Wolverhampton A large number of specialist and Joint Honours degrees are offered and many have work placements at home or abroad. Except for courses linked to specific professional requirements, programmes are modular providing flexibility of choice.

Admissions staff make decisions on the basis of the application, and may invite applicants for interview or audition. If an applicant cannot meet the entry requirements for the chosen course, the University may offer an alternative course, or give the applicant feedback about why it was unable to offer a place.

Worcester A wide range of undergraduate courses in Education, Health, Sport, Arts, Humanities, Sciences and Business are on offer with Single and Joint Honours degrees available. The University is close to Worcester city centre, and most of its halls of residence, many of which are en-suite, are right on campus.

The University accepts a wide range of qualifications including Access to HE Diplomas. The majority of offers are based on UCAS Tariff points but some courses have specific subject or GCSE requirements. Many courses require interviews before an offer is made, including Primary Education and Nursing courses. The personal statement is highly important and applicants are advised to reflect on interests, work experience, voluntary experience, extra-curricular activities and achievements relevant to their chosen course. If the applicant fails to receive an offer for their chosen course then an offer for an alternative course may be made.

Writtle (UC) The College is situated in Chelmsford, Essex and is one of the largest land-based colleges in the UK. Higher and further education courses include Agriculture, Animal Sciences, Bioveterinary Science, Equine Studies, Landscape and Garden Design and Veterinary Physiotherapy.

Application details for the full range of courses offered are available on the College's website.

York Thirty departments and centres cover a range of subjects in the arts and humanities, sciences, social sciences and medicine. The 'Languages for All' programme enables any student to take a course in any one of a number of languages, in addition to which there are several opportunities to build a period abroad into a degree course.

Decisions on offers are made in the following ways. Centralised decision making: Archaeology, Economics, Education, History, History of Art, Language and Linguistic Science, Management, PEP, Philosophy, Politics, Psychology, Social Policy, Social and Political Sciences, Sociology. Semi-centralised decision making: Law, Mathematics, Physics. Devolved decision making in academic departments: Biology, Biochemistry, Biomedical Science, Chemistry, Computer Science, Electronics, English, Environment, Hull York Medical School, Music, Nursing and Midwifery, Natural Sciences, Social Work, Theatre Film and Television. All candidates are interviewed for Biology, Chemistry, Health Sciences, Law, Medicine, Music, Natural Sciences, Physics, Social Work and Theatre Film and Television. There are optional interviews for Maths. Hull York Medical School offers a Medicine with a Gateway Year programme, allowing locally based UK applicants who meet Widening Participation requirements to apply for Medicine with lower expected grades.

York St John A city centre university with nine schools: Art and Design, Education, Health Sciences, Humanities, Religion and Philosophy, Languages and Linguistics, Performance and Media Production, Psychological and Social Sciences, Sport, and York Business School. These offer a range of specialist degrees with Joint Honours courses offered in Business, Counselling, Education, Health Studies, Information Technology, Languages and Linguistics, Management, Psychology and Sport.

Interviews are compulsory for Physiotherapy and Primary Education courses.

4 | APPLICATIONS

ENTRY REQUIREMENTS

Before applying to universities and colleges, be sure that you have the required subjects and qualifications for entry to your chosen course. Details of entry requirements are available direct from the universities and colleges. You will need to check:

 (i) the general entry requirements for courses
 (ii) any specific subject requirements to enter a particular course, for example, study of specified GCE A-levels and (where required) AS, Scottish Highers/Advanced Highers, GCSEs, Scottish Nationals, or BTEC qualifications (for example, Diploma, Certificate). The course requirements are set out in prospectuses and on websites
(iii) any age, health, Disclosure and Barring Service (DBS; formerly CRB) clearance or other requirements for entry to particular courses and universities and colleges. For entry to some specific courses such as Medicine and Nursing, offers are made subject to health screening for hepatitis B, for example, and immunisation requirements. Owing to government regulations, some universities will insist on a minimum age at entry of 18 years. Check university and college websites and prospectuses for these particular course requirements
(iv) admissions tests required by a number of universities for a range of subjects, including Dentistry, Law, Medicine and Veterinary Science/Medicine. Offers of places made by these universities are dependent on an applicant's performance in the relevant test. It is important to find out full details about universities' course requirements for possible admissions tests well before submitting the UCAS application and to make all the necessary arrangements for registering and taking any required admissions tests. See **Chapter 5** and check university/college and admissions tests websites for the latest information.

Potential applicants should ask the advice of teachers, careers advisers and university and college advisers before submitting their application.

APPLICATIONS FOR UNIVERSITY AND COLLEGE COURSES THROUGH UCAS

UCAS, the organisation responsible for managing applications to higher education courses in the UK, deals with applications for admission to full-time and sandwich first degrees, Foundation degrees, Diploma of Higher Education and Higher National Diploma courses and some full-time Higher National Certificate courses in nearly all universities (but not the Open University), university colleges, colleges and institutes of higher education, specialist colleges and some further education colleges. The UCAS Undergraduate scheme also is applicable for those applying for teacher training courses in Scotland.

The UCAS application process

Full details of application procedures and all course information can be found on the UCAS website (www.ucas.com).

Applications are made online at www.ucas.com using **Apply**. This is a secure web-based application system, which has been designed for all applicants whether they are applying through a UCAS-registered centre, such as a school or college, or applying independently from anywhere in the world.

Applications for 2021 entry can be sent to UCAS from 8 September 2020. The first deadline is 15 October by 18.00 (UK time) for applications to the universities of Oxford or Cambridge and applications for most courses in Medicine, Dentistry and Veterinary Science/Medicine. The deadline for UK and EU applicants to apply for all other courses is 15 January by 18.00 (UK time). You can still apply after this deadline up to 30 June, but institutions may not be able to consider you.

On the UCAS application, you have up to five course choices unless you are applying for Dentistry, Medicine or Veterinary Science/Medicine. For these courses only four choices are permitted; however, you can make another subject your fifth choice.

Each university or college makes any offer through the UCAS system. UCAS does not make offers, or recruit on behalf of universities and colleges. It does not advise applicants on their choice of subject although it does publish material which applicants may find useful.

Applicants may receive an 'unconditional' offer in the case of those who already hold the required qualifications, or, for those awaiting examination results, a 'conditional' offer or a rejection. When all decisions have been received from universities or colleges, applicants may finally hold up to two offers: a firm choice (first) offer and an insurance offer. Applicants who have made five choices and have no offers or have declined any offers received can use **Extra**. Applicants are told if they become eligible for **Extra** and can apply online for one further course at a time using **Track** at www.ucas.com. **Extra** runs from 25 February until 4 July. Courses available in **Extra** can be found in the search tool at www.ucas.com. Applicants not placed through this system will be eligible to contact institutions with vacancies in **Clearing** from 5 July. If you're holding a confirmed place and decide you no longer want it, from 5 July you can use online self-release into Clearing by using the 'decline your place' button in Track. You should only use this button if you no longer wish to take up your place at your firm choice and you have spoken to your university or college and/or an adviser at your school/centre.

If you already have your qualifications and are not waiting for any exam results, your place can be confirmed at any time after you send in your application. However, for thousands of applicants confirmation starts on the day when the A-level examination results are released. Clearing vacancies are listed in the search tool from early July to late-September. Applicants meeting the conditions of their offers for their firm choice will receive confirmation from their university or college and may still be accepted even if their results are slightly lower than those stipulated in the original offer. If rejected by their firm choice university/college, applicants will have their places confirmed by their insurance choice institution providing they have obtained the right grades. Applicants who are unsuccessful with both their institutions will be eligible to go into **Clearing** in which they can select an appropriate course in the same or a different institution where places are available. In 2019, a record high of 73,320 applicants obtained places through **Clearing**, and 4,635 applicants found a place though **Extra**.

Each year some applicants pass their exams with better results than expected. This may mean that some will not only have met the conditions of their firm choice, but will have exceeded them. UCAS introduced **Adjustment** for these applicants – it provides an opportunity to reconsider where and what to study while holding a confirmed place. The **Adjustment** process is available from A-level results day (19 August 2021) until 31 August.

UCAS timetable

8 September 2020	UCAS begins accepting applications.
15 October	Deadline for UCAS to receive applications to Oxford University or the University of Cambridge, and applications to most courses in Medicine, Dentistry or Veterinary Medicine/Science.
15 January 2021	Deadline for UCAS to receive applications from UK and EU applicants for all other courses.
16 January–30 June	Applications received by UCAS are forwarded to the institutions for consideration at their discretion. Applications received after 30 June are processed through **Clearing**.
25 February–4 July	Applicants who have made five choices and have no offers or who have declined any offers received can use **Extra** to apply for one further course at a time on **Track** at www.ucas.com. Institutions will show which courses have vacancies in **Extra** on the UCAS website. Details of the **Extra** service can be found at www.ucas.com/extra.
5 May	Applicants who have received all their decisions from universities and colleges by the end of March are asked to reply to their offers by this date.
3 June	Applicants receiving decisions from all their choices by 6 May must reply to their offers by this date.

30 June	Last date for receiving applications. Applications received after this date are entered directly into Clearing. On 6 July Clearing starts.
10 August	Scottish SQA results published.
19 August	GCE A-level and AS results published. (See **What To Do on Results Day ... and After** below.)

PLEASE NOTE

- You are not required to reply to any university/college offers until you have received your last decision.
- Do not send a firm acceptance to more than one offer.
- Do not try to alter a firm acceptance.
- If you decide not to go to university or college this year you can go to Track to completely cancel your application. But don't forget, you will not be able to reapply until next year.
- Remember to tell the institutions and UCAS if you change your address, or change your examination board, subjects or arrangements.

Information on the special arrangements for applications for Law, Medicine and Dentistry can be found under separate headings in Chapter 5.

APPLICATIONS FOR MUSIC COURSES AT CONSERVATOIRES

UCAS Conservatoires handles applications for practice-based music, dance, drama and musical theatre courses. Applications can be made simultaneously to a maximum of six of the conservatoires listed below and simultaneous applications can also be made through both UCAS Undergraduate and UCAS Conservatoires systems. Full details of UCAS Conservatoires are given on www.ucas.com/conservatoires. The conservatoires taking part in this online admissions system are:

- Bristol Old Vic Theatre School www.oldvic.ac.uk
- Leeds College of Music www.lcm.ac.uk
- Royal Academy of Music www.ram.ac.uk
- Royal Birmingham Conservatoire www.bcu.ac.uk/conservatoire
- Royal College of Music www.rcm.ac.uk
- Royal Conservatoire of Scotland www.rcs.ac.uk
- Royal Northern College of Music www.rncm.ac.uk
- Royal Welsh College of Music & Drama www.rwcmd.ac.uk
- Trinity Laban Conservatoire of Music & Dance www.trinitylaban.ac.uk

The Guildhall School of Music & Drama is not part of the UCAS Conservatoires scheme, so students wishing to apply will have to make their applications directly to the school. There is an application fee, which varies depending on the course for which you apply; the fee includes the audition fee, which is charged by all conservatoires. For more details, see the Guildhall website. Similarly, applications for the Conservatoire for Dance and Drama (a group of eight specialist colleges) and the Royal Central School of Speech and Drama should be made directly to the schools as they are not part of the UCAS Conservatoires scheme either.

APPLICATIONS FOR TEACHER TRAINING COURSES

Applicants intending to start a course of initial teacher training in England, Northern Ireland and Wales leading to Qualified Teacher Status can find information on the Get Into Teaching website https://getintoteaching.education.gov.uk. See also www.ucas.com/teaching-in-the-uk for full details of applying for undergraduate (and postgraduate) training courses. Scottish students should apply through UCAS Undergraduate for teacher training courses.

APPLICATIONS FOR DEGREE APPRENTICESHIP COURSES

Applications for degree apprenticeship courses in England are handled by GOV.UK (www.gov.uk/apply-apprenticeship). It is likely that the employer and university will jointly recruit for their vacancies, to ensure that both are satisfied that the applicant can meet their respective requirements. You can use UCAS' career finder tool to see details of a number of new degree apprenticeship vacancies. Deadlines for vacancies vary so you'll need to keep an eye on these. Please also see page 11.

THE UCAS APPLICATION

In the choices section of **Apply**, all your university/college choices (a maximum of five) are to be listed, but remember that you should not mix your subjects. For example, in popular subject areas such as English, History or Physiotherapy, it is safer to show total commitment by applying for all courses in the same subject and not to include second and/or third subject alternatives on the form. (See advice in separate tables in **Chapter 7** for **Medicine**, **Dentistry** and **Veterinary Science/Medicine**.)

A brief glance at the subject tables in **Chapter 7** will give you some idea of the popularity of various courses. In principle, institutions want the best applicants available so if there are large numbers of applicants the offers made will be higher. For Medicine and a number of other courses, offers in terms of A-level grades are now reaching AAA or A* grades, and sometimes with additional grades at AS, where school policy does not limit your opportunity to take AS subjects (in which case alternative A-level offers may be given). Conversely, for the less popular subjects, the offers can be much lower – down to CCC.

Similarly, some institutions are more popular (not necessarily better) than others. Again, this popularity can be judged easily in the tables in **Chapter 7**: the higher the offer, the more popular the institution. Popular universities often are located in attractive towns or cities such as Bristol, Exeter, Warwick, Bath or York. Because of the intense competition for places at the popular universities, applications to five of them could result in rejections from all of them! (If you are not good enough for one of them you won't be good enough for the other four!) Spread your choice of institutions.

When you have chosen your courses and your institutions, look again at the offers made and compare these with the grades projected by your teachers. It is most important to maximise your chances of a place by choosing institutions which might make you a range of offers. When all universities have considered your application you can hold only two offers (one firm and one insurance offer) and naturally it is preferable for one to be lower than the other in case you do not achieve the offer grades or equivalent points for your first choice of university or college.

The other section of the UCAS application that deserves careful thought is the personal statement. This seems simple enough but it is the only part of the application where you can put in a personal bid for a place! In short, you are asked to give relevant background information about yourself, your interests and your choice of course and career. Give yourself plenty of time to prepare your personal statement as this part of your application could make all the difference to getting an offer or not.

The personal statement

The statement is your only opportunity to make a personal bid for your chosen courses. The University of Surrey advises applicants to include the following information:

- Why you want to study the course you have chosen. Show why you are passionate about the field.
- How your current studies have helped you to prepare for university. Be reflective – explain why you have made certain choices and what you have learnt, but do not go into lots of detail.
- How you have gone above and beyond the curriculum to demonstrate your interest in the subject (for example, books you have read, taster sessions you have attended).
- Your skills and experiences (including work and placements) and how you feel they will help you to succeed on your chosen course.
- The achievements that you are particularly proud of. Be honest – you may be asked about them at interview!
- What you hope to gain from university, and your career aspirations.
- Your interests and hobbies. It is recommended that 75% of your statement be academic/course related, while the other 25% can focus on extra-curricular activities.

Motivation to undertake your chosen course is very important. You can show this by giving details of any work experience and work shadowing you have done (and for History courses, for example, details of visits to places of historical interest). It is a good idea to begin your statement with such evidence and explain how your interest in your chosen subject has developed. In the subject tables in **Chapter 7** under **Advice to applicants and planning the UCAS personal statement**, advice is given on what you might include in your personal statement. You should also include various activities in which you have been involved in the last three or four years. Get your parents and other members of the family to refresh your memory – it is easy to forget something quite important. You might consider planning out this section in a series of sub-sections – and if you have a lot to say, be brief. The sub-sections can include the following.

- **School activities** Are you a prefect, chairperson or treasurer of a society? Are you involved in supervisory duties of any kind? Are you in a school team? Which team? For how long? (Remember, team means any team: sports, chess, debating, even business.)
- **Intellectual activities** Have you attended any field or lecture courses in your main subjects? Where? When? Have you taken part in any school visits? Do you play in the school orchestra or have you taken part in a school drama production – on or off stage? Do you go to the theatre, art galleries or concerts?
- **Out-of-school activities** This category might cover many of the topics above, but it could also include any community or voluntary work you do, or Duke of Edinburgh Awards, the Combined Cadet Force (CCF), sport, music and drama activities etc. The countries you have visited might also be mentioned, for example, any exchange visits with friends living abroad.
- **Work experience** Details of part-time, holiday or Saturday jobs could be included here, particularly if they have some connection with your chosen course. Some applicants plan ahead and arrange to visit firms and discuss career interests with various people who already work in their chosen field. For some courses such as Veterinary Science, work experience is essential, and it certainly helps for others, for example Medicine and Business courses.
- **Functional/Essential Skills** These cover maths, English and information technology (the basics) and also advanced skills involving teamwork, communication, problem solving and improving your own learning. If you are not offering the qualifications then evidence of your strengths in these areas may be mentioned in the school or college reference or you may include examples in your personal statement relating to your out-of-school activities.

Finally, plan your personal statement carefully. Although you are not required to write in continuous prose, it is advisable to do so as this is likely to make a better impression on admissions tutors. Your statement should be written in good, clear English, and it is essential that your spelling and grammar be accurate throughout. Keep a copy of your complete application for reference if you are called for interview. Almost certainly you will be questioned on what you have written.

Admissions tutors always stress the importance of the confidential reference from your head teacher or form tutors. Most schools and colleges will make some effort to find out why you want to apply for a particular course, but if they do not ask, do not take it for granted that they will know! Consequently, although you have the opportunity to write about your interests on the form, it is still a good idea to tell your teachers about them. Also, if you have to work at home under difficult conditions or if you have any medical problems, your teachers must be told since these points should be mentioned on the reference.

Deferred entry

Although application is usually made in the autumn of the year preceding the proposed year of entry, admissions tutors may be prepared to consider an application made two years before entry, so that the applicant can, perhaps, gain work experience or spend a period abroad. Policies on deferred entry may differ from department to department, so you should check with admissions tutors before applying. Simply remember that there is no guarantee that you will get the grades you need or a place at the university of your first choice at the first attempt! If not, you may need to repeat A-levels and try again. It may be better not to apply for deferred entry until you are certain in August of your grades and your place.

APPLICATIONS TO THE UNIVERSITY OF CAMBRIDGE

The universities of Oxford and Cambridge offer a wealth of resources and opportunities to students, including highly personalised teaching in tutorials (at Oxford) or supervisions (at Cambridge), where groups of two or three students meet to discuss their work with a tutor (Oxford) or supervisor (Cambridge). The college system is also a key advantage of an Oxbridge education, as students gain all the benefits of studying at a large and internationally acclaimed university, as well as the benefits of life in the smaller college community.

If you are a UK or EU applicant applying to Cambridge, you need only complete the UCAS application. Your UCAS application listing Cambridge as one of your university choices must be sent to UCAS by 15 October, 18.00 (UK time). If you are applying for Medicine or Veterinary Medicine you must include your BMAT registration with your application. You can indicate your choice of college or make an Open application if you have no preference. Open applicants are allocated by a computer program to colleges that have had fewer applicants per place for your chosen subject.

Following the submission of your application to UCAS, you will receive an email from the University, confirming the arrival of your application and giving you the website address of their online Supplementary Application Questionnaire (SAQ), which you will then need to complete and return by the specified date. International students and prospective organ scholars also need to submit a Cambridge Online Preliminary Application (COPA) by the required deadline; further details are available on the Cambridge website. Check with the Admissions Office or on www.undergraduate.study.cam.ac.uk/applying for the latest information.

The Extenuating Circumstances Form (ECF) has been designed to ensure that the Cambridge colleges have the information they require in order to accurately assess any applicant who has experienced particular personal or educational disadvantage through health, personal problems, disability or difficulties with schooling. The ECF should normally be submitted by the applicant's school/college by 22 October. Further details can be obtained at www.undergraduate.study.cam.ac.uk/applying/decisions/extenuating-circumstances-form.

Interviews take place in Cambridge in the first three weeks of December, although some may be earlier. The colleges at the University of Cambridge use common format written assessments to be taken by all applicants for all subjects, except Mathematics and Music. Applicants will take the written assessments either pre-interview or at interview (or both for some courses), depending on the course for which they apply. Pre-interview assessments will take place on 30 October, on the same day as those set by the University of Oxford, while at-interview assessments will form part of the December interview period. Please see www.undergraduate.study.cam.ac.uk/applying/admission-assessments for further information on these assessments and **Chapter 5** for information you need to know before completing and submitting your application.

In January, applicants receive either an offer conditional upon certain grades in examinations to be taken the following summer, or a rejection. Alternatively, you may be placed in a pool for further consideration. Decisions are made on the basis of academic record, reference, personal statement, submitted work/test results and interviews. The conditions set are grades to be obtained in examinations such as A-levels, Scottish Highers/Advanced Highers or the International Baccalaureate. Offers made will include Sixth Term Examination Papers (STEP) in mathematics (see **Chapter 5** under *Mathematics*). The STEPs are taken in June and copies of past papers and full details are available from www.admissionstesting.org.

College policies

All colleges that admit undergraduates use the selection procedures described in **Chapter 5**. However, there will be some minor variations between the various colleges, within each college and also between subjects. Further information about the policies of any particular college can be found in the Cambridge Undergraduate Prospectus and may also be obtained from the admissions tutor of the college concerned. No college operates a quota system for any subject except Medicine and Veterinary Medicine, for which there are strict quotas for the University from which places are allocated to each college.

Full details of the admissions procedures are contained in the current Cambridge Undergraduate Prospectus. Copies of the prospectus are available from Cambridge Admissions Office, Student Services Centre, New Museums Site, Cambridge CB2 3PT, or via the website www.undergraduate.study.cam.ac.uk.

APPLICATIONS TO THE UNIVERSITY OF OXFORD

Applications for undergraduate courses at Oxford are made through UCAS in the same way as applications to other UK universities. Candidates must submit their application by 18:00 (UK time), 15 October for entry in the following year.

You can only apply to one undergraduate course at Oxford. You can also express a preference for a particular college if you wish, or you can make an Open application. This indicates that you don't mind which college you go to, meaning your application will be allocated to a college which has relatively fewer applications for your subject in that year. The colleges are generally similar – they all provide a high standard of academic teaching for all the courses they offer. However, once an application has been allocated to a college, this is final. If there are any colleges you do not want to go to, you should name a college preference rather than submitting an Open application.

Most Oxford courses require candidates to sit a written test by 30 October as part of their application, while some also ask candidates to submit examples of their written work by 10 November. See **Chapter 5** for more information and www.ox.ac.uk/tests and www.ox.ac.uk/writwork for more details. Separate registration is required for any tests, so it is really important to check the details for your subject in the summer before you apply.

When considering your application, tutors will take into account all the information that has been provided, in order to assess your suitability and potential for your chosen course. This includes your academic record, personal statement, academic reference and predicted grades, alongside any admissions tests or any written work required. Each application is considered carefully on its individual merits, including contextual information about candidates' educational background.

A shortlist of candidates will be invited to Oxford for interviews held in early to mid-December. The interview is a crucial part of the selection process (see www.ox.ac.uk/interviews for more details). Candidates will be interviewed by two tutors (occasionally more) at their college of preference (if they have specified one), or the college which they have been allocated to (if they submitted an Open application), and they may also be interviewed by other colleges. Those from outside Europe who are not able to travel may request to be interviewed by telephone or Skype or some other remote means. However, shortlisted candidates applying for Medicine and Fine Art will need to travel to Oxford for the interview. The University works hard to ensure that the best candidates are successful, whichever college you have applied to. This means a lot of successful applicants receive an offer from a college they did not specify on their application.

Successful candidates who have not completed their school-leaving examinations will be made conditional offers based on final grades. This will be probably be between A*A*A and AAA at A-level, 38–40 points in the International Baccalaureate (including core points) with 776–666 at Higher level, or other equivalent qualifications (see www.ox.ac.uk/enreqs). Decisions are notified to candidates via UCAS by the end of January.

To find out more
The University holds three Open Days a year: two in late June or early July, and one in mid-September. These are highly recommended as a great way to visit the city and the University, meet tutors and current students and find out more. Visit the website at www.ox.ac.uk/study for further information, and details of other events around the UK and beyond.

APPLICATIONS TO THE RUSSELL GROUP

The 24 Russell Group universities are:
University of Birmingham; University of Bristol; University of Cambridge; Cardiff University; Durham University; University of Edinburgh; University of Exeter; University of Glasgow; Imperial College London; King's College London; University of Leeds; University of Liverpool; London School of Economics and Political Science; University of Manchester; Newcastle University; University of Nottingham; University

of Oxford; Queen Mary University of London; Queen's University Belfast; University of Sheffield; University of Southampton; University College London; University of Warwick; University of York. (See also under London (LSE) in **Chapter 3**.)

The Russell Group has published information on what it terms 'Informed Choices', ie how subjects taken at sixth form and college can affect students' options at university and beyond, and which subject choices can open up various degrees. This information can be found at www.informedchoices.ac.uk.

APPLICATIONS TO IRISH UNIVERSITIES
All applications to universities, colleges of education and institutes of technology, along with some specialist colleges, in the Republic of Ireland are made through the Central Application Office, Tower House, Eglinton Street, Galway, Ireland; see www.cao.ie or telephone 091 509800. The CAO website gives full details of all institutions and details of the application procedure. Applications are made by 1 February. Individual institutions publish details of their entry requirements for courses, but unlike applications through UCAS in the UK, no conditional offers are made. Applicants are judged purely on their academic ability. Offers are made in August following the release of Leaving Certificate results, and successful students are required to quickly accept or decline the offer.

APPLICATIONS TO COMMONWEALTH UNIVERSITIES
Details of universities in 50 commonwealth countries (all charge fees) are published on the website of the Association for Commonwealth Universities, www.acu.ac.uk, or for those in Australia, on www.idp. com/australia, and for those in Canada, www.studyincanada.com.

APPLICATIONS TO AMERICAN UNIVERSITIES
There is a very large number of universities and colleges offering degree course programmes in the USA; some institutions are independent and others state-controlled. Students applying to study in the USA can apply to over 650 institutions through the Common Application, the central admissions system. However, unlike the UK, where UCAS controls nearly all university and college applications, it is still necessary to apply to American institutions directly; a full list of participating Common Application colleges can be downloaded from the website at www.commonapp.org. Most American universities will expect applicants to have A-levels or IB qualifications and usually require students to complete either the SAT or ACT admissions tests. The SAT Reasoning Test covers mathematical and evidence-based reasoning abilities. In some cases applicants may be required to complete a writing task as part of the reasoning test, as well as taking SAT II tests which are based on specific subjects. The ACT tests English, maths, comprehension and scientific reasoning. Some universities require applicants to take the ACT with writing, which includes an additional writing task. Both the SAT and the ACT can be taken at centres in the UK: see www.collegeboard.org and www.act.org respectively for details.

Unlike the usual specialised subject degrees at UK universities, in the USA you just apply as an undergraduate, rather than to a specific degree. 'Liberal Arts' programmes in the USA have considerable breadth and flexibility, although subjects requiring greater specialised knowledge such as Medicine and Law require further study at Medical or Law School.

While each institution has its own admissions requirements and timetable, in general early application deadlines are mid-November and regular application deadlines are between January and March.

Because of the complexities of an application to American universities, such as financial implications, visas, etc, students should initially refer to www.fulbright.co.uk. It is also important to be able to identify the differences between and the quality of institutions, and valuable guides can be sourced through www.petersons.com.

THE ERASMUS+ PROGRAMME
Many universities in the UK have formal agreements with partner institutions in Europe through the Erasmus+ programme which enables UK undergraduate students to apply for courses or work placements in one of 32 other European countries for periods of three to twelve months as part of their degree course. Some of these courses are taught in English and students can receive help with accommodation and other expenses through the Erasmus+ Student Grant scheme.

Most universities offer it, although it is not available with every course so students are advised to check with their chosen universities before making an application. Students do not pay any fees to the European university they visit and those who go for the full academic year (24 weeks) have their UK tuition fees reduced. Following Britain's departure from the European Union on 31 January 2020, the UK's future participation in the Erasmus+ programme is to be determined as part of formal discussions with the EU. Until the UK has finalised the terms of its withdrawal with the other Member States, students will continue to have access to the Erasmus+ scheme under the current terms of the programme, until the end of 2020 at least.

AND FINALLY ... BEFORE YOU SEND IN YOUR APPLICATION

CHECK that you have passes at grade 4/C or higher in the GCSE (or equivalent) subjects required for the course at the institutions to which you are applying. FAILURE TO HAVE THE RIGHT GCSE SUBJECTS OR THE RIGHT NUMBER OF GRADE 4/C OR ABOVE PASSES IN GCSE WILL RESULT IN A REJECTION.

CHECK that you are taking (or have taken) the GCE A-level subjects required for the course at the institution to which you are applying. FAILURE TO BE TAKING OR HAVE TAKEN THE RIGHT A-LEVELS WILL ALSO RESULT IN A REJECTION.

CHECK that the GCE A-levels and any other qualifications you are taking will be accepted for the course for which you are applying. Some subjects and institutions do not stipulate any specific A-levels, only that you are required to offer two or three subjects at GCE A-level. In the view of some admissions tutors NOT ALL GCE A-LEVELS CARRY THE SAME WEIGHT (see **Chapter 1**).

CHECK that you can meet the requirements for all relevant admissions/interview tests.

CHECK that you have made all the necessary arrangements for sitting any required admissions tests.

CHECK that you can meet any age, health and DBS requirements for entry to your listed courses.

WHAT TO DO ON RESULTS DAY ... AND AFTER

BE AT HOME! Do not arrange to be away when your results are published. If you do not achieve the grades you require, you will need to follow an alternative course of action and make decisions that could affect your life for the next few years. Do not expect others to make these decisions for you. If you achieve the grades or points of your offer you will receive confirmation of a place, but this may take a few days to reach you. Once your place is confirmed, contact the accommodation office at the university or college and inform them that you will need a place in a hall of residence or other accommodation.

From 5 July you can use online self-release into Clearing by using the 'decline your place' button in Track. You should only use this button if you no longer wish to take up your place at your firm choice and you have spoken to your university or college and/or an adviser at your school/centre.

If you achieve grades or points higher than your conditional firm (CF) choice you can reconsider where and what to study by registering with UCAS to use the **Adjustment** process in **Track**. This is available from A-level results day until 31 August and you have five days to register and secure an alternative course. You must check very carefully all the **Adjustment** information on the UCAS website (www.ucas.com/adjustment) to make sure you are eligible and that a vacancy is available. There is no guarantee of a vacancy on a course you are aiming for, and it is very unlikely that competitive courses will have places. If you decide definitely to change courses advise the university or college immediately, but check with www.ucas.com and your school/college adviser for the latest information.

If your grades or points are higher than you expected and you are not holding any offers you can telephone or email the admissions tutor at the universities and colleges which rejected you and request that they might reconsider you.

If you just miss your offers then telephone or email the universities and colleges to see if they can still offer you a place. ALWAYS HAVE YOUR UCAS PERSONAL ID AVAILABLE WHEN YOU CALL. Their decisions may take a few days. You should check the universities and colleges in your order of preference. Your first choice must reject you before you contact your second choice.

If you have not applied to any university or college earlier in the year then you can apply through the **Clearing** scheme which runs from early July. Check the tables in **Chapter 7** to identify which institutions normally make offers matching your results, check **Clearing** vacancy listings, and then telephone or email the institution before completing your application.

If you learn finally that you do not have a place because you have missed the grades in your offer you'll know you're in **Clearing** if your **Track** status says 'You are in **Clearing**' or '**Clearing** has started', and your **Clearing** number will be displayed.

If an institution has vacancies they will ask you for your grades. Get informal offers over the phone – maybe from a variety of universities and colleges – then decide which one you want to accept. If you're given an offer you want to accept, and you have permission from the university or college, you can add a **Clearing** choice in **Track**. You can only add one choice at a time, but if the university or college doesn't confirm your place, you'll be able to add another.

If you have to re-apply for a place, check the vacancies on the UCAS website (www.ucas.com). If there are vacancies in your subject, check with the university or college that these vacancies have not been taken.

REMEMBER – There are many thousands of students just like you. Admissions tutors have a mammoth task checking how many students will be taking up their places since not all students whose grades match their offers finally decide to do so!

IF YOU HAVE AN OFFER AND THE RIGHT GRADES BUT ARE NOT ACCEPTING THAT OR AN ALTERNATIVE PLACE – TELL THE UNIVERSITY OR COLLEGE. Someone else is waiting for your place! If you are applying for a place through **Clearing** it may even be late September before you know you have a place so BE PATIENT AND STAY CALM!

Good luck!

ADMISSIONS TESTS, SELECTION OF APPLICANTS AND INTERVIEWS

The selection of applicants by universities and colleges takes many forms. Competition for places is tough. Great importance is attached not only to applicants' predicted A-level grades and GCSE attainments, but also to other aspects of their applications, especially the school reference and the personal statement and, for some courses and some institutions, performance at interview, and performance in admissions tests.

ADMISSIONS TESTS
Admissions tests are now increasingly used for undergraduate entry to specific courses and specific institutions. These include national subject-based tests such as LNAT, BMAT and UCAT (see below) which are used for selecting applicants for entry to specified courses at particular institutions in subjects such as Law, Medicine, Dentistry and Veterinary Sciences. Admissions tests are also set by individual universities and colleges (or commercial organisations on their behalf) for entry, again, to particular courses in the individual institutions. Examples of these include the Thinking Skills Assessment (TSA) used by, for example, the University of Oxford, and the Health Professions Aptitude Test (HPAT) used by Ulster University for entry to some health-related courses. Other examples include the subject-based admissions tests used by many universities and colleges for entry to particular courses in subjects such as Art, Dance, Construction, Design, Drama and other Performance-based courses, Education and Teacher Training, Economics, Engineering, Journalism, Languages, Music, Nursing and Social Work.

Admissions tests are usually taken before or at interview and, except for courses requiring auditions or portfolio inspections, they are generally timed, unseen, written, or online tests. They can be used on their own, or alongside other selection methods used by university and college admissions staff, including:

- questionnaires or tests to be completed by applicants prior to interview and/or offer
- examples of school work to be submitted prior to interview and/or offer
- written tests at interview
- mathematical tests at interview
- practical tests at interview
- a response to a passage at interview
- performance-based tests (for example, for Music, Dance, Drama).

With regard to tests, applicants should check prospectuses and subject websites as soon as possible since, in some cases, early registration is required. This is especially important for applicants to Oxford and Cambridge and for those applying for Law, Medicine, Dentistry and Veterinary Science who may be required to take the LNAT, UCAT or BMAT.

Here is a list of commonly used admissions tests, and this is followed by degree subject lists showing subject-based and individual institutions' admissions tests.

English
English Literature Admissions Test (ELAT)
The ELAT is a pre-interview admissions test for applicants to English courses at the Universities of Oxford and Cambridge (see the ELAT pages on the Admissions Testing Service website www.admissionstesting.org).

Health Professions
Health Professions Admissions Test (HPAT)-Ulster
The HPAT-Ulster is used by Ulster University for entry to courses including Dietetics, Occupational Therapy, Physiotherapy, Diagnostic Radiography and Imaging, Radiotherapy and Oncology, and Speech and Language Therapy.

History
History Aptitude Test (HAT)
The HAT is a one-hour test sat by all candidates applying for History courses and joint schools at Oxford University (see *History* below). See www.history.ox.ac.uk/history-aptitude-test-hat.

Law
Cambridge Law Test (CLT)
This is a one-hour test designed and used by the University of Cambridge with Law applicants who are called for interview. No prior knowledge of law is required for the test. See http://ba.law.cam.ac.uk/applying/cambridge_law_test for full details.

Law National Aptitude Test (LNAT)
The LNAT is an on-screen test for applicants to specified undergraduate Law programmes at Bristol, Durham, Glasgow, London (King's), London (LSE), London (UCL), Nottingham, Oxford and SOAS universities. (See *Law* below, and **Law** in the subject tables in **Chapter 7**.) Applicants need to check universities' websites and the LNAT website (www.lnat.ac.uk) for the UCAS codes for courses requiring applicants to sit the LNAT. (**NB** Cambridge does not require Law applicants to take the LNAT but see above and the Cambridge entry under *Law* below.) Details of LNAT (which includes multiple-choice and essay questions), practice papers, registration dates, test dates, test centres and fees are all available on the LNAT website.

Mathematics
Mathematics Admissions Test (MAT)
The MAT is required by the University of Oxford for Mathematics, Computer Science courses and joint schools, and by Imperial London for its Mathematics course. Details of the test can be found on the MAT pages on the Admissions Testing Service website (www.admissionstesting.org).

Sixth Term Examination Paper (STEP)
Applicants with offers for Mathematics courses at Cambridge and Warwick universities are usually required to take STEP. Bath and Bristol universities, and Imperial London also encourage applicants for their Mathematics courses to take STEP. For details, see the STEP pages on the Admissions Testing Service website (www.admissionstesting.org).

Test of Mathematics for University Admission (TMUA)
The TMUA is (usually) an optional test that allows applicants to courses such as Mathematics, Economics or Computer Science to demonstrate their ability in mathematical reasoning and thinking, and can result in a reduced offer. It consists of two 75-minute, multiple-choice papers. The TMUA is accepted by Bath, Cardiff, Durham, Lancaster, LSE, Nottingham School of Mathematical Sciences, Sheffield, Southampton and Warwick universities. For more details, see the TMUA pages on the Admissions Testing Service website (www.admissionstesting.org).

Medicine, Dentistry, Veterinary Science/Medicine, and related subjects
Most medical schools require applicants to sit the University Clinical Aptitude Test (UCAT) or the BioMedical Admissions Test (BMAT) or, for graduate entry, the Graduate Australian Medical Schools Admissions Test (GAMSAT) for specified Medicine courses. Applicants are advised to check the websites of all universities and medical schools offering Medicine for their latest admissions requirements, including admissions and aptitude tests, to check the UCAT website www.ucat.ac.uk or the BMAT pages on www.admissionstesting.org (and for graduate entry www.gamsat.co.uk) for the latest information.

The BioMedical Admissions Test (BMAT)
This is a pen-and-paper admissions test taken by undergraduate applicants to Medicine at Cambridge, Medicine and Biomedical Sciences at Oxford, Medicine and Dentistry at Leeds, and Medicine courses at Imperial London, London (UCL), Brighton and Sussex (MS) and Lancaster. The test is also required for international applicants for Medicine courses at Keele University and the University of Manchester Medical School. Applicants for Graduate Medicine at Imperial and Oxford are also required to take the BMAT. A list of the courses requiring BMAT is available on the BMAT pages of the Admissions Testing Service website (www.admissionstesting.org) and also on university websites and in their prospectuses.

It is important to note BMAT's early closing date for entries and also the test dates. The two-hour test consists of three sections:

- aptitude and skills
- scientific knowledge and applications
- writing task.

Applicants sit the test only once and pay one entry fee no matter how many courses they apply for. However, if they re-apply to universities the following year they will need to re-take the BMAT and pay another fee. Past question papers are available (see website) and an official study guide *Preparing for the BMAT* is also available at www.pearsonschoolsandfecolleges.co.uk. Results of the BMAT are first sent to the universities, and then to the BMAT test centres. Candidates need to contact their test centres direct for their results. See **Dentistry**, **Medicine** and **Veterinary Science/Medicine** below and relevant subject tables in **Chapter 7**.

The University Clinical Aptitude Test (UCAT)
The UCAT is a clinical aptitude test used by the majority of medical and dental schools in the selection of applicants for Medicine and Dentistry, alongside their existing selection processes, for undergraduate entry. The tests are not curriculum-based and do not have a science component. No revision is necessary; there is no textbook and no course of instruction. In the first instance, the UCAT is a test of cognitive skills involving problem-solving and critical reasoning. With over 160 test centres, it is an on-screen test (not paper-based), and is marked electronically. Some bursaries are available to help towards the cost of the test. Applicants who require extra time due to a disability or medical condition should register for the UCATSEN. Further details (including the most recent list of universities requiring applicants to sit the UCAT) are found on the website www.ucat.ac.uk. See also the **Dentistry** and **Medicine** subject tables in **Chapter 7**, the entries for **Dentistry** and **Medicine** below, and **Chapter 4** for application details. See www.ucat.ac.uk.

Modern and Medieval Languages
The Modern and Medieval Languages Written Assessment (MML)
This written test is used by the University of Cambridge for selecting applicants for entry to courses involving modern and medieval languages. See www.mml.cam.ac.uk/applying/involve.

General Admissions Tests
Thinking Skills Assessment (TSA)
The TSA is a pen-and-paper test that tests applicants' critical thinking and problem-solving skills. The test is used by the University of Cambridge for applicants to Land Economy, by University College London for European, Social and Political Studies (ESPS) and International Social and Political Studies (ISPS), and by the University of Oxford for entry to several courses (see below and the TSA web pages on www.admissionstesting.org). Both the TSA Cambridge and TSA UCL tests consist of 50 multiple-choice questions, which applicants have 90 minutes to complete. However, the TSA Oxford has an additional section, the Writing Task, where candidates are given 30 minutes to answer one essay question out of a possible four questions.

LSE UG Admissions Assessment (UGAA)
The LSE UGAA is used by the London School of Economics for some applicants with non-traditional educational backgrounds. The test is not subject or course specific and consists of English comprehension exercises, essay questions and mathematical problems.

DEGREE SUBJECT EXAMPLES OF UNIVERSITIES AND COLLEGES USING TESTS AND ASSESSMENTS
Many universities and colleges set their own tests for specific subjects so it is important to check the websites for your preferred institutions and courses for the latest information about their applications and selection processes. The following list provides a guide to the subjects and some of the institutions requiring admissions tests and other forms of assessment. Due to the constant changes in admissions policies, this is not a complete list. However, applicants for these subjects should be guided as to the requirements of those universities requiring tests.

Accounting
Reading Interview.

Acting
Marjon Interview.
Queen Margaret Interview.

Adult Nursing
Bolton Numeracy and literacy test.

Agriculture Courses
Harper Adams Interview.

Anglo Saxon, Norse and Celtic
Cambridge ASNCAA pre-interview. Check college websites for submitted work requirements.

Animal Management
Kirklees (Coll) Mature applicants screening test.

Anthropology
Oxford See Archaeology.

Archaeology
Cambridge Shortlisted applicants take the ARCHAA at interview. Check college websites for submitted work requirements.
Oxford (Arch Anth) Two recent marked essays are required, preferably in different subjects, plus a statement of no more than 500 words in response to a set question – required before interview. No written test at interview. (Class Arch Anc Hist) Written work required. No written test at interview.

Architecture
Cambridge ARCHITAA taken at interview. Check college websites for details.
Cardiff (Archit, Archit Eng) Samples of work to be sent before interview.
Dundee Samples of work required before interview.
Huddersfield Portfolio of work required.
Liverpool Portfolio and selection workshop.
London Met Portfolio of work required.
London South Bank Samples of work to be sent before interview.
Manchester Met Portfolio of work required.
Nottingham Portfolio of work required.
Nottingham Trent Examples of work are required.
Plymouth Digital portfolio of work required.
Portsmouth Interview.
Reading Interview.
Sheffield Portfolio required.

Art
Huddersfield Interview.
Reading Interview.

Art and Design
Arts London Portfolio required.
Bolton (Fash) You may be required to attend for interview and provide a portfolio of appropriate work.
Bournemouth (Comp Animat Art) Portfolio of work required.
Brunel (Des Eng, Prod Des, Ind Des) All applicants are required to attend an interview including a portfolio review as part of the selection process.
Chester (Fash Des) Applicants may be required to attend a portfolio interview.
Hertfordshire (Fash Des) Portfolio interview required.

Oxford (Fn Art) No written work required. Portfolio to be submitted in November. Practical examination. Two pieces in different media from a number of possible subjects.
Plymouth Interview.
Portsmouth Interview.
Ravensbourne Univ Verbal examination. (Animat) Written test.
Sussex (Prod Des) Interview and portfolio review required.

Asian and Middle Eastern Studies
Cambridge AMESAA pre-interview. Check www.cam.ac.uk/assessment.

Biomedical Sciences
Oxford BMAT is required.
Portsmouth Test of motivation and knowledge of the subject, the degree and careers to which it leads.

Business
Portsmouth Interview.

Business Courses
Arts London (CFash) School work to be submitted before interview. Degree subject-based test and numeracy test at interview.
Buckingham (Bus Man) Informal interview required.

Business courses
Newcastle Some shortlisted applicants will be given a variety of assessment tests at interview.

Business Courses
Plymouth (Cru Mgt) Informal interview required.

Chemistry
Oxford No written work required. All candidates must take the TSA Chemistry (section 1 of the TSA Oxford).
Reading During the interview, applicants will be asked a series of chemistry-related questions from a select list. Applicants are required to discuss these in detail and may be asked to draw molecular formulas.

Classics (see also Archaeology)
Cambridge Shortlisted applicants take the CAA at interview, with separate tests for the three- and four-year courses. Check college websites for submitted work requirements.
Oxford For all Classics courses, two essays or commentaries required, normally in areas related to Classics, and submitted in November. CAT also required.

Classics and English
Oxford Two pieces of written work required, one relevant to Classics and one to English. CAT and ELAT also required.

Classics and Modern Languages
Oxford Two Classics essays and two modern language essays required, one in the chosen language and one in English. CAT and MLAT also required.

Classics and Oriental Studies
Oxford CAT; two pieces written work also required, at least one should be on a classical topic if already studying a classical subject.

Community Learning and Development
Dundee Written question response form.

Computer Science
Cambridge Shortlisted applicants take the CSAT. Check www.cam.ac.uk/assessment.
Oxford No written work required. MAT required. See also **Mathematics**.
Winchester (Comp Aid Des) Interview required.

Costume Design and Construction
Queen Margaret Interview.

Creative Writing and Drama
Winchester Interview.

Dance
Chichester (Perf Arts) Group practical test.
Plymouth Interview.
Winchester Audition.

Dental Nursing
Bolton (Dntl Tech) A manual dexterity test is taken at interview.
Portsmouth Interview.

Dentistry
Aberdeen Entrants must sit UCAT.
Glasgow UCAT.
Leeds BMAT.
Liverpool Entrants require UCAT.
London (King's) UCAT.
Manchester UCAT and interview.
Newcastle Entrants must sit the UCAT.
Plymouth Interview.

Design Engineering
Bournemouth Portfolio of work required.

Diagnostic Radiography
Robert Gordon Interview.

Dietetics
Hertfordshire Literacy and numeracy tests are used at interview.
London Met (Diet Nutr) Interview required.
Plymouth Interview.
Robert Gordon Interview.
Ulster HPAT: see www.hpat.org.uk and www.ulster.ac.uk before completing the UCAS application.

Drama
Brunel Interview.
Exeter Interview.
Glyndŵr Interview.
Huddersfield Interview.
Liverpool (LIPA) (Actg) Applicants will be expected to perform one devised piece, one Shakespearean piece and a song and give a short review of a performance they have seen recently.
London (Royal Central Sch SpDr) Written papers and/or tests.
Plymouth Interview.
Portsmouth Interview.
Reading (Thea) Applicants undertake a practical assessment and an interview.
Winchester Audition.

Economics
Cambridge ECAA pre-interview. Check college websites for submitted work requirements.
Oxford (Econ Mgt) No written work required. Oxford TSA required.

Education Studies (see also Teacher Training)
Cambridge Shortlisted applicants take the EAA at interview. Check www.cam.ac.uk/assessment and college websites for written work requirements.

Cumbria Literacy and numeracy Professional Skills tests.
Newman (P Educ) Basic numeracy and literacy tests.

Educational Studies
Plymouth Interview.

Engineering
Cambridge ENGAA pre-interview. Check www.cam.ac.uk/assessment.
Liverpool BTEC level 3 applicants sit a maths test.
Oxford No written work required. All candidates take the PAT.
Portsmouth Interview.
Southampton Mathematics test may be required for Foundation course applicants.

English
Cambridge ELAT pre-interview. Check college websites for submitted work requirements.
London (UCL) After interview, applicants are asked to write a critical commentary on an unseen passage of prose or verse.
Oxford (Engl Lang Lit) ELAT and one recent marked essay. (Engl Modn Langs) ELAT and MLAT. One English essay and two modern language essays required, one in the chosen language and one in English.
Portsmouth (Crea Writ) All applicants will be required to submit a short piece of creative writing to the admissions office.
European and Middle Eastern Languages (see also Modern and Medieval Languages)
Oxford Two pieces of written work, one in the chosen language and one in English. MLAT and OLAT required.

Film Production and Theatre
Brunel Interview.

Film Studies
Bournemouth Arts (Flm Prod) Portfolio including a five minute showreel of the applicant's work.
Creative Arts (Flm Prod) Portfolio at interview.
Huddersfield Interview.
Reading There are three stages to the interview process: a practical, a film seminar and an interview.
South Wales Piece of written work required at interview.

Film, TV and Radio
Glyndŵr Interview.
Portsmouth (Film Prod) Applicants without relevant qualifications may be asked to submit a digital portfolio.
Staffordshire Interview with portfolio required.

Fine Art
Chichester Interview+Portfolio.

Food Science
Reading Interview.

Geography
Cambridge GAA pre-interview. Check college websites for submitted work requirements.
Cardiff Test for some Joint Honours courses.

Healthcare Science
Hertfordshire Literacy and numeracy tests are used at interview.

History
Cambridge HAA pre-interview. Check college websites for submitted work requirements.
Liverpool John Moores Mature students not in education must submit an essay.
London (Gold) Samples of written work from non-standard applicants and from those without academic qualifications.

Oxford An essay on a historical topic is required as well as the HAT. (Hist Modn Langs) Written work; HAT and MLAT required.

History of Art
Cambridge Shortlisted applicants take the HAAA at interview. Check college websites for submitted work requirements.
Oxford Two pieces of work required: (a) a marked essay from an A-level or equivalent course and (b) no more than 750 words responding to an item of art, architecture or design to which the applicant has had first-hand access with a photograph or photocopy of the item provided if possible. No written test at interview.

Human Sciences
Oxford No written work required. All candidates must take the Oxford TSA.

Human, Social and Political Sciences
Cambridge HSPSAA pre-interview. Check college websites for submitted work requirements.

Industrial Design
Brunel Interview.

Journalism
Huddersfield Interview.
Marjon Interview.
Portsmouth Test.

Journalism (see also Media Studies)
Brighton (Spo Jrnl) Test for those called to interview: contact admissions tutor.
City Written test.
Edinburgh Napier (Jrnl) Samples of work before interview.
Kent English language and academic tests for all candidates, relating to requirements of the accrediting professional bodies.
South Wales Test and interview.

Land Economy
Cambridge Shortlisted applicants take the TSA Cambridge at interview. Check college websites for individual requirements.

Law
Bradford College UC Academic tests at interview may be required for mature students.
Cambridge Shortlisted applicants take the CLT at interview. Check college websites for submitted work requirements.
Durham LNAT.
Glasgow LNAT.
London (King's) LNAT.
London (UCL) LNAT.
London LSE LNAT.
Nottingham LNAT.
Oxford No written work required. All applicants take the LNAT. (Law; Law St Euro) LNAT plus, at interview, a possible oral test in the modern language for students taking a joint language, except for those taking Dutch Law options.

Linguistics
Cambridge Shortlisted applicants take the LAA. Check college websites for submitted work requirements.

Materials Science
Oxford No written work required. All candidates must take the PAT.

Mathematics
Cambridge STEP. Check www.cam.ac.uk/assessment.
Imperial London MAT. The paper takes two and a half hours and sample tests are available online. Students unable to sit the MAT must complete the STEP.
London LSE TMUA is recommended but not mandatory.
Oxford No written work required. MAT required.

Media Studies
Coventry Interview and portfolio.
Huddersfield Interview.
Hull (Coll) Essay required before interview.
Liverpool John Moores Questionnaire to be completed before interview. Degree subject-based test at interview.
Portsmouth Interview and admissions test.

Medical Imaging
Exeter Interview.

Medicine
Aberdeen Entrants must sit UCAT.
Aston UCAT 5-year course.
Birmingham UCAT.
Brighton Interview+UCAT.
Brighton and Sussex (MS) Entrants must sit UCAT
Bristol Entrants must sit UCAT.
Buckingham Entrants must sit UCAT.
Cambridge BMAT test required. Check www.cam.ac.uk/assessment.
Cardiff Entrants must sit UCAT.
Dundee Entrants must sit UCAT.
East Anglia Entrants must sit UCAT.
Edinburgh Entrants must sit UCAT.
Exeter UCAT or GAMSAT required.
Glasgow UCAT.
Hull UCAT required.
Hull York (MS) Entrants must sit UCAT (formerly UKCAT).
Imperial London BMAT and UCAT.
Keele Entrants must sit UCAT.
Kent Medway Med Sch UCAT required.
Lancaster BMAT.
Leeds BMAT.
Leicester Entrants must sit UCAT.
Liverpool Entrants require UCAT. Graduate entrants to Medicine must complete GAMSAT.
London (King's) UCAT.
London (QM) Entrants must sit UCAT.
London (St George's) GAMSAT is required for the four-year Graduate Stream course. UCAT is required for the five-year course.
London (UCL) (Six-year course) BMAT+UCAT
Manchester UCAT and interview.
Newcastle Entrants must sit the UCAT.
Nottingham UCAT.
Oxford No written work required. BMAT test required.
Plymouth Interview.
Queen's Belfast Entrants must sit UCAT.
Sheffield Entrants must sit UCAT.
Southampton Entrants must sit UCAT.
St Andrews Entrants must sit UCAT.

Meteorology
Reading (Meteor Clim (MMet)) All applicants will be asked to attend an interview prior to an offer being made.

Midwifery
Bournemouth Interview.
Bradford Interview.
Canterbury Christ Church Literacy test at interview.
Cumbria Tests.
Hertfordshire Literacy and numeracy tests are used at interview.
Huddersfield Interview.
Hull Short written tests at interview.
Leicester Interview.
Liverpool John Moores Literacy and numeracy tests.
Teesside No offers without interview.

Modern and Medieval Languages (see also Asian and Middle Eastern Studies, Oriental Studies and separate languages)
Cambridge Shortlisted applicants take the MMLAA. Check college websites for submitted work requirements.
Oxford (Modn Langs; Modn Lang Ling) MLAT. Two marked essays, one in chosen language and one in English. (Euro Mid E Langs) MLAT and OLAT required. One essay required in English and for the European language but none for the Middle Eastern language.

Music
Bath Spa (Commer Mus) Interview requirements include performance of an original piece of work.
Birmingham City Portfolio required for some courses.
Brunel Interview.
Cambridge Check college websites for assessment details and submitted work requirements.
Cardiff Interview requirements include performance or extracts for analysis.
Chichester Interview requirements include performance.
City Interview requirements include performance.
Colchester (UC) Interview requirements include performance, aural, keyboard skills and essay.
Coventry Audition held alongside an interview.
Derby Interview requirements include performance.
Edinburgh Interview requirements include performance, harmony and counterpoint (written), essay and sight-singing.
Edinburgh Napier Audition and theory test.
Glasgow Interview requirements include performance and sight-singing.
Guildhall (Sch Mus Dr) Interviews mostly held at the School but also at Newcastle and in the USA.
Huddersfield Audition.
Liverpool Audition.
Liverpool Hope Interview requirements include performance, keyboard tests and harmony and counterpoint (written).
London (Gold) Interview requirements include performance.
London (King's) Only borderline applicants or candidates with non-standard qualifications are interviewed.
London (RAcMus) (Mus) Interview requirements include performance, keyboard skills, harmony and counterpoint (written), and extracts for analysis.
Oxford Interview requirements include the performance of a piece/s on the candidate's principal instrument or voice. Candidates without keyboard skills to grade 5 may be asked to take a keyboard sight-reading test. Two pieces of marked work (with at least one on music), plus one or two examples of marked harmony and counterpoint required, plus examples of composition (optional).
RCMus Interview requirements include performance and sight-singing.
RConsvS Interview requirements include performance, sight-singing and aural.
Royal Welsh (CMusDr) Interview requirements include performance and essay.

West London Students required to produce a portfolio of work and attend an audition: see www.
uwl.ac.uk.
Wolverhampton Interview requirements include performance and a musical theory test.
York Interview requirements include performance.

Musical Theatre
Chichester Interview.
Portsmouth Interview.
Winchester Audition.

Natural Sciences
Cambridge NSAA pre-interview. Check www.cam.ac.uk/assessment.

Nursing
Birmingham City Literacy and numeracy tests prior to interview.
Bournemouth Tests.
Brighton Literacy and numeracy tests and interview.
Bucks New Tests for BSc Nursing.
City Written test.
Coventry Literacy and numeracy tests.
Cumbria (Nurs; Midwif) Numeracy test.
Derby Literacy and numeracy tests at interview.
East Anglia Tests.
Essex Numeracy and literacy test alongside an interview.
Glyndŵr Interview.
Hertfordshire Literacy and numeracy tests are used at interview.
Huddersfield Interview.
Keele Interview.
Leicester Interview.
Liverpool Interview.
London South Bank (Nurs A/C/MH) On-campus literacy and numeracy tests before interview.
Portsmouth Interview.
Queen Margaret Interview.
Stirling Interviews.
Suffolk Interview and tests.
Teesside No offers without interview.
UWE Bristol Selection event involving numeracy and literacy test, group activity and individual interview.
West London Numeracy and literacy tests.
Winchester Numeracy test at interview.
Wolverhampton Tests.

Nursing (Adult, Child and Mental Health)
Canterbury Christ Church Literacy and numeracy tests at interview.

Nursing and Midwifery
Cardiff Multiple Mini Interview (MMI).
Plymouth Interview.

Occupational Therapy
Bournemouth Interview.
Brunel Interview.
Essex Numeracy and literacy test alongside an interview.
Glyndŵr Interview.
Huddersfield Interview.
Plymouth Interview.
Queen Margaret Interview.
Robert Gordon Interview.

Ulster HPAT: see www.hpat.org.uk and www.ulster.ac.uk before completing the UCAS application.
UWE Bristol Interview.

Operating Department Practice
Bournemouth Interview.
Canterbury Christ Church Written assessment at interview.
Leicester Interview.

Optometry
Hertfordshire Literacy and numeracy tests are used at interview.
Huddersfield Interview.
Plymouth Interview.

Oral Health Science
Essex Literacy and numeracy test alongside interview.

Oriental Studies
Oxford Two essays required. OLAT required for certain course combinations.

Orthoptics
Liverpool Interview.

Paramedic Practitioner
Plymouth Interview.

Paramedic Science
Anglia Ruskin Literacy and numeracy tests.
Bournemouth Interview.
Bradford Interview.
Hertfordshire Literacy and numeracy tests are used at interview.
Portsmouth Tests.

Performing Arts
Winchester Interview.

Pharmacology/Pharmaceutical Sciences
Portsmouth Test of motivation, knowledge of the subject, degree course and the careers to which it leads.

Pharmacy
Brighton Numeracy test alongside interview.
Hertfordshire Literacy and numeracy tests are used at interview.
Keele Interview.
Liverpool John Moores Aptitude test.
Portsmouth (A-level students) Test of motivation and knowledge of pharmacy as a profession. (Other applicants) Test of chemistry and biology, plus literacy and numeracy tests.
Reading Values-based admissions tests and numeracy test.

Philosophy
Cambridge Shortlisted applicants take the PAA at interview. Check college websites for submitted work requirements.
Oxford (Phil Modn Langs) MLAT. Two pieces of written work required; one in English and one in the chosen language. (Phil Theol) Philosophy Test and one piece of written work. (Phil Pol Econ (PPE)) Oxford TSA; no written work required.

Photography
Huddersfield Interview.
Plymouth Interview.
Portsmouth Interview.

Physical Education
Chichester Physical test.

Physics
Exeter Interview.
Oxford PAT; no written work required.

Physiotherapy
Bournemouth Interview.
Bradford Interview.
Brighton Interview.
Brunel Interview.
Cardiff Multiple Mini Interview (MMI).
East Anglia Tests.
Essex Numeracy and literacy test alongside an interview.
Glyndŵr Interview.
Hertfordshire Literacy and numeracy tests are used at interview.
Huddersfield Interview.
Keele Interview.
Leicester Interview.
Liverpool Interview.
Plymouth Interview.
Robert Gordon Interview.
Ulster HPAT: see www.hpat.org.uk and www.ulster.ac.uk before completing the UCAS application.
Winchester Anatomy test at interview.

Podiatry
Brighton Interview.
Huddersfield Interview.
Ulster HPAT: see www.hpat.ac.uk and www.ulster.ac.uk before completing the UCAS application.

Podiatry (Chiropody)
Plymouth Interview.

Politics
Oxford See (Phil Pol Econ (PPE)) under Philosophy.

Popular Music
South Wales Audition.

Product Design
Bournemouth Portfolio of work required.
Brunel Interview.
Dundee Portfolio and interview will determine the appropriate entry point for candidate (Level 1 or 2).

Psychological and Behavioural Sciences
Cambridge PBSAA pre-interview. Check college websites for submitted work requirements.

Psychology
Exeter (App Psy Clin) Interview.
London (UCL) Questionnaire may be required.
Oxford (Expmtl Psy) Oxford TSA; no written work required.
Reading (App Psy (Clin)) Interview.

Radiography
Hertfordshire Literacy and numeracy tests are used at interview.
Keele Interview.
Liverpool Interview.
Ulster HPAT: see www.hpat.ac.uk and www.ulster.ac.uk before completing the UCAS application.

Social Work
Birmingham Shortlisted applicants may be required to complete a written test.
Birmingham City Written test at interview.
Bournemouth Interview.
Brighton Tests.
Bucks New Tests.
Cardiff Met Group task, individual interview and written test.
Derby Literacy and numeracy tests at interview.
Dundee Written question response form.
Durham New (Coll) Written test at interview.
East Anglia Test.
Essex Literacy test alongside an interview.
Glyndŵr Interview.
Hertfordshire Literacy and numeracy tests are used at interview.
Hull Short written tests at interview.
Keele Tests.
Kent Written test followed by an interview and observed group discussions.
London (Gold) Questions on social work practice and the applicant's experience of working in the social work/social care field.
London Met Pre-interview literacy test and, if successful, an interview.
Plymouth Interview.
Portsmouth Test.
Robert Gordon Numeracy tests carried out at interview, but only for those who do not already meet minimum numeracy standards.
Stirling Assessments.
Suffolk Interview and test.
UWE Bristol Written test and interview.
Winchester Written task required at interview.
Wolverhampton Tests.

Speech and Language Therapy
Marjon Interview.
Reading Interview.

Speech Pathology
Essex Literacy and numeracy test alongside interview.

Speech Pathology/Sciences/Therapy
Ulster HPAT: see www.hpat.ac.uk and www.ulster.ac.uk before completing the UCAS application.

Sports and Exercise Science
Robert Gordon Interview.

Sports Therapy
Bournemouth Interview.

Sports, PE & Education
Stirling Interviews.

Surgery
Kent Medway Med Sch UCAT required.

Teacher Training
Bishop Grosseteste Literacy and numeracy tests are part of the selection criteria at interview.
Brighton Written test at interview.
Canterbury Christ Church All candidates are interviewed in groups of 8-10 and assessments are made based on the results of a written English test and performance in the group interview.

Cardiff Met Literacy and numeracy tests.
Chester Literacy and numeracy tests.
Chichester Written test at interview.
Dundee Literacy and numeracy tests.
Durham Literacy and numeracy tests.
Hertfordshire Admissions test.
Hull Government specified literacy and numeracy tests.
Liverpool John Moores (P Educ) Literacy and numeracy tests.
Plymouth Professional Skills Tests in literacy and numeracy required. Applicants may also be required to take the ITT (Initial Teacher Training) Skills Test.
Reading Applicants are required to take part in both a group activity and an individual interview as well as completing a short essay-based written test.
Roehampton Written test at interview.
Sheffield Hallam Interview with numeracy and literacy tests.
St Mary's National Skills Test in English and mathematics.
UWE Bristol Literacy test at interview.
Winchester Literacy test at interview.

Theatre and Performance
Glyndŵr Audition.

Theatre Courses
Brunel Interview.

Theology and Religious Studies
Cambridge TAA pre-interview. Check college websites for submitted work requirements.
Oxford (Theol Relgn) No test; one piece of marked written work required or response to a marked unseen exam question. (Theol Orntl St) OLAT for certain strands; two pieces of written work required, one on religious studies and one on any subject.

Veterinary Nursing
Harper Adams Interview required.

Veterinary Physiotherapy
Harper Adams Interview.

Veterinary Science
Liverpool Interview.

Veterinary Science/Medicine
Cambridge BMAT test required. Check www.cam.ac.uk/assessment.
Glasgow (Vet Med) Computer-based ethical reasoning test for candidates attending interviews.
Myerscough (Coll) (Vet Nurs) Subject-based test at interview.

Youth & Community Work
Marjon Interview.

SELECTION OF APPLICANTS
University and college departmental admissions tutors are responsible for selecting candidates, basing their decisions on the policies of acceptable qualifications established by each institution and, where required, applicants' performance in admissions tests. There is little doubt that academic achievement, aptitude and promise are the most important factors although other subsidiary factors may be taken into consideration. The outline which follows provides information on the way in which candidates are selected for degree and diploma courses.

- Grades obtained by the applicant in GCE A-level and equivalent examinations and the range of subjects studied may be considered. Some universities require an additional AS grade for certain courses, such as Medicine. Where school policy limits a student's opportunity to take AS subjects, alternative A-level offers may be given (check websites).

- Applicant's performance in aptitude and admissions tests, as required by universities and colleges.
- Academic record of the applicant throughout his or her school career, especially up to A-level, Highers, Advanced Highers or other qualifications and the choice of subjects. If you are taking general studies at A-level confirm with the admissions tutor that this is acceptable.
- Time taken by the applicant to obtain good grades at GCSE/Scottish Nationals and A-level/Scottish Highers/Advanced Highers.
- Forecast or the examination results of the applicant at A-level (or equivalent) and headteacher's report.
- The applicant's intellectual development; evidence of ability and motivation to follow the chosen course.
- The applicant's range of interests, both in and out of school; aspects of character and personality.
- The vocational interests, knowledge and experience of the applicant particularly if they are choosing vocational courses.

INTERVIEWS

Fewer applicants are now interviewed than in the past but even if you are not called you should make an effort to visit your chosen universities and/or colleges before you accept any offer. Interviews may be arranged simply to give you a chance to see the institution and the department and to meet the staff and students. Alternatively, interviews may be an important part of the selection procedure for specific courses such as Law, Medicine and Teaching. If they are, you need to prepare yourself well. Most interviews last approximately 20–30 minutes and you may be interviewed by more than one person. For practical subjects such as Music and Drama almost certainly you will be asked to perform, and for artistic subjects, to take examples of your work. For some courses you may also have a written or other test at interview (see above).

How best can you prepare yourself?
- Prepare well – interviewers are never impressed by applicants who only sit there with no willingness to take part.
- Read up the prospectus and course details. Know how their course differs from any others you have applied for and be able to say why you prefer theirs.
- Show enthusiasm and, for vocational courses, the ability to work with others.
- Take a moment to think before rushing your answers at interview.
- You will always be asked if you have any questions for the interviewers, so prepare some!

Questions which you could ask might focus on the ways in which work is assessed, the content of the course, field work, work experience, teaching methods, accommodation and, especially for vocational courses, contacts with industry, commerce or the professions. Examples include: How many students are admitted to the course each year? What are the job prospects for graduates? How easy is it to change from your chosen course to a related course? Don't ask questions that are already answered in the prospectus!

These are only a few suggestions and other questions may come to mind during the interview, which, above all, should be a two-way flow of information. It is also important to keep a copy of your UCAS application (especially your personal statement) for reference since your interview will probably start with a question about something you have written.

Usually interviewers will want to know why you have chosen the subject and why you have chosen their particular institution. They will want to see how motivated you are, how much care you have taken in choosing your subject, how much you know about your subject, what books you have read. If you have chosen a vocational course they will want to find out how much you know about the career it leads to, and whether you have visited any places of work or had any work experience. If your chosen subject is also an A-level subject you will be asked about your course and the aspects of the course you like the most.

Try to relax. For some people interviews can be an ordeal; most interviewers know this and will make allowances. The following extract from the University of Manchester's website will give you some idea of what admissions tutors look for.

- 'You should remember that receiving an interview invite means that the admissions tutors are impressed with your application so far and you are in the running for an offer of a place at that university. It is an opportunity for you to discuss a subject that you and the interviewer share an interest in.'
- 'Interviewers will be looking for you to demonstrate how you met the criteria advertised in the prospectus and UCAS entry profiles, but will not always ask you about them directly. Some examples of criteria used by admissions tutors include: interest, motivation and commitment to the subject; the ability to study independently; the ability to work with others; the ability to manage time effectively; an interest in the university.'

In the tables in **Chapter 7** (**Selection interviews**, **Interview advice and questions** and **Reasons for rejection**) you will also find examples of questions which have been asked in recent years for which you might prepare, and non-academic reasons why applicants have been rejected! **Chapter 4**, **Applications**, provides a guide through the process of applying to your chosen universities and courses and highlights key points for your action.

Try to turn up looking smart (it may not matter, but it can't be wrong). A previous applicant was more specific: 'Dress smartly but sensibly so you are comfortable for travelling and walking round the campus.'

MULTIPLE MINI INTERVIEWS (MMIs)
MMIs involve the applicants participating in a number of small interviews and tasks. An example of the structure of an MMI could be eight seven-minute interviews (also called stations), with interviewees having a minute between stations. The format of each station will vary, but you will receive instructions explaining what you will be required to do, so ensure you listen carefully and read any written instructions to give you a good idea of what you will be facing.

MMIs are often used in the belief that they can provide the interviewers with a more accurate indication of an applicant's personality and character attributes than the traditional panel interview, which can be heavily coached for.

Some universities divulge very little about the exact detail of the MMI they offer, while others will provide some detail about what the interviewees will face. Students should be prepared to be tested on their ability to communicate and interact with others; to undertake basic observation and memory tasks; to undertake manual dexterity tasks, depending on the chosen course; to analyse different methods of data presentation, eg tables and graphs; to make a presentation.

The subject tables in the next chapter represent the core of the book, listing degree courses offered by all UK universities and colleges. These tables are designed to provide you with the information you need so that you can match your abilities and interests with your chosen degree subject, prepare your application and find out how applicants are selected for courses.

At the top of each table there is a brief overview of the subject area, together with a selection of websites for organisations that can provide relevant careers or course information. This is then followed by the subject tables themselves in which information is provided in sequence under the following headings.

Course offers information
- Subject requirements/preferences (GCSE/A-level/other requirements)
- NB Offers statement
- Your target offers and examples of degree courses
- Alternative offers

Examples of colleges offering courses in this subject field

Choosing your course
- Universities and colleges teaching quality
- Top universities and colleges (research)
- Examples of sandwich degree courses

Admissions information
- Number of applicants per place
- Advice to applicants and planning the UCAS personal statement
- Misconceptions about this course
- Selection interviews
- Interview advice and questions
- Reasons for rejection (non-academic)

After-results advice
- Offers to applicants repeating A-levels

Graduate destinations and employment (Higher Education Statistics Agency (HESA))
- HESA data on graduate destinations
- Career note

Other degree subjects for consideration

When selecting a degree course it is important to try to judge the points score or grades that you are likely to achieve and compare them with the offers listed under **Your target offers and examples of degree courses**. However, even though you might be capable of achieving the indicated grades or UCAS Tariff points, it is important to note that these are likely to be the minimum grades or points required and that there is no guarantee that you will receive an offer: other factors in your application, such as the personal statement, references, and admissions test performance will be taken into consideration (see also **Chapters 3** and **5**).

University departments frequently adjust their offers, depending on the numbers of candidates applying, so you must not assume that the offers and policies published now will necessarily apply to courses starting in 2021 or thereafter. Even though offers may change during the 2020/21 application cycle, you can assume that the offers published in this book represent the typical academic levels at which you should aim.

Below are explanations of the information given under the headings in the subject tables. It is important that you read these carefully so that you understand how they can help you to choose and apply for courses that are right for you.

COURSE OFFERS INFORMATION

Subject requirements/preferences

Brief information is given on the GCSE and A-level requirements. Specific A-level subject requirements for individual institutions are listed separately. Other requirements are sometimes specified, where these are relevant to the course subject area, for example, medical requirements for health-related courses and Disclosure and Barring Service (DBS) clearance. Check prospectuses and websites of universities and colleges for course requirements.

GCSE reforms Under the reformed GCSEs, the grading system has changed from letter to numerical grading, with students no longer receiving their results graded as A*–G but as 9–1. We have included the numerically adjusted GCSEs alongside the letter grading for reference, but please check university websites for their exact requirements. For further details about the reforms, see the government website.

Your target offers and examples of degree courses

Universities and colleges offering degree courses in the subject area are listed in descending order according to the number of UCAS Tariff points and/or A-level grades they are likely to require applicants to achieve. The UCAS Tariff points total is listed down the left-hand side of the page, and to the right appear all the institutions (in alphabetical order) likely to make offers in this Tariff point range. (Information on the UCAS Tariff is given in **Appendix 1** and guidance on how to calculate your offers is provided on every other page of the subject tables in this book. Please also read the information in the **Important Note** box on page 80.)

The courses included on the offers line are examples of the courses available in the subject field at that university or college. You will need to check prospectuses and websites for a complete list of the institution's Single, Joint, Combined or Major/Minor Honours degree courses available in the subject. For each institution listed, the following information may be given.

Name of institution

Note that the name of an institution's university college or campus may be given in brackets after the institution title, for example London (King's) or Kent (Medway Sch Pharm). Where the institution is not a university, further information about its status may also be given to indicate the type of college – for example (UC) to mean University College or (CAg) to mean College of Agriculture. This is to help readers to differentiate between the types of colleges and to help them identify any specialisation a college may have, for example art or agriculture. A full list of abbreviations used is given under the heading **INSTITUTION ABBREVIATIONS** later in this chapter.

Grades/points offer

After the institution's name, a line of offers information is given, showing a typical offer made by the institution for the courses indicated in brackets. **Offers, however, may vary between applicants and the published grades and/or points offers should be regarded as targets to aim for and not necessarily the actual grades or points required**. Offers may be reduced after the publication of A-level results, particularly if a university or college is left with spare places. However, individual course offers listed in the tables in **Chapter 7** are abridged and should be used as a first source of reference and comparison only. It is not possible to publish all the variables relevant to each offer: applicants must check prospectuses and websites for full details of all offers and courses. All offers listed in the tables in **Chapter 7** refer to degree courses only. Applicants should note however that some courses in the same subject areas are also available at lower levels with lower offers, eg Foundation courses, Diplomas of Higher Education and Certificates; these are published on university and college websites.

Depending on the details given by institutions, the offers may provide information as follows.

- **Grades** The specific grades, or average grades, required at GCE A-level or at A-level plus AS in some cases, where available, or, if specified, EPQ for the listed courses. (**NB** Graded offers may require specific grades for specific subjects.) A-level grades are always presented in capital letters; AS and EPQ grades are shown in lower case. The offer BBBc would indicate three grade Bs at A-level, plus an additional AS at grade c. The offer AAB+aEPQ would indicate two grade As and one grade B at A-level, plus an additional EPQ at grade a. Where necessary, the abbreviation 'AL' is used to indicate

A-level, 'AS' to indicate AS and EPQ to indicate that an Extended Project Qualification is part of the offer. Offers are usually shown in terms of three A-level grades although some institutions accept two grades with the same points total or, alternatively, two A-level grades accompanied by AS grades.

NB Unit grade and module information, now introduced into the admissions system, is most likely to be required by universities where a course is competitive, or where taking a specific unit is necessary or desirable for entry. Check with institutions' websites for their latest information.

- **The UCAS Tariff points system** A-levels, AS, International Baccalaureate (IB), Scottish Highers, the Progression Diploma and a range of other qualifications have a unit value in the UCAS Tariff system (see **UCAS 2021 Entry Tariff Points Tables** in **Appendix 1**). Where a range of Tariff points is shown, for example 112–120 points, offers are usually made within this points range for these specified courses. Note that, in some cases, an institution may require a points score which is higher than the specified grade offer given. This can be for a number of reasons – for example, you may not be offering the standard subjects that would have been stipulated in a grades offer. In such cases additional points may be added by way of AS grades, Functional/Essential Skills, the Extended Project Qualification, etc.

Unit value of A-level grades in the UCAS Tariff points system:

A* = 56 pts; A = 48 pts; B = 40 pts; C = 32 pts; D = 24 pts; E = 16 pts

Some universities make offers for entry to each course by way of A-level grades, others make Tariff points offers while others will make offers in both A-level grades and in Tariff points. Applicants should be sure that the A-level subjects they are taking are acceptable for their chosen course and for A-level grades and points offers.

A Tariff points offer will not usually discriminate between the final year exam subjects being taken by the applicant unless otherwise stated, although certain GCSE subjects may be stipulated eg English or mathematics.

Admission tutors have the unenviable task of trying to assess the number of applicants who will apply for their courses against the number of places available and so judging the offers to be made. However, since the government removed the cap on the number of places that universities in England are able to offer, English universities can admit an unlimited number of home and EU undergraduates, though not every institution has adopted these reforms. Nevertheless, it is still important when reading the offers tables to be aware that variations occur each year. Lower offers or equivalents may be made to disadvantaged students, mature and international applicants.

The offers published in this edition therefore are based on expected admission policies operating from September to January 2020/21. They are targets to be achieved and in the case of popular courses at popular universities they should be regarded as minimum entry qualifications.

See **Chapter 3** for information from universities about their admissions policies including, for example, information about their expected use of A*, unit grades, the Progression Diploma, the Extended Project Qualification and the Cambridge Pre-U in their offers for applicants. See **Appendix 1** for **UCAS 2021 Entry Tariff Points** tables.

- **Admissions tests for Law, Medicine and Veterinary Science/Medicine** Where admissions tests form part of a university's offer for any of these subjects, this is indicated on the offers line in the subject tables for the relevant university. This is shown by '+LNAT' (for Law), '+BMAT' or '+UCAT' (for Medicine), and '+BMAT' (for Veterinary Science/Medicine). For example, the offers lines could read as follows:

    Cardiff – AAA incl chem+biol+interview+UCAT (Med 5 yrs) (IB 36 pts HL 666 incl chem/biol+sci/maths)
    Durham – A*AA +LNAT (Law) (IB 38 pts)
    London (RVC) – AAA–AAB incl chem+biol +BMAT (Vet Med)

    Entry and admissions tests will be required for 2021 by a number of institutions for a wide range of subjects: see **Chapter 5** and the subject tables in **Chapter 7** for more information and check university websites and prospectuses.

Course title(s)

After the offer, an abbreviated form of the course title(s) to which the offers information refers is provided in brackets. Unless otherwise indicated, this course title represents all other courses in this subject offered by the institution, including joint courses. The abbreviations used (see **COURSE ABBREVIATIONS** at the end of this chapter) closely relate to the course titles shown in the institutions' prospectuses. When the course gives the opportunity to study abroad this can be indicated on the offers line by including 'St Abrd' after the abbreviated course title. For example:

Lancaster – AAB incl maths (Econ (St Abrd)) (IB 35 pts HL 6 maths)

When experience in industry is provided as part of the course (not necessarily a sandwich course) this can be indicated on the offers line by including 'Yr Ind' after the abbreviated course title. For example:

Liverpool – ABB (Bus Mgt (Yr Ind)) (IB 33 pts)

Sometimes the information in the offers line relates to more than one course (see **Worcester** below). In such cases, each course title is separated with a semicolon.

Worcester – 112 pts (PE Spo St; PE Dance)

When a number of joint courses exist in combination with a Major subject, they may be presented using a list separated by slashes – for example '(Int Bus Fr/Ger/Span)' indicates International Business with French or German or Spanish. Some titles may be followed by the word 'courses' – for example, (Hist courses):

Bishop Grosseteste – 96–112 pts (Hist courses; Arch Hist)

This means that the information on the offers line refers not only to the Single Honours course in Archaeology History, but also to the range of History courses. For some institutions with extensive Combined or Joint Honours programmes, the information given on the offers line may specify (Comb Hons) or (Comb courses).

For Engineering courses, BSc is included as an abbreviation in the subject line if the course is also offered at the same institution as a BEng degree with different entry requirements. For example:

Anglia Ruskin – 96 pts (Civ Eng (BSc)) (IB 24 pts)

Sometimes, where relevant, the offers line shows integrated master's degree courses (four year courses which combine three years of undergraduate study with a fourth year of postgraduate level study). In such cases, an abbreviation showing the type of degree course appears at the end of the course offer. For example:

Bristol – AAA–ABB incl maths (Elec Electron Eng (MEng)) (IB 36–32 pts HL 6 maths)

Courses awaiting validation are usually publicised in prospectuses and on websites. However, these are not included in the tables in **Chapter 7** since there is no guarantee that they will run. You should check with the university that a non-validated course will be available.

To help you understand the information provided under the **Your target offers and examples of degree courses** heading, the box below provides a few examples with their meaning explained underneath.

OFFERS LINES EXPLAINED

136 pts [University/University College name] – AAB (Acc Fin)
For the Accounting Finance course the University requires grades of AAB (136 pts) at A-level.

152 pts [University/University College name] – A*AA incl chem+biol +BMAT (Med 6 yrs)
For the 6 year Medicine course the University requires one A* and two A grades at A-level, with two of these subjects in Chemistry and Biology, plus the BMAT.

104 pts [University/University College name] – 104–120 pts (Geog)
For Geography, the University usually requires 104 UCAS Tariff points, but offers may range up to 120 UCAS Tariff points.

Alternative offers
In each of the subject tables, offers are shown in A-level grades or equivalent UCAS Tariff points, and in some cases as points offers of the International Baccalaureate Diploma (see below). However, applicants taking Scottish Highers/Advanced Highers, the Advanced Welsh Baccalaureate – Skills Challenge Certificate, the International Baccalaureate Diploma, BTEC, the Extended Project, Music examinations and Art and Design Foundation Studies should refer to **Appendix 1 – UCAS 2021 Entry Tariff Points**. For more information, see www.ucas.com/undergraduate/what-and-where-study/entry-requirements/ucas-tariff-points or contact the institution direct.

IB offers
A selection of IB points offers appears at the end of some university/subject entries, along with any requirements for points gained from specific Higher Level (HL) subjects. Where no specific subjects are named for HL, the HL points can be taken from any subject. For comparison of entry requirements, applicants with IB qualifications should check the A-level offers required for their course and then refer to **Appendix 1** which gives the revised IB UCAS Tariff points for 2021 entry. The figures under this subheading indicate the number or range of International Baccalaureate (IB) Diploma points likely to be requested in an offer. A range of points indicates variations between Single and Joint Honours courses. Applicants offering the IB should check with prospectuses and websites and, if in doubt, contact admissions tutors for the latest information on IB offers.

Scottish offers
Scottish Honours degrees normally take four years. However, students with very good qualifications may be admitted into the second year of courses (Advanced entry). In some cases it may even be possible to enter the third year.

This year we have included some offers details for Advanced entry. Any student with sufficient A-levels or Advanced Highers considering this option should check with the university to which they are applying. The policies at some Scottish universities are listed below:

Aberdeen Advanced entry possible for many courses, but not for Education, Law or Medicine.
Abertay Possibility of advanced entry largely dependent on content of current course.
Dundee Advanced entry possible for many courses, but not Education or Medicine.
Edinburgh Advanced entry possible for Science, Engineering, and Art and Design courses.
Edinburgh Napier Advanced entry to Stages 2, 3 or 4 of a programme, particularly for those with an HNC/HND or those with (or expecting to obtain) good grades in Advanced Highers or A-levels.
Glasgow Advanced entry possible in a range of subjects, including Neuroscience, Sociology and Civil Engineering.
Glasgow Caledonian Advanced entry available in a wide range of courses, including Business, Journalism and Biological Sciences.
Queen Margaret Advanced entry for some courses.
St Andrews Advanced entry for some courses.
Stirling Advanced entry for some courses.
Strathclyde Advanced entry for some courses.
West Scotland Advanced entry for some courses.

For others not on this list, please check individual university and college websites.

Contextual offers
These offers are made by most universities to disadvantaged students wishing to be considered for university places. In most cases these are lower offers by one or two grades compared to the standard offers.

DEGREE APPRENTICESHIPS
Examples of degree apprenticeships offered by some universities, designed in partnerships with employers. To check degree apprenticeship vacancies and details, refer to GOV.UK (www.findapprenticeship.service.gov.uk/apprenticeshipsearch).

IMPORTANT NOTE ON THE COURSE OFFERS INFORMATION

The information provided in **Chapter 7** is presented as a first reference source as to the target levels required. Institutions may alter their standard offers in the light of the qualifications offered by applicants.

The offers they publish do not constitute a contract and are not binding on prospective students: changes may occur between the time of publication and the time of application in line with market and student demand.

The points levels shown on the left-hand side of the offers listings are for ease of reference for the reader: not all universities will be making offers using the UCAS Tariff points system and it cannot be assumed that they will accept a points equivalent to the grades they have stipulated. Check university and college prospectuses, and also their websites, for their latest information before submitting your application.

EXAMPLES OF COLLEGES OFFERING COURSES IN THIS SUBJECT FIELD

Examples of courses offered by some local colleges – but also check your local college. To check details of courses, refer to college websites and **Chapter 9** Sections 2 and 3.

CHOOSING YOUR COURSE

The information under this heading (to be read in conjunction with **Chapter 1**) covers factors that are important to consider in order to make an informed decision on which courses to apply for. The information is organised under the following subheadings.

Universities and colleges teaching quality

The Unistats website (https://unistats.ac.uk) provides official information where available for different subjects and universities and colleges in the UK to help prospective students and their advisers make comparisons between them and so make informed choices about what and where to study. Information is updated annually and is available for each subject taught at each university and college (and for some further education colleges). The Quality Assurance Agency (www.qaa.ac.uk) reviews the quality and standards of all universities and colleges and official reports of their reviews are available on their website but it is important to note their dates of publication.

Top research universities and colleges (REF 2014)

In December 2014 the latest Research Excellence Framework was undertaken covering certain subject areas. The leading universities in the relevant subject areas are listed in the order of achievement. It should be noted that not all subjects were assessed. The next REF is due in 2021.

Examples of sandwich degree courses

This section lists examples of institutions that offer sandwich placements for some of their courses in the subject field shown. The institutions listed offer placements of one-year duration and do not include language courses or work experience or other short-term placements. Check with the institutions too, since new courses may be introduced and others withdrawn depending on industrial or commercial arrangements. Further information on sandwich courses with specific information on the placements of students appears in **Chapter 1**.

NB During a period of economic uncertainty, universities and colleges may have problems placing students on sandwich courses. Applicants applying for courses are therefore advised to check with admissions tutors that these courses will run, and that placements will be available.

ADMISSIONS INFORMATION

Under this heading, information gathered from the institutions has been provided. This will be useful when planning your application.

Number of applicants per place (approx)

These figures show the approximate number of applicants initially applying for each place before any offers are made. It should be noted that any given number of applicants represents candidates who have also applied for up to four other university and college courses.

Advice to applicants and planning the UCAS personal statement
This section offers guidelines on information that could be included in the personal statement section of your UCAS application. In most cases, applicants will be required to indicate why they wish to follow a particular course and, if possible, to provide positive evidence of their interest. See also **Chapters 4** and **5**.

Misconceptions about this course
Admissions tutors are given the opportunity in the research for this book to set the record straight by clarifying aspects of their course they feel are often misunderstood by students, and in some cases, advisers!

Selection interviews
A sample of institutions that normally use the interview as part of their selection procedure is listed here. Those institutions adopting the interview procedure will usually interview only a small proportion of applicants. It is important to use this section in conjunction with **Chapters 3** and **5**.

Interview advice and questions
This section includes information from institutions on what candidates might expect in an interview to cover, and examples of the types of interview questions posed in recent years. Also refer to **Chapters 3** and **5**: these chapters provide information on tests and assessments which are used in selecting students.

Reasons for rejection (non-academic)
Academic ability and potential to succeed on the course are the major factors in the selection (or rejection) of applicants. Under this subheading, admissions tutors give other reasons for rejecting applicants.

AFTER-RESULTS ADVICE
Under this heading, information for helping you decide what to do after the examination results are published is provided (see also the section on **What to do on Results Day ... and After** in **Chapter 4**). Details refer to the main subject area unless otherwise stated in brackets.

Offers to applicants repeating A-levels
This section gives details of whether second-time offers made to applicants repeating their exams may be 'higher', 'possibly higher' or the 'same' as those made to first-time applicants. The information refers to Single Honours courses. It should be noted that circumstances may differ between candidates – some will be repeating the same subjects taken in the previous year, while others may be taking different subjects. Offers will also be dictated by the grades you achieved on your first sitting of the examinations. Remember, if you were rejected by all your universities and have achieved good grades, contact them by telephone on results day – they may be prepared to revise their decision. This applies particularly to medical schools.

GRADUATE DESTINATIONS AND EMPLOYMENT (2016/17 HESA)
The information under this heading has been provided by the Higher Education Statistics Agency (HESA) and is taken from their most recent report *Destinations of Leavers from Higher Education 2016/17*, released in July 2018. The report can be obtained from www.hesa.ac.uk.

Details are given of the total number of graduates surveyed whose destinations have been recorded – not the total number who graduated in that subject. Employment figures relate to those in full-time permanent paid employment after six months in a variety of occupations not necessarily related to their degree subject (part-time employment figures are not included). Figures are also given for those in voluntary, unpaid work. 'Further study' includes research into a subject-related field, higher degrees, private study or, alternatively, career training involving work and further study. The 'Assumed unemployed' category refers to those students who were believed to be unemployed for various reasons (eg travelling, personal reasons) or those students still seeking permanent employment six months after graduating. The figures given do not equal the total number of graduates surveyed as we have chosen only to include the most relevant or interesting areas.

Career note
Short descriptions of the career destinations of graduates in the subject area are provided.

OTHER DEGREE SUBJECTS FOR CONSIDERATION
This heading includes some suggested alternative courses that have similarities to the courses listed in the subject table.

ABBREVIATIONS USED IN THE SUBJECT TABLES IN CHAPTER 7

INSTITUTION ABBREVIATIONS

The following abbreviations are used to indicate specific institutions or types of institution:

Ac	Academy
AI	Arts Institute
ALRA	Academy of Live and Recorded Arts
AMD	Academy of Music and Drama
Birk	Birkbeck (London University)
BITE	British Institute of Technology, England
CA	College of Art(s)
CAD	College of Art and Design
CAFRE	College of Agriculture, Food and Rural Enterprise
CAg	College of Agriculture
CAgH	College of Agriculture and Horticulture
CAT	College of Advanced Technology or Arts and Technology
CComm	College of Communication
CDC	College of Design and Communication
CECOS	London College of IT and Management
CFash	College of Fashion
CHort	College of Horticulture
CmC	Community College
CMus	College of Music
CMusDr	College of Music and Drama
Coll	College/Collegiate
Consv	Conservatoire
Court	Courtauld Institute (London University)
CT	College of Technology
CTA	College of Technology and Arts
Educ	Education
Gold	Goldsmiths (London University)
GSA	Guildford School of Acting
HOW	Heart of Worcestershire College
IA	Institute of Art(s)
IFHE	Institute of Further and Higher Education
Inst	Institute
King's	King's College (London University)
LeSoCo	Lewisham Southwark College
LIBF	London Institute of Banking and Finance
LIPA	Liverpool Institute of Performing Arts
LIS	London Interdisciplinary School
LSE	London School of Economics and Political Science
LSST	London School of Science and Technology
Met	Metropolitan
MS	Medical School
NCC	New City College
NCH	New College of the Humanities
QM	Queen Mary (London University)
RAc Dance	Royal Academy of Dance
RAcMus	Royal Academy of Music
RConsvS	Royal Conservatoire of Scotland
RCMus	Royal College of Music

Reg Coll	Regional College
Reg Fed	Regional Federation (Staffordshire)
RH	Royal Holloway (London University)
RNCM	Royal Northern College of Music
RVC	Royal Veterinary College (London University)
SA	School of Art
SAD	School of Art and Design
Sch	School
Sch SpDr	School of Speech and Drama
SMO	Sabhal Mòr Ostaig
SOAS	School of Oriental and African Studies (London University)
SRUC	Scotland's Rural College
UC	University College
UCEM	University College of Estate Management
UCFB	University College of Football Business
UCL	University College (London University)
UCO	University College of Osteopathy
UHI	University of the Highlands and Islands
Univ	University

COURSE ABBREVIATIONS

The following abbreviations are used to indicate course titles and admissions tests:

Ab	Abrahamic	**Agribus**	Agribusiness
Abrd	Abroad	**Agric**	Agriculture/Agricultural
Acc	Accountancy/Accounting	**Agrofor**	Agroforestry
Accs	Accessories	**Agron**	Agronomy
Acoust	Acoustics/Acoustical	**Aid**	Aided
Acq	Acquisition	**Aircft**	Aircraft
Act	Actuarial	**Airln**	Airline
Actg	Acting	**Airpt**	Airport
Actn	Action	**Airvhcl**	Airvehicle
Actr	Actor	**Akkdn**	Akkadian
Actv	Active	**ALN**	Additional Learning Needs
Actvsm	Activism	**Am**	America(n)
Actvt(s)	Activity/Activities	**Amen**	Amenity
Acu	Acupuncture	**AMESAA**	Asian and Middle Eastern
Add	Additional		Studies Admissions Assessment
Adlscn	Adolescence	**Analys**	Analysis
Adlt	Adult	**Analyt**	Analytical/Analytics
Admin	Administration/Administrative	**Anat**	Anatomy/Anatomical
Adt	Audit	**Anc**	Ancient
Adv	Advertising	**Anim**	Animal
Advc	Advice	**Animat**	Animation
Advnc	Advanced	**Animatron**	Animatronics
Advntr	Adventure	**Anth**	Anthropology
Aero	Aeronautical/Aeronautics	**Antq**	Antique(s)
Aerodyn	Aerodynamics	**App(s)**	Applied/Applicable/Applications
Aero-Mech	Aero-mechanical	**Appar**	Apparel
Aerosp	Aerospace	**Appr**	Appropriate
Aeroth	Aerothermal	**Apprsl**	Appraisal
Af	Africa(n)	**Aqua**	Aquaculture/Aquatic
Affrs	Affairs	**Ar**	Area(s)
Age	Ageing	**Arbc**	Arabic
Agncy	Agency	**Arbor**	Arboriculture

Arch	Archaeology/Archaeological	**Bioarch**	Bioarchaeology
ARCHAA	Archaeology Admissions Assessment	**Bioch**	Biochemistry/Biochemical
		Biocomp	Biocomputing
Archit	Architecture/Architectural	**Biodiv**	Biodiversity
ARCHITAA	Architecture Admissions Assessment	**Bioelectron**	Bioelectronics
		Bioeng	Bioengineering
Archvl	Archival	**Biogeog**	Biogeography
Aroma	Aromatherapy	**Biogeosci**	Biogeoscience
Arst	Artist	**Bioinform**	Bioinformatics
Artfcts	Artefacts	**Biokin**	Biokinetics
Artif	Artificial	**Biol**	Biological/Biology
As	Asia(n)	**Biom**	Biometry
ASNCAA	Anglo-Saxon, Norse and Celtic Admissions Assessment	**Biomat**	Biomaterials
		Biomed	Biomedical/Biomedicine
Ass	Assessment	**Biomol**	Biomolecular
Assoc	Associated	**Biophys**	Biophysics
Asst	Assistant	**Bioproc**	Bioprocess
Assyr	Assyriology	**Biorg**	Bio-organic
Ast	Asset	**Biosci**	Bioscience(s)
Astnaut	Astronautics/Astronautical	**Biotech**	Biotechnology
Astro	Astrophysics	**Biovet**	Bioveterinary
Astron	Astronomy	**Bkbnd**	Bookbinding
A-Sxn	Anglo-Saxon	**Bld**	Build(ing)
Ated	Accelerated	**Bldstck**	Bloodstock
Atel	Atelier	**Blksmthg**	Blacksmithing
Atlan	Atlantic	**Blt**	Built
Atmos	Atmospheric/Atmosphere	**Bngli**	Bengali
Attrctns	Attractions	**Braz**	Brazilian
Auc	Auctioneering	**Brew**	Brewing
Aud	Audio	**Brit**	British
Audiol	Audiology	**Brnd**	Brand(ing)
Audtech	Audiotechnology	**Broad**	Broadcast(ing)
Aus	Australia(n)	**Bspk**	Bespoke
Austr	Australasia	**Bty**	Beauty
Auth	Author/Authoring/Authorship	**Bulg**	Bulgarian
Auto	Automotive	**Burm**	Burmese
Autom	Automated/Automation	**Bus**	Business
Automat	Automatic	**Buy**	Buying
Autombl	Automobile	**Byz**	Byzantine
Autsm	Autism		
AV	Audio Video	**CAA**	Classics Admissions Assessment
Avion	Avionic(s)	**CAD**	Computer Aided Design
Avn	Aviation	**Callig**	Calligraphy
Ay St	Ayurvedic Studies	**Can**	Canada/Canadian
		Canc	Cancer
Bank	Banking	**Cap**	Capital
Bch	Beach	**Cardio**	Cardiology
Bd	Based	**Cardiov**	Cardiovascular
Bdwk	Bodywork	**Carib**	Caribbean
Bev	Beverage	**Cart**	Cartography
BHS	British Horse Society	**Cat**	Catering
Bhv	Behaviour(al)	**Cat**	Classics Admissions Test
Bib	Biblical	**CATS**	Credit Accumulation and Transfer Scheme
Bio Ins	Bio Instrumentation		

Cell	Cellular	**Col**	Colour
Celt	Celtic	**Coll**	Collaborative
Cent	Century	**Comb**	Combined
Ceram	Ceramics	**Combus**	Combustion
Cert	Certificate	**Comm(s)**	Communication(s)
Ch Mgt	Chain Management	**Commer**	Commerce/Commercial
Chart	Chartered	**Commun**	Community
Chc	Choice	**Comp**	Computation/Computer(s)/
Chch	Church		Computerised/Computing
Chem	Chemistry	**Compar**	Comparative
Cheml	Chemical	**Complem**	Complementary
Chin	Chinese	**Con**	Context
Chiro	Chiropractic	**Conc**	Concept
Chld	Child/Children/Childhood	**Concur**	Concurrent
Chn	Chain	**Cond**	Conductive
Chng	Change	**Condit**	Conditioning
Choreo	Choreography	**Cons**	Conservation
Chr	Christian(ity)	**Conslt**	Consultant
Chrctr	Character	**Constr**	Construction
Chtls	Chattels	**Consum**	Consumer
Cits	Cities	**Cont**	Contour
Civ	Civil(isation)	**Contemp**	Contemporary
Class	Classical/Classics	**Contnl**	Continental
Clim	Climate/Climatic	**Contr**	Control
Clin	Clinical	**Conv**	Conveyancing
Cllct	Collect(ing)	**Cord**	Cordwainers
Clnl	Colonial	**Corn**	Cornish
Cloth	Clothing	**Corp**	Corporate/Corporation
Clsrm	Classroom	**Cos**	Cosmetic
CLT	Cambridge Law Test	**Cosmo**	Cosmology
Cmbt	Combat	**Cr**	Care
Cmc	Comic	**Crcs**	Circus
Cmdy	Comedy	**Crdc**	Cardiac
Cmn	Common	**Crea**	Creative/Creation
Cmnd	Command	**Crft(s)**	Craft(s)/Craftsmanship
Cmplrs	Compilers	**Crim**	Criminal
Cmpn	Companion	**Crimin**	Criminological/Criminology
Cmpsn	Composition	**Crit**	Criticism/Critical
Cmpste(s)	Composite(s)	**Crm**	Crime
Cmwlth	Commonwealth	**Cro**	Croatian
Cncr	Cancer	**Crr**	Career
Cnflct	Conflict	**Crsn**	Corrosion
Cnma	Cinema/Cinematics/	**Crtn**	Cartoon
	Cinematography	**Cru**	Cruise
Cnslg	Counselling	**Crypt**	Cryptography
Cnsltncy	Consultancy	**CSAT**	Computer Science
Cnt	Central		Admissions Test
Cntnt	Content	**Cstl**	Coastal
Cntrms	Countermeasures	**Cstm**	Costume
Cntry	Country(side)	**Cstmd**	Customised
Cntxt	Context	**Ctln**	Catalan
Cnty	Century	**Ctlys**	Catalysis
Coach	Coaching	**Ctzn**	Citizenship
Cog	Cognitive	**Culn**	Culinary

Cult	Culture(s)/Cultural		Dth	Death
Cur	Curation		Dvc	Device
Cy	Cyber		Dvnc	Deviance
Cyber	Cybernetics/Cyberspace		Dvsd	Devised
Cybercrim	Cybercrime		Dynmcs	Dynamics
Cyberscrty	Cybersecurity			
Cybertron	Cybertronics		E	East(ern)
Cym	Cymraeg		EAA	Education Admissions
Cz	Czech			Assessment
			ECAA	Economics Admissions
Dan	Danish			Assessment
Decn	Decision		Ecol	Ecology/Ecological
Decr	Decoration/Decorative		Ecomet	Econometrics
Def	Defence		e-Commer	E-Commerce
Defer	Deferred Choice		Econ	Economic(s)
Deg	Degree		Econy	Economy/Economies
Demcr	Democratic		Ecosys	Ecosystem(s)
Dept	Department		Ecotech	Ecotechnology
Des	Design(er)		Ecotour	Ecotourism
Desr	Desirable		Ecotox	Ecotoxicology
Dest	Destination(s)		Edit	Editorial/Editing
Dev	Development(al)		Educ	Education(al)
Devsg	Devising		Educr	Educare
Df	Deaf		Efcts	Effects
Diag	Diagnostic		EFL	English as a Foreign
Diet	Diet/Dietetics/Dietitian			Language
Dif	Difficulties		Egypt	Egyptian/Egyptology
Dig	Digital		ELAT	English Literature
Dip	Diploma			Admissions Test
Dip Ing	Diplom Ingeneur		Elec	Electrical
Dipl	Diplomacy		Elecacoust	Electroacoustics
Dir	Direct/Direction/		Electromech	Electromechanical
	Director/Directing		Electron	Electronic(s)
Dis	Disease(s)		ELT	English Language Teaching
Disab	Disability		Ely	Early
Disas	Disaster		Emb	Embryo(logy)
Discip	Disciplinary		Embd	Embedded
Diso	Disorders		Embr	Embroidery
Disp	Dispensing		Emer	Emergency
Dist	Distributed/Distribution		Emp	Employment
Distil	Distillation/Distilling		Ener	Energy
Div	Divinity		Eng	Engineer(ing)
d/l	distance learning		ENGAA	Engineering Admissions
Dlvry	Delivery			Assessment
Dnstry	Dentistry		Engl	English
Dntl	Dental		Engmnt	Engagement
Doc	Document(ary)		Engn	Engine
Dom	Domestic(ated)		Ent	Enterprise
Dr	Drama		Enter	Entertainment
Drg	Drawing		Entomol	Entomology
Drs	Dress		Entre	Entrepreneur(ship)
Dscrt	Discrete		Env	Environment(s)/Environmental
Dscvry	Discovery		EPQ	Extended Project
Dsply	Display			Qualification
Dtbs	Databases		Eql	Equal

Eqn	Equine/Equestrian
Equip	Equipment
Equit	Equitation
Ergon	Ergonomics
Est	Estate
Eth	Ethics
Ethl	Ethical
Eth-Leg	Ethico-Legal
Ethn	Ethnic
Ethnol	Ethnology
Ethnomus	Ethnomusicology
EU	European Union
Euro	Europe/European
Eval	Evaluation
Evnglstc	Evangelistic
Evnt(s)	Event(s)
Evol	Evolution(ary)
Ex	Executing
Excl	Excellence
Exer	Exercise
Exhib	Exhibition
Exmp	Exempt(ing)
Exp	Export
Explor	Exploration
Explsn	Explosion
Expltn	Exploitation
Expmtl	Experimental
Expnc	Experience
Expr	Expressive
Ext	Extended
Extr	Exterior
Extrm	Extreme
Fabs	Fabric(s)
Fac	Faculty
Fact	Factor(s)
Facil	Facilities
Fash	Fashion
Fbr	Fibre
Fctn	Fiction
Fd	Food
Fdn	Foundation
Fd Sc	Foundation degree in Science
Filmm	Filmmaking
Fin	Finance/Financial
Finn	Finnish
Fish	Fishery/Fisheries
Fit	Fitness
Fl	Fluid
Fld	Field
Flex	Flexible
Flm	Film
Flor	Floristry
Fmaths	Further Mathematics
Fmly	Family

Fn	Fine
Foot	Footwear
For	Foreign
Foren	Forensic
Foss	Fossil(s)
Fr	French
Frchd	Franchised
Frcst	Forecasting
Frm	Farm
Frmwk	Framework
Frshwtr	Freshwater
Frst	Forest
Frsty	Forestry
Frtlty	Fertility
Fst Trk	Fast Track
Fstvl	Festival(s)
Ftbl	Football
Ftre	Feature(s)
Ftwr	Footwear
Furn	Furniture
Fut	Futures
GAA	Geography Admissions Assessment
Gael	Gaelic
Gam	Gambling
GAMSAT	Graduate Australian Medical School Admission Test
Gdn	Garden
Gdnc	Guidance
Gem	Gemmology
Gen	General
Genet	Genetics
Geochem	Geochemistry
Geog	Geography
Geoinform	Geoinformatics
Geol	Geology/Geological
Geophys	Geophysics
Geophysl	Geophysical
Geopol	Geopolitics
Geosci	Geoscience
Geosptl	Geospatial
Geotech	Geotechnics
Ger	German(y)
Gerc	Germanic
GIS	Geographical Information Systems
Gk	Greek
Glf	Golf
Gllry	Gallery/Galleries
Glob	Global(isation)
Gls	Glass
Gm(s)	Game(s)
Gmg	Gaming
Gmnt	Garment

Gmtc	Geomatic	**Hydrog**	Hydrography
Gndr	Gender	**Hydrol**	Hydrology
Gnm	Genome/Genomics	**Hyg**	Hygiene
Gold	Goldsmithing		
Gov	Government	**Iber**	Iberian
Govn	Governance	**Ice**	Icelandic
Gr	Grade	**ICT**	Information and
Graph	Graphic(s)		Communications Technology
Grgn	Georgian	**Id**	Idea(s)
Grn	Green	**Idnty**	Identity
Guji	Gujerati	**Illus**	Illustration
		Imag	Image/Imaging/Imaginative
HAA	History Admissions Assessment	**Immun**	Immunology/Immunity
HAAA	History of Art Admissions	**Impair**	Impairment
	Assessment	**Incl**	Including
Hab	Habitat	**Incln**	Inclusion
Hack	Hacking	**Inclsv**	Inclusive
Hard	Hardware	**Ind**	Industrial/Industry/Industries
HAT	History Aptitude Test	**Indep St**	Independent Study
Haz	Hazard(s)	**Indiv**	Individual(s)
Heal	Healing	**Indsn**	Indonesian
Heb	Hebrew	**Inf**	Information
Herb	Herbal	**Infec**	Infectious/Infection
Herit	Heritage	**Infml**	Informal
Hi	High	**Inform**	Informatics
Hisp	Hispanic	**Infra**	Infrastructure
Hist	History/Historical	**Inftq**	Informatique
HL	IB Higher level	**Injry**	Injury
Hlcst	Holocaust	**Innov**	Innovation
Hlnds	Highlands	**Ins**	Insurance
Hlth	Health	**Inst**	Institute/Institution(al)
Hlthcr	Healthcare	**Instln**	Installation
Hm	Home	**Instr**	Instrument(ation)
Hnd	Hindi	**Int**	International
Hol	Holistic	**Integ**	Integrated/Integration
Hom	Homeopathic	**Intel**	Intelligent/Intelligence
Homin	Hominid	**Inter**	Interior(s)
Horol	Horology	**Interact**	Interaction/Interactive
Hort	Horticulture	**Intercult**	Intercultural
Hosp	Hospital	**Interd**	Interdisciplinary
Hous	Housing	**Intermed**	Intermedia
HPAT	Health Professions	**Interp**	Interpretation/Interpreting
	Admissions Test	**Intlctl**	Intellectual
HR	Human Resource(s)	**Intnet**	Internet
Hrdrs	Hairdressing	**Intr**	Interest(s)
Hrs	Horse	**Intrmdl**	Intermodal
Hse	House	**Inv**	Investment
HSPSAA	Human, Social and Political	**Invstg**	Investigating/Investigation(s)/
	Sciences Admissions		Investigative
	Assessment	**IPML**	Integrated Professional Master
Hspty	Hospitality		in Language
Htl	Hotel	**Ir**	Irish
Hum	Human(ities)	**Is**	Issues
Hung	Hungarian	**Isl**	Islands

Islam	Islamic	**Ltg**	Lighting
Isrl	Israel/Israeli	**Ltr**	Later
IT	Information Technology	**Lv**	Live
Ital	Italian	**Lvstk**	Livestock
ITE	Initial Teacher Education		
ITT	Initial Teacher Training	**Mach**	Machine(ry)
		Mag	Magazine
Jap	Japanese	**Mait**	Maitrise Internationale
Jew	Jewish	**Mak**	Making/Maker
Jewel	Jewellery	**Mand**	Mandarin
Jrnl	Journalism	**Manuf**	Manufacture/Manufacturing
Jud	Judaism	**Map**	Map(ping)
Juris	Jurisprudence	**Mar**	Marine
Just	Justice	**Marit**	Maritime
		Mark	Market(ing)
Knit	Knit(ted)	**Masch**	Maschinenbau
Kntwr	Knitwear	**Mat**	Material(s)
Knwl	Knowledge	**Mat**	Mathematics Admissions Test
Kor	Korean	**Mathem**	Mathematical
KS	Key Stage	**Maths**	Mathematics
		Mbl	Mobile
LAA	Linguistics Admissions	**Measur**	Measurement
	Assessment	**Mech**	Mechanical
Lab	Laboratory	**Mecha**	Mechatronic(s)
Lang(s)	Language(s)	**Mechn**	Mechanisation
Las	Laser	**Mechnsms**	Mechanisms
Lat	Latin	**Med**	Medicine/Medical
Lcl	Local	**Medcnl**	Medicinal
LD	Learning Disabilities	**Mediev**	Medieval
Ldrshp	Leadership	**Medit**	Mediterranean
Lea	Leather	**Ment**	Mentoring
Leg	Legal	**Metal**	Metallurgy/Metallurgical
Legis	Legislative	**Meteor**	Meteorology/Meteorological
Leis	Leisure	**Meth**	Method(s)
Lf	Life	**Mgr**	Manager
Lfstl	Lifestyle	**Mgrl**	Managerial
Lgc	Logic	**Mgt**	Management
Lib	Library	**Microbiol**	Microbiology/Microbiological
Librl	Liberal	**Microbl**	Microbial
Libshp	Librarianship	**Microcomp**	Microcomputer/
Lic	Licensed		Microcomputing
Lic de Geog	Licence de Geographie	**Microelec**	Microelectronics
Lic de Let	Licence de Lettres	**Mid E**	Middle Eastern
Ling	Linguistics	**Midwif**	Midwifery
Lit	Literature/Literary/Literate	**Min**	Mining
Litcy	Literacy	**Miner**	Minerals
Lnd	Land(scape)	**Mix**	Mixed
Lndbd	Land-based	**Mkup**	Make-up
Lns	Lens	**MLAT**	Modern Languages
Log	Logistics		Admissions Test
Lrn	Learn	**Mling**	Multilingual
Lrng	Learning	**Mltry**	Military
Ls	Loss	**MMath**	Master of Mathematics
Lsr	Laser		

MMLAA	Medieval and Modern Languages Admissions Assessment	**Neg**	Negotiated
		Net	Networks/Networking
		Neur	Neural
Mnd	Mind	**Neuro**	Neuroscience
Mndrn	Mandarin	**Neuropsy**	Neuropsychology
Mnrts	Minorities	**News**	Newspaper
Mnstry	Ministry	**NGO**	Non-Governmental Organisation(s)
Mnswr	Menswear		
Mntl Hlth	Mental Health	**NI**	Northern Ireland/Northern Irish
Mntn	Mountain		
Mntnce	Maintenance	**Nnl**	National
Mny	Money	**Norw**	Norwegian
Mod	Modular	**Npli**	Nepali
Modl	Modelling/Modelmaking	**Nrs**	Norse
Modn	Modern	**NSAA**	Natural Sciences Admissions Assessment
Modnty	Modernity		
Mol	Molecular	**Ntv**	Native
Monit	Monitoring	**Nucl**	Nuclear
MORSE	Mathematics, Operational Research, Statistics and Economics	**Num**	Numerate
		Nurs	Nursing
		Nursy	Nursery
MOst	Master's in Osteopathy	**Nutr**	Nutrition(al)
Mov	Movement/Moving	**Nvl**	Naval
Mrchnds	Merchandise/Merchandising	**NZ**	New Zealand
Mrchnt	Merchant		
Mrl	Moral	**Obj(s)**	Object(s)
Msg	Massage	**Obs**	Observational
Mslm	Muslim	**Occ**	Occupational
Mtl	Metal(s)	**Ocean**	Oceanography
Mtlsmth	Metalsmithing	**Ocn**	Ocean
Mtlwk	Metalwork(ing)	**Ocnc**	Oceanic
Mtn	Motion	**Oeno**	Oenology
Mtr	Motor	**Ofce**	Office
Mtrcycl	Motorcycle	**Off**	Offshore
Mtrg	Motoring	**Offrd**	Off-road
Mtrspo	Motorsport(s)	**Okl**	Oklahoma
Multid	Multi-disciplinary	**OLAT**	Oriental Languages Aptitude Test
Multim	Multimedia		
Mus	Music(ian)	**Onc**	Oncology
Muscskel	Musculoskeletal	**Onln**	Online
Musl	Musical	**Op(s)**	Operation(s)
Musm	Museum(s)	**Oph**	Ophthalmic
Mushp	Musicianship	**Oprtg**	Operating
Myan	Myanmar	**Opt**	Optical
		Optim	Optimisation
N	New	**Optn/s**	Optional/Options
N Am	North America	**Optoel**	Optoelectronics
Nanoelectron	Nanoelectronics	**Optom**	Optometry
Nanosci	Nanoscience	**OR**	Operational Research
Nanotech	Nanotechnology	**Ord**	Ordinary
Nat	Nature/Natural	**Org**	Organisation(s)/Organisational
Natpth	Naturopathy	**Orgnc**	Organic
Navig	Navigation	**Orgnsms**	Organisms
Nbrhd	Neighbourhood	**Orn**	Ornithology
Nds	Needs	**Orntl**	Oriental

Orth	Orthoptics	Phys	Physics
Orthot	Orthotics	Physio	Physiotherapy
Oseas	Overseas	Physiol	Physiology/Physiological
Ost	Osteopathy	Physl	Physical
Out	Outdoor	Pks	Parks
Out Act	Outdoor Activity	Plan	Planning
Outsd	Outside	Planet	Planetary
Ovrs	Overseas	Plas	Plastics
		Play	Playwork
P	Primary	Plcg	Police/Policing
PAA	Philosophy Admissions	Plcy	Policy
	Assessment	Plmt	Placement
P Cr	Primary Care	Plnt	Plant
Pacif	Pacific	Plntsmn	Plantsmanship
Pack	Packaging	Plt	Pilot
PActv	Physical Activity	Pltry	Poultry
Pal	Palaeobiology	PMaths	Pure Mathematics
Palae	Palaeoecology/Palaeontology	Pntg	Painting
Palaeoenv	Palaeoenvironments	Pod	Podiatry/Podiatric
Paramed	Paramedic(al)	Pol	Politics/Political
Parasit	Parasitology	Polh	Polish
Parl	Parliamentary	Pollut	Pollution
Part	Participation	Poly	Polymer(ic)
Pat	Patent	Pop	Popular
Pat	Physics Aptitude Test	Popn	Population
Path	Pathology	Port	Portuguese
Pathobiol	Pathobiological	Postcol	Postcolonial
Pathogen	Pathogenesis	PPE	Philosophy, Politics and
Patt	Pattern		Economics or Politics,
Pblc	Public		Philosophy and Economics
PBSAA	Psychological and Behavioural	PPI	Private Pilot Instruction
	Sciences Admissions	Ppl	People
	Assessment	Ppr	Paper
Pce	Peace	Pptry	Puppetry
PE	Physical Education	PR	Public Relations
Ped	Pedagogy	Prac	Practice(s)/Practical
Per	Person(al)	Practnr	Practitioner
Perf	Performance/Performed	Prchsng	Purchasing
Perfum	Perfumery	Prcrmt	Procurement
Pers	Personnel	Prdcl	Periodical
Persn	Persian	Precsn	Precision
Petrol	Petroleum	Pref	Preferable/Preferred
PGCE	Postgraduate Certificate	Prehist	Prehistory
	in Education	Prelim	Preliminary
Pharm	Pharmacy	Prem	Premises
Pharmacol	Pharmacology	Proc	Process(ing)
Pharml	Pharmaceutical	Prod	Product(s)/Production/Produce
Phil	Philosophy/Philosophies/	Prodg	Producing
	Philosophical	Prof	Professional/Proffesiynol/
Philgy	Philology		Professions
Phn	Phone	Prog	Programme/Programming
Phon	Phonetics	Proj	Project
Photo	Photography/Photographic	Prom	Promotion
Photojrnl	Photojournalism	Prop	Property/ies
Photon	Photonic(s)	Pros	Prosthetics

Prot	Protection/Protected	**Repro**	Reproductive
Proto	Prototyping	**Reqd**	Required
Prplsn	Propulsion	**Res**	Resource(s)
Prsts	Pursuits	**Resid**	Residential
Prt	Print	**Resoln**	Resolution
Prtcl	Particle	**Resp**	Response
Prtd	Printed	**Respir**	Respiratory
Prtg	Printing/Printmaking	**Restor**	Restoration
Prtshp	Partnership	**Rev**	Revenue
Prvntn	Prevention	**Rflxgy**	Reflexology
Pst	Post	**Rgby**	Rugby
Pstrl	Pastoral	**Rgstrn**	Registration
Psy	Psychology/Psychological	**Rl**	Real
Psychobiol	Psychobiology	**Rlblty**	Reliability
Psyling	Psycholinguistics	**Rlwy**	Railway
Psysoc	Psychosocial	**Rmnc**	Romance
Psytrpy	Psychotherapy	**RN**	Registered Nurse
Pt	Port	**Rnwl**	Renewal
p/t	part-time	**Robot**	Robotic(s)
Ptcl	Particle	**Rom**	Roman
Pub	Publishing/Publication	**Romn**	Romanian
Pvt	Private	**Rsch**	Research
Pwr	Power	**Rspnsb**	Responsibility
Pwrcft	Powercraft	**Rsrt**	Resort
		Rstrnt	Restaurant
Qntm	Quantum	**Rtl**	Retail(ing)
Qry	Quarry	**Rts**	Rights
Qtrnry	Quaternary	**Rur**	Rural
QTS	Qualified Teacher Status	**Russ**	Russian
Qual	Quality	**Rvr**	River
Qualif	Qualification		
Quant	Quantity/Quantitative	**S**	Secondary
		S As	South Asian
Rad	Radio	**Sansk**	Sanskrit
Radiog	Radiography	**Sat**	Satellite
Radiothera	Radiotherapy	**Sbstnce**	Substance
Rbr	Rubber	**Scand**	Scandinavian
Rce	Race	**Sch**	School
Rcycl	Recycling	**Schlstc**	Scholastic
Rdtn	Radiation	**Schm**	Scheme
Realsn	Realisation	**Sci**	Science(s)/Scientific
Rec	Recording(s)	**Scn**	Scene
Reclam	Reclamation	**Scnc**	Scenic
Recr	Recreation	**Scngrph**	Scenographic/Scenography
Reg	Regional	**Scot**	Scottish
Regn	Regeneration	**Scr**	Secure
Rehab	Rehabilitation	**Script**	Scriptwriting
Rel	Relations	**Scrn**	Screen
Relgn	Religion(s)	**Scrnwrit**	Sreenwriting
Relig	Religious	**Scrts**	Securities
Reltd	Related	**Scrty**	Security
Rem Sens	Remote Sensing	**Sctr**	Sector
Ren	Renaissance	**Sculp**	Sculpture/Sculpting
Renew	Renewable(s)	**Sdlry**	Saddlery
Rep	Representation	**SE**	South East

Sec	Secretarial
Semicond	Semiconductor
SEN	Special Educational Needs
Serb Cro	Serbo-Croat
Serv	Services
Set	Settings
Sex	Sexual
Sfty	Safety
Sgnl	Signal
Ship	Shipping
Silver	Silversmithing
Simul	Simulation
Sit Lrng	Situated Learning
Sk	Skills
Slav	Slavonic
Slf	Self
Sln	Salon
Slovak	Slovakian
Slp	Sleep
Sls	Sales
Sml	Small
Smt	Smart
Smtc	Semitic
Snc	Sonic
Snd	Sound
Sndtrk	Soundtrack
Sndwch	Sandwich
Sng	Song
Soc	Social
Sociol	Sociology
SocioLeg	Socio-Legal
Socling	Sociolinguistics
Soft	Software
Sol	Solution(s)
Solic	Solicitors
Soty	Society
Sov	Soviet
Sp	Speech
Span	Spanish
Spat	Spatial
Spc	Space
Spcrft	Spacecraft
Spec	Special/Specialism(s)/ Specialist
Spec Efcts	Special Effects
Sply	Supply
Spn	Spain
Spo	Sport(s)
Spotrf	Sportsturf
Spowr	Sportswear
Sppt(d)	Support(ed)
Sprtng	Supporting
Sqntl	Sequential
Srf	Surf(ing)

Srgy	Surgery
SS	Solid-state
St	Studies/Study
St Reg	State Registration
Stats	Statistics/Statistical
Std	Studio
STEM	Science, Technology, Engineering and Mathematics
Stg	Stage
Stgs	Settings
Stnds	Standards
STQ	Scottish Teaching Qualification
Str	Stringed
Strat	Strategic/Strategy
Strf	Stratified
Strg	Strength
Strt	Street
Struct	Structural/Structures
Stry	Story
Stt	State
Stwdshp	Stewardship
Styl	Styling
Sub	Subject
Surf	Surface
Surv	Surveying
Sust	Sustainability/Sustainable
Swed	Swedish
Swli	Swahili
Sxlty	Sexuality
Sys	System(s)
Systmtc	Systematic
TAA	Theology Admissions Assessment
Tam	Tamil
Tap	Tapestry
Tax	Taxation
Tax Rev	Taxation and Revenue
Tbtn	Tibetan
Tcnqs	Techniques
Teach	Teaching
Tech	Technology/Technologies/ Technician/Technical
Technol	Technological
TEFL	Teaching English as a Foreign Language
Telecomm	Telecommunication(s)
Ter	Terrestrial
TESOL	Teaching English to Speakers of Other Languages
Testmt	Testament
Tex	Textile(s)
Thbred	Thoroughbred
Thea	Theatre
Theol	Theology

Theor	Theory/Theoretical
Ther	Therapeutic
Thera	Therapy
Thngs	Things
Tht	Thought
Tiss	Tissue
Tlrg	Tailoring
Tm	Time
Tmbr	Timber
TMUA	Test of Mathematics for University Admission
Tnnl	Tunnel(ling)
Tns	Tennis
Topog	Topographical
Tour	Tourism
Tox	Toxicology
TQ	Teaching Qualification
Tr	Trade
Tr Stands	Trading Standards
Trad	Traditional
Trans	Transport(ation)
Transat	Transatlantic
Transl	Translation
Transnl Med Sci	Translational Medical Science
Trav	Travel
Trfgrs	Turfgrass
Trg	Training
Trnrs	Trainers
Trpcl	Tropical
Trpl	Triple
Trstrl	Terrestrial
Tstmnt	Testament
Ttl	Total
Turk	Turkish
TV	Television
Twn	Town
Typo	Typographical/Typography
Ukr	Ukrainian
Un	Union
Undwtr	Underwater
Unif	Unified
Up	Upland
Urb	Urban
USA	United States of America
Util	Utilities/Utilisation
Val	Valuation
Vcl	Vocal
Veh	Vehicle

Vert	Vertebrate
Vet	Veterinary
Vib	Vibration
Vict	Victorian
Vid	Video
Viet	Vietnamese
Virol	Virology
Vis	Visual(isation)
Vit	Viticulture
Vkg	Viking
Vntr	Venture
Vnu	Venue
Voc	Vocational
Vol	Voluntary
Vrtl Rlty	Virtual Reality
Vsn	Vision
Vstr	Visitor
Wdlnd	Woodland
Welf	Welfare
Wk	Work
Wkg	Working
Wkplc	Workplace
Wlbng	Well-being
Wldlf	Wildlife
Wls	Wales
Wmnswr	Womenswear
Wn	Wine
Wrbl	Wearable
Writ	Writing/Writer
Wrld	World
Wrlss	Wireless
Wst	Waste(s)
Wstn	Western
Wtr	Water
Wtrspo	Watersports
Wvn	Woven
www	World Wide Web
Ycht	Yacht
Ychtg	Yachting
Yng	Young
Yrs	Years
Yth	Youth
Zool	Zoology
3D	Three-dimensional

ACCOUNTANCY/ACCOUNTING
(see also Finance)

Accountancy and Accounting degree courses include accounting, finance, economics, law, management, qualitative methods and information technology. Depending on your chosen course, other topics will include business law, business computing, a study of financial institutions and markets, management accountancy, statistics, taxation and auditing, while at some institutions an optional language might be offered. Many, but not all, Accountancy and Accounting degrees give exemptions from the examinations of some or all of the accountancy professional bodies. Single Honours courses are more likely to give full exemptions, while Joint Honours courses are more likely to lead to partial exemptions. Students should check with universities and colleges about which professional bodies offer exemptions for their courses before applying. Most courses are strongly vocational and many offer sandwich placements or opportunities to study Accountancy/Accounting with a second subject.

Useful websites www.accaglobal.com/uk; www.cimaglobal.com; www.cipfa.org; www.tax.org.uk; www.icaew.com; www.ifa.org.uk

NB The points totals shown to the left of the institutions are for ease of reference only. It must not be assumed that Tariff points are always used by institutions or that they can be substituted for an offer in grades. The level of an offer is not necessarily indicative of the quality of a course.

COURSE OFFERS INFORMATION

Subject requirements/preferences GCSE English and mathematics required: popular universities may require A or A* (7 or 8/9). **AL** Mathematics (A or B) or accounting (A or B) required or preferred for some courses.

Your target offers and examples of degree courses

144 pts **Bath** – AAA–AAB +aEPQ incl maths (Acc Fin) (IB 36 pts HL 666)

Bristol – AAA–ABB incl maths (Acc Mgt) (IB 32–36 pts HL 16–18 pts); (Acc Fin) (IB 32–36 pts HL 6 maths)

City – AAA (Acc Fin; Acc Fin (Yr Ind)) (IB 35 pts)

Exeter – AAA (Acc Bus; Acc Fin (Euro St); Acc Fin (Yr Ind)) (IB 36 pts HL 666)

Glasgow – AAA/A*AB incl maths (Acc Fin; Acc Maths) (IB 38 pts HL 666 incl Engl/maths)

Leeds – AAA (Acc Fin) (IB 35 pts HL 17 pts incl 5 maths)

London (QM) – AAA (Acc Mgt) (IB 36 pts HL 666)

London LSE – AAA (Acc Fin) (IB 38 pts HL 666)

Manchester – AAA (Acc) (IB 36 pts HL 666)

Reading – AAA–AAB (Acc Fin) (IB 35–34 pts)

Strathclyde – AAA incl maths (Acc; Acc Hspty Tour Mgt; Acc Mark) (IB 38 pts HL 6 maths)

Warwick – AAA incl maths (Acc Fin) (IB 38 pts HL 5 maths)

136 pts **Birmingham** – AAB (Acc Fin) (IB 32 pts HL 665)

Cardiff – AAB–ABB (Acc; Acc (Yr Ind)) (IB 33–35 pts)

Durham – AAB (Acc Fin; Acc Mgt) (IB 36 pts HL 665 incl 5 maths)

Lancaster – AAB (Acc Fin; Acc Mgt St) (IB 35 pts HL 16 pts)

Liverpool – AAB (Acc Fin) (IB 35 pts)

Nottingham – AAB (Acc; Fin Acc Mgt) (IB 34 pts)

Queen's Belfast – AAB (Acc; Acc Fr/Span) (IB 34 pts HL 665)
Reading – AAB +interview (Acc Bus) (IB 34 pts)
Southampton – AAB/ABB +aEPQ (Acc Fin; Acc Fin (Yr Ind)) (IB 34 pts HL 17 pts)
York – AAB (Acc Bus Fin Mgt) (IB 35 pts)

128 pts **Cardiff** – AAB–ABB (Acc Fin) (IB 32–34 pts HL 665–655)
Coventry – ABB–BBB (Acc Fin) (IB 30 –31 pts)
East Anglia – ABB (Acc Fin) (IB 32 pts)
Edinburgh – AAB–ABB (Acc Bus; Acc Fin) (IB 40–34 pts HL 776–655)
Leicester – ABB–BBB +bEPQ (Acc Fin) (IB 30 pts HL 16 incl 4 maths)
London (Birk) – ABB–BBC 112 pts (Acc)
London (RH) – AAB–ABB (Acc Fin) (IB 32 pts HL 655 incl maths)
Loughborough – AAB–ABB (Acc Fin Mgt) (IB 35–34 pts HL 665)
Nottingham Trent – ABB 128 pts (Acc Fin)
Reading – ABB (Acc Mgt) (IB 32 pts)
Sheffield – ABB (Acc Fin Mgt) (IB 33 pts)
Surrey – ABB (Acc Fin) (IB 32 pts)
Sussex – AAB–ABB (Acc Fin; Acc Fin (Yr Ind)) (IB 34–32 pts)

120 pts **Aberdeen** – BBB (Acc Bus Mgt) (IB 32 pts HL 555)
Abertay – BBB (3 yr course) CCC (4 yr course) (Acc Fin) (IB 28 pts)
Aberystwyth – BBB (Acc Fin) (IB 28 pts)
BPP – ABB (2 yr course) BBB (3 yr course) 128–120 pts (Acc Fin) (IB 30 pts HL 555)
Brunel – BBB (Bus Mgt (Acc)) (IB 30 pts HL 4 Maths)
Derby – 120 pts (Acc Comb Hons; Acc Fin)
Essex – BBB (Acc Fin; Acc courses) (IB 30 pts)
Greenwich – BBB 120 pts (Acc Fin)
Heriot-Watt – ABB (3 yr course) BBB (4 yr course) (Acc Fin) (IB 34 pts (3 yr course) 29 pts (4 yr course) HL 5 maths)
Huddersfield – BBB 120 pts (Acc; Acc Fin)
Kent – BBB (Acc Fin) (IB 34 pts HL 16)
Kingston – ABC 120 pts (Acc Fin) (IB 27 pts HL 4 Engl lang)
Lincoln – BBB (Acc Fin) (IB 30 pts)
London South Bank – BBB 120 pts (Acc Fin)
Northumbria – 120 pts (Acc)
Roehampton – 120 pts (Acc)
Sheffield Hallam – 120 pts (Acc Fin; Foren Acc)
Staffordshire – BBB 120 pts (Acc Fin)
Stirling – ABB incl acc+econ (3 yr course) BBB (4 yr course) (Acc) (IB 35 pts (3 yr course) 32 pts (4 yr course))
Swansea – ABB–BBB (Acc; Acc Fin (Yr Ind)) (IB 33–32 pts HL 4 Engl)
Ulster – ABB–BBB incl maths (Acc; Acc Law) (IB 27 pts HL 13 pts)
Westminster – AAB–BBB (Acc) (IB 27 pts HL 4 Engl)

112 pts **Bangor** – 112 pts (Acc Econ)
Birmingham City – BBC 112 pts (Bus Acc) (IB 28 pts HL 14 pts)
Bradford – 112 pts (Acc Fin; Acc Fin (Yr Ind))
Cardiff Met – 112 pts (Acc)
Central Lancashire – 112 pts (Acc Fin)
De Montfort – 112 pts (Acc Fin) (IB 26 pts)
East London – BBC 112 pts (Acc Fin) (IB 26 pts HL 15 pts)
Edge Hill – BBB–BBC (Acc)
Gloucestershire – BBC 112 pts (Acc Fin)
Glyndŵr – BBC 112 pts (Acc Fin)
Hull – 112 pts (Acc) (IB 28 pts)
Keele – (Acc Comb Hons) (IB 30 pts HL 5 maths)
Leeds Beckett – 112 pts (Acc Fin) (IB 25 pts)
Liverpool Hope – BBC (Acc Fin) (IB 26 pts)

Liverpool John Moores – BBC 112 pts (Acc Fin) (IB 28 pts)
Middlesex – 112 pts (Acc Fin)
Northampton – BBC (Acc Comb Hons)
Portsmouth – 112–120 pts (Acc Fin) (IB 30 pts HL 754–655)
Robert Gordon – BBC (Acc Fin) (IB 29 pts)
Salford – (Acc Fin) (IB 31 pts)
Suffolk – BBC (Acc Fin Mgt)
UWE Bristol – 112 pts (Acc Fin)
Univ Law – BBC (Acc Fin)
West London – BBB–BBC 112–120 pts (Acc Fin) (IB 26 pts)
Winchester – 112–120 pts (Acc Fin) (IB 26 pts)
Worcester – 112 pts (Acc Fin)

104 pts **Bolton** – 104 pts (Acc)
Bournemouth – 104–120 pts (Acc Bus; Acc Fin) (IB 28–31 pts HL 55)
Chester – BBC–BCC (Acc Fin) (IB 26 pts)
Dundee – BBB–BCC (Acc) (IB 30 pts HL 555)
Glasgow Caledonian – BCC (Acc) (IB 25 pts HL Engl/maths)
Hertfordshire – BCC 104 pts (Acc)
Manchester Met – BBC–BCC 104–112 pts (Acc Fin; Bank Fin) (IB 26 pts)
Oxford Brookes – 104 pts (Acc Fin) (IB 29 pts); BBC 104 pts (Acc Econ) (IB 29 pts)

96 pts **Anglia Ruskin** – 96 pts (Acc Fin) (IB 24 pts)
Bath Spa – CCC (Bus Mgt (Acc)) (IB 26 pts)
Bedfordshire – BBB–CCC 96–120 pts (Acc)
Brighton – BBB–CCC 96–120 pts (Acc Fin) (IB 26 pts HL incl maths)
Buckingham – BBC–CCC +interview (Acc Fin) (IB 29–31 pts)
Chichester – 96–112 pts (Acc Fin) (IB 28 pts)
Edinburgh Napier – CCC (Acc) (IB 28 pts HL 654)
London Met – CCC 96 pts (Acc Fin) (IB 28 pts HL 15)
Middlesex – 96 pts (Bus Acc)
Newman – 96–144 pts (Acc Fin)
Plymouth – 96–112 pts (Acc Fin) (IB 28 pts HL 4)
Wolverhampton – CCC (Acc Fin; Acc Law)
York St John – 96–112 pts (Acc Fin)

88 pts **Canterbury Christ Church** – 88–112 pts (Acc)
Trinity Saint David – 88 pts +interview (Acc)

80 pts **Bucks New** – 80 pts (Acc Fin)
South Wales – BCC–CDD 80–104 pts (Acc Fin)
Teesside – 80–104 pts (Acc Fin)

60 pts **UHI** – D (Acc Fin)

Alternative offers
See **Chapter 6** and **Appendix 1** for grades/UCAS Tariff points information for other examinations.

DEGREE APPRENTICESHIPS
Robert Gordon (Acc).

EXAMPLES OF COLLEGES OFFERING COURSES IN THIS SUBJECT FIELD
Accrington and Rossendale (Coll); Barking and Dagenham (Coll); Bath (Coll); Blackburn (Coll); Blackpool and Fylde (Coll); Bournemouth and Poole (Coll); Bradford College UC; Bridgwater and Taunton (Coll); Bury (Coll); Chesterfield (Coll); Cornwall (Coll); Craven (Coll); Derby (Coll); East Riding (Coll); East Sussex (Coll); Exeter (Coll); Farnborough (CT); Hartlepool (CFE); HOW (Coll); Leeds City (Coll); LeSoCo; London City (Coll); London South East (Coll); Macclesfield (Coll); Manchester (Coll); Mont Rose (Coll); NCC Redbridge; Neath Port Talbot (Coll); Nescot; North Notts (Coll); North West London (Coll); Norwich City (Coll); Nottingham (Coll); Oldham (Univ Campus); Pearson (Coll); Peterborough (Coll); Plymouth City (Coll); Redcar and Cleveland (Coll); Richmond-upon-Thames (Coll);

South City Birmingham (Coll); South Gloucestershire and Stroud (Coll); St Helens (Coll); Tameside (Coll); TEC Partnership; Telford (Coll); Westminster Kingsway (Coll); Weymouth (Coll); Yeovil (Coll).

CHOOSING YOUR COURSE (SEE ALSO CH.1)

Universities and colleges teaching quality See www.qaa.ac.uk; https://unistats.ac.uk.

Examples of sandwich degree courses Aston; Bath; Bedfordshire; Birmingham City; Bournemouth; Bradford; Brighton; Brunel; Canterbury Christ Church; Cardiff Met; Central Lancashire; Chester; Chichester; Coventry; De Montfort; Derby; Durham; Gloucestershire; Greenwich; Hertfordshire; Huddersfield; Hull; Kent; Lancaster; Leeds Beckett; Liverpool John Moores; Loughborough; Manchester Met; Middlesex; Northumbria; Nottingham Trent; Oxford Brookes; Portsmouth; Reading; Salford; Sheffield Hallam; South Wales; Surrey; Sussex; Teesside; Ulster; UWE Bristol; West London; Westminster; Wolverhampton; Worcester; York.

ADMISSIONS INFORMATION

Number of applicants per place (approx) Bath 15; Birmingham 8; Bristol 10; Dundee 5; Durham 5; East Anglia 6; Essex 7; Exeter 18; Glasgow 10; Heriot-Watt 6; Hull 5; Lancaster 5; Leeds 25; London LSE 14; Manchester 11; Oxford Brookes 8; Salford 8; Sheffield 6; Staffordshire 3; Stirling 7; Strathclyde 10; Ulster 10; Warwick 14.

Advice to applicants and planning the UCAS personal statement Universities look for good numerical and communication skills, interest in the business and financial world, teamwork, problem-solving and computing experience. On the UCAS application you should be able to demonstrate your interest in and understanding of accountancy and to give details of any work experience or work shadowing undertaken. Try to arrange meetings with accountants, work shadowing or work experience in accountants' offices, commercial or industrial firms, town halls, banks or insurance companies and describe the work you have done. Obtain information from the main accountancy professional bodies (see **Appendix 3**). Refer to current affairs which have stimulated your interest from articles in the*Financial Times*, *The Economist* or the business and financial sections of the weekend press. **Bath** Gap year welcomed. Extracurricular activities are important and should be described on the personal statement. There should be no gaps in your chronological history. **Bristol** Deferred entry accepted.

Misconceptions about this course Buckingham Some students think it's a maths course. **Salford** Some applicants believe the course is limited to financial knowledge when it also provides an all-round training in management skills.

Selection interviews Yes Newcastle, Reading; **Some** Cardiff Met, Liverpool John Moores, Warwick, Wolverhampton; **No** Birmingham, Bristol, Cardiff, East Anglia, Essex, London LSE, Staffordshire, Surrey.

Interview advice and questions Be prepared to answer questions about why you have chosen the course, the qualities needed to be an accountant, and why you think you have these qualities! You should also be able to discuss any work experience you have had and to describe the differences in the work of chartered, certified, public finance and management accountants. See also **Chapter 5**. **Buckingham** Students from a non-English-speaking background are asked to write an essay. If their maths results are weak they may be asked to do a simple arithmetic test. Mature students with no formal qualifications are usually interviewed and questioned about their work experience.

Reasons for rejection (non-academic) Poor English. Lack of interest in the subject because they realise they have chosen the wrong course! No clear motivation. Course details not researched. **London South Bank** Punctuality, neatness, enthusiasm and desire to come to London South Bank not evident.

AFTER-RESULTS ADVICE

Offers to applicants repeating A-levels
Higher Manchester Met; **Possibly higher** Brighton; Central Lancashire; Leeds; Sheffield Hallam; **Same** Abertay; Aberystwyth; Anglia Ruskin; Bangor; Birmingham City; Bolton; Bradford; Brunel; Buckingham; Cardiff; Cardiff Met; Chichester; De Montfort; Derby; Dundee; Durham; East Anglia; East

London; Edinburgh Napier; Heriot-Watt; Huddersfield; Hull; Liverpool John Moores; Loughborough; Northumbria; Oxford Brookes; Salford; Staffordshire; Stirling; Trinity Saint David; West London; Wolverhampton; **No** Glasgow.

GRADUATE DESTINATIONS AND EMPLOYMENT (2016/17 HESA)
Graduates surveyed 4,370 **Employed** 2,610 **In voluntary employment** 100 **In further study** 905 **Assumed unemployed** 265

Career note Most Accountancy/Accounting graduates enter careers in finance.

OTHER DEGREE SUBJECTS FOR CONSIDERATION
Actuarial Studies; Banking; Business Studies; Economics; Financial Services; Insurance; International Securities and Investment Banking; Mathematics; Quantity Surveying; Statistics.

ACTUARIAL SCIENCE/STUDIES

Actuaries deal with the evaluation and management of financial risks, particularly those associated with insurance companies and pension funds. Studies focus on business economics, financial mathematics, probability and statistics, computer mathematics, statistics for insurance, and mathematics in finance and investment. Most courses include compulsory and optional subjects. Although Actuarial Science/Studies degrees are vocational and give full or partial exemptions from some of the examinations of the Institute and Faculty of Actuaries, students are not necessarily committed to a career as an actuary on graduation. However, many graduates go on to be actuary trainees, leading to one of the highest-paid careers.

Useful websites www.actuaries.org.uk; www.soa.org; www.beanactuary.org

NB The points totals shown to the left of the institutions are for ease of reference only. It must not be assumed that Tariff points are always used by institutions or that they can be substituted for an offer in grades. The level of an offer is not necessarily indicative of the quality of a course.

COURSE OFFERS INFORMATION
Subject requirements/preferences GCSE Most institutions require grades A or B (7 or 5/6) in English and mathematics. **AL** Mathematics at a specified grade required.

Your target offers and examples of degree courses
152 pts **Queen's Belfast** – A*AA–AAA incl maths (Act Sci Risk Mgt) (IB 37 pts HL 666 incl maths)
144 pts **City** – AAA incl maths (Act Sci) (IB 35 pts HL 6 maths)
      Heriot-Watt – AAA incl maths (3 yr course) AAB incl maths (4 yr course) (Act Sci; Act Sci Dip Ind Trg) (IB 30 pts (3 yr course) 28 pts (4 yr course) HL 7 maths (3 yr course) 6 maths (4 yr course))
      Kent – AAA incl maths (Act Sci (Yr Ind)) (IB 34 pts HL 6 maths); AAA incl maths/AAB incl maths+fmaths (Act Sci) (IB 34 pts HL 17 pts incl 6 maths)
      London LSE – AAA incl maths (Act Sci) (IB 38 pts HL 766 incl maths)
      Manchester – A*AA–AAA incl maths (Act Sci Maths) (IB 36 pts HL 666 incl maths)
      Southampton – AAA incl maths (Maths Act Sci) (IB 36 pts HL18 pts incl 6 maths)
136 pts **Leeds** – AAA–A*AB incl maths/AAB–A*BB incl maths+fmaths (Act Maths) (IB 35 pts HL 17 pts incl 6 maths)
      Liverpool – AAB incl maths (Act Maths) (IB 35 pts HL 6 maths)
128 pts **East Anglia** – ABB incl A maths (Act Sci (Yr Ind)) (IB 32 pts HL 6 incl maths); ABB incl maths (Act Sci) (IB 32 pts HL 6 incl maths)
      Leicester – ABB/ABC +bEPQ incl maths (Maths Act Sci) (IB 30 pts HL 16 incl 6 maths)
120 pts **Essex** – BBB incl maths/fmaths (Act Sci) (IB 30 pts HL 5 maths); (Act Sci (Yr Ind)) (IB 30 pts HL 6 maths)

Alternative offers
See **Chapter 6** and **Appendix 1** for grades/UCAS Tariff points information for other examinations.

CHOOSING YOUR COURSE (SEE ALSO CH.1)
Universities and colleges teaching quality See www.qaa.ac.uk; https://unistats.ac.uk.

Top research universities and colleges (REF 2014) See **Mathematics**.

Examples of sandwich degree courses East Anglia; Essex; Heriot-Watt; Kent; Kingston; Queen's Belfast.

ADMISSIONS INFORMATION
Number of applicants per place (approx) City 3; Heriot-Watt 4; London LSE 8; Southampton (Maths Act Sci) 9.

Advice to applicants and planning the UCAS personal statement
Demonstrate your knowledge of this career and its training, and mention any contacts you have made with an actuary. (See **Appendix 3** for contact details of professional associations for further information.) Any work experience or shadowing in insurance companies should be mentioned, together with what you have learned about the problems facing actuaries. It is important to show motivation and sheer determination for training as an actuary as it is long and tough (up to three or four years after graduation). Mathematical flair, an ability to communicate and an interest in business are paramount.

Selection interviews No East Anglia, Southampton.

Interview advice and questions In view of the demanding nature of the training, it is important to have spent some time discussing this career with an actuary in practice. Questions, therefore, may focus on the roles of the actuary and the qualities you need to succeed. You should also be ready to field questions about your AL mathematics course and the aspects of it you most enjoy. See also **Chapter 5**.

Reasons for rejection (non-academic) Kent Poor language skills.

AFTER-RESULTS ADVICE
Offers to applicants repeating A-levels Higher City; Heriot-Watt; Southampton.

GRADUATE DESTINATIONS AND EMPLOYMENT (2016/17 HESA)
See **Finance**.

Career note Graduates commonly enter careers in finance, many taking further examinations to qualify as actuaries.

OTHER DEGREE SUBJECTS FOR CONSIDERATION
Accountancy; Banking; Business Studies; Economics; Financial Risk Management; Financial Services; Insurance; Mathematics; Money, Banking and Finance; Statistics.

AFRICAN, ASIAN AND MIDDLE-EASTERN STUDIES
(including **Arabic, Ancient Near Eastern Studies, East Asian Studies, South Asian Studies, Swahili, Thai, Vietnamese;** see also **Chinese, History (ancient), Japanese, Religious Studies**)

These courses allow students to specialise in the language, history, religion and culture of one or two of a vast range of nations and people-groups. Arabic is one of the world's most widely used languages, spoken by more than 300 million people in over 20 countries in the Middle East and North Africa. Study of the language also includes Islamic and modern Middle Eastern history, while a course in Middle Eastern Studies will include an optional language such as Arabic, Persian or Turkish

(Edinburgh, Exeter). Links between Britain and Arabic-speaking countries have increased considerably in recent years and most of the larger UK organisations with offices in the Middle East have only a relatively small pool of Arabic-speaking graduates from which to recruit future employees each year. African Studies courses also tend to be multi-disciplinary and cover several subject areas, including anthropology, history geography, sociology and languages. Students may learn a language such as Yoruba (Nigeria), Amharic (Ethiopia) or Zulu (South Africa). Asian Studies courses offer the opportunity to study languages such as Korean, Japanese, Vietnamese and Thai. Both African and Asian studies are often studied as a Joint Honours with another subject.

Useful websites www.ciol.org.uk; www.bbc.co.uk/languages; www.languageadvantage.com; www.languagematters.co.uk; www.upi.com; www.merip.org; www.memri.org; www.mei.edu

NB The points totals shown to the left of the institutions are for ease of reference only. It must not be assumed that Tariff points are always used by institutions or that they can be substituted for an offer in grades. The level of an offer is not necessarily indicative of the quality of a course.

COURSE OFFERS INFORMATION
Subject requirements/preferences GCSE English, mathematics and a foreign language usually required. A high grade in Arabic may be required. **AL** A modern language is usually required or preferred.

Your target offers and examples of degree courses
160 pts   **St Andrews** – A*A*A incl maths (Arbc Maths) (IB 38 pts HL 666 incl 6 maths)
152 pts   **Cambridge** – A*AA +interview +AMESAA (As Mid E St) (IB 42–40 pts HL 776)
          Durham – A*AA (Comb Hons Soc Sci) (IB 38 pts HL 666)
144 pts   **Exeter** – AAA–ABB (Arbc Islam St Comb Hons) (IB 36–34 pts HL 666–665)
          Oxford – AAA +interview +CAT (Class Orntl St) (IB 39 pts HL 666); AAA+interview +OLAT (Orntl St incl Jap/Arab/Chin) (IB 39 pts HL 666)
          St Andrews – AAA (Arbc Mid E St) (IB 36 pts HL 6 hist); (Art Hist Mid E St) (IB 36 pts HL 665); (Arbc Econ) (IB 38 pts HL 666)
136 pts   **Exeter** – AAA–AAB (Mid E St) (IB 36–34 pts)
          London (UCL) – AAB incl Fr (Fr As Af Lang) (IB 36 pts HL 17 incl 6 Fr)
128 pts   **Edinburgh** – AAB–ABB (Islam St; Mid E St; Persn Soc Anth; Persn St) (IB 40–34 pts HL 766–655); (Arbc courses) (IB 40–34pts HL 766–655); ABB (Class Mid E St) (IB 37–34 pts HL 665–666)
          Exeter – AAB–ABB (Modn Langs Arbc) (IB 34–32 pts HL 665–655)
          Leeds – AAB–ABB 128–136 pts (Jap courses) (IB 35–34 pts HL 16 pts); ABB (Arbc Islam St; Arbc Mid E St; As Pacif St; As Pacif St (Int); Mid E St; Thai St) (IB 34 pts HL 16 pts)
          London (SOAS) – AAB–ABB (Af St; Anc Near E St; Arbc Comb Hons; Arbc Islam St; Heb Comb Hons; Kor; Mid E St; Persn Comb Hons; SE As St courses) (IB 35 pts HL 665); ABB (S As St) (IB 35 pts HL 665)
          Manchester – ABB (Arbc St; Mid E St) (IB 34 pts HL 655)
          Sheffield – ABB–BBB +bEPQ (E As St; Kor St; Kor St Jap) (IB 33 pts)
          Sussex – ABB 128 pts (Anth Lang) (32 pts)
          Warwick – ABB incl Fr/Ger (Fr/Ger St Arbc) (IB 34 pts HL 5 Fr/Ger)
120 pts   **Birmingham** – BBB (Af St; Af St Anth; Af St Dev) (IB 32 pts HL 555)
104 pts   **Central Lancashire** – 104–112 pts (As Pacif St; Int Bus Comm Modn For Lang; Modn Langs Arbc); 104–112 pts incl lang (Modn Langs (2 Lang) (Fr/Ger/Span/Jap/Russ/Ital/Kor))
          Westminster – ABB–BCC (Arbc Ling) (IB 27 pts HL 4 Engl/maths)
96 pts   **Islamic (Coll)** – CCC (Hawza St; Islam St)

Alternative offers
See **Chapter 6** and **Appendix 1** for grades/UCAS Tariff points information for other examinations.

CHOOSING YOUR COURSE (SEE ALSO CH.1)
Universities and colleges teaching quality See www.qaa.ac.uk; https://unistats.ac.uk.

ADMISSIONS INFORMATION

Number of applicants per place (approx) Cambridge 2; Durham 5; Leeds 6; London (SOAS) 5.

Advice to applicants and planning the UCAS personal statement Describe any visits to, or your experience of living in, Arabic-speaking countries. Develop a knowledge of Middle Eastern cultures, history and politics and mention these topics on the UCAS application. Provide evidence of language-learning skills and experience.

Selection interviews Yes Cambridge, Oxford (Orntl St) 24%); **No** Leeds.

Interview advice and questions For Arabic, the applicant will need to be able to justify their reasons for wanting to study Arabic or other languages and to discuss their interest in, and awareness of, cultural, social and political aspects of the Middle East. Applicants interviewing for a place on an African or Asian Studies course should describe any visits they have made to African or Asian countries and why they wish to study particular regions in more depth. It is expected that applicants will be up to date with political developments in relevant countries and willing to discuss any aspects which interest them. **Cambridge** See **Chapter 5** under**Modern and Medieval Languages**. **Oxford** See **Chapter 5** under**Modern and Medieval Languages**.

AFTER-RESULTS ADVICE

Offers to applicants repeating A-levels Higher Leeds; St Andrews; **Same** Exeter.

GRADUATE DESTINATIONS AND EMPLOYMENT (2016/17 HESA)

Graduates surveyed 115 **Employed** 40 **In voluntary employment** 5 **In further study** 35 **Assumed unemployed** 5

Career note Graduates of African and Asian studies work in a wide range of areas, including education, public relations, the third sector, journalism and consultancy. A significant number pursue further study. Arabic-language skills are currently sought after in areas such as cyber-security, national intelligence and security (GCHQ) and by the charity sector.

OTHER DEGREE SUBJECTS FOR CONSIDERATION

Anthropology; Archaeology; Classical Studies; Hebrew; History; Persian; Politics; Turkish.

AGRICULTURAL SCIENCES/AGRICULTURE

(including **Forestry**; see also**Animal Sciences, Food Science/Studies and Technology, Horticulture, Landscape Architecture, Surveying and Real Estate Management, Zoology**)

Courses in Agriculture recognise that modern farming practice requires sound technical and scientific knowledge, together with appropriate management skills, and most courses focus to a greater or lesser extent on all these requirements. Your choice of course depends on your particular interest and aims: some courses will give greater priority than others to practical application. Most graduates enter the agriculture industry while others move into manufacturing, wholesale and retail work. Agricultural courses specialise in crop and animal production and will also include agri-business and environmental issues. Forestry courses cover all aspects of the importance of forests from the biological, ecological, environmental, economic and sociological aspects with practical involvement in the establishment of forests and their control, growth, health and quality. Rural Estate and Land Management courses relate to the purchase and sale of country property, residential agency in towns, the management of commercial property, portfolios, investment funds and the provision of valuation and technical services. Countryside management courses cover the uses of the countryside including tourism, land use, and ecosystems and environmental aspects.

Useful websites www.gov.uk/government/organisations/department-for-environment-food-rural-affairs; www.gov.uk/government/organisations/natural-england; www.lantra.co.uk; www.forestryengland.uk; www.nfuonline.com; www.nfyfc.org.uk; http://iagre.org; www.bbsrc.ac.uk; www.wwoof.org.uk

NB The points totals shown to the left of the institutions are for ease of reference only. It must not be assumed that Tariff points are always used by institutions or that they can be substituted for an offer in grades. The level of an offer is not necessarily indicative of the quality of a course.

COURSE OFFERS INFORMATION

Subject requirements/preferences GCSE English and mathematics usually required; chemistry sometimes required. Practical experience may be required. **AL** One or two maths/biological science subjects may be required or preferred. Geography may be accepted as a science subject. Similar requirements apply for Agricultural Business Management courses. (Crop Sci) Two science subjects may be required. (Cntry Mgt) Geography or biology may be preferred.

Your target offers and examples of degree courses

120 pts **CAFRE** – BBB (Agric Tech)
     Edinburgh – BBB incl biol/chem (Agric Sci (Anim Sci); Agric Sci (Glob Agric Fd Scrty)) (IB 30 pts HL 5 biol/chem)
     Newcastle – ABB–BBB (Agric; Agric Agron) (IB 32–30 pts HL biol/chem)
     Nottingham – ABB–BBB incl sci (Agric; Agric Crop Sci; Agric Lvstk Sci) (IB 32–30 pts)
     Queen's Belfast – ABB–BBB (Agric Tech) (IB 33–32 pts HL 655)
     Reading – BBB (Agric Bus Mgt) (IB 30 pts); BBB incl sci (Agric) (IB 30 pts)
104 pts **Bangor** – 104 pts incl sci (Cons Frsty; Frsty)
     Myerscough (Coll) – 104 pts (Arbor Urb Frsty) (IB 24 pts)
     Royal Agricultural Univ – BCC (Agric; Rur Lnd Mgt) (IB 26 pts)
96 pts **Aberystwyth** – BBB–CCC incl sci 96–120 pts (Agric Anim Sci) (IB 30–26 pts HL 5 sci); CCC–BBB incl sci 96–120 pts (Agric) (IB 28–30 pts HL 5 sci)
     Cumbria – 96–112 pts (Frst Mgt); BBC–CCC 96–112 pts (Wdlnd Ecol Cons)
     Harper Adams – 96–112 pts (Agric courses); 96–112 pts+interview (Agric Mechn) (IB 28 pts)
     Royal Agricultural Univ – CCC (Bldstck Perf Hrs Mgt) (IB 26 pts)
     Writtle (UC) – 96 pts (Agric) (IB 24 pts)

Alternative offers
See **Chapter 6** and **Appendix 1** for grades/UCAS Tariff points information for other examinations.

EXAMPLES OF COLLEGES OFFERING COURSES IN THIS SUBJECT FIELD

Askham Bryan (Coll); Bicton (Coll); Bishop Burton (Coll); Bridgend (Coll); Bridgwater and Taunton (Coll); Craven (Coll); Duchy Coll UC; Easton Otley (Coll); Hadlow (UC); Hartpury (Coll); Moulton (Coll); Myerscough (Coll); Northumberland (Coll); Plumpton (Coll); Reaseheath (UC); Sir Gâr (Coll); Sparsholt (Coll).

CHOOSING YOUR COURSE (SEE ALSO CH.1)

Universities and colleges teaching quality See www.qaa.ac.uk; https://unistats.ac.uk.

Top research universities and colleges (REF 2014) (Agriculture, Veterinary and Food Science) Warwick; Cambridge; Nottingham; Aberdeen; Glasgow; East Anglia; Bristol; Stirling; Queen's Belfast; Liverpool; Reading.

Examples of sandwich degree courses Aberystwyth; Bangor Forestry; CAFRE; Cumbria Forestry; Harper Adams; Newcastle; Nottingham; Queen's Belfast; Reading.

ADMISSIONS INFORMATION

Number of applicants per place (approx) Bangor (Frstry) 6;Newcastle 3;Nottingham 6;Royal Agricultural Univ (Agric) 2.

Advice to applicants and planning the UCAS personal statement First-hand farming experience is essential for most courses and obviously important for all. Check prospectuses and websites. Describe the work done. Details of experience of work with agricultural or food farms (production and laboratory work), garden centres, even with landscape architects, could be appropriate. Keep up-to-date with European agricultural and fishing policies and mention any interests you have in these areas. Read farming magazines and discuss any articles which have interested you. You may even have had first-hand experience of the serious problems facing farmers. Discuss your interest or experience in practical conservation work. Ability to work both independently or as a member of a team is important. (See also **Appendix 3**.) **Forestry** Contact the Forestry Commission and the Woodland Trust and try to arrange visits to forestry centres, local community woodlands and forests and to the Woodland Trust's sites. Discuss the work with forest officers and learn about future plans for specific forest areas and describe any visits made. Mention any experience of forestry or wood processing industries (for example, visits to forests and mills, work experience in relevant organisations). (See also **Appendix 3**.) **Harper Adams** Applicants should be aware that our courses are academic and not necessarily totally vocational.

Misconceptions about this course Bangor Forestry That the course provides practical training in forestry (for example, in the use of chainsaws and pesticides) or wood processing. It does not: it is intended to educate future managers, for example. It is not intended to train forestry or mill workers. **Royal Agricultural Univ** The focus of the BSc Rural Land Management is not specifically about managing land. The course focuses on the key concepts, principles and practice influencing activities in rural land and property management, the context in which rural surveying operates, and the linkages and inter-relationships between elements of the rural surveying discipline and related surveying disciplines.

Selection interviews Yes Bishop Burton (Coll), Harper Adams; **No** Reading, Royal Agricultural Univ.

Interview advice and questions You should be up-to-date with political and scientific issues concerning the farming community in general and how these problems might be resolved. You are likely to be questioned on your own farming background (if relevant) and your farming experience. Questions asked in the past have included: What special agricultural interests do you have? What types of farms have you worked on? What farming publications do you read and which agricultural shows have you visited? What is meant by the term 'sustainable development'? Are farmers custodians of the countryside? What are the potential sources of non-fossil-fuel electricity generation? See also **Chapter 5**. **Forestry** Work experience or field courses attended are likely to be discussed and questions asked such as: What is arboriculture? On a desert island how would you get food from wood? How do you see forestry developing in the next hundred years? What aspects of forestry are the most important? See also **Chapter 5**.

Reasons for rejection (non-academic) Insufficient motivation. Too immature. Unlikely to integrate well. Lack of practical experience with crops or animals.

AFTER-RESULTS ADVICE

Offers to applicants repeating A-levels Possibly higher Harper Adams; Newcastle; **Same** Bangor (Forestry); Nottingham; Royal Agricultural Univ.

GRADUATE DESTINATIONS AND EMPLOYMENT (2016/17 HESA)

Agriculture graduates surveyed 1,300 **Employed** 680 **In voluntary employment** 5 **In further study** 330 **Assumed unemployed** 70

Career note The majority of graduates entered the agricultural industry while others moved into manufacturing, the wholesale and retail trades and property development. For Forestry, opportunities exist with the Forestry Commission as supervisors, managers and in some cases, scientists. Other employers include private landowners (especially in Scotland), co-operative forest societies, local authorities and commercial firms.

OTHER DEGREE SUBJECTS FOR CONSIDERATION

Agroforestry; Animal Sciences; Biochemistry; Biological Sciences; Biology; Biotechnology; Chemistry; Conservation Management; Ecology (Biological Sciences); Environmental Sciences; Estate Management (Surveying); Food Science and Technology; Forestry; Horticulture; Land Surveying; Landscape Architecture; Plant Sciences; Veterinary Science; Zoology.

AMERICAN STUDIES

Courses normally cover American history, politics and literature, although there are opportunities to study specialist fields such as drama, film studies, history of art, linguistics, politics or sociology. In some universities, a year, term or semester spent in the USA (or Canada) is compulsory or optional while at other institutions the course lasts three years without a placement abroad.

Useful websites www.historynet.com; www.americansc.org.uk; www.theasa.net

NB The points totals shown to the left of the institutions are for ease of reference only. It must not be assumed that Tariff points are always used by institutions or that they can be substituted for an offer in grades. The level of an offer is not necessarily indicative of the quality of a course.

COURSE OFFERS INFORMATION

Subject requirements/preferences GCSE Specific grades in some subjects may be specified by some popular universities. **AL** English, a modern language, humanities or social science subjects preferred.

Your target offers and examples of degree courses

128 pts	**Birmingham** – ABB (Am Can St) (IB 32 pts HL 655)
	East Anglia – ABB (Am Lit Crea Writ) (IB 32 pts HL 5 Engl)
	Manchester – ABB incl Engl lit/hist (Am St) (IB 34 pts HL 655)
	Nottingham – ABB (Am Can Lit Hist Cult; Flm TV St Am St) (IB 32 pts); ABB incl Engl (Am St Engl) (IB 32 pts HL 5 Engl); ABB incl hist (Am St Hist) (IB 32 pts HL 5 hist)
	Sussex – AAB–ABB (Am St courses) (IB 34–32 pts)
120 pts	**Essex** – BBB (Am (US) St Flm; Crimin Am St) (IB 30 pts HL 5)
	Kent – BBB (Am St) (IB 34 pts HL 16 incl 5 hist)
	Leicester – BBB (Am St) (IB 28 pts)
	Northumbria – 120 pts (Am St)
	Swansea – BBB 120 pts (Am St) (IB 32 pts)
112 pts	**Hull** – BBC 112 pts (Am St) (IB 28 pts)
104 pts	**Hertfordshire** – BCC 104 pts (Am St Comb Hons)
	Winchester – 104–120 pts (Am St) (HL 4)
96 pts	**Derby** – 96–128 pts (Am St Comb Hons)
	Portsmouth – 96–112 pts (Am St)
	Richmond (Am Int Univ) – CCC (Am St) (IB 24 pts)
	York St John – 96–112 pts (Am St courses)
88 pts	**Canterbury Christ Church** – 88–112 pts (Am St courses)

Alternative offers See **Chapter 6** and **Appendix 1** for grades/UCAS Tariff points information for other examinations.

CHOOSING YOUR COURSE (SEE ALSO CH.1)

Universities and colleges teaching quality See www.qaa.ac.uk; https://unistats.ac.uk.

ADMISSIONS INFORMATION

Number of applicants per place (approx) Birmingham 6; East Anglia 5; Essex 6; Hull 5; Keele 7; Leicester 7; Manchester 6; Nottingham 4; Swansea 2.

Advice to applicants and planning the UCAS personal statement Visits to America should be described, and any knowledge or interests you have of the history, politics, economics and the culture of the USA should be included on the UCAS application. The US Embassy in London may be a useful source of information. American magazines and newspapers are good reference sources and also give a good insight to life in the USA. Applicants should demonstrate an intelligent interest in both North American literature and history in their personal statement. State why you are interested in the subject and dedicate at least half of your personal statement to how and why your interest has developed – for example through extra-curricular reading, projects, films and academic study.

Manchester Due to the detailed nature of entry requirements for American Studies courses, the prospectus is unable to include full details. For complete and up-to-date information on entry requirements for these courses, please visit the website at www.manchester.ac.uk/study/undergraduate/courses.

Misconceptions about this course Swansea Some candidates feel that American Studies is a soft option. While we study many topics which students find interesting, we are very much a humanities-based degree course incorporating more traditional subjects such as history, literature and English. Our graduates also find that they are as employable in the same jobs as those students taking other degrees.

Selection interviews No Birmingham, Derby, East Anglia, Essex, Hull, Kent, Winchester.

Interview advice and questions Courses often focus on history and literature so expect some questions on any American literature you have read and also on aspects of American history, arts and culture. You may also be questioned on visits you have made to America (or Canada) and your impressions. Current political issues might also be raised, so keep up-to-date with the political scene. See also **Chapter 5**.

Reasons for rejection (non-academic) If personal reasons prevent year of study in America. **Birmingham** Lack of commitment to the course. **Swansea** Lack of knowledge covering literature, history and politics.

AFTER-RESULTS ADVICE
Offers to applicants repeating A-levels Same Birmingham; Derby; East Anglia; Essex; Hull; Nottingham; Swansea; Winchester.

GRADUATE DESTINATIONS AND EMPLOYMENT (2016/17 HESA)
Graduates surveyed 445 **Employed** 205 **In voluntary employment** 20 **In further study** 125 **Assumed unemployed** 30

Career note All non-scientific careers are open to graduates. Start your career planning during your degree course and obtain work experience.

OTHER DEGREE SUBJECTS FOR CONSIDERATION
Business Studies; Cultural Studies; English Literature; Film Studies; Government; History; International History; International Relations; Latin-American Literature/Studies; Politics.

ANIMAL SCIENCES

(including **Equine Science**; see also **Agricultural Sciences/Agriculture, Biological Sciences, Biology, Physiology, Psychology, Veterinary Science/Medicine, Zoology**)

Animal Science is a broad-based subject including the study of farm and companion animals and wildlife conservation and management. The more specialised courses include a range of specialisms including animal biology, nutrition and health, behavioural studies and welfare. Equine Science involves specialised studies in areas such as breeding, equine business, horsemanship, performance, stud management, event management, veterinary techniques and injuries. Some scholarships are available.

Useful websites www.rspca.org.uk; www.bhs.org.uk; www.wwf.org.uk; www.bsas.org.uk

NB The points totals shown to the left of the institutions are for ease of reference only. It must not be assumed that Tariff points are always used by institutions or that they can be substituted for an offer in grades. The level of an offer is not necessarily indicative of the quality of a course.

COURSE OFFERS INFORMATION

Subject requirements/preferences GCSE Mathematics/science subjects required. Also check any weight limits on equitation modules. **AL** One or two science subjects usually required for scientific courses; biology and chemistry preferred.

Your target offers and examples of degree courses

128 pts **Exeter** – AAB–ABB incl sci/maths (Anim Bhv (Cornwall)) (IB 34–32 pts HL 5 sci/maths)
Manchester – AAA–ABB (Zool Modn Lang) (IB 36–33 pts HL 6–5 sci)
Sussex – AAB–ABB (Zool) (IB 34–32 pts HL 5 sci)

120 pts **Aberdeen** – BBB incl maths/sci (Anim Bhv) (IB 32 pts HL 5 maths/sci)
Kent – BBB incl sci (Wldlf Cons; Wldlf Cons (Yr Prof Prac)) (IB 34 pts HL 15 incl 5 sci)
Lincoln – BBB incl biol (Anim Bhv Welf) (IB 30 pts HL 5 biol)
Newcastle – ABB–BBB incl biol+sci (Anim Sci) (IB 32 pts HL 6 biol)
Nottingham – ABB–BBB incl sci/maths (Anim Sci) (IB 32–30 pts)
Reading – BBB incl biol+sci (Anim Sci) (IB 30 pts incl biol+sci)
Stirling – BBB incl biol+sci (Anim Biol) (IB 32 pts)

112 pts **Anglia Ruskin** – 112 pts incl biol/psy (Anim Bhv) (IB 24 pts HL biol/psy)
Bangor – 112 pts incl biol+sci (Zool Anim Bhv)
Chester – BBC–BCC incl biol/chem (Anim Bhv Welf) (IB 26 pts HL 5 biol); BBC–BCC incl biol/chem/psy (Anim Bhv) (IB 26 pts HL 5 biol)
Gloucestershire – BBC 112 pts (Anim Biol)
Glyndŵr – 112 pts (Anim Bhv Welf Cons Sci); BBC 112 pts (Eqn Sci Welf Mgt)
Liverpool John Moores – BBC incl biol/geog/sci 112 pts (Wldlf Cons) (IB 26 pts); BBC incl biol 112 pts (Anim Bhv) (IB 26 pts)
Nottingham Trent – BBC incl biol 112 pts incl biol (Anim Biol); BBC incl sci 112 pts (Eqn Spo Sci; Wldlf Cons)
Oxford Brookes – BBC 112 pts (Eqn Sci; Eqn Sci Thbred Mgt) (IB 30 pts)
Plymouth – 112–128 pts incl biol+C sci (Anim Bhv Welf) (IB 30 pts HL 5 biol+sci)

104 pts **Aberystwyth** – BBB–BCC incl B biol 104–120 pts (Eqn Sci) (IB 30–28 pts HL 5 biol); BBB–BCC incl biol 104–120 pts (Anim Bhv; Anim Sci) (IB 30–28 pts HL 5 biol)
Bournemouth – 104–120 pts (Ecol Wldlf Cons) (IB 28–31 pts)
Edinburgh Napier – BCC incl sci (Anim Cons Biol) (IB 28 pts HL 654 incl 5 biol)
Harper Adams – 104–120 pts (Anim Prod Sci) (IB 28 pts HL 5 pts)
Manchester Met – BBC–BCC incl biol 104–112 pts (Anim Bhv) (IB 26 pts HL 5 biol)
Oxford Brookes – BCC 104 pts (Anim Biol Cons) (IB 29 pts HL sci)
SRUC – BCC incl biol/chem (App Anim Sci)

96 pts **CAFRE** – 96 pts incl sci (Eqn Mgt)
Cumbria – BBC–CCC 96–112 pts +interview +portfolio (Wldlf Media); BBC–CCC incl biol 96–112 pts (Anim Cons Sci)
Royal Agricultural Univ – CCC (Bldstck Perf Hrs Mgt) (IB 26 pts); CCC 96 pts (App Eqn Sci Bus) (IB 26 pts)
Worcester – 96–104 pts incl biol/sci (Anim Biol)
Writtle (UC) – 96 pts (Eqn courses)

88 pts **Canterbury Christ Church** – 88–112 pts (Anim Sci)
Harper Adams – 88–104 pts (Anim Bhv Welf (Clin); Anim Bhv Welf (Non Clin); Anim Hlth Welf) (IB 28 pts HL 5 pts)

80 pts **South Wales** – BCC–CDD incl sci 80–112 pts (Nat Hist); BCC–CDD incl biol+sci 80–112 pts (Int Wldlf Biol)
Wolverhampton – CDD incl sci (Anim Bhv Wldlf Cons)

Alternative offers See **Chapter 6** and **Appendix 1** for grades/UCAS Tariff points information for other examinations.

EXAMPLES OF COLLEGES OFFERING COURSES IN THIS SUBJECT FIELD

Barnsley (Coll); Bedford (Coll); Bicton (Coll); Bishop Burton (Coll); Brooksby Melton (Coll); Bury (Coll);

Calderdale (Coll); Canterbury (Coll); Central Bedfordshire (Coll); Cornwall (Coll); Craven (Coll); Derby (Coll); Duchy Coll UC; Easton Otley (Coll); Guildford (Coll); Hadlow (UC); Hartpury (Coll); Kingston Maurward (Coll); Kirklees (Coll); Lancaster and Morecambe (Coll); Moulton (Coll); Myerscough (Coll); Northumberland (Coll); Pembrokeshire (Coll); Petroc; Plumpton (Coll); Reaseheath (UC); Sir Gâr (Coll); South Devon (Coll); South Gloucestershire and Stroud (Coll); South Staffordshire (Coll); Sparsholt (Coll); Stamford New (Coll); TEC Partnership; Warwickshire (Coll); West Anglia (Coll); Weston (Coll); Wiltshire (Coll); Wirral Met (Coll).

CHOOSING YOUR COURSE (SEE ALSO CH.1)

Universities and colleges teaching quality See www.qaa.ac.uk; https://unistats.ac.uk.

Top research universities and colleges (REF 2014) See **Agricultural Sciences/Agriculture** and **Biological Sciences**.

Examples of sandwich degree courses Aberystwyth; Anglia Ruskin; Cumbria; Harper Adams; Liverpool John Moores; Manchester Met; Nottingham Trent; Reading; Royal Agricultural Univ.

ADMISSIONS INFORMATION

Number of applicants per place (approx) Harper Adams 4; Newcastle 3; Nottingham 6; Nottingham Trent (Eqn Spo Sci) 4; Reading 10; Royal Agricultural Univ 4.

Advice to applicants and planning the UCAS personal statement Describe any work you have done with animals which generated your interest in this subject. Work experience in veterinary practices, on farms or with agricultural firms would be useful. Read agricultural/scientific journals for updates on animal nutrition or breeding. For equine courses, details of practical experience with horses (eg BHS examinations, Pony Club tests) should be included.

Misconceptions about this course Bishop Burton (Coll) (Eqn Sci) Some students wrongly believe that riding skills and a science background are not required for this course which, in fact, is heavily focused on the scientific principles and practice of horse management.

Selection interviews Yes Bishop Burton (Coll), SRUC; **Some** Cumbria; **No** Anglia Ruskin, Harper Adams, Newcastle, Nottingham, Plymouth, Royal Agricultural Univ, Stirling, Writtle (UC).

Interview advice and questions Questions are likely about your experience with animals and your reasons for wishing to follow this science-based subject. Other questions asked in recent years have included: What do your parents think about your choice of course? What are your views on battery hens and the rearing of veal calves? The causes of blue-tongue disease, foot and mouth disease and BSE may also feature. (Eqn courses) Students should check the level of riding ability expected (eg BHS Level 2 or PC B-test level). Check the amount of riding, jumping and competition work on the course. (See also **Chapter 5**.)

Reasons for rejection (non-academic) Uncertainty as to why applicants chose the course. Too immature. Unlikely to integrate well.

AFTER-RESULTS ADVICE

Offers to applicants repeating A-levels Same Anglia Ruskin; Bishop Burton (Coll); Chester; Harper Adams; Liverpool John Moores; Nottingham; Royal Agricultural Univ; Stirling.

GRADUATE DESTINATIONS AND EMPLOYMENT (2016/17 HESA)

Graduates surveyed 1,220 **Employed** 540 **In voluntary employment** 40 **In further study** 405 **Assumed unemployed** 55

Career note The majority of graduates obtained work with animals while others moved towards business and administration careers. This is a specialised subject area and undergraduates should start early to make contacts with organisations and gain work experience.

OTHER DEGREE SUBJECTS FOR CONSIDERATION

Agriculture; Biological Sciences; Biology; Food Science; Natural Sciences; Veterinary Science; Zoology.

ANTHROPOLOGY

(including **Social Anthropology**; see also **Archaeology, Sociology**)

Anthropology is the study of people's behaviour, beliefs and institutions and the diverse societies in which they live, and is concerned with the biological evolution of human beings. It also involves our relationships with other primates, the structure of communities and the effects of diet and disease on human groups. Alternatively, social or cultural anthropology covers aspects of social behaviour regarding family, kinship, marriage, gender, religion, political structures, law, psychology and language. Anthropology is also offered in combination with several other subjects such as Archaeology (London (UCL) and Southampton) and the study of forensics (Dundee and Bradford).

Useful websites www.britishmuseum.org; www.therai.org.uk; www.theasa.org

NB The points totals shown to the left of the institutions are for ease of reference only. It must not be assumed that Tariff points are always used by institutions or that they can be substituted for an offer in grades. The level of an offer is not necessarily indicative of the quality of a course.

COURSE OFFERS INFORMATION

Subject requirements/preferences GCSE English and mathematics usually required. A foreign language may be required. **AL** Biology and geography preferred for some biological anthropological courses. (Soc Anth) No specific subjects required.

Your target offers and examples of degree courses

152 pts **Cambridge** – A*AA +interview +HSPSAA (Hum Soc Pol Sci) (IB 42–40 pts HL 777–776)

144 pts **Oxford** – AAA +interview (Arch Anth) (IB 38 pts HL 666)

136 pts **Bristol** – AAB (Anth) (IB 34–31 pts HL 17 pts)
Durham – AAB (Anth; Anth Arch; Anth Sociol) (IB 36 pts HL 665)
Exeter – AAB (Anth; Arch Anth; Sociol Anth) (IB 34 pts HL 665)
London (SOAS) – AAB–ABB (Soc Anth) (IB 35 pts HL 665)
London (UCL) – AAB (Arch Anth) (IB 36 pts HL 17 pts)
London LSE – AAB (Anth Law; Soc Anth) (IB 37 pts HL 666)
St Andrews – AAB (Soc Anth courses) (IB 35 pts)

128 pts **Birmingham** – ABB (Anth courses) (IB 32 pts HL 655)
East Anglia – ABB (Arch Anth Art Hist) (IB 32 pts)
Edinburgh – ABB (Arch Soc Anth) (IB 36–34 pts HL 665–655); (Soc Anth courses) (IB 40 pts HL 766)
Manchester – ABB (Relgn Anth; Soc Anth Crimin) (IB 34 pts HL 655)
Queen's Belfast – ABB (Anth courses) (IB 33 pts HL 655)
Southampton – ABB/BBB +aEPQ (Sociol Anth) (IB 32 pts HL 16 pts); ABB–BBB +aEPQ (Arch Anth) (IB 32–30 pts HL 16 pts)
Sussex – ABB (Anth courses) (IB 32 pts); ABB 128 pts (Anth Lang) (32 pts)

120 pts **Aberdeen** – BBB (Anth; Anth Fr/Ger) (IB 32 pts HL 555)
Brunel – BBB (Anth; Anth Sociol) (IB 30 pts)
Essex – BBB (Soc Anth) (IB 30 pts)
Kent – BBB (Anth; Soc Anth) (IB 34 pts HL 15 pts); BBB incl sci/maths (Biol Anth) (IB 34 pts HL 15 pts)
Liverpool – BBB (Evol Anth) (IB 30 pts)
London (Gold) – BBB (Anth courses) (IB 33 pts HL 655)

112 pts **Bradford** – BBC incl sci 112 pts (Foren Arch Anth) (HL 3 Engl/maths)
Liverpool John Moores – BBC incl sci/soc sci 112 pts (Foren Anth) (IB 26 pts)
Roehampton – 112 pts (Anth)

104 pts **Bournemouth** – 104–120 pts (Anth; Arch Anth; Arch Anth Foren Sci) (IB 28–31 pts); (Sociol Soc Anth) (IB 28–31 pts HL 555)
Central Lancashire – 104 pts (Arch Anth)

Dundee – BBB–BCC incl biol (Foren Anth) (IB 30 pts HL 555)
Oxford Brookes – (Anth) (IB 29 pts); 104 pts (Biol Anth; Soc Anth) (IB 29 pts)
Portsmouth – 104–120 pts incl sci (Palae) (IB 27 pts)
Winchester – 104–120 pts (Anth)
96 pts **Trinity Saint David** – Variable, contact admissions tutor 96 pts (Anth)

Alternative offers
See **Chapter 6** and **Appendix 1** for grades/UCAS Tariff points information for other examinations.

CHOOSING YOUR COURSE (SEE ALSO CH.1)
Universities and colleges teaching quality See www.qaa.ac.uk; https://unistats.ac.uk.

Top research universities and colleges (REF 2014) (Anthropology and Development Studies) London LSE (Int Dev); Manchester (Anth); Oxford (Int Dev); Manchester (Dev St); London (Gold); Durham; East Anglia; Cambridge; Edinburgh.

Examples of sandwich degree courses Bournemouth; Bradford; Brunel; Liverpool John Moores.

ADMISSIONS INFORMATION
Number of applicants per place (approx) Bristol 9; Cambridge 2; Durham 3; Hull 5; Liverpool John Moores 4; London (Gold) 7; London (SOAS) 10; London (UCL) 5; London LSE 7; Manchester 5; Oxford Brookes 7; Queen's Belfast 10; Southampton 6; Sussex 10.

Advice to applicants and planning the UCAS personal statement Visits to museums should be discussed; for example, museums of anthropology (London, Oxford, Cambridge). Describe any aspect of the subject which interests you (including books you have read) and how you have pursued this interest. Give details of any overseas travel. Give reasons for choosing course: since this is not a school subject, you will need to convince the selectors of your knowledge and interest. **Bristol** Deferred entry acceptable. **Oxford** See **Archaeology**.

Selection interviews Yes Cambridge, Oxford ((Arch Anth) 28%); **Some** Bristol; **No** Dundee, East Anglia, Hull, London (Gold), London (UCL), London LSE, Oxford Brookes, Roehampton.

Interview advice and questions This is a broad subject and questions will tend to emerge as a result of your interests in aspects of anthropology or social anthropology and your comments on your personal statement. Past questions have included: What stresses are there among the nomads of the North African desert? What is a society? What is speech? If you dug up a stone axe, what could you learn from it? What are the values created by a capitalist society? Discuss the role of women since the beginning of this century. **Cambridge** See Chapter 5 and **Archaeology**. **Oxford** See **Chapter 5** and **Archaeology**.

Reasons for rejection (non-academic) Lack of commitment. Inability to deal with a more philosophical (less positivist) approach to knowledge.

AFTER-RESULTS ADVICE
Offers to applicants repeating A-levels Same Cambridge; Durham; East Anglia; Liverpool John Moores; London (UCL); Oxford Brookes; Roehampton.

GRADUATE DESTINATIONS AND EMPLOYMENT (2016/17 HESA)
Graduates surveyed 1,415 **Employed** 670 **In voluntary employment** 55 **In further study** 395 **Assumed unemployed** 90

Career note All non-scientific careers are open to graduates. However, career planning should start early and efforts made to contact employers and gain work experience.

OTHER DEGREE SUBJECTS FOR CONSIDERATION
Archaeology; Egyptology; Heritage Studies; History; Human Sciences; Political Science; Psychology; Religious Studies; Social Science; Sociology.

ARCHAEOLOGY

(see also **Anthropology, History (ancient)**)

Courses in Archaeology differ between institutions but the majority focus on the archaeology of Europe, the Mediterranean and Middle Eastern countries and on the close examination of discoveries of prehistoric communities and ancient, medieval and post-medieval societies. Hands-on experience is involved in all courses as well as a close study of the history of the artefacts themselves. All courses will involve excavations in the UK or abroad. A number of universities combine Archaeology with History and Anthropology while Bournemouth combines it with Forensic Sciences. Southampton also has a Centre for Maritime Archaeology.

Useful websites http://new.archaeologyuk.org; www.english-heritage.org.uk; www.britishmuseum. org; www.archaeologists.net

NB The points totals shown to the left of the institutions are for ease of reference only. It must not be assumed that Tariff points are always used by institutions or that they can be substituted for an offer in grades. The level of an offer is not necessarily indicative of the quality of a course.

COURSE OFFERS INFORMATION

Subject requirements/preferences GCSE English and mathematics or science usually required for BSc courses. **AL** history, geography, English or a science subject may be preferred for some courses and two science subjects for Archaeological Science courses.

Your target offers and examples of degree courses

152 pts   **Cambridge** – A*AA +interview +ARCHAA (Arch) (IB 40–42 pts HL 776)

144 pts   **Oxford** – AAA +interview (Arch Anth) (IB 38 pts HL 666); (Class Arch Anc Hist) (IB 39 pts HL 666)

St Andrews – AAA incl hist (Mediev Hist Arch) (IB 36 pts HL 666 incl hist)

136 pts   **Bristol** – AAB (Arch Anth) (IB 34 pts HL 17 pts)

Durham – AAB (Anc Hist Arch; Anth Arch; Arch) (IB 36 pts HL 665)

Exeter – AAB (Arch Anth) (IB 34 pts HL 665)

Glasgow – AAB incl sci (Arch) (IB 36 pts HL 665 incl sci)

London (King's) – AAB (Class Arch) (IB 35 pts HL 665)

London (UCL) – AAB (Arch Anth) (IB 36 pts HL 17 pts)

128 pts   **Birmingham** – ABB (Arch courses) (IB 32 pts HL 655)

East Anglia – ABB (Arch Anth Art Hist (St Abrd)) (IB 32 pts)

Edinburgh – ABB (Archit Hist Arch; Celt Arch) (IB 34 pts HL 655); (Arch; Arch Anc Hist; Arch Soc Anth) (IB 36–34 pts HL 665–655)

Exeter – AAB–ABB (Arch) (IB 34–32 pts HL 665–655)

Leicester – ABB (Anc Hist Arch) (IB 30 pts)

London (SOAS) – AAB–ABB (Hist Art Arch courses) (IB 35 pts HL 665)

London (UCL) – ABB (Arch; Class Arch Class Civ; Egypt Arch) (IB 34 pts HL 16 pts)

Manchester – ABB (Arch; Arch Anth) (IB 34 pts HL 655)

Nottingham – ABB (Anc Hist Arch) (IB 32 pts); ABB incl hist (Arch Hist) (IB 32 pts HL 6 hist); ABB–BBB incl geog (Arch Geog) (IB 32–30 pts HL 5 geog); ABB–BBB incl sci (Arch) (IB 32–30 pts)

Sheffield – ABB (Arch; Arch Comb Hons; Class Hist Arch) (IB 33 pts)

Southampton – AAB–ABB incl hist (Arch Hist) (IB 34–32 pts HL 17–16 pts incl 5 hist)

Warwick – ABB (Anc Hist Class Arch) (IB 34 pts)

120 pts   **Aberdeen** – BBB incl maths/sci (Arch) (IB 32 pts HL 5 pts incl maths/sci)

Kent – BBB (Class Arch St) (IB 34 pts HL 15 pts)

Liverpool – BBB (Arch; Arch Anc Civ; Egypt) (IB 30 pts)

Newcastle – ABB–BBB (Arch) (IB 32 pts HL 555)

Queen's Belfast – BBB (Arch; Arch Palae) (IB 32 pts HL 655)

Reading – BBB (Arch Sci; Arch courses) (IB 30 pts)
Sheffield – BBB/BBC+bEPQ incl lang (Arch Modn Langs Cult (Yr Abrd)) (IB 32 pts HL 5 lang)
Southampton – ABB-BBB (Arch) (IB 32–30 pts HL 16 pts)
Swansea – BBB (Egypt Anc Hist) (IB 32 pts)
York – ABB-BBB (Arch; Hist Arch) (IB 34–31 pts); ABB-BBB incl sci (Bioarch) (IB 34–31 pts incl sci)

112 pts **Bangor** – 112 pts (Herit Arch Hist; Welsh Hist Arch)
Bradford – BBC 112 pts (Arch courses) (HL 3 Engl/maths)
Cardiff – BBB-BBC (Cons Objs Musm Arch) (HL 665–655)

104 pts **Bournemouth** – 104–120 pts (Arch Anth; Arch Anth Foren Sci) (IB 28–31 pts); (Arch) (IB 28–31 pts HL 55)
Cardiff – BBB-BCC +interview (Arch courses) (HL 665–655)
Central Lancashire – 104 pts (Arch)
Chester – BBC-BCC (Arch courses) (IB 26 pts)
London (Birk) – BBB-BCC 104–120 pts (Arch)
Portsmouth – 104–120 pts incl sci (Palae) (IB 27 pts)
Winchester – 104–120 pts (Arch)

96 pts **Bishop Grosseteste** – 96–112 pts (Arch Hist)
Trinity Saint David – 96 pts (Arch)
Winchester – 96–112 pts (Arch Prac)
Worcester – 96–112 pts (Arch Herit St courses)

88 pts **Canterbury Christ Church** – 88–112 pts (Arch courses)
72 pts **UHI** – BC (Arch; Scot Hist Arch)
64 pts **UHI** – CC (Arch Env St)

Alternative offers
See **Chapter 6** and **Appendix 1** for grades/UCAS Tariff points information for other examinations.

EXAMPLES OF COLLEGES OFFERING COURSES IN THIS SUBJECT FIELD
Truro and Penwith (Coll).

CHOOSING YOUR COURSE (SEE ALSO CH.1)
Universities and colleges teaching quality See www.qaa.ac.uk; https://unistats.ac.uk.

Top research universities and colleges (REF 2014) (Geography, Environmental Studies and Archaeology) Southampton (Geog); London (UCL) (Geog); Reading (Arch); Sheffield (Geog); Oxford (Arch); London (RH); London LSE; Bristol (Geog); Cambridge (Geog); Oxford (Geog Env St); London (QM); St Andrews; Newcastle (Geog).

Examples of sandwich degree courses Bradford; Reading.

ADMISSIONS INFORMATION
Number of applicants per place (approx) Bangor 4; Birmingham 7; Bradford 4; Bristol 7; Cambridge 8; Cardiff 6; Durham 3; Leicester 5; Liverpool 6; London (UCL) 3; Manchester (Arch) 4; Newcastle 3; Nottingham 4; Sheffield 7; Southampton 6; Trinity Saint David 2; York 4

Advice to applicants and planning the UCAS personal statement First-hand experience of digs and other fieldwork should be described. The Council for British Archaeology (see **Appendix 3**) can provide information on where digs are taking place. Describe any interests in fossils and any museum visits as well as details of visits to current archaeological sites. Your local university archaeological department or central library can also provide information on contacts in your local area (each county council employs an archaeological officer). Since this is not a school subject, the selectors will be looking for good reasons for your choice of subject. Gain practical field experience and discuss this in the personal statement. Show your serious commitment to archaeology through your out-of-school activities (eg fieldwork, museum experience) (see **Chapter 5**). (See also **Anthropology**.) **Bristol** Deferred entry accepted. **Cambridge** Many colleges require a school/college essay.

Misconceptions about this course Bristol We are not an elitist course: 75% of applicants and students come from state schools and non-traditional backgrounds. **Liverpool** (Egypt) Some students would have been better advised looking at courses in Archaeology or Ancient History and Archaeology which offer major pathways in the study of Ancient Egypt.

Selection interviews Yes Cambridge, Oxford ((Arch Anth) 28%, (Class Arch Anc Hist) 25%), Southampton, Trinity Saint David, Winchester; **Some** Bristol; **No** Bangor, Birmingham, Bournemouth, Bradford, Cardiff, East Anglia, Leicester, London (UCL), Newcastle, Nottingham, Reading.

Interview advice and questions Questions will be asked about any experience you have had in visiting archaeological sites or taking part in digs. Past questions have included: How would you interpret archaeological evidence, for example a pile of flints, coins? What is stratification? How would you date archaeological remains? What recent archaeological discoveries have been made? How did you become interested in archaeology? With which archaeological sites in the UK are you familiar? See also **Chapter 5**. **Cambridge** See Chapter 5. **Oxford** Interviews involve artefacts, maps and other material to be interpreted. Successful entrants average 28% (see **Chapter 5**).

Reasons for rejection (non-academic) (Mature students) Inability to cope with essay-writing and exams. **Liverpool** (Egypt) Applicant misguided on choice of course – Egyptology used to fill a gap on the UCAS application.

AFTER-RESULTS ADVICE
Offers to applicants repeating A-levels Same Birmingham; Bradford; Cambridge; Chester; Durham; East Anglia; Leicester; Liverpool; London (UCL); Sheffield; Trinity Saint David; Winchester.

GRADUATE DESTINATIONS AND EMPLOYMENT (2016/17 HESA)
Graduates surveyed 590 **Employed** 200 **In voluntary employment** 30 **In further study** 210 **Assumed unemployed** 45

Career note Vocational opportunities closely linked to this subject are limited. However, some graduates aim for positions in local authorities, libraries and museums. A number of organisations covering water boards, forestry, civil engineering and surveying also employ field archaeologists.

OTHER DEGREE SUBJECTS FOR CONSIDERATION
Ancient History; Anthropology; Classical Studies; Classics; Geology; Heritage Studies; History; History of Art and Architecture; Land Economy; Medieval History.

ARCHITECTURE

(including **Architectural Technology and Architectural Engineering**; see also **Art And Design (interior, Product And Industrial Design), Building And Construction, Landscape Architecture)**

Courses in Architecture provide a broad education consisting of technological subjects covering structures, construction, materials and environmental studies. Project-based design work is an integral part of all courses and in addition, history and social studies will also be incorporated into degree programmes. After completing the first three years leading to a BA (Hons), students aiming for full professional status take a further two-year course leading to, for example, a BArch, MArch or Diploma, and after a year in an architect's practice, the final professional examinations are taken. There is also a close link between architecture and civil engineering in the construction of large projects eg The Shard, Sydney Opera House and the construction of bridges and other major projects. Several architectural engineering courses are offered, for example Bath, Loughborough and Glasgow offer courses which, while focussing on civil engineering, also introduce creative design elements working on inventive and imaginative design solutions.

Useful websites www.ciat.org.uk; www.architecture.com; www.rias.org.uk; www.ciob.org; www.citb.co.uk

NB The points totals shown to the left of the institutions are for ease of reference only. It must not be assumed that Tariff points are always used by institutions or that they can be substituted for an offer in grades. The level of an offer is not necessarily indicative of the quality of a course.

COURSE OFFERS INFORMATION

Subject requirements/preferences GCSE English and mathematics, in some cases at certain grades, are required in all cases. A science subject may also be required. AL Mathematics and/or physics required or preferred for some courses. Art and design may be preferable to design and technology. Art is sometimes a requirement and many schools of architecture prefer it; a portfolio of art work is often requested and, in some cases, a drawing test will be set. MEng courses not listed below unless otherwise stated.

Your target offers and examples of degree courses

152 pts   **Bath** – A*AA (Archit) (IB 36 pts HL 766); A*AA/AAA +aEPQ incl maths (Civ Archit Eng (MEng)) (IB 36 pts HL 766)

Cambridge – A*AA +interview +ARCHITAA +portfolio (Archit) (IB 42–40 pts HL 776)

Southampton – A*AA/A*AB +aEPQ incl maths+sci/geog (Civ Eng Archit (MEng)) (IB 38 pts HL 18 pts incl 6 maths)

144 pts   **Leeds** – AAA incl maths (Archit Eng) (IB 35 pts HL 18 pts incl 5 maths)

Liverpool – AAA +portfolio (Archit) (IB 36 pts)

Manchester – AAA (Archit) (IB 36 pts HL 666)

Manchester Met – AAA 144 pts +portfolio (Archit) (IB 36 pts HL 666)

Newcastle – AAA +portfolio (Archit) (IB 36 pts)

Nottingham – AAA (Archit) (IB 36 pts); AAA incl maths/phys (Archit Env Des (MEng)) (IB 36 pts HL 6 maths/phys)

Queen's Belfast – AAA +interview (Archit) (IB 36 pts HL 666); AAA incl maths+sci/tech/geog (Struct Eng Archit (MEng)) (IB 36 pts HL 666)

Sheffield – AAA (Archit) (IB 36 pts); AAA–AAB +aEPQ incl maths (Archit Eng (MEng); Struct Eng Archit (MEng)) (IB 36 pts HL 6 maths)

UWE Bristol – 144 pts (Archit)

136 pts   **Arts London** – AAB 136 pts +interview +portfolio (Archit) (IB 35 pts)

Birmingham City – AAB 136 pts (Archit) (IB 34 pts)

Cardiff – AAA–AAB +interview +portfolio (Archit) (HL 665 incl 6 art/des)

Coventry – AAB (Archit) (IB 34 pts)

De Montfort – 136 pts +portfolio +interview (Archit) (IB 32 pts)

Glasgow – AAB incl maths+phys (Civ Eng Archit) (IB 36 pts HL 665 incl maths+phys)

Huddersfield – AAB 136 pts +interview +portfolio (Archit; Archit (Int))

Liverpool – AAB incl maths (Archit Eng (MEng)) (IB 35 pts HL 5 maths)

London (UCL) – AAB +interview +portfolio (Archit; Archit Interd St) (IB 36 pts HL 17 pts)

Northumbria – +interview +portfolio (Archit)

Oxford Brookes – +portfolio (Archit) (IB 33 pts)

UWE Bristol – 136 pts (Archit Plan)

128 pts   **Bournemouth Arts** – ABB (Archit)

Central Lancashire – 128–136 pts +portfolio (Archit)

Edinburgh – A*AA–ABB (Archit) (IB 40–34 pts HL 766–655); AAA–ABB incl maths+phys/eng/ des tech (Struct Eng Archit) (IB 37–32 pts HL 555); ABB (Archit Hist Arch; Archit Hist Herit) (IB 34 pts HL 655)

Glasgow (SA) – ABB +interview +portfolio (Archit)

Greenwich – ABB 128 pts +interview +portfolio (Archit)

Kent – ABB +interview +portfolio (Archit) (IB 34 pts HL 16 pts)

Kingston – 128 pts +portfolio (Archit)

Leeds Beckett – 128 pts +interview +portfolio (Archit)

Liverpool – ABB incl maths (Archit Eng) (IB 33 pts HL 5 maths)

Liverpool John Moores – ABB 128 pts (Archit) (IB 27 pts)

Loughborough – ABB incl maths (Archit Eng) (IB 34 pts HL 655 incl maths)

Newcastle – ABB (Archit Urb Plan) (IB 32 pts HL 555)
Nottingham – AAB–ABB incl maths (Archit Env Eng) (IB 34–32 pts)
Reading – ABB+ portfolio (Archit) (IB 32 pts)
Westminster – AAB–ABB 128–136 pts +portfolio (Archit) (IB 27 pts HL 4 art+Engl)
Wolverhampton – ABB/AAC +interview +portfolio (Archit)
120 pts   Cardiff – ABB–BBB incl maths (Archit Eng) (IB 34–32 pts HL 655 incl 5 maths)
East London – BBB 120 pts incl art des +interview +portfolio (Archit) (IB 28 pts HL 15 pts)
Falmouth – 120–136 pts (Archit) (IB 24 pts)
London Met – BBB 120 pts +interview +portfolio (Archit) (IB 28 pts HL 15 pts)
Norwich Arts – BBB +interview +portfolio (Archit) (IB 27 pts)
Nottingham Trent – BBB 120 pts +portfolio (Archit)
Portsmouth – 120–136 pts +interview (Archit) (IB 27–25 pts)
Strathclyde – ABB–BBB 120 pts +interview +portfolio (Archit St) (IB 34 pts HL 5 Engl/maths/
        phys)
UWE Bristol – 120 pts incl maths (Archit Env Eng) (HL 5 maths)
Ulster – BBB +portfolio (Archit) (IB 26 pts HL 13 pts)
112 pts   Anglia Ruskin – 112 pts +portfolio (Archit) (IB 24 pts)
Birmingham City – BBC 112 pts (Archit Tech) (IB 28 pts HL 14 pts)
Coventry – BBB–BBC +interview (Archit Tech) (IB 30 pts)
Creative Arts – 112 pts +portfolio (Archit)
Derby – BBC 112 pts (Archit Tech Prac)
East London – 112 pts (Archit Des Tech) (IB 26 pts HL 15 pts)
Glyndŵr – BBC 112 pts (Archit Des Tech)
Heriot-Watt – BBC incl maths (Archit Eng) (IB 31 pts HL 5 maths)
Leeds Beckett – 112 pts (Archit Tech) (IB 24 pts)
Lincoln – BBC 112 pts +portfolio (Archit) (IB 29 pts)
London South Bank – BBC 112–128 pts +interview +portfolio (Archit)
Portsmouth – 112–120 pts +interview (Inter Archit Des) (IB 25 pts)
Robert Gordon – BBC incl maths/sci +portfolio (Archit MArch) (IB 29 pts)
Salford – 112 pts +portfolio (Archit) (IB 30 pts)
Sheffield Hallam – 112 pts +interview +portfolio (Archit Tech)
UWE Bristol – 112 pts (Archit Tech Des)
Ulster – (Archit Tech Mgt)
West London – BBB–BBC 112–120 pts (Archit Des Tech)
Westminster – ABB–BBC 112–128 pts (Archit Tech) (IB 27 pts HL 4 Engl)
104 pts   Anglia Ruskin – 104 pts (Archit Tech)
Dundee – BBB–BCC (Archit) (IB 30 pts HL 555)
Liverpool John Moores – BCC 104 pts (Archit Tech) (IB 24 pts)
Northampton – BCC 104 pts (Archit Tech) (IB 25 pts)
Nottingham Trent – BCC 104 pts (Archit Tech)
Plymouth – 104–136 pts +portfolio (Archit) (IB 34–26 pts)
UHI – BCC incl maths/phys/tech (Archit Tech)
96 pts   Brighton – AAB–CCC 96–136 pts +portfolio (Archit) (IB 27 pts)
Cardiff Met – BBB–CCC 96–120 pts (Archit Des Tech) (IB 24 pts)
Derby – 96–128 pts (Archit Des Comb Hons)
London South Bank – CCC 96–112 pts (Archit Tech)
Robert Gordon – CCC (Archit Tech) (IB 26 pts)
Solent – CCC 96–112 pts (Archit Des Tech) (IB 28 pts)
Trinity Saint David – 96 pts (Archit Tech)
88 pts   Edinburgh Napier – CCD (Archit Tech) (IB 26 pts HL 555)
80 pts   Wolverhampton – CCE +interview +portfolio (Archit Des Tech)
64 pts   Archit Assoc Sch London – CC +portfolio (Archit)
Ravensbourne Univ – CC +interview +portfolio (Archit) (IB 28 pts)

Alternative offers
See **Chapter 6** and **Appendix 1** for grades/UCAS Tariff points information for other examinations.

DEGREE APPRENTICESHIPS
Oxford Brookes (Arch, Completion of RIBA/ARB Part 1).

EXAMPLES OF COLLEGES OFFERING COURSES IN THIS SUBJECT FIELD
Bournemouth and Poole (Coll); Hull (Coll); London South East (Coll); Weymouth (Coll).

CHOOSING YOUR COURSE (SEE ALSO CH.1)
Universities and colleges teaching quality See www.qaa.ac.uk; https://unistats.ac.uk.

Top research universities and colleges (REF 2014) (Architecture, Built Environment and Planning) Bath; Reading; London (UCL); Sheffield Hallam; Glasgow; Cambridge; Loughborough; Aberdeen; Newcastle; Sheffield; Cardiff (Plan Geog); Liverpool.

Examples of sandwich degree courses Coventry; Derby; Glasgow (SA); Leeds Beckett; London South Bank; Loughborough; Northumbria; Nottingham Trent; Plymouth; Robert Gordon; Sheffield Hallam; Ulster; UWE Bristol; Wolverhampton.

ADMISSIONS INFORMATION
Number of applicants per place (approx) Archit Assoc Sch London 2; Bath 8; Bournemouth Arts 4; Cambridge 7; Cardiff 12; Cardiff Met 2; Creative Arts 4; Dundee 8; Edinburgh 10; Glasgow 16; London (UCL) 14; London Met 13; Manchester 7; Manchester Met 25; Newcastle 5; Nottingham 7; Oxford Brookes 6; Queen's Belfast 9; Robert Gordon 8; Sheffield 9; Southampton 10; Strathclyde 10.

Admissions tutors' advice The following universities require a portfolio and evidence of art/design ability – East London, Greenwich, Huddersfield, Liverpool, London South Bank, Nottingham, Nottingham Trent, Strathclyde. Check with other universities.

Bath Preference for applicants with high proportion of GCSEs at A* (8/9). A-level mathematics, physics and art or design technology highly desirable.
Cambridge Art provides a better preparation than design technology.
Liverpool A lower grade offer if portfolio impressive.
Manchester Two art and/or design A-levels not advised.
UWE Bristol Architecture and Environmental Engineering degree gives RIBA status.

Advice to applicants and planning the UCAS personal statement You should describe any visits to historical or modern architectural sites and give your opinions. Contact architects in your area and try to obtain work shadowing or work experience in their practices. Describe any such work you have done. Develop a portfolio of drawings and sketches of buildings and parts of buildings (you will probably need this for your interview). Show evidence of your reading on the history of architecture in Britain and modern architecture throughout the world. Discuss your preferences among the work of leading 20th and 21st century world architects (see **Chapter 4** and also **Appendix 3**). **Cambridge** Check College requirements for preparatory work.

Selection interviews
Yes Archit Assoc Sch London, Cambridge, De Montfort, Dundee, East London, Glasgow (SA), Huddersfield, Kingston, London (UCL), London Met, London South Bank; **Some** Bath, Cardiff Met, Coventry, Leeds Beckett, Queen's Belfast; **No** Anglia Ruskin, Birmingham City, Cardiff, Derby, Edinburgh, Falmouth, Kent, Liverpool, Manchester Met, Newcastle, Northumbria, Nottingham, Oxford Brookes, Portsmouth, Sheffield, Ulster, West London.

Interview advice and questions Most Architecture departments will expect to see evidence of your ability to draw; portfolios are often requested at interview and, in some cases, drawing tests are set prior to the interview. You should have a real awareness of architecture with some knowledge of historical styles as well as examples of modern architecture. If you have gained some work experience then you will be asked to describe the work done in the architect's office and any site visits you have made. Questions in the past have included the following: What is the role of the architect in society? Is the London Eye an eyesore? Discuss one historic and one 21st century building you admire. Who is your favourite architect? What sort of buildings do you want to design? How would you make a place peaceful? How would you reduce crime through architecture? Do you like the University buildings? Do you read any architectural journals? Which? What is the role of an architectural technologist? See also **Chapter 5**. **Archit Assoc Sch London** The interview assesses the student's potential and ability to benefit from the course. Every portfolio we see at interview will be different; sketches, models, photographs and paintings all help to build up a picture of the student's interests. Detailed portfolio guidelines are available on the website. **Cambridge** All candidates should bring with them their portfolio of work. We are interested to see any graphic work in any medium that you would like to show us – please do not feel you should restrict your samples to only those with architectural reference. All evidence of sketching ability is helpful to us. (NB All colleges at Cambridge and other university departments of architecture will seek similar evidence.) **Sheffield** Some Architecture and Landscape courses have portfolio requirements.

Reasons for rejection (non-academic) Weak evidence of creative skills. Portfolio of artwork does not give sufficient evidence of design creativity. Insufficient evidence of interest in architecture. Unwillingness to try freehand sketching. **Archit Assoc Sch London** Poor standard of work in the portfolio.

AFTER-RESULTS ADVICE
Offers to applicants repeating A-levels Higher Huddersfield; **Possibly higher** Brighton; De Montfort; Newcastle; **Same** Archit Assoc Sch London; Bath; Birmingham City; Cambridge; Cardiff; Cardiff Met; Creative Arts; Derby; Dundee; Greenwich; Kingston; Liverpool John Moores; London Met; London South Bank; Manchester Met; Nottingham; Nottingham Trent; Oxford Brookes; Queen's Belfast; Robert Gordon; Sheffield; **No** Glasgow.

GRADUATE DESTINATIONS AND EMPLOYMENT (2016/17 HESA)
Graduates surveyed 2,460 **Employed** 1615 **In voluntary employment** 110 **In further study** 310 **Assumed unemployed** 150

Career note Further study is needed to enter architecture as a profession. Opportunities exist in local government or private practice – areas include planning, housing, environmental and conservation fields. Architectural technicians support the work of architects and may be involved in project management, design presentations and submissions to planning authorities.

OTHER DEGREE SUBJECTS FOR CONSIDERATION
Building; Building Surveying; Civil Engineering; Construction; Heritage Management; History of Art and Architecture; Housing; Interior Architecture; Interior Design; Landscape Architecture; Property Development; Quantity Surveying; Surveying; Town and Country Planning; Urban Studies.

ART AND DESIGN (GENERAL)

(including **Drawing and Painting**; see also **Art and Design (3d Design)**, **Art and Design (Graphic Design)**, **Combined And Liberal Arts Courses**, **Communication Studies/Communication**, **Drama**, **Media Studies**, **Photography**)

Art and Design and all specialisms remain one of the most popular subjects. Many of the courses listed here cover aspects of fine art, graphic or three-dimensional design, but to a less specialised extent than those listed in the other Art and Design tables. Travel and visits to art galleries and museums are strongly recommended by many universities and colleges. Note that for entry to many Art and Design courses it is often necessary to follow an Art and Design Foundation course first: check with your chosen institution. Art and Design degree courses cover a wide range of subjects. These are grouped together in six tables: Art and Design (General), Art and Design (Fashion and Textiles), Art and Design (Fine Art), Art and Design (Graphic Design), Art and Design (Interior, Product and Industrial Design), Art and Design (3D Design). (History of Art and Photography are listed in separate tables.)

Useful websites www.artscouncil.org.uk; www.designcouncil.org.uk; www.theatredesign.org.uk; www.arts.ac.uk; www.dandad.org; www.csd.org.uk; www.creativefuture.org.uk

NB The points total shown to the left of the institutions are for ease of reference only. It must not be assumed that Tariff points are always used by institutions or that they can be substituted for an offer in grades. The level of an offer is not necessarily indicative of the quality of a course.

COURSE OFFERS INFORMATION

Subject requirements/preferences Entry requirements for Art and Design courses vary between institutions and courses (check prospectuses and websites). Most courses require an Art and Design Foundation course and a portfolio of work demonstrating potential and visual awareness. **GCSE** Five subjects at grades A–C (7–4), or a recognised equivalent. **AL** Grades or points may be required. (Des Tech) Design technology or a physical science may be required or preferred. (Crea Arts courses) Music/ art/drama may be required. All institutions will require candidates to attend, usually with portfolios.

Your target offers and examples of degree courses

128 pts	**Edinburgh** – ABB +portfolio (Pntg) (IB 34 pts HL 655)
	Leeds – ABB incl art/des (Art Des) (IB 34 pts HL 16 pts incl 5/6 art/des)
120 pts	**Bournemouth Arts** – BBB 120 pts +interview (Crea Evnts Mgt) (IB 30 pts)
	De Montfort – B art des 120 pts incl art des +interview +portfolio (Gm Art) (IB 30 pts HL 6 art des)
	Huddersfield – BBB 120 pts +interview +portfolio (Contemp Art)
	Reading – BBB +interview +portfolio (Art courses) (IB 30 pts); BBB incl Engl +interview +portfolio (Art Crea Writ) (IB 30 pts HL 5 Engl)
112 pts	**Birmingham City** – BBC 112 pts (Art Des) (IB 28 pts HL 14 pts)
	Coventry – BBC incl art/des +portfolio (Gm Art) (IB 29 pts)
	Lincoln – BBC (Des Evnt Exhib Perf) (IB 29 pts)
	Nottingham Trent – BBC 112 pts +interview +portfolio (Decr Arts)
	Portsmouth – 112 pts (Comp Animat Vis Efcts) (IB 25 pts)
	Staffordshire – BBC 112 pts (Gms Art)
	UWE Bristol – 112 pts (Drg Prt) (+interview +portfolio)
104 pts	**Falmouth** – 104–120 pts +interview +portfolio (Drg) (IB 24 pts)
96 pts	**Bolton** – 96 pts +interview +portfolio (Art Des)
	Cardiff Met – BBB–CCC 96–120 pts +interview +portfolio (Arst Des (Mak)) (IB 24 pts)
	Hertfordshire – CCC 96 pts +interview +portfolio (Contemp Des Crfts courses)
	Rose Bruford (Coll) – 96 pts +interview +portfolio (Scnc Arts (Constr Props Pntg))
	Westminster – BBB–CCC 96–120 pts +interview (Illus Vis Comm) (IB 27 pts HL 4 Engl)
80 pts	**Hereford (CA)** – 80 pts +interview +portfolio (Contemp Des Crfts; Illus)
	South Wales – BCC–CDD 80–104 pts +interview +portfolio (Crea Ther Arts) (IB 29 pts incl Engl)
72 pts	**Robert Gordon** – BC incl art/des +Engl +interview/portfolio (Contemp Art Prac) (IB 24 pts); BC incl art/des +Engl +portfolio +interview (Pntg) (IB 24 pts)

Alternative offers

See **Chapter 6** and **Appendix 1** for grades/UCAS Tariff points information for other examinations.

EXAMPLES OF COLLEGES OFFERING COURSES IN THIS SUBJECT FIELD

Banbury and Bicester (Coll); Barnet and Southgate (Coll); Barnsley (Coll); Blackburn (Coll); Blackpool and Fylde (Coll); Bradford College UC; Chelmsford (Coll); Chesterfield (Coll); Chichester (Coll); Cornwall (Coll); Doncaster (Coll); Ealing, Hammersmith and West London (Coll); East Coast (Coll); East Surrey (Coll); East Sussex (Coll); Exeter (Coll); Furness (Coll); Greater Brighton Met (Coll); Grŵp Llandrillo Menai; Highbury Portsmouth (Coll); Hugh Baird (Coll); Hull (Coll); Kingston (Coll); London UCK (Coll); Loughborough (Coll); Manchester (Coll); NCC Redbridge; North Notts (Coll); North Warwickshire and South Leicestershire (Coll);

M|P|W

Mander Portman Woodward

ART AND DESIGN

Make your
mark

MPW is one of the UK's best known groups of independent sixth-form colleges. We offer a range of specialist services to those who have chosen a career in art or design related fields.

Two-year and one-year
A level courses

Fine Art, Ceramics, Photography, Textiles and History of Art

Specialist Art Portfolio
Preparation Programmes

London
020 7835 1355

Birmingham
0121 454 9637

Cambridge
01223 350158

Getting into Art and Design Courses by MPW is published by Trotman Publishing

Northumberland (Coll); Norwich City (Coll); Nottingham (Coll); Pembrokeshire (Coll); Peter Symonds (Coll); Portsmouth (Coll); Richmond-upon-Thames (Coll); South Devon (Coll); South Essex (Coll); Southampton City (Coll); Southport (Coll); Stockport (Coll); Sunderland (Coll); TEC Partnership; Totton (Coll); Truro and Penwith (Coll); Tyne Coast (Coll); Wakefield (Coll); West Cheshire (Coll); West Herts (Coll); West Kent (Coll); Westminster City (Coll); Windsor Forest (Coll); Wirral Met (Coll); Yeovil (Coll).

CHOOSING YOUR COURSE (SEE ALSO CH.1)

Top research universities and colleges (REF 2014) (Art and Design: History, Practice and Theory) London (Court); Newcastle; York; Birmingham; Lancaster; Leeds (Art); London (SOAS); Sheffield Hallam; Reading (Typo/Graph Comm); St Andrews; Westminster; Essex; Open University; London (UCL) (Hist Art); Manchester; Arts London.

ADMISSIONS INFORMATION

Number of applicants per place (approx) Dundee 6; Manchester Met 10.

Advice to applicants and planning the UCAS personal statement Admissions tutors look for a wide interest in aspects of art and design. Discuss the type of work and the range of media you have explored through your studies to date. Refer to visits to art galleries and museums and give your opinions of the styles of paintings and sculpture, both historical and present day. Mention art-related hobbies. Good drawing skills and sketchbook work, creative and analytical thinking will be needed.

Misconceptions about this course Bournemouth Arts (Animat Prod) This is not a computer design or programming course. This course has an emphasis on drawing for animation and we expect portfolios to demonstrate strong life drawing skills, observational work, painting, character design and storyboards. **Lincoln** (Des Musm Exhib) This is a design course, not a museum course.

Selection interviews Yes Bath Spa, Bolton, Dundee, Hertfordshire, Huddersfield, Reading, Robert Gordon, South Wales; **Some** Westminster; **No** Lincoln, Staffordshire.

Interview advice and questions Admissions tutors will want to see both breadth and depth in the applicant's work and evidence of strong self-motivation. They will also be interested to see any sketchbooks or notebooks. However, they do not wish to see similar work over and over again! A logical, ordered presentation helps considerably. Large work, especially three-dimensional work, can be presented by way of photographs. Video or film work should be edited to a running time of no more than 15 minutes. Examples of written work may also be provided. Past questions have included: How often do you visit art galleries and exhibitions? Discuss the last exhibition you visited. What are the reactions of your parents to your choice of course and career? Do you think that modern art has anything to contribute to society compared with earlier art? Is a brick a work of art? Show signs of life – no apathy! Be eager and enthusiastic. **Bournemouth** Bring a portfolio of your work, which may be used as the basis of your discussion with one of our academics. For Product Design, this should be a good overview of your creative work, for example, drawings and school projects which demonstrate creative ability, problem solving and maybe some evidence of model making or workshop activity. For Industrial Design, bring life drawings and 3D modelling that demonstrates skills with wood, metal or plastics. For Design Engineering, examples of any technical work you have created should be included in the portfolio.

Reasons for rejection (non-academic) Lack of enthusiasm for design issues or to acquire design skills. Poorly presented practical work. Lack of interest or enthusiasm in contemporary visual arts. Lack of knowledge and experience of the art and design industry.

GRADUATE DESTINATIONS AND EMPLOYMENT (2016/17 HESA)

Graduates surveyed 29,090 **Employed** 13,330 **In voluntary employment** 1,235 **In further study** 4,595 **Assumed unemployed** 1,650

Career note Many Art and Design courses are linked to specific career paths which are achieved through freelance consultancy work or studio work. Some graduates enter teaching and many find other areas such as retail and management fields. Opportunities for fashion and graphic design specialists exceed those of other areas of art and design. Opportunities in industrial and product design and three-dimensional design are likely to be limited and dependent on the contacts that students establish during their degree courses. Only a very limited number of students committed to painting and sculpture can expect to succeed without seeking alternative employment.

OTHER DEGREE SUBJECTS FOR CONSIDERATION

Animation; Architecture; Art Gallery Management; Communication Studies; Computer Studies; Education; Film Studies; History of Art; Media Studies; Photography; see other **Art and Design** tables.

ART AND DESIGN (FASHION AND TEXTILES)

(including Printed Textiles and Surface Pattern Design)

Fashion Design courses involve drawing and design, research, pattern cutting and garment construction for clothing for menswear and womenswear, with specialisation often offered later in the course. First year Textiles courses will involve the study of constructed textile technology techniques such as knitting and stitching, leading to specialisation later. Within digital textiles, the focus is on fashion for interiors and students will experiment with techniques such as laser knitting and digital fabric printing. Courses may also cover design for textiles, commercial production and marketing. Some institutions have particularly good contacts with industry and are able to arrange sponsorships for students.

Useful websites www.fashion.net; www.londonfashionweek.co.uk; www.texi.org; www.creativefuture.org.uk; www.britishfashioncouncil.co.uk; www.designcouncil.org.uk

NB The points totals shown to the left of the institutions are for ease of reference only. It must not be assumed that Tariff points are always used by institutions or that they can be substituted for an offer in grades. The level of an offer is not necessarily indicative of the quality of a course.

COURSE OFFERS INFORMATION

Subject requirements/preferences AL A textile-related subject may be required.

Your target offers and examples of degree courses

144 pts **Manchester** – AAA incl maths/phys/chem +interview (Mat Sci Eng (MEng)) (IB 36 pts HL 666)

128 pts **Edinburgh** – ABB +portfolio (Fash; Jewel Silver; Perf Cstm; Tex) (IB 34 pts HL 655)
Glasgow (SA) – ABB +interview +portfolio (Fash Des)
Kingston – 128 pts +interview +portfolio (Fash)
Leeds – ABB incl art/des (Fash Des; Tex Des) (IB 34 pts HL 16 pts incl 5/6 art/vis/des)
Loughborough – ABB +interview +portfolio (Tex (Innov Des)) (IB 34 pts HL 655)

120 pts **Bournemouth Arts** – BBB 120 pts +interview +portfolio (Fash Brnd Comm) (IB 30 pts)
Huddersfield – BBB 120 pts +interview +portfolio (Fash Brnd Mark; Int Fash Buy Mgt; Tex)
Northumbria – 120 pts +portfolio (Fash; Fash Des Mark)
Norwich Arts – BBB +interview +portfolio (Fash; Tex Des) (IB 27 pts)
Nottingham Trent – BBB 120 pts (Fash Comm Prom; Fash Mark Brnd)
Southampton (Winchester SA) – BBB (Fash Mark Mgt) (IB 30 pts HL 16 pts); BBB +interview +portfolio (Fash Des) (IB 30 pts HL 16 pts)
Trinity Saint David – 120 pts +interview +portfolio (Surf Patt Des (Fash Obj); Surf Patt Des (Tex Inter)) (IB 32 pts)

112 pts **Arts London (CFash)** – 112 pts (Fash Mgt) (IB 25 pts); 112 pts +interview +portfolio (Fash Jrnl)
Birmingham City – BBC 112 pts+portfolio (Fash Bus Prom) (HL 14 pts); (Fash Des courses) (IB 28 pts HL 14 pts)
Bournemouth Arts – BBB 112–120 pts +portfolio +interview (Mkup Media Perf) (IB 30 pts); BBC–BBB 112–120 pts (Cstm Perf Des) (IB 30 pts); BBC–BBB 112–120 pts +interview +portfolio (Fash; Tex) (IB 30 pts)

Coventry – BBC incl art/des +portfolio +interview (Fash) (IB 29 pts)

Creative Arts – 112 pts+interview +portfolio (Hand Embr) (IB 30–27 pts HL 15 pts); 112 pts+portfolio (Fash Atel; Fash Jrnl; Fash Prom Imag; Tex Des) (IB 30–27 pts HL 15 pts)

De Montfort – 112 pts+interview +portfolio (Fash Buy courses) (IB 26 pts); 112 pts incl art des +interview (Fash Tex Des) (IB 26 pts incl art des); 112 pts incl art des +interview +portfolio (Cont Fash; Tex Des) (IB 26 pts incl art des)

Derby – BBC 112 pts +interview +portfolio (Fash Des; Tex Des)

East London – BBC 112 pts +interview +portfolio (Fash Des) (IB 25 pts HL 15 pts)

Heriot-Watt – BBC (Fash Tech) (IB 29 pts); BBC +portfolio (Fash; Fash Comm) (IB 29 pts)

Leeds Arts – BBC incl art des 112 pts+interview +portfolio (Fash Brnd Comm; Fash Des; Tex Des)

Lincoln – BBC+interview +portfolio (Fash) (IB 29 pts)

Liverpool John Moores – BBC 112 pts +interview +portfolio (Fash Des Comm) (IB 28 pts)

Manchester Met – BBC 112 pts (Fash Buy Mrchnds) (IB 26 pts); BBC 112 pts +interview +portfolio (Fash; Fash Des Tech courses; Tex Prac) (IB 26 pts); BBC 112 pts +portfolio (Fash Prom) (IB 26 pts)

Middlesex – 112 pts +interview +portfolio (Fash Des; Fash Tex)

Northern SA – BBC 112 pts +interview +portfolio (Fash Body Cont; Tex Surf Des)

Nottingham Trent – BBC 112 pts +interview +portfolio (Cstm Des Mak; Fash Des; Fash Kntwr Des Knit Tex; Tex Des)

Salford – 112 pts incl art des +interview +portfolio (Fash Des) (IB 31 pts)

Sheffield Hallam – BBC 112 pts +portfolio (Fash Des)

Staffordshire – BBC 112 pts +interview +portfolio (Surf Patt Tex Des) (IB 24 pts)

Sunderland – BBB–BBC 112–120 pts (Fash Jrnl); BBC 112 pts +interview +portfolio (Fash Des Prom)

UWE Bristol – 112 pts +interview +portfolio (Fash Comm)

West London – BBC 112 pts (Fash Brnd Mark; Fash Prom Imag); BBC 112 pts +portfolio (Fash Tex)

Winchester – 112–120 pts (Fash Bus)

Wolverhampton – BBC 112 pts +portfolio (Fash)

104 pts **Bolton** – 104 pts +interview +portfolio (Spec Mkup FX Flm TV)

Central Lancashire – 104–112 pts +interview +portfolio (Fash Prom)

Falmouth – 104–120 pts +interview +portfolio (Fash Photo; Tex Des) (IB 24 pts); 104–120 pts +portfolio (Fash Des; Spowr Des) (IB 24 pts)

Northampton – BCC (Fash Mark); BCC +interview (Fash; Fash (Tex Fash); Ftwr Accs) (IB 25 pts)

Portsmouth – 104–112 pts +interview +portfolio (Fash Tex Des) (IB 25 pts)

Robert Gordon – BCC (Fash Mgt) (IB 28 pts)

Ulster – BBB–BCC +interview +portfolio (Tex Art Des Fash) (IB 24 pts HL 12 pts)

Westminster – ABB–BCC 104–128 pts (Fash Mrchnds Mgt) (IB 27 pts)

Winchester – 104–120 pts (Fash Jrnl)

96 pts **Anglia Ruskin** – 96 pts incl art/des/media +interview +portfolio (Fash Des) (IB 24 pts)

Arts London (CFash) – 96 pts +interview +portfolio (Cstm Perf; Fash PR Comm); CCC 96 pts +interview +portfolio (Hair Mkup Pros Perf)

Bath Spa – CCC +interview +portfolio (Fash Des) (IB 26 pts HL 6 art); CCC incl art des +interview +portfolio (Tex Des Fash Inter) (IB 26 pts HL 6 art)

Bolton – 96 pts +interview +portfolio (Fash); 96 pts incl art +interview +portfolio (Tex Surf Des)

Brighton – BBB–CCC 96–120 pts +interview +portfolio (Fash Des Bus St; Tex Des Bus St) (IB 26 pts); BCC–CCC 96–104 pts (Fash Drs Hist) (IB 26 pts)

Cardiff Met – BBB–CCC 96–120 pts +interview +portfolio (Tex) (IB 24 pts)

Hertfordshire – CCC 96 pts +interview +portfolio (Fash Des; Fash Fash Bus)

London Met – CCC 96 pts (Fash Mark Bus Mgt) (IB 28 pts HL 15 pts)

Plymouth (CA) – C art 96–120 pts +interview +portfolio (Fash; Fash Media Mark; Prtd Tex Des Surf Patt) (IB 30–28 pts)

Solent – CCC 96–112 pts +interview +portfolio (Fash Styl Crea Dir) (IB 28 pts)

88 pts   **Queen Margaret** – CCD +interview +portfolio (Cstm Des) (IB 28 pts)
80 pts   **Bedfordshire** – CCC–CCE 80–96 pts +interview +portfolio (Fash Des)
             Bradford College UC – CCD 80 pts +interview +portfolio (Fash)
             Bucks New – 80 pts +interview (Fash Des)
             Hereford (CA) – 80 pts +interview +portfolio (Jewel Des; Tex Des)
             South Wales – BCC–CDD 80–112 pts +interview +portfolio (Fash Mark Rtl Des); BCC–CDD incl
             art des 80–112 pts +interview +portfolio (Fash Des; Fash Prom)
72 pts   **Robert Gordon** – BC incl art/des +interview +portfolio (Fash Tex Des) (IB 24 pts)
             Solent – DDD 72–96 pts (Fash Mgt Mark; Fash courses) (IB 28 pts); DDD 72–96 pts
             +interview +portfolio (Fash Graph) (IB 28 pts)
64 pts   **Arts London (CFash)** – CC +interview +portfolio (Cord Ftwr Prod Des Innov); CC 64 pts
             +interview +portfolio (Bspk Tlrg; Cord Fash Bags Accs (Prod Des Innov); Crea Dir Fash;
             Fash Cont; Fash Des Dev; Fash Des Tech (Mnswr); Fash Des Tech (Wmnswr); Fash Imag
             Illus; Fash Jewel; Fash Photo; Fash Spowr; Fash Tex courses)
             Colchester (UC) – 64 pts +interview +portfolio (Fash Prtd Tex)
             London (Royal Central Sch SpDr) – 64–120 pts +interview +portfolio (Thea Prac (Cstm
             Constr))
             Ravensbourne Univ – CC +interview +portfolio (Fash; Fash Accs Tex Fut; Fash Prom) (IB
             28 pts)
             UHI – CC +interview +portfolio (Fn Art Tex); CC incl Engl +portfolio (Contemp Tex)
**40 pts and below, or other selection criteria (Foundation course, interview and portfolio
             inspection)** Arts London; Arts London (CFash); Arts London (Chelsea CA); Arts London
             (Wimb CA); Bath Spa; Bolton; Cardiff Met; East London; Hertfordshire; Kent; Kingston;
             Lincoln; Liverpool John Moores; London Met; Loughborough; Middlesex; Robert Gordon;
             South Wales; Southampton (Winchester SA); Suffolk; UWE Bristol

Alternative offers
See **Chapter 6** and **Appendix 1** for grades/UCAS Tariff points information for other examinations.

EXAMPLES OF COLLEGES OFFERING COURSES IN THIS SUBJECT FIELD
Barnet and Southgate (Coll); Barnfield (Coll); Basingstoke (CT); Bath (Coll); Blackburn (Coll); Blackpool
and Fylde (Coll); Bournemouth and Poole (Coll); Bradford College UC; Bury (Coll); Central Bedfordshire
(Coll); Central Campus, Sandwell (Coll); Chelmsford (Coll); City and Islington (Coll); Doncaster (Coll);
Dudley (Coll); East Coast (Coll); Gloucestershire (Coll); Harrogate (Coll); Havering (Coll); HOW (Coll); Hull
(Coll); Leicester (Coll); LeSoCo; Liverpool City (Coll); NCC Hackney; Newcastle (Coll); North Warwickshire
and South Leicestershire (Coll); Rotherham (CAT); Sir Gâr (Coll); South City Birmingham (Coll); South
Devon (Coll); South Essex (Coll); South Gloucestershire and Stroud (Coll); South Thames (Coll); Tresham
(CFHE); Walsall (Coll); West Herts (Coll); West Kent (Coll); Wigan and Leigh (Coll); York (Coll).

CHOOSING YOUR COURSE (SEE ALSO CH.1)
Universities and colleges teaching quality See www.qaa.ac.uk; https://unistats.ac.uk.

Top research universities and colleges (REF 2014) See **Art and Design (General)**.

Examples of sandwich degree courses Arts London; Birmingham City; Brighton; Central Lancashire;
Coventry; De Montfort; East London; Hertfordshire; Huddersfield; Manchester Met; Northumbria;
Nottingham Trent; Portsmouth; South Wales; Ulster; Westminster; Wolverhampton.

ADMISSIONS INFORMATION
Number of applicants per place (approx) Arts London 5; Arts London (CFash) (Fash Mgt) 20;
Bournemouth Arts 4; Central Lancashire 4; Creative Arts 8; De Montfort 5; Derby 4; Heriot-Watt 6;
Huddersfield 4; Kingston 5; Leeds Arts 4; Liverpool John Moores 6; Manchester Met 3; Middlesex 5;
Northampton 4; Nottingham Trent 8, (Tex Des) 3; Southampton (Winchester SA) 6; Staffordshire 3;
Wolverhampton 2.

Advice to applicants and planning the UCAS personal statement A well-written statement is
sought, clearly stating an interest in fashion and how prior education and work experience relate to

your application. You should describe any visits to exhibitions and, importantly, your views and opinions. Describe any work you have done ('making' and 'doing' skills, if any, for example, pattern cutting, sewing) or work observation in textile firms, fashion houses, even visits to costume departments in theatres can be useful. These contacts and visits should be described in detail, showing your knowledge of the types of fabrics and production processes. Give opinions on trends in haute couture, and show awareness of the work of others. Provide evidence of materials handling (see also **Appendix 3**). Show good knowledge of the contemporary fashion scene. See also **Art and Design (Graphic Design)**.

Misconceptions about this course
Bournemouth Arts Make-up for Media and Performance is not a beauty course and competition for places is very high. Successful applicants have to meet a wide range of criteria and hold at least the minimum entry requirements. Portfolios for our courses should evidence a visual understanding of the human body, life drawing, portrait studies, observational drawing and experimental ideas.

Selection interviews
Yes Bolton, Huddersfield, Leeds Beckett, Liverpool John Moores, Manchester, Northumbria, Salford; **Some** Chester, Westminster; **No** Falmouth, UWE Bristol, West London.

Interview advice and questions Questions mostly originate from student's portfolio. See also **Art and Design (General)** and **Chapter 5**. **Birmingham City** (Tex Des) What do you expect to achieve from a degree in Fashion? **Creative Arts** Describe in detail a specific item in your portfolio and why it was selected.

Reasons for rejection (non-academic) Portfolio work not up to standard. Not enough research. Not articulate at interview. Lack of sense of humour, and inflexibility. Narrow perspective. Lack of resourcefulness, self-motivation and organisation. Complacency, lack of verbal, written and self-presentation skills. Not enough experience in designing or making clothes. See also **Art and Design (General)**.

AFTER-RESULTS ADVICE
Offers to applicants repeating A-levels Same Birmingham City; Bournemouth Arts; Creative Arts; Huddersfield; Manchester Met; Nottingham Trent; South Essex (Coll); Staffordshire.

GRADUATE DESTINATIONS AND EMPLOYMENT (2016/17 HESA)
Graduates surveyed See **Art and Design (General)**.

Career note See **Art and Design (General)**.

OTHER DEGREE SUBJECTS FOR CONSIDERATION
History of Art; Retail Management; Theatre Design.

ART AND DESIGN (FINE ART)
(including **Painting and Printmaking and Sculpture and Environmental Art**; see also **Art and Design (Graphic Design), Photography**)

Fine Art courses are essentially practice-based courses encouraging students to find their own direction through additional intellectual and theoretical studies. The work will involve a range of activities which cover painting, illustration and sculpture. Additional studies can also involve electronic media, film, video, photography and print, although course options will vary between institutions. A more specialised study in the field of Sculpture and Environmental Art is offered at Glasgow School of Art, taking sculpture outside art galleries and museums and into the public domain where students focus on drawing, wood and metal fabrication, photography, video, computers and sound. As in the case of most Art degrees, admission to courses usually requires a one-year Foundation Art course before applying.

Useful websites www.artcyclopedia.com; www.nationalgallery.org.uk; www.britisharts.co.uk; www.
tate.org.uk; www.creativefuture.org.uk; www.a-n.co.uk/news; www.artscouncil.org.uk

*NB The points totals shown to the left of the institutions are for ease of reference only. It must not
be assumed that Tariff points are always used by institutions or that they can be substituted for an
offer in grades. The level of an offer is not necessarily indicative of the quality of a course.*

COURSE OFFERS INFORMATION
Subject requirements/preferences See **Art and Design (General)**.

Your target offers and examples of degree courses

144 pts **Oxford** – AAA +interview +portfolio (Fn Art) (IB 38 pts HL 666)

136 pts **Leeds** – AAB +portfolio (Fn Art) (IB 35–34 pts)

128 pts **Dundee** – ABB incl art des +portfolio (Fn Art) (IB 34 pts HL 665)
    Edinburgh – ABB +portfolio (Fn Art; Illus) (IB 34 pts HL 655)
    Glasgow (SA) – ABB +interview +portfolio (Fn Art Photo; Pntg Prtg; Sculp Env Art)
    Lancaster – ABB +portfolio (Fn Art) (IB 32 pts HL 16 pts)
    London (UCL) – ABB +interview +portfolio (Fn Art) (IB 34 pts HL 16 pts)
    London (UCL/Slade SA) – ABB +interview +portfolio (Fn Art) (IB 34 pts HL 16 pts)
    Loughborough – ABB +interview +portfolio (Fn Art) (IB 34 pts HL 655)

120 pts **Bournemouth Arts** – BBB (Art Des Hist) (IB 30 pts); BBB 120 pts +interview +portfolio (Fn
    Art) (IB 30 pts)
    Huddersfield – BBB 120 pts +interview +portfolio (Contemp Art)
    Newcastle – AAB–BBB +interview +portfolio (Fn Art) (IB 35–32 pts HL 555)
    Northumbria – 120 pts +interview +portfolio (Fn Art)
    Norwich Arts – BBB +interview +portfolio (Fn Art) (IB 27 pts)
    Reading – BBB +Art Fdn +interview +portfolio (Fn Art) (IB 30 pts); BBB +interview +portfolio
    (Art courses) (IB 30 pts)
    Southampton (Winchester SA) – BBB +interview +portfolio (Fn Art) (IB 30 pts HL 16 pts)
    Trinity Saint David – 120 pts +interview +portfolio (Fn Art (Std Site Con)) (IB 32 pts)

112 pts **Birmingham City** – BBC 112 pts +portfolio +interview (Fn Art) (IB 28 pts HL 14 pts)
    Chester – 112 pts incl art des+Fr (Fn Art Fr) (IB 26 pts HL 5 vis arts+Fr)
    Coventry – BBC incl art/des +interview +portfolio (Fn Art; Fn Art Illus) (IB 29 pts)
    Creative Arts – 112 pts +portfolio (Fn Art courses) (IB 30–27 pts HL 15 pts)
    De Montfort – 112 pts incl art des +interview +portfolio (Fn Art) (IB 26 pts incl art des)
    Derby – BBC 112 pts +interview +portfolio (Fn Art)
    Glyndŵr – BBC 112 pts +portfolio +interview (Fn Art)
    Kingston – 112 pts +interview +portfolio (Fn Art)
    Leeds Arts – BBC 112 pts +interview +portfolio (Fn Art)
    Leeds Beckett – 112 pts +interview +portfolio (Fn Art) (IB 25 pts)
    Liverpool Hope – BBC 112–120 pts +interview +portfolio (Fn Art) (IB 26 pts)
    Liverpool John Moores – BBC incl art/des 112 pts +interview +portfolio (Fn Art) (IB 26 pts)
    London Met – BBC 112 pts +interview +portfolio (Fn Art) (IB 28 pts HL 15 pts)
    Manchester Met – BBC 112 pts +interview +portfolio (Fn Art) (IB 26 pts)
    Middlesex – 112 pts +interview +portfolio (Fn Art)
    Nottingham Trent – BBC 112 pts +portfolio +interview (Fn Art)
    Oxford Brookes – BBC incl art +interview +portfolio (Fn Art) (IB 30 pts)
    Sheffield Hallam – BBC 112 pts incl art des +interview +portfolio (Fn Art)
    Staffordshire – BBC 112 pts +interview +portfolio (Fn Art) (IB 24 pts)
    Sunderland – BBC 112 pts +portfolio +interview (Fn Art)
    UWE Bristol – 112 pts +portfolio +interview (Fn Art)
    Wolverhampton – BBC 112 pts +portfolio (Fn Art)
    Worcester – 112 pts (Fn Art Psy)

104 pts **Aberystwyth** – BBB–BCC incl art 104–120 pts +portfolio (Fn Art; Fn Art Art Hist) (IB
    30–28 pts)
    Central Lancashire – 104–112 pts +interview +portfolio (Fn Art)

Chester – BBC–BCC incl art des/fn art 104–112 pts +interview +portfolio (Fn Art) (IB 26 pts HL 5 vis arts)

Falmouth – 104–120 pts +interview +portfolio (Fn Art) (IB 24 pts)

Lincoln – BCC +interview +portfolio (Fn Art) (IB 28 pts)

Northampton – BCC +interview +portfolio (Fn Art; Fn Art Pntg Drg) (IB 25 pts)

Ulster – BBB–BCC +portfolio +interview (Fn Art) (IB 24 pts HL 12 pts)

Worcester – 104 pts +interview +portfolio (Fn Art)

York St John – 104–120 pts +interview +portfolio (Fn Art)

96 pts **Anglia Ruskin** – 96 pts +interview +portfolio (Fn Art) (IB 24 pts)

Bath Spa – CCC +interview +portfolio (Fn Art) (IB 27 pts HL 6 art)

Bolton – 96 pts incl art +interview +portfolio (Fn Art)

Brighton – BBB–CCC 96–120 pts +interview +portfolio (Fn Art; Fn Art Crit Prac; Fn Art Pntg) (IB 26 pts)

Cardiff Met – BBB–CCC 96–120 pts +interview +portfolio (Fn Art) (IB 24 pts)

Chichester – 96–120 pts incl art/photo/tex +interview +portfolio (Fn Art courses)

Cumbria – BBC–CCC 96–112 pts +interview +portfolio (Fn Art)

East London – CCC 96 pts +interview +portfolio (Fn Art) (IB 24 pts HL 15 pts)

Hertfordshire – CCC 96 pts incl art +interview +portfolio (Fn Art)

Plymouth – 96–144 pts +interview +portfolio (Fn Art Art Hist) (IB 26-3625 pts)

Plymouth (CA) – C art 96–120 pts +interview +portfolio (Fn Art) (IB 30–28 pts)

Solent – CCC 96–112 pts +portfolio (Fn Art)

Teesside – 96–112 pts +interview +portfolio (Fn Art)

Westminster – BBB–CCC 96–120 pts +interview +portfolio (Fn Art Mix Media) (IB 27 pts HL 4 Engl)

80 pts **Hereford (CA)** – 80 pts+interview +portfolio (Fn Art)

64 pts **Colchester (UC)** – 64 pts+interview +portfolio (Fn Art)

UHI – CC+interview +portfolio (Fn Art; Fn Art Tex)

40 pts and below, or other selection criteria (Foundation course, interview and portfolio inspection) Arts London; Arts London (Camberwell CA); Arts London (Chelsea CA); Arts London (Wimb CA); Bath Spa; Bedfordshire; Cardiff Met; Central Lancashire; Creative Arts; De Montfort; Gloucestershire; Glyndŵr; Hertfordshire; Kent; Kingston; London (Gold); Middlesex; Trinity Saint David; UWE Bristol

Alternative offers

See **Chapter 6** and **Appendix 1** for grades/UCAS Tariff points information for other examinations.

EXAMPLES OF COLLEGES OFFERING COURSES IN THIS SUBJECT FIELD

Bath (Coll); Blackpool and Fylde (Coll); Bradford College UC; Bury (Coll); Central Bedfordshire (Coll); City and Islington (Coll); City of Oxford (Coll); Cornwall (Coll); Craven (Coll); Doncaster (Coll); Exeter (Coll); Grŵp Llandrillo Menai; Harrogate (Coll); Havering (Coll); Leicester (Coll); Liverpool City (Coll); Newcastle (Coll); Sheffield (Coll); South Gloucestershire and Stroud (Coll); St Helens (Coll); Stamford New (Coll); Sunderland (Coll); TEC Partnership; Tyne Coast (Coll); Weymouth (Coll).

CHOOSING YOUR COURSE (SEE ALSO CH.1)

Universities and colleges teaching quality See www.qaa.ac.uk; https://unistats.ac.uk.

Top research universities and colleges (REF 2014) See **Art and Design (General)**.

Examples of sandwich degree courses Coventry; Huddersfield; Plymouth; Ulster; Wolverhampton.

ADMISSIONS INFORMATION

Number of applicants per place (approx) Arts London (Chelsea CA) 5; Arts London (Wimb CA) (Sculp) 3; Bath Spa 8; Birmingham City 6; Bournemouth Arts 5; Cardiff Met 3; Central Lancashire 4; Creative Arts 2; Cumbria 4; De Montfort 5; Derby 4; Dundee 6; Gloucestershire 5; Kingston 9; Lincoln 4; Liverpool John Moores 3; London (Gold) 10; London (UCL) 23; London Met 11; Manchester Met 4; Middlesex 3; Newcastle 8; Northampton 3; Nottingham Trent 5; Sheffield Hallam 4; Solihull (Coll) 4;

Southampton (Winchester SA) 6; Staffordshire 3; Sunderland 3; UHI 2; Wirral Met (Coll) 3.

Advice to applicants and planning the UCAS personal statement Since this is a subject area that can be researched easily in art galleries, you should discuss not only your own style of work and your preferred subjects but also your opinions on various art forms, styles and periods. Keep up to date with public opinion on controversial issues. Give your reasons for wishing to pursue a course in Fine Art. Visits to galleries and related hobbies, for example reading, cinema, music, literature should be mentioned. Show the nature of your external involvement in art. (See also **Appendix 3**.) **Oxford** No deferred applications are accepted for this course; successful applicants average 10%.

Misconceptions about this course
Bournemouth Arts Applicants need to make the distinction between fine art and illustration. **Oxford** Some applicants think that this course will not have the same academic requirements as other subjects. The course has a strong practical element but academic ability is also important and AAA (or equivalent) will be required.

Selection interviews Yes Arts London (Chelsea CA), Bolton, Brighton, Cardiff Met, Chichester, Leeds Beckett, Liverpool John Moores, Newcastle, Northumbria, Oxford (10%), Plymouth; **Some** Chester, Cumbria; **No** Falmouth, Kent, York St John.

Interview advice and questions Questions asked on portfolio of work. Be prepared to answer questions on your stated opinions on your UCAS application and on current art trends and controversial topics reported in the press. Discussion covering the applicant's engagement with contemporary fine art practice. Visits to exhibitions, galleries etc. Ambitions for their own work. How do you perceive the world in a visual sense? Who is your favourite living artist and why? See also **Art and Design (General)** and **Chapter 5**.

Reasons for rejection (non-academic) Lack of a fine art specialist portfolio. No intellectual grasp of the subject – only interested in techniques.

AFTER-RESULTS ADVICE
Offers to applicants repeating A-levels Same Anglia Ruskin; Arts London; Birmingham City; Cumbria; Manchester Met; Nottingham Trent; Staffordshire; Sunderland; UHI; **No** Oxford.

GRADUATE DESTINATIONS AND EMPLOYMENT (2016/17 HESA)
Graduates surveyed 2,645 **Employed** 960 **In voluntary employment** 130 **In further study** 530 **Assumed unemployed** 170

Career note See **Art and Design (General)**.

OTHER DEGREE SUBJECTS FOR CONSIDERATION
Art Gallery Management; History of Art; see other **Art and Design** tables.

ART AND DESIGN (GRAPHIC DESIGN)

(including **Advertising, Animation, Design, Graphic Communication, Illustration and Visual Communication;** see also **Art And Design (fine Art), Art And Design (general), Film, Radio, Video And Tv Studies**)

Graphic Design ranges from the design of websites, books, magazines and newspapers to packaging and advertisements. Visual communication uses symbols as teaching aids and also includes TV graphics. An Art Foundation course is usually taken before entry to degree courses. Graphic Design students are probably the most fortunate in terms of the range of career opportunities open to them on graduation. These include advertising, animation, book and magazine illustration, film, interactive media design, typography, packaging, photography and work in publishing and television. Courses cover the essential element of creative thinking alongside the normal industrial practices of scriptwriting, character design, storyboarding, animation, and sound design.

Useful websites www.thoughtco.com/graphic-design-4133467; www.graphic-design.com; www.creativefuture.org.uk; www.designcouncil.org.uk

NB The points totals shown to the left of the institutions are for ease of reference only. It must not be assumed that Tariff points are always used by institutions or that they can be substituted for an offer in grades. The level of an offer is not necessarily indicative of the quality of a course.

COURSE OFFERS INFORMATION
Subject requirements/preferences See **Art and Design (General)**.

Your target offers and examples of degree courses

128 pts **Dundee** – ABB incl art des +interview +portfolio (Animat; Graph Des) (IB 34 pts HL 665)
Edinburgh – ABB +portfolio (Graph Des; Intermed Art) (IB 34 pts HL 655)
Leeds – ABB incl art/des (Graph Comm Des) (IB 34 pts HL 16 pts incl 5/6 art/vis art/des)
Loughborough – ABB +interview +portfolio (Graph Comm Illus) (IB 34 pts HL 655)
Oxford Brookes – 128 pts (Des) (IB 32 pts)

120 pts **Birmingham City** – BBB 120 pts (Vis Efcts) (IB 30 pts)
Bournemouth Arts – BBB 120 pts +interview +portfolio (Vis Comm) (IB 30 pts); BBB 120 +interview +portfolio (Animat Prod) (HL 555)
East Anglia – BBB (Comp Graph Imag Multim) (IB 31 pts HL 5 maths/comp sci/phys/econ)
Huddersfield – BBB 120 pts +interview +portfolio (Animat; Contemp Art Illus; Graph Des; Illus)
Kent – BBB (Dig Art) (IB 34 pts HL 15 pts)
Northumbria – 120 pts +portfolio (Graph Des)
Norwich Arts – BBB +interview +portfolio (Animat; Flm Mov Imag Prod; Graph Comm; Graph Des; Illus) (IB 27 pts)
Reading – BBB +interview +portfolio (Graph Comm) (IB 30 pts)
Southampton (Winchester SA) – BBB incl art/des +interview +portfolio (Graph Arts) (IB 30 pts HL 16 pts)
Trinity Saint David – 120 pts +interview +portfolio (Comp Animat; Graph Des; Illus) (IB 32 pts)

112 pts **Bournemouth** – 112–128 pts +portfolio (Comp Animat Art Des) (IB 32–30 pts)
Bournemouth Arts – BBB–BBC 112–120 pts +interview +portfolio (Graph Des) (IB 3032-3230 pts)
Coventry – BBC incl art/des +interview +portfolio (Graph Des; Illus Animat; Illus Graph) (IB 29 pts)
Creative Arts – 112 pts +interview +portfolio (Graph Des); 112 pts +portfolio (Animat)
Derby – BBC 112 pts +interview +portfolio (Graph Des; Illus); BBC 112 pts +portfolio (Animat)
East London – BBC 112 pts +interview +portfolio (Animat) (IB 25 pts HL 15 pts)
Edge Hill – BBB–BBC 112–120 pts +interview (Animat)
Glyndŵr – BBC 112 pts +interview +portfolio (Graph Des); BBC 112 pts +interview/portfolio (Chld Bks; Comics; Illus)
Greenwich – BBC 112 pts +interview +portfolio (Graph Dig Des)
Hertfordshire – BBC 112 pts +interview +portfolio (2D Animat Chrctr Dig Media); BBC incl art +interview +portfolio (3D Comp Animat Modl)
Hull – 112 pts +interview +portfolio (Dig Des) (IB 28 pts)
Kingston – 112 pts +interview +portfolio (Graph Des)
Leeds Arts – BBC incl art/des 112 pts +interview +portfolio (Animat; Graph Des; Vis Comm)
Lincoln – BBC +interview +portfolio (Animat Vis Efcts; Graph Des; Illus) (IB 29 pts)
Liverpool John Moores – BBC 112 pts +interview +portfolio (Graph Des Illus) (IB 26 pts)
London Met – BBC 112 pts +interview +portfolio (Graph Des) (IB 28 pts HL 15 pts)
Manchester Met – BBC 112 pts +interview +portfolio (Graph Des; Illus Animat) (IB 26 pts)
Middlesex – 112 pts +interview +portfolio (Animat; Graph Des; Illus)
Nottingham Trent – BBC 112 pts +interview +portfolio (Graph Des)
Oxford Brookes – BBC 112 pts +portfolio +interview (Graph Des) (IB 30 pts)
Portsmouth – 112 pts +interview +portfolio (Animat) (IB 25 pts)

Sheffield Hallam – BBC 112 pts +portfolio (Animat); BBC 112 pts +portfolio (Graph Des)
Staffordshire – BBC 112 pts +interview +portfolio (Crtn Cmc Arts; Graph Des; Illus) (IB 24 pts)
Suffolk – BBC (Graph Comm Des); BBC +interview +portfolio (Graph Des; Graph Des (Graph Illus))
Sunderland – BBC 112 pts +interview +portfolio (Graph Des; Illus Des)
UWE Bristol – 112 pts +interview +portfolio (Animat; Graph Des)
104 pts **Central Lancashire** – 104 pts +interview (Animat); 104–112 pts +interview +portfolio (Crea Adv); 104–112 pts +portfolio (Graph Des)
Chester – BBC–BCC 104–112 pts +interview +portfolio (Graph Des) (IB 26 pts HL 5 vis arts)
Chichester – 104–120 pts (3D Anim Vis Efcts) (IB 28 pts)
De Montfort – C art des 104 pts incl art des +portfolio (Animat; Graph Des; Graph Des (Illus)) (IB 24 pts HL 5 art des)
Edinburgh Napier – BCC incl Engl+art/des +interview +portfolio (Graph Des) (IB 28 pts HL 654)
Falmouth – 104–120 pts +interview +portfolio (Animat Vis Efcts; Graph Des; Illus) (IB 24 pts)
Northampton – BCC 104–112 pts +interview (Graph Comm; Illus) (IB 25 pts)
Portsmouth – 104–112 pts +interview +portfolio (Graph Des; Illus) (IB 25 pts)
Ulster – BBB–BCC +interview +portfolio (Animat) (IB 24 pts HL 12 pts); BBB–BCC +portfolio +interview (Graph Des Illus) (IB 24 pts HL 12 pts)
Winchester – 104–120 pts (Crea Adv)
Worcester – 104 pts +interview +portfolio (Animat courses; Crea Media Graph Des)
96 pts **Anglia Ruskin** – 96 pts incl art/des/media +interview +portfolio (Graph Des; Illus; Illus Animat) (IB 24 pts)
Bath Spa – CCC +interview +portfolio (Graph Comm) (IB 26 pts HL 6 art)
Bolton – 96 pts +interview +portfolio (Animat Illus)
Brighton – BBB–CCC 96–120 pts +interview +portfolio (Graph Des) (IB 26 pts)
Cardiff Met – BBB–CCC 96–120 pts +interview +portfolio (Graph Comm) (IB 24 pts)
Cumbria – BBC–CCC 96–112 pts +interview +portfolio (Graph Des; Illus)
East London – CCC 96 pts +interview +portfolio (Graph Des) (IB 24 pts HL 15 pts)
Hertfordshire – CCC 96 pts +interview +portfolio (Graph Des)
Plymouth – 96–120 pts (Gm Arts Des) (IB 28–26 pts); 96–120 pts +portfolio (Graph Des Typo) (IB 28–26 pts)
Plymouth (CA) – 96–120 pts +interview +portfolio (Illus) (IB 30–28 pts); C art 96–120 pts +interview +portfolio (Animat; Graph Comm) (IB 30–28 pts)
Solent – 96–112 pts +interview (Animat) (IB 28 pts); CCC 96–112 pts +portfolio (Graph Des) (IB 28 pts)
Teesside – 96–112 pts +interview (Graph Des Mark); 96–112 pts +interview +portfolio (Comp Animat; Comp Gms Art); 96–112 pts +portfolio +interview (Graph Des Illus)
Westminster – BBB–CCC 96–120 pts +interview (Illus Vis Comm) (IB 27 pts HL 4 Engl); BBB–CCC 96–120 pts+interview +portfolio (Animat; Graph Comm Des) (IB 27 pts HL 4 Engl)
York St John – 96–112 pts+interview (Graph Des)
88 pts **Canterbury Christ Church** – 88–112 pts (Animat Prod); 88–112 pts +interview +portfolio (Graph Des)
West Scotland – CCD incl art 88–102 pts (Comp Animat Arts) (IB 24 pts)
80 pts **Bedfordshire** – CCC–CCE 80–96 pts +interview +portfolio (Adv Brnd Des); CCC–CCE 80–96 pts +portfolio +interview (Animat; Graph Des)
Blackburn (Coll) – 80 pts +interview +portfolio (Illus Animat)
Bucks New – 80 pts +interview +portfolio (Animat; Crea Adv)
Hereford (CA) – 80 pts +interview +portfolio (Graph Media Des; Illus)
South Wales – BCC–CDD incl art des 80–112 pts +interview +portfolio (Adv Des; Graph Comm)
64 pts **Colchester (UC)** – 64 pts +interview +portfolio (Graph Des Dig Comm)
Creative Arts – CC 64 pts +interview +portfolio (Graph Des Comm)

Ravensbourne Univ – CC +interview +portfolio (Graph Des) (IB 28 pts); CC +portfolio (Animat) (IB 28 pts); CC +portfolio +interview (Adv Brnd Des) (IB 24-28 pts)

40 pts and below, or other selection criteria (Foundation course, interview and portfolio inspection) Arden; Arts London; Arts London (Camberwell CA); Arts London (Chelsea CA); Bucks New; Gloucestershire (Adv; Graph Des); Greenwich; Hertfordshire; Kingston; Liverpool John Moores; Loughborough; Southampton (Winchester SA); UWE Bristol

Alternative offers

See **Chapter 6** and **Appendix 1** for grades/UCAS Tariff points information for other examinations.

EXAMPLES OF COLLEGES OFFERING COURSES IN THIS SUBJECT FIELD

Banbury and Bicester (Coll); Barking and Dagenham (Coll); Barnet and Southgate (Coll); Birmingham Met (Coll); Blackburn (Coll); Bristol City (Coll); Bury (Coll); Canterbury (Coll); Cornwall (Coll); Craven (Coll); Doncaster (Coll); Durham New (Coll); Exeter (Coll); Farnborough (CT); Harlow (Coll); Havering (Coll); Hugh Baird (Coll); Kirklees (Coll); Leicester (Coll); London UCK (Coll); Milton Keynes (Coll); NCC Redbridge; Newcastle (Coll); Northern SA; Nottingham (Coll); Oldham (Coll); Rotherham (CAT); Sheffield (Coll); South Cheshire (Coll); South Gloucestershire and Stroud (Coll); Southport (Coll); St Helens (Coll); Stamford New (Coll); Stockport (Coll); Truro and Penwith (Coll); Tyne Coast (Coll); West Kent (Coll); West Suffolk (Coll); Weston (Coll); Wigan and Leigh (Coll); York (Coll).

CHOOSING YOUR COURSE (SEE ALSO CH.1)

Universities and colleges teaching quality See www.qaa.ac.uk; https://unistats.ac.uk.

Top research universities and colleges (REF 2014) See **Art and Design (General)**.

Examples of sandwich degree courses Aberystwyth; Arts London; Central Lancashire; Coventry; Hertfordshire; Huddersfield; Loughborough; Northumbria; Portsmouth; South Wales; Ulster; Wolverhampton.

ADMISSIONS INFORMATION

Number of applicants per place (approx) Anglia Ruskin (Illus) 3; Arts London 4; Bath Spa 9; Bournemouth Arts 4; Cardiff Met 5; Central Lancashire 5; Colchester (UC) 3; Creative Arts 5; Derby 4; Edinburgh Napier 10; Hertfordshire 6; Kingston 8; Lincoln 5; Liverpool John Moores 7; Manchester Met 8; Middlesex 3; Northampton 3; Nottingham Trent 6; Ravensbourne Univ 9; Solihull (Coll) 3; Staffordshire 3; Teesside 5; Trinity Saint David 10; Wolverhampton 5.

Advice to applicants and planning the UCAS personal statement Discuss your special interest in this field and any commercial applications that have impressed you. Discuss the work you are enjoying at present and the range of media that you have explored. Show your interests in travel, architecture, the arts, literature, film, current affairs (see also **Appendix 3** for contact details of relevant professional associations). Have an awareness of the place of design in society.

Misconceptions about this course Bath Spa Some students think that illustration is simply 'doing small drawings' and that Graphic Design is a soft option with little academic work. **Bournemouth** You need to have a good mix of artistic and mathematical/technical ability. **Plymouth** These courses also involve typography.

Selection interviews Yes Bolton, Brighton, Chester, Cumbria, Huddersfield, Leeds Beckett, Liverpool John Moores, Plymouth, Reading, Salford; **Some** Edge Hill, Northumbria; **No** Falmouth, UWE Bristol, West London, York St John.

Interview advice and questions Questions may be asked on recent trends in graphic design from the points of view of methods and designers and, particularly, art and the computer. Questions are usually asked on applicant's portfolio of work. See also **Art and Design (General)** and **Chapter 5**.

Reasons for rejection (non-academic) Not enough work in portfolio. Inability to think imaginatively. Lack of interest in the arts in general. Lack of drive. Tutor's statement indicating problems. Poorly constructed personal statement. Inability to talk about your work. Lack of knowledge about the chosen course. See also **Art and Design (General)**.

AFTER-RESULTS ADVICE

Offers to applicants repeating A-levels Same Bath Spa; Bournemouth Arts; Cardiff Met; Creative Arts; Lincoln; Manchester Met; Nottingham Trent; Staffordshire.

GRADUATE DESTINATIONS AND EMPLOYMENT (2016/17 HESA)

Graduates surveyed See Art and Design (General).

Career note See **Art and Design (General)**.

OTHER DEGREE SUBJECTS FOR CONSIDERATION

Art Gallery Management; Film and Video Production; History of Art; Multimedia Design, Photography and Digital Imaging. See also other **Art and Design** tables.

ART AND DESIGN (INTERIOR, PRODUCT AND INDUSTRIAL DESIGN)

(including **Footwear Design, Furniture Design, Interior Design, Product Design, Product Design Technology, Theatre Design and Transport Design**; see also **Architecture, Art And Design (3d Design)**)

The field of industrial design is extensive and degree studies are usually preceded by an Art Foundation course. Product Design is one of the most common courses in which technological studies (involving materials and methods of production) are integrated with creative design in the production of a range of household and industrial products. Other courses on offer include Furniture Design, Interior, Theatre, Automotive and Transport Design. It should be noted that some Product Design courses have an engineering bias. Interior Design courses involve architectural considerations and courses will include aspects of building practices, materials, products and finishes. Historical studies of period designs and styles will also be included: see **Subject requirements/preferences** below. These are stimulating courses but graduate opportunities in this field are very limited. Good courses will have good industrial contacts for sandwich courses or shorter work placements – check with course leaders (or students) before applying.

Useful websites www.ergonomics.org.uk; www.creativefuture.org.uk; www.productdesignforums. com; www.carbodydesign.com; www.bild.org.uk; www.csd.org.uk; www.designcouncil.org.uk; www. theatredesign.org.uk

NB The points totals shown to the left of the institutions are for ease of reference only. It must not be assumed that Tariff points are always used by institutions or that they can be substituted for an offer in grades. The level of an offer is not necessarily indicative of the quality of a course.

COURSE OFFERS INFORMATION

Subject requirements/preferences Interior Architecture Design courses require an art portfolio. **AL** Check Product Design, Industrial Design and Engineering Design course requirements since these will often require mathematics and/or physics.

Your target offers and examples of degree courses

144 pts   **Glasgow** – AAA incl maths+phys (Prod Des Eng (MEng)) (IB 38 pts HL 666 incl maths+phys)
            Leeds – AAA +interview +portfolio (Prod Des) (IB 35 pts HL 18 pts)
            Queen's Belfast – AAA incl maths+sci/des tech (Prod Des Eng (MEng)) (IB 36 pts HL 666 incl maths+sci)

136 pts   **Glasgow** – AAB incl maths+phys (Prod Des Eng) (IB 36 pts HL 665 incl maths+phys)
            Liverpool – AAB/ABB +aEPQ incl maths+sci (Ind Des (MEng)) (IB 35 pts HL 5 maths+phys)
            Strathclyde – AAB incl maths+phys (4 yr course) BBB (5 yr course) (Prod Eng Mgt (MEng)) (IB 36 pts HL 5 maths/phys)

128 pts **Brunel** – ABB incl art/des/tech +interview +portfolio (Ind Des Tech) (IB 31 pts HL 5 art/des/tech); ABB incl art/des/tech+maths/phys +interview +portfolio (Prod Des; Prod Des Eng) (IB 31 pts HL 5 art/des/tech+maths/phys)

Edinburgh – ABB +portfolio (Inter Des; Prod Des) (IB 34 pts HL 655)

Glasgow (SA) – ABB +interview +portfolio (Inter Des) (IB 30 pts HL 18 pts); ABB +portfolio +interview (Prod Des) (IB 30 pts HL 18 pts)

Liverpool – ABB/BBB +aEPQ incl maths+sci/des tech (Ind Des) (IB 33 pts HL 5 maths+phys)

Loughborough – ABB +portfolio (Ind Des Tech) (IB 34 pts HL 655); ABB incl maths/phys +portfolio (Prod Des Tech) (IB 34 pts HL 655 incl 5 maths/phys)

Nottingham – AAB–ABB incl maths (Prod Des Manuf) (IB 36–34 pts HL 5 maths)

Oxford Brookes – 128 pts (Des) (IB 32 pts); 128 pts incl art des +portfolio (Inter Archit) (IB 32 pts)

Strathclyde – ABB (3 yr course) BBB (4 yr course) (Prod Des Innov) (IB 34 pts HL 5 maths/phys)

UWE Bristol – 128 pts (Inter Archit)

120 pts **Bournemouth Arts** – BBB 120 pts (Inter Archit Des) (IB 30 pts)

Coventry – BBB incl art/des +portfolio +interview (Inter Archit Des) (IB 29 pts)

Huddersfield – BBB 120 pts +interview +portfolio (Inter Des); BBB 120 pts +portfolio/interview (Prod Des)

Leeds Beckett – 120 pts +interview +portfolio (Inter Archit Des)

London South Bank – BBB incl art/des 120–128 pts +portfolio (Prod Des)

Nottingham Trent – BBB 120 pts +portfolio (Inter Archit Des)

Queen's Belfast – ABB incl maths+sci/des tech (Prod Des Eng) (IB 33 pts HL 655 incl maths+sci)

Strathclyde – AAB–BBB (Prod Des Eng (MEng)) (IB 36 pts HL 5 maths+phys)

Sussex – ABB–BBB incl art/des +portfolio (Prod Des) (IB 32–30 pts)

Trinity Saint David – 120 pts +interview +portfolio (Auto Des; Prod Des)

Ulster – BBB +portfolio +interview (Prod Des) (IB 26 pts HL 13 pts)

Westminster – AAB–BBB 120–136 pts+portfolio (Inter Archit) (IB 27 pts HL 4 Engl)

112 pts **Aston** – BBB–BBC incl sci/tech (Prod Des Tech) (IB 29 pts HL 554 incl sci/tech)

Birmingham City – BBC 112 pts (Inter Archit Des) (IB 28 pts); (Prod Furn Des) (IB 28 pts HL 14 pts)

Coventry – BBC incl art/des +portfolio +interview (Prod Des) (IB 29 pts)

De Montfort – 112 pts incl art des +interview +portfolio (Ftwr Des; Inter Des; Prod Des; Prod Furn Des) (IB 26 pts incl art des)

Derby – BBC 112 pts +interview +portfolio (Prod Des)

Kingston – 112 pts +portfolio +interview (Prod Furn Des); 112 pts incl art des +portfolio +interview (Inter Des)

Leeds Beckett – 112 pts +interview +portfolio (Prod Des) (IB 24 pts)

Lincoln – BBC (Inter Archit Des; Prod Des) (IB 29 pts)

London Met – BBC 112 pts +interview +portfolio (Furn Prod Des; Inter Archit Des) (IB 28 pts HL 15 pts)

Manchester Met – BBC 112 pts +portfolio (Inter Des; Prod Des Tech) (IB 26 pts)

Middlesex – 112 pts+interview +portfolio (Inter Des)

Nottingham Trent – BBC 112 pts +interview +portfolio (Furn Prod Des; Prod Des); BBC 112 pts+portfolio +interview (Thea Des)

Portsmouth – 112–120 pts +interview (Inter Archit Des) (IB 25 pts)

Salford – 112 pts incl art des/tech +interview +portfolio (Inter Des) (IB 31 pts)

Sheffield Hallam – 112 pts +interview +portfolio (Prod Des); BBC 112 pts +interview +portfolio (Inter Archit Des)

Staffordshire – BBC 112 pts (Ind Des Prod Trans)

UWE Bristol – 112 pts +portfolio (Prod Des; Prod Des Tech); 112 pts +portfolio +interview (Inter Des)

Wolverhampton – BBC +portfolio (Inter Des; Prod Des)

104 pts   **Bournemouth** – 104–120 pts +interview +portfolio (Prod Des) (IB 31–28 pts)
Central Lancashire – 104–112 pts +interview +portfolio (Inter Des) (IB 28 pts)
Falmouth – 104–120 pts +interview +portfolio (Inter Des) (IB 24 pts)
Hertfordshire – BCC 104 pts +interview +portfolio (Inter Archit Des; Prod Ind Des)
Northampton – BCC 104–112 pts +interview (Inter Archit Spat Des; Prod Des) (IB 25 pts)
Worcester – 104 pts (Prod Des)

96 pts   **Anglia Ruskin** – C art/des 96 pts incl art/des/media +interview +portfolio (Inter Des) (IB 24 pts)
Brighton – BBB–CCC 96–120 pts +portfolio (Prod Des (Prof Expnc)) (IB 27 pts)
Cardiff Met – BBB–CCC 96–120 pts +interview +portfolio (Prod Des) (IB 24 pts)
Chichester – 96–112 pts +portfolio (Prod Des)
Dundee – BCC–CCC incl art/des +portfolio +interview (Inter Env Des) (IB 30 pts); BCC–CCC incl art/des/sci/tech 96–104 pts +portfolio +interview (Prod Des) (IB 30 pts)
East London – CCC 96 pts incl art des +interview +portfolio (Inter Des; Prod Des) (IB 25 pts HL 15 pts)
Edinburgh Napier – CCC incl Engl+art/des +interview +portfolio (Inter Spat Des; Prod Des) (IB 27 pts HL 654)
Plymouth – C art 96–120 pts +interview +portfolio (3D Des courses) (IB 30–28 pts)
Portsmouth – 96–120 pts +portfolio (Prod Des Innov) (IB 25 pts)
Rose Bruford (Coll) – 96 pts +interview +portfolio (Ltg Des)
Solent – CCC 96–112 pts +interview +portfolio (Inter Des Decr; Prod Des) (IB 28 pts)
Teesside – 96–112 pts +interview +portfolio (Inter Des; Prod Des Crea Innov)
York St John – 96–112 pts +interview +portfolio (Inter Des; Prod Des)

88 pts   **Canterbury Christ Church** – 88–112 pts (Prod Des)

80 pts   **Bangor** – 80 pts +interview (Prod Des)
Bedfordshire – CCC–CCE 80–96 pts +portfolio (Inter Des)
South Wales – BCC–CDD 80–112 pts +interview +portfolio (Inter Des)

64 pts   **Liverpool (LIPA)** – CC 64 pts +interview +portfolio (Thea Perf Des; Thea Perf Tech)
London (Royal Central Sch SpDr) – 64–120 pts +interview+portfolio (Thea Prac (Prod Ltg)); 64–120 pts +interview +portfolio (Thea Prac (Prop Mak); Thea Prac (Scnc Art); Thea Prac (Scnc Constr); Thea Prac (Thea Ltg Des))
London Regent's – CC +interview +portfolio (Inter Des)
Ravensbourne Univ – CC +interview +portfolio (Inter Des Env Archit; Prod Des) (IB 28 pts)

40 pts and below, or other selection criteria (Foundation course, interview and portfolio inspection) (all Prod Ind Des) Arts London; Arts London (Chelsea CA); Arts London (Wimb CA); Bath Spa; Brighton; Heriot-Watt; Kingston; Solent

Alternative offers
See **Chapter 6** and **Appendix 1** for grades/UCAS Tariff points information for other examinations.

EXAMPLES OF COLLEGES OFFERING COURSES IN THIS SUBJECT FIELD
Accrington and Rossendale (Coll); Banbury and Bicester (Coll); Barking and Dagenham (Coll); Bradford College UC; Bury (Coll); Calderdale (Coll); Chichester (Coll); Doncaster (Coll); East Riding (Coll); Gloucestershire (Coll); Harrogate (Coll); Hartlepool (CFE); Havering (Coll); Hull (Coll); Manchester (Coll); Moulton (Coll); Newcastle (Coll); North Warwickshire and South Leicestershire (Coll); Sir Gâr (Coll); South Essex (Coll); Stockport (Coll); TEC Partnership; Truro and Penwith (Coll); West Suffolk (Coll).

CHOOSING YOUR COURSE (SEE ALSO CH.1)
Universities and colleges teaching quality See www.qaa.ac.uk; https://unistats.ac.uk.

Top research universities and colleges (REF 2014) See **Art and Design (General)**.

Examples of sandwich degree courses Aston; Bournemouth; Brighton; Brunel; Coventry; De Montfort; Huddersfield; Lincoln; London South Bank; Loughborough; Manchester Met; Middlesex; Nottingham Trent; Portsmouth; Queen's Belfast; Sheffield Hallam; Sussex; UWE Bristol; Wolverhampton.

ADMISSIONS INFORMATION

Number of applicants per place (approx) Arts London 2; Arts London (Chelsea CA) 2; Aston 6; Bath Spa 4; Birmingham City (Inter Des) 9; Cardiff Met 6; Central Lancashire 7; Creative Arts 4; De Montfort 5; Derby 4; Edinburgh Napier 5; Manchester Met 2; Northampton (Prod Des) 2; Nottingham Trent (Inter Archit Des) 7, (Prod Des) 5; Ravensbourne Univ (Inter Des) 4; Salford 6; Staffordshire 3; Teesside 3; Trinity Saint David 3.

Advice to applicants and planning the UCAS personal statement Your knowledge of design in all fields should be described, including any special interests you may have, for example in domestic, rail and road aspects of design, and visits to exhibitions, motor shows. **School/college reference**: Tutors should make it clear that the applicant's knowledge, experience and attitude match the chosen course – not simply higher education in general. Admissions tutors look for knowledge of interior design and interior architecture, experience in three-dimensional design projects (which include problem-solving and sculptural demands), model-making experience in diverse materials, experience with two-dimensional illustration and colour work, and computer skills. Knowledge of computer-aided design (CAD) and photography is also helpful. See also **Art and Design (Graphic Design)**.

Misconceptions about this course Birmingham City (Inter Des) Some applicants believe that it is an interior decorating course (carpets and curtains).

Selection interviews Yes Bournemouth, Brunel, Cardiff Met, Chester, Dundee, Huddersfield, Northumbria, Salford, Staffordshire, Sussex; **Some** UWE Bristol; **No** Falmouth, York St John.

Interview advice and questions Applicants' portfolios of artwork form an important talking-point throughout the interview. Applicants should be able to discuss examples of current design and new developments in the field and answer questions on the aspects of industrial design which interest them. See also **Art and Design (General)** and **Chapter 5**. **Creative Arts** No tests. Discuss any visits to modern buildings and new developments, eg British Museum Great Court or the Louvre Pyramid.

Reasons for rejection (non-academic) Mature students without formal qualifications may not be able to demonstrate the necessary mathematical or engineering skills. Poor quality and organisation of portfolio. Lack of interest. Inappropriate dress. Lack of enthusiasm. Insufficient portfolio work (eg exercises instead of projects). Lack of historical knowledge of interior design. Weak oral communication. See also **Art and Design (General)**. **Creative Arts** Not enough three-dimensional model-making. Poor sketching and drawing.

AFTER-RESULTS ADVICE

Offers to applicants repeating A-levels Same Birmingham City; Creative Arts; Nottingham Trent; Salford; Staffordshire.

GRADUATE DESTINATIONS AND EMPLOYMENT (2016/17 HESA)

Graduates surveyed See **Art and Design (General)**.

Career note See **Art and Design (General)**.

OTHER DEGREE SUBJECTS FOR CONSIDERATION

Architectural Studies; Architecture; Art Gallery Management; Design (Manufacturing Systems); History of Art; Manufacturing Engineering; Multimedia and Communication Design and subjects in other **Art and Design** tables.

ART AND DESIGN (3D DESIGN)

(including Ceramics, Design Crafts, Glass and Ceramics, Jewellery and Metalwork, Modelmaking and Silversmithing and Jewellery; see also Art and Design (General), Art and Design (interior, Product and Industrial Design))

This field covers a range of specialisations which are involved in the manufacture of products in metal, ceramics, glass and wood and also digital design. Some courses approach the study in a broad, comprehensive manner while other universities offer specialised courses in subjects such as Silversmithing and Jewellery (Glasgow School of Art and Sheffield Hallam), or Contemporary Jewellery and Fashion Accessories (Staffordshire University). The Birmingham City University course in Horology is the only course in the UK offering the study of time measurement and watches and clocks, both mechanical and electronic.

Useful websites www.ergonomics.org.uk; www.creativefuture.org.uk; www.glassassociation.org.uk; www.naj.co.uk; www.cpaceramics.com; http://ccskills.org.uk; www.dandad.org; www.designcouncil.org.uk

NB The points totals shown to the left of the institutions are for ease of reference only. It must not be assumed that Tariff points are always used by institutions or that they can be substituted for an offer in grades. The level of an offer is not necessarily indicative of the quality of a course.

COURSE OFFERS INFORMATION
Subject requirements/preferences See **Art and Design (General)**.

Your target offers and examples of degree courses

128 pts   **Dundee** – ABB incl art des +portfolio (Jewel Metal Des) (IB 34 pts HL 665)
Edinburgh – ABB (Sculp) (IB 34 pts HL 655); ABB +portfolio (Jewel Silver) (IB 34 pts HL 655)
Glasgow (SA) – ABB +interview +portfolio (Silver Jewel)

120 pts   **Bournemouth Arts** – BBB 120 pts +interview +portfolio (Modl) (IB 30 pts HL 555)
Northumbria – 120 pts +portfolio (3D Des)

112 pts   **Birmingham City** – BBC 112 pts +interview (Horol) (IB 28 pts HL 14 pts); BBC 112 pts +portfolio (Jewel Objs) (IB 28 pts HL 14 pts)
Creative Arts – 112 pts (Jewel Silver)
De Montfort – 112 pts incl art des +interview +portfolio (Des Crfts) (IB 26 pts)
Glyndŵr – BBC 112 pts +interview +portfolio (App Art; Vis Efcts)
Hertfordshire – BBC incl art +interview +portfolio (3D Comp Animat Modl)
Liverpool Hope – BBC 112 pts +interview +portfolio (Des) (IB 26 pts)
Nottingham Trent – BBC 112 pts +interview +portfolio (Decr Arts)
Sheffield Hallam – BBC 112 pts +interview +portfolio (Jewel Mtlwk)
Staffordshire – BBC (3D Des Mak) (IB 24 pts)
Sunderland – BBC 112 pts +interview +portfolio (Gls Ceram)

104 pts   **Bolton** – 104 pts +interview +portfolio (Spec FX Modl Flm TV)

96 pts   **Cardiff Met** – BBB–CCC 96–120 pts +interview +portfolio (Ceram) (IB 24 pts)
Plymouth – C art 96–120 pts +interview +portfolio (3D Des courses) (IB 30–28 pts)
Plymouth (CA) – 96–120 pts +interview +portfolio (3D Des Crfts) (IB 30–28 pts)

80 pts   **Hereford (CA)** – 80 pts +interview +portfolio (Arst Blksmthg; Jewel Des)

72 pts   **Robert Gordon** – BC incl art/des +interview +portfolio (3D Des) (IB 24 pts)

40 pts and below, or other selection criteria (Foundation course, interview and portfolio inspection) (all 3D Des) Arts London; Arts London (Camberwell CA); Bath Spa; Hertfordshire-Watt

Alternative offers
See **Chapter 6** and **Appendix 1** for grades/UCAS Tariff points information for other examinations.

EXAMPLES OF COLLEGES OFFERING COURSES IN THIS SUBJECT FIELD

Barking and Dagenham (Coll); Bedford (Coll); Bury (Coll); Gloucestershire (Coll); Havering (Coll); HOW (Coll); London UCK (Coll); Oldham (Coll); Sir Gâr (Coll); York (Coll).

CHOOSING YOUR COURSE (SEE ALSO CH.1)

Universities and colleges teaching quality See www.qaa.ac.uk; https://unistats.ac.uk.

Top research universities and colleges (REF 2014) See **Art and Design (General)**.

ADMISSIONS INFORMATION

Number of applicants per place (approx) Bath Spa 3; Birmingham City 4, (Jewel) 5; Creative Arts 4; De Montfort 3; Dundee 6; Manchester Met 5.

Advice to applicants and planning the UCAS personal statement Describe your art studies and your experience of different types of materials used. Discuss your special interest in your chosen field. Compare your work with that of professional artists and designers and describe your visits to museums, art galleries, exhibitions etc. Portfolios of recent work should demonstrate drawing skills, visual awareness, creativity and innovation, showing examples of three-dimensional work in photographic or model form. See also **Art and Design (Graphic Design)**.

Selection interviews Yes Anglia Ruskin;

Interview advice and questions Questions focus on the artwork presented in the student's portfolio. See also **Art and Design (General)** and **Chapter 5**.

Reasons for rejection (non-academic) Lack of pride in their work. No ideas. See also **Art and Design (General)**.

AFTER-RESULTS ADVICE

Offers to applicants repeating A-levels Same Brighton; Creative Arts; Dundee; Manchester Met.

GRADUATE DESTINATIONS AND EMPLOYMENT (2016/17 HESA)

Graduates surveyed See **Art and Design (General)**.

Career note See **Art and Design (General)**.

OTHER DEGREE SUBJECTS FOR CONSIDERATION

Design Technology; see other **Art and Design** tables.

ASTRONOMY AND ASTROPHYSICS

(including **Planetary Science with Astronomy and Space Science and Robotics**; see also Geology/Geological Sciences, Physics)

All Astronomy-related degrees are built on a core of mathematics and physics which, in the first two years, is augmented by an introduction to the theory and practice of astronomy or astrophysics. Astronomy emphasises observational aspects of the science and includes a study of the planetary system while Astrophysics tends to pursue the subject from a more theoretical standpoint. Some universities have onsite observatories (Central Lancashire and Lancaster). Courses often combine Mathematics or Physics with Astronomy.

Useful websites www.ras.org.uk; www.scicentral.com; www.iop.org; www.britastro.org

NB The points totals shown to the left of the institutions are for ease of reference only. It must not be assumed that Tariff points are always used by institutions or that they can be substituted for an offer in grades. The level of an offer is not necessarily indicative of the quality of a course.

COURSE OFFERS INFORMATION

Subject requirements/preferences GCSE English and a foreign language may be required by some universities; specified grades may be stipulated for some subjects. **AL** Mathematics and physics usually required.

Your target offers and examples of degree courses

160 pts **Cambridge** – A*A*A incl sci/maths +interview +NSAA (Nat Sci (Astro)) (IB 42–40 pts HL 776)

Durham – A*A*A incl maths+phys (Phys Astron (MPhys)) (IB 38 pts HL 776 incl maths+phys)

152 pts **Birmingham** – A*AA incl maths+phys (Phys Astro) (IB 32 pts HL 766 incl 7 maths/phys)

Bristol – A*AA incl maths+phys (Phys Astro) (IB 38 pts HL 76 maths+phys)

Exeter – A*AA incl maths+phys +interview (Phys Astro (MPhys)) (IB 38 pts HL 766 incl maths+phys)

Manchester – A*A*A–A*AA incl maths+phys +interview (Phys Astro) (IB 38–37 pts HL 776–766 incl maths+phys)

144 pts **Exeter** – AAA incl maths+sci (Nat Sci) (IB 36 pts HL 666 incl 6 maths+sci)

Lancaster – AAA incl maths+phys (Phys Ptcl Phys Cosmo (MPhys)) (IB 36 pts HL 16 pts incl maths+phys)

London (UCL) – AAA incl maths+phys (Astro) (IB 38 pts HL 18 incl 6 maths+phys)

Nottingham – A*AA–AAA incl maths+phys (Phys Astron; Phys Theor Astro) (IB 38 pts HL 666 incl maths+phys)

St Andrews – AAA incl maths+phys (Astro) (IB 38 pts HL 6 maths+phys)

Sussex – AAA incl maths+phys (Astro) (IB 36 pts HL 6 maths)

136 pts **Cardiff** – AAA–A*BB incl maths+phys +interview (Astro MPhys; Phys Astron (MPhys)) (IB 36–34 pts HL 665 incl 6 maths+phys)

Glasgow – AAB incl maths (Astron courses) (IB 36 pts); AAB incl maths+phys (Phys Astro) (IB 36–32 pts)

Lancaster – AAB incl maths+phys (Phys Astro Cosmo; Phys Ptcl Phys Cosmo) (IB 35 pts HL 16 incl 6 maths+phys)

Leeds – AAB incl maths+phys (Phys Astro) (IB 35 pts HL 15 pts incl 5 maths+phys)

London (QM) – AAB incl maths+phys (Astro (MSci)) (IB 34 pts HL 665 incl 6 maths+phys)

London (RH) – AAA–AAB incl maths+phys (Astro) (IB 32 pts HL 665 incl 6 maths+ 5 phys)

Manchester – AAB incl sci +interview (Earth Planet Sci) (IB 34 pts HL 655)

York – AAB incl maths+phys +interview (Phys Astro) (IB 35 pts HL 6 maths+phys)

128 pts **Cardiff** – AAB–ABB incl maths+phys +interview (Astro; Phys Astron) (IB 34–32 pts HL 665 incl 6 maths+phys)

Edinburgh – AAA–ABB incl maths+phys (Astro) (IB 37–32 pts HL 666–655)

Kingston – ABB incl maths+sci 128 pts incl maths+sci (Aerosp Eng Astnaut Spc Tech (MEng)) (IB 32 pts HL 5 maths+phys)

Leicester – ABB incl maths+phys (Phys Astro; Phys Spc Sci) (IB 30 pts HL 5 maths+phys)

Liverpool – ABB incl maths+phys (Phys Astron) (IB 33 pts HL 6 maths+phys)

Liverpool John Moores – ABB incl maths+phys 128 pts (Phys Astron)

London (QM) – ABB incl maths+phys (Astro) (IB 32 pts HL 655 incl maths+phys)

Queen's Belfast – ABB incl maths+phys (Phys Astro) (IB 33 pts HL 655 incl maths+phys)

Sheffield – ABB incl maths+phys (Phys Astro) (IB 33 pts HL 5 maths+phys)

Surrey – ABB incl maths+phys (Phys Astron; Phys Nucl Astro) (IB 32 pts HL 5 maths+phys)

Sussex – AAB–ABB incl maths (Phys Astro) (IB 34–32 pts HL 5 maths)

120 pts **Central Lancashire** – B phys/maths 120 pts incl maths+phys (Astro) (IB 30 pts HL 5 maths+phys)

Kent – BBB incl maths (Astron Spc Sci Astro) (IB 34 pts HL 14 incl 5 maths); (Phys Astro) (IB 34 pts HL 5 maths)

Swansea – AAB–BBB incl maths+phys (Phys Ptcl Phys Cosmo) (IB 34–32 pts HL 6 maths 6/5 phys)

112 pts **Aberystwyth** – BBB–BBC incl phys+maths 112–120 pts (Spc Sci Robot) (IB 30–28 pts HL 5 maths+phys)

Hertfordshire – C maths+phys 112 pts incl maths+phys (Astro) (HL 555 incl maths+phys)

Hull – B phys+maths 112 pts (Phys Astro) (IB 28 pts HL 6 maths+phys)

Keele – BBC incl maths+phys (Astro Comb Hons) (IB 30 pts HL 5 maths+5/4 phys)

Kingston – BBC incl maths+sci 112 pts (Aerosp Eng Astnaut Spc Tech) (IB 30 pts HL 5 maths+phys)

Nottingham Trent – B phys+maths 112 pts incl maths+phys (Phys Astro)

96 pts **London (Birk)** – BBB–CCC 96–120 pts+interview (Planet Sci Astron)

Alternative offers
See **Chapter 6** and **Appendix 1** for grades/UCAS Tariff points information for other examinations.

CHOOSING YOUR COURSE (SEE ALSO CH.1)
Universities and colleges teaching quality See www.qaa.ac.uk; https://unistats.ac.uk.

Top research universities and colleges (REF 2014) See **Physics**.

Examples of sandwich degree courses Cardiff; Hertfordshire; Surrey.

ADMISSIONS INFORMATION
Number of applicants per place (approx) Cardiff 6; Durham 5; Hertfordshire 5; London (QM) 6; London (RH) 5; London (UCL) 7; Southampton 6.

Advice to applicants and planning the UCAS personal statement Books and magazines on astronomy and astrophysics are an obvious source of information. Describe your interests and why you have chosen this subject. Visits to observatories would also be important. (See also **Appendix 3**.)

Selection interviews Yes Cambridge; **No** Cardiff, London (QM), London (UCL).

Interview advice and questions You will probably be questioned on your study of physics and the aspects of the subject you most enjoy. Questions in the past have included: Can you name a recent development in physics which will be important in the future? Describe a physics experiment, indicating any errors and exactly what it was intended to prove. Explain weightlessness. What is a black hole? What are the latest discoveries in space? See also **Chapter 5**.

AFTER-RESULTS ADVICE
Offers to applicants repeating A-levels Higher St Andrews; **Same** Cardiff; Durham; London (UCL); **No** Cambridge.

GRADUATE DESTINATIONS AND EMPLOYMENT (2016/17 HESA)
Graduates surveyed 280 **Employed** 95 **In voluntary employment** 5 **In further study** 95 **Assumed unemployed** 25

Career note The number of posts for professional astronomers is limited although some technological posts are occasionally offered in observatories. However, degree courses include extensive mathematics and physics so many graduates can look towards related fields including telecommunications and electronics.

OTHER DEGREE SUBJECTS FOR CONSIDERATION
Aeronautical/Aerospace Engineering; Computer Science; Earth Sciences; Geology; Geophysics; Mathematics; Meteorology; Mineral Sciences; Oceanography; Physics.

BIOCHEMISTRY

(see also Biological Sciences, Chemistry, Food Science/Studies and Technology, Pharmacy and Pharmaceutical Sciences)

Biochemistry is the study of life at molecular level – how genes and proteins regulate cells, tissues and ultimately whole organisms – you! It's a subject which provides the key to understanding how diseases arise and how they can be treated, it is the core of many areas of biology and it is responsible for a large number of breakthroughs in medicine and biotechnology. At Newcastle, Year 1 of the course consists of modules in cell biology, biochemistry, microbiology and immunology, genetics, pharmacology and physiology with transfers between degrees possible at the end of the year. This is a pattern reflected in many other university courses. Many courses also allow for a placement in industry in the UK or in Europe or North America.

Useful websites www.biochemistry.org; www.bioworld.com; www.annualreviews.org; www.ibms.org; www.acb.org.uk; see also **Biological Sciences** and **Biology**.

NB The points totals shown to the left of the institutions are for ease of reference only. It must not be assumed that Tariff points are always used by institutions or that they can be substituted for an offer in grades. The level of an offer is not necessarily indicative of the quality of a course.

COURSE OFFERS INFORMATION

Subject requirements/preferences GCSE English, mathematics and science usually required; leading universities often stipulate A–B grades (7–5/6). **AL** Chemistry required and biology usually preferred by most universities; one or two mathematics/science subjects usually required.

Your target offers and examples of degree courses

160 pts **Cambridge** – A*A*A incl sci/maths +interview +NSAA (Nat Sci (Bioch)) (IB 42–40 pts HL 776)

152 pts **Oxford** – A*AA incl maths/sci +interview (Bioch (Mol Cell)) (IB 39 pts HL 766 incl 7 chem)

144 pts **Bristol** – A*AB–AAA incl chem+sci/maths (Bioch; Bioch Med Bioch) (IB 36–32 pts HL 18 pts incl 6 chem+ 5 sci/maths)

　　　　 Imperial London – AAA incl chem+sci/maths (Bioch; Bioch (Yr Ind/Rsch)) (IB 38 pts HL 6 chem+biol/maths); (Bioch courses) (IB 38 pts HL 6 chem+sci/maths)

　　　　 London (UCL) – AAA incl chem¦sci+maths (Bioch) (IB 38 pts HL 18 pts incl 5 chem+sci+maths)

136 pts **Bath** – AAB incl chem+biol (Bioch) (IB 36 pts HL 665 incl 6 chem+biol)

　　　　 Birmingham – AAB incl chem+sci (Bioch; Bioch (Genet); Med Bioch) (IB 32 pts HL 665)

　　　　 Glasgow – AAB incl biol/chem (Bioch) (IB 36 pts HL 665 incl biol/chem+sci)

　　　　 Lancaster – AAB incl chem+sci (Bioch) (IB 35 pts HL 16 pts incl 6 chem+sci/maths)

　　　　 Leeds – AAA–AAB incl chem+sci (Bioch) (IB 35–34 pts HL 18–17 pts incl 6 chem+sci); AAA–AAB incl chem+sci +interview (Med Bioch) (IB 35–34 pts HL 18–17 pts incl 6 chem+sci)

　　　　 London (King's) – AAB incl chem+biol (Bioch) (IB 35 pts HL 665 incl chem+biol)

　　　　 Loughborough – AAB incl chem+sci (Bioch) (IB 35 pts HL 665 incl chem+sci)

　　　　 Newcastle – AAA–AAB incl biol/chem+maths/sci (Bioch) (IB 35–34 pts HL 5 biol/chem+sci)

　　　　 Nottingham – AAB incl chem+sci (Bioch Biol Chem) (IB 34 pts HL 5 chem+sci); (Bioch; Bioch Genet; Bioch Mol Med) (IB 34 pts HL 5/6 chem+sci)

　　　　 Sheffield – AAB incl chem+sci (Med Bioch) (IB 34 pts HL 6 chem+sci); (Bioch; Bioch Comb Hons) (IB 34 pts HL 65 chem+sci)

　　　　 Southampton – AAB incl chem+sci (Bioch) (IB 34 pts HL 17 pts incl 6 chem+sci)

　　　　 St Andrews – AAB incl biol+chem (Bioch) (IB 36 pts HL 665 incl 6 chem+biol)

　　　　 York – A*AA–AAB incl chem+sci/maths+interview (Chem Biol Medcnl Chem) (IB 37–35 pts HL 6 chem+sci/maths); AAB incl chem+sci/maths (Bioch) (IB 35 pts HL 6 chem+sci)

128 pts **Bristol** – A*AB–AAC incl chem+sci/maths (Bioch Mol Biol Biotech) (IB 36–32 pts HL 18 pts incl 6 chem+sci/maths)

　　　　 Cardiff – AAB–ABB incl biol+chem (Bioch) (IB 34–32 pts HL 655 incl 6 biol+chem)

　　　　 Dundee – AAB–ABB incl biol+chem (Bioch) (IB 30 pts HL 555 incl biol+chem)

　　　　 Edinburgh – AAA–ABB incl biol+chem (Biol Sci Bioch) (IB 37–32 pts HL 666–555)

　　　　 Exeter – AAB–ABB incl biol+chem (Bioch) (IB 34–32 pts HL 665–655 incl 5 biol+chem)

　　　　 Keele – ABB incl sci (Bioch) (IB 34 pts HL 6 chem/sci)

　　　　 Leicester – ABB incl sci (Biol Sci (Bioch); Med Bioch) (IB 30 pts HL 65 sci)

　　　　 Liverpool – ABB incl biol+chem (Bioch) (IB 33 pts HL 6/5 biol/chem)

　　　　 London (QM) – ABB incl chem (Bioch) (IB 34 pts HL 655 incl chem)

Manchester – AAA–ABB incl sci/maths +interview (Bioch; Bioch (Yr Ind); Med Bioch) (IB 36–33 pts HL 666–655 incl chem+sci)

Sussex – AAB–ABB incl biol+chem (Bioch) (IB 34–32 pts HL 5 biol+chem)

Warwick – AAB–ABB incl biol+chem (Bioch) (IB 36–34 pts HL 5 biol+chem)

120 pts **Aberdeen** – BBB incl maths/sci (Bioch courses) (IB 32 pts HL 5 maths/sci)

Aston – ABB–BBB incl biol+chem (Bioch (Yr Ind)) (IB 32–31 pts HL 555 incl biol+chem)

Brunel – BBB incl sci (Biomed Sci (Bioch)) (IB 30 pts HL 5 sci)

East Anglia – BBB incl chem (Bioch; Bioch (Yr Ind)) (IB 31 pts HL 5 chem)

Keele – ABC/BBB incl chem+sci (Bioch Comb Hons) (IB 32 pts HL 6 sci/maths)

Lincoln – BBB incl biol/chem (Bioch) (IB 30 pts HL 5 biol/chem)

London (RH) – ABB–BBB incl biol+sci (Bioch; Med Bioch; Mol Biol) (IB 32 pts HL 555 incl biol+sci)

Nottingham Trent – BBB incl biol 120 pts (Bioch)

Queen's Belfast – ABB–BBB incl chem+sci/maths (Bioch) (IB 33–32 pts HL 655 incl sci/maths)

Reading – BBB incl biol+chem (Bioch) (IB 30 pts HL 5 biol+chem)

Strathclyde – ABB–BBB incl sci (Bioch courses) (IB 34 pts HL 55 sci)

Surrey – ABB–BBB incl biol/chem+sci (Bioch) (IB 32 pts HL 5 biol/chem)

Swansea – AAB–BBB incl biol+chem 120–136 pts (Bioch; Bioch Genet) (IB 33–32 pts)

112 pts **East London** – BBC incl biol/chem 112 pts (Bioch) (IB 25 pts HL 15 pts incl biol+chem)

Heriot-Watt – BBC incl chem+maths (Chem Bioch) (IB 30 pts HL 5 chem+maths)

Hertfordshire – BBC incl chem+sci 112 pts (Bioch; Bioch (St Abrd))

Huddersfield – BBC incl chem+sci 112 pts (Bioch; Med Bioch)

Kent – BBC incl chem+biol (Bioch) (IB 34 pts HL 15 pts incl 5 chem+biol)

Kingston – BBC incl chem+biol 112 pts (Bioch) (IB 27 pts HL 5 biol/chem+sci)

Portsmouth – 112 pts incl biol+chem (Bioch) (IB 27 pts HL 6 biol/chem)

104 pts **Aberystwyth** – BBB–BCC incl chem 104–120 pts (Bioch; Genet Bioch) (IB 30–28 pts HL 5 chem)

Chester – BBC–BCC incl chem 104–112 pts (Bioch) (IB 26 pts HL 5 chem)

Essex – BCC incl chem+sci/maths +interview (Bioch) (IB 28 pts HL 5 chem+sci/maths)

Liverpool John Moores – BCC incl biol/chem 104 pts (Bioch) (IB 26 pts)

Salford – 104–120 pts incl biol+chem (Bioch) (IB 30 pts HL 4 biol+chem)

Sheffield Hallam – 104 pts incl biol+chem (Bioch)

96 pts **Westminster** – BBB–CCC incl sci 96–120 pts (Bioch) (IB 27 pts HL 4 sci)

Worcester – 96–104 pts incl biol+chem (Bioch)

88 pts **London Met** – CCD 88 pts (Bioch) (IB 28 pts HL 15 pts)

Reading – BBB–CCD (Bioch Fdn) (IB 30–24 pts)

80 pts **Wolverhampton** – CDD incl biol/chem (Bioch)

Alternative offers

See **Chapter 6** and **Appendix 1** for grades/UCAS Tariff points information for other examinations.

CHOOSING YOUR COURSE (SEE ALSO CH.1)

Universities and colleges teaching quality See www.qaa.ac.uk; https://unistats.ac.uk.

Top research universities and colleges (REF 2014) See **Biological Sciences**.

Examples of sandwich degree courses Aston; Bath; Bristol; Brunel; Cardiff; East London; Essex; Hertfordshire; Huddersfield; Imperial London; Kent; Kingston; Leeds; Lincoln; Liverpool John Moores; Manchester; Nottingham Trent; Queen's Belfast; Reading; Sheffield Hallam; Sussex; York.

ADMISSIONS INFORMATION

Number of applicants per place (approx) Bath 10; Birmingham 5; Bradford 7; Bristol 7; Cardiff 6; Dundee 8; East Anglia 5; East London 5; Edinburgh 8; Essex 5; Imperial London 6; Keele 7; Leeds 10; Leicester (Med Bioch) 5; London (RH) 5; London (UCL) 8; Nottingham 10; Salford 4; Southampton 8; Strathclyde 7; Warwick 6; York 6.

Advice to applicants and planning the UCAS personal statement It is important to show by reading scientific journals that you have interests in chemistry and biology beyond the exam syllabus. Focus on one or two aspects of biochemistry that interest you. Attend scientific lectures (often arranged by universities on Open Days), find some work experience if possible, and use these to show your understanding of what biochemistry is. Give evidence of your communication skills and time management. (See **Appendix 3**.) **Bristol** Deferred entry accepted. **Oxford** No written or work tests; successful entrants 19%. Further information may be obtained from the Royal Society of Biology and the Royal Society of Chemistry.

Misconceptions about this course York Students feel that being taught by two departments could be a problem but actually it increases their options.

Selection interviews Yes Cambridge, Kent, Manchester, Oxford (75% (success rate 19%)), Sheffield; **Some** Aberystwyth (mature students only), Bath, Warwick; **No** Birmingham, Cardiff, Dundee, East Anglia, East London, Essex, Keele, Kingston, Leeds, Liverpool John Moores, London (RH), London (UCL), Salford, Surrey, Wolverhampton.

Interview advice and questions Questions will be asked on your study of chemistry and biology and any special interests. They will also probe your understanding of what a course in Biochemistry involves and the special features offered by the university. In the past questions have been asked covering Mendel, genetics, RNA and DNA. See also **Chapter 5**.

Reasons for rejection (non-academic) Borderline grades plus poor motivation. Failure to turn up for interviews or answer correspondence. Inability to discuss subject. Not compatible with A-level predictions or references. **Birmingham** Lack of total commitment to Biochemistry, for example intention to transfer to Medicine without completing the course.

AFTER-RESULTS ADVICE
Offers to applicants repeating A-levels Higher Leeds; Leicester; St Andrews; Strathclyde; Warwick; **Possibly higher** Bath; Bristol; Keele; Lancaster; **Same** Aberystwyth; Birmingham; Brunel; Cardiff; Dundee; East Anglia; Heriot-Watt; Liverpool; Liverpool John Moores; London (RH); London (UCL); Nottingham; Salford; Sheffield; Wolverhampton; York; **No** Cambridge.

GRADUATE DESTINATIONS AND EMPLOYMENT (2016/17 HESA)
Biochemistry, Biophysics and Molecular Biology graduates surveyed 2,175 **Employed** 830 **In voluntary employment** 45 **In further study** 920 **Assumed unemployed** 130

Career note Biochemistry courses involve several specialities which offer a range of job opportunities. These include the application of biochemistry in industrial, medical and clinical areas with additional openings in pharmaceuticals and agricultural work, environmental science and in toxicology.

OTHER DEGREE SUBJECTS FOR CONSIDERATION
Agricultural Sciences; Agriculture; Biological Sciences; Biology; Biotechnology; Botany; Brewing; Chemistry; Food Science; Genetics; Medical Sciences; Medicine; Microbiology; Neuroscience; Nursing; Nutrition; Pharmaceutical Sciences; Pharmacology; Pharmacy; Plant Science.

BIOLOGICAL SCIENCES

(including **Biomedical Materials Science, Biomedical Science, Brewing and Distilling, Forensic Science, Immunology, Medical Science and Virology and Immunology**; see also **Animal Sciences, Biochemistry, Biology, Biotechnology, Environmental Sciences, Genetics, Marine/Maritime Studies, Medicine, Microbiology, Natural Sciences, Neuroscience, Nursing And Midwifery, Pharmacology, Plant Sciences, Psychology, Zoology**)

Biological Science (in some universities referred to as Biosciences) is a fast-moving, rapidly expanding and wide subject area, ranging from, for example, conservation biology to molecular genetics. Boundaries between separate subjects are blurring and this is reflected in the content and variety of the courses offered. Many universities offer a common first year allowing final decisions to be made later in the course. Since most subjects are research-based, students undertake their own projects in the final year. It should be noted that some Medical Science courses provide a foundation for graduate entry to medical schools. Check with universities.

Useful websites www.ibms.org; www.scicentral.com; www.bbsrc.ac.uk; www.csofs.org; www. immunology.org; see also Biochemistry and **Biology**.

NB The points totals shown to the left of the institutions are for ease of reference only. It must not be assumed that Tariff points are always used by institutions or that they can be substituted for an offer in grades. The level of an offer is not necessarily indicative of the quality of a course.

COURSE OFFERS INFORMATION

Subject requirements/preferences GCSE English, mathematics and science usually required. **AL** Chemistry usually required plus one or two other mathematics/science subjects, biology preferred. (Ecol) Biology and one other science subject may be required or preferred. (Neuro) Mathematics/ science subjects with chemistry and/or biology required or preferred.

Your target offers and examples of degree courses

160 pts **Cambridge** – A*A*A incl sci/maths +interview +NSAA (Nat Sci (Biol Biomed Sci)) (IB 42–40 pts HL 776)

152 pts **Bath** – A*AA incl maths/sci (Nat Sci) (IB 36 pts HL 766 incl maths/sci)
Nottingham – A*AA incl sci/maths (Nat Sci) (IB 38 pts HL 6/7 sci/maths)
Oxford – A*AA incl sci/maths +interview (Biol) (IB 39 pts HL 7 sci/maths); A*AA incl sci/ maths +interview +BMAT (Biomed Sci) (IB 39 pts HL 766)

144 pts **Bath** – AAA/A*AB–AAB +aEPQ incl biol+chem (Biomed Sci) (IB 36 pts HL 765–666 incl 6 biol+chem)
Durham – AAA incl biol/chem+sci (Biol Sci) (IB 37 pts HL 666 incl 6 biol)
Imperial London – AAA incl biol+sci/maths (Biol Sci; Med Biosci) (IB 38 pts HL 6 biol+sci/ maths); AAA incl sci/maths (Biol Sci Span Sci) (IB 38 pts HL 66 incl biol+chem/maths/ phys)
London (UCL) – AAA incl biol+chem (Bioproc N Med (Sci Eng)) (IB 38 pts HL 18 pts incl biol+chem); AAA incl biol+chem+maths (Biomed Sci) (IB 38 pts HL 18 pts incl 5 biol+chem+maths); AAA incl biol+sci/maths (Biol Sci) (IB 38 pts HL 18 pts incl 6 biol 5 sci/maths); AAA incl sci (Bioproc N Med (Bus Mgt)) (IB 38 pts HL 18 pts incl sci)

136 pts **Birmingham** – AAB/ABB+aEPQ incl biol/chem+sci (Biomed Mat Sci) (IB 32 pts HL 665 incl chem+biol); AAB incl biol+sci (Biol Sci; Biol Sci (Genet)) (IB 32 pts HL 665)
Bristol – AAB incl biol+sci (Palae Evol) (IB 34–32 pts HL 17–16 pts incl 65 sci/maths); AAB incl chem+sci/maths (Virol Immun) (IB 34–31 pts HL 15 pts incl 5 chem+sci/maths); (Canc Biol Immun) (IB 34–31 pts HL 17 pts incl 5 chem+sci/maths); (Cell Mol Med) (IB 34–31 pts HL 6–5 chem+sci/maths)
Glasgow – AAB incl biol/chem (Immun) (IB 36 pts HL 665 incl biol/chem+sci)
Lancaster – AAB incl biol+sci/maths (Biomed Sci) (IB 35 pts HL 16 pts incl 6 sci)
Leeds – AAA–AAB incl biol+sci (Biol Sci) (IB 35–34 pts HL 18–17 pts incl 6 biol+sci); AAA–AAB incl biol/chem+sci (Biol Sci (Biotech Ent); Med Sci) (IB 35–34 pts HL 18–17 pts incl 6 biol/ chem+sci)
London (King's) – AAB incl chem+biol (Biomed Sci) (IB 35 pts HL 665 incl chem+biol)
London (QM) – AAB incl biol+sci (Biomed Sci) (IB 35 pts HL 665 biol+sci/maths)
London (UCL) – AAB incl biol+chem (App Med Sci) (IB 36 pts HL 17 pts incl biol+chem)
Newcastle – AAA–AAB incl biol (Psy Biol) (IB 35 pts HL 6 biol); AAA–AAB incl biol/ chem+maths/sci (Biomed Genet; Biomed Sci; Med Sci (Defer)) (IB 35–34 pts HL 5 biol/ chem+maths/sci)
Sheffield – AAA–AAB incl sci/maths +interview (Ecol Cons Biol) (IB 36 pts HL 6 sci); AAB incl chem+sci (Med Bioch) (IB 34 pts HL 6 chem+sci); AAB–ABB+ bEPQ incl sci (Biomed Sci) (IB 34 pts HL 65 sci/maths)

Southampton – AAB incl biol/chem+sci (Biomed Sci) (IB 34 pts HL 17 pts incl 56 chem/biol+sci)

York – AAB incl biol+chem (Biomed Sci) (IB 35 pts HL 6 biol+chem)

128 pts **Aberdeen** – ABB incl chem/biol+maths/sci (Biomed Sci courses) (IB 34 pts HL 6 chem/biol+maths/sci)

Cardiff – AAB–ABB incl biol+chem (Biomed Sci (Anat)) (IB 34–32 pts HL 6 biol+chem); AAB–ABB incl biol/chem (Biol Sci (Zool)) (IB 34-32 pts HL 655 incl 6 biol/chem); (Biomed Sci; Biomed Sci (Physiol); Neuro) (IB 34–32 pts HL 655 incl 6 biol/chem)

Dundee – AAB–ABB incl biol+chem (Biol Sci) (IB 30 pts HL 555 incl biol+chem)

East Anglia – ABB incl biol (Biol Sci (Yr Abrd)) (IB 32 pts HL 5 biol); ABB incl biol+maths/sci (Biomed) (IB 32 pts HL 5 biol+sci/maths)

Edinburgh – AAA–ABB incl biol+chem (Biol Sci; Biol Sci (Immun); Biol Sci (Zool)) (IB 37–32 pts HL 666–555 incl biol+chem); AAB–ABB incl biol+chem (Infec Dis) (IB 36–32 pts HL 6 biol+chem); ABB incl biol+chem (Med Sci) (IB 36–32 pts HL 56 biol+chem)

Exeter – AAB–ABB incl biol+sci (Biol Sci; Hum Biosci) (IB 34–32 pts HL 665–655 incl 5 biol+sci); ABB incl biol+sci (Med Sci) (IB 32 pts HL 655 incl 6 biol/sci)

Leicester – ABB incl sci/maths (Biol Sci; Biol Sci (Genet)) (IB 30 pts HL 56 sci/maths)

Liverpool – ABB/BBB+aEPQ incl biol+chem (Biol Med Sci) (IB 33 pts HL 6/5 biol/chem); ABB/BBB +aEPQ incl biol+sci (Biol Sci) (IB 33 pts HL 65 incl 6 biol)

London (St George's) – ABB incl biol+chem (Biomed Sci) (IB 34 pts HL 16 pts incl 6/5 biol+chem)

Manchester – AAA–ABB (Zool Modn Lang) (IB 36–33 pts HL 6–5 sci); AAA–ABB incl sci/maths+interview (Biomed Sci; Biomed Sci (Yr Ind)) (IB 36–33 pts HL 666–655 incl chem+sci)

Queen's Belfast – AAB–ABB incl biol/chem+sci (Biomed Sci) (IB 34–33 pts HL 6 biol/chem)

Reading – ABB incl biol+sci (Med Sci) (IB 32 pts HL 5 biol+sci)

Sussex – AAB–ABB incl biol+sci/maths (Biomed Sci) (IB 34–32 pts HL 5 biol+sci/maths)

Warwick – AAB–ABB incl biol (Biomed Sci) (IB 36–34 pts HL 5 biol); AAB–ABB incl biol+sci (Biol Sci) (IB 36–34 pts HL 5 biol+sci/maths)

120 pts **Aberdeen** – BBB incl maths/sci (Immun) (IB 32 pts HL 5 maths/sci); BBB incl sci/maths (Biol Sci) (IB 32 pts HL 5 sci/maths)

Aston – ABB–BBB incl biol (Biomed Sci) (IB 32-31 pts HL 555 incl biol); (Biol Sci) (IB 32-31 pts HL 655–555 incl biol)

Bradford – BBB incl biol+chem 120 pts (Clin Sci) (HL 665 incl 6 chem+biol); (Biomed Sci) (HL 665 incl 6 chem/biol)

Brunel – BBB incl maths/sci (Lf Sci) (IB 30 pts HL 5 sci); BBB incl sci (Biomed Sci; Biomed Sci (Genet)) (IB 30 pts HL 5 sci)

Central Lancashire – BBB (Med Sci)

Coventry – BBB incl biol (Biomed Sci) (IB 32 pts HL 5 biol)

De Montfort – 120 pts incl biol/chem (Med Sci) (IB 28 pts HL 6 chem/biol); (Biomed Sci) (IB 30 pts HL 6 biol/chem)

Derby – BBB incl biol/chem 120 pts incl biol/chem (Foren Sci); BBB incl biol 120 pts incl biol/chem (Foren Sci Psy)

East Anglia – BBB/ABC incl biol (Biol Sci; Biol Sci (Yr Ind)) (IB 31 pts HL 5 biol)

Keele – ABC–BBB incl chem/biol (Foren Sci) (IB 32 pts HL 6 chem/biol)

Kent – BBB incl chem/biol (Foren Sci) (IB 34 pts HL 14 pts incl 5 chem/biol)

Leicester – ABB–BBB incl chem (Chem Foren Sci) (IB 30–28 pts HL 5 chem)

Lincoln – BBB incl biol/chem (Biomed Sci) (IB 30 pts HL 5 biol/chem)

London (RH) – ABB–BBB incl biol+sci (Biomed Sci; Mol Biol) (IB 32 pts HL 555 incl biol+sci)

Newcastle – ABB–BBB incl biol (App Plnt Sci) (IB 32 pts HL 6 biol)

Northumbria – 120 pts incl biol (Biomed Sci); 120 pts incl chem/biol/app sci (Foren Sci)

Nottingham Trent – BBB incl biol 120 pts (Biomed Sci); BBB incl chem+sci 120 pts (Foren Sci)

Queen's Belfast – ABB–BBB incl biol/sci (Biol Sci) (IB 33–32 pts HL 655 incl biol)

Reading – BBB incl biol+sci (Biol Sci; Biol Sci (Yr Ind); Biomed Sci) (IB 30 pts HL 5 biol+sci)

Roehampton – 120 pts incl biol/chem (Biomed Sci)
South Wales – BBB incl biol (Med Sci) (IB 32 pts HL 5 biol)
Strathclyde – ABB–BBB incl biol/chem (Biomed Sci; Immun) (IB 34 pts HL 5 sci)
Surrey – ABB–BBB incl biol/chem+sci/maths (Biomed Sci) (IB 32 pts HL 5 biol/chem)
Swansea – ABB–BBB incl biol (Biol Sci Defer) (IB 33–32 pts HL 5 biol)
UWE Bristol – 120 pts incl biol/chem (Foren Sci) (HL 6 biol/chem); 120 pts incl biol/chem+sci (Biomed Sci) (HL 6 biol/chem 5 sci)
Ulster – BBB incl sci (Biomed Sci; Strf Med) (IB 26 pts HL 13 pts)

112 pts **Anglia Ruskin** – 112 pts incl biol/chem (Foren Sci) (IB 26 pts HL biol/chem)
Bangor – 112 pts incl biol (Biomed Sci); 112 pts incl biol+sci/maths (Med Sci)
Bedfordshire – BBB–BBC incl sci 112–120 pts incl sci (Biomed Sci)
Bradford – BBC incl chem/biol 112 pts (Foren Med Sci) (HL 655 incl 6 chem/biol); BBC incl chem 112 pts (Foren Sci) (HL 655 incl 6 chem)
Cardiff Met – BBC incl biol+sci 112 pts incl biol+sci (Biomed Sci) (IB 25 pts)
Coventry – BBC incl biol (Biol Foren Sci; Med Pharmacol Sci) (IB 30 pts HL 5 biol)
De Montfort – 112 pts incl sci (Foren Sci) (IB 26 pts HL 6 sci)
East London – BBC incl biol/chem 112 pts incl biol/chem (Biomed Sci) (IB 25 pts HL 15 pts incl biol+chem)
Glasgow Caledonian – BBC (Biol Sci); BBC incl chem (Biomed Sci) (IB 28 pts HL 5 chem)
Glyndŵr – BBC 112 pts incl sci (Foren Sci)
Heriot-Watt – BBC incl chem/biol/maths (Brew Distil) (IB 27 pts HL 5 sci); BBC incl sci (Biol Sci) (IB 27 pts HL 5 sci)
Huddersfield – BBC incl chem+sci 112 pts (Med Bioch); BBC incl chem 112 pts (Foren Analyt Sci) (HL 5 chem); BBC incl sci 112 pts (Biomed Sci)
Hull – C biol/app sci 112 pts incl biol/app sci (Biomed Sci) (IB 28 pts HL 5 biol)
Kent – BBC incl biol (Biomed Sci) (IB 34 pts HL 15 incl 5 biol)
Kingston – BBC incl biol+sci 112 pts incl sci (Biomed Sci) (IB 26 pts HL 5 biol); BBC incl biol/chem 112 pts (Foren Sci) (IB 27 pts HL 5 biol/chem)
Leeds Beckett – 112 pts incl sci (Biomed Sci) (IB 25 pts HL 6 biol)
Lincoln – BBC incl biol/chem/app sci (Foren Sci) (IB 29 pts HL 4 biol/chem)
Liverpool John Moores – BBC incl biol/chem 112 pts (Foren Sci) (IB 26 pts); BBC incl chem/biol 112 pts incl sci (Biomed Sci) (IB 26 pts); BBC incl sci/soc sci 112 pts (Foren Anth) (IB 26 pts)
London Met – BBC incl biol+chem 112 pts (Biomed Sci) (IB 28 pts HL 15 pts incl biol+chem)
Middlesex – 112 pts (Biomed Sci)
Plymouth – 112–128 pts incl biol+sci (Biomed Sci) (IB 27 pts HL 5 biol+sci); (Biol Sci) (IB 30 pts HL 5 biol+sci)
Roehampton – 112 pts incl biol/chem (Biol Sci)
Sheffield Hallam – 112 pts incl biol (Biomed Sci)
Staffordshire – BBC 112 pts (Biol Sci; Biomed Sci) (IB 24 pts); BBC incl biol/chem 112 pts (Foren Sci) (IB 24 pts)
Suffolk – BBC incl biol +interview (Biosci)
Sunderland – BBC 112 pts (Biomed Sci; Cos Sci)
West London – BBC incl sci 112–120 pts (Biomed Sci)

104 pts **Bournemouth** – 104–120 pts (Arch Anth Foren Sci) (IB 2831-3128 pts); (Biol Sci; Foren Sci; Med Sci) (IB 31–28 pts HL 55)
Central Lancashire – 104–112 pts incl biol/chem/app sci (Foren Sci)
Chester – BBC–BCC incl biol/chem/app sci 104–112 pts (Biomed Sci) (IB 26 pts HL 5 biol); BBC–BCC incl biol/chem/env sci/app sci 104–112 pts (Foren Biol) (IB 26 pts HL 5 biol/chem); BBC–BCC incl sci 104–112 pts (Immun) (IB 26 pts HL 5 biol/chem)
Cumbria – BBB–BBD 104–120 pts incl sci (Foren Sci)
De Montfort – 104 pts incl chem+sci (Pharml Cos Sci) (IB 24 pts HL 6 chem+sci)
Dundee – BBB–BCC incl biol (Foren Anth) (IB 30 pts HL 555)
Edinburgh Napier – BCC incl sci (Biomed Sci) (IB 28 pts HL 5 sci); (Biol Sci) (IB 28 pts HL 654 incl 5 sci)

Essex – BCC incl biol +interview (Biol Sci) (IB 28 pts HL 5 biol); BCC incl chem/biol+sci/maths +interview (Biomed Sci) (IB 28 pts HL 5 chem/biol+sci/maths)

Greenwich – 104 pts (Biomed Sci); BCC 104 pts incl biol+chem +interview (App Biomed Sci); BCC incl chem 104 pts+interview (Foren Sci; Foren Sci Crimin)

Hertfordshire – BCC incl sci 104 pts (Biol Sci; Biol Sci (St Abrd); Biomed Sci)

Manchester Met – BBC–BCC incl biol/app sci 104–112 pts (Biomed Sci) (IB 26 pts HL 5 biol)

Northampton – BCC 104–112 pts (Hum Biosci) (IB 25 pts)

Nottingham Trent – BCC incl biol 104 pts (Biol Sci)

Oxford Brookes – 104 pts incl sci (Biol Sci Genet Gnm; Biol Sci Hum Biosci; Biomed Sci; Med Sci) (IB 29 pts); (Biol Sci) (IB 29 pts HL 4 sci)

Portsmouth – ABB–BCC incl biol+sci/maths (Biomed Sci) (IB 30–28 pts HL 655–654)

Robert Gordon – BCC incl biol+sci (App Biomed Sci) (IB 28 pts HL 5 biol+sci); BCC incl chem+sci/maths (Foren Analyt Sci) (IB 26 pts HL 5 chem+sci/maths)

West London – BBB–BCC 104–120 pts (Foren Sci)

96 pts **Abertay** – CCC incl biol (Biomed Sci) (IB 28 pts HL 4 biol); CCC incl sci (Foren Sci) (IB 28 pts HL 4 sci)

Brighton – BBC–CCC incl biol+chem 96–112 pts (Biomed Sci) (IB 26 pts HL 4 biol+sci); BCC–CCC incl biol 96–104 pts (Biol Sci) (IB 26 pts HL 4 biol+sci)

Glasgow Caledonian – CCC incl chem (Foren Invstg) (IB 24 pts)

Kingston – CCC incl biol 96 pts (Biol Sci) (IB 27 pts HL 5 biol)

London (Birk) – BBB–CCC 96–120 pts (Biomed)

London Met – CCC incl biol+chem 96 pts (Biol Sci; Med Biosci) (IB 28 pts HL 15 pts incl biol+chem)

Salford – 96–112 pts incl biol (Hum Biol Infec Dis) (IB 29 pts HL 4 biol)

Teesside – C biol/app sci 96–112 pts +interview (Biol Sci; Foren Sci)

UWE Bristol – C biol/app sci 96–112 pts +interview (Biol Sci)

Westminster – BBB–CCC incl sci 96–120 pts (Biol Sci; Biomed Sci) (IB 27 pts HL 4 sci)

Wolverhampton – CCC incl biol/chem (Foren Sci); CCC incl sci (Biomed Sci)

Worcester – 96–104 pts incl biol (Foren App Biol); 96–104 pts incl biol/chem (Biomed Sci)

88 pts **Canterbury Christ Church** – 88–112 pts (Biol; Foren Invstg)

London Met – CCD incl biol+chem (Foren Sci) (IB 28 pts HL 15 pts incl biol+chem)

London South Bank – CCD incl sci 88–96 pts (Biosci; Foren Sci)

Reading – BBB–CCD (Biol Sci Fdn; Biomed Sci Fdn) (IB 30–24 pts)

West Scotland – CCD incl biol 88–102 pts (App Biosci Zool; Biomed Sci) (IB 24 pts); CCD incl chem 88–102 pts (Foren Sci) (IB 24 pts incl chem)

80 pts **Bedfordshire** – CCC–CCE 80–96 pts (Biol Sci; Foren Sci)

Stirling – BB incl biol/chem (App Biol Sci) (IB 28 pts)

West Scotland – CDD incl biol 80–102 pts (App Biosci) (IB 24 pts)

64 pts **Greenwich** – DDE 64 pts (Biol (Ext))

Alternative offers
See **Chapter 6** and **Appendix 1** for grades/UCAS Tariff points information for other examinations.

DEGREE APPRENTICESHIPS
Hull (Lab Asst); Brighton (Biomed Sci).

EXAMPLES OF COLLEGES OFFERING COURSES IN THIS SUBJECT FIELD
Birmingham Met (Coll); Furness (Coll); Greater Brighton Met (Coll); Haringey, Enfield and North East London (Coll); Liverpool City (Coll); Nescot; Peterborough (Coll); Petroc; South Devon (Coll); Sunderland (Coll); Weymouth (Coll).

CHOOSING YOUR COURSE (SEE ALSO CH.1)
Universities and colleges teaching quality See www.qaa.ac.uk; https://unistats.ac.uk.

Examples of sandwich degree courses Brighton; Plymouth; Reading; Robert Gordon; Stirling.

ADMISSIONS INFORMATION

Number of applicants per place (approx) Aston (Biomed Sci) 8; Bangor (Biol Sci) 4, (Med Sci) 5; Bath 7; Cardiff 5; Durham 8; East Anglia 5; Edinburgh 10; Essex 8; Lancaster (Biomed Sci) 5; Leeds (Med Sci) 25; Leicester 8; London (King's) 7; London (QM) 8; London (St George's) 15; London (UCL) 8; Newcastle 5; Nottingham 6; Southampton 8; York 9.

Advice to applicants and planning the UCAS personal statement Read scientific journals and try to extend your knowledge beyond the A-level syllabus. Discuss your special interests, for example, ecology, microbiology, genetics or zoology (read up thoroughly on your interests since questions could be asked at interview). Mention any voluntary attendance on courses, work experience, voluntary work, or holiday jobs. Demonstrate good oral and written communication skills and be competent at handling numerical data. Interest in the law for Forensic Science courses. See **Appendix 3**.

Misconceptions about this course Anglia Ruskin (Foren Sci) Some students are not aware that modules in management and quality assurance are taken as part of the course. **Birmingham** We offer a range of degree labels each with different UCAS codes, for example Biological Sciences Genetics, Biological Sciences Microbiology: all have the same first year and students can freely transfer between them. (Med Sci) Applicants often use this course as an insurance for a vocational course (usually Medicine). If they are unsuccessful for their first choice, they occasionally find it difficult to commit themselves to Medical Sciences and do not perform as well as their academic performance would predict. **Cardiff** Some students mistakenly believe that they can transfer to Medicine. **De Montfort** (Foren Sci) Students are often unaware of how much of the work is analytical biology and chemistry: they think they spend their time visiting crime scenes. **London (St George's)** It is not possible to transfer to Medicine after the first year of the Biomedical Science course. Students may be able to transfer to Year 3 of the Medical course on completion of the BSc degree. **Swansea** (Med Sci Hum) Some applicants think the course is a form of medical training – it isn't, but it is relevant to anyone planning graduate entry for courses in Medicine or paramedical careers. (Biol Sci Defer) Some applicants think that this is a degree in its own right. In fact, after the first year, students have to choose one of the other degrees offered by the School of Biological Sciences. This course allows students an extra year in which to consider their final specialisation.

Selection interviews Yes Manchester, Oxford ((Bio Sci) 21%, (Biomed Sci) 12%), Sheffield, Stirling, Sunderland; **Some** Cardiff Met, East Anglia, Imperial London, Warwick; **No** Anglia Ruskin, Aston, Bangor, Birmingham, Cardiff, Derby, Dundee, Essex, Greenwich, Hull, Kent, Liverpool John Moores, London (RH), London (St George's), London (UCL), Newcastle, Nottingham, Nottingham Trent, Oxford Brookes, Reading, Roehampton, Salford, Sheffield Hallam, Staffordshire, Strathclyde, Surrey, Swansea, UWE Bristol, Wolverhampton.

Interview advice and questions You are likely to be asked about your main interests in biology and your choice of specialisation in the field of biological sciences or, for example, about the role of the botanist, specialist microbiologist in industry, your understanding of biotechnology or genetic engineering. Questions likely to be asked on any field courses attended. If you have a field course workbook, take it to interview. See also **Chapter 5**. **Oxford** No written or work tests. Interviews are rigorous but sympathetic; successful entrants average 21%. Applicants are expected to demonstrate their ability to understand whatever facts they have encountered and to discuss a particular aspect of biology in which they are interested. What problems does a fish face under water? Are humans still evolving?

Reasons for rejection (non-academic) Oxford Applicant appeared to have so much in his head that he tended to express his ideas in too much of a rush. He needs to slow down a bit and take more time to select points that are really pertinent to the questions. **Ulster** Reasons relating to health and/or police checks.

AFTER-RESULTS ADVICE

Offers to applicants repeating A-levels Higher London (St George's); Newcastle; Sheffield; **Possibly higher** Lancaster; Manchester Met; **Same** Abertay; Anglia Ruskin; Aston; Birmingham; Cardiff; Cardiff

Met; De Montfort; Derby; Durham; East Anglia; East London; Edinburgh Napier; Essex; Exeter; Heriot-Watt; Huddersfield; Hull; Kingston; Leeds; Lincoln; Liverpool Hope; Liverpool John Moores; London (RH); Oxford Brookes; Plymouth; Robert Gordon; Roehampton; Salford; Sheffield Hallam; Stirling; West London; West Scotland; Wolverhampton; Worcester; York; **No** Cambridge; Glasgow.

GRADUATE DESTINATIONS AND EMPLOYMENT (2016/17 HESA)
Graduates surveyed See **Biology**.

Career note Degrees in biological science subjects often lead graduates into medical, pharmaceutical, veterinary, food and environmental work, research and education, in both the public and private sectors (see also **Biology**). Sandwich courses are offered at a number of institutions enabling students to gain paid experience in industry and commerce, often resulting in permanent employment on graduation. In recent years there has been a considerable increase in the number of Biomedical Science courses designed for students interested in taking a hands-on approach to studying the biology of disease. However, students should be warned that the ever-popular Forensic Science courses may not always pave the way to jobs in this highly specialised field.

OTHER DEGREE SUBJECTS FOR CONSIDERATION
Biochemistry; Biology; Biotechnology; Botany; Chemistry; Consumer Sciences; Ecology; Environmental Health; Environmental Science; Genetics; Genomics; Immunology; Microbiology; Pharmaceutical Sciences; Pharmacology; Pharmacy; Physiology; Plant Sciences; Psychology; Sport and Exercise Science; Toxicology; Virology; Zoology.

BIOLOGY

(including **Marine Biology**; see also **Animal Sciences, Biological Sciences, Biotechnology, Environmental Sciences, Microbiology, Plant Sciences, Zoology**)

The science of biology is a broad and rapidly developing subject that increasingly affects our lives. Biologists address the challenges faced by human populations such as disease, conservation and food production, and the continuing advances in such areas as genetics and molecular biology that have applications in medicine and agriculture. (See also under **Biological Sciences**.)

Useful websites www.rsb.org.uk; www.mba.ac.uk; www.bbsrc.ukri.org; see also **Biochemistry**.

NB The points totals shown to the left of the institutions are for ease of reference only. It must not be assumed that Tariff points are always used by institutions or that they can be substituted for an offer in grades. The level of an offer is not necessarily indicative of the quality of a course.

COURSE OFFERS INFORMATION
Subject requirements/preferences GCSE Mathematics and English stipulated in some cases. **AL** Biology and chemistry important, other science subjects may be accepted. Two and sometimes three mathematics/science subjects required including biology.

Your target offers and examples of degree courses
152 pts   **Durham** – A*AA (Nat Sci) (IB 38 pts)
           Oxford – A*AA incl sci/maths +interview (Biol) (IB 39 pts HL 7 sci/maths)
144 pts   **Imperial London** – AAA incl biol+sci/maths (Biol Sci Ger Sci; Ecol Env Biol) (IB 38 pts HL 6 biol+sci/maths)
           Lancaster – AAA incl sci (Biology (Yr Abrd)) (IB 36 pts HL 16 pts)
           Sheffield – AAA/AAB +bEPQ incl biol+sci (Biol (MBiolSci)) (IB 36 pts HL 6 biol+sci); AAA/AAB+bEPQ incl biol+sci +interview (Biol (Yr Abrd)) (IB 36 pts HL 6 biol+sci)
136 pts   **Bath** – AAB/ABB +aEPQ incl biol+sci/maths (Biol) (IB 36 pts HL 665 incl 6 biol+sci/maths)
           Birmingham – AAB incl biol+sci (Hum Biol) (IB 32 pts HL 665)
           Bristol – AAB incl chem+sci/maths (Canc Biol Immun) (IB 34–31 pts HL 17 pts incl 5 chem+sci/maths); AAB incl sci/maths (Biol) (IB 34 pts HL 17 pts incl 6/5 sci/maths)

Glasgow – AAB incl biol/chem 136 pts (Mar Frshwtr Biol) (IB 36 pts HL 665 incl biol/chem+sci)
Lancaster – AAB incl sci (Biol courses) (IB 35 pts HL 16 pts incl 6 sci)
Leeds – AAA–AAB incl biol (Biol) (IB 35–34 pts HL 18–17 pts incl 6 biol+sci)
London (King's) – AAB incl chem+biol (Anat Dev Hum Biol) (IB 35 pts HL 665 chem+biol)
Newcastle – AAA–AAB incl biol+sci (Biol) (IB 34 pts HL 6 biol)
Nottingham – AAB incl biol+sci/maths (Biol) (IB 34 pts HL 5/6 biol+sci)
Sheffield – AAA–AAB/ABB +bEPQ incl biol/sci (Biol) (IB 36–34 pts HL 6/5 biol+sci)
Southampton – AAB incl biol+sci (Biol) (IB 34 pts HL 17 pts incl 65 biol+sci)
St Andrews – AAB incl biol+sci/maths (Biol Arbc; Biol courses) (IB 36 pts HL 665 incl 6 biol+sci)
York – AAB incl biol+sci (Biol; Mol Cell Biol) (IB 35 pts HL 6 biol+sci)
128 pts **Bangor** – B biol+sci 128 pts incl biol (App Mar Biol) (HL 6 biol+sci)
Edinburgh – AAA–ABB incl biol+chem (Biol Sci (Evol Biol)) (IB 37–32 pts HL 666–555 incl biol+chem); AAB–ABB incl biol+chem (Repro Biol) (IB 36–32 pts HL 65 biol+chem)
Exeter – AAB–ABB incl sci/maths (Cons Biol Ecol; Evol Biol) (IB 34–32 pts HL 665–655 incl 5 sci/maths)
Keele – ABB incl sci/maths (Biol) (IB 34 pts HL 6 sci/maths)
Leeds – ABB incl biol (Biol Hist Phil Sci) (IB 34 pts HL 6 biol)
Liverpool – ABB/BBB +aEPQ incl biol+sci (Trpcl Dis Biol) (IB 33 pts HL 6 biol 5 sci); ABB/BBB+aEPQ incl biol+sci/maths/geog (Mar Biol) (IB 33 pts HL 6 biol 5 sci)
London (QM) – ABB incl biol (Biol) (IB 34 pts HL 655 incl biol)
Loughborough – ABB incl sci (Hum Biol) (IB 34 pts HL 655 incl 5 biol+sci)
Manchester – AAA–ABB (Zool Modn Lang) (IB 36–33 pts HL 6–5 sci); AAA–ABB incl sci/maths +interview (Biol; Biol (Yr Ind); Biol Modn Lang; Biol Sci Soty; Cell Biol; Cell Biol (Yr Ind); Cell Biol Modn Lang; Dev Biol; Mol Biol) (IB 36–33 pts HL 666–655 incl chem+sci)
Southampton – ABB incl biol+sci/maths/geog (Mar Biol) (IB 32 pts HL 16 pts incl 5 biol+sci/maths/geog); ABB incl biol+sci/maths/geog +interview (Mar Biol Ocean) (IB 32 pts HL 16 pts incl 6 biol+sci/maths/geog)
Sussex – AAB–ABB incl sci (Biol) (IB 34–32 pts HL 5 sci)
120 pts **Aberdeen** – BBB incl maths/sci (Biol; Cons Biol; Mar Biol) (IB 32 pts HL 5 maths/sci)
Bangor – 120 pts (App Trstl Mar Ecol); 120 pts incl biol (Mar Biol; Mar Biol Zool)
Derby – 120 pts incl biol (Biol)
Hull – C biol 120 pts (Biol) (IB 30 pts HL 5 biol)
Lincoln – BBB incl biol/chem (Biol) (IB 30 pts HL 5 biol/chem)
London (RH) – ABB–BBB incl biol (Biol) (IB 32 pts HL 555 incl biol); ABB–BBB incl biol+sci (Mol Biol) (IB 32 pts HL 555 incl biol+sci)
Middlesex – 120 pts (Biol)
Newcastle – ABB–BBB incl biol+sci +interview (Mar Biol) (IB 32 pts HL 6 biol)
Nottingham – ABB–BBB incl sci/maths/geog (Env Biol) (IB 32–30 pts)
Queen's Belfast – ABB–BBB incl biol (Mar Biol) (IB 33–32 pts HL 655 incl biol)
Stirling – BBB incl sci/maths (Biol) (IB 32 pts)
Strathclyde – ABB–BBB incl sci (Microbiol) (IB 34 pts HL 5 sci)
Swansea – ABB–BBB incl biol (Biol) (IB 33–32 pts HL 5 biol)
112 pts **Anglia Ruskin** – 112 pts incl biol (Mar Biol Biodiv Cons) (IB 24 pts)
Bangor – C biol+sci 112 pts incl biol (Biol) (HL 5 biol)
Chester – BBC–BCC incl biol/chem/app sci (Biol courses) (IB 26 pts HL 5 biol)
Coventry – BBC incl biol (Hum Biosci) (IB 30 pts HL 5 biol)
Edge Hill – BBB–BBC 112–120 pts (Biol)
Glasgow Caledonian – BBC incl chem (Cell Mol Biol) (IB 28 pts)
Gloucestershire – BBC 112 pts (Anim Biol; Biol)
Heriot-Watt – BBC incl sci (Mar Biol) (IB 27 pts HL 5 sci)
Huddersfield – BBC incl sci 112 pts (Biol (Mol Cell); Med Biol)
Kent – BBC incl biol (Biol courses) (IB 34 pts HL 15 pts incl 5 biol)
Liverpool John Moores – BBC incl sci (Biol) (IB 26 pts)
Nottingham Trent – BBC incl biol 112 pts (Zoo Biol)

UCAS points Tariff: A* = 56 pts; A = 48 pts; B = 40 pts; C = 32 pts; D = 24 pts; E = 16 pts

Portsmouth – 112 pts incl biol (Biol; Mar Biol) (IB 27 pts HL 6 biol)

104 pts **Aberystwyth** – BBB–BCC incl biol 104–120 pts (Biol; Mar Frshwtr Biol; Plnt Biol) (IB 30–28 pts HL 5 biol)

Central Lancashire – 104–112 pts incl biol/chem/app sci (Foren Sci Mol Biol (MSci))

Chester – BBC–BCC incl biol/chem/env sci/app sci 104–112 pts (Foren Biol) (IB 26 pts HL 5 biol/chem); BBC–BCC incl biol 104–112 pts (Cell Mol Biol) (IB 26 pts HL 5 biol)

Dundee – BBB–BCC incl maths+sci (Mathem Biol) (IB 30 pts HL 555 incl maths+sci)

Edinburgh Napier – BCC incl sci (Anim Cons Biol) (IB 28 pts HL 654 incl 5 biol); (Mar Frshwtr Biol) (IB 28 pts HL 654 incl 5 sci)

Essex – BCC incl biol (Hum Biol) (IB 28 pts HL 544 incl biol)

Manchester Met – BBC–BCC incl biol/app sci 104–112 pts (Biol (Yr Abrd/Yr Ind)) (IB 26 pts HL 5 biol)

Northampton – BCC 104–112 pts (Biol) (IB 25 pts)

Salford – C biol 104–112 pts (Biol) (IB 30 pts HL 4 biol)

Sheffield Hallam – 104 pts incl biol (Biol; Hum Biol)

Ulster – BCC incl sci/maths (Biol) (IB 24 pts HL 12 pts incl 5 sci)

96 pts **Bath Spa** – CCC incl biol/env sci (Biol) (IB 26 pts HL 5 incl biol)

Bolton – 96 pts +interview (Med Biol)

Cumbria – 96–112 pts incl biol/geog (Cons Biol)

South Wales – 96–104 pts incl biol+sci (Biol)

Worcester – 96–104 pts incl biol (Biol)

88 pts **Canterbury Christ Church** – 88–112 pts (Biol)

80 pts **South Wales** – BCC–CDD incl biol+sci 80–112 pts (Int Wldlf Biol); (Hum Biol) (IB 29 pts HL 5 biol+sci)

Wolverhampton – CDD incl sci (Genet Mol Biol)

Alternative offers

See **Chapter 6** and **Appendix 1** for grades/UCAS Tariff points information for other examinations.

EXAMPLES OF COLLEGES OFFERING COURSES IN THIS SUBJECT FIELD

Bishop Burton (Coll); Blackpool and Fylde (Coll); Bournemouth and Poole (Coll); Greater Brighton Met (Coll); HOW (Coll); Leeds City (Coll); Liverpool City (Coll); Manchester (Coll); North Hertfordshire (Coll); Solihull (Coll); South Devon (Coll); Sparsholt (Coll); SRUC; Sunderland (Coll); Truro and Penwith (Coll); Walsall (Coll); Warrington and Vale Royal (Coll).

CHOOSING YOUR COURSE (SEE ALSO CH.1)

Universities and colleges teaching quality See www.qaa.ac.uk; https://unistats.ac.uk.

Top research universities and colleges (REF 2014) See **Biological Sciences**.

Examples of sandwich degree courses Aston; Bath; Birmingham; Coventry; Dundee; Huddersfield; Kent; Leeds; Lincoln; Liverpool John Moores; Loughborough; Manchester; Manchester Met; Middlesex; Newcastle; Northumbria; Nottingham Trent; Queen's Belfast; Sheffield Hallam; Sussex; Teesside; Ulster; York.

ADMISSIONS INFORMATION

Number of applicants per place (approx) Aston 6; Bath 8; Bath Spa 8; Birmingham 9; Bristol 5; Dundee 6; Durham 8; Exeter 6; Heriot-Watt 4; Hull 5; Imperial London 4; Kent 8; Leeds 6; London (RH) 5; Newcastle (Mar Biol) 3; Nottingham 8; Oxford Brookes 7; Salford 3; Southampton 7; Stirling 8; Sussex 4; Swansea (Mar Biol) 8, (Biol) 4; York 8.

Advice to applicants and planning the UCAS personal statement See **Biochemistry**, **Biological Sciences** and **Appendix 3**.

Misconceptions about this course Sussex Many students think that a Biology degree limits you to being a professional scientist which is not the case. **York** Mature students often lack the confidence to consider the course.

Selection interviews Yes Manchester, SRUC; **Some** Bath, Southampton, York; **No** Anglia Ruskin, Aston, Bangor, Birmingham, Derby, Dundee, Essex, Kent, Liverpool John Moores, London (RH), Nottingham, Sheffield, Sheffield Hallam, Staffordshire, Stirling, Swansea, Wolverhampton.

Interview advice and questions Questions are likely to focus on your studies in biology, on any work experience or any special interests you may have in biology outside school. In the past, questions have included: Is the computer like a brain and, if so, could it ever be taught to think? What do you think the role of the environmental biologist will be in the next 40–50 years? Have you any strong views on vivisection? You have a micro-organism in the blood: you want to make a culture. What conditions should be borne in mind? What is a pacemaker? What problems will a giraffe experience? How does water enter a flowering plant? Compare an egg and a potato. Discuss a family tree of human genotypes. Discuss fish farming in Britain today. What problems do fish face underwater? See also **Chapter 5**. **York** Why Biology? How do you see your future?

Reasons for rejection (non-academic) Bath Spa Poor mathematical and scientific knowledge.

AFTER-RESULTS ADVICE

Offers to applicants repeating A-levels Higher East London; St Andrews; Strathclyde; **Possibly higher** Bath; Durham; Leeds; London (RH); **Same** Aberystwyth; Anglia Ruskin; Bangor; Chester; Derby; Dundee; Edinburgh Napier; Heriot-Watt; Hull; Liverpool John Moores; Loughborough; Manchester Met; Newcastle; Nottingham; Oxford Brookes; Plymouth; Sheffield; Southampton; Staffordshire; Stirling; Teesside; Wolverhampton; York.

GRADUATE DESTINATIONS AND EMPLOYMENT (2016/17 HESA)

Graduates surveyed 4,715 **Employed** 1,735 **In voluntary employment** 140 **In further study** 1835 **Assumed unemployed** 290

Career note Some graduates go into research, but many will go into laboratory work in hospitals, food laboratories, agriculture, the environment and pharmaceuticals. Others go into teaching, management and other professional and technical areas.

OTHER DEGREE SUBJECTS FOR CONSIDERATION

Anatomy; Biochemistry; Biological Sciences; Biotechnology; Chemistry; Dentistry; Ecology; Environmental Health; Environmental Science/Studies; Food Science; Genomics; Health Studies; Medicine; Midwifery; Nursing; Nutrition; Optometry; Orthoptics; Pharmaceutical Sciences; Pharmacology; Pharmacy; Physiology; Physiotherapy; Plant Sciences; Radiography; Speech and Language Therapy; Zoology.

BIOTECHNOLOGY

(including **Prosthetics and Orthotics**; see also **Biological Sciences, Biology, Engineering (medical), Microbiology**)

Biotechnology is basically the application of biology to improve the quality of life. It is a multi-disciplinary subject which can involve a range of scientific disciplines covering chemistry, the biological sciences, microbiology and genetics. At Bangor for example, the course involves medical and industrial applications, the environment, the food industry, and because of its very favourable coastal location it can add marine biotechnology and fisheries genetics to its programme. Medical engineering involves the design, installation, maintenance and provision of technical support for diagnostic, therapeutic and other clinical equipment used by doctors, nurses and other clinical healthcare workers.

Useful websites www.bbsrc.ukri.org; www.bioindustry.org; www.abcinformation.org

NB The points totals shown to the left of the institutions are for ease of reference only. It must not be assumed that Tariff points are always used by institutions or that they can be substituted for an offer in grades. The level of an offer is not necessarily indicative of the quality of a course.

COURSE OFFERS INFORMATION

Subject requirements/preferences GCSE Mathematics and science subjects required. **AL** Courses vary but one, two or three subjects from chemistry, biology, physics and mathematics may be required.

Your target offers and examples of degree courses

152 pts **Leeds** – A*AA incl maths+phys (Med Eng; Med Eng (MEng)) (IB 36 pts HL 18 pts incl 6 maths+phys)

144 pts **Imperial London** – AAA incl chem+sci/maths (Biotech; Biotech (Yr Ind/Rsch)) (IB 38 pts HL 6 chem+biol/maths); AAA incl maths+phys/chem +interview (Biomat Tiss Eng (MEng)) (IB 38 pts HL 6 maths+phys+chem)

London (UCL) – AAA incl chem+biol+maths (Biotech) (IB 38 pts HL 18 pts incl 5 maths+biol+chem)

136 pts **Glasgow** – AAB incl biol/chem (Mol Cell Biol (Biotech)) (IB 36 pts HL 665 incl biol/chem+sci)

Leeds – AAA–AAB incl biol/chem+sci (Biol Sci (Biotech Ent)) (IB 35–34 pts HL 18–17 pts incl 6 biol/chem+sci)

York – AAB incl biol+sci (Biotech Microbiol) (IB 35 pts HL 6 biol+sci)

128 pts **Bristol** – A*AB–AAC incl chem+sci/maths (Bioch Mol Biol Biotech) (IB 36–32 pts HL 18 pts incl 6 chem+sci/maths)

Edinburgh – AAA–ABB incl biol+chem (Biol Sci (Biotech)) (IB 37–32 pts HL 666–555)

Manchester – AAA–ABB incl sci/maths +interview (Biotech) (IB 36–33 pts HL 666–655)

120 pts **Aberdeen** – BBB incl maths/sci (Biotech (App Mol Biol)) (IB 32 pts HL 5 maths/sci)

Nottingham – ABB–BBB incl biol+sci/maths (Biotech) (IB 32–30 pts)

Strathclyde – ABB–BBB incl maths+sci +interview (Pros Orthot) (IB 34 pts HL 6 maths)

112 pts **Bangor** – 112 pts incl biol (Biol Biotech)

Robert Gordon – BBC incl maths+phys/eng/des tech (Mech Biomed Tech) (IB 29 pts)

104 pts **Chester** – BBC–BCC incl sci 104–112 pts (Biotech) (IB 26 pts HL 5 biol); (Genet Evol) (IB 26 pts HL 5 biol/chem)

Robert Gordon – BCC incl maths+phys/eng/des tech (Elec Biomed Tech) (IB 28 pts)

80 pts **Wolverhampton** – CDD incl sci (Microbiol Biotech)

Alternative offers
See **Chapter 6** and **Appendix 1** for grades/UCAS Tariff points information for other examinations.

CHOOSING YOUR COURSE (SEE ALSO CH.1)

Universities and colleges teaching quality See www.qaa.ac.uk; https://unistats.ac.uk.

Examples of sandwich degree courses Imperial London; Manchester; Surrey; York.

ADMISSIONS INFORMATION

Number of applicants per place (approx) Bristol 9; Imperial London 4; Leeds 7; London (UCL) 8; Strathclyde 4.

Advice to applicants and planning the UCAS personal statement See **Biological Sciences**, **Biochemistry** and **Appendix 3**.

Selection interviews Yes Manchester, Strathclyde; **No** Imperial London, Leeds, Surrey, Wolverhampton.

Interview advice and questions See **Biology**, **Biological Sciences** and **Chapter 5**.

AFTER-RESULTS ADVICE

Offers to applicants repeating A-levels Same Leeds; Nottingham; Wolverhampton.

GRADUATE DESTINATIONS AND EMPLOYMENT (2016/17 HESA)

Graduates surveyed 1390 **Employed** 1195 **In voluntary employment** 0 **In further study** 75 **Assumed unemployed** 35

Career note Biotechnology, biomedical and biochemical engineering opportunities exist in medical, agricultural, food science and pharmaceutical laboratories. Some Bioengineering graduates apply for graduate medical courses and obtain both engineering and medical qualifications.

OTHER DEGREE SUBJECTS FOR CONSIDERATION

Agriculture; Biochemistry; Biological Sciences; Biomedicine; Chemistry; Food Technology; Genetics; Materials Science and Technology; Microbiology; Molecular Biology; Pharmacology.

BUILDING AND CONSTRUCTION

(including **Building Services Engineering and Construction and Project Management**; see also**Architecture, Engineering (civil), Housing, Surveying And Real Estate Management**)

The building and construction industry covers a wide range of specialisms and is closely allied to civil, municipal and structural engineering (see under **Engineering (Civil)**). The specialisms include Construction Management involving accountancy, economics, law and estimating in addition to main studies in building materials and methods, construction techniques, and health and safety. Then there is Building Surveying which not only involves modules on building technology but also the study of the history of building techniques and styles and enables the surveyor to diagnose and test all aspects of a building's performance and construction. Quantity Surveying is another specialism which relates to the financial planning of a building project covering costs (which can constantly change during the period of the project) as well as modifications which might be required to the original architect's plans. (See under **Surveying and Real Estate Management**.) Finally, there is Building Services Engineering, a career which involves specialised areas such as heating, lighting, acoustics, refrigeration and air conditioning. All university courses in these subjects will offer work placements.

Useful websites www.ciob.org; www.cibse.org; www.citb.co.uk; www.rics.org; www.cstt.org.uk; www.cbuilde.com

NB The points totals shown to the left of the institutions are for ease of reference only. It must not be assumed that Tariff points are always used by institutions or that they can be substituted for an offer in grades. The level of an offer is not necessarily indicative of the quality of a course.

COURSE OFFERS INFORMATION

Subject requirements/preferences GCSE English, mathematics and science usually required. **AL** Physics, mathematics or a technical subject may be required for some courses.

Your target offers and examples of degree courses
128 pts **London (UCL)** – ABB (Proj Mgt Constr) (IB 34 pts HL 16 pts)
120 pts **London South Bank** – BBB 120–128 pts (Bld Surv)
Loughborough – BBB/ABC +interview (Constr Eng Mgt) (IB 32 pts HL 555)
Northumbria – 120 pts (Constr Eng Mgt)
Nottingham Trent – BBB 120 pts (Bld Surv)
Reading – BBB (Constr Mgt) (IB 30 pts)
Ulster – BBB incl maths/sci (Constr Eng Mgt) (IB 26 pts HL 13 pts)
112 pts **Aston** – BBB–BBC (Constr Proj Mgt) (IB 29 pts HL 554)
Birmingham City – BBC 112 pts +interview (Constr Mgt) (IB 28 pts)
Coventry – BBB–BBC (Constr Mgt) (IB 30 pts); BBB–BBC incl maths (Bld Serv Eng) (IB 30 pts)
Derby – BBC 112 pts (Constr Mgt Prop Dev)
Glyndŵr – BBC 112 pts (Constr Mgt)
Greenwich – BBC 112 pts (Quant Surv)
Heriot-Watt – ABB (3 yr course) BBC (4 yr course) (Constr Proj Mgt) (IB 34 pts (3 yr course)
    29 pts (4 yr course))

Liverpool John Moores – BBC incl maths/sci 112 pts (Bld Serv Eng) (IB 25 pts HL 5 maths)

Nottingham Trent – BBC 112 pts (Quant Surv Commer Mgt)

Oxford Brookes – BBC 112 pts +interview (Constr Proj Mgt) (IB 30 pts)

Portsmouth – 112–120 pts (Constr Eng Mgt) (IB 25 pts)

West London – BBB–BBC 112–120 pts (Constr Proj Mgt)

Westminster – ABB–BBC 112–128 pts (Constr Mgt) (IB 27 pts HL 4 Engl)

104 pts Anglia Ruskin – 104 pts (Constr Mgt)

Leeds Beckett – 104 pts (Constr Mgt)

Plymouth – BBC–BCC 104–112 pts +interview (Constr Proj Mgt) (IB 27–26 pts)

Sheffield Hallam – 104 pts (Constr Proj Mgt)

UWE Bristol – 104 pts (Constr Proj Mgt)

96 pts Brighton – BBC–CCC 96–112 pts (Constr Mgt) (IB 26 pts)

Central Lancashire – 96 pts (Constr Proj Mgt); 96 pts incl maths (Bld Serv Sust Eng)

Glasgow Caledonian – CCC (Constr Mgt) (IB 24 pts); CCC incl maths+phys (Bld Serv Eng) (IB 24 pts)

Kingston – CCC 96 pts (Constr Mgt) (IB 24 pts HL 4 Engl)

London South Bank – CCC 96–112 pts (Commer Mgt (Quant Surv); Constr Mgt)

Nottingham Trent – CCC 96 pts (Constr Mgt)

Teesside – 96–112 pts+interview (Constr Mgt)

Trinity Saint David – 96 pts (Constr Mgt)

UCEM – 96 pts (Bld Surv)

80 pts Colchester (UC) – 80 pts (Constr Mgt (Quant Surv); Constr Mgt (Site Mgt))

Wolverhampton – BB/CCE (Constr Mgt)

72 pts Solent – DDD 72–96 pts (Constr Mgt)

Alternative offers

See **Chapter 6** and **Appendix 1** for grades/UCAS Tariff points information for other examinations.

DEGREE APPRENTICESHIPS

Robert Gordon (Constr Blt Env).

EXAMPLES OF COLLEGES OFFERING COURSES IN THIS SUBJECT FIELD

Accrington and Rossendale (Coll); Banbury and Bicester (Coll); Barnfield (Coll); Barnsley (Coll); Basingstoke (CT); Bath (Coll); Bedford (Coll); Birmingham Met (Coll); Blackpool and Fylde (Coll); Bournemouth and Poole (Coll); Bradford College UC; Bury (Coll); Canterbury (Coll); Carshalton (Coll); Chelmsford (Coll); Chesterfield (Coll); Croydon (Univ Centre); Darlington (Coll); Doncaster (Coll); Dudley (Coll); Durham New (Coll); Ealing, Hammersmith and West London (Coll); East Kent (Coll); East Riding (Coll); East Surrey (Coll); East Sussex (Coll); Eastleigh (Coll); Exeter (Coll); Furness (Coll); Gateshead (Coll); Gloucestershire (Coll); Gower Swansea (Coll); Hartlepool (CFE); Hull (Coll); Leicester (Coll); LeSoCo; Lincoln (Coll); London UCK (Coll); MidKent (Coll); Nescot; North West London (Coll); Norwich City (Coll); Plymouth City (Coll); Redcar and Cleveland (Coll); Richmond-upon-Thames (Coll); South Cheshire (Coll); South City Birmingham (Coll); South Essex (Coll); Southampton City (Coll); St Helens (Coll); Stamford New (Coll); Stephenson (Coll); Stockport (Coll); Tameside (Coll); TEC Partnership; Trafford (Coll); Wakefield (Coll); Warrington and Vale Royal (Coll); West Cheshire (Coll); West Kent (Coll); West Suffolk (Coll); Westminster City (Coll); Wigan and Leigh (Coll); Windsor Forest (Coll); Wirral Met (Coll); York (Coll).

CHOOSING YOUR COURSE (SEE ALSO CH.1)

Universities and colleges teaching quality See www.qaa.ac.uk; https://unistats.ac.uk.

Top research universities and colleges (REF 2014) See **Architecture**.

Examples of sandwich degree courses Aston; Brighton; Brunel; Coventry; Greenwich; Kingston; Leeds Beckett; Liverpool John Moores; London South Bank; Loughborough; Nottingham Trent; Portsmouth; Sheffield Hallam; Ulster; UWE Bristol; Wolverhampton.

ADMISSIONS INFORMATION
Number of applicants per place (approx) Edinburgh Napier 7; Heriot-Watt 5; Kingston 4.

Advice to applicants and planning the UCAS personal statement Details of work experience with any levels of responsibility should be included. Make contact with any building organisation to arrange a meeting with staff to discuss careers in building. Give evidence of your ability to work in a team and give details of any personal achievements in technological areas and work experience. Building also covers civil engineering, surveying, quantity surveying etc and these areas should also be explored. See also **Appendix 3**.

Selection interviews Yes Birmingham City, Loughborough, Plymouth; **Some** Greenwich; **No** Derby, Kingston, Liverpool John Moores, Northumbria, Oxford Brookes, Reading, Westminster, Wolverhampton.

Interview advice and questions Work experience in the building and civil engineering industries is important and you could be expected to describe any building project you have visited and any problems experienced in its construction. A knowledge of the range of activities to be found on a building site will be expected, for example the work of quantity and land surveyors and of the various building trades. See also **Chapter 5**.

Reasons for rejection (non-academic) Inability to communicate. Lack of motivation. Indecisiveness about reasons for choosing the course. **Loughborough** Applicant more suited to a hands-on course rather than an academic one.

AFTER-RESULTS ADVICE
Offers to applicants repeating A-levels
Same Birmingham City; Brighton; Coventry; Heriot-Watt; Huddersfield; Kingston; Liverpool John Moores; London (UCL); Loughborough; Northumbria; Trinity Saint David.

GRADUATE DESTINATIONS AND EMPLOYMENT (2016/17 HESA)
Graduates surveyed 2,700 **Employed** 2,000 **In voluntary employment** 20 **In further study** 430 **Assumed unemployed** 85

Career note There is a wide range of opportunities within the building and construction industry for building technologists and managers. This subject area also overlaps into surveying, quantity surveying, civil engineering, architecture and planning and graduates from all these subjects commonly work together as members of construction teams.

OTHER DEGREE SUBJECTS FOR CONSIDERATION
Architectural Technology; Architecture; Civil Engineering; Property Planning and Development; Quantity Surveying; Surveying.

BUSINESS AND MANAGEMENT COURSES

(see also **Business and Management Courses (international and European), Business and Management Courses (Specialised), Economics, Hospitality and Event Management, Human Resource Management, Leisure and Recreation Management/Studies, Marketing, Retail Management, Tourism and Travel**)

Business degrees attract more applicants than any other degree subject, and students should try to assess the balance between theoretical studies and hands-on approaches offered by courses. Most universities offer a range of courses such as at Durham University, where in the first year of the Business and Management course, accounting, marketing and business management are covered. Transfers between business courses is a common feature at most institutions. As for the course content, financial studies form part of all courses with additional modules which may include marketing, business law and human resources. In the following table, there is also a section focusing

PREPARING YOU FOR THE REAL WORLD OF BUSINESS

Our range of practical Business Management programmes will help you think and act like the next generation of business leaders from day one of your course. You'll learn from commercially experienced tutors in small workshops, more closely aligned to how you'll work in business than a crowded lecture hall.

FREE MASTER'S

On completion of your business degree, you'll be able to progress onto a business Masters course at no extra cost.

CHOICES OF UK AND INTERNATIONAL LOCATIONS

Study in the UK at our 5 city centre locations in London, Birmingham, Leeds, Manchester and Nottingham.

Alternatively, gain a global business experience by studying at our campuses in Berlin and Hong Kong.

You'll have access to talks, guest lectures and networking sessions with a range of employers and professional bodies.

*See law.ac.uk for full terms and conditions of the Free Masters Offer

INTERNATIONAL SUMMER SCHOOL

Attend our International Leadership Summer School in Berlin to boost your leadership skills and sample Berlin.

For more information
law.ac.uk/business

on European and International Business courses for those with a language ability, and a further section on more specialised courses which cover advertising, airports, engineering, music, transport, travel and sport. Since this is a vocational subject, some work experience in the field is generally required prior to application.

Useful websites www.faststream.gov.uk; www.icsa.org.uk; www.adassoc.org.uk; www.cipr.co.uk; www.ismprofessional.com; www.export.org.uk; www.ipsos.com; www.capitaresourcing.co.uk; www.tax.org.uk; www.gov.uk/government/organisations/hm-revenue-customs; www.camfoundation.com; www.iconsulting.org.uk; www.managers.org.uk; www.cipd.co.uk; www.instam.org

NB The points totals shown to the left of the institutions are for ease of reference only. It must not be assumed that Tariff points are always used by institutions or that they can be substituted for an offer in grades. The level of an offer is not necessarily indicative of the quality of a course.

COURSE OFFERS INFORMATION
Subject requirements/preferences GCSE Mathematics and English often at grade A or B (7 or 5/6) required. **AL** Mathematics required for some courses. In some cases grades A, B or C may be required.

Your target offers and examples of degree courses

152 pts **Durham** – A*AA incl maths (Econ Mgt) (IB 38 pts)
  London (King's) – A*AA incl hum/soc sci (Bus Mgt) (IB 35 pts HL 766)
  Warwick – A*AA incl maths+phys (Phys Bus St) (IB 38 pts HL 6 maths+phys)

144 pts **Bath** – AAA/A*AB (Mgt courses) (IB 36 pts HL 666/765)
  Bristol – AAA–ABB incl maths (Acc Mgt) (IB 32–36 pts HL 16–18 pts)
  City – AAA 144 pts (Bus Mgt) (IB 35 pts)
  Exeter – AAA (Acc Bus; Bus Mgt) (IB 36 pts HL 666)
  Leeds – AAA (Bus Econ; Bus Mgt Mark) (IB 35 pts HL 17 pts)
  London (QM) – AAA (Bus Mgt) (IB 36 pts HL 666)
  London (UCL) – AAA incl maths (Mgt Sci) (IB 38 pts HL 18 pts incl 6 maths)
  London LSE – AAA incl maths (Maths Stats Bus) (IB 38 pts HL 766 incl 7 maths); (Mgt) (IB 38 pts HL 766 incl maths)
  St Andrews – AAA incl sci/maths (Mgt Sci; Mgt courses) (IB 38 pts)
  Warwick – AAA (Law Bus St; Mgt) (IB 38 pts)

136 pts **Birmingham** – AAB (Bus Mgt courses) (IB 32 pts HL 665)
  Durham – AAB (Bus Mgt) (IB 36 pts HL 665)
  Exeter – AAA–AAB incl maths (Maths Mgt) (IB 36–34 pts HL 666–665 incl 6 maths)
  Glasgow – AAB incl arts/hum (Bus Mgt Comb Hons) (IB 38 pts HL 666 incl Engl+hum/lang)
  Lancaster – AAB (Acc Mgt St; Bus Mgt; Mgt courses) (IB 35 pts HL 16 pts)
  Leeds – AAB (Bus Mgt) (IB 35 pts HL 16 pts)
  Manchester – AAB (Mgt courses) (IB 35 pts HL 665)
  Newcastle – AAB (Bus Mgt) (IB 35 pts)
  Nottingham – AAB (Mgt) (IB 34 pts)
  Reading – AAB (Bus Mgt) (IB 32 pts)
  Southampton – AAB/ABB +aEPQ (Bus Mgt; Econ Mgt Sci) (IB 34 pts HL 17 pts)
  Surrey – AAB (Bus Econ) (IB 34 pts)
  Sussex – AAA–AAB (Law Bus Mgt) (IB 36–34 pts)

128 pts **Cardiff** – AAB–ABB (Bus Mgt) (IB 34–32 pts HL 665–655); AAB–ABB+interview (Bus St Jap) (IB 35–32 pts HL 665–655 incl maths+Engl)
  East Anglia – ABB (Bus Econ; Mark Mgt) (IB 32 pts)
  Edinburgh – AAB–ABB (Acc Bus) (IB 40–34 pts HL 776–655); AAB–ABB incl maths (Bus courses) (IB 40–34 pts HL 766–655 incl maths)
  Leicester – ABB/BBB +bEPQ (Mgt St) (IB 30 pts HL 16 pts)
  Liverpool – ABB (Bus Mgt; Bus Mgt (Yr Ind)) (IB 33 pts); ABB incl maths (Maths Bus St) (IB 33 pts HL 6 maths)
  Liverpool John Moores – ABB (Bus Mgt) (IB 33 pts)

158 | BUSINESS and MANAGEMENT COURSES

London (RH) – AAB–ABB (Econ Mgt; Mgt Acc) (IB 32 pts HL 655)
Loughborough – AAB–ABB (Mgt courses) (IB 35–34 pts HL 665)
Nottingham – ABB incl lang (Modn Langs Bus) (IB 32 pts)
Queen's Belfast – ABB (Bus Mgt (Yr Ind)) (IB 33 pts HL 665)
Reading – ABB (Entre Mgt; Int Bus Mgt) (IB 32 pts)
Sheffield – ABB (Bus Mgt) (IB 33-34 pts)
Surrey – ABB (Bus Mgt) (IB 32 pts)
Sussex – AAB–ABB (Bus Mgt St; Comp Bus Mgt; Econ Mgt St; Fin Bus; Mark Mgt) (IB 34–32 pts)
York – ABB (Bus Crea Ind) (IB 34 pts)

120 pts **Aston** – ABB–BBB (Psy Bus) (IB 32–31 pts HL 555); BBB (Bus Mgt) (IB 31 pts HL 555)
Brunel – BBB (Bus Mgt; Bus Mgt (Mark); Bus Mgt Entre Innov) (IB 30 pts); (Bus Mgt (Acc)) (IB 30 pts HL 4 Maths)
Coventry – ABB–BBB (Bus Mgt) (IB 30 pts); BBB (Glob Bus Mgt) (IB 27 pts)
Derby – BBB 120 pts (Bus Mgt; Bus St)
Essex – BBB (Bus Mgt) (IB 30 pts)
Heriot-Watt – BBB (Int Bus Mgt HR Mgt; Int Bus Mgt Mark) (IB 29 pts)
Huddersfield – BBB 120 pts (Bus Data Analyt; Bus Law; Bus Mgt; Bus Mgt Fin)
Northumbria – 120 pts (Bus Econ; Bus Log Sply Chn Mgt; Bus Mark Mgt; Bus Mgt; Bus Tour Mgt)
Nottingham Trent – BBB 120 pts (Bus; Bus Mgt Comb Hons)
Portsmouth – 120 pts (Law Bus) (IB 29 pts HL 664)
Southampton – ABB–BBB incl mus+gr 8 (Mus Bus Mgt) (IB 32–30 pts HL 16 incl 5 mus)
Stirling – BBB (Bus St) (IB 32 pts)
Strathclyde – ABB–BBB (Bus; Bus Ent courses) (IB 36 pts)
Swansea – ABB–BBB (Bus Mgt; Bus Mgt (Fin)) (IB 33–32 pts)
Ulster – AAB–BBB (Bus St) (IB 28–26 pts HL 14–13 pts)

112 pts **Bangor** – 112 pts (Bus; Bus St Ital; Bus St courses)
Birmingham City – BBC 112 pts (Bus courses) (IB 28 pts HL 14 pts); BBC 112 pts+portfolio (Fash Bus Prom) (HL 14 pts)
Bradford – BBC 112 pts (Bus Mgt)
Buckingham – BBB–BBC (Bus Mgt courses) (IB 32–31 pts)
Cardiff Met – BBC 112 pts (Bus Mgt Fin; Bus Mgt HR Mgt; Bus Mgt Law; Bus Mgt courses) (IB 24 pts HL 12 pts)
De Montfort – 112 pts (Bus Mgt courses; Bus courses) (IB 26 pts)
East London – 112 pts (Bus Mgt) (IB 25 pts HL 15 pts)
Edge Hill – BBC 112 pts (Bus Mgt)
Gloucestershire – BBC 112 pts (Bus Mgt)
Glyndŵr – BBC 112 pts (Bus)
Greenwich – BBC 112 pts (Bus Entre Innov; Bus Mgt; Bus Prchsng Sply Chn Mgt; PR Comms)
Hull – 112 pts (Bus Mgt Fin Mgt; Bus courses) (IB 28 pts)
Leeds Beckett – 112 pts (Bus Mgt)
Leeds Trinity – 112 pts (Acc Bus; Bus Mark; Bus Mgt)
Lincoln – BBC 112 pts (Bus Mark; Bus Mgt; Bus St) (IB 29 pts)
Liverpool Hope – BBC 112 pts (Bus Mgt) (IB 26 pts)
Liverpool John Moores – BBC 112 pts (Bus Fin; Bus Mark) (IB 28 pts)
London (Birk) – ABB–BBC 112–128 pts (Mgt)
London Regent's – BBC (Glob Mgt courses)
Middlesex – 112 pts (Bus Mgt; Bus Mgt (Mark))
Nottingham Trent – BBC 112 pts (Law Bus)
Oxford Brookes – 112 pts (Bus Mgt) (IB 30 pts)
Portsmouth – 112–120 pts+interview (Bus Mgt) (IB 29 pts HL 655/754)
Robert Gordon – BBC (Mgt) (IB 29 pts)
Sheffield Hallam – 112 pts (Bus HR Mgt; Bus St; Bus courses)
Staffordshire – 112 pts (Bus Mgt)

Suffolk – BBC (Psy Bus Mgt); BBC 112 pts (Bus Mgt Law); BBC 112 pts +interview (Bus Mgt)
Sunderland – BBC 112 pts (Bus Fin Mgt; Bus HR Mgt; Bus Mark Mgt; Bus Mgt)
UWE Bristol – 112 pts (Bus Mgt Ldrshp; Bus Mgt courses; Bus courses)
Univ Law – BBC (Bus Mgt; Bus Mgt Mark) (IB 27 pts)
West London – BBC 112 pts (Bus St; Bus St Fin)
Westminster – ABB–BBC 112–128 pts (Bus Mgt (Mark); Bus Mgt courses) (IB 27 pts HL 4 Engl)
Worcester – 112 pts (Bus courses)

104 pts **Bolton** – 104 pts (Bus Mgt)
Bournemouth – 104–120 pts (Acc Bus) (IB 28–31 pts HL 55); (Bus Mgt) (IB 31–28 pts)
Buckingham – BBB–BCC +interview (Law Bus Mgt) (IB 32 pts)
Central Lancashire – 104–112 pts (Bus Mgt Chin)
Chester – BBC–BCC 104–112 pts (Bus Mgt) (IB 26 pts)
Dundee – BBB–BCC (Bus Mgt) (IB 30 pts HL 555)
Edinburgh Napier – BCC (Bus Mgt; Bus St) (IB 28 pts HL 654); BCC 104 pts (Bus Inf Tech) (IB 28 pts HL 654)
Glasgow Caledonian – BCC (Bus Mgt) (IB 25 pts)
Kent – BBC–BCC +interview (Bus Inf Tech) (IB 34 pts HL 14 pts)
Kingston – 104 pts (Bus Mgt) (IB 25 pts HL 4 Engl)
Leeds Beckett – 104 pts (Bus St)
London South Bank – BCC 104–112 pts (Bus Mgt Comb Hons)
Manchester Met – BBC-BCC 104–112 pts (Bus Mgt) (IB 26 pts); BBC–BCC 104–112 pts (Bus HR Mgt) (IB 26 pts)
Northampton – BCC 104–112 pts (Bus Comp (Sys); Bus Entre; Bus courses) (IB 25 pts)
Queen Margaret – BCC (Bus Mgt) (IB 28 pts)
SRUC – BCC (Rur Bus Mgt)
Salford – 104–112 pts (Bus Mgt) (IB 30 pts HL 5 Engl 4 maths)
Sheffield Hallam – BCC 104 pts (Bus Econ)
Winchester – 104–120 pts (Bus Mgt courses) (HL 44)

102 pts **West Scotland** – CCC (Bus) (IB 24 pts)
96 pts **Abertay** – CCC (Bus Mgt; Mark Bus) (IB 28 pts)
Aberystwyth – BBB–CCC 96–120 pts (Bus Mgt) (IB 30–26 pts)
Anglia Ruskin – 96 pts (Bus Mgt) (IB 24 pts)
Bath Spa – CCC (Bus Mgt (Acc); Bus Mgt courses) (IB 26 pts)
Bedfordshire – BBB–CCC 96–120 pts (Bus Mgt)
Brighton – BBB–CCC 96–120 pts (Law Bus) (IB 26 pts); BBB–CCC 96–120 pts +interview +portfolio (Fash Des Bus St) (IB 26 pts); BBC–CCC incl maths 96–112 pts (Maths Bus) (IB 26 pts HL 6 maths); BCC–CCC 96–104 pts (Bus Mgt Fin; Bus Mgt courses) (IB 26 pts)
Chichester – BBC–CCC 96–112 pts (Bus Mgt) (IB 28 pts)
Cumbria – BBC–CCC 96–112 pts (Bus Mgt)
Hertfordshire – CCC 96 pts (Bus St)
Keele – BBC–CCC (Bus Mgt Comb Hons) (IB 30–26 pts)
Leeds Beckett – 96 pts (Int Tour Mgt)
London Met – CCC 96 pts (Bus Econ) (IB 28 pts HL 15 pts)
Newman – 96–144 pts (Bus Mgt)
Roehampton – 96–112 pts (Bus Mgt) (IB 24 pts)
Royal Agricultural Univ – CCC +interview (Int Bus Mgt) (IB 26 pts)
Solent – CCC 96–112 pts (Bus Mgt) (IB 28 pts)
St Mary's – BCC–CCC 96–104 pts (Bus Law courses; Bus Mgt) (IB 28–24 pts)
Wolverhampton – CCC 96 pts (Bus Mgt)
York St John – 96–112 pts (Bus Mgt)

88 pts **Canterbury Christ Church** – 88–112 pts (Bus Mgt)
Harper Adams – 88–104 pts (Bus Mgt Mark) (IB 28 pts)
London Met – CCD 88 pts (Bus Inf Tech) (IB 28 pts HL 15 pts)
Plymouth – 88–96 pts (Bus) (IB 26–24 pts HL 4)
Teesside – 88–112 pts (Law Bus Mgt)

160 | BUSINESS and MANAGEMENT COURSES

Trinity Saint David – 88 pts +interview (Bus Mgt)
80 pts   **Bucks New** – 80 pts (Bus Mgt)
South Wales – BCC–CDD 80–104 pts (Bus Mgt) (IB 29 pts)
Teesside – 80–96 pts (Team Entre); 80–104 pts (Bus Mgt)
64 pts   **Worcester** – 64 pts (Bus St)
60 pts   **UHI** – D (Bus Mgt)
32 pts   **Arden** – EE (Bus Fin)

Open University – contact 0300 303 0073 or www.open.ac.uk/contact/new (Bus Mgt)

Alternative offers
See **Chapter 6** and **Appendix 1** for grades/UCAS Tariff points information for other examinations.

DEGREE APPRENTICESHIPS
Bolton (Rtl Bus Mgt); Chester (Bus Mgt); Queen Margaret (Bus Mgt); Robert Gordon (Bus Mgt, Bus Mgt Fin Serv); Kent (Mgt); Teesside (Bus Mgt) Portsmouth (Bus Ldrshp, Proj Mgt); Hull (Bus); Reading (Bus, (App Mgt-Chartered Manager Degree Apprenticeship).

CHOOSING YOUR COURSE (SEE ALSO CH.1)
Universities and colleges teaching quality See www.qaa.ac.uk; https://unistats.ac.uk.

Top research universities and colleges (REF 2014) (Business and Management Studies) Imperial London; London Bus Sch; Reading; Sheffield; Warwick; East Anglia; Lancaster; London LSE; Cambridge; Oxford; Cardiff; Bath; City; London (King's); Leeds.

Examples of sandwich degree courses Aston; Bangor; Bath; Bedfordshire; Birmingham City; Bournemouth; Bradford; Brighton; Brunel; Buckingham; Central Lancashire; Chester; Chichester; Coventry; De Montfort; Derby; Glasgow Caledonian; Gloucestershire; Greenwich; Harper Adams; Hertfordshire; Huddersfield; Hull; Keele; Kingston; Liverpool; Liverpool John Moores; Loughborough; Manchester Met; Newcastle; Nottingham Trent; Oxford Brookes; Plymouth; Portsmouth; Reading; Robert Gordon; Royal Agricultural Univ; Sheffield Hallam; Staffordshire; Surrey; Teesside; Trinity Saint David; Ulster; UWE Bristol; Westminster; Wolverhampton.

ADMISSIONS INFORMATION
Number of applicants per place (approx) Abertay (Bus St) 3; Anglia Ruskin 5; Aston (Bus Mgt) 12; Bangor 3; Bath 7; Birmingham 8; Blackpool and Fylde (Coll) 2; Bolton 3; Bradford 12; Bristol 10; Buckingham 5; Cardiff 8; Central Lancashire 15; City (Bus St) 9, (Mgt) 7; Colchester (UC) 2; De Montfort (Bus Mgt) 5; Durham 10; Edge Hill 4; Heriot-Watt 5; Hertfordshire 10; Huddersfield 4; Hull (Bus St) 5, (Mgt) 5; Kent 9; Kingston 50; Lancaster 6; Leeds 27, (Mgt St) 16; Leeds Trinity 6; Liverpool 7; London (King's) 25, (Mgt Sci) 12; London (RH) 9; London LSE 11; London Met 10; London Regent's 25; London South Bank 4; Manchester 7; Manchester Met (Bus St) 26; Middlesex 12; Newcastle 9; Oxford Brookes 7; Plymouth 21; Robert Gordon 5; Salford (Bus St) 9, (Mgt Sci) 2; Stirling 13; Strathclyde 12; Sunderland 20; Trinity Saint David 7; Warwick 22; West Scotland 5; Westminster 12; Winchester 5; Wolverhampton 7; York St John 3.

Admissions tutors' advice Buckingham Try to demonstrate that you have a genuine interest in business and explain why it fascinates you. Why have you decided to choose this particular course and how do you think it will add value to you in your pursuit of your career goals? **Leeds** Applicants taking the BTEC Extended Diploma may be required to take an additional Maths A-level paper.

Advice to applicants and planning the UCAS personal statement There are many different kinds of businesses and any work experience is almost essential for these courses. This should be described in detail: for example, size of firm, turnover, managerial problems, sales and marketing aspects, customers' attitudes. Any special interests in business management should also be included, for example, personnel work, purchasing, marketing. Give details of travel or work experience abroad and, for international courses, language expertise and examples of leadership and organising skills. Reference can be made to any particular business topics you have studied in the *Financial Times*, *The Economist* and the business sections in the weekend press. Applicants need to be sociable and ambitious team players. Say why you are interested in the course, identify your academic strengths, your personal strengths and interests. Check information on the websites of the Chartered Institute of Public Relations, the Chartered Institute of Marketing and the Chartered Institute of Personnel and Development. See **Appendix 3**; see also **Accountancy/Accounting**. **Bournemouth** Link your experiences, achievements and passions back to the subject area you are interested in. For example, take some time to think about why being a good communicator could help on a business degree.

Misconceptions about this course Aberystwyth Students are unaware that the course addresses practical aspects of business.

Selection interviews Yes Buckingham, Trinity Saint David; **Some** Bath, Blackpool and Fylde (Coll), Cardiff Met, Liverpool John Moores, Southampton, Warwick; **No** Aberystwyth, Anglia Ruskin, Birmingham, Birmingham City, Bradford, Brighton, City, Coventry, De Montfort, Derby, Dundee, East Anglia, Edge Hill, Essex, Glasgow Caledonian, Greenwich, Harper Adams, Hull, Kent, Leeds, London Met, Manchester Met, Middlesex, Northumbria, Nottingham, Nottingham Trent, Plymouth, Portsmouth, Robert Gordon, Roehampton, Salford, Sheffield Hallam, Staffordshire, Stirling, Strathclyde, Sunderland, Swansea, Teesside, West London, West Scotland, Winchester, Wolverhampton.

Interview advice and questions Any work experience you describe on the UCAS application will probably be the focus of questions which could include topics covering marketing, selling, store organisation and management and customer problems. Personal qualities are naturally important in a career in business, so be ready for such questions as: What qualities do you have which are suitable and important for this course? Describe your strengths and weaknesses. Why should we give you a place on this course? Is advertising fair? What qualities does a person in business require to be successful? What makes a good manager? What is a cash-flow system? What problems can it cause? How could supermarkets improve customer relations? See also **Chapter 5**. **Buckingham** Why Business? How do you see yourself in five years' time? Have you had any work experience? If so, discuss. **Wolverhampton** Mature students with no qualifications will be asked about their work experience.

Reasons for rejection (non-academic) Hadn't read the prospectus. Lack of communication skills. Limited commercial interest. Weak on numeracy and problem-solving. Lack of interview preparation (no questions). Lack of outside interests. Inability to cope with a year abroad. The candidate brought his parent who answered all the questions. See also **Marketing**. **Aberystwyth** Would have trouble fitting into the unique environment of Aberystwyth. Casual approach to learning. **Buckingham** Applicants are requested to attend an Open Day/Evening or a Tutorial Taster Day. The University believes it is very important for applicants to visit its campus. Candidates who do not respond to these invitations may be rejected, irrespective of academic achievement, as the University looks for committed, well-motivated students.

AFTER-RESULTS ADVICE
Offers to applicants repeating A-levels Higher Bradford; Greenwich; Hertfordshire; Kingston; Lancaster; Liverpool; Manchester Met; Sheffield; St Andrews; Strathclyde; Teesside; UWE Bristol; **Same** Abertay; Aberystwyth; Anglia Ruskin; Aston; Bath; Bath Spa; Birmingham City; Bolton; Brighton; Brunel; Buckingham; Cardiff; Cardiff Met; Chester; De Montfort; Derby; Durham; East Anglia; East London; Gloucestershire; Harper Adams; Huddersfield; Hull; Leeds; Lincoln; Liverpool Hope; Liverpool John Moores; Loughborough; Newman; Northumbria; Oxford Brookes; Robert Gordon; Roehampton; Royal Agricultural Univ; Salford; Sheffield Hallam; Staffordshire; Stirling; Suffolk; Sunderland; Trinity Saint David; Ulster; West London; West Scotland; Winchester; Wolverhampton; Worcester; York St John; **No** Glasgow.

GRADUATE DESTINATIONS AND EMPLOYMENT (2016/17 HESA)
Business Studies graduates surveyed 17,390 **Employed** 10,710 **In voluntary employment** 390 **In further study** 2,980 **Assumed unemployed** 920

Career note The majority of graduates enter trainee management roles in business-related and administrative careers, many specialising in some of the areas listed in Other degree subjects for consideration below. The main graduate destinations are in finance, property development, wholesale, retail and manufacturing.

OTHER DEGREE SUBJECTS FOR CONSIDERATION

Accountancy; Banking; Business Information Technology; E-Business; Economics; Estate Management; Finance; Hospitality Management; Housing Management; Human Resource Management; Insurance; Leisure Management; Logistics; Marketing; Public Administration; Retail Management; Sports Management; Surveying.

BUSINESS AND MANAGEMENT COURSES (INTERNATIONAL AND EUROPEAN)

(including **Business Management with a European Language**; see also **Business and Management Courses, Business and Management Courses (Specialised), Hospitality and Event Management, Human Resource Management, Leisure and Recreation Management/Studies, Marketing, Retail Management, Tourism and Travel**)

Useful websites See **Business and Management Courses**.

NB The points totals shown to the left of the institutions are for ease of reference only. It must not be assumed that Tariff points are always used by institutions or that they can be substituted for an offer in grades. The level of an offer is not necessarily indicative of the quality of a course.

COURSE OFFERS INFORMATION

Subject requirements/preferences GCSE Mathematics and English often at grade A or B (7 or 5/6) required. **AL** A language will be stipulated for most courses in this subject area. In some cases grades A, B or C may be required.

Your target offers and examples of degree courses

144 pts **Bath** – AAA/A*AB (Int Mgt) (IB 36 pts HL 765/666)
Exeter – AAA (Bus Mgt (Int St)) (IB 36 pts HL 666)
Leeds – AAA (Int Bus; Int Bus Fin) (IB 35 pts HL 17 pts)
London (UCL) – AAA incl maths (Econ Bus E Euro St) (IB 38 pts HL 18 pts incl 6 maths)
Warwick – AAA (Int Mgt) (IB 38 pts); AAA incl lang (Int Bus courses) (IB 38 pts HL 5 lang)

136 pts **Bath** – AAB/ABB +aEPQ incl Ger (Int Mgt Ger) (IB 35 pts HL 665 incl 6 Ger); AAB–ABB+aEPQ incl Fr (Int Mgt Fr) (IB 36 pts HL 665 incl 6 Fr); AAB–ABB+aEPQ incl Span (Int Mgt Span) (IB 36 pts HL 665 incl 6 Span)
Birmingham – AAB (Int Bus; Int Bus Lang) (IB 32 pts HL 665)
Lancaster – AAB incl lang (Int Bus Mgt (Yr Abrd)) (IB 35 pts HL 16 pts)
London (King's) – AAB (Mgt Modn Lang (Yr Abrd)) (IB 35 pts HL 665)
Manchester – AAB (Int Mgt; Int Mgt Am Bus St) (IB 35 pts HL 665)
Newcastle – AAB (Int Bus Mgt) (IB 35 pts)
Southampton – AAB/ABB +aEPQ incl Fr/Ger/Span (Bus Mgt Fr/Ger/Span) (IB 34 pts HL 17 pts incl 6 Fr/Ger/Span)

128 pts **Cardiff** – AAB–ABB (Bus Mgt (Int Mgt)) (IB 34–32 pts HL 665–655); AAB–ABB incl lang (Bus Mgt Euro Lang) (IB 34–32 pts HL 665–655 incl 6 lang)
Edinburgh – AAB–ABB (Int Bus; Int Bus Fr/Ger/Span) (IB 40–34 pts HL 766–655)
Liverpool – ABB (Int Bus; Modn Lang St Bus) (IB 33 pts)
London (QM) – ABB incl hum/soc sci (Russ Bus Mgt) (IB 32 pts HL 655)
London (RH) – AAB–ABB (Mgt Int Bus; Modn Lang Mgt) (IB 32 pts HL 655)
London (SOAS) – AAB–ABB (Int Mgt courses) (IB 35 pts HL 665)
Loughborough – AAB–ABB (Int Bus) (IB 35–34 pts HL 665)
Northumbria – 128 pts (Int Bus Mgt)
Nottingham Trent – ABB 128 pts (Int Bus Comb Hons)
Queen's Belfast – ABB (Int Bus Fr/Ger/Mand Chin) (IB 33 pts HL 665 incl lang)
Reading – ABB (Int Bus Mgt; Int Mgt Bus Admin Fr/Ger/Ital) (IB 32 pts)
Sheffield – ABB (Int Bus Mgt (St Abrd)) (IB 33 pts); ABB 128 pts (Bus Mgt Jap St) (IB 33 pts)

Surrey – ABB (Int Bus Mgt) (IB 32 pts); ABB incl Fr/Ger/Span (Bus Mgt Fr/Ger/Span) (IB 32 pts HL 5 lang)

Sussex – AAB–ABB (Int Bus) (IB 34–32 pts)

120 pts **Aston** – ABB–BBB (Int Bus Fr/Ger/Span) (IB 32 pts HL 665–655)

Brunel – BBB (Int Bus) (IB 30 pts)

Coventry – ABB–BBB (Int Bus Mgt) (IB 31-30 pts)

Essex – BBB (Int Bus Entre) (IB 30 pts)

Heriot-Watt – BBB (Int Bus Mgt (Econ/Ops Mgt)) (IB 29 pts); BBB incl lang (Int Bus Mgt Fr/Ger/Span/Chin) (IB 30 pts HL 5 lang)

Huddersfield – BBB 120 pts (Int Bus)

Kent – BBB (Int Bus) (IB 34 pts HL 16 pts)

Stirling – BBB (Int Mgt St Euro Langs Soty) (IB 32 pts)

112 pts **Bradford** – BBC 112 pts (Int Bus Mgt)

Cardiff Met – BBC 112 pts (Int Bus Mgt) (IB 24 pts HL 12 pts)

Coventry – BBC (Int Fash Bus) (IB 30 pts)

De Montfort – 112 pts (Int Bus) (IB 26 pts)

Gloucestershire – BBC 112 pts (Int Bus Mgt)

Greenwich – BBC 112 pts (Int Bus)

Hertfordshire – BBC 112 pts (Int Bus)

Hull – 112 pts (Int Bus) (IB 28 pts)

Kingston – 112 pts (Int Bus)

Liverpool John Moores – BBC 112 pts (Bus Int Bus Mgt) (IB 28 pts)

London Regent's – BBC (Glob Mgt courses; Int Bus)

Middlesex – 112 pts (Bus Mgt Mand); BBC 112 pts (Int Bus)

Oxford Brookes – BBC 112 pts (Int Bus Mgt) (IB 30 pts)

Portsmouth – 112–120 pts (Int Bus) (IB 29 pts HL 655/754)

Robert Gordon – BBC (Int Bus Mgt) (IB 29 pts)

Roehampton – 112 pts+interview (Int Bus)
Salford – BBC 112 pts (Int Bus) (IB 30 pts)
Sheffield Hallam – 112 pts incl Fr/Ger/Span (Langs Int Bus (Fr/Ger/Span))
UWE Bristol – 112 pts (Int Bus)
Westminster – ABB–BBC 112–128 pts (Int Bus) (IB 27 pts HL 4 Engl)

104 pts **Central Lancashire** – 104–112 pts (Int Bus)
Chester – BBC–BCC 104–112 pts (Int Bus Mgt) (IB 26 pts)
Dundee – BBB–BCC (Int Bus) (IB 30 pts HL 555)
Glasgow Caledonian – BCC (Int Bus) (IB 25 pts)
Leeds Beckett – 104 pts (Int Bus)
Lincoln – BCC (Int Bus Mgt) (IB 28 pts)
Manchester Met – BBC–BCC 104–112 pts (Int Bus Mgt) (IB 26 pts); BBC–BCC 104–112 pts incl lang (Int Bus/Fr/Span) (IB 26 pts)
Sheffield Hallam – 104 pts (Int Bus)
Westminster – ABB–BCC 104–128 pts (Int Bus (Arbc/Chin/Fr/Span)) (IB 27 pts HL 4 Engl)

96 pts **Anglia Ruskin** – 96 pts (Int Bus Mgt) (IB 24 pts)
Bedfordshire – BBB–CCC 96–120 pts (Bus St (Int))
Brighton – BBC–CCC 96–112 pts (Int Bus Mgt) (IB 26 pts)
Edinburgh Napier – CCC incl lang (Int Bus Mgt Lang) (IB 27 pts HL 654 incl 5 lang)
Keele – BBC–CCC (Int Bus Comb Hons) (IB 30–26 pts)
London Met – CCC 96 pts (Int Bus Mgt) (IB 28 pts HL 15 pts)
Middlesex – 96 pts (Int Tour Mgt (Span))
Wolverhampton – CCC 96 pts (Int Bus Mgt)
York St John – 96–112 pts (Int Bus)

88 pts **Plymouth** – 88–96 pts (Int Bus) (IB 26–24 pts HL 4)

Alternative offers
See **Chapter 6** and **Appendix 1** for grades/UCAS Tariff points information for other examinations.

EXAMPLES OF COLLEGES OFFERING COURSES IN THIS SUBJECT FIELD

Blackburn (Coll); Bristol City (Coll); Cornwall (Coll); Doncaster (Coll); Durham New (Coll); Ealing, Hammersmith and West London (Coll); HOW (Coll); Newcastle (Coll); Nottingham (Coll); Riverside (Coll); South Essex (Coll).

CHOOSING YOUR COURSE (SEE ALSO CH.1)

Universities and colleges teaching quality See www.qaa.ac.uk; https://unistats.ac.uk.

Top research universities and colleges (REF 2014) See **Business and Management Courses**.

Examples of sandwich degree courses Anglia Ruskin; Aston; Bath; Bournemouth; Bradford; Brighton; Brunel; De Montfort; Greenwich; Hertfordshire; Leeds Beckett; Loughborough; Manchester Met; Middlesex; Northumbria; Nottingham Trent; Oxford Brookes; Plymouth; Portsmouth; Robert Gordon; Sheffield Hallam; Staffordshire; Sussex.

ADMISSIONS INFORMATION

Number of applicants per place (approx) Anglia Ruskin 5; Aston (Int Bus) 6; Bath 26; Birmingham 28; Blackpool and Fylde (Coll) 2; Bradford 12; Cardiff 8; Central Lancashire 15; Colchester (UC) 2; Derby 4; Heriot-Watt 6; Hertfordshire 10; Huddersfield 2; Kingston 50; Leeds 27; London (King's) 25; London (RH) 9; London Met 10; London Regent's 25; Manchester Met (Int Bus) 8; Middlesex 12; Newcastle 8; Oxford Brookes 7; Plymouth 39; Robert Gordon 5; Sheffield Hallam (Int Bus) 6; Warwick 22; Westminster 12; Wolverhampton 7; York St John 3.

Advice to applicants and planning the UCAS personal statement See **Business and Management Courses**.

Misconceptions about this course Aston (Int Bus Fr) Not two separate disciplines – the two subjects are integrated involving the study of language in a business and management context.

Selection interviews Some Bath, Cardiff Met, Warwick; **No** Anglia Ruskin, Birmingham, Bradford, Brighton, Coventry, De Montfort, Derby, Glasgow Caledonian, Greenwich, Hull, Leeds, London Met, Manchester Met, Middlesex, Northumbria, Nottingham Trent, Plymouth, Robert Gordon, Roehampton, Salford, Sheffield Hallam, Staffordshire, Stirling, Wolverhampton.

Interview advice and questions See **Business and Management Courses**.

Reasons for rejection (non-academic) See **Business and Management Courses**.

AFTER-RESULTS ADVICE
Offers to applicants repeating A-levels Higher Bradford; Greenwich; Hertfordshire; Kingston; Liverpool; Manchester Met; Sheffield; **Same** Anglia Ruskin; Aston; Bath; Brighton; Cardiff; Cardiff Met; Chester; De Montfort; Derby; Gloucestershire; Huddersfield; Hull; Leeds; Lincoln; Loughborough; Northumbria; Oxford Brookes; Robert Gordon; Roehampton; Salford; Sheffield Hallam; Staffordshire; Stirling; Wolverhampton; York St John.

GRADUATE DESTINATIONS AND EMPLOYMENT (2016/17 HESA)
Graduates surveyed See **Business and Management Courses**.

Career note See **Business and Management Courses**.

OTHER DEGREE SUBJECTS FOR CONSIDERATION
Accountancy; Banking; Business Information Technology; E-Business; Economics; Estate Management; Finance; Hospitality Management; Housing Management; Human Resource Management; Insurance; Leisure Management; Logistics; Marketing; Public Administration; Retail Management; Sports Management; Surveying.

BUSINESS AND MANAGEMENT COURSES (SPECIALISED)

(including **Advertising, Agri-Business Management, Business, Marketing and Consumer Behaviour, Food Science with Business, Public Relations and Publishing**; see also **Business and Management Courses, Business and Management Courses (international and European), Hospitality and Event Management, Human Resource Management, Leisure and Recreation Management/Studies, Marketing, Retail Management, Tourism and Travel**)

Useful websites See **Business and Management Courses**.

NB The points totals shown to the left of the institutions are for ease of reference only. It must not be assumed that Tariff points are always used by institutions or that they can be substituted for an offer in grades. The level of an offer is not necessarily indicative of the quality of a course.

COURSE OFFERS INFORMATION
Subject requirements/preferences GCSE Mathematics and English often at grade A or B (7 or 5/6) required. **AL** Mathematics required for some courses. In some cases grades A, B or C may be required. (Publ) English required for some courses.

Your target offers and examples of degree courses
152 pts **Southampton** – A*AA/A*AB +aEPQ incl maths+phys (Aero Astnaut (Eng Mgt) (MEng)) (IB 38 pts HL 18 pts incl 6 maths+phys)
144 pts **London (UCL)** – AAA incl chem+sci/maths (Chem Mgt St) (IB 38 pts HL 18 pts incl 6 chem+sci/maths)
        Warwick – AAA incl maths+phys (Eng Bus Mgt) (IB 38 pts HL 6 maths+phys)
136 pts **Lancaster** – AAB (Adv Mark; Int Bus Mgt (Fr)) (IB 35 pts HL 16 pts)
        Loughborough – AAB (Geog Mgt) (IB 35 pts HL 665)

Ulster – AAA–AAB (Comm Adv Mark) (IB 29–28 pts HL 14 pts)

128 pts **Cardiff** – AAB–ABB (Bus Mgt (Log Ops)) (IB 34–32 pts HL 665–655)
Edinburgh – AAA–ABB incl sci/maths (Ecol Env Sci Mgt) (IB 37–32 pts HL 555)
Leeds – ABB (Env Bus) (IB 34 pts HL 16 pts)
London (SOAS) – AAB–ABB (Int Mgt SE As St) (IB 35 pts HL 665)
Reading – ABB incl sci/maths +interview (Fd Sci Bus) (IB 32 pts HL 5 sci/maths)

120 pts **Coventry** – ABB–BBB (Bus Mark) (IB 31–30 pts)
Derby – BBB 120 pts (Bus Mgt Comb Hons)
East Anglia – BBB (Intercult Comm Bus Mgt) (IB 31 pts)
Essex – BBB (Lat Am St Bus Mgt) (IB 30 pts)
Heriot-Watt – BBB (Bus Fin) (IB 29 pts)
Huddersfield – BBB 120 pts (Air Trans Log Mgt)
Newcastle – ABB–BBB (Agribus Mgt) (IB 32 pts)
Nottingham Trent – BBB 120 pts (Fash Mgt)
Ulster – BBB incl sci/maths/tech (Eng Mgt) (IB 26 pts HL 13 pts incl 5 maths+sci)

112 pts **Arts London (CFash)** – 112 pts (Fash Mgt) (IB 25 pts)
Coventry – BBC (Int Fash Bus) (IB 30 pts)
Creative Arts – 112 pts+interview (Fash Bus Mgt) (IB 30–27 pts)
De Montfort – 112 pts (Adv Mark Comms) (IB 26 pts)
Derby – BBC 112 pts (Int Tour Mgt)
East London – BBC 112 pts (Adv; HR Mgt) (IB 25 pts HL 15 pts)
Leeds Beckett – 112 pts (Spo Bus Mgt) (IB 25 pts)
Liverpool John Moores – BBC 112 pts (Marit Bus Mgt) (IB 26 pts)
London (Birk) – ABB–BBC 112–128 pts (Env Mgt)
Middlesex – 112 pts (Mus Bus Arts Mgt) (IB -28 pts)
Nottingham Trent – BBC 112 pts (Quant Surv Commer Mgt)
Oxford Brookes – 112 pts (Quant Surv Commer Mgt) (IB 30 pts)
Sheffield Hallam – BBC 112 pts (Bus Fin Mgt; IT Bus St)
Sunderland – BBC 112 pts (Tour Mgt)
West London – BBC 112 pts (Adv PR; Airln Airpt Mgt; Culn Arts Mgt)

104 pts **Bournemouth** – 104–120 pts (Bus Mgt (Fin)) (IB 31–28 pts)
Buckingham – BBB–BCC (Bus Mgt App Comp) (IB 32–31 pts)
Central Lancashire – 104 pts (Pub); 104–112 pts +interview +portfolio (Crea Adv)
Coventry – ABB–BCC (Disas Emer Mgt) (IB 30 pts)
Glasgow Caledonian – BCC (Risk Mgt) (IB 25 pts)
Manchester Met – BBC–BCC 104–112 pts (Bus Mgt (Rtl); Spo Bus Mgt) (IB -26 pts)
Northampton – BCC 104–112 pts (Bus Entre) (IB 25 pts)
Robert Gordon – BCC (Fash Mgt) (IB 28 pts)
Royal Agricultural Univ – BCC (Rur Lnd Mgt) (IB 26 pts)

96 pts **Arts London (CFash)** – 96 pts +interview +portfolio (Fash PR Comm)
Birmingham (UC) – CCC 96 pts (Bus Ent)
Harper Adams – 96–112 pts +interview (Agric Frm Bus Mgt) (IB 28 pts)
Hertfordshire – CCC 96 pts (Mus Ind Mgt)
Liverpool (LIPA) – CCC 96 pts +interview (Mgt Mus Enter Thea Evnts)
London Met – CCC 96 pts (Mus Bus) (IB 28 pts HL 15 pts)
Nottingham Trent – CCC 96 pts (Constr Mgt)
Plymouth – 96–112 pts (Marit Bus Log; Marit Bus Marit Law) (IB 28 pts HL 4)
Royal Agricultural Univ – CCC (Int Bus Mgt (Fd Agribus)) (IB 26 pts)
Solent – 96–112 pts (Marit Bus); CCC 96–112 pts (Advntr Out Mgt) (IB 28 pts)
UCEM – 96 pts (Rl Est Mgt)

88 pts **Plymouth** – 88–96 pts +interview (Cru Mgt) (IB 26–24 pts HL 4)
Trinity Saint David – 88 pts +interview (Int Trav Tour Mgt; Spo Mgt)

80 pts **Arts London** – 80 pts (PR)
Bedfordshire – 80–96 pts (Adv Mark Comms)
Bucks New – 80–96 pts (Airln Airpt Mgt)

Colchester (UC) – 80 pts (Constr Mgt (Site Mgt))
South Wales – BCC–CCD 80–104 pts (Bus Mgt Evnt Mgt) (IB 29 pts)
Sparsholt (Coll) – CCE incl sci (Aqua Fish Mgt) (IB 24 pts HL 4 sci)
Trinity Saint David – 80 pts +interview (Tour Mgt)
72 pts   **Solent** – DDD 72–96 pts (Fash Mgt Mark) (IB 28 pts)
64 pts   **London (Royal Central Sch SpDr)** – 64–120 pts +interview +portfolio (Thea Prac (Stg Mgt);
      Thea Prac (Tech Prod Mgt))
Trinity Saint David – 64 pts +interview (Mtrspo Mgt)
UHI – CC (Glf Mgt)
32 pts   **Plymouth** – 32–80 pts (Marit Bus Log Fdn Yr) (IB 25–24 pts HL 4)
24 pts   **UHI** – D +interview (Mus Bus)

Alternative offers
See **Chapter 6** and **Appendix 1** for grades/UCAS Tariff points information for other examinations.

CHOOSING YOUR COURSE (SEE ALSO CH.1)
Universities and colleges teaching quality See www.qaa.ac.uk; https://unistats.ac.uk.

Top research universities and colleges (REF 2014) See **Business and Management Courses**.

Examples of sandwich degree courses Birmingham (UC); Bournemouth; Central Lancashire; Coventry; De Montfort; Harper Adams; Hertfordshire; Huddersfield; Lancaster; Leeds Beckett; Liverpool John Moores; Loughborough; Manchester Met; Newcastle; Nottingham Trent; Oxford Brookes; Portsmouth; Reading; Sheffield Hallam; Solent; Trinity Saint David; Ulster.

ADMISSIONS INFORMATION
Number of applicants per place (approx) Birmingham (UC) 5; Blackpool and Fylde (Coll) 2; Cardiff 8; Central Lancashire 15; Colchester (UC) 2; Edge Hill 4; Heriot-Watt 5; Hertfordshire 10; Huddersfield 4; Leeds 27; London (UCL) 8; London South Bank 4; Middlesex 12; Newcastle 8; Oxford Brookes 7; Plymouth 57; Robert Gordon 5; Trinity Saint David 7; Warwick 22; West Scotland 5.

Advice to applicants and planning the UCAS personal statement See **Business and Management Courses**.

Misconceptions about this course Bournemouth Advertising is not mainly a creative course but also includes strategy, planning, finance and the management of the advertising process.

Selection interviews Yes Trinity Saint David; **Some** Blackpool and Fylde (Coll), Cardiff Met, Coventry, Plymouth, Warwick; **No** De Montfort, Derby, East Anglia, Edge Hill, Glasgow Caledonian, Greenwich, Harper Adams, Leeds, Liverpool John Moores, Manchester Met, Middlesex, Nottingham Trent, Robert Gordon, Sheffield Hallam, Stirling, Sunderland, West London.

Interview advice and questions For Consumer Studies/Science, questions will stem from your special interests in this subject and in the past have included: What interests you in consumer behaviour? What are the advantages and disadvantages of measuring consumer behaviour? What is ergonomics? What do you understand by the term sustainable consumption? What world or national news has annoyed, pleased or upset you? What relevance do textiles and dress have to home economics? How would you react in a room full of fools?

Reasons for rejection (non-academic) Buckingham Applicants are requested to attend an Open Day/Evening or a Tutorial Taster Day. The University believes it is very important for applicants to visit its campus. Candidates who do not respond to these invitations may be rejected, irrespective of academic achievement, as the University looks for committed, well-motivated students.

AFTER-RESULTS ADVICE
Offers to applicants repeating A-levels Higher Hertfordshire; Lancaster; Manchester Met; **Same** Cardiff; Cardiff Met; De Montfort; Derby; East Anglia; Huddersfield; Leeds; Liverpool John Moores; Loughborough; Oxford Brookes; Robert Gordon; Royal Agricultural Univ; Sheffield Hallam; Ulster; West London; Worcester.

GRADUATE DESTINATIONS AND EMPLOYMENT (2016/17 HESA)
Graduates surveyed See **Business and Management Courses**.

Career note See **Business and Management Courses**.

OTHER DEGREE SUBJECTS FOR CONSIDERATION
Accountancy; Banking; Business Information Technology; E-Business; Economics; Estate Management; Finance; Hospitality Management; Housing Management; Human Resource Management; Insurance; Leisure Management; Logistics; Marketing; Public Administration; Retail Management; Sports Management; Surveying.

CELTIC, IRISH, SCOTTISH AND WELSH STUDIES

(including Celtic and Linguistics and Gaelic Studies)

Strong evidence of Celtic civilisation and language exists in Ireland, Scotland, Wales, Cornwall, the Isle of Man and across the Celtic Sea in Brittany, although the Celts are believed to have inhabited much of Great Britain prior to the arrival of the Saxons and afterwards. In Great Britain, the Welsh language is spoken by 19% of the Welsh population, mainly in the border counties and Gwynedd, where it is reported that 70% of the population are fluent speakers. Scottish Gaelic is native to Scotland and bears strong similarities to the Irish language. The 'Scots' dialect of English is also spoken in the Lowlands and the Northern Isles. In Ireland, the native Irish language is taught in schools throughout the island. In the Gaeltacht areas of the Republic of Ireland, the language is used on an everyday basis. The content of courses in each of these languages, such as the Celtic option at Aberystwyth (the largest department of Welsh in the UK), will cover the history, literature and the language and its place in the modern world. Cambridge also offers a degree in Anglo Saxon, Norse and Celtic, unique in the UK for those fascinated by medieval history, literature, languages and archaeology. It is offered by all colleges and there are no specific subject requirements.

Useful websites http://gov.wales; www.bbc.co.uk/wales; www.daltai.com; www.eisteddfod.cymru; www.digitalmedievalist.com

NB The points totals shown to the left of the institutions are for ease of reference only. It must not be assumed that Tariff points are always used by institutions or that they can be substituted for an offer in grades. The level of an offer is not necessarily indicative of the quality of a course.

COURSE OFFERS INFORMATION
Subject requirements/preferences GCSE A foreign language or Welsh may be required. **AL** Welsh may be required for some courses.

Your target offers and examples of degree courses
152 pts   **Cambridge** – A*AA (A-Sxn Nrs Celt) (IB 42–40 pts HL 776)
144 pts   **St Andrews** – AAA incl hist (Scot Hist courses) (IB 38 pts HL 666 incl hist)
136 pts   **Glasgow** – AAB incl arts/hum (Celt Civ courses) (IB 36 pts HL 665 incl Eng+hum/lang); (Celt St courses; Gael; Scot Lit) (IB 36 pts HL 665 incl Engl+hum/lang)
128 pts   **Edinburgh** – AAB–ABB incl Engl (Engl Scot Lit) (IB 40–34 pts HL 766–655 incl 5 Engl); ABB (Celt; Celt Arch; Celt Ling; Celt Scot Hist; Scot Ethnol; Scot St) (IB 34 pts HL 655); (P Educ Gael) (IB 34 pts HL 655 incl 5 Engl); ABB incl Engl (Celt Engl Lit; Celt Scot Lit; Scot Lit) (IB 34 pts HL 655 incl 5 Engl)
           Queen's Belfast – ABB incl Ir (Ir)
120 pts   **Aberdeen** – BBB (Celt A-Sxn St; Celt A-Sxn St Comb Hons; Engl Scot Lit; Gael St) (IB 32 pts HL 555)
           Liverpool – BBB (Ir St Comb Hons) (IB 30 pts)
           Stirling – BBB (Scot Hist) (IB 32 pts)
           Swansea – ABB–BBB 120 pts (Welsh courses) (IB 33–32 pts)

112 pts   **Bangor** – 112 pts (Welsh Hist Comb Hons; Welsh Hist Mus); 112 pts incl Welsh (Prof Welsh (Cym Prof))

104 pts   **Aberystwyth** – BBB–BCC 104–120 pts (Ir Comb Hons; Welsh courses) (IB 30–28 pts)
           Cardiff – BBC–BCC incl Welsh (Welsh) (HL 665)

96 pts   **Aberystwyth** – BBB–CCC 96–120 pts (Celt St; Hist Welsh Hist) (IB 30–26 pts)

72 pts   **UHI** – BC (Scot Hist; Scot Hist Arch); BC+interview (Gael Dev; Gael Media St); BC+interview +audition (Gael Trad Mus)

Alternative offers
See **Chapter 6** and **Appendix 1** for grades/UCAS Tariff points information for other examinations.

CHOOSING YOUR COURSE (SEE ALSO CH.1)
Universities and colleges teaching quality See www.qaa.ac.uk; https://unistats.ac.uk.

ADMISSIONS INFORMATION
Number of applicants per place (approx) Bangor (Welsh) 5; Cambridge 3; Cardiff 2; Swansea 7.

Advice to applicants and planning the UCAS personal statement Interests in this field largely develop through literature, museum visits or archaeology which should be fully described in the UCAS application.

Selection interviews Yes Cambridge; **No** Aberystwyth.

Interview advice and questions Past questions have included: Why do you want to study this subject? What specific areas of Celtic culture interest you? What do you expect to gain by studying unusual subjects? See **Chapter 5**.

AFTER-RESULTS ADVICE
Offers to applicants repeating A-levels Same Aberystwyth; Bangor; Cardiff; Swansea; **No** Glasgow.

GRADUATE DESTINATIONS AND EMPLOYMENT (2016/17 HESA)
Celtic Studies graduates surveyed 170 **Employed** 55 **In voluntary employment** 0 **In further study** 60 **Assumed unemployed** 5

Career note See **Combined Courses** and **Languages**.

OTHER DEGREE SUBJECTS FOR CONSIDERATION
Anthropology; Archaeology; English; History; Linguistics.

CHEMISTRY

(see also **Biochemistry, Engineering (Chemical), Pharmacy and Pharmaceutical Sciences**)

There is a shortage of applicants for this subject despite the fact that it's the basis of many careers in the manufacturing industries, such areas as pharmaceuticals, medicine, veterinary science and health, agriculture, petroleum, cosmetics, plastics, the food industry, colour chemistry and aspects of the environment such as pollution and recycling. Most courses will offer a range of compulsory modules (possibly up to 75% of a course) and a series of optional modules. For example, at the University of York, compulsory modules will include organic, inorganic and physical chemistry. Optional modules on offer cover air quality and human health, analytical and forensic science, atmospheric chemistry and climate, biological chemistry, environmental chemistry, green chemistry, industrial management, materials chemistry and medical chemistry. These options at all universities enable students to begin to focus on special studies and lay a foundation for possible future careers.

Useful websites www.rsc.org; www.chem.ox.ac.uk/vrchemistry

NB The points totals shown to the left of the institutions are for ease of reference only. It must not be assumed that Tariff points are always used by institutions or that they can be substituted for an offer in grades. The level of an offer is not necessarily indicative of the quality of a course.

COURSE OFFERS INFORMATION

Subject requirements/preferences GCSE English, mathematics/science subjects usually required. A/B (7/5 or 6) grades often stipulated by popular universities. **AL** Two science subjects including chemistry usually required.

Your target offers and examples of degree courses

160 pts **Cambridge** – A*A*A incl sci/maths +interview +NSAA (Nat Sci (Chem)) (IB 42–40 pts HL 776)

Oxford – A*A*A incl chem+maths +interview +TSA (Chem) (IB 40 pts HL 7 chem+6/7 sci/maths)

152 pts **Durham** – A*AA incl chem+maths (Chem) (IB 38 pts HL 666)

144 pts **Bath** – AAA/AAB+aEPQ incl chem+sci/maths (Chem courses) (IB 36 pts HL 666 incl chem+sci/maths)

Bristol – AAA incl chem (Chem) (IB 36 pts HL 18 pts incl 6 chem)

Imperial London – AAA incl chem+maths +interview (Chem (Yr Ind/Rsch); Chem Fr/Ger/Span Sci; Chem Medcnl Chem; Chem Mol Phys (MSci); Chem courses) (IB 38 pts HL 6 chem+maths)

London (UCL) – AAA incl chem+maths+phys (Cheml Phys) (IB 38 pts HL 18 pts incl 5 chem+maths+phys); AAA incl chem+sci/maths (Chem; Chem Euro Lang; Chem Mgt St; Medcnl Chem) (IB 38 pts HL 18 pts incl 6 chem+sci/maths); AAA incl maths+chem (Chem Maths) (IB 38 pts HL 18 pts incl 6 chem+maths)

Manchester – AAA incl chem+sci/maths +interview (Chem; Chem Medcnl Chem) (IB 36 pts HL 666 incl chem+sci/maths)

Queen's Belfast – AAA incl chem+sci+Fr/Span (Chem Fr/Span/Yr Abrd (MSci)) (IB 36 pts HL 666 incl chem+sci+Fr/Span)

St Andrews – AAA incl chem (Chem) (IB 38 pts HL 666 incl chem)

136 pts **Glasgow** – AAB incl chem+maths (Chem) (IB 36 pts HL 665 incl 6 chem+maths)

Leeds – AAB incl chem (Chem courses; Medcnl Chem) (IB 35 pts HL 16 pts incl 6 chem)

London (King's) – AAB incl chem+sci/maths (Chem; Chem Biomed) (IB 35 pts HL 665 incl 6 chem+sci/maths)

Newcastle – AAB incl chem (Chem (MChem)) (IB 33 pts HL 6 chem)

Nottingham – AAB incl chem+sci (Bioch Biol Chem) (IB 34 pts HL 5 chem+sci); AAB incl maths+phys+chem +interview (Chem Mol Phys) (IB 34 pts HL 6 maths 6/5 phys+chem)

Southampton – AAA–AAB incl chem+maths (Chem Maths (MChem)) (IB 36–34 pts HL 18–17 pts incl 6 chem+maths); AAA–AAB incl chem+sci/maths (Chem Medcnl Sci (MChem)) (IB 36–34 pts HL 18–17 pts incl 6 chem+sci/maths)

Warwick – AAB incl chem+sci/maths (Chem; Chem Medcnl Chem) (IB 36 pts HL 6 chem 5 maths/sci)

York – A*AA–AAB incl chem+sci/maths (Chem; Chem Atmos Env) (IB 37–35 pts HL 6 chem+sci/maths); A*AA–AAB incl chem+sci/maths +interview (Chem Biol Medcnl Chem) (IB 37–35 pts HL 6 chem+sci/maths)

128 pts **Birmingham** – AAB–ABB incl chem (Chem; Chem Modn Lang) (IB 32 pts HL 665–655 incl chem)

Cardiff – AAB–ABB incl chem +interview (Chem) (IB 34–30 pts)

Dundee – AAB–ABB incl biol+chem (Biol Chem Drug Dscvry) (IB 30 pts HL 555 incl biol+chem)

Edinburgh – AAA–ABB incl chem+maths (Chem; Medcnl Biol Chem) (IB 37–32 pts HL 666–555)

Hull – B chem 128 pts incl chem (Chem) (IB 32 pts HL 6 chem)

Lancaster – ABB incl chem+sci (Chem) (IB 32 pts HL 16 pts incl 6 chem+sci)

Liverpool – ABB/BBB +aEPQ incl chem+sci (Chem; Chem (Yr Ind); Medcnl Chem) (IB 33 pts HL 6 chem 5 sci)

London (QM) – ABB incl chem (Chem) (IB 34 pts HL 655 incl chem)

Loughborough – ABB incl chem (Chem; Chem (MChem); Medcnl Pharml Chem) (IB 34 pts HL 655 incl chem)

Newcastle – ABB incl chem (Chem; Chem (Yr Ind); Chem Medcnl Chem) (IB 32 pts HL 6 chem)

Nottingham – AAB–ABB incl chem (Chem) (IB 34–32 pts HL 6 chem); AAB–ABB incl chem+interview (Medcnl Biol Chem) (IB 34–32 pts Hl 6 chem)

Nottingham Trent – ABB incl chem 128 pts (Chem (MChem))

Reading – ABB incl chem +interview (Chem (MChem)) (IB 32 pts HL 6 chem)

Sheffield – ABB incl chem (Chem) (IB 33 pts HL 5 chem)

Southampton – AAB–ABB incl chem (Chem) (IB 34–32 pts HL 17–16 pts incl 6 chem)

Strathclyde – AAA–ABB incl sci/maths (Foren Analyt Chem (MChem)) (IB 34 pts); AAB–ABB incl sci/maths (Chem Teach (MChem)) (IB 34 pts)

Sussex – ABB incl chem (Chem) (IB 34–32 pts HL 5 chem)

120 pts **Aberdeen** – BBB incl sci/maths (Chem) (IB 32 pts HL 5 sci/maths)

Aston – ABB–BBB incl chem (App Chem) (IB 31 pts HL 555 incl chem)

East Anglia – BBB incl chem (Chem; Chem Educ) (IB 31 pts HL 5 chem)

Kent – BBB incl chem/biol (Chem) (IB 34 pts HL 14 pts incl 5 chem/6 biol)

Leicester – ABB–BBB incl chem (Chem; Chem Foren Sci; Pharml Chem) (IB 30–28 pts HL 5 chem)

Manchester Met – BBB incl chem 120 pts (Pharml Chem (MChem)) (IB 26 pts HL 5 chem)

Northumbria – B chem 120 pts incl chem (Chem)

Queen's Belfast – BBB incl chem+sci (Chem; Medcnl Chem) (IB 32 pts HL 655 incl chem+sci)

Reading – BBB incl chem (Chem Cos Sci) (IB 30 pts HL 5 chem); BBB incl chem+interview (Chem) (IB 30 pts HL 5 chem)

Strathclyde – AAB–BBB incl sci/maths (Chem (MChem)) (IB 30 pts)

Surrey – ABB–BBB incl chem+sci (Chem) (IB 32 pts HL 5 chem); (Medcnl Chem) (IB 32 pts HL 5 chem+sci)

Swansea – AAB–BBB incl chem+sci/maths (Chem) (IB 34–32 pts HL 6 chem)

112 pts **Aston** – BBB–BBC incl chem (Chem) (IB 29 pts HL 554 incl 5 chem)

Bradford – BBC incl chem 112 pts (Chem) (HL 6 chem)

Central Lancashire – 112 pts incl chem (Chem) (HL 5 chem)

Chester – BBB–BBC incl chem 112–120 pts (Chem) (IB 28 pts HL 5 chem)

Coventry – BBC incl chem/biol (Analyt Chem Foren Sci) (IB 30 pts HL 5 biol/chem)

Heriot-Watt – BBC incl chem+maths (Chem Bioch; Chem courses) (IB 30 pts HL 5 chem+maths); BBC incl chem+maths+phys (Chem Mat Nanosci) (IB 30 pts HL 5 chem+maths+phys)

Huddersfield – BBC incl chem 112 pts (Chem) (HL 5 chem)

Keele – BBC incl chem (Chem) (IB 30 pts HL 6 chem)

Kingston – BBC incl chem sci 112 pts (Chem) (IB 28 pts)

Lincoln – BBC incl chem (Chem) (IB 29 pts HL 5 chem)

Nottingham Trent – BBC incl chem (Chem); BBC incl chem 112 pts incl chem (Medcnl Chem)

Sheffield Hallam – BBC incl chem 112 pts (Chem)

104 pts **Greenwich** – 104 pts+interview (Chem)

Liverpool John Moores – BCC incl chem 104 pts (Chem) (IB 26 pts)

London Met – BCC incl chem+sci/maths 104 pts (Chem) (IB 28 pts HL 15 pts)

Manchester Met – BBC–BCC incl chem 104–112 pts (Chem; Medcnl Biol Chem) (IB 26 pts HL 5 chem)

96 pts **Brighton** – BCC–CCC incl chem 96–104 pts (Chem) (IB 26 pts HL 4 chem)

Canterbury Christ Church – 96 pts incl sci (Chem Drug Dscvry)

Plymouth – 96–112 pts incl chem (Chem) (IB 27–26 pts HL 5/4 chem+sci)

Teesside – C chem 96–112 pts +interview (Chem)

Wolverhampton – CCC incl chem (Chem)

88 pts **Reading** – BBB–CCD (Chem Fdn)

West Scotland – CCD incl chem (Chem) (IB 24 pts)

80 pts **South Wales** – BCC–CDD incl chem+biol 80–112 pts (Foren Sci) (IB 29 pts HL 5 biol+chem); BCC–CDD incl sci/maths 80–112 pts (Chem) (IB 29 pts HL 5 chem+sci)

Open University – contact 0300 303 0073 or www.open.ac.uk/contact/new (Nat Sci)

Alternative offers
See **Chapter 6** and **Appendix 1** for grades/UCAS Tariff points information for other examinations.

EXAMPLES OF COLLEGES OFFERING COURSES IN THIS SUBJECT FIELD
Birmingham Met (Coll); Cornwall (Coll); Harrow (Coll); Leeds City (Coll); Liverpool City (Coll); Warrington and Vale Royal (Coll); Wirral Met (Coll).

CHOOSING YOUR COURSE (SEE ALSO CH.1)
Universities and colleges teaching quality See www.qaa.ac.uk; https://unistats.ac.uk.

Examples of sandwich degree courses Aston; Bangor; Bath; Brighton; Cardiff; Dundee; East Anglia; Huddersfield; Kent; Kingston; Liverpool; Loughborough; Manchester; Manchester Met; Northumbria; Nottingham Trent; Plymouth; Queen's Belfast; Reading; Sheffield Hallam; St Andrews; Surrey; Teesside; West Scotland; York.

ADMISSIONS INFORMATION
Number of applicants per place (approx) Bangor 3; Bath 9; Birmingham 8; Bradford 10; Bristol 6; Cardiff 4; Durham 6; Edinburgh 14; Heriot-Watt 7; Hull 5; Imperial London 3; Kingston 4; Lancaster 6; Leeds 3; Leicester 6; Liverpool 5; London (QM) 3; London (UCL) 7; Newcastle 4; Nottingham (Chem Mol Phys) 3, (Chem) 7; Oxford 4; Southampton 7; York 5.

Advice to applicants and planning the UCAS personal statement Extend your knowledge beyond your exam studies by reading scientific journals and keeping abreast of scientific developments in the news. Discuss any visits to chemical firms and laboratories, for example, pharmaceutical, food science, rubber and plastic, paper, photographic, environmental health. See also **Appendix 3**. **Bristol** Deferred entry accepted.

Misconceptions about this course Durham Students fail to realise that they require mathematics and that physics is useful. **Plymouth** Our course is accredited by the Royal Society of Chemistry, something that is highly important to employers.

Selection interviews Yes Cambridge, Imperial London, Manchester, Oxford (84% (success rate 25%)), Teesside, York; **Some** Bath, Sheffield, Southampton, Warwick; **No** Aston, Bangor, Birmingham, Bristol, Cardiff, Coventry, Dundee, East Anglia, Greenwich, Huddersfield, Hull, Keele, Kingston, Leicester, Liverpool John Moores, London (QM), London (UCL), Loughborough, Newcastle, Northumbria, Nottingham, Nottingham Trent, Plymouth, Reading, Surrey, Wolverhampton.

Interview advice and questions Be prepared for questions on your chemistry syllabus and aspects that you enjoy the most. In the past a variety of questions have been asked, for example: Why is carbon a special element? Discuss the nature of forces between atoms with varying intermolecular distances. Describe recent practicals. What is acid rain? What other types of pollution are caused by the human race? What is an enzyme? What are the general properties of benzene? What can a mass spectrometer be used for? What would you do if a river turned bright blue and you were asked how to test a sample? What would be the difference between metal and non-metal pollution? What is 'turning you on' in chemistry at the moment? See also **Chapter 5**. **Bath** Non-selective and informal interview. Why Chemistry? Discuss the practical work you are doing. **Oxford** No written work required. Evidence required of motivation, further potential, and a capacity to analyse and use information to form opinions and a willingness to discuss them. **York** Discuss your favourite areas of chemistry, some of your extra-curricular activities, your preferred learning styles – for example, small tutorials of four or fewer, or lectures.

Reasons for rejection (non-academic) Didn't attend interview. Rude and uncooperative. Arrived under influence of drink. Poor attitude and poor commitment to chemistry. Incomplete, inappropriate, illiterate personal statements. **Southampton** Applicants called for interview are not normally rejected.

AFTER-RESULTS ADVICE
Offers to applicants repeating A-levels
Higher Leeds; St Andrews; Warwick; **Possibly higher** Edinburgh; Newcastle; **Same** Aston; Bangor;

Bath; Bristol; Cardiff; Coventry; Dundee; Durham; East Anglia; Greenwich; Heriot-Watt; Huddersfield; Hull; Keele; Kingston; Liverpool John Moores; London (UCL); London Met; Loughborough; Northumbria; Nottingham; Plymouth; Sheffield; **No** Cambridge.

GRADUATE DESTINATIONS AND EMPLOYMENT (2016/17 HESA)
Graduates surveyed 3,195 **Employed** 1,450 **In voluntary employment** 60 **In further study** 1,235 **Assumed unemployed** 205

Career note A large number of Chemistry graduates choose to go on to further study as well as into scientific careers in research, analysis or development. Significant numbers also follow careers in a wide range of areas in management, teaching and retail work.

OTHER DEGREE SUBJECTS FOR CONSIDERATION
Agriculture; Biochemistry; Biological Sciences; Biomedical Science; Chemical Engineering; Environmental Science; Forensic Science; Genetics; Materials Science; Medicine; Microbiology; Oceanography; Pharmacology; Pharmacy.

CHINESE

(including Korean; see also Languages)

Oriental languages are not necessarily difficult languages but they differ considerably in their writing systems which present their own problems for the new student. Even so, Chinese is not a language to be chosen for its novelty and students should have a strong interest in China and its people. In all courses, students should prepare for intensive language learning, the focus being on the written and spoken word supported by studies covering the history, politics and culture of China, and at the University of Leeds, additional studies of the Asia Pacific region. At Oxford (Oriental Studies), it is possible to take an additional language from Japanese, Korean or Tibetan. The course in Chinese Studies at Durham also allows students to take modules in Japanese. It is customary in all universities to spend either the second or third year at a university in China. Several universities offer joint courses with Chinese universities.

Useful websites www.ciol.org.uk; www.bbc.co.uk/languages; www.china.org.cn; www. languageadvantage.com; www.languagematters.co.uk; www.thoughtco.com/asian-history-4133325

NB The points totals shown to the left of the institutions are for ease of reference only. It must not be assumed that Tariff points are always used by institutions or that they can be substituted for an offer in grades. The level of an offer is not necessarily indicative of the quality of a course.

COURSE OFFERS INFORMATION
Subject requirements/preferences GCSE A language is required. **AL** A modern language is usually required.

Your target offers and examples of degree courses
152 pts **Cambridge** – A*AA +interview +AMESAA (As Mid E St) (IB 42–40 pts HL 776)
144 pts **Oxford** – AAA +interview +OLAT (Orntl St incl Jap/Arab/Chin) (IB 39 pts HL 666)
136 pts **Durham** – AAB (Chin St (Yr Abrd)) (IB 36 pts HL 17 pts)
128 pts **Birmingham** – ABB incl lang (Modn Langs (Chin)) (IB 32 pts HL 655)
        Edinburgh – ABB (Chin) (IB 38–34 pts HL 666–655)
        Leeds – ABB (Chin (Modn); Chin courses) (IB 34 pts HL 16 pts)
        London (SOAS) – AAB–ABB (Chin (Modn Class); Chin St; Kor) (IB 35 pts HL 665)
        Manchester – ABB +interview (Chin St) (IB 34 pts HL 655); ABB incl Chin/Jap +interview (Chin Jap) (IB 34 pts HL 655); ABB incl lang +interview (Chin courses; Russ Chin) (IB 34 pts HL 655)
        Newcastle – AAA–ABB (Ling Chin/Jap) (IB 36–34 pts)

Nottingham – ABB incl Span (Span Contemp Chin St) (IB 32 pts HL 5 Span); ABB incl hist (Hist Contemp Chin St) (IB 32 pts HL 5 hist)
Sheffield – ABB (Chin St courses) (IB 33 pts); ABB–BBB +bEPQ (Kor St) (IB 33 pts)
Sussex – ABB 128 pts (Anth Lang) (32 pts)
Warwick – ABB incl lang (Chin Comb Hons) (IB 34 pts HL 5 lang)

120 pts   **De Montfort** – 120 pts (Educ St Mand) (IB 28 pts)
London (Gold) – BBB (Int Rel Chin) (IB 33 pts HL 655)
Newcastle – ABB–BBB (Chin St) (IB 32 pts)

112 pts   **Hull** – 112 pts (Chin St) (IB 28 pts)
Middlesex – 112 pts (Bus Mgt Mand)

104 pts   **Central Lancashire** – 104–112 pts (Bus Mgt Chin)
Chester – BBC–BCC 104–112 pts (Chin St Comb Hons) (26 pts)
Hertfordshire – BCC 104 pts (Eng Lang Jap/Mand; Mand Comb Hons)
Manchester Met – BBC–BCC 104–112 pts (Ling Mand Chin/Fr/Ger/Ital/Span) (IB 26 pts)
Nottingham Trent – 104 pts (Mand Chin Comb Hons)
Westminster – ABB–BCC 104–128 pts (Chin Engl Lang) (IB 27 pts HL 4 Engl)

96 pts   **Bangor** – 96 pts (Chin Comb)
Trinity Saint David – 96 pts +interview (Chin St courses)

Alternative offers
See **Chapter 6** and **Appendix 1** for grades/UCAS Tariff points information for other examinations.

CHOOSING YOUR COURSE (SEE ALSO CH.1)
Universities and colleges teaching quality See www.qaa.ac.uk; https://unistats.ac.uk.

Examples of sandwich degree courses Westminster.

ADMISSIONS INFORMATION
Number of applicants per place (approx) Durham 5; Leeds 5; London (SOAS) 8; Westminster 18.

Advice to applicants and planning the UCAS personal statement It will be necessary to demonstrate a knowledge of China, its culture, political and economic background. Visits to the Far East should be mentioned, with reference to any features which have influenced your choice of degree course. See also **Appendix 3** under Languages.

Selection interviews Yes Cambridge, Oxford; **Some** London (SOAS); **No** Leeds.

Interview advice and questions You will be expected to convince the admissions tutor why you want to study the language. Your knowledge of Chinese culture, politics and society in general, and of Far Eastern problems, could also be tested. See also **Chapter 5**.

Reasons for rejection (non-academic) Oxford Applicant's language background seemed a little weak and his written work not as strong as that of other applicants. At interview he showed himself to be a dedicated hard-working young man but lacking in the imagination, flexibility and the intellectual liveliness needed to succeed on the course.

AFTER-RESULTS ADVICE
Offers to applicants repeating A-levels Higher Leeds; **No** Cambridge.

GRADUATE DESTINATIONS AND EMPLOYMENT (2016/17 HESA)
Graduates surveyed 135 **Employed** 65 **In voluntary employment** 5 **In further study** 30 **Assumed unemployed** 10

Career note China is a country with a high economic growth rate and there are good opportunities for graduates, an increasing number being recruited by firms based in East Asia. Other opportunities exist in diplomacy, aid work and tourism throughout China, Taiwan and Mongolia as well as most non-scientific career areas in the UK. See also **Languages**.

OTHER DEGREE SUBJECTS FOR CONSIDERATION
Traditional Chinese Medicine; other Oriental languages.

CLASSICS AND CLASSICAL STUDIES/CIVILISATION
(see also **Archaeology, Greek, History (Ancient), Latin**)

Classics courses tend to focus on the study of Greek and Latin literature and language alongside topics such as the history, art, archaeology, drama and philosophy of Ancient Greece and Rome. Generally speaking, Classical Studies and Civilisation courses tend to focus more heavily on the wider life of the ancient world as revealed through these topics, whereas Classics courses seek to engage particularly with literature. Course entry requirements vary and Classics is by no means limited to those with prior knowledge of Greek and Latin. At Oxford, home of the largest Classics department in the UK, two courses which do not require a previous knowledge of Latin or Greek are offered. Many Classical Studies degree courses offer these languages at beginner or advanced level, but applicants should check subject requirements carefully before applying.

Useful websites www.users.globalnet.co.uk/~loxias; www.classics.ox.ac.uk; www.cambridgescp.com; www.bbc.co.uk/history/ancient/greeks; www.bbc.co.uk/history/ancient/romans

NB The points totals shown to the left of the institutions are for ease of reference only. It must not be assumed that Tariff points are always used by institutions or that they can be substituted for an offer in grades. The level of an offer is not necessarily indicative of the quality of a course.

COURSE OFFERS INFORMATION
Subject requirements/preferences GCSE English and a foreign language usually required. Grades A*/A/B (8-9/7/5-6) may be stipulated. **AL** Check courses for Latin/Greek requirements.

Your target offers and examples of degree courses
152 pts **Cambridge** – A*AA +interview +CAA (Class) (IB 42-40 pts HL 776)
144 pts **Bristol** – AAA (Class) (IB 36 pts HL 18 pts); AAA incl Engl (Engl Class St) (IB 36 pts HL 6 Engl)
Durham – AAA (Class; Class Civ) (IB 37 pts HL 18 pts)
Oxford – AAA +interview +CAT (Class; Class Orntl St) (IB 39 pts HL 666); AAA+interview +CAT +ELAT (Class Engl) (IB 39 pts HL 666); AAA+interview +CAT +MLAT (Class Modn Langs) (IB 39 pts HL 666)
St Andrews – AAA (Class) (IB 36 pts HL 66); (Art Hist Class St) (IB 36 pts HL 665); (Class St courses) (IB 36 pts HL 666)
136 pts **Bristol** – AAB (Class St) (IB 34 pts HL 17 pts)
Exeter – AAA–AAB (Class St Theol/Phil (Emp Expnc)) (IB 36-34 pts HL 666-665); AAA–AAB incl Engl (Class St Engl courses) (IB 36-34 pts HL 6 Engl); AAA–AAB incl Lat/class Gk (Class) (IB 36-34 pts HL 5 Lat/class Gk); AAA–AAB incl class Gk/Lat (Class (Emp Expnc)) (IB 36-34 pts HL 666-665 incl class Gk/Lat)
Leeds – AAB incl Engl (Class Lit courses) (IB 35 pts HL 16 pts incl 6 Engl)
London (King's) – AAB (Class Arch; Class St) (IB 35 pts HL 665); (Class (Gk Lat)) (IB 35 pts HL 665 incl 6 Lat/Gk); AAB incl Engl (Class St Engl) (IB 35 pts HL 665)
London (UCL) – AAB incl Gk/Lat (Class) (IB 36 pts HL 17 pts incl 6 Gk/Lat)
Warwick – AAB (Class Civ) (IB 36 pts); AAB incl Lat/Anc Gk (Class) (IB 36 pts HL 6 Lat/Anc Gk)
128 pts **Birmingham** – ABB (Class Lit Civ) (IB 32 pts HL 655)
Edinburgh – ABB (Anc Medit Civ) (IB 36-34 pts HL 665-655); (Class Mid E St) (IB 37-34 pts HL 665-666); (Class Engl Lang; Class St) (IB 37-34 pts HL 666-655); ABB 128 pts (Class Ling) (IB 37-34 pts HL 666-655); ABB incl Lat/Gk (Class) (IB 37-34 pts HL 666-655 incl Lat/Gk)
Exeter – AAB–ABB incl lang (Class St Modn Langs) (IB 34-32 pts HL 665-655)
Leeds – AAB–ABB (Class Civ) (IB 35-34 pts HL 16 pts)
Liverpool – ABB/BBB +aEPQ +interview (Class; Class St) (IB 33 pts)

London (UCL) – ABB (Class Arch Class Civ) (IB 34 pts HL 16 pts)
Manchester – ABB+interview (Class; Class St) (IB 34 pts HL 655)
Newcastle – AAB–ABB (Class; Class St) (IB 35–32 pts HL 555)
Nottingham – AAB–ABB (Class Civ) (IB 34–32 pts); ABB (Arch Class Civ; Class) (IB 32 pts)

120 pts **Kent** – BBB (Class Arch St; Class St) (IB 34 pts HL 15 pts)
London (RH) – ABB–BBB (Class St) (IB 32 pts HL 555); ABB–BBB incl Lat/Gk (Class) (IB 32 pts HL 555 incl Lat/Gk)
Reading – BBB (Class Mediev St; Class St) (IB 30 pts)
Swansea – BBB 120 pts (Class; Class Civ) (IB 32 pts)

112 pts **Roehampton** – BBC 112 pts (Class Civ)
104 pts **London (Birk)** – 104–120 pts (Class)
96 pts **Trinity Saint David** – +interview (Class Civ)
88 pts **Reading** – CCD (Class Fdn) (IB 24 pts)

Alternative offers
See **Chapter 6** and **Appendix 1** for grades/UCAS Tariff points information for other examinations.

CHOOSING YOUR COURSE (SEE ALSO CH.1)

Universities and colleges teaching quality See www.qaa.ac.uk; https://unistats.ac.uk.

Examples of sandwich degree courses Reading.

ADMISSIONS INFORMATION

Number of applicants per place (approx) Bristol 9; Cambridge 2; Durham 7; Leeds 4; London (King's) 6; London (RH) 5; London (UCL) 5; Manchester 6; Newcastle 6; Nottingham 4; Oxford 3; Swansea 6; Trinity Saint David 5.

Advice to applicants and planning the UCAS personal statement Describe any visits made to classical sites or museums, or literature which you have read and enjoyed. Discuss any significant aspects which impressed you. Classics is an interdisciplinary subject and universities are looking for people who are versatile, imaginative and independently minded, so all types of extra-curricular activities (drama, music, philosophy, creative arts, politics, other languages and cultures) will be relevant.

Misconceptions about this course Oxford You do not have to have studied Latin or Greek to apply for Classics at Oxford, we welcome beginners.

Selection interviews Yes Cambridge, Oxford (Class) 37%, (Class Engl) 26%, (Class Modn Langs) 25%, (Class Orntl St) 56%); **Some** Bristol, Warwick; **No** Leeds, London (RH), London (UCL), Newcastle, Nottingham, Swansea.

Interview advice and questions What do you think it means to study Classics? Do you think Classics is still a vital and central cultural discipline? What made you apply to study Classics at this university? There are often detailed questions on the texts which the students have read, to find out how reflective they are in their reading. See **Chapter 5**. **Cambridge** What would happen if the Classics department burned down? Do you think feminism is dead? Emma has become a different person since she took up yoga. Therefore she is not responsible for anything she did before she took up yoga. Discuss. **Oxford** Candidates studying Latin or Greek at A-level are required to demonstrate competence in translation as part of the Classics Admissions Test. Use of dictionaries not permitted. Classics and English applicants take both the Classics Admissions Test and the English Literature Admissions Test.

Reasons for rejection (non-academic) Did not demonstrate a clear sense of why they wanted to study Classics rather than anything else.

AFTER-RESULTS ADVICE

Offers to applicants repeating A-levels Higher Leeds; St Andrews; **Same** Cambridge; Durham; Newcastle; Nottingham; Swansea.

GRADUATE DESTINATIONS AND EMPLOYMENT (2016/17 HESA)

Graduates surveyed 915 **Employed** 350 **In voluntary employment** 30 **In further study** 305
Assumed unemployed 230

Career note As with other non-vocational subjects, graduates enter a wide range of careers. In a small number of cases, this may be subject-related, such as work in museums and art galleries. However, much will depend on how the student's interests develop during the undergraduate years and career planning should be started at an early stage.

COMBINED AND LIBERAL ARTS COURSES

(see also **Art and Design (General)**, **Social Sciences/Studies**)

Many different subjects are offered in Combined and Liberal Arts courses which are now becoming increasingly popular. These courses are particularly useful for those applicants who have difficulty in deciding on one specialist subject to follow, allowing students to mix and match according to their interests and often enabling them to embark on new subjects.

Useful websites www.artscouncil.org.uk; www.creativescotland.com; www.artsprofessional.co.uk

NB The points totals shown to the left of the institutions are for ease of reference only. It must not be assumed that Tariff points are always used by institutions or that they can be substituted for an offer in grades. The level of an offer is not necessarily indicative of the quality of a course.

COURSE OFFERS INFORMATION

Subject requirements/preferences The offers listed below are average offers. Specific offers will vary depending on the relative popularity of each subject. Check with the admissions tutor of your selected institution. **GCSE** English, mathematics or science and a foreign language may be required by some universities. **AL** Some joint courses may require a specified subject.

Your target offers and examples of degree courses

160 pts   **Cambridge** – A*A*A incl sci/maths +interview +NSAA (Nat Sci) (IB 42–40 pts HL 776)

152 pts   **Durham** – A*AA (Comb Hons Soc Sci) (IB 38 pts HL 666)
           London (UCL) – A*AA (Arts Sci) (IB 39 pts HL 19 pts)

144 pts   **Birmingham** – A*AA–AAA +admissions essay (Librl Arts Sci) (IB 36–35 pts)
           Exeter – AAA (Librl Arts) (IB 36 pts HL 666)
           Imperial London – AAA incl chem+sci/maths (Bioch courses) (IB 38 pts HL 6 chem+sci/maths)
           Leeds – AAA (Librl Arts) (IB 35 pts HL 17 pts)
           London (King's) – AAA (Librl Arts) (IB 35 pts HL 666)
           Nottingham – AAA incl Engl/maths (Librl Arts) (IB 36 pts HL 6 Engl/maths)
           Warwick – AAA (Librl Arts) (IB 38 pts)

136 pts   **Exeter** – A*AA–AAB +interview (Flex Comb Hons) (IB 38–34 pts HL 766–665)
           Leeds – AAB (Flm St Comb Hons) (IB 35 pts HL 16 pts)
           Newcastle – AAA–AAB incl Engl (Engl Lit Comb Hons) (IB 36–35 pts HL 6 Engl); AAB (Comb Hons) (IB 34 pts)
           Sheffield – AAB incl chem+sci (Bioch Comb Hons) (IB 34 pts HL 65 chem+sci)

128 pts   **Bristol** – AAA–ABB incl arts/hum/lang (Librl Arts) (IB 36–32 pts HL 18 pts incl 6 arts/hum/lang)
           Liverpool – ABB (Flm St Comb Hons) (IB 33 pts)
           London (RH) – AAB–ABB (Librl Arts) (IB 32 pts HL 655)
           London (SOAS) – AAB–ABB (Glob Librl Arts) (IB 35 pts HL 665)
           Newcastle – ABB (Flm Prac) (IB 32 pts)

120 pts   **Cardiff** – ABB–BBB (Anc Hist Comb Hons; Welsh Comb Hons) (HL 665)
           East Anglia – BBB (Int Rel Comb Hons) (IB 31 pts)
           Essex – BBB (Librl Arts) (IB 30 pts)

Kent – BBB (Cult St courses; Librl Arts) (IB 34 pts HL 15 pts)

112 pts   **Heriot-Watt** – BBC incl maths+sci (Comb St) (IB 31 pts HL 5 maths+sci)

Hull – BBC 112 pts (Am St) (IB 28 pts)

104 pts   **Dundee** – BBB–BCC (Librl Arts) (IB 30 pts HL 555)

Keele – BCC (Librl Arts) (IB 28 pts)

Winchester – 104–120 pts (Librl Arts; Librl Arts Engl Lit; Librl Arts Sociol)

96 pts   **Bath Spa** – CCC (Psy Comb Hons; Sociol Comb Hons) (IB 26 pts)

Brighton – BCC–CCC 96–104 pts (Hum) (IB 26 pts)

Leeds (CMus) – 96 pts +audition +gr 5 (Mus (Comb))

Winchester – 96–112 pts (Librl Arts Dr; Librl Arts Hist)

Open University – contact 0300 303 0073 or www.open.ac.uk/contact/new (Hum Engl/Fr/ Ger/Span)

Alternative offers
See **Chapter 6** and **Appendix 1** for grades/UCAS Tariff points information for other examinations.

CHOOSING YOUR COURSE (SEE ALSO CH.1)

Universities and colleges teaching quality See www.qaa.ac.uk; https://unistats.ac.uk.

Top research universities and colleges (REF 2014) See individual subject tables.

ADMISSIONS INFORMATION

Number of applicants per place (approx) Birmingham 9; Heriot-Watt 5; Newcastle 4.

Advice to applicants and planning the UCAS personal statement Refer to tables for those subjects you've chosen.

Selection interviews Some Bristol; **No** Liverpool.

Interview advice and questions Questions will focus on your chosen subjects. See under individual subject tables. See also **Chapter 5**.

Reasons for rejection (non-academic) Lack of clarity of personal goals.

AFTER-RESULTS ADVICE

Offers to applicants repeating A-levels Higher St Andrews; **Possibly higher** Newcastle; **Same** Bath Spa; Birmingham; Durham; Liverpool; Manchester Met.

GRADUATE DESTINATIONS AND EMPLOYMENT

Career note Graduates enter a wide range of careers covering business and administration, retail work, education, transport, finance, community and social services. Work experience during undergraduate years will help students to focus their interests.

OTHER DEGREE SUBJECTS FOR CONSIDERATION

See **Social Sciences/Studies**

COMMUNICATION STUDIES/COMMUNICATION

(including **Communication and Media, Marketing Communication Management and Public Relations**; see also **Art and Design (General), Computer Science and Information Technology, Engineering (Communications), Film, Radio, Video And TV Studies, Journalism, Media Studies, Speech Pathology/Sciences/Therapy**)

Communication Studies courses are often linked with Media Studies and as such attract large numbers of applicants; however the course content of your chosen course should be checked since there are several variations. Some courses are purely academic.

Useful websites www.camfoundation.com; www.aejmc.org

NB The points totals shown to the left of the institutions are for ease of reference only. It must not be assumed that Tariff points are always used by institutions or that they can be substituted for an offer in grades. The level of an offer is not necessarily indicative of the quality of a course.

COURSE OFFERS INFORMATION

Subject requirements/preferences GCSE English and mathematics grade A–C (7–4) may be required. **AL** No specific subjects required.

Your target offers and examples of degree courses
144 pts London (King's) – AAA (Librl Arts) (IB 35 pts HL 666)
136 pts Leeds – AAB (Comm Media) (IB 35 pts HL 16 pts incl 5 Engl)
　　　　Newcastle – AAB (Media Comm Cult St) (IB 34 pts)
　　　　Ulster – AAA–AAB (Comm Adv Mark) (IB 29–28 pts HL 14 pts)
128 pts Leeds – ABB incl art/des (Graph Comm Des) (IB 34 pts HL 16 pts incl 5/6 art/vis art/des)
　　　　Liverpool – ABB/BBB +aEPQ (Comm Media) (IB 33 pts)
　　　　Loughborough – ABB (Media Comm) (IB 34 pts HL 655)
　　　　Nottingham – ABB (Span Int Media Comms St) (IB 32 pts)
　　　　Sussex – ABB (Media Comms) (IB 32 pts)
120 pts East Anglia – BBB (Intercult Comm Bus Mgt) (IB 31 pts)
　　　　London (Gold) – BBB (Media Comms) (IB 33 pts HL 655)
　　　　Northumbria – 120 pts +interview +portfolio (Fash Comm)
112 pts Birmingham City – BBC 112 pts +interview +portfolio (Media Comm) (IB 28 pts HL 14 pts)
　　　　Brunel – BBC (Comm Media St) (IB 29 pts)
　　　　Buckingham – BBB–BBC (Mark Media Comms) (IB 32–31 pts)
　　　　Coventry – BBC +interview (Media Comms) (IB 29 pts)
　　　　Greenwich – BBC 112 pts +interview +portfolio (Media Comms)
　　　　Leeds Beckett – 112 pts (Media Comm Cult) (IB 24 pts)
　　　　Liverpool Hope – BBC 112 pts (Media Comm) (IB 26 pts)
　　　　Sheffield Hallam – 112 pts (Jrnl PR Media; Mark Comms Adv)
　　　　Sunderland – BBC 112 pts (Media Cult Comm)
　　　　UWE Bristol – 112 pts (Media Cult Comm)
　　　　Ulster – BBB–BBC (Comm Mgt PR) (IB 26–25 pts HL 13–12 pts)
　　　　Wolverhampton – BBC (Media)
104 pts Bournemouth – 104–120 pts (Comm Media; Mark Comm) (IB 31–28 pts)
　　　　De Montfort – 104 pts (Media Comm) (IB 24 pts)
　　　　Glasgow Caledonian – BCC (Media Comm) (IB 25 pts)
　　　　Hertfordshire – BCC 104 pts (Eng Lang Jap/Mand)
　　　　Manchester Met – BCC 104–112 pts (Dig Media Comms) (IB 26 pts)
　　　　Nottingham Trent – 104 pts (Comm Soty (Comb Hons) + Phil/Ling/Media)
　　　　Oxford Brookes – 104 pts (Comm Media Cult) (IB 29 pts)
　　　　Winchester – 104–120 pts (Comm Vid Gms)
96 pts Aberystwyth – BBB–CCC 96–120 pts (Media Comm St) (IB 30–26 pts)
　　　　Bath Spa – CCC (Media Comms) (IB 26 pts)
　　　　Buckingham – BBC–CCC +interview (Comm Media Jrnl) (IB 24 pts)
　　　　Keele – BCC–CCC (Media Comms Crea Prac) (IB 28–26 pts)
　　　　St Mary's – BBC–BCC 96–112 pts (Comm Media Mark) (IB 28–24 pts)
88 pts Canterbury Christ Church – 88–112 pts (Media Comms)
80 pts Bedfordshire – CCC–CCE 80–96 pts (Media Comms)

Alternative offers
See **Chapter 6** and **Appendix 1** for grades/UCAS Tariff points information for other examinations.

CHOOSING YOUR COURSE (SEE ALSO CH.1)

Universities and colleges teaching quality See www.qaa.ac.uk; https://unistats.ac.uk.

Top research universities and colleges (REF 2014) (Communication, Cultural and Media Studies, Literary and Information Management) London LSE; London (RH); East Anglia; Leeds; Leicester (Media Comm); Newcastle; Leicester (Musm St); Wolverhampton; Cardiff; London (Gold); Loughborough (Comm Media St); Westminster; De Montfort; Nottingham.

Examples of sandwich degree courses Bournemouth; Brunel; Liverpool; Loughborough; Plymouth; Ulster; Westminster.

ADMISSIONS INFORMATION
Number of applicants per place (approx) Liverpool 6.

Advice to applicants and planning the UCAS personal statement Applicants should be able to give details of any work experience/work shadowing/discussions they have had in the media including, for example, in newspaper offices, advertising agencies, local radio stations or film companies (see also **Media Studies**). **London (Gold)** Interest in a study in depth of media theory plus some experience in media practice. **Manchester Met** Motivation more important than grades.

Selection interviews Yes Buckingham; **No** Glasgow Caledonian, Sheffield Hallam, Ulster.

Interview advice and questions Courses differ in this subject and, depending on your choice, the questions will focus on the type of course, either biased towards the media, or towards human communication by way of language, psychology, sociology or linguistics. See also separate subject tables and Chapter 5.

Reasons for rejection (non-academic) Unlikely to work well in groups. Poor writing. Misguided application, for example more practical work wanted. Poor motivation. Inability to give reasons for choosing the course. More practice needed in academic writing skills. Wrong course choice, wanted more practical work.

AFTER-RESULTS ADVICE
Offers to applicants repeating A-levels Same Brunel; Coventry; Loughborough; Nottingham Trent; Robert Gordon; Sheffield Hallam.

GRADUATE DESTINATIONS AND EMPLOYMENT (2016/17 HESA)
Graduates surveyed See **Business and Management Courses (Specialised)**, **Marketing** and **Media Studies**.

Career note Graduates have developed a range of transferable skills in their courses which open up opportunities in several areas. There are obvious links with openings in the media, public relations and advertising.

OTHER DEGREE SUBJECTS FOR CONSIDERATION
Advertising; Art and Design; Cultural Studies; Digital Communications; English; Film, Radio, Video and TV Studies; Information Studies; Journalism; Languages; Linguistics; Marketing; Media Studies; Psychology; Public Relations; Speech Sciences.

COMMUNITY STUDIES/DEVELOPMENT
(see also **Health Sciences/Studies, Nursing and Midwifery, Social and Public Policy and Administration, Social Work**)

These courses cover aspects of community social issues, for example housing, food, health, the elderly, welfare rights and counselling and features of community development such as education, arts, sport and leisure. Many courses are vocational in nature and often linked with youth work. Courses are in Education, Housing, Social Sciences and Public Policy. Work experience always forms part of these courses and should also take place before you apply. Most courses will lead to professional qualifications.

Useful websites www.volunteeringmatters.org.uk; www.infed.org/mobi/developing-community

NB The points totals shown to the left of the institutions are for ease of reference only. It must not be assumed that Tariff points are always used by institutions or that they can be substituted for an offer in grades. The level of an offer is not necessarily indicative of the quality of a course.

COURSE OFFERS INFORMATION

Subject requirements/preferences GCSE English and mathematics grade A–C (7–4) may be required at some institutions. **AL** No specific subjects required. Other Minimum age 19 plus youth work experience for some courses. Health and Disclosure and Barring Service (DBS) checks required for some courses.

Your target offers and examples of degree courses

120 pts	**Glasgow** – BBB +interview (Commun Dev) (IB 30 pts HL 655)	
	Sussex – ABB–BBB (Chld Yth (Theor Prac)) (IB 32–30 pts)	
112 pts	**Derby** – BBC 112 pts +interview (Yth Wk Commun Dev)	
	Glyndŵr – BBC 112 pts +interview (Yth Commun Wk)	
	Huddersfield – BBC 112 pts (Yth Commun Wk)	
	London (Birk) – ABB–BBB 112–128 pts (Commun Dev Pblc Plcy)	
	London Met – BBC 112 pts (Commun Dev Ldrshp) (IB 28 pts HL 15 pts)	
	Sunderland – BBC 112 pts (Pblc Hlth)	
104 pts	**De Montfort** – 104 pts +interview (Yth Wk Commun Dev) (IB 24 pts)	
	West Scotland – BCC 104 pts +interview (Commun Educ) (IB 24 pts)	
	Winchester – 104–120 pts (Chld Yth Commun St)	
96 pts	**Cumbria** – BBC–CCC 96–112 pts (Wkg Chld Fmly)	
	Dundee – CCC/AB (Commun Edu) (IB 29 pts HL 554)	
	Leeds Beckett – 96 pts +interview (Yth Wk Commun Dev) (IB 24 pts)	
	Newman – CCC 96–144 pts (Wk Chld Yng Ppl Fmly); CCC 96–144 pts+interview (Yth Commun Wk)	
	Sunderland – CCC 96 pts +interview (Commun Yth Wk St)	
88 pts	**Marjon** – CCD 88 pts +interview (Yth Commun Wk)	
	Winchester – 88–104 pts (Hlth Commun Soc Cr St)	
80 pts	**Bedfordshire** – 80 pts +interview (Yth Commun Wk)	
	Cardiff Met – 80 pts incl CC +interview (Yth Commun Wk courses) (IB 24 pts)	
	South Wales – BCC–CDD 80–104 pts +interview (Yth Commun Wk) (IB 29 pts)	
	Trinity Saint David – 80 pts +interview (Yth Commun Wk)	
	Ulster – CDD +interview (Commun Yth Wk) (IB 24 pts HL 12 pts)	
64 pts	**London (Gold)** – CC+interview (App Soc Sci Commun Dev Yth Wk)	

Alternative offers
See **Chapter 6** and **Appendix 1** for grades/UCAS Tariff points information for other examinations.

EXAMPLES OF COLLEGES OFFERING COURSES IN THIS SUBJECT FIELD

Blackburn (Coll); Bradford College UC; Cornwall (Coll); East Kent (Coll); North Notts (Coll); Oldham (Univ Campus); TEC Partnership; Truro and Penwith (Coll); Weston (Coll); York (Coll).

CHOOSING YOUR COURSE (SEE ALSO CH.1)

Universities and colleges teaching quality See www.qaa.ac.uk; https://unistats.ac.uk.

ADMISSIONS INFORMATION

Number of applicants per place (approx) Manchester Met 8; Marjon 7.

Advice to applicants and planning the UCAS personal statement You should describe work you have done with people (elderly or young), particularly in a caring capacity, such as social work, or with the elderly or young children in schools, nursing, hospital work, youth work, community or charity work. You should also describe any problems arising and how staff dealt with them. See **Appendix 3**. **Marjon** Strong multicultural policy.

Selection interviews Yes Bedfordshire, De Montfort, Manchester Met, Marjon.

Interview advice and questions This subject has a vocational emphasis and work experience, or even full-time work in the field, will be expected. Community work varies considerably, so, depending on your experiences, you could be asked about the extent of your work and how you would solve the problems which occur. See also **Chapter 5**.

Reasons for rejection (non-academic) Insufficient experience. Lack of understanding of community and youth work. Uncertain career aspirations. Incompatibility with values, methods and aims of the course. No work experience.

AFTER-RESULTS ADVICE
Offers to applicants repeating A-levels Same Marjon.

GRADUATE DESTINATIONS AND EMPLOYMENT (2016/17 HESA)
Graduates surveyed See **Social Work**.

Career note Social and welfare areas of employment provide openings for those wanting to specialise in their chosen field of social work. Other opportunities will also exist in educational administration, leisure and outdoor activities.

OTHER DEGREE SUBJECTS FOR CONSIDERATION
Communication Studies; Education; Health and Social Care; Nursing; Politics; Psychology; Social Policy and Administration; Social Work; Sociology; Youth Studies.

COMPUTER GAMES DEVELOPMENT

(including **Games Technology, Computer Science (Games), Games Design**; see also **Art and Design (3D Design), Computer Science and Information Technology**)

The UK gaming industry is the sixth largest in the world and the second largest in Europe, currently worth around £4.3 billion. There are now over 2,000 game companies based in the UK, which continue to create a wide range of internationally acclaimed titles. Game Design courses train students to plan, develop and test video games. Courses typically include programming, coding, 3D modelling, sound-editing and game mechanics. Computer Science courses with a focus on games tend to introduce general computer programming skills in Year 1, before building on this foundation by introducing modules specific to games development in Years 2 and 3. Many courses partner with gaming events, linking students with future employers and staying up to date with developments in the industry.

Useful websites www.ukie.org.uk/research; www.tiga.org/about-tiga-and-our-industry/about-uk-video-games-industry; www.thecreativeindustries.co.uk/industries/games

NB The points totals shown to the left of the institutions are for ease of reference only. It must not be assumed that Tariff points are always used by institutions or that they can be substituted for an offer in grades. The level of an offer is not necessarily indicative of the quality of a course.

COURSE OFFERS INFORMATION
Subject requirements/preferences GCSE Mathematics usually required. A*/A/B (8-9/7/5-6) grades may be stipulated for some subjects. **AL** Mathematics, a science or computer science required for some courses.

Your target offers and examples of degree courses
128 pts   **City** – ABB 128 pts (Comp Sci Gms Tech) (IB 32 pts HL 666)
          Sussex – AAB–ABB (Gms Multim Env) (IB 34–32 pts)
120 pts   **Brunel** – BBB (Comp Sci (Dig Media Gms); Gms Des) (IB 30 pts)
          Derby – BBB 120 pts (Comp Gms Modl Animat; Comp Gms Prog)

Huddersfield – BBB 120 pts (Comp Sci Gms Prog)
Northumbria – 120 pts (Comp Sci Gms Dev)
Norwich Arts – BBB (Gms Art Des) (IB 27 pts)
Trinity Saint David – 120 pts (Comp Gms Des) (IB 32 pts)
UWE Bristol – 120 pts (Gms Tech)

112 pts **Abertay** – BBC incl maths (Comp Gms Tech) (IB 30 pts)
Birmingham City – BBC incl sci/tech/maths/comp 112 pts (Comp Gms Tech) (IB 28 pts HL 5 maths)
Bradford – BBC 112 pts (Comp Sci Gms)
East London – BBC 112 pts +portfolio (Comp Gm Dev; Comp Gms Des Stry Dev) (IB 25 pts HL 15 pts)
Hull – 112 pts (Comp Sci Gms Dev) (IB 28 pts)
Lincoln – BBC (Gms Comp) (IB 29 pts)
Liverpool John Moores – BBC 112 pts (Comp Gms Dev) (IB 26 pts)
Middlesex – 112 pts (Gms Des)
Plymouth – 112–120 pts (Comp Gms Dev) (IB 30–27 pts)
Plymouth (CA) – 112–120 pts +interview (Gm Arts)
Staffordshire – BBC 112 pts (Gms Art) (IB -24 pts)
Suffolk – BBC 112 pts (Comp Gms Tech)
Sunderland – BBC 112 pts +interview +portfolio (Animat Gms Art)
West London – BBC 112 pts (Gms Des Animat)

104 pts **Central Lancashire** – 104–112 pts (Comp Gms Dev)
Chichester – 104–120 pts (Elec Spo) (IB 28 pts)
Falmouth – 104–120 pts (Comp Gms) (IB 24 pts)
Manchester Met – BBC–BCC 104–112 pts (Comp Gms Tech) (IB 26 pts HL 5 IT)
Northampton – BCC 104–112 pts (Gms Des) (IB 25 pts)
Teesside – 104–120 pts (Comp Gms Prog)
Trinity Saint David – 104 pts (Comp Gms Dev)
Ulster – BBB–BCC 104–120 pts (Gms Des) (IB 24 pts HL 12 pts)

96 pts **Aberystwyth** – BBB–CCC 96–120 pts (Comp Graph Vsn Gms) (IB 30–26 pts)
Anglia Ruskin – 96 pts (Comp Gmg Tech) (IB 24 pts)
Bangor – 96 pts (Comp Sci Gms Des)
Brighton – BBC–CCC 96–112 pts (Comp Sci Gms; Comp Sci Gms) (IB 26 pts); BBC–CCC 96–112 pts+interview (Dig Gms Dev) (IB 26 pts)
Glasgow Caledonian – CCC (Comp Gms courses) (IB 24 pts); CCC incl art des+portfolio (Comp Gms (Art Animat)) (IB 24 pts)
Leeds Beckett – 96 pts (Comp Animat Vis Efcts); CCC 96 pts (Gms Des)
London Met – CCC 96 pts (Gms Prog)
Sunderland – CCC 96 pts (Gm Dev)
Teesside – 96–112 pts (Comp Gms Des); 96–112 pts +interview +portfolio (Comp Animat; Comp Gms Art)
Worcester – 96 pts (Comp Gms Des Dev)

88 pts **West Scotland** – CCD 88 pts (Comp Gms Dev) (IB 24 pts)
Wolverhampton – CCD +interview (Comp Sci (Gms Dev))

Alternative offers
See **Chapter 6** and **Appendix 1** for grades/UCAS Tariff points information for other examinations.

ADMISSIONS INFORMATION

Number of applicants per place (approx) See **Computer Science and Information Technology.**

Advice to applicants and planning the UCAS personal statement See **Computer Science and Information Technology.**

Selection interviews See **Computer Science and Information Technology.**

Interview advice and questions See **Computer Science and Information Technology.**

UCAS Tariff points for A-level equivalent qualifications appear in **Appendix 1.**

AFTER-RESULTS ADVICE
Offers to applicants repeating A-levels See **Computer Science and Information Technology.**

GRADUATE DESTINATIONS AND EMPLOYMENT (2016/17 HESA)
Career note See **Computer Science and Information Technology.**

OTHER DEGREE SUBJECTS FOR CONSIDERATION
Business Studies; Communications Engineering; Computer Engineering; Computer Science and Information Technology; Electrical and Electronic Engineering; Geographical Information Systems; Information Studies; Mathematics; Physics; Software Engineering.; Electrical and Electronic Engineering; Geographical Informati on Systems; Information Studies; Mathematics; Physics; Software Engineering.

COMPUTER SCIENCE AND INFORMATION TECHNOLOGY

(including **Artificial Intelligence, Business Information Systems, Computing, Computer Networks, Computer Science, Information Systems and Web Design and Development;** see also **Communication Studies/Communication, Information Management and Librarianship, Media Studies**)

Most universities and also colleges of further education offer Computer courses. The specialisms are many and varied, which can cause a problem when deciding which course to follow. For example, at Brunel University London, the Computer Science course has four specialisms with a choice from Artificial Intelligence, Digital Media and Games, Network Computing or Software Engineering, all with sandwich placements. At Plymouth University, there are over 17 computer courses including Computer and Information Security and Computer Science, while at Kingston, Liverpool John Moores and other institutions, Cyber Security and Computer Forensics courses are on offer. At all universities, there are considerable opportunities for financial support and future employment by choosing sandwich courses. Courses vary in content and in the specialisations offered, which may include software engineering, programming languages, artificial intelligence, data processing and graphics.
Useful websites www.bcs.org; www.techuk.org; www.iap.org.uk; www.tpdegrees.com/tech-partnership-legacy/

NB The points totals shown to the left of the institutions are for ease of reference only. It must not be assumed that Tariff points are always used by institutions or that they can be substituted for an offer in grades. The level of an offer is not necessarily indicative of the quality of a course.

COURSE OFFERS INFORMATION
Subject requirements/preferences GCSE Mathematics usually required. A*/A/B (8–9/7/5–6) grades may be stipulated for some subjects. **AL** Mathematics, a science subject or computer science required for some courses.

Your target offers and examples of degree courses
160 pts Cambridge – A*A*A incl maths +interview +CSAT (Comp Sci) (IB 42–40 pts HL 776 incl maths)
        Imperial London – A*A*A incl maths+fmaths +interview (Maths Comp Sci) (IB 40 pts HL 7 maths); A*A*A incl maths +interview (Comp) (IB 39 pts HL 7 maths)
        London (UCL) – A*A*A incl maths (Comp Sci; Mathem Comput (MEng)) (IB 40 pts HL 7 maths)
152 pts Bath – A*AA incl maths (Comp Sci) (IB 36 pts HL 766 incl maths)
        Birmingham – A*AA incl maths (Comp Sci/Soft Eng (MEng)) (IB 32 pts HL 766 incl 6 maths)
        Bristol – A*A*A–A*AA incl maths+fmaths (Maths Comp Sci) (IB 40 pts HL 18 pts incl 7 maths); A*AA incl maths (Comp Sci) (IB 38 pts HL 18 pts incl 7 maths)
        Durham – A*AA incl maths (Comp Sci) (IB 38 pts HL 766 incl maths)

Imperial London – A*A*A*– A*AA incl maths +interview (Comp (Artif Intel Mach Lrng) (MEng); Comp (Soft Eng) (MEng)) (IB 39 pts HL 7 maths)

Oxford – A*AA incl maths/fmaths/comp +interview +MAT (Comp Sci) (IB 39 pts HL 766 incl 7 maths)

Southampton – A*AA incl maths (Comp Sci; Comp Sci Artif Intel (MEng); Comp Sci Cy Scrty (MEng)) (IB 38 pts HL 18 pts incl 6 maths); A*AA incl maths+phys/fmaths/tech (Electron Eng Comp Sys (MEng)) (IB 38 pts HL 18 pts incl 6 maths+phys)

Warwick – A*AA incl maths (Comp Sci) (IB 38 pts HL 666 incl maths)

144 pts **Birmingham** – AAA incl maths (Comp Sci) (IB 32 pts HL 666 incl 6 maths)

Leeds – AAA incl maths/comp (Comp Sci; Comp Sci Artif Intel) (IB 35 pts HL 18 pts incl 5 maths/comp)

London (King's) – AAA incl maths/phys/comp (Comp Sci Intel Sys; Comp Sci Mgt) (IB 35 pts HL 666 incl maths/phys/comp)

Queen's Belfast – AAA/A*AB incl maths (Maths Comp Sci (MSci)) (IB 36 pts HL 666 incl maths)

Sheffield – AAA incl maths (Comp Sci) (IB 36 pts HL 6 maths)

St Andrews – AAA incl maths (Comp Sci courses) (IB 38 pts HL 666 incl maths); AAA incl maths+phys (Comp Sci Phys) (IB 38 pts HL 666 incl maths+phys)

136 pts **Exeter** – AAA–AAB incl maths (Comp Sci) (IB 36–34 pts HL 666–665 incl 5 maths)

Glasgow – AAB incl maths (Comp Sci courses) (IB 36 pts HL 665 incl sci)

Lancaster – AAB (Comp Sci courses) (IB 35 pts HL 16 pts)

London (QM) – AAB (Comp Sci courses) (IB 34 pts HL 665)

Manchester – AAB (IT Mgt Bus; IT Mgt Bus (Yr Ind)) (IB 35 pts HL 665)

Newcastle – AAB (Comp Sci courses) (IB 35–34 pts)

Nottingham – AAA–AAB incl comp (Comp Sci) (IB 34 pts)

Queen's Belfast – AAA–AAB incl chem/phys/maths/tech/comp (Comp Sci (MEng)) (IB 36–34 pts HL 666–665 incl maths/chem/phys)

128 pts **City** – ABB 128 pts (Comp Sci; Comp Sci Gms Tech) (IB 32 pts HL 666)

Edinburgh – AAA–ABB incl maths (Artif Intel; Comp Sci courses; Inform (MInf)) (IB 37–32 pts HL 666–655 incl 6 maths)

Leicester – ABB/BBB +bEPQ (Comp Sci) (IB 30 pts HL 4 maths)

Liverpool – ABB incl maths/fmaths/phys/comp (Comp Sci) (IB 33 pts HL 5 maths/phys/comp); ABB incl maths/phys/comp sci (Comp Sci (Yr Ind); Fin Comp) (IB 33 pts HL 5 maths/phys/comp sci)

London (RH) – AAB–ABB (Mgt Dig Innov) (IB 32 pts HL 655); AAB–ABB incl maths/phys/comp (Comp Sci) (IB 32 pts HL 655 incl maths/phys/comp)

Loughborough – ABB (IT Mgt Bus) (IB 34 pts HL 655); ABB incl maths (Comp Sci; Comp Sci Artif Intel) (IB 34 pts HL 655 incl maths)

Queen's Belfast – ABB (Bus IT) (IB 33 pts HL 655)

Reading – ABB (Comp Sci courses; Mgt IT) (IB 32 pts)

Surrey – ABB incl maths (Comp Sci) (IB 32 pts HL 5 maths); ABB incl maths/phys/comp (Comp IT) (IB 32 pts HL 5 maths)

Sussex – AAB–ABB (Comp Dig Media; Comp Sci; Comp Sci Artif Intel) (IB 34–32 pts)

York – AAB–ABB incl maths (Comp Sci) (IB 35–34 pts HL 6 maths)

120 pts **Aberdeen** – BBB incl maths+sci (Comp Sci) (IB 32 pts HL 5 maths+sci)

Aston – BBB (Bus Comp IT; Comp Sci) (IB 31 pts HL 555)

Brunel – BBB (Bus Comp; Comp Sci; Comp Sci (Artif Intel); Comp Sci (Net Comp)) (IB 30 pts)

Cardiff – ABB–BBB (Comp Sci; Comp Sci Scrty Foren) (IB 32–30 pts HL 655)

Coventry – ABB–BBB incl maths/phys/chem/tech/comp (Comp Sci) (IB 29 pts)

Derby – 120 pts (Dig Foren Scrty); BBB 120 pts (Comp Net Scrty; Comp Sci; IT); BBB incl maths 120 pts (Maths Comp Sci)

East Anglia – BBB incl maths/comp/phys/electron/econ (Comp Sci) (IB 31 pts HL 5 maths/comp sci/phys/econ); BBB incl maths/comp sci/phys/econ/bus (Bus Inf Sys) (IB 31 pts HL 5 maths/comp sci/phys/econ/bus)

Heriot-Watt – BBB (Inf Sys courses) (IB 28 pts); BBB incl maths (Comp Sci) (IB 28 pts HL 5 maths)

Huddersfield – BBB 120 pts (Bus Data Analyt; Comp; Comp Sci; IT; Web Prog)

Kent – AAB–BBB +interview (Comp Sci Artif Intel; Comp Sci Net; Comp Sci courses) (IB 34 pts HL 15 pts); BBB (Multim Tech Des) (IB 34 pts HL 15 pts)

London (Gold) – BBB (Comp Sci; Crea Comp) (IB 33 pts HL 655)

London South Bank – BBB 120–128 pts (Comp Sci)

Northumbria – 120 pts (Comp Sci; IT Mgt Bus)

Nottingham Trent – BBB incl IT/maths/sci 120 pts (Comp Sci courses)

Queen's Belfast – ABB–BBB incl chem/phys/math/tech/comp (Comp Sci (Yr Ind)) (IB 33–32 pts Hl 655 incl chem/phys/maths)

Stirling – BBB (Bus Comp; Comp Sci) (IB 32 pts)

Strathclyde – ABB–BBB incl maths (Comp Sci) (IB 34 pts HL 5 maths)

Swansea – AAB–BBB incl sci/maths/comp (Comp Sci) (IB 34–32 pts HL 5 sci/maths/comp)

UWE Bristol – 120 pts (Comp Sci; Comp courses)

Ulster – BBB (Comp Sci; Comp Sci (Soft Sys Dev)) (IB 26 pts HL 13 pts)

112 pts   **Abertay** – BBC incl art/des/comp +portfolio (Comp Arts) (IB 30 pts HL 4 art)

Anglia Ruskin – 112 pts (Comp Sci)

Birmingham City – BBC incl sci/tech/maths/comp 112 pts (Bus Inf Tech; Comp Foren; Comp Net Scrty; Comp Sci) (IB 28 pts HL 5 maths)

Bournemouth – 112–128 pts +portfolio (Comp Animat Art Des) (IB 32–30 pts)

Bradford – BBC 112 pts (Comp Sci) (HL 3 Engl+maths)

De Montfort – 112 pts (Comp Sci) (IB 26 pts)

Edge Hill – BBC 112 pts (Comp courses)

Gloucestershire – BBC 112 pts (Comp)

Glyndŵr – BBC 112 pts (Comp; Comp Net Scrty)

Greenwich – BBC 112 pts (Comp Scrty Foren)

Hull – 112 pts (Comp Sci) (IB 28 pts)

Keele – BBC (Comp Sci) (IB 30 pts)

Kingston – BBC 112 pts (Comp Sci; Cyberscrty Comp Foren) (IB 25 pts)

Lincoln – BBC (Comp Sci) (IB 29 pts)

Liverpool Hope – BBC 112 pts (Comp Sci; IT courses) (IB 26 pts)

Liverpool John Moores – BBC 112 pts (Comp Foren; Comp St) (IB 26 pts)

London (Birk) – ABB–BBC 112–128 pts (Inf Sys Mgt)

Nottingham Trent – BBC incl IT/sci/maths 112 pts (Comp Sys (Net)); BBC incl IT/sci 112 pts (Inf Sys)

Oxford Brookes – BBC (Comp Sci) (IB 30 pts); BBC +interview (IT Mgt Bus) (IB 30 pts)

Plymouth – 112–120 pts (Comp Inf Scrty; Comp Sci) (IB 30–27 pts)

Salford – 112–120 pts incl maths/sci/comp (Comp Sci) (IB 30 pts HL 14 pts incl eng/sci/tech)

Sheffield Hallam – BBC 112 pts (Comp Sci)

Staffordshire – 112 pts (Comp Sci)

Suffolk – BBC 112 pts (Soft Dev)

West London – BBB–BBC 112–120 pts (Comp Sci; Cy Scrty; IT Mgt Bus)

104 pts   **Bolton** – 104 pts (Comp Net Scrty)

Bournemouth – 104–120 pts (Bus IT; Comp) (IB 31–28 pts)

Buckingham – BBB–BCC (Comp courses) (IB 32–30 pts)

Central Lancashire – 104 pts (Web Des Dev); 104–112 pts (Comp)

Chester – BBC–BCC 104–112 pts (App Comp) (IB 26 pts); BBC–BCC incl comp sci/maths 104–112 pts (Comp Sci) (IB 26 pts)

De Montfort – 104 pts (Bus Inf Sys; Comp) (IB 24 pts)

Edinburgh Napier – BCC (Web Des Dev) (IB 27 pts HL 654); BCC incl maths/phys (Comp) (IB 28 pts HL 654 incl maths/phys)

Greenwich – BCC 104 pts +interview (Maths Comp)

Hertfordshire – BCC 104 pts (Inf Tech)

Kent – BBC–BCC +interview (Bus Inf Tech; Comp) (IB 34 pts HL 14 pts)

UCAS points Tariff: A* = 56 pts; A = 48 pts; B = 40 pts; C = 32 pts; D = 24 pts; E = 16 pts

Leeds Beckett – 104 pts (Comp Foren) (IB 24 pts)

London South Bank – BCC (Bus IT)

Manchester Met – BBC–BCC 104–112 pts (Comp Sci) (IB 26 pts HL 5 IT); BBC–BCC incl comp sci/maths/sci 104–112 pts (Comp Foren Scrty) (IB 26 pts HL 5 IT)

Northampton – BCC 104–112 pts (Bus Comp (Sys)) (IB 25 pts)

Portsmouth – 104–120 pts (Bus Inf Sys; Comp Sci) (IB 25 pts); 104–120 pts+interview (Comp) (IB 25 pts)

Robert Gordon – BCC (Comp Sci; Cy Scrty) (IB 27 pts)

Teesside – 104–120 pts (Comp Sci)

Trinity Saint David – 104 pts (Comp (Comp Net Cy Scrty); Comp (Web Dev); Comp Data Inf Sys)

Ulster – BBB–BCC (Bus Inf Sys) (IB 26–24 pts HL 13–12 pts)

Westminster – ABB–BCC 104–128 pts (Bus Inf Sys; Comp Sci) (IB 27 pts HL 4 Engl); ABB–BCC 104–128 pts +interview (Comp Net Scrty) (IB 27 pts HL 4 Engl)

96 pts   **Aberystwyth** – BBB–CCC 96–120 pts (Bus IT; Comp Sci; Comp Sci Artif Intel; Web Dev) (IB 30–26 pts)

Bangor – 96 pts (Comp Sci; Comp Sci Bus; Comp Sci Gms Des)

Bath Spa – CCC (Crea Comp courses) (IB 26 pts)

Bolton – 96 pts incl maths/comp (Comp (Cyb Sec)); 96 pts incl maths/comp+interview (Comp (Data Analys))

Brighton – BBC–CCC 96–112 pts (Bus Comp; Bus Comp Cy Sec; Comp Sci; Comp Sci Artif Intel) (IB 26 pts)

Canterbury Christ Church – 96–120 pts (Comp Sci)

Cardiff Met – CCC 96 pts (Bus Inf Sys; Comp Sci) (IB 24 pts HL 12 pts)

Chichester – BBC–CCC 96–112 pts (IT Mgt Bus) (IB 28 pts); BBC–CCC incl maths 96–112 pts (Comp Sci) (IB 28 pts)

Dundee – BBB–CCC incl maths+sci (Comp Sci) (IB 30 pts HL 555 incl maths+sci)

East London – CCC 96 pts (Comp Bus) (IB 24 pts HL 15 pts); CCC 96 pts incl maths (Comp Sci) (IB 25 pts HL 15 pts incl maths)

Glasgow Caledonian – CCC incl comp/maths (IT Mgt Bus) (IB 24 pts)

Greenwich – CCC 96 pts (Inf Tech Mgt Bus)

Hertfordshire – CCC 96 pts (Bus St Inf Sys)

Leeds Beckett – 96 pts (Comp Foren Scrty; Comp Sci) (IB 24-25 pts)

Middlesex – 96 pts (Bus Inf Sys)

Solent – CCC 96–112 pts (Cyb Scrty Mgt) (IB 28 pts)

Sunderland – CCC 96 pts (Comp Sci; Cyberscrty Dig Foren; Net Cyberscrty)

Teesside – 96–112 pts (Artif Intel; Comp; Data Analyt Bus Intel; IT); BBC incl maths/comp/IT 96–112 pts (Comp Dig Foren)

Winchester – 96–112 pts (Comp Aid Des)

Wolverhampton – CCC (Comp IT; Comp Sci)

Worcester – 96 pts (Comp); 96 pts +interview (Bus IT); 96 pts incl maths (Maths Comp Sci)

88 pts   **Canterbury Christ Church** – 88–112 pts (Bus Inf Sys; Comp)

London Met – CCD 88 pts (Bus Inf Tech) (IB 28 pts HL 15 pts)

West Scotland – CCD (Web Mbl Dev) (IB 24 pts); (Comp Net; Comp Sci) (IB 24 pts HL 44)

80 pts   **Bangor** – 80 pts (Comp Inf Sys)

Bedfordshire – CCC–CCE 80–96 pts (Inf Data Sys)

Bucks New – 80 pts (Comp courses)

Colchester (UC) – 80 pts +interview (IT Sys Apps)

London Met – CCE 80 pts (Comp courses) (IB 28 pts HL 15 pts)

South Wales – BBC 80–112 pts (Comp Sci) (IB 29 pts); BCC–CDD 80–104 pts (ICT) (IB 29 pts)

72 pts   **Wolverhampton** – CDE (Cyberscrty)

24 pts   **UHI** – D (Comp)

Gloucestershire – +interview (Dig Media)

Open University – contact 0300 303 0073 or www.open.ac.uk/contact/new (Comp IT)

Alternative offers
See **Chapter 6** and **Appendix 1** for grades/UCAS Tariff points information for other examinations.

DEGREE APPRENTICESHIPS
Bangor (Comp Sci); Bolton (Dig Tech Sol-Soft Eng/Net Eng/Data Analys/Cyber Security); Chichester (Dig Tech Sol, Cyberscrty Analys); Essex (Dig Tech Sol); Glasgow (Soft Eng); Portsmouth (Dig Tech Sol); Robert Gordon (IT Soft Dev, IT Mgt Bus).

CHOOSING YOUR COURSE (SEE ALSO CH.1)
Universities and colleges teaching quality See www.qaa.ac.uk; https://unistats.ac.uk.

Top research universities and colleges (REF 2014) (Computer Science and Informatics) Liverpool; Cambridge; London (King's); Nottingham; Bristol; Newcastle; Oxford; Warwick; London (UCL); Imperial London; Manchester; Sheffield; Lancaster; London (QM); York.

Examples of sandwich degree courses Aston; Bath; Birmingham City; Bournemouth; Bradford; Brighton; Brunel; Cardiff; City; Coventry; De Montfort; Derby; East Anglia; Edinburgh Napier; Gloucestershire; Greenwich; Huddersfield; Kent; Kingston; Leeds Beckett; Lincoln; Liverpool; Liverpool John Moores; London (QM); London (RH); London South Bank; Loughborough; Manchester Met; Middlesex; Newcastle; Northumbria; Nottingham Trent; Oxford Brookes; Plymouth; Portsmouth; Queen's Belfast; Reading; Robert Gordon; Salford; Sheffield Hallam; Solent; South Wales; Stirling; Sunderland; Surrey; Teesside; Ulster; UWE Bristol; Westminster; Wolverhampton; York.

ADMISSIONS INFORMATION
Number of applicants per place (approx) Abertay 5; Aston (Bus Comp IT) 12; Bangor 5; Bath 10; Birmingham 9; Bradford 13; Bristol 8; Buckingham 5; Cambridge 3; Cardiff 5; City 8; Derby 5; Dundee 5; Durham 9; Edinburgh 4; Exeter 10; Heriot-Watt 9; Hull (Comp Sci) 5; Imperial London 6; Kingston 10; Lancaster 5; Leeds 10; Leicester 10; Lincoln 5; Liverpool 5; Liverpool John Moores 3; London (King's) 20; London (QM) 6; London (RH) 8; London (UCL) 12; Manchester Met 10, (Bus IT) 8; Newcastle 6; Nottingham 8; Nottingham Trent 4; Oxford Brookes 6; Plymouth 24; Robert Gordon 3; Sheffield Hallam 5; Southampton 9; Stirling 10; Strathclyde 16; Swansea 5; Teesside 4; Warwick 11; York 6.

Admissions tutors' advice Bournemouth It can be difficult for applicants to know when applying for courses what specialism they wish to follow. Our course offers a common first year with specialisms following in Years 2 and 3.

Advice to applicants and planning the UCAS personal statement Your computer and programming interests in and outside school or college should be described. It is also useful to give details of any visits, work experience and work shadowing relating to industrial or commercial organisations and their computer systems. (See **Appendix 3**.) Give details of your interests in, and knowledge of, computer hardware, software and multimedia packages. Contact the Chartered Institute for IT for information. **Bristol** Deferred entry accepted.

Misconceptions about this course Bournemouth For computer animation courses, being a good artist is not all that is required. Students typically need to have a mix of artistic and technical/mathematical abilities. Therefore, a good mix of subjects, eg art and maths can be the best background for these types of courses. However, we do have a range of animation courses, one of which is accessible to students with an arts subject but without a 'technical' A-level. For Computing Courses, applicants should not be concerned if they initially do not know what area they want to specialise in. The computing courses share a common first year, allowing students to specialise later in the course. **London (QM)** There are many misconceptions – among students, teachers and careers advisers – about what computer science entails. The main one is to confuse it with what schools call information and communication technology, which is about the use of computer applications. Computer science is all about software – ie programming – and will generally only cover a limited study of hardware. **Oxford** Applicants may think that a background in computing is required for this course but mathematics is the only essential subject at A level (or equivalent). **Plymouth** Paid placements are part of some Computing courses and can lead to employment.

Selection interviews Yes Buckingham, Cambridge, Imperial London, Kent, Manchester, Oxford ((Comp Sci) 9%), St Andrews, Winchester; **Some** Bath, Birmingham City, Bournemouth, Cardiff, Loughborough, Warwick; **No** Anglia Ruskin, Bradford, Brighton, Coventry, Dundee, East Anglia, Edinburgh, Falmouth, Hull, Kingston, Liverpool Hope, Liverpool John Moores, London (Gold), London (QM), London (UCL), London Met, London South Bank, Manchester Met, Newcastle, Northampton, Nottingham, Nottingham Trent, Plymouth, Portsmouth, Salford, Sheffield Hallam, Southampton, Sunderland, Surrey, UWE Bristol, West London, West Scotland.

Interview advice and questions While A-level computer studies is not usually required, you will be questioned on your use of computers and aspects of the subject which interest you. How do you organise your homework/social life? What are your strengths and weaknesses? Do you have any idea of the type of career you would like? See also **Chapter 5**. **York** Applicants are given the opportunity to attend an interview. It is not part of the selection process, but offers may be lowered if candidates perform well.

Reasons for rejection (non-academic) Little practical interest in computers/electronics. Inability to work as part of a small team. Mismatch between referee's description and performance at interview. Unsatisfactory English. Can't communicate. Inability to convince interviewer of the candidate's worth. Incoherent, unmotivated, arrogant and without any evidence of good reason. **London (QM)** Misunderstanding of what computer science involves as an academic subject – especially in personal statements where some suggest that they are interested in a course with business and administrative skills. Lack of sufficient mathematics. Computer science is a mathematical subject and we cannot accept applicants who are unable to demonstrate good mathematical skills. **Southampton** Lack of motivation, incoherence and/or carelessness.

AFTER-RESULTS ADVICE
Offers to applicants repeating A-levels Higher Brighton; De Montfort; Greenwich; Kingston; St Andrews; Sussex; Warwick; **Possibly higher** Bath; Edinburgh; Lancaster; Leeds; Newcastle; Sheffield; Teesside; **Same** Abertay; Anglia Ruskin; Aston; Brunel; Buckingham; Cambridge; Cardiff; Cardiff Met; City; Derby; Dundee; Durham; East Anglia; East London; Exeter; Huddersfield; Hull; Lincoln; Liverpool; Liverpool Hope; Liverpool John Moores; London (RH); London (UCL); London South Bank; Loughborough; Manchester Met; Northumbria; Nottingham Trent; Oxford Brookes; Robert Gordon; Salford; Sheffield Hallam; Sunderland; West London; Wolverhampton; Worcester; York.

GRADUATE DESTINATIONS AND EMPLOYMENT (2016/17 HESA)
Computer Science graduates surveyed 9,860 **Employed** 6,245 **In voluntary employment** 210 **In further study** 1,550 **Assumed unemployed** 870

Career note A high proportion of graduates go to work in the IT sector with some degrees leading towards particular fields (usually indicated by the course title). Significant areas include software design and engineering, web and internet-based fields, programming, systems analysis and administration.

OTHER DEGREE SUBJECTS FOR CONSIDERATION
Business Studies; Communications Engineering; Computer Engineering; Electrical and Electronic Engineering; Geographical Information Systems; Information Studies; Mathematics; Physics; Software Engineering.

DANCE/DANCE STUDIES
(see also **Drama**)

Dance courses abound, most offering a balance of theoretical and practical studies across a range of dance styles. The Royal Academy of Dance for example offers ballet, adult ballet, boys' ballet, creative and contemporary dance, West End jazz, street dance, and song and dance. Other institutions offer Dance combined with other subjects equally. Some universities offer Performance Arts with many courses covering the study of choreography, acting and directing, and acting and dance. While entry to Dance courses usually requires A-level grades, competitive entry to the most popular courses, such as the Contemporary Dance course at Trinity Laban, is by a demanding audition.

Useful websites www.cdmt.org.uk; www.onedanceuk.org; www.royalacademyofdance.org; www. royalballetschool.org.uk

NB The points totals shown to the left of the institutions are for ease of reference only. It must not be assumed that Tariff points are always used by institutions or that they can be substituted for an offer in grades. The level of an offer is not necessarily indicative of the quality of a course.

COURSE OFFERS INFORMATION

Subject requirements/preferences GCSE English usually required. **AL** No specific subjects required. Other Disclosure and Barring Service (DBS) checks required for some courses: check websites. Practical dance experience essential.

Your target offers and examples of degree courses

128 pts **East London** – ABB 128 pts +interview +audition (Dance (Urb Prac)) (IB 27 pts HL 15 pts)

120 pts **Leeds Beckett** – 120 pts +interview +audition (Dance) (IB 26 pts)

Roehampton – 120 pts +interview +audition (BFA Dance; Dance)

West London – ABB–BBB 120–128 pts +interview +audition (Musl Thea)

112 pts **Bedfordshire** – BBB–BBC 112–120 pts +interview +audition (Dance Prof Prac)

Chester – BBC–BCC +interview +audition (Dance) (IB 26 pts)

De Montfort – 112 pts +interview +audition (Dance) (IB 26 pts)

Derby – 112–128 pts (Dance Mov St Comb Hons)

Edge Hill – BBB–BBC 112–120 pts +audition workshop (Dance; Dance Dr)

Kingston – BBC incl dance/perf arts/Engl lit 112 pts +interview +audition (Dance)

Liverpool Hope – BBC 112 pts +interview +audition (Dance courses) (IB 26 pts)

Middlesex – 112 pts +interview +audition (Dance Perf)

RAc Dance – BBC +RAD Intermediate +interview +audition (Ballet Educ)

Wolverhampton – BBC +audition (Dance; Dance Dr)

Worcester – 112 pts +interview (PE Dance)

104 pts **Central Lancashire** – 104 pts +audition (Dance Perf Teach)

Chichester – 104–120 pts +interview +audition (Dance)

Falmouth – 104–120 pts +audition +portfolio (Dance Choreo) (IB 24 pts)

Lincoln – BCC+interview +audition (Dance) (IB 28 pts)

Plymouth – 104 pts +interview +audition (Dance) (IB 26 pts)

Salford – BCC 104 pts +interview +audition (Dance) (IB 31 pts HL 6/5)

96 pts **Bath Spa** – CCC incl dance/perf arts +interview +audition (Dance) (IB 26 pts)

Birmingham City – CCC 96 pts incl dr +interview (App Thea (Commun Educ)) (IB 24 pts)

Cardiff Met – BB 96–112 pts (Spo Physl Educ Hlth Dance) (IB 25 pts HL 13 pts)

Cumbria – BBC–CCC 96–112 pts +interview +audition (Dance)

Winchester – 96–112 pts +interview +audition (Dance)

88 pts **Canterbury Christ Church** – 88–112 pts +interview +audition (Dance Educ; Dance courses)

London Met – CCD 88 pts (Spo Dance Thera) (IB 28 pts HL 15 pts)

80 pts **Bucks New** – 80 pts +interview +audition (Dance Perf)

64 pts **Greenwich** – 64 pts +audition (Prof Dance Musl Thea)

Liverpool (LIPA) – CC 64 pts +interview +audition (Dance)

32 pts **Trinity Laban Consv** – EE +interview +audition (Contemp Dance)

Northern (Sch Contemp Dance) – interview +audition (Dance (Contemp))

RConsvS – interview +audition (Modn Ballet)

Alternative offers
See **Chapter 6** and **Appendix 1** for grades/UCAS Tariff points information for other examinations.

EXAMPLES OF COLLEGES OFFERING COURSES IN THIS SUBJECT FIELD
Barking and Dagenham (Coll); Bournemouth and Poole (Coll); Brooksby Melton (Coll); City and Islington (Coll); Coventry (Coll); Doncaster (Coll); Ealing, Hammersmith and West London (Coll); East Durham (Coll); Gateshead (Coll); Havering (Coll); Hull (Coll); Kingston (Coll); Leeds City (Coll); Leicester (Coll); LeSoCo; Liverpool City (Coll); Manchester (Coll); Nottingham (Coll); Petroc; South Essex (Coll); South Gloucestershire and Stroud (Coll); Southampton City (Coll); Stratford-upon-Avon (Coll); Sunderland (Coll); TEC Partnership; Wakefield (Coll); West Thames (Coll).

CHOOSING YOUR COURSE (SEE ALSO CH.1)
Universities and colleges teaching quality See www.qaa.ac.uk; https://unistats.ac.uk.

Top research universities and colleges (REF 2014) (Music, Drama, Dance and Performing Arts) Open University; Birmingham (Mus); City; London (King's) (Film); Manchester (Dr); London (RH) (Dr Thea); Huddersfield; Manchester (Mus); Cardiff; Roehampton (Dance); London (QM); Warwick; London (SOAS); Durham; London (RH) (Mus); Southampton; Oxford.

Examples of sandwich degree courses Coventry; Surrey.

ADMISSIONS INFORMATION
Number of applicants per place (approx) De Montfort (Dance) 13; Derby 4; Liverpool (LIPA) 24; Liverpool John Moores 3; Middlesex 12; Northern (Sch Contemp Dance) 6; Roehampton 8; Trinity Laban Consv 5.

Advice to applicants and planning the UCAS personal statement Full details should be given of examinations taken and practical experience in contemporary dance or ballet. Refer to your visits to the theatre and your impressions. You should list the dance projects in which you have worked, productions in which you have performed and the roles. State any formal dance training you have had and the grades achieved. Applicants need to have dedication, versatility, inventiveness and individuality, practical experience of dance, theoretical ability and language competency. **Bath Spa** Dance experience outside education should be mentioned.

Selection interviews Yes Bedfordshire, Bucks New, Cardiff Met, Chester, Chichester, Kingston, Northern (Sch Contemp Dance), Plymouth, Winchester, Worcester; **Some** Cumbria, RAc Dance; **No** Falmouth.

Interview advice and questions Nearly all institutions will require auditions or interviews or attendance at a workshop. The following scheme required by **Liverpool (LIPA)** may act as a guide:
1 Write a short essay (500 words) on your own views and experience of dance. You should take into account the following.
(i) Your history and how you have developed physically and intellectually in your run-up to applying to LIPA.
(ii) Your main influences and what inspires you.
(iii) What you want to gain from training as a dancer.
(iv) Your ideas on health and nutrition as a dancer, taking into account gender and physicality.
2 All candidates must prepare **two** practical audition pieces.
(i) Whatever you like, in whatever style you wish, as long as the piece does not exceed two minutes (please note: panel will stop anyone exceeding this time limit). There will be no pianist at this part of the session, so if you're using music please bring it with you. This devised piece should be created by you and this means that you should feel comfortable with it and that it expresses something personal about you. You should wear your regular practice clothes for your presentation.
(ii) You are asked to sing a musical theatre solo as part of the audition and will be accompanied by a pianist. An accompanist is provided, but you must provide the sheet music for your song, fully written out for piano accompaniment and in the key you wish to sing (the accompanist will **not** transpose at sight). **Important** Do NOT choreograph your song. You should expect to sit on a high stool or stand when singing for the audition.
3 Additionally, all candidates will participate in a class given on the day of audition.

(i) Please ensure that you are dressed appropriately for class with clothing you are comfortable in but allows your movement to be seen. In preparing the practical elements of the audition, please remember that audition panels are not looking for a polished performance. The panel will be looking for candidates' ability to make a genuine emotional and physical connection with the material that they are presenting which shows clear intent and focus.

Remember that it is in your best interest to prepare thoroughly. Nerves inevitably play a part in any audition and can undermine even the best-prepared candidate. Your best defence is to feel confident in your preparation.

See also **Chapter 5**. **Salford** Audition and interview. **Wolverhampton** Audition.

Reasons for rejection (non-academic) Applicants more suitable for an acting or dance school course than a degree course. No experience of dance on the UCAS application. Limited dance skills.

AFTER-RESULTS ADVICE

Offers to applicants repeating A-levels Same Chester; Chichester; De Montfort; Liverpool John Moores; Salford; Trinity Laban Consv; Winchester; Wolverhampton.

GRADUATE DESTINATIONS AND EMPLOYMENT (2016/17 HESA)

Graduates surveyed 910 **Employed** 355 **In voluntary employment** 30 **In further study** 230 **Assumed unemployed** 20

Career note Teaching is the most popular career destination for the majority of graduates. Other opportunities exist as dance animators working in education or in the community to encourage activity and participation in dance. There is a limited number of openings for dance or movement therapists who work with the emotionally disturbed, the elderly or physically disadvantaged.

OTHER DEGREE SUBJECTS FOR CONSIDERATION

Arts Management; Drama; Education (Primary); Music; Performance Studies; Physical Education; Sport and Exercise Science.

DENTISTRY

(including Dental Hygiene and Dental Therapy and Oral Health Science)

Dentistry involves the treatment and prevention of a wide range of mouth diseases from tooth decay and gum disease to mouth cancer. Courses in Dentistry/Dental Surgery cover the basic medical sciences, human disease, clinical studies and clinical dentistry. The amount of patient contact will vary between institutions but will be considerable in all dental schools. Intercalated courses in other science subjects are offered on most courses. Courses in Oral Health Science and Dental Therapy and Hygiene lead to professional qualifications as therapists and hygienists providing advice and non-surgical treatment for children and adults to prevent tooth decay. Dental Technology courses similarly lead to a professional qualification to prepare crowns, bridges, partial and complete sets of dentures, and other orthodontic devices to replace and correct teeth.

Useful websites www.badn.org.uk; www.bsdht.org.uk; www.dla.org.uk

NB The points totals shown to the left of the institutions are for ease of reference only. It must not be assumed that Tariff points are always used by institutions or that they can be substituted for an offer in grades. The level of an offer is not necessarily indicative of the quality of a course.

COURSE OFFERS INFORMATION

Subject requirements/preferences GCSE English, mathematics and science subjects required in most cases for Dentistry courses. A*/A/B (8–9/7/5–6) grades stipulated in certain subjects by many dental schools. **AL** Chemistry plus biology or another science subject usually required for Dentistry: see offers lines below. (Dntl Tech, Oral Hlth Sci) Science subject required or preferred. Many dental schools use admissions tests (eg UCAT: see Chapter 5). Evidence of non-infectivity or hepatitis B immunisation required and all new dental students screened for hepatitis C. Disclosure and Barring Service (DBS) check at enhanced level is also required. **London (King's) GCSE** English and maths grade B (6) if not offered at a higher level. **Manchester GCSE** Six subjects at grade A (7).

Your target offers and examples of degree courses

152 pts **London (King's)** – A*AA incl biol+chem +UCAT (Dnstry) (IB 35 pts HL 766 incl biol/chem+sci/maths)

London (QM) – A*AA incl chem/biol+sci/maths +UCAT +interview (Dnstry) (IB 38 pts HL 666 incl chem/biol+sci/maths)

144 pts **Birmingham** – AAA incl chem+biol +UCAT +interview (Dntl Srgy) (IB 32 pts HL 666 incl chem+biol)

Bristol – AAA incl chem+biol/phys +UCAT +interview (Dnstry) (IB 36 pts HL 18 pts incl 6 chem+sci)

Cardiff – AAA incl chem+biol +UCAT (Dntl Srgy) (IB 36 pts HL 6 chem+biol)

Dundee – AAA incl chem+sci +UCAT +interview (Dnstry) (IB 37 pts HL 666 incl chem+sci)

Glasgow – AAA incl biol+chem +UCAT +interview (Dnstry) (IB 36 pts HL 666 incl chem+biol)

Leeds – AAA incl biol+chem +BMAT +interview (Dntl Srgy) (IB 35 pts HL 666 incl biol+chem)

Liverpool – AAA incl chem+biol +UCAT +interview (Dntl Srgy) (IB 36 pts HL 6 chem+biol)

Manchester – AAA incl chem+biol +UCAT +interview (Dnstry) (IB 37 pts HL 766)

Newcastle – AAA incl chem+biol +UCAT +interview (Dntl Srgy) (IB 37 pts HL 6 chem+biol)

Queen's Belfast – AAA incl biol+chem +UCAT +interview (Dnstry)

Sheffield – AAA incl chem+biol +UCAT +interview (Dntl Srgy)

136 pts **Plymouth** – A*AA–AAB incl biol+sci/maths +interview +UCAT (Dntl Srgy) (IB 38–36 pts HL 6 biol+sci/maths)

128 pts **Birmingham** – ABB incl biol +interview (Dntl Hyg Thera) (IB 32 pts HL 655 incl biol)

London (QM) – ABB incl maths/phys/chem (Dntl Mat) (IB 32 pts HL 655 incl maths/phys/chem)

Newcastle – ABB incl biol +interview (Oral Dntl Hlth Sci) (IB 34 pts HL 5 biol)

120 pts **Dundee** – BBB incl biol +interview (Oral Hlth Sci) (IB 30 pts HL 555 incl biol)

Edinburgh – BBB incl biol +interview (Oral Hlth Sci) (IB 32 pts HL 55 incl biol)

Portsmouth – 120 pts +interview (Dntl Hyg) (IB 29 pts HL 664 incl 6 sci); 120 pts incl sci +interview (Dntl Hyg Dntl Thera) (IB 29 pts HL 664 incl 6 sci)

112 pts **Cardiff** – BBB–BBC incl biol +interview (Dntl Thera Dntl Hyg) (IB 31–30 pts HL 665 incl 6 biol)

104 pts **Glasgow Caledonian** – BCC incl biol +interview (Oral Hlth Sci) (IB 24 pts)

Teesside – 104–112 pts +interview (Dntl Hyg Dntl Thera)

UHI – BCC incl sci +interview (Oral Hlth Sci)

96 pts **Cardiff Met** – CC incl sci/maths 96 pts (Dntl Tech) (IB 24 pts)

Portsmouth – 96 pts +interview (Advnc Dntl Nurs) (IB 26 pts HL 5 sci)

Alternative offers
See **Chapter 6** and **Appendix 1** for grades/UCAS Tariff points information for other examinations.

EXAMPLES OF COLLEGES OFFERING COURSES IN THIS SUBJECT FIELD
Birmingham Met (Coll); Bury (Coll); Neath Port Talbot (Coll); Plumpton (Coll).

CHOOSING YOUR COURSE (SEE ALSO CH.1)
Universities and colleges teaching quality See www.qaa.ac.uk; https://unistats.ac.uk.

Top research universities and colleges (REF 2014) (Allied Health Professions, Dentistry, Nursing and Pharmacy) Birmingham; Glasgow; Nottingham (Pharm); Bradford; East Anglia (Allied Hlth); London (QM); Queen's Belfast (Pharm); Bath; London (King's) (Pharm); Leeds; Sheffield (Biomed Sci), (Dnstry); Bangor; Swansea (Allied Hlth); Aston; Coventry; Southampton; Cardiff; Surrey.

Examples of sandwich degree courses London (QM).

ADMISSIONS INFORMATION

Number of applicants per place (approx) Birmingham 7, (Dntl Hyg Thera) 8; Bristol 13; Cardiff 4; Cardiff Met 1; Dundee 8, (Pre-Dntl) 5; Edinburgh (Oral Hlth Sci) 10 places every 2nd yr; Glasgow 7; Leeds 11; Liverpool 7; London (King's) 128 (offers to 1 in 9); London (QM) 4; Manchester 12, (Pre-Dntl) 21, (Oral Hlth Sci) 26; Newcastle 10; Queen's Belfast 5; Sheffield 12.

Advice to applicants and planning the UCAS personal statement UCAS applications listing four choices only should be submitted by 15 October. Applicants may add one alternative (non-Dentistry) course. On your UCAS application, show evidence of your manual dexterity, work experience and awareness of problems experienced by dentists. Details should be provided of discussions with dentists and work shadowing in dental surgeries. Employment (paid or voluntary) in any field, preferably dealing with people in an environment widely removed from your home or school, could be described. Discuss any specialised fields of dentistry in which you might be interested. See also **Appendix 3**. **Aberdeen** Information is provided in the prospectus and on our web pages. As we are a Scottish institution, we admit students applying for a specific subject to an overall area of study, for example Engineering, Science, Arts or Social Sciences. **Bristol** Applications are not segregated by type of educational institution. Candidates are assessed on general presentation. Work experience is expected, if possible in different fields of dentistry. Re-sit candidates are considered, but only one re-sit is allowed in each subject unless there are mitigating circumstances. **Cardiff** Applicants must be able to demonstrate: (a) evidence of, and potential for, high academic achievement, (b) an understanding of the demands of dental training and practice, (c) a caring and committed attitude towards people, (d) a willingness to accept responsibility, (e) an ability to communicate effectively, (f) evidence of broad social, cultural or sporting interests. **London (King's)** School activities desirable, for example, general reading, debating, theological interests. Community activities very desirable. General activities desirable, for example, sport, first-aid, handiwork (which can be used to demonstrate manual dexterity). Work shadowing and paid or voluntary work very desirable (check website). **Manchester** Re-sit offers A*AA. Applicants are required to have observed a general dental practitioner at work before applying; a minimum of two weeks' work experience is expected.

Misconceptions about this course Cardiff Met (Dntl Tech) Some think that the course allows them to practise as a dentist. Some think the degree is entirely practical.

Selection interviews Yes Aberdeen (Applicants are required to sit the UCAT test), Birmingham, Bristol, Cardiff, Dundee, Edinburgh, Glasgow, Leeds, Liverpool, London (King's), London (QM), Manchester, Newcastle, Portsmouth, Queen's Belfast, Sheffield; **No** Cardiff Met.

Interview advice and questions Dental work experience or work shadowing is essential (check with university websites) and, as a result, questions will be asked on your reactions to the work and your understanding of the different types of treatment that a dentist can offer. In the past, questions at interview have included: What is conservative dentistry? What does integrity mean? Do you think the first-year syllabus is a good one? What qualities are required by a dentist? What are prosthetics, periodontics, orthodontics? What causes tooth decay? Questions asked on the disadvantages of being a dentist, the future of dentistry and how you could show that you are manually dexterous. Other questions on personal attributes and spare time activities. What are the careers within the profession open to dentists? Questions on the future of dentistry (preventative and cosmetic dentistry), the problems facing dentists, the skills needed and the advantages and disadvantages of fluoride in water. How do you relax? How do you cope with stress? See also **Chapter 5**. **Aberdeen** We provide information in our prospectus and in the invite for interview, as well as on web pages. **Bristol** All candidates called for interview must attend in order to be considered for a place. The University uses the Multiple Mini Interview system and interviewees are asked to fill in a form detailing their work experience. Candidates are assessed on general presentation, response to questions, knowledge of dentistry, evidence of teamwork and leadership, general interests and manual dexterity. **Leeds** The interview assesses personality, verbal and communication skills and knowledge of dentistry. **London (King's)** Approximately 180 offers are made each year. All applicants receiving offers will have been interviewed. The interviews will normally take the MMI format.

Reasons for rejection (non-academic) Lack of evidence of a firm commitment to dentistry. Lack of breadth of interests. Lack of motivation for a health care profession. Unprofessional attitude. Poor manual dexterity. Poor communication skills. Poor English. Lack of evidence of ability to work in groups. Not for the faint-hearted! More interested in running a business and making money than in caring for people. **Aberdeen** When applicants apply and we are unable to make them an offer of admission, the reason for the rejection is indicated to the applicant via UCAS. **Cardiff Met** (Dntl Tech) Target numbers need to be precise so the course fills at a late stage.

Mature students The following universities/dental schools offer shortened (usually four-year) courses in Dentistry/Dental Surgery for graduates with at least 2.1 degrees in specified subjects. GCE A-level subjects and grades are also specified. Check with universities: Liverpool, London (King's), (QM).

AFTER-RESULTS ADVICE
Offers to applicants repeating A-levels Higher Leeds (very few); Manchester (AAA for applicants who firmly accepted offer of a place); **Same** Cardiff Met (Dntl Tech); Queen's Belfast; **No** Cardiff; **Rare** Dundee.

GRADUATE DESTINATIONS AND EMPLOYMENT (2016/17 HESA)
Clinical Dentistry graduates surveyed 870 **Employed** 800 **In voluntary employment** 10 **In further study** 25 **Assumed unemployed** 0

Career note The great majority of Dental Technology graduates gain employment in this career with job opportunities excellent in both the UK and Europe. There are openings in the NHS, commercial dental laboratories and the armed services.

OTHER DEGREE SUBJECTS FOR CONSIDERATION
Anatomy; Biochemistry; Biological Sciences; Biomedical Materials Science; Chemistry; Medical Sciences; Medicine; Nursing; Optometry; Pharmacy; Physiology; Physiotherapy; Radiography; Speech Therapy/Sciences; Veterinary Medicine/Science.

DEVELOPMENT STUDIES
(see also **International Relations, Politics, Town and Urban Planning**)

Development Studies courses are multi-disciplinary and cover a range of subjects including economics, geography, sociology, social anthropology, politics, natural resources, with special reference to countries overseas. Courses obviously overlap with International Relations degrees which should also be checked. The main focus of Development Studies is to identify and recognise problems arising overseas and how countries may be assisted in terms of poverty and health, as well as exploring wider issues concerning social and political perspectives. The unique degree course in this category is Charity Development at the University of Chichester with either Single Honours or Joint Honours. The course covers fund-raising practices, through events and campaigns, marketing and planning.

Useful websites www.devstud.org.uk; www.gov.uk/government/organisations/department-for-international-development; www.ids.ac.uk; see also **Politics**.

NB The points totals shown to the left of the institutions are for ease of reference only. It must not be assumed that Tariff points are always used by institutions or that they can be substituted for an offer in grades. The level of an offer is not necessarily indicative of the quality of a course.

COURSE OFFERS INFORMATION
Subject requirements/preferences GCSE Mathematics, English and a foreign language may be required. **AL** Science or social science subjects may be required or preferred for some courses.

Your target offers and examples of degree courses

144 pts   **London (King's)** – AAA (Int Dev) (IB 35 pts HL 666)
   Warwick – AAA (Glob Sust Dev Bus) (IB 38 pts)

136 pts   **Bath** – AAB/ABB +aEPQ (Int Dev Econ) (IB 36 pts HL 665)
   London (SOAS) – AAA–AAB (Dev St) (IB 37 pts HL 666)
   Manchester – AAB (Dev St) (IB 35 pts HL 665)
   Sussex – AAB (Int Dev; Int Rel Dev) (IB 34 pts)
   York – AAB (Glob Dev) (IB 35 pts)

128 pts   **East Anglia** – ABB (Int Dev; Int Dev Anth; Int Dev Pol) (IB 32 pts)
   Leeds – ABB (Int Dev courses) (IB 34 pts HL 655)
   Sussex – AAB–ABB (Econ Int Dev) (IB 34–32 pts)

120 pts   **Birmingham** – BBB (Af St Dev) (IB 32 pts HL 555)
   Sussex – ABB–BBB (Sociol Int Dev) (IB 32–30 pts)

112 pts   **East London** – BBC 112 pts (Int Dev NGO Mgt) (IB 25 pts HL 15 pts)

104 pts   **Northampton** – BCC 104–112 pts (Int Dev courses) (IB 25 pts)

96 pts   **Bath Spa** – CCC (Glob Dev Sust) (IB 26 pts)
   Chichester – BCC–CCC 96–112 pts +interview (Charity Dev) (IB 28 pts)
   Portsmouth – 96–112 pts (Int Dev) (IB 25 pts)
   Westminster – BBB–CCC 96–120 pts (Int Rel Dev) (IB 27 pts HL 4 Engl)

72 pts   **UHI** – BC+interview (Gael Dev)

64 pts   **UHI** – CC (Sust Dev)

Alternative offers
See **Chapter 6** and **Appendix 1** for grades/UCAS Tariff points information for other examinations.

CHOOSING YOUR COURSE (SEE ALSO CH.1)

Universities and colleges teaching quality See www.qaa.ac.uk; https://unistats.ac.uk.

Top research universities and colleges (REF 2014) (Anthropology and Development Studies) London LSE (Int Dev); Manchester (Anth); Oxford (Int Dev); Manchester (Dev St); London (Gold); Durham; East Anglia; Cambridge; Edinburgh.

Examples of sandwich degree courses Reading.

ADMISSIONS INFORMATION

Number of applicants per place (approx) Bradford 6; East Anglia 5; Leeds 8.

Admissions tutors' advice Discuss aspects of development studies which interest you, for example in relation to geography, economics, politics. Interests in Third World countries should be mentioned. Knowledge of current events.

Advice to applicants and planning the UCAS personal statement Some students think that Development Studies has something to do with property, with plants or with childhood. It is none of these and is about international processes of change, development, progress and crisis.

Interview advice and questions Since this is a multi-disciplinary subject, questions will vary considerably. Initially they will stem from your interests and the information given on your UCAS application and your reasons for choosing the course. In the past, questions at interview have included: Define a Third World country. What help does the United Nations provide in the Third World? Could it do too much? What problems does the United Nations face in its work throughout the world? Why Development Studies? What will you do in your gap year, and what do you want to achieve? See also **Chapter 5**.

AFTER-RESULTS ADVICE

Offers to applicants repeating A-levels Same East Anglia.

GRADUATE DESTINATIONS AND EMPLOYMENT

Career note The range of specialisms offered on these courses will encourage graduates to make contact with and seek opportunities in a wide range of organisations, not necessarily limited to non-governmental organisations and government agencies.

OTHER DEGREE SUBJECTS FOR CONSIDERATION
Economics; Environmental Science/Studies; Geography; Government; International Relations; Politics; Sociology; Sustainable Development.

DIETETICS
(see also Food Science/Studies and Technology, Health Sciences/Studies, Nutrition)

Courses are often linked with nutrition and train students for a career as a dietitian. In addition to the scientific aspects of dietetics covering biochemistry, human physiology, food and clinical medicine, students are also introduced to health promotion, psychology, counselling and management skills. (See **Appendix 3**.)

Useful websites www.nutrition.org; www.bda.uk.com; www.dietetics.co.uk; www.skillsforhealth.org.uk

NB The points totals shown to the left of the institutions are for ease of reference only. It must not be assumed that Tariff points are always used by institutions or that they can be substituted for an offer in grades. The level of an offer is not necessarily indicative of the quality of a course.

COURSE OFFERS INFORMATION
Subject requirements/preferences GCSE English, mathematics and science usually required. **AL** Biology and/or chemistry may be required. Other Health and Disclosure and Barring Service (DBS) checks required and possible immunisation against hepatitis B for practice placements.

Your target offers and examples of degree courses

136 pts London (King's) – AAB incl chem+biol +interview (Nutr Diet) (IB 35 pts HL 665 incl chem+biol)

128 pts Coventry – ABB incl biol +interview (Diet Hum Nutr) (IB 32 pts HL 7 biol)
Leeds – ABB incl sci (Fd Sci Nutr) (IB 34 pts HL 16 pts); ABB incl sci/maths (Fd Sci) (IB 34 pts HL 16 pts)
Nottingham – AAB-ABB incl sci +interview (Nutr Diet (MNutr)) (IB 34-32 pts)
Surrey – ABB incl biol+sci/maths +interview (Nutr Diet) (IB 32 pts HL 5 hiol+sci/maths)

120 pts Cardiff Met – BBB incl biol+chem 120 pts +interview (Hum Nutr Diet) (IB 26 pts HL 15 pts incl 6 biol+chem)
Hertfordshire – BBB incl biol+chem 120 pts +interview (Diet)
Leeds Beckett – BBB incl chem+sci +interview (Diet) (IB 26 pts HL 6 chem)
London Met – BBB incl biol+chem 120 pts +interview (Diet Nutr) (IB 28 pts HL 15 pts)
Ulster – BBB incl sci/maths +HPAT (Diet) (IB 26 pts HL 13 pts incl sci/maths)

112 pts Chester – BBB-BBC incl biol+sci 112-120 pts +interview (Nutr Diet) (IB 28 pts HL 5 biol+chem)
Plymouth – ABB-BBC incl biol+sci/maths 112-128 pts +interview (Diet) (IB 31 pts HL 5 biol+sci/maths)

104 pts Glasgow Caledonian – BCC incl chem +interview (Hum Nutr Diet) (IB 28 pts)
Robert Gordon – BCC incl biol+chem +interview (Diet) (IB 27 pts HL 5 biol+chem)

96 pts Bath Spa – CCC incl biol+sci (Hum Nutr) (IB 26 pts)

88 pts Queen Margaret – AB incl chem/biol (Diet) (IB 28 pts)

Alternative offers
See **Chapter 6** and **Appendix 1** for grades/UCAS Tariff points information for other examinations.

CHOOSING YOUR COURSE (SEE ALSO CH.1)
Universities and colleges teaching quality See www.qaa.ac.uk; https://unistats.ac.uk.

Top research universities and colleges (REF 2014) See **Health Sciences/Studies**.

Examples of sandwich degree courses Glasgow Caledonian; Surrey; Ulster.

ADMISSIONS INFORMATION
Number of applicants per place (approx) Nottingham 8.

Advice to applicants and planning the UCAS personal statement Discuss the work with a hospital dietitian and describe fully work experience gained in hospital dietetics departments or with the schools meals services, and the problems of working in these fields. Admissions tutors expect applicants to have at least visited a dietetics department, and to be outgoing with good oral and written communication skills. Contact the British Dietetic Association (see **Appendix 3**).

Selection interviews Yes Chester, Coventry, Leeds Beckett; **Some** Cardiff Met; **No** Ulster.

Interview advice and questions Your knowledge of a career in dietetics will be fully explored and questions will be asked on your work experience and how you reacted to it. See also **Chapter 5**.

GRADUATE DESTINATIONS AND EMPLOYMENT (2016/17 HESA)
Graduates surveyed See **Nutrition**.

Career note Dietitians are professionally trained to advise on diets and aspects of nutrition and many degree courses combine both subjects. They may work in the NHS as hospital dietitians collaborating with medical staff on the balance of foods for patients, or in local health authorities working with GPs, or in health centres or clinics dealing with infant welfare and antenatal problems. In addition, dietitians advise consumer groups in the food industry and government and may be involved in research. Courses can lead to professional registration: check with admissions tutors.

OTHER DEGREE SUBJECTS FOR CONSIDERATION
Biological Sciences; Biochemistry; Biology; Consumer Studies; Food Science; Health Studies; Hospitality Management; Human Nutrition; Nursing; Nutrition.

DRAMA

(including **Performing Arts/Studies, Theatre Arts, Theatre Studies and Theatre Design**; see also Art and Design (General), Dance/Dance Studies)

Drama courses are popular, with twice as many women as men applying each year. Lack of confidence in securing appropriate work at the end of the course, however, tends to encourage many applicants to bid for joint courses, although these are usually far more competitive since there are fewer places available. Most schools of acting and drama provide a strong vocational bias while university drama departments offer a broader field of studies combining theory and practice. For example, at London (Goldsmiths) the Drama and Theatre Arts degree offers a balance between acting and production.

Useful websites www.equity.org.uk; www.abtt.org.uk; www.thestage.co.uk; www.uktw.co.uk; www.stagecoach.co.uk; www.rada.ac.uk; www.artscouncil.org.uk

NB The points totals shown to the left of the institutions are for ease of reference only. It must not be assumed that Tariff points are always used by institutions or that they can be substituted for an offer in grades. The level of an offer is not necessarily indicative of the quality of a course.

COURSE OFFERS INFORMATION
Subject requirements/preferences GCSE English usually required. **AL** English, drama, theatre studies may be required or preferred. (Thea Arts) English, theatre studies or drama may be required for some courses. Other Disclosure and Barring Service (DBS) clearance required for some courses: check websites.

Your target offers and examples of degree courses

152 pts **Cambridge** – A*AA +interview +EAA (Educ Engl Dr Arts) (IB 42–40 pts HL 776)

144 pts **Bristol** – AAA incl Engl (Thea Engl) (IB 36 pts HL 18 pts incl 6 Engl)

136 pts **Bristol** – AAB (Thea Perf St) (IB 34 pts HL 17 pts); AAB incl lang (Thea Modn Lang) (IB 34 pts HL 17 pts incl 5 lang)

Exeter – AAA–AAB incl Engl lit +interview (Engl Drama courses) (IB 36–34 pts HL 666–665 incl 6 Engl lit)

Glasgow – AAB incl arts/hum (Thea St) (IB 36 pts HL 665 incl Engl+lang/hum)

Lancaster – AAB incl Engl (Thea Engl Lit) (IB 35 pts HL 16 pts incl 6 Engl)

Leeds – AAB incl arts/hum +interview (Thea Perf) (IB 34 pts)

Manchester – AAB +interview (Dr Engl Lit) (IB 35 pts HL 665); AAB incl essay sub+interview (Dr) (IB 35 pts HL 665)

Warwick – AAB incl Engl +interview (Engl Thea St) (IB 36 pts HL 6 Engl)

York – AAB +interview (Thea Writ Dir Perf) (IB 35 pts)

128 pts **Birmingham** – AAB–ABB +workshop (Dr Thea Arts) (IB 32 pts HL 665–655)

Exeter – AAB–ABB +interview +workshop (Dr) (IB 34–32 pts HL 665–655)

Lancaster – ABB (Dr Thea Perf; Thea Crea Writ) (IB 32 pts HL 16 pts)

London (RH) – AAB–ABB (Dr Phil; Dr Thea St) (IB 32 pts HL 655); AAB–ABB incl 6 mus (Dr Mus) (IB 32 pts HL 655 incl mus); AAB–ABB incl Engl (Engl Dr) (IB 32 pts HL 655 incl Engl); AAB–ABB incl Engl lit +portfolio (Dr Crea Writ) (IB 32 pts HL 655 incl 6 Engl); AAB–ABB incl lang (Modn Lang Dr) (IB 32 pts HL 655)

Manchester – ABB incl essay sub (Dr Flm St) (IB 34 pts HL 655)

Sussex – AAB–ABB (Dr Flm St) (IB 34–32 pts); AAB–ABB +workshop (Dr Thea Perf) (IB 34–32 pts)

Warwick – ABB +interview (Thea Perf St) (IB 34 pts)

120 pts **Bournemouth Arts** – BBB 112–120 pts +interview +audition (Actg)

Brunel – BBB+audition workshop (Thea) (IB 30 pts); BBB incl Engl+audition workshop (Thea Crea Writ; Thea Engl) (IB 30 pts HL 5 Engl)

East Anglia – BBB incl dr/thea st/Engl lit +interview +audition (Dr; Script Perf) (IB 31 pts HL 5 thea st/Engl)

Essex – BBB +workshop (Dr Lit) (IB 30 pts); BBB incl essay sub +workshop (Dr) (IB 30 pts HL 5 essay sub)

Huddersfield – BBB 120 pts +audition workshop (Dr; Dr Engl Lang/Lit)

Kent – BBB (Dr Thea) (IB 34 pts HL 15 pts)

Leeds Beckett – 120 pts +interview +workshop (Perf Arts) (IB 26 pts)

London (Gold) – BBB (Dr Thea Arts) (IB 33 pts HL 655)

London (QM) – BBB incl art/hum/soc sci (Dr) (IB 32 pts HL 655 incl 6 art/hum/soc sci)

Northumbria – 120 pts +interview +audition (Dr)

Queen Margaret – BBB (Dr) (IB 30 pts)

Queen's Belfast – BBB +interview +workshop (Dr) (IB 32 pts HL 655)

Reading – BBB +interview (Thea Perf) (IB 30 pts); BBB incl Engl/thea st (Engl Lit Flm Thea) (IB 30 pts HL 5 Engl/thea st)

West London – ABB–BBB 120–128 pts +audition (Actg); ABB–BBB 120–128 pts +interview +audition (Musl Thea)

112 pts **Bangor** – 112 pts incl Engl (Engl Lit Thea Perf)

Birmingham City – BBC 112 pts +portfolio (Des Perf Thea Flm Lv Evnts) (IB 28 pts HL 14 pts); BBC incl Engl 112 pts (Engl Dr) (IB 28 pts HL 14 pts)

Chester – BBC incl dr/thea st 112 pts +interview +audition (Musl Thea) (IB 26 pts HL 5 thea arts)

Coventry – BBC incl dr/thea/perf arts +portfolio +interview (Thea Prof Prac) (IB 29 pts)

Cumbria – ABB–BBC 112–128 pts +interview +audition (Perf Arts)

De Montfort – 112 pts +interview +workshop (Perf Arts) (IB 26 pts)

Derby – 112–128 pts +interview +audition (Thea Comb Hons)

East London – BBC 112 pts +interview +audition (Dr App Thea Perf) (IB 25 pts HL 15 pts)

Edge Hill – BBB–BBC 112–120 pts +audition workshop (Dr)

Glyndŵr – BBC 112 pts +interview +audition (Thea TV Perf)
Hull – 112 pts (Dr Engl) (IB 28 pts)
Liverpool Hope – BBC 112 pts +audition (Dr Thea St) (IB 26 pts)
London (Birk) – ABB–BBC 112–128 pts +interview (Thea Dr St)
London Met – BBC 112 pts +audition (Thea Perf Prac) (IB 28 pts HL 15 pts)
London South Bank – BBC +audition (Dr Perf)
Manchester Met – BBC 112 pts +audition (Actg) (IB 26 pts)
Middlesex – 112 pts +interview (Thea Arts)
Northampton – BBC +audition (Actg)
Roehampton – 112 pts +interview +audition (Dr Thea Perf St)
Rose Bruford (Coll) – 112 pts +interview +audition (Am Thea Arts; Euro Thea Arts)
Sunderland – BBC 112 pts +interview +audition (Perf Arts)
UWE Bristol – 112 pts +interview +workshop (Dr)
Wolverhampton – BBC +audition (Dance Dr; Dr)
Worcester – 112 pts (Dr Psy); 112 pts +workshop (Dr Perf)

104 pts **Bolton** – 104 pts +interview +audition (Thea Perf)
Cardiff Met – 104 pts (Engl Dr) (IB 24 pts)
Central Lancashire – 104 pts +interview +audition (Actg; Mus Thea; Thea Perf)
Chester – BBC–BCC incl dr/thea st 104–112 pts +interview +audition (Dr Thea St courses) (IB 26 pts HL 5 thea)
Chichester – 104–120 pts +audition (Thea) (IB 28 pts); BBC–BCC 104–112 pts +audition (Scrn Actg Crea Tech) (IB 28 pts)
Falmouth – 104–120 pts +portfolio +interview (Actg) (IB 24 pts)
Greenwich – BCC 104 pts +audition (Dr)
Kingston – 104–112 pts incl dr/perf arts/Engl lit +interview +workshop (Dr courses)
Lincoln – BCC +interview (Dr Thea) (IB 28 pts)
Liverpool John Moores – BCC 104 pts +interview +audition (Dr) (IB 24 pts)
Northampton – BCC 104–112 pts +interview +audition (Dr courses) (IB 25 pts)
Plymouth – 104 pts +interview +audition workshop (Dr Thea Prac) (IB 26 pts)
Portsmouth – 104–112 pts +interview +workshop (Dr Perf; Musl Thea) (IB 25 pts)
Salford – 104–120 pts (Engl Dr) (IB 31–30 pts)
Sheffield Hallam – BCC 104 pts (Perf Stg Scrn)

96 pts **Aberystwyth** – BBB–CCC 96–120 pts (Dr Thea St; Scngrph Thea Des) (IB 30–26 pts)
Anglia Ruskin – 96 pts +interview +audition (Dr Engl Lit) (IB 24 pts); 96 pts incl dr/thea st +interview +audition (Dr) (IB 24 pts)
Bath Spa – CCC incl dr/thea st/Engl +interview +audition (Dr) (IB 26 pts)
Birmingham City – CCC incl dr 96 pts +interview (Stg Mgt)
Bishop Grosseteste – 96–112 pts (App Dr courses; Sociol Dr)
Chichester – BCC–CCC 96–112 pts +audition (Actg Flm) (IB 28 pts)
Colchester (UC) – 96 pts +interview +audition (Musl Thea)
Cumbria – BBB–CCC 96–120 pts +interview +audition (Musl Thea)
Liverpool (LIPA) – CCC 96 pts +interview (Mgt Mus Enter Thea Evnts)
London (Royal Central Sch SpDr) – 96–120 pts +interview (Dr App Thea Educ); 96–120 pts +interview +portfolio (Thea Prac (Perf Arts))
Marjon – CCC +audition +interview (Actg)
Newman – 96 pts +audition (Dr Thea App Perf)
Solent – CCC 96–112 pts +audition (Actg Perf) (IB 28 pts)
St Mary's – BBC–CCC 96–112 pts +interview +audition (Actg) (IB 28–24 pts)
Surrey (GSA) – CCC +interview +audition (Actg; Musl Thea) (IB 30 pts)
Trinity Saint David – 96–120 pts+interview +workshop (Perf)
Winchester – 96–112 pts (Actg); 96–112 pts +interview (Crea Writ Dr; Dr Eng Lit; Musl Thea); 96–112 pts +interview +workshop (Dr)

88 pts **Canterbury Christ Church** – 88–112 pts (Musl Thea; Perf Arts; Thea Tech Prod)
York St John – 88–104 pts (Dr Thea)
80 pts **Bedfordshire** – 80 pts +interview +audition (Thea Prof Prac)

Bucks New – 80 pts +interview +audition (Perf Arts (Film TV Stg))

Essex – CDD 80 pts +audition (Actg; Actg Contemp Thea)

South Wales – BCC–CDD 80–112 pts +audition workshop (Perf Media; Thea Dr)

72 pts   **Liverpool (LIPA)** – BC 72–80 pts +interview +audition (App Thea Commun Dr)

64 pts   **Arts London** – CC +interview +portfolio (Perf Des Prac) (IB -28 pts); CC 64 pts +audition +interview (Actg Perf)

Birmingham City – 64 pts +audition (Actg)

Liverpool (LIPA) – CC 64 pts +audition (Actg); CC 64 pts +interview +portfolio (Thea Perf Des; Thea Perf Tech)

London (Royal Central Sch SpDr) – 64–120 pts +interview +portfolio (Thea Prac (Des Perf); Thea Prac (Stg Mgt); Thea Prac (Tech Prod Mgt); Thea Prac (Thea Snd)); CC +audition (Actg; Actg (Coll Dvsd Thea); Actg (Musl Thea))

London Regent's – CC +interview +audition (Actg Stg Scrn)

Rose Bruford (Coll) – CC 64 pts +audition (Actg; Actr Mushp); CC 64 pts +interview +portfolio (Cstm Prod; Stg Evnts Mgt)

Trinity Saint David – audition (Actg)

32 pts   **Arts Educ Sch** – EE +audition (Actg); EE +audition (Musl Thea)

Bristol Old Vic (Thea Sch) – audition (Prof Actg)

Guildhall (Sch Mus Dr) – 32 pts +audition (Actg) (IB 24 pts); 32 pts +interview (Prod Arts) (IB 24 pts)

RConsvS – EE+ audition (Actg; Contemp Perf Prac) (IB 24 pts); EE +interview (Prod Arts Des) (IB 24 pts)

LAMDA – interview +audition (Prof Actg)

London (RADA) – audition (Actg)

London Mountview (Ac Thea Arts) – audition (Perf (Actg); Perf (Musl Thea))

Royal Welsh (CMusDr) – audition (Actg); interview (Stg Mgt Tech Thea)

Alternative offers

See **Chapter 6** and **Appendix 1** for grades/UCAS Tariff points information for other examinations.

EXAMPLES OF COLLEGES OFFERING COURSES IN THIS SUBJECT FIELD

Blackpool and Fylde (Coll); Bradford College UC; Brooksby Melton (Coll); Buckinghamshire (Coll Group); Bury (Coll); Calderdale (Coll); Chichester (Coll); Coventry (Coll); Craven (Coll); Croydon (Univ Centre); Doncaster (Coll); Ealing, Hammersmith and West London (Coll); East Durham (Coll); Exeter (Coll); Gateshead (Coll); Gloucestershire (Coll); Guildford (Coll); Havering (Coll); Hopwood Hall (Coll); Hull (Coll); Kingston (Coll); Leicester (Coll); Liverpool City (Coll); Manchester (Coll); Middlesbrough (Coll); NCC Redbridge; Nescot; Newcastle (Coll); North Notts (Coll); North Shropshire (Coll); Nottingham (Coll); Oldham (Univ Campus); Peterborough (Coll); Plymouth City (Coll); Richmond-upon-Thames (Coll); Rotherham (CAT); Sheffield (Coll); South Devon (Coll); South Gloucestershire and Stroud (Coll); Southampton City (Coll); St Helens (Coll); Stamford New (Coll); Stratford-upon-Avon (Coll); Sunderland (Coll); TEC Partnership; Tresham (CFHE); Wakefield (Coll); Warrington and Vale Royal (Coll); West Herts (Coll); West Thames (Coll); Westminster City (Coll); Weymouth (Coll); Wigan and Leigh (Coll).

CHOOSING YOUR COURSE (SEE ALSO CH.1)

Universities and colleges teaching quality See www.qaa.ac.uk; https://unistats.ac.uk.

Top research universities and colleges (REF 2014) (Music, Drama, Dance and Performing Arts) Open University; Birmingham (Mus); City; London (King's) (Film); Manchester (Dr); London (RH) (Dr Thea); Huddersfield; Manchester (Mus); Cardiff; Roehampton (Dance); London (QM); Warwick; London (SOAS); Durham; London (RH) (Mus); Southampton; Oxford.

ADMISSIONS INFORMATION

Number of applicants per place (approx) Arts London (Actg) 32, (Dir) 10; Bath Spa 10; Birmingham 15; Bristol 19; Cumbria 4; De Montfort (Perf Arts) 5; East Anglia 6; Edge Hill 8; Essex 15; Exeter 20; Huddersfield 5; Hull 5; Hull (Coll) 2; Kent 6; Leeds 10; Liverpool (LIPA) (Actg) 48; Liverpool John Moores

10; London (Gold) 28; London (RH) 7; London (Royal Central Sch SpDr) (Thea Prac) 5; London Met 20; London Mountview (Ac Thea Arts) (Musl Thea) 8; Manchester (Dr) 6, (Dr Engl Lit) 7; Manchester (Coll) 10; Manchester Met 48; Middlesex 26; Northampton 3; Reading 17; Roehampton 6; Royal Welsh (CMusDr) (Actg) 50, (Stg Mgt) 10; Warwick 18; Winchester 5; Worcester 4; York 4; York St John 9.

Admissions tutors' advice Emphasis is placed on academic and practical abilities.

Advice to applicants and planning the UCAS personal statement List the plays in which you have performed and specify the characters played. Indicate any experience in other areas of theatre, especially directing or writing. Add any information on projects you have initiated or developed or worked on in theatre craft, such as set design, costume design, lighting design, prop-making, scene painting. List any community arts projects such as work with youth clubs, hospital radio, amateur dramatics, music/drama workshops and voluntary work within the arts. Show your strengths in dance and theatre, and your commitment to drama in all its aspects. See **Chapter 5** and also **Appendix 3**. **Bournemouth** For Make-up, a portfolio is required with evidence including portraits and life drawings. **Bristol** Deferred entry accepted. **London (Royal Central Sch SpDr)** (Dr App Thea Educ) We look for an interest in theatre and performance in different social and cultural settings, for example, community, schools, prisons. We also look for an enquiring mind, practical drama skills, flexibility and focus. **Manchester** Due to the detailed nature of entry requirements for Drama courses, the University is unable to include full details in the prospectus. For complete and up-to-date information on the entry requirements for these courses, please visit the website at www.manchester.ac.uk/study/undergraduate/courses. **Warwick** Applications for deferred entry considered, but candidates should bear in mind the competition for places. **York** (Thea (Writ Dir Perf)) Strong analytical ability plus experience in a related field, eg stage management/design, drama, writing are important factors.

Misconceptions about this course Arts London Provides a long-established classical conservatoire-type training for actors, and not Theatre Studies or Performance Arts courses, contrary to the views of some students. It is no longer a private school and home and EU students pay the standard degree fee. **De Montfort** (Perf Arts) Students are unaware that the course involves music. **York St John** This is not a course for intending actors.

Selection interviews Yes Anglia Ruskin, Arts London, Bath Spa, Bedfordshire, Birmingham City, Bolton (Thea), Cambridge, Central Lancashire, Chester, Chichester, Cumbria, East Anglia, East London, Edge Hill, Exeter, Greenwich, Huddersfield, Hull, Kingston, Liverpool John Moores, Loughborough, Manchester, Middlesex, Northumbria, Plymouth, Portsmouth, Queen Margaret, Sussex, UWE Bristol, Warwick, Winchester; **Some** Bristol, London (Gold), London (Royal Central Sch SpDr), Royal Welsh (CMusDr), Wolverhampton, York; **No** Bishop Grosseteste, Bucks New, Falmouth, London (QM), Reading, St Mary's.

Interview advice and questions See also **Chapter 5**. **Arts London** (Actg) Two three-minute speeches or scenes, one of which must be from the classical repertoire. (Dir) Interview and practical workshop which may involve directing actors. **Bristol** Assesses each case on its merits, paying attention to candidate's educational and cultural opportunities. Particularly interested in applicants who have already shown some evidence of commitment in their approach to drama in practical work, theatre-going, film viewing or reading. **Brunel** All applicants to whom an offer may be made will be auditioned, involving a practical workshop, voice, movement improvisation and a short prepared speech. Offers unlikely to be made to those with less than a grade B in drama or theatre studies. **De Montfort** (Perf Arts) What do you hope to gain on a three-year course in Performing Arts? Interviews involve practical workshops in drama and theatre. **East Anglia** Looks for candidates with a sound balance of academic and practical skills. Applicants will be expected to analyse performance and to understand what is entailed in the production of a drama. **Kent** No Single Honours candidate accepted without interview/group audition. Equal emphasis placed on academic and practical abilities. Questions asked to probe the applicant's creative and analytical grasp of theatre. **Loughborough** Candidates judged as individuals. Applicants with unconventional subject combinations and mature students considered. Final selection based on interview and audition. Applicants ought to show experience of practical drama, preferably beyond school plays. **Royal Welsh (CMusDr)** (Actg) Audition; (Stg Mgt) interview; (Thea Des) interview and portfolio presentation. All applicants are charged an audition/interview fee. **Warwick** Interview is important to assess academic potential and particularly commitment to, and suitability for, teaching; offers therefore variable.

Reasons for rejection (non-academic) Poor ambition. Wrong expectations of the course. Several students clearly want drama school acting training rather than a degree course. Not enough background reading. **Arts London** Insufficient clarity about career aims. **De Montfort** (Perf Arts) Candidate more suitable for a drama or dance school than for a degree course. No genuine engagement with the subject. Evidence of poor attendance at school.

AFTER-RESULTS ADVICE
Offers to applicants repeating A-levels Higher Bristol; Warwick; **Possibly higher** London (RH); **Same** Brunel; Chichester; De Montfort (Perf Arts); East Anglia; Huddersfield; Hull; Leeds (further audition required); Liverpool Hope; Liverpool John Moores; Loughborough; Manchester (Coll); Newman; Roehampton; Royal Welsh (CMusDr); St Mary's; Sunderland; Surrey (GSA); Winchester; York St John; **No** Glasgow.

GRADUATE DESTINATIONS AND EMPLOYMENT (2016/17 HESA)
Graduates surveyed 4,340 **Employed** 1,955 **In voluntary employment** 135 **In further study** 755 **Assumed unemployed** 230

Career note Some graduates develop careers in performance, writing, directing and producing as well as wider roles within the theatre. Others go on to careers such as teaching, media management and retail where their creativity and communication skills are valued.

OTHER DEGREE SUBJECTS FOR CONSIDERATION
Art and Design (Costume Design, Stage Design); Arts Management; Dance; Education (Primary); English; Performance Studies.

ECONOMICS

(see also **Business and Management Courses, Mathematics, Philosophy, Politics and Economics (PPE), Statistics**)

Economics is about how society makes good use of the limited resources available. Degree courses cover all aspects of finance, taxation and monetary union between countries, aiming to equip the student to analyse economic problems in a systematic way and thus acquire an understanding of how economic systems work. Economics involves mathematics and statistics, and applicants without economics at AS or A-level should be prepared for this, although for BA courses mathematics is not required at A-level. All courses are quite flexible with specialisms coming later in the course, leading to a range of career choices. Many joint courses are often offered with combinations such as Politics, Management and Finance. The course at Cambridge in Land Economy focuses on the legal and economic aspects relative to the natural environment, covering business regulations and the financial aspects of real estate and development; the course is accredited by the Royal Institution of Chartered Surveyors and has a high success rate of graduate employment. (See also the **Surveying and Real Estate Management** table.)

Useful websites www.iea.org.uk; www.res.org.uk; www.economist.com; www.neweconomics.org; see also **Finance**.

NB The points totals shown to the left of the institutions are for ease of reference only. It must not be assumed that Tariff points are always used by institutions or that they can be substituted for an offer in grades. The level of an offer is not necessarily indicative of the quality of a course.

COURSE OFFERS INFORMATION
Subject requirements/preferences GCSE English, mathematics and occasionally a foreign language required. A*/A/B (8–9/7/5–6) may be stipulated by some universities. **AL** Mathematics, economics or business studies may be required or preferred. Business studies may be preferred if economics is

not offered. Applicants should note that many courses will accept students without economics (check prospectuses and websites).

Your target offers and examples of degree courses

160 pts **Cambridge** – A*A*A incl maths +interview +ECAA (Econ) (IB 42–40 pts HL 776 incl maths)

152 pts **Bath** – A*AA incl maths (Econ) (IB 36 pts HL 766 incl maths); A*AA–AAA +aEPQ incl maths (Econ Pol) (IB 36 pts HL 766 incl maths)

Bristol – A*AA incl maths (Econ courses) (IB 38 pts HL 18 pts)

Cambridge – A*AA +interview +TSA (Lnd Econ) (IB 42–40 pts HL 776)

Durham – A*AA incl maths (Econ Mgt) (IB 38 pts); (Econ; Econ Pol) (IB 38 pts HL 666)

London (UCL) – A*AA incl geog+maths (Econ Geog) (IB 39 pts HL 19 pts incl 7 maths 6 geog); A*AA incl maths (Econ; Econ Stats; Stats Econ Fin) (IB 39 pts HL 19 pts incl 7 maths)

London LSE – A*AA incl maths (Ecomet Mathem Econ; Econ; Econ Econ Hist; Maths Econ) (IB 38 pts HL 766 incl 7 maths)

Nottingham – A*AA (Econ Fr; Econ Ger; Econ Hisp St) (IB 38-3836 pts); A*AA incl maths (Econ courses) (IB 38 pts)

Oxford – A*AA incl maths +interview +TSA (Econ Mgt) (IB 39 pts HL 766 incl maths)

Warwick – A*AA (Econ Pol Int St) (IB 38 pts); A*AA incl maths (Econ; Econ Ind Org) (IB 38 pts HL 6 maths)

144 pts **Birmingham** – AAA incl maths (Mathem Econ Stats) (IB 32 pts HL 666)

Bristol – AAA incl maths (Econ Acc; Phil Econ) (IB 36 pts HL 18 pts)

Exeter – A*AA–AAA (Bus Econ; Bus Econ (Euro St); Econ; Econ Ecomet; Econ Pol (Euro St)) (IB 38–36 pts HL 766–666)

Leeds – AAA (Bus Econ; Econ; Econ Fin) (IB 35 pts HL 17 pts)

London (QM) – AAA incl maths (Econ; Econ Comb Hons; Econ Fin Mgt) (IB 36 pts HL 666)

London (UCL) – AAA incl maths (Econ Bus E Euro St) (IB 38 pts HL 18 pts incl 6 maths)

London LSE – AAA incl maths (Pol Econ) (IB 38 pts HL 766 incl maths)

Oxford – AAA +interview +HAT +TSA (Hist Econ) (IB 38 pts HL 666)

Sheffield – AAA incl maths (Econ Fin) (IB 36 pts HL 5 maths)

Southampton – AAA–AAB +aEPQ incl maths (Maths OR Stats Econ (MORSE)) (IB 36 pts HL 18 pts incl 6 maths)

St Andrews – AAA incl sci/maths (Econ courses) (IB 38 pts HL 666)

York – AAA incl hist/class civ+maths (Hist Econ) (IB 36 pts HL 666 incl hist+maths); AAA incl maths (Econ Maths) (IB 36 pts HL 6 maths)

136 pts **Birmingham** – AAA–AAB (Econ; Econ Lang) (IB 32 pts HL 666–665); AAB (Plcy Pol Econ; Pol Econ) (IB 32 pts HL 665); AAB 136 pts (Econ Pol Sci) (IB 32 pts HL 665)

City – AAB (Econ) (IB 30 pts); AAB incl maths 136 pts (Fin Econ) (IB 30 pts HL 5 maths)

Edinburgh – AAA–AAB incl maths (Econ Stats) (IB 43–34 pts HL 766–655 incl 6 maths)

Exeter – AAA–AAB incl maths (Maths Econ) (IB 36–34 pts HL 666–665 incl 6 maths)

Glasgow – AAB incl arts/hum (Econ Comb Hons) (IB 38 pts HL 666)

Lancaster – AAB incl maths/fmaths (Econ; Econ (St Abrd); Econ (Yr Ind); Econ Comb Hons; Fin Econ) (IB 35 pts HL 16 pts incl 6 maths)

Liverpool – AAB incl maths (Econ) (IB 36 pts HL 6 maths)

London (SOAS) – AAA–AAB (Econ) (IB 37 pts HL 666)

London LSE – AAB (Env Plcy Econ) (IB 37 pts HL 666); AAB incl maths (Int Soc Pblc Plcy Econ) (IB 37 pts HL 666 incl maths)

Loughborough – AAB (Bus Econ Fin; Econ; Geog Econ) (IB 35 pts HL 665)

Manchester – AAB (Econ Pol; Econ Sociol) (IB 35 pts HL 665); AAB incl maths (Econ) (IB 35 pts HL 665 incl 6 maths)

NCH London – AAB (Econ courses) (IB 35 pts HL 665)

Newcastle – AAB (Econ; Econ Bus Mgt; Econ Fin) (IB 35 pts)

Nottingham – AAB (Ind Econ; Ind Econ Ins) (IB 34 pts)

Sheffield – AAB incl maths (Econ Comb Hons) (IB 34 pts HL 5 maths)

Southampton – AAA–AAB incl maths/fmaths (Econ Act Sci) (IB 36 pts HL 18 pts incl 6 maths); AAB/ABB +aEPQ (Econ Mgt Sci) (IB 34 pts HL 17 pts); AAB incl maths (Econ Fin)

(IB 34 pts HL 17 pts incl 5 maths); AAB–ABB+aEPQ incl maths (Econ) (IB 34 pts HL 17 pts incl 5 maths); AAB–ABB +aEPQ incl maths/phys (Acc Econ) (IB 34 pts HL 17 pts)

Surrey – AAB (Bus Econ; Econ; Econ Fin) (IB 34 pts)

York – AAB incl maths (Econ; Econ Ecomet Fin; Econ Fin) (IB 35 pts HL 6 maths)

128 pts **Cardiff** – AAB–ABB (Bus Econ) (IB 34–32 pts HL 665–655); AAB–ABB incl Fr/Ger/Span (Bus Econ Euro Lang (Fr/Ger/Span)) (IB 34–32 pts incl 6 Fr/Ger/Span); AAB–ABB incl maths (Econ) (IB 34–32 pts HL 665–655 incl 6 maths)

City – AAB–ABB 128–136 pts (Econ Acc) (IB 30 pts)

East Anglia – ABB (Bus Econ; Bus Fin Econ; Econ; Econ Acc) (IB 32 pts)

Edinburgh – AAA–ABB (Econ Fin; Econ courses) (IB 43–34 pts HL 776–655)

Leicester – ABB (Econ Courses) (IB 30 pts)

Liverpool – ABB (Bus Econ) (IB 33 pts)

London (RH) – AAB–ABB (Econ Mgt; Econ Pol Int Rel) (IB 32 pts HL 655); AAB–ABB incl maths (Econ) (IB 32 pts HL 655); (Econ Maths) (IB 32 pts HL 655 incl 6 maths)

Loughborough – ABB (Econ Pol) (IB 34 pts HL 655)

Newcastle – AAA–ABB (Pol Econ) (IB 34–32 pts)

Nottingham Trent – ABB 128 pts (Econ; Econ Bus; Econ Int Fin Bank)

Queen's Belfast – ABB (Econ courses) (IB 33 pts HL 665)

Reading – ABB (Bus Econ; Econ) (IB 32 pts)

Southampton – AAB–ABB (Econ Phil) (IB 34–32 pts HL 17–16 pts); ABB incl maths/phys (Pol Econ) (IB 32 pts HL 16 pts)

Sussex – AAB–ABB (Econ; Econ Int Dev; Econ Int Rel; Econ Mgt St; Econ Pol) (IB 34–32 pts)

120 pts **Aberdeen** – BBB (Econ) (IB 32 pts HL 555)

Aston – ABB–BBB (Econ Mgt) (IB 32 pts HL 665–655)

Brunel – BBB (Econ Bus Fin) (IB 30 pts); BBB incl maths (Econ) (IB 30 pts HL 5 maths)

Coventry – BBB (Bus Econ; Econ courses) (IB 30 pts)

Essex – BBB (Bus Econ; Econ; Econ Modn Lang; Econ Pol; Fin Econ; Int Econ; Mgt Econ; Psy Econ) (IB 30 pts)

Greenwich – BBB 120 pts (Econ)

Heriot-Watt – BBB (Econ) (IB 29 pts)

Huddersfield – BBB 120 pts (Econ; Econ courses)

Hull – 120 pts (Bus Econ; Econ) (IB 30 pts)

Kent – BBB (Econ) (IB 34 pts HL 15 pts)

London (Gold) – BBB (Econ) (IB 33 pts HL 655)

London (RH) – AAB–BBB (Fin Bus Econ) (IB 32 pts HL 555)

Reading – BBB (Fd Mark Bus Econ) (IB 30 pts)

Stirling – BBB (Econ) (IB 32 pts)

Strathclyde – ABB–BBB (Maths Stats Econ) (IB 32 pts HL 6 maths); (Econ; Econ Psy; Soc Plcy Econ) (IB 36 pts)

Swansea – ABB–BBB (Econ courses) (IB 33–32 pts)

Westminster – AAB–BBB 120–136 pts (Bus Econ) (IB 27 pts HL 4 Engl)

112 pts **Bangor** – 112 pts (Acc Econ; Bus Econ); 112–120 pts (Econ Comb Hons)

Birmingham City – BBC 112 pts (Fin Econ) (HL 14 pts)

Bradford – BBC 112 pts (Econ; Fin Econ)

Buckingham – BBB–BBC (Econ) (IB 33–32 pts)

Cardiff Met – BBC 112 pts (Econ; Int Econ Fin) (IB 24 pts HL 12 pts)

De Montfort – 112 pts (Econ Fin) (IB 26 pts)

East London – BBC 112 pts (Econ) (IB 25 pts HL 15 pts)

Hertfordshire – BBC 112 pts (Bus Econ; Econ)

Kingston – BBC 112 pts (Bus Econ; Econ; Fin Econ) (IB 25 pts)

Leeds Beckett – 112 pts (Bus Econ) (IB 25-26 pts)

London (Birk) – ABB–BBC 112–128 pts (Econ Soc Pol)

Manchester Met – BBB–BBC 112–120 pts (Econ) (IB 26 pts)

Portsmouth – 112–120 pts (Econ) (IB 29 pts HL 655/754)

Salford – BBC 112 pts (Bus Econ) (IB 30 pts)

UWE Bristol – C maths 112 pts (Econ) (HL 5 maths)

Worcester – 112 pts (Bus Econ Fin)

104 pts   **Bournemouth** – 104–120 pts (Econ) (IB 31–28 pts)

Central Lancashire – 104–112 pts (Econ)

Chester – BBC–BCC 104–112 pts (Econ (Comb Hons)) (IB 26 pts)

Dundee – BBB–BCC incl sci/maths (Econ) (IB 30 pts HL 555 incl sci/maths)

Hertfordshire – BCC 104 pts (Acc Econ)

Manchester Met – BBC–BCC 104–112 pts (Econ Comb Hons) (IB 26 pts)

Northampton – BCC 104–112 pts (Econ courses) (IB 25 pts)

Oxford Brookes – BBC 104 pts (Acc Econ) (IB 29 pts)

Sheffield Hallam – BCC 104 pts (Bus Econ)

Winchester – 104–120 pts (Econ; Econ Fin)

96 pts   **Aberystwyth** – BBB–CCC 96–120 pts (Bus Econ; Econ) (IB 30–26 pts)

Anglia Ruskin – (Bus Econ)

Keele – BBC–CCC (Bus Mgt Econ; Econ Comb Hons) (IB 30–26 pts)

London Met – CCC (Econ) (IB 28 pts HL 15 pts); CCC 96 pts (Bus Econ) (IB 28 pts HL 15 pts)

Plymouth – 96–112 pts (Econ courses) (IB 28–26 pts)

Open University – contact 0300 303 0073 or www.open.ac.uk/contact/new (Comb Soc Sci (Econ/Geog/Psy/Sociol); Econ Mathem Sci)

Alternative offers

See **Chapter 6** and **Appendix 1** for grades/UCAS Tariff points information for other examinations.

EXAMPLES OF COLLEGES OFFERING COURSES IN THIS SUBJECT FIELD

Plymouth City (Coll).

CHOOSING YOUR COURSE (SEE ALSO CH.1)

Universities and colleges teaching quality See www.qaa.ac.uk; https://unistats.ac.uk.

Top research universities and colleges (REF 2014) (Economics and Econometrics) London (UCL); Edinburgh; Cambridge; Warwick; Essex; London LSE; Nottingham; Oxford; Bristol; East Anglia.

Examples of sandwich degree courses Aston; Bangor; Bath; Birmingham City; Bournemouth; Brighton; Brunel; Coventry; De Montfort; Essex; Greenwich; Hertfordshire; Leeds Beckett; Liverpool; London (QM); Loughborough; Manchester Met; Newcastle; Nottingham Trent; Plymouth; Portsmouth; Queen's Belfast; Reading; Salford; Sheffield Hallam; Surrey; UWE Bristol; Westminster.

ADMISSIONS INFORMATION

Number of applicants per place (approx) Anglia Ruskin 10; Aston 8; Bangor 5; Bath 8; Birmingham 3; Birmingham City 16; Bradford 5; Bristol 8; Buckingham 7; Cambridge 6; Cardiff 8; Central Lancashire 5; City 8, (Econ Acc) 6; Dundee 5; Durham 7; East Anglia 4; Essex 6; Exeter 12; Greenwich 8; Heriot-Watt 6; Hull 5; Kingston 9; Lancaster 5; Leeds 16; Leicester 8; Liverpool 7; London (RH) 6; London (UCL) 11; London LSE (Econ) 12, (Ecomet Mathem Econ) 12; Manchester 8; Manchester Met 5; Newcastle 7; Northampton 8; Nottingham (Econ) 9; Nottingham Trent 2; Oxford 13; Plymouth 52; Queen's Belfast 10; Salford 6; Sheffield 6; Southampton 6; Stirling 8; Swansea 7; Warwick 16; York 4.

Advice to applicants and planning the UCAS personal statement Visits, work experience and work shadowing in banks, insurance companies, accountants' offices, etc should be described. Keep up-to-date with economic issues by reading *The Economist* and the *Financial Times* and find other sources of information. Describe any particular aspects of economics which interest you – and why. Make it clear on the statement that you know what economics is and why you want to study it. Give evidence of your interest in economics and your reasons for choosing the course and provide information about your sport/extracurricular activities and positions of responsibility.

Misconceptions about this course Bradford That the Economics course is very mathematical and that students will not get a good job, eg management. **London (UCL)** Some think the Economics course is a Business course. **Oxford** Students think that Economics and Management is a business studies course but this is not the case. The programme is taught as an academic subject and students learn through traditional academic means of problem sets, reading, discussion and essay-writing.

Selection interviews Yes Buckingham, Cambridge, Oxford ((Econ Mgt) 25% (success rate 8%)); **Some** Southampton; **No** Aberystwyth, Anglia Ruskin, Bangor, Birmingham, Bristol, Coventry, Dundee, East Anglia, East London, Edinburgh, Essex, Keele, Kent, Leeds, London (RH), London (UCL), London LSE, London Met, Loughborough, Manchester Met, Nottingham, Nottingham Trent, Reading, Surrey, Swansea, UWE Bristol.

Interview advice and questions If you have studied economics at A-level or in other examinations, expect to be questioned on aspects of the subject. Economics is constantly in the news, so keep abreast of developments and be prepared to be asked questions such as: What is happening to sterling at present? What is happening to the dollar? How relevant is economics today? What are your views on the government's economic policy? Do you think that the family is declining as an institution? Discuss Keynesian economics. Is the power of the Prime Minister increasing? What is a recession? How would you get the world out of recession? What causes a recession? See also **Chapter 5**. **Cambridge** What is the point of using NHS money to keep old people alive? **Oxford** (Econ Mgt) 'I was asked questions on a newspaper article I had been given to read 45 minutes beforehand, followed by a few maths problems and an economics question.' Explain why teachers might be changing jobs to become plumbers. What is the difference between the buying and selling of slaves and the buying and selling of football players? Should a Wal-Mart store be opened in the middle of Oxford?

Reasons for rejection (non-academic) Lack of knowledge about the course offered and the subject matter; lack of care in preparing personal statement; poor written English; the revelation on the statement that they want a course different from that for which they have applied! **Aberystwyth** Would have trouble fitting into the unique environment at Aberystwyth.

AFTER-RESULTS ADVICE
Offers to applicants repeating A-levels Higher Birmingham City; City; Leeds; Newcastle; Queen's Belfast; St Andrews; Warwick; York; **Possibly higher** Bradford; Durham; Lancaster; **Same** Aberystwyth; Anglia Ruskin; Bangor; Bath; Brunel; Buckingham; Cambridge; Cardiff; Coventry; Dundee; East Anglia; East London; Essex; Heriot-Watt; Hull; Kingston; Liverpool; London (RH); London Met; Loughborough; Nottingham; Nottingham Trent; Salford; Sheffield; Swansea.

GRADUATE DESTINATIONS AND EMPLOYMENT (2016/17 HESA)
Graduates surveyed 4,805 **Employed** 2,880 **In voluntary employment** 135 **In further study** 990 **Assumed unemployed** 300

Career note Most graduates work within areas of business and finance, and in a range of jobs including management and administration posts across both public and private sectors.

OTHER DEGREE SUBJECTS FOR CONSIDERATION
Accountancy; Actuarial Studies; Administration; Banking; Business Studies; Development Studies; Estate Management; Financial Services; Government; Politics; Management Sciences/Studies; Property Development; Quantity Surveying; Social Sciences; Sociology; Statistics.

EDUCATION STUDIES

(see also **Physical Education, Social Sciences/Studies, Teacher Training**)

There are four types of degree courses in Education. Firstly, there are those universities providing an academic study of the subject at Single Honours level, covering the study of childhood and aspects of education such as psychology, sociology, philosophy and history. Secondly, there are institutions offering degrees in Education with a professional practice qualification to teach, as in the degree course in Early Years Education at Edge Hill University. Thirdly, as in all degree subjects, there are many Joint Honours and combined degrees in which Education is taken with another academic subject. Finally, there are specific degree courses in teacher training and professional practice leading directly to the classroom (see the **Teacher Training** table).

Useful websites www.gtcs.org.uk; www.ucas.com/teaching-in-the-uk; www.gov.uk/government/organisations/department-for-education; www.set.et-foundation.co.uk; www.et-foundation.co.uk

NB The points totals shown to the left of the institutions are for ease of reference only. It must not be assumed that Tariff points are always used by institutions or that they can be substituted for an offer in grades. The level of an offer is not necessarily indicative of the quality of a course.

COURSE OFFERS INFORMATION

Subject requirements/preferences GCSE English and mathematics usually required. **AL** No subjects specified.

Plymouth Maths, English and Science at **GCSE** Grade C/4 or above. Plus interview, DBS checks (including overseas checks) and Fit2teach.

Your target offers and examples of degree courses

152 pts Cambridge – A*AA +interview +EAA (Educ Engl Dr Arts; Educ Plcy Int Dev; Educ Psy Lrng) (IB 42–40 pts HL 776)

136 pts Durham – AAB (Educ St (Engl St/Geog/Hist/Phil/Psy/Sociol/Theol Relgn)) (IB 36 pts HL 665)
Glasgow – AAB incl tech/sci/maths +interview (Technol Educ) (IB 36 pts HL 665 incl Engl+sci/maths)

128 pts Bath – ABB/BBB +aEPQ (Educ Psy) (IB 35 pts HL 655)
Birmingham – ABB (Educ) (IB 32 pts HL 655)
Sheffield – ABB (Educ Cult Chld) (IB 33 pts)
Southampton – ABB/BBB +aEPQ (Educ) (IB 32 pts HL 16 pts)
York – ABB (Sociol Educ) (IB 34 pts)

120 pts Cardiff – BBB (Educ) (HL 17 pts); (Sociol Educ) (IB 32 pts HL 17–16 pts)
De Montfort – 120 pts (Educ St; Educ St Mand; Educ St Psy) (IB 28 pts)
East Anglia – BBB (Educ) (IB 31 pts)
Edge Hill – BBB 120 pts +interview (Ely Yrs Educ)
Kent – BBB (Autsm St) (IB 34 pts HL 15 pts)
Liverpool John Moores – BBB 120 pts+interview (P Educ)
Newcastle – BBB (Educ) (IB 32 pts HL 555)
Northumbria – 120 pts +interview (P Educ)
Reading – BBB (Educ St) (IB 30 pts)
Stirling – BBB (Prof Educ P courses) (IB 32 pts HL 5 Engl)
York – BBB (Educ; Engl Educ) (IB 31 pts)

112 pts Canterbury Christ Church – 112 pts (Arts Educ; Ely Chld St)
Cardiff – BBB–BBC incl B Welsh (Educ Welsh) (HL 665)
Cardiff Met – BBC 112 pts +interview (P Educ QTS) (IB 24 pts)
Derby – BBC 112 pts (Educ St; Ely Chld St)
Dundee – BBC +interview (Educ) (IB 30 pts)
East London – BBC 112 pts (Educ St; Spec Educ) (IB 25 pts HL 15 pts); BBC 112 pts incl soc sci/hum (Ely Chld St) (IB 25 pts HL 15 pts)
Essex – BBC (Chld St) (IB 30 pts)
Gloucestershire – BBC 112 pts (Physl Educ)
Glyndŵr – BBC 112 pts (Educ (ALN/SEN))
Huddersfield – BBC 112 pts (Educ)
Keele – BBC incl B phys/maths (Educ Phys) (IB 30 pts HL 5 phys/maths)
Liverpool Hope – BBC 112 pts (Educ; SEN courses) (IB 26 pts)
London (Gold) – BBC (Educ Cult Soty) (IB 31 pts HL 655)
London Met – BBC 112 pts (Educ)
Manchester Met – BBC +interview (P Educ) (IB 25 pts)
Queen Margaret – BBC 112 pts (Educ St P) (IB 30 pts HL 5 Engl)

Roehampton – 112 pts (Educ St)
Suffolk – BBC 112 pts (Ely Chld St)
West London – BBC 112 pts (Ely Yrs Educ)

104 pts Cardiff Met – 104 pts (Educ Psy SEN) (IB 24 pts)
Central Lancashire – 104–112 pts (Educ courses)
Chester – BBC–BCC 104–112 pts (Educ St courses) (IB 26 pts)
Chichester – BBC–BCC 104–112 pts (Educ) (IB 28 pts)
Edge Hill – BBC–BCC 104–112 pts (Educ)
Hull – 104 pts (Educ St courses) (IB 26 pts)
Leeds Beckett – 104 pts (Chld St) (IB 24 pts)
Leeds Trinity – 104 pts (Educ Relig St; Educ St)
Liverpool John Moores – BCC 104 pts (Educ SEN; Educ St Ely Yrs)
Manchester Met – BBC–BCC 104–112 pts (Educ St) (IB 25 pts)
Northampton – BCC (Educ St courses) (IB 24 pts)
Nottingham Trent – BCC 104 pts (Chld (Psy); Chld Lrng Dev; Educ; Ely Yrs; Yth St)
Oxford Brookes – BCC (Educ St) (IB 29 pts)
Sheffield Hallam – BCC 104 pts (Educ Psy Cnslg; Educ St)

96 pts Aberystwyth – BBB–CCC 96–120 pts (Chld St; Educ Comb Hons) (IB 30–26 pts)
Anglia Ruskin – 96 pts (P Educ St) (IB 24 pts)
Bangor – 96 pts (Chld Yth St)
Bath Spa – CCC (Educ St) (IB 26 pts)
Bedfordshire – BBB–CCC 96–120 pts (Educ; Ely Chld Educ)
Birmingham (UC) – 96 pts (Ely Chld St)
Bishop Grosseteste – 96–112 pts (Educ St courses)
Brighton – BBC–CCC 96–112 pts (Educ) (IB 26 pts)
Brunel – CCC (Educ) (IB 27 pts)
Cardiff Met – BB 96–112 pts (Spo Physl Educ Hlth Dance) (IB 25 pts HL 13 pts)
Chester – BCC–CCC 96–104 pts (P Educ St) (IB 26 pts)
Chichester – BBC–CCC 96–112 pts+interview (Out Advntr Educ) (IB 28 pts)
Gloucestershire – CCC 96 pts (Ely Chld St)
Hertfordshire – CCC 96 pts (Educ St); (Ely Chld Educ) (HL 44)
Keele – CCC (Educ) (IB 28–26 pts)
Marjon – CCC (Out Advntr Educ); CCC 96 pts (Educ St)
Middlesex – 96 pts (Educ St)
Newman – 96 pts (Ely Chld Educ Cr; St P Educ)
Northampton – CCC (Ely Chld St) (IB 24 pts)
Plymouth – 96–112 pts (Ely Chld St) (IB 26-27 pts)
Portsmouth – 96–112 pts (Ely Chld St) (IB 25-26 pts)
St Mary's – 96–104 pts (Educ St)
Staffordshire – CCC 96 pts+interview (Ely Chld St)
Sunderland – CCC 96 pts (Educ St)
Trinity Saint David – 96 pts (Educ St; P Educ QTS)
York St John – 96–112 pts (Educ St)

88 pts Canterbury Christ Church – 88–112 pts (Educ St)
Marjon – CCD 88 pts (SEN Disab St)
Oldham (Univ Campus) – 88–96 pts +interview (Ely Yrs)
Queen Margaret – CCD (Educ St) (IB 26 pts)
Trinity Saint David – 88–104 pts (Ely Yrs Educ Cr)
Worcester – 88 pts (Educ St courses)

80 pts Bradford College UC – CDD 80 pts (Educ St)
Cardiff Met – 80 pts incl CC +interview (Yth Commun Wk courses) (IB 24 pts)
South Wales – BCC–CDD 80–104 pts (Ely Yrs Educ Prac) (IB 29 pts)

72 pts Teesside – 72–96 pts (Chld Yth St; Ely Chld St)

64 pts Colchester (UC) – 64 pts +interview (Ely Yrs)
South Essex (Coll) – 64 pts (Ely Yrs Educ)

Alternative offers
See **Chapter 6** and **Appendix 1** for grades/UCAS Tariff points information for other examinations.

DEGREE APPRENTICESHIPS
Chichester (Wk Chld).

EXAMPLES OF COLLEGES OFFERING COURSES IN THIS SUBJECT FIELD
Barnet and Southgate (Coll); Barnfield (Coll); Barnsley (Coll); Blackburn (Coll); Blackpool and Fylde (Coll); Bournville (Coll); Bridgwater and Taunton (Coll); Bristol City (Coll); Buckinghamshire (Coll Group); Calderdale (Coll); Chesterfield (Coll); Cornwall (Coll); Craven (Coll); Derby (Coll); Duchy Coll UC; East Riding (Coll); Exeter (Coll); Farnborough (CT); Grŵp Llandrillo Menai; Guildford (Coll); Harrogate (Coll); Havering (Coll); Hopwood Hall (Coll); Hull (Coll); Kensington and Chelsea (Coll); Kirklees (Coll); Lakes (Coll); Lincoln (Coll); Liverpool City (Coll); Macclesfield (Coll); Nescot; Newcastle (Coll); Newham (CFE); Norland (Coll); North Lindsey (Coll); Norwich City (Coll); Nottingham (Coll); Peter Symonds (Coll); Peterborough (Coll); Petroc; RAc Dance; Sheffield (Coll); South Cheshire (Coll); South City Birmingham (Coll); South Devon (Coll); Stockport (Coll); Sunderland (Coll); TEC Partnership; Truro and Penwith (Coll); Wakefield (Coll); Warrington and Vale Royal (Coll); Warwickshire (Coll); West Anglia (Coll); Westminster City (Coll); Wirral Met (Coll); Yeovil (Coll).

CHOOSING YOUR COURSE (SEE ALSO CH.1)
Universities and colleges teaching quality See www.qaa.ac.uk; https://unistats.ac.uk.

Top research universities and colleges (REF 2014) (Education) Sheffield; York; Stirling; Bristol; Oxford; London (King's); Queen's Belfast; Loughborough; Exeter; Nottingham; Cardiff; Durham.

ADMISSIONS INFORMATION
Number of applicants per place (approx) Anglia Ruskin 1; Bangor 5; Bath 5; Bath Spa 5; Birmingham 8; Bishop Grosseteste 12; Cambridge 2; Cardiff (Educ) 8; Cardiff Met 3; Central Lancashire 5; Derby 4; Dundee 13; Durham 3; Edge Hill 17; Gloucestershire 20; Hull 5; Hull (Coll) 4; Liverpool John Moores 3; London (Gold) 5; Manchester Met 23; Marjon 5; Nottingham Trent 11; Oxford Brookes 6; Plymouth 14; Roehampton 3; Sheffield Hallam 7; Southampton 8; St Mary's 19; Trinity Saint David 10; Worcester 21; York 3.

Advice to applicants and planning the UCAS personal statement Liverpool John Moores (P Educ) Deciding to pursue a career in teaching should be based on a real commitment and passion and this should be demonstrated through your personal statement. You should have at least two weeks' recent work experience in a school or related setting before applying. In addition, we would like to see some evidence of work in the community (not as part of your course). This may be helping in sports clubs, Brownies, youth clubs or volunteering. This experience may be linked to a hobby or interest you have. Personal statements should have a clear structure with use of paragraphs and good use of grammar.

Misconceptions about this course Bath Spa (Educ St) Applicants should note that this is not a teacher training course – it leads on to PGCE teacher training (this applies to other Education Studies courses).

Selection interviews Yes Bangor, Brunel, Cambridge, Chichester, Glasgow, Stockport (Coll); **Some** Cardiff, Worcester; **No** Anglia Ruskin, Bishop Grosseteste, Chester, Derby, East Anglia, Glyndŵr, Manchester Met, Marjon, Newman, Nottingham Trent, Oxford Brookes, Plymouth, Reading, Roehampton, Sheffield Hallam, Stirling, York St John.

Interview advice and questions
Cambridge The stage is a platform for opinions or just entertainment? **Derby** Applicants are asked about an aspect of education. **Worcester** Interviewees are asked to write a statement concerning their impressions of the interview.

Reasons for rejection (non-academic) Unable to meet the requirements of written standard English. Ungrammatical personal statements.

AFTER-RESULTS ADVICE
Offers to applicants repeating A-levels Same Anglia Ruskin; Bangor; Bishop Grosseteste; Brighton; Brunel; Cambridge; Canterbury Christ Church; Cardiff; Chester; Chichester; De Montfort; Derby; Dundee; Durham; East Anglia; Liverpool Hope; Liverpool John Moores; London (Gold); Manchester Met; Marjon; Newman; Northumbria; Nottingham Trent; Oxford Brookes; Roehampton; St Mary's; Sunderland; Worcester; York; York St John.

GRADUATE DESTINATIONS AND EMPLOYMENT (2016/17 HESA)
Academic Studies in Education graduates surveyed 9,760 **Employed** 3,760 **In voluntary employment** 145 **In further study** 3,560 **Assumed unemployed** 280

Career note Education Studies degrees prepare graduates for careers in educational administration although many will move into more general areas of business or into aspects of work with Social Services. Prospects are generally good. Courses in Childhood Studies could lead to work in health or childcare-related posts, in social work or administration.

OTHER DEGREE SUBJECTS FOR CONSIDERATION
Psychology; Social Policy; Social Sciences; Social Work.

ENGINEERING/ENGINEERING SCIENCES

(including **General Engineering, Integrated Engineering, Engineering Design and Product Design**; see also **Engineering (Manufacturing and Production), Transport Management and Planning**)

Mathematics and physics provide the basis of all Engineering courses, although several universities and colleges now provide one-year Foundation courses for applicants without science A-levels. Many of the Engineering courses listed below enable students to delay the decision of their final engineering specialism. Engineering courses at most universities offer a range of specialisms in which, after a common first or second year, the choice of specialism is made. The flexibility of these courses is considerable, for example, it is sometimes possible to transfer from the BEng degree to the MEng degree at the end of the first or second year. At some universities, eg Durham, the first two years of the course cover a broad engineering education for all students enabling them to decide on their specialism in Year 3 from Civil, Electronic or Mechanical Engineering. A similar scheme operates at Lancaster University, while at Bath, the Mechanical Engineering department offers a choice of five courses at the end of Year 2. Many institutions offer sandwich courses and firms also offer valuable sponsorships.

Engineering Council UK (ECUK) Statement
Recent developments in the engineering profession and the regulations that govern registration as a professional engineer (UK-SPEC) mean that MEng and bachelor's degrees are the typical academic routes to becoming registered.

Chartered Engineers (CEng) develop solutions to engineering problems, using new or existing technologies, through innovation, creativity and change. They might develop and apply new technologies, promote advanced designs and design methods, introduce new and more efficient production techniques, marketing and construction concepts, and pioneer new engineering services and management methods.

Incorporated Engineers (IEng) act as exponents of today's technology through creativity and innovation. They maintain and manage applications of current and developing technology, and may be involved in engineering design, development, manufacture, construction and operation. Both Chartered and Incorporated Engineers are variously engaged in technical and commercial leadership and possess effective interpersonal skills.

Most courses offer BEng and MEng degrees. MEng confers the minimum requirements to take the Initial Professional Development (IPD) training with an employer in order to obtain Chartered Engineer status, while the BEng does not. However, students taking a BEng may be able to switch onto an MEng course, as the first three years of an MEng are broadly similar to a BEng. Another route for BEng students is to subsequently undertake an MSc, which also allows access to IPD and Chartered Engineer status.

You should confirm with universities whether their courses are accredited for CEng or IEng by relevant professional engineering institutions. To become a Chartered or Incorporated Engineer, you will have to demonstrate competence and commitment appropriate to the registration category. On top of your academic knowledge, you will also need to demonstrate your professional development and experience. Most of this will come after you graduate but placements in industry during your degree course are also available. Both Chartered and Incorporated Engineers usually progress to become team leaders or to take other key management roles. For full information check www.engc.org. uk/ukspec.

Useful websites www.scicentral.com; www.engc.org.uk; https://epsrc.ukri.org; www.etrust.org.uk

NB The points totals shown to the left of the institutions are for ease of reference only. It must not be assumed that Tariff points are always used by institutions or that they can be substituted for an offer in grades. The level of an offer is not necessarily indicative of the quality of a course.

COURSE OFFERS INFORMATION

Subject requirements/preferences GCSE English, mathematics and a science subject required. **AL** Mathematics and/or physics, engineering or another science usually required. Design technology may be acceptable or in some cases required. Offers shown below refer to BEng or BSc courses unless otherwise stated; BSc only appears as an abbreviation if the course is offered at the same institution as a BEng with different requirements. **Cambridge** (Peterhouse, Trinity) STEP may be used as part of conditional offer. **Oxford AL** Mathematics and mechanics modules are recommended; further mathematics is helpful.

Your target offers and examples of degree courses

160 pts **Cambridge** – A*A*A incl maths+phys +interview +ENGAA (Eng) (IB 42–40 pts HL 776 incl maths+phys)

Oxford – A*A*A incl maths+phys +interview +PAT (Eng Sci) (IB 40 pts HL 776 incl 7 maths+phys)

152 pts **Bath** – A*AA–AAA +aEPQ incl maths+phys (Mech Eng (MEng)) (IB 36 pts HL 766 incl maths+phys)

Bristol – A*AA incl maths+sci+interview (Eng Des (MEng) (Yr Ind)) (IB 38 pts HL 18 pts incl 76 maths+sci)

Durham – A*AA incl maths+phys (Gen Eng) (IB 38 pts HL 666 incl maths+phys)

144 pts **Bristol** – AAA incl maths (Eng Maths) (IB 36 pts HL 18 pts incl 6 maths)

Exeter – AAA incl maths+sci (Eng (MEng); Eng Mgt (MEng); Eng Mgt (MEng) (Yr Ind)) (IB 36 pts HL 666 incl maths+sci)

Lancaster – AAA incl maths+physl sci (Eng (MEng) (St Abrd)) (IB 36 pts HL 16 pts incl 6 maths+physl sci)

Liverpool – AAA incl maths+sci (Eng (MEng)) (IB 35 pts HL 5 maths+phys)

London (QM) – AAA incl maths/phys (Des Innov Crea Eng (MEng)) (IB 36 pts HL 665 incl maths/phys/chem/des tech)

Nottingham – A*AA–AAA incl maths+chem/phys (Cheml Eng Env Eng (Yr Ind); Env Eng) (IB 36 pts HL 6 maths+chem/phys)

Southampton – AAA–AAB +aEPQ incl maths+phys/chem/fmaths (Ship Sci (MEng)) (IB 36 pts HL 18 pts incl 6 maths+phys/chem/fmaths)

Warwick – AAA incl maths+phys (Eng; Eng Bus Mgt) (IB 38 pts HL 6 maths+phys)

York – AAA incl maths (Eng) (IB 36 pts HL 6 maths)

136 pts **Dyson** – AAB incl maths+sci/tech/eng (Eng Tech) (IB 34 pts HL 665 incl maths+sci/tech/eng)

Lancaster – AAB incl maths+physl sci (Eng) (IB 35 pts HL 16 pts incl 6 maths+physl sci)

Southampton – AAB–ABB+aEPQ incl maths+phys/chem/fmaths (Ship Sci) (IB 34 pts HL 17 pts incl 6 maths+phys/chem/fmaths)

128 pts **Brunel** – ABB incl art/des/tech+maths/phys +interview +portfolio (Prod Des Eng) (IB 31 pts HL 5 art/des/tech+maths/phys)

Cardiff – AAB–ABB incl maths (Integ Eng courses) (IB 34–32 pts HL 655 incl maths)

City – ABB incl maths 128 pts (Eng (MEng)) (IB 34 pts HL 6 maths)

Coventry – AAB–ABB incl maths (Civ Env Eng (MEng)) (IB 30 pts)

Edinburgh – AAA–ABB incl maths+phys/eng/des tech (Eng) (IB 37–32 pts HL 666–555 incl maths+phys/des tech)

Exeter – AAB–ABB incl maths+sci (Eng; Eng Entre; Eng Mgt) (IB 34–32 pts HL 665–655 incl maths+sci)

Leicester – ABB incl maths+physl sci (Gen Eng) (IB 30 pts HL 5 maths+phys)

Liverpool – ABB incl maths+sci (Aero Eng Plt St; Eng) (IB 33 pts HL 5 maths+phys)

Loughborough – ABB incl maths/phys +interview (Eng Mgt) (IB 34 pts HL 655 incl maths/ phys); ABB incl maths/phys +portfolio (Prod Des Tech) (IB 34 pts HL 655 incl 5 maths/ phys); ABB incl maths/phys/des tech/eng +interview (Prod Des Eng) (IB 34 pts HL 655 incl maths+phys/des tech)

Newcastle – ABB incl maths+phys/chem/fmaths (Mar Tech Off Eng) (IB 32 pts HL 5 maths+phys/chem)

120 pts **Aberdeen** – BBB incl maths+phys/des tech/eng (Eng) (IB 32 pts HL 5 maths+phys)

City – BBB incl maths (Eng) (IB 32 pts HL 5 maths)

London South Bank – BBB incl maths/phys+art/des 120–128 pts +portfolio (Eng Prod Des)

Portsmouth – 120–144 pts (Innov Eng (MEng)) (IB 28–27 pts HL 6 maths)

Queen's Belfast – ABB incl maths+sci/des tech (Prod Des Eng) (IB 33 pts HL 655 incl maths+sci)

Strathclyde – ABB–BBB (Prod Des Eng) (IB 34 pts HL 5 maths/phys)

UWE Bristol – 120 pts incl maths (Archit Env Eng) (HL 5 maths)

Ulster – BBB incl sci/maths/tech (Eng Mgt) (IB 26 pts HL 13 pts incl 5 maths+sci)

112 pts **Aston** – BBC incl maths+physl sci/tech (Des Eng) (IB 29 pts HL 554 incl 5 maths+phys)

Coventry – BBB–BBC incl maths (Civ Env Eng) (IB 30 pts)

Derby – BBC 112 pts +interview +portfolio (Prod Des)

Greenwich – 112 pts incl maths/physl sci (Eng Mgt)

Heriot-Watt – BBC incl maths +sci (Eng) (IB 31 pts HL 5 maths+sci)

Manchester Met – BBC 112 pts +portfolio (Prod Des Tech) (IB 26 pts)

Portsmouth – 112–128 pts incl maths (Innov Eng) (IB 26 pts HL 5 maths)

Staffordshire – BBC 112 pts (Ind Des Prod Trans)

UWE Bristol – 112 pts +portfolio (Prod Des Tech)

104 pts **Bournemouth** – 104–120 pts +interview +portfolio (Des Eng) (IB 31–28 pts)

Central Lancashire – C maths+phys/STEM 104–112 pts incl maths+phys/STEM (Robot Eng) (IB 28 pts HL 5 maths+phys/STEM)

Hertfordshire – BCC 104 pts +interview +portfolio (Prod Ind Des)

96 pts **Cardiff Met** – BBB–CCC 96–120 pts +interview +portfolio (Prod Des) (IB 24 pts)

East London – CCC 96 pts incl art des +interview +portfolio (Prod Des) (IB 25 pts HL 15 pts)

Portsmouth – 96–120 pts +portfolio (Prod Des Innov) (IB 25 pts)

64 pts **Northampton** – DDE (Eng)

UHI – CC incl maths (Ener Eng)

Open University – contact 0300 303 0073 or www.open.ac.uk/contact/new (Eng)

Alternative offers
See **Chapter 6** and **Appendix 1** for grades/UCAS Tariff points information for other examinations.

EXAMPLES OF COLLEGES OFFERING COURSES IN THIS SUBJECT FIELD

Blackburn (Coll); Blackpool and Fylde (Coll); Bristol City (Coll); Bury (Coll); City and Islington (Coll); Cornwall (Coll); Coventry (Coll); East Kent (Coll); East Surrey (Coll); Grŵp Llandrillo Menai; Harlow (Coll); Highbury Portsmouth (Coll); Lancaster and Morecambe (Coll); Loughborough (Coll); Manchester

(Coll); Middlesbrough (Coll); Newcastle (Coll); North Kent (Coll); Northumberland (Coll); Redcar and Cleveland (Coll); Richmond-upon-Thames (Coll); Selby (Coll); South Devon (Coll); South Essex (Coll); St Helens (Coll); Stockport (Coll); Trafford (Coll); Tyne Coast (Coll); Warwickshire (Coll); West Nottinghamshire (Coll); West Suffolk (Coll); Westminster City (Coll); Windsor Forest (Coll).

CHOOSING YOUR COURSE (SEE ALSO CH.1)
Universities and colleges teaching quality See www.qaa.ac.uk; https://unistats.ac.uk.

Top research universities and colleges (REF 2014) (General Engineering) London (King's); Cardiff; Oxford; Sheffield; Cambridge; Imperial London; Liverpool; London (UCL); Glasgow.

Examples of sandwich degree courses Aston; Brunel; Cardiff; Central Lancashire; East London; Leicester; London (QM); London South Bank; Loughborough; Manchester Met; Nottingham; Portsmouth; Ulster.

ADMISSIONS INFORMATION
Number of applicants per place (approx) Aston 8; Bristol (Eng Des) 3, (Eng Maths) 5; Cambridge 7; Cardiff 5; Durham 7; Edinburgh 12; Exeter 6; Heriot-Watt 4; Lancaster 9; Leicester 8; Liverpool 7; Manchester Met 2; Northampton 3; Oxford Brookes 5; Strathclyde 5; Warwick 10.

Admissions tutors' advice Leeds Applicants taking the BTEC Extended Diploma may be required to take an additional Maths A-level paper.

Advice to applicants and planning the UCAS personal statement Details of careers in the various engineering specialisms should be obtained from the relevant engineering institutions (see Appendix 3). This will enable you to describe your interests in various aspects of engineering. Contact engineers to discuss their work with them. Try to visit an engineering firm relevant to your choice of specialism.

Selection interviews Yes Bournemouth, Cambridge, Loughborough, Oxford (47% (success rate 15%)); **Some** Cardiff, Leicester; **No** Bristol, London (QM), Manchester Met, Strathclyde.

Interview advice and questions Since mathematics and physics are important subjects, it is probable that you will be questioned on the applications of these subjects too, for example, the transmission of electricity, nuclear power, aeronautics, mechanics, etc. Past questions have included: Explain the theory of an arch; what is its function? What is the connection between distance and velocity and acceleration and velocity? How does a car ignition work? See also separate **Engineering** tables and **Chapter 5.**

Reasons for rejection (non-academic) Made no contribution whatsoever to the project discussions during the UCAS interview. Forged reference! Poor work ethic. Lack of motivation towards the subject area. Better suited to an alternative Engineering course. Failure to attend interview. Poor interview preparation.

AFTER-RESULTS ADVICE
Offers to applicants repeating A-levels Higher Loughborough; Warwick; **Possibly higher** Edinburgh; Lancaster; Manchester Met; **Same** Brunel; Cambridge; Cardiff; Derby; Durham; Exeter; Heriot-Watt; Liverpool.

GRADUATE DESTINATIONS AND EMPLOYMENT (2016/17 HESA)
Graduates surveyed 1,605 **Employed** 1,050 **In voluntary employment** 20 **In further study** 330 **Assumed unemployed** 75

Career note A high proportion of Engineering graduates go into industry as engineers, technicians, IT specialists or managers, irrespective of their engineering speciality. However, the transferable skills gained during their courses are also valued by employers in other sectors.

OTHER DEGREE SUBJECTS FOR CONSIDERATION
Computer Science; Materials Science; Mathematics; Physics; Technology; all branches of Engineering (see also other **Engineering** tables).

indigo

Combining Trotman's 50-year legacy of careers education with engaging technology for schools

Not every student knows what they want to be "when they grow up". Even those that do have an idea will still need some help and support along the way. Guiding students through can be a real challenge, particularly when you add in a requirement to meet the Gatsby Benchmarks.

Trotman have recently launched Indigo, the gold standard online resource combining the best from HEAP Degree Course Offers with easy to use tools for students and teachers.

✔ Investigate careers, industry sectors and employers with our search, filter and compare functions.

✔ Research and select university courses, powered by our *HEAP* guide, read about and compare subjects, unis and courses.

✔ Make the most of Indigo with our free and growing collection of careers lesson plans and resources.

✔ Stay abreast of career and industry news via our Indigo newsletter – a curated collection of essential news updated weekly and delivered direct to your inbox.

To find out more, download some free resources and learn how Indigo helps you meet the Gatsby Benchmarks visit: https://indigo.careers

ENGINEERING (ACOUSTICS AND SOUND)

(including **Audio Engineering and Sound Technology**; see also **Engineering (electrical And Electronic), Film, Radio, Video And Tv Studies, Media Studies, Music**)

These courses, such as the one at the University of Southampton, focus on sound and vibration engineering, which covers many aspects of society, such as the motor industry, airlines, the environment, underwater communication, ultrasound, as used in medicine, and all communication systems. Courses also involve sound measurement, hearing, environmental health, and legal aspects of sound and vibration. Acoustics and sound are also extensively involved in the music industry, perhaps the most prestigious course being the Music and Sound Recording (Tonmeister) degree at the University of Surrey, which comprises music theory and practice, sound, acoustics, electronics and computer systems. The department has good links with and a high reputation in the music industry.

Most courses offer BEng and MEng degrees. MEng confers the minimum requirements to take the Initial Professional Development (IPD) training with an employer in order to obtain Chartered Engineer status, while the BEng does not. However, students taking a BEng may be able to switch onto an MEng course, as the first three years of an MEng are broadly similar to a BEng. Another route for BEng students is to subsequently undertake an MSc, which also allows access to IPD and Chartered Engineer status.

Engineering Council statement See **Engineering/Engineering Sciences**.

Useful websites www.ioa.org.uk; www.engc.org.uk

NB The points totals shown to the left of the institutions are for ease of reference only. It must not be assumed that Tariff points are always used by institutions or that they can be substituted for an offer in grades. The level of an offer is not necessarily indicative of the quality of a course.

COURSE OFFERS INFORMATION
Subject requirements/preferences AL Mathematics and physics usually required; music is also required for some courses. See also **Engineering/Engineering Sciences**. Offers shown below refer to BEng or BSc courses unless otherwise stated; BSc only appears as an abbreviation if the course is offered at the same institution as a BEng with different requirements.

Your target offers and examples of degree courses

144 pts **Glasgow** – AAA incl maths+mus+phys (Electron Mus (MEng)) (IB 38 pts HL 666 incl maths+mus+phys)

Surrey – AAA incl maths+mus+phys +interview (Mus Snd Rec (Tonmeister)) (IB 34 pts HL 666 incl maths+mus+phys)

York – AAA incl maths +interview (Electron Eng Mus Tech Sys (MEng); Mus Tech Sys (MEng)) (IB 36 pts HL 6 maths)

136 pts **Glasgow** – AAB incl maths+mus+phys (Electron Mus) (IB 36 pts HL 665 incl maths+mus+phys)

Southampton – AAB incl maths+phys (Acoust Eng) (IB 34 pts HL 17 pts incl 6 maths+phys); AAB incl maths+phys +interview (Acoust Mus) (IB 34 pts HL 17 pts incl 6 maths+phys)

128 pts **York** – ABB incl maths +interview (Electron Eng Mus Tech Sys; Mus Tech Sys) (IB 34 pts HL 6 maths)

120 pts **Birmingham City** – BBB incl sci/tech/maths/comp 120 pts (Snd Eng Prod) (IB 30 pts HL 15 pts)

Huddersfield – BBB incl maths/tech/comp/sci/eng 120 pts (Mus Tech Aud Sys)

112 pts **Glyndŵr** – BBC 112 pts (Snd Tech)

Lincoln – BBC (Snd Mus Prod) (IB 29 pts)

Liverpool (LIPA) – BBC 112 pts +interview (Snd Tech)

Liverpool John Moores – BBC 112 pts (Aud Mus Prod) (IB 26 pts)

Salford – 112–120 pts incl maths/sci (Acoust Aud Eng) (IB 30 pts HL 5 maths/sci)

West London – BBB–BBC 112–120 pts (App Snd Eng)

104 pts **Bournemouth** – 104–120 pts incl sci/maths/mus/tech (Mus Snd Prod Tech) (IB 31–28 pts)

Chichester – BBC–BCC 104–112 pts (Aud Prod Mus Tech) (IB 28 pts)
De Montfort – 104 pts (Aud Rec Tech) (IB 24 pts)
96 pts **Hertfordshire** – CCC 96 pts (Aud Rec Prod; Mus Snd Des Tech)
Solent – CCC 96–112 pts (Pop Mus Prod) (IB -28 pts)
80 pts **Arts London** – BB 80 pts +portfolio (Snd Arts)
64 pts **London (Royal Central Sch SpDr)** – 64–120 pts +interview +portfolio (Thea Prac (Thea Snd))
24 pts **UHI** – D +interview (Aud Eng)

Alternative offers
See **Chapter 6** and **Appendix 1** for grades/UCAS Tariff points information for other examinations.

EXAMPLES OF COLLEGES OFFERING COURSES IN THIS SUBJECT FIELD
Barnsley (Coll); Buckinghamshire (Coll Group); Calderdale (Coll); Leicester (Coll); Newcastle (Coll); Plymouth City (Coll); St Helens (Coll); Truro and Penwith (Coll).

CHOOSING YOUR COURSE (SEE ALSO CH.1)
Universities and colleges teaching quality See www.qaa.ac.uk; https://unistats.ac.uk.

Examples of sandwich degree courses Birmingham City; Huddersfield; Portsmouth; Surrey; York.

ADMISSIONS INFORMATION
Number of applicants per place (approx) Salford 4; Southampton 4.

Advice to applicants and planning the UCAS personal statement See **Engineering/Engineering Sciences**. See also **Appendix 3**.

Selection interviews No Salford, Southampton.

Interview advice and questions What interests you about acoustics engineering? What career do you have in mind on graduating? See also **Chapter 5**.

Reasons for rejection (non-academic) See **Engineering/Engineering Sciences**.

AFTER-RESULTS ADVICE
Offers to applicants repeating A-levels Same Salford.

GRADUATE DESTINATIONS AND EMPLOYMENT (2016/17 HESA)
Graduates surveyed See **Engineering/Engineering Sciences**.

Career note Specialist topics on these courses will enable graduates to make decisions as to their future career destinations.

OTHER DEGREE SUBJECTS FOR CONSIDERATION
Audiology; Broadcast Engineering; Communications Engineering; Computer Engineering; Computer Science; Media Technology; Music; Radio and TV; Technology; Telecommunications Engineering and Electronic Engineering.

ENGINEERING (AERONAUTICAL AND AEROSPACE)
(see also Engineering (Electrical and Electronic))

Courses cover the manufacture of military and civil aircraft, theories of mechanics, thermodynamics, electronics, computing and engine design. Avionics courses include flight and energy control systems, airborne computing, navigation, optical and TV displays, airborne communications, and radar systems for navigation and power. Aeronautical Engineering involves the design, construction and powering of aircraft, and similarly Aerospace Engineering covers aerodynamics, flight design and control propulsion, and communications. Pilot training, with an additional fee, is also included in some courses as at the universities of Brunel, Leeds, Kingston, Hertfordshire and Liverpool. Some courses also include spaceflight studies and the Electronic Engineering course at Bath can be combined with Space Science and Technology. (See also under **Business and Management Courses (Specialised)** and **Transport Management and Planning** for details of Aviation Management degrees.)

Most courses offer BEng and MEng degrees. MEng confers the minimum requirements to take the Initial Professional Development (IPD) training with an employer in order to obtain Chartered Engineer status, while the BEng does not. However, students taking a BEng may be able to switch onto an MEng course, as the first three years of an MEng are broadly similar to a BEng. Another route for BEng students is to subsequently undertake an MSc, which also allows access to IPD and Chartered Engineer status.

Engineering Council statement See **Engineering/Engineering Sciences**.

Useful websites www.aerosociety.com; www.engc.org.uk; www.theiet.org

NB The points totals shown to the left of the institutions are for ease of reference only. It must not be assumed that Tariff points are always used by institutions or that they can be substituted for an offer in grades. The level of an offer is not necessarily indicative of the quality of a course.

COURSE OFFERS INFORMATION
Subject requirements/preferences See **Engineering/Engineering Sciences**. Offers shown below refer to BEng or BSc courses unless otherwise stated; BSc only appears as an abbreviation if the course is offered at the same institution as a BEng with different requirements.

Your target offers and examples of degree courses

160 pts **Cambridge** – A*A*A incl maths+phys +interview +ENGAA (Eng (Aerosp Aeroth Eng)) (IB 42–40 pts HL 776)

Imperial London – A*A*A incl maths+phys +interview (Aero Eng (MEng); Aero Eng (Yr Abrd)) (IB 40 pts HL 7 maths+phys)

152 pts **Bath** – A*AA/AAA +aEPQ incl maths+phys (Aerosp Eng) (IB 36 pts HL 766 incl maths+phys)

Bristol – A*AA incl maths+phys (Aerosp Eng; Aerosp Eng (St Abrd) (MEng)) (IB 38 pts HL 18 pts incl 7,6 maths+phys)

Leeds – A*AA incl maths+phys (Aero Aerosp Eng) (IB 36 pts HL 18 pts incl 6 maths+phys)

Southampton – A*AA/A*AB +aEPQ incl maths+phys (Aero Astnaut (Airvhcl Sys Des) (MEng); Aero Astnaut (Eng Mgt) (MEng); Aero Astnaut (Mat Struct) (MEng); Aero Astnaut (Spcrft Eng) (MEng); Mech Eng (Aerosp) (MEng)) (IB 38 pts HL 18 pts incl 6 maths+phys); (Aero Astnaut; Aero Astnaut (Aerodyn) (MEng)) (IB 38 pts HL 6 maths+phys); A*AA incl maths+phys (Aero Astnaut (MEng)) (IB 38 pts HL 18 pts incl 6 math+phys)

144 pts **Bath** – A*AB/AAA incl maths+sci/tech (Electron Eng Spc Sci Tech) (IB 36 pts HL 666/765 incl 6 maths+sci/tech)

Glasgow – AAA incl maths+phys (Aerosp Sys (MEng); Mech Eng Aero (MEng)) (IB 38 pts HL 666 incl maths+phys)

Leeds – AAA incl maths/phys (Avn Tech Plt St Mgt) (IB 35 pts HL 18 pts incl 5 maths/phys)

Liverpool – AAA/AAB +aEPQ incl maths+sci (Aerosp Eng (MEng); Aerosp Eng Plt St (MEng)) (IB 35 pts HL 5 maths+phys)

London (QM) – AAA incl maths+phys/chem (Aerosp Eng (MEng)) (IB 36 pts HL 666 incl maths+phys/chem)

Manchester – AAA incl maths+phys +interview (Aerosp Eng (MEng); Aerosp Eng Mgt (MEng)) (IB 36 pts HL 666 incl maths+phys)

Queen's Belfast – AAA incl maths+sci (Aerosp Eng (MEng)) (IB 36 pts HL 666 incl maths+sci); AAA incl maths+sci/des tech (Prod Des Eng (MEng)) (IB 36 pts HL 666 incl maths+sci)

Sheffield – AAA/AAB +aEPQ incl maths+sci (Aerosp Eng (MEng)) (IB 36 pts HL 6 maths+sci)

136 pts **Glasgow** – AAB incl maths+phys (Aero Eng; Aerosp Sys) (IB 36 pts HL 665 incl maths+phys)

London (QM) – AAB incl maths+phys (Aerosp Eng) (IB 34 pts HL 665 incl maths+phys)

Loughborough – AAB incl maths+phys +interview (Aero Eng) (IB 35 pts HL 665 incl maths+phys)

Manchester – AAB incl maths+phys +interview (Aerosp Eng) (IB 35 pts HL 665 maths+phys)

Nottingham – AAA-AAB incl maths (Aerosp Eng) (IB 36-34 pts)

Sheffield – AAB/ABB +aEPQ incl maths+sci (Aerosp Eng (PPI)) (IB 34 pts HL 6 maths+sci); AAB/ABB +bEPQ incl maths+sci (Aerosp Eng) (IB 34 pts HL 6 maths+phys); (Aerosp Eng (PPI) (MEng); Aerosp Eng (Yr Ind)) (IB 34 pts HL 6 maths+sci)

Surrey – AAA-AAB incl maths+phys (Aerosp Eng (MEng)) (IB 34 pts)

128 pts **Brunel** – ABB incl maths+sci (Aerosp Eng (MEng)) (IB 31 pts HL 5 maths+sci)

City – ABB incl maths 128 pts (Aero Eng (MEng)) (IB 33 pts HL 5 maths)

Kingston – ABB incl maths+sci 128 pts (Aerosp Eng (MEng)) (IB 32 pts HL 5 maths+phys+sci); ABB incl maths+sci 128 pts incl maths+sci (Aerosp Eng Astnaut Spc Tech (MEng)) (IB 32 pts HL 5 maths+phys)

Leicester – ABB-BBB +bEPQ incl maths+sci (Aerosp Eng) (IB 30 pts HL 5 maths+phys)

Liverpool – ABB/BBB +aEPQ incl maths+sci (Aerosp Eng) (IB 33 pts HL 5 maths+phys)

Queen's Belfast – ABB incl maths+sci/fmaths/tech des (Aerosp Eng) (IB 33 pts HL 655 incl maths+sci)

Surrey – AAB-ABB incl maths+phys (Aerosp Eng) (IB 34-32 pts)

Swansea – AAB-ABB incl maths (Aerosp Eng (MEng)) (IB 34 pts)

120 pts **Brunel** – BBB (Aerosp Eng) (IB 30 pts HL 5 maths+sci)

City – BBB incl maths 120 pts (Aero Eng) (IB 32 pts HL 5 maths)

Coventry – ABB-BBB (Avn Mgt) (IB 31 pts); ABB-BBB incl maths+phys/des tech (Aerosp Sys Eng) (IB 31 pts)

Hertfordshire – BBB incl maths+phys/tech/eng 120 pts (Aerosp Eng (MEng); Aerosp Sys Eng (MEng); Aerosp Sys Eng Plt St (MEng))

Strathclyde – AAB-BBB +interview (Mech Eng Aero (MEng)) (IB 36 pts HL 6 maths+phys); AAB-BBB incl maths+phys +interview (Aero-Mech Eng (MEng)) (IB 36 pts HL 6 maths+phys); ABB-BBB incl maths+phys +interview (Aero-Mech Eng) (IB 32 pts HL 5 maths+phys)

Swansea – ABB-BBB incl maths (Aerosp Eng) (IB 32 pts)

UWE Bristol – C maths 120 pts (Aerosp Eng (MEng)) (HL 6 maths)

112 pts **Glyndŵr** – BBC 112 pts incl maths/sci (Aero Mech Eng)

Kingston – BBC incl maths+sci 112 pts (Aerosp Eng; Aerosp Eng Astnaut Spc Tech) (IB 30 pts HL 5 maths+phys)

Sheffield Hallam – 112 pts (Aerosp Eng)

UWE Bristol – C maths 112 pts (Aerosp Eng) (HL 5 maths)

104 pts **Brighton** – BBB-BCC incl maths+sci 104-120 pts (Aero Eng (MEng)) (IB 26 pts HL 5 maths+phys)

Hertfordshire – BCC incl maths+phys/tech/eng 104 pts (Aerosp Eng; Aerosp Sys Eng; Aerosp Sys Eng Plt St)

96 pts **Brighton** – BBC-CCC incl maths+sci 96-112 pts (Aero Eng) (IB 26 pts HL 5 maths+phys)

Hertfordshire – CCC 96 pts (Aerosp Tech Mgt; Aerosp Tech Plt St)

Teesside – C maths 96-112 pts +interview (Aerosp Eng) (HL 5 maths)

80 pts **South Wales** – BCC-CDD incl maths+sci 80-104 pts (Aero Eng) (IB 29 pts HL 5 maths+sci); BCC-CDD incl num sub (Aircft Mntnce Sys Mgt)

64 pts **UHI** – CC incl maths (Aircft Eng)

Alternative offers

See **Chapter 6** and **Appendix 1** for grades/UCAS Tariff points information for other examinations.

EXAMPLES OF COLLEGES OFFERING COURSES IN THIS SUBJECT FIELD

Blackpool and Fylde (Coll); Bristol City (Coll); Exeter (Coll); Farnborough (CT); Macclesfield (Coll); Newcastle (Coll); Solihull (Coll); Yeovil (Coll).

CHOOSING YOUR COURSE (SEE ALSO CH.1)

Universities and colleges teaching quality See www.qaa.ac.uk; https://unistats.ac.uk.

Top research universities and colleges (REF 2014) (Aeronautical, Mechanical, Chemical and Manufacturing Engineering) Cambridge; London (UCL); Manchester (Chem Eng); Bath; Imperial London; Sheffield (Mech Eng Advnc Manuf), (Chem Biol Eng); Queen's Belfast; Birmingham (Chem Eng).

Examples of sandwich degree courses Bath; Brighton; Brunel; City; Coventry; Hertfordshire; Kingston; Leeds; London (QM); Loughborough; Queen's Belfast; Sheffield Hallam; South Wales; Surrey; Teesside; UWE Bristol.

ADMISSIONS INFORMATION
Number of applicants per place (approx) Bath 10; Bristol 7; City 11; Farnborough (CT) 7; Hertfordshire 17; Kingston 9; London (QM) 8; Queen's Belfast 6; Southampton 10.

Advice to applicants and planning the UCAS personal statement Interest in engineering and aerospace. Work experience in engineering. Flying experience. Personal attainments. Relevant hobbies. Membership of Air Training Corps. See also **Engineering/Engineering Sciences**. **Bristol** Deferred entry accepted. **Imperial London** Deferred entry acceptable.

Selection interviews Yes Cambridge, Farnborough (CT), Imperial London; **Some** Loughborough; **No** Bristol, Hertfordshire, Kingston, London (QM), Southampton.

Interview advice and questions Why Aeronautical Engineering? Questions about different types of aircraft and flight principles of helicopters. Range of interests in engineering. See also **Chapter 5**.

Reasons for rejection (non-academic) See **Engineering/Engineering Sciences**.

AFTER-RESULTS ADVICE
Offers to applicants repeating A-levels Higher Bristol; Queen's Belfast; **Possibly higher** Hertfordshire; **Same** Bath; City; Farnborough (CT); Kingston; Liverpool; Loughborough; Southampton; **No** Cambridge.

GRADUATE DESTINATIONS AND EMPLOYMENT (2016/17 HESA)
Aerospace Engineering graduates surveyed 1030 **Employed** 545 **In voluntary employment** 10 **In further study** 300 **Assumed unemployed** 100

Career note Specialist areas of study on these courses will open up possible career directions. See also **Engineering/Engineering Sciences**.

OTHER DEGREE SUBJECTS FOR CONSIDERATION
Astronomy; Astrophysics; Computer Science; Electronics and Systems Engineering; Materials Science; Mathematics; Naval Architecture; Physics.

ENGINEERING (CHEMICAL)

(including **Fire Engineering, Nuclear Engineering** and **Petrol Engineering**; see also **Chemistry**)

Chemical engineers explore solutions to problems across the whole spectrum of industries involving oil and gas, petroleum, pharmaceuticals, cosmetics, food and drink, biotechnology, bioengineering and biomedical engineering, their role being concerned with the chemical properties of materials and also the safety aspects of projects. Petroleum engineers work in oil and gas projects which can include exploration, excavation and refining, and courses include the study of geology. Another branch is Fire Risk Engineering which invariably overlaps to some extent with Civil Engineering, as in the Fire and Leadership Studies course at the University of Central Lancashire. Finally, Nuclear Engineering focuses on the uses of nuclear energy, such as the provision of non-fossil fuels, and also covers power generation and the decommissioning of nuclear waste.

Most courses offer BEng and MEng degrees. MEng confers the minimum requirements to take the Initial Professional Development (IPD) training with an employer in order to obtain Chartered Engineer status, while the BEng does not. However, students taking a BEng may be able to switch onto an MEng course, as the first three years of an MEng are broadly similar to a BEng. Another route for BEng students is to subsequently undertake an MSc, which also allows access to IPD and Chartered Engineer status.

Engineering Council statement See **Engineering/Engineering Sciences**.

Useful websites www.icheme.org; www.engc.org.uk; www.bceca.org.uk; https://semta.org.uk

NB The points totals shown to the left of the institutions are for ease of reference only. It must not be assumed that Tariff points are always used by institutions or that they can be substituted for an offer in grades. The level of an offer is not necessarily indicative of the quality of a course.

COURSE OFFERS INFORMATION

Subject requirements/preferences AL Mathematics and chemistry usually required. See also **Engineering/Engineering Sciences**. Offers shown below refer to BEng or BSc courses unless otherwise stated; BSc only appears as an abbreviation if the course is offered at the same institution as a BEng with different requirements.

Your target offers and examples of degree courses

160 pts **Cambridge** – A*A*A incl chem+maths+phys +interview +ENGAA/NSAA (Cheml Eng) (IB 42–40 pts HL 776 incl chem+maths+phys)

Imperial London – A*A*A incl maths+chem+sci +interview (Cheml Eng (MEng)) (IB 39 pts HL 7 maths+chem 6 sci/econ); A*A*A incl maths+chem+sci/econ +interview (Cheml Nucl Eng (MEng)) (IB 39 pts HL 7 maths+chem 6 sci/econ)

Oxford – A*A*A incl maths+phys +interview +PAT (Cheml Eng (MEng)) (IB 40 pts HL 776 incl 7 maths+phys)

152 pts **Bath** – A*AA/AAA+aEPQ incl maths+chem (Cheml Eng; Cheml Eng (MEng)) (IB 36 pts HL 766 incl maths+chem)

Birmingham – A*AA incl chem+maths (Cheml Eng; Cheml Eng (MEng); Cheml Eng (MEng) (Yr Abrd)) (IB 32 pts HL 766 incl 6 chem+maths)

144 pts **Birmingham** – AAA incl maths+phys (Nucl Eng (MEng)) (IB 32 pts HL 666 incl maths+phys)

Lancaster – AAA incl maths+sci (Cheml Eng (MEng)) (IB 36 pts HL 16 pts incl 6 maths+chem)

Leeds – AAA incl maths+phys/chem (Chem Nucl Eng; Cheml Eng courses) (IB 35 pts HL 18 pts incl 5 maths+phys/chem)

London (UCL) – AAA incl chem+maths (Chem Eng) (IB 38 pts HL 665 incl maths+chem); AAA incl maths+chem (Eng (Cheml)) (IB 38 pts HL 18 pts incl 6 maths+chem); AAA incl maths+sci (Eng (Bioch); Eng (Bioch) (MEng)) (IB 38 pts HL 18 pts incl 6 maths+sci)

Loughborough – AAA incl maths+chem/phys (Cheml Eng (MEng)) (IB 37 pts HL 666 incl maths+chem/phys)

Nottingham – A*AA–AAA incl maths+chem/phys (Cheml Eng; Cheml Eng (MEng); Cheml Eng Env Eng) (IB 36 pts)

Sheffield – AAA incl maths+sci (Cheml Eng; Cheml Eng (MEng) Comb Hons) (IB 36 pts HL 6 maths+sci)

136 pts **Lancaster** – AAB incl maths+sci (Cheml Eng) (IB 35 pts HL 16 pts incl 6 maths+chem); (Nucl Eng) (IB 35 pts HL 16 pts incl 6 maths+sci)

Manchester – AAB incl maths+phys/chem +interview (Cheml Eng) (IB 35 pts HL 665 incl maths+phys/chem)

Newcastle – AAB incl maths+chem (Cheml Eng) (IB 34 pts HL 6 maths+chem)

128 pts **Aston** – ABB incl chem+maths (Cheml Eng (MEng)) (IB 32 pts HL 655 incl maths+chem)

Brunel – ABB incl maths+sci/geog/geol/des (Cheml Eng (MEng)) (IB 31 pts HL 5 maths+sci/geog/geol/des)

Edinburgh – AAA–ABB incl maths+chem (Cheml Eng) (IB 37–32 pts HL 666–555 incl maths+chem); AAA–ABB incl maths+phys/eng/des tech (Struct Fire Sfty Eng) (IB 37–32 pts HL 555 incl maths+phys/des tech)

Liverpool – ABB/BBB+aEPQ incl phys+maths (Phys Nucl Sci) (IB 33 pts HL 6 phys+maths)

120 pts **Aberdeen** – BBB incl maths+chem+phys/des tech/eng (Petrol Eng) (IB 32 pts HL 5 maths+phys); BBB incl maths+phys/des tech/eng (Cheml Eng) (IB 32 pts HL 5 maths+phys)

Aston – BBB incl chem+maths (Cheml Eng) (IB 31 pts HL 555 incl maths+chem)

Brunel – BBB incl maths+sci/geog/geol/env/des (Cheml Eng) (IB 30 pts HL 5 maths+sci/geog/geol/env/des)

Huddersfield – BBB incl maths+phys/chem 120 pts (Cheml Eng Chem)

Queen's Belfast – BBB incl maths+sci/tech/geog (Cheml Eng) (IB 32 pts HL 655 incl maths+sci)

Strathclyde – ABB–BBB (Cheml Eng) (IB 32 pts HL 6 maths 5 chem+phys)

Surrey – ABB–BBB (Cheml Eng) (IB 32 pts)

Swansea – ABB–BBB incl maths (Cheml Eng) (IB 32 pts)

112 pts **Bradford** – BBC incl maths+chem 112 pts (Cheml Eng)

Heriot-Watt – BBC incl maths+chem (Cheml Eng; Cheml Eng Ener Eng (MEng); Cheml Eng Oil Gas Tech (MEng)) (IB 31 pts)

Hull – 112 pts incl maths+chem (Cheml Eng) (IB 28 pts HL 5 maths+chem)

Teesside – 112–128 pts incl maths +interview (Cheml Eng (MEng))

104 pts **Nottingham Trent** – 104 pts incl phys+maths (Phys Nucl Tech)

96 pts **Central Lancashire** – 96 pts incl maths/sci (Fire Eng; Fire Eng (MEng))

Portsmouth – 96–120 pts (Petrol Eng) (IB 27 pts HL 6 maths)

Teesside – 96–112 pts incl maths +interview (Cheml Eng)

88 pts **West Scotland** – CCD incl maths+chem (Cheml Eng) (IB 24 pts)

Alternative offers
See **Chapter 6** and **Appendix 1** for grades/UCAS Tariff points information for other examinations.

DEGREE APPRENTICESHIPS
Chester (Chem Eng); Kent (Chem Sci Tech Sci, Chem Sci Lab Sci).

EXAMPLES OF COLLEGES OFFERING COURSES IN THIS SUBJECT FIELD
Lakes (Coll).

CHOOSING YOUR COURSE (SEE ALSO CH.1)
Universities and colleges teaching quality See www.qaa.ac.uk; https://unistats.ac.uk.

Top research universities and colleges (REF 2014) See **Engineering (Aeronautical and Aerospace)**.

Examples of sandwich degree courses Aston; Bath; Bradford; Huddersfield; Hull; London (QM); Loughborough; Manchester; Queen's Belfast; Surrey; Teesside.

ADMISSIONS INFORMATION
Number of applicants per place (approx) Aston 4; Bath 10; Birmingham 6; Heriot-Watt 6; Huddersfield 7; Imperial London 4, (MEng) 4; Leeds 9; London (UCL) 7; Newcastle 4; Nottingham 19; Sheffield 7; Strathclyde 6; Swansea 3.

Selection interviews Yes Cambridge, Imperial London, Loughborough, Manchester, Oxford; **Some** Bath, Teesside; **No** Birmingham, Leeds, London (UCL), Newcastle, Nottingham, Surrey.

Interview advice and questions Past questions have included the following: How would you justify the processing of radioactive waste to people living in the neighbourhood? What is public health engineering? What is biochemical engineering? What could be the sources of fuel and energy in the year 2020? Discuss some industrial applications of chemistry. Regular incidents occur in which chemical spillage and other problems affect the environment – be prepared to discuss these social issues. See also **Chapter 5**. **Imperial London** Interviews can be conducted in South East Asia if necessary.

Reasons for rejection (non-academic) See **Engineering/Engineering Sciences**.

AFTER-RESULTS ADVICE
Offers to applicants repeating A-levels Higher Swansea; **Possibly higher** Bath; Leeds; Queen's Belfast; **Same** Aston; Birmingham; Cambridge; Loughborough; Newcastle; Nottingham; Sheffield; Teesside.

GRADUATE DESTINATIONS AND EMPLOYMENT (2016/17 HESA)
Chemical, Process and Energy Engineering graduates surveyed 3,545 **Employed** 1,440 **In voluntary employment** 20 **In further study** 385 **Assumed unemployed** 130

Career note Chemical engineering is involved in many aspects of industry and scientific development. In addition to the oil and chemical-based industries, graduates enter a wide range of careers including the design and construction of chemical process plants, food production, pollution control, environmental protection, energy conservation, waste recovery and recycling, medical science, health and safety, and alternative energy sources.

OTHER DEGREE SUBJECTS FOR CONSIDERATION
Biochemistry; Biotechnology; Chemistry; Cosmetic Science; Environmental Science; Food Science and Technology; Materials Science; Mathematics; Nuclear Engineering; Physics.

ENGINEERING (CIVIL)

(including **Architectural Engineering, Civil and Coastal Engineering, Civil and Environmental Engineering, Marine Technology with Offshore Engineering, Civil and Transportation Engineering**; see also **Building And Construction, Environmental Sciences**)

Civil engineers translate the work of architectural designs into reality, dealing with large scale projects such as high rise buildings, bridges, dock and harbour projects, roads, railways, dams, water supplies and reservoirs. In all major projects, civil engineers and architects work in close liaison as demonstrated at the University of Bath which has the only interdisciplinary Architecture and Civil Engineering department in the UK in which students following either degree work together. The University of Leeds also offers a common first Engineering year for all students, who can switch courses with a choice from Architectural Engineering or Civil Engineering with specialisms in either Environmental Engineering, Project Management or Structural Engineering, which focuses on the materials used in construction.

Most courses offer BEng and MEng degrees. MEng confers the minimum requirements to take the Initial Professional Development (IPD) training with an employer in order to obtain Chartered Engineer status, while the BEng does not. However, students taking a BEng may be able to switch onto an MEng course, as the first three years of an MEng are broadly similar to a BEng. Another route for BEng students is to subsequently undertake an MSc, which also allows access to IPD and Chartered Engineer status.

Engineering Council statement See **Engineering/Engineering Sciences**.

Useful websites www.ice.org.uk; www.engc.org.uk; www.wisecampaign.org.uk; www.istructe.org

NB The points totals shown to the left of the institutions are for ease of reference only. It must not be assumed that Tariff points are always used by institutions or that they can be substituted for an offer in grades. The level of an offer is not necessarily indicative of the quality of a course.

COURSE OFFERS INFORMATION
Subject requirements/preferences See **Engineering/Engineering Sciences**. Offers shown below refer to BEng or BSc courses unless otherwise stated; BSc only appears as an abbreviation if the course is offered at the same institution as a BEng with different requirements.

Your target offers and examples of degree courses

160 pts **Cambridge** – A*A*A incl maths+phys +interview +ENGAA (Eng (Civ Struct Env Eng)) (IB 42–40 pts HL 776)

Imperial London – A*A*A incl maths+phys +interview (Civ Eng (MEng)) (IB 39 pts HL 7 maths 6 phys)

Oxford – A*A*A incl maths+phys +interview +PAT (Civ Eng (MEng)) (IB 40 pts HL 776 incl 7 maths+phys)

152 pts **Bath** – A*AA/AAA +aEPQ incl maths (Civ Archit Eng (MEng)) (IB 36 pts HL 766); (Civ Eng) (IB 36 pts HL 766 incl maths)

Bristol – A*AA incl maths+sci (Civ Eng; Civ Eng (MEng)) (IB 38 pts HL 18 pts incl 76 maths+sci)

London (UCL) – A*AA (Eng (Civ)) (IB 39 pts HL 19 pts)

Southampton – A*AA/A*AB +aEPQ incl maths+sci/geog (Civ Eng Archit (MEng)) (IB 38 pts HL 18 pts incl 6 maths); (Civ Eng (MEng)) (IB 38 pts HL 18 pts incl 6 maths+sci); (Civ Eng) (IB 38 pts HL 6 maths+sci)

144 pts **Birmingham** – AAA incl maths (Civ Eng (MEng)) (IB 32 pts HL 666 incl maths)

Exeter – AAA incl maths+sci (Civ Eng (MEng)) (IB 36 pts HL 6 maths+sci); (Renew Ener Eng (MEng); Renew Ener Eng (MEng) (Yr Ind)) (IB 36 pts HL 666 incl 6 maths+sci); (Civ Eng (MEng) (Yr Ind)) (IB 36 pts HL 666 incl maths+sci)

Glasgow – AAA incl maths+phys (Civ Eng (MEng)) (IB 38 pts HL 666 incl maths+phys)

Leeds – AAA incl maths (Civ Env Eng) (IB 35 pts HL 18 pts incl 5 maths)

Nottingham – AAA incl maths+sci/tech/geog/fmaths (Civ Eng (MEng)) (IB 36 pts HL 6 maths+sci)

Queen's Belfast – AAA incl maths+sci/tech/geog (Struct Eng Archit (MEng)) (IB 36 pts HL 666); (Civ Eng (MEng); Env Civ Eng (MEng)) (IB 36 pts HL 666 incl maths+sci/tech/geog)

Sheffield – AAA/AAB +aEPQ incl maths (Civ Eng; Civ Eng Modn Lang (MEng); Civ Struct Eng (MEng)) (IB 36 pts HL 6 maths)

Warwick – AAA incl maths+phys (Civ Eng) (IB 38 pts HL 6 maths+phys)

136 pts **Birmingham** – AAB incl maths (Civ Eng) (IB 32 pts HL 665 incl maths)

Glasgow – AAB incl maths+phys (Civ Eng; Civ Eng Archit) (IB 36 pts HL 665 incl maths+phys)

Liverpool – AAB incl maths (Archit Eng (MEng); Civ Eng (MEng); Civ Struct Eng (MEng)) (IB 35 pts HL 5 maths)

Manchester – AAB incl maths+phys (Civ Eng) (IB 35 pts HL 665 incl maths+phys)

Newcastle – AAB incl maths (Civ Eng (MEng); Civ Eng (MEng) (Yr Ind); Civ Struct Eng (MEng)) (IB 34 pts HL 6 maths); AAB incl maths+phys/chem/fmaths (Mar Tech Off Eng (MEng)) (IB 34 pts HL 6 maths+phys/chem)

Nottingham – AAB incl maths+sci/tech/geog/fmaths (Civ Eng) (IB 34 pts HL 6 maths+sci)

128 pts **Aberdeen** – ABB incl maths+phys/des tech/eng (Civ Eng (MEng); Civ Env Eng (MEng); Civ Struct Eng (MEng)) (IB 34 pts HL 6 maths+phys)

Brunel – ABB incl maths+sci/geog/env/des tech (Civ Eng (MEng)) (IB 31 pts HL 5 maths+sci/geog/env/des tech)

City – ABB incl maths 128 pts (Civ Eng (MEng)) (IB 33 pts HL 5 maths)

Coventry – AAB–ABB incl maths (Civ Eng (MEng)) (IB 30 pts)

Edinburgh – AAA–ABB incl maths+phys/eng/des tech (Struct Eng Archit) (IB 37–32 pts HL 555); (Civ Eng) (IB 37–32 pts HL 555 incl maths+phys/des tech)

Exeter – AAB–ABB incl maths+sci (Civ Eng; Renew Ener Eng) (IB 34–32 pts HL 665–655 incl 5 maths+sci)

Liverpool – ABB incl maths (Civ Eng) (IB 33 pts HL 5 maths)

Liverpool John Moores – ABB 128 pts (Civ Eng (MEng)) (IB 27 pts)

Loughborough – ABB incl maths (Civ Eng) (IB 34 pts HL 655 incl maths)

Newcastle – ABB incl maths (Civ Eng; Civ Eng (Yr Ind); Civ Struct Eng) (IB 32 pts HL 5 maths)

Queen's Belfast – ABB incl maths+sci/tech/geog (Civ Eng) (IB 33 pts HL 655 incl maths+sci/tech/geog)

Swansea – ABB–BBB incl maths (Civ Eng) (IB 32 pts)

120 pts **Brunel** – BBB incl maths+sci/geog/env/des tech (Civ Eng; Civ Eng Sust) (IB 30 pts HL 5 maths+sci/geog/env/des tech)

Cardiff – ABB–BBB incl maths (Civ Eng; Civ Env Eng) (IB 34–32 pts HL 5 maths); (Archit Eng) (IB 34–32 pts HL 655 incl 5 maths)

City – BBB incl maths 120 pts (Civ Eng) (IB 32 pts HL 5 maths)

Derby – BBB incl maths 120 pts (Civ Eng)

Hertfordshire – BBB incl maths 120 pts (Civ Eng (MEng))

Leeds Beckett – 120 pts incl maths+sci (Civ Eng) (IB 25 pts)

Nottingham Trent – BBB 120 pts (Civ Eng)

Strathclyde – ABB–BBB incl maths+phys (Civ Eng) (IB 32 pts HL 5 maths+phys/eng)

Surrey – ABB–BBB incl maths+sci/tech/fmaths (Civ Eng) (IB 32 pts)

Ulster – BBB incl maths+sci/tech (Civ Eng) (IB 26 pts HL 13 pts)

112 pts **Bradford** – BBC incl maths 112 pts (Civ Struct Eng) (HL 5 maths)

Coventry – BBB–BBC incl maths (Civ Eng) (IB 30 pts)

Greenwich – BBC incl maths/sci 112 pts (Civ Eng)

Heriot-Watt – BBC incl maths (Civ Eng; Civ Eng Int St (MEng)) (IB 31 pts HL 5 maths)

Kingston – BBC incl maths 112 pts (Civ Infra Eng) (IB 26 pts HL 6 maths)

Liverpool John Moores – BBC 112 pts (Civ Eng) (IB 26 pts); BBC incl maths/sci 112 pts (Bld Serv Eng) (IB 25 pts HL 5 maths)

London South Bank – BBC incl maths+sci 112–128 pts (Civ Eng)

Portsmouth – 112–120 pts (Civ Eng) (IB 25 pts)

Salford – BBB–BBC incl maths+phys/des tech 112–120 pts (Civ Eng) (IB 30 pts HL 5 maths+phys)

UWE Bristol – C maths 112 pts (Civ Env Eng) (HL 5 maths)

West London – BBB–BBC 112–120 pts (Civ Env Eng)

104 pts **Anglia Ruskin** – 104 pts (Civ Eng) (IB 24 pts)

Bolton – 104 pts incl maths+sci (Civ Eng)

Brighton – BBB–BCC incl maths 104–120 pts (Civ Eng) (IB 26 pts HL 5 maths)

Dundee – BBB–BCC incl maths+sci/eng (Civ Eng) (IB 30 pts HL 555 incl maths+sci/eng)

Edinburgh Napier – BCC incl maths (Civ Eng (MEng); Civ Trans Eng (MEng)) (IB 29 pts HL 655)

Hertfordshire – BCC incl maths 104 pts (Civ Eng)

Nottingham Trent – BCC 104 pts (Civ Eng (BSc))

Plymouth – 104–120 pts incl maths+sci/tech (Civ Cstl Eng; Civ Eng) (IB 30–26 pts HL 5 maths)

96 pts **Abertay** – CCC incl maths (Civ Env Eng) (IB 28 pts)

Coventry – BCC–CCC incl maths 96–104 pts (Civ Eng (BSc)) (IB 30 pts)

East London – CCC incl maths 96 pts (Civ Eng) (IB 27 pts HL 15 pts incl maths+phys)

Edinburgh Napier – CCC incl maths (Civ Eng) (IB 28 pts HL 654)

Glasgow Caledonian – CCC incl maths/phys (Env Civ Eng) (IB 24 pts incl maths+phys)

Teesside – C maths 96–112 pts incl maths +interview (Civ Eng)

Trinity Saint David – 96 pts +interview (Civ Eng Env Mgt)

Wolverhampton – CCC incl maths (Civ Eng)

88 pts **West Scotland** – CCD incl maths+sci 88 pts (Civ Eng) (IB 24 pts)

80 pts **South Wales** – BCC–CDD incl maths+sci 80–104 pts (Civ Eng) (IB 29 pts HL 5 maths+sci)

Alternative offers

See **Chapter 6** and **Appendix 1** for grades/UCAS Tariff points information for other examinations.

DEGREE APPRENTICESHIPS

Bolton (Civ Eng); Portsmouth (Civ Eng); Reading (Civ Eng).

EXAMPLES OF COLLEGES OFFERING COURSES IN THIS SUBJECT FIELD

Birmingham Met (Coll); Blackburn (Coll); Bolton (Coll); Bradford College UC; Chelmsford (Coll); Chesterfield (Coll); Exeter (Coll); Guildford (Coll); Lakes (Coll); Leeds Building (Coll); Lincoln (Coll); London UCK (Coll); MidKent (Coll); Moulton (Coll); Norwich City (Coll); Plymouth City (Coll); Sheffield (Coll); South Devon (Coll); Wakefield (Coll); Wigan and Leigh (Coll).

CHOOSING YOUR COURSE (SEE ALSO CH.1)

Universities and colleges teaching quality See www.qaa.ac.uk; https://unistats.ac.uk.

Top research universities and colleges (REF 2014) (Civil and Construction Engineering) Cardiff; Imperial London; Sheffield; Manchester; Dundee.

Examples of sandwich degree courses Bath; Bradford; Brighton; Cardiff; City; Coventry; East London; Kingston; Liverpool John Moores; London South Bank; Loughborough; Nottingham Trent; Plymouth; Portsmouth; Queen's Belfast; Salford; Surrey; Teesside; Ulster; UWE Bristol; West Scotland; Wolverhampton.

ADMISSIONS INFORMATION

Number of applicants per place (approx) Abertay 3; Bath 7; Birmingham 11; Bradford 5; Bristol 8; Cardiff 5; City 6; Dundee 9; Edinburgh Napier 5; Greenwich 11; Heriot-Watt 7; Imperial London 4; Kingston 8; Leeds 10; Liverpool John Moores 16; London (UCL) 5; London South Bank 5; Newcastle 4, (Off Eng) 4; Nottingham 9; Nottingham Trent 11; Plymouth 3; Queen's Belfast 6; Salford 5; Sheffield 4; South Wales 6; Southampton 10; Strathclyde 4; Swansea 3; Teesside 6; West Scotland 4; Wolverhampton 3.

Advice to applicants and planning the UCAS personal statement See **Engineering/Engineering Sciences**. Also read the magazine *New Civil Engineer* and discuss articles which interest you on your application. See also **Appendix 3**. **Bristol** Deferred entry accepted.

Selection interviews Yes Cambridge, Imperial London, Oxford; **Some** Bath, Cardiff, Southampton, Warwick; **No** Anglia Ruskin, Birmingham, Brighton, Bristol, Coventry, Dundee, Edinburgh Napier, Greenwich, Heriot-Watt, Kingston, Leeds, London (UCL), Loughborough, Newcastle, Nottingham, Nottingham Trent, Salford, Surrey.

Interview advice and questions Past questions have included: Why have you chosen Civil Engineering? Have you contacted the Institution of Civil Engineers/Institution of Structural Engineers? How would you define the difference between the work of a civil engineer and the work of an architect? What would happen to a concrete beam if a load were applied? Where would it break and how could it be strengthened? The favourite question: Why do you want to be a civil engineer? What would you do if you were asked to build a concrete boat? Do you know any civil engineers? What problems were faced in building the Channel Tunnel? See also **Chapter 5**. **Cambridge** Why did they make mill chimneys so tall?

Reasons for rejection (non-academic) Lack of vitality. Lack of interest in buildings, the built environment or in civil engineering. Poor communication skills. See also **Engineering/ Engineering Sciences**.

AFTER-RESULTS ADVICE

Offers to applicants repeating A-levels Higher East London; Kingston; Queen's Belfast; Teesside; Warwick; **Possibly higher** Southampton; **Same** Abertay; Bath; Birmingham; Bradford; Brighton; Bristol; Cardiff; City; Coventry; Dundee; Greenwich; Heriot-Watt; Leeds; Liverpool John Moores; London (UCL); London South Bank; Loughborough; Newcastle; Nottingham; Nottingham Trent; Salford; Sheffield; Wolverhampton; **No** Cambridge.

GRADUATE DESTINATIONS AND EMPLOYMENT (2016/17 HESA)

Graduates surveyed 2,365 **Employed** 1,615 **In voluntary employment** 30 **In further study** 435 **Assumed unemployed** 100

Career note The many aspects of this subject will provide career directions for graduates with many openings with local authorities and commercial organisations.

OTHER DEGREE SUBJECTS FOR CONSIDERATION

Architecture; Building; Surveying; Town and Country Planning.

ENGINEERING (COMMUNICATIONS)

(including **Business Information Systems**; see also **Communication Studies/Communication, Engineering (Electrical and Electronic)**)

Communications engineering impacts on many aspects of the engineering and business world. Courses overlap considerably with Electronic, Computer, Digital, Media and Internet Engineering and provide graduates with expertise in such fields as telecommunications, mobile communications and microwave engineering, optoelectronics, radio engineering and internet technology. Sandwich courses and sponsorships are offered by several universities.

Most courses offer BEng and MEng degrees. MEng confers the minimum requirements to take the Initial Professional Development (IPD) training with an employer in order to obtain Chartered Engineer status, while the BEng does not. However, students taking a BEng may be able to switch onto an MEng course, as the first three years of an MEng are broadly similar to a BEng. Another route for BEng students is to subsequently undertake an MSc, which also allows access to IPD and Chartered Engineer status.

Engineering Council statement See **Engineering/Engineering Sciences**.

Useful websites See **Computer Science and Information Technology** and **Engineering (Electrical and Electronic)**.

NB The points totals shown to the left of the institutions are for ease of reference only. It must not be assumed that Tariff points are always used by institutions or that they can be substituted for an offer in grades. The level of an offer is not necessarily indicative of the quality of a course.

COURSE OFFERS INFORMATION

Subject requirements/preferences See **Engineering/Engineering Sciences**. Offers shown below refer to BEng or BSc courses unless otherwise stated; BSc only appears as an abbreviation if the course is offered at the same institution as a BEng with different requirements.

Your target offers and examples of degree courses

152 pts **Southampton** – A*AA incl maths+phys (Electron Eng Wrlss Comms (MEng)) (IB 38 pts HL 18 pts incl 6 maths+phys)

144 pts **Bath** – A*AB/AAA/AAB +aEPQ incl maths+sci/tech (Electron Sys Eng (MEng)) (IB 36 pts HL 765/666 incl 6 maths+sci/tech); A*AB/AAA/ABB +aEPQ incl maths+sci/tech (Comp Sys Eng) (IB 36 pts HL 765/666 incl 6 maths+sci/tech); AAA/A*AB/AAB +aEPQ incl maths+sci/tech (Comp Sys Eng (MEng)) (IB 36 pts HL 765/666 incl 6 maths+sci/tech)

Leeds – AAA incl maths (Electron Comms Eng) (IB 35 pts HL 18 pts incl 5 maths)

Sheffield – AAA/AAB +aEPQ incl maths+phys/chem/electron +interview (Electron Comms Eng (MEng)) (IB 36 pts HL 6 maths+phys/chem/electron)

York – AAA incl maths +interview (Electron Comm Eng (MEng)) (IB 36 pts HL 6 maths)

136 pts **Newcastle** – AAB incl maths+phys/chem/electron (Electron Comms (MEng) (Yr Abrd/Ind)) (IB 37 pts HL 6 maths+phys/chem)

Sheffield – AAB/ABB +bEPQ incl maths+phys/chem/electron +interview (Electron Comms Eng) (IB 34 pts HL 6/5 maths+phys/chem/electron)

128 pts **Kent** – ABB incl maths+sci/tech +interview (Electron Comms Eng (MEng)) (IB 34 pts HL 15 pts incl 5 maths+sci)

London (QM) – ABB incl maths+sci (Electron Eng Telecomm) (IB 32 pts HL 655 incl maths+sci)

Newcastle – ABB incl maths+phys/chem/electron (Electron Comms) (IB 32 pts HL 5 maths+phys/chem)

York – ABB incl maths +interview (Electron Comm Eng) (IB 34 pts HL 6 maths)

120 pts **Aston** – BBB (Bus Comp IT) (IB 31 pts HL 555)

Brunel – BBB incl maths+sci/tech (Electron Elec Eng Comm Sys) (IB 30 pts HL 5 maths+sci/tech)

Essex – BBB incl maths +interview (Comms Eng) (IB 30 pts HL 5 maths)
Kent – BBB incl maths+sci +interview (Electron Comms Eng) (IB 34 pts HL 15 pts incl 5 maths+sci)

112 pts **Birmingham City** – BBC incl sci/tech/maths/comp 112 pts (Bus Inf Tech) (IB 28 pts HL 5 maths)
Huddersfield – BBB–BBC incl maths+sci/tech 112–120 pts (Electron Comm Eng)
Liverpool Hope – BBC 112 pts (IT courses) (IB 26 pts)
Nottingham Trent – BBC incl IT/sci 112 pts (ICT)

104 pts **Northampton** – BCC 104–112 pts (Comp (Comp Net Eng)) (IB 25 pts)
96 pts **Brighton** – BBC–CCC 96–112 pts (Bus Comp) (IB 26 pts)
88 pts **London Met** – CCD (Electron Intnet Thngs)
80 pts **Bedfordshire** – CCC–CCE 80–96 pts (Inf Data Sys); CCC–CCE incl maths/sci/eng 80–96 pts (Telecomms Net Eng)
South Wales – BCC–CDD 80–104 pts (ICT) (IB 29 pts)
Wolverhampton – CDD incl maths+sci/tech (Electron Telecomm Eng)

Alternative offers

See **Chapter 6** and **Appendix 1** for grades/UCAS Tariff points information for other examinations.

EXAMPLES OF COLLEGES OFFERING COURSES IN THIS SUBJECT FIELD
Birmingham Met (Coll).

CHOOSING YOUR COURSE (SEE ALSO CH.1)
Universities and colleges teaching quality See www.qaa.ac.uk; https://unistats.ac.uk.

Examples of sandwich degree courses Aston; Brunel; Kent; Kingston; Wolverhampton; York.

ADMISSIONS INFORMATION
Number of applicants per place (approx) Bradford 9; London Met 5; London South Bank 3; York 8.

Advice to applicants and planning the UCAS personal statement See **Engineering (Electrical and Electronic)** and **Appendix 3**.

Selection interviews No Hertfordshire, Kent, London Met.

Interview advice and questions See **Engineering (Electrical and Electronic)**.

Reasons for rejection (non-academic) See **Engineering (Electrical and Electronic)**.

GRADUATE DESTINATIONS AND EMPLOYMENT (2016/17 HESA)
Graduates surveyed See **Engineering (Electrical and Electronic)** and **Engineering/ Engineering Sciences**.

Career note Many commercial organisations offer opportunities in the specialist areas described at the top of this table. Work placements and sandwich courses have, in the past, resulted in over 60% of graduates gaining employment with their firms.

OTHER DEGREE SUBJECTS FOR CONSIDERATION
Computer Science; Engineering (Computer, Control, Electrical, Electronic, Systems); Physics.

ENGINEERING (COMPUTER, CONTROL, SOFTWARE AND SYSTEMS)

The design and application of modern computer systems is fundamental to a wide range of disciplines which also include electronic, software and computer-aided engineering. Most courses give priority to reinforcing the essential transferable skills consisting of management techniques, leadership skills, literacy, presentation skills, business skills and time management. At many universities, Computer Engineering is offered as part of a range of Electronics degree programmes where the first and even the second year courses are common to all students, who then choose to specialise later. A year in industry is a common feature of many of these courses.

Most courses offer BEng and MEng degrees. MEng confers the minimum requirements to take the Initial Professional Development (IPD) training with an employer in order to obtain Chartered Engineer status, while the BEng does not. However, students taking a BEng may be able to switch onto an MEng course, as the first three years of an MEng are broadly similar to a BEng. Another route for BEng students is to subsequently undertake an MSc, which also allows access to IPD and Chartered Engineer status.

Engineering Council statement See **Engineering/Engineering Sciences**.

Useful websites See **Computer Science and Information Technology** and **Engineering/ Engineering Sciences**.

NB The points totals shown to the left of the institutions are for ease of reference only. It must not be assumed that Tariff points are always used by institutions or that they can be substituted for an offer in grades. The level of an offer is not necessarily indicative of the quality of a course.

COURSE OFFERS INFORMATION

Subject requirements/preferences See **Engineering/Engineering Sciences**. Offers shown below refer to BEng or BSc courses unless otherwise stated; BSc only appears as an abbreviation if the course is offered at the same institution as a BEng with different requirements.

Your target offers and examples of degree courses

160 pts **Cambridge** – A*A*A incl maths+sci +interview +ENGAA (Eng (Inf Comp Eng)) (IB 42–40 pts HL 776)

Oxford – A*A*A incl maths+phys +interview +PAT (Inf Eng) (IB 40 pts HL 776 incl 7 maths+phys)

152 pts **Birmingham** – A*AA incl maths (Comp Sci/Soft Eng (MEng)) (IB 32 pts HL 766 incl 6 maths)

Imperial London – A*A*A*– A*AA incl maths +interview (Comp (Soft Eng) (MEng)) (IB 39 pts HL 7 maths); A*AA incl maths+phys +interview (Electron Inf Eng; Electron Inf Eng (MEng) (St Abrd)) (IB 38 pts HL 6 maths+phys)

Manchester – A*AA incl maths +interview (Comp Sys Eng) (IB 37 pts HL 766 incl 7 maths)

Southampton – A*AA incl maths (Soft Eng) (IB 38 pts HL 18 pts incl 6 maths)

144 pts **Bath** – A*AB/AAA/ABB +aEPQ incl maths+sci/tech (Comp Sys Eng) (IB 36 pts HL 765/666 incl 6 maths+sci/tech); AAA/A*AB/AAB +aEPQ incl maths+sci/tech (Comp Sys Eng (MEng)) (IB 36 pts HL 765/666 incl 6 maths+sci/tech); AAA/AAB +aEPQ incl maths+sci/tech (Elec Electron Eng (MEng); Electron Sys Eng) (IB 36 pts HL 666/765 incl 6 maths+sci/tech)

Liverpool – AAA/AAB +aEPQ incl maths+sci/tech (Avion Sys (MEng)) (IB 36 pts HL 5 maths+sci)

Loughborough – AAA incl maths+sci/tech/fmaths (Electron Comp Sys Eng (MEng)) (IB 37 pts HL 666 incl maths+sci)

Warwick – AAA incl maths (Comp Sys Eng) (IB 38 pts HL 6 maths)

136 pts **Dyson** – AAB incl maths+sci/tech/eng (Eng Tech) (IB 34 pts HL 665 incl maths+sci/tech/eng)

Glasgow – AAB incl maths+phys (Electron Soft Eng) (IB 36 pts HL 665 incl maths+phys)

Liverpool – AAB/ABB +aEPQ incl maths+sci/tech (Avion Sys) (IB 35 pts HL 5 maths+phys/ electron); (Comp Sci Electron Eng (MEng)) (IB 35 pts HL 5 maths+sci)

Queen's Belfast – AAA–AAB incl chem/phys/tech des/IT (Soft Eng (MEng)) (IB 36–34 pts HL 666–655 incl maths/chem/phys)

Sheffield – AAB/ABB +bEPQ incl maths+sci (Comp Sys Eng; Intel Sys Contr Eng; Intel Sys Contr Eng (Eng Mgt); Mecha Robot Eng) (IB 34 pts HL 65 maths+sci)

128 pts **Brunel** – ABB incl maths+sci/geog/env/des tech (Comp Sys Eng (MEng); Electron Comp Eng (MEng)) (IB 31 pts HL 6 maths 5 sci/geog/des tech)

Edinburgh – AAA–ABB incl maths (Electron Comp Sci (MEng)) (IB 37–32 pts HL 666–655 incl 6 maths)

Leicester – ABB (Soft Eng courses) (IB 30 pts)

Liverpool – AAB–ABB incl maths/phys/comp sci (Comp Sci Soft Dev) (IB 35–33 pts HL 5 maths/phys/comp sci); ABB/BBB +aEPQ incl maths+sci/tech (Comp Sci Electron Eng) (IB 33 pts HL 5 maths+phys/electron)

London (RH) – AAB–ABB incl comp sci/maths/phys (Comp Sci (Soft Eng)) (IB 32 pts HL 655 incl maths/comp sci/phys)

Loughborough – ABB incl maths+sci/tech/fmaths (Electron Comp Sys Eng) (IB 34 pts HL 655 incl maths+sci)

Newcastle – ABB incl maths+phys/chem/electron (Electron Comp Eng) (IB 32 pts HL 5 maths+phys/chem)

Oxford Brookes – ABB incl maths+phys/chem/elec/eng/sci 128 pts (Robot Eng (MEng)) (IB 32 pts HL 5 maths+phys)

120 pts **Aberdeen** – BBB incl maths+phys/des tech/eng (Eng Electron Soft Eng) (IB 32 pts HL 5 maths+phys)

Bangor – C maths+phys 120 pts incl maths+phys (Comp Sys Eng (MEng)) (HL 5 maths+phys)

Brunel – BBB (Comp Sci (Soft Eng)) (IB 30 pts); BBB incl maths+sci/geog/env/des tech (Comp Sys Eng) (IB 30 pts HL 5 maths+sci/geog/des tech)

Cardiff – ABB–BBB (App Soft Eng) (32–30 pts HL 655)

East Anglia – BBB incl maths/comp/electron/econ/phys (Comp Sys Eng (Yr Ind)) (IB 31 pts HL 5 maths/comp/econ/phys); BBB incl maths/comp/electron/econ/phys (Comp Sys Eng) (IB 31 pts HL 5 maths/comp/econ/phys)

Essex – BBB (Comp Net; Comp Sys Eng) (IB 30 pts); (Comp Electron) (IB 30 pts HL 555)

Kent – BBB incl maths+sci +interview (Comp Sys Eng) (IB 34 pts HL 15 pts)

London South Bank – BBB (Comp Sys Net Eng)

Northumbria – 120 pts (Comp Net Cy Scrty) (HL 444)

Nottingham Trent – BBB incl IT/maths/sci 120 pts (Soft Eng)

Oxford Brookes – 120 pts (Robot Eng) (IB 31 pts)

Stirling – BBB (Soft Eng) (IB 32 pts)

Strathclyde – AAB–BBB incl maths+phy +interview (Comp Electron Sys (MEng)) (IB 36 pts HL 6 maths+phys); ABB–BBB incl maths (Soft Eng) (IB 34 pts HL 5 maths); ABB–BBB incl maths+phys +interview (Comp Electron Sys) (IB 32 pts HL 5 maths+phys)

112 pts **Aberystwyth** – BBB–BBC incl phys+maths 112–120 pts (Spc Sci Robot) (IB 30–28 pts HL 5 maths+phys)

Bradford – BBC 112 pts (Soft Eng)

Coventry – BBB–BBC incl maths+sci/tech/eng (Comp Hard Soft Eng) (IB 29 pts)

De Montfort – 112 pts (Soft Eng) (IB 26 pts)

Greenwich – 112 pts incl sci/maths (Comp Eng); BBC 112–120 pts (Soft Eng)

Heriot-Watt – BBC incl maths+phys (Comp Electron) (IB 29 pts HL 5 maths+phys)

Huddersfield – BBB–BBC incl maths+sci/tech 112–120 pts (Comp Sys Eng)

Hull – 112 pts (Comp Sci (Soft Eng)) (IB 28 pts)

Liverpool John Moores – BBC 112 pts (Soft Eng) (IB 26 pts)

Nottingham Trent – BBC incl IT/maths/sci 112 pts (Comp Sys Eng)

Sheffield Hallam – BBC 112 pts (Soft Eng)

Staffordshire – BBC 112 pts (Comp Gms Prog) (IB 24 pts)

Teesside – B maths 112–128 pts incl maths+phys +interview (Instr Contr Eng (MEng)) (HL 5 maths)

104 pts **Bolton** – 104 pts (Soft Eng); 104 pts incl maths/comp (Dig Tech Sol Net Eng)

Bournemouth – 104–120 pts (Soft Eng) (IB 31–28 pts)

Central Lancashire – 104–112 pts incl maths+phys/STEM (Comp Aid Eng (MEng)) (HL 5 maths+phys/STEM); 104–112 pts incl maths/phys/STEM (Comp Aid Eng)

Hertfordshire – BCC 104 pts (Comp Sci (Soft Eng))

Manchester Met – BBC–BCC incl IT/comp sci/maths/sci 104–112 pts (Soft Eng) (IB 26 pts HL 5 IT)

Northampton – BCC (Comp (Comp Sys Eng)) (IB 25 pts)
Trinity Saint David – 104 pts +interview (Comp Soft Eng)
Winchester – 104–112 pts (Soft Eng)

96 pts **Aberystwyth** – BBB–CCC 96–120 pts (Soft Eng (Yr Ind)) (IB 30–26 pts)
Bangor – C maths+phys 96 pts (Comp Sys Eng) (HL 5 maths+phys)
Cardiff Met – CCC 96 pts (Soft Eng) (IB 24 pts HL 12 pts)
Edinburgh Napier – CCC (Comp Sys Net) (IB 27 pts HL 654)
Solent – CCC 96–112 pts (Cyb Scrty Mgt) (IB 28 pts)
Sunderland – CCC 96 pts (Gm Dev)
Teesside – C maths 96–112 pts incl maths +interview (Instr Contr Eng)

88 pts **Glasgow Caledonian** – CCD incl maths+phys (Comp Aid Mech Eng) (IB 24 pts)
London Met – CCD 88 pts (Comp Sys Eng Robot)
Wolverhampton – CCD/BCD 88–96 pts (Comp Sci (Soft Eng))

80 pts **Bedfordshire** – 80 pts (Comp Sci Soft Eng); CCC–CCE 80–96 pts (Comp Sys Eng)
Bucks New – 80 pts (Soft Eng)

72 pts **Solent** – 72–96 pts (Comp Sys Net Eng)

Alternative offers
See **Chapter 6** and **Appendix 1** for grades/UCAS Tariff points information for other examinations.

DEGREE APPRENTICESHIPS
Bangor (Soft Eng); Robert Gordon (Soft Dev, IT Mgt Bus); Chichester (Soft Eng).

EXAMPLES OF COLLEGES OFFERING COURSES IN THIS SUBJECT FIELD
Accrington and Rossendale (Coll); Barking and Dagenham (Coll); Barnfield (Coll); Birmingham Met (Coll); Blackburn (Coll); Blackpool and Fylde (Coll); Bristol City (Coll); Cornwall (Coll); Doncaster (Coll); Farnborough (CT); Gateshead (Coll); Highbury Portsmouth (Coll); Manchester (Coll); Newcastle (Coll); North Lindsey (Coll); Nottingham (Coll); Tyne Coast (Coll).

CHOOSING YOUR COURSE (SEE ALSO CH.1)
Universities and colleges teaching quality See www.qaa.ac.uk; https://unistats.ac.uk.

Top research universities and colleges (REF 2014) See **Computer Science and Information Technology**.

Examples of sandwich degree courses Aberystwyth; Bath; Bradford; Brunel; Chester; Greenwich; Huddersfield; Kent; London (QM); London (RH); London South Bank; Loughborough; Manchester; Manchester Met; Northumbria; Nottingham Trent; Sheffield Hallam; Stirling; Westminster; York.

ADMISSIONS INFORMATION
Number of applicants per place (approx) Bath 8; Birmingham 9; Cardiff 6; Central Lancashire 12; East Anglia 5; Edinburgh 3; Huddersfield 3; Imperial London 5; Liverpool John Moores 2; London South Bank 3; Sheffield 4; Sheffield Hallam 8; Southampton 4; Staffordshire 5; Stirling 10; Strathclyde 7; Teesside 3; Trinity Saint David 4; Westminster 5; York 3.

Advice to applicants and planning the UCAS personal statement See **Computer Science and Information Technology**, **Engineering (Electrical and Electronic)** and **Appendix 3**.

Selection interviews Yes Cambridge, Manchester, Trinity Saint David; **Some** Bath, Cardiff; **No** Bradford, East Anglia, Hertfordshire, Huddersfield, Kent, Liverpool John Moores, Loughborough, Nottingham Trent, Sheffield Hallam, Westminster.

Interview advice and questions See **Computer Science and Information Technology**, **Engineering (Electrical and Electronic)** and Chapter 5.

Reasons for rejection (non-academic) Lack of understanding that the course involves engineering. See also **Computer Science and Information Technology** and **Engineering (Electrical and Electronic)**.

AFTER-RESULTS ADVICE
Offers to applicants repeating A-levels Higher Strathclyde; Warwick; York; **Possibly higher** City; Sheffield; **Same** Bath; Birmingham; Coventry; East Anglia; Huddersfield; Liverpool John Moores; London South Bank; Loughborough; Teesside; **No** Cambridge.

GRADUATE DESTINATIONS AND EMPLOYMENT (2016/17 HESA)
Software Engineering graduates surveyed 690 **Employed** 460 **In voluntary employment** 10 **In further study** 90 **Assumed unemployed** 70

Career note Career opportunities extend right across the whole field of electronics, telecommunications, control and systems engineering.

OTHER DEGREE SUBJECTS FOR CONSIDERATION
Computer Science; Computing; Engineering (Aeronautical, Aerospace, Communications, Electrical and Electronic); Mathematics; Media (Systems/Engineering/Technology); Physics.

ENGINEERING (ELECTRICAL AND ELECTRONIC)

(see also **Engineering (acoustics And Sound)**, **Engineering (aeronautical And Aerospace)**, **Engineering (communications)**)

Electrical and Electronic Engineering courses provide a sound foundation for those looking for a career in electricity generation and transmission, communications or control systems, including robotics. All courses cater for students wanting a general or more specialist engineering education and options should be considered when choosing degree courses. These could include optoelectronics and optical communication systems, microwave systems, radio frequency engineering and circuit technology. Many courses have common first years, allowing transfer in Year 2. Electronic Engineering courses also overlap closely with Information Technology and Information Systems Engineering, which involves electronic and digital information. This includes the internet and mobile phones. Most institutions have good industrial contacts and applicants should look closely at sandwich courses.

Most courses offer BEng and MEng degrees. MEng confers the minimum requirements to take the Initial Professional Development (IPD) training with an employer in order to obtain Chartered Engineer status, while the BEng does not. However, students taking a BEng may be able to switch onto an MEng course, as the first three years of an MEng are broadly similar to a BEng. Another route for BEng students is to subsequently undertake an MSc, which also allows access to IPD and Chartered Engineer status.

Engineering Council statement See **Engineering/Engineering Sciences**.

Useful websites www.theiet.org; www.engc.org.uk

NB The points totals shown to the left of the institutions are for ease of reference only. It must not be assumed that Tariff points are always used by institutions or that they can be substituted for an offer in grades. The level of an offer is not necessarily indicative of the quality of a course.

COURSE OFFERS INFORMATION
Subject requirements/preferences See **Engineering/Engineering Sciences**. Offers shown below refer to BEng or BSc courses unless otherwise stated; BSc only appears as an abbreviation if the course is offered at the same institution as a BEng with different requirements.

Your target offers and examples of degree courses
160 pts   Cambridge – A*A*A incl maths+phys +interview +ENGAA (Eng (Elec Inf Sci/Elec Electron Eng)) (IB 42–40 pts HL 776)
          Oxford – A*A*A incl maths+phys +interview +PAT (Elec Eng) (IB 40 pts HL 776 incl 7 maths+phys)

152 pts   **Imperial London** – A*AA incl maths+phys +interview (Elec Electron Eng Mgt (MEng); Electron Inf Eng; Electron Inf Eng (MEng) (St Abrd)) (IB 38 pts HL 6 maths+phys); A*AA–A*A*A incl maths+phys +interview (Elec Electron Eng (MEng)) (IB 38–39 pts HL 6 maths+phys)

   Manchester – A*AA incl maths +interview (Comp Sys Eng) (IB 37 pts HL 766 incl 7 maths)

   Southampton – A*AA incl maths+phys (Electron Eng Wrlss Comms (MEng)) (IB 38 pts HL 18 pts incl 6 maths+phys); A*AA incl maths+phys/fmaths/tech (Electron Eng Artif Intel (MEng); Electron Eng Comp Sys (MEng); Electron Eng Mbl Scr Sys (MEng); Electron Eng Nanotech (MEng)) (IB 38 pts HL 18 pts incl 6 maths+phys)

144 pts   **Bath** – A*AB/AAA/AAB +aEPQ incl maths+sci/tech (Electron Sys Eng (MEng)) (IB 36 pts HL 765/666 incl 6 maths+sci/tech); A*AB/AAA incl maths+sci/tech (Electron Eng Spc Sci Tech) (IB 36 pts HL 666/765 incl 6 maths+sci/tech); AAA/AAB +aEPQ incl maths+sci/tech (Elec Electron Eng; Elec Electron Eng (MEng); Elec Pwr Eng (MEng); Electron Sys Eng) (IB 36 pts HL 666/765 incl 6 maths+sci/tech); AAA–AAB +aEPQ incl maths+sci/tech (Elec Pwr Eng) (IB 36 pts HL 666/765 incl 6 maths+sci/tech)

   Bristol – AAA incl maths (Elec Electron Eng (MEng)) (IB 36 pts HL 18 pts incl 6 maths)

   Exeter – AAA incl maths+sci (Electron Eng (MEng)) (IB 36 pts HL 666 incl maths+sci)

   Glasgow – AAA incl maths+mus+phys (Electron Mus (MEng)) (IB 38 pts HL 666 incl maths+mus+phys); AAA incl maths+phys (Electron Elec Eng (MEng)) (IB 38 pts HL 666 incl maths+phys)

   Leeds – AAA incl maths (Electron Comms Eng; Electron Elec Eng; Electron Eng (MEng)) (IB 35 pts HL 18 pts incl 5 maths)

   London (UCL) – AAA incl maths (Eng (Electron Elec)) (IB 38 pts HL 18 pts incl 6 maths)

   Loughborough – AAA incl maths+comp sci/fmaths/phys (Electron Elec Eng (MEng)) (IB 37 pts HL 666 incl maths+comp sci/phys); AAA incl maths+sci/tech/fmaths (Electron Comp Sys Eng (MEng)) (IB 37 pts HL 666 incl maths+sci)

   Queen's Belfast – AAA incl maths+sci/tech/fmaths (Elec Electron Eng (MEng)) (IB 36 pts HL 666 incl maths+sci)

   Sheffield – AAA/AAB +aEPQ incl maths+phys/chem/electron (Electron Elec Eng Modn Lang (MEng)) (IB 36 pts HL 6 maths+phys/chem/electron); AAA/AAB +aEPQ incl maths+phys/chem/electron +interview (Electron Comms Eng (MEng)) (IB 36 pts HL 6 maths+phys/chem/electron); AAA/AAB +aEPQ incl maths+sci/electron (Elec Eng (MEng); Electron Comp Eng (MEng); Microelec (MEng)) (IB 36 pts HL 6 maths+sci/electron); AAA–AAB +aEPQ incl maths+sci/electron (Electron Eng (MEng)) (IB 36 pts HL 6 maths+sci/electron)

   Southampton – AAA incl maths+phys/electron/fmaths (Elec Eng) (IB 36 pts HL 18 pts incl 6 maths+phys); AAA incl maths+phys/fmaths/tech (Electron Eng) (IB 36 pts HL 18 pts incl 6 maths+phys)

   Warwick – AAA incl maths+phys (Electron Eng) (IB 38 pts HL 6 maths+phys)

   York – AAA incl maths (Electron Eng (MEng); Electron Eng Nanotech (MEng)) (IB 36 pts HL 6 maths); AAA incl maths+interview (Electron Comm Eng (MEng)) (IB 36 pts HL 6 maths)

136 pts   **Birmingham** – AAB incl maths+sci (Electron Elec Eng) (IB 32 pts HL 665 incl maths)

   Dyson – AAB incl maths+sci/tech/eng (Eng Tech) (IB 34 pts HL 665 incl maths+sci/tech/eng)

   Glasgow – AAB incl maths+mus+phys (Electron Mus) (IB 36 pts HL 665 incl maths+mus+phys); AAB incl maths+phys (Electron Elec Eng) (IB 36 pts HL 665 incl maths+phys)

   Lancaster – AAB incl maths+physl sci (Electron Elec Eng; Electron Elec Eng (MEng)) (IB 35 pts HL 16 pts incl 6 maths+physl sci)

   Liverpool – AAB incl maths+sci (Elec Eng Electron (MEng)) (IB 35 pts HL 5 maths+sci)

   London (King's) – AAB (Electron Eng) (IB 35 pts HL 665 incl 6 maths)

   Manchester – AAB incl maths+phys/electron/fmaths/chem+interview (Elec Electron Eng) (IB 35 pts HL 6 maths+phys/chem)

   Newcastle – AAB incl maths+phys/chem/electron (Electron Comms (MEng) (Yr Abrd/Ind)) (IB 37 pts HL 6 maths+phys/chem)

   Sheffield – AAB/ABB +bEPQ incl maths+phys/chem/electron +interview (Electron Comms Eng) (IB 34 pts HL 6/5 maths+phys/chem/electron); AAB/ABB +bEPQ incl maths+sci/

electron (Elec Eng) (IB 34 pts HL 6 maths 5 sci/electron); AAB incl maths+sci/electron (Electron Eng) (IB 34 pts HL 6 maths 5 sci/electron)

Surrey – AAA–AAB incl maths+phys/electron/comp/fmaths (Electron Eng (MEng); Electron Eng Comp Sys (MEng)) (IB 34 pts)

128 pts **Aberdeen** – ABB incl maths+phys/des tech/eng (Elec Electron Eng (MEng)) (IB 34 pts HL 6 maths+phys)

Brunel – ABB incl maths+sci/geog/env/comp/des tech (Electron Elec Eng (MEng)) (IB 31 pts HL 5 maths+sci/geog/env/comp/des tech); ABB incl maths+sci/geog/env/des tech (Electron Comp Eng (MEng)) (IB 31 pts HL 6 maths 5 sci/geog/des tech)

City – ABB incl maths 128 pts (Elec Electron Eng (MEng)) (IB 34 pts HL 6 maths)

Edinburgh – AAA–ABB incl maths (Electron Elec Eng) (IB 37–32 pts HL 666–555 incl maths); (Electron Comp Sci) (IB 37–32 pts HL 666–655 incl 6 maths); AAA–ABB incl maths+phys/eng/des tech (Elec Mech Eng) (IB 37–32 pts HL 666–555 incl maths+phys/des tech)

Exeter – AAA–ABB incl maths+sci (Electron Eng (Yr Ind)) (IB 34–32 pts HL 665–655 incl maths+sci)

Kent – ABB incl maths+sci/tech +interview (Electron Comms Eng (MEng)) (IB 34 pts HL 15 pts incl 5 maths+sci)

Leicester – ABB/BBB +bEPQ incl maths+physl sci (Electron Elec Eng) (IB 30 pts HL 5 maths+phys)

Liverpool – ABB incl maths+sci (Elec Electron Eng; Elec Eng Electron (Yr Ind)) (IB 35 pts HL 5 maths+sci)

London (QM) – ABB incl maths+sci (Elec Electron Eng; Electron Eng Telecomm) (IB 32 pts HL 655 incl maths+sci)

Loughborough – ABB incl maths+sci/tech/fmaths (Electron Comp Sys Eng) (IB 34 pts HL 655 incl maths+sci)

Newcastle – ABB incl maths+phys/chem/electron (Elec Electron Eng; Electron Comms; Electron Comp Eng) (IB 32 pts HL 5 maths+phys/chem)

Nottingham – AAA–ABB incl maths+sci/electron (Elec Electron Eng; Elec Eng; Electron Comp Eng; Electron Eng) (IB 36–32 pts HL 5 maths+sci)

Plymouth – B maths+sci/tech 128 pts incl maths+sci/tech (Elec Electron Eng (MEng)) (IB 32 pts HL 5 maths+sci/tech)

Queen's Belfast – ABB incl maths+sci/tech/fmaths (Elec Electron Eng) (IB 33 pts HL 655 incl maths+sci)

Surrey – AAB–ABB incl maths+phys/electron/comp/fmaths (Electron Eng; Electron Eng Comp Sys) (IB 34–32 pts)

York – ABB incl maths (Electron Eng; Electron Eng Nanotech) (IB 34 pts HL 6 maths); ABB incl maths+interview (Electron Comm Eng) (IB 34 pts HL 6 maths)

120 pts **Aston** – ABB–BBB incl maths+physl sci/tech (Elec Electron Eng (MEng)) (IB 31 pts HL 555 incl maths+phys)

Bangor – C maths+phys/electron 120 pts incl maths+phys/electron (Electron Eng (MEng)) (HL 5 maths+phys)

Brunel – BBB incl maths+sci/tech (Electron Elec Eng Comm Sys) (IB 30 pts HL 5 maths+sci/tech)

Cardiff – ABB–BBB incl maths (Elec Electron Eng) (IB 34–32 pts HL 655 incl maths)

City – BBB incl maths 120 pts (Elec Electron Eng) (IB 32 pts HL 5 maths)

Coventry – ABB–BBB incl maths+sci/des tech/electron/eng (Elec Electron Eng) (IB 29 pts)

Derby – C maths 120 pts incl maths+sci/tech (Elec Electron Eng)

Essex – BBB (Comp Electron) (IB 30 pts HL 555); BBB incl maths (Electron Eng) (IB 30 pts HL 555 incl maths)

Hull – BBB incl maths 120 pts (Elec Electron Eng (MEng)) (IB 30 pts HL 5 maths)

Kent – BBB incl maths+sci +interview (Electron Comms Eng) (IB 34 pts HL 15 pts incl 5 maths+sci)

London South Bank – BBB incl maths+physl sci 120–128 pts (Elec Electron Eng)

Northumbria – 120 pts incl maths+sci/tech/comp sci (Elec Electron Eng)

Plymouth – C maths+sci/tech 120 pts incl maths+sci/tech (Elec Electron Eng) (IB 30 pts HL 4 maths+sci/tech)

Strathclyde – AAB–BBB incl maths+phys +interview (Electron Dig Sys (MEng)) (IB 36 pts HL 6 maths+phys); ABB–BBB incl maths+phys +interview (Electron Elec Eng) (IB 32 pts HL 5 maths+phys)

Sussex – ABB–BBB incl maths (Elec Electron Eng) (IB 32–30 pts HL 5 maths)

Swansea – ABB–BBB incl maths (Electron Elec Eng) (IB 32 pts)

Ulster – BBB incl sci/maths/tech/eng (Electron Eng (Yr Ind)) (IB 26 pts HL 13 pts incl 5 maths+sci)

112 pts **Aston** – BBB–BBC incl maths+physl sci/tech (Electron Eng Comp Sci) (IB 29 pts HL 554 incl maths+phys); BBC incl maths+physl sci/tech (Elec Electron Eng) (IB 29 pts HL 554 incl maths+phys)

Bedfordshire – BBB–BBC 112 pts (Electron Eng)

Birmingham City – BBC incl maths 112 pts (Electron Eng) (IB 28 pts HL 5 maths)

Central Lancashire – 112 pts incl maths/phys/STEM (Electron Eng)

Chester – BBC incl maths+sci/geog/env/comp/des tech (Electron Elec Eng) (IB 28 pts HL 5 maths+physl sci)

De Montfort – 112 pts incl maths/phys (Elec Electron Eng) (IB 26 pts)

Glyndŵr – 112 pts incl maths/phys (Elec Electron Eng)

Greenwich – 112 pts incl maths/physl sci (Elec Electron Eng)

Heriot-Watt – BBC incl maths+phys (Comp Electron; Elec Electron Eng) (IB 29 pts HL 5 maths+phys)

Huddersfield – BBB–BBC incl maths+sci/tech 112–120 pts (Electron Comm Eng; Electron Eng)

Hull – BBC incl maths 112 pts (Elec Electron Eng) (IB 28 pts HL 5 maths)

Liverpool John Moores – BBC incl maths+sci/tech/eng/fmaths 112 pts (Elec Electron Eng) (HL 5 maths+phys)

Oxford Brookes – BBC 112 pts (Elec Mech Eng) (IB 30 pts)

Robert Gordon – BBC incl maths+phys/eng/des tech (Electron Elec Eng (MEng)) (IB 29 pts HL 6/5 maths+phys)

Sheffield Hallam – BBC 112 pts incl maths+sci (Elec Electron Eng)

Staffordshire – BBC incl maths/phys/eng 112 pts (Elec Electron Eng)

Sunderland – 112 pts incl maths/phys (Electron Elec Eng)

UWE Bristol – 112 pts incl maths+sci/tech/eng (Electron Eng) (HL 5 maths+sci/tech)

104 pts **Hertfordshire** – BCC incl maths+phys/tech/eng 104 pts (Elec Electron Eng)

Manchester Met – BBC–BCC incl maths+sci/eng/tech 104–112 pts (Elec Electron Eng) (IB 26 pts)

Robert Gordon – BCC incl maths+phys/eng/des tech (Electron Elec Eng) (IB 28–27 pts HL 65 maths+phys)

96 pts **Bangor** – C maths+phys/electron 96 pts incl maths+phys/elec/electron eng (Electron Eng) (HL 5 maths+phys); C maths+phys 96 pts (Comp Sys Eng) (HL 5 maths+phys)

Brighton – BBC–CCC incl maths+physl sci 96–112 pts (Elec Electron Eng) (IB 26 pts HL 5 maths+phys)

Chichester – BBC–CCC incl maths 96–112 pts (Electron Elec Eng) (IB 28 pts)

Edinburgh Napier – CCC incl maths+sci/tech (Electron Elec Eng) (IB 28 pts HL 654 incl sci/tech)

Portsmouth – 96–120 pts incl maths (Electron Eng) (IB 25 pts HL 5 maths)

Solent – 96–112 pts incl maths/sci (Electron Eng)

Teesside – C maths 96–112 pts incl maths +interview (Elec Electron Eng) (HL 5 maths)

88 pts **Glasgow Caledonian** – CCD incl maths+phys (Elec Pwr Eng) (IB 24 pts)

80 pts **South Wales** – BCC–CDD incl maths+sci/geog 80–104 pts (Elec Electron Eng) (IB 29 pts HL 5 maths+sci); BCC–CDD incl maths/sci/tech 80–104 pts (Ltg Des Tech) (IB 29 pts HL 5 maths/sci/tech)

Wolverhampton – CDD incl maths+sci/tech (Electron Telecomm Eng)

Alternative offers
See **Chapter 6** and **Appendix 1** for grades/UCAS Tariff points information for other examinations.

DEGREE APPRENTICESHIPS
Bolton (Elec Eng); Essex (Elec Sys Des); Chichester (Elec Tech Suppt Eng); Portsmouth (Elec Eng); Reading (Elec Eng).

EXAMPLES OF COLLEGES OFFERING COURSES IN THIS SUBJECT FIELD
Banbury and Bicester (Coll); Barking and Dagenham (Coll); Basingstoke (CT); Bedford (Coll); Birmingham Met (Coll); Blackburn (Coll); Blackpool and Fylde (Coll); Bournemouth and Poole (Coll); Bradford College UC; Canterbury (Coll); Carshalton (Coll); Chesterfield (Coll); Darlington (Coll); Doncaster (Coll); Dudley (Coll); Ealing, Hammersmith and West London (Coll); East Surrey (Coll); East Sussex (Coll); Exeter (Coll); Farnborough (CT); Furness (Coll); Gateshead (Coll); Gloucestershire (Coll); Gower Swansea (Coll); Hartlepool (CFE); Havering (Coll); Highbury Portsmouth (Coll); Hopwood Hall (Coll); Hull (Coll); Leeds City (Coll); Lincoln (Coll); Liverpool City (Coll); London City (Coll); London UCK (Coll); Loughborough (Coll); MidKent (Coll); Milton Keynes (Coll); Newcastle (Coll); North Lindsey (Coll); North Notts (Coll); North Warwickshire and South Leicestershire (Coll); Norwich City (Coll); Pembrokeshire (Coll); Plymouth City (Coll); Solihull (Coll); Southport (Coll); St Helens (Coll); Stephenson (Coll); Stockport (Coll); Stoke-on-Trent (Coll); Sunderland (Coll); Tameside (Coll); TEC Partnership; Tyne Coast (Coll); Uxbridge (Coll); Wakefield (Coll); Warrington and Vale Royal (Coll); Wigan and Leigh (Coll); York (Coll).

CHOOSING YOUR COURSE (SEE ALSO CH.1)
Universities and colleges teaching quality See www.qaa.ac.uk; https://unistats.ac.uk.

Top research universities and colleges (REF 2014) (Electrical and Electronic Engineering, Metallurgy and Materials) Leeds; London (QM) (Electron Elec Comp Eng); Oxford; Cambridge; Imperial London (Metal Mat); London (UCL); Sheffield (Electron Elec Comp Eng); Southampton.

Examples of sandwich degree courses Aston; Bath; Birmingham City; Brighton; Brunel; Cardiff; Central Lancashire; City; Coventry; Glasgow Caledonian; Greenwich; Hertfordshire; Huddersfield; Kent; Leicester; Liverpool; Liverpool John Moores; London (QM); London (RH); London South Bank; Loughborough; Manchester Met; Northumbria; Plymouth; Portsmouth; Queen's Belfast; Robert Gordon; Sheffield Hallam; South Wales; Staffordshire; Sunderland; Surrey; Teesside; Ulster; UWE Bristol; Westminster; Wolverhampton; York.

ADMISSIONS INFORMATION
Number of applicants per place (approx) Aston 6; Bangor 7; Bath 8; Birmingham 10; Birmingham City 11; Bradford (Elec Electron Eng) 8; Bristol 10; Cardiff 7; Central Lancashire 4; City 3; Derby 5; Dundee 9; Edinburgh Napier 7; Greenwich 10; Heriot-Watt 7; Hertfordshire 7; Huddersfield 3; Hull 5; Lancaster 7; Leeds 15; Leicester 8; Liverpool John Moores 2; London (UCL) 7; London South Bank 5; Manchester Met 5; Newcastle 3; Nottingham 14; Plymouth 22; Robert Gordon 3; Sheffield 6; Sheffield Hallam 2; South Wales 2; Southampton 8; Staffordshire 7; Strathclyde 7; Sunderland 6; Swansea 3; Teesside 4; Warwick 8; Westminster 5; York 5.

Advice to applicants and planning the UCAS personal statement Applicants should show enthusiasm for the subject, for example, through career ambitions, hobbies, work experience, attendance at appropriate events, competitions, etc, and evidence of good ability in mathematics and a scientific mind. Applicants should also show that they can think creatively and have the motivation to succeed on a demanding course. See also **Engineering/Engineering Sciences** and **Appendix 3**. **Bristol** Deferred entry accepted.

Selection interviews Yes Cambridge, Imperial London, Manchester, Oxford, Strathclyde; **Some** Bath, Cardiff, Leicester; **No** Aston, Bangor, Birmingham, Brighton, Bristol, Brunel, Central Lancashire, Derby, Dundee, Essex, Heriot-Watt, Hertfordshire, Huddersfield, Hull, Kent, Liverpool, Liverpool John Moores, London (UCL), Loughborough, Newcastle, Nottingham, Plymouth, Portsmouth, Southampton, Staffordshire, Sunderland, Surrey, UWE Bristol, Westminster.

Interview advice and questions Past questions have included: How does a combustion engine work? How does a trumpet work? What type of position do you hope to reach in five to 10 years' time? Could you sack an employee? What was your last physics practical? What did you learn from it? What are the methods of transmitting information from a moving object to a stationary observer? Wire bending exercise – you are provided with an accurate diagram of a shape that could be produced by bending a length of wire in a particular way. You are supplied with a pair of pliers and the exact length of wire required and you are given 10 minutes to reproduce as accurately as possible the shape drawn. A three-minute talk has to be given on one of six subjects (topics given several weeks before the interview), such as 'The best is the enemy of the good'. Is there a lesson here for British industry? 'I was asked to take my physics file and discuss some of my conclusions in certain experiments.' Explain power transmission through the National Grid. How would you explain power transmission to a friend who hasn't done physics? See also **Chapter 5**. **York** Technical questions asked.

Reasons for rejection (non-academic) Poor English. Inability to communicate. Frightened of technology or mathematics. Poor motivation and work ethic. Better suited to a less specialised engineering/science course. See also **Engineering/Engineering Sciences**.

AFTER-RESULTS ADVICE
Offers to applicants repeating A-levels Higher Brighton; Central Lancashire; Greenwich; Huddersfield; Newcastle; Queen's Belfast; Strathclyde; Warwick; **Possibly higher** Aston; City; Hertfordshire; London Met; Sheffield; **Same** Bangor; Bath; Birmingham; Cardiff; Coventry; Derby; Dundee; Hull; Leeds; Liverpool; Liverpool John Moores; London South Bank; Loughborough; Northumbria; Nottingham; Robert Gordon; Southampton; Staffordshire; Wolverhampton; York; **No** Cambridge; Glasgow.

GRADUATE DESTINATIONS AND EMPLOYMENT (2016/17 HESA)
Graduates surveyed 3,140 **Employed** 2,045 **In voluntary employment** 65 **In further study** 590 **Assumed unemployed** 185

Career note Electrical and electronic engineering is divided into two main fields – heavy current (electrical machinery, distribution systems, generating stations) and light current (computers, control engineering, telecommunications). Opportunities exist with many commercial organisations.

OTHER DEGREE SUBJECTS FOR CONSIDERATION
Computer Science; Engineering (Aeronautical, Communications, Computer, Control); Mathematics; Physics.

ENGINEERING (MANUFACTURING AND PRODUCTION)
(see also **Engineering/Engineering Sciences**)

Manufacturing engineering is sometimes referred to as production engineering. It is a branch of the subject concerned with management aspects of engineering such as industrial organisation, purchasing, and the planning and control of operations. Manufacturing Engineering courses are therefore geared to providing the student with a broad-based portfolio of knowledge in both the technical and business areas. Mechanical, product and design engineers develop systems and production processes relating to the overall progress and management of a product from its design to its final completion, including the materials used, the efficiency of the production line and development costs. For those students from an artistic background who wish to combine their design skills with the technical aspects of engineering, the BA Industrial Design and Technology course at Brunel University London is ideal. This course is taught by a cross-disciplinary team including mechanical and electrical engineers, practical designers and psychologists, and students are expected to discuss solutions to design problems. As in all Engineering courses, those offering industrial placements through sandwich courses provide many financial benefits (see Chapter 1).

Most courses offer BEng and MEng degrees. MEng confers the minimum requirements to take the Initial Professional Development (IPD) training with an employer in order to obtain Chartered Engineer status, while the BEng does not. However, students taking a BEng may be able to switch onto an MEng course, as the first three years of an MEng are broadly similar to a BEng. Another route for BEng students is to subsequently undertake an MSc, which also allows access to IPD and Chartered Engineer status.

Useful websites www.engc.org.uk; www.imeche.org; www.theiet.org; www.semta.org.uk

NB The points totals shown to the left of the institutions are for ease of reference only. It must not be assumed that Tariff points are always used by institutions or that they can be substituted for an offer in grades. The level of an offer is not necessarily indicative of the quality of a course.

COURSE OFFERS INFORMATION
Subject requirements/preferences See **Engineering/Engineering Sciences**. Offers shown below refer to BEng or BSc courses unless otherwise stated; BSc only appears as an abbreviation if the course is offered at the same institution as a BEng with different requirements.

Your target offers and examples of degree courses
160 pts **Cambridge** – A*A*A incl maths+phys +interview +ENGAA (Eng (Manuf Eng)) (IB 42–40 pts HL 776)
152 pts **Bath** – A*AA/AAA +aEPQ incl maths+phys (Mech Eng Manuf Mgt (MEng)) (IB 36 pts HL 766 incl maths+phys)
144 pts **Glasgow** – AAA incl maths+phys (Prod Des Eng (MEng)) (IB 38 pts HL 666 incl maths+phys)
Manchester – AAA incl maths/phys/chem +interview (Mat Sci Eng (MEng)) (IB 36 pts HL 666)
Warwick – AAA incl maths+phys (Manuf Mech Eng) (IB 38 pts HL 6 maths+phys)
136 pts **Liverpool** – AAB/ABB +aEPQ incl maths+sci (Ind Des (MEng)) (IB 35 pts HL 5 maths+phys)
Newcastle – AAB incl maths+chem/phys/fmaths +interview (Mech Des Manuf Eng (MEng)) (IB 34 pts HL 6 maths+phys/chem)
Nottingham – AAB incl maths+phys (Manuf Eng) (IB 34 pts HL 6 maths)
128 pts **Brunel** – ABB incl art/des/tech +interview +portfolio (Ind Des Tech) (IB 31 pts HL 5 art/des/tech)
Liverpool – ABB/BBB +aEPQ incl maths+sci/des tech (Ind Des) (IB 33 pts HL 5 maths+phys)
Loughborough – ABB incl maths+phys/des/eng +interview (Manuf Eng) (IB 34 pts HL 655)
120 pts **Derby** – C maths 120 pts (Mech Manuf Eng)
South Wales – BBB incl maths+sci +interview (Mech Eng) (IB 29 pts HL 5 maths+sci)
Strathclyde – AAB–BBB (Prod Des Eng (MEng)) (IB 36 pts HL 5 maths+phys); ABB–BBB (Prod Des Eng) (IB 34 pts HL 5 maths/phys)
112 pts **Aston** – BBC incl sci/tech (Prod Des Mgt) (IB 29 pts HL 554 incl sci/tech)
Liverpool John Moores – BBC 112 pts (Prod Des Eng)
Trinity Saint David – 112 pts (Mech Manuf Eng)
96 pts **Solent** – CCC 96–112 pts (Eng Des Manuf) (IB 28 pts)
80 pts **Portsmouth** – 80–96 pts incl maths (Mech Manuf Eng) (IB 25 pts)

Alternative offers
See **Chapter 6** and **Appendix 1** for grades/UCAS Tariff points information for other examinations.

DEGREE APPRENTICESHIPS
Robert Gordon (Eng Des Manuf, Eng Instr Measur Cont); Chichester (Manuf Eng).

EXAMPLES OF COLLEGES OFFERING COURSES IN THIS SUBJECT FIELD
Basingstoke (CT); Birmingham Met (Coll); Blackpool and Fylde (Coll); Bristol City (Coll); Central Bedfordshire (Coll); City and Islington (Coll); Darlington (Coll); Doncaster (Coll); Dudley (Coll); Exeter (Coll); Farnborough (CT); Hartlepool (CFE); Leeds City (Coll); Newcastle (Coll); North Warwickshire and South Leicestershire (Coll); Petroc; Solihull (Coll); Sunderland (Coll); Tyne Coast (Coll); Warwickshire (Coll); Weymouth (Coll); Wigan and Leigh (Coll).

CHOOSING YOUR COURSE (SEE ALSO CH.1)

Universities and colleges teaching quality See www.qaa.ac.uk; https://unistats.ac.uk.

Top research universities and colleges (REF 2014) See **Engineering (Aeronautical and Aerospace)**.

Examples of sandwich degree courses Aston; Bath; Brunel; Loughborough.

ADMISSIONS INFORMATION

Number of applicants per place (approx) Aston 6; Bath 10; Nottingham 6; Strathclyde 8; Warwick 8.

Advice to applicants and planning the UCAS personal statement Work experience or work shadowing in industry should be mentioned. See **Engineering/Engineering Sciences** and **Appendix 3**.

Selection interviews Yes Cambridge, Loughborough; **No** Nottingham, Strathclyde.

Interview advice and questions Past questions include: What is the function of an engineer? Describe something interesting you have recently done in your A-levels. What do you know about careers in manufacturing engineering? Discuss the role of women engineers in industry. Why is a disc brake better than a drum brake? Would you be prepared to make people redundant to improve the efficiency of a production line? See also **Chapter 5**.

Reasons for rejection (non-academic) Mature students failing to attend interview are rejected. One applicant produced a forged reference and was immediately rejected. See also **Engineering/ Engineering Sciences**.

AFTER-RESULTS ADVICE

Offers to applicants repeating A-levels Higher Strathclyde; **Same** Cambridge; Loughborough; Nottingham.

GRADUATE DESTINATIONS AND EMPLOYMENT (2016/17 HESA)

Production and Manufacturing Engineering graduates surveyed 570 **Employed** 370 **In voluntary employment** 5 **In further study** 90 **Assumed unemployed** 25

Career note Graduates with experience in both technical and business skills have the flexibility to enter careers in technology or business management.

OTHER DEGREE SUBJECTS FOR CONSIDERATION

Business Studies; Computer Science; Engineering (Electrical, Mechanical); Physics; Technology.

ENGINEERING (MECHANICAL)

(including Automotive Engineering, Mechatronics and Motorsport Engineering)

Mechanical engineering is one of the most wide-ranging engineering disciplines. All courses involve the design, installation and maintenance of equipment used in industry. While Automotive Engineering deals with all forms of transport, specialisms are also offered in Motorsport Engineering at several universities, such as in Mining Engineering at the University of Exeter. Several universities include a range of Engineering courses with a common first year allowing students to specialise from Year 2. Agricultural Engineering involves all aspects of off-road vehicle design and maintenance of other machinery used in agriculture.

Most courses offer BEng and MEng degrees. MEng confers the minimum requirements to take the Initial Professional Development (IPD) training with an employer in order to obtain Chartered Engineer status, while the BEng does not. However, students taking a BEng may be able to switch onto an MEng course, as the first three years of an MEng are broadly similar to a BEng. Another route for BEng students is to subsequently undertake an MSc, which also allows access to IPD and Chartered Engineer status.

Engineering Council statement: See **Engineering/Engineering Sciences**.

Useful websites www.imeche.org; www.engc.org.uk; http://iagre.org

NB The points totals shown to the left of the institutions are for ease of reference only. It must not be assumed that Tariff points are always used by institutions or that they can be substituted for an offer in grades. The level of an offer is not necessarily indicative of the quality of a course.

COURSE OFFERS INFORMATION

Subject requirements/preferences See **Engineering/Engineering Sciences**. Offers shown below refer to BEng or BSc courses unless otherwise stated; BSc only appears as an abbreviation if the course is offered at the same institution as a BEng with different requirements.

Your target offers and examples of degree courses

160 pts **Cambridge** – A*A*A incl maths+phys +interview +ENGAA (Eng (Mech Eng) (MEng)) (IB 42–40 pts HL 776)

Imperial London – A*A*A incl maths+phys +interview (Mech Eng (MEng)) (IB 40 pts HL 666 incl maths+phys)

Oxford – A*A*A incl maths+phys +interview +PAT (Mech Eng) (IB 40 pts HL 776 incl maths+phys)

152 pts **Bath** – A*AA–AAA +aEPQ incl maths+phys (Mech Auto Eng (MEng); Mech Eng (MEng)) (IB 36 pts HL 766 incl maths+phys)

Bristol – A*AA incl maths+phys (Mech Eng) (IB 38 pts HL 18 pts incl 76 maths+phys)

Leeds – A*AA incl maths+phys (Auto Eng; Mech Eng) (IB 36 pts HL 18 pts incl 6 maths+phys)

London (UCL) – A*AA incl maths+phys (Eng (Mech Bus Fin) (MEng)) (IB 39 pts HL 19 pts incl 7 maths+phys); (Eng (Mech) (MEng)) (IB 39 pts HL 19 pts incl maths+phys)

Loughborough – A*AA incl maths+phys +interview (Mech Eng (MEng)) (IB 38 pts HL 776 incl maths+phys)

Southampton – A*AA/A*AB +aEPQ incl maths+phys (Mech Eng (Aerosp) (MEng)) (IB 38 pts HL 18 pts incl 6 maths+phys); A*AA incl maths+phys (Mech Eng (Eng Mgt) (MEng)) (IB 38 pts HL 18 pts incl 6 maths+phys); A*AA–A*AB+aEPQ incl maths+phys (Mech Eng; Mech Eng (Auto) (MEng); Mech Eng (Biomed Eng) (MEng); Mech Eng (Mat) (MEng); Mech Eng (Mecha) (MEng); Mech Eng (Nvl Eng) (MEng); Mech Eng (Sust Ener Sys) (MEng)) (IB 38 pts HL 18 pts incl 6 maths+phys)

144 pts **Bath** – AAA–AAB+aEPQ incl maths+phys (Integ Mech Elec Eng (MEng)) (IB 36 pts HL 666/765 incl 6 maths+phys)

Birmingham – AAA incl maths (Mech Eng (MEng)) (IB 32 pts HL 666 incl maths)

Exeter – AAA incl maths+sci (Mech Eng (MEng) (Yr Ind)) (IB 36 pts HL 666 incl maths+sci); AAA incl sci+maths (Mech Eng (MEng)) (IB 36 pts HL 6 sci+maths)

Leeds – AAA incl maths (Mecha Robot) (IB 35 pts HL 18 pts incl 5 maths)

Liverpool – AAA incl maths+sci (Mech Eng (MEng)) (IB 35 pts HL 5 maths+phys)

London (QM) – AAA incl maths+phys/chem (Mech Eng (MEng)) (IB 36 pts HL 666 maths+phys/chem)

Manchester – AAA incl maths+phys (Mech Eng (MEng)) (IB 36 pts HL 666 incl maths+phys)

Nottingham – A*AA–AAA incl maths (Mech Eng (MEng)) (IB 38–36 pts)

Queen's Belfast – AAA incl maths+sci/fmaths (Mech Eng (MEng)) (IB 36 pts HL 666 incl maths+sci)

Sheffield – AAA incl maths+phys/chem (Mech Eng; Mech Eng (MEng); Mech Eng Fr/Ger/Ital (MEng)) (IB 36 pts HL 6 maths+phys/chem)

Warwick – AAA incl maths+phys (Auto Eng; Manuf Mech Eng; Mech Eng) (IB 38 pts HL 6 maths+phys)

York – AAA incl maths (Micro-Mech Eng; Robot Eng) (IB 36 pts HL 6 maths)

136 pts **Birmingham** – AAB incl maths (Mech Eng; Mech Eng (Auto)) (IB 32 pts HL 665 incl maths)

Dyson – AAB incl maths+sci/tech/eng (Eng Tech) (IB 34 pts HL 665 incl maths+sci/tech/eng)

Glasgow – AAB incl maths+phys (Mech Des Eng; Mech Eng; Mech Eng Aero) (IB 36 pts HL 665 incl maths+phys)

Glasgow (SA) – AAB incl maths+phys (Prod Des Eng) (IB 36 pts HL 665 incl maths+phys)

Huddersfield – AAB incl maths+sci/tech 136 pts (Auto Mtrspo Eng (MEng); Mech Eng (MEng))

Lancaster – AAB incl maths+physl sci (Mech Eng (MEng)) (IB 35 pts HL 16 pts incl 6 maths+physl sci); (Mech Eng) (IB 35 pts HL16 pts incl 6 maths+physl sci)

Leicester – AAB incl maths+physl sci (Mech Eng (MEng)) (IB 32 pts HL 6/5 maths+phys)

Liverpool – AAB incl maths+sci/tech (Mecha Robot Sys (MEng)) (IB 35 pts HL 5 maths+sci)

London (QM) – AAB incl math+phys/chem (Mech Eng) (IB 34 pts HL 665)

Loughborough – AAB incl maths+phys (Mech Eng) (IB 35 pts HL 665 incl maths+phys)

Manchester – AAB incl maths+phys (Mech Eng; Mech Eng Mgt) (IB 35 pts HL 665 incl maths+phys); AAB incl maths+phys/electron/fmaths +interview (Mecha Eng) (IB 35 pts HL 6 maths+phys)

Nottingham – AAB incl maths (Mech Eng) (IB 34 pts)

Surrey – AAA–AAB incl maths+phys (Auto Eng (MEng)) (IB 34 pts)

Ulster – AAB incl maths+sci/tech/eng (Mech Eng (MEng)) (IB 28 pts HL 14 pts incl 6 maths 5 sci)

128 pts **Aberdeen** – ABB incl maths+phys/des tech/eng (Mech Eng Mgt (MEng)) (IB 34 pts HL 6 maths+phys)

Brunel – ABB incl maths+sci/geog/env/comp/des tech (Mech Eng (MEng)) (IB 31 pts HL 5 maths+sci/geog/env/comp/des tech)

Cardiff – AAB–ABB incl maths (Mech Eng) (IB 34–32 pts HL 666–665 incl maths)

City – ABB incl maths 128 pts (Mech Eng (MEng)) (IB 34 pts HL 6 maths/sci)

Edinburgh – AAA–ABB incl maths+phys/eng/des tech (Elec Mech Eng; Mech Eng) (IB 37–32 pts HL 666–555 incl maths+phys/des tech)

Exeter – AAB–ABB incl phys/chem+sci (Min Eng) (IB 34–32 pts HL 5 phys/chem/maths+sci); AAB–ABB incl sci+maths (Mech Eng) (IB 34–32 pts HL 5 sci+maths)

Leicester – ABB incl maths+physl sci (Mech Eng) (IB 30 pts HL 5 maths+phys)

Liverpool – ABB incl maths+sci (Mech Eng) (IB 33 pts HL 5 maths+phys)

Liverpool John Moores – ABB 128 pts (Mech Eng (MEng)) (HL 6 maths+phys)

Newcastle – ABB incl maths+phys/chem/fmaths (Mech Eng) (IB 32 pts HL 5 maths+phys/chem)

Oxford Brookes – B maths+phys 128 pts (Mech Eng (MEng)) (IB 32 pts HL 5 maths+phys)

Queen's Belfast – ABB incl maths+sci/tech/fmaths (Mech Eng) (IB 33 pts HL 655 incl maths+sci)

Salford – B maths+sci 128 pts incl maths+sci (Mech Eng (MEng)) (IB 32 pts HL 6 maths+phys)

Sheffield Hallam – ABB incl maths+sci 128 pts incl maths+sci (Mech Eng (MEng))

Surrey – ABB incl maths+phys (Auto Eng) (IB 34–32 pts); ABB incl maths+phys (Mech Eng) (IB 32 pts)

Swansea – AAB–ABB incl maths (Mech Eng (MEng)) (IB 34 pts)

120 pts **Aberdeen** – BBB incl maths+phys/des tech/eng (Eng (Mech)) (IB 32 pts HL 5 maths+phys)

Aston – ABB–BBB incl maths+physl sci/tech (Mech Eng (MEng)) (IB 31 pts HL 555 incl maths+phys)

Brunel – BBB incl maths+sci/geog/env/comp/des tech (Mech Eng) (IB 30 pts HL 5 maths+sci/geog/env/comp/des tech)

City – BBB incl maths 120 pts (Mech Eng) (IB 32 pts HL 5 sci)

Coventry – ABB–BBB incl maths+sci/tech/eng (Mech Eng; Mtrspo Eng) (IB 31 pts)

Derby – C maths+sci/tech 120 pts (Mech Eng; Mtrspo Eng)

Essex – BBB incl maths (Mecha Sys) (IB 30 pts HL 555 incl maths)

Hull – C maths 120 pts (Mech Med Eng (MEng)) (IB 30 pts HL 5 maths)

London South Bank – BBB incl maths/physl sci (Mech Eng)

Northumbria – 120 pts incl maths+sci/tech (Mech Auto Eng; Mech Eng)

Oxford Brookes – BBB incl maths+sci 120 pts (Auto Eng; Mech Eng; Mtrspo Eng) (IB 31 pts HL 5 maths+phys)

Portsmouth – 120–144 pts incl maths (Mech Eng (MEng)) (IB 28–27 pts HL 6 maths)

Robert Gordon – BBB incl maths+phys/eng/des tech (Mech Elec Eng (MEng); Mech Eng (MEng)) (IB 30 pts HL 6/5 maths+phys)

South Wales – BBB incl maths+sci +interview (Mech Eng) (IB 29 pts HL 5 maths+sci)

Strathclyde – ABB–BBB incl maths+phys (Mech Eng) (IB 32 pts HL 5 maths+phys)

Sussex – ABB–BBB incl maths (Auto Eng; Mech Eng) (IB 32–30 pts HL 5 maths)

Swansea – ABB–BBB incl maths (Mech Eng) (IB 32 pts)

Ulster – BBB incl maths+sci/tech/eng (Mech Eng) (IB 26 pts HL 13 pts incl 5 maths+sci)

112 pts   **Aston** – BBB–BBC incl maths+physl sci/tech (Mech Eng) (IB 31 pts HL 555 incl maths+phys)

Birmingham City – BBC incl maths 112 pts (Auto Eng; Mech Eng) (IB 28 pts HL 5 maths)

Bradford – BBC incl maths 112 pts (Mech Eng) (HL 5 maths)

De Montfort – C maths/phys 112 pts incl maths/phys (Mech Eng; Mecha) (IB 26 pts)

Glyndŵr – BBC 112 pts incl maths/sci (Aero Mech Eng)

Greenwich – 112 pts incl maths/physl sci (Mech Eng)

Heriot-Watt – BBC incl maths+phys (Mech Ener Eng; Mech Eng) (IB 30 pts HL 5 maths+phys)

Huddersfield – BBB–BBC incl maths+sci/tech 112–120 pts (Auto Mtrspo Eng; Mech Eng)

Hull – 112 pts (Mech Eng) (IB 28 pts HL 5 maths); BBC incl maths 112 pts (Mech Eng (MEng)) (IB 28 pts HL 5 maths); C maths 112 pts (Mech Med Eng) (IB 28 pts HL 5 maths)

Kingston – BBC incl maths/phys/chem 112 pts (Mech Eng) (IB 26 pts HL 4 maths+sci); BBC incl maths/phys/chem 112 pts incl maths+sci (Mech Eng (Auto)) (IB 26 pts HL 4 maths+sci)

Lincoln – BBC incl maths (Mech Eng) (IB 29 pts HL 5 maths)

Liverpool John Moores – BBC incl maths+sci/tech/eng 112 pts (Mech Eng) (IB 26 pts HL 5 maths+phys)

Oxford Brookes – BBC 112 pts (Elec Mech Eng) (IB 30 pts)

Robert Gordon – BBC incl maths+phys/eng/des tech (Mech Elec Eng; Mech Eng) (IB 29 pts HL 6/5 maths+phys)

Sheffield Hallam – 112 pts incl maths+sci (Mech Eng); 112 pts incl maths+sci/eng/tech (Auto Eng)

Staffordshire – BBC 112 pts (Auto Mtrspo Eng); BBC incl maths/phys/eng 112 pts (Mech Eng)

Sunderland – BBC incl maths/phys 112 pts incl maths/phys (Auto Eng; Mech Eng)

Trinity Saint David – 112 pts incl maths/phys (Auto Eng; Mech Eng; Mtrcycl Eng; Mtrspo Eng)

UWE Bristol – C maths 112 pts (Auto Eng; Mech Eng) (HL 5 maths)

104 pts   **Anglia Ruskin** – 104 pts incl maths (Mech Eng) (IB 24 pts)

Brighton – BBB–BCC incl maths+physl sci 104–120 pts (Auto Eng (MEng)) (IB 26 pts HL 5 maths+phys)

Central Lancashire – 104–112 pts incl maths+phys/STEM (Mtrspo Eng) (HL 5 maths+phys/STEM)

Dundee – BBB–BCC incl maths+sci/eng (Mech Eng) (IB 30 pts HL 555 incl maths+sci/eng)

Hertfordshire – BCC incl maths+phys/tech/eng 104 pts incl maths+phys/tech/eng (Auto Eng; Auto Eng Mtrspo; Mech Eng)

Manchester Met – BBC–BCC incl maths+sci/eng/tech 104–112 pts (Mech Eng) (IB 26 pts HL 5 maths+sci/eng/tech)

Plymouth – 104–120 pts incl maths+sci/tech (Mech Eng; Mech Eng Cmpstes) (IB 30–26 pts HL 5 maths 4 sci/tech)

Portsmouth – 104–120 pts incl maths (Mech Eng) (IB 26 pts HL 5 maths)

Robert Gordon – BCC incl maths+phys/eng/des tech (Mech Off Eng) (IB 28–27 pts HL 6/5 maths+phys)

96 pts   **Bolton** – 96 pts incl maths+phys (Auto Perf Eng (Mtrspo)); 96 pts incl maths+sci (Mech Eng; Mtrspo Tech)

Brighton – BBC–CCC incl maths+physl sci 96–112 pts (Auto Eng; Mech Eng) (IB 26 pts HL 5 maths+phys)

Chichester – BBC–CCC incl maths 96–112 pts (Mech Eng) (IB 28 pts)

Edinburgh Napier – CCC incl maths+sci/tech (Mech Eng) (IB 28 pts HL 654 incl sci/tech)

Solent – CCC 96–112 pts (Eng Des Manuf) (IB 28 pts)

Teesside – 96–112 pts incl maths (Mech Eng) (HL 5 maths)

Wolverhampton – CCC/BCD incl maths+sci/tech 96 pts (Auto Eng; Mech Eng)

88 pts   **Glasgow Caledonian** – CCD incl maths+phys (Comp Aid Mech Eng; Mech Sys Eng) (IB 24 pts)

West Scotland – CCD incl maths+phys (Mech Eng) (IB 28 pts)

80 pts   **Portsmouth** – 80–96 pts incl maths (Mech Manuf Eng) (IB 25 pts)

Alternative offers

See **Chapter 6** and **Appendix 1** for grades/UCAS Tariff points information for other examinations.

EXAMPLES OF COLLEGES OFFERING COURSES IN THIS SUBJECT FIELD

Banbury and Bicester (Coll); Barking and Dagenham (Coll); Barnet and Southgate (Coll); Basingstoke (CT); Bath (Coll); Bedford (Coll); Blackburn (Coll); Blackpool and Fylde (Coll); Bradford College UC; Bridgwater and Taunton (Coll); Canterbury (Coll); Chesterfield (Coll); Cornwall (Coll); Darlington (Coll); Doncaster (Coll); Dudley (Coll); East Surrey (Coll); East Sussex (Coll); Exeter (Coll); Farnborough (CT); Furness (Coll); Gateshead (Coll); Gloucestershire (Coll); Gower Swansea (Coll); Hartlepool (CFE); Highbury Portsmouth (Coll); Lincoln (Coll); Loughborough (Coll); MidKent (Coll); Newcastle (Coll); North Lindsey (Coll); North Warwickshire and South Leicestershire (Coll); Norwich City (Coll); Pembrokeshire (Coll); Petroc; Plymouth City (Coll); South Devon (Coll); South Gloucestershire and Stroud (Coll); Southampton City (Coll); Southport (Coll); Stephenson (Coll); Tameside (Coll); TEC Partnership; Tyne Coast (Coll); Uxbridge (Coll); Wakefield (Coll); Wigan and Leigh (Coll); Wiltshire (Coll); Wirral Met (Coll); Yeovil (Coll).

CHOOSING YOUR COURSE (SEE ALSO CH.1)

Universities and colleges teaching quality See www.qaa.ac.uk; https://unistats.ac.uk.

Top research universities and colleges (REF 2014) See **Engineering (Aeronautical and Aerospace)**.

Examples of sandwich degree courses Aston; Bath; Birmingham City; Bradford; Brighton; Cardiff; Central Lancashire; City; Coventry; De Montfort; Glasgow Caledonian; Harper Adams; Hertfordshire; Huddersfield; Kingston; Leicester; Liverpool John Moores; London South Bank; Loughborough; Manchester Met; Northumbria; Oxford Brookes; Plymouth; Portsmouth; Queen's Belfast; Salford; Sheffield Hallam; South Wales; Staffordshire; Sunderland; Surrey; Teesside; Ulster; UWE Bristol; West Scotland; Wolverhampton.

ADMISSIONS INFORMATION

Number of applicants per place (approx) Aston 8; Bath 10; Birmingham 9; Bradford 4; Bristol 9; Cardiff 8; City 11; Dundee 9; Heriot-Watt 10; Hertfordshire 10; Huddersfield 1; Hull 5; Kingston 8; Lancaster 8; Leeds 15; Leicester 8; Liverpool John Moores 2; London (QM) 6; London (UCL) 10; London South Bank 4; Manchester Met 6, (Mech Eng) 6; Newcastle 4; Nottingham 7; Plymouth 12; Sheffield 7; South Wales 6; Southampton 9; Staffordshire 6; Strathclyde 6; Teesside 7; Warwick 8.

Advice to applicants and planning the UCAS personal statement Work experience. Hands-on skills. An interest in solving mathematical problems related to physical concepts. Enjoyment in designing mechanical devices or components. Interest in engines, structures, dynamics or fluid flow and efficient use of materials or energy. Apply to the Year in Industry Scheme (www.etrust.org.uk) for placement. Scholarships are available to supplement the scheme. See **Engineering/Engineering Sciences** and **Appendix 3**.

Misconceptions about this course Harper Adams Our engineering courses are not vocational training.

Selection interviews Yes Cambridge, Harper Adams, Imperial London, Loughborough, Oxford; **Some** Blackpool and Fylde (Coll), Cardiff, Leicester; **No** Aston, Birmingham, Bolton, Bradford, Brighton,

Bristol, Dundee, Hertfordshire, Huddersfield, Kingston, Leeds, Liverpool, Liverpool John Moores, London (QM), Manchester Met, Newcastle, Nottingham, Sheffield, Sheffield Hallam, Staffordshire, Strathclyde, Sunderland, Surrey.

Interview advice and questions Past questions include: What mechanical objects have you examined and/or tried to repair? How do you see yourself in five years' time? What do you imagine you would be doing (production, management or design engineering)? What engineering interests do you have? What qualities are required to become a successful mechanical engineer? Do you like sixth-form work? Describe the working of parts on an engineering drawing. How does a fridge work? What is design in the context of mechanical engineering? What has been your greatest achievement to date? What are your career plans? See also **Engineering/Engineering Sciences** and **Chapter 5.**

Reasons for rejection (non-academic) See **Engineering/Engineering Sciences**.

AFTER-RESULTS ADVICE
Offers to applicants repeating A-levels Higher Brighton; Kingston; Newcastle; Queen's Belfast; Swansea; Warwick; **Possibly higher** City; Huddersfield; **Same** Aston; Bath; Bradford; Bristol; Coventry; Derby; Dundee; Edinburgh Napier; Harper Adams; Heriot-Watt; Leeds (usually); Lincoln; Liverpool; Liverpool John Moores; London South Bank; Loughborough; Manchester Met; Northumbria; Nottingham; Oxford Brookes; Sheffield; Sheffield Hallam; Southampton; Staffordshire; Sunderland; Teesside; Wolverhampton; **No** Cambridge.

GRADUATE DESTINATIONS AND EMPLOYMENT (2016/17 HESA)
Graduates surveyed 4,675 **Employed** 2,980 **In voluntary employment** 95 **In further study** 875 **Assumed unemployed** 300

Career note Mechanical Engineering graduates have a wide choice of career options. Apart from design and development of plant and machinery, they are also likely to be involved in production processes and working at various levels of management. Mechanical engineers share interests such as structures and stress analysis with civil and aeronautical engineers, and electronics and computing with electrical and software engineers.

OTHER DEGREE SUBJECTS FOR CONSIDERATION
Engineering (Aeronautical/Aerospace, Building, Computer (Control, Software and Systems), Electrical/ Electronic, Manufacturing, Marine); Materials Science; Mathematics; Physics; Product Design; Technologies.

ENGINEERING (MEDICAL)
(including **Biomedical Engineering, Mechanical and Medical Engineering and Medical Physics;** see also **Biotechnology**)

Biomedical engineering lies at the interface between engineering, mathematics, physics, chemistry, biology and clinical practice. This makes it a branch of engineering that has the most direct effect on human health. It is a rapidly expanding interdisciplinary field that applies engineering principles and technology to medical and biological problems. Biomedical engineers work in fields as diverse as neurotechnology, fluid mechanics of the blood and respiratory systems, bone and joint biomechanics, biosensors, medical imaging, synthetic biology and biomaterials. These can lead to the creation of novel devices such as joint replacements and heart valves, new surgical instruments, rehabilitation protocols and even prosthetic limbs.

Useful websites www.assclinsci.org; www.ipem.ac.uk; www.healthcareers.nhs.uk

NB The points totals shown to the left of the institutions are for ease of reference only. It must not be assumed that Tariff points are always used by institutions or that they can be substituted for an offer in grades. The level of an offer is not necessarily indicative of the quality of a course.

COURSE OFFERS INFORMATION

Subject requirements/preferences GCSE/AL Subjects taken from mathematics, physics, chemistry and biology. Offers shown below refer to BEng or BSc courses unless otherwise stated; BSc only appears as an abbreviation if the course is offered at the same institution as a BEng with different requirements.

Your target offers and examples of degree courses

152 pts   Imperial London – A*AA incl maths+phys+fmaths/chem/biol +interview (Biomed Eng (MEng)) (IB 38 pts HL 666 incl maths+phys)

Leeds – A*AA incl maths+phys (Med Eng; Med Eng (MEng)) (IB 36 pts HL 18 pts incl 6 maths+phys)

144 pts   Glasgow – AAA incl maths+phys (Biomed Eng (MEng)) (IB 38 pts HL 666 incl maths+phys)

London (QM) – AAA incl maths+phys/chem (Biomed Eng (MEng)) (IB 36 pts HL 666 incl maths+phys/chem)

London (UCL) – AAA incl maths+phys (Med Phys (MSci)) (IB 38 pts HL 18 pts incl 6 maths+phys)

Queen's Belfast – AAA/A*AB incl maths+phys (Phys Med Apps (MSci)) (IB 36 pts HL 666 incl maths+phys)

Sheffield – AAA incl maths+sci (Bioeng (MEng)) (IB 36 pts HL 6 maths+sci)

York – AAA incl maths (Med Eng) (IB 36 pts HL 6 maths)

136 pts   Glasgow – AAB incl maths+phys (Biomed Eng) (IB 36 pts HL 665 incl maths+phys)

London (King's) – AAB incl maths+phys (Biomed Eng) (IB 35 pts HL 665 incl maths+phys)

London (QM) – AAB incl maths+phys/chem (Biomed Eng) (IB 34 pts HL 665 incl maths+phys/chem)

Sheffield – AAB incl maths+sci (Bioeng) (IB 34 pts HL 6 maths 5 sci)

Surrey – AAA–AAB incl maths+phys/sci (Biomed Eng (MEng)) (IB 34 pts HL 6 maths 5 phys/sci)

128 pts   Cardiff – AAB–ABB incl maths (Med Eng) (IB 34–32 pts HL 5 maths)

Kent – ABB incl maths+sci +interview (Biomed Eng) (IB 34 pts HL 15 pts incl 5 maths+sci)

Queen's Belfast – ABB incl maths+phys (Phys Med Apps) (IB 33 pts HL 655 incl maths+phys)

Reading – ABB incl maths+sci (Biomed Eng (MEng)) (IB 32 pts HL 5 maths+sci)

Surrey – AAB–ABB incl maths+phys+sci (Biomed Eng) (IB 34–32 pts HL 6 maths 5 phys/sci)

120 pts   City – BBB incl maths 120 pts (Biomed Eng) (IB 32 pts HL 5 maths)

Hull – C maths 120 pts (Mech Med Eng (MEng)) (IB 30 pts HL 5 maths)

Reading – BBB incl maths+sci (Biomed Eng) (IB 30 pts HL 5 maths+sci)

Swansea – ABB–BBB incl maths (Med Eng) (IB 32 pts HL 5 maths)

112 pts   Bradford – BBC incl maths 112 pts (Biomed Eng) (HL 5 maths)

Hull – C maths 112 pts (Mech Med Eng) (IB 28 pts HL 5 maths)

104 pts   Dundee – BBB–BCC incl maths+sci/eng (Biomed Eng) (IB 30 pts HL 555 incl maths+sci/eng)

Alternative offers
See **Chapter 6** and **Appendix 1** for grades/UCAS Tariff points information for other examinations.

CHOOSING YOUR COURSE (SEE ALSO CH.1)

Universities and colleges teaching quality See www.qaa.ac.uk; https://unistats.ac.uk.

Examples of sandwich degree courses Cardiff; City; Hull; Leeds; London (QM); Surrey.

ADMISSIONS INFORMATION

Number of applicants per place (approx) Cardiff 4; London (UCL) 8; Swansea 5.

Advice to applicants and planning the UCAS personal statement Cardiff An appreciation of the typical careers available within medical engineering and an interest in engineering and anatomy would be preferable. **London (UCL)** Evidence of interest in medical physics/physics, eg visits to hospitals or internships.

Selection interviews **Yes** Imperial London, Kent; **No** Glasgow, Leeds, Swansea.

AFTER-RESULTS ADVICE
Offers to applicants repeating A-levels Same Cardiff; London (UCL); Swansea.

GRADUATE DESTINATIONS AND EMPLOYMENT (2016/17 HESA)
Graduates surveyed See **Biotechnology**.

Career note High rate of graduate employment. *Money* magazine ranks Biomedical Engineering number 1 for job growth prospects for the next 10 years.

OTHER DEGREE SUBJECTS FOR CONSIDERATION
Biological Sciences; Prosthetics; Orthotics.

ENGLISH

(including **Creative Writing**; see also **Journalism, Languages, Linguistics, Literature**)

English courses continue to be extremely popular and competitive and include English Literature, English and English Language. Bear in mind that the content of courses can vary considerably. English Literature courses are popular because they are often an extension of A-level or equivalent studies and will offer a wide range of modules. At the University of Sheffield, the course covers the study of literature, poetry, fiction and drama from Old English to the 21st century along with modules such as American Literature, Gothic Literature and Renaissance Literature. However, English Language courses break the mould and offer a broader interpretation of English with studies in the use of language, grammar, the meaning of words, language in the workplace, in broadcasting and other aspects of society, Pidgin and Creole English, methods of communication and linguistics. Admissions tutors will expect students to have read widely outside their A-level syllabus.

Useful websites www.bl.uk; www.lrb.co.uk; www.3ammagazine.com/3am; www.bibliomania.com

NB The points totals shown to the left of the institutions are for ease of reference only. It must not be assumed that Tariff points are always used by institutions or that they can be substituted for an offer in grades. The level of an offer is not necessarily indicative of the quality of a course.

COURSE OFFERS INFORMATION
Subject requirements/preferences GCSE English language and English literature required and a foreign language may be preferred. Grades may be stipulated. **AL** English with specific grades usually stipulated. Modern languages required for joint courses with languages.

Your target offers and examples of degree courses

152 pts **Cambridge** – A*AA (A-Sxn Nrs Celt) (IB 42–40 pts HL 776); A*AA +interview +EAA (Educ Engl Dr Arts) (IB 42–40 pts HL 776); A*AA incl Engl+interview +ELAT (Engl) (IB 42–40 pts HL 776 incl Engl)

Durham – A*AA incl Engl (Engl Lit) (IB 38 pts HL 666 incl Engl)

144 pts **Bristol** – AAA incl Engl (Engl; Thea Engl) (IB 36 pts HL 18 pts incl 6 Engl); (Engl Class St) (IB 36 pts HL 6 Engl)

East Anglia – AAA incl Engl +portfolio (Engl Lit Crea Writ) (IB 34 pts HL 6 Engl)

London (UCL) – AAA incl Engl (Engl) (IB 38 pts HL 6 Engl)

Oxford – AAA incl Engl +interview +ELAT (Engl Lang Lit) (IB 38 pts HL 666 incl Engl); AAA incl Engl +interview +ELAT +MLAT (Engl Modn Langs) (IB 38 pts HL 666 incl Engl)

St Andrews – AAA incl Engl (Engl courses) (IB 38 pts HL 666 incl Engl)

Warwick – A*AB/AAA incl Engl (Engl Lit) (IB 38 pts HL 6 Engl); AAA/A*AB incl Engl (Engl Lit Crea Writ) (IB 38 pts HL 6 Engl)

York – AAA/A*AB incl Engl (Engl) (IB 36 pts HL 666 incl Engl); AAA incl Engl+hist (Engl Hist) (IB 36 pts HL 666 incl Engl+hist)

136 pts **Birmingham** – AAB incl Engl (Engl; Engl Lang) (IB 32 pts HL 665); (Engl Crea Writ) (IB 32 pts HL 665 incl Engl)

Exeter – AAA-AAB incl Engl (Class St Engl courses) (IB 36-34 pts HL 6 Engl); AAA-AAB incl Engl lit +interview (Engl Drama courses) (IB 36-34 pts HL 666-665 incl 6 Engl lit)

Glasgow – AAB (Engl Lang Ling) (IB 36 pts HL 665 incl 6 Engl+hum/lang); (Engl Lit) (IB 36 pts HL 665 incl Engl+hum/lang)

Lancaster – AAB (Engl Lang) (IB 35 pts HL 16 pts); AAB incl Engl (Engl Lang Lit; Engl Lit) (IB 35 pts HL 16 pts incl 6 lit); AAB incl Engl/lang (Engl Lang Crea Writ) (IB 35 pts HL 16 pts incl 6 lit)

Leeds – AAA-AAB incl Engl (Engl Lang Lit) (IB 35 pts HL 17-16 pts incl 6 Engl)

London (King's) – AAB incl Engl (Class St Engl) (IB 35 pts HL 665); (Compar Lit) (IB 35 pts HL 665 incl 6 Engl lit); AAB incl Engl/lang/psy (Engl Lang Ling) (IB 35 pts HL 665 incl 6 Engl/lang/psy)

Loughborough – AAB incl Engl (Engl; Engl Spo Sci) (IB 35 pts HL 665 incl Engl)

Manchester – AAA-AAB incl Engl (Engl Lit courses) (IB 36 pts HL 666)

NCH London – AAB +interview (Engl courses) (IB 35 pts HL 665)

Newcastle – AAA-AAB incl Engl (Engl Lang Lit) (IB 36-35 pts HL 6 Engl)

Nottingham – AAA-AAB incl Engl (Engl; Engl Crea Writ; Engl Lang Lit) (IB 36-34 pts HL 6 Engl)

Sheffield – AAB incl art/hum (Engl Lang Lit) (IB 34 pts HL 5 art/hum); AAB-ABB+bEPQ (Engl Comb Hons; Engl Lang Ling) (IB 34 pts); (Engl Lit) (IB 34 pts HL 5 art/hum)

Southampton – AAB/ABB +aEPQ incl Engl+Fr/Ger/Span (Engl Fr/Ger/Span) (IB 34 pts HL 17 pts incl 65 Engl+Fr/Ger/Span); AAB incl Engl (Engl) (IB 34 pts HL 17 pts incl 6 Engl); AAB-ABB +aEPQ incl Engl+hist (Engl Hist) (IB 34 pts HL 17 pts incl 6/5 Engl+hist); AAB-ABB +aEPQ incl Engl+mus+gr 8 (Engl Mus) (IB 34 pts HL 17 pts incl 6/5 Engl+mus)

Warwick – AAB incl Engl lit+Fr (Engl Fr) (IB 36 pts HL 5 Engl lit+Fr)

York – AAB incl Engl (Engl Hist Art; Engl Ling; Engl Phil) (IB 35 pts HL 6 Engl); AAB-ABB +aEPQ incl Engl (Engl Pol) (IB 35 pts HL 6 Engl)

128 pts **East Anglia** – ABB incl Engl (Engl Lit) (IB 32 pts HL 5 Engl)

Edinburgh – A*AA-ABB incl Engl (Engl Lit) (IB 43-34 pts HL 776-655 incl Engl); AAB-ABB (Engl Lang) (IB 36-34 pts HL 665-655); AAB-ABB incl Engl (Engl Scot Lit) (IB 40-34 pts HL 766-655 incl 5 Engl); ABB (Class Engl Lang) (IB 37-34 pts HL 666-655)

Exeter – AAA-ABB incl Engl lit (Engl; Engl (St Abrd)) (IB 36-32 pts HL 5/6 Engl); (Engl (Emp Exp)) (IB 36-32 pts HL 6/5 Engl); AAB-ABB incl Engl (Engl Film TV St) (IB 34-32 pts HL 6 Engl)

Huddersfield – ABB 128 pts (Engl Lang Lit; Engl Lang courses)

Liverpool – ABB incl Engl (Engl) (IB 33 pts HL 6 Engl)

London (QM) – ABB (Engl Lang Ling) (IB 32 pts HL 655); ABB incl Engl lit/Engl lang lit (Engl; Engl Lit Ling) (IB 32 pts HL 655 incl 6 Engl)

London (RH) – AAB-ABB incl Engl (Engl; Engl Dr) (IB 32 pts HL 655 incl Engl); AAB-ABB incl Engl lit +portfolio (Dr Crea Writ) (IB 32 pts HL 655 incl 6 Engl)

Newcastle – AAB-ABB (Engl Lang) (IB 35-34 pts)

Nottingham – ABB incl Engl (Engl Hisp St) (IB 32 pts HL 5 Engl)

Queen's Belfast – ABB incl Engl (Engl courses) (IB 33 pts HL 655 incl Engl)

Sheffield – ABB (Engl Lang Sociol) (IB 33 pts)

Southampton – AAB-ABB incl Engl (Flm Engl) (IB 32 pts HL 16 pts incl 5 Engl); (Phil Engl) (IB 34-32 pts HL 17-16 pts incl 5 Engl)

Sussex – AAB-ABB incl Engl (Engl; Engl Comb Hons; Engl Lang Lit) (IB 34-32 pts HL 6 Engl)

120 pts **Aberdeen** – BBB (Engl; Engl Scot Lit) (IB 32 pts HL 555)

Aston – ABB-BBB (Engl Lit Int Rel; Pol Engl Lang) (IB 32 pts HL 655); (Engl Lang) (IB 32 pts HL 655 incl Engl)

Bangor – B mus 120 pts (Mus Crea Writ) (HL 6 mus)

Bournemouth Arts – BBB 120 pts (Crea Writ) (HL 555)

Brunel – BBB incl Engl (Engl; Engl Crea Writ) (IB 30 pts HL 5 Engl); BBB incl Engl +audition workshop (Thea Crea Writ; Thea Engl) (IB 30 pts HL 5 Engl)

Cardiff – ABB-BBB incl Engl (Engl Lit) (HL 665 incl 6 Engl)

Coventry – BBB (Engl Jrnl) (IB 31 pts)

Derby – C Engl 120 pts (Crea Prof Writ; Engl)

Dundee – BBB (Engl Flm St) (IB 30 pts HL 555 incl Engl); BBB incl Engl lit (Engl) (IB 30 pts HL 555)

East Anglia – BBB incl Engl (Am Engl Lit; Engl Lit Comb Hons; Flm St Engl Lit) (IB 31 pts HL 5 Engl); BBB incl dr/thea st/Engl lit +interview +audition (Script Perf) (IB 31 pts HL 5 thea st/Engl)

Essex – BBB (Crea Writ; Engl Lang Lit; Engl Lang courses; Engl Lit) (IB 30 pts HL 555)

Huddersfield – BBB 120 pts +audition workshop (Dr Engl Lang/Lit); BBB incl Engl 120 pts (Engl Lit)

Hull – BBB 120 pts (Engl) (IB 30 pts)

Kent – BBB (Engl Lang Ling) (IB 34 pts HL 15 pts); BBB incl Engl (Engl Am Postcol Lit courses) (IB 34 pts HL 15 pts); (Eng Am Lit) (IB 34 pts HL 15 pts incl Engl)

Leicester – ABB–BBB incl Engl (Engl courses) (IB 30 pts HL 6 Engl)

London (Gold) – BBB incl Engl (Engl; Engl Compar Lit) (IB 33 pts HL 655); BBB incl Engl+portfolio (Engl Crea Writ) (IB 33 pts HL 655)

Northumbria – 120 pts (Engl Lang Lit; Engl Lit Crea Writ)

Reading – BBB (Engl Lang courses) (IB 30 pts); BBB incl Engl (Engl Lang Lit; Engl Lit Crea Writ) (IB 30 pts HL 5 Engl); BBB incl Engl/hist/soc/phil/dr +interview (P Educ Engl Spec) (IB 30 pts HL 5 Engl/hist/soc/phil/dr)

Stirling – BBB (Engl St) (IB 32 pts)

Strathclyde – ABB–BBB (Engl courses) (IB 36 pts)

Surrey – BBB incl Engl (Engl Lit; Engl Lit Crea Writ) (IB 32 pts); BBB incl Engl+Fr/Ger/Span (Engl Lit Fr/Ger/Span) (IB 32 pts)

Swansea – BBB (Engl Lang Engl Lit; Engl courses; Pol Engl Lit) (IB 32 pts)

York – BBB (Engl Educ) (IB 31 pts)

112 pts **Bangor** – 112 pts (Engl Lang Engl Lit; Engl Lang courses); (Engl Lit courses) (HL 6 Engl); 112 pts incl Engl (Engl Lit Thea Perf)

Bedfordshire – 112 pts (Engl Lit)

Birmingham City – BBC incl Engl 112 pts (Engl; Engl Crea Writ; Engl Lang Lit) (IB 28 pts HL 14 pts)

Buckingham – BBB–BBC (Engl Lit) (IB 32–31 pts)

Cardiff – BBB–BBC (Engl Lang) (HL 665–655)

Chester – BBB–BBC incl Engl 112–120 pts (Engl Lang; Engl Lang Lit courses; Engl Lit) (IB 28 pts HL 5 Engl)

City – BBC (Engl) (IB 29 pts HL 55)

Coventry – BBC (Engl) (IB 31 pts)

De Montfort – C Engl 112 pts (Engl Lit) (IB 26 pts)

Derby – 112 pts (Writ Pub); 112–128 pts (Crea Prof Writ Comb Hons)

East London – 112 pts incl Engl (Crea Prof Writ) (IB 25 pts HL 15 pts)

Edge Hill – BBB–BBC 112–120 pts (Engl; Engl Flm St; Engl Lang; Engl Lit; Engl Lit Hist); BBB–BBC 112–120 pts +portfolio (Crea Writ)

Gloucestershire – BBC 112 pts (Crea Writ)

Glyndŵr – 112 pts (Crea Writ Engl)

Hull – 112 pts (Dr Engl) (IB 28 pts)

Kingston – 112 pts (Engl Lit)

Leeds Beckett – 112 pts (Engl Lit) (IB 25 pts)

Liverpool Hope – BBC 112 pts (Engl Lang; Engl Lit) (IB 28 pts)

Liverpool John Moores – BBC 112 pts (Crea Writ Flm St) (IB 26 pts)

London (Birk) – ABB–BBC 112–128 pts +interview (Engl)

London Met – BBC 112 pts (Crea Writ Engl Lit)

Middlesex – 112 pts (Engl)

Nottingham Trent – C Engl 112 pts (Engl)

Roehampton – 112 pts (Engl Lang Ling); C Engl/hum 112 pts (Crea Writ; Engl Lit)

Sheffield Hallam – BBC 112 pts (Crea Writ; Engl; Engl Lang; Engl Lit)

Staffordshire – BBC 112 pts (Engl Lit Crea Writ)
Suffolk – BBC (Engl Hist); BBC 112 pts (Engl App Sociol)
Sunderland – 112 pts (Engl)
UWE Bristol – 112 pts (Engl Lit; Engl Lit Writ)
Winchester – 112–128 pts (Crea Writ) (HL 44)
Worcester – C Engl 112 pts (Engl Lit courses)

104 pts   **Aberystwyth** – BBB–BCC incl B Engl 104–120 pts (Engl Lit) (IB 30–28 pts HL 5 Engl)
Bournemouth – 104–120 pts (Engl) (IB 31–28 pts)
Cardiff Met – 104 pts (Engl Crea Writ; Engl Media) (IB -24 pts)
Central Lancashire – 104 pts (Engl Lang Crea Writ; Engl Lang Lit; Engl Lit)
Chester – BBC–BCC incl Engl/crea writ 104–112 pts (Crea Writ courses) (IB 26 pts HL 5 Engl)
Chichester – BBB–BCC 104–120 pts (Engl Lit) (IB 28 pts HL 4 Engl)
De Montfort – 104 pts (Crea Writ Comb Hons; Engl Lang Comb Hons) (IB 24 pts)
Edinburgh Napier – BCC incl Engl (Engl; Engl Flm) (IB 29 pts HL 655 incl Engl)
Falmouth – 104–120 pts +interview (Engl Crea Writ)
Gloucestershire – BCC 104 pts (Engl Crea Writ; Engl Lit Crea Writ)
Greenwich – BCC 104 pts (Crea Writ; Engl Lang Lit)
Hertfordshire – BCC 104 pts (Eng Lang Jap/Mand; Engl Lit)
Leeds Trinity – 104 pts (Engl Flm; Engl Media)
Liverpool John Moores – BCC 104 pts (Crea Writ) (IB 24 pts); BCC incl B Engl 104 pts (Engl Lit) (HL incl lit and lang); BCC incl Engl 104 pts (Hist Engl Lit)
Manchester Met – 104–112 pts (Engl; Engl Am Lit; Engl Crea Writ) (IB 26 pts)
Northampton – BCC incl Engl (Engl courses)
Portsmouth – 104–112 pts +portfolio (Crea Writ) (IB 25 pts)
Westminster – ABB–BCC 104–128 pts (Chin Engl Lang) (IB 27 pts HL 4 Engl); ABB–BCC incl Engl/hum (Engl Lang courses) (IB 27 pts HL 5 Engl/hum)
Winchester – 104–120 pts incl Engl/art/hum/soc sci (Engl Am Lit; Engl courses) (HL 44)
Worcester – 104 pts (Engl Lang courses)

96 pts   **Anglia Ruskin** – 96 pts (Engl Lang) (IB 24 pts); 96 pts incl Engl (Writ Engl Lit) (IB 24 pts); C Engl 96 pts (Engl Lit) (IB 24 pts HL 4 Engl)
Bath Spa – CCC incl Engl (Crea Writ; Engl Lit) (IB 26 pts HL 5 Engl)
Bishop Grosseteste – 96–112 pts (Engl courses)
Bolton – 96 pts incl Engl +interview/portfolio (Engl); 96 pts incl Engl lang +interview/portfolio (Crea Writ)
Brighton – BCC–CCC incl Engl 96–104 pts (Engl Lit) (IB 26 pts)
Chichester – 96–120 pts incl Engl/dr/crea writ (Crea Writ Engl) (IB 28 pts HL 4 Engl)
Cumbria – 96–120 pts (Crea Writ; Engl Lit)
Keele – CCC incl Engl/dr (Engl Lit; Engl Lit Comb Hons) (IB 26 pts HL 6 Engl)
Marjon – CCC incl Engl/hum 96 pts (Engl)
Newman – CC incl hum/soc sci 96 pts (Engl)
Portsmouth – 96–112 pts incl Engl (Engl Lang Ling) (IB 25 pts)
Solent – 96–112 pts +interview (Engl Crea Writ; Engl Flm)
St Mary's – BBC–CCC 96–112 pts (Crea Prof Writ; Engl Lit)
Teesside – 96–112 pts (Engl Crea Writ; Engl St)
Wolverhampton – CCC/BCD 96 pts (Crea Prof Writ courses; Engl courses)
York St John – 96 pts (Crea Writ; Engl Lang Ling; Engl Lit)

88 pts   **Canterbury Christ Church** – 88–112 pts (Engl Lang; Engl Lit)

80 pts   **Arts London** – 80 pts (Mag Jrnl Pub) (IB 24 pts)
Bedfordshire – CC 80 pts (Crea Writ)
Norwich City (Coll) – 80 pts (Engl Soc Sci)
South Wales – BCC–CDD incl Engl 80–104 pts (Engl; Engl Crea Writ) (IB 29 pts)

72 pts   **Anglia Ruskin** – 72 pts (Hist Engl Lit)
UHI – BC incl Engl (Lit)

48 pts   **Bolton** – 48 pts+interview/portfolio (Engl Fdn); 48 pts incl Engl +interview/portfolio (Crea Writ Fdn)

UCAS points Tariff: A* = 56 pts; A = 48 pts; B = 40 pts; C = 32 pts; D = 24 pts; E = 16 pts

Alternative offers
See **Chapter 6** and **Appendix 1** for grades/UCAS Tariff points information for other examinations.

EXAMPLES OF COLLEGES OFFERING COURSES IN THIS SUBJECT FIELD
Accrington and Rossendale (Coll); Birmingham Met (Coll); Blackburn (Coll); Blackpool and Fylde (Coll); Bournemouth and Poole (Coll); Bradford College UC; Craven (Coll); Doncaster (Coll); Farnborough (CT); Newham (CFE); South Devon (Coll); TEC Partnership; Truro and Penwith (Coll); West Suffolk (Coll); Yeovil (Coll).

CHOOSING YOUR COURSE (SEE ALSO CH.1)
Universities and colleges teaching quality See www.qaa.ac.uk; https://unistats.ac.uk.

Top research universities and colleges (REF 2014) (English Language and Literature) Warwick; Liverpool; London (UCL); Oxford Brookes; Aberdeen; Durham; Newcastle; London (QM); York; Birmingham; Cardiff; St Andrews.

Examples of sandwich degree courses Aston; Brighton; Coventry; Hertfordshire; Huddersfield; Loughborough; Plymouth; Solent; Surrey.

ADMISSIONS INFORMATION
Number of applicants per place (approx) Bangor (Engl Lit) 4, (Ling Engl Lang) 5; Bath Spa 8; Birmingham 7; Birmingham City 9; Blackpool and Fylde (Coll) 2; Bristol 7; Buckingham 5; Cambridge 4; Cardiff (Engl Lit) 6; Central Lancashire 10; Cumbria 24; De Montfort 7; Derby 6; Dundee 11; Durham 8; East Anglia (Engl Lit Crea Writ) 2; Edge Hill 4; Exeter 13; Gloucestershire 35; Hertfordshire 6; Huddersfield 4; Hull 5; Kingston 6; Lancaster 4; Leeds 10; Leeds Trinity 6; Leicester 5; Liverpool 8; London (Gold) 9; London (QM) 9; London (RH) 7; London (UCL) 10; London South Bank 5; Manchester 10; Manchester Met 7; Middlesex 8; Newman 3; Northampton 3; Nottingham 6; Nottingham Trent 21; Oxford 5; Oxford Brookes 6; Reading 11; Roehampton 6; Sheffield 6; Sheffield Hallam 4; South Wales 8; Southampton 8; Stirling 9; Sunderland 10; Teesside 5; Trinity Saint David 4; Warwick 15; Winchester 5; York 8; York St John 3.

Admissions tutors' advice Buckingham In a situation where everyone is trying to show off, it's amazing how powerful sincerity is. What poems, novels, or drama have really excited you? English Literature is a great subject, but why do you really want to read it?

Advice to applicants and planning the UCAS personal statement Applicants should read outside their subject. Details of any writing you have done (for example poetry, short stories) should be provided. Theatre visits and play readings are also important. Keep up-to-date by reading literary and theatre reviews in the national newspapers (keep a scrapbook of reviews for reference). Evidence is needed of a good writing style. Favourite authors, spare-time reading. Ability to write lucidly, accurately and succinctly. Evidence of literary enthusiasm. General interest in communications – verbal, visual, media. **Bristol** Deferred entry accepted in some cases. Late applications may not be accepted. **Manchester** Due to the detailed nature of entry requirements for English Literature courses, we are unable to include full details in the prospectus. For complete and up-to-date information on our entry requirements for these courses, please visit our website at www.manchester.ac.uk/study/undergraduate/courses.

Misconceptions about this course Birmingham City The study of English language means descriptive linguistics – the course won't necessarily enable students to speak or write better English. **Buckingham** Native speakers of English often do not realise that the EFL degree courses are restricted to non-native speakers of English.

Selection interviews Yes Anglia Ruskin, Cambridge, Cardiff Met, East Anglia, Leeds, London (UCL), Oxford (Engl Lang Lit) 22%, (Engl Modn Langs) 19%), Trinity Saint David; **Some** Blackburn (Coll), Blackpool and Fylde (Coll), Bristol, Kingston, London (Gold), Loughborough, Southampton, Truro and Penwith (Coll), Warwick; **No** Bangor, Birmingham, Birmingham City, Bishop Grosseteste, Canterbury Christ Church, Chester, Chichester, Cumbria, De Montfort, Derby, Dundee, Essex, Falmouth,

Gloucestershire, Huddersfield, Hull, Leeds Trinity, London (King's), London (QM), London (RH), London Met, Middlesex, Newcastle, Nottingham, Portsmouth, Reading, Roehampton, Wolverhampton.

Interview advice and questions Questions will be asked on set A-level texts and any essays that have been submitted prior to the interview. You will also be expected to have read outside your A-level subjects and to answer questions about your favourite authors, poets, dramatists, etc. Questions in the past have included: Do you think that class discussion plays an important part in your English course? What is the value of studying a text in depth rather than just reading it for pleasure? What is the difference between satire and comedy? Are books written by women different from those written by men? Why would you go to see a production of *Hamlet*? What are your views on the choice of novels for this year's Booker Prize? What books are bad for you? If you could make up a word, what would it be? Short verbal tests and a précis may be set. See also **Chapter 5**. **Buckingham** It is useful to know if there is any particular reason why students want a particular programme; for example, for the TEFL degree is a member of the family a teacher? **Cambridge** We look for interviewees who respond positively to ideas, can think on their feet, engage intelligently with critical issues and sustain an argument. If they don't evince any of these, we reject them. **Leeds** Interview questions based on information supplied in the personal statement, academic ability and current reading interests. **London (King's)** Interview questions are based on the information in the personal statement. **London (UCL)** The interview will focus on an ability to discuss literature in terms of language, plot, characters and genre. Following the interview applicants will be asked to write a critical commentary on an example of unseen prose or verse. **Oxford** Is there a difference between innocence and naivety? If you could make up a word, what would it be? Why? Do you think *Hamlet* is a bit long? No? Well I do. Is the Bible a fictional work? Was Shakespeare a rebel? **Warwick** We may ask students to sight-read or to analyse a text. **York** Only mature candidates and applicants with special circumstances and/or qualifications will usually be interviewed. Examples of recent essays are required at interview.

Reasons for rejection (non-academic) Some are well-informed about English literature – others are not. Inability to respond to questions about their current studies. Lack of enthusiasm for the challenge of studying familiar subjects from a different perspective. Must be able to benefit from the course. Little interest in how people communicate with each other. **Bristol** Not enough places to make offers to all those whose qualifications deserve one. **Buckingham** Applicants are requested to attend an Open Day/Evening or a Tutorial Taster Day. The University believes it is very important for applicants to visit its campus. Candidates who do not respond to these invitations may be rejected, irrespective of academic achievement, as the University looks for committed, well-motivated students. **Cambridge** See Interview advice and questions. **Leeds** Unsuitable predictions. **Oxford** (1) The essay she submitted was poorly written, careless and reductive and, in general, lacking in attention to the subject. She should be encouraged to write less and think more about what she is saying. She seems to put down the first thing that comes into her head. (2) We had the feeling that he rather tended to dismiss texts which did not satisfy the requirements of his personal canon and that he therefore might not be happy pursuing a course requiring the study of texts from all periods. (3) In her essay on Brontë, she took a phrase from Arnold which was metaphorical (to do with hunger) and applied it literally, writing at length about the diet of the characters. **Reading** None. If they have reached the interview we have already eliminated all other factors. **Sheffield Hallam** Apparent lack of eagerness to tackle all three strands of the course (literature, language and creative writing). **Southampton** Insufficient or patchy academic achievement. Applicants coming from non-standard academic backgrounds are assessed in terms of their individual situations.

AFTER-RESULTS ADVICE
Offers to applicants repeating A-levels Higher Sheffield Hallam; Southampton (varies); Warwick; **Possibly higher** Lancaster; Newcastle; Stirling; **Same** Bangor; Birmingham City; Blackpool and Fylde (Coll); Bristol; Cambridge; Cardiff; Cardiff Met; Chester; Chichester; Cumbria; De Montfort; Derby; Dundee; Durham; East Anglia; Edge Hill; Hull; Leeds; Leeds Trinity; Liverpool; Liverpool Hope; London (Gold); London (RH); Loughborough; Manchester Met; Newman; Nottingham; Nottingham Trent; Oxford Brookes; Reading; Roehampton; Sheffield; St Mary's; Suffolk; Trinity Saint David; Winchester; Wolverhampton; York; York St John.

GRADUATE DESTINATIONS AND EMPLOYMENT (2016/17 HESA)

English Studies graduates surveyed 8,180 **Employed** 3,440 **In voluntary employment** 330 **In further study** 2,560 **Assumed unemployed** 440

Career note English graduates work in the media, publishing, management, public and social services, business, administration and IT, retail sales, the cultural industries and the teaching profession. Those who have undertaken courses in Creative Writing could aim for careers in advertising, public relations or journalism.

OTHER DEGREE SUBJECTS FOR CONSIDERATION

Communication Studies; Drama; Language courses; Linguistics; Literature; Media Studies.

ENVIRONMENTAL SCIENCES

(including **Climate Change, Ecology, Environmental Hazards, Environmental Health, Environmental Management and Meteorology and Climate Science;** see also **Biological Sciences, Biology, Engineering (Civil), Geography, Geology/Geological Sciences, Health Sciences/Studies, Marine/Maritime Studies, Town and Urban Planning**)

Environmental Sciences courses need to be researched carefully since the content offered by different institutions can vary considerably. The emphasis may be biological or geographical and courses can cover marine, legal, social and political issues. Some courses focus on ecological issues, either environmental or industrial, while others focus on environmental hazards and health, so expect some overlap in many courses. There are some vocational courses in this category with professional status which allow graduates to progress into certain professions. For example, they may choose to become an environmental health officer whose role is concerned with all aspects of public health, covering food safety, housing, health and safety, and environmental protection.

Useful websites www.cieh.org; www.endsreport.com; www.enn.com; http://iagre.org; www.gov.uk/government/organisations/department-for-environment-food-rural-affairs; http://socenv.org.uk; www.the-ies.org; www.noc.ac.uk; www.britishecologicalsociety.org; www.rmets.org

NB The points totals shown to the left of the institutions are for ease of reference only. It must not be assumed that Tariff points are always used by institutions or that they can be substituted for an offer in grades. The level of an offer is not necessarily indicative of the quality of a course.

COURSE OFFERS INFORMATION

Subject requirements/preferences GCSE English, mathematics and a science (often chemistry or biology) usually required. **AL** One or two science subjects are usually stipulated; mathematics may be required. (Meteor) Mathematics, physics and another science may be required sometimes with specified grades, eg mathematics and physics grade B.

Your target offers and examples of degree courses

144 pts   **Imperial London** – AAA incl biol+sci/maths (Ecol Env Biol) (IB 38 pts HL 6 biol+sci/maths)

       Leeds – AAA incl sci/maths/geog/econ/sociol/hist/law/Engl (Sust Env Mgt (Int)) (IB 35 pts HL 17 pts)

       Sheffield – AAA incl biol+sci (Ecol Cons Biol (MBiolSci)) (IB 36 pts HL 6 biol+sci)

136 pts   **Leeds** – AAA–AAB incl biol (Ecol Cons Biol) (IB 35–34 pts HL 18–17 pts incl 6 biol+sci)

       London (UCL) – AAB (Env Geosci) (IB 36 pts HL 17 pts)

       London LSE – AAB (Env Plcy Econ) (IB 37 pts HL 666)

       Sheffield – AAA–AAB incl sci/maths +interview (Ecol Cons Biol) (IB 36 pts HL 6 sci)

       St Andrews – AAB incl biol+sci/maths (Env Earth Sci) (IB 36 pts HL 665 incl maths/sci)

       York – A*AA–AAB incl chem+sci/maths (Chem Atmos Env) (IB 37–35 pts HL 6 chem+sci/maths); AAB incl biol+sci (Ecol) (IB 35 pts HL 6 biol+chem/maths)

128 pts   **Birmingham** – ABB incl sci/maths/geog/psy/comp (Env Sci) (IB 32 pts HL 655)

Edinburgh – AAA–ABB incl maths+phys (Geophys Meteor) (IB 37–32 pts HL 555 incl maths+phys); (Phys Meteor) (IB 37–32 pts HL 666–655 incl maths+phys); AAA–ABB incl sci/maths (Ecol Env Sci Mgt) (IB 37–32 pts HL 555); AAA–ABB incl sci/maths/geog (Ecol Env Sci) (IB 37–32 pts HL 555 incl sci/maths)

Exeter – AAB–ABB incl sci/maths (Cons Biol Ecol) (IB 34–32 pts HL 665–655 incl 5 sci/maths); AAB–ABB incl sci/maths/geog/tech/psy/PE (Env Sci; Renew Ener) (IB 34–32 pts HL 5 sci/maths/geog/tech/psy/PE)

Lancaster – ABB incl sci/maths (Ecol Cons; Env Sci) (IB 32 pts HL 16 pts incl 6 sci)

Leeds – ABB incl maths/sci/geog (Env Sci) (IB 34 pts HL 16 pts incl 5 maths/sci); ABB incl sci/maths/geog/econ/sociol/hist/law/pol/Engl (Sust Env Mgt) (IB 34 pts HL 16 pts)

Liverpool – ABB incl sci/maths/geog (Env Sci) (IB 33 pts HL 4 sci)

London (QM) – ABB incl sci/maths/geog/geol/psy (Env Sci) (IB 32 pts HL 655 incl sci/maths/geog/geol/psy)

Manchester – ABB (Env Mgt) (IB 34 pts HL 655); ABB incl sci (Env Sci) (IB 34 pts HL 655 incl sci)

Newcastle – ABB incl maths/sci/geog/psy (Env Sci (Yr Ind)) (IB 32 pts HL 5 maths/sci/geo/psy); ABB incl sci/maths/geog/psy (Env Sci) (IB 32 pts HL 5 sci/maths/geog/psy)

Reading – ABB incl biol/geog/env sci/maths (Ecol Wldlf Cons) (IB 32 pts HL 5 biol/geog/env sci/maths); ABB incl maths (Meteor Clim) (IB 32 pts HL 5 maths)

Sheffield – ABB (Lnd Archit) (IB 33 pts); ABB incl geog/sci (Env Sci) (IB 33 pts HL 5 geog/sci)

Southampton – ABB incl sci/maths/geog/psy (Env Mgt Bus; Env Sci) (IB 32 pts HL 16 pts incl 5 sci)

Sussex – AAB–ABB incl sci/env st (Ecol Cons Env) (IB 34–32 pts HL 5 sci)

York – ABB incl sci/maths/geog/psy (Env Sci) (IB 34 pts)

120 pts **Aberdeen** – BBB incl maths/sci (Ecol; Env Sci) (IB 32 pts HL 555 incl maths/sci)

Bangor – 120 pts (App Trstl Mar Ecol)

Coventry – ABB–BBB (Geog Nat Haz) (IB 29 pts)

Derby – C sci 120 pts incl sci (Env Haz Comb Hons)

East Anglia – BBB/ABC incl geog/maths/econ/sci (Env Sci) (IB 31 pts HL 5 geog/maths/econ/sci); BBB/ABC incl maths (Meteor Ocean) (IB 31 pts HL 5 maths)

Glasgow – BBB (Env Sci Sust) (IB 30 pts HL 655 incl sci)

Kent – BBB (Env Soc Sci; Env Soc Sci (Yr Ind)) (IB 34 pts HL 15 pts)

Leicester – ABB–BBB incl sci/maths/geog (App Env Geol) (IB 30 pts)

Liverpool – BBB (Env Plan) (IB 31 pts)

London (RH) – ABB–BBB incl biol/geog/env sci+sci/maths (Ecol Cons) (IB 32 pts HL 555 incl biol/geog/env+sci)

Northumbria – 120 pts (Env Sci)

Nottingham – ABB–BBB incl sci/maths (Env Sci) (IB 32–30 pts HL 5 sci); ABB–BBB incl sci/maths/geog (Env Biol) (IB 32–30 pts)

Plymouth – 120–144 pts incl biol (Mar Biol Cstl Ecol) (IB 36–30 pts HL biol)

Reading – ABC incl maths (Maths Meteor) (IB 30 pts HL 6 maths); BBB (Env Mgt) (IB 30 pts); BBB incl sci (Env Sci) (IB 30 pts HL 5 sci)

Stirling – BBB incl sci/geog/geol/maths (Cons Biol Mgt; Env Sci) (IB 32 pts HL 5 sci/geog/geol/maths); BBB incl sci/maths (Ecol) (IB 32 pts); BBB incl sci/maths/geog (Env Sci Out Educ) (IB 32 pts HL 5 sci/maths/geog)

Ulster – ABC incl sci/maths/geog/hm econ/hlth soc cr (Env Hlth) (IB 26 pts HL 13 pts incl sci)

112 pts **Bangor** – C sci 112 pts incl sci/maths/geog/econ (Env Cons; Env Sci) (HL 5 sci)

Brunel – BBC incl sci/env/maths (Env Sci) (IB 29 pts HL 5 sci/eng/maths)

Gloucestershire – BBC 112 pts (Ecol Env Sci)

Keele – BBC (Env Sci; Env Sust) (IB 30 pts)

Liverpool Hope – BBC 112 pts (Env Sci) (IB 28 pts)

London (Birk) – ABB–BBC 112–128 pts (Env Mgt)

Nottingham Trent – BBC 112 pts (Ecol Cons); BBC incl sci 112 pts (Env Sci)
Sheffield Hallam – BBC 112 pts (Env Sci)
UWE Bristol – C sci 112 pts (Env Sci; Wldlf Ecol Cons Sci) (HL 5 sci)

104 pts **Aberystwyth** – BBB–BCC incl biol 104–120 pts (Ecol) (IB 30–28 pts HL 5 biol)
Bangor – BC sci/geog/maths/econ/psy 104 pts incl sci (Mar Env St) (HL 5 sci)
Bournemouth – 104–120 pts (Env Sci) (IB 31–28 pts)
Cardiff Met – 104 pts (Env Hlth) (IB 24 pts)
Chester – BBC–BCC incl geog/soc sci/app sci 104–112 pts (Nat Haz Mgt courses) (IB 26 pts HL 5 geog)
Dundee – BBB–BCC (Env Sust) (IB 30 pts HL 555); BBB–BCC incl sci (Env Sci) (IB 30 pts HL 555 incl sci)
Greenwich – 104 pts incl sci/geog (Env Sci)
Leeds Beckett – 104 pts (Env Hlth) (IB 24 pts)
Manchester Met – BBC–BCC incl geog/sci/maths 104–112 pts (Env Sci (St Abrd)) (IB 26 pts HL 5 geog/sci); BBC–BCC incl geog 104–112 pts (Physl Geog) (IB 26 pts HL 5 geog)
Northampton – BCC (Env Sci)
Plymouth – 104–112 pts (Env Mgt Sust; Env Sci) (IB 27–26 pts)
Portsmouth – 104–120 pts incl sci/maths/geog (Mar Env Sci) (IB 26 pts HL 5 sci/maths/geog)
Ulster – BCC incl sci/maths/geog/econ/tech/PE (Env Sci) (IB 26 pts HL 13 pts incl sci/maths/geog/econ/tech/PE)

96 pts **Bath Spa** – CCC incl sci/geog (Env Sci) (IB 26 pts HL 5 sci/geog)
Brighton – BBC–CCC incl sci 96–112 pts (Env Sci) (IB 26 pts); BCC–CCC incl sci 96–104 pts (Ecol Cons) (IB 26 pts HL 5 biol)
Glasgow Caledonian – CCC (Env Mgt) (IB 24 pts)
Hertfordshire – CCC 96 pts (Env Mgt courses)
Kingston – CCC incl sci/geog 96 pts (Env Sci)
Teesside – 96–112 pts (Env Sci)
Trinity Saint David – 96 pts (Env Cons)
Wolverhampton – CCC/BCD incl sci 96 pts (Env Hlth)

88 pts **Canterbury Christ Church** – 88–112 pts incl sci (Ecol)
Reading – BBB–CCD (Ecol Wldf Cons Fdn) (IB 30–24 pts)

80 pts **Sparsholt (Coll)** – CCE incl sci (Aqua Fish Mgt) (IB 24 pts HL 4 sci)
West Scotland – CDD incl sci 80 pts (Env Hlth) (IB 24 pts)

64 pts **UHI** – CC (Arch Env St); CC incl sci (Env Sci)

Open University – contact 0300 303 0073 or www.open.ac.uk/contact/new (Env St)

Alternative offers
See **Chapter 6** and **Appendix 1** for grades/UCAS Tariff points information for other examinations.

EXAMPLES OF COLLEGES OFFERING COURSES IN THIS SUBJECT FIELD
Askham Bryan (Coll); Bedford (Coll); Birmingham Met (Coll); Bishop Burton (Coll); Cornwall (Coll); Duchy Coll UC; Durham New (Coll); Easton Otley (Coll); Hadlow (UC); Hartpury (Coll); Kingston Maurward (Coll); Leeds City (Coll); Moulton (Coll); Myerscough (Coll); Petroc; Plymouth City (Coll); Sparsholt (Coll); Truro and Penwith (Coll); Weston (Coll); York (Coll).

CHOOSING YOUR COURSE (SEE ALSO CH.1)
Universities and colleges teaching quality See www.qaa.ac.uk; https://unistats.ac.uk.

Top research universities and colleges (REF 2014) (Earth Systems and Environmental Sciences) Bristol; Manchester; Leeds; Cambridge; Oxford; London (RH); Birmingham; Southampton; London (Birk); London (UCL); Leicester.

Examples of sandwich degree courses Brighton; Coventry; Glasgow Caledonian; Greenwich; Hertfordshire; Keele; Kingston; Leeds; Manchester Met; Nottingham Trent; Reading; Teesside; Ulster; UWE Bristol.

ADMISSIONS INFORMATION

Number of applicants per place (approx) Bangor 4; Bath Spa 2; Birmingham 5; Cardiff Met 4; Dundee 13; East Anglia 5; Edinburgh 1; Gloucestershire 11; Greenwich 2; Hertfordshire 5; Hull 5; Kingston 3; Lancaster 5; London LSE 8; Manchester Met (Env Sci) 5; Northampton 4; Nottingham 7; Nottingham Trent 3; Oxford Brookes 7; Plymouth 13; Sheffield Hallam 8; Southampton 4; Stirling 7; Trinity Saint David 3; Ulster 16; Wolverhampton 2; Worcester 7; York 4.

Advice to applicants and planning the UCAS personal statement 'We want doers, not just thinkers' is one comment from an admissions tutor. Describe any field courses you have attended; make an effort to visit National Parks. Discuss these visits and identify any particular aspects that impressed you. Outline travel interests. Give details of work as a conservation volunteer and other outside-school activities. Strong communication skills, people-oriented work experience. Watch your spelling and grammar! What sparked your interest in environmental science? Discuss your field trips. (Env Hlth courses) A basic knowledge of environmental health as opposed to environmental sciences. Work experience in an environmental health department is looked upon favourably. See also **Appendix 3**. **Lancaster** (Env Sci) One A-level subject required from biology, human biology, chemistry, computing, environmental science, information technology, mathematics, physics, psychology or geography.

Misconceptions about this course Bangor Students should note that only simple mathematical skills are required for this course. **Southampton** This is not just a course for environmentalists, for example links with BP, IBM etc. **Wolverhampton** This is a course in environmental science, not environmental studies: there is a difference.

Selection interviews Yes Trinity Saint David; **Some** Cardiff Met, Plymouth; **No** Bangor, Birmingham, Coventry, Derby, Dundee, East Anglia, Gloucestershire, Greenwich, Hertfordshire, Kingston, Manchester Met, Newcastle, Nottingham, Nottingham Trent, Oxford Brookes, Reading, Sheffield Hallam, Southampton, UWE Bristol.

Interview advice and questions Environmental issues are constantly in the news, so keep abreast of developments. You could be asked to discuss particular environmental problems in the area in which you live and to justify your stance on any environmental issues on which you have strong opinions. See also **Chapter 5**.

Reasons for rejection (non-academic) Inability to be aware of the needs of others.

AFTER-RESULTS ADVICE

Offers to applicants repeating A-levels Higher Greenwich; Lancaster; Nottingham Trent; **Possibly higher** Aberystwyth; **Same** Bangor; Birmingham; Brighton; Cardiff Met; Derby; Dundee; East Anglia; Leeds; Manchester Met; Northumbria; Nottingham; Plymouth; Southampton; Wolverhampton.

GRADUATE DESTINATIONS AND EMPLOYMENT (2016/17 HESA)
Graduates surveyed See **Biological Sciences**.

Career note Some graduates find work with government departments, local authorities, statutory and voluntary bodies in areas like land management and pollution control. Others go into a range of non-scientific careers.

OTHER DEGREE SUBJECTS FOR CONSIDERATION
Biological Sciences; Biology; Chemistry; Earth Sciences; Environmental Engineering; Geography; Geology; Meteorology; Ocean Sciences/Oceanography; Town and Country Planning.

EUROPEAN STUDIES

(see also **French, German, International Relations, Languages, Russian and East European Studies**)

European Studies courses provide the opportunity to study one or two main languages along with a broad study of economic, political, legal, social and cultural issues within the broad context of the European community. Other similar specific courses such as European History or European Politics allow the student to focus on an individual subject area.

Useful websites www.europa.eu; www.erasmusplus.org.uk; see also **Languages**.

NB The points totals shown to the left of the institutions are for ease of reference only. It must not be assumed that Tariff points are always used by institutions or that they can be substituted for an offer in grades. The level of an offer is not necessarily indicative of the quality of a course.

COURSE OFFERS INFORMATION

Subject requirements/preferences GCSE English and a foreign language for all courses and possibly mathematics. Grades may be stipulated. **AL** A modern language usually required.

Your target offers and examples of degree courses
152 pts   **London (UCL)** – A*AA (Euro Soc Pol St) (IB 39 pts HL 19 pts)
136 pts   **Bath** – AAB–ABB +aEPQ incl lang (Int Pol Modn Langs) (IB 35 pts HL 665 incl 7 lang)
           Glasgow – AAB incl art/hum (Cnt E Euro St) (IB 38 pts HL 666 incl Engl+lang/hum)
           London (King's) – AAB (Euro St (Fr/Ger/Span) (Yr Abrd)) (IB 35 pts HL 665)
           London (UCL) – AAB (Lang Cult; Pol Sociol E Euro St) (IB 36 pts HL 17 pts)
           Southampton – AAB/ABB +aEPQ incl lang (Langs Contemp Euro St) (IB 34 pts HL 17 pts incl 6 lang)
128 pts   **Kent** – AAA–ABB (Euro Leg St (Fr/Ger/Span)) (IB 34 pts HL 17 pts)
           Leicester – ABB/BBB +bEPQ incl Fr/Ital/Span (Euro St) (IB 30 pts HL 6 Fr/Ital/Span)
           London (RH) – AAB–ABB (Euro Int St Fr/Ger/Ital/Span) (IB 32 pts HL 655)
           Nottingham – ABB (Modn Euro St) (IB 32 pts)
120 pts   **Essex** – BBB (Euro St (Yr Abrd); Euro St Fr/Ger/Ital/Span) (IB 30 pts)
           Kent – BBB incl lang (Euro St (Comb Langs)) (IB 34 pts HL 15 pts)

Alternative offers
See **Chapter 6** and **Appendix 1** for grades/UCAS Tariff points information for other examinations.

CHOOSING YOUR COURSE (SEE ALSO CH.1)

Universities and colleges teaching quality See www.qaa.ac.uk; https://unistats.ac.uk.

Top research universities and colleges (REF 2014) See **Languages**.

ADMISSIONS INFORMATION

Number of applicants per place (approx) Bath 6; Dundee 14; Leicester 6; London (King's) 7; London (UCL) 8; Nottingham 1; Nottingham Trent 12.

Advice to applicants and planning the UCAS personal statement Try to identify an interest you have in the country relevant to your studies. Visits to that country should be described. Read the national newspapers and magazines and keep up-to-date with political and economic developments. Show your interest in the culture and civilisation of Europe as a whole, through, for example, European travel. Show your motivation for choosing the course and give details of your personal achievements and any future career plans, showing your international awareness and perspective.

Selection interviews Yes Southampton; **No** Essex.

Interview advice and questions While your interest in studying a language may be the main reason for applying for this subject, the politics, economics and culture of European countries are constantly in the news. You should keep up-to-date with any such topics concerning your chosen country and be prepared for questions. A language test may occupy part of the interview. See also **Chapter 5**.

Reasons for rejection (non-academic) Poor powers of expression. Lack of ideas on any issues. Lack of enthusiasm.

AFTER-RESULTS ADVICE
Offers to applicants repeating A-levels Same Dundee.

GRADUATE DESTINATIONS AND EMPLOYMENT (2016/17 HESA)
Graduates surveyed 150 **Employed** 75 **In voluntary employment** 10 **In further study** 35 **Assumed unemployed** 15

Career note See **Languages**.

OTHER DEGREE SUBJECTS FOR CONSIDERATION
Business and Management; History; International Relations; Politics; Language courses.

FILM, RADIO, VIDEO AND TV STUDIES

(see also **Art and Design (Graphic Design), Communication Studies/Communication, Engineering (Acoustics And Sound), Media Studies, Photography**)

Many course are offered in Film, Radio, Video and TV Studies. The Film, Photography and Media course at the University of Leeds combines theory with practice, covering digital film and photography with options in TV production, film editing, and documentary production. By contrast, the Exeter course presents a broad chronological and geographical coverage from the silent film to the Hollywood classics. It's therefore important to choose courses with care, particularly the theoretical and practical content of courses. At Brunel University, practical studies occupy up to 40% of the Film and Television Studies course. It is often possible to study Film, Radio, Video and TV Studies as part of a combined degree. For example, at the University of Chester, it is possible to study Radio Production with Business Management or Television Production.

Useful websites www.bfi.org.uk; www.mtv.com/news/movies; www.allmovie.com; www.societyinmotion.com; www.imdb.com; www.fwfr.com; www.bafta.org; www.movingimage.us; http://film.britishcouncil.org; www.filmsite.org; www.festival-cannes.com/en; www.bbc.co.uk/careers; www.rogerebert.com; www.bectu.org.uk

NB The points totals shown to the left of the institutions are for ease of reference only. It must not be assumed that Tariff points are always used by institutions or that they can be substituted for an offer in grades. The level of an offer is not necessarily indicative of the quality of a course.

COURSE OFFERS INFORMATION
Subject requirements/preferences GCSE English usually required. Courses vary, check prospectuses. **AL** English may be stipulated for some courses.

Your target offers and examples of degree courses
136 pts **Bristol** – AAB (Flm TV) (IB 34 pts HL 17 pts)
Glasgow – AAB (Flm TV St Comb Hons) (IB 36 pts HL 665 incl 6 Engl+hum/lang)
Lancaster – AAB incl Engl (Flm Engl Lit) (IB 35 pts HL 16 pts incl 6 lit)
Leeds – AAB (Flm Photo Media; Flm St Comb Hons) (IB 35 pts HL 16 pts)
London (King's) – AAB incl Engl (Compar Lit Flm St) (IB 35 pts HL 665 incl Engl)
Manchester – AAB incl Engl/hist/pol (Flm St courses) (IB 35 pts HL 665)

St Andrews – AAB (Flm St courses) (IB 36 pts HL 665)

York – AAB (Flm TV Prod) (IB 35 pts)

128 pts **Edinburgh** – ABB +portfolio (Flm TV) (IB 34 pts HL 655)

Exeter – AAB–ABB (Flm St (Emp Exp); Flm TV St) (IB 34–32 pts HL 665–655)

Lancaster – ABB (Flm Sociol; Flm St) (IB 32 pts HL 16 pts)

Leeds Beckett – 128 pts +portfolio (Filmm) (IB 27 pts)

Liverpool – ABB (Flm St Comb Hons) (IB 33 pts)

London (QM) – ABB incl hum/soc sci (Flm St) (IB 32 pts HL 655 incl hum/soc sci)

Manchester – ABB incl essay sub (Dr Flm St) (IB 34 pts HL 655)

Newcastle – ABB (Flm Media; Flm Prac) (IB 32 pts)

Nottingham – ABB (Flm TV St; Flm TV St Am St) (IB 32 pts)

Southampton – AAB–ABB (Flm; Flm Phil) (IB 32 pts HL 16 pts); AAB–ABB incl Engl (Flm Engl) (IB 32 pts HL 16 pts incl 5 Engl); AAB–ABB incl hist (Flm Hist) (IB 32 pts HL 16 pts incl 5 hist)

Surrey – AAB–ABB incl maths+interview (Flm Vid Prod Tech) (IB 34–32 pts)

Sussex – AAB–ABB (Dr Flm St) (IB 34–32 pts); ABB (Flm St) (IB 32 pts)

UWE Bristol – 128 pts +interview +portfolio (Filmm)

Warwick – ABB +interview +portfolio (Flm St) (IB 34 pts); ABB incl Engl +interview +portfolio (Flm Lit) (IB 34 pts HL 5 Engl)

Westminster – AAB–ABB 128–136 pts +interview +portfolio (Flm) (IB 27 pts)

120 pts **Aberdeen** – BBB (Flm Vis Cult) (IB 32 pts HL 555)

Birmingham City – BBB 120 pts (Flm Prod Tech; Vis Efcts) (IB 30 pts)

Bournemouth Arts – BBB 120 pts +portfolio +interview (Flm Prod); BBB 120 +interview +portfolio (Animat Prod) (HL 555)

Creative Arts – BBB 120 pts +interview +portfolio (Flm Prod) (HL 555)

Dundee – BBB (Engl Flm St) (IB 30 pts HL 555 incl Engl)

East Anglia – BBB/ABC (Flm TV St) (IB 31 pts); BBB incl Engl (Flm St Engl Lit) (IB 31 pts HL 5 Engl)

Essex – BBB (Flm St; Flm St Lit) (IB 30 pts HL 555)

Kent – BBB (Flm; Flm courses) (IB 34 pts HL 15 pts)

Leicester – BBB–BBC +bEPQ (Flm Media St) (IB 28 pts)

London (RH) – ABB–BBB (Flm St) (IB 32 pts HL 555)

Northumbria – 120 pts (Flm TV St)

Norwich Arts – BBB +interview +portfolio (Flm Mov Imag Prod) (IB 27 pts)

Queen Margaret – BBB (Thea Flm) (IB 30 pts)

Queen's Belfast – BBB (Flm St courses) (IB 32 pts HL 655)

Reading – BBB +interview (Flm TV; Flm Thea) (IB 30 pts); BBB +interview +portfolio (Art Flm Thea) (IB 30 pts); BBB incl Engl/thea st (Engl Lit Flm Thea) (IB 30 pts HL 5 Engl/thea st)

Stirling – BBB (Flm Media) (IB 32 pts)

112 pts **Bedfordshire** – 112 pts (TV Prod)

Bournemouth – 112–128 pts (Flm Prod Cnma) (IB 32–30 pts)

Bradford – BBC 112 pts (Flm TV Prod)

Brunel – BBC (Flm Prod; Flm TV St) (IB 29 pts); BBC +audition workshop (Flm Prod Thea) (IB 29 pts); BBC incl Engl (Flm TV St Engl) (IB 29 pts)

Derby – 112 pts +interview (Flm Prod); 112 pts+portfolio (Media Prod); 112–128 pts (Flm TV St Comb Hons)

East London – 112 pts (Flm) (IB 25 pts HL 15 pts)

Edge Hill – BBB–BBC 112–120 pts (Engl Flm St; Flm St; Flm TV Prod; Media Flm TV)

Greenwich – BBC 112 pts (Flm St; Flm TV Prod)

Huddersfield – BBC 112 pts (Flm St courses)

Hull – BBC 112 pts (Flm St) (IB 28 pts)

Kent – BBC (Art Hist Flm) (IB 34 pts HL 14 pts)

Kingston – 112 pts +interview +portfolio (Filmm)

Leeds Trinity – 112 pts (Flm; TV Prod)

Lincoln – BBC (Flm TV St) (IB 29 pts)
Liverpool John Moores – BBC 112 pts (Crea Writ Flm St; Flm St) (IB 26 pts)
London Met – BBC 112 pts (Jrnl Flm TV St); BBC 112 pts+interview +portfolio (Flm TV St)
Manchester Met – 112 pts +interview +portfolio (Filmm) (IB 26 pts)
Middlesex – 112 pts (Flm)
Nottingham Trent – BBC 112 pts +portfolio (Des Flm TV)
Oxford Brookes – BBC 112 pts (Flm) (IB 30 pts)
Plymouth (CA) – 112–120 pts +portfolio +interview (Flm St)
Roehampton – 112 pts (Flm)
Sheffield Hallam – BBC 112 pts (Flm Media Prod)
Staffordshire – BBC 112 pts (Flm Media Prod); BBC 112 pts +interview +portfolio (Flm TV Rad)
Suffolk – BBC 112 pts +interview +portfolio (Dig Flm Prod)
Sunderland – 112 pts (Flm Media; Photo Vid Dig Imag); 112–120 pts (Flm Prod)
Winchester – 112–120 pts (Flm Prod) (HL 44)

104 pts **Arts London** – 104 pts +portfolio (Flm TV)
Bangor – 104–120 pts (Flm St courses); B mus 104–120 pts (Mus Flm St) (HL 6 mus)
Bournemouth – 104–120 pts (TV Prod) (IB 31–28 pts)
Central Lancashire – 104 pts (Flm Media Pop Cult; Scrnwrit Flm TV Rad; TV Prod); 104
pts+portfolio (Flm Prod)
Chichester – BBC–BCC 104–112 pts (Dig Flm Tech) (IB 28 pts)
De Montfort – 104 pts (Aud Rec Tech; Flm St Comb Hons) (IB 24 pts)
Edinburgh Napier – BCC incl Engl (Engl Flm) (IB 29 pts HL 655 incl Engl)
Falmouth – 104–120 pts +interview (Flm)
Hertfordshire – BCC 104 pts (Engl Lang Flm; Flm TV (Prod))
Leeds Trinity – 104 pts (Engl Flm)
London South Bank – BCC (Flm Prac; Flm St)
Manchester Met – 104–112 pts (Flm Media St) (IB 26 pts)
Northampton – BCC (Flm Scrn St Comb Hons)
Nottingham Trent – 104 pts (Flm TV Comb Hons)
Portsmouth – 104–112 pts (Flm Ind courses)
Queen Margaret – BCC (Flm Media) (IB 28 pts)
Sheffield Hallam – BCC 104 pts (Flm St; Scrnwrit Flm)
West Scotland – BCC 104 pts (Filmm Scrnwrit) (IB 24 pts HL 3 pts)
Worcester – 104 pts (Flm St Scrnwrit); 104 pts +interview +portfolio (Flm Prod)

96 pts **Aberystwyth** – BBB–CCC 96–120 pts (Flm TV St) (IB 30–26 pts)
Anglia Ruskin – 96 pts (Flm St) (IB 24 pts); 96 pts+portfolio (Flm TV Prod) (IB 24 pts)
Bath Spa – CCC (Flm Scrn St courses) (IB 26 pts)
Chester – BCC–CCC 96–104 pts (Flm St courses; Rad Prod courses; TV Prod courses) (IB 26 pts)
Cumbria – 96–120 pts +interview +portfolio (Flm TV)
Keele – CCC (Flm St) (IB 26 pts)
Solent – 96–112 pts +interview (Engl Flm; Flm; Flm TV; TV Prod)
St Mary's – BBC–CCC 96–112 pts (Flm Scrn Media)
Teesside – 96–112 pts (Flm TV Prod)
West London – CCC 96 pts (Cntnt Media Flm Prod)
West Scotland – CCC (Broad Prod (TV Rad)) (IB 24 pts HL 3 pts)
Winchester – 96–112 pts (Flm Media); (Flm St) (HL 44)
Wolverhampton – CCC/BCD 96 pts (Media Flm TV St)
York St John – 96 pts (Flm St)

88 pts **Canterbury Christ Church** – 88–112 pts (Flm Prod; Flm Rad TV St)
80 pts **Bucks New** – 80 pts +portfolio (Flm TV Prod)
South Wales – BCC–CDD incl art/des 80–104 pts +interview +portfolio (Flm) (IB 29 pts)
64 pts **Ravensbourne Univ** – CC +portfolio (Dig Flm Prod) (IB 28 pts)
32 pts **RConsvS** – EE +interview +audition (Filmm) (IB 24 pts)

Gloucestershire – interview (Flm Prod)

Alternative offers
See **Chapter 6** and **Appendix 1** for grades/UCAS Tariff points information for other examinations.

EXAMPLES OF COLLEGES OFFERING COURSES IN THIS SUBJECT FIELD
Accrington and Rossendale (Coll); Barking and Dagenham (Coll); Barnsley (Coll); Birmingham Met (Coll); Bournemouth and Poole (Coll); Bournville (Coll); Bradford College UC; Brooksby Melton (Coll); Buckinghamshire (Coll Group); Bury (Coll); Central Film Sch; Chesterfield (Coll); Chichester (Coll); Cornwall (Coll); Croydon (Univ Centre); Doncaster (Coll); East Surrey (Coll); Exeter (Coll); Farnborough (CT); Gloucestershire (Coll); Harrow (Coll); Hereford (CA); Hull (Coll); Kensington and Chelsea (Coll); Manchester (Coll); Northern SA; Nottingham (Coll); Rotherham (CAT); South Devon (Coll); South Staffordshire (Coll); TEC Partnership; Truro and Penwith (Coll); Warwickshire (Coll); West Thames (Coll); Weston (Coll); Wiltshire (Coll).

CHOOSING YOUR COURSE (SEE ALSO CH.1)
Universities and colleges teaching quality See www.qaa.ac.uk; https://unistats.ac.uk.

Top research universities and colleges (REF 2014) See **Drama**.

Examples of sandwich degree courses Bangor; Birmingham City; Bradford; Greenwich; Hertfordshire; Huddersfield; Portsmouth; Solent; Surrey; Wolverhampton.

ADMISSIONS INFORMATION
Number of applicants per place (approx) Bournemouth Arts 8; Bristol 15; Central Lancashire 5; East Anglia (Film Engl St) 4, (Film Am St) 5; Kent 6; Leicester 9; Liverpool John Moores 17; London Met 7; Sheffield Hallam 60; Southampton 6; Staffordshire 31; Stirling 11; Warwick 18; Westminster 41; York 4; York St John 6.

Advice to applicants and planning the UCAS personal statement Bournemouth Arts Any experience in film making (beyond home videos) should be described in detail. Knowledge and preferences of types of films and the work of some producers should be included on the UCAS application. Read film magazines and other appropriate literature to keep informed of developments. Show genuine interest in a range of film genres and be knowledgeable about favourite films, directors and give details of work experience or film projects undertaken. You should also be able to discuss the ways in which films relate to broader cultural phenomena, social, literary, historical. It takes many disciplines to make a film. Bournemouth Film School is home to all of them.

Misconceptions about this course Bournemouth Arts (Animat Prod) This is not a Film Studies course but a course based on traditional animation with supported computer image processing. **De Montfort** Some believe that this is a course in practical film making: it is not, it is for analysts and historians.

Selection interviews Yes Bournemouth Arts, Reading; **Some** Bournemouth, Bristol, Cumbria, East Anglia, Liverpool John Moores, Southampton, Staffordshire, Warwick, York; **No** Birmingham City, Canterbury Christ Church, Chichester, Essex, Falmouth, Hertfordshire, Leeds Beckett, London South Bank, Middlesex, Nottingham, Wolverhampton.

Interview advice and questions Questions will focus on your chosen field. In the case of films, be prepared to answer questions not only on your favourite films but on the work of one or two directors you admire and early Hollywood examples. See also **Chapter 5**. **Bournemouth Arts** Applicants will be required to bring a five minute show reel of their work. **Staffordshire** We assess essay-writing skills.

Reasons for rejection (non-academic) Not enough drive or ambition. No creative or original ideas. Preference for production work rather than practical work. Inability to articulate the thought process behind the work in the applicant's portfolio. Insufficient knowledge of media affairs. Lack of knowledge of film history. Wrong course choice, wanted more practical work.

AFTER-RESULTS ADVICE
Offers to applicants repeating A-levels Higher Manchester Met; **Same** Bournemouth Arts; De Montfort; East Anglia; St Mary's; Staffordshire; Stirling; Winchester; Wolverhampton; York St John; **No** Glasgow.

GRADUATE DESTINATIONS AND EMPLOYMENT (2016/17 HESA)
Graduates surveyed See **Media Studies**.

Career note Although this is a popular subject field, job opportunities in film, TV and radio are limited. Successful graduates frequently have gained work experience with companies during their undergraduate years. The transferable skills (verbal communication etc) will open up other career opportunities.

OTHER DEGREE SUBJECTS FOR CONSIDERATION
Animation; Communication Studies; Creative Writing; Media Studies; Photography.

FINANCE

(including **Finance and Investment Banking, Financial Services and Property, Finance and Investment**; see also **Accountancy/Accounting**)

Courses involving finance are wide ranging and can involve accountancy, actuarial work, banking, economics, financial services, insurance, international finance, marketing, quantity surveying, real estate management, and risk management. Some courses are theoretical, others, such as accountancy and real estate management, are vocational, providing accreditation to professional bodies. A large number of courses are offered with commercial and industrial placements over six months or a year (which includes paid employment) and many students have found that their connection with a firm has led to offers of full-time employment upon graduation.

Useful websites www.cii.co.uk; www.financialadvice.co.uk; www.fnlondon.com; www.worldbank.org; www.libf.ac.uk; www.ft.com

NB The points totals shown to the left of the institutions are for ease of reference only. It must not be assumed that Tariff points are always used by institutions or that they can be substituted for an offer in grades. The level of an offer is not necessarily indicative of the quality of a course.

COURSE OFFERS INFORMATION
Subject requirements/preferences GCSE Most institutions will require English and mathematics grade C (4) minimum. **AL** Mathematics may be required or preferred.

Your target offers and examples of degree courses

160 pts **Imperial London** – A*A*A incl maths+fmaths +MAT/STEP (Maths Stats Fin) (IB 39 pts HL 7 maths)

152 pts **London (UCL)** – A*AA incl maths (Stats Econ Fin) (IB 39 pts HL 19 pts incl 7 maths); A*AA incl maths+phys (Eng (Mech Bus Fin) (MEng)) (IB 39 pts HL 19 pts incl 7 maths+phys)

144 pts **Bath** – AAA–AAB +aEPQ incl maths (Acc Fin) (IB 36 pts HL 666)
Birmingham – AAA incl maths (Mny Bank Fin) (IB 32 pts HL 666)
Bristol – AAA–ABB incl maths (Acc Fin) (IB 32–36 pts HL 6 maths)
City – AAA (Bank Int Fin; Inv Fin Risk Mgt) (IB 35 pts)
Exeter – A*AA–AAA incl maths (Econ Fin; Econ Fin (Int St)) (IB 38–36 pts HL 766–666 incl maths); AAA (Acc Fin) (IB 36 pts HL 666)
Glasgow – AAA/A*AB incl maths (Acc Fin) (IB 38 pts HL 666 incl Engl/maths); (Fin Stats) (IB 38 pts HL 666 incl maths)
Leeds – AAA (Econ Fin; Int Bus Fin) (IB 35 pts HL 17 pts); (Acc Fin) (IB 35 pts HL 17 pts incl 5 maths)
London LSE – AAA (Acc Fin) (IB 38 pts HL 666)
Manchester – A*AA–AAA incl maths +interview (Maths Fin Maths) (IB 36 pts HL 666 incl 6 maths); (Maths Fin) (IB 36 pts HL 666 incl maths)
Nottingham – A*AA–AAA/A*AB incl maths (Fin Maths) (IB 36 pts HL 6 maths)
Reading – AAA–AAB (Acc Fin) (IB 35–34 pts)

YOUR FIRST GREAT BUSINESS DECISION

Aspire to a career in accounting or finance? Our BSc (Hons) Accounting and Finance will equip you with the knowledge and skills you need to succeed.

FREE MASTER'S
On completion of your business degree, you'll be able to progress onto a business Masters course at no extra cost.

CHOICE OF LOCATIONS
City centre locations in London, Birmingham, Leeds, Manchester and Nottingham.

TEF Silver

FREE MASTERS OFFER*

*See law.ac.uk for full terms and conditions of the Free Masters Offer

The University of **Law**

BUSINESS SCHOOL

For more information
law.ac.uk/business

Sheffield – AAA incl maths (Econ Fin) (IB 36 pts HL 5 maths)
Southampton – AAA incl maths (Maths Fin) (IB 36 pts HL 18 pts incl 6 maths)
St Andrews – AAA (Fin Econ) (IB 38 pts HL 666)
Strathclyde – AAA incl maths (Acc Fin) (IB 38 pts HL 6 maths)
Warwick – AAA incl maths (Acc Fin) (IB 38 pts HL 5 maths)

136 pts **Birmingham** – AAB (Acc Fin) (IB 32 pts HL 665)
City – AAB incl maths 136 pts (Fin Econ) (IB 30 pts HL 5 maths)
Durham – AAB (Acc Fin) (IB 36 pts HL 665 incl 5 maths)
Lancaster – AAA–AAB incl maths/fmaths (Fin Maths) (IB 36 pts HL 16 pts incl 6 maths); AAB (Acc Fin; Fin) (IB 35 pts HL 16 pts); AAB incl maths (Acc Fin Maths) (IB 35 pts HL 16 pts incl 6 maths); AAB incl maths/fmaths (Fin Econ) (IB 35 pts HL 16 pts incl 6 maths)
Leeds – AAA/A*AB–AAB/A*BB incl maths (Fin Maths) (IB 35 pts HL 17 pts incl 6 maths)
Liverpool – AAB (Acc Fin; Acc Fin (Yr Ind)) (IB 35 pts); AAB incl maths (Maths Fin) (IB 35 pts HL 6 maths)
London (QM) – AAB incl maths (Maths Fin Acc) (IB 34 pts HL 665 incl maths)
Loughborough – AAB (Bus Econ Fin) (IB 35 pts HL 665); (Fin Mgt) (IB 35–34 pts HL 665)
Manchester – AAB (Acc Fin; Fin) (IB 35 pts HL 665)
Newcastle – AAB (Acc Fin; Bus Acc Fin; Econ Fin) (IB 35 pts); AAB–A*BB incl maths (Maths Fin) (IB 34 pts HL 6 maths)
Nottingham – AAB (Fin Acc Mgt; Ind Econ Ins) (IB 34 pts)
Sheffield – AAB incl maths (Fin Maths) (IB 34 pts HL 6 maths)
Southampton – AAB/ABB +aEPQ (Acc Fin; Acc Fin (Yr Ind)) (IB 34 pts HL 17 pts); AAB incl maths (Econ Fin) (IB 34 pts HL 17 pts incl 5 maths)
Surrey – AAB (Econ Fin) (IB 34 pts)
York – AAB (Acc Bus Fin Mgt) (IB 35 pts); AAB incl maths (Econ Ecomet Fin; Econ Fin) (IB 35 pts HL 6 maths)

UCAS Tariff points for A-level equivalent qualifications appear in **Appendix 1**.

128 pts **Cardiff** – AAB–ABB (Acc Fin) (IB 32–34 pts HL 665–655); (Bank Fin) (IB 34–32 pts HL 665–655); AAB–ABB incl lang (Bank Fin Euro Lang) (IB 34–32 pts HL 665–655 incl 6 lang)

East Anglia – ABB (Bus Fin Econ) (IB 32 pts)

Edinburgh – AAA–ABB (Econ Fin) (IB 43–34 pts HL 776–655); AAB–ABB (Acc Fin) (IB 40–34 pts HL 776–655)

Leicester – ABB/BBB +bEPQ (Fin Econ Bank) (IB 30 pts); ABB–BBB +bEPQ (Acc Fin) (IB 30 pts HL 16 incl 4 maths)

Liverpool – ABB (Law Acc Fin) (IB 33 pts); ABB incl maths/phys/comp sci (Fin Comp) (IB 33 pts HL 5 maths/phys/comp sci)

London (Institute of Banking and Finance) – AAB–ABB (Fin Inv Risk) (IB 32–30 pts)

London (RH) – AAB–ABB (Acc Fin) (IB 32 pts HL 655 incl maths)

Loughborough – AAB–ABB (Acc Fin Mgt) (IB 35–34 pts HL 665)

Nottingham Trent – ABB 128 pts (Acc Fin; Econ Int Fin Bank)

Queen's Belfast – ABB incl maths (Fin (Yr Ind)) (IB 33 pts HL 655 incl maths)

Reading – ABB incl maths (Fin Inv Bank) (IB 32 pts)

Sheffield – ABB (Acc Fin Mgt) (IB 33 pts)

Surrey – AAB–ABB incl maths (Fin Maths) (IB 34–32 pts HL 6 maths); ABB (Acc Fin) (IB 32 pts)

Sussex – AAB–ABB (Acc Fin; Fin Bus) (IB 34–32 pts)

120 pts **Aberdeen** – BBB (Fin courses) (IB 32 pts HL 555)

Abertay – BBB (3 yr course) CCC (4 yr course) (Acc Fin) (IB 28 pts)

Aberystwyth – BBB (Acc Fin) (IB 28 pts)

Brunel – BBB (Econ Bus Fin) (IB 30 pts); BBB incl maths (Fin Acc) (IB 30 pts HL 5 maths)

Dundee – BBB (Fin; Int Fin) (IB 30 pts HL 555)

Essex – BBB (Acc Fin; Fin Econ) (IB 30 pts); (Bank Fin; Fin; Law Fin) (IB 30 pts HL 555)

Greenwich – 120 pts (Fin Inv Bank); BBB 120 pts (Acc Fin)

Heriot-Watt – ABB (3 yr course) BBB (4 yr course) (Acc Fin) (IB 34 pts (3 yr course) 29 pts (4 yr course) HL 5 maths); BBB (Bus Fin) (IB 29 pts)

Huddersfield – BBB 120 pts (Acc Fin; Bus Fin Serv)

Kent – BBB (Fin Econ) (IB 34 pts HL 15 pts); (Acc Fin) (IB 34 pts HL 16)

Kingston – ABC 120 pts (Acc Fin) (IB 27 pts HL 4 Engl lang)

Lincoln – BBB (Acc Fin) (IB 30 pts)

London (RH) – AAB–BBB (Fin Bus Econ) (IB 32 pts HL 555)

London South Bank – BBB 120 pts (Acc Fin)

Northumbria – 120 pts (Fin Inv Mgt)

Nottingham Trent – BBB (Prop Fin Inv)

Sheffield Hallam – 120 pts (Acc Fin)

Staffordshire – BBB 120 pts (Acc Fin)

Stirling – BBB (Fin) (IB 32 pts)

Strathclyde – AAB–BBB incl maths+phys (Mech Eng Fin Mgt (MEng)) (IB 36 pts HL 6 maths+phys); ABB–BBB (Fin courses) (IB 36 pts)

Swansea – ABB–BBB (Bus Mgt (Fin)) (IB 33–32 pts); (Acc Fin; Acc Fin (Yr Ind)) (IB 33–32 pts HL 4 Engl)

112 pts **Bangor** – 112 pts (Bank Fin)

Birmingham City – BBC 112 pts (Acc Fin) (28 pts HL 14 pts); (Fin Econ) (HL 14 pts); (Bus Fin) (IB 28 pts HL 14 pts)

Bradford – 112 pts (Acc Fin; Acc Fin (Yr Ind))

Cardiff Met – BBC 112 pts (Bus Mgt Fin; Int Econ Fin) (IB 24 pts HL 12 pts)

De Montfort – 112 pts (Econ Fin) (IB 26 pts)

East London – BBC 112 pts (Acc Fin) (IB 26 pts HL 15 pts)

Gloucestershire – BBC 112 pts (Acc Fin)

Greenwich – 112 pts (Bus Fin)

Hertfordshire – BBC incl maths 112 pts (Fin Maths) (HL 4 maths)

Hull – 112 pts (Bus Mgt Fin Mgt) (IB 28 pts); BBC 112 pts (Fin Mgt) (IB 28 pts)

Leeds Beckett – 112 pts (Acc Fin) (IB 25 pts)

Lincoln – BBC (Bus Fin) (IB 29 pts)

Liverpool Hope – BBC (Acc Fin) (IB 26 pts)
Liverpool John Moores – BBC 112 pts (Acc Fin) (IB 28 pts)
London (Institute of Banking and Finance) – ABB–BBC (Bank Fin) (IB 32–28 pts)
London Regent's – BBC (Glob Mgt courses)
Middlesex – 112 pts (Acc Fin)
Plymouth – 112–128 pts incl maths (Maths Fin) (IB 30 pts HL 5 maths)
Portsmouth – 112–120 pts (Econ Fin Bank) (IB 29 pts HL 655/754–664); (Acc Fin) (IB 30 pts
   HL 754–655); 112–128 pts incl maths (Maths Fin Mgt) (IB 26–25 pts)
Robert Gordon – BBC (Acc Fin) (IB 29 pts)
Sheffield Hallam – BBC 112 pts (Bus Fin Mgt)
Sunderland – 112 pts (Acc Fin); BBC 112 pts (Bus Fin Mgt)
UWE Bristol – 112 pts (Acc Fin; Bank Fin)
West London – BBB–BBC 112–120 pts (Acc Fin) (IB 26 pts); BBC 112 pts (Bus St Fin)
Westminster – ABB–BBC 112–128 pts (Fin) (IB 27 pts)
Winchester – 112–120 pts (Acc Fin) (IB 26 pts)

104 pts **Aston** – BBB–BCC (Fin) (IB 31 pts HL 555)
Bournemouth – 104–120 pts (Acc Fin) (IB 28–31 pts HL 55); (Bus Mgt (Fin)) (IB 31–28 pts)
Chester – BBC–BCC 104–112 pts (Bus Fin) (IB 26 pts)
Coventry – 104 pts (Fin Serv)
Glasgow Caledonian – BCC (Fin Inv Risk) (IB 25 pts)
Greenwich – BCC incl maths 104 pts (Fin Maths)
Hertfordshire – BCC 104 pts (Fin)
Manchester Met – BBC–BCC 104–112 pts (Acc Fin; Bank Fin) (IB 26 pts)
Northampton – BCC (Bank Fin Plan)
Oxford Brookes – 104 pts (Acc Fin) (IB 29 pts); BCC 104 pts (Econ Fin Int Bus) (IB 29 pts)
Winchester – 104–120 pts (Econ Fin); 104–120 pts incl maths (Maths Fin) (HL 44)

96 pts **Aberystwyth** – BBB–CCC 96–120 pts (Bus Fin) (IB 30–26 pts)
Anglia Ruskin – 96 pts (Bank Fin; Bus Mgt Fin) (IB 24 pts)
Brighton – BBB–CCC 96–120 pts (Acc Fin) (IB 26 pts HL incl maths); BBC–CCC 96–112 pts (Fin
   Inv) (IB 26 pts); BBC–CCC incl maths 96–112 pts (Maths Fin) (IB 26 pts HL 6 maths)
Buckingham – BBC–CCC+interview (Acc Fin) (IB 29–31 pts)
Chichester – 96–112 pts (Acc Fin) (IB 28 pts)
Edinburgh Napier – CCC (Fin Serv) (IB 28 pts HL 654)
Keele – CCC (Acc Fin; Fin Comb Hons) (IB 26 pts)
London Met – CCC 96 pts (Bank Fin)
Middlesex – 96 pts (Bank Fin)
Plymouth – 96–112 pts (Acc Fin) (IB 28 pts HL 4)
Solent – 96–112 pts (Acc Fin)
Wolverhampton – CCC (Acc Fin)
York St John – 96–112 pts (Acc Fin)

88 pts **Plymouth** – 88–104 pts (Fin Econ) (IB 28–26 pts HL 4)
80 pts **Bucks New** – 80 pts (Bus Fin)
South Wales – BCC–CDD 80–104 pts (Acc Fin)
Teesside – 80–104 pts (Acc Fin)

Alternative offers
See **Chapter 6** and **Appendix 1** for grades/UCAS Tariff points information for other examinations.

EXAMPLES OF COLLEGES OFFERING COURSES IN THIS SUBJECT FIELD
Barnet and Southgate (Coll); Blackburn (Coll); Bradford College UC; Croydon (Univ Centre); Manchester (Coll); Newcastle (Coll); Norwich City (Coll); Pearson (Coll); Peterborough (Coll); Plymouth City (Coll).

CHOOSING YOUR COURSE (SEE ALSO CH.1)
Universities and colleges teaching quality See www.qaa.ac.uk; https://unistats.ac.uk.

Examples of sandwich degree courses Aston; Bath; Birmingham City; Bournemouth; Bradford; Brighton; Brunel; Chichester; City; Coventry; De Montfort; Durham; Greenwich; Hertfordshire; Huddersfield; Kent; Kingston; Lancaster; Leeds Beckett; Liverpool; Liverpool John Moores; London Met; Loughborough; Manchester Met; Middlesex; Nottingham Trent; Oxford Brookes; Plymouth; Portsmouth; Queen's Belfast; Reading; Sheffield Hallam; Surrey; Sussex; Teesside; Trinity Saint David; UWE Bristol; West London; Westminster; Wolverhampton; York.

ADMISSIONS INFORMATION
Number of applicants per place (approx) Bangor 5; Birmingham 3; Birmingham City 13; Buckingham 4; Cardiff 10; Central Lancashire 6; City 9; Dundee 8; Durham 5; Manchester 11; Middlesex 3; Northampton 3; Sheffield Hallam 4.

Advice to applicants and planning the UCAS personal statement Visits to banks or insurance companies should be described, giving details of any work experience or work shadowing done in various departments. Discuss any particular aspects of finance etc which interest you. See also **Appendix 3**.

Selection interviews Yes Buckingham; **No** City, Dundee, Huddersfield, Staffordshire, Stirling.

Interview advice and questions Banking involves both high street and merchant banks, so a knowledge of banking activities in general will be expected. In the past mergers have been discussed and also the role of the Bank of England in the economy. The work of the accountant may be discussed. See also **Chapter 5**.

Reasons for rejection (non-academic) Lack of interest. Poor English. Lacking in motivation and determination to complete the course.

AFTER-RESULTS ADVICE
Offers to applicants repeating A-levels Same Bangor; Birmingham; Birmingham City; Bradford; Cardiff; City; Dundee; Edinburgh Napier; London Met; Loughborough; Northumbria; Stirling; **No** Glasgow.

GRADUATE DESTINATIONS AND EMPLOYMENT (2016/17 HESA)
Graduates surveyed 2,135 **Employed** 1,310 **In voluntary employment** 60 **In further study** 415 **Assumed unemployed** 125

Career note Most graduates enter financial careers. Further study is required to qualify as an accountant and to obtain other professional qualifications, eg Institute of Banking.

OTHER DEGREE SUBJECTS FOR CONSIDERATION
Accountancy; Actuarial Studies; Business Studies; Economics.

FOOD SCIENCE/STUDIES AND TECHNOLOGY

(see also **Agricultural Sciences/Agriculture, Biochemistry, Dietetics, Hospitality and Event Management, Nutrition**)

Food Science courses are purely scientific and technical in their approach with the study of food composition and storage in order to monitor food quality, safety and preparation. Scientific elements cover biochemistry, chemistry and microbiology, focussing on human nutrition and, in some courses, dietetics, food processing and management. However, these courses are not to be confused with Culinary Arts subjects which lead to careers in food preparation. There are also several business courses specialising in food, such as Food Product Management and Marketing options. The unique course in this category, however, is the Viticulture and Oenology course offered at Plumpton College in partnership with the University of Brighton, which involves the study of grape growing and wine-making.

Useful websites www.sofht.co.uk; www.ifst.org; www.gov.uk/government/organisations/department-for-environment-food-rural-affairs; http://iagre.org

NB The points totals shown to the left of the institutions are for ease of reference only. It must not be assumed that Tariff points are always used by institutions or that they can be substituted for an offer in grades. The level of an offer is not necessarily indicative of the quality of a course.

COURSE OFFERS INFORMATION

Subject requirements/preferences GCSE English, mathematics and a science. **AL** One or two mathematics/science subjects; chemistry may be required.

Your target offers and examples of degree courses

136 pts   Newcastle – AAB incl sci (Fd Hum Nutr) (IB 34 pts); (Nutr Fd Mark) (IB 34 pts HL 6 biol)

128 pts   Leeds – ABB incl sci/maths (Fd Sci) (IB 34 pts HL 16 pts)
   Nottingham – AAB–ABB incl sci/maths (Fd Sci; Fd Sci Nutr) (IB 34–32 pts)
   Reading – ABB incl sci/maths +interview (Fd Sci; Fd Sci Bus; Fd Tech Bioproc; Nutr Fd Sci) (IB 32 pts HL 5 sci/maths)

120 pts   Newcastle – ABB–BBB (Fd Bus Mgt Mark) (IB 32 pts)
   Northumbria – 120 pts incl sci/fd tech/hm econ (Fd Sci Nutr)
   Queen's Belfast – ABB–BBB incl sci (Fd Qual Sfty Nutr) (IB 33–32 pts HL 655 incl biol+chem)
   Reading – BBB (Fd Mark Bus Econ) (IB 30 pts)
   Surrey – ABB–BBB incl biol/chem+sci/maths (Fd Sci Nutr) (IB 32 pts HL 5 biol/chem+maths/sci)

112 pts   Cardiff Met – BBC 112 pts incl sci/fd tech (Fd Sci Tech) (IB 24 pts)
   Coventry – BBC incl biol/chem/fd tech (Fd Sci; Fd Sfty Insp Cntrl) (IB 30 pts HL 5 biol/chem)
   Glasgow Caledonian – BBC incl chem (Fd Biosci) (IB 24 pts HL 4 biol+chem)
   Sheffield Hallam – 112 pts (Fd Mark Prod Dev; Fd Nutr)

104 pts   Abertay – BCC incl sci/maths (Fit Nutr Hlth) (IB 29 pts HL 4 sci+maths)
   CAFRE – 104 pts incl sci/hm econ (Fd Innov Nutr; Food Tech)
   Liverpool John Moores – BCC incl sci 104 pts (Nutr)
   Ulster – BBB–BCC (Consum Mgt Fd Innov) (IB 26–24 pts HL 13–12 pts)

96 pts   Abertay – CCC (Fd Consum Sci) (IB 28 pts)
   Bath Spa – CCC (Fd Nutr) (IB 26 pts)
   Birmingham (UC) – CCC 96 pts (Fd Dev Innov)
   Royal Agricultural Univ – CCC (Int Bus Mgt (Fd Agribus)) (IB 26 pts)
   Teesside – C sci/fd tech/biol 96–112 pts+interview (Fd Nutr)
   Ulster – CCC incl sci/maths/env tech/hm econ (Fd Nutr) (IB 24 pts HL 12 pts incl 5 sci/maths/hm econ)

72 pts   Harper Adams – 72–88 pts (Agri-Fd Mark Bus) (IB 24 pts)

Alternative offers
See **Chapter 6** and **Appendix 1** for grades/UCAS Tariff points information for other examinations.

EXAMPLES OF COLLEGES OFFERING COURSES IN THIS SUBJECT FIELD
Bridgwater and Taunton (Coll); CAFRE; Cornwall (Coll); Duchy Coll UC; Plumpton (Coll); TEC Partnership; Westminster Kingsway (Coll).

CHOOSING YOUR COURSE (SEE ALSO CH.1)
Universities and colleges teaching quality See www.qaa.ac.uk; https://unistats.ac.uk.

Top research universities and colleges (REF 2014) See **Agricultural Sciences/Agriculture**.

Examples of sandwich degree courses Birmingham (UC); Cardiff Met; Coventry; Huddersfield; London South Bank; Northumbria; Queen's Belfast; Reading; Sheffield Hallam.

ADMISSIONS INFORMATION
Number of applicants per place (approx) Bath Spa 4; Birmingham (UC) 2; Cardiff Met 1; Leeds 5; Liverpool John Moores 2; London South Bank 3; Nottingham 8; Queen's Belfast 10; Sheffield Hallam 4.

Advice to applicants and planning the UCAS personal statement Visits, work experience or work shadowing in any food manufacturing firm, or visits to laboratories, should be described on your UCAS application. Keep up-to-date with developments by reading journals relating to the industry.

Misconceptions about this course Leeds Food Science is not food technology, catering or cooking. It aims to understand why food materials behave in the way they do, in order to improve the nutritive value, safety and quality of the food we eat.

Selection interviews Yes Harper Adams; **No** Leeds, Liverpool John Moores, Nottingham, Reading, Surrey.

Interview advice and questions Food science and technology is a specialised field and admissions tutors will want to know your reasons for choosing the subject. You will be questioned on any experience you have had in the food industry. More general questions may cover the reasons for the trends in the popularity of certain types of food, the value of junk food and whether scientific interference with food is justifiable. See also **Chapter 5**. **Leeds** Questions asked to ensure that the student understands, and can cope with, the science content of the course.

Reasons for rejection (non-academic) Too immature. Unlikely to integrate well. Lack of vocational commitment.

AFTER-RESULTS ADVICE
Offers to applicants repeating A-levels Higher Heriot-Watt; Leeds; **Same** Abertay; Liverpool John Moores; Nottingham; Queen's Belfast; Sheffield Hallam.

GRADUATE DESTINATIONS AND EMPLOYMENT (2016/17 HESA)
Food and Beverage Studies graduates surveyed 595 **Employed** 315 **In voluntary employment** 0 **In further study** 190 **Assumed unemployed** 20

Career note Employment levels for food science/studies and technology graduates are high mainly in manufacturing and retailing and increasingly with large companies.

OTHER DEGREE SUBJECTS FOR CONSIDERATION
Biochemistry; Biological Sciences; Biology; Biotechnology; Chemistry; Consumer Studies; Crop Science; Dietetics; Health Studies; Hospitality Management; Nutrition; Plant Science.

FRENCH
(see also European Studies, Languages)

Applicants should select courses according to the emphasis which they prefer. Courses could focus on literature or language (or both), or on the written and spoken word, as in the case of interpreting and translating courses, or on the broader study of French culture, political and social aspects found on European Studies courses.

Useful websites http://europa.eu; www.bbc.co.uk/languages; www.languageadvantage.com; www.languagematters.co.uk; www.ciol.org.uk; www.lemonde.fr; www.institut-francais.org.uk; www.academie-francaise.fr; www.institut-de-france.fr; www.sfs.ac.uk; https://academic.oup.com/fs

NB The points totals shown to the left of the institutions are for ease of reference only. It must not be assumed that Tariff points are always used by institutions or that they can be substituted for an offer in grades. The level of an offer is not necessarily indicative of the quality of a course.

COURSE OFFERS INFORMATION
Subject requirements/preferences GCSE French, mathematics (for business courses), grade levels may be stipulated. **AL** French is usually required at a specific grade and in some cases a second language may be stipulated.

Your target offers and examples of degree courses

152 pts **Nottingham** – A*AA (Econ Fr) (IB 38 pts)

144 pts **Durham** – AAA incl lang (Modn Langs Cult (Yr Abrd)) (IB 37 pts HL 666 incl lang)

Imperial London – AAA incl chem+maths +interview (Chem Fr/Ger/Span Sci) (IB 38 pts HL 6 chem+maths)

Oxford – AAA incl Fr +interview +MLAT (Fr) (IB 38 pts HL 666 incl Fr)

Southampton – AAA incl maths+Fr/Ger/Span (Maths Fr/Ger/Span) (IB 36 pts HL 18 pts incl 6 maths+Fr/Ger/Span)

136 pts **Bath** – AAB–ABB +aEPQ incl Fr (Int Mgt Fr) (IB 36 pts HL 665 incl 6 Fr); AAB–ABB+aEPQ incl lang (Int Pol Modn Langs) (IB 35 pts HL 665 incl 7 lang)

Birmingham – AAB incl Fr (Fr St Comb Hons) (IB 32 pts HL 665); AAB incl hist (Modn Langs Hist) (IB 32 pts HL 665)

Bristol – AAB incl Fr (Fr courses) (IB 34 pts HL 17 pts incl 5 Fr)

Dundee – AAB incl Engl (Law Langs) (IB 36 pts HL 665 incl Engl)

Glasgow – AAB incl arts/hum (Fr) (IB 36 pts HL 665 incl Engl+lang/hum)

London (King's) – AAB (Euro St (Fr/Ger/Span) (Yr Abrd); Fr Phil (Yr Abrd); Mgt Modn Lang (Yr Abrd)) (IB 35 pts HL 665); AAB incl Fr (Fr) (IB 35 pts HL 665 incl Fr); AAB incl Fr/Ger (Fr Ger (Yr Abrd)) (IB 35 pts HL 665); AAB incl Fr/Span (Fr Span (Yr Abrd)) (IB 35 pts HL 665); AAB incl hist (Fr Hist (Yr Abrd)) (IB 35 pts HL 665 incl hist)

London (UCL) – AAB incl Fr (Fr As Af Lang) (IB 36 pts HL 17 incl 6 Fr); (Fr) (IB 36 pts HL 17 pts incl 6 Fr)

Southampton – AAB/ABB +aEPQ incl Engl+Fr/Ger/Span (Engl Fr/Ger/Span) (IB 34 pts HL 17 pts incl 65 Engl+Fr/Ger/Span); AAB/ABB +aEPQ incl Fr (Fr) (IB 34 pts HL 17 pts incl 6 Fr); AAB incl sci/maths/geog+interview (Ocean Fr (MSci)) (IB 34 pts HL 17 pts incl 6 sci/maths/geog)

St Andrews – AAB incl Fr (Fr courses) (IB 36 pts HL 665 incl 6 Fr)

Warwick – AAB incl Fr (Fr Comb Hons; Fr Ger (Yr Abrd)) (IB 36 pts HL 5 Fr)

York – AAB incl Fr (Fr Ger Lang (Yr Abrd); Fr Span Lang (Yr Abrd)) (IB 35 pts HL 6 Fr)

128 pts **Edinburgh** – AAB–ABB (Int Bus Fr/Ger/Span) (IB 40–34 pts HL 766–655); ABB incl lang (Fr) (IB 40–34 pts HL 766–655 incl 5 lang)

Exeter – AAB–ABB incl Fr (Fr Arbc) (IB 34–32 pts HL 5 Fr); AAB–ABB incl Lat (Fr Lat) (IB 34–32 pts HL 665–655 incl Lat); AAB–ABB incl lang (Class St Modn Langs) (IB 34–32 pts HL 665–655)

Lancaster – ABB (Fr St) (IB 32 pts HL 16 pts)

Leeds – ABB incl Fr (Fr) (IB 34 pts HL 16 pts incl 6 Fr)

Leicester – ABB/BBB +bEPQ (Fr Comb Hons) (IB 30 pts)

Liverpool – ABB incl Fr (Fr; Fr Comb Hons) (IB 33 pts HL 6 Fr)

London (Inst Paris) – ABB incl Fr+interview (Fr St) (IB 34 pts HL 6 Fr)

London (RH) – AAB–ABB (Euro Int St Fr/Ger/Ital/Span; Modn Lang Mgt; Modn Lang Mus) (IB 32 pts HL 655); AAB–ABB incl lang (Modn Lang Dr) (IB 32 pts HL 655)

Manchester – ABB (Fr courses) (IB 34 pts HL 655)

Newcastle – AAA–ABB incl Fr (Ling Fr) (IB 36–34 pts HL 5 Fr)

Northumbria – 128 pts (Int Bus Mgt Fr)

Nottingham – ABB incl Fr (Fr Comb Hons; Fr St) (IB 32 pts HL 5 Fr)

Queen's Belfast – ABB incl Fr (Fr; Fr Comb Hons) (IB 33 pts HL 655 incl 6 Fr)

Sheffield – ABB (Modn Langs Cult) (IB 33 pts HL 5 lang)

Southampton – AAB–ABB incl Fr/Ger/Span (Flm Fr/Ger/Span) (IB 32 pts HL 6 Fr/Ger/Span)

Sussex – ABB 128 pts (Anth Lang) (32 pts)

Warwick – ABB incl Fr (Fr St) (IB 34 pts HL 5 Fr)

York – AAB–ABB incl Fr (Fr Ital Lang (Yr Abrd); Fr Ling (Yr Abrd)) (IB 35–34 pts HL 6 Fr)

120 pts **Aberdeen** – BBB (Anth Fr/Ger; Fr St) (IB 32 pts HL 555)

Aston – ABB–BBB (Int Bus Fr/Ger/Span) (IB 32 pts HL 665–655); ABB–BBB incl Fr (Fr courses) (IB 33–32 pts HL 6 Fr)

Cardiff – ABB–BBB incl lang (Fr courses) (IB 32–30 pts HL 665–655)

Essex – BBB (Fr St Modn Langs) (IB 30 pts)

        Heriot-Watt – BBB incl lang (App Langs Transl (Fr/Span)/(Ger/Span)) (IB 30 pts HL 5 lang)
        Kent – BBB (Fr) (IB 34 pts HL 15 pts)
        London (QM) – BBB incl hum/soc sci (Fr courses) (IB 30 pts HL 555 incl hum/soc sci)
        London (RH) – ABB–BBB (Modn Lang Lat; Modn Langs) (IB 32 pts HL 555)
        Nottingham Trent – BBB incl Fr 120 pts (Fr Comb Hons)
        Reading – BBB (Fr courses) (IB 30 pts)
        Stirling – BBB (Fr) (IB 32 pts)
        Strathclyde – ABB–BBB incl Fr (Fr courses) (IB 36 pts)
        Surrey – BBB incl Fr (Fr courses) (IB 32 pts)
        Swansea – BBB (Modn Langs) (IB 32 pts); BBB incl lang 120 pts (Fr)
112 pts   **Chester** – 112 pts incl art des+Fr (Fn Art Fr) (IB 26 pts HL 5 vis arts+Fr)
        Hull – BBC incl lang 112 pts (App Modn Lang (Fr/Ger/Span)) (IB 28 pts HL 5 lang)
        London (Birk) – ABB–BBC 112–128 pts (Fr Mgt; Modn Langs (Fr/Ger/Ital/Jap/Port/Span));
          ABB–BBC incl Fr 112–128 pts (Fr St)
104 pts   **Aberystwyth** – BBB–BCC 104–120 pts (Fr Comb Hons) (IB 30–28 pts HL 5 Fr)
        Central Lancashire – 104–112 pts (Int Bus Comm Modn For Lang); 104–112 pts incl lang
          (Modn Langs (2 Lang) (Fr/Ger/Span/Jap/Russ/Ital/Kor))
        Chester – BBC–BCC incl Fr 104–112 pts (Fr) (IB 26 pts HL 5 Fr)
        Hertfordshire – BCC 104 pts (Engl Lit Fr; Fr Comb Hons)
        Manchester Met – BBC–BCC 104–112 pts (Ling Mand Chin/Fr/Ger/Ital/Span) (IB 26 pts); BBC–
          BCC incl B Fr 104–112 pts incl Fr (Fr St) (IB 26 pts HL 6 Fr)
        Westminster – ABB–BCC 104–128 pts (Fr courses) (IB 27 pts)
96 pts   **Bangor** – 96–104 pts incl lang (Fr courses)
        Portsmouth – 96–112 pts (Modn Langs) (IB 25 pts)

Alternative offers
See **Chapter 6** and **Appendix 1** for grades/UCAS Tariff points information for other examinations.

EXAMPLES OF COLLEGES OFFERING COURSES IN THIS SUBJECT FIELD
Richmond-upon-Thames (Coll).

CHOOSING YOUR COURSE (SEE ALSO CH.1)
Universities and colleges teaching quality See www.qaa.ac.uk; https://unistats.ac.uk.

Top research universities and colleges (REF 2014) See **Languages**.

Examples of sandwich degree courses Bangor; Plymouth.

ADMISSIONS INFORMATION
Number of applicants per place (approx) Aston 6; Bangor 5; Bath (Modn Langs Euro St) 6;
Birmingham 5; Bristol 4; Cardiff 6; Central Lancashire 5; Durham 5; Exeter 8; Hull 5; Kent 6; Lancaster
7; Leicester (Fr Ital) 6; Liverpool 6; London (Inst Paris) 9; London (King's) 9; London (RH) 7; London
(UCL) 5; Manchester Met 13; Newcastle (Modn Langs) 7; Nottingham 8; Warwick 7; York 8.

Advice to applicants and planning the UCAS personal statement Visits to France (including
exchange visits) should be described, with reference to any particular cultural or geographical features
of the region visited. Providing information about your contacts with French friends and experience in
speaking the language are also important. Express your willingness to work/live/travel abroad and
show your interests in French life and culture. Read French newspapers and magazines and keep
up-to-date with news stories etc. See also **Appendix 3**. **Bristol** Deferred entry accepted in some cases.
Late applications may not be accepted. **London (Inst Paris)** On the personal statement candidates
must indicate their interest in and the value of spending an extended stay in the country of their
target language. At interview candidates must be prepared to speak in both French and English.

Misconceptions about this course Leeds See **Languages**. **London (Inst Paris)** Students do not
need to be fully fluent in French to study on this course, but a B in A-level French or B1 French
certification is required. **Swansea** Some applicants are not aware of the range of subjects that can

be combined with French in our flexible modular system. They sometimes do not know that linguistics and area studies options are also available as well as literature options in French.

Selection interviews Yes Leeds, London (Inst Paris), Oxford; **Some** London (UCL), Warwick; **No** Bangor, Birmingham, Canterbury Christ Church, Essex, Heriot-Watt, Hull, Liverpool, Nottingham, Portsmouth, Reading, Surrey.

Interview advice and questions Questions will almost certainly be asked on your A-level texts, in addition to your reading outside the syllabus – books, magazines, newspapers etc. Part of the interview may be conducted in French and written tests may be involved. See also **Chapter 5**. **Leeds** See **Languages**. **London (Inst Paris)** Candidates should be prepared to speak both in French and in English.

Reasons for rejection (non-academic) Candidate unenthusiastic, unmotivated, ill-informed about the nature of the course (had not read the prospectus). Not keen to spend a year abroad. **London (Inst Paris)** Lack of communicative competence and/or maturity required to survive the experience of living independently in a foreign country.

AFTER-RESULTS ADVICE
Offers to applicants repeating A-levels Higher Aberystwyth; Leeds; Warwick; **Possibly higher** Aston; **Same** Chester; Durham; Lancaster; Liverpool; Newcastle; Nottingham; Sheffield; Sussex; **No** Glasgow.

GRADUATE DESTINATIONS AND EMPLOYMENT (2016/17 HESA)
Graduates surveyed 1,075 **Employed** 560 **In voluntary employment** 50 **In further study** 255 **Assumed unemployed** 55

Career note See **Languages**.

OTHER DEGREE SUBJECTS FOR CONSIDERATION
European Studies; International Business Studies; Literature; other language.

GENETICS
(See also Biological Sciences, Microbiology)

Genetics is at the cutting edge of modern biology, as demonstrated by the recent developments in genomics and biotechnology leading to considerable advances in the treatment of disease and genetic engineering. Studies can cover such fields as genetic counselling, population genetics, pharmaceuticals, pre-natal diagnoses, cancer biology, evolution, forensic genetics, plant biology and food quality. Possibly an ideal option for keen science students looking for a degree allied to medicine.

Useful websites www.genetics.org; www.nature.com/subjects/genetics; www.genetics.org.uk; see also **Biological Sciences**.

NB The points totals shown to the left of the institutions are for ease of reference only. It must not be assumed that Tariff points are always used by institutions or that they can be substituted for an offer in grades. The level of an offer is not necessarily indicative of the quality of a course.

COURSE OFFERS INFORMATION

Subject requirements/preferences GCSE English, mathematics and science subjects. **AL** Chemistry and/or biology are usually required or preferred.

Your target offers and examples of degree courses
160 pts   **Cambridge** – A*A*A incl sci/maths +interview +NSAA (Nat Sci (Genet)) (IB 42–40 pts HL 776)
136 pts   **Birmingham** – AAB incl biol+sci (Biol Sci (Genet)) (IB 32 pts HL 665); AAB incl chem+sci
            (Bioch (Genet)) (IB 32 pts HL 665)
          Glasgow – AAB incl biol/chem (Genet) (IB 36 pts HL 665 incl 6 biol/chem)
          Leeds – AAA–AAB incl biol (Genet) (IB 35–34 pts HL 18–17 pts incl 6 biol+sci)

London (King's) – AAB incl chem+biol (Mol Genet) (IB 35 pts HL 665); (Pharmacol Mol Genet) (IB 35 pts HL 665 incl chem+biol)

Newcastle – AAA–AAB incl biol/chem+maths/sci (Biomed Genet) (IB 35–34 pts HL 5 biol/chem+maths/sci)

Nottingham – AAB incl biol+sci/geog/psy (Genet) (IB 34 pts HL 5/6 biol+sci); AAB incl chem+sci (Bioch Genet) (IB 34 pts HL 5/6 chem+sci)

Sheffield – AAB incl sci (Genet; Genet Microbiol; Med Genet) (IB 34 pts HL 65 sci)

York – AAB incl biol+sci/maths (Genet) (IB 35 pts HL 6 biol+sci/maths)

128 pts Cardiff – AAB–ABB incl biol/chem (Biol Sci (Genet)) (IB 34–32 pts HL 655 incl 6 biol/chem)

Dundee – AAB–ABB incl biol+chem (Mol Genet) (IB 30 pts HL 555 incl biol+chem)

Leicester – ABB incl sci/maths (Biol Sci (Genet)) (IB 30 pts HL 56 sci/maths); (Med Genet) (IB 30 pts HL 65 sci/maths)

Liverpool – ABB/BBB +aEPQ incl biol+sci (Genet) (IB 33 pts HL 6 biol 5 sci)

London (QM) – ABB incl biol (Genet) (IB 34 pts HL 655 incl biol)

Manchester – AAA–ABB incl sci/maths +interview (Genet; Genet (Yr Ind)) (IB 36–33 pts HL 666–655 incl chem+sci); (Genet Modn Lang) (IB 36–33 pts HL 666–655 incl sci)

120 pts Aberdeen – BBB incl maths/sci (Genet; Genet (Immun)) (IB 32 pts HL 5 maths/sci)

Brunel – BBB incl sci (Biomed Sci (Genet)) (IB 30 pts HL 5 sci)

East Anglia – BBB incl biol (Mol Biol Genet) (IB 31 pts HL 5 biol)

Swansea – AAB–BBB incl biol (Genet) (IB 33–32 pts); AAB–BBB incl biol+chem (Med Genet) (IB 33–32 pts); AAB–BBB incl biol+chem 120–136 pts (Bioch Genet) (IB 33–32 pts)

112 pts Hertfordshire – BBC incl biol/chem+sci/maths/geog/psy 112 pts (Mol Biol)

Huddersfield – BBC incl sci 112 pts (Med Genet)

104 pts Aberystwyth – BBB–BCC incl biol 104–120 pts (Genet) (IB 30–28 pts HL 5 biol)

Essex – BCC incl biol +interview (Genet) (IB 28 pts HL 544 incl biol)

80 pts Wolverhampton – CDD incl sci (Genet Mol Biol)

Alternative offers
See **Chapter 6** and **Appendix 1** for grades/UCAS Tariff points information for other examinations.

CHOOSING YOUR COURSE (SEE ALSO CH.1)

Universities and colleges teaching quality See www.qaa.ac.uk; https://unistats.ac.uk.

Top research universities and colleges (REF 2014) See **Biological Sciences**.

Examples of sandwich degree courses Brunel; Essex; Huddersfield; Leeds; Manchester; York.

ADMISSIONS INFORMATION

Number of applicants per place (approx) Bath 8; Dundee 8; Leeds 7; Leicester (Biol Sci) 10; Nottingham 8; Swansea 7; Wolverhampton 4; York 9.

Advice to applicants and planning the UCAS personal statement See **Biological Sciences**.

Misconceptions about this course York Some fail to realise that chemistry (beyond **GCSE**) is essential to an understanding of genetics.

Selection interviews Yes Cambridge, Manchester; **No** Dundee, Liverpool, Swansea, Wolverhampton.

Interview advice and questions Likely questions will focus on your A-level science subjects, particularly biology, why you wish to study genetics, and on careers in genetics. See also **Chapter 5.**

AFTER-RESULTS ADVICE

Offers to applicants repeating A-levels Higher Aberystwyth; Leeds; Swansea; **Same** Dundee; Nottingham; Wolverhampton; York; **No** Cambridge.

GRADUATE DESTINATIONS AND EMPLOYMENT (2016/17 HESA)

Graduates surveyed 295 **Employed** 100 **In voluntary employment** 0 **In further study** 135 **Assumed unemployed** 15

Career note See **Biological Sciences**.

OTHER DEGREE SUBJECTS FOR CONSIDERATION

Biochemistry; Biological Sciences; Biology; Biotechnology; Human Sciences; Immunology; Life Sciences; Medical Biochemistry; Medical Biology; Medicine; Microbiology; Molecular Biology; Natural Sciences; Physiology; Plant Sciences.

GEOGRAPHY

(See also **Environmental Sciences**)

The content and focus of Geography courses will vary between universities, although many similarities exist between BA and BSc courses apart from entry requirements. For example, at the University of Birmingham, the course is flexible offering topics from migration and urban and social changes, to natural hazards and global environmental changes, with decisions on the paths to take between human and physical geography being delayed. At Leeds, the BA course focuses on human geography and the BSc course on physical aspects. This is a subject deserving real research between the offerings of a wide range of institutions in view of the variety of topics on offer, for example, rural, historical, political or cultural geography at Exeter, environmental geography and climate change at East Anglia, and physical oceanography as part of the BSc course at Plymouth.

Useful websites www.metoffice.gov.uk; www.rgs.org; www.ordnancesurvey.co.uk; http://geographical.co.uk; www.nationalgeographic.com; www.cartography.org.uk; www.gov.uk/government/organisations/natural-england; www.geography.org.uk; www.publicprofiler.org; www.esri.com/en-us/what-is-gis/overview

NB The points totals shown to the left of the institutions are for ease of reference only. It must not be assumed that Tariff points are always used by institutions or that they can be substituted for an offer in grades. The level of an offer is not necessarily indicative of the quality of a course.

COURSE OFFERS INFORMATION

Subject requirements/preferences GCSE Geography usually required. Mathematics/sciences often required for BSc courses. **AL** Geography is usually required for most courses. Mathematics/science subjects required for BSc courses.

Your target offers and examples of degree courses
152 pts   **Cambridge** – A*AA +interview +GAA (Geog) (IB 42–40 pts HL 776)
        Durham – A*AA (Comb Hons Soc Sci; Geog courses) (IB 38 pts HL 666)
        London (UCL) – A*AA incl geog+maths (Econ Geog) (IB 39 pts HL 19 pts incl 7 maths 6 geog)
        Oxford – A*AA +interview +GAT (Geog) (IB 39 pts HL 766)
144 pts   **Lancaster** – AAA (Hum Geog (Yr Abrd)) (IB 36 pts HL 16 pts incl 6 geog)
        Leeds – AAA (Geog courses) (IB 35 pts HL 17 pts incl 5 geog)
        London (UCL) – AAA incl geog (Geog) (IB 38 pts HL 18 pts incl 6 geog)
        London LSE – AAA (Geog) (IB 38 pts HL 766); AAA incl maths (Geog Econ) (IB 38 pts HL 766 incl maths)
        St Andrews – AAA (Geog Int Rel; Geog Lang) (IB 38 pts); (Geog) (IB 38 pts HL 666)
136 pts   **Birmingham** – AAB (Geog) (IB 32 pts HL 665)
        Bristol – AAA–AAB (Geog) (IB 36–34 pts HL 17 pts)
        Glasgow – AAB incl sci (Geog) (IB 36 pts HL 665 incl sci)
        Lancaster – AAB incl geog (Geog; Physl Geog) (IB 35 pts HL 16 pts incl 6 geog)
        Leeds – AAB incl geog (Geog Trans St) (IB 35 pts HL 16 pts incl 5 geog)
        London (King's) – AAB (Geog) (IB 35 pts HL 665)
        Loughborough – AAB (Geog; Geog Econ; Geog Mgt; Geog Spo Sci) (IB 35 pts HL 665)
        Manchester – AAB (Geog) (IB 35 pts HL 665)
        Nottingham – AAB (Geog Bus) (IB 34 pts)

Department
Of
Landscape
Architecture.

SHAPE YOUR WORLD.

Study at the UK's only independent Department of Landscape Architecture.

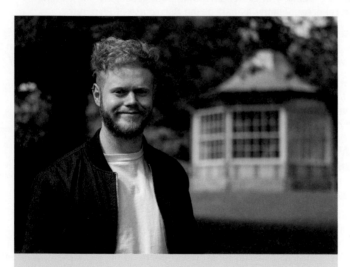

Why study Landscape Architecture?

"I was initially looking into Architecture, but discovered Landscape Architecture at a careers meeting in year 12 and as soon as I visited the department I knew this is where I wanted to go. The course is so varied and dynamic beyond anything I really expected, you learn about everything across the whole Landscape Architecture discipline.

The best thing about the course at Sheffield is how it has encouraged my graphic skills. I had no idea how to use Photoshop or Indesign before I started and now I would consider my graphic skills as one of my main strengths."

Daniel Bilsborough, BA Landscape Architecture

Landscape Architecture involves the design, planning and management of places that benefit people and nature. Landscape Architects create spaces between buildings that are both functional and inspirational. If you have a flair for creativity and a passion for improving the environment and people's lives, this could be the subject for you.

Join us and you will be joining one of the world's leading departments for landscape education and research. Our staff are involved in some of the most exciting landscape design projects and are committed to developing the next generation of Landscape Architects.

*DLHE 2016-17

Sheffield is the ideal place to study Landscape Architecture, whether large-scale urban renewal, complex planning issues or natural habitat.

Our students are highly sought after within the Landscape profession. We aim to develop graduates with outstanding skills, who are able to take the lead in multidisciplinary projects. Study with us and you will develop design skills as well as the ability to understand the cultural, social and ecological drivers that underpin successful landscapes.

Our courses also equip students with excellent transferable skills. Through working in teams, undertaking live projects for community groups and developing your personal portfolio, you will acquire professional standards in communication, graphic design, report writing and presentation.

Our graduates are in demand. Alumni work in the private sector, where many have set up their own companies. Others work in the public or Third sectors, helping to improve local communities.

Whatever path you choose, a degree in Landscape Architecture from Sheffield will set you up to make a positive and lasting difference to the world around you.

100% of students went on to employment or further study within 6 months of graduation*

Contact Us

Email: landscape@sheffield.ac.uk

Telephone: +44 (0)114 222 0600

Website: www.sheffield.ac.uk/landscape

Twitter/Facebook/Instagram: @LandscapeSheff

SHEFFIELD
LANDSCAPE
ARCHITECTURE

Sheffield – AAB–ABB +bEPQ incl sci/geog (Geog) (IB 34 pts HL 5 sci/geog)
Southampton – AAB/ABB +aEPQ incl geog (Geog) (IB 34 pts HL 17 pts)
York – AAB incl geog/geol+sci/maths/env st/psy (Env Geog) (IB 35 pts HL 6 geog/geol+sci/
maths/env st/psy)

128 pts **Birmingham** – ABB (Geog Urb Reg Plan Comb Hons) (IB 32 pts HL 655)
Cardiff – AAB–ABB (Hum Geog) (HL 666–665)
Edinburgh – AAA–ABB incl maths/sci (Geol Physl Geog) (IB 37–32 pts HL 555 incl maths/sci)
Exeter – AAB–ABB incl hum/soc sci (Geog) (IB 34–32 pts)
Leicester – ABB–BBB +bEPQ (Geog; Hum Geog; Physl Geog) (IB 30 pts)
Liverpool – ABB (Geog) (IB 33 pts)
London (QM) – ABB (Geog; Hum Geog) (IB 32 pts HL 655)
London (RH) – AAB–ABB (Geog; Hum Geog; Physl Geog) (IB 32 pts HL 655)
Newcastle – AAB–ABB incl geog+maths/sci (Geog) (IB 35–32 pts HL 6 geog+maths/sci);
AAB–ABB incl sci/maths/geog (Earth Sci) (IB 35–33 pts); ABB incl geog+sci/maths/geol
(Physl Geog) (IB 32 pts HL 6 geog+sci/maths)
Nottingham – ABB–BBB incl geog (Arch Geog) (IB 32–30 pts HL 5 geog)
Queen's Belfast – ABB incl geog (Geog) (IB 33 pts HL 655 incl geog)
Southampton – ABB (Popn Geog) (IB 32 pts HL 16 pts); ABB incl geog/sci/maths (Geol
Physl Geog) (IB 32 pts HL 16 pts incl 5 geog/sci/maths); ABB incl geog/sci/maths
+interview (Ocean Physl Geog) (IB 32 pts HL 16 pts incl 6 geog/sci/maths)
Sussex – AAB–ABB (Geog Anth) (IB 34–32 pts); AAB–ABB incl geog/sci (Geog) (IB 34–32 pts
HL 5 geog/sci)

120 pts **Aberdeen** – BBB incl maths/sci (Geog) (IB 32 pts HL 555 incl maths/sci)
Bangor – C geog 120 pts (Geog) (HL 5 geog)
Cardiff – ABB–BBB (Hum Geog Plan) (HL 665)
Coventry – ABB–BBB (Geog; Geog Nat Haz) (IB 29 pts)
Derby – C sci/soc sci 120 pts (Geog)
East Anglia – BBB/ABC incl geog/maths/econ/sci (Geog; Geog (Yr Ind)) (IB 31 pts HL 5
geog/maths/econ/sci)
Hull – BBB 120 pts (Geog; Hum Geog; Physl Geog) (IB 30 pts); BBB 120 pts incl sci/maths/
geol (Geol Physl Geog) (IB 30 pts HL 5 sci/maths/geol)
Kent – BBB incl geog/maths/sci (Hum Geog) (IB 34 pts HL 15 pts)
Newcastle – ABB–BBB (Geog Info Sci) (IB 32 pts); ABB–BBB incl geog (Geog Plan) (IB
32–30 pts)
Northumbria – 120 pts (Geog)
Nottingham Trent – BBB incl geog/sci/maths 120 pts (Geog; Geog (Physl))
Reading – BBB incl geog (Geog (Hum Physl); Geog (Hum); Geog (Physl); Geog Econ (Reg
Sci)) (IB 30 pts HL 5 geog)
Stirling – BBB incl sci/maths/geog (Env Geog) (IB 32 pts HL 5 sci/maths/geog)
Swansea – AAB–BBB incl geog (Geog; Geog Geoinform) (IB 34–32 pts HL 5 geog)

112 pts **Chester** – BBB–BBC incl geog/soc sci/app sci 112 pts (Geog) (IB 26 pts HL 5 geog)
Edge Hill – BBB–BBC 112–120 pts incl geog/geol/env sci (Geog Geol); BBC incl geog/env sci
112 pts incl geog/env sci (Geog)
Gloucestershire – BBC 112 pts (Geog courses)
Heriot-Watt – BBC (Geog) (IB 29 pts)
Keele – BBC (Geog; Hum Geog; Physl Geog) (IB 30 pts)
Leeds Beckett – 112 pts (Hum Geog Plan) (IB 25 pts)
Liverpool Hope – BBC 112 pts (Geog) (IB 28 pts)
Liverpool John Moores – BBC incl sci/geog 112 pts (Geog) (IB 26 pts)
London (Birk) – ABB–BBC 112–128 pts (Geog)
Plymouth – 112–128 pts incl sci/maths/geog/tech (Physl Geog Geol) (IB 30–28 pts)
Portsmouth – 112–120 pts (Geog) (IB 25 pts)
Sheffield Hallam – BBC incl geog/env sci 112 pts incl geog/env sci (Geog); BBC incl geog/
soc sci 112 pts incl geog/soc sci (Hum Geog)
Staffordshire – BBC 112 pts (Geog)

UCAS points Tariff: A* = 56 pts; A = 48 pts; B = 40 pts; C = 32 pts; D = 24 pts; E = 16 pts

UWE Bristol – 112 pts (Geog)

104 pts   **Bangor** – BC geog/sci/maths 104 pts (Physl Geog Ocean)

Bournemouth – 104–120 pts (Geog) (IB 31–28 pts)

Central Lancashire – 104–112 pts (Geog)

Coventry – ABB–BCC (Disas Emer Mgt) (IB 30 pts)

Dundee – BBB–BCC incl geog/sci (Geog) (IB 30 pts HL 555 incl sci)

Greenwich – 104 pts incl geog/sci (Physl Geog)

Leeds Beckett – 104 pts (Hum Geog) (IB 25 pts)

Manchester Met – BBC–BCC incl geog 104–112 pts (Geog (St Abrd); Hum Geog (St Abrd); Physl Geog) (IB 26 pts HL 5 geog)

Northampton – BCC (Geog; Geog (Physl Geog))

Oxford Brookes – BCC incl geog 104 pts (Geog) (IB 29 pts)

Plymouth – 104–112 pts (Geog) (IB 27 pts)

Ulster – BCC incl geog (Geog) (IB 24 pts HL 12 pts incl geog)

Winchester – 104–120 pts (Geog) (HL 44)

Worcester – 104–120 pts (Geog; Hum Geog)

96 pts   **Aberystwyth** – BBB–CCC 96–120 pts (Geog; Hum Geog; Physl Geog) (IB 30–26 pts)

Bath Spa – CCC incl geog/sociol/econ/sci (Geog) (IB 26 pts)

Brighton – BBC–CCC 96–112 pts (Geog) (IB 26 pts)

Hertfordshire – CCC 96 pts (Geog; Hum Geog)

Kingston – 96 pts (Hum Geog); CC incl sci/soc sci 96 pts (Geog Comb Hons)

Teesside – 96–112 pts (Geog)

80 pts   **South Wales** – BCC–CDD 80–104 pts (Geog) (IB 29 pts); BCC–CDD incl sci/geog/maths 80–104 pts (Geol Physl Geog) (IB 29 pts HL 5 sci)

Open University – contact 0300 303 0073 or www.open.ac.uk/contact/new (Comb Soc Sci (Econ/Geog/Psy/Sociol); Geog Env Sci)

Alternative offers
See **Chapter 6** and **Appendix 1** for grades/UCAS Tariff points information for other examinations.

EXAMPLES OF COLLEGES OFFERING COURSES IN THIS SUBJECT FIELD
Hopwood Hall (Coll); Truro and Penwith (Coll).

CHOOSING YOUR COURSE (SEE ALSO CH.1)
Universities and colleges teaching quality See www.qaa.ac.uk; https://unistats.ac.uk.

Top research universities and colleges (REF 2014) (Geography, Environmental Studies and Archaeology) Glasgow (Geog); Southampton (Geog); London (UCL) (Geog); Reading (Arch); Sheffield (Geog); Oxford (Arch); London (RH); London LSE; Bristol (Geog); Cambridge (Geog); Oxford (Geog Env St); London (QM); St Andrews; Newcastle (Geog).

Examples of sandwich degree courses Brighton; Cardiff; Coventry; Hertfordshire; Kingston; Loughborough; Manchester Met; Northumbria; Nottingham Trent; Plymouth; Reading; Sheffield Hallam; Ulster.

ADMISSIONS INFORMATION
Number of applicants per place (approx) Birmingham 5; Bristol 6; Cambridge 3; Cardiff 5; Central Lancashire 3; Derby 5; Dundee 9; Durham 4; Edge Hill 8; Edinburgh 9; Exeter 10; Gloucestershire 40; Greenwich 2; Hull 5; Kingston 7; Lancaster 13; Leeds 12; Leicester 7; Liverpool 6; Liverpool John Moores 6; London (King's) 5; London (QM) 5; London (RH) 5; London (SOAS) 5; London (UCL) 4; London LSE 8; Manchester 6; Newcastle 7; Northampton 4; Nottingham 9; Oxford Brookes 9; Sheffield 6; South Wales 5; Southampton 7; Staffordshire 10; Swansea 5; Worcester 5.

Advice to applicants and planning the UCAS personal statement Visits to, and field courses in, any specific geographical region should be fully described. Study your own locality in detail and get in touch with the area planning office to learn about any future developments. Read geographical magazines and describe any special interests you have – and why. Be aware of world issues and have travel experience. **Bristol** Deferred entry accepted.

Misconceptions about this course Birmingham Some students think that the BA and BSc Geography courses are very different; in fact they do not differ from one another. All course options are available for both degrees. **Liverpool** Some applicants assume that a BSc course restricts them to physical geography modules. This is not so since human geography modules can be taken. Some students later specialise in human geography. **Plymouth** Our course has shared BA and BSc modules in the first year, allowing students to choose between courses and degrees at a later stage.

Selection interviews Yes Cambridge, Oxford (26%), Worcester; **Some** Cardiff, Coventry, London (SOAS), Loughborough, Nottingham; **No** Birmingham, Bristol, Canterbury Christ Church, Central Lancashire, Dundee, East Anglia, Edge Hill, Greenwich, Kingston, Liverpool, London (King's), London (RH), London (UCL), Manchester, Manchester Met, Newcastle, Northumbria, Reading, Southampton, Staffordshire.

Interview advice and questions Geography is a very broad subject and applicants can expect to be questioned on their syllabus and those aspects which they find of special interest. Some questions in the past have included: What fieldwork have you done? What are your views on ecology? What changes in the landscape have you noticed on the way to the interview? Explain in simple meteorological terms today's weather. Why are earthquakes almost unknown in Britain? What do you enjoy about geography and why? Are there any articles of geographical importance in the news at present? Discuss the current economic situation in Britain and give your views. Questions on the Third World, on world ocean currents and drainage and economic factors worldwide. What do you think about those people who consider global warming nonsense? Expect to comment on local geography and on geographical photographs and diagrams. See also **Chapter 5. Cambridge** Are Fairtrade bananas really fair? Imagine you are hosting the BBC radio show on New Year's day, what message would you send to listeners? **Oxford** Is nature natural? **Southampton** Applicants selected on academic ability only.

Reasons for rejection (non-academic) Lack of awareness of the content of the course. Failure to attend interview. Poor general knowledge. Lack of geographical awareness. **Liverpool** Personal statement gave no reason for choosing Geography.

AFTER-RESULTS ADVICE
Offers to applicants repeating A-levels Higher Kingston; St Andrews; **Possibly higher** Edinburgh; **Same** Aberystwyth; Birmingham; Brighton; Bristol; Cardiff; Chester; Coventry; Derby; Dundee; Durham; East Anglia; Edge Hill; Hull; Lancaster; Leeds; Liverpool; Liverpool Hope; Liverpool John Moores; London (RH); London (SOAS); Loughborough; Manchester Met; Newcastle; Northumbria; Nottingham; Oxford Brookes; Southampton; Staffordshire; **No** Cambridge; Glasgow.

GRADUATE DESTINATIONS AND EMPLOYMENT (2016/17 HESA)
Human and Social Geography graduates surveyed 5,025 **Employed** 2,375 **In voluntary employment** 170 **In further study** 1,480 **Assumed unemployed** 235

Career note Geography graduates enter a wide range of occupations, many in business and administrative careers. Depending on specialisations, areas could include agriculture, forestry, hydrology, transport, market research and retail. Teaching is also a popular option.

OTHER DEGREE SUBJECTS FOR CONSIDERATION
Agriculture; Anthropology; Civil Engineering; Countryside Management; Development Studies; Environmental Engineering/Science/Studies; Forestry; Geology; Geomatic Engineering; Surveying; Town Planning; Urban Land Economics; Urban Studies.

GEOLOGY/GEOLOGICAL SCIENCES

(including **Earth Sciences, Geophysics and Geoscience**; See also **Astronomy and Astrophysics, Environmental Sciences**)

Topics in Geology courses include the physical and chemical constitution of the earth, exploration geophysics, oil and marine geology (oceanography) and seismic interpretation. Earth Sciences covers geology, environmental science, physical geography and can also include business studies and language modules. No previous knowledge of geology is required for most courses.

Useful websites www.geolsoc.org.uk; www.bgs.ac.uk; www.noc.ac.uk; www.scicentral.com; http://britgeophysics.org

NB The points totals shown to the left of the institutions are for ease of reference only. It must not be assumed that Tariff points are always used by institutions or that they can be substituted for an offer in grades. The level of an offer is not necessarily indicative of the quality of a course.

COURSE OFFERS INFORMATION

Subject requirements/preferences GCSE English, mathematics and a science required. **AL** One or two mathematics/science subjects usually required. Geography may be accepted as a science subject.

Your target offers and examples of degree courses

160 pts **Cambridge** – A*A*A incl sci/maths +interview +NSAA (Nat Sci (Earth Sci)) (IB 42–40 pts HL 776)

152 pts **Oxford** – A*AA/AAAA +interview (Earth Sci (Geol)) (IB 39 pts HL 766)

144 pts **Birmingham** – AAA incl sci (Geol (MSci) (Yr Abrd)) (IB 32 pts HL 666)

Durham – AAA incl sci (Earth Sci (MSci)) (IB 37 pts HL 666 incl sci)

Imperial London – A*AA–AAA incl maths/geog/sci +interview (Geol Geophys (MSci)) (IB 39–38 pts HL 666 incl sci/maths/geog); AAA incl maths+phys +interview (Geophys) (IB 38 pts HL 6 maths+phys); AAA incl sci/maths/geog +interview (Geol) (IB 38 pts HL 6 sci/maths/geog)

Leeds – AAA incl maths+phys (Geophys (Int) (MGeophys)) (IB 35 pts HL 17 pts incl 5 maths+phys); AAA incl sci/maths/geog (Geol (Int) (MGeol)) (IB 35 pts HL 17 pts)

136 pts **Bristol** – AAB incl maths/sci (Env Geosci; Geol) (IB 34 pts HL 17 pts incl 6/5 maths/sci)

Durham – AAB incl sci (Geol; Geosci) (IB 36 pts HL 665 incl sci); AAB incl sci+maths (Geophys Geol) (IB 36 pts HL 665 incl sci)

Glasgow – AAB incl sci (Earth Sci) (IB 36 pts HL 665 incl sci)

Leicester – AAB incl sci/maths/geog (Geol (MGeol); Geol Palae (MGeol)) (IB 32 pts HL 5 sci)

Liverpool – AAB incl maths+phys (Geol Geophys (MESci)) (IB 35 pts HL 4 maths+phys); AAB incl sci (Geol (MESci); Geol Physl Geog (MESci)) (IB 35 pts HL 4 sci)

London (UCL) – AAB (Env Geosci) (IB 36 pts HL 17 pts); AAB incl maths+phys (Geophys) (IB 36 pts HL 17 pts incl maths+phys); AAB incl sci (Earth Sci; Geol) (IB 36 pts HL 17 pts incl sci); AAB incl sci/maths (Earth Sci (Int) (MSci)) (IB 36 pts HL 17 pts incl 5 sci/maths)

Manchester – AAB incl sci+interview (Earth Planet Sci) (IB 34 pts HL 655)

Southampton – AAB incl maths+phys (Geophys (MSci)) (IB 34 pts HL 17 pts incl 5 maths+phys)

St Andrews – AAB incl biol+sci/maths (Env Earth Sci) (IB 36 pts HL 665 incl maths/sci); AAB incl sci/maths/geog (Geol) (IB 36 pts HL 665 incl sci/maths/geog)

128 pts **Birmingham** – ABB incl sci (Geol) (IB 32 pts HL 655)

Edinburgh – AAA–ABB incl maths+phys (Geophys; Geophys Geol; Geophys Meteor) (IB 37–32 pts HL 555 incl maths+phys); AAA–ABB incl maths/sci (Geol Physl Geog) (IB 37–32 pts HL 555 incl maths/sci); AAA–ABB incl maths/sci/geog (Geol) (IB 37–32 pts HL 555 incl maths/sci/geog)

Exeter – AAB–ABB incl sci/geol (App Geol; Geol) (IB 34–32 pts HL 665–655 incl sci)

Lancaster – ABB incl sci (Earth Env Sci) (IB 32 pts HL 16 pts incl 6 sci)

Leeds – ABB incl sci/maths/geog (Geol) (IB 34 pts HL 16 pts incl 5 maths/sci)
Liverpool – ABB incl sci (Geol; Geol Physl Geog) (IB 33 pts HL 4 sci)
Southampton – ABB incl geog/sci/maths (Geol Physl Geog) (IB 32 pts HL 16 pts incl 5 geog/sci/maths); ABB incl maths+phys (Geophysl Sci) (IB 32 pts HL 5 maths+phys); ABB incl sci/maths/geog (Geol) (IB 32 pts HL 16 pts incl 5 sci)

120 pts   **Aberdeen** – BBB incl maths/sci (Geol Petrol Geol) (IB 32 pts HL 555 incl maths/sci)
Derby – 120 pts incl sci/maths/geog (Geol)
Hull – BBB 120 pts incl sci/maths/geol (Geol Physl Geog) (IB 30 pts HL 5 sci/maths/geol)
Leicester – ABB–BBB incl maths/phys (Geol Geophys) (IB 30 pts HL 5 sci); ABB–BBB incl sci/maths/comp sci/geog (Geol) (IB 30 pts HL 5 sci); ABB–BBB incl sci/maths/geog (App Env Geol) (IB 30 pts)
London (RH) – ABB–BBB incl sci (Geosci (MSci)) (IB 32 pts HL 555 incl sci); ABB–BBB incl sci+interview (Geol) (IB 32 pts HL 555 incl sci); ABB–BBB incl sci/maths+interview (Geol (Yr Ind)) (IB 32 pts HL 555 incl sci)
Swansea – AAB–BBB incl sci (Physl Earth Sci) (IB 34–32 pts HL 5 geog)

112 pts   **Bangor** – BB sci/maths/geog 112 pts incl sci/maths/geog (Geol Ocean) (HL 6 sci)
Cardiff – ABB–BBC incl sci (Explor Geol (MSci)) (IB 34–30 pts HL 665–655); (Env Geosci; Env Geosci (MSci); Explor Geol; Geol; Geol (MSci)) (IB 34–30 pts HL 665–655 incl sci)
Edge Hill – BBB–BBC 112–120 pts incl geog/geol/env sci (Geog Geol)
Keele – BBC (Geol Comb Hons) (IB 30 pts)
Plymouth – 112–128 pts incl sci/maths/geog (Geol; Geol Ocn Sci) (IB 30–28 pts); 112–128 pts incl sci/maths/geog/tech (Physl Geog Geol) (IB 30–28 pts)
Portsmouth – 112–136 pts incl sci/maths/geog/tech (Eng Geol Geotech) (IB 27–25 pts)

104 pts   **Aberystwyth** – BBB–BCC incl sci 104–120 pts (Env Earth Sci) (IB 30–28 pts HL 5 sci)
Portsmouth – 104–120 pts incl sci/maths/geog (Geol) (IB 27 pts)

96 pts   **Brighton** – BBC–CCC 96–112 pts (Geol) (IB 26 pts); BBC–CCC incl geog/sci 96–112 pts (Physl Geog Geol) (IB 26 pts)
London (Birk) – BBB–CCC 96–120 pts (Geol)
Teesside – 96–112 pts incl sci/geog (Geol)

80 pts   **South Wales** – BCC–CDD incl sci/maths/geog 80–104 pts (Geol) (IB 29 pts HL 5 sci)

Open University – contact 0300 303 0073 or www.open.ac.uk/contact/new (Nat Sci (Earth Sci))

Alternative offers
See **Chapter 6** and **Appendix 1** for grades/UCAS Tariff points information for other examinations.

CHOOSING YOUR COURSE (SEE ALSO CH.1)

Universities and colleges teaching quality See www.qaa.ac.uk; https://unistats.ac.uk.

Top research universities and colleges (REF 2014) See **Environmental Sciences**.

Examples of sandwich degree courses Brighton; Cardiff; Leeds; London (RH); Portsmouth.

ADMISSIONS INFORMATION

Number of applicants per place (approx) Bangor 5; Birmingham 4; Bristol 6; Cardiff 5; Derby 5; Durham 3; Edinburgh 19; Exeter 5; Imperial London 5; Leeds 8; Leicester 5; Liverpool 8; London (RH) 5; London (UCL) 5; Oxford 4; Plymouth 14; Southampton 5.

Advice to applicants and planning the UCAS personal statement Visits to any outstanding geological sites and field courses you have attended should be described in detail. Apart from geological formations, you should also be aware of how geology has affected humankind in specific areas in the architecture of the region and artefacts used. Evidence of social skills could be given. See also **Appendix 3. Bristol** Only accepting a limited number of deferred applicants in fairness to next year's applicants. Apply early.

Misconceptions about this course London (UCL) Environmental geoscience is sometimes mistaken for environmental science; they are two different subjects.

Selection interviews Yes Cambridge, Imperial London, Oxford (86% (success rate 27%)), Southampton; **Some** Aberystwyth (mature students only); **No** Birmingham, Bristol, Derby, East Anglia, Edinburgh, Liverpool, London (RH).

Interview advice and questions Some knowledge of the subject will be expected and applicants could be questioned on specimens of rocks and their origins. Past interviews have included questions on the field courses attended, and the geophysical methods of exploration in the detection of metals. How would you determine the age of this rock (sample shown)? Can you integrate a decay curve function and would it help you to determine the age of rocks? How many planes of crystallisation could this rock have? What causes a volcano? What is your local geology? See also **Chapter 5. Oxford** (Earth Sci (Geol)) Candidates may be asked to comment on specimens of a geological nature, based on previous knowledge of the subject.

Reasons for rejection (non-academic) Exeter Outright rejection uncommon but some applicants advised to apply for other programmes.

AFTER-RESULTS ADVICE
Offers to applicants repeating A-levels Higher Bristol; St Andrews; **Possibly higher** Cardiff; **Same** Aberystwyth; Derby; Durham; East Anglia; Leeds; London (RH); Plymouth; Southampton; **No** Cambridge.

GRADUATE DESTINATIONS AND EMPLOYMENT (2016/17 HESA)
Graduates surveyed 1,340 **Employed** 520 **In voluntary employment** 25 **In further study** 540 **Assumed unemployed** 80

Career note Areas of employment include mining and quarrying, the oil and gas industry, prospecting and processing.

OTHER DEGREE SUBJECTS FOR CONSIDERATION
Archaeology; Civil and Mining Engineering; Environmental Science; Geography; Meteorology; Oceanography; Physics.

GERMAN
(See also **European Studies, Languages**)

There are fewer Single Honours German courses than formerly, although the subject is offered jointly with other subjects, particularly other languages and business and management studies, at many universities. German courses range from those which focus on language and literature (eg Edinburgh), those which emphasise fluency of language and communication (eg Hull) and those offering translation studies (eg Heriot-Watt).

Useful websites www.goethe.de; www.bbc.co.uk/languages; www.ciol.org.uk; www.languageadvantage.com; www.languagematters.co.uk; www.faz.net; www.sueddeutsche.de; http://europa.eu; www.gslg.org.uk; https://womeningermanstudies.wordpress.com

NB The points totals shown to the left of the institutions are for ease of reference only. It must not be assumed that Tariff points are always used by institutions or that they can be substituted for an offer in grades. The level of an offer is not necessarily indicative of the quality of a course.

COURSE OFFERS INFORMATION
Subject requirements/preferences GCSE English and German are required. **AL** German required usually at a specified grade.

Your target offers and examples of degree courses
152 pts   Bristol – A*AA/A*A*B incl Ger +LNAT (Law Ger) (IB 38 pts HL 18 pts incl 6 Ger)
   Cambridge – A*AA incl lang +interview +MMLAA (Modn Mediev Langs) (IB 42–40 pts HL 776 incl lang)

Nottingham – A*AA (Econ Ger) (IB 38 pts)

144 pts   **Birmingham** – AAA incl Ger (Law Ger Law) (IB 32 pts HL 666 incl Ger)

Imperial London – AAA incl biol+sci/maths (Biol Sci Ger Sci) (IB 38 pts HL 6 biol+sci/maths); AAA incl chem+maths +interview (Chem Fr/Ger/Span Sci) (IB 38 pts HL 6 chem+maths)

Oxford – AAA +interview +MLAT (Ger courses) (IB 38 pts HL 666)

Southampton – AAA incl maths+Fr/Ger/Span (Maths Fr/Ger/Span) (IB 36 pts HL 18 pts incl 6 maths+Fr/Ger/Span)

136 pts   **Bath** – AAB/ABB +aEPQ incl Ger (Int Mgt Ger) (IB 35 pts HL 665 incl 6 Ger); AAB–ABB +aEPQ incl lang (Int Pol Modn Langs) (IB 35 pts HL 665 incl 7 lang)

Birmingham – AAB incl hist (Modn Langs Hist) (IB 32 pts HL 665)

Bristol – AAB incl Ger (Ger) (IB 34 pts HL 17 pts incl 5 Ger); AAB incl lang (Ger courses) (IB 34 pts HL 17 pts incl 5 lang)

Dundee – AAB incl Engl (Law Langs) (IB 36 pts HL 665 incl Engl)

Exeter – AAB–BBB incl Ger (Ger) (IB 34–30 pts HL 5 Ger)

Glasgow – AAB (Ger Comb Hons) (IB 36 pts HL 665 incl Engl/lang/hum)

London (King's) – AAB (Euro St (Fr/Ger/Span) (Yr Abrd)) (IB 35 pts HL 665); AAB incl Fr/Ger (Fr Ger (Yr Abrd)) (IB 35 pts HL 665)

Southampton – AAB/ABB +aEPQ incl Engl+Fr/Ger/Span (Engl Fr/Ger/Span) (IB 34 pts HL 17 pts incl 65 Engl+Fr/Ger/Span)

St Andrews – AAB (Ger courses) (IB 36 pts HL 665)

Warwick – AAB incl Engl lit+lang (Engl Ger) (IB 36 pts HL 5 Engl lit+lang); AAB incl Fr (Fr Ger (Yr Abrd)) (IB 36 pts HL 5 Fr); AAB incl lang (Ger Comb Hons) (IB 36 pts HL 5 lang)

York – AAB +interview (Ger courses) (IB 35 pts); AAB incl Fr (Fr Ger Lang (Yr Abrd)) (IB 35 pts HL 6 Fr)

128 pts   **Birmingham** – ABB incl lang (Modn Langs) (IB 32 pts HL 655)

Edinburgh – AAB–ABB (Ger; Int Bus Fr/Ger/Span) (IB 40–34 pts HL 766–655)

Exeter – AAB–ABB incl lang (Class St Modn Langs) (IB 34–32 pts HL 665–655)

Lancaster – ABB (Ger St courses) (IB 32 pts HL 16 pts)

Leeds – ABB incl Ger (Ger courses) (IB 34 pts HL 16 pts incl 6 Ger)

Liverpool – ABB (Ger courses) (IB 33 pts)

London (QM) – ABB incl hum/soc sci (Ger courses) (IB 32 pts HL 655 incl hum/soc sci)

London (RH) – AAB–ABB (Euro Int St Fr/Ger/Ital/Span; Modn Lang Mgt; Modn Lang Mus) (IB 32 pts HL 655); AAB–ABB incl lang (Modn Lang Dr) (IB 32 pts HL 655)

Manchester – ABB (Ger St; Ger courses) (IB 34 pts HL 655)

Nottingham – ABB (Ger; Ger Comb Hons) (IB 32 pts)

Sheffield – ABB (Modn Langs Cult) (IB 33 pts HL 5 lang); ABB incl lang (Ger St Comb Hons) (IB 33 pts HL 5 lang)

Southampton – AAB–ABB incl Fr/Ger/Span (Flm Fr/Ger/Span) (IB 32 pts HL 6 Fr/Ger/Span)

Sussex – ABB 128 pts (Anth Lang) (32 pts)

Warwick – ABB incl Ger (Ger Ital) (IB 34 pts HL 5 Ger)

120 pts   **Aberdeen** – BBB (Anth Fr/Ger; Ger St) (IB 32 pts HL 555)

Aston – ABB–BBB (Int Bus Fr/Ger/Span) (IB 32 pts HL 665–655)

Cardiff – ABB–BBB (Ger) (IB 32–30 pts HL 665–655)

Dundee – BBB (Ger courses; Phil Ger) (IB 30 pts HL 555)

Heriot-Watt – BBB incl lang (App Langs Transl (Fr/Span)/(Ger/Span)) (IB 30 pts HL 5 lang)

Kent – BBB (Ger; Ger courses) (IB 34 pts HL 15 pts)

London (QM) – BBB incl hum/soc sci (Ger Compar Lit; Ger Ling) (IB 30 pts HL 555 incl hum/soc sci)

London (RH) – ABB–BBB (Modn Lang Lat; Modn Langs) (IB 32 pts HL 555)

Reading – BBB (Ger courses) (IB 30 pts)

Surrey – BBB incl Ger (Ger courses) (IB 32 pts)

Swansea – BBB (Ger courses; Modn Langs) (IB 32 pts)

112 pts   **Hull** – BBC incl lang 112 pts (App Modn Lang (Fr/Ger/Span); Ger Comb Hons) (IB 28 pts HL 5 lang)

London (Birk) – ABB–BBC 112-128 pts (Ger; Modn Langs (Fr/Ger/Ital/Jap/Port/Span))

104 pts **Aberystwyth** – BBB–BCC 104 pts (Ger Comb Hons) (IB 30–28 pts)
Central Lancashire – 104–112 pts (Int Bus Comm Modn For Lang); 104–112 pts incl lang
(Modn Langs (2 Lang) (Fr/Ger/Span/Jap/Russ/Ital/Kor))
Chester – BBC–BCC incl Ger 104–112 pts (Ger courses) (IB 26 pts HL 5 Ger)
Hertfordshire – BCC 104 pts (Ger Comb Hons)
Manchester Met – BBC–BCC 104–112 pts (Ling Mand Chin/Fr/Ger/Ital/Span) (IB 26 pts)
96 pts **Aston** – BBC–CCC (Ger courses) (IB 29 pts HL 554)
Bangor – C Ger 96 pts (Ger courses) (HL 5 Ger)
Portsmouth – 96–112 pts (Modn Langs) (IB 25 pts)

Alternative offers
See **Chapter 6** and **Appendix 1** for grades/UCAS Tariff points information for other examinations.

CHOOSING YOUR COURSE (SEE ALSO CH.1)
Universities and colleges teaching quality See www.qaa.ac.uk; https://unistats.ac.uk.

Top research universities and colleges (REF 2014) See **Languages**.

Examples of sandwich degree courses Bangor.

ADMISSIONS INFORMATION
Number of applicants per place (approx) Aston 4; Bath 6 (Mod Langs Eur St); Birmingham 6; Bristol 4; Cardiff 6; Central Lancashire 2; Exeter 4; Heriot-Watt 10; Hull 5; Kent 5; Lancaster 7; Leeds (Comb Hons) 8; London (King's) 5; London (QM) 6; London (RH) 7; London (UCL) 5; Nottingham 5; Swansea 4; Warwick 8; York 6.

Advice to applicants and planning the UCAS personal statement Describe visits to Germany or a German-speaking country and the particular cultural and geographical features of the region. Contacts with friends in Germany and language experience should also be mentioned, and if you are bilingual, say so. Read German newspapers and magazines and keep up-to-date with national news.

Misconceptions about this course Leeds See **Languages**. **Swansea** Some students are afraid of the year abroad, which is actually one of the most enjoyable parts of the course.

Selection interviews Yes Cambridge, Leeds, Oxford, Southampton; **Some** Cardiff, London (UCL); **No** Bangor, Birmingham, Heriot-Watt, Hull, Liverpool, Nottingham, Portsmouth, Sheffield, Surrey, Swansea.

Interview advice and questions Questions asked on A-level syllabus. Part of the interview may be in German. What foreign newspapers and/or magazines do you read? Questions on German current affairs, particularly politics and reunification problems, books read outside the course, etc. See also **Chapter 5. Leeds** See **Languages**.

Reasons for rejection (non-academic) Unstable personality. Poor motivation. Insufficient commitment. Unrealistic expectations. Not interested in spending a year abroad.

AFTER-RESULTS ADVICE
Offers to applicants repeating A-levels Higher Birmingham; Leeds; Warwick; **Same** Aston; Cardiff; Chester; Nottingham; Swansea; York; **No** Cambridge; Glasgow.

GRADUATE DESTINATIONS AND EMPLOYMENT (2016/17 HESA)
Graduates surveyed 380 **Employed** 195 **In voluntary employment** 20 **In further study** 105 **Assumed unemployed** 20

Career note See **Languages**.

OTHER DEGREE SUBJECTS FOR CONSIDERATION
East European Studies; European Studies; International Business Studies.

GREEK

(See also Classics and Classical Studies/Civilisation, Languages, Latin)

Courses are offered in Ancient and Modern Greek, covering the language and literature from ancient times to the present day. Some Classics and Classical Studies courses (see separate tables) also provide the opportunity to study Greek from scratch.

Useful websites www.greek-language.com; www.greek-gods.org; www.fhw.gr; www.culture.gr; www.greeklanguage.gr

NB The points totals shown to the left of the institutions are for ease of reference only. It must not be assumed that Tariff points are always used by institutions or that they can be substituted for an offer in grades. The level of an offer is not necessarily indicative of the quality of a course.

COURSE OFFERS INFORMATION

Subject requirements/preferences GCSE English and a foreign language required. Greek required by some universities. **AL** Latin, Greek or a foreign language may be specified by some universities.

Your target offers and examples of degree courses

152 pts   Cambridge – A*AA +interview (Modn Mediev Langs (Class Gk)) (IB 42–40 pts HL 776); A*AA +interview +CAA (Class) (IB 42–40 pts HL 776)

144 pts   Oxford – AAA +interview +MLAT (Modn Langs (Modn Gk)) (IB 38 pts HL 666)
St Andrews – AAA (Gk courses) (IB 36 pts HL 665 incl 6 lang)

136 pts   Glasgow – AAB incl arts/hum (Gk) (IB 36 pts HL 665 incl Engl+lang/hum)
London (UCL) – AAB incl Gk (Gk Lat) (IB 36 pts HL 17 pts incl 6 Gk); AAB incl Lat (Lat Gk) (IB 36 pts HL 17 pts incl 6 Lat)

128 pts   Edinburgh – AAB–ABB (Gk St) (IB 36–34 pts HL 665–655); ABB (Anc Hist Gk) (IB 36–34 pts HL 666–655)

120 pts   London (RH) – ABB–BBB (Gk) (IB 32 pts HL 555)

Alternative offers
See **Chapter 6** and **Appendix 1** for grades/UCAS Tariff points information for other examinations.

CHOOSING YOUR COURSE (SEE ALSO CH.1)

Universities and colleges teaching quality See www.qaa.ac.uk; https://unistats.ac.uk.

Top research universities and colleges (REF 2014) See **Classics and Classical Studies/Civilisation**.

ADMISSIONS INFORMATION

Number of applicants per place (approx) London (King's) 3; London (UCL) 5.

Advice to applicants and planning the UCAS personal statement See **Classics and Classical Studies/Civilisation**.

Selection interviews Yes Cambridge; **No** London (RH).

Interview advice and questions Questions asked on A-level syllabus. Why do you want to study Greek? What aspects of this course interest you? (Questions will develop from answers.) See also **Chapter 5.**

Reasons for rejection (non-academic) Poor language ability.

AFTER-RESULTS ADVICE

Offers to applicants repeating A-levels Higher St Andrews; **Same** Leeds; **No** Cambridge.

GRADUATE DESTINATIONS AND EMPLOYMENT (2016/17 HESA)
See **Languages**.

Career note See **Languages**.

OTHER DEGREE SUBJECTS FOR CONSIDERATION
Ancient History; Classical Studies; Classics; European Studies; Philosophy.

HEALTH SCIENCES/STUDIES

(including **Deaf Studies, Nutrition, Orthoptics, Osteopathy, Paramedic Science, Prosthetics and Orthotics and Public Health**; See also **Community Studies/Development, Dietetics, Environmental Sciences, Nursing And Midwifery, Nutrition, Pharmacology, Pharmacy And Pharmaceutical Sciences, Physiotherapy, Radiography, Social Sciences/Studies, Speech Pathology/Sciences/Therapy**)

Health Sciences/Studies is a broad subject field which includes courses covering both practical applications concerning health and well-being (some of which border on nursing) and also the administrative activities involved in the promotion of health in the community. Also included are some specialised courses which include chiropractic, involving the healing process by way of manipulation, mainly in the spinal region, and osteopathy in which joints and tissues are manipulated to correct abnormalities. See **Physiotherapy**. Audiology is concerned with the treatment and diagnosis of hearing and balance disorders while prosthetics involves the provision and fitting of artificial limbs and orthotics is concerned with making and fitting braces, splints and special footwear to ease pain and to assist movement.

Useful websites www.rsph.org.uk; www.bmj.com; www.aor.org.uk; www.baap.org.uk; https:// chiropractic-uk.co.uk; www.osteopathy.org.uk; www.who.int; www.csp.org.uk; www.baaudiology.org; www.thebsa.org.uk; www.healthcareers.nhs.uk; www.gcc-uk.org; www.uco.ac.uk; www.osteopathy. org.uk; www.collegeofparamedics.co.uk

NB The points totals shown to the left of the institutions are for ease of reference only. It must not be assumed that Tariff points are always used by institutions or that they can be substituted for an offer in grades. The level of an offer is not necessarily indicative of the quality of a course.

COURSE OFFERS INFORMATION
Subject requirements/preferences GCSE English, mathematics and a science important or essential for some courses. **AL** Mathematics, chemistry or biology may be required for some courses. Other Health checks and Disclosure and Barring Service (DBS) clearance required for many courses. (Paramed Sci) Full clean manual UK driving licence with at least a provisional C1 category required by some universities.

Your target offers and examples of degree courses
136 pts **Durham** – AAB (Hlth Hum Sci) (IB 36 pts HL 665)
128 pts **Aston** – ABB incl biol/phys (Hlthcr Sci (Audiol)) (IB 32 pts HL 655 incl biol/phys)
Exeter – ABB incl biol+sci (Med Sci) (IB 32 pts HL 655 incl 6 biol/sci)
Leeds – ABB incl sci/maths +interview (Hlthcr Sci (Audiol)) (IB 34 pts HL 555 incl sci/maths)
London (UCL) – ABB (Popn Hlth) (IB 34 pts HL 16 pts)
Manchester – ABB incl sci/maths/psy +interview (Hlthcr Sci (Audiol)) (IB 34 pts HL 655 incl sci/maths/psy)
Southampton – ABB (Crdc Physiol); ABB incl sci (Audio) (IB 32 pts HL 16 pts incl 5 sci)
UWE Bristol – B sci/soc sci 128 pts +interview (Paramed Sci) (HL 6 sci/soc sci)
120 pts **Bolton** – 120 pts +Active entry on part 1 or part 2 of the Nursing and Midwifery Council (Spec Comm Pblc Hlth Nurs)
Bradford – BBB incl biol+chem 120 pts (Clin Sci) (HL 665 incl 6 chem+biol)
Brighton – BBB incl sci/soc sci +interview (Paramed Sci) (IB 27 pts)
Brunel – BBB incl sci (Biomed Sci (Hum Hlth)) (IB 30 pts HL 5 sci)
Cardiff Met – BB biol+sci 120 pts +interview (Hlthcr Sci)

Dundee – BBB incl biol +interview (Oral Hlth Sci) (IB 30 pts HL 555 incl biol)
East Anglia – BBB/ABC incl biol/chem/PE +interview (Paramed Sci) (IB 31 pts HL 5 sci)
Glasgow – BBB (Hlth Soc Sctr Ldrshp) (IB 30 pts HL 655)
Glasgow Caledonian – BBB incl sci (Orth) (IB 28 pts HL 6 sci+maths)
Kent – BBB (Hlth Soc Cr) (IB 34 pts HL 15 pts)
Liverpool – BBB incl sci/maths +interview (Orth) (IB 30 pts HL 6 biol)
London (St George's) – BBB incl biol+sci/maths +interview (Hlthcr Sci) (IB 32 pts HL 15 pts)
Manchester Met – BBB incl biol 120 pts +interview (Hlthcr Sci (Physiol Sci)) (IB 26 pts HL 5 biol)
Salford – B maths/phys/eng 120 pts incl maths/phys/eng +interview (Pros Orthot) (IB 28 pts)
Sheffield – BBB (Hlth Hum Sci) (IB 32 pts); BBB incl sci/maths +interview (Orth) (IB 32 pts HL 5 sci/maths)
Strathclyde – ABB–BBB incl maths+sci +interview (Pros Orthot) (IB 34 pts HL 6 maths)
Surrey – BBB incl sci +interview (Paramed Sci) (IB 32 pts)
Swansea – BBB incl biol sci/physl educ +interview (Ost) (IB 32 pts); BBB incl sci/maths (Hlthcr Sci (Audiol))
Worcester – BBB 120 pts +interview (Paramed Sci) (IB 24 pts)

112 pts **Bournemouth** – 112–128 pts incl sci/physl educ +interview (Paramed Sci)
Brit Coll Ost Med – 112 pts incl biol +interview (Ost (MOst))
Canterbury Christ Church – BBC +interview (Paramed Sci)
Cardiff Met – CC biol+sci 112 pts (Biomed Sci Hlth Exer Nutr)
Chester – 112 pts (Hlth Soc Cr) (IB 26 pts)
Derby – 112 pts (Hlth Soc Cr)
East London – 112 pts (Publc Hlth) (IB 25 pts HL 15 pts)
European Sch Ost – BBC incl sci/maths/PE/psy 112 pts +interview (Ost (MOst)) (IB 31 pts HL 5 sci)
Greenwich – 112 pts (Pblc Hlth)
Hertfordshire – BBC incl sci 112 pts (Paramed Sci)
Liverpool Hope – BBC 112 pts (Hlth Wlbng Comb Hons) (IB 28 pts)
Liverpool John Moores – BBC 112 pts (Pblc Hlth)
London (St George's) – BBC incl sci +interview (Paramed Sci) (HL 554 incl 5 biol/chem)
London Met – BBC 112 pts (Hlth Soc Cr)
Marjon – BBC incl biol 112 pts (Ost Med (MOst))
Middlesex – C sci 112 pts +interview (Hlthcr Sci (Audiol))
Nottingham Trent – BBC incl sci/PE 112 pts (Exer Nutr Hlth)
Plymouth – ABB–BBC incl sci 112–128 pts +interview (Paramed Sci) (IB 30 pts HL 5 biol/chem)
Portsmouth – 112 pts incl sci +interview (Paramed Sci) (IB 26 pts HL 5 sci)
Salford – 112 pts incl sci/spo/sociol/psy (Exer Nutr Hlth) (IB 31 pts)
South Wales – ABB–BBC incl biol+sci (MChiro) (IB 32 pts HL 5 biol+sci)
Sunderland – 112 pts +interview (Hlthcr Sci (Physiol/Lf Sci)); BBC 112 pts (Pblc Hlth)
Swansea – BBB–BBC (Hlth Soc Cr) (IB 32–30 pts)
UCO – BBC incl biol+sci (MOst)
Ulster – BBC (Hlth Soc Cr Plcy) (IB 25 pts HL 12 pts); BBC incl sci/maths (Hlth Physiol/Hlthcr Sci)

104 pts **AECC (UC)** – BCC (MChiro) (IB 28 pts)
Bournemouth – 104–120 pts (Med Sci) (IB 31–28 pts HL 55)
Edge Hill – BBC–BCC 104–112 pts (Hlth Soc Wlbng)
Lincoln – BCC+interview (Hlth Soc Cr) (IB 28 pts)
Northampton – BCC (Hlth St Comb Hons)
Nottingham Trent – BCC 104 pts (Hlth Soc Cr)
Sunderland – 104 pts (Hlth Soc Cr)
UHI – BCC incl sci +interview (Oral Hlth Sci)

96 pts **BPP** – CCC incl sci/maths +interview (MChiro) (IB 26 pts HL 5 biol+sci/maths)
Bangor – 96 pts (Hlth Soc Cr)

Bolton – 96 pts +interview (Med Biol; Prof St Hlth Soc Care)
Cardiff Met – 96 pts +interview (Hlth Soc Cr)
Keele – CCC 96 pts (Pblc Hlth) (IB 26 pts)
Kingston – C sci/psy/PE 96 pts (Nutr (Exer Hlth))
Nescot – 96 pts incl sci (Ost Med)
Solent – 96–112 pts (Hlth Nutr Exer Sci)
Teesside – BBC 96–112 pts (Hlth Sci) (C sci)
Trinity Saint David – 96 pts +interview (Hlth Nutr Lfstl)
West London – CCC 96 pts (Hlth Prom Pblc Hlth)
Wolverhampton – CCC/BCD 96 pts (Df St courses; Hlth St; Soc Cr Hlth St)
88 pts Canterbury Christ Church – 88–112 pts (Pblc Hlth Hlth Prom)
Winchester – 88–104 pts (Hlth Commun Soc Cr St)
80 pts Anglia Ruskin – 80 pts (Pblc Hlth) (IB 24 pts)
Bucks New – 80 pts (Hlth Soc Sci)
West Scotland – CDD incl sci 80 pts (Env Hlth) (IB 24 pts)
64 pts UHI – CC (Hlth Soc St)

Open University – contact 0300 303 0073 or www.open.ac.uk/contact/new (Hlth Soc Cr)

Alternative offers
See **Chapter 6** and **Appendix 1** for grades/UCAS Tariff points information for other examinations.

DEGREE APPRENTICESHIPS
Brighton (Hlthcr); Essex (Hlthcr Asst Prac).

EXAMPLES OF COLLEGES OFFERING COURSES IN THIS SUBJECT FIELD
Accrington and Rossendale (Coll); Bedford (Coll); Blackburn (Coll); Blackpool and Fylde (Coll); Bradford College UC; Bridgwater and Taunton (Coll); Bristol City (Coll); Buckinghamshire (Coll Group); Chesterfield (Coll); City of Oxford (Coll); Cornwall (Coll); Doncaster (Coll); Duchy Coll UC; Durham New (Coll); Exeter (Coll); Grŵp Llandrillo Menai; Hugh Baird (Coll); Hull (Coll); Leeds City (Coll); Lincoln (Coll); London South East (Coll); Manchester (Coll); Myerscough (Coll); Newcastle (Coll); Norwich City (Coll); Petroc; Sir Gâr (Coll); Sparsholt (Coll); St Helens (Coll); Stockport (Coll); TEC Partnership; Tresham (CFHE); Truro and Penwith (Coll); Wakefield (Coll); Warwickshire (Coll); West Cheshire (Coll); Westminster City (Coll); Weston (Coll); Wigan and Leigh (Coll); York (Coll).

CHOOSING YOUR COURSE (SEE ALSO CH.1)
Universities and colleges teaching quality See www.qaa.ac.uk; https://unistats.ac.uk.

Top research universities and colleges (REF 2014) (Public Health, Health Services and Primary Care) Cambridge; Birmingham; Glasgow; London (QM); Nottingham (Pharm); Bradford; East Anglia (Allied Hlth); London (QM); Sheffield (Dnstry); Queen's Belfast (Pharm); Bath; London (King's) (Pharm); Leeds; Liverpool; Sheffield (Biomed Sci); Bangor; Oxford; Imperial London; Swansea (Allied Hlth); Aston; Keele; Coventry; London (UCL); Southampton; Southampton; Bristol; Cardiff; London (King's); Surrey.

ADMISSIONS INFORMATION
Number of applicants per place (approx) Bangor 5; Brit Coll Ost Med 5; Central Lancashire 6; European Sch Ost 3; Liverpool John Moores 10; London Met 7; Manchester 18; Manchester Met 10; Northampton 3; Salford 8; Southampton 4; Swansea 1.

Admissions tutors' advice You should describe any work with people you have done, particularly in a caring capacity, for example, working with the elderly, nursing, hospital work. Show why you wish to study this subject. You should give evidence of your ability to communicate and to work in a group. Evidence needed of applicants' understanding of the NHS and health care systems. Osteopathy applicants should provide clear evidence of why they want to work as an osteopath: work shadowing in an osteopath's practice is important and should be described. Give details of any work using your hands. **London (St George's)** Work experience required.

Advice to applicants and planning the UCAS personal statement Bournemouth Link your experiences, achievements and passions back to the subject area you are interested in. For example, take some time to think about why your attention to detail will be a brilliant attribute as a scientist.

Misconceptions about this course Bangor (Hlth Soc Cr) This is an administration course, not a nursing course. **Bournemouth** Many think that being passionate about babies is what midwifery is all about, but really it is about the care of the adult (ie mothers through pregnancy), not the child. **Brit Coll Ost Med** Some students think that we offer an orthodox course in medicine. **European Sch Ost** Some applicants think we teach in French: we do not although we do have a franchise with a French school based in St Etienne and a high percentage of international students. All lectures are in English. Applicants should note that cranial osteopathy – one of our specialisms – is only one aspect of the programme.

Selection interviews Yes Anglia Ruskin, Bolton, Brighton, Dundee, European Sch Ost, London (St George's), Portsmouth, Worcester; **Some** Cardiff Met, Nottingham Trent; **No** Canterbury Christ Church, Derby, Lincoln, Liverpool John Moores, Southampton, Swansea, West Scotland.

Interview advice and questions Courses vary considerably and you are likely to be questioned on your reasons for choosing the course at that university or college. If you have studied biology, then questions on the A-level syllabus are possible and you could also be asked to discuss any work experience you have had. (Ost) What personal qualities would you need to be a good osteopath? What have you done that you feel demonstrates a sense of responsibility? What would you do if you were not able to secure a place on an Osteopathy course this year? See also **Chapter 5. Bournemouth** Be prepared to speak about your strengths and weaknesses, what it is you like most about the course, why you want to work with people and what you will bring to group work. Don't dominate in the group interview, make sure you listen to others.

Reasons for rejection (non-academic) Some students are mistakenly looking for a professional qualification in, for example, occupational therapy or nursing.

AFTER-RESULTS ADVICE
Offers to applicants repeating A-levels Same Bangor; Brighton; Chester; Derby; European Sch Ost; Lincoln; Liverpool John Moores; Salford; Swansea.

GRADUATE DESTINATIONS AND EMPLOYMENT (2016/17 HESA)
Graduates surveyed 945 **Employed** 585 **In voluntary employment** 0 **In further study** 130 **Assumed unemployed** 25

Career note Graduates enter a very broad variety of careers depending on their specialism. Opportunities exist in the public sector, for example, management and administrative positions with health and local authorities and in health promotion.

OTHER DEGREE SUBJECTS FOR CONSIDERATION
Audiology; Biological Sciences; Biology; Community Studies; Consumer Studies; Dentistry; Dietetics; Medicine; Environmental Health; Nursing; Nutrition; Occupational Therapy; Optometry; Physiotherapy; Psychology; Podiatry; Radiography; Speech Therapy; Sport Science.

HISTORY

(including **Heritage Studies and Medieval Studies**; See also **History (Ancient)**, **History (Economic and Social)**, **History of Art**)

Degrees in History cover a very broad field with many courses focusing on British and European history. However, specialised History degrees are available which cover other regions of the world and all courses will offer a wide range of modules.

Useful websites www.english-heritage.org.uk; www.historytoday.com; www.archives.com; www. historynet.com; www.archives.org.uk; http://royalhistsoc.org; www.nationalarchives.gov.uk; www. history.ac.uk

NB The points totals shown to the left of the institutions are for ease of reference only. It must not be assumed that Tariff points are always used by institutions or that they can be substituted for an offer in grades. The level of an offer is not necessarily indicative of the quality of a course.

COURSE OFFERS INFORMATION
Subject requirements/preferences GCSE English and a foreign language may be required or preferred. **AL** History usually required at a specified grade. (Mediev St) History or English Literature required for some courses.

Your target offers and examples of degree courses
152 pts **Cambridge** – A*AA +interview +HAA (Hist) (IB 42–40 pts HL 776)
         Durham – A*AA incl hist (Hist) (IB 38 pts HL 666 incl hist)
144 pts **Bristol** – AAA incl hist (Hist) (IB 36 pts HL 18 pts incl 6 hist)
         Exeter – A*AA–AAA (Hist; Hist (Emp Expnc)) (IB 38–36 pts HL 766–666)
         Leeds – AAA incl hist (Hist) (IB 35 pts HL 17 pts incl 6 hist)
         London (King's) – AAA incl hist (Hist) (IB 35 pts HL 666 incl hist); AAA incl hist +interview
            (War St Hist) (IB 35 pts HL 666 incl hist)
         London (UCL) – AAA incl hist (Hist; Hist (Yr Abrd)) (IB 38 pts HL 18 pts incl 6 hist); AAA incl
            hist+Euro lang (Hist Euro Lang) (IB 38 pts HL 18 pts incl 6 hist+Euro lang)
         London LSE – AAA (Hist; Int Rel Hist; Pol Hist) (IB 38 pts HL 766)
         Nottingham – AAA incl Engl+hist (Engl Hist) (IB 36–34 pts HL 6 Engl+hist)
         Oxford – AAA +interview (Class Arch Anc Hist) (IB 39 pts HL 666); AAA +interview +HAT (Anc
            Modn Hist; Hist; Hist Pol) (IB 38 pts HL 666); AAA +interview +HAT +MLAT (Hist Modn
            Langs) (IB 38 pts HL 666); AAA +interview +HAT +TSA (Hist Econ) (IB 38 pts HL 666)
         St Andrews – AAA incl hist (Mediev Hist Arch) (IB 36 pts HL 666 incl hist); (Mediev Hist
            courses; Modn Hist courses; Scot Hist courses) (IB 38 pts HL 666 incl hist)
         Warwick – AAA incl hist (Hist (Ren/Modn Modn)) (IB 38 pts HL 6 hist)
         York – AAA/A*AB incl hist (Hist) (IB 36 pts HL 6 hist); AAA incl Engl+hist (Engl Hist) (IB 36
            pts HL 666 incl Engl+hist)
136 pts **Birmingham** – AAB incl hist (Hist Comb Hons; Modn Langs Hist) (IB 32 pts HL 665)
         Glasgow – AAB (Hist; Scot Hist) (IB 36 pts HL 665 incl Engl+hum/lang)
         Lancaster – AAB (Hist; Hist Int Rel; Hist Phil; Hist Pol; Mediev Ely Modn St) (IB 35 pts HL
            16 pts)
         Liverpool – AAA–AAB (Hist) (IB 36–35 pts)
         London (King's) – AAB incl hist (Fr Hist (Yr Abrd)) (IB 35 pts HL 665 incl hist)
         London (UCL) – AAB (Hist Phil Sci) (IB 36 pts HL 17 pts)
         Manchester – AAA–AAB incl hist (Hist) (IB 36 pts HL 666 incl hist); AAB incl hist/pol/gov
            (Pol Modn Hist) (IB 35 pts HL 665 incl hist/pol/gov)
         NCH London – AAB+interview (Hist courses) (IB 35 pts HL 665)
         Newcastle – AAA–AAB incl hist (Hist) (IB 37–35 pts HL 6 hist)
         Nottingham – AAA–AAB incl hist (Hist) (IB 36–34 pts HL 6 hist); AAB incl hist (Anc Hist Hist)
            (IB 34 pts HL 6 hist)
         Sheffield – AAB incl hist/class civ (Hist Comb Hons) (IB 34 pts HL 5 hist); AAB–ABB +bEPQ
            incl hist/class civ (Hist; Hist Pol) (IB 34 pts HL 6 hist)
         Southampton – AAB incl hist (Hist; Modn Hist Pol) (IB 34 pts HL 17 pts incl 5 hist); AAB–
            ABB +aEPQ incl Engl+hist (Engl Hist) (IB 34 pts HL 17 pts incl 6/5 Engl+hist)
         York – AAB incl Fr+hist/class civ (Hist Fr) (IB 35 pts HL 6 Fr+hist)
128 pts **East Anglia** – ABB incl hist (Hist Hist Art) (IB 32 pts HL 5 hist)
         Edinburgh – A*A*A–ABB (Hist Pol) (IB 43–34 pts HL 776–655); AAA–ABB (Hist) (IB 40–34 pts
            HL 766–655); ABB (Archit Hist Herit; Celt Scot Hist) (IB 34 pts HL 655)
         Exeter – AAB–ABB (Hist Int Rel) (IB 34–32 pts HL 665–655)

Leeds – ABB (Hist Phil Sci courses) (IB 34 pts HL 16 pts); ABB incl biol (Biol Hist Phil Sci) (IB 34 pts HL 6 biol); ABB incl hist (Hist Hist Phil Sci) (IB 34 pts HL 16 pts incl 6 hist)

Leicester – ABB–BBB +bEPQ (Anc Hist Hist) (IB 30 pts); (Contemp Hist; Hist; Hist Am St) (IB 30 pts HL 6)

Liverpool – ABB (Hist Comb Hons)

London (QM) – ABB incl hist (Hist; Hist Compar Lit; Hist Pol; Mediev Hist) (IB 32 pts HL 655 incl hist)

London (RH) – AAB–ABB (Hist) (IB 32 pts HL 655)

London (SOAS) – AAB–ABB (Hist) (IB 35 pts HL 665)

London (UCL) – ABB (Scand St Hist) (IB 34 pts HL 16 pts); ABB incl hist (Russ Hist) (IB 34 pts HL 16 pts incl 5 hist)

Loughborough – ABB (Hist; Hist Int Rel; Hist Pol) (IB 34 pts HL 655)

Manchester – ABB incl hist (Hist courses) (IB 34 pts HL 655 incl 6 hist)

Nottingham – ABB (Am Can Lit Hist Cult) (IB 32 pts); ABB incl hist (Am St Hist; Hist Contemp Chin St; Hist E Euro Cult St) (IB 32 pts HL 5 hist); (Hist Hist Art) (IB 32 pts HL 6 hist)

Queen's Belfast – ABB (Hist courses) (IB 33 pts HL 655); ABB incl Fr (Fr Comb Hons) (IB 33 pts HL 655 incl 6 Fr)

Southampton – AAB–ABB incl hist (Flm Hist) (IB 32 pts HL 16 pts incl 5 hist); (Arch Hist; Phil Hist) (IB 34–32 pts HL 17–16 pts incl 5 hist)

Sussex – AAB–ABB (Hist; Hist Comb Hons) (IB 34–32 pts)

120 pts   **Aberdeen** – BBB (Hist) (IB 32 pts HL 555)

Brunel – BBB (Mltry Int Hist; Modn Hist) (IB 30 pts)

Cardiff – ABB–BBB (Hist) (HL 665 incl 6 hist); (Modn Hist Pol) (IB 34–32 pts HL 665–655)

City – BBB (Hist) (IB 29 pts HL 55)

Coventry – BBB (Hist courses) (IB 31 pts)

Derby – C class st/hist/pol 120 pts (Hist)

Dundee – BBB (Hist; Scot Hist St) (IB 30 pts HL 555)

East Anglia – BBB/ABC incl Engl+hist (Lit Hist) (IB 31 pts HL 5 Engl+hist); BBB/ABC–BBC +aEPQ incl hist (Am Hist; Hist; Hist Pol; Modn Hist; Phil Hist) (IB 31 pts HL 5 hist)

Essex – BBB (Hist; Modn Hist) (IB 30 pts HL 555)

Huddersfield – BBB incl hist 120 pts (Hist; Hist Comb Hons)

Hull – BBB 120 pts (Hist) (IB 30 pts)

Kent – BBB incl hist/hum (Hist courses; Mltry Hist) (IB 34 pts HL 15 pts)

Leicester – BBB–BBC +bEPQ (Int Rel Hist) (IB 28 pts)

London (Birk) – ABB–BBB 120–128 pts (Pol Phil Hist)

London (Gold) – BBB (Hist; Hist Pol) (IB 33 pts HL 655)

Northumbria – 120 pts (Hist; Hist Pol)

Reading – BBB incl hist (Hist; Span Hist) (IB 30 pts HL 5 hist)

Stirling – BBB (Scot Hist) (IB 32 pts); BBB incl hist (Hist) (IB 32 pts)

Strathclyde – ABB–BBB (Hist) (IB 36 pts)

Swansea – BBB 120 pts (Hist) (IB 32 pts)

112 pts   **Bangor** – 112 pts (Herit Arch Hist; Hist; Mediev Ely Modn Hist; Modn Contemp Hist; Welsh Hist Comb Hons)

Buckingham – BBB–BBC (Engl Lit Hist) (IB 32–31 pts)

Chester – BBB–BBC incl hist/class civ/pol/sociol 112–120 pts (Hist) (IB 28 pts HL 5 hist)

Coventry – BBC (Hist Pol) (IB 29 pts)

De Montfort – 112 pts incl hist (Hist) (IB 26 pts)

Edge Hill – BBB–BBC 112–120 pts (Engl Lit Hist; Hist; Hist Pol)

Leeds Beckett – 112 pts (Hist) (IB 25 pts)

Lincoln – BBC (Engl Hist) (IB 29 pts)

Liverpool Hope – BBC 112 pts (Hist) (IB 28 pts)

Liverpool John Moores – BBC 112 pts (Hist) (IB 26 pts)

Manchester Met – BBC 112 pts (Hist) (IB 26 pts)

Nottingham Trent – 112 pts (Hist)

Roehampton – 112 pts (Hist)
Sheffield Hallam – BBC 112 pts (Hist)
Suffolk – BBC incl hist 112 pts (Hist)
Sunderland – 112 pts (Hist courses)
UWE Bristol – 112 pts (Hist)
104 pts **Central Lancashire** – 104 pts (Hist)
Chichester – BBB–BCC 104–120 pts (Hist; Modn Hist) (IB 28 pts)
Greenwich – BCC 104 pts (Hist)
Hertfordshire – BCC 104 pts (Hist)
London (Birk) – BBB–BCC 104–120 pts (Hist)
Manchester Met – 104–112 pts (Hist Comb Hons) (IB 26 pts)
Northampton – BCC incl hist (Hist courses)
Nottingham Trent – 104 pts (Hist Pol)
Oxford Brookes – BCC 104 pts (Hist) (IB 29 pts)
Plymouth – B hist/class civ/econ/law 104–112 pts (Hist Pol; Hist courses) (IB 28–26 pts HL 5 hist/class civ/econ/law)
Westminster – ABB–BCC incl Engl/hum (Engl Lit Hist) (IB 27 pts HL 5 Engl)
Winchester – 104–120 pts incl hist/arch/econ/pol (Hist; Mediev Hist) (HL 44)
Worcester – 104–112 pts (Hist courses)
96 pts **Aberystwyth** – BBB–CCC 96–120 pts (Hist; Hist Welsh Hist; Mediev Ely Modn Hist; Modn Contemp Hist) (IB 30–26 pts)
Anglia Ruskin – 96 pts (Hist) (IB 24 pts)
Bath Spa – CCC incl hist (Hist) (IB 26 pts HL 5 hist)
Bishop Grosseteste – 96–112 pts (Arch Hist; Hist courses)
Brighton – BCC–CCC 96–104 pts (Hist Lit Cult) (IB 26 pts)
Gloucestershire – BBC 96–112 pts (Hist)
Keele – CCC (Hist) (IB 26 pts)
Newman – CC 96 pts (Hist)
Portsmouth – 96–112 pts incl hist (Hist) (IB 25 pts HL 17 pts)
St Mary's – BBC–CCC 96–112 pts (Hist)
Teesside – 96–112 pts (Hist)
Wolverhampton – CCC/BCD 96 pts (Hist; Pol Hist)
York St John – 96 pts (Hist)
88 pts **Canterbury Christ Church** – 88–112 pts (Hist)
80 pts **South Wales** – BCC–CDD 80–104 pts (Hist) (IB 29 pts)
72 pts **Anglia Ruskin** – 72 pts (Hist Engl Lit)
UHI – BC (Hist Pol; Scot Hist; Scot Hist Arch)

Trinity Saint David – interview (Hist courses; Mediev St Comb Hons)

Alternative offers
See **Chapter 6** and **Appendix 1** for grades/UCAS Tariff points information for other examinations.

EXAMPLES OF COLLEGES OFFERING COURSES IN THIS SUBJECT FIELD
North Lindsey (Coll); Peterborough (Coll); Petroc; South Devon (Coll); Stockton Riverside (Coll); Truro and Penwith (Coll).

CHOOSING YOUR COURSE (SEE ALSO CH.1)
Universities and colleges teaching quality See www.qaa.ac.uk; https://unistats.ac.uk.

Examples of sandwich degree courses Bangor; Plymouth.

ADMISSIONS INFORMATION
Number of applicants per place (approx) Anglia Ruskin 4; Bangor 4; Bath Spa 6; Birmingham 8; Bristol 7; Buckingham 10; Cambridge 3; Cardiff 7; Central Lancashire 5; De Montfort 10; Dundee 8; Durham 7; East Anglia 3; Edge Hill 8; Exeter 9; Gloucestershire 26; Huddersfield 3; Hull 5; Kent 5;

Kingston 6; Lancaster 4; Leeds 12; Leeds Trinity 6; Leicester 5; Liverpool 4; London (Gold) 6; London (King's) 10; London (QM) 5; London (RH) 6; London (UCL) 5; London LSE 11; Manchester 6; Manchester Met 8; Newcastle 5; Newman 2; Northampton 4; Nottingham 5; Oxford Brookes 9; Roehampton 4; Sheffield Hallam 21; Southampton 8; St Mary's 5; Staffordshire 8; Stirling 10; Teesside 4; Trinity Saint David 6; Warwick 17; York 5; York St John 3.

Advice to applicants and planning the UCAS personal statement Show your passion for the past! Visits to places of interest should be mentioned, together with any particular features which impressed you. Read historical books and magazines outside your A-level syllabus. Mention these and describe any special areas of study which interest you. (Check that these areas are covered in the courses for which you are applying!) **Bristol** Only accepting a limited number of deferred applicants in fairness to next year's applicants. Apply early. **Manchester** Due to the detailed nature of entry requirements for History courses, we are unable to include full details in the prospectus. For complete and up-to-date information on our entry requirements for these courses, please visit our website at www.manchester.ac.uk/study/undergraduate/courses.

Misconceptions about this course Lincoln Some students expect the subject to be assessed only by exams and essays. It is not – we use a wide range of assessment methods. **Stirling** Some applicants think that we only teach British history. We also cover European, American, African and environmental history.

Selection interviews Yes Brighton, Buckingham, Cambridge, Oxford ((Hist) 23%, (Hist Econ) 11%, (Hist Modn Lang) 21%, (Hist Pol) 13%), Trinity Saint David; **Some** Bristol, Cardiff, Leeds Trinity, London (QM), Southampton, Warwick, Wolverhampton; **No** Anglia Ruskin, Bangor, Birmingham, Bishop Grosseteste, Canterbury Christ Church, Chichester, De Montfort, Dundee, East Anglia, Edge Hill, Essex, Hertfordshire, Huddersfield, Hull, Kent, Liverpool, London (King's), London (RH), London (UCL), London LSE, Nottingham, Oxford Brookes, Portsmouth, Reading, Roehampton, Sheffield Hallam, Staffordshire, Winchester.

Interview advice and questions Questions are likely to be asked on those aspects of the history A-level syllabus which interest you. Examples of questions in previous years have included: Why did imperialism happen? If a Martian arrived on Earth what aspect of life would you show him/her to sum up today's society? Has the role of class been exaggerated by Marxist historians? What is the difference between power and authority and between patriotism and nationalism? Did Elizabeth I have a foreign policy? What is the relevance of history in modern society? Who are your favourite monarchs? How could you justify your study of history to the taxpayer? See also **Chapter 5.** **Cambridge** How would you compare Henry VIII to Stalin? In the 1920s did the invention of the Henry Ford car lead to a national sub-culture or was it just an aspect of one? Is there such a thing as 'race'? Should historians be allowed to read sci-fi novels? **Oxford** Questions on submitted work and the capacity to think independently. What are the origins of your name? Why are you sitting in this chair?

Reasons for rejection (non-academic) Personal statements which read like job applications, focusing extensively on personal skills and saying nothing about the applicant's passion for history. Poor use of personal statement combined with predicted grades. Little commitment and enthusiasm. No clear reason for choice of course. Little understanding of history. Absence or narrowness of intellectual pursuits. Deception or concealment on the UCAS application. Knowledge of 19th century history (chosen subject) did not have any depth. Unwillingness to learn. Narrow approach to subject. Failure to submit requested information. **Birmingham** Commitment insufficient to sustain interest over three years. **London (King's)** Inability to think analytically and comparatively. **London (UCL)** The vast majority of applications are of a very high standard, many applicants being predicted AAA grades. We view each application as a complete picture, taking into account personal statement, reference and performance at any interview as well as actual and predicted academic performance. There is no single rule by which applicants are selected and therefore no single reason why they are rejected.

AFTER-RESULTS ADVICE
Offers to applicants repeating A-levels Higher Exeter; Huddersfield; Leeds; Liverpool; St Andrews; Trinity Saint David; Warwick; **Possibly higher** Aberystwyth; Birmingham; Cambridge; **Same** Anglia Ruskin; Bangor; Bristol; Buckingham; Cardiff; Chester; Chichester; De Montfort; Dundee; Durham;

East Anglia; Edge Hill; Hull; Lancaster; Lincoln; Liverpool Hope; Liverpool John Moores; London (QM); London (RH); London (SOAS); Newcastle; Newman; Nottingham Trent; Oxford Brookes; Roehampton; St Mary's; Staffordshire; Stirling; Suffolk; Winchester; Wolverhampton; York; York St John; **No** Glasgow.

GRADUATE DESTINATIONS AND EMPLOYMENT (2016/17 HESA)
Graduates surveyed 8,660 **Employed** 3,540 **In voluntary employment** 390 **In further study** 2,895 **Assumed unemployed** 495

Career note Graduates enter a broad spectrum of careers. While a small number seek positions with museums and galleries, most will enter careers in management, public and social services and retail as well as the teaching profession.

OTHER DEGREE SUBJECTS FOR CONSIDERATION
Ancient History; Anthropology; Archaeology; Economic and Social History; Government; History of Art; International Relations; Medieval History; Politics.

HISTORY (ANCIENT)
(See also **African, Asian and Middle-eastern Studies, Archaeology, History**)

Ancient History covers the Greek and Roman world, the social, religious, political and economic changes taking place in the Byzantine period and the medieval era which followed.

Useful websites http://royalhistsoc.org; www.guardians.net; www.ancientworlds.net; www.bbc.co.uk/history/ancient

NB The points totals shown to the left of the institutions are for ease of reference only. It must not be assumed that Tariff points are always used by institutions or that they can be substituted for an offer in grades. The level of an offer is not necessarily indicative of the quality of a course.

COURSE OFFERS INFORMATION
Subject requirements/preferences GCSE A foreign language or classical language may be required. **AL** History or Classical Civilisation may be preferred subjects.

Your target offers and examples of degree courses
144 pts **Durham** – AAA (Anc Hist) (IB 37 pts HL 18 pts)
      London (UCL) – AAA incl hist/class civ (Anc Hist) (IB 38 pts HL 18 pts incl 6 hist)
      Oxford – AAA +interview +HAT (Anc Modn Hist) (IB 38 pts HL 666)
      St Andrews – AAA (Anc Hist Comb Hons) (IB 36 pts HL 666)
136 pts **Bristol** – AAB (Anc Hist) (IB 34 pts HL 17 pts)
      Durham – AAB (Anc Hist Arch) (IB 36 pts HL 665)
      Exeter – AAA–AAB (Anc Hist) (IB 36–34 pts HL 666–665)
      London (King's) – AAB (Anc Hist) (IB 35 pts HL 665)
      London (UCL) – AAB (Anc Wrld) (IB 36 pts HL 17 pts)
      Nottingham – AAB incl hist (Anc Hist Hist) (IB 34 pts HL 6 hist)
128 pts **Birmingham** – ABB (Anc Hist; Anc Mediev Hist; Arch Anc Hist) (IB 32 pts HL 655)
      Edinburgh – AAB–ABB (Anc Hist) (IB 36–34 pts HL 665–655); ABB (Anc Medit Civ; Arch Anc Hist) (IB 36–34 pts HL 665–655); (Anc Hist Gk; Anc Hist Lat) (IB 36–34 pts HL 666–655)
      Leicester – ABB (Anc Hist Arch) (IB 30 pts); ABB–BBB+bEPQ (Anc Hist Hist) (IB 30 pts)
      Liverpool – ABB (Anc Hist) (IB 33 pts)
      Manchester – ABB +interview (Anc Hist) (IB 34 pts HL 655)
      Nottingham – AAB–ABB (Anc Hist) (IB 34–32 pts); ABB (Anc Hist Arch) (IB 32 pts)
      Warwick – ABB (Anc Hist Class Arch) (IB 34 pts)
120 pts **Cardiff** – ABB–BBB (Anc Hist Comb Hons) (HL 665)
      Kent – BBB (Anc Hist) (IB 34 pts HL 15 pts)
      Liverpool – BBB (Arch Anc Civ) (IB 30 pts)

London (RH) – ABB–BBB (Anc Hist; Anc Hist Phil) (IB 32 pts HL 555)

Swansea – BBB (Egypt Anc Hist) (IB 32 pts); BBB 120 pts (Anc Hist Hist; Anc Mediev Hist) (IB 32 pts)

96 pts **Trinity Saint David** – 96 pts +interview (Anc Civ; Anc Hist; Mediev St)

Alternative offers
See **Chapter 6** and **Appendix 1** for grades/UCAS Tariff points information for other examinations.

CHOOSING YOUR COURSE (SEE ALSO CH.1)
Universities and colleges teaching quality See www.qaa.ac.uk; https://unistats.ac.uk.

Top research universities and colleges (REF 2014) See **Classics and Classical Studies/Civilisation.**

Examples of sandwich degree courses Reading.

ADMISSIONS INFORMATION
Number of applicants per place (approx) Birmingham 7; Bristol 6; Cardiff 4; Durham 6; Leicester 5; London (RH) 5; London (UCL) 5; Manchester 7; Nottingham 4; Oxford 4.

Advice to applicants and planning the UCAS personal statement Any information about experience of excavation or museum work should be given. Visits to Greece and Italy to study archaeological sites should be described. Show how your interest in, for example, Ancient Egypt developed through, for example, reading, television and the internet. Be aware of the work of the career archaeologist, for example, sites and measurement officers, field officers and field researchers (often specialists in pottery, glass, metalwork). See also **History**.

Misconceptions about this course Liverpool (Egypt) Some students would have been better advised looking at V400 Archaeology or VV16 Ancient History and Archaeology, both of which offer major pathways in the study of Ancient Egypt.

Selection interviews Yes Oxford (23%); **Some** Bristol, Cardiff; **No** Birmingham, London (RH).

Interview advice and questions See **History**.

AFTER-RESULTS ADVICE
Offers to applicants repeating A-levels Same Birmingham; Cardiff; Durham; Newcastle.

GRADUATE DESTINATIONS AND EMPLOYMENT (2016/17 HESA)
Graduates surveyed See **History**.

Career note See **History**.

OTHER DEGREE SUBJECTS FOR CONSIDERATION
Anthropology; Archaeology; Classical Studies; Classics; Greek; History of Art; Latin.

HISTORY (ECONOMIC AND SOCIAL)

(See also **History**)

Economic and Social History is a study of societies and economies and explores the changes that have taken place in the past and the causes and consequences of those changes. The study can cover Britain, Europe and other major powers.

Useful websites http://royalhistsoc.org; www.ehs.org.uk; see also **Economics** and **History**.

NB The points totals shown to the left of the institutions are for ease of reference only. It must not be assumed that Tariff points are always used by institutions or that they can be substituted for an offer in grades. The level of an offer is not necessarily indicative of the quality of a course.

COURSE OFFERS INFORMATION

Subject requirements/preferences GCSE Mathematics usually required and a language may be preferred. **AL** History preferred.

Your target offers and examples of degree courses

152 pts   **London LSE** – A*AA incl maths (Econ Econ Hist) (IB 38 pts HL 766 incl 7 maths)

144 pts   **York** – AAA incl hist/class civ+maths (Hist Econ) (IB 36 pts HL 666 incl hist+maths)

136 pts   **Glasgow** – AAB incl Engl/hum (Econ Soc Hist courses) (IB 36 pts HL 665 incl Engl+lang/hum)

128 pts   **Edinburgh** – AAB–ABB 128–136 pts (Econ Hist) (IB 36–34 pts HL 665–655)

            Manchester – ABB incl hist/sociol (Hist Sociol) (IB 34 pts HL 655 incl 6 hist/sociol)

112 pts   **Glyndŵr** – BBC 112 pts (Soc Cult Hist)

Alternative offers

See **Chapter 6** and **Appendix 1** for grades/UCAS Tariff points information for other examinations.

CHOOSING YOUR COURSE (SEE ALSO CH.1)

Universities and colleges teaching quality See www.qaa.ac.uk; https://unistats.ac.uk.

ADMISSIONS INFORMATION

Number of applicants per place (approx) London LSE (Econ Hist) 7, (Econ Hist Econ) 12; York 8.

Advice to applicants and planning the UCAS personal statement See **History**.

Interview advice and questions See **History**.

AFTER-RESULTS ADVICE

Offers to applicants repeating A-levels Higher York.

GRADUATE DESTINATIONS AND EMPLOYMENT (2016/17 HESA)

Graduates surveyed See **History**.

Career note See **History**.

OTHER DEGREE SUBJECTS FOR CONSIDERATION

Economics; Government; History; Politics; Social Policy and Administration; Sociology.

HISTORY OF ART

(See also **History**)

History of Art (and Design) courses differ slightly between universities although most will focus on the history and appreciation of European art and architecture from the 14th to 20th centuries. Some courses also cover the Egyptian, Greek and Roman periods and at London (SOAS), Asian, African and European Art. The history of all aspects of design and film can also be studied in some courses.

Useful websites www.artchive.com; www.artcyclopedia.com; http://theartguide.com; www.galleries. co.uk; https://cryptoart.com; www.nationalgallery.org.uk; www.britisharts.co.uk; www.tate.org.uk

NB The points totals shown to the left of the institutions are for ease of reference only. It must not be assumed that Tariff points are always used by institutions or that they can be substituted for an offer in grades. The level of an offer is not necessarily indicative of the quality of a course.

COURSE OFFERS INFORMATION

Subject requirements/preferences GCSE English required and a foreign language usually preferred. **AL** History is preferred for some courses.

Your target offers and examples of degree courses

152 pts **Cambridge** – A*AA +interview +HAAA (Hist Art) (IB 42–40 pts HL 776)
144 pts **London (UCL)** – AAA (Hist Art) (IB 38 pts HL 18 pts)
   Oxford – AAA +interview (Hist Art) (IB 38 pts HL 666)
   St Andrews – AAA (Art Hist; Art Hist Class St; Art Hist Mid E St; Art Hist Psy) (IB 36 pts HL 665); AAA incl lang (Art Hist Lang) (IB 36 pts HL 665 incl 6 lang)
136 pts **Bristol** – AAB (Hist Art) (IB 34 pts HL 17 pts); AAB incl lang (Hist Art Modn Lang) (IB 34 pts HL 17 pts incl 5 lang)
   Glasgow – AAB incl arts/hum (Hist Art) (IB 36 pts HL 665 incl 6 Engl/hum/lang)
   Nottingham – AAB incl Engl (Hist Art Engl) (IB 34 pts HL 6 Engl)
   York – AAB incl Engl (Engl Hist Art) (IB 35 pts HL 6 Engl); AAB incl hist/class civ (Hist Hist Art) (IB 35 pts HL 6 hist)
128 pts **Birmingham** – ABB (Hist Art) (IB 32 pts HL 655); ABB incl lang (Modn Langs Hist Art) (IB 32 pts HL 655)
   East Anglia – ABB (Arch Anth Art Hist (St Abrd); Hist Art Gllry Musm St) (IB 32 pts); ABB incl hist (Hist Hist Art) (IB 32 pts HL 5 hist); ABB–BBB +aEPQ (Hist Art) (IB 32 pts)
   Edinburgh – ABB (Hist Art) (IB 40–34 pts HL 766–655); ABB incl mus (Hist Art Hist Mus) (IB 40–34 pts HL 766–655)
   Exeter – AAB–ABB (Art Hist Vis Cult; Art Hist courses) (IB 34–32 pts HL 665–655)
   Leeds – AAB–ABB (Hist Art) (IB 35–34 pts)
   London (Court) – AAA–ABB +interview (Hist Art) (IB 35 pts)
   London (SOAS) – AAB–ABB (Hist Art; Hist Art (As Af Euro); Hist Art Arch courses) (IB 35 pts HL 665)
   Manchester – ABB (Hist Art) (IB 34 pts HL 655)
   Nottingham – ABB (Hist Art) (IB 32 pts); ABB incl hist (Hist Hist Art) (IB 32 pts HL 6 hist)
   Sussex – AAB–ABB (Art Hist) (IB 34–32 pts)
   Warwick – ABB (Hist Art) (IB 34 pts)
   York – AAB–ABB (Hist Art) (IB 35–34 pts)
120 pts **Aberdeen** – BBB (Hist Art) (IB 32 pts HL 555)
   Bournemouth Arts – BBB (Art Des Hist) (IB 30 pts)
   Essex – BBB (Art Hist; Lit Art Hist) (IB 30 pts)
   Nottingham – ABB–BBB (Arch Hist Art) (IB 32–30 pts)
112 pts **Buckingham** – BBB–BBC +interview (Hist Art Herit Mgt) (IB 32–31 pts)
   Kent – BBC (Art Hist; Art Hist Flm) (IB 34 pts HL 14 pts)
   Liverpool John Moores – BBC 112 pts (Hist Art Musm St) (IB 26 pts)
   London (Birk) – ABB–BBC 112–128 pts (Hist Art; Hist Art Cur)
   Manchester Met – BBB–BBC 112–120 pts (Art Hist) (IB 26 pts)
104 pts **Aberystwyth** – BBB–BCC incl art 104–120 pts +portfolio (Fn Art Art Hist) (IB 30–28 pts)
   Plymouth – 104–112 pts (Art Hist) (IB 26 pts)
96 pts **Aberystwyth** – BBB–CCC 96–120 pts (Art Hist) (IB 30–26 pts)
   Brighton – BCC–CCC 96–104 pts (Fash Drs Hist; Hist Art Des) (IB 26 pts)
   Plymouth – 96–144 pts +interview +portfolio (Fn Art Art Hist) (IB 26 pts)

Alternative offers
See **Chapter 6** and **Appendix 1** for grades/UCAS Tariff points information for other examinations.

EXAMPLES OF COLLEGES OFFERING COURSES IN THIS SUBJECT FIELD
South Gloucestershire and Stroud (Coll).

CHOOSING YOUR COURSE (SEE ALSO CH.1)
Universities and colleges teaching quality See www.qaa.ac.uk; https://unistats.ac.uk.

Top research universities and colleges (REF 2014) See **Art and Design (General)**.

Examples of sandwich degree courses Plymouth.

ADMISSIONS INFORMATION

Number of applicants per place (approx) Birmingham 14; Bristol 4; Cambridge 4; East Anglia 5; Essex 5; Leeds 29; Leicester 9; London (Court) 320; London (SOAS) 4; London (UCL) 6; Manchester 3; Manchester Met 10; Nottingham 2; York 4.

Advice to applicants and planning the UCAS personal statement Applicants for History of Art courses should have made extensive visits to art galleries, particularly in London, and should be familiar with the main European schools of painting. Evidence of lively interest required. Discuss your preferences and say why you prefer certain types of work or particular artists. You should also describe any visits to museums and any special interests in furniture, pottery or other artefacts. **Bristol** Deferred entry may be considered. **London (Court)** Everyone is surrounded by visual materials, from buildings and works of art to films, photography, fashion, advertisements and computer games. Ideally, your personal statement includes an explanation of why some visual materials you have seen really interest you. Admissions tutors look for an expression and explanation of enthusiasm for the topic of art history and for the study of the visual material as evidence of historical circumstances and human activity. You might include an account of how your understanding of visual materials has been affected by an article or book you have read (not necessarily art history). Admissions tutors also want a clear picture of the applicant as an individual with the motivation and potential to benefit from a degree course in art history.

Misconceptions about this course London (Court) The BA History of Art programme does not have fine art/practice based components. **York** Students do not need a background in art or art history. It is not a course with a studio element in it.

Selection interviews Yes Buckingham, Cambridge, Manchester, Oxford (10%), Warwick; **Some** Bristol; **No** Birmingham, Brighton, East Anglia, Essex, Kent, London (UCL), Manchester Met, Nottingham.

Interview advice and questions Some universities set slide tests on painting and sculpture. Those applicants who have not taken History of Art at A-level will be questioned on their reasons for choosing the subject, their visits to art galleries and museums and their reactions to the art work which has impressed them. See **Chapter 5**. **Kent** Do they visit art galleries? Have they studied art history previously? What do they expect to get out of the degree? Sometimes they are given images to compare and discuss. **London (Court)** If selected for interview, candidates are asked to attend an interview day, first completing a 30 minute test comparing two images, then an informal interview with two members of academic staff. This exercise is a chance for our academic members of staff to assess candidates' visual comprehension. Candidates are not expected to exercise specific history of art knowledge at this stage.

Reasons for rejection (non-academic) Poorly presented practical work. Students who do not express any interest or enthusiasm in contemporary visual arts are rejected.

AFTER-RESULTS ADVICE

Offers to applicants repeating A-levels Possibly higher St Andrews; **Same** Aberystwyth; East Anglia; Leeds; Warwick; York; **No** Cambridge.

GRADUATE DESTINATIONS AND EMPLOYMENT

Career note Work in galleries, museums and collections will be the objective of many graduates, who should try to establish contacts by way of work placements and experience during their undergraduate years. The personal skills acquired during their studies, however, open up many opportunities in other careers.

OTHER DEGREE SUBJECTS FOR CONSIDERATION

Art; Archaeology; Architecture; Classical Studies; Photography.

HORTICULTURE

(including Garden Design; See also Agricultural Sciences/Agriculture, Landscape Architecture, Plant Sciences)

Horticulture is a broad subject area covering amenity or landscape horticulture, production horticulture and retail horticulture.

Useful websites http://iagre.org; www.rhs.org.uk; www.horticulture.org.uk; www.sgd.org.uk

NB The points totals shown to the left of the institutions are for ease of reference only. It must not be assumed that Tariff points are always used by institutions or that they can be substituted for an offer in grades. The level of an offer is not necessarily indicative of the quality of a course.

COURSE OFFERS INFORMATION

Subject requirements/preferences GCSE Mathematics sometimes required. **AL** A science subject may be required or preferred for some courses.

Your target offers and examples of degree courses
104 pts   SRUC – BCC incl sci (Hort; Hort Plntsmn)
96 pts   Writtle (UC) – 96 pts (Hort) (IB 24 pts)
64 pts   Hadlow (UC) – 64 pts (Hort (Commer))

Alternative offers
See **Chapter 6** and **Appendix 1** for grades/UCAS Tariff points information for other examinations.

EXAMPLES OF COLLEGES OFFERING COURSES IN THIS SUBJECT FIELD

Askham Bryan (Coll); Bicton (Coll); Bishop Burton (Coll); Bridgend (Coll); Bridgwater and Taunton (Coll); Brooksby Melton (Coll); CAFRE; Capel Manor (Coll); Craven (Coll); Myerscough (Coll); Warwickshire (Coll).

CHOOSING YOUR COURSE (SEE ALSO CH.1)

Universities and colleges teaching quality See www.qaa.ac.uk; https://unistats.ac.uk.

ADMISSIONS INFORMATION

Number of applicants per place (approx) Sparsholt (Coll) 1; SRUC 1; Writtle (UC) 3.

Advice to applicants and planning the UCAS personal statement Practical experience is important and visits to botanical gardens (the Royal Botanic Gardens, Kew or Edinburgh and the Royal Horticultural Society gardens at Wisley) could be described. Contact your local authority offices for details of work in parks and gardens departments. See also **Appendix 3.**

Selection interviews Some SRUC; **No** Greenwich.

Interview advice and questions Past questions have included: How did you become interested in horticulture? How do you think this course will benefit you? Could you work in all weathers? What career are you aiming for? Are you interested in gardening? Describe your garden. What plants do you grow? How do you prune rose trees and fruit trees? Are there any EU policies at present affecting the horticulture industry? Topics relating to the importance of science and horticulture. See also **Chapter 5.**

AFTER-RESULTS ADVICE

Offers to applicants repeating A-levels Same SRUC.

GRADUATE DESTINATIONS AND EMPLOYMENT (2016/17 HESA)

Graduates surveyed See **Agricultural Sciences/Agriculture**.

Career note Graduates seeking employment in horticulture will look towards commercial organisations for the majority of openings. These will include positions as growers and managers with fewer vacancies for scientists involved in research and development and advisory services.

OTHER DEGREE SUBJECTS FOR CONSIDERATION

Agriculture; Biology; Crop Science; Ecology; Forestry; Landscape Architecture; Plant Sciences.

HOSPITALITY AND EVENT MANAGEMENT

(See also **Business and Management Courses, Business and Management Courses (international and European), Business and Management Courses (Specialised), Food Science/Studies and Technology, Leisure and Recreation Management/Studies, Tourism and Travel**)

Courses cover the full range of skills required for those working in the industry. Specific studies include hotel management, food and beverage supplies, equipment design, public relations and marketing. Depending on the course, other topics may include events management, tourism and the international trade.

Useful websites www.thebapa.org.uk; www.cordonbleu.edu; www.instituteofhospitality.org; www.people1st.co.uk; www.abpco.org

NB The points totals shown to the left of the institutions are for ease of reference only. It must not be assumed that Tariff points are always used by institutions or that they can be substituted for an offer in grades. The level of an offer is not necessarily indicative of the quality of a course.

COURSE OFFERS INFORMATION

Subject requirements/preferences GCSE English and mathematics usually required together with a foreign language for International Management courses. **AL** No specified subjects.

Your target offers and examples of degree courses

144 pts   Strathclyde – AAA incl maths (Acc Hspty Tour Mgt) (IB 38 pts HL 6 maths)

120 pts   Bournemouth Arts – BBB 120 pts+interview (Crea Evnts Mgt) (IB 30 pts)
   Strathclyde – ABB–BBB (Hspty Tour Mgt) (IB 36 pts)
   Surrey – BBB (Int Hspty Mgt; Int Hspty Tour Mgt) (IB 32 pts)

112 pts   Coventry – BBC (Evnt Mgt) (IB 29 pts)
   De Montfort – 112 pts (Arts Fstvl Mgt) (IB 26 pts)
   Derby – 112 pts (Evnts Mgt; Int Hspty Mgt)
   East London – 112 pts (Hspty Mgt) (IB 25 pts HL 15 pts)
   Greenwich – 112 pts (Evnt Mgt)
   Huddersfield – BBC 112 pts (Evnts Mgt courses; Hspty Bus Mgt)
   Lincoln – BBC 112 pts (Evnts Mgt) (IB 29 pts)
   Liverpool Hope – BBC 112 pts (Tour Mgt) (IB 28 pts)
   Liverpool John Moores – BBC 112 pts (Evnts Mgt)
   Salford – BBC 112 pts (Int Evnts Mgt) (IB 30 pts)
   Suffolk – BBC 112 pts+interview (Evnt Tour Mgt)
   Sunderland – 112 pts (Int Tour Hspty Mgt)
   West London – BBC 112 pts (Evnt Mgt; Hspty Mgt)

104 pts   Birmingham (UC) – BCC 104 pts (Evnts Mgt)
   Bournemouth – 104–120 pts (Evnts Mgt) (IB 31–28 pts)
   CAFRE – 104 pts incl bus/sci/hm econ (Fd Bus Mgt)
   Chester – BBC–BCC 104–112 pts (Evnts Mgt) (IB 26 pts)
   Coventry – 104 pts (Int Hspty Tour Mgt)
   Gloucestershire – BCC 104 pts (Evnts Mgt)
   Manchester Met – BBC–BCC 104–112 pts (Evnts Mgt; Int Hspty Bus Mgt) (IB 26 pts)
   Northampton – BCC (Evnts Mgt; Evnts Mgt Comb Hons)

Oxford Brookes – BCC 104 pts (Int Hspty Mgt) (IB 29 pts)
Queen Margaret – BCC (Evnts Fstvl Mgt) (IB 28 pts)
Robert Gordon – BCC (Evnts Mgt) (IB 28 pts HL 5 Engl)
Ulster – BBB–BCC (Leis Evnts Mgt) (IB 26–24 pts HL 13–12 pts); BCC (Int Hspty Mgt) (IB 26–25 pts HL 13–12 pts)

96 pts **Birmingham (UC)** – CCC 96 pts (Hspty courses; Spec Hair Media Mkup)
Cardiff Met – 96–112 pts (Evnts Mgt; Int Tour Evnts Mgt)
Central Lancashire – 96–104 pts (Evnt Mgt; Int Hspty Mgt)
Chichester – BBC–CCC 96–112 pts (Evnt Mgt) (IB 28 pts)
Edinburgh Napier – CCC (Int Fstvl Evnt Mgt) (IB 27 pts HL 654)
Essex – CCC 96 pts (Evnt Mgt; Evnt Mgt Hspty; Htl Mgt) (IB 26 pts HL 444)
Hertfordshire – CCC 96 pts (Evnt Mgt)
Leeds Beckett – 96 pts (Evnts Mgt; Spo Evnt Mgt) (IB 24 pts)
London Met – CCC/BC 96 pts (Evnts Mgt)
Plymouth – 96–112 pts (Evnts Mgt) (IB 28–26 pts HL 4)
Robert Gordon – CCC (Int Hspty Mgt) (IB 26 pts)
Sheffield Hallam – BBC 96–112 pts (Int Htl Mgt)
Solent – 96–112 pts (Evnts Mgt)
Staffordshire – 96 pts (Evnts Mgt)
West Scotland – CCC 96 pts (Evnts Mgt) (IB 24 pts HL 44)
Winchester – 96–112 pts (Evnt Mgt) (HL 44)
Wolverhampton – CCC/BCD 96 pts (Evnt Vnu Mgt; Int Hspty Mgt)

88 pts **Canterbury Christ Church** – 88–112 pts (Evnts Mgt)
Plymouth – 88–96 pts (Hspty Mgt) (IB 26–24 pts HL 4); 88–96 pts +interview (Cru Mgt) (IB 26–24 pts HL 4)
Trinity Saint David – 88 pts +interview (Evnts Fstvl Mgt)

80 pts **Bedfordshire** – 80–120 pts (Evnt Mgt)
Bucks New – 80 pts (Evnts Fstvl Vnu Mgt)
South Wales – BCC–CCD 80–104 pts (Bus Mgt Evnt Mgt) (IB 29 pts)

64 pts **UHI** – CC (Hspty Mgt)

Alternative offers
See **Chapter 6** and **Appendix 1** for grades/UCAS Tariff points information for other examinations.

EXAMPLES OF COLLEGES OFFERING COURSES IN THIS SUBJECT FIELD

Accrington and Rossendale (Coll); Barnsley (Coll); Bedford (Coll); Birmingham Met (Coll); Bishop Burton (Coll); Blackburn (Coll); Blackpool and Fylde (Coll); Bournemouth and Poole (Coll); Bournville (Coll); Bradford College UC; Bury (Coll); Cornwall (Coll); Craven (Coll); Darlington (Coll); Derby (Coll); Doncaster (Coll); Durham New (Coll); Ealing, Hammersmith and West London (Coll); East Riding (Coll); Furness (Coll); Greater Brighton Met (Coll); Grŵp Llandrillo Menai; Guildford (Coll); Hartlepool (CFE); Highbury Portsmouth (Coll); Hull (Coll); Leicester (Coll); Liverpool City (Coll); London City (Coll); London UCK (Coll); Loughborough (Coll); LSST; Macclesfield (Coll); Manchester (Coll); MidKent (Coll); NCC Redbridge; Neath Port Talbot (Coll); Nescot; Newcastle (Coll); North Notts (Coll); Northumberland (Coll); Norwich City (Coll); Petroc; Plymouth City (Coll); Reaseheath (UC); Richmond-upon-Thames (Coll); Sheffield (Coll); South Cheshire (Coll); South Devon (Coll); South Essex (Coll); Stratford-upon-Avon (Coll); TEC Partnership; Walsall (Coll); Warwickshire (Coll); West Cheshire (Coll); West Herts (Coll); West Suffolk (Coll); Westminster Kingsway (Coll); Weymouth (Coll); Wirral Met (Coll).

CHOOSING YOUR COURSE (SEE ALSO CH.1)

Universities and colleges teaching qualit y See www.qaa.ac.uk; https://unistats.ac.uk.

Examples of sandwich degree courses Birmingham (UC); Bournemouth; Brighton; Cardiff Met; Central Lancashire; Derby; Gloucestershire; Huddersfield; Leeds Beckett; Manchester Met; Oxford Brookes; Portsmouth; Robert Gordon; Salford; Sheffield Hallam; Staffordshire; Sunderland; Surrey; Ulster; Wolverhampton.

ADMISSIONS INFORMATION
Number of applicants per place (approx) Cardiff Met 12; Central Lancashire 8; Edinburgh Napier 10; London Met 10; Manchester Met (Hspty Mgt) 12; Oxford Brookes 5; Robert Gordon 3; Strathclyde 8.

Advice to applicants and planning the UCAS personal statement Experience in dealing with members of the public is an important element in this work which, coupled with work experience in cafés, restaurants or hotels, should be described fully. All applicants are strongly recommended to obtain practical experience in catering or hotel work. Admissions tutors are likely to look for experience in industry and for people who are ambitious, sociable and team players. See also **Appendix 3.**

Misconceptions about this course Cardiff Met The course is not about cooking! We are looking to create managers, not chefs.

Selection interviews No Bucks New, Cardiff Met, Manchester Met, Portsmouth, Robert Gordon, Salford, Surrey.

Interview advice and questions Past questions have included: What books do you read? What do you know about hotel work and management? What work experience have you had? What kind of job do you have in mind when you have qualified? How did you become interested in this course? Do you eat in restaurants? What types of restaurants? Discuss examples of good and bad restaurant organisation. What qualities do you have which make you suitable for management? See also **Chapter 5.**

Reasons for rejection (non-academic) Lack of suitable work experience or practical training. Inability to communicate. Lack of awareness of workload, for example shift working, weekend work. **Cardiff Met** Students looking specifically for licensed trade courses or a cookery course.

AFTER-RESULTS ADVICE
Offers to applicants repeating A-levels Same Brighton; Cardiff Met; Huddersfield; Manchester Met; Oxford Brookes; Salford; Strathclyde; Suffolk; Ulster; West London; Wolverhampton.

GRADUATE DESTINATIONS AND EMPLOYMENT (2016/17 HESA)
Including Leisure, Tourism and Transport graduates surveyed 4,105 **Employed** 2,425 **In voluntary employment** 85 **In further study** 735 **Assumed unemployed** 200

Career note These business-focused hospitality programmes open up a wide range of employment and career opportunities in both hospitality and other business sectors. The demand for employees has been high in recent years. Events management is currently a growth area with graduates working in sports and the arts, tourist attractions, hospitality, business and industry.

OTHER DEGREE SUBJECTS FOR CONSIDERATION
Business; Consumer Studies; Dietetics; Food Science; Health Studies; Leisure and Recreation Management; Management; Tourism and Travel.

HOUSING

(See also Building and Construction, Surveying and Real Estate Management, Town and Urban Planning)

These courses prepare students for careers in housing management although topics covered will also be relevant to other careers in business and administration. Modules will be taken in housing, law, finance, planning policy, public administration and construction.

Useful websites www.gov.uk/housing-local-and-community/housing; www.rtpi.org.uk; www.freeindex.co.uk/categories/property/construction/Property_Development

NB The points totals shown to the left of the institutions are for ease of reference only. It must not be assumed that Tariff points are always used by institutions or that they can be substituted for an offer in grades. The level of an offer is not necessarily indicative of the quality of a course.

COURSE OFFERS INFORMATION
Subject requirements/preferences GCSE English and mathematics required. **AL** No specified subjects.

Your target offers and examples of degree courses
112 pts   Leeds Beckett – 112 pts (Hous St)
104 pts   Central Lancashire – 104–112 pts (Commun Soc Cr Plcy Prac)
88 pts   Cardiff Met – CCD 88 pts (Hous St) (IB 24 pts)

Alternative offers
See **Chapter 6** and **Appendix 1** for grades/UCAS Tariff points information for other examinations.

EXAMPLES OF COLLEGES OFFERING COURSES IN THIS SUBJECT FIELD
Blackburn (Coll); St Helens (Coll).

CHOOSING YOUR COURSE (SEE ALSO CH.1)
Universities and colleges teaching quality See www.qaa.ac.uk; https://unistats.ac.uk.

ADMISSIONS INFORMATION
Number of applicants per place (approx) Cardiff Met 1.

Advice to applicants and planning the UCAS personal statement An interest in people, housing problems, social affairs and the built environment is important for this course. Contacts with local housing managers (through local authority offices or housing associations) are important. Describe any such contacts and your knowledge of the housing types and needs in your area. The planning department in your local council office will be able to provide information on the various types of developments taking place in your locality and how housing needs have changed during the past 50 years. See also **Appendix 3.**

Selection interviews Yes Cardiff Met.

Interview advice and questions Since the subject is not studied at school, questions are likely to be asked on reasons for choosing this degree. Other past questions include: What is a housing association? Why were housing associations formed? In which parts of the country would you expect private housing to be expensive and, by comparison, cheap? What is the cause of this? Have estates of multi-storey flats fulfilled their original purpose? If not, why not? What causes a slum? What is an almshouse? See also **Chapter 5.**

Reasons for rejection (non-academic) Lack of awareness of current social policy issues.

AFTER-RESULTS ADVICE
Offers to applicants repeating A-levels Same Cardiff Met; London South Bank.

GRADUATE DESTINATIONS AND EMPLOYMENT (2016/17 HESA)
Graduates surveyed See **Building and Construction**.

Career note Graduates aiming for openings in housing will be employed mainly as managers with local authorities; others will be employed by non-profit-making housing associations and trusts and also by property companies owning blocks of flats.

OTHER DEGREE SUBJECTS FOR CONSIDERATION
Architecture; Building; Business Studies; Community Studies; Environmental Planning; Estate Management; Property Development; Social Policy and Administration; Social Studies; Surveying; Town Planning; Urban Regeneration.

HUMAN RESOURCE MANAGEMENT

(See also **Business and Management Courses, Business and Management Courses (international and European), Business and Management Courses (Specialised)**)

This is one of the many branches of the world of business and has developed from the role of the personnel manager. HR managers may be involved with the induction and training of staff, disciplinary and grievance procedures, redundancies and equal opportunities issues. In large organisations, some HR staff may specialise in one or more of these areas. Work experience dealing with the public should be stressed in the UCAS personal statement.

Useful websites www.hrmguide.co.uk; www.cipd.co.uk

NB The points totals shown to the left of the institutions are for ease of reference only. It must not be assumed that Tariff points are always used by institutions or that they can be substituted for an offer in grades. The level of an offer is not necessarily indicative of the quality of a course.

COURSE OFFERS INFORMATION
Subject requirements/preferences GCSE English and mathematics at C (4) or above. **AL** No subjects specified.

Your target offers and examples of degree courses
136 pts **Lancaster** – AAB (Mgt HR) (IB 35 pts HL 16 pts)
Leeds – AAB (HR Mgt) (IB 35 pts HL 16 pts)
Manchester – AAB (Mgt HR) (IB 35 pts HL 665)
128 pts **Cardiff** – AAB-ABB (Bus Mgt (HR Mgt)) (IB 34-32 pts HL 665-655)
London (RH) – AAB-ABB (Mgt HR) (IB 32 pts HL 655)
120 pts **Aston** – BBB (HR Bus Mgt) (IB 31 pts HL 555)
Coventry – ABB-BBB (Bus HR Mgt) (IB 31-30 pts)
Derby – 120-128 pts (HR Mgt Comb Hons)
Heriot-Watt – BBB (Int Bus Mgt HR Mgt) (IB 29 pts)
Huddersfield – BBB 120 pts (Bus HR Mgt)
Northumbria – 120 pts (HR Mgt)
Nottingham Trent – BBB 120 pts (Bus Mgt HR)
Stirling – BBB (HR Mgt) (IB 32 pts)
Swansea – ABB-BBB (Bus Mgt (HR Mgt)) (IB 33-32 pts)
Ulster – BBB (HR Mgt) (IB 26 pts HL 13 pts)
112 pts **Birmingham City** – BBC 112 pts (HR Mgt) (IB 28 pts HL 14 pts)
Bradford – BBC 112 pts (HR Mgt)
Cardiff Met – BBC 112 pts (Bus Mgt HR Mgt) (IB 24 pts HL 12 pts)
De Montfort – 112 pts (HR Mgt) (IB 26 pts)
East London – BBC 112 pts (HR Mgt) (IB 25 pts HL 15 pts)
Greenwich – BBC 112 pts (HR Mgt)
Middlesex – 112 pts (Bus Mgt (HR); HR Mgt)
Robert Gordon – BBC 112 pts (Mgt Hum Res Mgt) (IB 29 pts)
Sheffield Hallam – 112 pts (Bus HR Mgt)
Sunderland – BBC 112 pts (Bus HR Mgt)
West London – BBC 112 pts (Hum Res Mgt)
Westminster – ABB-BBC 112-128 pts (Bus Mgt HR Mgt) (IB 27 pts HL 4 Engl)
104 pts **Leeds Beckett** – 104 pts (HR Mgt Bus) (IB 24 pts)
Liverpool John Moores – BCC 104 pts (HR Mgt) (IB 24 pts)
Northampton – BCC (HR Mgt courses) (IB 25 pts)
96 pts **Anglia Ruskin** – 96 pts (Bus HR Mgt)
Bath Spa – CCC (Bus Mgt (HR Mgt)) (IB 26 pts)
Brighton – BCC-CCC 96-104 pts (Bus Mgt HR Mgt) (IB 26 pts)

Hertfordshire – CCC 96 pts (Bus HR; HR Mgt)
Keele – BBC–CCC (Bus HR Mgt) (IB 30–26 pts)
Wolverhampton – CCC (HR Mgt)
York St John – 96 pts (HR Mgt)

88 pts **Trinity Saint David** – 88 pts +interview (Bus Mgt (HR Mgt))
80 pts **Bedfordshire** – BBB–CCE 80–120 pts (HR Mgt)
Bucks New – 80 pts (Bus HR Mgt)
South Wales – BCC–CDD 80–104 pts (HR Mgt)
64 pts **Canterbury Christ Church** – 64 pts (HR Mgt)

Alternative offers
See **Chapter 6** and **Appendix 1** for grades/UCAS Tariff points information for other examinations.

EXAMPLES OF COLLEGES OFFERING COURSES IN THIS SUBJECT FIELD
Barking and Dagenham (Coll); Basingstoke (CT); Bath (Coll); Birmingham Met (Coll); Bournemouth and Poole (Coll); Croydon (Univ Centre); London City (Coll); Manchester (Coll); Newcastle (Coll); North Lindsey (Coll); Plymouth City (Coll); South Gloucestershire and Stroud (Coll); St Helens (Coll).

CHOOSING YOUR COURSE (SEE ALSO CH.1)
Universities and colleges teaching quality See www.qaa.ac.uk; https://unistats.ac.uk.

Examples of sandwich degree courses Aston; Bath Spa; Bedfordshire; Birmingham City; Bournemouth; Bradford; Brighton; Chichester; Coventry; De Montfort; Hertfordshire; Huddersfield; Leeds; Leeds Beckett; Liverpool John Moores; Manchester Met; Northampton; Northumbria; Portsmouth; Sheffield Hallam; Ulster; Westminster; Wolverhampton; Worcester.

ADMISSIONS INFORMATION
Number of applicants per place (approx) Anglia Ruskin 10; Aston 10.

Advice to applicants and planning the UCAS personal statement See **Business and Management Courses**.

Selection interviews No Anglia Ruskin, De Montfort.

Interview advice and questions See **Business and Management Courses**.

Reasons for rejection (non-academic) See **Business and Management Courses**.

AFTER-RESULTS ADVICE
Offers to applicants repeating A-levels Higher Anglia Ruskin.

GRADUATE DESTINATIONS AND EMPLOYMENT (2016/17 HESA)
Graduates surveyed 680 **Employed** 425 **In voluntary employment** 15 **In further study** 125 **Assumed unemployed** 45

Career note See under **Business and Management Courses**.

OTHER DEGREE SUBJECTS FOR CONSIDERATION
Business Studies; Information Systems; Management Studies/Sciences; Marketing; Psychology; Retail Management; Sociology; Sports Management.

HUMAN SCIENCES/HUMAN BIOSCIENCES
(See also **Medicine, Neuroscience**)

Human Sciences is a multi-disciplinary study relating to biological and social sciences and focuses on social and cultural behaviour. Topics range from genetics and evolution to health, disease, social behaviour and industrial societies. A typical course may include anatomy, physiology, bio-mechanics, anthropology and psychology.

Useful websites https://bbsrc.ukri.org; www.becominghuman.org; see also **Biology** and **Geography**.

NB The points totals shown to the left of the institutions are for ease of reference only. It must not be assumed that Tariff points are always used by institutions or that they can be substituted for an offer in grades. The level of an offer is not necessarily indicative of the quality of a course.

COURSE OFFERS INFORMATION
Subject requirements/preferences GCSE Science essential and mathematics usually required. **AL** Chemistry/biology usually required or preferred for some courses.

Your target offers and examples of degree courses
144 pts   **London (UCL)** – AAA incl sci (Hum Sci) (IB 38 pts HL 18 pts incl 6 sci)
             Oxford – AAA +interview +TSA (Hum Sci) (IB 38 pts HL 666)
136 pts   **Durham** – AAB (Hlth Hum Sci) (IB 36 pts HL 665)
             Sussex – AAA–AAB (Psy Cog Sci; Psy Neuro) (IB 36–34 pts)
128 pts   **Cardiff** – ABB (Hum Soc Sci) (HL 17 pts)
             Exeter – AAB–ABB (Hum Sci (Cornwall)) (IB 34–32 pts HL 665–655)
             Swansea – AAB–ABB incl biol+STEM (App Med Sci)
120 pts   **Aberdeen** – BBB incl sci/maths (Hum Emb Dev Biol) (IB 32 pts HL 5 sci/maths)
             Sheffield – BBB (Hlth Hum Sci) (IB 32 pts)
112 pts   **Coventry** – BBC incl biol (Hum Biosci) (IB 30 pts HL 5 biol)
104 pts   **Oxford Brookes** – 104 pts incl sci (Biol Sci Hum Biosci) (IB 29 pts)
             Plymouth – 104–120 pts incl biol+maths/sci (Hum Biosci) (IB 27 pts HL 5 biol/chem)
88 pts   **West Scotland** – CCD incl biol 88–102 pts (App Biomed Sci; Biomed Sci) (IB 24 pts)

Alternative offers
See **Chapter 6** and **Appendix 1** for grades/UCAS Tariff points information for other examinations.

DEGREE APPRENTICESHIPS
Kent (App Biosci Tech Sci, App Biosci, Lab Sci).

EXAMPLES OF COLLEGES OFFERING COURSES IN THIS SUBJECT FIELD
Blackpool and Fylde (Coll).

CHOOSING YOUR COURSE (SEE ALSO CH.1)
Universities and colleges teaching quality See www.qaa.ac.uk; https://unistats.ac.uk.

ADMISSIONS INFORMATION
Number of applicants per place (approx) London (UCL) 4; Oxford 8.

Advice to applicants and planning the UCAS personal statement See **Biology** and **Anthropology**.

Selection interviews Yes Oxford (11%); **No** London (UCL).

Interview advice and questions Past questions have included: What do you expect to get out of a degree in Human Sciences? Why are you interested in this subject? What problems do you think you will be able to tackle after completing the course? Why did you drop PE as an A-level given that it's relevant to Human Sciences? How do you explain altruism, given that we are surely programmed by our genes to be selfish? How far is human behaviour determined by genes? What do you think are the key differences between animals and human beings? See also **Chapter 5. Oxford** Are there too many people in the world?

GRADUATE DESTINATIONS AND EMPLOYMENT (2016/17 HESA)
Graduates surveyed See **Biology**.

Career note As a result of the multi-disciplinary nature of these courses, graduates could focus on openings linked to their special interests or look in general at the scientific and health sectors. Health administration, social services work and laboratory-based careers are some of the more common career destinations of graduates.

OTHER DEGREE SUBJECTS FOR CONSIDERATION

Anthropology; Biology; Community Studies; Environmental Sciences; Life Sciences; Psychology; Sociology.

INFORMATION MANAGEMENT AND LIBRARIANSHIP

(including **Informatics**; See also **Computer Science And Information Technology, Media Studies**)

Information Management and Library Studies covers the very wide field of information. Topics covered include retrieval, indexing, computer and media technology, classification and cataloguing.

Useful websites www.emerald.com/insight/publication/issn/2050-3806; www.cilip.org.uk; www.bl.uk

NB The points totals shown to the left of the institutions are for ease of reference only. It must not be assumed that Tariff points are always used by institutions or that they can be substituted for an offer in grades. The level of an offer is not necessarily indicative of the quality of a course.

COURSE OFFERS INFORMATION

Subject requirements/preferences GCSE English, mathematics and occasionally a foreign language. **AL** No specified subjects.

Your target offers and examples of degree courses

144 pts   **London (UCL)** – AAA (Inf Mgt Bus) (IB 38 pts HL 18 pts)
136 pts   **Lancaster** – AAB (Mgt IT) (IB 35 pts HL 16 pts)
          Manchester – AAB (IT Mgt Bus; IT Mgt Bus (Yr Ind)) (IB 35 pts HL 665)
128 pts   **East Anglia** – ABB (Hist Art Gllry Musm St) (IB 32 pts)
          Edinburgh – AAA–ABB incl maths (Inform (MInf)) (IB 37–32 pts HL 666–655 incl 6 maths)
          Loughborough – ABB (IT Mgt Bus) (IB 34 pts HL 655)
          Reading – ABB (Mgt IT) (IB 32 pts)
120 pts   **Essex** – BBB (Cur St) (IB 30 pts)
          Huddersfield – BBB 120 pts (IT)
          London (Gold) – BBB (Cur) (IB 33 pts HL 655)
          Northumbria – 120 pts (IT Mgt Bus)
          Reading – BBB (Musm Class St) (IB 30 pts)
112 pts   **Cardiff** – BBB–BBC (Cons Objs Musm Arch) (HL 665–655)
          Edge Hill – BBC (Inf Tech Mgt); BBC 112 pts (IT Mgt Bus)
          Kingston – 112 pts +interview +portfolio (Crea Cult Ind Cur Exhibit Evnt)
          Lincoln – BBC (Des Evnt Exhib Perf) (IB 29 pts)
          Liverpool John Moores – BBC 112 pts (Hist Art Musm St) (IB 26 pts)
          London (Birk) – ABB–BBC 112–128 pts (Hist Art Cur; Inf Sys Mgt)
          Oxford Brookes – BBC +interview (IT Mgt Bus) (IB 30 pts)
          UWE Bristol – 112 pts (IT Mgt Bus)
104 pts   **Bournemouth** – 104–120 pts (IT Mgt) (IB 31–28 pts)
          Kent – BBC–BCC +interview (Comp) (IB 34 pts HL 14 pts)
96 pts   **Chichester** – BBC–CCC 96–112 pts (IT Mgt Bus) (IB 28 pts)

Alternative offers
See **Chapter 6** and **Appendix 1** for grades/UCAS Tariff points information for other examinations.

EXAMPLES OF COLLEGES OFFERING COURSES IN THIS SUBJECT FIELD
Birmingham Met (Coll); Grŵp Llandrillo Menai; Totton (Coll).

CHOOSING YOUR COURSE (SEE ALSO CH.1)
Universities and colleges teaching quality See www.qaa.ac.uk; https://unistats.ac.uk.

Top research universities and colleges (REF 2014) (Communication, Cultural and Media Studies, Library and Information Management) London LSE; London (RH); East Anglia; Leeds; Leicester (Media Comm); Newcastle; Leicester (Musm St); Wolverhampton; Cardiff; London (Gold); Loughborough (Comm Media St); Westminster; De Montfort; Nottingham.

Examples of sandwich degree courses Bournemouth; Huddersfield; Kent; Lancaster; Loughborough; Manchester; Reading; UWE Bristol.

ADMISSIONS INFORMATION
Number of applicants per place (approx) London (UCL) 8; Southampton 5.

Advice to applicants and planning the UCAS personal statement Work experience or work shadowing in local libraries is important but remember that reference libraries provide a different field of work. Visit university libraries and major reference libraries and discuss the work with librarians. Describe your experiences in the personal statement. See also **Appendix 3.**

Selection interviews Yes London (UCL); **Some** Loughborough; **No** Southampton.

Interview advice and questions Past questions include: What is it about librarianship that interests you? Why do you think you are suited to be a librarian? What does the job entail? What is the role of the library in school? What is the role of the public library? What new developments are taking place in libraries? Which books do you read? How often do you use a library? What is the Dewey number for the history section in the library? (Applicant studying A-level history.) See also **Chapter 5.**

AFTER-RESULTS ADVICE
Offers to applicants repeating A-levels Higher Loughborough.

GRADUATE DESTINATIONS AND EMPLOYMENT
Career note Graduates in this subject area and in communications enter a wide range of public and private sector jobs where the need to process information as well as to make it easily accessible and user-friendly is very high. Areas of work could include web content, design and internet management and library management.

OTHER DEGREE SUBJECTS FOR CONSIDERATION
Business Information Systems; Communication Studies; Computer Science; Geographic Information Systems; Media Studies.

INTERNATIONAL RELATIONS

(including **International Development, Peace Studies and International Relations and War Studies**; See also **Development Studies, Economics, European Studies, History (Economic and Social), Philosophy, Philosophy, Politics and Economics (PPE), Politics**)

International Relations (IR) is a well-established field of study which encompasses aspects of political science, philosophy, global history and economics. A strong interest in international affairs and a desire to think, write and persuade using a range of political theories are prerequisites. Courses will typically build on a foundation of IR theories introduced in the first year (eg Realist, Liberal and Constructivist schools of thought) which draw upon political thinking spanning from the Ancient Greeks (eg Thucydides) to the twentieth century (eg Morgenthau, Buzan). Most universities offer modules which focus on specific areas of the world, such as South and Central Asia, as well as global issues such as terrorism, civil conflict and nuclear weapons. In recent years, IR has begun to focus more on feminist voices and non-western scholarship, with the need for truly global perspectives now recognised widely in the field.

Useful websites www.sipri.org; www.un.org; www.un.int; https://militarist-monitor.org; see also **Politics**.

NB The points totals shown to the left of the institutions are for ease of reference only. It must not be assumed that Tariff points are always used by institutions or that they can be substituted for an offer in grades. The level of an offer is not necessarily indicative of the quality of a course.

COURSE OFFERS INFORMATION

Subject requirements/preferences GCSE English; a foreign language usually required. **AL** No specified subjects. (War St) History may be required.

Your target offers and examples of degree courses

152 pts **Warwick** – A*AA (Econ Pol Int St) (IB 38 pts)

144 pts **Bath** – AAA-AAB +aEPQ (Pol Int Rel) (IB 36 pts HL 666/765)
 Bristol – AAA (Pol Int Rel) (IB 36 pts HL 18 pts)
 Durham – AAA incl soc sci/hum (Int Rel) (37 pts HL 666 incl soc sci/hum)
 London (King's) – AAA (War St; War St Phil) (IB 35 pts HL 666); AAA incl hist +interview (War St Hist) (IB 35 pts HL 666 incl hist)
 London LSE – AAA (Int Rel; Int Rel Hist) (IB 38 pts HL 766)
 Nottingham – AAA (Int Rel Glob Is (MSci)) (IB 36 pts)
 St Andrews – AAA (Geog Int Rel) (IB 38 pts); (Int Rel courses) (IB 38 pts HL 666)

136 pts **Birmingham** – AAB (Int Rel; Pol Sci Int Rel) (IB 32 pts HL 665)
 Exeter – AAA (Pol Int Rel) (IB 36 pts)
 Lancaster – AAB (Hist Int Rel) (IB 35 pts HL 16 pts)
 Leeds – AAB (Int Rel) (IB 35 pts HL 655)
 Manchester – AAB (Pol Int Rel) (IB 35 pts HL 665)
 Sheffield – AAB-ABB +bEPQ (Int Rel Pol) (IB 34 pts); AAB-ABB +bEPQ incl hist/class civ (Hist Pol) (IB 34 pts HL 6 hist)
 Sussex – AAA-AAB (Law Int Rel) (IB 36-34 pts); AAB (Int Rel; Int Rel Dev) (IB 34 pts)
 York – AAB (Int Rel; Pol Int Rel) (IB 35 pts)

128 pts **Edinburgh** – A*AA-ABB (Int Rel) (IB 43-34 pts HL 776-655); AAA-ABB incl Engl (Law Int Rel) (IB 43-34 pts HL 776-655 incl Engl)
 Exeter – AAB-ABB (Hist Int Rel; Hist Int Rel (St Abrd)) (IB 34-32 pts HL 665-655); AAB-ABB incl lang (Int Rel Modn Langs) (IB 34-32 pts HL 665-655)
 Lancaster – ABB (Pce St Int Rel; Pol Int Rel) (IB 32 pts HL 16 pts)
 London (QM) – ABB (Int Rel Bus Mgt); (Int Rel) (IB 32 pts HL 655)
 London (RH) – AAB-ABB (Econ Pol Int Rel; Pol Int Rel) (IB 32 pts HL 655)
 Loughborough – ABB (Hist Int Rel; Int Rel) (IB 34 pts HL 655)
 Queen's Belfast – ABB (Int Pol Cnflct St)
 Reading – AAB-ABB (Pol Int Rel Modn Langs (Fr/Ger/Ital/Span)) (IB 32 pts HL 655)
 Sussex – AAB-ABB (Econ Int Rel) (IB 34-32 pts)

120 pts **Aberdeen** – BBB (Int Rel courses) (IB 32 pts HL 555)
 Aston – ABB-BBB (Engl Lit Int Rel) (IB 32 pts HL 655)
 Brunel – BBB (Int Pol; Mltry Int Hist) (IB 30 pts)
 Cardiff – ABB-BBB incl lang (Int Rel Pol (Lang)) (IB 34-32 pts HL 665-655)
 Dundee – BBB (Int Rel Pol) (IB 30 pts HL 555)
 East Anglia – BBB (Int Rel Comb Hons) (IB 31 pts); BBB/ABC-BBC +aEPQ (Int Rel) (IB 31 pts)
 Essex – BBB (Int Rel; Pol Hum Rts; Sociol Hum Rts) (IB 30 pts HL 555)
 Hull – BBB 120 pts (Pol Int Rel) (IB 30 pts)
 Kent – BBB (War Cnflct) (IB 34 pts HL 15 pts)
 Leicester – BBB-BBC +bEPQ (Int Rel; Int Rel Hist) (IB 28 pts)
 London (Birk) – ABB-BBB 120-128 pts (Glob Pol Int Rel)

London (Gold) – BBB (Int Rel) (IB 33 pts HL 655)
Nottingham Trent – BBB 120 pts (Int Law)
Portsmouth – 120 pts (Law Int Rel) (IB 29 pts HL 664)
Reading – BBB (Int Dev; Pol Int Rel; War Pce Int Rel) (IB 30 pts)
Southampton – ABB–BBB incl pol (Int Rel; Pol Int Rel) (IB 32 pts HL 16 pts)
Stirling – BBB (Pol (Int)) (IB 32 pts)
Surrey – ABB–BBB (Law Int St) (IB 32 pts); BBB (Int Rel) (IB 32 pts)
Swansea – BBB 120 pts (Int Rel; Int Rel Am St; War Soty) (IB 32 pts)

112 pts **Aston** – BBC (Bus Int Rel; Pol Int Rel) (IB 29 pts HL 554)
Bradford – BBC 112 pts (Int Rel Pol Scrty St)
Buckingham – BBB–BBC (Int St) (IB 32–31 pts)
Coventry – BBC (Int Rel) (IB 29 pts)
De Montfort – 112 pts (Int Rel) (IB 26 pts)
Derby – 112 pts (Int Rel Dipl Comb Hons)
Heriot-Watt – BBC incl maths (Civ Eng Int St (MEng)) (IB 31 pts HL 5 maths)
Lincoln – BBC 112 pts (Int Rel) (IB 29 pts)
Liverpool Hope – BBC 112 pts (Int Rel Comb Hons) (IB 28 pts)
London Met – BBC/BC 112 pts (Int Rel); BBC 112 pts (Law (Int Rel))
Middlesex – 112 pts (Int Pol)
Nottingham Trent – BBC 112 pts (Int Rel Comb Hons)

104 pts **Aberystwyth** – ABB–BCC 104–128 pts (Int Pol) (IB 30–28 pts)
Chester – BBC–BCC 104–112 pts (Int Dev St courses) (IB 26 pts)
De Montfort – 104 pts (Int Rel Pol) (IB 24 pts)
Greenwich – 104 pts +interview (Pol Int Rel); BCC 104 pts +interview (Langs Int Rel)
Leeds Beckett – 104 pts (Int Rel courses) (IB 24 pts)
Manchester Met – 104–112 pts (Int Rel) (IB 26 pts)
Nottingham Trent – 104 pts (Glob St Comb Hons); BCC 104 pts (Pol Int Rel)
Oxford Brookes – BCC 104 pts (Int Rel) (IB 29 pts)

96 pts **Brighton** – BCC–CCC 96–104 pts (Hum) (IB 26 pts)
Keele – CCC (Int Rel) (IB 26 pts)
London Met – CCC/BC 96–112 pts (Int Rel Pce Cnflct St)
Portsmouth – 96–112 pts (Int Rel) (IB 25 pts)
Westminster – BBB–CCC 96–120 pts (Int Rel) (IB 27 pts)
Wolverhampton – CCC/BCD 96 pts (War St; War St Phil)

88 pts **Canterbury Christ Church** – 88–112 pts (Int Rel)
Plymouth – 88–104 pts (Pol Int Rel; Pol Law) (IB 26–24 pts HL 4); (Int Bus Econ) (IB 28–26 pts HL 4)

80 pts **Plymouth** – 80–104 pts (Int Rel) (IB 26–24 pts HL 4)

Open University – contact 0300 303 0073 or www.open.ac.uk/contact/new (Int St)

Alternative offers
See **Chapter 6** and **Appendix 1** for grades/UCAS Tariff points information for other examinations.

CHOOSING YOUR COURSE (SEE ALSO CH.1)

Universities and colleges teaching quality See www.qaa.ac.uk; https://unistats.ac.uk.

Top research universities and colleges (REF 2014) See **Politics**.

Examples of sandwich degree courses Aston; Bath; Brunel; Coventry; Nottingham Trent; Oxford Brookes; Plymouth; Portsmouth; Westminster.

ADMISSIONS INFORMATION

Number of applicants per place (approx) Bath 7; Birmingham 10; De Montfort 6; Derby 3; Exeter 8; Leeds 13; London (King's) 6; London (RH) 8; London LSE 14; Nottingham 5; Reading 5; Southampton (Int Rel) 6.

Advice to applicants and planning the UCAS personal statement Describe any special interests you have in the affairs of any particular country. Contact embassies for information on cultural, economic and political developments. Follow international events through newspapers and magazines. Give details of any voluntary work you have done. **London (King's)** Substantial experience required in some area of direct relevance to War Studies.

Misconceptions about this course Bradford The teaching and research in Peace Studies aims to be applied to real-life problems such as the control of Weapons of Mass Destruction, sexual violence in conflict and the influence of environmental threats.

Selection interviews Some Nottingham Trent, Wolverhampton; **No** Birmingham, De Montfort, East Anglia, London (King's), London Met, Nottingham.

Interview advice and questions Applicants are likely to be questioned on current international events and crises between countries. See also **Chapter 5. Nottingham Trent** Be prepared to be challenged on your existing views!

AFTER-RESULTS ADVICE
Offers to applicants repeating A-levels Same Chester; De Montfort; Lincoln; Wolverhampton.

GRADUATE DESTINATIONS AND EMPLOYMENT (2016/17 HESA)
Graduates surveyed See **Politics**.

Career note See **Politics**.

OTHER DEGREE SUBJECTS FOR CONSIDERATION
Development Studies; Economics; European Studies; Government; Politics.

ITALIAN
(See also **Languages**)

The language and literature of Italy will feature strongly on most Italian courses. The majority of applicants have no knowledge of Italian, and will need to give convincing reasons for their interest and to show an ability to assimilate language quickly. See also **Appendix 3** under **Languages**.

Useful websites http://europa.eu; www.governo.it; www.bbc.co.uk/languages; www.languageadvantage.com; http://italianstudies.org.uk; www.languagematters.co.uk; see also **Languages**.

NB The points totals shown to the left of the institutions are for ease of reference only. It must not be assumed that Tariff points are always used by institutions or that they can be substituted for an offer in grades. The level of an offer is not necessarily indicative of the quality of a course.

COURSE OFFERS INFORMATION
Subject requirements/preferences GCSE English and a foreign language required. **AL** Italian may be required for some courses.

Your target offers and examples of degree courses
152 pts   **Cambridge** – A*AA incl lang +interview +MMLAA (Modn Mediev Langs) (IB 42–40 pts HL 776 incl lang)
144 pts   **Durham** – AAA incl lang (Modn Langs Cult (Yr Abrd)) (IB 37 pts HL 666 incl lang)
             Oxford – AAA +interview +MLAT (Ital courses) (IB 38 pts HL 666)
136 pts   **Bristol** – AAB incl lang (Ital) (IB 34 pts HL 17 pts incl 5 lang)
             Glasgow – AAB incl arts/hum (Ital Comb Hons) (IB 36 pts HL 665 incl 6 Engl/hum/lang)
             London (UCL) – AAB (Ital) (IB 36 pts HL 17 pts)
             St Andrews – AAB (Ital courses) (IB 36 pts)
             Sussex – AAB (Int Dev Lang) (IB 34 pts)

Warwick – AAB incl Engl lit+lang (Engl Ital) (IB 36 pts HL 5 Engl lit+lang); AAB incl lang (Ital Comb Hons) (IB 36 pts HL 5 lang)

128 pts   **Edinburgh** – ABB (Ital; Ital Ling) (IB 34 pts HL 655)

Leeds – ABB (Ital; Ital Comb Hons) (IB 34 pts HL 16 pts)

Leicester – ABB-BBB +aEPQ incl Ital/lang (Ital Comb Hons) (IB 30 pts HL 6 Ital/lang)

London (RH) – AAB-ABB (Euro Int St Fr/Ger/Ital/Span; Modn Lang Mgt; Modn Lang Mus) (IB 32 pts HL 655); AAB-ABB incl lang (Modn Lang Dr) (IB 32 pts HL 655)

Manchester – ABB +interview (Ital St; Ital courses) (IB 34 pts HL 655)

Sheffield – ABB (Modn Langs Cult) (IB 33 pts HL 5 lang)

Sussex – ABB 128 pts (Anth Lang) (32 pts)

Warwick – ABB incl Ger (Ger Ital) (IB 34 pts HL 5 Ger)

York – AAB-ABB incl Fr (Fr Ital Lang (Yr Abrd)) (IB 35-34 pts HL 6 Fr)

120 pts   **Cardiff** – ABB-BBB incl lang (Ital) (IB 32-30 pts HL 665-655)

Kent – BBB (Ital courses) (IB 34 pts HL 15 pts)

London (RH) – ABB-BBB (Modn Langs) (IB 32 pts HL 555)

Reading – BBB (Ital courses) (IB 30 pts)

Swansea – BBB (Modn Langs) (IB 32 pts)

112 pts   **Bangor** – 112 pts (Bus St Ital); 112 pts incl lang (Law Ital (Euro Expnc)) (HL 5 lang)

London (Birk) – ABB-BBC 112-128 pts (Modn Langs (Fr/Ger/Ital/Jap/Port/Span))

104 pts   **Cardiff** – BBC-BCC (Relig St Ital) (HL 655)

Central Lancashire – 104-112 pts incl lang (Modn Langs (2 Lang) (Fr/Ger/Span/Jap/Russ/Ital/Kor))

Manchester Met – BBC-BCC 104-112 pts (Ling Mand Chin/Fr/Ger/Ital/Span) (IB 26 pts)

96 pts   **Bangor** – 96-104 pts (Hist Ital)

Portsmouth – 96-112 pts (Modn Langs) (IB 25 pts)

Alternative offers

See **Chapter 6** and **Appendix 1** for grades/UCAS Tariff points information for other examinations.

CHOOSING YOUR COURSE (SEE ALSO CH.1)

Universities and colleges teaching quality See www.qaa.ac.uk; https://unistats.ac.uk.

Top research universities and colleges (REF 2014) See **Languages**.

Examples of sandwich degree courses Bangor.

ADMISSIONS INFORMATION

Number of applicants per place (approx) Birmingham 5; Bristol 4; Cardiff 3; Durham 5; Hull 5; Leeds 3; London (RH) 7; London (UCL) 5.

Advice to applicants and planning the UCAS personal statement Describe any visits to Italy and experience of speaking the language. Interests in Italian art, literature, culture, society and architecture could also be mentioned. Read Italian newspapers and magazines and give details if you have a bilingual background. Give evidence of your interest and your reasons for choosing the course. See also **Appendix 3** under **Languages**.

Misconceptions about this course Leeds See **Languages**.

Selection interviews Yes Cambridge, Oxford; **No** Birmingham, Reading.

Interview advice and questions Past questions include: Why do you want to learn Italian? What foreign newspapers or magazines do you read (particularly if the applicant has taken A-level Italian)? Have you visited Italy? What do you know of the Italian people, culture, art? See also **Chapter 5. Leeds** See **Languages**.

AFTER-RESULTS ADVICE

Offers to applicants repeating A-levels Higher Birmingham; Warwick; **Same** Cardiff; Hull; Leeds; **No** Glasgow.

GRADUATE DESTINATIONS AND EMPLOYMENT (2016/17 HESA)
Graduates surveyed 175 **Employed** 90 **In voluntary employment** 0 **In further study** 40 **Assumed unemployed** 10

Career note See **Languages**.

OTHER DEGREE SUBJECTS FOR CONSIDERATION
European Studies; International Business Studies; other languages.

JAPANESE
(See also **Languages**)

A strong interest in Japan and its culture is expected of applicants. A number of four-year joint courses are now offered, all of which include a period of study in Japan. Potential employers are showing an interest in Japanese. Students report that 'it is not a soft option'. They are expected to be firmly committed to a Japanese degree (for example, by listing only Japanese on the UCAS application), to have an interest in using their degree in employment and to be prepared for a lot of hard work. See Appendix 3 under **Languages**.

Useful websites www.ciol.org.uk; www.bbc.co.uk/languages; www.languageadvantage.com; www.languagematters.co.uk; www.japanese-online.com; http://thejapanesepage.com; www.japanesestudies.org.uk

NB The points totals shown to the left of the institutions are for ease of reference only. It must not be assumed that Tariff points are always used by institutions or that they can be substituted for an offer in grades. The level of an offer is not necessarily indicative of the quality of a course.

COURSE OFFERS INFORMATION
Subject requirements/preferences GCSE A foreign language usually required. **AL** Modern language required for some courses.

Your target offers and examples of degree courses
152 pts **Cambridge** – A*AA +interview +AMESAA (As Mid E St) (IB 42–40 pts HL 776)
144 pts **Oxford** – AAA +interview +CAT (Class Orntl St) (IB 39 pts HL 666); AAA +interview +OLAT (Orntl St incl Jap/Arab/Chin) (IB 39 pts HL 666)
136 pts **Durham** – AAB (Jap St) (IB 36 pts HL 665)
128 pts **Birmingham** – ABB incl lang (Modn Langs) (IB 32 pts HL 655)
    Cardiff – AAB–ABB +interview (Bus St Jap) (IB 35–32 pts HL 665–655 incl maths+Engl)
    Edinburgh – ABB (Jap; Jap Ling) (IB 38–34 pts HL 666–655)
    Leeds – AAB–ABB 128–136 pts (Jap courses) (IB 35–34 pts HL 16 pts)
    Manchester – ABB +interview (Jap St) (IB 34 pts HL 655); ABB incl Chin/Jap +interview (Chin Jap) (IB 34 pts HL 655); ABB incl Russ/Jap +interview (Russ Jap) (IB 34 pts HL 655 incl Russ/Jap)
    Sheffield – ABB 128 pts (Bus Mgt Jap St) (IB 33 pts); ABB–BBB +bEPQ (Jap St; Kor St Jap) (IB 33 pts)
    Sussex – ABB 128 pts (Anth Lang) (32 pts)
120 pts **Cardiff** – ABB–BBB (Jap+Ger/Fr/Ital/Span) (IB 32–30 pts HL 665–655)
    East Anglia – BBB (Modn Langs) (IB 31 pts)
    Newcastle – ABB–BBB (Jap St) (IB 32 pts)
112 pts **London (Birk)** – ABB–BBC 112–128 pts (Modn Langs (Fr/Ger/Ital/Jap/Port/Span))
104 pts **Central Lancashire** – 104–112 pts (Int Bus Comm Modn For Lang); 104–112 pts incl lang (Modn Langs (2 Lang) (Fr/Ger/Span/Jap/Russ/Ital/Kor))
    Hertfordshire – BCC 104 pts (Eng Lang Jap/Mand)
    Manchester Met – BBC–BCC 104–112 pts (TESOL Jap) (IB 26 pts)
    Oxford Brookes – BCC 104 pts (Jap St) (IB 29 pts)

Alternative offers
See **Chapter 6** and **Appendix 1** for grades/UCAS Tariff points information for other examinations.

CHOOSING YOUR COURSE (SEE ALSO CH.1)
Universities and colleges teaching quality See www.qaa.ac.uk; https://unistats.ac.uk.

ADMISSIONS INFORMATION
Number of applicants per place (approx) Cardiff 8; Sheffield 6.

Advice to applicants and planning the UCAS personal statement Discuss your interest in Japan and your reasons for wishing to study the language. Know Japan, its culture and background history. Discuss any visits you have made or contacts with Japanese nationals. See also **Appendix 3** under **Languages**. **Leeds** See **Languages**.

Selection interviews Yes Cambridge, Oxford; **No** Leeds.

Interview advice and questions Japanese is an extremely demanding subject and applicants are most likely to be questioned on their reasons for choosing this degree. They will be expected also to have some knowledge of Japanese culture, history and current affairs. See also **Chapter 5.**

Reasons for rejection (non-academic) Insufficient evidence of genuine motivation.

AFTER-RESULTS ADVICE
Offers to applicants repeating A-levels No Cambridge.

GRADUATE DESTINATIONS AND EMPLOYMENT (2016/17 HESA)
Graduates surveyed 125 **Employed** 55 **In voluntary employment** 0 **In further study** 25 **Assumed unemployed** 5

Career note See **Languages**.

OTHER DEGREE SUBJECTS FOR CONSIDERATION
Asia-Pacific Studies; International Business Studies; Oriental Languages; South East Asia Studies.

JOURNALISM

(See also **Communication Studies/Communication, English, Media Studies**)

A passion for writing, good spelling, grammar and punctuation and the ability to work under pressure are some of the qualities which all journalists require. The opportunities within journalism range from covering day-to-day news stories in the local and national press to periodicals and magazines covering specialist subjects. Journalism is also the foundation for work in local radio.

Useful websites www.journalism.co.uk; www.bjtc.org.uk; www.nctj.com; www.nuj.org.uk

The points totals shown to the left of the institutions are for ease of reference only. It must not be assumed that Tariff points are always used by institutions or that they can be substituted for an offer in grades. The level of an offer is not necessarily indicative of the quality of a course.

COURSE OFFERS INFORMATION
Subject requirements/preferences GCSE English and maths often required. **AL** No specific subjects required.

Your target offers and examples of degree courses
136 pts **Leeds** – AAB (Jrnl) (IB 35 pts HL 16 pts)
Newcastle – AAB (Jrnl Media Cult) (IB 34 pts)
128 pts **Cardiff** – ABB (Jrnl Media Sociol) (HL 17 pts)
City – ABB 128 pts +interview (Jrnl) (IB 33 pts)

Sheffield – ABB (Jrnl St) (IB 33 pts)
Sussex – ABB (Jrnl) (IB 32 pts)

120 pts
Cardiff – ABB–BBB incl Engl (Jrnl Media Engl Lit) (HL 665 incl 6 Engl)
Coventry – BBB (Engl Jrnl) (IB 31 pts)
Kent – BBB +interview (Jrnl) (IB 34 pts HL 16 pts)
Leicester – BBB/BBC +bEPQ (Jrnl) (IB 28 pts)
London (Gold) – BBB +interview (Jrnl) (IB 33 pts HL 655)
Northumbria – 120 pts (Jrnl Engl Lit)
Stirling – BBB (Jrnl St) (IB 32 pts)
Strathclyde – ABB–BBB (Jrnl Media Comm courses) (IB 36 pts)
Trinity Saint David – 120 pts +interview (Doc Photo Vis Actvsm) (IB 32 pts)
UWE Bristol – 120 pts (Broad Jrnl; Jrnl PR)

112 pts
Birmingham City – BBC 112 pts (Jrnl) (IB 28 pts)
Brunel – BBC incl Engl/hist/soc sci (Jrnl Cult) (IB 29 pts HL 5 Engl/hist/soc sci)
Coventry – BBC (Jrnl) (IB 29 pts)
Creative Arts – 112 pts +portfolio (Fash Jrnl) (IB 30–27 pts HL 15 pts)
Derby – 112 pts +interview (Jrnl; Mag Jrnl; Spec Spo Jrnl)
East London – 112 pts (Jrnl; Spo Jrnl) (IB 25 pts HL 15 pts)
Huddersfield – BBC 112 pts (Broad Jrnl; Jrnl; Spo Jrnl)
Leeds Beckett – 112 pts (Jrnl) (IB 25 pts)
Leeds Trinity – 112 pts (Spo Jrnl); 112 pts +interview (Broad Jrnl; Jrnl)
Lincoln – BBC (Jrnl) (IB 29 pts)
Liverpool John Moores – BBC 112 pts (Jrnl) (IB 26-27 pts)
London Met – BBC 112 pts (Fash Mark Jrnl; Jrnl Flm TV St); BBC 112 pts +interview (Jrnl)
Middlesex – 112 pts (Crea Writ Jrnl)
Nottingham Trent – BBC 112 pts (Broad Jrnl; Jrnl)
Roehampton – 112 pts incl hum (Jrnl)
Sheffield Hallam – 112 pts (Jrnl PR Media); BBC 112 pts (Jrnl)
Staffordshire – BBC 112 pts (Spo Jrnl)
Sunderland – 112–120 pts (Jrnl; Spo Jrnl); BBB–BBC 112–120 pts (Fash Jrnl)
West London – BBC 112 pts (Broad Dig Jrnl)
Westminster – ABB–BBC (Jrnl) (IB 27 pts)

104 pts
Bangor – 104–120 pts (Jrnl Media St)
Bournemouth – 104–120 pts (Multim Jrnl) (IB 31–28 pts)
Central Lancashire – 104 pts +interview (Multim Jrnl; Spo Jrnl)
Chester – BBC–BCC 104–112 pts (Jrnl) (IB 26 pts)
De Montfort – 104 pts +interview (Jrnl) (IB 24 pts)
Edinburgh Napier – BCC incl Engl (Jrnl) (IB 28 pts HL 654 incl 5 Engl)
Falmouth – 104–120 pts +interview (Jrnl; Spo Jrnl)
Glasgow Caledonian – BCC +interview (Multim Jrnl) (IB 25 pts)
Hertfordshire – BCC 104 pts (Jrnl Comb Hons)
London South Bank – BCC (Jrnl)
Northampton – BCC incl Engl/hum (Multim Jrnl)
Portsmouth – 104–112 pts +interview +portfolio (Jrnl) (IB 25 pts)
Robert Gordon – BCC incl Engl (Jrnl) (IB 28 pts HL 5 Engl)
Winchester – 104–120 pts (Enter Jrnl; Mus Jrnl); (Jrnl; Media Comm Jrnl) (HL 44)
Worcester – 104 pts (Jrnl)

96 pts
Arts London – CCC 96 pts (Jrnl)
Brighton – BBC–CCC 96–112 pts (Jrnl; Spo Jrnl) (IB 26 pts)
Buckingham – BBC–CCC (Jrnl Comm St) (IB 31–29 pts)
Chester – BCC–CCC 96–104 pts (Spo Jrnl) (IB 26 pts)
Leeds Beckett – 96 pts (PR Jrnl) (IB 24 pts)
Marjon – CCC (Jrnl; Spo Jrnl)
Solent – 96–112 pts (Jrnl; Spo Jrnl)
Teesside – 96–112 pts (Broad Media Prod; Jrnl)

Wolverhampton – CCC/BCD 96 pts +interview (Multim Jrnl)
88 pts **Canterbury Christ Church** – 88–112 pts +interview (Multim Jrnl)
80 pts **Bedfordshire** – 80 pts (Jrnl)
South Wales – BCC–CDD 80–104 pts +interview (Jrnl) (IB 29 pts)
72 pts **Anglia Ruskin** – 72–96 pts (Jrnl (Multim))

Gloucestershire – interview (Jrnl; Photojrnl Doc Photo)

Alternative offers
See **Chapter 6** and **Appendix 1** for grades/UCAS Tariff points information for other examinations.

EXAMPLES OF COLLEGES OFFERING COURSES IN THIS SUBJECT FIELD
Cornwall (Coll); Darlington (Coll); Exeter (Coll); Harlow (Coll); Peterborough (Coll); South Essex (Coll).

CHOOSING YOUR COURSE (SEE ALSO CH.1)
Universities and colleges teaching quality See www.qaa.ac.uk; https://unistats.ac.uk.

Examples of sandwich degree courses Bangor; City; Coventry; Hertfordshire; Huddersfield; Leeds; Portsmouth; Robert Gordon; Solent.

ADMISSIONS INFORMATION
Number of applicants per place (approx) Strathclyde (Jrnl) 20.

Admissions tutors' advice Buckingham As far as journalism and media are concerned you can't be just a wannabe any more. Keeping a blog (on any theme) is great; so is producing video for YouTube. Writing for school magazine or newspaper is also well regarded. Active knowledge of current affairs and a wide frame of reference is to be commended. Having an interest in people is absolutely key.

Advice to applicants and planning the UCAS personal statement Buckingham Do not begin your personal statement with 'I've always been fascinated by media...' This is now a cliché and suggests slack-jawed drooling on a sofa rather than engaging actively.

Include the URLs of your blogs, YouTube channels, Tableau projects, Instagram albums or anything that will show me that you engage with media as a producer rather than a consumer. Make me really want to watch, see or read it. I will have a look at your content for sure. It will give you a firm base for discussion when I call you for interview.

Tell me whether your content lived up to your expectations. Trying, failing and learning a lesson are signs of character.

Tell me about what you've done outside the classroom – that will reveal to me what kind of person you are and create an opportunity for meaningful conversation at interview.

Tell me the kind of news media you love: whose byline thrills you, whose journalism takes you there, who you love to read in order to disagree with.]

Show me a wide range of reference – sometimes as journalists we have to become instant experts.

City In your personal statement you should demonstrate a clear passion and enthusiasm for Journalism. This can be shown in a variety of ways, particularly demonstrated by the extra-curricular activities you do. Try and have an online presence through writing or blogging about a topic that interests you, or writing for your school's student paper or magazine. Immerse yourself in different types of media by reading newspapers, listening to news reports on TV and radio, and understanding how news is portrayed through different forms of social media. Try and get some relevant work experience with a radio station, TV company or local news provider, or make your own work experience by running your own website or blog. We are also interested in hearing about your influences, such as journalists and foreign correspondents who inspire you; let us know why their work interests you. It is also important to view and read news critically, as this will be something you will do while studying at university.

From a Journalism applicant we are looking for the following qualities:

- be curious and interested in news;
- be determined – don't take no for an answer;
- good communication skills;
- be keen to find out more;
- enjoy writing and develop a style.

Also, do not be afraid to aim high with your university choices; you might be surprised where you receive offers from. Some universities, such as City, will invite you to a Selection Day as part of the application process, so you will have another opportunity to show why you are suitable for the degree, and have a chance to see the University and find out more details about the course.

Hertfordshire Many of the tutors who teach Journalism have also been journalists and they will expect students to listen to/watch the news or read articles. So when you write your personal statement, do make sure you refer to news stories or documentaries you have read. A vague statement such as 'I enjoy reading news tweets' tells the reader nothing. A much better example would be: 'Since my grandmother became ill I have been following stories about the NHS with great interest, particularly ones about bed-blocking. A news item on my local radio station about a woman who had been waiting to leave hospital for a month was really interesting because...'

If your passion is fashion journalism, then, again, give examples of articles you have read and why they have interested you or what you like about particular fashion magazines or fashion bloggers. Be specific and make sure you watch/read/listen to the news regularly as well.

Tutors won't expect professional experience but if you have a blog, make videos about things that interest you, or if you have written for the school or community website or magazine, then tell them about it. If you have researched a particular project, write about that research. This is because writing and research are important journalistic skills. Similarly, if you've watched a TV programme being made or spent a day shadowing a local journalist, mention this. Journalism tutors hope to teach the journalists of the future and showing that you have already taken the time to learn about some aspects of journalism shows the sort of enthusiasm they like to see.

Robert Gordon In regard to their personal statements we would be looking for applicants to display their passion for Journalism and the media in general – what sparked their interest in the field? What understanding do they have of the role of a journalist? Why would they like to work in this industry? Any work or shadowing experience they may have is certainly a plus, though this is not mandatory.

Winchester We are typically looking for applicants to demonstrate a keen interest in becoming a journalist in their personal statement, ideally by talking about any relevant work experience that they may have had or whether they write on a daily basis, for example in a blog. We see a lot of applicants who have their own blogs which provide a very helpful starting point for discussions at interview.

Selection interviews Yes Brunel, Canterbury Christ Church, Edinburgh Napier, Kent, Leeds Trinity, Worcester; **Some** Sussex, Winchester; **No** Bedfordshire, Falmouth, London South Bank, Northumbria.

Interview advice and questions Buckingham I will ask you to tell me a funny story because:
- it shows me you can tell a story – what we do every day of our journalistic lives;
- it shows me you keep a narrative thread;
- it breaks the ice;
- I like a chuckle/laughter can be a potent journalistic weapon.

I will ask you about all the practical efforts you describe in your personal statement. I will ask you in detail about the content of the A-levels/BTECs you are taking. I will ask you what makes you angry in life. Good journalists always carry a little fire in their bellies.

Hertfordshire Questions you might meet at interview include the following.
- Tell me about some news stories or documentaries you've read/listened to/watched in the past week. Which have interested you and why?
- What do you think a journalist does?
- What skills do you think you will learn?
- Here is an article. How do you think the writer might have found out these facts?

Winchester During interviews we are looking for students to be fully aware of current events and understand the power of the media for social change. Some applicants may talk about who or what (for example, a particular news story) inspired them to consider journalism as a profession and this is also helpful.

During the course of the interview applicants are also expected to perform a short piece in front of a camera, in addition to the more formal question and answer section.

Finally, interviews are as much about the applicants selecting the right university as the University selecting the right applicants, so there are always opportunities to ask the programme team questions about the course and life at the University.

Reasons for rejection (non-academic) Buckingham Applicants are requested to attend an Open Day/Evening or Tutorial Taster Days. The University believes it is very important for applicants to visit its campus. Candidates who do not respond to these invitations may be rejected, irrespective of academic achievement, as the University looks for committed, well-motivated students.

GRADUATE DESTINATIONS AND EMPLOYMENT (2016/17 HESA)
Graduates surveyed 1,830 **Employed** 1,005 **In voluntary employment** 100 **In further study** 240 **Assumed unemployed** 120

Career note Some graduates go on to work directly in journalism for local, regional and national newspapers, magazines, broadcasting corporations and creative digital media agencies as journalists, press editors and publishing copy-editors. Many enter other areas, including PR, advertising, marketing, management, charity work, education, law and politics.

OTHER DEGREE SUBJECTS FOR CONSIDERATION
Communication Studies; English; Media Studies

LANDSCAPE ARCHITECTURE

(including **Garden Design**; See also **Agricultural Sciences/Agriculture, Architecture, Horticulture**)

Landscape architects shape the world you live in. They are responsible for urban design, the integration of ecology and the quality of the built environment. Courses in Landscape Architecture include project-based design, landscape theory, management, planning and design, ecology, construction, plant design and design practice. After completing the first three years leading to a BSc (Hons) or BA (Hons), students aiming for full professional status take a further one year in practice and one year to achieve their Master of Landscape Architecture (MLA).

Useful websites www.landscapeinstitute.org; www.chooselandscape.org; www.bali.org.uk

NB The points totals shown to the left of the institutions are for ease of reference only. It must not be assumed that Tariff points are always used by institutions or that they can be substituted for an offer in grades. The level of an offer is not necessarily indicative of the quality of a course.

COURSE OFFERS INFORMATION
Subject requirements/preferences GCSE English, geography, art and design, mathematics and at least one science usually required. **AL** Preferred subjects for some courses include biology, geography and environmental science. A portfolio may also be required.

Your target offers and examples of degree courses
144 pts   **Sheffield** – AAA +portfolio (Archit Lnd) (IB 36 pts)
128 pts   **Edinburgh** – ABB (Lnd Archit) (IB 34 pts HL 655)
          Sheffield – ABB (Lnd Archit) (IB 33 pts)
120 pts   **Leeds Beckett** – 120 pts +interview +portfolio (Lnd Archit Des) (IB 26 pts)
112 pts   **Birmingham City** – BBC 112 pts +portfolio (Lnd Archit) (IB 28 pts)

The University Of Sheffield.

Department Of Landscape Architecture.

SHAPE YOUR WORLD

www.sheffield.ac.uk/landscape

100% of students went on to employment or further study within 6 months of graduation*

DLHE 2016-17

Study Landscape Architecture with a specialism in ecology or planning

Our undergraduate courses in Landscape Architecture are unique. They combine training in Landscape Architecture with an opportunity to choose specialist modules in ecology or planning. This allows you to follow your interests and specialise in the subjects that really excite you.

It also ensures that Sheffield students graduate with an attractive blend of broad professional skills and specialist knowledge. Students have the opportunity to transfer between BA and BSc Landscape Architecture at the end of first year. All our undergraduate courses are fully accredited by the Landscape Institute – the Royal Chartered Body for Landscape Architects.

Student work: Lucy Wilson

Student work: Zoe Dobson

BA Landscape Architecture
UCAS code: K3K4

This course aims to educate Landscape Architects who, as well as being skilled designers, have a sound understanding of landscape issues at the large scale. If you enjoy geography, politics, economics or history you will appreciate the scope and challenge of this course. You'll learn about urban design theory, planning and practice and will acquire a better understanding of the context in which design takes place and the wider implications of your design proposals.

BSc Landscape Architecture
UCAS code: KC39

This course aims to educate Landscape Architects to have an in-depth understanding of ecology and habitat creation. If you are interested in the natural world or biology, you will enjoy the focus of this course. You'll learn about ecological processes and the impact that design proposals have on habitat. In a world facing a climate crisis, this course will give you specialist training to protect and restore existing habitats and create new places in which nature thrives.

Greenwich – BBC 112 pts +interview +portfolio (Lnd Archit)

104 pts **Myerscough (Coll)** – BCC (Lnd Archit) (IB 24 pts)

96 pts **Reaseheath (UC)** – CCC (Lnd Archit)

Writtle (UC) – 96 pts +interview +portfolio (Lnd Archit; Lnd Gdn Des) (IB 24 pts)

64 pts **Ravensbourne Univ** – CC (Urb Lnd Archit) (IB 28 pts)

Gloucestershire – interview (Lnd Archit)

Alternative offers
See **Chapter 6** and **Appendix 1** for grades/UCAS Tariff points information for other examinations.

EXAMPLES OF COLLEGES OFFERING COURSES IN THIS SUBJECT FIELD
Craven (Coll); Duchy Coll UC.

CHOOSING YOUR COURSE (SEE ALSO CH.1)
Universities and colleges teaching quality See www.qaa.ac.uk; https://unistats.ac.uk.

ADMISSIONS INFORMATION
Number of applicants per place (approx) Edinburgh 19; Gloucestershire 9; Greenwich 3; Writtle (UC) 5.

Advice to applicants and planning the UCAS personal statement Knowledge of the work of landscape architects is important. Arrange a visit to a landscape architect's office and try to organise some work experience. Read up on historical landscape design and visit country house estates with examples of outstanding designs. Describe these visits in detail and your preferences. Membership of the National Trust could be useful. See also **Appendix 3.**

Selection interviews Yes Greenwich, Writtle (UC); **No** Birmingham City, Gloucestershire, Sheffield.

Interview advice and questions Applicants will be expected to have had some work experience and are likely to be questioned on their knowledge of landscape architectural work and the subject. Historical examples of good landscaping could also be asked for. See also **Chapter 5.**

Reasons for rejection (non-academic) Lack of historical knowledge and awareness of current developments. Poor portfolio.

AFTER-RESULTS ADVICE
Offers to applicants repeating A-levels Same Birmingham City; Edinburgh; Greenwich.

GRADUATE DESTINATIONS AND EMPLOYMENT (2016/17 HESA)
Landscape Design graduates surveyed 125 **Employed** 70 **In voluntary employment** 5 **In further study** 30 **Assumed unemployed** 5

Career note Opportunities at present in landscape architecture are good. Openings exist in local government or private practice and may cover planning, housing, and conservation.

OTHER DEGREE SUBJECTS FOR CONSIDERATION
Architecture; Art and Design; Environmental Planning; Forestry; Horticulture.

LANGUAGES

(including **British Sign Language, European Studies, Modern Languages and Translation Studies;** see separate language tables; See also **Chinese, English, European Studies, French, German, Greek, Italian, Japanese, Latin, Linguistics, Russian And East European Studies, Scandinavian Studies, Spanish, Portuguese And Latin American Studies**)

Modern language courses usually offer three main options: a single subject degree commonly based on literature and language, a European Studies course, or two-language subjects which can often include languages different from those available at school (such as Scandinavian Studies, Russian and the languages of Eastern Europe, the Middle and Far East).

Useful websites www.ciol.org.uk; www.iti.org.uk; http://europa.eu; www.bbc.co.uk/languages; www.languageadvantage.com; www.omniglot.com; www.languagematters.co.uk

NB The points totals shown to the left of the institutions are for ease of reference only. It must not be assumed that Tariff points are always used by institutions or that they can be substituted for an offer in grades. The level of an offer is not necessarily indicative of the quality of a course.

COURSE OFFERS INFORMATION
Subject requirements/preferences GCSE English and a modern language required. In some cases grades A (7) and/or B (5 or 6) may be stipulated. **AL** A modern foreign language required usually with a specified grade.

Your target offers and examples of degree courses
152 pts **Cambridge** – A*AA +interview +AMESAA (As Mid E St) (IB 42–40 pts HL 776); A*AA incl lang +interview +MMLAA (Modn Mediev Langs) (IB 42–40 pts HL 776 incl lang)
144 pts **Bristol** – AAA incl lang (Modn Langs) (IB 36 pts HL 18 pts incl 6 langs)
   Durham – AAA incl lang (Modn Langs Cult (Yr Abrd)) (IB 37 pts HL 666 incl lang); AAA incl lang+hist (Modn Euro Langs Hist (Yr Abrd)) (IB 37 pts HL 666)
   Imperial London – AAA incl chem+maths +interview (Chem Fr/Ger/Span Sci) (IB 38 pts HL 6 chem+maths)
   London (UCL) – AAA incl hist+Euro lang (Hist Euro Lang) (IB 38 pts HL 18 pts incl 6 hist+Euro lang)
   Nottingham – A*AA–AAA incl maths+phys (Phys Euro Lang) (IB 38 pts HL 6 maths+phys)
   Oxford – AAA +interview +CAT +MLAT (Class Modn Langs) (IB 39 pts HL 666); AAA +interview +HAT +MLAT (Hist Modn Langs) (IB 38 pts HL 666); AAA +interview +MLAT (Modn Langs Ling) (IB 38 pts HL 666); (Phil Modn Langs) (IB 39 pts HL 666); AAA +interview +OLAT (Orntl St incl Jap/Arab/Chin) (IB 39 pts HL 666); AAA incl Engl +interview +ELAT +MLAT (Engl Modn Langs) (IB 38 pts HL 666 incl Engl)
   Sheffield – AAA/AAB +aEPQ incl maths (Civ Eng Modn Lang (MEng)) (IB 36 pts HL 6 maths); AAA/AAB +aEPQ incl maths+phys/chem/electron (Electron Elec Eng Modn Lang (MEng)) (IB 36 pts HL 6 maths+phys/chem/electron)
   St Andrews – A*AB incl maths (Maths Langs) (IB 36 pts HL 655 incl 6 maths); AAA (Heb courses) (IB 36 pts HL 665); AAA incl lang (Art Hist Lang) (IB 36 pts HL 665 incl 6 lang)
136 pts **Bath** – AAB–ABB +aEPQ incl lang (Int Pol Modn Langs) (IB 35 pts HL 665 incl 7 lang)
   Birmingham – AAA–AAB (Econ Lang) (IB 32 pts HL 666–665)
   Bristol – AAB (Russ Comb Hons) (IB 34 pts HL 17 pts incl 5 lang); AAB incl lang (Hist Art Modn Lang; Phil Modn Lang; Pol Modn Lang) (IB 34 pts HL 17 pts incl 5 lang); AAB incl mus+lang (Mus Modn Lang) (IB 34 pts HL 17 pts incl 5 mus+lang)
   London (UCL) – AAB (Lang Cult) (IB 36 pts HL 17 pts)
   Southampton – AAB/ABB +aEPQ incl Fr/Ger/Span (Bus Mgt Fr/Ger/Span) (IB 34 pts HL 17 pts incl 6 Fr/Ger/Span); AAB/ABB +aEPQ incl lang (Langs Contemp Euro St) (IB 34 pts HL 17 pts incl 6 lang)
   Sussex – AAB (Int Dev Lang) (IB 34 pts)
128 pts **Birmingham** – ABB incl lang (Modn Langs) (IB 32 pts HL 655)
   Edinburgh – AAA–ABB incl Span/Port (Span Port) (IB 40–34 pts HL 766–655 incl Span/Port)
   Exeter – AAB–ABB (Modn Langs Arbc) (IB 34–32 pts HL 665–655); AAB–ABB incl Lat (Fr Lat) (IB 34–32 pts HL 665–655 incl Lat); AAB–ABB incl lang (Int Rel Modn Langs) (IB 34–32 pts HL 665–655)
   Lancaster – ABB incl lang (Modn Langs) (IB 32 pts HL 16 pts incl lang)
   Leeds – AAB–ABB (Lang, Cult, Pol); ABB incl Russ (Port Russ) (IB 34 pts HL 16 pts incl 6 Russ)

Liverpool – ABB (Modn Lang St Bus) (IB 33 pts); ABB incl lang +interview (Modn Langs) (IB 33 pts HL 6 lang); ABB incl maths (Maths Langs) (IB 33 pts HL 6 maths)

London (SOAS) – AAB–ABB (Kor) (IB 35 pts HL 665)

Manchester – AAA–ABB incl sci/maths +interview (Biol Modn Lang) (IB 36–33 pts HL 666–655 incl chem+sci); (Anat Sci Modn Lang; Genet Modn Lang; Microbiol Modn Lang; Plnt Sci Modn Lang) (IB 36–33 pts HL 666–655 incl sci)

Newcastle – AAA–ABB incl Fr (Ling Fr) (IB 36–34 pts HL 5 Fr); ABB incl Fr/Ger/Span (Mod Langs Transl Interp) (IB 32 pts HL 6 Fr/Ger/Span); ABB–BBB incl Fr/Ger/Span (Modn Langs) (IB 32 pts HL 6 Fr/Ger/Span)

Nottingham – ABB (Modn Euro St) (IB 32 pts); ABB incl lang (Modn Lang St; Modn Langs Bus) (IB 32 pts)

Sheffield – ABB (Modn Langs Cult) (IB 33 pts HL 5 lang)

120 pts **Aberdeen** – BBB (Lang Ling) (IB 32 pts HL 555)

East Anglia – BBB (Modn Langs) (IB 31 pts); BBB/ABC (Transl Media Modn Langs) (IB 31 pts); BBB/ABC incl Fr/Span/Jap (Transl Interp Modn Langs (Yr Abrd)) (IB 31 pts HL 5 Fr/Span/Jap)

Essex – BBB (Euro St Fr/Ger/Ital/Span) (IB 30 pts); (Lang St; Modn Langs; Span St Modn Langs) (IB 30 pts HL 555)

Heriot-Watt – BBB incl lang (App Langs Transl (Fr/Span)/(Ger/Span); Brit Sign Lang (Interp Transl App Lang St); Langs (Interp Transl) (Fr/Ger)/(Ger/Span)) (IB 30 pts HL 5 lang)

London (RH) – ABB–BBB (Modn Lang Lat; Modn Langs) (IB 32 pts HL 555)

Newcastle – ABB–BBB incl Fr/Ger/Span (Modn Langs Ling) (IB 32 pts HL 6 Fr/Ger/Span)

North East Scot (Coll) – BBB (Modn Langs) (IB 30 pts)

Nottingham Trent – BBB incl Fr 120 pts (Fr Comb Hons)

Stirling – BBB (Int Mgt St Euro Langs Soty; Modn Langs) (IB 32 pts)

Swansea – BBB (Modn Langs; Modn Langs Transl Inter) (IB 32 pts)

112 pts **Greenwich** – 112 pts (Adv Dig Mark Comm Lang)

Hull – BBC incl lang 112 pts (App Modn Lang (Fr/Ger/Span)) (IB 28 pts HL 5 lang)

London Met – BBC 112 pts (Transl)

104 pts **Aberystwyth** – BBB–BCC incl lang 104–120 pts (Modn Langs) (IB 30–28 pts HL 5 lang)

Central Lancashire – 104–112 pts (Int Bus Comm Modn For Lang; Modn Langs)

Chester – BBC–BCC incl lang 104–112 pts (Modn Langs) (IB 26 pts HL 5 Span/Fr/Ger)

Greenwich – BCC 104 pts+interview (Langs Int Rel)

London (Birk) – BBB–BCC 104–120 pts (Ling Lang)

Westminster – ABB–BCC incl Fr (Transl (Fr)) (IB 27 pts HL 4 Fr); ABB–BCC incl Span (Transl (Span)) (IB 27 pts HL 4 Span)

96 pts **Edinburgh Napier** – CCC incl lang (Int Bus Mgt Lang) (IB 27 pts HL 654 incl 5 lang)

Portsmouth – 96–112 pts (Modn Langs) (IB 25 pts)

Wolverhampton – CCC 96 pts (Interp (Brit Sign Lang/Engl))

York St John – 96 pts (Glob Lang)

Open University – contact 0300 303 0073 or www.open.ac.uk/contact/new (Lang St)

Alternative offers

See **Chapter 6** and **Appendix 1** for grades/UCAS Tariff points information for other examinations.

CHOOSING YOUR COURSE (SEE ALSO CH.1)

Universities and colleges teaching quality See www.qaa.ac.uk; https://unistats.ac.uk.

Top research universities and colleges (REF 2014) (Modern Languages and Linguistics) London (QM) (Ling); Warwick; Glasgow (Celt St); Cambridge; Manchester; London (RH); Queen Margaret; Edinburgh (Ling); Kent; York; Queen's Belfast; Southampton; Cardiff; Essex.

Examples of sandwich degree courses Bangor.

ADMISSIONS INFORMATION

Number of applicants per place (approx) Aston 4; Bangor 6; Bath 6 (Mod Langs Eur St); Birmingham 5; Bristol 15; Cambridge 2; Durham 5; East Anglia 5; Heriot-Watt 6; Lancaster 7; Leeds 8;

LATIN | 321

Leicester 6; Liverpool 6; London (SOAS) (Thai) 2, (Burm) 1; London (UCL) 5; Newcastle 7; Swansea 4; Wolverhampton 10.

Advice to applicants and planning the UCAS personal statement Discuss any literature studied outside your course work. Students applying for courses in which they have no previous knowledge (for example, Italian, Portuguese, Modern Greek, Czech, Russian) would be expected to have done a considerable amount of language work on their own in their chosen language before starting the course. See also **Appendix 3.**

Misconceptions about this course Leeds Some applicants think that studying languages means studying masses of literature – wrong. At Leeds, generally speaking, it's up to you; you study as much or as little literature as you choose. Residence abroad does not inevitably mean a university course (except where you are taking a language from scratch). Paid employment is usually another option.

Selection interviews Yes Cambridge, Oxford ((Modn Lang) 34%, (Modn Lang Ling) 33%), Southampton; **No** Aston, Dundee, East Anglia, Heriot-Watt, Leeds, Liverpool, London (RH), Swansea.

Interview advice and questions See also **Chapter 5. Cambridge** Think of a painting of a tree. Is the tree real? **Leeds** Give an example of something outside your studies that you have achieved over the past year.

Reasons for rejection (non-academic) Lack of commitment to spend a year abroad. Poor references. Poor standard of English. No reasons for why the course has been selected. Poor communication skills. Incomplete applications, for example missing qualifications and reference.

AFTER-RESULTS ADVICE
Offers to applicants repeating A-levels Possibly higher Aston; **Same** Birmingham; Bristol; Durham; East Anglia; Leeds; Liverpool; Newcastle; Nottingham Trent; Stirling; Wolverhampton; **No** Cambridge.

GRADUATE DESTINATIONS AND EMPLOYMENT (2016/17 HESA)
Graduates surveyed See separate language tables.

Career note The only career-related fields for language students are teaching, which attracts some graduates, and the demanding work of interpreting and translating, to which only a small number aspire. The majority will be attracted to work in management and administration, financial services and a host of other occupations which may include the social services, law and property development.

OTHER DEGREE SUBJECTS FOR CONSIDERATION
Communication Studies; Linguistics; Modern Languages Education/Teaching.

LATIN
(See also Classics And Classical Studies/Civilisation, Greek, Languages)

Latin courses provide a study of the language, art, religion and history of the Roman world. This table should be read in conjunction with the **Classics and Classical Studies/Civilisation** table.

Useful websites www.thelatinlibrary.com; www.arlt.co.uk; www.cambridgescp.com

NB The points totals shown to the left of the institutions are for ease of reference only. It must not be assumed that Tariff points are always used by institutions or that they can be substituted for an offer in grades. The level of an offer is not necessarily indicative of the quality of a course.

COURSE OFFERS INFORMATION
Subject requirements/preferences GCSE English, a foreign language and Latin may be stipulated. **AL** Check courses for Latin requirement.

Your target offers and examples of degree courses

152 pts **Cambridge** – A*AA +interview +CAA (Class) (IB 42–40 pts HL 776); A*AA +interview +test
(Modn Mediev Langs (Class Lat)) (IB 42–40 pts HL 776)

144 pts **St Andrews** – AAA incl hist+lang (Lat Mediev Hist) (IB 38 pts HL 666 incl hist+lang); AAA
incl lang (Lat courses) (IB 36 pts HL 665 incl 6 lang)

136 pts **Glasgow** – AAB incl arts/hum (Lat Comb Hons) (IB 36 pts HL 665 incl 6 Engl+hum/lang)
London (UCL) – AAB incl Gk (Gk Lat) (IB 36 pts HL 17 pts incl 6 Gk); AAB incl Lat (Lat Gk)
(IB 36 pts HL 17 pts incl 6 Lat)

128 pts **Edinburgh** – ABB (Anc Hist Lat; Lat St) (IB 36–34 pts HL 666–655)
Exeter – AAB–ABB incl Lat (Fr Lat) (IB 34–32 pts HL 665–655 incl Lat)
Manchester – ABB (Lat courses) (IB 34 pts HL 655)
Nottingham – ABB (Lat)

120 pts **London (RH)** – ABB–BBB (Lat; Modn Lang Lat) (IB 32 pts HL 555)
Swansea – BBB 120 pts (Lat Comb Hons) (IB 32 pts)

Alternative offers
See **Chapter 6** and **Appendix 1** for grades/UCAS Tariff points information for other examinations.

CHOOSING YOUR COURSE (SEE ALSO CH.1)
Universities and colleges teaching quality See www.qaa.ac.uk; https://unistats.ac.uk.

Top research universities and colleges (REF 2014) See **Classics and Classical Studies/Civilisation**.

ADMISSIONS INFORMATION
Number of applicants per place (approx) London (UCL) 5; Nottingham 4; Trinity Saint David 6.

Advice to applicants and planning the UCAS personal statement See **Classics and Classical
Studies/Civilisation.**

Selection interviews Yes Cambridge, London (UCL), Trinity Saint David; **No** London (RH), Nottingham.

Interview advice and questions See **Classics and Classical Studies/Civilisation**.

AFTER-RESULTS ADVICE
Offers to applicants repeating A-levels Higher St Andrews; Warwick.

GRADUATE DESTINATIONS AND EMPLOYMENT (2016/17 HESA)
Graduates surveyed 10 **Employed** 5 **In voluntary employment** 0 **In further study** 5 **Assumed
unemployed** 0

Career note Graduates enter a broad range of careers within management, the media, commerce
and tourism as well as social and public services. Some graduates choose to work abroad and
teaching is a popular option.

OTHER DEGREE SUBJECTS FOR CONSIDERATION
Ancient History; Archaeology; Classical Studies; Classics.

LAW

(including **Criminology**; See also **Social Sciences/Studies**)

Law courses are usually divided into two parts. Part I occupies the first year and introduces the
student to criminal and constitutional law and the legal process. Thereafter, many different
specialised topics can be studied in the second and third years. Consult the subsection Interview
advice and questions in order to gain a flavour of the types of questions raised in studying this
subject. The course content is very similar for most courses. Applicants are advised to check with

universities for their current policies concerning their use of the National Admissions Test for Law (LNAT). See Subject requirements/preferences below and also Chapter 5.

Useful websites www.barcouncil.org.uk; www.cilex.org.uk; www.lawcareers.net; www.lawsociety.org. uk; www.cps.gov.uk; www.gov.uk/government/organisations/hm-courts-and-tribunals-service; www. lawscot.org.uk; www.lawsoc-ni.org; www.rollonfriday.com; www.lnat.ac.uk

NB The points totals shown to the left of the institutions are for ease of reference only. It must not be assumed that Tariff points are always used by institutions or that they can be substituted for an offer in grades. The level of an offer is not necessarily indicative of the quality of a course.

COURSE OFFERS INFORMATION
Subject requirements/preferences GCSE Many universities will expect high grades. **AL** Arts, humanities, social sciences and sciences plus languages for courses combined with a foreign language. **All universities** Applicants offering art and music A-levels should check whether these subjects are acceptable.

Your target offers and examples of degree courses
152 pts   Bristol – A*AA/A*A*B +LNAT (Law) (IB 38 pts HL 18 pts); A*AA/A*A*B incl Fr +LNAT (Law Fr) (IB 38 pts HL 18 pts incl 5 Fr); A*AA/A*A*B incl Ger +LNAT (Law Ger) (IB 38 pts HL 18 pts incl 6 Ger)
Cambridge – A*AA +interview +CLT (Law) (IB 42–40 pts HL 776); A*AA +interview +TSA (Lnd Fron) (IB 42–40 pts HL 776)
Durham – A*AA +LNAT (Law) (IB 38 pts HL 666)
London (King's) – A*AA +LNAT (Law; Pol Phil Law) (IB 35 pts HL 766); A*AA incl Fr/Ger +LNAT (Engl Law Fr Law/Ger Law) (IB 35 pts HL 766 incl 6 Fr/Ger)
London (QM) – A*AA (Law) (IB 36 pts HL 666)
London (UCL) – A*AA +LNAT (Law) (IB 39 pts HL 19 pts); A*AA incl Fr/Ger/Span +LNAT (Law Fr Law/Ger Law/Hisp Law) (IB 39 pts HL 19 pts incl 6 Fr/Ger/Span)
London LSE – A*AA +LNAT (Law) (IB 38 pts HL 776)
144 pts   Birmingham – AAA (Law) (IB 32 pts HL 666); AAA +LNAT (Law Bus St) (IB 32 pts HL 666); AAA incl Ger (Law Ger Law) (IB 32 pts HL 666 incl Ger)
East Anglia – AAA (Law Am Law) (IB 34 pts)
Exeter – AAA (Law; Law (Euro St)) (IB 36 pts HL 666)
Glasgow – AAA incl Engl +LNAT (Cmn Law Comb Hons) (IB 38 pts HL 666 incl Engl)
Kent – AAA (Int Legal St (Yr Abrd)) (IB 34 pts HL 17 pts)
Leeds – AAA (Law) (IB 35 pts HL 665)
London (QM) – AAA (Law Pol) (IB 36 pts HL 666)
Manchester – AAA (Law; Law Crimin; Law Pol) (IB 36 pts HL 666)
Newcastle – AAA (Law) (IB 34 pts)
Nottingham – AAA +LNAT (Law) (IB 36 pts); AAA incl Fr/Ger/Span +LNAT (Law Fr Fr Law/Ger Ger Law/Span Span Law) (IB 36 pts HL 6 Fr/Ger/Span)
Oxford – AAA +interview +LNAT (Law; Law Euro Law) (IB 38 pts HL 666)
Queen's Belfast – AAA (Law) (IB 36 pts HL 666)
Sheffield – AAA/AAB +aEPQ (Law; Law (Euro Int)) (IB 36 pts)
Southampton – AAA (Euro Leg St; Int Leg St; Law) (IB 36 pts HL 18 pts)
Warwick – AAA (Law; Law (St Abrd); Law Bus St) (IB 38 pts); AAA incl Fr/Ger (Law Fr Law/Ger Law) (IB 38 pts HL 6 Fr/Ger)
York – AAA/A*AB/A*A*C +interview (Law) (IB 36 pts)
136 pts   Dundee – AAB incl Engl (Law Langs) (IB 36 pts HL 665 incl Engl)
Lancaster – AAB (Law; Law (St Abrd); Law Crimin) (IB 35 pts HL 16 pts)
Leicester – AAB (Law) (IB 33 pts); AAB incl Fr (Engl Fr Law (Mait)) (IB 33 pts HL 6 Fr); AAB incl lang (Law Modn Lang (Fr/Span/Ital)) (IB 33 pts)
London (SOAS) – A*AA–AAB (Law) (IB 37 pts HL 666)
London LSE – AAB (Anth Law) (IB 37 pts HL 666)
NCH London – AAB +interview (Law) (IB 35 pts HL 665)

Reading – AAB (Law) (IB 34 pts)
Sheffield – AAB/ABB +bEPQ (Law Crimin) (IB 34 pts)
Sussex – AAA–AAB (Law; Law Am St; Law Bus Mgt; Law Int Rel; Law Lang (Yr Abrd); Law
   Pol) (IB 36–34 pts)
Warwick – AAB (Law Sociol) (IB 36 pts)

128 pts   **Aberdeen** – ABB (Law) (IB 34 pts)
Brunel – ABB (Law) (IB 31 pts)
Cardiff – AAB–ABB (Law Crimin) (IB 35–33 pts HL 666–655); (Law) (IB 35–33 pts HL 666–665)
City – ABB 128 pts (Law) (IB 29 pts)
Dundee – ABB (Law (Scot Engl); Law Scot) (IB 32 pts HL 655)
East Anglia – AAB–ABB (Law; Law Euro Leg Sys) (IB 33 pts)
Edinburgh – AAA–ABB incl Engl (Law courses) (IB 43–34 pts HL 776–655 incl Engl); (Law Acc)
   (IB 43–34 pts HL 776–655 incl Engl)
Essex – ABB incl Fr (Engl Fr Law (Mait)) (IB 32 pts HL 655 incl 6 Fr)
Kent – AAA–ABB (Law; Law Comb Hons) (IB 34 pts HL 17 pts); AAA–ABB incl Fr (Engl Fr Law)
   (IB 34 pts HL 17 pts)
Liverpool – ABB (Law; Law Acc Fin) (IB 33 pts)
London (RH) – AAB–ABB (Law) (IB 32 pts HL 655)
London South Bank – ABB (Law)
Northumbria – 128 pts (Law)
Portsmouth – 128 pts (Law) (IB 30 pts HL 665)
Stirling – ABB (Law) (IB 36 pts)
Ulster – ABB (Law) (IB 27 pts HL 13 pts)

120 pts   **Bangor** – 120 pts (Law Crea Media Writ; Law courses)
Chester – BBC–BBB 120 pts (Law Crimin) (IB 28 pts)
Coventry – BBB (Law) (IB 31 pts)
De Montfort – 120 pts (Law) (IB 28 pts)
Derby – 120 pts (Law; Law Crimin)
Essex – BBB (Law; Law Crimin; Law Fin; Law Hum Rts; Phil Law) (IB 30 pts HL 555)
Gloucestershire – BBB 120 pts (Law)
Greenwich – 120 pts +interview (Law)
Huddersfield – BBB 120 pts (Bus Law; Law)
Hull – BBB 120 pts (Law Pol) (IB 30 pts); BBB 120 pts +interview (Law) (IB 30 pts)
Keele – BBB/ABC (Law courses) (IB 32 pts)
Kingston – 120 pts (Law)
Leeds Beckett – 120 pts (Law) (IB 25 pts)
Liverpool John Moores – BBB 120 pts (Law; Law Crim Just) (IB 26 pts)
Manchester Met – BBB 120 pts (Law) (IB 26 pts)
Middlesex – 120 pts (Law)
Nottingham Trent – BBB 120 pts (Law)
Portsmouth – 120 pts (Law Bus; Law Crimin) (IB 29 pts HL 664)
Robert Gordon – BBB incl Engl (Law) (IB 30 pts HL 5 Engl)
Sheffield Hallam – BBB 120 pts (Law; Law Crimin)
Strathclyde – AAB–BBB (Scots Engl Law (Clin)) (IB 38 pts HL 5 Engl)
Surrey – ABB–BBB (Law; Law Crimin; Law Int St) (IB 32 pts)
Swansea – AAB–BBB (Bus Law)
Ulster – BBB incl Ir (Law Ir) (IB 26 pts HL 13 pts)
Univ Law – BBB (Law; Law Bus) (IB 29 pts)
Worcester – BBB 120 pts +interview (Law; Law Crimin; Law Foren Psy)

112 pts   **Bangor** – 112 pts (Law Crimin; Law Media St)
Birmingham City – BBC 112 pts (Law; Law Am Leg St; Law Crimin; Sociol Crimin) (IB 28 pts
   HL 14 pts)
Bradford – 112 pts (Bus St Law; Law)
Buckingham – BBB–BBC +interview (Law) (IB 32-3231 pts)

I LOVE THE FACT THAT OUR LECTURERS ARE PRACTISING LAWYERS

Olasubomi Oke, Student

99

The University of

Law

I WAS VERY ATTRACTED TO THE DIVERSITY AT ULAW, AS THEY HAVE STUDENTS FROM ALL AROUND THE WORLD

Megi Zego, Student

99

With a choice of seven campuses nationwide and online options we're closer than you think. Now offering courses in Business, Law, Criminology, Policing and Politics.

WE SUPPORT

YOUR AMBITION

TEF Silver

OUR LLB
92%
SECURED EMPLOYMENT
OR FURTHER STUDY*

FIND OUT MORE
law.ac.uk/undergraduate

*92% of our full-time UK LLB students graduating in 2017 secured employment or further study within six months of successfully completing their course.

The University of Law is one of the UK's longest-established specialist providers of legal education. In fact, we've trained more practising lawyers than anyone else. With a reputation for innovation and contemporary teaching practices, our courses have a practical focus and are taught by professionals. We now apply our approach to quality teaching and employability to business education through our Business School, as well as Criminology, Policing and Politics degrees

WE SUPPORT
YOUR AMBITION

OUR DEGREES

With courses designed by experienced academics and professionals, you can learn real-world skills on our business, criminology, law, policing and politics courses.

CAMPUSES ACROSS THE UK

With campuses based in seven of the UK's most vibrant and interesting cities, choose from the bustling cities of Birmingham, Bristol, Leeds, London, Nottingham and Manchester, the heritage-rich Guildford or LLB online courses that allow you to study anyplace, anytime, anywhere. All of our campuses provide the same first-class professional learning environment.

BERLIN SUMMER SCHOOL

All undergraduate students have the opportunity to attend our International Leadership Summer School in Berlin*.

FOLLOW US:

 liveprospectus.com

SWITCH IT UP

If you want to experience life in a new city, with CampuSwitch you can start your degree at one campus and then move to another to continue or complete your studies*. If you find your true calling mid-studies with our CourseSwitch offer you can change the course you're on part way through your degree*.

INNOVATIVE TEACHING

We specialise in teaching and focus our energy on developing innovative, highly effective teaching and learning methods that equip students for their professional career.

Our tutors are highly experienced. Over 90% of our law tutors are lawyers, who know the skills you need to learn to succeed. All of our business tutors also possess commercial experience.

I CHOSE TO STUDY AT THE UNIVERSITY OF LAW BECAUSE OF THE HIGH QUALITY OF TEACHING

Benjamin Yip, Student

*Subject to limitations, terms and conditions. See our website for full details.

The University of Law

ENHANCED EMPLOYABILITY

What really sets us apart from other universities is the belief that our students should learn in a realistic, professional and contemporary context. For our law courses we focus on practice-based training and give students access to our extensive careers service and jobs database. Through our pro bono programme, law students can hone their skills by working on real cases before they graduate. Our business, criminology, policing and politics degrees also have a firm focus on developing the skills demanded by employers.

FREE MASTER'S DEGREE

Existing and future Business School students have the opportunity to undertake a business Master's course on successful completion of their undergraduate degree at no additional cost†.

STIMULATING ENVIRONMENT

From business games to mock trials and negotiation competitions, you can enhance your learning and boost your CV without it feeling like work. Of course, you'll need time to switch off from studying too and our campuses have a range of activities such as debating societies, sports teams, fundraising events, balls, parties and social activities to make sure you have a full and well-rounded student experience.

FIND OUT MORE
law.ac.uk/undergraduate

**92% of our full-time UK LLB students graduating in 2017 secured employment or further study within six months of successfully completing their course.

†T&Cs apply, details at law.ac.uk/freemasters

Cardiff Met – BBC 112 pts (Bus Mgt Law) (IB 24 pts HL 12 pts)
Chester – BBB–BBC 112–120 pts (Law) (IB 28 pts)
Cumbria – BBC 112–128 pts (Law)
De Montfort – 112 pts (Law Hum Rts Soc Just) (IB 26 pts)
Derby – 112 pts (Law Comb Hons)
East London – 112 pts (Law) (IB 26 pts HL 15 pts)
Edge Hill – BBB–BBC 112–120 pts (Law; Law Crimin)
Hertfordshire – BBC 112 pts (Law)
Lincoln – BBC (Law) (IB 29 pts)
Liverpool Hope – BBC 112 pts (Law Comb Hons) (IB 28 pts)
London (Birk) – BBB–BBC 112–120 pts (Law)
London Met – BBC 112 pts (Law; Law (Int Rel))
Northampton – BBC (Law courses)
Nottingham Trent – BBC 112 pts (Law Bus; Law Crimin; Law Psy)
Staffordshire – BBC 112 pts (Law)
Sunderland – 112 pts (Law)
UWE Bristol – 112 pts (Crimin Law; Law)
West London – BBC 112–128 pts (Law)
Westminster – ABB–BBC 112–128 pts (Euro Leg St; Law) (IB 27 pts); ABB–BBC incl Fr 112–128 pts (Law Fr Law) (IB 27 pts HL 6 Fr)
Winchester – 112–120 pts (Law) (HL 44)

104 pts **Abertay** – BCC (Law) (IB 29 pts)
Aberystwyth – ABB–BCC 104–128 pts (Crim Law; Euro Law; Law) (IB 30–28 pts)
Aston – BBB–BCC (Law) (IB 31 pts HL 555)
Bournemouth – 104–120 pts (Law) (IB 31–28 pts)
Buckingham – BBB–BCC +interview (Law Bus Mgt) (IB 32 pts)
Central Lancashire – 104–112 pts (Law; Law Crimin)
Chester – BBC–BCC 104–112 pts (Law Comb Hons) (IB 26 pts)
De Montfort – 104 pts (Bus Mgt Law) (IB 24 pts)
Edinburgh Napier – BCC incl Engl (Law) (IB 29 pts HL 654 incl Engl)
Oxford Brookes – BCC 104 pts (Law) (IB 29 pts)
Plymouth – 104–120 pts (Law) (IB 30–27 pts)
Winchester – 104–120 pts (Law Comb Hons) (HL 44)

96 pts **Anglia Ruskin** – 96 pts (Law) (IB 24 pts)
Brighton – BBB–CCC 96–120 pts (Law Bus) (IB 26 pts)
Bucks New – 96 pts (Bus Law; Law)
Canterbury Christ Church – BBB 96–120 pts (Law)
Chichester – BBB–CCC 96–120 pts (Law) (IB 28 pts)
Cumbria – 96–112 pts (Crimin Law)
Plymouth – 96–112 pts (Marit Bus Marit Law) (IB 28 pts HL 4)
Solent – 96–112 pts (Law)
St Mary's – BBC–CCC 96–112 pts (Law); BCC–CCC 96–104 pts (Bus Law courses) (IB 28–24 pts)
West Scotland – CCC (Law) (IB 24 pts HL 4)
Wolverhampton – CCC/BCD (Law); CCC/BCD 96 pts (Law Phil)

88 pts **Plymouth** – 88–104 pts (Pol Law) (IB 26–24 pts HL 4)
Teesside – 88–112 pts (Law; Law Bus Mgt)

80 pts **Bedfordshire** – 80 pts (Law)
South Wales – BCC–CDD 80–104 pts (Law; Law Crimin Crim Just) (IB 29 pts)

Open University – contact 0300 303 0073 or www.open.ac.uk/contact/new (Law)

Alternative offers
See **Chapter 6** and **Appendix 1** for grades/UCAS Tariff points information for other examinations.

EXAMPLES OF COLLEGES OFFERING COURSES IN THIS SUBJECT FIELD
Barnsley (Coll); Birmingham Met (Coll); Blackburn (Coll); Blackpool and Fylde (Coll); Bury (Coll);

Croydon (Univ Centre); Nottingham (Coll); Pearson (Coll); Petroc; South Devon (Coll); South Thames (Coll); St Helens (Coll); Truro and Penwith (Coll).

CHOOSING YOUR COURSE (SEE ALSO CH.1)

Universities and colleges teaching quality See www.qaa.ac.uk; https://unistats.ac.uk.

Examples of sandwich degree courses Aston; Bournemouth; Bradford; Brighton; Brunel; Coventry; De Montfort; Essex; Greenwich; Hertfordshire; Huddersfield; Leeds; London (RH); Nottingham Trent; Plymouth; Portsmouth; Surrey; UWE Bristol; Westminster.

ADMISSIONS INFORMATION

Number of applicants per place (approx) Abertay 4; Anglia Ruskin 10; Aston 10; Bangor 5; Birmingham 6; Birmingham City 20; Bradford 2; Bristol 5; Buckingham 10; Cambridge 5; Cardiff 12; Central Lancashire 36; City 6; De Montfort 6; Derby 7; Dundee 6; Durham 7; East Anglia 7; East London 13; Edinburgh 9; Edinburgh Napier 11; Essex 26; Exeter 15; Glasgow 8; Huddersfield 6; Hull 5; Kent 6; Kingston 25; Lancaster 4; Leeds 15; Leicester 6; Liverpool 12; Liverpool John Moores 10; London (King's) 14; London (QM) 17; London (RH) 6; London (SOAS) 8; London (UCL) 14; London LSE 15; London Met 13; London South Bank 4; Manchester 7; Manchester Met 21; Middlesex 25; Newcastle 7; Northampton 4; Nottingham 7; Nottingham Trent 15; Oxford Brookes 7; Plymouth 21; Robert Gordon 4; Sheffield 6; Sheffield Hallam 6; Southampton 7; Staffordshire 16; Stirling 11; Strathclyde 10; Sussex 10; Teesside 3; Warwick 20; Westminster 29; Wolverhampton 12; York 8.

Admissions tutors' advice Buckingham A personal statement should demonstrate (at least a potential for) some of the key skills for the study of law: a passion or desire to study the subject, interest in other people and the world around us, powers of synthesis and analysis. Above all a statement should be articulate and succinct and show the applicant has an aptitude for effective communication. **London LSE** LNAT required.

Advice to applicants and planning the UCAS personal statement Visit the law courts and take notes on cases heard. Follow leading legal arguments in the press. Read the law sections in *The Independent*, *The Times* and the *Guardian*. Discuss the career with lawyers and, if possible, obtain work shadowing in lawyers' offices. Describe these visits and experiences and indicate any special areas of law which interest you. (Read *Learning the Law* by Glanville Williams.) Commitment is essential to the study of law as an academic discipline, not necessarily with a view to taking it up as a career. When writing to admissions tutors, especially by email, take care to present yourself well. You should use communication as an opportunity to demonstrate your skill in the use of English. Spelling mistakes, punctuation errors and bad grammar suggest that you will struggle to develop the expected writing ability (see Misconceptions about this course) and may lead to your application being rejected. When writing to an admissions tutor, do not demand an answer immediately or by return or urgently. If your query is reasonable, the tutor will respond without such urging. Adding these demands is bad manners and suggests that you are doing everything at the last minute and increases your chances of a rejection. The criteria for admission are: motivation and capacity for sustained and intense work; the ability to analyse and solve problems using logical and critical approaches; the ability to draw fine distinctions, to separate the relevant from the irrelevant; the capacity for accurate and critical observation, for sustained and cogent argument; creativity and flexibility of thought and lateral thinking; competence in English; the ability to express ideas clearly and effectively; a willingness to listen and to be able to give considered responses. See also **Appendix 3. Deferred entry** Check with your university choices since deferred entry will not necessarily be accepted. **Bristol** Deferred entry is limited. Second time applicants rarely considered. **Manchester** Deferred entry is accepted. **Warwick** Deferred entry is usually acceptable.

Misconceptions about this course Aberystwyth Some applicants believe that all Law graduates enter the legal profession – this is incorrect. **Birmingham** Students tend to believe that success in Law centres on the ability to learn information. While some information does necessarily have to be learnt, the most important skills involve (a) developing an ability to select the most relevant pieces of information and (b) developing the ability to write tightly argued, persuasively reasoned essays on the basis of such information. **Bournemouth** You don't have to know exactly which specialism to study before you start. You can specialise after your first semester. **Bristol** Many applicants think that most of our applicants have been privately educated: the reverse is true. **Derby** Many applicants do not realise the amount of work involved to get a good degree classification.

Selection interviews Yes Anglia Ruskin, Buckingham, Cambridge, Oxford ((Law) 15%, (Law Law St Euro) 11%), York; **Some** Cardiff, Liverpool John Moores, London (King's), London (UCL), Solent, Warwick; **No** Aberystwyth, Bangor, Birmingham, Bristol, Canterbury Christ Church, Central Lancashire, Coventry, Derby, Dundee, East Anglia, East London, Essex, Huddersfield, Kent, Liverpool, Northumbria, Nottingham, Nottingham Trent, Oxford Brookes, Reading, Sheffield Hallam, Southampton, Staffordshire, Sunderland, Surrey, Teesside, UWE Bristol, West London.

Interview advice and questions Law is a highly competitive subject and applicants will be expected to have a basic awareness of aspects of law and to have gained some work experience, on which they are likely to be questioned. It is almost certain that a legal question will be asked at interview and applicants will be tested on their responses. Questions in the past have included: What interests you in the study of law? What would you do to overcome the problem of prison overcrowding if you were (a) a judge, (b) a prosecutor, (c) the Prime Minister? What legal cases have you read about recently? What is jurisprudence? What are the causes of violence in society? Have you visited any law courts? What cases did you see? A person arrives in England unable to speak the language. He lights a cigarette in a restaurant where smoking is not allowed. Can he be charged and convicted? What, in your opinion, would be the two basic laws in Utopia? What would happen if there were no law? Should we legalise euthanasia? If you could change any law, what would it be? How would you implement the changes? Where does honesty fit into law? For joint courses: What academic skills are needed to succeed? Why have you applied for a joint degree? See also **Chapter 5. Cambridge** Logic questions. If I returned to the waiting room and my jacket had been taken and I then took another one, got home and actually discovered it was mine, had I committed a crime? If the interviewer pulled out a gun and aimed it at me, but missed as he had a bad arm, had he committed a crime? If the interviewer pulled out a gun and aimed it at me, thinking it was loaded but, in fact, it was full of blanks and fired it at me with the intention to kill, had he committed a crime? Which of the three preceding situations are similar and which is the odd one out? If a law is immoral, is it still a law and must people abide by it? For example, when Hitler legalised the systematic killing of Jews, was it still law? **Oxford** Should the use of mobile phones be banned on public transport? Is wearing school uniform a breach of human rights? If you could go back in time to any period of time, when would it be and why? Would you trade your scarf for my bike, even if you have no idea what state it's in or if I even have one? Is someone guilty of an offence if they did not set out to commit a crime but ended up doing so? Does a girl who joins the Scouts have a political agenda?

Reasons for rejection (non-academic) Poorly informed about the subject. Badly drafted application. Underestimated workload. Poor communication skills. **Buckingham** Applicants are requested to attend an Open Day/Evening or a Tutorial Taster Day. The University believes it is very important for applicants to visit its campus. Candidates who do not respond to these invitations may be rejected, irrespective of academic achievement, as the University looks for committed, well-motivated students. **Manchester Met** Some were rejected because they were obviously more suited to Psychology.

AFTER-RESULTS ADVICE
Offers to applicants repeating A-levels Higher Aberystwyth; Leeds; London Met; Manchester Met; Newcastle; Queen's Belfast; Sheffield; Sheffield Hallam; Strathclyde; Warwick; **Possibly higher** Liverpool; **Same** Anglia Ruskin; Bangor; Birmingham; Bradford; Brighton; Bristol; Brunel; Cardiff; Coventry; De Montfort; Derby; Dundee; Durham; East Anglia; Essex; Huddersfield; Hull; Kingston; Lincoln; Liverpool Hope; Liverpool John Moores; Northumbria; Nottingham; Nottingham Trent; Oxford Brookes; Staffordshire; Stirling; Sunderland; Wolverhampton; **No** Cambridge; Glasgow.

GRADUATE DESTINATIONS AND EMPLOYMENT (2016/17 HESA)
Graduates surveyed 10,160 **Employed** 3,880 **In voluntary employment** 250 **In further study** 4,370 **Assumed unemployed** 445

Career note Training places for the bar and solicitors' examinations remain extremely competitive. There are, however, alternative legal careers such as legal journalism, patent law, legal publishing and teaching. The course also proves a good starting point for careers in industry, commerce and the public service, while the study of consumer protection can lead to qualification as a Trading Standards officer.

OTHER DEGREE SUBJECTS FOR CONSIDERATION
Criminology; Economics; Government; History; International Relations; Politics; Social Policy and Administration; Sociology.

LEISURE AND RECREATION MANAGEMENT/STUDIES

(See also **Business and Management Courses, Business and Management Courses (international And European), Business and Management Courses (Specialised), Hospitality and Event Management, Sports Sciences/Studies, Tourism and Travel**)

The courses cover various aspects of leisure and recreation and in particular, a wide range of outdoor activities. Specialist options include Recreation Management, Tourism and Countryside Management, all of which are offered as individual degree courses in their own right. Look out for other 'outdoor' activities in sport such as the two-year Foundation course in Surf Science and Technology offered at Cornwall College in partnership with Plymouth University. There is also an obvious link with Sports Studies, Physical Education and Tourism and Travel courses. See also **Appendix 3.**

Useful websites www.cimspa.co.uk; www.leisuremanagement.co.uk; www.thebapa.org.uk; www.leisureopportunities.co.uk; www.recmanagement.com; www.uksport.gov.uk

NB The points totals shown to the left of the institutions are for ease of reference only. It must not be assumed that Tariff points are always used by institutions or that they can be substituted for an offer in grades. The level of an offer is not necessarily indicative of the quality of a course.

COURSE OFFERS INFORMATION
Subject requirements/preferences GCSE Normally English and mathematics grades A–C (7–4). **AL** No specified subjects. Other Disclosure and Barring Service (DBS) clearance and health checks required for some courses.

Your target offers and examples of degree courses
128 pts   **Edinburgh** – ABB (Spo Recr Mgt) (IB 36–34 pts HL 666–655)
           Manchester – ABB (Mgt Ldrshp Leis) (IB 34 pts HL 655)
120 pts   **Stirling** – BBB incl sci/maths/geog (Env Sci Out Educ) (IB 32 pts HL 5 sci/maths/geog)
112 pts   **Gloucestershire** – BBC 112 pts (Spo Bus Mgt)
104 pts   **Central Lancashire** – 104–112 pts (Out Advntr Ldrshp)
           Cumbria – 104–120 pts (Out Advntr Env; Out Ldrshp)
           Stranmillis (UC) – BCC (Hlth Physl Actvt Spo)
           Ulster – BBB–BCC (Leis Evnts Mgt) (IB 26–24 pts HL 13–12 pts)
96 pts   **Solent** – CCC 96–112 pts (Advntr Out Mgt) (IB 28 pts)
           Worcester – 96 pts (Out Advntr Ldrshp Mgt)
88 pts   **Trinity Saint David** – 88 pts+interview (Int Leis Rsrt Mgt)
64 pts   **UHI** – CC (Advntr Tour Mgt; Glf Mgt)

Alternative offers
See **Chapter 6** and **Appendix 1** for grades/UCAS Tariff points information for other examinations.

EXAMPLES OF COLLEGES OFFERING COURSES IN THIS SUBJECT FIELD
Bedford (Coll); Blackburn (Coll); Bradford College UC; Cornwall (Coll); Durham New (Coll); Exeter (Coll);

Greater Brighton Met (Coll); Leicester (Coll); Loughborough (Coll); Manchester (Coll); MidKent (Coll); Myerscough (Coll); Newcastle (Coll); Norwich City (Coll); South Devon (Coll); SRUC; TEC Partnership; Totton (Coll); Wakefield (Coll); West Herts (Coll); Wirral Met (Coll).

CHOOSING YOUR COURSE (SEE ALSO CH.1)

Universities and colleges teaching quality See www.qaa.ac.uk; https://unistats.ac.uk.

Top research universities and colleges (REF 2014) See **Sports Sciences/Studies**.

Examples of sandwich degree courses Bournemouth; Trinity Saint David; Ulster.

ADMISSIONS INFORMATION

Number of applicants per place (approx) Gloucestershire 7.

Advice to applicants and planning the UCAS personal statement Work experience, visits to leisure centres and national parks and any interests you have in particular aspects of leisure should be described, for example, art galleries, museums, countryside management, sport. An involvement in sports and leisure as a participant or employee is an advantage. See also **Appendix 3.**

Interview advice and questions In addition to sporting or other related interests, applicants will be expected to have had some work experience and can expect to be asked to discuss their interests. What do you hope to gain by going to university? See also **Chapter 5.**

Reasons for rejection (non-academic) Poor communication or presentation skills. Relatively poor sporting background or knowledge.

GRADUATE DESTINATIONS AND EMPLOYMENT (2016/17 HESA)

Graduates surveyed See **Hospitality and Event Management**.

Career note Career opportunities exist in public and private sectors within leisure facilities, health clubs, the arts, leisure promotion, marketing and events management. Some graduates work in sports development and outdoor activities.

OTHER DEGREE SUBJECTS FOR CONSIDERATION

Business Studies; Events Management; Hospitality Management; Sports Studies; Tourism.

LINGUISTICS

(See also **English, Languages**)

Hi/Hello/Good day/Good morning – Linguistics is the study of language, the way we speak to our friends, or at an interview, the expressions we use, how we express ideas or emotions. The way in which children speak, the types of language used in advertising, or in sports reporting. Courses will include morphology (the formation of words), phonetics (the study of sounds), and semantics (the study of meanings). OK?/Understand?/Cheers! Linguistics graduates are well-equipped to undertake a variety of careers involving communication and language, including teaching, speech therapy and publishing.

Useful websites www.ciol.org.uk; www.cal.org; https://academic.oup.com/applij; www.linguisticsociety.org; www.sil.org; www.baal.org.uk

NB The points totals shown to the left of the institutions are for ease of reference only. It must not be assumed that Tariff points are always used by institutions or that they can be substituted for an offer in grades. The level of an offer is not necessarily indicative of the quality of a course.

COURSE OFFERS INFORMATION

Subject requirements/preferences GCSE English required and a foreign language preferred. **AL** English may be required or preferred for some courses.

Your target offers and examples of degree courses

152 pts   **Cambridge** – A*AA +interview +LAA (Ling) (IB 42–40 pts HL 776)

136 pts   **Glasgow** – AAB (Engl Lang Ling) (IB 36 pts HL 665 incl 6 Engl+hum/lang)

      Lancaster – AAB (Ling; Ling (St Abrd); Ling Phil; Ling Psy) (IB 35 pts HL 16 pts)

      Leeds – AAB (Ling Comb Hons) (IB 35 pts HL 16 pts)

      Sheffield – AAB–ABB +bEPQ (Engl Lang Ling) (IB 34 pts)

      Warwick – AAB (Ling Russ) (IB 36 pts)

      York – AAB (Phil Ling) (IB 35 pts)

128 pts   **Edinburgh** – AAB–ABB (Ling Engl Lang) (IB 37–34 pts HL 666–655); ABB (Ital Ling) (IB 34 pts HL 655); (Ling) (IB 37–34 pts HL 666–655); (Jap Ling) (IB 38–34 pts HL 666–655); ABB 128 pts (Class Ling) (IB 37–34 pts HL 666–655)

      Huddersfield – ABB 128 pts (Ling)

      Leeds – AAB–ABB (Ling Phon) (IB 35–34 pts HL 16 pts)

      London (QM) – ABB (Engl Lang Ling) (IB 32 pts HL 655); ABB incl Engl lit/Engl lang lit (Engl Lit Ling) (IB 32 pts HL 655 incl 6 Engl)

      London (SOAS) – AAB–ABB (Ling Comb Hons) (IB 35 pts HL 665)

      Manchester – ABB (Ling courses) (IB 34 pts HL 655)

      Newcastle – AAA–ABB (Ling; Ling Chin/Jap) (IB 36–34 pts); AAA–ABB incl Fr (Ling Fr) (IB 36–34 pts HL 5 Fr)

      Queen's Belfast – ABB incl Engl (Engl Ling) (IB 33 pts HL 655 incl Engl)

      Reading – ABB 128 pts (Psy Lang Sci) (IB 32 pts)

      Sheffield – ABB (Ling Comb Hons) (IB 33 pts)

      York – AAB–ABB (Linq) (IB 35–34 pts); AAB–ABB incl Fr (Fr Ling (Yr Abrd)) (IB 35–34 pts HL 6 Fr)

120 pts   **Aberdeen** – BBB (Lang Ling) (IB 32 pts HL 555)

      Essex – BBB (Ling) (IB 30 pts)

      Kent – BBB (Engl Lang Ling) (IB 34 pts HL 15 pts)

      London (QM) – BBB incl hum/soc sci (Ger Ling) (IB 30 pts HL 555 incl hum/soc sci)

      Newcastle – ABB–BBB incl Fr/Ger/Span (Modn Langs Ling) (IB 32 pts HL 6 Fr/Ger/Span)

112 pts   **Bangor** – 112 pts (Ling; Ling Engl Lang; Ling Engl Lit)

      Roehampton – 112 pts (Engl Lang Ling)

      UWE Bristol – 112 pts (Engl Lang Ling)

104 pts   **Central Lancashire** – 104 pts (Engl Lang Ling)

      London (Birk) – BBB–BCC 104–120 pts (Ling Lang)

      Manchester Met – BBC–BCC 104–112 pts (Ling Mand Chin/Fr/Ger/Ital/Span) (IB 26 pts)

      Nottingham Trent – 104 pts (Ling Comb Hons)

      Ulster – BBC–BCC (Lang Ling) (IB 25–24 pts HL 12 pts)

      Westminster – ABB–BCC (Arbc Ling) (IB 27 pts HL 4 Engl/maths); ABB–BCC incl Engl/hum 104–128 pts (Engl Lang Ling) (IB 27 pts HL 5 Engl)

      Winchester – 104–120 pts (Engl Ling; Engl Ling Foren Ling) (HL 44)

96 pts   **Anglia Ruskin** – 96 pts (Engl Lang Ling)

      Bangor – 96 pts (Chin Comb)

      Brighton – BCC–CCC incl Engl 96–104 pts (Engl Lang Ling) (IB 26 pts)

      Wolverhampton – CCC (Ling courses)

80 pts   **Bedfordshire** – 80 pts (Engl Lang Ling)

Alternative offers

See **Chapter 6** and **Appendix 1** for grades/UCAS Tariff points information for other examinations.

CHOOSING YOUR COURSE (SEE ALSO CH.1)

Universities and colleges teaching quality See www.qaa.ac.uk; https://unistats.ac.uk.

Top research universities and colleges (REF 2014) (Modern Languages and Linguistics) London (QM) (Ling); Warwick; Glasgow (Celt St); Cambridge; Manchester; London (RH); Queen Margaret; Edinburgh (Ling); Kent; York; Queen's Belfast; Southampton; Cardiff; Essex.

Examples of sandwich degree courses Bangor; Leeds; Nottingham Trent; Westminster.

ADMISSIONS INFORMATION
Number of applicants per place (approx) Bangor 5; Cambridge 3; Essex 1; Lancaster 6; Leeds 12; York 11.

Advice to applicants and planning the UCAS personal statement Give details of your interests in language and how it works, and about your knowledge of languages and their similarities and differences.

Selection interviews Yes Cambridge; No Brighton, Essex, Newcastle, Sheffield.

Interview advice and questions Past questions include: Why do you want to study linguistics? What does the subject involve? What do you intend to do at the end of your degree course? What answer do you give to your parents or friends when they ask why you want to study the subject? How and why does language vary according to sex, age, social background and regional origins? See also **Chapter 5.**

Reasons for rejection (non-academic) Lack of knowledge of linguistics. Hesitation about the period to be spent abroad.

AFTER-RESULTS ADVICE
Offers to applicants repeating A-levels Same Brighton; Essex; Leeds; Newcastle; York.

GRADUATE DESTINATIONS AND EMPLOYMENT (2016/17 HESA)
Graduates surveyed 555 Employed 260 In voluntary employment 25 In further study 150 Assumed unemployed 20

Career note Students enter a wide range of careers, with information management and editorial work in publishing offering some interesting and useful outlets.

OTHER DEGREE SUBJECTS FOR CONSIDERATION
Cognitive Science; Communication Studies; Education Studies; English; Psychology; Speech Sciences.

LITERATURE
(See also **English**)

This is a very broad subject introducing many aspects of the study of literature and aesthetics. Courses will vary in content. Degree courses in English and foreign languages will also include a study of literature.

Useful websites www.lrb.co.uk; www.3ammagazine.com/3am; www.bibliomania.com; www.bl.uk; www.acla.org

NB The points totals shown to the left of the institutions are for ease of reference only. It must not be assumed that Tariff points are always used by institutions or that they can be substituted for an offer in grades. The level of an offer is not necessarily indicative of the quality of a course.

COURSE OFFERS INFORMATION
Subject requirements/preferences GCSE English and a foreign language usually required. AL English may be required or preferred for some courses.

Your target offers and examples of degree courses
152 pts   **Durham** – A*AA incl Engl (Engl Lit; Engl Lit Phil) (IB 38 pts HL 666 incl Engl); A*AA incl Engl+hist (Engl Lit Hist) (IB 38 pts HL 666 incl Engl+hist)
144 pts   **Oxford** – AAA incl Engl +interview +ELAT (Engl Lang Lit) (IB 38 pts HL 666 incl Engl)
          Warwick – A*AB/AAA incl Engl (Engl Lit) (IB 38 pts HL 6 Engl); AAA/A*AB incl Engl (Engl Lit Crea Writ) (IB 38 pts HL 6 Engl)

136 pts **Glasgow** – AAB (Compar Lit Comb Hons) (IB 36 pts HL 665 incl 6 Engl/hum/lang); (Engl Lit) (IB 36 pts HL 665 incl Engl+hum/lang); AAB incl arts/hum (Scot Lit) (IB 36 pts HL 665 incl Engl+hum/lang)

Lancaster – AAB incl Engl (Thea Engl Lit) (IB 35 pts HL 16 pts incl 6 Engl); (Engl Lang Lit; Engl Lit; Flm Engl Lit) (IB 35 pts HL 16 pts incl 6 lit)

Leeds – AAA–AAB incl Engl (Engl Lang Lit) (IB 35 pts HL 17–16 pts incl 6 Engl); AAB incl Engl (Class Lit courses) (IB 35 pts HL 16 pts incl 6 Engl)

London (King's) – AAB incl Engl (Compar Lit) (IB 35 pts HL 665 incl 6 Engl lit); (Compar Lit Flm St) (IB 35 pts HL 665 incl Engl)

Manchester – AAA–AAB incl Engl (Engl Lit courses) (IB 36 pts HL 666)

Newcastle – AAA–AAB incl Engl (Engl Lang Lit; Engl Lit; Engl Lit Comb Hons) (IB 36–35 pts HL 6 Engl)

Nottingham – AAA–AAB incl Engl (Engl Lang Lit) (IB 36–34 pts HL 6 Engl)

Sheffield – AAB incl art/hum (Engl Lang Lit) (IB 34 pts HL 5 art/hum); AAB–ABB+bEPQ (Engl Lit) (IB 34 pts HL 5 art/hum)

Warwick – AAB incl Engl lit+lang (Engl Ger; Engl Ital) (IB 36 pts HL 5 Engl lit+lang)

128 pts **East Anglia** – ABB (Am Lit Crea Writ) (IB 32 pts HL 5 Engl); ABB incl Engl (Engl Lit) (IB 32 pts HL 5 Engl)

Edinburgh – A*AA–ABB incl Engl (Engl Lit) (IB 43–34 pts HL 776–655 incl Engl); ABB incl Engl (Celt Scot Lit; Scot Lit) (IB 34 pts HL 655 incl 5 Engl)

London (QM) – ABB incl Engl lit/Engl lang lit (Engl Lit Ling) (IB 32 pts HL 655 incl 6 Engl); ABB incl hist (Hist Compar Lit) (IB 32 pts HL 655 incl hist)

Nottingham – ABB (Am Can Lit Hist Cult) (IB 32 pts)

Sussex – AAB–ABB incl Engl (Engl Lang Lit) (IB 34–32 pts HL 6 Engl)

Warwick – ABB incl Engl +interview +portfolio (Flm Lit) (IB 34 pts HL 5 Engl)

120 pts **Aberdeen** – BBB (Engl Scot Lit) (IB 32 pts HL 555)

Cardiff – ABB–BBB incl Engl (Engl Lit; Jrnl Media Engl Lit) (HL 665 incl 6 Engl)

East Anglia – BBB/ABC incl Engl (Cult Lit Pol) (IB 31 pts HL 5 Engl); BBB/ABC incl Engl+hist (Lit Hist) (IB 31 pts HL 5 Engl+hist); BBB incl Engl (Am Engl Lit; Engl Lit Comb Hons) (IB 31 pts HL 5 Engl)

Essex – BBB (Lit Art Hist) (IB 30 pts); (Engl Lang Lit; Engl Lit; Flm St Lit) (IB 30 pts HL 555); BBB +workshop (Dr Lit) (IB 30 pts)

Huddersfield – BBB incl Engl 120 pts (Engl Lit; Engl Lit Crea Writ)

Hull – BBB 120 pts (Engl Am Lit Cult) (IB 30 pts)

Kent – BBB (Compar Lit) (IB 34 pts HL 15 pts); BBB incl Engl (Engl Am Postcol Lit courses) (IB 34 pts HL 15 pts); (Contemp Lit) (IB 34 pts HL 15 pts incl Engl)

London (Gold) – BBB incl Engl (Engl Am Lit; Engl Compar Lit) (IB 33 pts HL 655)

London (QM) – BBB incl hum/soc sci (Ger Compar Lit) (IB 30 pts HL 555 incl hum/soc sci)

London (RH) – ABB–BBB (Compar Lit Cult) (IB 32 pts HL 555)

Northumbria – 120 pts (Engl Lang Lit; Engl Lit Crea Writ; Engl Lit Hist; Jrnl Engl Lit)

Reading – BBB incl Engl (Engl Lang Lit) (IB 30 pts HL 5 Engl); BBB incl Engl/thea st (Engl Lit Flm Thea) (IB 30 pts HL 5 Engl/thea st)

Surrey – BBB incl Engl (Engl Lit; Engl Lit Crea Writ) (IB 32 pts)

Swansea – BBB (Engl Lang Engl Lit) (IB 32 pts)

York – BBB (Engl Educ) (IB 31 pts)

112 pts **Bangor** – 112 pts (Engl Lang Engl Lit; Ling Engl Lit)

Birmingham City – BBC incl Engl 112 pts (Engl Lit courses) (IB 28 pts HL 14 pts)

Buckingham – BBB–BBC (Engl Lit; Engl Lit Hist) (IB 32–31 pts)

De Montfort – C Engl 112 pts (Engl Lit) (IB 26 pts)

Edge Hill – BBB–BBC 112–120 pts (Engl Lit)

Kingston – 112 pts (Engl Lit)

Leeds Beckett – 112 pts (Engl Lit) (IB 25 pts)

Liverpool Hope – BBC 112 pts (Engl Lit) (IB 28 pts)

Roehampton – C Engl/hum 112 pts (Engl Lit)

Sheffield Hallam – BBC 112 pts (Engl Lit)

Worcester – C Engl 112 pts (Engl Lit courses)

104 pts **Aberystwyth** – BBB–BCC incl B Engl 104–120 pts (Engl Lit) (IB 30–28 pts HL 5 Engl); BBB–BCC incl Engl 104–120 pts (Engl Lit Crea Writ) (IB 30–28 pts HL 5 Engl)

Central Lancashire – 104 pts (Engl Lit)

Gloucestershire – BCC 104 pts (Engl Lit Crea Writ)

Greenwich – 104 pts (Engl Lit)

Hertfordshire – BCC 104 pts (Engl Lit; Engl Lit Fr)

Manchester Met – 104–112 pts (Engl Am Lit) (IB 26 pts)

Westminster – ABB–BCC incl Engl/hum (Engl Lit Hist) (IB 27 pts HL 5 Engl)

Winchester – 104–120 pts incl Engl/art/hum/soc sci (Engl Am Lit) (HL 44)

96 pts **Anglia Ruskin** – 96 pts (Phil Engl Lit) (IB 24 pts); 96 pts +interview +audition (Dr Engl Lit) (IB 24 pts); 96 pts incl Engl (Writ Engl Lit) (IB 24 pts)

Bath Spa – CCC incl Engl (Engl Lit) (IB 26 pts HL 5 Engl)

Bishop Grosseteste – 96–112 pts (Engl courses)

Brighton – BCC–CCC 96–104 pts (Hist Lit Cult) (IB 26 pts); BCC–CCC incl Engl 96–104 pts (Engl Lit; Media Engl Lit) (IB 26 pts)

Portsmouth – 96–112 pts incl Engl (Engl Lit)

York St John – 96 pts (Crea Writ; Engl Lit)

72 pts **UHI** – BC incl Engl (Lit)

Alternative offers

See **Chapter 6** and **Appendix 1** for grades/UCAS Tariff points information for other examinations.

CHOOSING YOUR COURSE (SEE ALSO CH.1)

Universities and colleges teaching quality See www.qaa.ac.uk; https://unistats.ac.uk.

Top research universities and colleges (REF 2014) See **English**.

Examples of sandwich degree courses Bangor.

ADMISSIONS INFORMATION

Number of applicants per place (approx) Bangor 4; East Anglia 5; Essex 4.

Advice to applicants and planning the UCAS personal statement See **English**. **Kent** An interest in literatures other than English.

Interview advice and questions See **English**. See also **Chapter 5**. **Kent** Which book would you take on a desert island, and why? What is the point of doing a Literature degree in the 21st century?

AFTER-RESULTS ADVICE

GRADUATE DESTINATIONS AND EMPLOYMENT (2016/17 HESA)

Graduates surveyed See **English**.

Career note Students enter a wide range of careers, with information management and editorial work in publishing offering some interesting and useful outlets. See also **English**, **Linguistics** and **Celtic, Irish, Scottish and Welsh Studies**.

MARINE/MARITIME STUDIES

(including Marine Biology, Naval Architecture, Marine Geography and Oceanography; see also Environmental Sciences)

A wide range of courses come under this category. These include Marine Business; Marine Law (world shipping, transport of goods, shipbroking, salvage rights, piracy); Marine Technology (marine engineering/nautical design); Marine Technology Offshore Engineering (marine structures, oil rigs, offshore engineering); Navigation Marine Science (merchant navy, yachts, superyachts); Naval

Architecture with High Performance Crafts (design, construction, operation, large and small vessels, hydrofoils, hovercrafts); Shipping Port Management (international shipping, shipbroking, ship agency work) and Yacht and Powercraft Design (powerboats, yachts, superyachts). Other scientific courses cover marine applications with biology, chemistry, freshwater biology and geography.

Useful websites www.ukchamberofshipping.com; http://uksa.org; www.rya.org.uk; www.royalnavy. mod.uk; www.sstg.org; www.noc.ac.uk; www.nautinst.org; www.mcsuk.org; www.nmm-stena.com; www.imo.org; www.gov.uk/government/organisations/maritime-and-coastguard-agency; www.gov.uk/ government/organisations/centre-for-environment-fisheries-and-aquaculture-science; www.mba.ac.uk

NB The points totals shown to the left of the institutions are for ease of reference only. It must not be assumed that Tariff points are always used by institutions or that they can be substituted for an offer in grades. The level of an offer is not necessarily indicative of the quality of a course.

COURSE OFFERS INFORMATION
Subject requirements/preferences GCSE Mathematics and science are required for several courses. **AL** Science or mathematics will be required or preferred for some courses.

Your target offers and examples of degree courses

144 pts **Southampton** – AAA–AAB +aEPQ incl maths+phys/chem/fmaths (Ship Sci (MEng)) (IB 36 pts HL 18 pts incl 6 maths+phys/chem/fmaths)

136 pts **East Anglia** – AAB incl maths (Meteor Ocean (Yr Abrd)) (IB 32 pts HL 5 maths)
Glasgow – AAB incl biol/chem 136 pts (Mar Fishwtr Biol) (IB 36 pts HL 665 incl biol/chem+sci)
Newcastle – AAB incl maths+phys/chem/fmaths (Mar Tech Mar Eng (MEng)) (IB 34 pts HL 6 maths+phys/chem); (Mar Tech Off Eng (MEng); Mar Tech Sml Crft Tech (MEng)) (IB 34 pts HL 6 maths+phys/chem)
Southampton – AAB incl sci/maths/geog +interview (Ocean Fr (MSci)) (IB 34 pts HL 17 pts incl 6 sci/maths/geog); AAB–ABB +aEPQ incl maths+phys/chem/fmaths (Ship Sci) (IB 34 pts HL 17 pts incl 6 maths+phys/chem/fmaths)
St Andrews – AAB incl biol+sci/maths (Mar Biol) (IB 36 pts HL 665 incl biol+sci/maths)

128 pts **Bangor** – B biol+sci 128 pts incl biol (App Mar Biol) (HL 6 biol+sci)
East Anglia – ABB incl maths (Meteor Ocean (MSci)) (IB 32 pts HL 5 maths)
Liverpool – ABB incl biol+sci/maths/geog (Mar Biol Ocean) (IB 33 pts HL 5 biol+sci); ABB incl maths/sci (Ocn Sci) (IB 33 pts HL 5 maths/sci)
Liverpool John Moores – ABB incl maths+sci/tech/eng 128 pts (Mar Mech Eng (MEng)) (HL 6 maths+phys)
Newcastle – ABB incl maths+phys/chem/fmaths (Mar Tech Mar Eng; Mar Tech Sml Crft Tech) (IB 32 pts HL 5 maths+phys/chem)
Southampton – ABB incl biol+sci/maths/geog (Mar Biol) (IB 32 pts HL 16 pts incl 5 biol+sci/ maths/geog); ABB incl biol+sci/maths/geog +interview (Mar Biol Ocean) (IB 32 pts HL 16 pts incl 6 biol+sci/maths/geog); ABB incl geog/sci/maths +interview (Ocean Physl Geog) (IB 32 pts HL 16 pts incl 6 geog/sci/maths); ABB incl sci/maths/geog +interview (Ocean) (IB 32 pts HL 16 pts incl 5 sci)

120 pts **Aberdeen** – BBB incl maths/sci (Mar Biol) (IB 32 pts HL 5 maths/sci)
Bangor – 120 pts (App Trstl Mar Ecol)
East Anglia – BBB/ABC incl maths (Meteor Ocean) (IB 31 pts HL 5 maths)
Hull – BBB incl biol/app sci 120 pts (Mar Biol) (IB 30 pts HL 5 biol)
Newcastle – ABB–BBB incl biol+sci+interview (Mar Biol) (IB 32 pts HL 6 biol)
Plymouth – 120–144 pts incl biol (Mar Biol Cstl Ecol) (IB 36–30 pts HL biol); 120–144 pts incl biol+sci (Mar Biol Ocean) (IB 36–30 pts)
Queen's Belfast – ABB–BBB incl biol (Mar Biol) (IB 33–32 pts HL 655 incl biol)
Stirling – BBB incl sci/maths (Mar Biol) (IB 32 pts)
Strathclyde – ABB–BBB incl maths+phys (Nvl Archit Hi Perf Mar Veh; Nvl Archit Mar Eng; Nvl Archit Ocn Eng) (IB 32 pts HL 5 maths+phys)

112 pts **Anglia Ruskin** – 112 pts incl biol (Mar Biol Biodiv Cons) (IB 24 pts)
Bangor – BB sci/maths/geog 112 pts incl sci/maths/geog (Geol Ocean) (HL 6 sci)

Cardiff – ABB–BBC incl sci (Mar Geog (MSci)) (IB 34-30 pts HL 665-655); (Mar Geog) (IB 34-30 pts HL 665-655 incl sci)

Heriot-Watt – BBC incl sci (Mar Biol) (IB 27 pts HL 5 sci)

Liverpool John Moores – BBC 112 pts (Marit Bus Mgt) (IB 26 pts); BBC incl maths+phys/eng/tech 112 pts (Mar Mech Eng) (IB 26 pts HL 5 maths+phys)

Plymouth – 112-128 pts incl sci/maths/geog/psy/des tech (Ocn Explor Surv) (IB 28-26 pts)

Portsmouth – 112 pts incl biol (Mar Biol) (IB 27 pts HL 6 biol)

104 pts **Aberystwyth** – BBB–BCC incl biol 104-120 pts (Mar Frshwtr Biol) (IB 30-28 pts HL 5 biol)

Bangor – BB sci/maths/geog 104 pts (Ocn Sci) (HL 6 sci); BC geog/sci/maths 104 pts (Physl Geog Ocean); BC sci/geog/maths/econ/psy 104 pts incl sci (Mar Env St) (HL 5 sci)

Edinburgh Napier – BCC incl sci (Mar Frshwtr Biol) (IB 28 pts HL 654 incl 5 sci)

Falmouth – 104-120 pts +portfolio +interview (Mar Nat Hist Photo)

Plymouth – C maths+sci/tech 104-120 pts (Mar Tech) (IB 30-28 pts HL 5 maths+sci/tech)

Portsmouth – 104-120 pts incl sci/maths/geog (Mar Env Sci) (IB 26 pts HL 5 sci/maths/geog)

UHI – BCC incl sci (Mar Sci)

96 pts **Plymouth** – 96-112 pts (Marit Bus Log; Marit Bus Marit Law) (IB 28 pts HL 4)

Solent – 96-112 pts (Marit Bus; Ship Pt Mgt; Ycht Des Prod)

80 pts **Plymouth** – 80-112 pts incl sci (Navig Marit Sci) (IB 26 pts HL 4 sci)

32 pts **Plymouth** – 32-80 pts (Marit Bus Log Fdn Yr) (IB 25-24 pts HL 4)

Alternative offers
See **Chapter 6** and **Appendix 1** for grades/UCAS Tariff points information for other examinations.

EXAMPLES OF COLLEGES OFFERING COURSES IN THIS SUBJECT FIELD
Blackpool and Fylde (Coll); Cornwall (Coll); Plymouth City (Coll); South Devon (Coll); Southampton City (Coll); Sparsholt (Coll).

CHOOSING YOUR COURSE (SEE ALSO CH.1)
Universities and colleges teaching quality See www.qaa.ac.uk; https://unistats.ac.uk.

Examples of sandwich degree courses Anglia Ruskin; Bangor; Cardiff; Essex; Liverpool John Moores; Portsmouth; Solent.

ADMISSIONS INFORMATION
Number of applicants per place (approx) Bangor 4; Glasgow 2; Liverpool John Moores (Marit St) 3; Southampton 3 (Intake 40-45).

Advice to applicants and planning the UCAS personal statement This is a specialised field and, in many cases, applicants will have experience of marine activities. Describe these experiences, for example, sailing, snorkelling, fishing. See also **Appendix 3.**

Selection interviews No Southampton, UHI.

Interview advice and questions Most applicants will have been stimulated by their studies in science or will have strong interests or connections with marine activities. They are likely to be questioned on their reasons for choosing the course. See also **Chapter 5.**

AFTER-RESULTS ADVICE
Offers to applicants repeating A-levels Same Bangor; Liverpool John Moores; Plymouth; UHI.

GRADUATE DESTINATIONS AND EMPLOYMENT (2016/17 HESA)
Maritime Technology graduates surveyed 210 **Employed** 135 **In voluntary employment** 10 **In further study** 35 **Assumed unemployed** 10

Career note This subject area covers a wide range of vocational courses, each offering graduates an equally wide choice of career openings in either purely scientific or very practical areas.

OTHER DEGREE SUBJECTS FOR CONSIDERATION

Biology; Civil Engineering; Environmental Studies/Sciences; Geography; Marine Engineering; Marine Transport; Naval Architecture; Oceanography.

MARKETING

(including **Public Relations**; see also **Business and Management Courses,**
Business and Management Courses (International And European),
Business and Management Courses (Specialised), Retail Management)

Marketing courses are very popular and applications should include evidence of work experience or work shadowing. While marketing is also a subject included in all Business Studies courses, specialist marketing courses are also available focusing on Advertising (also included in Marketing and Graphic Design courses), Agriculture, Consumer Behaviour, Design, Fashion, Food, Leisure, Retail and Sport.

Useful websites www.adassoc.org.uk; www.cim.co.uk; www.camfoundation.com; www.ipa.co.uk; www.ipsos.com/ipsos-mori; www.marketingtoday.com

NB The points totals shown to the left of the institutions are for ease of reference only. It must not be assumed that Tariff points are always used by institutions or that they can be substituted for an offer in grades. The level of an offer is not necessarily indicative of the quality of a course.

COURSE OFFERS INFORMATION

Subject requirements/preferences GCSE English and mathematics. **AL** No specified subjects required.

Your target offers and examples of degree courses

144 pts **Exeter** – AAA (Mark Mgt) (IB 36 pts HL 666)
Leeds – AAA (Bus Mgt Mark) (IB 35 pts HL 17 pts)

136 pts **Durham** – AAB (Mark Mgt) (IB 36 pts HL 665)
Lancaster – AAB (Adv Mark; Mark; Mark (St Abrd); Mark Des; Mark Mgt; Mark Mgt (St Abrd)) (IB 35 pts HL 16 pts)
Liverpool – AAB (Mark) (IB 35 pts)
Manchester – AAB (Mgt (Mark)) (IB 35 pts HL 665); AAB +interview (Fash Mgt) (IB 35 pts HL 665)
Newcastle – AAB (Mark; Mark Mgt) (IB 35 pts)
Southampton – AAB/ABB +aEPQ (Mark (Yr Ind)) (IB 34 pts HL 17 pts)
Ulster – AAA-AAB (Comm Adv Mark) (IB 29-28 pts HL 14 pts)

128 pts **Cardiff** – AAB-ABB (Bus Mgt (Mark)) (IB 34-32 pts HL 665-655)
Coventry – ABB (Mark) (IB 31 pts)
London (RH) – AAB-ABB (Mgt Mark) (IB 32 pts HL 655)
Loughborough – AAB-ABB (Mark Mgt) (IB 35-34 pts HL 665)
Northumbria – 128 pts (Mark Mgt)
Nottingham Trent – ABB 128 pts (Mark)
Sussex – AAB-ABB (Mark Mgt) (IB 34-32 pts)

120 pts **Bournemouth Arts** – BBB 120 pts +interview +portfolio (Fash Brnd Comm) (IB 30 pts)
Coventry – ABB-BBB (Adv Mark) (IB 31-30 pts)
Derby – 120 pts (Mark (PR Adv); Mark courses)
Essex – BBB (Mark; Mgt Mark) (IB 30 pts HL 555)
Heriot-Watt – BBB (Int Bus Mgt Mark) (IB 29 pts)
Huddersfield – BBB 120 pts (Adv Mark Comm; Mark; Mark PR)
Kent – BBB (Mark) (IB 34 pts HL 16 pts)
Northumbria – 120 pts (Bus Mark Mgt); 120 pts +portfolio (Fash Des Mark)
Nottingham Trent – BBB 120 pts (Fash Comm Prom; Fash Mark Brnd)
Oxford Brookes – BBB 120 pts (Bus Mark Mgt) (IB 31 pts)
Reading – BBB (Consum Bhv Mark; Fd Mark Bus Econ) (IB 30 pts)

Southampton (Winchester SA) – BBB (Fash Mark Mgt) (IB 30 pts HL 16 pts)
Stirling – BBB (Mark; Rtl Mark) (IB 32 pts)
Strathclyde – ABB–BBB (Mark courses) (IB 36 pts)
Swansea – ABB–BBB (Bus Mgt (Mark); Mark) (IB 33–32 pts)
Trinity Saint David – 120 pts +interview +portfolio (Crea Adv) (IB 32 pts)
Ulster – BBB (HR Mgt) (IB 26 pts HL 13 pts)

112 pts
Birmingham City – BBC 112 pts (Mark; Mark Adv PR) (IB 28 pts HL 14 pts)
Bradford – 112 pts (Mark)
Buckingham – BBB–BBC (Mark Media Comms) (IB 32–31 pts)
Cardiff Met – 112 pts (Mark Mgt)
Creative Arts – 112 pts +interview (Adv) (IB 30–27 pts HL 15 pts); 112 pts +portfolio (Fash Prom Imag) (IB 30–27 pts HL 15 pts)
De Montfort – 112 pts (Adv Mark Comms; Mark) (IB 26 pts)
East London – 112 pts (Mark) (IB 25 pts HL 15 pts); 112 pts +interview +portfolio (Fash Mark) (IB 25 pts HL 15 pts)
Edge Hill – BBB–BBC 112–120 pts (Mark; Mark Adv)
Greenwich – 112 pts (Adv Dig Mark Comm Lang; Adv Dig Mark Comms; Mark Mgt)
Hull – BBC 112 pts (Mark) (IB 28 pts)
Leeds Arts – BBC incl art/des 112 pts +portfolio (Crea Adv)
Leeds Beckett – 112 pts (Mark Adv Mgt; Mark Mgt) (IB 25 pts)
Lincoln – BBC 112 pts (Adv Mark; Bus Mark; Mark Mgt) (IB 29 pts)
Liverpool Hope – BBC 112 pts (Mark) (IB 28 pts)
Liverpool John Moores – BBC 112 pts (Mark) (IB 26-28 pts)
London Met – BBC 112 pts (Fash Mark Jrnl)
Manchester Met – BBC 112 pts +portfolio (Fash Prom) (IB 26 pts)
Middlesex – 112 pts (Mark) (IB -28 pts)
Portsmouth – 112–120 pts (Mark) (IB 29 pts HL 655/754–664)
Robert Gordon – BBC (Mgt Mark) (IB 29 pts)
Roehampton – 112 pts (Mark)
Sheffield Hallam – 112 pts (Mark Comms Adv); BBC 112 pts (Bus Mark; Mark)
Staffordshire – BBC 112 pts (Mark Mgt)
Sunderland – BBC 112 pts (Bus Mark Mgt); BBC 112 pts +interview +portfolio (Fash Des Prom)
Ulster – BBC (Mark) (IB 27–26 pts HL 13 pts)
West London – BBC 112 pts (Fash Brnd Mark)
Westminster – ABB–BBC (PR Adv) (IB 27 pts); ABB–BBC 112–128 pts (Mark Comms; Mark Mgt) (IB 27 pts); (Bus Mgt (Mark)) (IB 27 pts HL 4 Engl)
Winchester – 112–120 pts (Mark)
Worcester – 112 pts (Mark Adv PR)

104 pts
Anglia Ruskin – BCC 104 pts (Bus Mark) (IB 24 pts)
Aston – BBB–BCC (Mark) (IB 32 pts HL 665–655)
Bournemouth – 104–120 pts (Mark; Mark Comm) (IB 31–28 pts)
Central Lancashire – 104–112 pts (Bus Mark)
Chester – BBC–BCC 104–112 pts (Mark Mgt) (IB 26 pts)
De Montfort – 104 pts (Int Mark Bus) (IB 24 pts)
Falmouth – 104–120 pts +interview (Crea Adv)
Glasgow Caledonian – BCC (Int Mark) (IB 25 pts)
London South Bank – BCC (Bus Mgt Mark; Mark)
Manchester Met – BBC–BCC 104–112 pts (Mark; Spo Mark Mgt) (IB 26 pts)
Northampton – BCC (Adv Comb Hons; Evnts Mgt Comb Hons; Fash Mark; Mark Comb Hons; Psy Mark Comb Hons)
Queen Margaret – BCC incl Engl/media (PR Mark Comms) (IB 28 pts)
Robert Gordon – BCC (Dig Mark) (IB 27 pts)
Winchester – 104–120 pts (Media Comm Adv) (HL 44)

96 pts
Abertay – CCC (Mark Bus) (IB 28 pts)
Aberystwyth – BBB–CCC 96–120 pts (Mark) (IB 30–26 pts)

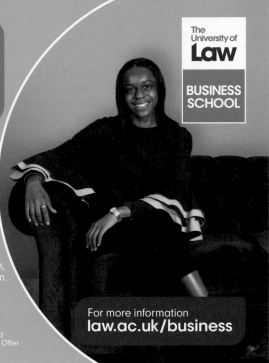
Bath Spa – CCC (Bus Mgt (Mark)) (IB 26 pts)
Birmingham (UC) – CCC 96 pts (Mark Mgt)
Brighton – BCC–CCC 96–104 pts (Mark Mgt) (IB 26 pts)
Bucks New – CC 96 pts (Ftbl Bus Mark) (IB 28 pts)
Chester – BCC–CCC 96–104 pts (Mark Adv Mgt) (IB 26 pts)
Chichester – BBC–CCC 96–112 pts (Mark) (IB 28 pts)
Edinburgh Napier – CCC (Mark Dig Media; Mark Mgt) (IB 27 pts HL 654)
Hertfordshire – CCC 96 pts (Mark Adv); (Mark) (HL 44)
Keele – CCC (Mark Comb Hons) (IB 26 pts)
London Met – CCC 96 pts (Adv Mark Comms PR); (Fash Mark Bus Mgt) (IB 28 pts HL 15 pts)
Plymouth – 96–112 pts (Mark) (IB 28–26 pts)
Plymouth (CA) – C art 96–120 pts +interview +portfolio (Fash Media Mark) (IB 30–28 pts)
Solent – 96–112 pts (Mark; Mark Adv; PR Comm)
St Mary's – BBC–BCC 96–112 pts (Comm Media Mark) (IB 28–24 pts)
Teesside – 96–112 pts +interview (Graph Des Mark)
Wolverhampton – CCC/BCD 96 pts (Mark Mgt)
York St John – 96 pts (Mark)
88 pts   **Canterbury Christ Church** – 88–112 pts (Adv; Mark)
Harper Adams – 88–104 pts (Bus Mgt Mark) (IB 28 pts)
Trinity Saint David – 88 pts +interview (Bus Mgt (Mark))
80 pts   **Bedfordshire** – 80–96 pts (Adv Mark Comms); CC 80 pts (Mark)
Bucks New – 80 pts (Mark)
South Wales – BCC–CDD 80–104 pts (Mark Mgt) (IB 29 pts); BCC–CDD 80–112 pts +interview +portfolio (Fash Mark Rtl Des); BCC–CDD incl art des 80–112 pts +interview +portfolio (Adv Des; Fash Prom)
Teesside – 80–104 pts (Mark)
72 pts   **Harper Adams** – 72–88 pts (Agri-Fd Mark Bus) (IB 24 pts)

64 pts **Ravensbourne Univ** – CC +interview +portfolio (Fash Prom) (IB 28 pts)
40 pts **Gloucestershire** – interview (Adv)

Alternative offers
See **Chapter 6** and **Appendix 1** for grades/UCAS Tariff points information for other examinations.

EXAMPLES OF COLLEGES OFFERING COURSES IN THIS SUBJECT FIELD

Arts London (CFash); Bath (Coll); Birmingham Met (Coll); Blackpool and Fylde (Coll); Bradford College UC; Croydon (Univ Centre); Doncaster (Coll); ESE; Kensington Bus (Coll); Leeds City (Coll); Loughborough (Coll); LSST; Manchester (Coll); Newcastle (Coll); Nottingham (Coll); Pearson (Coll); Petroc; Plymouth City (Coll); South City Birmingham (Coll); South Essex (Coll); TEC Partnership; Yeovil (Coll).

CHOOSING YOUR COURSE (SEE ALSO CH.1)

Universities and colleges teaching quality See www.qaa.ac.uk; https://unistats.ac.uk.

Examples of sandwich degree courses Aston; Bangor; Bath Spa; Bedfordshire; Birmingham City; Bournemouth; Bradford; Cardiff Met; Central Lancashire; Chester; Chichester; Coventry; De Montfort; Derby; Durham; Greenwich; Harper Adams; Hertfordshire; Huddersfield; Lancaster; Leeds Beckett; Liverpool John Moores; London (RH); London South Bank; Loughborough; Manchester Met; Newcastle; Northumbria; Nottingham Trent; Oxford Brookes; Plymouth; Portsmouth; Reading; Sheffield Hallam; Solent; Staffordshire; Sussex; Teesside; Trinity Saint David; Ulster; UWE Bristol; Westminster; Wolverhampton; Worcester.

ADMISSIONS INFORMATION

Number of applicants per place (approx) Abertay 3; Anglia Ruskin 5; Aston 9; Birmingham City 4; Central Lancashire 13; De Montfort 3; Derby 4; Harper Adams 3; Huddersfield 4; Lancaster 5; Lincoln 3; London Met 10; Manchester 7; Northampton 4; Nottingham Trent 2; Plymouth 7; Staffordshire 6; Stirling 13; Teesside 3.

Advice to applicants and planning the UCAS personal statement See **Business and Management Courses** and Appendix 3.

Misconceptions about this course Bournemouth These courses aren't just creative courses. We offer a range of Marketing options, with a focussed Marketing BSc and also a Marketing Communications degree which has pathways for specialisation in Advertising, Digital Media or Public Relations. Our Business Studies course also offers a Marketing Specialism.

Selection interviews Yes Buckingham; **No** Aberystwyth, Anglia Ruskin, Aston, De Montfort, Essex, Harper Adams, Manchester Met, Middlesex, Staffordshire.

Interview advice and questions Past questions include: What is marketing? Why do you want to take a Marketing degree? Is sales pressure justified? How would you feel if you had to market a product which you considered to be inferior? See also **Chapter 5. Buckingham** What job do you see yourself doing in five years' time?

Reasons for rejection (non-academic) Little thought of reasons for deciding on a Marketing degree. Weak on numeracy and problem solving. Limited commercial awareness. Poor interpersonal skills. Lack of leadership potential. No interest in widening their horizons, either geographically or intellectually. Limited understanding of the career. No clear reasons for wishing to do the course.

AFTER-RESULTS ADVICE

Offers to applicants repeating A-levels Same Abertay; Aberystwyth; Anglia Ruskin; Aston; Buckingham; De Montfort; Lincoln; Manchester Met; Queen Margaret; Staffordshire. GRADUATE DESTINATIONS AND EMPLOYMENT (2016/17 HESA) **Graduates surveyed** 3,285 **Employed** 2,320 **In voluntary employment** 100 **In further study** 325 **Assumed unemployed** 175

Career note See **Business and Management Courses**.

OTHER DEGREE SUBJECTS FOR CONSIDERATION

Advertising; Art and Design; Business courses; Communications; Graphic Design; Psychology; Public Relations.

MATERIALS SCIENCE/METALLURGY

Materials Science is a broad subject which covers physics, chemistry and engineering at one and the same time! From its origins in metallurgy, materials science has now moved into the processing, structure and properties of materials – ceramics, polymers, composites and electrical materials. Materials science and metallurgy are perhaps the most misunderstood of all careers and applications for degree courses are low with very reasonable offers. Valuable bursaries and scholarships are offered by the Institute of Materials, Minerals and Mining (check with Institute – see Appendix 3). Polymer science is a branch of materials science and is often studied in conjunction with chemistry. It covers such topics as polymer properties and processing relating to industrial applications with, for example, plastics, paints, adhesives. Other courses under this heading include Fashion and Leather Technology. See also **Appendix 3.**

Useful websites www.makeuk.org/uksteel; www.iom3.org; https://epsrc.ukri.org; www.imm.org; www.icme.org.uk

NB The points totals shown to the left of the institutions are for ease of reference only. It must not be assumed that Tariff points are always used by institutions or that they can be substituted for an offer in grades. The level of an offer is not necessarily indicative of the quality of a course.

COURSE OFFERS INFORMATION

Subject requirements/preferences GCSE (Eng/Sci courses) Science/mathematics subjects. **AL** Mathematics, physics and/or chemistry required for most courses. (Poly Sci) Mathematics and/or physics usually required; design technology encouraged.

Your target offers and examples of degree courses

160 pts **Cambridge** – A*A*A incl sci/maths +interview +NSAA (Nat Sci (Mat Sci)) (IB 42–40 pts HL 776)

152 pts **Loughborough** – A*AA incl maths+phys +interview (Auto Mat (MEng)) (IB 38 pts HL 766 incl maths+phys)

Oxford – A*AA incl maths+phys +interview +PAT (Mat Sci) (IB 40 pts HL 766 incl 7 maths/phys/chem)

Southampton – A*AA–A*AB +aEPQ incl maths+phys (Mech Eng (Mat) (MEng)) (IB 38 pts HL 18 pts incl 6 maths+phys)

144 pts **Birmingham** – AAA incl maths+phys/chem/des tech (Mat Sci Eng (MEng)) (IB 32 pts HL 666 incl maths+phys/chem/des tech)

Imperial London – AAA incl maths+phys/chem +interview (Biomat Tiss Eng (MEng)) (IB 38 pts HL 6 maths+phys+chem); (Mat Mgt; Mat Nucl Eng (MEng); Mat Sci Eng) (IB 38 pts HL 6 maths+phys/chem)

London (QM) – AAA incl maths/phys/chem (Dntl Mat (MEng); Mat Sci Eng (MEng) (Yr Ind)) (IB 36 pts HL 665 incl maths/phys/chem)

Loughborough – AAA incl maths/phys/chem +interview (Mat Sci Eng (MEng)) (IB 37 pts HL 666 incl maths/phys/chem)

Sheffield – AAA incl maths/phys/chem (Mat Sci Eng (MEng); Metal (MEng)) (IB 36 pts HL 6 maths/phys/chem); AAA–AAB +bEPQ incl sci/maths (Biomat Sci Eng (MEng)) (IB 36 pts HL 6 sci/maths)

St Andrews – AAA incl chem (Mat Chem) (IB 38 pts HL 666 incl chem+maths/sci)

136 pts **Birmingham** – AAB incl maths+phys (Nucl Sci Mat) (IB 32 pts HL 665 incl maths+phys); AAB incl maths+phys/chem/des tech (Metal) (IB 32 pts HL 665 incl maths+phys/chem/des tech)

Manchester – AAB incl maths/phys/chem +interview (Mat Sci Eng) (IB 35 pts HL 665 incl maths/phys/chem)

Sheffield – AAB incl maths/phys/chem (Mat Sci Eng) (IB 34 pts HL 6/5 maths/phys/chem); AAB incl sci/maths (Biomat Sci Eng) (IB 34 pts HL 6/5 sci/maths)

128 pts **Exeter** – AAB–ABB incl phys/chem+sci (Min Eng) (IB 34–32 pts HL 5 phys/chem/maths+sci)

London (QM) – ABB incl maths/phys/chem (Dntl Mat; Mat Sci Eng) (IB 32 pts HL 655 incl maths/phys/chem); ABB incl sci/maths/des tech (Mat Des) (IB 32 pts HL 655 incl sci/maths/des tech)

Loughborough – ABB incl maths+sci +interview (Biomat Eng) (IB 34 pts HL 655 incl maths+sci); ABB incl maths/phys/chem +interview (Auto Mat; Mat Sci Eng) (IB 34 pts HL 655 incl maths/phys/chem)

Swansea – AAB–ABB incl sci/maths (Mat Sci Eng (MEng)) (IB 34 pts)

120 pts **Strathclyde** – AAB–BBB incl maths+phys (Mech Eng Mat Eng (MEng)) (IB 36 pts HL 6 maths+phys)

Swansea – ABB–BBB incl sci/maths (Mat Sci Eng) (IB 32 pts)

112 pts **Heriot-Watt** – BBC incl chem+maths+phys (Chem Mat Nanosci) (IB 30 pts HL 5 chem+maths+phys)

Sheffield Hallam – BBC incl maths 112 pts (Mat Eng)

96 pts **Northampton** – CCC incl sci (Lea Tech)

Alternative offers
See **Chapter 6** and **Appendix 1** for grades/UCAS Tariff points information for other examinations.

EXAMPLES OF COLLEGES OFFERING COURSES IN THIS SUBJECT FIELD
Hereford (CA).

CHOOSING YOUR COURSE (SEE ALSO CH.1)
Universities and colleges teaching quality See www.qaa.ac.uk; https://unistats.ac.uk.

Top research universities and colleges (REF 2014) See **Engineering (Electrical and Electronic)**.

Examples of sandwich degree courses Exeter; London (QM); Loughborough; Sheffield Hallam; St Andrews.

ADMISSIONS INFORMATION
Number of applicants per place (approx) Birmingham 8; Imperial London 3; Southampton 8; Swansea 4.

Advice to applicants and planning the UCAS personal statement Read scientific and engineering journals and describe any special interests you have. Try to visit chemical or technological installations (rubber, plastics, glass, etc) and describe your visits. See also **Appendix 3.**
Selection interviews Yes Imperial London, Oxford (22%); **No** Birmingham.

Interview advice and questions Questions are likely to be based on AS/A-level science subjects. Recent examples include: Why did you choose Materials Science? How would you make each part of this table lamp (on the interviewer's desk)? Identify this piece of material. How was it manufactured? How has it been treated? (Questions related to metal and polymer samples.) What would you consider the major growth area in materials science? See also **Chapter 5. Oxford** Tutors look for an ability to apply logical reasoning to problems in physical science and an enthusiasm for thinking about new concepts in science and engineering.

AFTER-RESULTS ADVICE
Offers to applicants repeating A-levels Higher Swansea; **Same** Birmingham; **No** Cambridge.

GRADUATE DESTINATIONS AND EMPLOYMENT (2016/17 HESA)
Metallurgy graduates surveyed 125 **Employed** 80 **In voluntary employment** 5 **In further study** 35 **Assumed unemployed** 5

Career note Materials scientists are involved in a wide range of specialisms in which openings are likely in a range of industries. These include manufacturing processes in which the work is closely linked with that of mechanical, chemical, production and design engineers.

OTHER DEGREE SUBJECTS FOR CONSIDERATION

Aerospace Engineering; Biotechnology; Chemistry; Dentistry; Engineering Sciences; Mathematics; Mechanical Engineering; Medical Engineering; Plastics Technology; Physics; Product Design and Materials; Prosthetics and Orthotics; Sports Technology.

MATHEMATICS

(including **Mathematical Sciences**; see also **Economics, Statistics**)

Mathematics at degree level is an extension of A-level mathematics, covering pure and applied mathematics, statistics, computing, mathematical analysis and mathematical applications. Mathematics is of increasing importance and is used in the simplest of design procedures and not only in applications in the physical sciences and engineering. It also plays a key role in management, economics, medicine and the social and behavioural sciences.

Useful websites www.ima.org.uk; www.theorsociety.com; www.m-a.org.uk; www.mathscareers.org.uk; www.imo-official.org; http://bmos.ukmt.org.uk; http://maths.org; www.ukmt.org.uk

NB The points totals shown to the left of the institutions are for ease of reference only. It must not be assumed that Tariff points are always used by institutions or that they can be substituted for an offer in grades. The level of an offer is not necessarily indicative of the quality of a course.

COURSE OFFERS INFORMATION

Subject requirements/preferences GCSE English often required and mathematics is obviously essential at a high grade for leading universities. **AL** Mathematics, in several cases with a specified grade, required for all courses. Other Mathematics AEA or STEP papers may be required by some universities (eg Imperial, Warwick). See also **Chapter 4**. NB The level of an offer may depend on whether an applicant is taking AS/A-level further maths; check websites.

Your target offers and examples of degree courses

168 pts **Warwick** – A*A*A* incl maths+fmaths (Maths; Maths (MMath)) (IB 39 pts HL 766–666 incl maths)

160 pts **Cambridge** – A*A*A incl math s+interview +STEP (Maths) (IB 42–40 pts HL 776 incl maths); A*A*A incl maths+phys +interview +STEP (Maths Phys) (IB 42–40 pts HL 776 incl maths+phys)

Imperial London – A*A*A incl maths+fmaths +MAT/STEP (Maths; Maths Mathem Comp; Maths Optim Stats; Maths Stats; Maths Stats Fin; PMaths) (IB 39 pts HL 7 maths); A*A*A incl maths+fmaths +interview (Maths Comp Sci) (IB 40 pts HL 7 maths)

London (UCL) – A*A*A incl maths (Mathem Comput (MEng)) (IB 40 pts HL 7 maths)

Oxford – A*A*A incl maths +interview +MAT (Maths; Maths Phil; Maths Stats) (IB 39 pts HL 766 incl 7 maths)

St Andrews – A*A*A incl maths (Arbc Maths) (IB 38 pts HL 666 incl 6 maths); (App Maths; Maths; Maths Span; PMaths (MMath)) (IB 38 pts HL 666 incl maths)

Warwick – A*A*A incl maths+fmaths (Maths Comb Hons) (IB 39 pts HL 666 incl maths)

152 pts **Bath** – A*AA incl maths+fmaths (Mathem Sci) (IB 36 pts HL 766/765 incl 7/6 maths); A*AA-AAA +aEPQ incl maths+phys (Maths Phys) (IB 36 pts HL 766 incl maths+phys)

Bristol – A*A*A-A*AA incl maths+fmaths (Maths Comp Sci) (IB 40 pts HL 18 pts incl 7 maths); A*A*A-A*AA incl maths+fmaths/sci/econ/comp (Maths Stats) (IB 40 pts HL 18 pts incl 7 maths 6 sci/econ/comp); A*A*A-A*AA incl maths+fmaths/sci/econ/comp sci (Maths) (IB 40 pts HL 18 pts incl 7 maths 6 sci/econ/comp sci); A*AA incl maths (Maths Phil) (IB 38 pts HL 18 pts incl 7 maths)

Durham – A*A*A–A*AA incl maths+fmath s+TMUA (Maths) (IB 38 pts HL 776–766)

London (UCL) – A*A*A–A*AA incl maths+fmaths +STEP (Maths) (IB 39 pts HL 20–19 pts incl 7 maths)

London LSE – A*AA incl maths (Ecomet Mathem Econ; Maths Econ) (IB 38 pts HL 766 incl 7 maths)

Manchester – A*A*A–A*AA incl maths+phys +interview (Maths Phys) (IB 38–37 pts HL 776–766 incl maths+phys); A*AA incl maths (Comp Sci Maths) (IB 37 pts HL 766 incl 7 maths)

Warwick – A*A*A*–A*AA incl maths (MORSE) (IB 38 pts HL 7 maths); A*AA incl maths (Dscrt Maths) (IB 38 pts HL 666 incl maths); A*AA incl maths+fmaths (Maths Stats) (IB 38 pts HL7 maths)

144 pts **Birmingham** – AAA incl maths/fmaths (Maths; Maths Bus Mgt) (IB 32 pts HL 666 incl maths)

Bristol – AAA incl maths (Eng Maths) (IB 36 pts HL 18 pts incl 6 maths)

Glasgow – AAA/A*AB incl maths (Acc Maths) (IB 38 pts HL 666 incl Engl/maths)

London (King's) – AAA/A*AB incl maths+fmaths (Maths) (IB 35 pts HL 666/765 incl 6 maths); AAA incl maths+fmaths (Maths Phil) (IB 35 pts HL 666 incl maths)

London (QM) – AAA incl maths (Maths (MSci); Maths Stats Fin Econ) (IB 36 pts HL 666 incl maths)

London (UCL) – AAA incl maths+chem (Chem Maths) (IB 38 pts HL 18 pts incl 6 chem+maths)

Loughborough – AAA/A*AB incl maths (Maths; Maths Stats) (IB 37 pts HL 666 incl maths)

Manchester – A*AA–AAA incl maths (Act Sci Maths) (IB 36 pts HL 666 incl maths); A*AA–AAA incl maths +interview (Maths Fin Maths) (IB 36 pts HL 666 incl 6 maths); (Maths; Maths Fin; Maths Phil) (IB 36 pts HL 666 incl maths)

Newcastle – AAA/A*AB incl maths (Maths (MMath)) (IB 36 pts HL 6 maths)

Nottingham – A*AA–AAA/A*AB incl maths (Fin Maths; Maths) (IB 36 pts HL 6 maths); A*AA–AAA incl maths+phys (Mathem Phys) (IB 38 pts HL 6 maths+phys)

Queen's Belfast – AAA/A*AB incl maths (Maths (MSci); Maths Comp Sci (MSci); Maths Stats OR (MSci)) (IB 36 pts HL 666 incl maths); AAA/A*AB incl maths+phys (App Maths Phys (MSci)) (IB 36 pts HL 666 incl maths+phys)

Sheffield – AAA/AAB +aEPQ incl maths (Maths (MMath)) (IB 36 pts HL 6 maths)

Southampton – AAA incl maths (Maths; Maths (MMath); Maths Comp Sci; Maths Fin; Maths Stats) (IB 36 pts HL 18 pts incl 6 maths); (Maths Act Sci) (IB 36 pts HL18 pts incl 6 maths); AAA incl maths+Fr/Ger/Span (Maths Fr/Ger/Span) (IB 36 pts HL 18 pts incl 6 maths+Fr/Ger/Span); AAA incl maths+phys (Mathem Phys (MMath)) (IB 36 pts HL 18 pts incl 6 maths+phys); AAA–AAB +aEPQ incl maths (Maths OR Stats Econ (MORSE)) (IB 36 pts HL 18 pts incl 6 maths)

St Andrews – A*AB incl maths (Maths Langs) (IB 36 pts HL 655 incl 6 maths)

Sussex – AAA incl maths+fmaths (Maths (MMath)) (IB 36 pts HL 6 maths)

Swansea – AAA incl maths (Maths (MMath)) (IB 36 pts HL 6 maths)

York – AAA incl maths (Econ Maths; Maths; Maths Fin; Maths Stats) (IB 36 pts HL 6 maths)

136 pts **City** – AAB incl maths/fmaths 136 pts (Maths Fin) (IB 34 pts HL 6 maths)

Edinburgh – A*AA–AAB incl maths (Maths Stats) (IB 37–32 pts HL 666–655 incl 6 maths); (App Maths; Maths; Maths (MA); Maths Mgt; Maths Mus) (IB 37–32 pts HL 666–655 incl maths)

Exeter – AAA–AAB incl maths (Maths; Maths Acc; Maths Econ; Maths Fin; Maths Mgt) (IB 36–34 pts HL 666–665 incl 6 maths); AAA–AAB incl maths+phys +interview (Maths Phys) (IB 36–34 pts HL 666–665 incl 6 maths 5 phys)

Glasgow – AAB incl maths (Maths) (IB 36 pts HL 665 incl 6 sci)

Lancaster – AAA–AAB incl maths/fmaths (Maths OR Stats Econ (MORSE)) (IB 35 pts HL 16 pts incl 6 maths); (Fin Maths; Maths; Maths Phil; Maths Stats) (IB 36 pts HL 16 pts incl 6 maths); AAB incl maths (Acc Fin Maths) (IB 35 pts HL 16 pts incl 6 maths); AAB incl phys+maths +interview (Theor Phys Maths) (IB 35 pts HL 16 pts incl 6 maths+phys)

Leeds – AAA/A*AB–AAB/A*BB incl maths (Fin Maths; Maths; Maths Stats) (IB 35 pts HL 17 pts incl 6 maths); AAA–A*AB incl maths/AAB–A*BB incl maths+fmaths (Act Maths) (IB 35 pts HL 17 pts incl 6 maths)

Liverpool – AAB/ABB +aEPQ incl maths+phys (Mathem Phys (MMath)) (IB 35 pts HL 6 maths+phys); AAB incl maths (Maths Fin) (IB 35 pts HL 6 maths)

London (QM) – AAB incl maths (Maths; Maths Fin Acc; Maths Stats) (IB 34 pts HL 665 incl maths)

Newcastle – AAB/A*BB incl maths (Maths; Maths Stats) (IB 34 pts HL 6 maths); AAB-A*BB incl maths (Maths Fin) (IB 34 pts HL 6 maths)

Nottingham – AAA-AAB incl comp (Comp Sci) (IB 34 pts)

Queen's Belfast – AAB/A*BB incl maths (Maths; Maths Stats OR) (IB 34 pts HL 665 incl maths); AAB/A*BB incl maths+lang (Maths Ext St Euro) (IB 33 pts HL 655 incl maths+lang); AAB/A*BB incl maths+phys (App Maths Phys) (IB 34 pts HL 665 incl maths+phys)

Sheffield – AAB/ABB +bEPQ incl maths (Maths; Maths Comb Hons) (IB 34 pts HL 6 maths); AAB incl maths (Fin Maths) (IB 34 pts HL 6 maths)

Southampton – AAA-AAB incl maths/fmaths+phys (Phys Maths (MPhys)) (IB 36-34 pts HL 18-17 pts incl 6 maths/fmaths+phys); AAB-ABB +aEPQ incl maths (Phil Maths) (IB 34-32 pts HL 17-16 pts incl 6 maths)

York – AAB incl maths+phys +interview (Maths Phys) (IB 35 pts HL 6 maths+phys)

128 pts **Brunel** – ABB incl maths/fmaths (Fin Maths (MMath)) (IB 31 pts HL 6 maths)

Cardiff – AAB-ABB incl maths (Maths) (IB 36-34 pts HL 6 maths); (Maths OR Stats) (IB 36-34 pts HL 666-655 incl maths)

City – ABB incl maths/fmaths 128 pts (Maths) (IB 33 pts HL 6 maths)

East Anglia – AAB-ABB incl maths (Maths (MMath)) (IB 33 pts HL 6 maths); ABB incl maths (Maths) (IB 32 pts HL 6 maths)

Edinburgh – AAA-ABB incl maths+phys (Mathem Phys) (IB 37-32 pts HL 666-655 incl 6 maths+phys)

Leicester – ABB/BBB +bEPQ incl maths (Maths) (IB 30 pts HL 5 maths)

Liverpool – ABB/BBB +aEPQ incl maths (Maths; Maths Econ; Maths Stats) (IB 33 pts HL 6 maths); ABB incl maths (Maths Bus St; Maths Langs) (IB 33 pts HL 6 maths)

London (RH) – AAB-ABB incl maths (Econ Maths; Maths; Maths Stats) (IB 32 pts HL 655 incl 6 maths)

Loughborough – ABB incl maths+phys (Phys Maths) (IB 34 pts HL 655 incl maths+phys)

Portsmouth – 128-144 pts incl maths (Maths (MMath)) (IB 28-27 pts HL 6 maths)

Queen's Belfast – ABB incl maths (Maths Comp Sci)

Surrey – AAB-ABB incl maths (Maths (MMath)) (IB 34 pts HL 6 maths); (Fin Maths; Maths Stats) (IB 34-32 pts HL 6 maths); ABB incl maths (Maths courses) (IB 32 pts HL 6 maths)

Sussex – AAB-ABB incl maths (Maths Econ; Maths courses) (IB 34-32 pts HL 5 maths)

Swansea – AAB-ABB incl maths (Maths) (IB 34-32 pts HL 6 maths)

120 pts **Aberdeen** – BBB incl maths+sci (App Maths; Maths) (IB 32 pts HL 555 incl maths+sci)

Brunel – BBB incl maths/fmaths (Maths; Maths Comp Sci; Maths Stats Mgt) (IB 30 pts HL 5 maths)

Central Lancashire – 120 pts incl maths (Maths) (HL 6 maths)

Coventry – ABB-BBB incl maths (Maths courses) (IB 29 pts HL 5 maths)

Derby – BBB incl maths 120 pts (Maths Comp Sci); C maths 120 pts (Maths)

Dundee – BBB incl maths (Maths) (IB 30 pts HL 555)

Essex – BBB incl maths (Maths) (IB 30 pts HL 555 incl maths)

Heriot-Watt – BBB incl maths (Maths; Maths Comb Hons; Maths Stats) (IB 28 pts HL 5 maths); BBB incl maths+Span (Maths Span) (IB 28 pts HL 5 maths+Span)

Huddersfield – BBB incl maths 120 pts (Maths)

Kent – ABC incl maths (Fin Maths; Maths) (IB 34 pts HL 16 pts incl 6 maths)

Northumbria – B maths 120 pts (Maths)

Nottingham Trent – 120 pts incl maths (Maths)

Reading – ABC incl A maths (Maths; Maths Stats) (IB 30 pts HL 6 maths); ABC incl maths (Maths Meteor) (IB 30 pts HL 6 maths)

South Wales – BBB incl maths +interview (Maths) (IB 29 pts HL 6 maths)

Stirling – BBB incl maths (App Maths) (IB 32 pts)

Strathclyde – ABB-BBB (Maths Stats Econ) (IB 32 pts HL 6 maths); ABB-BBB incl maths (Maths courses) (IB 32 pts HL 6 maths)

UWE Bristol – B maths 120 pts (Maths) (HL 6 maths)

112 pts **Chester** – BBC–BCC 112 pts (Maths) (IB 26 pts HL 5 maths)
Coventry – BBB–BBC (Maths Stats) (IB 29 pts HL 5 maths)
De Montfort – 112 pts incl maths (Maths) (IB 26 pts HL 6 maths)
Hertfordshire – BBC incl maths 112 pts (Fin Maths; Maths) (HL 4 maths)
Hull – BBC incl maths 112 pts (Maths) (IB 28 pts HL 6 maths)
Keele – B maths 112 pts (Maths) (IB 30 pts HL 5 maths)
Kingston – C maths 112 pts (Maths)
Liverpool Hope – BBC 112 pts (Maths) (IB 28 pts)
Liverpool John Moores – BBC incl maths 112 pts (Maths; Maths Fin) (IB 26 pts)
London (Birk) – ABB–BBC incl B maths 112–128 pts (Maths Stats)
Nottingham Trent – 112 pts incl maths (Spo Sci Maths)
Oxford Brookes – BBC 112 pts (Maths courses) (IB 30 pts HL 5 maths)
Plymouth – 112–128 pts incl maths (Maths Fin) (IB 30 pts HL 5 maths)
Portsmouth – 112–128 pts incl maths (Maths; Maths Fin Mgt; Maths Stats) (IB 26–25 pts)
Sheffield Hallam – BBC incl maths 112 pts (Maths)
West London – BBC 112–120 pts (Maths Stats)

104 pts **Aberystwyth** – BBB–BCC incl B maths 104–120 pts (App Maths PMaths; App Maths Stats; Maths) (IB 30–28 pts HL 5 maths)
Aston – BBB–BCC incl B maths (Maths; Maths Comb Hons) (IB 31 pts HL 555 incl maths)
Bolton – 104 pts incl maths (Maths S Educ)
Canterbury Christ Church – 104–112 pts incl maths (Maths S Educ QTS)
Dundee – BBB–BCC incl maths+sci (Mathem Biol) (IB 30 pts HL 555 incl maths+sci)
Greenwich – BCC 104 pts (Maths); BCC 104 pts+interview (Maths Comp); BCC incl maths 104 pts (Fin Maths)
Kent – B maths 104–112 pts (Maths S Educ) (IB 24 pts)
Manchester Met – BBC–BCC incl maths 104–112 pts (Maths) (IB 26 pts HL 5 maths)
Winchester – 104–120 pts incl maths (Maths; Maths Fin) (HL 44)

96 pts **Bishop Grosseteste** – D maths 96–112 pts (Spo Maths)
Brighton – BBC–CCC incl maths 96–112 pts (Maths) (IB 26 pts HL 5 maths); (Maths Bus; Maths Fin) (IB 26 pts HL 6 maths)
Wolverhampton – BCD incl B maths 96 pts (Maths)
Worcester – 96 pts incl maths (Maths Comp Sci)

80 pts **Bedfordshire** – CC 80 pts (Comp Maths)
London Met – CCE incl maths (Maths)

72 pts **London Met** – CDE/BC 72 pts (Mathem Sci)

Open University – contact 0300 303 0073 or www.open.ac.uk/contact/new (Maths)

Alternative offers
See **Chapter 6** and **Appendix 1** for grades/UCAS Tariff points information for other examinations.

EXAMPLES OF COLLEGES OFFERING COURSES IN THIS SUBJECT FIELD
Accrington and Rossendale (Coll); Bournemouth and Poole (Coll); Bradford College UC; Bury (Coll).

CHOOSING YOUR COURSE (SEE ALSO CH.1)
Universities and colleges teaching quality See www.qaa.ac.uk; https://unistats.ac.uk.

Top research universities and colleges (REF 2014) (Mathematical Sciences) Oxford; Cardiff; Sheffield; Glasgow; Bath; Newcastle; Nottingham; Dundee; Cambridge; Warwick; Imperial London; Lancaster; London (RH); St Andrews; Manchester.

Examples of sandwich degree courses Aston; Bath; Brighton; Brunel; Cardiff; Coventry; East Anglia; Greenwich; Hertfordshire; Kent; Kingston; Lancaster; Liverpool; Liverpool John Moores; London (QM); Loughborough; Northumbria; Nottingham Trent; Plymouth; Portsmouth; Reading; Surrey; UWE Bristol; Wolverhampton; York.

ADMISSIONS INFORMATION

Number of applicants per place (approx) Aston 8; Bath 7; Birmingham 6; Bristol 8; Cambridge 5; Cardiff 5; Central Lancashire 7; City 5; Derby 5; Dundee 8; Durham 6; East Anglia 5; Edinburgh 13; Exeter 6; Greenwich 2; Heriot-Watt 6; Hertfordshire 9; Lancaster 6; Leeds (Maths) 5, (Maths Fin) 4; Leicester 6; Liverpool 6; London (King's) 8; London (QM) 5; London (RH) 7; London (UCL) 8; London LSE 8; London Met 3; Manchester Met 3; Newcastle 5; Nottingham Trent 7; Oxford Brookes 6; Plymouth 10; Sheffield 6; Sheffield Hallam 3; Southampton 10; Stirling 6; Strathclyde 6; Warwick 6; York 6.

Admissions tutors' advice Leeds Applicants taking the BTEC Extended Diploma may be required to take an additional Maths A-level paper.

Advice to applicants and planning the UCAS personal statement Any interests you have in careers requiring mathematical ability could be mentioned, for example, engineering, computers (hardware and software) and business applications. Show determination, love of mathematics and an appreciation of the rigour of the course. Give details of your skills, work experience, positions of responsibility. A variety of non-academic interests to complement the applicant's academic abilities preferred. For non-UK students, fluency in oral and written English required. **Manchester** Unit grades may form part of an offer. **Warwick** Offers for courses in Statistics (eg MORSE) include achievement requirements in STEP and other requirements. Check University website for latest information. See also **Appendix 3.**

Misconceptions about this course London (QM) Some believe that a study of mechanics is compulsory – it is not. **York** Further maths is not required.

Selection interviews Yes Cambridge, Manchester, Oxford ((Maths) 15%, (Maths Phil) 14%, (Maths Stats) 7%); **Some** Bath, Cardiff, London (UCL), Warwick, York; **No** Aberystwyth, Birmingham, Bishop Grosseteste, Brighton, Bristol, Central Lancashire, City, Coventry, Dundee, East Anglia, Essex, Greenwich, Heriot-Watt, Imperial London, Kent, Kingston, Leeds, Liverpool, Liverpool John Moores, London (King's), London (RH), London LSE, London Met, Loughborough, Manchester Met, Newcastle, Nottingham, Reading, Sheffield, Southampton, UWE Bristol.

Interview advice and questions Questions are likely to be asked arising from the information you have given in your UCAS application and about your interests in the subject. Questions in recent years have included: How many ways are there of incorrectly setting up the back row of a chess board? A ladder on a rough floor leans against a smooth wall. Describe the forces acting on the ladder and give the maximum possible angle of inclination possible. There are three particles connected by a string; the middle one is made to move – describe the subsequent motion of the particles. What mathematics books have you read outside your syllabus? Why does a ball bounce? Discuss the work of any renowned mathematician. Balance a pencil on your index fingers and then try to move both towards the centre of the pencil. Explain what is happening in terms of forces and friction. See also **Chapter 5. Cambridge** If you could spend half an hour with any mathematician past or present, who would it be? **Oxford** What makes you think I'm having thoughts? What was the most beautiful proof in A-level mathematics? I am an oil baron in the desert and I need to deliver oil to four different towns which happen to lie in a straight line. In order to deliver the correct amount to each town I must visit each town in turn, returning to my warehouse in between each visit. Where would I position my warehouse in order to drive the shortest possible distance? Roads are no problem since I have a friend who will build me as many roads as I like for free. **Southampton** Personal statements generate discussion points. Our interviews are informal chats and so technical probing is kept low key.

Reasons for rejection (non-academic) Usually academic reasons only. Lack of motivation. Uneasiness about how much mathematics will be remembered after a gap year. **Birmingham** A poorly written and poorly organised personal statement.

AFTER-RESULTS ADVICE

Offers to applicants repeating A-levels Higher Brighton; London Met; Strathclyde; Swansea; Warwick; **Possibly higher** Durham; Lancaster; Leeds; Newcastle; Sheffield; **Same** Aberystwyth; Aston;

Bath; Birmingham; Bristol; Brunel; Chester; Coventry; East Anglia; Essex; Liverpool; Liverpool Hope; London (RH); Loughborough (usually); Manchester Met; Nottingham; Nottingham Trent; Sheffield Hallam; Southampton; Stirling; Wolverhampton; York; **No** Cambridge (Hom); Glasgow.

GRADUATE DESTINATIONS AND EMPLOYMENT (2016/17 HESA)
Graduates surveyed 5,380 **Employed** 2,605 **In voluntary employment** 115 **In further study** 1,605 **Assumed unemployed** 405

Career note Graduates enter a range of careers. While business, finance and retail areas are popular options, mathematicians also have important roles in the manufacturing industries. Mathematics offers the pleasure of problem-solving, the satisfaction of a rigorous argument and the most widely employable non-vocational degree subject. A student's view: 'Maths trains you to work in the abstract, to think creatively and to come up with concrete conclusions.' These transferable skills are much sought-after by employers. Employment prospects are excellent, with high salaries.

OTHER DEGREE SUBJECTS FOR CONSIDERATION
Accountancy; Actuarial Studies; Astronomy; Astrophysics; Computer Science; Economics; Engineering Sciences; Operational Research; Physics; Statistics.

MEDIA STUDIES

(including **Broadcast Media Technologies**; see also **Art and Design (General),
Communication Studies/Communication, Computer Science and Information Technology,
Engineering (Acoustics and Sound), Film, Radio, Video And TV Studies,
Information Management and Librarianship, Journalism, Photography**)

Intending Media applicants need to check course details carefully since this subject area can involve graphic design, illustration and other art courses as well as the media in the fields of TV, radio and journalism.

Useful websites www.bbc.co.uk/careers; www.newsmediauk.org; www.ppa.co.uk; www.thomsonreuters.com/en/careers.html; www.nctj.com; https://ipa.co.uk; www.camfoundation.com; www.mediastudies.com

NB The points totals shown to the left of the institutions are for ease of reference only. It must not be assumed that Tariff points are always used by institutions or that they can be substituted for an offer in grades. The level of an offer is not necessarily indicative of the quality of a course.

COURSE OFFERS INFORMATION
Subject requirements/preferences GCSE English and mathematics often required. **AL** No specified subjects required.

Your target offers and examples of degree courses
136 pts **Leeds** – AAB (Comm Media) (IB 35 pts HL 16 pts incl 5 Engl)
        Newcastle – AAB (Jrnl Media Cult; Media Comm Cult St) (IB 34 pts)
        York – AAB +interview (Interact Media) (IB 35 pts)
128 pts **Cardiff** – ABB (Jrnl Media Sociol) (HL 17 pts)
        East Anglia – ABB (Media Int Dev) (IB 32 pts)
        Lancaster – ABB (Media Cult St) (IB 32 pts HL 16 pts)
        Leicester – ABB/BBB +bEPQ (Media Soty) (IB 30 pts); ABB–BBB+bEPQ (Media Comm) (IB 30 pts)
        Liverpool – ABB/BBB +aEPQ (Comm Media) (IB 33 pts)
        Loughborough – ABB (Media Comm) (IB 34 pts HL 655)
        Nottingham – ABB (Int Media Comm St; Span Int Media Comms St) (IB 32 pts)
120 pts **Brunel** – BBB incl art/tech +portfolio (Vis Efcts Mtn Graph) (IB 30 pts HL 5 art/tech)
        East Anglia – BBB/ABC (Media St; Transl Media Modn Langs) (IB 31 pts)

Kent – BBB (Media St; Multim Tech Des) (IB 34 pts HL 15 pts)
Leicester – BBB–BBC +bEPQ (Flm Media St) (IB 28 pts)
London (Gold) – BBB (Media Comms) (IB 33 pts HL 655)
Northumbria – 120 pts (Media Jrnl)
Oxford Brookes – BBB 120 pts (Media Jrnl Pub) (IB 31 pts)
Surrey – BBB 120 pts (Media Comm) (IB 32 pts)
Swansea – BBB 120 pts (Media courses) (IB 32 pts)

112 pts   **Arts London (CFash)** – 112 pts +interview +portfolio (Fash Jrnl)
Birmingham City – BBC 112 pts (Jrnl) (IB 28 pts)
Bournemouth – 112–128 pts (Flm Prod Cnma) (IB 32–30 pts)
Brunel – BBC (Comm Media St; Sociol (Media)) (IB 29 pts)
Coventry – BBC+interview (Media Comms) (IB 29 pts)
Derby – 112 pts (Media Comm); 112 pts+portfolio (Media Prod)
East London – 112 pts (Media Comm) (IB 25 pts HL 15 pts)
Greenwich – BBC 112 pts +interview +portfolio (Media Comms)
Huddersfield – BBC 112 pts (Media Pop Cult)
Hull – BBC 112 pts (Media St) (IB 28 pts)
Leeds Beckett – 112 pts (Media Comm Cult) (IB 24 pts)
Leeds Trinity – 112 pts (Media)
Lincoln – BBC (Media Prod) (IB 29 pts)
Liverpool Hope – BBC 112 pts (Media Comm) (IB 26 pts)
London Met – BBC 112 pts (Media Comms)
Nottingham Trent – 112 pts (Media Prod)
Portsmouth – 112 pts (Dig Media) (IB 25 pts)
Sheffield Hallam – 112 pts (Jrnl PR Media); BBC 112 pts (Media); BBC 112 pts +portfolio (Dig Media Prod)
Sunderland – BBC 112 pts (Media Cult Comm)
UWE Bristol – 112 pts (Media Cult Comm; Media Cult Prod; Media Jrnl)
West London – BBC 112 pts (Mark Soc Media; Media Comms)
Wolverhampton – BBC (Media)

104 pts   **Bangor** – 104–120 pts (Jrnl Media St; Media St courses)
Bournemouth – 104–120 pts (Comm Media; Media Prod) (IB 31–28 pts)
Cardiff Met – 104 pts (Engl Media)
Central Lancashire – 104 pts (Flm Media Pop Cult; Media Prod; Pub)
Chichester – BBC–BCC 104–112 pts (Media Comms; Spo Media) (IB 28 pts)
De Montfort – 104 pts (Media Comm) (IB 24 pts); 104 pts +interview (Jrnl) (IB 24 pts)
Falmouth – 104–120 pts +interview (Jrnl)
Glasgow Caledonian – BCC (Media Comm) (IB 25 pts)
Kingston – 104 pts (Media Comm)
Leeds Beckett – 104 pts (Broad Media Tech; Crea Media Tech) (IB 24 pts)
Leeds Trinity – 104 pts (Engl Media)
Liverpool John Moores – BCC 104 pts (Media Cult Comm)
Manchester Met – 104–112 pts (Flm Media St) (IB 26 pts); BCC 104–112 pts (Dig Media Comms) (IB 26 pts)
Northampton – BCC (Crea Flm TV Dig Media Prod)
Nottingham Trent – 104 pts (Media Comb Hons)
Oxford Brookes – 104 pts (Comm Media Cult) (IB 29 pts)
Portsmouth – 104–112 pts (Media St) (IB 25 pts)
Queen Margaret – BCC incl Eng/media (Media Comms) (IB 28 pts)
Robert Gordon – BCC incl Engl (Media) (IB 28 pts HL 5 Engl)
Winchester – 104–120 pts (Comm Vid Gms); (Media Comm Adv; Media Comm Jrnl; Media Comm courses) (HL 44)
Worcester – 104 pts (Media Cult)

96 pts   **Aberystwyth** – BBB–CCC 96–120 pts (Media Comm St) (IB 30–26 pts)
Anglia Ruskin – 96 pts (Media St courses) (IB 24 pts)

Bath Spa – CCC (Media Comms) (IB 26 pts)

Bolton – 96 pts +interview +portfolio (Scrnwrit Media Prod)

Brighton – BBC–CCC 96–112 pts (Media Env Comm; Media St) (IB 26 pts); BCC–CCC incl Engl 96–104 pts (Media Engl Lit) (IB 26 pts)

Buckingham – BBC–CCC (Jrnl Comm St) (IB 31–29 pts); BBC–CCC +interview (Comm Media Jrnl) (IB 24 pts)

Chester – BCC–CCC 96–104 pts (Media) (IB 26 pts)

Cumbria – BBC–CCC 96–112 pts +interview +portfolio (Wldlf Media)

Edinburgh Napier – CCC incl des/mus/media (Dig Media Interact Des Glob) (IB 28 pts HL 654 incl des/mus/mark)

Keele – BCC–CCC (Media Comms Crea Prac) (IB 28–26 pts)

Plymouth – 96–112 pts (Media Arts) (IB 28 pts)

Plymouth (CA) – C art 96–120 pts +interview +portfolio (Fash Media Mark) (IB 30–28 pts)

Roehampton – 96 pts (Media Cult Idnty)

St Mary's – BBC–BCC 96–112 pts (Comm Media Mark) (IB 28–24 pts)

Teesside – 96–112 pts (Broad Media Prod)

West London – CCC 96 pts (Cntnt Media Flm Prod)

Winchester – 96–112 pts (Dig Media Des courses) (HL 44)

Wolverhampton – CCC/BCD 96 pts (Media Engl)

York St John – 96 pts (Media courses)

88 pts   **Canterbury Christ Church** – 88–112 pts (Media Comms)

80 pts   **Arts London** – 80 pts (Contemp Media Cult; Mag Jrnl Pub) (IB 24 pts)

Bedfordshire – 80 pts (Media Prod courses); CCC–CCE 80–96 pts (Media Comms)

South Wales – BCC–CDD 80–112 pts +audition workshop (Perf Media); BCC–CDD incl art/des 80–104 pts +interview +portfolio (Media Prod) (IB 29 pts)

72 pts   **UHI** – BC +interview (Gael Media St)

64 pts   **Ravensbourne Univ** – CC +portfolio (Edit Pst Prod) (IB 24 pts)

Alternative offers

See **Chapter 6** and **Appendix 1** for grades/UCAS Tariff points information for other examinations.

EXAMPLES OF COLLEGES OFFERING COURSES IN THIS SUBJECT FIELD

Accrington and Rossendale (Coll); Blackpool and Fylde (Coll); Bridgwater and Taunton (Coll); Brooksby Melton (Coll); Central Film Sch; East Riding (Coll); Farnborough (CT); Gloucestershire (Coll); HOW (Coll); Hugh Baird (Coll); Kingston (Coll); Leeds City (Coll); Macclesfield (Coll); Newcastle (Coll); Peterborough (Coll); South Essex (Coll); Stratford-upon-Avon (Coll); TEC Partnership; Truro and Penwith (Coll); Westminster Kingsway (Coll); Weston (Coll); Yeovil (Coll).

CHOOSING YOUR COURSE (SEE ALSO CH.1)

Universities and colleges teaching quality See www.qaa.ac.uk; https://unistats.ac.uk.

Top research universities and colleges (REF 2014) See **Communication Studies/Communication**.

Examples of sandwich degree courses Bangor; Bedfordshire; Bournemouth; Brighton; Brunel; Coventry; De Montfort; Huddersfield; Leeds; Leeds Beckett; Liverpool John Moores; Manchester Met; Nottingham Trent; Plymouth; Portsmouth; Sheffield Hallam; Stirling; Surrey.

ADMISSIONS INFORMATION

Number of applicants per place (approx) Bath Spa 4; Bradford 13; Cardiff 11; Cardiff Met 3; Central Lancashire 33; Cumbria 4; De Montfort 11; East London 27; Falmouth 4; Greenwich 12; Lincoln 4; London (Gold) 13; Northampton 4; Nottingham Trent 5; Oxford Brookes (Pub) 5; Sheffield Hallam 56; South Essex (Coll) 10; Teesside 33; Winchester 5.

Advice to applicants and planning the UCAS personal statement Work experience or work shadowing is important. Contact local newspaper offices to meet journalists and to discuss their work. Contact local radio stations and advertising agencies, read newspapers (all types) and be able to describe the different approaches of newspapers. Watch TV coverage of news stories and the way in which the interviewer deals with politicians or members of the public. Give your opinions on the various forms of media. School magazine and/or any published work should be mentioned. A balance of academic and practical skills preferred. Creativity, problem-solving, cultural awareness, communication skills and commitment required. (International students: Fluency in written and spoken English required.) See also **Communication Studies/Communication** and Appendix 3.

Misconceptions about this course Birmingham City That Media courses are soft options: they are not! **Cardiff Met** Some applicants believe that the course will automatically lead to a job in the media: it won't. This depends on the student developing other employment skills and experience. **Cumbria** This is not a Media Studies course: it is a highly practical media production course. **Lincoln** (Media Prod) BTEC applicants may think that this is a technology-based course.

Selection interviews Yes Anglia Ruskin, Bolton, Cardiff Met, East Anglia; **Some** Bournemouth, Edge Hill, Liverpool John Moores, Solent, Westminster, Winchester, Wolverhampton; **No** Birmingham City, Cardiff, Huddersfield, London (Gold), Nottingham, Nottingham Trent, Portsmouth, Sheffield Hallam, South Essex (Coll), Sunderland, West London.

Interview advice and questions Past questions include: Which newspapers do you read? Discuss the main differences between the national daily newspapers. Which radio programmes do you listen to each day? Which television programmes do you watch? Should the BBC broadcast advertisements? What do you think are the reasons for the popularity of *EastEnders*? Film or video work, if required, should be edited to a running time of 15 minutes unless otherwise stated. See also **Chapter 5. Cardiff Met** What is your favourite area in respect of popular culture? Are you considering taking up the work placement module? If so where would you plan to go? **Cumbria** Role of journalism in society. What is today's main news story? Who is Rupert Murdoch?

Reasons for rejection (non-academic) No clear commitment (to Broadcast Journalism) plus no evidence of experience (now proving to be essential). Mistaken expectations of the nature of the course. Can't write and doesn't work well in groups. Too specific and narrow areas of media interest, for example, video or scriptwriting. Lack of knowledge of current affairs. **Cardiff Met** Lack of experience in the field. Application arrived too late.

AFTER-RESULTS ADVICE
Offers to applicants repeating A-levels Same Birmingham City; Cardiff; Cardiff Met; Chester; De Montfort; Huddersfield; Lincoln; Loughborough; Manchester Met; Nottingham Trent; South Essex (Coll); St Mary's; Sunderland; Winchester; Wolverhampton.

GRADUATE DESTINATIONS AND EMPLOYMENT (2016/17 HESA)
Graduates surveyed 4,415 **Employed** 2,215 **In voluntary employment** 185 **In further study** 685 **Assumed unemployed** 340

Career note See **Film, Radio, Video and TV Studies**.

OTHER DEGREE SUBJECTS FOR CONSIDERATION
Advertising; Communication; English; Film, Radio, Video and TV Studies; Journalism; Photography; Public Relations.

MEDICINE

(including **Medical Sciences**; see also **Biological Sciences, Human Sciences/Human Biosciences**)

Medicine is a highly popular choice of degree subject and career. All courses listed below include the same areas of study and all lead to a qualification and career in medicine. Medical schools aim to produce doctors who are clinically competent, who are able to see patients as people and have a holistic and ethical approach (including the ability to understand and manage each patient's case in a family and social context as well as in hospital), who treat patients and colleagues with respect, dignity and sensitivity, are skilled at teamwork and are prepared for continual learning. In several ways, these aims reflect the qualities selectors seek when interviewing applicants. In all cases, close attention will be paid to the confidential report on the UCAS application to judge the applicant's personality, communication skills, academic potential and commitment to a medical career. Methods of teaching may vary slightly, depending on the medical school. To achieve these aims, some medical schools adopt the system of self-directed learning (SDL) in which objectives are set to assess students' progress, and problem-based learning (PBL) which helps students to develop critical thinking and clinical problem-solving skills.

While there is a core curriculum of knowledge, the first three years integrate scientific and clinical experience, and there are fewer formal lectures than before, with more group and individual work. For outstanding students without science A-levels, some pre-medical courses are available. Most medical schools also offer an extra year of study, usually in the middle of the medical degree, to enable students to research a scientific subject leading to an 'intercalated' BSc degree. Additionally, elective periods abroad in the final year can sometimes be taken.

Medical students' and doctors' advice to applicants
'I did not fully appreciate how diverse medicine is as a career. Everyone has their own particular reasons for wishing to pursue it, but these will change as you progress through your career. There are many different pathways you can take which makes it all the more exciting... and daunting! Choose your university carefully; in most medical degrees, you will only be based at university for the first two years, and thereafter you will be in hospitals around the area so choose a city or an area you want to work and live in.'

'Medicine is a career which can open many doors – as a family or hospital doctor, working in Africa treating children with infectious diseases, in a war zone, in a laboratory, in sport, in journalism, and in law, going on to study law, to specialise in medical law, I have friends who have done all of these things.'

'Get to know what the real working lives of doctors are. The attributes needed to see sick and needy people. The fact that the NHS is a public and not a private organisation and what this means in the changing world of medical knowledge. Some of this is very difficult to learn in sixth form but periods of work experience will help. In addition to talking to medical students and family friends who are doctors, browse through medical journals and medical websites. Every doctor has had their own individual experiences, good and bad, but the majority would still apply to medicine again if they were 17!'

Useful websites www.scicentral.com; www.ipem.ac.uk; www.bmj.com; www.admissionstesting.org; www.gmc-uk.org; www.healthcareers.nhs.uk; www.bma.org.uk; www.rcgp.org.uk; www.rcpath.org

NB The points totals shown to the left of the institutions are for ease of reference only. It must not be assumed that Tariff points are always used by institutions or that they can be substituted for an offer in grades. The level of an offer is not necessarily indicative of the quality of a course.

COURSE OFFERS INFORMATION
Subject requirements/preferences Check the university's website. Many universities stipulate that applicants must hold certain GCSE grades.
Aberdeen GCSE grade 5 in English and mathematics. Biology and physics or dual award science recommended.
Aston Grade B (6) or above in English language, mathematics, chemistry, biology or double science (or overseas equivalent).
Birmingham Minimum of grade B (6) in **GCSE** English language, mathematics, biology and chemistry. Dual science award acceptable as an alternative to biology and chemistry.
Brighton Applicants should hold **GCSE** English Language/English and Maths at Grade B (6) or above.
Brighton and Sussex (MS) Mathematics and English at grade B or grade 6, or above.
Bristol Mathematics grade A (7) and English grade C (4).
Buckingham Grade C (4) in English and mathematics.
Cambridge Mathematics and dual science award (or biology and physics).

Cardiff B in nine subjects (minimum). English or Welsh at grade B (6), mathematics at grade B (6), grades BB in dual science.

Central Lancashire GCSE or equivalent to include English language at grade B (6) or higher with a broad study of sciences and mathematics.

Dundee Grade B/6 (minimum) in biology, mathematics and English.

East Anglia All applicants must have a minimum of six GCSEs (or two EU/International equivalent) passes at grade A/7 or above, to include English, mathematics and either two science subjects or double science. **GCSE** short courses are not accepted. Repeat GCSEs are accepted.

Edge Hill Check the university's website.

Edinburgh English, mathematics, biology, chemistry or dual science award at grade B/6 or higher.

Exeter Minimum grade C (4) in English language. Higher grades may be specified for individual programmes of study. International students should view requirements on the website.

Glasgow Grade B or grade 6 or above in English.

Hull York (MS) Eight subjects at grades 9–4 including English language and mathematics at grade 6 or higher.

Imperial London For advice on the requirements please contact the School of Medicine.

Keele Five A (7)s and maths, science and English at grade B(6) as a minimum requirement.

Kent Check the university's website.

Kent Medway Med Sch Normally A* to B (9–6) in English language, mathematics and biology, chemistry or physics/double award science.

Lancaster Applicants must provide evidence of excellent attainment in GCSEs. See the university's website for further details.

Leeds Six subjects at grade B minimum including English language, mathematics, chemistry and biology or dual science award.

Leicester You must have achieved at least a grade B (6) in English language, mathematics, and two sciences, including chemistry and biology, or double science achieved at first sitting, unless significant mitigating circumstances have been previously accepted by the admissions tutors. Leicester do not specify a minimum number of A* or 8/9 grades at **GCSE**. However, we do take **GCSE** performance into consideration when selecting applicants for interview, as competition for our places is so intense.

Lincoln For the University of Nottingham Lincoln Medical School, check the university's website.

Liverpool Five **GCSE** subjects at grade B or higher, including science, English and mathematics.

London (King's) Grade B/6 (minimum) in English and mathematics.

London (QM) Six subjects at A–B (7–6) minimum grades including English, mathematics and science subjects.

London (St George's) Typically five subjects at grade B (6) are required including English language, mathematics and science subjects. Contact the admissions team for a more detailed breakdown of grade requirements.

London (UCL) English and mathematics at grade B or 6 minimum plus grade C or 5 in a foreign language.

Manchester Seven subjects at grades A/A* or 7/8. English language, mathematics and at least two science subjects at grade B minimum.

Newcastle Grade A or 7 in biology/chemistry (or dual science award) if not offered as AS or A-level.

Nottingham Minimum of six GCSEs at grade A (7) including chemistry, physics and biology or dual science award. Grade B (6) in English and mathematics. For the University of Nottingham Lincoln Medical School, check the university's website.

Oxford Mathematics, biology and physics or dual science award if not taken at A-level.

Queen's Belfast GCSE mathematics and physics (or dual science award) at grade C (4) (or CC).

Southampton A minimum of six subjects at grade A (7) including mathematics with biology and chemistry or equivalent. (Widening Access course BM6) Five at grade C (4) including mathematics with biology and chemistry or equivalent. (Students join the five-year programme on completion of Year Zero.)

St Andrews Five subjects at Grade A (Grade 7) at one sitting. A level holders may be considered with fewer grades than five at Grade A (Grade 7).

UCAS points Tariff: A* = 56 pts; A = 48 pts; B = 40 pts; C = 32 pts; D = 24 pts; E = 16 pts

Sunderland Check the university's website.
Swansea Mathematics and English/Welsh at grade C (4) or above.
Warwick GCSE results not considered; this is a graduate entry course.

Your target offers and examples of degree courses

164 pts **Queen's Belfast** – AAAa/A*AAb/AAA +aEPQ incl chem+sci/maths +interview +UCAT (Med 5 yrs)

160 pts **Cambridge** – A*A*A incl chem+sci/maths +interview +BMAT (Med 6 yrs) (IB 42–40 pts HL 776 incl chem+sci/maths)

152 pts **London (King's)** – A*AA incl chem+biol +MMI +UCAT (Med 6 yrs) (IB 35 pts HL 766 incl chem/biol)

London (QM) – A*AA incl chem/biol+sci/maths +interview +UCAT (Med 5 yrs) (IB 38 pts HL 666 incl chem/biol+sci/maths)

London (UCL) – A*AA incl chem+biol +interview +BMAT (Med 6 yrs) (IB 39 pts HL 19 pts incl 6 biol/chem)

Oxford – A*AA incl chem+sci/maths +interview +BMAT (Med 6 yrs) (IB 39 pts HL 766 incl chem+sci/maths)

144 pts **Aberdeen** – AAA incl chem+sci/maths +interview +UCAT (Med 5 yrs) (IB 36 pts HL 666 incl chem+sci/maths)

Birmingham – AAA incl chem+biol +interview +UCAT (Med Srgy 5 yrs) (IB 32 pts HL 666 incl chem+biol)

Brighton and Sussex (MS) – AAA incl biol+chem +interview +BMAT (Med 5 yrs) (IB 36 pts HL 6 biol+chem)

Bristol – AAA incl chem+sci/maths +MMI +UCAT (Med 5 yrs) (IB 36 pts HL 18 pts incl 6 chem+sci/maths)

Cardiff – AAA incl chem+biol +MMI +UCAT (Med 5 yrs) (IB 36 pts HL 19 pts incl chem/biol+sci/maths)

Dundee – AAA incl chem+sci/maths 144 pts +interview +UCAT (Med 5 yrs) (IB 37 pts HL 666 incl chem+sci/maths)

East Anglia – AAA incl biol/chem +MMI +UCAT (Med 5 yrs) (IB 36 pts HL 666 incl biol/chem)

Edinburgh – AAA incl chem+maths/sci +UCAT +interview (Med 6 yrs) (IB 37 pts HL 766 incl chem+sci)

Exeter – AAA incl biol+chem +MMI +UCAT (Med) (IB 36 pts HL 6 biol+chem)

Glasgow – AAA incl chem+sci/maths +interview +UCAT (Med 5 yrs) (IB 38 pts HL 666 incl chem+biol)

Hull York (MS) – AAA incl chem+biol +interview +UCAT (Med 5 yrs) (IB 36 pts HL 665 incl chem+biol)

Imperial London – AAA incl biol+chem +MMI +BMAT (Med 6 yrs) (IB 38 pts HL 6 biol+chem)

Keele – AAA incl chem/biol +interview +UCAT (Med 5 yrs) (IB 35 pts HL 666 incl chem/biol)

Lancaster – AAA–AAB+bEPQ incl biol/chem/psy +MMI +BMAT (Med Srgy 5 yrs) (IB 36 pts HL 6 biol/chem/psy)

Leeds – AAA incl chem/biol +interview +BMAT (Med Srgy 5 yrs) (IB 35 pts HL 666 incl chem)

Leicester – AAA incl chem/biol+sci +interview +UCAT (Med 5 yrs) (IB 36 pts HL 666 incl chem/biol+sci)

Liverpool – AAA incl chem+sci/maths +MMI +UCAT (Med Srgy 5 yrs) (IB 36 pts HL 666 incl biol+chem)

London (St George's) – AAA incl chem+biol +interview +UCAT (Med 5 yrs) (IB 36 pts HL 18 pts incl 6 chem+biol)

Manchester – AAA incl art/hum+interview +UCAT (Med 6 yrs) (IB 36 pts HL 666 incl art/hum); AAA incl chem/biol+sci/maths +interview +UCAT (Med 5 yrs) (IB 37 pts HL 766 incl chem/biol+sci/maths)

Newcastle – AAA+interview +UCAT (Med Srgy 5 yrs) (IB 38 pts)

Nottingham – AAA incl chem+biol +interview +UCAT (Med 5 yrs) (IB 36 pts HL 666 incl chem+biol)

Sheffield – AAA incl chem/biol+sci +UCAT (Med 5 yrs) (IB 36 pts HL 666 incl chem/biol+sci)
Southampton – AAA incl chem+biol +interview +UCAT (Med 5 yrs) (IB 36 pts HL 18 pts incl 6 chem+biol)
St Andrews – AAA incl chem+sci/maths +interview +UCAT (Med 6 yrs) (IB 38 pts HL 666 incl chem+sci/maths)
136 pts **Aston** – AAA–AAB incl chem+biol +interview +UCAT (Med 5 yrs) (IB 35 pts HL 665 incl chem+biol)
Buckingham – AAB incl chem+maths/biol +MMI (Med) (IB 34 pts HL 6 chem+biol)
Kent Medway Med Sch – AAB incl chem/biol +UCAT +MMI (Med 5 yrs) (IB 34 pts HL 6 chem/biol)
Plymouth – A*AA–AAB incl biol+sci/maths +UCAT +interview (Med Srgy 5 yrs) (IB 38–36 pts HL 6 biol+sci/maths)
128 pts **Exeter** – ABB incl biol+sci (Med Sci) (IB 32 pts HL 655 incl 6 biol/sci)
120 pts **South Wales** – BBB incl biol (Med Sci) (IB 32 pts HL 5 biol)
112 pts **Hull** – BBC incl biol+chem +UCAT +interview (Med (Gateway)) (IB 29 pts HL 14 pts incl 5 biol+chem)

Alternative offers
See **Chapter 6** and **Appendix 1** for grades/UCAS Tariff points information for other examinations.

CHOOSING YOUR COURSE (SEE ALSO CH.1)
Universities and colleges teaching quality See www.qaa.ac.uk; https://unistats.ac.uk.

Top research universities and colleges (REF 2014) (Clinical Medicine) London (King's); Manchester; Oxford; London (QM); Cardiff; Edinburgh; Cambridge; Imperial London; Leeds.

ADMISSIONS INFORMATION
Number of applicants per place (approx) Brighton and Sussex (MS) 10; Bristol 15; Cambridge 6; Cardiff 10; Dundee 7; East Anglia 9; Edinburgh 8; Glasgow 4; Hull York (MS) 5; Imperial London 9; Keele 10; Lancaster 8; Leicester 5; Liverpool 7; London (King's) 11; London (QM) 5; London (UCL) 7; Manchester 5; Newcastle 10; Nottingham 10; Oxford 8.
Numbers of applicants (a UK **b** EU (non-UK) **c** non-EU **d** mature) Birmingham **a**5 **b**25, (Grad entry) 12 Brighton **a**7 Cambridge **c**21 Exeter **a**7 Leeds **a**17 London (St George's) **a**4 Queen's Belfast **a**4 **c** (a small number of places are allocated) Southampton **a**5 St Andrews **a**4 Warwick **a**8.

Admissions tutors' advice Policies adopted by all medical schools are very similar, although some medical schools use the Multiple Mini-Interview (MMI, see Chapter 5) format in which candidates rotate around different question stations, each one devoted to one question. Each interview lasts seven minutes. However, a brief outline of the information provided by admissions tutors is given below. Further information should be obtained direct from institutions. Applicants wishing to contact medical schools should do so by telephone and not by email.

Aberdeen Applicants must take the UCAT in the year of application. A cut-off score is not used. Overseas applicants may be interviewed abroad or in Aberdeen. The University uses the MMI format (see **Admissions tutors' advice**) and interviews last up to an hour. Total intake for 2017 was 178 including 16 international students. Most offers are made by end of March. Points equivalent results not accepted. Re-sits only accepted in exceptional circumstances. These must be submitted in good time to be considered. Feedback for unsuccessful applicants upon request. International students English language entry requirement (or equivalent): IELTS 7.0 and 7.0 in speaking.

Aston Deferred entry and gap years are accepted, however interviews, UCAT and academic qualifications must be obtained in the year of the application. General studies and critical thinking not accepted.

Birmingham UCAT required. Non-academic interests and extra-curricular activities noted in addition to academic factors. General studies and critical thinking not accepted. MMI format used (see **Admissions tutors' advice**). Approximately 1,200 called for interview. Approximately 10% take a year off which does not jeopardise the chances of an offer, but candidates must be available for interview. Re-sit candidates who failed by a small margin are only considered in exceptional circumstances. Transfers of undergraduates from other medical schools not considered. International applicants must show a good standard of written and spoken English. Second time applicants considered if not previously rejected at interview.

Brighton and Sussex (MS) BMAT used to assess each applicant. All applicants required to have grade B (grade 6) in maths and English **GCSE**. Candidates are interviewed if they have passed the first two stages of assessment (academic and personal statement if international; academic and BMAT score if a Home/EU applicant). Work experience necessary, but this does not need to be any given length and does not have to be in particular health sector. Interviews for Medicine are MMIs (see **Admissions tutors' advice**) and are currently held in January, February and March. Resit applicants are welcome to apply but only if they have dropped in one grade and one subject (eg AAB). Applicants with lower grades but resitting can apply to us once they have re-sat their subjects and obtained AAA. All Year 1 medical school students are guaranteed accommodation as long as they apply by the deadline (some students who live in the local area may not be able to apply for accommodation due to more applicants requiring housing than rooms available). Teaching is 'systems integrated' so students are exposed to the clinical environment from Year 1. Cadaver dissection is also part of the course from Year 1, so students get a real understanding of human anatomy, enhancing their learning experience. As the medical school is small, so are class sizes, meaning that students have a strong relationship with academic and support staff.

Bristol No places are offered without an interview. MMI interview format (see **Admissions tutors' advice**). Second time applicants rarely considered. The top applicants are called for an interview lasting an hour; the remainder grouped into two categories: 'hold' and 'unsuccessful' – some from the first two categories will be interviewed. Full details of the interview process are offered on the Bristol website. Widening participation panel considers appropriate candidates. Criteria for selection: UCAT, realistic and academic interest in medicine, commitment to helping others, wide range of interests, contribution to school/college activities, personal achievements. Interview criteria: reasons for wanting to study Medicine, awareness of current developments, communication skills, self-confidence, enthusiasm and determination to study, ability to cope with stress, awareness of the content of the course and career. General studies and critical thinking not acceptable. Subject content overlap (eg biology/PE/sports science) not allowed. Deferred entry welcomed (except for A101 (Graduate Entry)), but applicants must be available for interview. Points equivalent results not accepted. International students English language requirement (or equivalent): IELTS 7.5. Some candidates are still applying without the right subjects or grade predictions. Visit www.bristol.ac.uk/study/undergraduate for up-to-date course and entry information.

Cambridge Most applicants for Medicine at Cambridge have at least three science/mathematics A-levels and some colleges require this or ask for particular A-level subject(s). BMAT used to assess each applicant. The standard undergraduate course is offered at all colleges except Hughes Hall. Normally two interviews lasting 20 minutes each. Films of interviews can be found on www.undergraduate.study.cam.ac.uk/applying/interviews. Approximately 80% of applicants are interviewed. Applicants are not usually required to submit examples of written work. Gap year acceptable but for positive reasons. Clinical studies from Year 4 at the Cambridge Clinical School (Addenbrooke's Hospital).

Cardiff Admission is determined by a combination of academic performance, non-academic skills, knowledge and completion of the UCAT test. Applications can be made in the Welsh language. Approximately 1,500 of the 3,500 applicants are called for interview. Cardiff uses the MMI format for interviews (see **Admissions tutors' advice**). Applications are assessed and scored as follows: 1. Medical motivation and awareness of career. 2. Caring ethos. 3. Sense of responsibility. 4. Evidence of a balanced approach to life. 5. Evidence of self-directed learning. 6. Referee's report.

Central Lancashire Interview format is MMI with 10 activity stations (see Admissions tuors' advice above). All applicants invited to interview must provide a satisfactory enhanced DBS check or international equivalent and proof of ID. All applicants successful at interview will need to undergo occupational health screening as part of the enrolment process.

Dundee No minimum UCAT cut-off score used, although candidates receiving offers in recent years have typically achieved around 2,720 pts. A fully integrated hospital and medical school. Preference given to candidates who achieve the right grades at the first sitting. MMIs (see **Admissions tutors' advice**) have been introduced to give students separate opportunities to sell themselves. Deferred entry acceptable. Clinical attachments in Year 4. World-wide experience in final year electives.

East Anglia Criteria include academic requirements and UCAT. MMI format (see **Admissions tutors' advice**) are used for the interviews, candidates visit each station for one question with five minutes at each station. English entry requirement IELTS 7.5. Clinical experience from Year 1.

Edge Hill For entry requirements to the university's new access to medicine course, see the university's website.

Edinburgh All examination grades must be achieved at the first sitting; only in extenuating circumstances will re-sits be considered. All UCAT scores considered. The situation judgement section of the UCAT test is also considered. Equal weighting given to academic and non-academic criteria. Non-academic criteria score based on personal qualities and skills, evidence of career exploration prior to application, breadth and level of non-academic achievements and interests. Work experience and work shadowing, particularly in a hospital, viewed positively but the admissions panel recognises that not all applicants have equal opportunities to gain such experience. School-leaving applicants are not normally interviewed so references are important. Shortlisted graduate and mature applicants will be interviewed; 190 UK/EU fee rate places available, around one in eleven receive an offer. International applicants not normally called for interview. Some clinical experience from Year 1. The six-year programme includes an intercalated research Honours year in Year 3.

Exeter Selection procedures include the assessment of UCAT or GAMSAT. MMIs are used (see **Admissions tutors' advice**).

Glasgow The initial screening process considers the applicant's academic achievement, personal statement and reference. The UCAT is the final part of the screening process and is used for allocation of interview. The range of UCAT scores considered changes each year as the performance of each admissions cohort varies. Approximately 750 applicants are interviewed. The interview session will last around 30 minutes and candidates are made aware of what to expect on the day in the invite to interview. Normally applicants will be interviewed by two panels, with two interviewers on each panel. Candidates will be given the option to select one of two scenarios immediately prior to their interview and will be expected to discuss the issues around the scenario with their panel. Obtaining work experience in a medical setting is not necessary to study or obtain entry to Medicine at Glasgow, but it is expected that candidates will have a realistic understanding of what a career in medicine entails and be aware of current issues facing the medical profession. Given the competitive nature of entry to medicine, unsuccessful applicants are welcome to reapply to Glasgow in future admissions cycles, providing they meet minimum academic entry requirements within seven years of entry. All potential applicants should be encouraged to visit the Medical School prior to applying.

Hull York (MS) Students apply to HYMS, not to either the University of Hull or York. Students allocated places at Hull or York by ballot for Years 1 and 2. Transfers from other medical schools not accepted. Disabilities listed on UCAS application do not affect the assessment of the application. UCAT required; approximately 670 called for interview, 440 offered places. MMI system (see **Admissions tutors' advice**) involving a group interview of 20 minutes and two semi-structured individual interviews of 10 minutes, plus a 'scenario station' used. During the interview process, applicants will be scored on their motivation for a medical career, critical thinking skills, awareness and understanding of healthcare issues, communication skills, empathy, tolerance and resilience. A-level resits not usually accepted. Clinical placements from Year 1. Non-EU applicants English language (or equivalent requirement) IELTS 7.5 with at least 7 in each component. Students with band 4 in the Situational Judgement test will be rejected. The Medicine with a Gateway Year course (which requires widening participation criteria) is for UK applicants only and gives priority to applicants from the area around the Medical School.

Imperial London Approximately 850 candidates interviewed. Fifteen-minute interviews with panel of four or five selectors. Not aimed at being an intimidating experience – an evaluation of motivation, capacity to deal with stress, evidence of commitment to the values of the NHS constitution, evidence of working as a leader and team member, ability to multitask, likely contribution to university life, communication skills and maturity. BMAT test cut-off scores calculated each year depending on applications. Admissions tutor's comment: 'We look for resourceful men and women with wide interests and accomplishments, a practical concern for others and for those who will make a contribution to the life of the school and hospital.' Results within two weeks. Re-sits are only considered for candidates with extenuating circumstances. Approximately 600 offers made. Clinical contact in Year 1.

Keele Please check our website for details of our application process: www.keele.ac.uk/medicine/undergraduate/howtoapply.

Kent For entry requirements for the new medical school, check the university's website.

Lancaster The University delivers the curriculum at the academic base at Lancaster University and clinical placements in Years 2–5 at acute hospitals and primary care settings in Lancashire and Cumbria. BMAT required. Interviews in the MMI format with 12–14 different stations (see **Admissions tutors' advice**).

Leeds BMAT required. No cut-off point when assessing the results. 219 home students plus 18 non-EU students. Admissions tutor's comment: 'We use the MMI format for interviews [see **Admissions tutors' advice**]. Consider your motivation carefully – we do!' Good verbal, non-verbal and presentational skills required. Candidates should: (i) be able to report on some direct experience of what a career in medicine is about; (ii) show evidence of social activities on a regular basis (eg part-time employment, organised community experiences); (iii) show evidence of positions of responsibility and interests outside medical and school activities. Disabled students should indicate their disability status on the UCAS form. Candidates must be available for interview; approximately 1,000 applicants interviewed. Points-equivalent results not accepted. International students' English language requirement (or equivalent): IELTS 7.5 including 7.5 in spoken English. Re-applications accepted from students who have achieved the right grades. Resits only considered in exceptional circumstances and with good supporting evidence; offer AAA. Transfers from other medical schools not encouraged. Ward based attachments begin in Years 1 and 2; clinical practice from Year 3. Applicants should hold the required A-level grades or a high class science or medically related degree.

Leicester UCAT required. Interview is MMI format (see **Admissions tutors' advice**) – 8 stations assessing verbal and written communication, listening skills, compassion and respect, emotional intelligence, problem solving skills, motivation and ethical judgement. Deferred entry considered. Resits rarely considered and only on prior agreement from the admissions tutors. Transfers from other medical schools not considered. Patient contact in first semester, full body dissection. Integrated course.

Lincoln For entry requirements for the University of Nottingham Lincoln Medical School, see the university website.

Liverpool UCAT is required for all non-graduate applicants applying to the A100 programme. Graduate applicants to the A100 programme must offer GAMSAT. 255 Home/EU places are available on the A100 Liverpool medical programme. Evidence of healthcare insight and awareness, caring contribution to the community, excellent communication and values that embody and underpin good healthcare practice is necessary. Interview is via MMI (see **Admissions tutors' advice**). Applicants wishing to take a gap year may be considered, but applicants must be available for interview. The Liverpool A100 medical programme usually has 23 places available for international students. Under-qualified international students may be able to apply to Liverpool International College prior to placing an application for the Liverpool A100 medical programme. The selection process at Liverpool is a three stage process which is competitive at each stage. Applications are placed via UCAS. For international students, certain minimum language requirements for the course may exist (IELTS of no less than 7.0 in each component).

London (King's) UCAT required. Personal statement a significant factor in selection. Emphasis placed on appreciation of academic, physical and emotional demands of the course, commitment, evidence of working in a caring environment, communication skills and interaction with the general public. Approximately 400 out of 6,000 applications are successful. The University interviews around 1,300 applicants every year using the MMI format (see **Admissions tutors' advice**) and makes offers to approximately a third of them. Clinical contact in Year 1.

London (St George's) Applicants must be taking A-level chemistry and biology or human biology. You will be required to complete your A-levels within two years of study and the standard offer is AAA. Applicants must have an average grade of B (6) across their top five GCSEs including English language, maths and dual award or the three single sciences. Applicants are also required to take the UCAT test in the year of application. Applicants who meet our A-level and **GCSE** requirements and achieve our required overall and section scores in UCAT will be offered an interview. All offers are made post-interview. Applicants are expected to have relevant work experience which is assessed at interview. The value of work experience lies with reflection. What have you gained? How has the experience affected your journey to study Medicine? What skills do you need to work on as a result of carrying out this experience? The English language requirement for international students is IELTS 7.0 with 7.0 in writing and no section less than 6.5. Deferred entry welcome. Medicine (six years, including Foundation year) is for mature non-graduate students only. Medicine (four years, Graduate stream) is for graduates with a 2.1 Hons degree in any discipline. Graduates are not eligible for the five-year Medicine programme.

London (UCL) All candidates are required to take the BMAT. Two or three selectors interview applicants, each interview lasting 15–20 minutes; approximately 30% of applicants interviewed. Qualities sought include motivation, awareness of scientific and medical issues, ability to express and defend opinions, maturity and individual strengths. Deferred entry for good reason is acceptable. Minimum age of entry 18 years. Transfers from other medical schools considered. International students may take the University Preparation Certificate for Science and Engineering (UPCSE) which is the minimum entry requirement for entry to Medicine. 24 places for non-EU applicants. Patient contact starts in Year 1.

Manchester 372 places for around 2,000 applicants. UCAT scores important. Threshold not disclosed. Seven interviews based on the MMI format (see **Admissions tutors' advice**). Mitigating circumstances regarding the health or disposition of the candidate should appear in the referee's report. Any applicant who feels unwell before the interview should inform the admissions team and the interview will be re-scheduled; pleas of infirmity cannot be accepted after the interview! Candidates should be aware of the advantages and disadvantages of enquiry-based learning and opinions may be asked. Ethical questions may be raised. Decisions will be made by the end of March. Resit offers only made to applicants with extenuating circumstances; having AAB at first attempt A-level. Clinical attachments from Year 3. Application details on www.bmh.manchester.ac.uk/study/undergraduate.

Newcastle 367 places. The University runs MMIs (see **Admissions tutors' advice**). It does not stipulate its UCAT threshold until after the recruitment cycle has ended, and it only accepts resits in extenuating circumstances. Decisions on resits are made on an individual basis by the Sub-Dean of Admissions. The University accepts deferred entry. Clinical placements start in Year 3. Check the website for the latest up-to-date information before applying. Unlike many universities, Newcastle does not consider GCSEs as part of its entry requirements for Medicine.

Nottingham Up to date information on the Medicine programmes at the University of Nottingham and the application process is provided on the University's website, including for the University of Lincoln Medical School.

Oxford Your chances of being shortlisted rest on a number of factors although we do rely heavily on BMAT scores and the **GCSE** performances (where available) during shortlisting. A slightly weaker performance may be compensated by a very good BMAT score and vice versa. On average, our applicants hold about 80% of GCSEs at Grade A and A* (8.5) grades (the University treats the new grades 8 and 9 as equivalent to A*). Critical thinking and general studies are not acceptable. Approximately 30% of applicants called for interview on the basis of academic performance, test score and information on the application form. Ratio of interviewees to places approximately 2.5 to 1. No student admitted without an interview. All colleges use a common set of selection criteria: 11% success rate. Candidate's comment (Lincoln College): 'Two interviewers and two interviews. Questions covered my hobbies and social life, and scientific topics to test my logical train of thought. A great university, but it's not the be-all and end-all if you don't get in.' Clinical experience commences in Year 4.

Queen's Belfast Majority of applicants are school-leavers. When considering applicants' **GCSE** performance, the best nine subjects will be scored on the basis of 4 points for an A* and 3 points for an A. Points will also be given or deducted on each UCAT paper. Offers for re-sitting applicants will be restricted. These applicants will have been expected to have missed their offer by one grade. A proportion of candidates will be called for interview. Interviews based on the MMI format (see **Admissions tutors' advice**). A small number of places are allocated to non-EU applicants. Number of places restricted for resit applicants who have narrowly missed an offer at Queen's. Clinical experience from Year 1.

Sheffield Applications processed between October and end of March. Candidates may send additional information concerning extenuating circumstances or health problems via the University's Disrupted Studies form, which can be found at: www.sheffield.ac.uk/study/policies/disrupted-studies. UCAT required. MMI format used (see Admissions tuors' advice above). A-level resits are not accepted. Gap year acceptable; medicine-related work very helpful. Clinical experience from Year 1. For more information, please see: www.sheffield.ac.uk/medicine/undergraduate/medicine-admissions.

Southampton 202 places available for five-year course. Please refer to the website for further information: www.southampton.ac.uk/medicine.

St Andrews Medicine students take a full three-year programme leading to BSc (Hons), followed by clinical medicine at one of its partner medical schools. UCAT required. MMI format (see **Admissions tutors' advice**) with six or more mini interviews or stations. Special attention given to international students and those who achieve qualifications at more than one sitting. As far as possible, the interview panel will reflect the gender and ethnic distribution of candidates for interview.

Sunderland For entry requirements for the School of Medicine, see the university's website.

Swansea Graduate entry only.

Warwick Selection includes interview and group activities. UCAT, work experience and a reference required. You should have, or be predicted to gain, a minimum of a 2.1 degree or overseas equivalent in any subject. Candidates with a 2.2 degree should hold a master's or doctoral qualification to be considered for entry.

Advice to applicants and planning the UCAS personal statement (see also **Admissions tutors' advice**) Nearly all universities now require either the UCAT (formerly UCAT) or BMAT entry tests to be taken before applying for Medicine. Check websites (www.ucat.ac.uk; www.admissionstesting.org) for details of test dates and test centres and with universities for their requirements. It is essential that you check for the latest information before applying and that you give yourself plenty of time to make arrangements for sitting these tests (see also **Chapter 5**). Admissions tutors look for certain personal qualities (see **Admissions tutors' advice**) and these will emerge in your personal statement, at the interview and on your school or college reference. There should be evidence of scientific interest, commitment, enthusiasm, determination, stability, self-motivation, ability to organise your own work, interest in the welfare of others, communication skills, modesty (arrogance and over-confidence could lead to rejection!), breadth of interest, leadership skills, stamina, and good physical and mental health. Some kind of first-hand experience in a medical setting is almost obligatory for those applying for Medicine (see **Admissions tutors' advice**). Depending on your personal contacts in the medical profession, this could include observing operations (for example, orthopaedic surgery), working in hospitals and discussing the career with your GP. Remember that your friends and relatives may have medical conditions that they would be willing to discuss with you – and all this will contribute to your knowledge and show that you are informed and interested. Read medical and scientific magazines and keep up-to-date with important current issues – AIDS, Ebola, assisted dying, abortion. Community work, clubs, societies, school and social activities should be mentioned. Show that you have an understanding of the role of health professionals in society and the social factors that influence health and disease. And finally, a comment from one admissions tutor: 'Don't rush around doing things just for your CV. If you are a boring student, be an incredibly well-read boring student! You can play netball, rugby, hockey, make beautiful music and paint with your feet, but if you fail to get the grades you'll be rejected.' **Bristol** Deferred places are limited. Late applications may not be accepted.

Misconceptions about this course Hull York (MS) The Medicine with a Gateway Year course requires Widening Participation criteria, is for UK applicants only and gives priority to applicants from the area around the medical school. **Liverpool** Some applicants think that three science subjects at A-level are required to study Medicine – wrong! **London (St George's)** That you should be white, middle class and male: 60% of medical students are now female and 53% of our students are not white. **Oxford** Students interested in a career in medicine may think that they must study for a degree in Medicine. In fact, there are many other degree courses which will prepare you for a career in this field.

Selection interviews Yes Aberdeen, Birmingham, Bristol, Cambridge, Dundee, East Anglia, Exeter, Glasgow, Hull York (MS), Keele, Lancaster, Liverpool (Shortlisted Medicine applicants will be invited to multiple mini interviews – info on https://liverpool.ac.uk/medicine/study-with-us/undergraduate/admissions-information.), London (King's), London (St George's), Manchester, Newcastle, Nottingham, Oxford (11%), Queen's Belfast, St Andrews, Sussex; **Some** Edinburgh.

Interview advice and questions Questions will vary between applicants, depending on their UCAS statements and their A-level subjects. Questions are likely to relate to A-level specific subjects, general medicine topics and unconnected topics (see also **Admissions tutors' advice**). The following questions will provide a guide to the range of topics covered in past interviews. Outline the structure of DNA. What is meant by homeostasis? Is a virus a living organism? What has been the most important advance in biology in the last 50 years? What interests you about (i) science, (ii) biology, (iii) chemistry? Why did you choose the particular A-level subjects you are doing? Why do you want to study Medicine/become a doctor? Do you expect people to be grateful? Why do you want to study here? Why should we take you? What do you do to relax? What do you do when you have three or four things to do, and they are all equally urgent? How do you balance work and all the outside activities you do? Do you agree with the concept of 'foundation trusts'? What do you think about polyclinics? Do you think NHS doctors and staff should be able to take private patients? If you were in charge of finances for a large health authority, what would be your priorities for funding? If you had to decide between saving the life of a young child and that of an old person, what would you do? Would you treat lung cancer patients who refuse to give up smoking? What do you understand by 'gene therapy'? Can you give any examples? In your opinion, what is the most serious cause for concern for the health of the UK? What do you want to do with your medical degree? What do you think the human genome project can offer medicine? Should we pay for donor organs? Where do you see yourself in 15 years' time? Who made the most valuable contribution to the 20th century? Why do you think research is important? Why is teamwork important? What do you think about the NHS's problems? Do you think that sport is important? What did you gain from doing work experience in a nursing home? What were the standards like? How does the medical profession deal with social issues? How could you compare your hobby of rowing to medicine? In doing a medical course, what would you find the most emotionally challenging aspect? How would you cope with emotional strain? Who should have priority for receiving drugs in a flu epidemic/pandemic? How would you deal with the death of a patient? What are stem cells? Why are they controversial? How is cloning done? What constitutes a human being? How can you measure intelligence? How do we combat genetic diseases? How are genes actually implanted? What do you want to talk about? If you were a cardiothoracic surgeon, would you perform a heart by-pass operation on a smoker? What are the negative aspects of becoming a doctor? At some interviews, essays may be set, eg (i) 'A scientific education is a good basis for a medical degree: discuss'; (ii) 'Only drugs that are safe and effective should be prescribed to patients: discuss'. Should someone sell their kidney? How would you describe a human to a person from Mars? Should obese people have treatment on the NHS? Occasionally applicants at interview may be given scenarios to discuss (see **Glasgow** under

Admissions tutors' advice). See also **Chapter 5. Oxford** Tell me about drowning. What do you think of assisted suicide? Would you give a 60-year-old woman IVF treatment? When are people dead?

Reasons for rejection (non-academic) Insufficient vocation demonstrated. No steps taken to gain practical experience relevant to medicine. Doubts as to the ability to cope with the stress of a medical career. Not enough awareness about the career. Lack of knowledge about the course. Applicant appears dull and lacking in enthusiasm and motivation. Lacking a caring, committed attitude towards people. No evidence of broad social, cultural or sporting interests or of teamwork. Poor or lack of communication skills. Arrogance. Over-confident at interview. Unrealistic expectations about being a doctor. **Buckingham** Applicants are requested to attend an Open Day/Evening or a Tutorial Taster Day. The University believes it is very important for applicants to visit its campus. Candidates who do not respond to these invitations may be rejected, irrespective of academic achievement, as the University looks for committed, well-motivated students. **Hull York (MS)** Applicants with a band 4 in the situational judgement test will be rejected.

Age at entry Applicants must be 17 years old on 30 September of the year of entry. However, some medical schools stipulate 17 years and six months, and a small number stipulate 18 years. Those considering entry at 17 would probably be advised to take a gap year.

Health requirements Medical schools require all students to have their immunity status for hepatitis B, tuberculosis and rubella checked on entry. Offers are usually made subject to satisfactory health screening for hepatitis B. In line with advice from the General Medical Council, students will not be admitted to courses who are found to be e-antigen positive when screened within the first week of the course. Candidates accepting offers should assure themselves of their immunity status.

Mature students Medical schools usually accept a small number of mature students each year. However, several, if not the majority, reject applicants over 30 years of age. Some medical schools accept non-graduates although A-level passes at high grades are usually stipulated. The majority of applicants accepted are likely to be graduates with a first or 2.1 degree. **Birmingham** Applications from mature candidates are welcomed, but the length of training which has be to taken will be considered when assessing applications. **Leeds** There is no upper age limit for the course. Applicants should hold the required A-level grades or a high class science degree. **Southampton** Applicants with nursing qualifications should hold two grade A A-levels including chemistry and biology.

Advice to graduate applicants Graduate applicants are considered by all medical schools. At some medical schools the Graduate Australian Medical Schools Admission Test (GAMSAT) is now being used to assess the aptitude of prospective applicants. Applicants at some institutions are selected on the basis of three criteria: (i) an Honours degree at 2.2 or above; (ii) the GAMSAT score; (iii) performance at interview. All applicants must be EU students. **London (St George's)** Some students think that science graduates are the only ones to do well in GAMSAT: 40% of those on the course do not have a science degree or A-levels; however, work experience is essential.

AFTER-RESULTS ADVICE
Offers to applicants repeating A-levels Same Brighton and Sussex (MS); **Rare** Dundee.

GRADUATE DESTINATIONS AND EMPLOYMENT (2016/17 HESA)
Clinical Medicine graduates surveyed 4,755 **Employed** 4,635 **In voluntary employment** 5 **In further study** 70 **Assumed unemployed** 5

Career note Applicants should also bear in mind that while most doctors do work in the NHS, either in hospital services or in general practice, many graduates choose to work in other fields such as public health, pharmacology, the environment, occupational medicine with industrial organisations, the armed services and opportunities abroad.

OTHER DEGREE SUBJECTS FOR CONSIDERATION
Biomedical/Medical Materials Science; Biology; Biotechnology; Clinical Sciences; Dentistry; Dietetics; Genetics; Health Sciences; Immunology; Medical Biochemistry; Medical Engineering; Medical Microbiology; Medical Physics; Medical Product Design; Medical Sciences; Medicinal Chemistry;

Midwifery; Nursing; Nutrition; Occupational Therapy; Optometry; Osteopathy; Pharmacology; Pharmacy; Physiology; Physiotherapy; Psychology; Radiography; Speech Sciences; Sports Medicine; Veterinary Medicine; Virology – and Law! (The work of doctors and lawyers is similar: both are required to identify the relevant information – clinical symptoms or legal issues!)

MICROBIOLOGY

(See also **Biological Sciences, Biology, Biotechnology, Genetics**)

Microbiology is a branch of biological science specialising in the study of micro-organisms: bacteria, viruses and fungi. The subject covers the relationship between these organisms and disease and industrial applications such as food and drug production, waste-water treatment and future biochemical uses.

Useful websites www.microbiologysociety.org; www.nature.com/subjects/microbiology; www.asm. org; www.microbiologynetwork.com; see also **Biochemistry**, **Biological Sciences** and **Biology**.

NB The points totals shown to the left of the institutions are for ease of reference only. It must not be assumed that Tariff points are always used by institutions or that they can be substituted for an offer in grades. The level of an offer is not necessarily indicative of the quality of a course.

COURSE OFFERS INFORMATION

Subject requirements/preferences GCSE English and mathematics and science subjects. **AL** One or two mathematics/science subjects including chemistry and/or biology required or preferred; grades sometimes specified.

Your target offers and examples of degree courses
144 pts **Imperial London** – AAA incl biol+sci/maths (Microbiol) (IB 38 pts HL 6 biol+sci/maths)
136 pts **Bristol** – AAB incl chem+sci/maths (Med Microbiol) (IB 34 pts HL 17 pts incl 6/5 chem+sci); (Cell Mol Med) (IB 34–31 pts HL 6–5 chem+sci/maths)
Dundee – AAB incl biol+chem (Microbiol) (IB 30 pts HL 555 incl biol+chem)
Glasgow – AAB incl biol/chem (Microbiol; Mol Cell Biol (Plnt Sci)) (IB 36 pts HL 665 incl 6 sci); (Mol Cell Biol (Biotech)) (IB 36 pts HL 665 incl biol/chem+sci)
Sheffield – AAB incl sci (Med Microbiol; Microbiol; Mol Biol) (IB 34 pts HL 65 chem+sci); (Genet Microbiol) (IB 34 pts HL 65 sci)
York – AAB incl biol+sci (Biotech Microbiol) (IB 35 pts HL 6 biol+sci)
128 pts **Edinburgh** – AAA–ABB incl biol+chem (Biol Sci (Dev Regn Stem Cells); Biol Sci (Mol Biol)) (IB 37–32 pts HL 666–555 incl biol+chem)
Leeds – AAA–ABB incl chem/biol+sci (Med Microbiol; Microbiol) (IB 35–33 pts HL 18–17 pts incl 6 chem/biol+sci)
Leicester – ABB–BBB +bEPQ incl sci/maths (Med Microbiol) (IB 30 pts HL 65 sci/maths)
Liverpool – ABB incl biol+sci (Microbiol) (IB 33 pts HL 6 biol)
Manchester – AAA–ABB incl sci/maths +interview (Microbiol (Yr Ind); Microbiol Modn Lang) (IB 36–33 pts HL 666–655 incl sci)
Nottingham – AAB–ABB incl sci/maths/geog (Microbiol) (IB 34–32 pts HL 5 sci)
120 pts **Aberdeen** – BBB incl maths/sci (Microbiol) (IB 32 pts HL 555)
Nottingham Trent – BBB incl biol 120 pts (Microbiol)
Queen's Belfast – BBB incl biol+sci/maths (Microbiol)
Reading – BBB incl biol+sci (Microbiol) (IB 30 pts HL 5 biol+sci)
Stirling – BBB incl sci/maths (Cell Biol) (IB 32 pts)
Strathclyde – ABB–BBB incl sci (Microbiol) (IB 34 pts HL 5 sci); BBB incl biol/chem+sci (Immun Microbiol) (IB 32 pts HL 5 biol/chem+sci)
Surrey – BBB incl biol+sci/maths (Microbiol) (IB 32 pts)
112 pts **Glasgow Caledonian** – BBC incl chem (Cell Mol Biol; Microbiol) (IB 28 pts)
Heriot-Watt – BBC incl sci/maths (Biol Sci (Microbiol)) (IB 27 pts HL 5 sci)

Hertfordshire – BBC incl biol/chem+sci/maths/geog/psy 112 pts (Mol Biol)
Huddersfield – BBC incl sci 112 pts (Biol (Mol Cell))
Leeds Beckett – 112 pts incl biol+sci (Biomed Sci (Med Microbiol)) (IB 25 pts HL 6 biol)
104 pts **Aberystwyth** – BBB–BCC incl B biol 104–120 pts (Microbiol) (IB 30–28 pts HL 5 biol)
Chester – BBC–BCC 104–112 pts (Microbiol) (IB 26 pts HL 5 biol/chem)
Edinburgh Napier – BCC incl sci (App Microbiol) (IB 28 pts HL 654 incl 5 sci)
Manchester Met – BBC–BCC incl biol 104–112 pts (Microbiol Mol Biol (St Abrd)) (IB 26 pts HL 5 biol)
80 pts **Wolverhampton** – CDD incl sci (Microbiol Biotech)

Alternative offers
See **Chapter 6** and **Appendix 1** for grades/UCAS Tariff points information for other examinations.

EXAMPLES OF COLLEGES OFFERING COURSES IN THIS SUBJECT FIELD
St Helens (Coll).

CHOOSING YOUR COURSE (SEE ALSO CH.1)
Universities and colleges teaching quality See www.qaa.ac.uk; https://unistats.ac.uk.

Top research universities and colleges (REF 2014) See **Biological Sciences**.

Examples of sandwich degree courses Aston; Leeds; Manchester; Manchester Met; Nottingham Trent; Queen's Belfast; Reading; Surrey; York.

ADMISSIONS INFORMATION
Number of applicants per place (approx) Bradford 6; Bristol 8; Cambridge 4; Dundee 8; Leeds 7; Liverpool (Lf Sci) 7; Nottingham 7; Strathclyde 10; Wolverhampton 4.

Advice to applicants and planning the UCAS personal statement Relevant experience, particularly for mature students. See **Biological Sciences** and also Appendix 3.

Selection interviews Yes Leeds, Manchester, Wolverhampton; **Some** Aberystwyth (mature students only); **No** Bristol, Dundee, Nottingham, Surrey.

Interview advice and questions Examples of past questions include: How much does the country spend on research and on the armed forces? Discuss reproduction in bacteria. What do you particularly like about your study of biology? What would you like to do after your degree? Do you have any strong views on vivisection? Discuss the differences between the courses you have applied for. What important advances have been made in the biological field recently? How would you describe microbiology? Do you know anything about the diseases caused by micro-organisms? What symptoms would be caused by which particular organisms? See also **Chapter 5.**

AFTER-RESULTS ADVICE
Offers to applicants repeating A-levels Higher Bristol; Strathclyde; **Same** Aberystwyth; Leeds; Liverpool; Nottingham; Wolverhampton.

GRADUATE DESTINATIONS AND EMPLOYMENT (2016/17 HESA)
Graduates surveyed 390 **Employed** 130 **In voluntary employment** 0 **In further study** 190 **Assumed unemployed** 25

Career note See **Biology**.

OTHER DEGREE SUBJECTS FOR CONSIDERATION
Animal Sciences; Biochemistry; Biological Sciences; Biology; Biotechnology; Genetics; Medical Sciences; Medicine; Molecular Biology; Pharmacology; Physiology.

MUSIC

(including Music Technology; See also Engineering (Acoustics and Sound))

Theory and practice are combined to a greater or lesser extent in most university Music courses, and about 50% or more of graduates will go on to non-music careers. However, courses are also offered by conservatoires and schools of music where the majority of applicants are aiming to become professional musicians. For these courses, the ability to perform on an instrument is more important than academic ability and offers are therefore likely to be lower. When choosing music courses, the applicant should also be aware of the specialisms offered, such as classical, jazz, new music, popular music and film music (Leeds College of Music) in addition to courses in music production and music business. Music Journalism is also an option on some courses. See also **Appendix 2**. Some applications are made through UCAS Conservatoires (formerly CUKAS): see Chapter 4 for details.

Useful websites www.ism.org; www.roh.org.uk; www.nyo.org.uk; www.ucas.com/conservatoires; www.artscouncil.org.uk; www.soundandmusic.org; http://gb.abrsm.org/en

NB The points totals shown to the left of the institutions are for ease of reference only. It must not be assumed that Tariff points are always used by institutions or that they can be substituted for an offer in grades. The level of an offer is not necessarily indicative of the quality of a course.

COURSE OFFERS INFORMATION

Subject requirements/preferences GCSE A foreign language and mathematics may be required. A good range of As and Bs (9-6) for popular universities. **AL** Music plus an instrumental grade usually required.

Your target offers and examples of degree courses

160 pts **Imperial London** – A*A*A incl maths+phys +interview +audition +gr 8 (Phys Mus Perf) (IB 39 pts HL 766 incl maths+phys)

152 pts **Cambridge** – A*AA incl mus +interview (Mus) (IB 42–40 pts HL 776 incl mus)

144 pts **Oxford** – AAA incl mus +interview (Mus) (IB 38 pts HL 666 incl mus)

Surrey – AAA incl maths+mus+phys +interview (Mus Snd Rec (Tonmeister)) (IB 34 pts HL 666 incl maths+mus+phys)

136 pts **Birmingham** – AAB (Mus) (IB 32 pts HL 665)

Bristol – AAB incl mus +gr 8 (Mus) (IB 34 pts HL 17 pts incl 5 mus)

Durham – AAB incl mus (Mus) (IB 36 pts HL 665 incl mus)

Edinburgh – A*AA–AAB incl maths (Maths Mus) (IB 37–32 pts HL 666–655 incl maths)

Glasgow – AAB incl mus +gr 5 (Mus) (IB 36 pts HL 665 incl Engl+hum/lang)

Leeds – AAB +gr 8 +interview (Mus) (IB 35 pts HL 6 mus); AAB+interview +audition +gr 8 (Mus (Perf)) (IB 35 pts HL 6 mus); AAB incl mus +gr 8 +interview (Mus Comb Hons) (IB 35 pts HL 6 music)

London (King's) – AAB incl mus +gr 6 (Mus) (IB 35 pts HL 665 incl mus)

London (RH) – AAA–AAB incl maths+phys +gr 7 (Phys Mus) (IB 32 pts HL 665 incl 6 maths+mus 5 phys)

Manchester – AAB incl A mus +gr 8 +interview (Mus) (IB 35 pts HL 665); AAB incl A mus +interview +gr 8 (Mus Dr) (IB 35 pts HL 665)

Southampton – AAB incl maths+phys+interview (Acoust Mus) (IB 34 pts HL 17 pts incl 6 maths+phys); AAB–ABB +aEPQ incl Engl+mus +gr 8 (Engl Mus) (IB 34 pts HL 17 pts incl 6/5 Engl+mus)

York – AAB incl mus +gr 8 +audition +interview (Mus) (IB 35 pts HL 6 mus)

128 pts **City** – ABB incl mus 128 pts +gr 7 (Mus) (IB 30 pts HL 555)

Edinburgh – ABB (Mus) (IB 38–34 pts HL 666–655); ABB incl mus (Hist Art Hist Mus) (IB 40–34 pts HL 766–655)

Glasgow – ABB incl mus +gr 8 +audition (BMus) (IB 34 pts HL 665)

Liverpool – ABB/BBB +aEPQ +interview +audition (Mus Pop Mus) (IB 33 pts HL 6 mus)

London (RH) – AAB–ABB (Modn Lang Mus) (IB 32 pts HL 655); AAB–ABB +gr 7 (Mus Phil) (IB 32 pts HL 655 incl 6 mus); AAB–ABB incl 6 mus (Dr Mus) (IB 32 pts HL 655 incl mus); AAB–ABB incl mus +gr 7 (Mus Pol St) (IB 32 pts HL 655 incl 6 mus)

London (SOAS) – AAB–ABB (Mus Comb Hons) (IB 35 pts HL 665)

Newcastle – AAB–ABB +interview (Mus) (IB 34 pts)

Nottingham – ABB incl mus (Mus Phil) (IB 32 pts HL 5 mus); ABB incl mus/mus tech +gr 8 (Mus) (IB 32 pts HL 5 mus)

Sheffield – ABB incl mus +gr 8 (Mus) (IB 34 pts HL 5 mus); ABB incl music +gr 8 (Mus Comb Hons) (IB 33 pts HL 5 mus)

Southampton – AAB–ABB incl mus +gr 8 +audition (Phil Mus) (IB 34–32 pts HL 17–16 pts incl 5 mus)

120 pts   **Aberdeen** – BBB (Mus St courses) (IB 32 pts HL 555)

Bangor – B mus 120 pts (Mus Crea Writ) (HL 6 mus); B mus 120 pts incl mus (Mus) (HL 6 mus)

Brunel – BBB +audition +interview (Mus) (IB 30 pts)

Cardiff – AAB–BBB incl mus +gr 8 +audition +interview (Mus courses) (IB 32–31 pts HL 6 music)

Coventry – BBB incl maths/phys/tech/mus (Mus Tech) (IB 31 pts)

Huddersfield – BBB incl maths/tech/comp/sci/eng 120 pts (Mus Tech Aud Sys); BBB incl mus/mus tech 120 pts (Mus)

Leeds Beckett – 120 pts +interview +workshop (Perf Arts) (IB 26 pts)

London (Gold) – BBB +interview (Mus; Pop Mus) (IB 33 pts HL 655)

Newcastle – AAB–BBB incl mus +interview +audition (Folk Trad Mus) (IB 34–32 pts)

Queen's Belfast – BBB incl mus (Mus) (IB 32 pts HL 655 incl mus)

Reading – BBB incl mus +gr 6 +interview (P Ed Mus Spec) (IB 30 pts HL 5 mus)

Southampton – AAB–BBB incl mus +gr 8 +audition +interview (Mus) (IB 32–30 pts HL 16 pts incl 5 mus); ABB–BBB incl mus +gr 8 (Mus Bus Mgt) (IB 32–30 pts HL 16 incl 5 mus)

Surrey – ABB–BBB incl mus +gr 5 +interview +portfolio (Crea Mus Tech) (IB 32 pts); ABB–BBB incl mus +interview (Mus) (IB 32 pts)

Sussex – ABB–BBB +gr 7 (Mus; Mus Tech) (IB 32–30 pts HL 5 mus)

Trinity Saint David – 120 pts +interview +portfolio (Crea Mus Tech) (IB 32 pts)

West London – ABB–BBB 120–128 pts +interview +audition (Musl Thea)

112 pts   **Bangor** – 112 pts (Welsh Hist Mus)

Birmingham City – BBC 112 pts (Mus Ind) (IB 28 pts)

Chester – 112 pts +gr 8 +audition (Pop Mus Perf) (IB 26 pts); BBC incl dr/thea st 112 pts +interview +audition (Musl Thea) (IB 26 pts HL 5 thea arts)

Coventry – BBC +gr 5 +interview +audition (Mus) (IB 29 pts)

Derby – 112 pts +gr 7 +interview +portfolio (Pop Mus); C comp/maths/sci/tech 112 pts +interview +portfolio (Mus Prod)

East London – 112 pts incl mus (Mus Perf Prod) (IB 25 pts HL 15 pts)

Edge Hill – BBB–BBC 112–120 pts (Mus Prod)

Glyndŵr – 112 pts (Mus Tech)

Huddersfield – BBC 112 pts (Mus Jrnl)

Hull – BBC incl mus/mus tech 112 pts+gr 6 (Mus) (IB 28 pts HL 5 mus)

Kent – BBC incl mus/mus tech (Mus Bus Prod; Mus Perf Prod; Mus Tech Aud Prod) (IB 34 pts HL 14 pts)

Kingston – 112 pts incl mus/mus tech +portfolio (Mus Tech)

Leeds Beckett – 112 pts (Mus Prod; Mus Tech) (IB 25 pts)

Liverpool (LIPA) – BBC 112 pts +interview (Snd Tech)

Liverpool Hope – BBC 112 pts +gr 5 +interview +audition (Mus) (IB 28 pts)

Middlesex – 112 pts (Mus Bus Arts Mgt)

Staffordshire – BBC 112 pts (Mus Tech)

Trinity Laban Consv – BBC incl mus/mus tech +audition +gr 8 (Mus Educ)

UWE Bristol – 112 pts incl mus/mus tech +audition (Crea Mus Tech) (HL 5 mus)

West London – BBC 112–128 pts +gr 6 +audition +interview (Perf Mus Mgt); BBC 112–128 pts incl mus +interview +portfolio (Cmpsn)

104 pts **Bangor** – B mus 104–120 pts (Mus Flm St) (HL 6 mus)

Central Lancashire – 104 pts +interview +audition (Mus Thea)

Chichester – BBC 104–120 pts +audition (Musl Thea (Trpl Threat)) (IB 28 pts); BBC–BCC 104–112 pts (Aud Prod Mus Tech) (IB 28 pts)

De Montfort – 104 pts (Mus Tech) (IB 24 pts); 104 pts incl mus/mus tech (Crea Mus Tech) (IB 24 pts HL 5 mus/mus tech); (Mus Tech Perf) (IB 28 pts HL 5 mus/mus tech)

Edinburgh Napier – BCC incl mus+Engl +gr 5 +interview +audition (Pop Mus) (IB 27 pts HL 654 incl mus+Engl); BCC incl mus+Engl +gr 5 +portfolio (Mus) (IB 27 pts HL 654 incl mus+Engl)

Falmouth – 104–120 pts +interview +audition (Crea Mus Tech; Mus; Pop Mus)

Middlesex – 104 pts +audition (Mus); 104 pts +interview (Pop Mus)

Northampton – BCC +interview (Pop Mus courses)

Oxford Brookes – BCC 104 pts +portfolio +interview (Mus) (IB 29 pts)

Plymouth – 104 pts incl mus/mus tech +gr 6 (Mus) (IB 26 pts HL 4 mus)

Portsmouth – 104–112 pts +interview +workshop (Musl Thea) (IB 25 pts)

Winchester – 104–120 pts (Mus Jrnl); (Mus Snd Prod) (HL 44)

96 pts **Anglia Ruskin** – 96 pts (Aud Mus Tech) (IB 24 pts); 96 pts incl mus/mus tech +audition (Mus) (IB 24 pts)

Bath Spa – CCC incl mus/mus tech +interview +portfolio (Commer Mus) (IB 26 pts)

Brighton – BBC–CCC 96–112 pts +interview +portfolio (Dig Mus Snd Arts) (IB 26 pts)

Central Lancashire – 96 pts +interview (Mus Prod)

Chichester – BCC–CCC 96–112 pts +audition (Mus) (IB 26 pts)

Colchester (UC) – 96 pts +interview +audition (Musl Thea)

Hertfordshire – CCC 96 pts (Mus Cmpsn Tech; Mus Snd Des Tech)

Keele – CCC (Mus Comb Hons; Mus Tech) (IB 26 pts)

Leeds (CMus) – 96 pts +audition +gr 5 (Mus (Comb)); 96 pts incl mus +audition +gr 8/6 (Mus (Class); Mus (Jazz); Mus (Pop Mus)); 96 pts incl mus +portfolio (Mus (Prod))

Liverpool (LIPA) – CCC 96 pts +interview (Mgt Mus Enter Thea Evnts); CCC incl mus/mus tech 96 pts +gr 5 +audition (Mus)

Middlesex – 96 pts +audition (Jazz)

Solent – 96–112 pts (Dig Mus); CCC 96–112 pts (Pop Mus Prod)

Teesside – 96–112 pts (Mus Tech)

West Scotland – CCC 96 pts (Commer Mus) (IB 24 pts)

Winchester – 96–112 pts +interview (Musl Thea)

Wolverhampton – CCC/BCD 96 pts +audition (Mus; Mus Tech)

88 pts **Canterbury Christ Church** – 88–112 pts (Musl Thea); 88–112 pts +interview (Mus (Commer Mus); Mus (Crea Mus Prod Tech)); 88–112 pts incl mus +gr 5 +interview +audition (Mus)

West Scotland – CCD incl mus+maths 88 pts (Mus Tech) (IB 24 pts)

York St John – 88 pts (Mus courses)

80 pts **Bedfordshire** – CC 80 pts +interview (Mus Tech)

Bucks New – 80 pts (Aud Mus Prod; Mus Perf Mgt)

South Wales – BCC–CDD incl art/des 80–104 pts +interview (Pop Commer Mus) (IB 29 pts)

72 pts **UHI** – BC +interview +audition (Gael Trad Mus)

64 pts **Ravensbourne Univ** – CC +portfolio (Mus Snd Des) (IB 24 pts)

Rose Bruford (Coll) – CC 64 pts +audition (Actr Mushp)

32 pts **London (RAcMus)** – EE incl mus +audition (BMus) (IB 24 pts)

RCMus – EE +audition +portfolio (BMus) (IB 24 pts)

RConsvS – EE +audition (BMus courses; Musl Thea) (IB 24 pts)

RNCM – EE +gr 5 +audition (Pop Mus)

Royal Welsh (CMusDr) – EE incl mus +gr 8 +interview/audition (BMus)

24 pts **UHI** – D +interview +audition (Pop Mus)

Gloucestershire – audition (Pop Mus); interview (Mus Bus)

Alternative offers
See **Chapter 6** and **Appendix 1** for grades/UCAS Tariff points information for other examinations.

EXAMPLES OF COLLEGES OFFERING COURSES IN THIS SUBJECT FIELD
Accrington and Rossendale (Coll); Barnfield (Coll); Barnsley (Coll); Bath (Coll); Bedford (Coll); Birmingham Met (Coll); Blackpool and Fylde (Coll); Bournemouth and Poole (Coll); Bradford College UC; Buckinghamshire (Coll Group); Calderdale (Coll); Canterbury (Coll); Carshalton (Coll); City and Islington (Coll); Colchester (UC); Cornwall (Coll); Coventry (Coll); Doncaster (Coll); Dudley (Coll); Ealing, Hammersmith and West London (Coll); East Surrey (Coll); Exeter (Coll); Fareham (Coll); Gateshead (Coll); Gloucestershire (Coll); Greater Brighton Met (Coll); Havant and South Downs (Coll); Havering (Coll); Hertford (Reg Coll); HOW (Coll); Hull (Coll); Kingston (Coll); Leicester (Coll); Liverpool City (Coll); Manchester (Coll); MidKent (Coll); Neath Port Talbot (Coll); Nescot; Newcastle (Coll); Oaklands (Coll); Petroc; Rotherham (CAT); Sheffield (Coll); South Essex (Coll); South Gloucestershire and Stroud (Coll); TEC Partnership; Telford (Coll); Tresham (CFHE); Truro and Penwith (Coll); Westminster City (Coll); Wigan and Leigh (Coll).

CHOOSING YOUR COURSE (SEE ALSO CH.1)
Universities and colleges teaching quality See www.qaa.ac.uk; https://unistats.ac.uk.

Top research universities and colleges (REF 2014) (Music, Drama, Dance and Performing Arts) Open University; Birmingham (Mus); City; London (King's) (Film); Manchester (Dr); London (RH) (Dr Thea); Huddersfield; Manchester (Mus); Cardiff; Roehampton (Dance); London (QM); Warwick; London (SOAS); Durham; London (RH) (Mus); Southampton; Oxford.

Examples of sandwich degree courses Birmingham City; Bournemouth; Coventry; Hertfordshire; Huddersfield; Leeds; Leeds Beckett; Oxford Brookes; Portsmouth; Reading; Staffordshire; Surrey; UWE Bristol.

ADMISSIONS INFORMATION
Number of applicants per place (approx) Anglia Ruskin 5; Bangor 4; Bath Spa 8; Birmingham 8; Bristol 8; Cambridge 2; Cardiff 6; City 7; Colchester (UC) 4; Cumbria 7; Durham 6; Edinburgh 6; Edinburgh Napier 8; Glasgow 4; Huddersfield 2; Hull 5; Kingston 18; Leeds 18; Liverpool 6; Liverpool (LIPA) 12; London (Gold) 7; London (King's) 10; London (RAcMus) 7; London (RH) 6; London (SOAS) 4; Manchester 6; Middlesex 23; Newcastle 3; Northampton 3; Nottingham 5; Oxford Brookes 7; Queen's Belfast 6; RCMus 10; RConsvS 6; RNCM 8; Rose Bruford (Coll) 15; Southampton 6; Trinity Laban Consv 4; Ulster 8; York 8; York St John 2.

Advice to applicants and planning the UCAS personal statement In addition to your ability and expertise with your chosen musical instrument(s), it is also important to know your composers and to take a critical interest in various kinds of music. Reference should be made to these, visits to concerts listed and any special interests indicated in types of musical activity, for example, opera, ballet. Work with orchestras, choirs and other musical groups should also be included and full details given of any competitions entered and awards obtained. See Chapter 4 for details of applications for Music courses at conservatoires. **Guildhall (Sch Mus Dr)** International applicants sending extra documentation from overseas must make sure that for Customs purposes they indicate that they will pay any import tax charged. **London (Gold)** We encourage students to bring examples of their written and creative work. **London (SOAS)** Candidates are judged on individual merits. Applicants are expected to have substantial practical experience of musical performance, but not necessarily Western music. **Royal Welsh (CMusDr)** Evidence of performance-related experience, eg youth orchestras, solo work, prizes, scholarships etc. Our course is a conservatoire course as opposed to a more academic university course. We offer a very high standard of performance tuition balanced with academic theory modules.

Misconceptions about this course Cardiff Some mistakenly think that the BMus scheme is either performance-based or something inferior to the principal music-based degree.

Selection interviews Yes Aberdeen, Anglia Ruskin, Bath Spa, Birmingham City, Bucks New, Cambridge, Cardiff, Chichester, Edinburgh Napier, Glasgow, Guildhall (Sch Mus Dr), Leeds, Liverpool (LIPA), London (Gold), Manchester, Oxford (36%), York; **Some** Bristol, Canterbury Christ Church, Coventry, Surrey, West London; **No** Birmingham, Chester, Edinburgh, Falmouth, Hertfordshire, Huddersfield, Leeds Beckett, Staffordshire.

Interview advice and questions See also **Chapter 4** under Applications for Music Courses at Conservatoires. **Bangor** Offer depends on proven ability in historical or compositional fields plus acceptable performance standard. Options include music therapy, recording techniques and jazz. **Bath Spa** Candidates are required to submit three examples of their work prior to audition and then perform an original piece at audition. Discussion of previous performing, composing and academic experience. **Bristol** (Mus Fr/Ger/Ital) No in-depth interviews; candidates invited to Open Days. **Cambridge** (St Catharine's) At interview, candidates have to undergo some simple keyboard or aural tests (including harmonisation of an unseen melody and memorisation of a rhythm). They will also have to comment on some unseen musical extracts from a stylistic and analytical point of view and a passage of musicological literature. Candidates are usually asked to submit some examples of work before the interview, which can be from the fields of harmony and counterpoint, history and analysis; they are also encouraged to send any other material such as compositions, programme notes or an independent essay on a subject of interest to the candidate. (Taking the STEP examination is not a requirement for admission.) Above all this, though, the main prerequisite for reading Music at St Catharine's is an academic interest in the subject itself. **Colchester (UC)** Great stress laid on candidate's ability to communicate love of the subject. **Durham** Grade 7 or 8 in first instrument and keyboard skills advisable. **Edinburgh Napier** Most candidates are called for interview, although very well-qualified candidates may be offered a place without interview. All are asked to submit samples of their work. Associated Board or Trinity Guildhall Grade 5 theory required. **Hull (Coll)** Good instrumental grades can improve chances of an offer and of confirmation in August. Students are not normally required to attend an audition/interview. Decisions will be made according to the information supplied on the UCAS application. Successful applicants will be invited to attend a departmental Open Day. We welcome applications from mature students and those with unconventional qualifications: in such cases an interview may be required. **Leeds** Intending students should follow an academic rather than practical-oriented A-level course. Interviews and auditions last approximately 20 minutes. Grade 8 Associated Board on an instrument is a normal expectation. **Liverpool (LIPA)** In addition to performing in orchestras etc, give details of any compositions you have completed (the number and styles). Instrumentalists (including vocalists) should describe any performance/gig experience together with any musical instrument grades achieved. (Mus) Candidates should prepare two pieces of contrasting music to play on their chosen instrument. They are likely to be asked to send three music tracks and a biography prior to audition. (Snd Tech) Applicants will be expected to analyse a sound recording of their choice, highlighting the technical and production values that they think are the most important. Examples of recorded work they have undertaken should also be available at interview, eg on CD. **London (Gold)** The interview will include a discussion of music and the personal interests of the applicant. **London (RAcMus)** All candidates are called for audition; places are usually offered later, subject to the minimum **GCSE** requirements being achieved. (BMus) Applicants sit a 50-minute written paper, and may also be tested on keyboard and aural performance. **RCMus** All UK and Eire candidates are required to attend an audition in person, but recordings are acceptable from overseas applicants. It must be stressed, however, that personal audition is preferable and those students offered places on the basis of a recorded audition may be required to take a confirmatory audition on arrival. Candidates are required to perform on the principal study instrument, and may also be required to undertake sight-reading, aural tests and paperwork. There is also an interview. Potential scholars sometimes proceed to a second audition, usually on the same day. The academic requirement for the BMus (RCM) course is two A-levels at pass grades. Acceptance is ultimately based on the quality of performance at audition, performing experience and perceived potential as a performer. As a guide, applicants should be of at least Grade 8 distinction standard. **RNCM** All applicants are called for audition. Successful applicants proceed to an academic interview which will include aural tests and questions on music theory and history. Student comment: 'A 45-minute interview with a panel of three. Focus was on portfolio of compositions sent in advance. Prior to interview was asked to harmonise a short passage and study an orchestral excerpt followed up at interview. Aural test waived.' **Royal Welsh (CMusDr)** All UK and Eire applicants are called to audition and/or interview in person; overseas candidates may audition by sending a recording. Candidates may be required to demonstrate their sight-reading ability or complete a short aural test. Composers are required to send recent examples of their work to discuss at interview. **Trinity Laban Consv** Applicants for the BMus degree must attend an audition and show that they have attained a certain level of competence in their principal and second studies, musical subjects and in musical theory. Grade 8 practical and theory can count as one A-level, but not if the second A-level is in music. Overseas applicants may submit a tape recording of their audition; video recordings are preferred. They must also show evidence of good aural perception in musical techniques and musical analysis. **Wolverhampton** The audition will involve playing/singing a piece of own-choice music (up to five minutes – no longer). Accompanists may be brought along or the department may be able to provide one if requested in advance. Candidates will be requested to produce a short piece of written work. It would be helpful to see any music certificates if available, together with examples of recent work in music (an essay, harmony, composition etc).

Reasons for rejection (non-academic) Usually academic (auditions, practical, aural/written test). Dull, unenthusiastic students, ignorant about their subject, showing lack of motivation and imagination. **Cambridge** Her harmony was marred by elementary technical errors and her compositions lacked formal and stylistic focus. **London (King's)** Apparent lack of interest, performance not good enough, lack of music history knowledge. Foreign students: language skills inadequate. **Royal Welsh (CMusDr)** Performing/technical ability not of the required standard.

AFTER-RESULTS ADVICE
Offers to applicants repeating A-levels Higher Leeds; **Same** Anglia Ruskin; Bath Spa; Bristol; Cardiff; City; Colchester (UC); De Montfort; Durham; Guildhall (Sch Mus Dr); Huddersfield; Hull; Kingston; Leeds (CMus); London (RAcMus); London (RH); Nottingham; Rose Bruford (Coll); Royal Welsh (CMusDr); Staffordshire; York; York St John.

GRADUATE DESTINATIONS AND EMPLOYMENT (2016/17 HESA)
Graduates surveyed 4,080 **Employed** 1,550 **In voluntary employment** 95 **In further study** 1,175 **Assumed unemployed** 175

Career note Some graduates go into performance-based careers, many enter the teaching profession and others go into a wide range of careers requiring graduate skills.

OTHER DEGREE SUBJECTS FOR CONSIDERATION
Acoustics; Drama; Musical Theatre; Performance Arts.

NATURAL SCIENCES
(See also **Biological Sciences**)

These are flexible courses allowing the student to gain a broad view of the origins and potential of sciences in general and then to focus in Years 2 and 3 on a specialist area of scientific study.

Useful websites www.scicentral.com; www.nature.com; see also **Biology**,**Chemistry** and **Physics**.

NB The points totals shown to the left of the institutions are for ease of reference only. It must not be assumed that Tariff points are always used by institutions or that they can be substituted for an offer in grades. The level of an offer is not necessarily indicative of the quality of a course.

COURSE OFFERS INFORMATION
Subject requirements/preferences GCSE Strong results, particularly in the sciences. **AL** Science subjects required.

Your target offers and examples of degree courses

160 pts **Cambridge** – A*A*A incl sci/maths +interview +NSAA (Nat Sci; Nat Sci (Astro); Nat Sci (Bioch); Nat Sci (Biol Biomed Sci); Nat Sci (Chem); Nat Sci (Earth Sci); Nat Sci (Genet); Nat Sci (Mat Sci); Nat Sci (Neuro); Nat Sci (Physiol Dev Neuro); Nat Sci (Zool)) (IB 42–40 pts HL 776)

152 pts **Bath** – A*AA incl maths/sci (Nat Sci; Nat Sci (St Abrd)) (IB 36 pts HL 766 incl maths/sci)
         Durham – A*AA (Nat Sci) (IB 38 pts)
         East Anglia – A*AA incl sci (Nat Sci (Yr Ind/St Abrd)) (IB 35 pts HL 6 sci); A*AA incl sci/maths (Nat Sci (MNatSci)) (IB 35 pts HL 6 sci/maths)
         Leeds – A*AA incl sci (Nat Sci) (IB 36 pts)
         London (UCL) – A*AA incl sci/maths (Nat Sci) (IB 39 pts HL 19 pts incl 6 sci/maths)
         Nottingham – A*AA incl sci/maths (Nat Sci) (IB 38 pts HL 6/7 sci/maths)

144 pts **Birmingham** – A*AA–AAA +admissions essay (Librl Arts Sci (Nat Sci)) (IB 36–35 pts)
         East Anglia – AAA incl sci/maths (Nat Sci) (IB 34 pts HL 6 sci/maths)
         Exeter – AAA incl maths+sci (Nat Sci) (IB 36 pts HL 666 incl 6 maths+sci)
         Lancaster – A*AA–AAA incl sci (Nat Sci) (IB 38–36 pts HL 16 pts incl 6 sci)

136 pts **Loughborough** – AAB incl sci (Nat Sci) (IB 35 pts HL 665 incl sci)

         Open University – contact 0300 303 0073 or www.open.ac.uk/contact/new (Nat Sci)

Alternative offers

See **Chapter 6** and **Appendix 1** for grades/UCAS Tariff points information for other examinations.

CHOOSING YOUR COURSE (SEE ALSO CH.1)

Universities and colleges teaching quality See www.qaa.ac.uk; https://unistats.ac.uk.

Top research universities and colleges (REF 2014) See separate science tables.

Examples of sandwich degree courses Bath; East Anglia; Leeds.

ADMISSIONS INFORMATION

Number of applicants per place (approx) Bath 8; Birmingham 10; Cambridge 4; Durham 6; Lancaster 4; London (UCL) 4; Nottingham 7.

Advice to applicants and planning the UCAS personal statement See **Biology**, **Chemistry**, **Physics** and **Appendix 3**.

Selection interviews Yes Cambridge, East Anglia; **Some** Bath; **No** Birmingham.

Interview advice and questions See also **Chapter 5**. **Cambridge** Questions depend on subject choices and studies at A-level and past questions have included the following: Discuss the setting up of a chemical engineering plant and the probabilities of failure of various components. Questions on the basic principles of physical chemistry, protein structure and functions and physiology. Questions on biological specimens. Comment on the theory of evolution and the story of the Creation in Genesis. What are your weaknesses? Questions on electro-micrographs. What do you talk about with your friends? How would you benefit from a university education? What scientific magazines do you read? Questions on atoms, types of bonding and structures. What are the problems of being tall? What are the differences between metals and non-metals? Why does graphite conduct? Questions on quantum physics and wave mechanics. How could you contribute to life here? What do you see yourself doing in five years' time? If it is common public belief that today's problems, for example industrial pollution, are caused by scientists, why do you wish to become one? Questions on the gyroscopic motion of cycle wheels, the forces on a cycle in motion and the design of mountain bikes. What do you consider will be the most startling scientific development in the future? What do you estimate is the mass of air in this room? If a carrot can grow from one carrot cell, why not a human?

AFTER-RESULTS ADVICE

Offers to applicants repeating A-levels No Cambridge.

GRADUATE DESTINATIONS AND EMPLOYMENT (2016/17 HESA)

Graduates surveyed See **Biology**, **Chemistry**, **Mathematics** and **Physics**.

Career note These courses offer a range of science and in some cases non-scientific subjects, providing students with the flexibility to develop particular interests as they progress through the course.

OTHER DEGREE SUBJECTS FOR CONSIDERATION

Anatomy; Anthropology; Archaeology; Astrophysics; Biochemistry; Biological Sciences; Biology; Chemistry; Earth Sciences; Ecology; Genetics; Geography; Geology; History and Philosophy of Science; Neuroscience; Pharmacology; Physics; Plant Sciences; Psychology; Zoology.

NEUROSCIENCE

(including **Anatomical Science**; see also **Biological Sciences, Human Sciences/Human Biosciences, Physiology, Psychology**)

Courses in Neuroscience include the study of biochemistry, cell and molecular biology, genetics and physiology and focus on the structure and functions of the brain. It also overlaps into neurobiology, neuroanatomy, neurophysiology, pharmacology and psychology which in turn can involve the study of behavioural problems and mental processes, both conscious and unconscious. It is a field of research contributing to the treatment of such medical conditions as Parkinson's disease, Alzheimer's, schizophrenia, epilepsy and autism. Studies will cover anatomical structures such as skeletal, muscular, cardiovascular and nervous systems and components such as muscle cells.

Useful websites www.innerbody.com; www.instantanatomy.net

NB The points totals shown to the left of the institutions are for ease of reference only. It must not be assumed that Tariff points are always used by institutions or that they can be substituted for an offer in grades. The level of an offer is not necessarily indicative of the quality of a course.

COURSE OFFERS INFORMATION

Subject requirements/preferences GCSE Mathematics usually required. **AL** One or two mathematics/science subjects usually required; biology and chemistry preferred.

Your target offers and examples of degree courses

160 pts   **Cambridge** – A*A*A incl sci/maths +interview +NSAA (Nat Sci (Neuro)) (IB 42–40 pts HL 776)

144 pts   **Birmingham** – AAA incl biol (Hum Neuro) (IB 32 pts HL 666 incl biol)

      Bristol – AAA/A*AB incl sci/maths (Neuro) (IB 36 pts HL 18 pts incl 65 sci/maths)

      London (UCL) – AAA incl chem+sci/maths (Neuro) (IB 38 pts HL 18 pts incl 5 chem+sci/maths)

136 pts   **Glasgow** – AAB incl biol/chem (Anat) (IB 36 pts HL 665 incl sci); AAB incl biol/chem 136 pts (Neuro) (IB 36 pts HL 665 incl sci)

      Leeds – AAA–AAB incl biol/chem+sci (Neuro) (IB 35–34 pts HL 18–17 pts incl 6 biol/chem+sci)

      Liverpool – AAB incl biol (Anat Hum Biol) (IB 34 pts HL 6 biol)

      London (King's) – AAB incl chem+biol (Anat Dev Hum Biol; Neuro) (IB 35 pts HL 665 chem+biol)

      London (RH) – AAA–AAB (Psy Clin Cog Neuro) (IB 32 pts HL 665)

      Nottingham – AAB (Psy Cog Neuro) (IB 34 pts); AAB incl biol/chem+sci/maths (Neuro) (IB 34 pts)

      St Andrews – AAB incl sci/maths (Neuro) (IB 36 pts HL 665 incl sci/maths)

      Sussex – AAA–AAB (Psy Cog Sci; Psy Neuro) (IB 36–34 pts)

128 pts   **Cardiff** – AAB–ABB incl biol+chem (Biomed Sci (Anat)) (IB 34–32 pts HL 6 biol+chem); AAB–ABB incl biol/chem (Biomed Sci; Neuro) (IB 34–32 pts HL 655 incl 6 biol/chem)

      Edinburgh – AAB–ABB (Neuro) (IB 36–32 pts HL 65 biol+chem)

      Keele – ABB incl sci/maths/stats (Neuro) (IB 34 pts HL 6 sci)

      Manchester – AAA–ABB incl sci/maths (Anat Sci; Anat Sci (Yr Ind); Cog Neuro Psy; Neuro) (IB 36–33 pts HL 666–655 incl sci)

Reading – ABB (Psy Neuro) (IB 32 pts)

Sussex – AAB–ABB incl sci/psy (Med Neuro; Neuro Cog Sci) (IB 34–32 pts HL 5 sci/psy)

120 pts   **Aberdeen** – BBB incl maths+sci (Neuro Psy) (IB 32 pts HL 555 incl maths+sci)

Dundee – BBB incl biol (Anat Sci) (IB 30 pts HL 555 incl biol)

Essex – BBB (Psy Cog Neuro) (IB 30 pts HL 555)

Leicester – ABB–BBB (Psy Cog Neuro) (IB 30–28 pts)

London (Gold) – BBB (Psy Cog Neuro) (IB 33 pts HL 655)

112 pts   **Bangor** – 112 pts (Psy Neuropsy)

Central Lancashire – 112–128 pts (Neuropsy)

Middlesex – C sci 112 pts (Neuro)

Alternative offers

See **Chapter 6** and **Appendix 1** for grades/UCAS Tariff points information for other examinations.

CHOOSING YOUR COURSE (SEE ALSO CH.1)

Universities and colleges teaching quality See www.qaa.ac.uk; https://unistats.ac.uk.

Top research universities and colleges (REF 2014) See **Biological Sciences**.

Examples of sandwich degree courses Bristol; Cardiff; Leeds; Manchester.

ADMISSIONS INFORMATION

Number of applicants per place (approx) Bristol 10; Cardiff 9; London (UCL) 7.

Advice to applicants and planning the UCAS personal statement Give reasons for your interest in this subject (usually stemming from school work in biology). Discuss any articles in medical and other scientific journals which have attracted your attention and any new developments in medicine related to neuroscience.

Selection interviews Yes Bristol, Liverpool; **Some** Cardiff.

Interview advice and questions Questions are likely on your particular interests in biology and anatomy, why you wish to study the subject and your future career intentions. See also **Chapter 5**.

AFTER-RESULTS ADVICE

Offers to applicants repeating A-levels Higher Bristol; **Same** Cardiff.

GRADUATE DESTINATIONS AND EMPLOYMENT (2016/17 HESA)

Including Pathology and Physiology Graduates surveyed 3,030 **Employed** 1,895 **In voluntary employment** 25 **In further study** 660 **Assumed unemployed** 130

Career note The subject leads to a range of careers in various laboratories, in government establishments, the NHS, pharmaceutical and food industries. It can also lead to postgraduate studies in physiotherapy, nursing, osteopathy and, in exceptional cases, in medicine, dentistry and veterinary science.

OTHER DEGREE SUBJECTS FOR CONSIDERATION

Biological Sciences; Biology; Genetics; Microbiology; Osteopathy; Physiology; Physiotherapy.

NURSING AND MIDWIFERY

(See also **Biological Sciences, Community Studies/Development, Health Sciences/Studies**)

Nursing and Midwifery courses are designed to equip students with the scientific and caring skills demanded by medical science in the 21st century. Courses follow a similar pattern with an introductory programme of study covering clinical skills, nursing practice and the behavioural and social sciences. Thereafter, specialisation starts in adult, child or mental health nursing, or with patients with learning disabilities. Throughout the three-year course, students gain extensive clinical experience in hospital wards, clinics, accident and emergency and high-dependency settings. UCAS handles applications for Nursing degree courses. Nursing is an all-graduate profession.

Useful websites www.scicentral.com; www.healthcareers.nhs.uk; www.nursingtimes.net; www.nmc. org.uk; www.rcn.org.uk; www.rcm.org.uk; see also **Health Sciences/Studies** and **Medicine**.

NB The points totals shown to the left of the institutions are for ease of reference only. It must not be assumed that Tariff points are always used by institutions or that they can be substituted for an offer in grades. The level of an offer is not necessarily indicative of the quality of a course.

COURSE OFFERS INFORMATION
Subject requirements/preferences GCSE English and a science subject. Mathematics required at several universities. **AL** Science subjects required for some courses. All applicants holding firm offers will require an occupational health check and Disclosure and Barring Service (DBS) clearance and are required to provide documentary evidence that they have not been infected with hepatitis B.

Your target offers and examples of degree courses
136 pts **Southampton** – AAB incl sci +interview (Midwif) (IB 34 pts HL 17 pts incl sci)
128 pts **Birmingham City** – ABB incl sci 128 pts +interview (Midwif) (IB 32 pts)
Bournemouth – 128–144 pts incl sci +interview (Midwif) (IB 34–32 pts HL 5 sci)
Bradford – 128 pts +interview (Midwif St) (HL 665)
City – ABB 128 pts +interview (Midwif) (IB 33 pts)
Coventry – ABB incl sci/soc sci +interview +test (Midwif) (IB 30 pts HL 15 pts)
East Anglia – ABB +interview (Midwif) (IB 32 pts)
Edinburgh – ABB +interview (Nurs St) (IB 36–34 pts HL 665–655)
Glasgow – ABB incl sci/maths (Nurs) (IB 36 pts HL 665 incl 6 chem/biol)
Huddersfield – ABB incl biol 128 pts +interview (Midwif St)
Keele – ABB incl biol/hlth soc cr/psy/sociol +interview (Midwif) (IB 27 pts)
Kingston – ABB 128 pts +interview (Midwif)
Leeds – ABB incl biol +interview (Midwif) (IB 34 pts HL 16 pts incl 5 biol)
Leicester – ABB incl sci +MMI (Midwif Ldrshp) (IB 30 pts HL 6 biol)
Liverpool John Moores – ABB incl sci 128 pts +interview (Midwif)
London (King's) – ABB +interview (Midwif Reg) (IB 34 pts HL 655)
Manchester – AAB–ABB incl sci +interview (Midwif) (IB 34 pts HL 655 biol/chem)
Sheffield Hallam – ABB incl nat/soc sci 128 pts +interview (Midwif)
Surrey – ABB +MMI (Midwif) (IB 32 pts)
UWE Bristol – B sci/soc sci 128 pts +interview (Midwif) (HL 6 sci/soc sci)
York – ABB (Midwif) (IB 34 pts)
120 pts **Anglia Ruskin** – 120 pts +interview (Midwif) (IB 26 pts)
Bangor – 120 pts +interview (Midwif; Nurs A/C/LD/MH)
Birmingham – BBB +interview (Nurs A/MH/C) (IB 32 pts HL 555)
Birmingham City – BBB incl sci 120 pts +interview (Nurs A/C/LD/MH) (IB 30 pts)
Brighton – BBB incl sci/soc sci +interview (Midwif) (IB 27 pts)
Canterbury Christ Church – BBB +interview (Midwif)
Cardiff – ABB–BBB +MMI (Midwif) (IB 32–31 pts HL 655)
Cumbria – B biol/PE 120–128 pts +interview (Midwif)
De Montfort – B sci/soc sci 120 pts +interview (Midwif) (IB 28 pts HL sci/psy)
Derby – 120 pts +interview (Nurs A/MH)
Edge Hill – ABB–BBB incl sci 120–128 pts +interview (Midwif)
Greenwich – 120 pts +interview (Midwif)
Huddersfield – BBB 120 pts +interview (Nurs A/C/MH)
Hull – BBB 120 pts +interview +test (Midwif) (IB 30 pts)
Leeds – BBB incl sci/maths/soc sci +interview (Nurs A/C/MH) (IB 34 pts HL 555)
Leicester – BBB incl sci +MMI (Nurs Ldrshp MH A/C) (IB 28 pts HL 6 sci)
Liverpool – BBB incl biol +interview (Nurs) (IB 30 pts HL 555)

Liverpool John Moores – BBB 120 pts +interview (Nurs C)
London (King's) – BBB +interview (Nurs A/C/MH) (IB 32 pts HL 555)
London South Bank – BBB 120 pts +MMI (Midwif)
Northumbria – 120 pts +interview (Nurs St A/C/LD/MH); 120 pts incl sci/hlth +interview (Midwif)
Nottingham – BBB incl sci +interview (Nurs A/C/MH) (IB 30 pts HL 5 sci)
Oxford Brookes – BBB incl sci 120 pts +interview (Midwif) (IB 31 pts)
South Wales – BBB +interview (Midwif; Nurs A/C/LD/MH) (IB 32 pts HL 17 pts)
Southampton – BBB +interview (Nurs A/C/MH) (IB 30 pts HL 16 pts)
Staffordshire – BBB 120 pts (Midwif Prac)
Swansea – BBB +interview (Nurs A/C/MH) (IB -32 pts)
UWE Bristol – C sci/soc sci 120 pts +interview (Nurs A/C/LD/MH) (HL 5 sci/soc sci)
West London – 120 pts +interview (Midwif)
Worcester – BBB incl sci/PE/sociol/hlth 120 pts +interview (Midwif)
York – BBB (Nurs A/C/LD/MH) (IB 31 pts)

112 pts   **Anglia Ruskin** – 112 pts +interview (Nurs A/C/MH) (IB 24 pts)
Bedfordshire – 112 pts +interview (Midwif; Nurs A/C/MH)
Bradford – BBC 112 pts +interview (Nurs A/C/MH)
Brighton – BBC incl sci/soc sci 112 pts +MMI (Nurs A/C/MH) (IB 27 pts)
Bucks New – 112–128 pts +interview (Nurs A/C/MH)
Cardiff – BBB–BBC +MMI (Nurs A/C/MH) (IB 31–30 pts HL 655)
Central Lancashire – 112–128 pts (Midwif)
Chester – BBB–BBC incl biol/app sci 112–120 pts (Midwif) (IB 28 pts HL 5 biol)
City – BBC 112 pts +interview (Nurs A/C/MH) (IB 32 pts)
De Montfort – 112 pts +interview (Nurs A/C/MH/LD) (IB 26 pts)
East Anglia – BBC–BCC +aEPQ +interview (Nurs A/LD/MH) (IB 30 pts)
Edinburgh Napier – BBC incl sci+Engl +interview (Nurs A/C/LD/MH)
Essex – BBC +interview (Nurs MH) (IB 29 pts HL 554); BBC 112 pts +interview (Nurs) (IB 29 pts HL 554)
Glyndŵr – 112 pts +interview +test (Nurs A)
Greenwich – 112 pts +interview (Nurs A/C/LD/MH)
Hertfordshire – BBC incl biol sci/bhv sci/soc sci 112 pts +interview (Midwif)
Hull – BBC 112 pts +interview (Nurs A/MH/LD) (IB 28 pts)
Keele – BBC +interview (Nurs A/C/LD/MH) (IB 25 pts)
Kingston – BBC 112 pts +MMI (Nurs A/C/LD/MH) (IB 26 pts)
Leeds Beckett – 112 pts +interview (Nurs A/MH) (IB 25 pts)
Lincoln – BBC 112 pts +interview (Nurs A/C/MH) (IB 29 pts)
Liverpool John Moores – BBC 112 pts +interview (Nurs (MH/A))
London South Bank – BBC/A*A* +MMI (Nurs A/C/MH)
Manchester – BBC incl sci/psy/hlth/app sci +interview (Nurs A) (IB 30 pts HL 555 incl sci)
Middlesex – 112 pts +interview (Midwif); 112 pts +interview (Nurs A/C/MH)
Northampton – BBC incl sci/psy/sociol (Midwif)
Salford – 112–128 pts +interview (Midwif) (IB 31 pts)
Staffordshire – BBC 112 pts +interview (Nurs Prac A/C/MH)
Teesside – 112 pts incl sci +interview (Midwif)
Ulster – BBC +interview (Nurs A/MH) (IB 25 pts HL 12 pts)
West London – BBC 112 pts +interview (Nurs A/C/LD/MH)
Wolverhampton – BBC 112 pts +interview (Nurs A/C/MH/LD); BBC incl sci 112 pts +interview (Midwif)
Worcester – 112 pts +interview (Nurs (A/C/MH))

104 pts   **Abertay** – BCC +interview (Nurs MH) (IB 29 pts)
Bournemouth – 104–120 pts +interview (Chld Yng Ppl Nurs; Nurs A/C/MH) (IB 31–28 pts)
Canterbury Christ Church – BCC +MMI (Nurs A/C/MH)
Chester – BBC–BCC 104–112 pts (Nurs A/C/LD/MH) (IB 26 pts)
Coventry – BCC +interview (Nurs A/LD/MH) (IB 27 pts HL 14 pts)

Cumbria – C sci/soc sci 104–120 pts +interview +test (Nurs A/C/LD/MH)

Edge Hill – BBC–BCC 104–112 pts +interview (Nurs A/C/LD/MH)

Edinburgh Napier – BCC incl biol/app sci +interview (Midwif)

Hertfordshire – BCC 104 pts +interview +test (Nurs (A/C/LD/MH))

Manchester Met – BBC–BCC 104–112 pts +interview (Nurs A/MH) (IB 29 pts)

Northampton – BCC +interview (Nurs A/C/MH/LD)

Oxford Brookes – BCC 104 pts +interview (Nurs A/C/MH) (IB 29 pts)

Plymouth – 104–120 pts +interview (Nurs A/C/MH) (IB 30–26 pts)

Portsmouth – 104 pts incl sci/soc sci +interview (Nurs A; Nurs MH) (IB 26 pts HL 5 sci/soc sci)

Queen Margaret – BCC incl sci +interview (Nurs) (IB 30 pts)

Queen's Belfast – BBC–BCC incl sci +interview (Nurs A/C/LD/MH); BBC–BCC incl sci/maths 104–112 pts +MMI (Midwif Sci)

Robert Gordon – BCC incl Engl+sci +interview (Midwif; Nurs A/C/MH) (IB 27 pts)

Sheffield Hallam – BCC 104 pts +interview (Nurs A/C/MH)

Winchester – 104–120 pts +interview (Nurs A/LD/MH) (HL 44)

96 pts **Central Lancashire** – 96 pts (Nurs (A/MH))

Stirling – CCC +interview (Nurs A/MH) (IB 28 pts)

Suffolk – CCC 96 pts +interview (Nurs A/C/MH)

Teesside – 96 pts +interview (Nurs St A/C/LD/MH)

72 pts **Glasgow Caledonian** – BC +interview (Nurs St (A/C/LD/MH)) (IB 24 pts)

West Scotland – BC 72 pts +interview (Nurs A/MH)

64 pts **Dundee** – CC +interview (Nurs A/C/MH) (IB 24 pts HL 44)

Open University – contact 0300 303 0073 or www.open.ac.uk/contact/new (Nurs A)

Alternative offers

See **Chapter 6** and **Appendix 1** for grades/UCAS Tariff points information for other examinations.

DEGREE APPRENTICESHIPS

Chester (Nurs); Essex (Reg Nurs); Oxford Brookes (Nursing Associate); Portsmouth (Nurs); Hull (Nurs); Brighton (Nurs); Chester (Nurs); Canterbury Christ Church (Hlth Soc Cr Nurs).

EXAMPLES OF COLLEGES OFFERING COURSES IN THIS SUBJECT FIELD

Central Campus, Sandwell (Coll); East Kent (Coll); MidKent (Coll); Norwich City (Coll); Oaklands (Coll).

CHOOSING YOUR COURSE (SEE ALSO CH.1)

Universities and colleges teaching quality See www.qaa.ac.uk; https://unistats.ac.uk.

Top research universities and colleges (REF 2014) (Allied Health Professions, Dentistry, Nursing, Pharmacy) Birmingham; Glasgow; Nottingham (Pharm); Bradford; East Anglia (Allied Hlth); London (QM); Sheffield (Dnstry); Queen's Belfast (Pharm); Bath; London (King's) (Pharm); Leeds; Sheffield (Biomed Sci); Bangor; Swansea (Allied Hlth); Aston; Coventry; Southampton; Cardiff; Surrey.

ADMISSIONS INFORMATION

Number of applicants per place (approx) Abertay 5; Anglia Ruskin 10; Bangor 4; Birmingham 8; Birmingham City 15; Cardiff 7; Central Lancashire (Midwif) 14; City (Nurs MH) 14, (Nurs C) 11, (Midwif) 9, (Nurs A) 12; Cumbria 8; De Montfort 10; Huddersfield (Midwif St) 8; Hull 10; Leeds (Midwif) 12; Liverpool John Moores (Nurs) 5; London (King's) 4; London South Bank 16; Middlesex 10; Northampton 17; Nottingham 9; Oxford Brookes 7; Salford 10; Sheffield Hallam 8; Southampton (Nurs) 15, (Midwif) 25; Staffordshire (Midwif Prac) 10; Stirling 5; Swansea 10; York (Midwif) 2.

Numbers of applicants (a UK **b** EU (non-UK) **c** non-EU **d** mature) Cardiff **c** 6

Advice to applicants and planning the UCAS personal statement Experience of care work – for example in hospitals, old people's homes, children's homes – is important. Describe what you have done and what you have learned. Read nursing journals in order to be aware of new developments in the treatment of illnesses. Note, in particular, the various needs of patients and the problems they experience. Try to compare different nursing approaches with, for example, children, people with learning disabilities, old people and terminally ill people. If you underperformed at **GCSE**, give reasons. If you have had work experience or a part-time job, describe how your skills have developed, for example responsibility, communication, team building, organisational skills. How do you spend your spare time? Explain how your interests help with stress and pressure. See also **Appendix 3**. Contact NHS Student Bursaries for information about financial support; tel 0300 330 1345. **Liverpool John Moores** (Nurs C) The candidate needs to have clear evidence of experience in caring for children/young people aged 0–17. This can be paid employment, voluntary work or work experience within a health or social care setting within the last three years. Their experience needs to include working with a variety of age ranges (not just one), such as babies through to young people, as well as those children and young people who have a range of physical and intellectual abilities. **West Scotland** Research the role of a nurse and the essential qualities needed.

Misconceptions about this course Bournemouth Many think that being passionate about babies is what midwifery is all about, but really it is about the care of the adult (ie mothers through pregnancy), not the child. Applicants might wish to consider the BSc in Children's and Young People's Nursing, which is focused on the care of the child and can lead to later specialisations as a health visitor. Applicants are advised to apply to one type of degree, eg all adult nursing courses, or all child nursing courses, rather than a mixture. This is because admissions are looking for students who are dedicated to a specific health career which they can demonstrate insight into. **Bradford** Mental Health nurses are not just trained to keep patients sedated with drugs. The work involves supporting a patient's recovery and enabling them to have involvement and control in their recovery. **City** Midwives are only involved at the birth stage and not at the antenatal and postnatal stages, or in education and support. **Winchester** This is an intensive programme with professional placements and students have more contact hours than those on other courses.

Selection interviews Yes Abertay, Anglia Ruskin, Bangor, Bedfordshire, Birmingham, Birmingham City, Bolton, Bournemouth, Brighton, Cardiff, Chester, City, Cumbria, Dundee, East Anglia, Edge Hill, Edinburgh, Edinburgh Napier, Greenwich, Hertfordshire, Huddersfield, Hull, Leeds Beckett, Lincoln, Liverpool John Moores, London (King's), London South Bank, Manchester, Middlesex, Nottingham, Oxford Brookes, Plymouth, Queen Margaret, Queen's Belfast, Robert Gordon, Salford, Sheffield Hallam, Southampton, Stirling, Suffolk, Surrey, Swansea, UWE Bristol, West London, West Scotland, Wolverhampton, Worcester; **Some** Bucks New, Coventry, Keele; **No** Central Lancashire.

Interview advice and questions Past questions have included: Why do you want to be a nurse? What experience have you had in nursing? What do you think of the nurses' pay situation? Should nurses go on strike? What are your views on abortion? What branch of nursing most interests you? How would you communicate with someone who can't speak English? What is the nurse's role in the community? How should a nurse react in an emergency? How would you cope with telling a patient's relative that the patient was dying? Admissions tutors look for communication skills, team interaction and the applicant's understanding of health/society-related subjects. See also **Chapter 5**. **London South Bank** What do you understand by equal opportunities? **Swansea** What is your perception of the role of the nurse? What qualities do you have that would be good for nursing?

Reasons for rejection (non-academic) Insufficient awareness of the roles and responsibilities of a midwife or nurse. Lack of motivation. Poor communication skills. Lack of awareness of nursing developments through the media. (Detailed knowledge of the NHS or nursing practice not usually required.) Failed medical. Unsatisfactory health record. Not fulfilling the hepatitis B requirements or police check requirements. Poor preparation for the interview. Too shy. Only wants nursing as a means to something else, for example commission in the armed forces. Too many choices on the UCAS application, for example Midwifery, Physiotherapy, Occupational Therapy. No care experience. Difficulty with maths – multiplication and division – used in calculating dosage for medicines. **De Montfort** No insight as to nursing as a career or the various branches of nursing.

AFTER-RESULTS ADVICE
Offers to applicants repeating A-levels Higher Cardiff; **Same** De Montfort; Huddersfield; Hull; Liverpool John Moores; London South Bank; Queen Margaret; Salford; Staffordshire; Stirling; Suffolk; Swansea; Wolverhampton; **No** Birmingham City.

GRADUATE DESTINATIONS AND EMPLOYMENT (2016/17 HESA)
Nursing Graduates surveyed 20,835 **Employed** 17,395 **In voluntary employment** 20 **In further study** 975 **Assumed unemployed** 215

Career note The majority of Nursing graduates aim to enter the nursing profession.

OTHER DEGREE SUBJECTS FOR CONSIDERATION
Audiology; Biological Sciences; Biology; Community Studies; Dietetics; Education; Health Studies; Medicine; Nutrition; Occupational Therapy; Optometry; Pharmacology; Pharmacy; Physiotherapy; Podiatry; Psychology; Radiography; Social Policy and Administration; Social Work; Sociology; Speech Therapy; Veterinary Nursing.

NUTRITION
(see also Dietetics, Food Science/Studies and Technology, Health Sciences/Studies)

Nutrition attracts a great deal of attention in society and while controversy, claim and counter-claim seem to focus daily on the merits and otherwise of food, it is, nevertheless, a scientific study in itself. Courses involve topics relating to diet, health, nutrition and food policy and are designed to prepare students to enter careers as specialists in nutrition and dietetics.

Useful websites www.nutrition.org.uk; www.nutritionsociety.org; see also under **Dietetics**.

NB The points totals shown to the left of the institutions are for ease of reference only. It must not be assumed that Tariff points are always used by institutions or that they can be substituted for an offer in grades. The level of an offer is not necessarily indicative of the quality of a course.

COURSE OFFERS INFORMATION
Subject requirements/preferences GCSE Mathematics and science usually required. **AL** Science subjects required for most courses, biology and/or chemistry preferred.

Your target offers and examples of degree courses
136 pts **Leeds** – AAB incl sci/maths (Nutr) (IB 35 pts HL 16 pts incl sci)
    London (King's) – AAB incl chem+biol +interview (Nutr Diet) (IB 35 pts HL 665 incl chem+biol)
    Newcastle – AAB incl sci (Fd Hum Nutr) (IB 34 pts); (Nutr Fd Mark) (IB 34 pts HL 6 biol)
128 pts **Leeds** – ABB incl sci (Fd Sci Nutr) (IB 34 pts HL 16 pts)
    London (King's) – ABB incl chem+biol (Nutr) (IB 34 pts HL 655 incl chem+biol)
    Nottingham – AAB–ABB incl sci +interview (Nutr Diet (MNutr)) (IB 34–32 pts); AAB–ABB incl sci/maths (Fd Sci Nutr) (IB 34–32 pts)
    Reading – ABB incl sci/maths (Nutr) (IB 32 pts HL 5 sci/maths); ABB incl sci/maths +interview (Nutr Fd Consum Sci) (IB 32 pts HL 5 sci); (Fd Sci; Nutr Fd Sci) (IB 32 pts HL 5 sci/maths)
    Surrey – ABB incl biol+sci/maths +interview (Nutr Diet) (IB 32 pts HL 5 biol+sci/maths)
120 pts **Cardiff Met** – BBB incl biol+chem 120 pts +interview (Hum Nutr Diet) (IB 26 pts HL 15 pts incl 6 biol+chem)
    Leeds Beckett – BBB incl chem+sci +interview (Diet) (IB 26 pts HL 6 chem)
    London Met – BBB incl biol+chem 120 pts +interview (Diet Nutr) (IB 28 pts HL 15 pts)
    Northumbria – 120 pts incl sci/fd tech/hm econ (Fd Sci Nutr)
    Nottingham – ABB–BBB incl sci (Nutr) (IB 32–30 pts HL 5 sci)
    Queen's Belfast – ABB–BBB incl sci (Fd Qual Sfty Nutr) (IB 33–32 pts HL 655 incl biol+chem)
    Surrey – ABB–BBB incl biol/chem+sci/maths (Fd Sci Nutr) (IB 32 pts HL 5 biol/chem+maths/sci); BBB incl biol+sci (Nutr) (IB 32 pts HL 5 biol+sci)
112 pts **Cardiff Met** – CC biol+sci 112 pts (Biomed Sci Hlth Exer Nutr)
    Chester – BBB–BBC incl biol+sci 112–120 pts +interview (Nutr Diet) (IB 28 pts HL 5 biol+chem)

Coventry – BBC incl biol/chem/fd tech (Nutr Hlth) (IB 30 pts HL 5 biol/chem)
Hull – BBC 112 pts (Spo Exer Nutr) (IB 28 pts)
Leeds Beckett – 112 pts (Nutr) (IB 25 pts)
Liverpool Hope – BBC 112 pts (Nutr) (IB 28 pts)
Manchester Met – BBC 112 pts (Nutr Sci) (IB 26 pts)
Nottingham Trent – BBC incl sci/PE 112 pts (Exer Nutr Hlth)
Roehampton – 112 pts (Nutr Hlth)
Sheffield Hallam – 112 pts (Fd Nutr); BBC 112 pts (Nutr Diet Wlbng)
West London – BBC 112–120 pts (Hum Nutr)

104 pts **Abertay** – BCC incl sci/maths (Fit Nutr Hlth) (IB 29 pts HL 4 sci+maths)
Bournemouth – 104–112 pts incl sci (Nutr) (IB 30–28 pts HL 55 incl sci)
CAFRE – 104 pts incl sci/hm econ (Fd Innov Nutr)
Central Lancashire – 104–112 pts (Nutr Exer Sci)
Chester – BBC–BCC incl biol/chem 104–112 pts (Hum Nutr; Nutr Exer Sci) (IB 26 pts HL 5 biol/chem)
Edge Hill – BBC–BCC 104–112 pts (Nutr Hlth)
Glasgow Caledonian – BCC incl chem +interview (Hum Nutr Diet) (IB 28 pts)
Greenwich – 104 pts incl biol+chem +interview (Hum Nutr)
Hertfordshire – BCC incl biol+sci 104 pts (Nutr)
Leeds Trinity – 104 pts (Spo Exer Sci (Spo Nutr))
Liverpool John Moores – BCC incl sci 104 pts (Nutr)
North East Scot (Coll) – 104–120 pts (Nutr Diet)
Oxford Brookes – BCC incl sci 104 pts (Nutr) (IB 29 pts)
Plymouth – B biol 104–120 pts (Nutr Exer Hlth) (IB 27 pts HL 5 biol+sci)
Ulster – BCC incl sci/maths/tech (Hum Nutr) (IB 24 pts HL 12 pts incl 65 sci/maths/tech)

96 pts **Bath Spa** – CCC (Fd Nutr) (IB 26 pts); CCC incl biol+sci (Hum Nutr) (IB 26 pts)
Bedfordshire – 96 pts (Hlth Nutr Exer)
Kingston – C sci/psy/PE 96 pts (Nutr (Exer Hlth))
London Met – CCC incl biol 96 pts (Hum Nutr)
Robert Gordon – CCC incl biol/chem+maths/sci (Fd Nutr Hum Hlth) (IB 26 pts HL 4 biol/chem+maths/sci)
St Mary's – BBC–CCC 96–112 pts (Nutr)
Teesside – C sci/fd tech/biol 96–112 pts +interview (Fd Nutr)
Trinity Saint David – 96 pts+interview (Hlth Nutr Lfstl)
Ulster – CCC incl sci/maths/env tech/hm econ (Fd Nutr) (IB 24 pts HL 12 pts incl 5 sci/maths/hm econ)
Westminster – BBB–CCC incl chem/biol+sci (Hum Nutr) (IB 27 pts HL 44 sci)
Worcester – 96–104 pts incl biol+sci/maths (Hum Nutr)

88 pts **London South Bank** – CCD 88–96 pts (Hum Nutr)
80 pts **Kingston** – C sci 80–96 pts (Nutr (Hum Nutr))
Queen Margaret – BB incl chem/biol 80 pts (Nutr) (IB 26 pts)

Alternative offers
See **Chapter 6** and **Appendix 1** for grades/UCAS Tariff points information for other examinations.

EXAMPLES OF COLLEGES OFFERING COURSES IN THIS SUBJECT FIELD
Bradford College UC; Truro and Penwith (Coll).

CHOOSING YOUR COURSE (SEE ALSO CH.1)
Universities and colleges teaching quality See www.qaa.ac.uk; https://unistats.ac.uk.

Top research universities and colleges (REF 2014) See **Agricultural Sciences/Agriculture**.

Examples of sandwich degree courses Bedfordshire; Coventry; Glasgow Caledonian; Harper Adams; Huddersfield; Kingston; Leeds; Leeds Beckett; Liverpool John Moores; Manchester Met; Newcastle; Northumbria; Queen's Belfast; Reading; Robert Gordon; Sheffield Hallam; Surrey; Teesside; Ulster.

ADMISSIONS INFORMATION
Number of applicants per place (approx) Cardiff Met 5; Liverpool John Moores 10; London (King's) 6; London Met 9; London South Bank 5; Newcastle 5; Nottingham 9; Robert Gordon 4.

Advice to applicants and planning the UCAS personal statement Information on relevant experience, reasons for wanting to do the degree and careers sought would be useful. See also **Dietetics** and **Appendix 3**.

Selection interviews Some Chester, London Met, Surrey; **No** Liverpool John Moores, Nottingham, Robert Gordon, Roehampton.

Interview advice and questions Past questions have focused on scientific A-level subjects studied and aspects of subjects enjoyed by the applicants. Questions then arise from answers. Extensive knowledge expected of nutrition as a career and candidates should have talked to people involved in this type of work, for example dietitians. They will also be expected to discuss wider problems such as food supplies in developing countries and nutritional problems resulting from famine. See also **Chapter 5**.

AFTER-RESULTS ADVICE
Offers to applicants repeating A-levels Same Liverpool John Moores; Manchester Met; Nottingham; Roehampton; St Mary's.

GRADUATE DESTINATIONS AND EMPLOYMENT (2016/17 HESA)
Graduates surveyed 865 **Employed** 485 **In voluntary employment** 20 **In further study** 175 **Assumed unemployed** 45

Career note Nutritionists work in retail, health promotion and sport; others specialise in dietetics.

OTHER DEGREE SUBJECTS FOR CONSIDERATION
Biological Sciences; Biology; Consumer Studies; Dietetics; Food Sciences; Health Studies/Sciences.

OCCUPATIONAL THERAPY
(see also Health Sciences/Studies, Physiotherapy)

Everyday life involves washing, dressing, eating, walking, driving, shopping and going to work, all aspects we take for granted – until we have an injury or illness. During the recovery period, patients realise the importance of the occupational therapist's role. They assist people of all ages, not only those being treated with physical injuries/illness, but others with mental health issues, the work being to identify the special problems they face and the practical solutions required to help them recover and maintain their daily living and working skills. The focus of the OT is on meaningful and functional activity. This may be achieved by advising on physical modifications to the home environment and potentially introducing new equipment and devices to make various activities easier along with task analysis. In the case of mental health OTs, they assist clients to re-establish routines and skills to allow them to return to living fulfilling lives. To achieve these results, occupational therapists often work with physiotherapists, psychologists, speech therapists and social workers among others. Most courses therefore involve anatomy, physiology, psychology, sociology, mental health and ethics. OTs can work in a very wide range of settings, acute care, long term care, social services and mental health plus many more. There are opportunities to specialise in burns, hand therapy, oncology and surgery, forensic psychology and prison rehabilitation to name but a few. Selectors look for maturity, initiative, tact, sound judgement, team work and organising ability.

Occupational therapy is often very poorly understood by the general public. The profession is actually very diverse with therapists working in hospitals, schools, prisons, charities, voluntary organisations and in private practice.

Useful websites www.rcot.co.uk

NB The points totals shown to the left of the institutions are for ease of reference only. It must not be assumed that Tariff points are always used by institutions or that they can be substituted for an offer in grades. The level of an offer is not necessarily indicative of the quality of a course.

COURSE OFFERS INFORMATION

Subject requirements/preferences GCSE English, mathematics and science grade A–C (7–4). **AL** A social science or science subjects required or preferred for most courses. Other All applicants need to pass an occupational health check and obtain Disclosure and Barring Service (DBS) clearance.

Your target offers and examples of degree courses

128 pts **Bournemouth** – 128–144 pts (Occ Thera) (IB 34–32 pts)

UWE Bristol – 128 pts +interview (Occ Thera)

120 pts **Bradford** – 120 pts (Occ Thera)

Brunel – BBB incl biol/chem/psy/sociol +interview (Occ Thera) (IB 30 pts HL 5 biol/chem/psy/sociol)

Cardiff – ABB–BBB (Occ Thera) (IB 32–31 pts HL 655)

Derby – 120 pts +interview (Occ Thera)

Huddersfield – BBB incl biol/psy 120 pts (Occ Thera)

Liverpool – BBB incl soc sci/biol/PE (Occ Thera) (IB 30 pts HL 444 incl biol)

London (St George's) – BBB (Occ Thera) (IB 32 pts HL 15 pts)

London South Bank – BBB 120–128 pts +interview (Occ Thera)

Northumbria – BBB 120–128 pts +interview (Occ Thera)

Southampton – BBB incl sci/soc sci (Occ Thera) (IB 30 pts HL 16 pts incl sci/soc sci)

Ulster – BBB +HPAT (Occ Thera)

Worcester – BBB +HPAT (Occ Thera)

York St John – BBB 120 pts (Occ Thera)

112 pts **Canterbury Christ Church** – BBC +interview (Occ Thera)

Cumbria – 112–120 pts +interview (Occ Thera)

Essex – BBC (Occ Thera) (IB 29 pts HL 554)

Northampton – BBC (Occ Thera)

Plymouth – 112–128 pts incl sci/soc sci +interview (Occ Thera) (IB 32–27 pts HL 5 sci/soc sci)

104 pts **East Anglia** – BBC–BCC (Occ Thera) (IB 30 pts)

Glasgow Caledonian – BCC (Occ Thera)

Oxford Brookes – BCC 104 pts +interview (Occ Thera) (IB 29 pts)

Queen Margaret – BCC +interview (Occ Thera) (IB 28 pts)

Robert Gordon – BCC incl Engl+sci/hum +interview (Occ Thera) (IB 27 pts)

96 pts **Coventry** – BBB–CCC +interview (Occ Thera) (IB 29 pts HL 16 pts)

Alternative offers

See **Chapter 6** and **Appendix 1** for grades/UCAS Tariff points information for other examinations.

CHOOSING YOUR COURSE (SEE ALSO CH.1)

Universities and colleges teaching quality See www.qaa.ac.uk; https://unistats.ac.uk.

Top research universities and colleges (REF 2014) See **Health Sciences/Studies**.

Examples of sandwich degree courses Robert Gordon.

ADMISSIONS INFORMATION

Number of applicants per place (approx) Cardiff 10; Cumbria 20; Derby 5; East Anglia 6; Northampton 4; Oxford Brookes 11; Robert Gordon 6; Southampton 7; Ulster 13; York St John 5.

Admissions tutors' advice London (St George's) Work experience required.

Advice to applicants and planning the UCAS personal statement Contact your local hospital to meet with occupational therapists. Try to obtain work shadowing experience and make notes of your observations. Describe any such visits in full (see also Reasons for rejection (non-academic)). Applicants are expected to have visited two occupational therapy departments, one in a physical or social services setting, one in the mental health field. Good interpersonal skills. Breadth and nature of health-related work experience is important. Also skills, interests (eg sport, design). Applicants should have excellent communication skills and experience of working with people with disabilities. **York St John** Contact with the profession essential; very competitive course. See also **Appendix 3**.

Selection interviews Yes Bournemouth, Brighton, Brunel, Canterbury Christ Church, Coventry, Cumbria, East Anglia, Huddersfield, Oxford Brookes, Queen Margaret, Robert Gordon, Worcester; **No** Glyndŵr, Ulster, York St John.

Interview advice and questions Since this is a vocational course, work experience is nearly always essential and applicants are likely to be questioned on the types of work involved and the career. Some universities may use admissions tests: check websites and see **Chapter 5**.

Reasons for rejection (non-academic) Poor communication skills. Lack of knowledge of occupational therapy. Little evidence of working with people. Uncertain about their future career. Lack of maturity. Indecision regarding the profession.

AFTER-RESULTS ADVICE
Offers to applicants repeating A-levels Same Derby; York St John.

GRADUATE DESTINATIONS AND EMPLOYMENT
Career note Occupational therapists (who work mostly in hospital departments) are involved in the rehabilitation of those who have required medical treatment and work with the young, aged and, for example, people with learning difficulties.

OTHER DEGREE SUBJECTS FOR CONSIDERATION
Audiology; Community Studies; Dietetics; Education; Health Studies/Sciences; Nursing; Nutrition; Physiotherapy; Podiatry; Psychology; Radiography; Social Policy and Administration; Social Work; Sociology; Speech Sciences.

OPERATING DEPARTMENT PRACTICE

This career involves working in areas involved in anaesthetics, intensive care, A&E, transplants and the air ambulance. In operating theatres high-quality care is essential for patients before, during and after surgery.

Useful websites www.healthcareers.nhs.uk

NB The points totals shown to the left of the institutions are for ease of reference only. It must not be assumed that Tariff points are always used by institutions or that they can be substituted for an offer in grades. The level of an offer is not necessarily indicative of the quality of a course.

COURSE OFFERS INFORMATION
Subject requirements/preferences GCSE English, mathematics and a science. **AL** At least one science.

Your target offers and examples of degree courses
112 pts   **Bedfordshire** – BBB–BBC +interview (Oprtg Dept Prac)
      Birmingham City – BBC +interview (Oprtg Dept Prac) (IB 28 pts)
      Bolton – 112 pts +interview (Oprtg Dept Prac)
      Bucks New – 112–128 pts (Oprtg Dept Prac)
      Canterbury Christ Church – BBC +interview (Oprtg Dept Prac)
      Central Lancashire – 112 pts +interview (Oprtg Dept Prac)
      Coventry – BBC 112 pts +interview (Oprtg Dept Prac)
      Huddersfield – BBC +interview (Oprtg Dept Prac)
      Hull – 112 pts +interview (Oprtg Dept Prac) (IB 28 pts)
      Leicester – 112 pts +interview (Oprtg Dept Prac)

London South Bank – BBC +interview (Oprtg Dept Prac)
Sheffield Hallam – BBC +interview (Oprtg Dept Prac)
Staffordshire – BBC (Oprtg Dept Prac)
104 pts   **Bournemouth** – 104–120 pts (Oprtg Dept Prac) (IB 28–31 pts)
Cardiff – BBC–CCC +interview (Oprtg Dept Prac)
Edge Hill – 104–112 pts +interview (Oprtg Dept Prac)
Portsmouth – 104 pts incl sci +interview (Oprtg Dept Prac) (IB 28 pts)
West London – BBB–BCC +interview (Oprtg Dept Prac)
96 pts   **East Anglia** – CCC +interview (Oprtg Dept Prac)
Teesside – 96–112 pts (Oprtg Dept Prac)
80 pts   **Anglia Ruskin** – 80 pts +interview (Oprtg Dept Prac)
Suffolk – CDD +interview (Oprtg Dept Prac)
72 pts   **Northumbria** – 72 pts +interview (Oprtg Dept Prac)

Alternative offers
See **Chapter 6** and **Appendix 1** for grades/UCAS Tariff points information for other examinations.

DEGREE APPRENTICESHIPS
Huddersfield (Op Dept Prac).

CHOOSING YOUR COURSE (SEE ALSO CH.1)
Universities and colleges teaching quality See www.qaa.ac.uk; https://unistats.ac.uk.

ADMISSIONS INFORMATION
Advice to applicants and planning the UCAS personal statement Applicants should have a scientific background and exhibit evidence of attention to detail.

OTHER DEGREE SUBJECTS FOR CONSIDERATION
Nursing and Midwifery; Occupational Therapy; Podiatry; Physiotherapy.

OPTOMETRY (OPHTHALMIC OPTICS)
(including Ophthalmic Dispensing and Orthoptics)

Optometry courses (which are becoming increasingly popular) lead to qualification as an optometrist (previously known as an ophthalmic optician). They provide training in detecting defects and diseases in the eye and in prescribing treatment with, for example, spectacles, contact lenses and other appliances to correct or improve vision. Orthoptics includes the study of general anatomy, physiology and normal child development and leads to a career as an orthoptist. This involves the investigation, diagnosis and treatment of defects of binocular vision and other eye conditions. The main components of degree courses include the study of the eye, the use of diagnostic and measuring equipment and the treatment of eye abnormalities. See also **Appendix 3**.

Useful websites www.optical.org; www.orthoptics.org.uk; www.abdo.org.uk; www.college-optometrists.org

NB The points totals shown to the left of the institutions are for ease of reference only. It must not be assumed that Tariff points are always used by institutions or that they can be substituted for an offer in grades. The level of an offer is not necessarily indicative of the quality of a course.

COURSE OFFERS INFORMATION
Subject requirements/preferences GCSE Good grades in English and science subjects usually required. **AL** Science subjects required for all Optometry courses. Mathematics usually acceptable.
Plymouth 5 GCSEs to include English, Maths and Science at B/6. Plus interview, DBS and Occupational Health, Overseas checks required.

Your target offers and examples of degree courses

136 pts   **Anglia Ruskin** – AAB incl sci/maths (Optom) (IB 33 pts HL 6 sci/maths)

      Aston – AAA–AAB incl sci/maths (Optom) (IB 32 pts HL 666 incl sci/maths)

      Bradford – AAB incl sci/maths 136 pts (Optom) (HL 666 incl sci)

      Glasgow Caledonian – AAB incl sci/maths (Optom) (IB 30 pts HL 665 incl sci+maths)

      Hertfordshire – AAB incl sci/maths 136 pts (Optom (MOptom))

      Huddersfield – AAB incl sci/maths (Optom)

      Manchester – AAB incl sci/maths (Optom) (IB 35 pts HL 665 incl sci/maths)

      Plymouth – AAA–AAB incl maths/sci 136–144 pts (Optom) (IB 36–34 pts HL 6 maths/sci)

      Ulster – AAB incl sci/maths (Optom) (IB 28 pts HL 14 pts incl sci/maths)

128 pts   **Cardiff** – AAA–ABB incl sci/maths (Optom) (IB 34–32 pts HL 665 incl sci/maths)

      City – ABB incl sci/maths 128 pts (Optom) (IB 34 pts HL 66 sci)

      Teesside – ABB incl sci/maths 128 pts +interview (Clin Optom)

120 pts   **Liverpool** – BBB incl sci/maths +interview (Orth) (IB 30 pts HL 6 biol)

      Sheffield – BBB incl sci/maths +interview (Orth) (IB 32 pts HL 5 sci/maths)

104 pts   **Anglia Ruskin** – 104 pts incl sci (Oph Disp) (IB 24 pts)

64 pts   **Bradford College UC** – 64 pts incl sci/maths (Oph Disp)

      Glasgow Caledonian – CC (Oph Disp Mgt)

Alternative offers

See **Chapter 6** and **Appendix 1** for grades/UCAS Tariff points information for other examinations.

EXAMPLES OF COLLEGES OFFERING COURSES IN THIS SUBJECT FIELD

Bradford College UC; City and Islington (Coll).

CHOOSING YOUR COURSE (SEE ALSO CH.1)

Universities and colleges teaching quality See www.qaa.ac.uk; https://unistats.ac.uk.

ADMISSIONS INFORMATION

Number of applicants per place (approx) Anglia Ruskin 12; Aston 7; Bradford 6; Cardiff 13; City 8.

Advice to applicants and planning the UCAS personal statement For Optometry courses, contact with optometrists is essential, either work shadowing or gaining some work experience. Make notes of your experiences and the work done and report fully on the UCAS application on why the career interests you. See also **Appendix 3**.

Selection interviews Yes Aston, Manchester, Sheffield; **Some** Cardiff; **No** Anglia Ruskin, Bradford, City, Glasgow Caledonian.

Interview advice and questions Optometry is a competitive subject requiring applicants to have had some work experience on which they will be questioned. See also **Chapter 5**.

AFTER-RESULTS ADVICE

Offers to applicants repeating A-levels Higher City; **Possibly higher** Aston; **Same** Anglia Ruskin; Cardiff.

GRADUATE DESTINATIONS AND EMPLOYMENT (2016/17 HESA)

Graduates surveyed 795 **Employed** 660 **In voluntary employment** 25 **In further study** 95 **Assumed unemployed** 5

Career note The great majority of graduates enter private practice either in small businesses or in larger organisations (which have been on the increase in recent years). A small number work in eye hospitals. Orthoptists tend to work in public health and education dealing with children and the elderly.

OTHER DEGREE SUBJECTS FOR CONSIDERATION

Health Studies; Nursing; Occupational Therapy; Physics; Physiotherapy; Radiography; Speech Studies.

PHARMACOLOGY

(including **Physiology and Pharmacology**; see also **Biological Sciences, Health Sciences/Studies**)

Pharmacology is the study of drugs and medicines and courses focus on physiology, biochemistry, toxicology, immunology, microbiology and chemotherapy. Pharmacologists are not qualified to work as pharmacists. Toxicology involves the study of the adverse effects of chemicals on living systems. See also **Appendix 3** under Pharmacology.

Useful websites www.thebts.org; www.bps.ac.uk

NB The points totals shown to the left of the institutions are for ease of reference only. It must not be assumed that Tariff points are always used by institutions or that they can be substituted for an offer in grades. The level of an offer is not necessarily indicative of the quality of a course.

COURSE OFFERS INFORMATION

Subject requirements/preferences GCSE English, science and mathematics. **AL** Chemistry and/or biology required for most courses.

Your target offers and examples of degree courses

160 pts **Cambridge** – A*A*A incl sci/maths +interview +NSAA (Nat Sci (Pharmacol)) (IB 42–40 pts HL 776)

136 pts **Bath** – AAB–ABB +aEPQ incl chem+sci/maths (Pharmacol) (IB 36 pts HL 665 incl chem+sci/maths)

Bristol – AAB incl chem+sci/maths (Pharmacol) (IB 34 pts HL 17 pts incl 6/5 chem+sci/maths)

Dundee – AAB incl biol+chem (Pharmacol) (IB 30 pts HL 555 incl biol+chem)

Glasgow – AAB incl biol/chem (Pharmacol) (IB 36 pts HL 665 incl biol/chem)

Leeds – AAA–AAB incl biol/chem+sci (Pharmacol) (IB 35–34 pts HL 18–17 pts incl 6 biol/chem+sci)

Liverpool – AAB incl chem+sci (Pharmacol) (IB 34 pts HL 6 chem)

London (King's) – AAB incl chem+biol (Pharmacol; Pharmacol Mol Genet) (IB 35 pts HL 665 incl chem+biol)

London (UCL) – AAB incl chem+sci/maths (Pharmacol) (IB 36 pts HL 17 pts incl 5 chem+sci/maths)

Newcastle – AAA–AAB incl biol/chem+maths/sci (Pharmacol) (IB 35–34 pts HL 5 biol/chem+maths/sci)

Southampton – AAB incl chem+sci/maths (Pharmacol) (IB 34 pts HL 17 pts incl 5/6 chem+sci/maths)

128 pts **Edinburgh** – AAB–ABB incl biol+chem (Pharmacol) (IB 36–32 pts HL 5/6 biol+chem)

Leicester – ABB/BBB +bEPQ incl sci/maths (Biol Sci (Physiol Pharmacol)) (IB 30 pts HL 6/5 sci/maths)

Manchester – AAA–ABB incl sci/maths (Pharmacol; Pharmacol Physiol) (IB 36–33 pts HL 666–655 incl sci)

120 pts **Aberdeen** – BBB incl maths/sci (Pharmacol) (IB 32 pts HL 555 incl maths/sci)

Nottingham Trent – BBB incl biol 120 pts (Pharmacol)

Reading – BBB incl biol+chem (Pharmacol) (IB 30 pts HL 5 biol+chem)

Strathclyde – ABB–BBB incl chem+biol (Pharmacol) (IB 34 pts HL 5 chem+biol)

112 pts **Coventry** – BBC incl biol (Med Pharmacol Sci) (IB 30 pts HL 5 biol)

East London – B biol/chem 112 pts (Pharmacol) (IB 25 pts HL 15 pts incl biol+chem)

Glasgow Caledonian – BBC incl chem+sci/Engl (Pharmacol) (IB 28 pts)

Hertfordshire – BBC incl biol/chem+sci/maths/geog/psy 112 pts (Pharmacol)

Kingston – C biol/chem 112 pts (Pharmacol)

West London – BBC incl sci 112–120 pts (Pharmacol)

104 pts **Central Lancashire** – C biol/chem 104–112 pts (Physiol Pharmacol) (HL 5 biol/chem)

Chester – BBC–BCC incl chem 104–112 pts (Pharmacol) (IB 26 pts HL 5 chem)

96 pts **Portsmouth** – BBB–CCC incl biol/chem+sci/maths (Pharmacol) (IB 29–27 pts HL 664–644 incl biol+chem/maths)

Westminster – BBB–CCC incl sci/maths (Pharmacol Physiol) (IB 27 pts)

Wolverhampton – CCC/BCD incl chem/biol 96 pts (Pharmacol)

Worcester – 96–104 pts incl sci (Pharmacol)

88 pts **London Met** – CCD incl biol+chem 88 pts (Pharmacol)

Alternative offers
See **Chapter 6** and **Appendix 1** for grades/UCAS Tariff points information for other examinations.

CHOOSING YOUR COURSE (SEE ALSO CH.1)

Universities and colleges teaching quality See www.qaa.ac.uk; https://unistats.ac.uk.

Examples of sandwich degree courses Bath; Bristol; East London; Kingston; Leeds; Manchester; Medway Sch Pharm; Nottingham Trent; Southampton.

ADMISSIONS INFORMATION

Number of applicants per place (approx) Bath 7; Birmingham 6; Bristol 7; Dundee 8; East London 4; Hertfordshire 10; Leeds 7; Liverpool 7; London (King's) 6; London (UCL) 8; Southampton 8; Strathclyde 10; Wolverhampton 4.

Advice to applicants and planning the UCAS personal statement Contact with the pharmaceutical industry is important in order to be aware of the range of work undertaken. Read pharmaceutical journals (although note that Pharmacology and Pharmacy courses lead to different careers). See also Pharmacy and Pharmaceutical Sciences. **Bath** Interests outside A-level studies. Important to produce evidence that there is more to the student than A-level ability. **Bristol** Be aware that a Pharmacology degree is mainly biological rather than chemical although both subjects are important.

Selection interviews Yes Cambridge, Manchester; **Some** Bath; **No** Birmingham, Dundee, Newcastle, Portsmouth.

Interview advice and questions Past questions include: Why do you want to do Pharmacology? Why not Pharmacy? Why not Chemistry? How are pharmacologists employed in industry? What are the issues raised by anti-vivisectionists on animal experimentation? Questions relating to the A-level syllabus in chemistry and biology. See also **Chapter 5**.

Reasons for rejection (non-academic) Confusion between pharmacology, pharmacy and pharmaceutical sciences. One university rejected two applicants because they had no motivation or understanding of the course (one had A-levels at AAB!). Insurance against rejection for Medicine. Lack of knowledge about pharmacology as a subject.

AFTER-RESULTS ADVICE

Offers to applicants repeating A-levels Higher Bristol; Leeds; **Same** Bath; Dundee; **No** Glasgow.

GRADUATE DESTINATIONS AND EMPLOYMENT (2016/17 HESA)

Pharmacology, Toxicology and Pharmacy Graduates surveyed 2,980 **Employed** 2,075 **In voluntary employment** 95 **In further study** 645 **Assumed unemployed** 80

Career note The majority of pharmacologists work with the large pharmaceutical companies involved in research and development. A small number are employed by the NHS in medical research and clinical trials. Some will eventually diversify and become involved in marketing, sales and advertising.

OTHER DEGREE SUBJECTS FOR CONSIDERATION

Biochemistry; Biological Sciences; Biology; Biotechnology; Chemistry; Life Sciences; Medical Biochemistry; Medicinal Chemistry; Microbiology; Natural Sciences; Pharmaceutical Sciences; Pharmacy; Physiology; Toxicology.

PHARMACY AND PHARMACEUTICAL SCIENCES

(including **Herbal Medicine**; see also **Biochemistry, Chemistry, Health Sciences/Studies**)

Pharmacy is the science of medicines, involving research into chemical structures and natural products of possible medicinal value, the development of dosage and the safety testing of products. This table also includes information on courses in Pharmaceutical Science (which should not be confused with Pharmacy) which is a multi-disciplinary subject covering chemistry, biochemistry, pharmacology and medical issues. Pharmaceutical scientists apply their knowledge of science and the biology of disease to the design and delivery of therapeutic agents. Note: All Pharmacy courses leading to MPharm are four years. Only Pharmacy degree courses accredited by the Royal Phamaceutical Society of Great Britain lead to a qualification as a pharmacist. Check prospectuses and websites.

Useful websites www.rpharms.com; www.chemistanddruggist.co.uk

NB The points totals shown to the left of the institutions are for ease of reference only. It must not be assumed that Tariff points are always used by institutions or that they can be substituted for an offer in grades. The level of an offer is not necessarily indicative of the quality of a course.

COURSE OFFERS INFORMATION

Subject requirements/preferences GCSE English, mathematics and science subjects. **AL** Chemistry and one or two other sciences required for most courses.

Your target offers and examples of degree courses

136 pts   Bath – AAB–ABB +aEPQ incl chem+sci/maths +interview (MPharm) (IB 36 pts HL 665 incl chem+sci/maths)

Birmingham – AAB incl chem+sci/maths (MPharm) (IB 32 pts HL 665 incl chem+sci/maths)

London (King's) – AAB incl chem+sci/maths (MPharm) (IB 35 pts HL 665 incl chem+sci/maths)

London (UCL) – AAB incl chem+sci/maths +interview (MPharm) (IB 36 pts HL 17 pts incl chem+sci/maths)

Newcastle – AAB incl chem+sci/maths (MPharm) (IB 36 pts HL 5 chem+sci/maths)

Nottingham – AAB incl chem+sci/maths +interview (MPharm) (IB 34 pts HL 665 incl 6 chem 6/5 sci/maths)

Queen's Belfast – AAB incl chem+sci/maths (MPharm) (IB 34 pts HL 665 incl chem+sci/maths)

Strathclyde – AAB incl chem+biol +interview (MPharm) (IB 36 pts HL 7 chem 6 biol)

Ulster – AAB incl chem+sci/maths (MPharm) (IB 28 pts HL 14 pts incl 6 chem 7 sci/maths)

128 pts   Bradford – AB chem/biol+sci 128 pts +interview (MPharm) (HL 665 incl 6 chem/biol+sci)

Cardiff – AAB–ABB incl chem+sci/maths +interview (MPharm) (IB 34–32 pts HL 665 incl 6 chem/biol 5 sci/maths)

East Anglia – ABB incl chem+sci/maths +interview (MPharm) (IB 32 pts HL 5 chem+sci/maths)

Huddersfield – ABB incl chem+sci/maths 128–136 pts +interview (MPharm) (HL 6 chem 6/5 maths+biol)

Keele – ABB incl biol/chem +interview (MPharm) (IB 34 pts HL 6 biol/chem)

London (QM) – ABB incl chem (Pharml Chem) (IB 34 pts HL 655 incl chem)

Loughborough – ABB incl chem (Medcnl Pharml Chem) (IB 34 pts HL 655 incl chem)

Manchester – AAB–ABB incl chem+maths/biol +interview (MPharm) (IB 35 pts HL 6 chem 6/5 maths/biol)

Medway Sch Pharm – ABB incl chem+sci (MPharm) (IB 32 pts HL 15 pts incl 5 chem+sci)

Reading – ABB incl chem+sci/maths +admissions test (MPharm) (IB 32 pts HL 6 chem 5 sci)

120 pts   Brighton – ABB–BBB incl chem+sci 120–128 pts +interview +test (MPharm) (IB 32 pts HL 5 chem+biol)

Central Lancashire – BBB incl chem/biol+sci +interview (MPharm)

De Montfort – 120 pts incl chem+sci/maths/psy +interview (MPharm) (IB 30 pts HL 6 chem+sci/maths/psy)

Hertfordshire – BBB incl chem+sci/maths 120 pts (MPharm)

Kingston – 120 pts incl chem+sci/maths +interview (MPharm)

Leicester – ABB–BBB incl chem (Pharml Chem) (IB 30–28 pts HL 5 chem)

Liverpool John Moores – BBB incl chem 120 pts (MPharm) (IB 27 pts)

Manchester Met – BBB incl chem 120 pts (Pharml Chem (MChem)) (IB 26 pts HL 5 chem)

Portsmouth – ABB–BBB incl chem+sci/maths +interview +test (MPharm) (IB 30–29 pts HL 665–655 incl chem+sci/maths)

Reading – BBB incl chem (Pharml Chem) (IB 30 pts HL 5 chem)

Sunderland – B chem+sci 120 pts +MMI (MPharm)

112 pts **Aston** – BBB–BBC incl chem+sci/maths +interview (MPharm) (IB 31 pts HL 555 incl chem+sci/maths)

East London – B biol/chem 112 pts (Pharml Sci) (IB 25 pts HL 15 pts incl biol+chem)

Huddersfield – BBC incl chem 112 pts (Pharml Chem) (HL 5 chem)

Kingston – C chem+sci/maths 112 pts (Pharml Sci)

Robert Gordon – BBB–BBC incl chem+sci/maths (MPharm) (IB 30–29 pts HL 6 chem 5 Engl+sci/maths)

Wolverhampton – BBC incl chem+sci 112 pts +interview (MPharm)

104 pts **De Montfort** – 104 pts incl chem+sci (Pharml Cos Sci) (IB 24 pts HL 6 chem+sci)

Greenwich – 104 pts incl chem +interview (Pharml Sci)

Hertfordshire – BCC incl chem 104 pts (Pharml Sci)

96 pts **London Met** – CCC incl biol+chem 96 pts (Pharml Sci)

Wolverhampton – CCC/BCD incl chem 96 pts (Pharml Sci)

88 pts **Reading** – BBB–CCD (Pharml Chem Fdn) (IB 30–24 pts)

80 pts **South Wales** – BCC–CDD incl chem+sci 80–104 pts (Pharml Sci) (IB 29 pts HL 5 chem+sci)

Alternative offers
See **Chapter 6** and **Appendix 1** for grades/UCAS Tariff points information for other examinations.

EXAMPLES OF COLLEGES OFFERING COURSES IN THIS SUBJECT FIELD
Birmingham Met (Coll).

CHOOSING YOUR COURSE (SEE ALSO CH.1)
Universities and colleges teaching quality See www.qaa.ac.uk; https://unistats.ac.uk.

Top research universities and colleges (REF 2014) (Allied Health Professions, Dentistry, Nursing and Pharmacy) Birmingham; Glasgow; Nottingham (Pharm); Bradford; East Anglia (Allied Hlth); London (QM); Queen's Belfast (Pharm); Bath; London (King's) (Pharm); Leeds; Sheffield (Biomed Sci), (Dnstry); Swansea (Allied Hlth); Coventry; Southampton; Cardiff; Surrey.

Examples of sandwich degree courses Bradford; De Montfort; Greenwich; Hertfordshire; Reading; Robert Gordon.

ADMISSIONS INFORMATION
Number of applicants per place (approx) Aston 10; Bath 7; Bradford 10; Cardiff 8; De Montfort 14; Liverpool John Moores (Pharm) 7; London (King's) 15, (Sch Pharm) 6; Manchester 9; Nottingham 10; Robert Gordon 11; Strathclyde 10; Sunderland 20.

Advice to applicants and planning the UCAS personal statement Work experience and work shadowing with a retail and/or hospital pharmacist is important, and essential for Pharmacy applicants. Read pharmaceutical journals, extend your knowledge of well-known drugs and antibiotics. Read up on the history of drugs. Attend Open Days or careers conferences. See also **Appendix 3**. **Manchester** Students giving preference for Pharmacy are likely to be more successful than those who choose Pharmacy as an alternative to Medicine or Dentistry.

Selection interviews Yes Aston, Bath, Bradford, Cardiff, East Anglia, Huddersfield, Liverpool John Moores, London (UCL), Manchester, Nottingham, Sussex; **Some** Brighton; **No** De Montfort, Keele, Portsmouth, Reading, Robert Gordon, Strathclyde, Wolverhampton.

Interview advice and questions As work experience is essential for Pharmacy applicants, questions are likely to focus on this and what they have discovered. Other relevant questions could include: Why do you want to study Pharmacy? What types of work do pharmacists do? What interests you about the Pharmacy course? What branch of pharmacy do you want to enter? Name a drug – what do you know about it (formula, use, etc)? Name a drug from a natural source and its use. Can you think of another way of extracting a drug? Why do fungi destroy bacteria? What is an antibiotic? Can you name one and say how it was discovered? What is insulin? What is its source and function? What is diabetes? What type of insulin is used in its treatment? What is a hormone? What drugs are available over the counter without prescription? What is the formula of aspirin? What is genetic engineering? See also **Chapter 5**. **Bath** Informal and relaxed; very few rejected at this stage. **Cardiff** Interviews cover both academic and vocational aspects; candidates must reach a satisfactory level in both areas. **Liverpool John Moores** Aptitude test and interview. No specific preparation required. **Manchester** Candidates failing to attend interviews will have their applications withdrawn. The majority of applicants who are called for interview are made offers.

Reasons for rejection (non-academic) Poor communication skills. Poor knowledge of pharmacy and the work of a pharmacist.

AFTER-RESULTS ADVICE
Offers to applicants repeating A-levels Higher Bradford; Cardiff; De Montfort; London (UCL); Queen's Belfast; Strathclyde; **Possibly higher** Aston; **Same** Bath; Brighton; East Anglia; Liverpool John Moores; Nottingham; Robert Gordon; Sunderland; Wolverhampton.

GRADUATE DESTINATIONS AND EMPLOYMENT (2016/17 HESA)
Graduates surveyed See **Pharmacology**.

Career note The majority of Pharmacy graduates proceed to work in the commercial and retail fields, although opportunities also exist with pharmaceutical companies and in hospital pharmacies. There are also opportunities in agricultural and veterinary pharmacy.

OTHER DEGREE SUBJECTS FOR CONSIDERATION
Biochemistry; Biological Sciences; Biology; Biotechnology; Chemistry; Drug Development; Life Sciences; Medicinal Chemistry; Microbiology; Natural Sciences; Pharmacology; Physiology.

PHILOSOPHY
(See also **Philosophy, Politics and Economics (PPE)**, **Psychology**)

Philosophy is one of the oldest and most fundamental disciplines, which examines the nature of the universe and humanity's place in it. Philosophy seeks to discover the essence of the mind, language and physical reality and discusses the methods used to investigate these topics.

Useful websites www.iep.utm.edu; www.philosophypages.com; http://royalinstitutephilosophy.org; see also **Religious Studies**.

NB The points totals shown to the left of the institutions are for ease of reference only. It must not be assumed that Tariff points are always used by institutions or that they can be substituted for an offer in grades. The level of an offer is not necessarily indicative of the quality of a course.

COURSE OFFERS INFORMATION
Subject requirements/preferences GCSE English and mathematics. A foreign language may be required. **AL** No specific subjects except for joint courses.

Your target offers and examples of degree courses

160 pts   **Oxford** – A*A*A incl maths +interview +MAT (Maths Phil) (IB 39 pts HL 766 incl 7 maths)

152 pts   **Bristol** – A*AA incl maths (Maths Phil) (IB 38 pts HL 18 pts incl 7 maths); A*AA incl maths+phys (Phys Phil) (IB 38 pts HL 18 pts incl 76 maths+phys)

          Cambridge – A*AA +interview +PAA (Phil) (IB 42–40 pts HL 776)

          Durham – A*AA incl Engl (Engl Lit Phil) (IB 38 pts HL 666 incl Engl)

          London (King's) – A*AA +LNAT (Pol Phil Law) (IB 35 pts HL 766)

          Oxford – A*AA +interview +TSA (Psy Phil Ling) (IB 39 pts HL 766)

144 pts   **Bristol** – AAA (Phil; Phil Theol) (IB 36 pts HL 18 pts); AAA incl maths (Phil Econ) (IB 36 pts HL 18 pts)

          Durham – AAA (Phil Psy) (IB 37 pts HL 666); AAA +interview (Phil) (IB 37 pts HL 666); AAA incl soc sci/hum (Phil Pol) (IB 37 pts HL 666)

          Exeter – AAA (Phil) (IB 36 pts); (Phil Pol) (IB 36 pts HL 666)

          London (King's) – AAA (Phil courses; War St Phil) (IB 35 pts HL 666); AAA incl maths+fmaths (Maths Phil) (IB 35 pts HL 666 incl maths)

          London (UCL) – AAA (Phil) (IB 38 pts HL 18 pts)

          London LSE – AAA (Phil Lgc Sci Meth; Pol Phil) (IB 38 pts HL 766); AAA incl maths (Phil Econ) (IB 38 pts HL 766 incl maths)

          Manchester – A*AA–AAA incl maths +interview (Maths Phil) (IB 36 pts HL 666 incl maths)

          Oxford – AAA +interview +MLAT (Phil Modn Langs) (IB 39 pts HL 666); AAA +interview +test (Phil Theol) (IB 39 pts HL 666)

          York – AAA (Phil Pol) (IB 36 pts)

136 pts   **Birmingham** – AAB (Phil) (IB 32 pts HL 665)

          Bristol – AAB (Sociol Phil) (IB 34 pts HL 17 pts); AAB incl lang (Phil Modn Lang) (IB 34 pts HL 17 pts incl 5 lang)

          Exeter – AAA–AAB (Class St Theol/Phil (Emp Expnc)) (IB 36–34 pts HL 666–665)

          Glasgow – AAB (Phil) (IB 36 pts HL 665 incl Engl+hum/lang)

          Lancaster – AAA–AAB incl maths/fmaths (Maths Phil) (IB 36 pts HL 16 pts incl 6 maths); AAB (Ling Phil) (IB 35 pts HL 16 pts)

          Leeds – AAB (Phil; Phil Comb Hons) (IB 35 pts HL 16 pts)

          Liverpool – AAB (Phil) (IB 35 pts)

          London (King's) – AAB (Fr Phil (Yr Abrd); Relgn Phil Eth) (IB 35 pts HL 665)

          London (UCL) – AAB (Hist Phil Sci) (IB 36 pts HL 17 pts)

          Manchester – AAB (Theol St Phil Eth) (IB 35 pts HL 665)

          NCH London – AAB +interview (Phil courses) (IB 35 pts HL 665)

          Nottingham – AAB (Relgn Phil Eth) (IB 34 pts); AAB/A*BB (Class Civ Phil; Phil; Phil Theol) (IB 34 pts); (Phil Psy) (IB 34 pts HL 665); AAB/A*BB incl Engl (Engl Phil) (IB 34 pts HL 6 Engl)

          Sheffield – AAB/ABB +aEPQ (Phil Comb Hons) (IB 34 pts); AAB–ABB+bEPQ (Phil; Pol Phil) (IB 34 pts)

          Southampton – AAB–ABB +aEPQ incl maths (Phil Maths) (IB 34–32 pts HL 17–16 pts incl 6 maths)

          St Andrews – AAB (Phil courses) (IB 36 pts HL 665)

          Warwick – AAB (Phil; Phil Comb Hons) (IB 36 pts)

          York – AAB (Phil; Phil Ling) (IB 35 pts); AAB incl Engl (Engl Phil) (IB 35 pts HL 6 Engl); AAB incl maths+phys +interview (Phys Phil) (IB 35 pts HL 6 maths+phys)

128 pts   **Edinburgh** – AAA–ABB (Phil) (IB 40–34 pts HL 766–655)

          Lancaster – ABB (Eth Phil Relgn; Phil; Phil Relig St) (IB 32 pts HL 16 pts)

          Leeds – ABB (Hist Phil Sci courses) (IB 34 pts HL 16 pts); ABB incl hist (Hist Hist Phil Sci) (IB 34 pts HL 16 pts incl 6 hist)

          Liverpool – ABB (Phil Comb Hons)

          London (RH) – AAB–ABB (Pol Phil) (IB 32 pts HL 655); AAB–ABB+gr 7 (Mus Phil) (IB 32 pts HL 655 incl 6 mus)

          Manchester – ABB (Phil) (IB 34 pts HL 655)

          Newcastle – AAB–ABB (Phil Comb Hons) (IB 32 pts HL 555)

          Queen's Belfast – ABB (Phil courses) (IB 33 pts HL 655)

Southampton – AAB–ABB (Phil) (IB 17–16 pts); (Flm Phil) (IB 32 pts HL 16 pts); (Econ Phil; Phil Pol; Phil Sociol) (IB 34–32 pts HL 17–16 pts); AAB–ABB incl Engl (Phil Engl) (IB 34–32 pts HL 17–16 pts incl 5 Engl); AAB–ABB incl hist (Phil Hist) (IB 34–32 pts HL 17–16 pts incl 5 hist); AAB–ABB incl mus +gr 8 +audition (Phil Mus) (IB 34–32 pts HL 17–16 pts incl 5 mus)

Sussex – AAB–ABB (Phil) (IB 34–32 pts)

Warwick – ABB (Class Civ Phil) (IB 34 pts)

120 pts **Aberdeen** – BBB (Phil Comb Hons) (IB 32 pts HL 555); BBB incl maths+phys (Nat Phil) (IB 32 pts HL 555 incl maths+phys)

Cardiff – ABB–BBB (Phil) (HL 665)

Dundee – BBB (Euro Phil) (IB 30 pts HL 555); BBB 120 pts (Phil) (IB 30 pts HL 555)

East Anglia – BBB/ABC/BBC +aEPQ (Phil) (IB 31 pts); BBB/ABC–BBC +aEPQ (Phil Pol) (IB 31 pts); BBB/ABC–BBC +aEPQ incl hist (Phil Hist) (IB 31 pts HL 5 hist)

Essex – BBB (Phil; Phil Hist; Phil Law) (IB 30 pts HL 555)

Hull – BBB 120 pts (Phil; Phil Pol) (IB 30 pts)

Kent – BBB/ABC (Phil courses) (IB 34 pts HL 15 pts)

London (Birk) – ABB–BBB 120–128 pts (Phil; Pol Phil Hist)

London (RH) – ABB–BBB (Phil) (IB 32 pts HL 555)

Reading – BBB (Phil courses) (IB 30 pts); BBB +interview +portfolio (Art Phil) (IB 30 pts)

Stirling – BBB (Phil) (IB 32 pts)

112 pts **Liverpool Hope** – BBC 112 pts (Phil Eth Comb Hons; Phil Eth Relgn) (IB 28 pts)

Roehampton – 112 pts (Phil)

UWE Bristol – 112 pts (Phil)

104 pts **Bangor** – 104 pts (Phil Relgn)

Central Lancashire – 104 pts (Pol Phil Soty) (IB -26 pts)

Hertfordshire – BCC 104 pts (Phil)

Leeds Trinity – 104 pts (Phil Eth Relgn)

Manchester Met – 104–112 pts (Phil; Pol Phil) (IB 26 pts)

Nottingham Trent – 104 pts (Phil Comb Hons)

Oxford Brookes – BCC 104 pts (Phil) (IB 29 pts)

Winchester – 104–120 pts (Phil)

96 pts **Anglia Ruskin** – 96 pts (Phil; Phil Engl Lit) (IB 24 pts)

Bath Spa – CCC (Relgn Phil Eth) (IB 26 pts)

Bishop Grosseteste – 96–112 pts (Theol Phil Eth)

Brighton – BCC–CCC 96–104 pts (Phil Pol Eth) (IB 26 pts)

Chichester – BBC–CCC 96–112 pts +interview (Phil Eth) (IB 28 pts)

Gloucestershire – BBC 96 pts (Relgn Phil Eth)

Keele – CCC (Phil) (IB 26 pts)

Newman – CC 96 pts (Theol Phil)

Wolverhampton – CCC/BCD 96 pts (Law Phil; Phil Sociol; Pol Phil; Relig St Phil; War St Phil)

York St John – 96 pts (Relgn Phil Eth)

88 pts **Canterbury Christ Church** – 88–112 pts (Relgn Phil Eth)

Open University – contact 0300 303 0073 or www.open.ac.uk/contact/new (Phil Psy St)

Trinity Saint David – interview (Phil; Phil Comb Hons)

Alternative offers
See **Chapter 6** and **Appendix 1** for grades/UCAS Tariff points information for other examinations.

CHOOSING YOUR COURSE (SEE ALSO CH.1)
Universities and colleges teaching quality See www.qaa.ac.uk; https://unistats.ac.uk.

ADMISSIONS INFORMATION
Number of applicants per place (approx) Bangor 4; Birmingham 4; Bristol 19; Cambridge 4; Cardiff 8; Dundee 10; Durham 5; East Anglia 6; Hull 5; Lancaster 6; Leeds 10; Liverpool 5; London (King's) 6; London (UCL) 6; London LSE 13; Manchester 6; Nottingham 5; Oxford (PPE) 7; Oxford Brookes 7; Sheffield 8; Southampton 6; Stirling 10; Trinity Saint David 4; Warwick 9; York 6.

Advice to applicants and planning the UCAS personal statement Read Bertrand Russell's *Problems of Philosophy*. Refer to any particular aspects of philosophy which interest you (check that these are offered on the courses for which you are applying). Selectors will expect applicants to have read around the subject. Explain what you know about the nature of studying philosophy. Say what you have read in philosophy and give an example of a philosophical issue that interests you. Universities do not expect applicants to have a wide knowledge of the subject, but evidence that you know what the subject is about is important. **Bristol** Deferred entry considered.

Selection interviews Yes Cambridge, Oxford ((Phil Mod Lang) 27%, (PPE) 14%, (Phil Theol) 22%), Trinity Saint David; **Some** Bristol, Cardiff, Southampton, Warwick; **No** Birmingham, Dundee, East Anglia, Essex, Hull, Leeds, Liverpool, London (UCL), London LSE, Newcastle, Nottingham, Reading.

Interview advice and questions Philosophy is a very wide subject and initially applicants will be asked for their reasons for their choice and their special interests in the subject. Questions in recent years have included: Is there a difference between being tactless and being insensitive? Can you be tactless and thin-skinned? Define the difference between knowledge and belief. Was the vertical distortion of El Greco's paintings a product of a vision defect? What is the point of studying philosophy? What books on philosophy have you read? Discuss the work of a renowned philosopher. What is a philosophical novel? Who has the right to decide your future – yourself or another? What do you want to do with your life? What is a philosophical question? What is the difference between a man's entitlements, his deserts and his attributes? What are morals? A good understanding of philosophy is needed for entry to degree courses, and applicants are expected to demonstrate this if they are called to interview. As one admissions tutor stated, 'If you find Bertrand Russell's *Problems of Philosophy* unreadable – don't apply!' See also **Chapter 5**. **Cambridge** If you were to form a government of philosophers, what selection process would you use? Is it moral to hook up a psychopath (whose only pleasure is killing) to a really stimulating machine so that he can believe he is in the real world and kill as much as he likes? **Oxford** If you entered a teletransporter and your body was destroyed and instantly recreated on Mars in exactly the same way with all your memories intact etc, would you be the same person? Tutors are not so much concerned with what you know as how you think about it. Evidence required concerning social and political topics and the ability to discuss them critically. (PPE) Is being hungry the same thing as wanting to eat? Why is there not a global government? What do you think of teleport machines? Should there be an intelligence test to decide who should vote? **York** Do human beings have free will? Do we perceive the world as it really is?

Reasons for rejection (non-academic) Lack of knowledge of philosophy. **Oxford** He was not able to explore his thoughts deeply enough or with sufficient centrality. **York** No evidence of having read any philosophical literature.

AFTER-RESULTS ADVICE
Offers to applicants repeating A-levels Higher Leeds; Warwick; **Same** Birmingham; Bristol (Phil Econ); Cardiff; Dundee; Durham; East Anglia; Essex; Hull; Liverpool Hope; Newcastle; Nottingham (in some cases); Nottingham Trent; Southampton; St Mary's; Stirling; Wolverhampton; York; **No** Cambridge; Glasgow.

GRADUATE DESTINATIONS AND EMPLOYMENT (2016/17 HESA)
Graduates surveyed 1,710 **Employed** 725 **In voluntary employment** 60 **In further study** 500 **Assumed unemployed** 140

Career note Graduates have a wide range of transferable skills that can lead to employment in many areas, eg management, public administration, publishing, banking and social services.

OTHER DEGREE SUBJECTS FOR CONSIDERATION
Divinity; History and Philosophy of Science; History of Art; Human Sciences; Psychology; Religious Studies; Science; Theology.

PHILOSOPHY, POLITICS AND ECONOMICS (PPE)
(see also **Economics, Philosophy, Politics**)

Philosophy, Politics and Economics is an interdisciplinary study combination. Graduates of this prestigious trio of disciplines include three Prime Ministers of the United Kingdom, including David Cameron, as well as leaders of Australia and Pakistan. These days, PPE attracts the interest of those interested in governance and a wide range of other careers, including business, media and human rights. Although originally pioneered by Oxford University, a broad range of British universities now offer PPE. Courses encourage reflection on how Philosophy, Politics and Economics interrelate and bear influence upon public and political life and enable students to approach issues critically from different angles.

Useful websites NB The points totals shown to the left of the institutions are for ease of reference only. It must not be assumed that Tariff points are always used by institutions or that they can be substituted for an offer in grades. The level of an offer is not necessarily indicative of the quality of a course.

COURSE OFFERS INFORMATION

Subject requirements/preferences GCSE Specific grades in some subjects may be specified by some popular universities. **AL** English, a modern language, humanities or social science subjects preferred.

Your target offers and examples of degree courses

152 pts **Durham** – A*AA incl maths+art/hum (PPE) (IB 38 pts HL 666 incl maths+art/hum)
London (King's) – A*AA (PPE) (IB 35 pts HL 766)
London (UCL) – A*AA incl maths (PPE) (IB 39 pts HL 19 pts incl 7 maths)
London LSE – A*AA incl A* maths (PPE) (IB 38 pts HL 766 incl 7 maths)
Nottingham – A*AA (PPE) (IB 38 pts)
Warwick – A*AA (PPE) (IB 38 pts HL 5 maths)

144 pts **Exeter** – AAA (PPE) (IB 36 pts HL 666)
Leeds – AAA (PPE) (IB 35 pts HL 17 maths)
Manchester – AAA (PPE) (IB 36 pts HL 666)
Oxford – AAA +interview +TSA (PPE) (IB 39 pts HL 766)
Queen's Belfast – AAA (PPE) (IB 36 pts HL 666)
York – A*AA-AAA incl maths (PPE) (IB 37–36 pts HL 6 maths)

136 pts **Lancaster** – AAB (PPE) (IB 35 pts HL 16 pts)
NCH London – AAB (PPE) (IB 35 pts HL 665)
Reading – AAB (PPE) (IB 32 pts)
Sussex – AAA-AAB (PPE) (IB 36–34 pts)

128 pts **East Anglia** – ABB (PPE) (IB 32 pts)
London (RH) – AAB-ABB (PPE) (IB 32 pts HL 655)
Southampton – AAB/ABB incl maths/phys/stats (PPE) (IB 34–32 pts HL 17–16 pts incl 5 maths)

120 pts **Essex** – BBB (PPE) (IB 30 pts HL 555)
Hull – BBB 120 pts (PPE) (IB 30 pts)
London (Gold) – BBB (PPE) (IB 33 pts HL 655)
Stirling – BBB (PPE) (IB 32 pts)

112 pts **Buckingham** – BBB-BBC (PPE) (IB 32–31 pts)
104 pts **Winchester** – 104-120 pts (PPE) (HL 44)
72 pts **UHI** – BC (PPE)

Open University – contact 0300 303 0073 or www.open.ac.uk/contact/new (PPE)

Alternative offers
See **Chapter 6** and **Appendix 1** for grades/UCAS Tariff points information for other examinations.

CHOOSING YOUR COURSE (SEE ALSO CH.1)
Universities and colleges teaching quality See www.qaa.ac.uk; https://unistats.ac.uk.

ADMISSIONS INFORMATION
Number of applicants per place (approx) See **Economics, Philosophy, Politics.**

Admissions tutors' advice Admissions tutors expect evidence of capacity for sustained study, motivation and interest as well as an independent and reflective approach to learning. Reasoning, as demonstrated by the ability to analyse and solve problems using logical and critical approaches and construct and critically assess arguments, is also sought after. Prospective students should show willingness and ability to express ideas clearly and effectively on paper and orally, and an ability to listen.

Advice to applicants and planning the UCAS personal statement See **Economics, Philosophy, Politics.**

Misconceptions about this course See **Economics, Philosophy, Politics.**

Selection interviews See **Economics, Philosophy, Politics.**

Interview advice and questions See **Economics, Philosophy, Politics.**

Reasons for rejection (non-academic) See **Economics, Philosophy, Politics.**

AFTER-RESULTS ADVICE
Offers to applicants repeating A levels See **Economics, Philosophy, Politics.**

GRADUATE DESTINATIONS AND EMPLOYMENT (2016/17 HESA)
Career note See **Economics, Philosophy, Politics.**

OTHER DEGREE SUBJECTS FOR CONSIDERATION
Economics; History; International Relations; Philosophy; Politics

---

PHOTOGRAPHY

(See also **Art And Design (Fine Art), Art And Design (General), Film, Radio, Video and TV Studies, Media Studies**)

Photography courses offer a range of specialised studies involving commercial, industrial and still photography, portraiture and film, digital and video work. Increasingly this subject is featuring in Media courses. See also **Appendix 3**.

Useful websites www.the-aop.org; https://rps.org; www.bjp-online.com; www.bipp.com

NB The points totals shown to the left of the institutions are for ease of reference only. It must not be assumed that Tariff points are always used by institutions or that they can be substituted for an offer in grades. The level of an offer is not necessarily indicative of the quality of a course.

COURSE OFFERS INFORMATION
Subject requirements/preferences GCSE Art and/or a portfolio usually required. **AL** One or two subjects may be required, including an art/design or creative subject. Most institutions will make offers on the basis of a portfolio of work.

Your target offers and examples of degree courses
136 pts   **Leeds** – AAB (Flm Photo Media) (IB 35 pts HL 16 pts)
128 pts   **Edinburgh** – ABB +portfolio (Photo) (IB 34 pts HL 655)
           Glasgow (SA) – ABB +interview +portfolio (Fn Art Photo)
120 pts   **Bournemouth Arts** – BBB 120 pts +portfolio +interview (Commer Photo; Photo) (HL 555)
           Coventry – BBB incl art/media/photo +interview +portfolio (Photo) (IB 31 pts)

Huddersfield – BBB 120 pts +interview +portfolio (Photo)
Norwich Arts – BBB +interview +portfolio (Photo) (IB 27 pts)
Trinity Saint David – 120 pts +interview (Doc Photo Vis Actvsm; Photo Arts) (IB 32 pts)

112 pts   **Birmingham City** – BBC 112 pts +portfolio (Photo) (IB 28 pts HL 14 pts)
Creative Arts – 112 pts +portfolio (Photo) (IB 30–27 pts HL 15 pts)
De Montfort – 112 pts incl art des +interview +portfolio (Photo Vid) (IB 26 pts)
Derby – 112 pts +interview (Photo)
Leeds Arts – BBC 112 pts +portfolio +interview (Photo)
Lincoln – BBC 112 pts (Photo) (IB 29 pts)
Manchester Met – 112 pts +portfolio (Photo) (IB 26 pts)
Middlesex – 112 pts +interview +portfolio (Photo)
Nottingham Trent – BBC 112 pts +portfolio +interview (Photo)
Oxford Brookes – BBC 112 pts +interview +portfolio (Photo) (IB 30 pts)
Plymouth (CA) – 112–120 pts +portfolio (Photo)
Roehampton – 112 pts +portfolio (Photo)
Sheffield Hallam – BBC 112 pts +interview +portfolio (Photo)
Staffordshire – BBC 112 pts +interview +portfolio (Photo)
Sunderland – 112 pts (Photo Vid Dig Imag)
UWE Bristol – 112 pts +interview +portfolio (Photo)
West London – BBC 112 pts +interview +portfolio (Photo)

104 pts   **Central Lancashire** – 104 pts +interview +portfolio (Photo); 104–112 pts +interview +portfolio (Fash Prom)
Chester – BBC–BCC incl art/des/photo 104–112 pts +interview (Photo) (IB 26 pts HL 5 vis arts)
Falmouth – 104–120 pts +interview +portfolio (Fash Photo) (IB 24 pts); 104–120 pts +portfolio +interview (Mar Nat Hist Photo; Photo; Press Edit Photo)
Kingston – 104 pts incl art des +interview +portfolio (Photo)
Northampton – BCC incl art/des/photo +portfolio (Photo)
Portsmouth – 104–112 pts +interview +portfolio (Photo) (IB 25 pts)
Ulster – BCC +interview +portfolio (Photo Vid) (IB 24 pts HL 12 pts)

96 pts   **Anglia Ruskin** – 96 pts incl art/des/media +portfolio (Photo) (IB 24 pts)
Bath Spa – CCC incl photo +portfolio +interview (Photo) (IB 26 pts HL 6 art)
Bolton – 96 pts incl art/des/photo +interview +portfolio (Photo)
Bournemouth – 96–104 pts (Photo) (IB 29–26 pts)
Brighton – BBB–CCC 96–120 pts +interview +portfolio (Photo) (IB 26 pts)
Cumbria – 96–112 pts incl photo +interview +portfolio (Photo)
East London – 96 pts +interview +portfolio (Photo) (IB 24 pts HL 15 pts)
Hertfordshire – CCC incl art/des 96 pts +portfolio +interview (Photo)
Northern SA – 96 pts (Commer Photo)
Plymouth – 96–120 pts +portfolio (Photo) (IB 28 pts)
Solent – 96–112 pts +interview +portfolio (Photo)
Teesside – 96–112 pts (Photo)
Westminster – BBB–CCC 96–120 pts +portfolio (Photo) (IB 27 pts)
Wolverhampton – CCC/BCD 96 pts +portfolio (Photo)

88 pts   **Canterbury Christ Church** – 88–112 pts +portfolio (Photo)
80 pts   **Arts London** – 80 pts +portfolio (Photo) (IB 24 pts)
Bedfordshire – 80–96 pts +portfolio (Photo)
Hereford (CA) – 80 pts +portfolio +interview (Photo)
South Wales – BCC–CDD 80–104 pts +interview +portfolio (Photo) (IB 29 pts); BCC–CDD incl art des 80–104 pts +interview +portfolio (Doc Photo) (IB 29 pts)

64 pts   **Arts London (CFash)** – CC 64 pts+interview +portfolio (Fash Photo)
Colchester (UC) – 64 pts +portfolio +interview (Photo)
Ravensbourne Univ – CC +portfolio (Dig Photo) (IB 24 pts)
Stockport (Coll) – 64 pts +interview (Contemp Photo)

Gloucestershire – interview (Photo; Photojrnl Doc Photo)

Alternative offers
See **Chapter 6** and **Appendix 1** for grades/UCAS Tariff points information for other examinations.

EXAMPLES OF COLLEGES OFFERING COURSES IN THIS SUBJECT FIELD
Barking and Dagenham (Coll); Bedford (Coll); Birmingham Met (Coll); Blackburn (Coll); Blackpool and Fylde (Coll); Bournemouth and Poole (Coll); Bradford College UC; Bristol City (Coll); Buckinghamshire (Coll Group); Canterbury (Coll); Central Bedfordshire (Coll); Central Campus, Sandwell (Coll); City and Islington (Coll); Coventry (Coll); Doncaster (Coll); East Coast (Coll); East Surrey (Coll); East Sussex (Coll); Exeter (Coll); Farnborough (CT); Gloucestershire (Coll); Greater Brighton Met (Coll); Grŵp Llandrillo Menai; Havering (Coll); Hugh Baird (Coll); Hull (Coll); Kensington and Chelsea (Coll); Kirklees (Coll); Leeds City (Coll); Leicester (Coll); LeSoCo; Lincoln (Coll); Manchester (Coll); Milton Keynes (Coll); Myerscough (Coll); Nescot; Newcastle (Coll); North Shropshire (Coll); North Warwickshire and South Leicestershire (Coll); Northumberland (Coll); Nottingham (Coll); Rotherham (CAT); Sheffield (Coll); Sir Gâr (Coll); Solihull (Coll); South Devon (Coll); South Essex (Coll); South Gloucestershire and Stroud (Coll); South Staffordshire (Coll); Southampton City (Coll); Southport (Coll); St Helens (Coll); Stamford New (Coll); Stockport (Coll); TEC Partnership; Tresham (CFHE); Truro and Penwith (Coll); Wakefield (Coll); Walsall (Coll); West Kent (Coll); Westminster City (Coll); Weston (Coll); Weymouth (Coll); Wiltshire (Coll); Wirral Met (Coll); Yeovil (Coll).

CHOOSING YOUR COURSE (SEE ALSO CH.1)
Universities and colleges teaching quality See www.qaa.ac.uk; http://unistats.direct.gov.uk.

Examples of sandwich degree courses Coventry; Hertfordshire; Leeds; Portsmouth; Wolverhampton.

ADMISSIONS INFORMATION
Number of applicants per place (approx) Arts London 10; Birmingham City 6; Blackpool and Fylde (Coll) 3; Bournemouth Arts 3; Derby 4; Falmouth 3; Northern SA 2; Nottingham Trent 4; Plymouth 6; Plymouth (CA) 7; Staffordshire 3; Stockport (Coll) 6; Trinity Saint David 12.

Advice to applicants and planning the UCAS personal statement Discuss your interest in photography and your knowledge of various aspects of the subject, for example, digital, video, landscape, medical, wildlife and portrait photography. Read photographic journals to keep up-to-date on developments, particularly in photographic technology. You will also need first-hand experience of photography and to be competent in basic skills. See also **Appendix 3**. **Derby** (Non-UK students) Fluency in written and spoken English important. Portfolio of work essential.

Misconceptions about this course Cumbria They didn't realise the facilities were so good!

Selection interviews Yes Brighton, Chester, Cumbria, Huddersfield, Plymouth, Solent; **No** Falmouth, West London.

Interview advice and questions Questions relate to the applicant's portfolio of work which, for these courses, is of prime importance. Who are your favourite photographers? What is the most recent exhibition you have attended? Have any leading photographers influenced your work? Questions regarding contemporary photography. Written work sometimes required. See **Chapter 5**.

Reasons for rejection (non-academic) Lack of passion for the subject. Lack of exploration and creativity in practical work. Poorly presented portfolio.

AFTER-RESULTS ADVICE
Offers to applicants repeating A-levels Same Birmingham City; Blackpool and Fylde (Coll); Chester; Cumbria; Manchester Met; Nottingham Trent; Staffordshire.

GRADUATE DESTINATIONS AND EMPLOYMENT (2016/17 HESA)
Cinematics and Photography Graduates surveyed 4,140 **Employed** 2,050 **In voluntary employment** 160 **In further study** 450 **Assumed unemployed** 290

Career note Opportunities for photographers exist in a range of specialisms, including advertising and editorial work, fashion, medical, industrial, scientific and technical photography. Some graduates also go into photojournalism and other aspects of the media.

OTHER DEGREE SUBJECTS FOR CONSIDERATION

Art and Design; Digital Animation; Film, Radio, Video and TV Studies; Media Studies; Moving Image; Radiography.

PHYSICAL EDUCATION

(see also **Education Studies, Sports Sciences/Studies, Teacher Training**)

Physical Education courses are very popular and unfortunately restricted in number. Ability in gymnastics or an involvement in sport are obviously important factors.

Useful websites www.afpe.org.uk; www.uksport.gov.uk; see also **Education Studies** and **Teacher Training**.

NB The points totals shown to the left of the institutions are for ease of reference only. It must not be assumed that Tariff points are always used by institutions or that they can be substituted for an offer in grades. The level of an offer is not necessarily indicative of the quality of a course.

COURSE OFFERS INFORMATION

Subject requirements/preferences GCSE English, mathematics and a science. **AL** PE, sports studies and science are preferred subjects and for some courses one of these may be required. Disclosure and Barring Service (DBS) check before starting the course. Declaration of Health usually required.

Your target offers and examples of degree courses

128 pts **Birmingham** – AAB–ABB (Spo PE Coach Sci) (IB 32 pts HL 665–655)
East Anglia – ABB (PE) (IB 32 pts)
Edinburgh – ABB +interview (PE) (IB 34 pts HL 655 incl 5 Engl)

112 pts **Bangor** – 112 pts (Spo Hlth PE)
Brunel – BBC incl maths/sci (PE Yth Spo; Spo Hlth Exer Sci (Spo Dev)) (IB 29 pts HL 5 maths/sci)
Canterbury Christ Church – 112 pts (PE Spo Exer Sci)
Cardiff Met – 112–120 pts (Spo PE St)
East London – 112 pts incl PE/spo/sci (Spo PE Dev) (IB 25 pts HL 15 pts)
Edge Hill – BBC 112 pts (PE Sch Spo)
Leeds Beckett – 112 pts incl sci (PE Out Educ) (IB 25 pts); 112 pts incl sci/PE (PE courses) (IB 25 pts)
Leeds Trinity – 112 pts (S Educ PE Spo)
Liverpool Hope – BBC 112 pts (Spo PE) (IB 28 pts)
Newman – CC 112 pts (PE Spo)
RAc Dance – BBC +RAD Intermediate +interview +audition (Ballet Educ)
Sheffield Hallam – BBC 112 pts (PE Sch Spo)
Staffordshire – BBC 112 pts (PE Yth Spo Coach)
Worcester – 112 pts (PE Spo Coach Sci); 112 pts +interview (PE Dance)

104 pts **Anglia Ruskin** – 104 pts (Spo Coach PE) (IB 24 pts)
Bedfordshire – 104 pts +interview (PE S)
Greenwich – 104 pts (PE Spo)
Leeds Trinity – 104 pts (PE)
Oxford Brookes – BCC 104 pts (Spo Coach PE) (IB 29 pts)

96 pts **Brighton** – BBC–CCC 96–112 pts (PE) (IB 26 pts)
Cardiff Met – BB 96–112 pts (Spo Physl Educ Hlth Dance) (IB 25 pts HL 13 pts)
Chichester – BBC–CCC 96–112 pts +interview (PE Spo Coach)

Cumbria – 96–112 pts (Spo Coach PE)
Greenwich – 96 pts incl sci (Spo Sci Coach)
London Met – BC/CCC incl biol/PE/spo sci 96 pts (Spo Psy Coach PE)
Marjon – CCC 96 pts (PE; Spo Coach PE)
Trinity Saint David – 96 pts +interview (PE)
York St John – 96 pts (PE Spo Coach)
80 pts   **Bedfordshire** – 80 pts (Spo Sci Coach; Spo Sci Per Trg; Spo St)

Alternative offers
See **Chapter 6** and **Appendix 1** for grades/UCAS Tariff points information for other examinations.

EXAMPLES OF COLLEGES OFFERING COURSES IN THIS SUBJECT FIELD
City and Islington (Coll); Doncaster (Coll); Hartpury (Coll); Peterborough (Coll).

CHOOSING YOUR COURSE (SEE ALSO CH.1)
Universities and colleges teaching quality See www.qaa.ac.uk; https://unistats.ac.uk.

Top research universities and colleges (REF 2014) See **Sports Sciences/Studies**.

Examples of sandwich degree courses Chichester.

ADMISSIONS INFORMATION
Number of applicants per place (approx) Bangor 4; Birmingham 5; Edge Hill 40; Leeds Trinity 6; Liverpool John Moores 4; Marjon 18; Newman 5; Sheffield Hallam 60; Worcester 31.

Advice to applicants and planning the UCAS personal statement Ability in gymnastics, athletics and all sports and games is important. Full details of these activities should be given on the UCAS application – for example, teams, dates and awards achieved, assisting in extra-curricular activities. Involvement with local sports clubs, health clubs, summer camps, gap year. Relevant experience in coaching, teaching, community and youth work. **Liverpool John Moores** Commitment to working with children and a good sports background.

Selection interviews Yes Worcester.

Interview advice and questions The applicant's interests in physical education will be discussed, with specific questions on, for example, sportsmanship, refereeing, umpiring and coaching. Questions in the past have also included: What qualities should a good netball goal defence possess? How could you encourage a group of children into believing that sport is fun? Do you think that physical education should be compulsory in schools? Why do you think you would make a good teacher? What is the name of the Education Minister?

Reasons for rejection (non-academic) Poor communication and presentational skills. Relatively poor sporting background or knowledge. Lack of knowledge about the teaching of physical education and the commitment required. Lack of ability in practicalities, for example, gymnastics, dance when relevant. Poor self-presentation. Poor writing skills.

AFTER-RESULTS ADVICE
Offers to applicants repeating A-levels Same Liverpool John Moores; Newman.

GRADUATE DESTINATIONS AND EMPLOYMENT (2016/17 HESA)
Graduates surveyed See **Sports Sciences/Studies**.

Career note The majority of graduates go into teaching although, depending on any special interests, they may also go on into the sport and leisure industry.

OTHER DEGREE SUBJECTS FOR CONSIDERATION
Coach Education; Exercise and Fitness; Exercise Physiology; Human Biology; Leisure and Recreation; Physiotherapy; Sport and Exercise Science; Sport Health and Exercise; Sport Studies/Sciences; Sports Coaching; Sports Development; Sports Engineering; Sports Psychology; Sports Therapy.

PHYSICS

(See also **Astronomy and Astrophysics**)

Physics is an increasingly popular subject and a wide variety of courses are available which enables students to follow their own interests and specialisations. Some course options are nanotechnology, medical physics, cosmology, environmental physics and biophysics.

Useful websites www.iop.org; www.physics.org; www.scicentral.com; www.ipem.ac.uk; https://epsrc. ukri.org; http://jobs.newscientist.com; www.nature.com/subjects/physics

NB The points totals shown to the left of the institutions are for ease of reference only. It must not be assumed that Tariff points are always used by institutions or that they can be substituted for an offer in grades. The level of an offer is not necessarily indicative of the quality of a course.

COURSE OFFERS INFORMATION

Subject requirements/preferences GCSE English, mathematics and science. **AL** Physics and mathematics are required for most courses.

Your target offers and examples of degree courses

160 pts **Cambridge** – A*A*A incl sci/maths +interview +NSAA (Nat Sci (Phys/Physl Sci/Astro)) (IB 42– 40 pts HL 776 incl sci/maths)

Durham – A*A*A incl maths+phys (Phys Astron (MPhys)) (IB 38 pts HL 776 incl maths+phys); A*A*A incl phys+maths (Phys; Theor Phys (MPhys)) (IB 38 pts HL 776 incl phys+maths)

Imperial London – A*A*A incl maths+phys +interview (Phys; Phys (Yr Abrd) (MSci)) (IB 39 pts HL 766 incl maths+phys); A*A*A incl maths+phys +interview +audition +gr 8 (Phys Mus Perf) (IB 39 pts HL 766 incl maths+phys)

152 pts **Bath** – A*AA–AAA +aEPQ incl maths+phys (Maths Phys; Phys) (IB 36 pts HL 766 incl maths+phys)

Birmingham – A*AA incl maths+phys (Phys) (IB 32 pts HL 766 incl maths+phys)

Bristol – A*AA incl maths+phys (Phys; Phys Phil) (IB 38 pts HL 18 pts incl 76 maths+phys); (Phys Astro) (IB 38 pts HL 76 maths+phys)

Durham – A*AA (Nat Sci) (IB 38 pts)

Exeter – A*AA incl maths+phys +interview (Phys Astro (MPhys)) (IB 38 pts HL 766 incl maths+phys)

Manchester – A*A*A–A*AA incl maths+phys +interview (Phys; Phys Astro) (IB 38–37 pts HL 776–766 incl maths+phys)

Oxford – A*AA incl maths+phys +interview +PAT (Phys) (IB 39 pts HL 766 incl maths+phys)

Warwick – A*AA incl maths+phys (Phys Bus St) (IB 38 pts HL 6 maths+phys); A*AA incl maths/fmaths+phys (Phys) (IB 38 pts HL 6 maths+phys)

144 pts **East Anglia** – AAA incl sci/maths (Nat Sci) (IB 34 pts HL 6 sci/maths)

Lancaster – AAA incl maths+phys (Phys Ptcl Phys Cosmo (MPhys)) (IB 36 pts HL 16 pts incl maths+phys); AAA incl maths+phys +interview (Phys (MPhys)) (IB 36 pts HL 16 pts incl 6 maths+phys)

London (UCL) – AAA incl chem+maths+phys (Cheml Phys) (IB 38 pts HL 18 pts incl 5 chem+maths+phys); AAA incl maths+phys (Phys Med Phys) (IB 38 pts HL 18 pts incl 5 maths+phys); (Med Phys (MSci); Phys) (IB 38 pts HL 18 pts incl 6 maths+phys)

Newcastle – AAA/A*AB incl maths+phys (Phys (MPhys)) (IB 36 pts HL 6 maths+phys)

Nottingham – A*AA–AAA incl maths+phys (Mathem Phys; Phys Euro Lang) (IB 38 pts HL 6 maths+phys); (Phys; Phys Astron; Phys Med Phys; Phys Theor Astro; Phys Theor Phys) (IB 38 pts HL 666 incl maths+phys)

Queen's Belfast – AAA/A*AB incl maths+phys (Phys (MSci); Phys Med Apps (MSci)) (IB 36 pts HL 666 incl maths+phys)

Sheffield – AAA incl maths+phys (Phys (MPhys)) (IB 36 pts HL 6 maths+phys)

Southampton – AAA incl maths+phys (Mathem Phys (MMath)) (IB 36 pts HL 18 pts incl 6 maths+phys)

St Andrews – AAA incl maths+phys (Comp Sci Phys; Phys) (IB 38 pts HL 666 incl maths+phys)

York – AAA incl maths+phys +interview (Phys (MPhys)) (IB 36 pts HL 6 maths+phys)

136 pts **Cardiff** – AAA–A*BB incl maths+phys +interview (Phys Astron (MPhys)) (IB 36–34 pts HL 665 incl 6 maths+phys); AAA–AAB incl phys+maths (Phys (MPhys)) (IB 36–34 pts HL 665 incl 6 phys+maths)

Exeter – AAA–AAB incl maths+phys +interview (Maths Phys) (IB 36–34 pts HL 666–665 incl 6 maths 5 phys); (Phys) (IB 36–34 pts HL 666–665 incl maths+phys)

Glasgow – AAB incl maths+phys (Phys) (IB 36 pts HL 665 incl maths+phys); (Phys Astro) (IB 36–32 pts)

Lancaster – AAB incl maths+phys (Phys Astro Cosmo; Phys Ptcl Phys Cosmo) (IB 35 pts HL 16 incl 6 maths+phys); AAB incl phys+maths +interview (Phys; Theor Phys Maths) (IB 35 pts HL 16 pts incl 6 maths+phys)

Leeds – AAB incl maths+phys (Phys Astro) (IB 35 pts HL 15 pts incl 5 maths+phys); AAB incl phys+maths +interview (Phys; Theor Phys) (IB 35 pts HL 15 pts incl 5 phys+maths)

Liverpool – AAB/ABB+aEPQ incl maths+phys (Mathem Phys (MMath)) (IB 35 pts HL 6 maths+phys); AAB incl maths+phys (Theor Phys (MPhys)) (IB 35 pts HL 6 phys+maths); AAB incl phys+maths (Phys (MPhys)) (IB 35 pts HL 6 phys+maths)

Liverpool John Moores – AAB incl maths+phys 136 pts (Astro (MPhys))

London (King's) – AAB incl maths+phys (Phys; Phys Phil; Phys Theor Phys) (IB 35 pts HL 665 incl 6 maths+phys)

London (QM) – AAB incl maths+phys (Astro (MSci); Theor Phys (MSci)) (IB 34 pts HL 665 incl 6 maths+phys); AAB incl maths+phys 136 pts (Phys (MSci)) (IB 34 pts HL 665 incl 6 maths+phys)

London (RH) – AAA–AAB incl maths+phys (Theor Phys) (IB 32 pts HL 6 maths 5 phys); (Phys; Phys Ptcl Phys) (IB 32 pts HL 665 incl 6 maths 5 phys); AAA–AAB incl maths+phys+gr 7 (Phys Mus) (IB 32 pts HL 665 incl 6 maths+mus 5 phys)

Newcastle – AAB/A*BB incl maths+phys (Theor Phys) (IB 34 pts HL 6 maths+phys)

Nottingham – AAB incl maths+phys+chem +interview (Chem Mol Phys) (IB 34 pts HL 6 maths 6/5 phys+chem)

Queen's Belfast – AAB/A*BB incl maths+phys (Theor Phys) (IB 34 pts HL 665 incl maths+phys)

Southampton – AAA–AAB incl maths/fmaths+phys (Phys Maths (MPhys); Phys Nanotech (MPhys); Phys Photon (MPhys); Phys Spc Sci (MPhys)) (IB 36–34 pts HL 18–17 pts incl 6 maths/fmaths+phys)

Swansea – AAA–AAB incl maths+phys (Phys (MPhys)) (IB 36–34 pts HL 6 maths+phys)

York – AAB incl maths+phys +interview (Maths Phys; Phys; Phys Astro; Phys Phil; Theor Phys) (IB 35 pts HL 6 maths+phys)

128 pts **Cardiff** – AAB–ABB incl maths+phys +interview (Phys Astron) (IB 34–32 pts HL 665 incl 6 maths+phys); AAB–ABB incl phys+maths (Phys) (IB 34–32 pts HL 6 maths+phys); (Phys Med Phys) (IB 34–32 pts HL 6 phys+maths)

East Anglia – ABB incl maths+phys (Phys (MPhys)) (IB 32 pts HL 5 maths+phys)

Edinburgh – AAA–ABB incl maths+phys (Geophys; Geophys Meteor) (IB 37–32 pts HL 555 incl maths+phys); (Mathem Phys; Theor Phys) (IB 37–32 pts HL 666–655 incl 6 maths+phys); (Comput Phys; Phys; Phys Meteor) (IB 37–32 pts HL 666–655 incl maths+phys)

Leicester – ABB incl maths+phys (Phys Astro; Phys Spc Sci) (IB 30 pts HL 5 maths+phys); ABB incl phys+maths (Phys) (IB 30 pts HL 5 phys+maths)

Liverpool – ABB/BBB +aEPQ incl maths+phys (Geophys (Geol/Phys)) (IB 33 pts HL 4 maths+phys); ABB/BBB +aEPQ incl phys+maths (Phys; Phys Med Apps; Phys Nucl Sci) (IB 33 pts HL 6 phys+maths)

Liverpool John Moores – ABB incl maths+phys 128 pts (Phys Astron)

London (QM) – ABB incl maths+phys (Phys Ptcl Phys) (IB 32 pts HL 655 incl 6 maths+phys); (Theor Phys) (IB 32 pts HL 655 incl 6 maths/phys); (Astro) (IB 32 pts HL 655 incl maths+phys)

Loughborough – ABB incl maths+phys (Eng Phys; Phys; Phys Maths) (IB 34 pts HL 655 incl maths+phys)

Queen's Belfast – ABB incl maths+phys (Phys; Phys Astro; Phys Med Apps) (IB 33 pts HL 655 incl maths+phys)

Reading – ABB incl maths+phys (Env Phys) (IB 32 pts HL 5 maths+phys)

Sheffield – ABB/BBB +bEPQ incl maths+phys (Phys Comb Hons) (IB 33 pts HL 5 maths+phys); ABB incl maths+phys (Phys; Phys Astro; Theor Phys) (IB 33 pts HL 5 maths+phys)

Southampton – AAB–ABB incl maths/fmaths+phys (Phys) (IB 34–32 pts HL 17–16 pts incl 6/5 maths/fmaths+phys)

Surrey – ABB incl maths+phys (Phys; Phys Qntm Tech) (IB 32 pts); (Phys Astron; Phys Nucl Astro) (IB 32 pts HL 5 maths+phys)

Sussex – AAB–ABB incl maths (Phys; Phys Astro; Theor Phys) (IB 34–32 pts HL 5 maths)

120 pts   **Aberdeen** – BBB incl maths+phys (Nat Phil; Phys) (IB 32 pts HL 555 incl maths+phys)

Central Lancashire – B maths+phys 120 pts (Phys) (HL 5 maths+phys)

Dundee – BBB incl maths+phys/eng (Phys) (IB 30 pts HL 555 incl maths+phys/eng); BBB incl maths/phys (App Phys) (IB 30 pts HL 555 incl maths+phys/eng)

East Anglia – BBB/ABC incl chem+maths (Cheml Phys) (IB 31 pts HL 5 chem+maths); BBB/ABC incl maths+phys (Phys) (IB 31 pts HL 5 maths+phys)

Keele – ABC/BBB incl phys+maths (Phys Comb Hons) (IB 32 pts HL 6 phys+maths)

Kent – BBB incl maths (Phys) (IB 34 pts HL 14 pts); (Phys Astro) (IB 34 pts HL 5 maths)

Strathclyde – BBB incl phys+maths (Phys) (IB 32 pts HL 5 phys+maths)

Swansea – AAB–BBB incl maths+phys (Phys; Theor Phys) (IB 34–32 pts HL 6 maths 5 phys); (Phys Ptcl Phys Cosmo) (IB 34–32 pts HL 6 maths 6/5 phys)

112 pts   **Aberystwyth** – BBB–BBC incl maths+phys 112–120 pts (Phys courses) (IB 30–28 pts HL 5 maths+phys); BBB–BBC incl phys+maths 112–120 pts (Spc Sci Robot) (IB 30–28 pts HL 5 maths+phys)

Heriot-Watt – BBC incl maths+phys (Phys courses) (IB 29 pts)

Hertfordshire – BBC incl maths+phys 112 pts (Phys) (HL 4 maths+phys)

Hull – BBC incl maths+phys 112 pts (Phys) (IB 28 pts HL 6 maths+phys); B phys+maths 112 pts (Phys Astro) (IB 28 pts HL 6 maths+phys)

Keele – BBC incl B phys/maths (Educ Phys) (IB 30 pts HL 5 phys/maths)

Nottingham Trent – B maths+phys 112 pts (Phys Maths); B phys+maths 112 pts incl maths+phys (Phys Astro)

Portsmouth – 112–128 pts incl maths+phys (Phys (MPhys)) (IB 29 pts HL 6 maths+phys)

104 pts   **Nottingham Trent** – 104 pts incl phys+maths (Phys Nucl Tech); B/C maths+phys 104 pts (Phys)

Salford – 104–112 pts incl maths+phys (Phys) (IB 30 pts HL 5 maths+phys); C maths+phys 104–112 pts (Phys Acoust) (IB 30 pts HL 5 maths+phys)

88 pts   **West Scotland** – CCD incl maths+phys 88 pts (Phys) (IB 24 pts)

Open University – contact 0300 303 0073 or www.open.ac.uk/contact/new (Nat Sci (Phys))

Alternative offers
See **Chapter 6** and **Appendix 1** for grades/UCAS Tariff points information for other examinations.

CHOOSING YOUR COURSE (SEE ALSO CH.1)
Universities and colleges teaching quality See www.qaa.ac.uk; https://unistats.ac.uk.

Examples of sandwich degree courses Bath; Bristol; Cardiff; East Anglia; Hertfordshire; Kent; Loughborough; Nottingham Trent; Portsmouth; Surrey; Sussex; West Scotland.

ADMISSIONS INFORMATION
Number of applicants per place (approx) Bath 7; Birmingham 6; Bristol 7; Cardiff 4, (Phys Astron) 6; Dundee 10; Durham 6; Edinburgh 10; Exeter 5; Heriot-Watt 5; Hull 5; Imperial London 3; Lancaster 4; Leeds 7; Leicester 5; Liverpool 10; London (King's) 7; London (QM) 6; London (RH) 5; London (UCL) 7; Manchester 4; Nottingham 4; Salford 5; Southampton 6; Strathclyde 5; Swansea 3; Warwick 8; York 5.

UCAS points Tariff: A* = 56 pts; A = 48 pts; B = 40 pts; C = 32 pts; D = 24 pts; E = 16 pts

Advice to applicants and planning the UCAS personal statement Admissions tutors look for potential, enthusiasm and interest in the subject so interests relating to maths and physics must be mentioned. An awareness of the range of careers in which physics is involved should also be mentioned on the UCAS application together with a demonstration of any particular interests, such as details on a physics or maths book you have read recently (not science fiction!). Make sure to mention if you have attended any courses, summer schools or day conferences on physics and engineering. See also **Appendix 3**. **Bristol** Deferred entry accepted.

Selection interviews Yes Cambridge, Exeter, Imperial London, Manchester, Oxford ((Phys) 17%), York; **Some** Bath, Heriot-Watt, Lancaster, St Andrews, Surrey, Warwick; **No** Aberystwyth, Birmingham, Bristol, Cardiff, Dundee, East Anglia, Hull, Liverpool, London (QM), London (RH), Loughborough, Nottingham, Salford, Sheffield, Strathclyde, Swansea.

Interview advice and questions Questions will almost certainly focus on those aspects of the physics A-level course that the student enjoys. See also **Chapter 5**. **Bristol** Why Physics? Questions on mechanics, physics and pure maths. Given paper and calculator and questions asked orally; best to take your own calculator. Tutors seek enthusiastic and highly motivated students and the physicist's ability to apply basic principles to unfamiliar situations.

AFTER-RESULTS ADVICE
Offers to applicants repeating A-levels Higher Bristol; St Andrews; Warwick; **Possibly higher** Aberystwyth; Leeds; Loughborough; York; **Same** Birmingham; Cardiff; Dundee; Durham; East Anglia; Exeter; Hull; Lancaster; Leicester; Liverpool; Salford; Swansea; **No** Cambridge; Glasgow.

GRADUATE DESTINATIONS AND EMPLOYMENT (2016/17 HESA)
Graduates surveyed 2,795 **Employed** 1,105 **In voluntary employment** 50 **In further study** 1,125 **Assumed unemployed** 220

Career note Many graduates go into scientific and technical work in the manufacturing industries. However, in recent years, financial work, management and marketing have also attracted many seeking alternative careers.

OTHER DEGREE SUBJECTS FOR CONSIDERATION
Astronomy; Astrophysics; Computer Science; Earth Sciences; Engineering subjects; Geophysics; Materials Science and Metallurgy; Mathematics; Meteorology; Natural Sciences; Oceanography; Optometry; Radiography.

PHYSIOLOGY
(see also Animal Sciences, Neuroscience, Psychology)

Physiology is the study of body function. Courses in this wide-ranging subject will cover the central nervous system, special senses and neuro-muscular mechanisms, and body-regulating systems such as exercise, stress and temperature regulation. The Bristol course is available for intercalation in which it is possible to follow a one-year stand-alone degree in any of the following subjects: Heart in Health and Disease/Sensational Neuroscience, Neuroscience of Pain/Future of Molecular Medicine, Cardiovascular Systems in Health and Disease/Brain Behaviour, Pharmacology of ion cells and synaptic transmission, Receptor signalling and non-drug therapies, Pharmacology of the Nervous System, Synaptic Plasticity, Synaptic Cell Biology, or Neurological and Psychiatric disorders.

Useful websites www.physoc.org; www.physiology.org; www.bases.org.uk; see also **Biological Sciences**.

NB The points totals shown to the left of the institutions are for ease of reference only. It must not be assumed that Tariff points are always used by institutions or that they can be substituted for an offer in grades. The level of an offer is not necessarily indicative of the quality of a course.

COURSE OFFERS INFORMATION

Subject requirements/preferences GCSE Science and mathematics at grade A (7). **AL** Two science subjects are usually required; chemistry and biology are the preferred subjects.

Your target offers and examples of degree courses

160 pts **Cambridge** – A*A*A incl sci/maths +interview +NSAA (Nat Sci (Physiol Dev Neuro)) (IB 42–40 pts HL 776)

136 pts **Bristol** – AAB incl sci/maths (Physiol Sci) (IB 34 pts HL 17 pts incl 6/5 maths/sci)
Dundee – AAB incl biol+chem (Physiol Sci) (IB 30 pts HL 555 incl biol+chem)
Glasgow – AAB incl biol/chem (Physiol) (IB 36 pts HL 665 incl sci)
Leeds – AAA–AAB (Hum Physiol) (IB 35–34 pts HL 18–17 pts incl 6 biol/chem+sci)
London (King's) – AAB incl chem+biol (Med Physiol) (IB 35 pts HL 665 incl biol+chem)
Newcastle – AAA–AAB incl biol/chem+maths/sci (Physiol Sci) (IB 35–34 pts HL 5 biol/chem+maths/sci)

128 pts **Aberdeen** – ABB incl chem+biol (Physiol (Yr Ind)) (IB 34 pts HL 6 chem+biol)
Edinburgh – AAB–ABB incl biol+chem (Physiol) (IB 36–32 pts HL 65 biol+chem)
Leeds – AAA–ABB incl sci (Spo Sci Physiol) (IB 35–33 pts HL 18–17 pts incl 6 sci); ABB incl sci+interview (Hlthcr Sci (Crdc Physiol)) (IB 34 pts HL 555 incl sci)
Leicester – ABB–BBB +bEPQ incl sci/maths (Med Physiol) (IB 30 pts HL 65 sci/maths)
Manchester – AAA–ABB incl sci/maths (Pharmacol Physiol) (IB 36–33 pts HL 666–655 incl sci); AAA–ABB incl sci/maths+interview (Med Physiol) (IB 36–33 pts HL 666–655 incl sci)

120 pts **Aberdeen** – BBB incl maths/sci (Physiol) (IB 32 pts HL 555 incl maths/sci)
Manchester Met – BBB incl biol 120 pts +interview (Hlthcr Sci (Physiol Sci)) (IB 26 pts HL 5 biol)

112 pts **East London** – B biol/chem 112 pts (Med Physiol) (IB 25 pts HL 15 pts incl biol+chem)
Sunderland – 112 pts incl biol/chem (Physiol Sci)
Ulster – BBC incl sci/maths (Hlth Physiol/Hlthcr Sci)

104 pts **Central Lancashire** – C biol/chem 104–112 pts (Physiol Pharmacol) (HL 5 biol/chem)
96 pts **Westminster** – BBB–CCC incl sci/maths (Pharmacol Physiol) (IB 27 pts)

Alternative offers
See **Chapter 6** and **Appendix 1** for grades/UCAS Tariff points information for other examinations.

CHOOSING YOUR COURSE (SEE ALSO CH.1)

Universities and colleges teaching quality See www.qaa.ac.uk; https://unistats.ac.uk.

Top research universities and colleges (REF 2014) See **Biological Sciences**.

Examples of sandwich degree courses Cardiff; Leeds; Manchester Met; Medway Sch Pharm.

ADMISSIONS INFORMATION

Number of applicants per place (approx) Bristol 6; Cardiff 8; Dundee 8; Leeds 4; Leicester 5; London (King's) 5.

Advice to applicants and planning the UCAS personal statement See **Neuroscience** and **Biological Sciences**.

Selection interviews Yes Cambridge, Manchester; **No** Bristol, Cardiff, Dundee, Leeds, Leicester, Newcastle.

Interview advice and questions Past questions include: What made you decide to do a Physiology degree? What experimental work have you done connected with physiology? What future career do you have in mind? What is physiology? Why not choose Medicine instead? What practicals do you do at school? See also **Chapter 5**.

AFTER-RESULTS ADVICE

Offers to applicants repeating A-levels Higher Bristol; Leeds; Leicester; **Same** Cardiff; Dundee; **No** Cambridge; Glasgow.

GRADUATE DESTINATIONS AND EMPLOYMENT (2016/17 HESA)
Graduates surveyed See **Neuroscience**.

Career note See **Biology**.

OTHER DEGREE SUBJECTS FOR CONSIDERATION
Anatomy; Biochemistry; Biological Sciences; Biotechnology; Dentistry; Genetics; Health Studies; Medicine; Microbiology; Neuroscience; Nursing; Optometry; Pharmacology; Radiography; Sports Science.

PHYSIOTHERAPY
(including Chiropractic, Sports Therapy and Veterinary Physiotherapy; see also Health Sciences/Studies)

Physiotherapists work as part of a multi-disciplinary team with other health professionals and are involved in the treatment and rehabilitation of patients of all ages and with a wide variety of medical problems. Degree courses include periods of clinical practice. On successful completion of the three-year course, graduates are eligible for State Registration and Membership of the Chartered Society of Physiotherapy. Courses are very competitive. A-levels in biology or human biology and PE are usually specified with high grades. Check websites. Tuition fees are paid by the NHS Bursary Scheme in England (and similar support is available in the rest of the UK, but arrangements differ so it is important to consult the relevant authority). Bursaries are available based on individual circumstances. All courses expect applicants to have gained some work experience which can include caring and voluntary work.

Useful websites www.csp.org.uk; www.local-physio.co.uk; www.healthcareers.nhs.uk; www.physio-pedia.com; www.hpc-uk.org

NB The points totals shown to the left of the institutions are for ease of reference only. It must not be assumed that Tariff points are always used by institutions or that they can be substituted for an offer in grades. The level of an offer is not necessarily indicative of the quality of a course.

COURSE OFFERS INFORMATION
Subject requirements/preferences GCSE English, mathematics and science subjects. Many universities stipulate A/B (7/5–6) grades in specific subjects. **AL** One or two science subjects are required. Other Occupational health check and Disclosure and Barring Service (DBS) clearance.

Your target offers and examples of degree courses
136 pts **Birmingham** – AAB incl biol/PE +interview (Physio) (IB 32 pts HL 665)
    Bradford – AAB 136 pts +interview (Physio) (HL 765 incl 6 biol)
    East Anglia – AAB incl biol/PE +interview (Physio) (IB 33 pts HL 6 biol)
    Glasgow Caledonian – AAB incl sci +MMI (Physio) (IB 30 pts HL 6 biol+sci)
    Liverpool – AAB incl biol/PE +interview (Physio) (IB 32 pts HL 655 incl 6 biol)
    London (King's) – AAB incl sci/maths/soc sci +MMI (Physio) (IB 35 pts HL 665 incl sci/maths/soc sci)
    Nottingham – AAB incl biol/PE +interview (Physio) (IB 34 pts HL 6 biol)
    Queen Margaret – AAB incl sci/maths (Physio) (IB 32 pts)
    Southampton – AAB incl sci +interview (Physio) (IB 34 pts HL 17 pts incl sci)
128 pts **Bournemouth** – 128–144 pts incl biol/PE +interview (Physio) (IB 33–32 pts HL 5 biol/PE)
    Brighton – ABB incl biol/PE +interview (Physio) (IB 27 pts)
    Brunel – AAB–ABB incl sci/maths +interview (Physio) (IB 33 pts HL 5 sci/maths)
    Canterbury Christ Church – ABB incl sci +interview (Physio)
    Cardiff – AAB–ABB incl biol +MMI (Physio) (IB 34–32 pts HL 665 incl biol)
    Central Lancashire – ABB incl biol/psy/PE (Physio)

Coventry – ABB inc biol +interview (Physio) (IB 34 pts HL 666 incl biol)
Hertfordshire – ABB incl sci 128 pts +interview (Physio)
Huddersfield – ABB incl biol/PE 128 pts +interview (Physio)
Keele – ABB/A*BC/AAC incl biol/PE +interview (Physio) (IB 34 pts HL 6 biol)
Leeds Beckett – 128 pts incl sci +interview (Physio) (IB 27 pts HL 6 sci)
Leicester – ABB incl biol/PE +interview (Physio) (IB 30 pts HL 6 biol)
London (St George's) – ABB +interview (Physio) (IB 34 pts HL 16 pts)
Manchester Met – ABB incl biol/spo +interview (Physio) (IB 29 pts)
Northumbria – C sci/hlth 128 pts +interview (Physio)
Oxford Brookes – ABB incl biol 128 pts +interview (Physio) (IB 32 pts)
Robert Gordon – ABB incl sci/maths +interview (Physio) (IB 32 pts HL 5 Engl+sci/maths)
Sheffield Hallam – ABB 128 pts incl biol/PE +interview (Physio)
Teesside – 128 pts incl sci/soc sci +interview (Physio)
UWE Bristol – B biol 128 pts +interview (Physio) (HL 6 biol)
York St John – ABB incl biol/PE +interview (Physio)
120 pts **Chichester** – ABB incl biol sci 120–136 pts +interview (Physio)
Cumbria – 120–136 pts incl biol/PE +interview (Physio)
East London – BBB incl biol/chem 120 pts +interview +test (Physio) (IB 28 pts HL 15 pts incl biol+chem)
Essex – BBB incl sci +interview +test (Physio) (IB 30 pts HL 555 incl sci)
Plymouth – AAB incl biol/PE/app sci 120–136 pts +interview (Physio) (IB 33 pts HL 6 biol)
Ulster – BBB incl sci/maths +HPAT (Physio)
Worcester – BBB incl biol/PE 120 pts +interview (Physio) (HL 6 biol)
112 pts **Chichester** – BBC–BCC incl sci/PE 112–120 pts (Spo Thera)
104 pts **AECC (UC)** – BCC (MChiro) (IB 28 pts)
Winchester – 104–120 pts incl sci +interview (Physio) (HL 44)
96 pts **Harper Adams** – C biol 96–112 pts +interview (Vet Physio) (IB 28 pts HL 6 biol)

Alternative offers
See **Chapter 6** and **Appendix 1** for grades/UCAS Tariff points information for other examinations.

EXAMPLES OF COLLEGES OFFERING COURSES IN THIS SUBJECT FIELD
Warwickshire (Coll).

CHOOSING YOUR COURSE (SEE ALSO CH.1)
Universities and colleges teaching quality See www.qaa.ac.uk; https://unistats.ac.uk.

Top research universities and colleges (REF 2014) See **Health Sciences/Studies**.

Examples of sandwich degree courses Robert Gordon.

ADMISSIONS INFORMATION
Number of applicants per place (approx) Birmingham 9; Bradford 22; Cardiff 17; East Anglia 16; East London 10; Hertfordshire 13; Huddersfield 12; Kingston 9; Liverpool 20; London (King's) 16; Oxford Brookes 14; Robert Gordon 13; Sheffield Hallam 12; Southampton 36; Teesside 33; Ulster 12.

Admissions tutors' advice London (St George's) Work experience required.

Advice to applicants and planning the UCAS personal statement Visits to, and work experience in, hospital physiotherapy departments are important, although many universities publicly state that this is not necessary. However, with the level of competition for this subject this is doubtful (see Reasons for rejection). Applicants must demonstrate a clear understanding of the nature of the profession. Give details of voluntary work activities. Take notes of the work done and the different aspects of physiotherapy. Explain your experience fully on the UCAS application. Outside interests and teamwork are considered important. Good communication skills are required. Observation placement within a physiotherapy department. See also **Appendix 3**. **Manchester Met** We need to know why you want to be a physiotherapist. We also look for work shadowing a physiotherapist or work experience in another caring role. Evidence is also required of good communication skills, ability to care for people and of teamwork and leadership.

Misconceptions about this course Winchester This is an intensive programme with professional placements and students have more contact hours than those on other courses.

Selection interviews Yes Birmingham, Bournemouth, Bradford, Brighton, Brunel, Cardiff, Coventry, Cumbria, East Anglia, East London, Huddersfield, Kingston, London (St George's), Nottingham, Oxford Brookes, Plymouth, Robert Gordon, Sheffield Hallam, Worcester, York St John; **Some** Keele; **No** Northumbria, Southampton, Ulster.

Interview advice and questions Physiotherapy is a very popular course and work experience is very important, if not essential. A sound knowledge of the career, types of treatment used in physiotherapy and some understanding of the possible problems experienced by patients will be expected. Past interview questions include: How does physiotherapy fit into the overall health care system? If one patient was a heavy smoker and the other not, would you treat them the same? What was the most emotionally challenging thing you have ever done? Give an example of teamwork in which you have been involved. Why should we make you an offer? What is chiropractic? What is osteopathy? See also **Chapter 5**.

Reasons for rejection (non-academic) Lack of knowledge of the profession. Failure to convince the interviewers of a reasoned basis for following the profession. Failure to have visited a hospital physiotherapy unit. Lack of awareness of the demands of the course. **Birmingham** Poor communication skills. Lack of career insight. **Cardiff** Lack of knowledge of physiotherapy; experience of sports injuries only.

AFTER-RESULTS ADVICE
Offers to applicants repeating A-levels Higher East Anglia; East London; Kingston; Teesside; **Same** Coventry; Queen Margaret; Southampton.

GRADUATE DESTINATIONS AND EMPLOYMENT (2016/17 HESA)
Graduates surveyed See **Health Sciences/Studies**.

Career note The professional qualifications gained on graduation enable physiotherapists to seek posts in the NHS where the majority are employed. A small number work in the community health service, particularly in rural areas, while others work in residential homes. In addition to private practice, there are also some opportunities in professional sports clubs.

OTHER DEGREE SUBJECTS FOR CONSIDERATION
Anatomy; Audiology; Biological Sciences; Health Studies; Leisure and Recreation; Nursing; Occupational Therapy; Osteopathy; Physical Education; Psychology; Sport Science/Studies.

PLANT SCIENCES
(see also **Biological Sciences, Biology, Horticulture**)

Plant Sciences cover such areas as plant biochemistry, plant genetics, plant conservation and plant geography. Botany encompasses all aspects of plant science and also other subject areas including agriculture, forestry and horticulture. Botany is basic to these subjects and others including pharmacology and water management. As with other biological sciences, some universities introduce Plant Sciences by way of a common first year with other subjects. Plant sciences has applications in the agricultural, biotechnological, horticultural and food industries.

Useful websites www.kew.org; www.anbg.gov.au; http://bsbi.org; www.theplantlist.org; https://cms. botany.org

NB The points totals shown to the left of the institutions are for ease of reference only. It must not be assumed that Tariff points are always used by institutions or that they can be substituted for an offer in grades. The level of an offer is not necessarily indicative of the quality of a course.

COURSE OFFERS INFORMATION

Subject requirements/preferences GCSE Mathematics if not offered at A-level. **AL** One or two science subjects are usually required.

Your target offers and examples of degree courses

160 pts **Cambridge** – A*A*A incl sci/maths +interview +NSAA (Nat Sci (Plnt Sci)) (IB 42–40 pts HL 776)

144 pts **Sheffield** – AAA (Plnt Sci (MBiolSci)) (IB 36 pts HL 6 biol+sci)

136 pts **Glasgow** – AAB incl biol/chem (Mol Cell Biol (Plnt Sci)) (IB 36 pts HL 665 incl 6 sci)
         Sheffield – AAA–AAB (Plnt Sci) (IB 36–34 pts HL 6 biol+sci)

128 pts **Manchester** – AAA–ABB incl sci/maths +interview (Plnt Sci; Plnt Sci (Yr Ind); Plnt Sci Modn Lang) (IB 36–33 pts HL 666–655 incl sci)
         Nottingham – AAB–ABB incl biol+sci (Plnt Sci) (IB 34–32 pts HL 5 sci)

120 pts **Aberdeen** – BBB incl maths+sci (Plnt Soil Sci) (IB 32 pts HL 555 incl maths+sci)
         Newcastle – ABB–BBB incl biol (App Plnt Sci) (IB 32 pts HL 6 biol)

112 pts **Edge Hill** – BBB–BBC 112–120 pts (Plnt Sci)

104 pts **Aberystwyth** – BBB–BCC incl biol 104–120 pts (Plnt Biol) (IB 30–28 pts HL 5 biol)

88 pts   **Canterbury Christ Church** – 88–112 pts (Plnt Sci)

Alternative offers
See **Chapter 6** and **Appendix 1** for grades/UCAS Tariff points information for other examinations.

CHOOSING YOUR COURSE (SEE ALSO CH.1)

Universities and colleges teaching quality See www.qaa.ac.uk; https://unistats.ac.uk.

Top research universities and colleges (REF 2014) See **Biological Sciences**.

Examples of sandwich degree courses Manchester.

ADMISSIONS INFORMATION

Number of applicants per place (approx) Edinburgh 6; Glasgow 4; Nottingham 6; Sheffield 8.

Advice to applicants and planning the UCAS personal statement Visit botanical gardens. See also **Biological Sciences** and **Appendix 4**.

Selection interviews Yes Cambridge; **No** Nottingham.

Interview advice and questions You are likely to be questioned on your biology studies, your reasons for wishing to study Plant Sciences and your ideas about a possible future career. In the past, questions have been asked about Darwin's theory of evolution, photosynthesis and DNA and the value of gardening programmes on TV! See also **Chapter 5**.

AFTER-RESULTS ADVICE

Offers to applicants repeating A-levels Same Birmingham; Nottingham; Sheffield; **No** Cambridge.

GRADUATE DESTINATIONS AND EMPLOYMENT (2016/17 HESA)

Botany Graduates surveyed 70 **Employed** 15 **In voluntary employment** 0 **In further study** 45 **Assumed unemployed** 0

Career note See **Biology** and **Horticulture**.

OTHER DEGREE SUBJECTS FOR CONSIDERATION

Agriculture; Biochemistry; Biological Sciences; Biology; Crop Science (Agronomy); Ecology; Food Science; Forestry; Herbal Medicine; Horticulture; Landscape Architecture; Traditional Chinese Medicine.

PODIATRY (CHIROPODY)

A podiatrist's primary aim is to improve the mobility, independence and quality of life for their patients. They are autonomous healthcare professionals who deliver preventative, palliative, biomechanical, pharmacological and surgical interventions for lower limb problems. They work alone or are part of a multidisciplinary team. Courses lead to the eligibility for registration with the Health and Care Professions Council and some work shadowing prior to application is preferred by admissions tutors.

Useful websites www.careersinpodiatry.com; www.healthcareers.nhs.uk; www.podiatrynetwork.com; www.podiatrytoday.com; www.healthcommunities.com/health-topics/foot-health.shtml; https://cop.org.uk

NB The points totals shown to the left of the institutions are for ease of reference only. It must not be assumed that Tariff points are always used by institutions or that they can be substituted for an offer in grades. The level of an offer is not necessarily indicative of the quality of a course.

COURSE OFFERS INFORMATION

Subject requirements/preferences GCSE Mathematics and science subjects. **AL** Biology usually required or preferred. Other Hepatitis B, tuberculosis and tetanus immunisation; Disclosure and Barring Service (DBS) clearance (a pre-existing record could prevent a student from participating in the placement component of the course and prevent the student from gaining state registration).

Your target offers and examples of degree courses
120 pts   **East London** – 120 pts incl sci/maths/PE (Pod) (IB 28 pts HL 15 pts incl biol+chem)
          Huddersfield – BBB incl biol/spo sci/PE 120 pts+interview (Pod)
          Southampton – BBB incl sci/soc sci (Pod) (IB 30 pts HL 16 pts incl sci/soc sci)
          Ulster – BBB incl sci/maths (Pod)
112 pts   **Brighton** – BBC (Pod) (IB 26 pts)
          Cardiff Met – 112 pts incl biol +interview (Pod)
          Northampton – BBC (Pod)
          Wolverhampton – BBC incl biol/hum biol/chem (Pod)
104 pts   **Plymouth** – C sci 104–120 pts +interview (Pod) (IB 28–26 pts HL 5 sci)
96 pts   **Glasgow Caledonian** – CCC incl sci (Pod) (IB 24 pts)
          Queen Margaret – CCC (Pod) (IB 28 pts)
64 pts   **Durham New (Coll)** – interview (Pod)

Alternative offers
See **Chapter 6** and **Appendix 1** for grades/UCAS Tariff points information for other examinations.

DEGREE APPRENTICESHIPS
Huddersfield (Pod).

EXAMPLES OF COLLEGES OFFERING COURSES IN THIS SUBJECT FIELD
Birmingham Met (Coll); Durham New (Coll).

CHOOSING YOUR COURSE (SEE ALSO CH.1)
Universities and colleges teaching quality See www.qaa.ac.uk; https://unistats.ac.uk.

ADMISSIONS INFORMATION
Number of applicants per place (approx) Birmingham Met (Coll) 4; Cardiff Met 8; Huddersfield 3; Northampton 2; Southampton 4.

Advice to applicants and planning the UCAS personal statement Visit a podiatrist's clinic to gain work experience/work shadowing experience. Applicants need the ability to communicate with all age ranges, to work independently, to be resourceful and to possess a focused approach to academic work. Admissions tutors look for evidence of an understanding of podiatry, some work experience, good people skills, and effective communication. Mature applicants must include an academic reference (not an employer reference). See also **Appendix 3**.

Misconceptions about this course Cardiff Met Prospective students are often not aware of the demanding requirements of the course: 1,000 practical clinical hours augmented by a rigorous academic programme. Applicants are often unaware that while the elderly are a significant sub-population of patients with a variety of foot problems, increasingly the role of the podiatrist is the diagnosis and management of biomechanical/developmental disorders as well as the management of the diabetic or rheumatoid patient and those who require surgical intervention for nail problems. **Huddersfield** Many people think that podiatry is limited in its scope of practice to treating toe nails, corns and calluses: FALSE. As professionals, we do treat such pathologies but the scope of practice is much wider. It now includes surgery, biomechanics, sports injuries, treating children and high-risk patients. Because offers are low it is considered an easier course than, for example, Physiotherapy: FALSE. The course is academically demanding in addition to the compulsory clinical requirement.

Selection interviews Yes Cardiff Met, Huddersfield, Plymouth; **No** Southampton, Ulster.

Interview advice and questions Past questions include: Have you visited a podiatrist's surgery? What do your friends think about your choice of career? Do you think that being a podiatrist could cause you any physical problems? With which groups of people do podiatrists come into contact? What are your perceptions of the scope of practice of podiatry? What transferable skills do you think you will need? See also **Chapter 5**. **Cardiff Met** What made you consider podiatry as a career? Have you researched your career choice and where did you find the information? What have you discovered and has this altered your original perception of podiatry? What personal characteristics do you think you possess which might be useful for this work? **Southampton** Applicants should show an interest in medical topics. Communication skills are important, as is an insight into the implications of a career in podiatry.

Reasons for rejection (non-academic) Unconvincing attitude; poor communication and interpersonal skills; lack of motivation; medical condition or physical disabilities which are incompatible with professional practice; no knowledge of chosen profession; lack of work experience.

AFTER-RESULTS ADVICE
Offers to applicants repeating A-levels Same Cardiff Met; Huddersfield.

GRADUATE DESTINATIONS AND EMPLOYMENT
Career note Many state-registered podiatrists are employed by the NHS while others work in private practice or commercially run clinics.

OTHER DEGREE SUBJECTS FOR CONSIDERATION
Audiology; Biological Sciences; Health Studies; Nursing; Occupational Therapy; Osteopathy; Physiotherapy.

POLITICS

(including **Government and European Politics**; see also **Development Studies, International Relations, Philosophy, Politics and Economics (PPE), Social Sciences/Studies**)

Politics is often described as the study of 'who gets what, where, when and how'. Courses have become increasingly popular in recent years and usually cover the politics and government of the major powers. Because of the variety of degree courses on offer, it is possible to study the politics of almost any country in the world.

Useful websites http://europa.eu; www.gov.uk/government/organisations/foreign-commonwealth-office; www.psa.ac.uk; www.parliament.uk; www.whitehouse.gov; www.amnesty.org; www.gov.uk; www.un.org; www.un.int

NB The points totals shown to the left of the institutions are for ease of reference only. It must not be assumed that Tariff points are always used by institutions or that they can be substituted for an offer in grades. The level of an offer is not necessarily indicative of the quality of a course.

COURSE OFFERS INFORMATION

Subject requirements/preferences GCSE English, mathematics and a foreign language may be required. **AL** No subjects specified; history useful but an arts or social science subject also an advantage.

Your target offers and examples of degree courses

152 pts   **Bath** – A*AA–AAA +aEPQ incl maths (Econ Pol) (IB 36 pts HL 766 incl maths)
Durham – A*AA incl maths (Econ Pol) (IB 38 pts HL 666)
London (King's) – A*AA +LNAT (Pol Phil Law) (IB 35 pts HL 766)
Warwick – A*AA (Econ Pol Int St) (IB 38 pts)

144 pts   **Bath** – AAA–AAB +aEPQ (Pol Int Rel) (IB 36 pts HL 666/765)
Bristol – AAA (Pol Int Rel) (IB 36 pts HL 18 pts)
Durham – AAA incl soc sci/hum (Phil Pol) (IB 37 pts HL 666); (Pol) (IB 37 pts HL 666 incl soc sci/hum)
Exeter – A*AA–AAA (Econ Pol (Euro St)) (IB 38–36 pts HL 766–666); AAA (Pol) (IB 36 pts)
London (King's) – AAA (Euro Pol; War St) (IB 35 pts HL 666)
London (QM) – AAA (Law Pol) (IB 36 pts HL 666)
London (SOAS) – AAA (Pol) (IB 37 pts HL 666)
London LSE – AAA (Int Rel; Pol; Pol Hist; Pol Phil) (IB 38 pts HL 766); AAA incl maths (Pol Econ) (IB 38 pts HL 766 incl maths)
Oxford – AAA +interview +HAT (Hist Pol) (IB 38 pts HL 666)
Queen's Belfast – AAA (Law Pol) (IB 36 pts HL 666)
Warwick – AAA (Pol courses) (IB 38 pts)
York – AAA (Phil Pol) (IB 36 pts)

136 pts   **Birmingham** – AAB (Plcy Pol Econ; Pol Econ; Pol Sci; Pol Sci Int Rel; Pol Sci Soc Plcy) (IB 32 pts HL 665); AAB 136 pts (Econ Pol Sci) (IB 32 pts HL 665)
Bristol – AAB (Pol Sociol; Soc Plcy Pol) (IB 34 pts HL 17 pts); AAB incl lang (Pol Modn Lang) (IB 34 pts HL 17 pts incl 5 lang)
Exeter – AAA (Pol Int Rel) (IB 36 pts)
Glasgow – AAB incl art/hum/lang (Pol) (IB 38 pts HL 666)
Lancaster – AAB (Hist Pol; Pol (St Abrd)) (IB 35 pts HL 16 pts)
Leeds – AAB (Pol) (IB 35 pts HL 655)
London (UCL) – AAB (Pol Sociol E Euro St) (IB 36 pts HL 17 pts)
London LSE – AAB (Int Soc Pblc Plcy Pol) (IB 37 pts HL 666)
NCH London – AAB (Pol Int Rel Comb Hons) (IB 35 pts HL 665)
Nottingham – AAB (Pol Int Rel) (IB 34 pts)
Sheffield – AAB–ABB +bEPQ (Int Rel Pol; Pol; Pol Phil) (IB 34 pts); AAB–ABB +bEPQ incl hist/class civ (Hist Pol) (IB 34 pts HL 6 hist)
Southampton – AAB incl Fr/Ger (Pol Fr/Ger) (IB 34 pts HL 17 pts incl 6 Fr/Ger); AAB incl Span+interview (Pol Span Lat Am St) (IB 34 pts HL 17 pts incl 6 Span); AAB incl hist (Modn Hist Pol) (IB 34 pts HL 17 pts incl 5 hist)
Sussex – AAA–AAB (Law Pol) (IB 36–34 pts); AAB–ABB (Pol courses) (IB 32 pts)
Warwick – AAB (Pol Sociol) (IB 36 pts)
York – AAB (Pol; Pol Int Rel; Soc Pol Sci) (IB 35 pts); AAB–ABB +aEPQ incl Engl (Engl Pol) (IB 35 pts HL 6 Engl)

128 pts   **Edinburgh** – A*A*A–ABB (Hist Pol) (IB 43–34 pts HL 776–655); AAA–ABB (Pol) (IB 43–34 pts HL 776–655)
Lancaster – ABB (Pol; Pol Int Rel; Pol Relig St; Pol Sociol) (IB 32 pts HL 16 pts)

Leeds – AAB–ABB (Lang, Cult, Pol)
Liverpool – ABB (Int Pol Plcy; Pol) (IB 33 pts)
London (QM) – ABB (Pol) (IB 32 pts HL 655); ABB incl hist (Hist Pol) (IB 32 pts HL 655 incl hist)
London (RH) – AAB–ABB (Econ Pol Int Rel; Pol; Pol Int Rel; Pol Phil) (IB 32 pts HL 655); AAB–ABB incl mus +gr 7 (Mus Pol St) (IB 32 pts HL 655 incl 6 mus)
Loughborough – ABB (Econ Pol; Hist Pol; Pol courses) (IB 34 pts HL 655)
Manchester – ABB (Pol Soc Anth; Pol Sociol) (IB 34 pts HL 655)
Newcastle – AAA–ABB (Pol Econ) (IB 34–32 pts); (Pol) (IB 34–32 pts HL 555); ABB (Pol Sociol) (IB 32 pts)
Nottingham – ABB (Int Rel As St) (32 pts)
Queen's Belfast – ABB (Pol Comb Hons) (IB 33 pts HL 655); ABB incl Fr (Fr Comb Hons) (IB 33 pts HL 655 incl 6 Fr)
Reading – AAB–ABB (Pol Int Rel Modn Langs (Fr/Ger/Ital/Span)) (IB 32 pts HL 655)
Sheffield – ABB–BBB +bEPQ (Pol Sociol) (IB 33 pts)
Southampton – AAB–ABB (Phil Pol) (IB 34–32 pts HL 17–16 pts); ABB incl maths/phys (Pol Econ) (IB 32 pts HL 16 pts)
Sussex – AAB–ABB (Econ Pol) (IB 34–32 pts)

120 pts **Aberdeen** – BBB (Pol courses) (IB 32 pts HL 555)
Aston – ABB–BBB (Pol Engl Lang) (IB 32 pts HL 655)
Brunel – BBB (Int Pol; Pol) (IB 30 pts)
Cardiff – ABB–BBB (Int Rel Pol; Pol) (IB 34–32 pts HL 665–655); ABB–BBB incl lang (Int Rel Pol (Lang)) (IB 34–32 pts HL 665–655)
City – BBB 120 pts (Int Pol) (IB 30 pts HL 555)
Dundee – BBB (Geopol; Pol) (IB 30 pts HL 555)
East Anglia – BBB/ABC (Pol) (IB 31 pts); BBB/ABC–BBC +aEPQ incl hist (Hist Pol) (IB 31 pts HL 5 hist)
Essex – BBB (Econ Pol) (IB 30 pts); (Pol; Pol Hum Rts) (IB 30 pts HL 555)
Hull – BBB 120 pts (Law Pol; Phil Pol) (IB 30 pts)
Kent – BBB (Econ Pol; Pol; Pol Int Rel) (IB 34 pts HL 15 pts)
Leicester – BBB–BBC +bEPQ (Pol; Pol Econ) (IB 28 pts)
London (Birk) – ABB–BBB 120–128 pts (Pol Phil Hist)
London (Gold) – BBB (Int Rel; Pol) (IB 33 pts HL 655)
Northumbria – 120 pts (Hist Pol)
Reading – BBB (Pol Int Rel; War Pce Int Rel) (IB 30 pts)
Southampton – ABB–BBB (Pol) (IB 32 pts HL 16 pts); ABB–BBB incl pol (Pol Int Rel) (IB 32 pts HL 16 pts)
Stirling – BBB (Pol; Pol (Int)) (IB 32 pts)
Strathclyde – ABB–BBB (Pol courses) (IB 36 pts)
Surrey – BBB (Pol) (IB 32 pts)
Swansea – BBB (Pol Engl Lit) (IB 32 pts); BBB 120 pts (Pol; Pol Soc Plcy; War Soty) (IB 32 pts)

112 pts **Aston** – BBC (Pol Int Rel; Pol Soc Plcy) (IB 29 pts HL 554)
Coventry – BBC (Hist Pol; Pol) (IB 29 pts)
De Montfort – 112 pts (Pol Comb Hons) (IB 26 pts)
Edge Hill – BBB–BBC 112–120 pts (Hist Pol)
Huddersfield – BBC 112 pts (Int Pol; Pol)
Kingston – 112 pts (Pol Int Rel)
Lincoln – BBC 112 pts (Pol) (IB 29 pts)
Liverpool Hope – BBC 112 pts (Pol Int Rel; Pol courses) (IB 28 pts)
London Met – BBC 112 pts (Pol)
Middlesex – 112 pts (Int Pol)
Nottingham Trent – BBC 112 pts (Pol)

104 pts **Aberystwyth** – ABB–BCC 104–128 pts (Int Pol; Pol) (IB 30–28 pts)
Central Lancashire – 104 pts (Pol Phil Soty; Pol courses)

Chester – BBC–BCC 104–112 pts (Pol) (IB 26 pts)
Chichester – BBB–BCC 104–120 pts (Pol; Pol Contemp Hist) (IB 28 pts)
De Montfort – 104 pts (Int Rel Pol) (IB 24 pts)
Greenwich – 104 pts +interview (Pol Int Rel)
Leeds Beckett – 104 pts (Pol) (IB 24 pts)
Lincoln – BCC 104 pts (Int Rel Pol)
London South Bank – BCC (Pol)
Manchester Met – 104–112 pts (Pol; Pol Phil) (IB 26 pts)
Northampton – BCC (Int Rel Pol)
Nottingham Trent – 104 pts (Hist Pol); BCC 104 pts (Pol Int Rel)
Oxford Brookes – BCC 104 pts (Econ Pol Int Rel; Int Rel Pol; Pol) (IB 29 pts)
Plymouth – B hist/class civ/econ/law 104–112 pts (Hist Pol) (IB 28–26 pts HL 5 hist/class civ/econ/law)
Sheffield Hallam – BCC 104 pts (Pol)
Ulster – BCC (Pol; Sociol Pol) (IB 24 pts HL 12 pts)
West London – BCC 104–120 pts (Pol Int Rel)
Worcester – 104 pts (Pol Comb Hons)

96 pts   **Aston** – BBC–CCC (Pol Sociol) (IB 29 pts HL 554)
Brighton – BCC–CCC 96–104 pts (Phil Pol Eth) (IB 26 pts)
Keele – CCC 96 pts (Pol) (IB 26 pts)
London Met – CCC/BC 96–112 pts (Int Rel Pce Cnflct St)
Portsmouth – 96–112 pts (Pol) (IB 25 pts)
Teesside – 96–112 pts (Pol)
Westminster – BBB–CCC 96–120 pts (Pol Int Rel) (IB 27 pts HL 4 Engl lang); (Pol) (IB 27 pts Hl 4 Engl lang)
Wolverhampton – CCC/BCD 96 pts (Pol Hist; Pol Phil; Sociol Pol)

88 pts   **Canterbury Christ Church** – 88–112 pts (Pol)
Plymouth – 88–104 pts (Pol Int Rel) (IB 26–24 pts HL 4)

72 pts   **UHI** – BC (Hist Pol; Sociol Pol); BC incl Engl/hist/pol (Scot Hist Pol)

Alternative offers
See **Chapter 6** and **Appendix 1** for grades/UCAS Tariff points information for other examinations.

EXAMPLES OF COLLEGES OFFERING COURSES IN THIS SUBJECT FIELD
Blackburn (Coll); Newham (CFE).

CHOOSING YOUR COURSE (SEE ALSO CH.1)
Universities and colleges teaching quality See www.qaa.ac.uk; https://unistats.ac.uk.

Top research universities and colleges (REF 2014) (Politics and International Studies) London LSE; London (UCL); Sheffield; Essex; Exeter; Oxford; Cardiff; Warwick; York.

Examples of sandwich degree courses Aston; Bath; Brunel; Coventry; De Montfort; Essex; Leeds; Loughborough; Middlesex; Oxford Brookes; Surrey.

ADMISSIONS INFORMATION
Number of applicants per place (approx) Aston 4; Bath 7; Birmingham 5; Bradford 10; Bristol 14; Cambridge 5; Cardiff 14; De Montfort 6; Dundee 13; Durham (Pol) 11, (PPE) 8; East Anglia 4; Exeter 8; Hull (Pol) 5, (PPE) 5; Kent 9; Lancaster 14; Leeds 18; Leicester 6; Liverpool 8; London (QM) 10; London (RH) 8; London (SOAS) 5; London LSE (Gov) 7, (Gov Econ) 8, (Gov Hist) 6; London Met 5; Newcastle 5; Northampton 4; Nottingham 5; Nottingham Trent 3; Oxford (PPE) 7; Oxford Brookes 7; Southampton 6; Stirling 10; Swansea 3; Warwick 10; York 6, (PPE) 9.

Advice to applicants and planning the UCAS personal statement Study the workings of government in the UK, Europe and other areas of the world, such as the Middle East, the Far East, America and Russia. Describe visits to the Houses of Commons and Lords and the debates taking place. Attend council meetings – county, town, district, village halls. Describe these visits and agendas. Read current affairs avidly. Be aware of political developments in the major countries and regions of the world including the Middle East, South America, the UK, Europe, USA, China, Korea and Russia. Keep abreast of developments in theatres of war, for example, Afghanistan. Explain your interests in detail. **Aberystwyth** We look for degree candidates with a strong interest in political and social issues and who want to inquire into the way in which the world is organised politically, socially and economically. **Bristol** Deferred entry accepted. **De Montfort** Demonstration of active interest in current affairs and some understanding of how politics affects our daily lives.

Misconceptions about this course Aberystwyth Many students believe that they need to study politics at A-level for Politics courses – this is not the case. **De Montfort** Some applicants believe that a Politics course only covers the mechanics of government and parliament.

Selection interviews Yes Cambridge, Kent, Oxford; **Some** Bath, Bristol, London (SOAS), Nottingham, Warwick; **No** Aberystwyth, Birmingham, De Montfort, Dundee, East Anglia, Essex, Huddersfield, Hull, Leeds, Leicester, Liverpool, London (Gold), London LSE, London Met, Loughborough, Portsmouth, Reading, Sheffield, Surrey, Swansea, Ulster.

Interview advice and questions Questions may stem from A-level studies but applicants will also be expected to be up-to-date in their knowledge and opinions of current events. Questions in recent years have included: What constitutes a 'great power'? What is happening at present in the Labour Party? Define capitalism. What is a political decision? How do opinion polls detract from democracy? Is the European Union a good idea? Why? What are the views of the present government on the European Union? What is a 'spin doctor'? Are politicians hypocrites? See also **Chapter 5**.

AFTER-RESULTS ADVICE
Offers to applicants repeating A-levels Higher Leeds; Newcastle; Warwick; York; **Possibly higher** Lancaster; Swansea; **Same** Aberystwyth; Birmingham; Bristol; De Montfort; Dundee; Durham; East Anglia; Essex; Hull; Lincoln; Liverpool Hope; London (SOAS); London Met; London South Bank; Loughborough; Nottingham; Nottingham Trent; Oxford Brookes; Stirling; Sussex; Wolverhampton; **No** Cambridge; Glasgow.

GRADUATE DESTINATIONS AND EMPLOYMENT (2016/17 HESA)
Graduates surveyed 4,530 **Employed** 2,170 **In voluntary employment** 200 **In further study** 1,360 **Assumed unemployed** 260

Career note The transferable skills gained in this degree open up a wide range of career opportunities. Graduates seek positions in management, public services and administration and in some cases in political activities.

OTHER DEGREE SUBJECTS FOR CONSIDERATION
Development Studies; Economics; Government; History; International Relations; Public Policy and Administration; Social Policy and Administration; Sociology.

PROFESSIONAL POLICING
(including Police Studies)

It is now a requirement for new police officers to be educated to degree level. The new Pre-join degree in Professional Policing is an academic knowledge-based degree covering the essential skills required to enter the police force. Graduates of the new degree course will still be required to undertake further work-based training on entering the force.

Useful websites www.college.police.uk

NB The points totals shown to the left of the institutions are for ease of reference only. It must not be assumed that Tariff points are always used by institutions or that they can be substituted for an offer in grades. The level of an offer is not necessarily indicative of the quality of a course.

COURSE OFFERS INFORMATION

Subject requirements/preferences GCSE English and mathematics at grade C or above (4 or above). **AL** No subjects specified.

Your target offers and examples of degree courses

144 pts **London (UCL)** – AAA (Prof Plcg) (IB 38 pts HL 555)

120 pts **Derby** – (Prof Plcg)
Northumbria – (Prof Plcg; Prof Plcg (Yr Ind))

112 pts **Birmingham City** – (Prof Plcg) (IB 28 pts)
East London – (Prof Plcg)
Edge Hill – BBB–BBC 112–120 pts (Prof Plcg)
Glyndŵr – (Prof Plcg)
Nottingham Trent – BBC (Prof Plcg)
Sheffield Hallam – (Prof Plcg)
Staffordshire – BBC (Prof Plcg)
Suffolk – BBC (Prof Plcg)
Univ Law – BBC (Prof Plcg)

104 pts **Bangor** – (Prof Plcg)
Central Lancashire – 104–112 pts (Prof Plcg)
Chester – (Prof Plcg) (IB 26 pts)
De Montfort – (Prof Plcg)
Gloucestershire – BCC (Prof Plcg)
Northampton – BCC (Prof Plcg)
Winchester – 104–120 pts (Prof Plcg)

96 pts **Anglia Ruskin** – (Prof Plcg)
Canterbury Christ Church – 96–120 pts (Prof Plcg)
Cumbria – 96–112 pts (Prof Plcg)
Liverpool John Moores – CCC (Prof Plcg)
Wolverhampton – BBC–CCC (Prof Plcg)
York St John – (Prof Plcg)

80 pts **Bucks New** – 80 pts (Plcg St Crim Invstg)
South Wales – BCC–CDD 80–104 pts (Prof Plcg)
Teesside – 80–104 pts (Prof Plcg)
Trinity Saint David – (Prof Plcg)

Alternative offers
See **Chapter 6** and **Appendix 1** for grades/UCAS Tariff points information for other examinations.

CHOOSING YOUR COURSE (SEE ALSO CH.1)

Universities and colleges teaching quality See www.qaa.ac.uk; https://unistats.ac.uk.

OTHER DEGREE SUBJECTS FOR CONSIDERATION

Criminal Justice; Criminology.

PSYCHOLOGY

(including **Autism Studies, Cognitive Science, Counselling Psychology and Forensic Psychology;** see also **Animal Sciences, Biological Sciences, Neuroscience, Philosophy, Physiology, Social Sciences/Studies**)

Psychology is a very popular subject, with the number of applications rising by 40,000 in the last 10 years. The study attracts three times more women than men. It covers studies in development, behaviour, perception, memory, language, learning and personality as well as social relationships and abnormal psychology. Psychology is a science and you will be involved in experimentation and statistical analysis. The degree is usually offered as a BSc or a BA course and there are many similarities between them; the differences are in the elective subjects which can be taken in the second and third years. Contrary to popular belief, psychology is not a study to enable you to psycho-analyse your friends – psychology is not the same as psychiatry! To qualify as a chartered psychologist (for which a postgraduate qualification is required), it is necessary to obtain a first degree (or equivalent) qualification which gives eligibility for both Graduate Membership (GM) and the Graduate Basis for Chartered Membership (GBC) of the British Psychological Society (BPS). A full list of courses accredited by the British Psychological Society is available on the Society's website www.bps.org.uk. Specialisms in the subject include Educational, Clinical, Occupational and Forensic Psychology (See **Appendix 3**). Behavioural Science covers the study of animal and human behaviour and offers an overlap between Zoology, Sociology, Psychology and Biological Sciences. Psychology, however, also crosses over into Education, Management Sciences, Human Resource Management, Counselling, Public Relations, Advertising, Artificial Intelligence, Marketing, Retail and Social Studies.

Useful websites www.psychology.org; www.bps.org.uk; www.socialpsychology.org; https://psychcentral.com

NB The points totals shown to the left of the institutions are for ease of reference only. It must not be assumed that Tariff points are always used by institutions or that they can be substituted for an offer in grades. The level of an offer is not necessarily indicative of the quality of a course.

COURSE OFFERS INFORMATION

Subject requirements/preferences GCSE English, mathematics and a science. **AL** A science subject is usually required. Psychology may be accepted as a science subject.

Your target offers and examples of degree courses

160 pts **Cambridge** – A*A*A incl sci/maths +interview +NSAA (Nat Sci (Psy)) (IB 42–40 pts HL 776 incl sci/maths)

152 pts **Bath** – A*AA-AAA +aEPQ (Psy) (IB 36 pts HL 766)
Bristol – A*AA incl sci/psy/geog (Psy) (IB 38 pts HL 18 pts incl 6 sci)
Cambridge – A*AA +interview +PBSAA (Psy Bhv Sci) (IB 42–40 pts HL 776)
Exeter – A*AA incl sci (Psy (Yr Abrd)) (IB 38 pts HL 766 incl sci)
London (UCL) – A*AA incl sci/maths/psy (Psy) (IB 39 pts HL 19 pts incl 6 sci/maths/psy)
Oxford – A*AA +interview +TSA (Psy (Expmtl); Psy Phil Ling) (IB 39 pts HL 766)

144 pts **Birmingham** – AAA (Psy) (IB 32 pts HL 666)
Durham – AAA (Psy) (IB 37 pts); (Phil Psy) (IB 37 pts HL 666)
Exeter – AAA incl sci (Psy) (IB 36 pts HL 666 incl sci); AAA incl sci +interview (App Psy (Clin) (MSci)) (IB 36 pts HL 6 sci)
Glasgow – AAA incl sci/maths (Psy) (IB 38 pts HL 666 incl sci/maths)
Leeds – AAA incl sci/maths (Psy) (IB 35 pts HL 6 sci/maths)
Liverpool – AAA/AAB +aEPQ incl sci/maths (Psy (MPsycholSci)) (IB 36 pts)
St Andrews – AAA (Art Hist Psy) (IB 36 pts HL 665)
York – AAA incl sci/maths (Psy) (IB 36 pts)

136 pts **Bangor** – 136–112 pts (Psy)
Cardiff – AAA-AAB (Psy) (IB 36–34 pts HL 666)
City – AAB/ABB +bEPQ 136 pts (Psy) (IB 30 pts HL 555)
Exeter – AAA-AAB incl sci (Psy Spo Exer Sci) (IB 36–34 pts HL 666–665 incl sci)
Kent – AAB (Psy; Psy Clin Psy; Psy St Euro; Soc Psy) (IB 34 pts HL 17 pts)
Lancaster – AAB (Ling Psy; Psy) (IB 35 pts HL 16 pts)
London (QM) – AAB incl sci/maths (Psy) (IB 35 pts Hl 665 incl sci/maths)
London (RH) – AAA-AAB (Psy; Psy Clin Cog Neuro) (IB 32 pts HL 665)
Loughborough – AAB (Psy; Spo Exer Psy) (IB 35 pts HL 665)
Manchester – AAB incl sci/maths (Psy) (IB 35 pts HL 665 incl sci/maths)
Newcastle – AAA-AAB incl biol (Psy Biol) (IB 35 pts HL 6 biol); AAA-AAB incl sci (Psy) (IB 35 pts HL 666); AAA-AAB incl sci/maths (Psy Nutr) (IB 35 pts HL 666)
Nottingham – AAB (Psy Cog Neuro) (IB 34 pts); AAB/A*BB (Phil Psy) (IB 34 pts HL 665); AAB incl sci (Psy) (IB 36–34 pts HL 665)

Reading – AAB (App Psy Clin) (IB 34 pts)
Sheffield – AAB incl sci/maths (Psy) (IB 34 pts HL 5 sci/maths)
Southampton – AAA–AAB incl psy/sci/maths (Psy) (IB 36–34 pts HL 666–665 incl psy/sci/maths); AAB (Educ Psy) (IB 34 pts HL 17 pts)
St Andrews – AAB (Psy) (IB 36 pts HL 665)
Sussex – AAA–AAB (Psy; Psy Cog Sci; Psy Neuro) (IB 36–34 pts)
Warwick – AAB (Psy) (IB 36 pts HL 5 maths)

128 pts **Aston** – ABB (Psy) (IB 32 pts HL 655)
Bangor – 128 pts (Spo Exer Psy)
Derby – 128 pts (Psy)
East Anglia – ABB/BBB +aEPQ (Psy) (IB 32 pts)
Edinburgh – AAA–ABB incl sci/maths (Psy) (IB 40–34 pts HL 766–655 incl sci/maths); ABB incl sci/maths (Cog Sci (Hum)) (IB 38–34 pts HL 666–655 incl sci/maths)
Kent – ABB (Bus Psy) (IB 34 pts HL 15 pts)
Lincoln – ABB incl sci/maths (Psy) (IB 32 pts HL 5 sci/maths); ABB incl sci/maths/econ/geog (Psy Clin Psy) (IB 32 pts HL 5 sci/maths/econ/geog)
Liverpool – ABB incl sci/maths (Psy) (IB 33 pts HL 6 sci/maths)
Liverpool John Moores – ABB 128 pts (Foren Psy Crim Just)
Manchester – AAA–ABB incl sci/maths (Cog Neuro Psy) (IB 36–33 pts HL 666–655 incl sci)
Northumbria – 128 pts (Psy)
Nottingham Trent – ABB 128 pts (Psy)
Queen's Belfast – ABB (Psy) (IB 33 pts HL 655)
Reading – ABB (Psy; Psy Lang Sci; Psy Neuro) (IB 32 pts); ABB 120 pts (Psy Lang Sci) (IB 32 pts)
Surrey – ABB (Psy) (IB 32 pts)
Sussex – AAB–ABB incl sci/psy (Neuro Cog Sci) (IB 34–32 pts HL 5 sci/psy)
Swansea – AAB–ABB incl sci/maths (Psy) (IB 34–33 pts)
UWE Bristol – 128 pts (Psy courses)
York – ABB (Sociol Soc Psy) (IB 34 pts)

120 pts **Aberdeen** – BBB (Psy) (IB 32 pts HL 555); BBB incl maths+sci (Neuro Psy) (IB 32 pts HL 555 incl maths+sci)
Aston – BBB (Psy Sociol) (IB 32 pts HL 655)
Brunel – BBB (Psy; Psy (Spo Hlth Exer)) (IB 30 pts)
Coventry – BBB (Psy; Spo Exer Psy) (IB 30 pts HL 15 pts)
De Montfort – 120 pts (Psy; Psy Crimin) (IB 28-30 pts)
Derby – BBB incl biol 120 pts incl biol/chem (Foren Sci Psy)
Dundee – BBB incl psy (Psy) (IB 30 pts HL 555)
Edge Hill – BBB 120 pts (Psy)
Essex – BBB (Psy Econ) (IB 30 pts); (Neur Eng Psy; Psy; Psy Cog Neuro) (IB 30 pts HL 555)
Greenwich – 120 pts (Psy)
Heriot-Watt – BBB (Psy courses) (IB 29 pts)
Huddersfield – BBB 120 pts (Psy; Psy Cnslg; Psy Crimin)
Hull – BBB 120 pts (Psy; Psy Crimin) (IB 30 pts)
Keele – ABC/BBB (Psy) (IB 32 pts)
Kent – BBB (Autsm St) (IB 34 pts HL 15 pts)
Kingston – 120 pts (Foren Psy)
Leicester – ABB–BBB (Psy; Psy Cog Neuro) (IB 30–28 pts)
Liverpool Hope – BBB 120 pts (Psy) (IB 28 pts)
Liverpool John Moores – BBB incl sci/soc sci 120 pts (Psy) (IB 26 pts)
London (Birk) – BBB 120 pts (Psy)
London (Gold) – BBB (Psy; Psy Cog Neuro) (IB 33 pts HL 655)
London South Bank – BBB (Psy; Psy (Chld Dev); Psy (Clin Psy))
Manchester Met – BBB 120 pts (Psy) (IB 26 pts)
Northumbria – 120 pts (Gdnc Cnslg)
Portsmouth – 120 pts (Foren Psy; Psy) (IB 29 pts HL 664)

Reading – BBB +interview +portfolio (Art Psy) (IB 30 pts)
Sheffield Hallam – BBB 120 pts (Psy)
Stirling – BBB (Psy) (IB 32 pts)
Strathclyde – ABB–BBB (Econ Psy; Psy) (IB 36 pts)
UWE Bristol – 120 pts (Crimin Psy)
Ulster – BBB (Psy courses) (IB 26 pts HL 13 pts)
Worcester – BBB 120 pts +interview (Law Foren Psy)
York St John – 120 pts (Psy)

112 pts **Bangor** – 112 pts (Psy Clin Hlth Psy; Psy Neuropsy)
Bedfordshire – 112 pts (Psy; Psy Crim Bhv)
Birmingham City – BBC 112 pts (Psy) (IB 28 pts HL 14 pts)
Bolton – 112 pts (Psy; Psy Psytrpy Cnslg)
Bournemouth – 112–128 pts (Psy) (IB 32–30 pts)
Bradford – 112 pts (Psy)
Buckingham – BBB–BBC (Psy Span) (IB 32–31 pts); BBB–BBC +interview (Psy) (IB 32–31 pts)
Cardiff Met – 112 pts (Psy)
Central Lancashire – 112–128 pts (Foren Psy; Neuropsy; Psy)
Chester – BBB–BBC 112–120 pts (Psy courses) (IB 28 pts)
East London – 112 pts (Foren Psy; Psy) (IB 25 pts HL 15 pts)
Glyndŵr – 112 pts (Psy)
Greenwich – 112 pts +interview (Crimin Crim Psy)
Hertfordshire – BBC 112 pts (Psy)
Kingston – 112 pts (Psy courses)
Leeds Beckett – 112 pts (Crimin Psy) (IB 24 pts); 112 pts incl sci/maths (Psy courses) (IB 25 pts HL 6 sci)
Leeds Trinity – 112 pts (Cnslg Psy; Foren Psy; Psy)
Liverpool John Moores – BBC 112 pts (Crimin Psy); BBC incl spo/sci/soc sci 112 pts (Spo Psy) (IB 26 pts)
Middlesex – 112 pts (Psy)
Northampton – BBC (Psy courses)
Nottingham Trent – BBC 112 pts (Law Psy)
Oxford Brookes – BBC 112 pts (Psy) (IB 30 pts)
Plymouth – 112–120 pts (Psy; Psy Sociol) (IB 26 pts)
Queen Margaret – BBC (Psy) (IB 30 pts)
Roehampton – 112 pts (Psy; Psy Cnslg)
Salford – 112 pts (Psy) (IB 31 pts)
Sheffield Hallam – BBC 112 pts (Crimin Psy)
Staffordshire – BBC 112 pts (Foren Psy; Psy; Psy Crimin)
Suffolk – BBC 112 pts (Psy Sociol)
Sunderland – 112 pts (Psy; Psy Cnslg)
Trinity Saint David – 112 pts (Psy)
West London – BBC 112–120 pts (Psy; Psy Crimin/Cnslg Theor)
Wolverhampton – BBC/CCA 112 pts (Psy; Psy (Cnslg Psy))
Worcester – 112 pts (Dr Psy; Fn Art Psy; Psy)

104 pts **Abertay** – BCC (Psy; Psy Cnslg) (IB 29 pts)
Anglia Ruskin – 104 pts (Psy; Psy Crimin) (IB 24 pts)
Chester – BBC–BCC 104–112 pts (Cnslg Sk Psy) (IB 26 pts)
Chichester – BBB–BCC 104–120 pts (Cnslg Psy) (IB 28 pts HL 5 sci); BBB–BCC incl psy/sci 104–120 pts (Psy) (IB 28 pts HL 4 sci); BBB–BCC incl sci/psy 104–120 pts (Educ Psy) (IB 28 pts HL 4 sci)
Cumbria – 104–128 pts (App Psy)
Edinburgh Napier – BCC incl Engl (Psy; Psy Sociol) (IB 28 pts HL 654 incl 5 Engl)
London Met – BCC 104 pts (Psy)
Newman – CC 104 pts (Psy)
Northampton – BCC (Psy Mark Comb Hons)

Nottingham Trent – BCC 104 pts (Chld (Psy))
Sheffield Hallam – BCC 104 pts (Educ Psy Cnslg)
St Mary's – BBB–BCC 104–120 pts (Psy)
West Scotland – BCC 104 pts (Psy) (IB 27 pts)
Westminster – ABB–BCC 104–128 pts (Psy; Psy Cnslg) (IB 27 pts HL 4 Engl lang)

96 pts **Aberystwyth** – BBB–CCC 96–120 pts (Psy; Psy Crimin) (IB 30–26 pts)
Bath Spa – CCC (Psy; Psy Comb Hons) (IB 26 pts)
Bishop Grosseteste – 96–112 pts (Psy Comb Hons)
Brighton – BBC–CCC 96–112 pts (Psy Crimin; Psy Sociol) (IB 26 pts)
Bucks New – 96 pts (Psy; Psy Crimin)
Canterbury Christ Church – 96–120 pts (Psy)
Portsmouth – 96–112 pts (Sociol Psy) (IB 25 pts)
Solent – 96–112 pts (Psy)

88 pts **Queen Margaret** – CCD (Psy Sociol) (IB 26 pts)
Teesside – 88–112 pts (Foren Psy; Psy; Psy Cnslg; Psy Crimin)
Trinity Saint David – 88 pts (Psy Cnslg)

80 pts **Bedfordshire** – 80 pts (Hlth Psy)
South Wales – BCC–CDD 80–104 pts (Psy; Psy Cnslg; Psy Dev Diso) (IB 29 pts)

72 pts **UHI** – BC +interview (Psy)

Open University – contact 0300 303 0073 or www.open.ac.uk/contact/new (Comb Soc Sci
(Econ/Geog/Psy/Sociol); Psy)

Alternative offers
See **Chapter 6** and **Appendix 1** for grades/UCAS Tariff points information for other examinations.

EXAMPLES OF COLLEGES OFFERING COURSES IN THIS SUBJECT FIELD
Barking and Dagenham (Coll); Bedford (Coll); Birmingham Met (Coll); Blackburn (Coll); Bradford
College UC; Bury (Coll); Canterbury (Coll); Chesterfield (Coll); Colchester (UC); Cornwall (Coll); Croydon
(Univ Centre); Doncaster (Coll); Durham New (Coll); East Coast (Coll); Eastleigh (Coll); Farnborough
(CT); Guildford (Coll); Haringey, Enfield and North East London (Coll); Harrogate (Coll); Havering (Coll);
Lambeth (Coll); Metanoia (Inst); Milton Keynes (Coll); Nescot; Newham (CFE); North Lindsey (Coll);
North Notts (Coll); Norwich City (Coll); Oldham (Coll); Oldham (Univ Campus); Peter Symonds (Coll);
Peterborough (Coll); Petroc; Riverside (Coll); South Devon (Coll); South Gloucestershire and Stroud
(Coll); Southport (Coll); TEC Partnership; Totton (Coll); Truro and Penwith (Coll); Tyne Coast (Coll);
Warwickshire (Coll); West Anglia (Coll); West Thames (Coll); Wirral Met (Coll).

CHOOSING YOUR COURSE (SEE ALSO CH.1)
Universities and colleges teaching quality See www.qaa.ac.uk; https://unistats.ac.uk.

Top research universities and colleges (REF 2014) (Psychology, Psychiatry and Neuroscience)
Oxford; London (Birk); Birmingham; Dundee; Bangor; York; Cambridge; London (RH); Imperial London;
Cardiff; Sussex; Warwick; Essex.

Examples of sandwich degree courses Aston; Bangor; Bath; Bedfordshire; Bournemouth; Brunel;
Cardiff; Coventry; Hertfordshire; Kent; Leeds; Loughborough; Middlesex; Newcastle; Nottingham Trent;
Plymouth; Portsmouth; Reading; Surrey; Ulster; UWE Bristol; Westminster.

ADMISSIONS INFORMATION
Number of applicants per place (approx) Abertay 4; Aston 6; Bangor 4; Bath 9; Bath Spa 10;
Birmingham 6; Bolton 5; Bradford 2; Bristol 8; Buckingham 7; Cambridge 7; Cardiff 5; Cardiff Met 5;
Central Lancashire 13; City 7; De Montfort 10; Derby 5; Dundee 8; Durham 8; Edinburgh Napier 13;
Exeter 14; Greenwich 8; Heriot-Watt 5; Hertfordshire 22; Huddersfield 3; Hull 5; Kent 7; Lancaster 6;
Leeds 12; Leeds Trinity 6; Leicester 6; Liverpool 6; Liverpool John Moores 8; London (RH) 7; London
(UCL) 10; London South Bank 7; Manchester 7; Manchester Met 14; Middlesex 10; Newcastle 9;
Newman 3; Northampton 4; Nottingham 11; Nottingham Trent 3; Oxford Brookes 11; Plymouth 17;
Roehampton 5; Salford 4; Sheffield 6; Sheffield Hallam 10; Southampton 10; Staffordshire 6; Stirling

8; Sussex 5; Swansea 7; Teesside 10; Ulster 4; Warwick 13; Westminster 6; Worcester 9; York 9; York St John 3.

Advice to applicants and planning the UCAS personal statement Psychology is heavily over-subscribed so prepare well in advance by choosing suitable A-level subjects. Contact the Education and Social Services departments in your local authority office to arrange meetings with psychologists to gain a knowledge of the work. Make notes during those meetings and of any work experience gained and describe these fully on the UCAS application. Reference to introductory reading in psychology is important (many students have a distorted image of it). Demonstrate your interest in psychology through, for example, voluntary or other work experience. See also **Appendix 3**. **Bristol** General scientific interests are important. Only consider this course if you have some aptitude and liking for scientific study (either in biological or physical sciences). Deferred entry accepted. **Leeds** One A-level subject must be taken from psychology, geography, maths, chemistry, physics, biology, geology, economics, statistics, environmental science or computing.

Misconceptions about this course Bath They think that they are going to learn about themselves. **Birmingham** Some applicants underestimate the scientific nature of the course. **Exeter** Students should be aware that it is a rigorous scientific discipline. **Lincoln** Applicants should be aware that this is a science-based course. Academic psychology is an empirical science requiring research methodologies and statistical analysis. **Reading** Not all applicants are aware that it is a science-based course and are surprised at the high science and statistics content. **Sussex** Applicants should note that the BSc course is not harder than the BA course. Many students mistakenly believe that Psychology consists of counselling and that there is no maths. Psychology is a science. **York** Some students think psychology means Freud, which it hasn't done for 50 years or more. They do not realise that psychology is a science in the same vein as biology, chemistry or physics. Only 20% of Psychology graduates become professional psychologists. This involves taking a postgraduate degree in a specialist area of psychology.

Selection interviews Yes Anglia Ruskin, Buckingham, Cambridge, Oxford ((Psy (Expmtl) 19%, (Psy Phil Ling) 16%); **Some** Cardiff, East Anglia, Exeter, Leeds Trinity, Liverpool John Moores, Nottingham Trent, Reading; **No** Aston, Bangor, Birmingham, Bishop Grosseteste, Bolton, Bristol, Chichester, Derby, Dundee, Essex, Glyndŵr, Huddersfield, Keele, Leeds, Leicester, London (QM), London (UCL), London Met, Manchester, Middlesex, Newcastle, Northampton, Nottingham, Oxford Brookes, Plymouth, Roehampton, Salford, Southampton, Sunderland, Surrey, Swansea.

Interview advice and questions Although some applicants will have studied the subject at A-level and will have a broad understanding of its coverage, it is still essential to have gained some work experience or to have discussed the career with a professional psychologist. Questions will focus on this and in previous years they have included: What have you read about psychology? What do you expect to gain by studying psychology? What are your parents' and teachers' views on your choice of subject? Are you interested in any particular branch of the subject? Is psychology an art or a science? Do you think you are well suited to this course? Why? Do you think it is possible that if we learn enough about the functioning of the brain we can create a computer that is functionally the same? What is counselling? Is it necessary? Know the differences between the various branches of psychology and discuss any specific interests, for example, in clinical, occupational, educational, criminal psychology and cognitive, neuro-, social or physiological psychology. What influences young children's food choices? What stereotypes do we have of people with mental illness? See also **Chapter 5**. **Oxford** Ability to evaluate evidence and to have the capacity for logical and creative thinking.

Reasons for rejection (non-academic) Lack of background reading and lack of awareness of psychology; poor communication skills; misunderstanding of what is involved in a degree course. Poor personal statement. Poor grades, especially in **GCSE** maths. **Exeter** Competition for places – we can only select those with exceptional grades. **Warwick** (BSc) Lack of science background.

AFTER-RESULTS ADVICE
Offers to applicants repeating A-levels Higher Birmingham; City; Loughborough; Newcastle; Southampton; Swansea; Warwick; York; **Possibly higher** Aston; Northampton; **Same** Bangor; Bolton;

Brunel; Cardiff; Cardiff Met; Chester; Derby; Dundee; Durham; East Anglia; Huddersfield; Hull; Lincoln; Liverpool Hope; Liverpool John Moores; London (RH); London South Bank; Manchester Met; Newman; Nottingham; Nottingham Trent; Oxford Brookes; Roehampton; Salford; Sheffield Hallam; Staffordshire; Stirling; Suffolk; Sunderland; West London; Wolverhampton; York St John; **No** Cambridge.

GRADUATE DESTINATIONS AND EMPLOYMENT (2016/17 HESA)

Graduates surveyed 12,110 **Employed** 4,945 **In voluntary employment** 425 **In further study** 3,865 **Assumed unemployed** 620

Career note Clinical, educational and occupational psychology are the three main specialist careers for graduate psychologists, all involving further study. Ergonomics, human/computer interaction, marketing, public relations, human resource management, advertising, the social services, the prison and rehabilitation services also provide alternative career routes.

OTHER DEGREE SUBJECTS FOR CONSIDERATION

Anthropology; Behavioural Science; Cognitive Sciences; Education; Health Studies; Neuroscience; Sociology.

RADIOGRAPHY

(including **Medical Imaging and Radiotherapy**; see also **Health Sciences/Studies**)

Many institutions offer both Diagnostic and Therapeutic Radiography but applicants should check this, and course entry requirements, before applying. Information on courses is also available from the Society of Radiographers (see **Appendix 3**). Diagnostic Radiography is the demonstration on film (or other imaging materials) of the position and structure of the body's organs using radiation or other imaging media. Therapeutic Radiography is the planning and administration of treatment for patients suffering from malignant and non-malignant disease using different forms of radiation. Courses lead to state registration.

Useful websites www.sor.org; http://radiographycareers.co.uk; www.healthcareers.nhs.uk

NB The points totals shown to the left of the institutions are for ease of reference only. It must not be assumed that Tariff points are always used by institutions or that they can be substituted for an offer in grades. The level of an offer is not necessarily indicative of the quality of a course.

COURSE OFFERS INFORMATION

Subject requirements/preferences GCSE Five subjects including English, mathematics and a science subject (usually at one sitting). **AL** One or two sciences required; mathematics may be acceptable. (Radiothera) One science subject required for some courses. Psychology may not be considered a science subject at some institutions. Other Applicants required to have an occupational health check and a Disclosure and Barring Service (DBS) clearance. Visit to, or work experience in, a hospital imaging department often required/expected.

Your target offers and examples of degree courses
128 pts **Derby** – B sci 128 pts +interview (Diag Radiog)
    Leeds – ABB incl sci +interview (Diag Radiog) (IB 34 pts HL 555 incl sci)
    Sheffield Hallam – ABB incl sci/maths 128 pts+interview (Diag Radiog)
120 pts **Bangor** – BBB incl biol/phys 120 pts +interview (Diag Radiog) (HL 6 biol/phys)
    Birmingham City – BBB incl sci 120 pts +interview (Diag Radiog; Radiothera) (IB 30 pts)
    City – BBB incl sci/maths 120 pts (Radiog (Diag Imag)) (IB 33 pts)
    Cumbria – 120–128 pts incl sci +interview (Diag Radiog)
    Exeter – BBB incl sci/maths/geog +interview (Med Imag (Diag Radiog)) (IB 32 pts HL 655 incl sci)
    Hertfordshire – BBB incl sci 120 pts (Diag Radiog Imag)

Keele – BBB incl sci +interview (Radiog (Diag Imag)) (IB 32 pts HL 6 sci)

Liverpool – BBB incl sci (Ther Radiog Onc) (IB 30 pts HL 5 maths+biol/phys); (Diag Radiog) (IB 30 pts HL 555 incl biol)

London (St George's) – BBB incl sci 120 pts (Diag Radiog) (IB 28 pts HL 554 incl sci); BBB incl sci 120 pts+interview (Ther Radiog) (HL 554 incl sci)

London South Bank – BBB +interview (Diag Radiog; Thera Radiog)

Sheffield Hallam – BBB incl sci 120 pts +interview (Radiothera Onc)

UWE Bristol – C sci 120 pts incl sci +interview (Diag Radiog) (HL 5 sci)

Ulster – BBB incl sci/maths +HPAT (Diag Radiog Imag; Radiothera Onc)

112 pts **Canterbury Christ Church** – 112 pts +interview (Diag Radiog)

Cardiff – BBB–BBC incl sci +interview (Diag Radiog Imag; Radiothera Onc) (IB 31–30 pts HL 655 incl sci)

City – BBC incl maths/sci 112 pts (Radiog (Radiothera Onc)) (IB 33 pts)

Hertfordshire – BBC incl maths/sci 112 pts (Radiothera Onc)

Portsmouth – 112 pts incl sci/maths +interview (Diag Radiog Med Imag) (IB 29 pts HL 754/655 incl 5 sci)

104 pts **Glasgow Caledonian** – BCC incl sci (Diag Imag; Radiothera Onc) (IB 24 pts)

Robert Gordon – BCC incl sci/maths +interview (Diag Radiog) (IB 27 pts HL 5 Engl)

Alternative offers

See **Chapter 6** and **Appendix 1** for grades/UCAS Tariff points information for other examinations.

EXAMPLES OF COLLEGES OFFERING COURSES IN THIS SUBJECT FIELD

Birmingham Met (Coll).

CHOOSING YOUR COURSE (SEE ALSO CH.1)

Universities and colleges teaching quality See www.qaa.ac.uk; https://unistats.ac.uk.

Top research universities and colleges (REF 2014) See **Health Sciences/Studies**.

Examples of sandwich degree courses Robert Gordon.

ADMISSIONS INFORMATION

Number of applicants per place (approx) Bangor 6; Birmingham City (Radiothera) 8; Cardiff 3; Derby 9; Hertfordshire (Diag Radiog Imag) 8; Leeds 10; London (St George's) 7; London South Bank 9; Robert Gordon 5; Sheffield Hallam 8, (Radiothera Onc) 3.

Admissions tutors' advice London (St George's) **WORK EXPERIENCE REQUIRED.**

Advice to applicants and planning the UCAS personal statement Contacts with radiographers and visits to the radiography departments of hospitals should be discussed in full on the UCAS application. See also **Appendix 3**. **Birmingham City** Evidence needed of a visit to at least one imaging department or oncology (radiotherapy) department before completing the UCAS application. Evidence of good research into the career. **Liverpool** Choice between therapeutic and diagnostic pathways should be made before applying.

Selection interviews Yes Bangor, Birmingham City, Cardiff, City, Cumbria, Derby, Exeter, Hertfordshire, London (St George's), London South Bank, Portsmouth, Queen Margaret, Sheffield Hallam;

Interview advice and questions All applicants should have discussed this career with a radiographer and visited a hospital radiography department. Questions follow from these contacts. Where does radiography fit into the overall healthcare system? See also **Chapter 5**.

Reasons for rejection (non-academic) Lack of interest in people. Poor communication skills. Occasionally students may be unsuitable for the clinical environment, for example, they express a fear of blood and needles; poor grasp of radiography as a career. Unable to meet criteria for employment in the NHS, for example, health factors, criminal convictions, severe disabilities.

AFTER-RESULTS ADVICE
Offers to applicants repeating A-levels **Higher** London (St George's); **Same** Derby.

GRADUATE DESTINATIONS AND EMPLOYMENT (2016/17 HESA)
Graduates surveyed See **Health Sciences/Studies**.

Career note Most radiographers work in the NHS in hospital radiography departments undertaking diagnostic or therapeutic treatment. Others work in private healthcare.

OTHER DEGREE SUBJECTS FOR CONSIDERATION
Audiology; Forensic Engineering; Health Studies; Medical Physics; Nursing; Occupational Therapy; Physics; Podiatry; Speech Sciences.

RELIGIOUS STUDIES

(including **Biblical Studies, Divinity, Hebrew, Islamic Studies and Theology;** see also **African, Asian and Middle-eastern Studies**)

The subject content of these courses varies and students should check prospectuses carefully. They are not intended as training courses for ministry; an adherence to a particular religious denomination is not a necessary qualification for entry. Courses offer the study of the major religions – Christianity, Judaism, Islam, Buddhism and Hinduism. The comprehensive Lancaster course offers optional modules covering theological, sociological, anthropological, psychological and philosophical perspectives.

Useful websites www.theguardian.com/world/religion; www.jewfaq.org; https://.virtualreligion.net; https://academic.oup.com/jis; www.sikhs.org; www.buddhanet.net; www.religionfacts.com/hinduism; www.islaminfocentre.org.uk; www.christianity.com

NB The points totals shown to the left of the institutions are for ease of reference only. It must not be assumed that Tariff points are always used by institutions or that they can be substituted for an offer in grades. The level of an offer is not necessarily indicative of the quality of a course.

COURSE OFFERS INFORMATION
Subject requirements/preferences GCSE English and mathematics. For teacher training, English, mathematics and science. **AL** Religious studies or theology may be required or preferred for some courses.

Your target offers and examples of degree courses
152 pts   **Cambridge** – A*AA +interview +TAA (Theol Relgn Phil Relgn) (IB 42–40 pts HL 776)
144 pts   **Durham** – AAA (Phil Theol) (IB 37 pts HL 666)
          Oxford – AAA +interview (Relig Orntl St; Theol Relgn) (IB 38 pts HL 666); AAA +interview +test (Phil Theol) (IB 39 pts HL 666)
          St Andrews – AAA (Bib St; Heb courses; Theol; Theol St) (IB 36 pts HL 665); AAA incl Engl (Bib St Engl) (IB 38 pts HL 666 incl Engl)
136 pts   **Birmingham** – AAB (Pol Relgn Phil) (IB 32 pts HL 665)
          Bristol – AAB (Relgn Theol) (IB 34 pts HL 17 pts)
          Durham – AAB incl soc sci/hum (Theol courses) (IB 36 pts HL 665)
          Exeter – AAB (Theol Relgn) (IB 34 pts HL 665)
          Glasgow – AAB (Theol Relig St) (IB 36 pts HL 665 incl Engl+hum/lang)
          London (King's) – AAB (Relgn Phil Eth; Relgn Pol Soty; Theol Relgn Cult) (IB 35 pts HL 665)
          Nottingham – AAB (Relgn Phil Eth) (IB 34 pts)
128 pts   **Birmingham** – ABB (Theol Relgn) (IB 32 pts HL 655)
          Edinburgh – AAB–ABB (Islam St) (IB 40–34 pts HL 766–655); ABB (Div Class; Relig St) (IB 34 pts HL 655)
          Lancaster – ABB (Phil Relig St; Pol Relig St; Relig St; Relig St Sociol) (IB 32 pts HL 16 pts)

Leeds – ABB (Islam St; Theol Relig St) (IB 34 pts HL 16 pts)
London (UCL) – ABB (Heb Jew St) (IB 34 pts HL 16 pts)
Manchester – ABB (Relgns Theol) (IB 34 pts HL 655)
Nottingham – ABB (Relgn Cult Eth) (IB 32 pts)
Sheffield – ABB-BBB +bEPQ (Phil Relgn Eth) (IB 33 pts)

120 pts   **Aberdeen** – BBB (Div; Theol; Theol Relgn) (IB 32 pts HL 555)
Essex – BBB (Phil Relgn Eth) (IB 30 pts HL 555)
Kent – BBB (Relig St) (IB 34 pts HL 15 pts)
Stirling – BBB (Relgn) (IB 32 pts)

112 pts   **Cardiff** – BBB-BBC (Relig St Span) (HL 655-555)
Liverpool Hope – BBC 112 pts (Phil Eth Relgn; Theol Relig St) (IB 28 pts)
Roehampton – 112 pts (Relgn Theol Cult)

104 pts   **Bangor** – 104 pts (Phil Relgn)
Cardiff – BBC-BCC (Relgn Theol; Relig St Ger; Relig St Ital) (HL 655)
Central Lancashire – 104 pts (Relgn Cult Soty)
Chester – BBC-BCC 104-112 pts (Relig St; Theol; Theol Relig St) (IB 26 pts)
Leeds Trinity – 104 pts (Phil Eth Relgn; Theol Relig St)
Winchester – 104-120 pts+interview (Theol Relgn Eth) (HL 44)

96 pts   **Bath Spa** – CCC (Relgn Phil Eth) (IB 26 pts)
Bishop Grosseteste – 96-112 pts (Theol Phil Eth)
Gloucestershire – BBC 96 pts (Relgn Phil Eth)
Islamic (Coll) – CCC (Hawza St; Islam St)
Newman – CC 96 pts (Theol Phil)
St Mary's – BBC-CCC 96-112 pts (Theol Relgn Eth)
Wolverhampton – CCC/BCD 96 pts (Relig St Phil; Relig St Sociol; Relig St courses)
York St John – 96 pts (Relgn Phil Eth; Theol Relig St)

88 pts   **Canterbury Christ Church** – 88-112 pts (Theol)
64 pts   **UHI** – CC (Theol St)

Trinity Saint David – interview (Relig St Comb Hons; Theol Comb Hons)

Alternative offers
See **Chapter 6** and **Appendix 1** for grades/UCAS Tariff points information for other examinations.

CHOOSING YOUR COURSE (SEE ALSO CH.1)
Universities and colleges teaching quality See www.qaa.ac.uk; https://unistats.ac.uk.

Top research universities and colleges (REF 2014) (Theology and Religious Studies) Durham; Exeter; Leeds; Cambridge; Birmingham; London (UCL); London (SOAS); Edinburgh.

ADMISSIONS INFORMATION
Number of applicants per place (approx) Bangor 4; Birmingham 4; Bristol 9; Cambridge 2; Durham 4; Edinburgh 3; Exeter 7; Glasgow 4; Hull 5; Kent 4; Lancaster 6; Leeds 4; Leeds Trinity 6; London (King's) 6; Manchester 4; Newman 2; Nottingham 4; Sheffield 8; Trinity Saint David 7; Winchester 5; York St John 2.

Advice to applicants and planning the UCAS personal statement An awareness of the differences between the main religions is important as is any special research you have done to help you decide on your preferred courses. Interests in the religious art and architecture of various periods and styles should be noted. Applicants should have an open-minded approach to studying a diverse range of religious traditions. **Bristol** Deferred entry accepted.

Misconceptions about this course Leeds Some applicants are not aware of the breadth of the subject. We offer modules covering New Testament, Christian theology, Islamic studies, Hinduism, Buddhism, Sikhism, Christian ethics and sociology of religion. **Newman** That the Theology course only concentrates on the Christian/Catholic religions – all major religions are covered.

Selection interviews Yes Cambridge, Manchester, Oxford ((Theol Relgn) 29%), Trinity Saint David, Winchester; **Some** Bristol, Cardiff, London (SOAS); **No** Birmingham, Bishop Grosseteste, Chester, Chichester, Edinburgh, Hull, Leeds, Leeds Trinity, Nottingham, Sheffield.

Interview advice and questions
Past questions have included: Why do you want to study Theology/Biblical Studies/Religious Studies? What do you hope to do after obtaining your degree? Questions relating to the A-level syllabus. Questions on current theological topics. Do you have any strong religious convictions? Do you think that your religious beliefs will be changed at the end of the course? Why did you choose Religious Studies rather than Biblical Studies? How would you explain the miracles to a 10-year-old? (BEd course.) Do you agree with the National Lottery? How do you think you can apply theology to your career? See also **Chapter 5**. **Cambridge** There is a Christian priest who regularly visits India and converted to a Hindu priest. When he is in England he still practises as a Christian priest. What problems might this pose? Do you believe we should eradicate Christmas on the basis that it offends other religious groups? **Oxford** The ability to defend one's opinions and willingness to engage in a lively dialogue are both important.

Reasons for rejection (non-academic) Students not attending Open Days may be rejected. Too religiously conservative. Failure to interact. Lack of motivation to study a subject which goes beyond A-level. **Cardiff** Insufficiently open to an academic study of religion.

AFTER-RESULTS ADVICE
Offers to applicants repeating A-levels Higher Manchester; St Andrews; **Same** Bangor; Birmingham, Cardiff, Chester, Durham, Hull, Lancaster, Leeds, Liverpool Hope, London (SOAS), Nottingham; Sheffield; St Mary's; Stirling; Trinity Saint David; Winchester; Wolverhampton; York St John; **No** Cambridge (Hom); Glasgow.

GRADUATE DESTINATIONS AND EMPLOYMENT (2016/17 HESA)
Theology and Religious Studies Graduates surveyed 1,155 **Employed** 415 **In voluntary employment** 70 **In further study** 410 **Assumed unemployed** 55

Career note Although a small number of graduates may regard these courses as a preparation for entry to religious orders, the great majority enter other careers, with teaching particularly popular.

OTHER DEGREE SUBJECTS FOR CONSIDERATION
Community Studies; Education; History; Philosophy; Psychology; Social Policy and Administration; Social Work.

RETAIL MANAGEMENT
(see also **Business and Management Courses, Business and Management Courses (International and European), Business and Management Courses (Specialised), Marketing**)

This subject attracts a large number of applicants each year and it is necessary to have work experience before applying. The work itself varies depending on the type of retail outlet. After completing their courses graduates in a large department store will be involved in different aspects of the business, for example supervising shop assistants, warehouse and packing staff. They could also receive special training in the sales of particular goods, for example food and drink, clothing, furniture. Subsequently there may be opportunities to become buyers. In more specialised shops, for example shoes, fashion and food, graduates are likely to work only with these products, with opportunities to reach senior management.

Useful websites http://brc.org.uk; www.retail-week.com; www.theretailbulletin.com; www.retailchoice.com; https://nrf.com

NB The points totals shown to the left of the institutions are for ease of reference only. It must not be assumed that Tariff points are always used by institutions or that they can be substituted for an offer in grades. The level of an offer is not necessarily indicative of the quality of a course.

COURSE OFFERS INFORMATION

Subject requirements/preferences GCSE English and mathematics at grade C or above (4 or above). **AL** No subjects specified.

Your target offers and examples of degree courses

120 pts **Huddersfield** – BBB 120 pts +interview +portfolio (Int Fash Buy Mgt)

Nottingham Trent – BBB 120 pts (Fash Mgt)

Stirling – BBB (Rtl Mark) (IB 32 pts)

112 pts **Arts London** – 112 pts (Fash Mgt) (IB 25 pts)

Birmingham City – BBC 112 pts +portfolio (Fash Bus Prom) (HL 14 pts)

Cardiff Met – 112 pts (Mark Mgt)

De Montfort – 112 pts +interview +portfolio (Fash Buy courses) (IB 26 pts)

Heriot-Watt – BBC (Fash Mark Rtl) (IB 29 pts)

104 pts **Manchester Met** – BBC–BCC 104–112 pts (Bus Mgt (Rtl))

Alternative offers

See **Chapter 6** and **Appendix 1** for grades/UCAS Tariff points information for other examinations.

EXAMPLES OF COLLEGES OFFERING COURSES IN THIS SUBJECT FIELD

Blackburn (Coll); Blackpool and Fylde (Coll); Durham New (Coll); Grŵp Llandrillo Menai; Hugh Baird (Coll); Hull (Coll); Leeds City (Coll); Newcastle (Coll).

CHOOSING YOUR COURSE (SEE ALSO CH.1)

Universities and colleges teaching quality See www.qaa.ac.uk; https://unistats.ac.uk.

Examples of sandwich degree courses Arts London; Birmingham City; Bournemouth; Brighton; Central Lancashire; Huddersfield; Leeds Beckett; Manchester Met; Surrey.

ADMISSIONS INFORMATION

Number of applicants per place (approx) Manchester Met 10.

Advice to applicants and planning the UCAS personal statement See also **Business and Management Courses**. **Manchester Met** (Rtl Mgt Mark) Evidence of working with people or voluntary work experience (department unable to assist with sponsorships).

Interview advice and questions See **Business and Management Courses**.

Reasons for rejection (non-academic) See **Business and Management Courses**.

GRADUATE DESTINATIONS AND EMPLOYMENT (2016/17 HESA)

Graduates surveyed See **Business and Management Courses**.

Career note Majority of graduates work in business involved in marketing and retail work. Employment options include brand design, product management, advertising, PR, sales and account management.

OTHER DEGREE SUBJECTS FOR CONSIDERATION

Business Studies; Consumer Sciences/Studies; E-Commerce; Human Resource Management; Psychology; Supply Chain Management.

RUSSIAN AND EAST EUROPEAN STUDIES

(including **Russian and Arabic, Russian and History and History and East European Cultural Studies;** see also **European Studies, Languages**)

East European Studies cover a wide range of the less popular language courses and should be considered by anyone with a love of and gift for languages. Many natural linguists often devote themselves to one of the popular European languages studied up to A-level, when their language skills could be extended to the more unusual languages, thereby increasing their future career opportunities.

Useful websites www.ciol.org.uk; www.bbc.co.uk/languages; www.languageadvantage.com; www.languagematters.co.uk

NB The points totals shown to the left of the institutions are for ease of reference only. It must not be assumed that Tariff points are always used by institutions or that they can be substituted for an offer in grades. The level of an offer is not necessarily indicative of the quality of a course.

COURSE OFFERS INFORMATION
Subject requirements/preferences GCSE A foreign language. **AL** One or two modern languages may be stipulated.

Your target offers and examples of degree courses

152 pts   Cambridge – A*AA incl lang +interview +MMLAA (Modn Mediev Langs) (IB 42–40 pts HL 776 incl lang)

Durham – A*AA (Comb Hons Soc Sci (Russ)) (IB 38 pts)

144 pts   Durham – AAA 144 pts (Modn Langs Cult Yr Abrd) (IB 37 pts HL 666)

Oxford – AAA +interview +MLAT (Modn Langs (Russ+2nd Lang)) (IB 38 pts HL 666); AAA +interview +MLAT +OLAT (Euro Mid E Langs (Cz/Russ)) (IB 38 pts HL 666)

136 pts   Birmingham – AAB incl hist (Modn Langs Hist) (IB 32 pts HL 665)

Bristol – AAB (Russ Comb Hons) (IB 34 pts HL 17 pts incl 5 lang); AAB incl lang (Russ) (IB 34 pts HL 17 pts incl 5 lang)

Glasgow – AAB (Russ) (IB 36 pts HL 665 incl Engl+hum/lang); AAB incl art/hum (Cnt E Euro St) (IB 38 pts HL 666 incl Engl+lang/hum)

St Andrews – AAB (Russ courses) (IB 36 pts HL 665)

Warwick – AAB (Ling Russ) (IB 36 pts)

128 pts   Birmingham – ABB incl lang (Modn Langs) (IB 32 pts HL 655)

Edinburgh – ABB (Russ St) (IB 34 pts HL 655)

Exeter – AAB–ABB (Russ Arbc) (IB 34–32 pts HL 665–655)

Leeds – ABB (Russ Comb Hons) (IB 34 pts HL 16 pts)

London (QM) – ABB incl hum/soc sci (Russ Bus Mgt) (IB 32 pts HL 655)

London (UCL) – ABB (Bulg/Czech/Finn/Hung/Polh/Romn/Slovak E Euro St; Russ St) (IB 34 pts HL 16 pts); ABB incl hist (Russ Hist) (IB 34 pts HL 16 pts incl 5 hist)

Manchester – ABB incl Russ/Jap +interview (Russ Jap) (IB 34 pts HL 655 incl Russ/Jap); ABB incl lang+interview (Russ Chin) (IB 34 pts HL 655)

Nottingham – ABB (Russ St) (IB 32 pts); ABB incl hist (Hist E Euro Cult St) (IB 32 pts HL 5 hist)

Sheffield – ABB (Modn Langs Cult) (IB 33 pts HL 5 lang)

112 pts   London Regent's – BBC (Int Bus (Russ))

104 pts   Central Lancashire – 104–112 pts incl Span/Russ (Span Russ); 104–112 pts incl lang (Modn Langs (2 Lang) (Fr/Ger/Span/Jap/Russ/Ital/Kor))

Alternative offers
See **Chapter 6** and **Appendix 1** for grades/UCAS Tariff points information for other examinations.

CHOOSING YOUR COURSE (SEE ALSO CH.1)
Universities and colleges teaching quality See www.qaa.ac.uk; https://unistats.ac.uk.

ADMISSIONS INFORMATION

Number of applicants per place (approx) Bath 6 (Modn Langs Eur St); Birmingham 3; Bristol 4; Durham 5; Leeds 3; London (UCL) 3; Nottingham 3.

Advice to applicants and planning the UCAS personal statement Visits to Eastern Europe should be mentioned, supported by your special reasons for wishing to study the language. A knowledge of the cultural, economic and political scene could be important. Fluent English important for non-UK students. Evidence of wide reading, travel and residence abroad. See also **Appendix 3** under Languages.

Selection interviews Yes Cambridge, Oxford ((Euro Mid E Langs) 41%); **No** London (UCL), Nottingham.

Interview advice and questions Since many applicants will not have taken Russian at A-level, questions often focus on their reasons for choosing a Russian degree, and their knowledge of, and interest in, Russia. Those taking A-level Russian are likely to be questioned on the course and on any reading done outside A-level work. East European Studies applicants will need to show some knowledge of their chosen country/countries and any specific reasons why they wish to follow the course. See also **Chapter 5**. **Leeds** See **Languages**.

Reasons for rejection (non-academic) Lack of perceived commitment for a demanding *ab initio* subject.

AFTER-RESULTS ADVICE

Offers to applicants repeating A-levels Higher Bristol; Leeds; St Andrews; **Same** Durham; **No** Cambridge; Glasgow.

GRADUATE DESTINATIONS AND EMPLOYMENT (2016/17 HESA)

Graduates surveyed 120 **Employed** 60 **In voluntary employment** 5 **In further study** 30 **Assumed unemployed** 10

Career note See **Languages**.

OTHER DEGREE SUBJECTS FOR CONSIDERATION

Economics; European Studies; International Relations; Linguistics; Politics; other languages.

SCANDINAVIAN STUDIES

(See also **Languages**)

Scandinavian Studies provides students who enjoy languages with the opportunity to extend their language expertise to learn a modern Scandinavian language – Danish, Norwegian or Swedish – from beginner's level to Honours level in four years, including a year in Scandinavia. The three languages are very similar to each other and a knowledge of one makes it possible to access easily the literature and cultures of the other two. Viking Studies includes Old Norse, runology and archaeology.

Useful websites www.ciol.org.uk; www.bbc.co.uk/languages; www.languageadvantage.com; www.languagematters.co.uk; www.scandinaviahouse.org; https://scandinavianstudy.org

NB The points totals shown to the left of the institutions are for ease of reference only. It must not be assumed that Tariff points are always used by institutions or that they can be substituted for an offer in grades. The level of an offer is not necessarily indicative of the quality of a course.

COURSE OFFERS INFORMATION

Subject requirements/preferences GCSE Foreign language preferred for all courses. **AL** A modern language may be required.

Your target offers and examples of degree courses
152 pts   Cambridge – A*AA (A-Sxn Nrs Celt) (IB 42–40 pts HL 776)

128 pts   **Edinburgh** – AAB–ABB (Scand St (Dan); Scand St (Norw); Scand St (Swed)) (IB 37–34 pts HL 666–655); ABB (Celt) (IB 34 pts HL 655)
        London (UCL) – ABB (Ice; Scand St; Vkg Old Nrs St) (IB 34 pts HL 16 pts)

Alternative offers
See **Chapter 6** and **Appendix 1** for grades/UCAS Tariff points information for other examinations.

CHOOSING YOUR COURSE (SEE ALSO CH.1)
Universities and colleges teaching quality See www.qaa.ac.uk; https://unistats.ac.uk.

ADMISSIONS INFORMATION
Number of applicants per place (approx) London (UCL) 5.

Advice to applicants and planning the UCAS personal statement Visits to Scandinavian countries could be the source of an interest in studying these languages. You should also be aware of cultural, political, geographical and economic aspects of Scandinavian countries. Knowledge of these should be shown in your statement.

Selection interviews Yes Cambridge.

Interview advice and questions Applicants have been asked wht they chose this subject area, about their visits to Scandinavia and on their knowledge of the country/countries and their people. Future career plans are likely to be discussed. See also **Chapter 5**.

Reasons for rejection (non-academic) One applicant didn't know the difference between a noun and a verb.

AFTER-RESULTS ADVICE
Offers to applicants repeating A-levels No Cambridge.

GRADUATE DESTINATIONS AND EMPLOYMENT (2016/17 HESA)
Graduates surveyed See **Languages**.

Career note See **Languages**.

OTHER DEGREE SUBJECTS FOR CONSIDERATION
Archaeology; European History/Studies; History; other modern languages, including, for example, Russian and East European languages.

SOCIAL AND PUBLIC POLICY AND ADMINISTRATION

(See also **Community Studies/Development, Social Work, Sociology**)

Social Policy is a multi-disciplinary degree that combines elements from sociology, political science, social and economic history, economics, cultural studies and philosophy. It is a study of the needs of society and how best to provide such services as education, housing, health and welfare services.

Useful websites www.local.gov.uk

NB The points totals shown to the left of the institutions are for ease of reference only. It must not be assumed that Tariff points are always used by institutions or that they can be substituted for an offer in grades. The level of an offer is not necessarily indicative of the quality of a course.

COURSE OFFERS INFORMATION
Subject requirements/preferences GCSE English and mathematics normally required. **AL** No subjects specified.

Your target offers and examples of degree courses

152 pts   **Cambridge** – A*AA +interview +HSPSAA (Hum Soc Pol Sci) (IB 42–40 pts HL 777–776)
           Durham – A*AA (Comb Hons Soc Sci) (IB 38 pts HL 666)

136 pts   **Bath** – AAB–ABB +aEPQ (Soc Plcy) (IB 35 pts HL 665)
           Birmingham – AAB (Plcy Pol Econ; Pol Sci Soc Plcy) (IB 32 pts HL 665)
           Bristol – AAB (Soc Plcy Pol) (IB 34 pts HL 17 pts)
           Glasgow – AAB incl art/hum/lang (Soc Pblc Plcy) (IB 38 pts HL 666 incl Engl)
           London LSE – AAB (Int Soc Pblc Plcy; Int Soc Pblc Plcy Pol) (IB 37 pts HL 666); AAB incl
              maths (Int Soc Pblc Plcy Econ) (IB 37 pts HL 666 incl maths)

128 pts   **Bristol** – ABB (Soc Plcy; Soc Plcy Sociol) (IB 32 pts HL 16 pts)
           Cardiff – ABB (Crimin Soc Plcy) (HL 17 pts)
           Edinburgh – ABB (Soc Plcy courses) (IB 40–34 pts HL 766–655)
           Leeds – ABB (Soc Plcy courses; Soc Pol Sociol) (IB 34 pts HL 655)
           Loughborough – ABB (Crimin Soc Plcy) (IB 34 pts HL 655)
           Nottingham – ABB (Sociol Soc Plcy) (IB 32 pts)

120 pts   **Birmingham** – BBB (Soc Plcy) (IB 32 pts HL 555 incl Engl)
           Cardiff – BBB (Sociol Soc Plcy) (HL 17–16 pts)
           Kent – BBB (Soc Plcy) (IB 34 pts HL 15 pts)
           Liverpool – BBB (Sociol Soc Plcy) (IB 30 pts)
           London (Gold) – BBB (Econ Pol Pblc Plcy) (IB 33 pts HL 655)
           Queen's Belfast – BBB (Soc Plcy courses) (IB 32 pts HL 655)
           Sheffield – BBB (Sociol Soc Plcy) (IB 32 pts)
           Stirling – BBB (Sociol Soc Plcy) (IB 32 pts)
           Strathclyde – ABB–BBB (Soc Plcy Econ) (IB 36 pts)
           Swansea – ABB–BBB (Soc Plcy) (IB -3332 pts)
           York – BBB (Soc Plcy) (IB 31 pts)

112 pts   **Aston** – BBC (Bus Mgt Pblc Plcy; Pol Soc Plcy; Sociol Soc Pol) (IB 29 pts HL 554)
           Liverpool Hope – BBC 112 pts (Soc Plcy courses) (IB 28 pts)
           London Met – BBC/BC 112 pts (Sociol Soc Plcy)

104 pts   **Lincoln** – BCC (Crimin Soc Plcy; Soc Plcy) (IB 28 pts)
           Ulster – BCC (Soc Plcy Sociol) (IB 25–24 pts HL 12 pts)

96 pts   **Bangor** – 96 pts (Soc Plcy Comb Hons; Sociol Soc Pol)
           Salford – 96 pts (Soc Plcy) (IB 28 pts)
           Wolverhampton – CCC/BCD 96 pts (Soc Plcy courses)

88 pts   **Canterbury Christ Church** – 88–112 pts (Sociol Soc Plcy)

80 pts   **Trinity Saint David** – 80 pts +interview (Pblc Serv)

Alternative offers
See **Chapter 6** and **Appendix 1** for grades/UCAS Tariff points information for other examinations.

DEGREE APPRENTICESHIPS
Portsmouth (Pblc Admin).

EXAMPLES OF COLLEGES OFFERING COURSES IN THIS SUBJECT FIELD
Barnfield (Coll); Blackburn (Coll); Canterbury (Coll); Central Bedfordshire (Coll); Chesterfield (Coll); Craven (Coll); Dearne Valley (Coll); Derby (Coll); Dudley (Coll); Durham New (Coll); East Surrey (Coll); Exeter (Coll); Grŵp Llandrillo Menai; Hull (Coll); Macclesfield (Coll); Manchester (Coll); Milton Keynes (Coll); Norwich City (Coll); Plymouth City (Coll); South Gloucestershire and Stroud (Coll); St Helens (Coll); Walsall (Coll); Weston (Coll).

CHOOSING YOUR COURSE (SEE ALSO CH.1)
Universities and colleges teaching quality See www.qaa.ac.uk; https://unistats.ac.uk.

Top research universities and colleges (REF 2014) See **Social Work**.

Examples of sandwich degree courses Aston; Bath; Leeds.

ADMISSIONS INFORMATION

Number of applicants per place (approx) Aston 8; Bangor 6; Bath 6; Birmingham 5; Bristol 3; Cardiff 4; Central Lancashire 6; Leeds 10; London LSE (Soc Plcy) 10, (Soc Plcy Sociol) 13, (Soc Plcy Econ) 18, (Soc Plcy Gov) 9; Manchester Met 4; Nottingham 5; Southampton 6; Swansea 6; York 3.

Advice to applicants and planning the UCAS personal statement Careers in public and social administration are covered by this subject; consequently a good knowledge of these occupations and contacts with the social services should be discussed fully on your UCAS application. Gain work experience if possible. (See **Appendix 3** for contact details of some relevant organisations.) **Bangor** Ability to communicate and work in a group. **Bristol** Deferred entry accepted.

Misconceptions about this course York Some applicants imagine that the course is vocational and leads directly to social work – it does not. Graduates in this field are well placed for a wide range of careers.

Selection interviews Some Bath, Cardiff, Southampton; **No** Anglia Ruskin, Bangor, Birmingham, Kent, Leeds, London LSE, Loughborough, Nottingham, Swansea.

Interview advice and questions Past questions have included: What relevance has history to social administration? What do you understand by 'public policy'? What advantage do you think studying social science gives when working in policy fields? How could the image of public management of services be improved? Applicants should be fully aware of the content and the differences between all the courses on offer, why they want to study Social Policy and their career objectives. See also **Chapter 5**.

Reasons for rejection (non-academic) Some universities require attendance when they invite applicants to Open Days (check). Lack of awareness of current social issues. See also **Social Work**. **Bath** Applicant really wanted Business Studies: evidence that teacher, careers adviser or parents are pushing the applicant into the subject or higher education.

AFTER-RESULTS ADVICE

Offers to applicants repeating A-levels Higher Leeds; **Same** Anglia Ruskin; Bangor; Bath; Birmingham; Cardiff; Loughborough; Southampton; York; **No** Glasgow.

GRADUATE DESTINATIONS AND EMPLOYMENT (2016/17 HESA)

Social Policy Graduates surveyed 1,280 **Employed** 575 **In voluntary employment** 30 **In further study** 340 **Assumed unemployed** 75

Career note See **Social Sciences/Studies**.

OTHER DEGREE SUBJECTS FOR CONSIDERATION

Behavioural Science; Community Studies; Criminology; Economic and Social History; Economics; Education; Government; Health Studies; Human Resource Management; Law; Politics; Psychology; Social Work; Sociology; Women's Studies.

SOCIAL SCIENCES/STUDIES

(including **Combined Social Sciences, Criminal Justice, Criminology and Human Rights;**
see also **Combined And Liberal Arts Courses, Education Studies, Health Sciences/Studies,
Law, Politics, Psychology, Teacher Training**)

Most Social Sciences/Studies courses take a broad view of aspects of society, for example, economics, politics, history, social psychology and urban studies. Applied Social Studies usually focuses on practical and theoretical preparation for a career in social work; these courses are popular with mature students and some institutions offer shortened degree courses for those with relevant work experience.

Useful websites http://volunteeringmatters.org.uk

NB The points totals shown to the left of the institutions are for ease of reference only. It must not be assumed that Tariff points are always used by institutions or that they can be substituted for an offer in grades. The level of an offer is not necessarily indicative of the quality of a course.

COURSE OFFERS INFORMATION

Subject requirements/preferences GCSE Usually English and mathematics; a science may be required. **AL** No subjects specified. Other A Disclosure and Barring Service (DBS) check and relevant work experience required for some courses.

Your target offers and examples of degree courses

152 pts **Durham** – A*AA (Comb Hons Soc Sci) (IB 38 pts HL 666)

144 pts **London (UCL)** – AAA (Soc Sci) (IB 38 pts HL 18 pts)
Manchester – AAA (Law Crimin) (IB 36 pts HL 666)

136 pts **Cardiff** – AAB (Crimin) (HL 18 pts)
Durham – AAB (Crimin) (IB 36 pts HL 665)
Exeter – AAB (Crimin) (IB 34 pts)
Lancaster – AAB (Crimin Psy; Law Crimin) (IB 35 pts HL 16 pts)
York – AAB (Soc Pol Sci) (IB 35-36 pts)

128 pts **Bath** – ABB–BBB+aEPQ (Soc Sci) (IB 35 pts HL 655)
Bristol – ABB (Chld St) (IB 32 pts HL 16 pts)
Cardiff – ABB (Crimin Soc Plcy; Crimin Sociol) (HL 17 pts)
Lancaster – ABB (Crimin) (IB 32 pts HL 16 pts)
Leeds – ABB (Chld St; Soc Plcy Crm) (IB 34 pts HL 655)
Leicester – ABB–BBB +bEPQ (Crimin) (IB 30 pts)
Liverpool John Moores – ABB 128 pts (Foren Psy Crim Just)
London (UCL) – ABB (Popn Hlth) (IB 34 pts HL 16 pts)
Loughborough – ABB (Crimin Soc Plcy) (IB 34 pts HL 655)
Manchester – AAA–ABB incl sci/maths +interview (Biol Sci Soty) (IB 36–33 pts HL 666–655 incl chem+sci); ABB (Crimin; Soc Anth Crimin) (IB 34 pts HL 655)
Queen's Belfast – ABB (Crimin) (IB 33 pts HL 655)

120 pts **Cardiff** – BBB (Soc Sci) (HL 17–16 pts)
Chester – BBC–BBB 120 pts (Law Crimin) (IB 28 pts)
City – BBB 120 pts (Crimin Sociol)
Derby – BBB incl biol 120 pts incl biol/chem (Foren Sci Psy)
Essex – BBB (Crimin Am St) (IB 30 pts HL 5); (Crimin; Law Crimin; Law Hum Rts; Sociol Crimin) (IB 30 pts HL 555)
Huddersfield – BBB 120 pts (Psy Crimin)
Hull – BBB 120 pts (Psy Crimin) (IB 30 pts)
Kent – BBB (Crimin; Crimin Comb Hons) (IB 34 pts HL 15 pts)
Liverpool – BBB (Crimin) (IB 30 pts)
Liverpool John Moores – BBB 120 pts (Law Crim Just) (IB 26 pts)
London (RH) – ABB–BBB (Crimin Sociol; Soc Sci) (IB 32 pts HL 555)
Northumbria – 120 pts (Crimin; Crimin Foren Sci; Integ Hlth Soc Cr)
Stirling – BBB (Crimin Sociol) (IB 32 pts)
Stranmillis (UC) – BBB +interview (Ely Chld St)
Surrey – ABB–BBB (Law Crimin) (IB 32 pts); BBB (Crimin Sociol) (IB 32 pts)
UWE Bristol – 120 pts (Crimin; Crimin Psy)
Ulster – BBB (Crimin Crim Just) (IB 26 pts HL 13 pts)
York – BBB (App Soc Sci) (IB 31 pts)

112 pts **Birmingham City** – BBC 112 pts (Crimin Plcg Invstg; Crimin courses) (IB 28 pts HL 14 pts)
Bolton – 112 pts+interview (Crm Crim Just)
Coventry – BBC (Sociol Crimin) (IB 29 pts)
De Montfort – 112 pts (Law Hum Rts Soc Just) (IB 26 pts)
Derby – 112 pts (Crimin)
East London – 112 pts (Crimin Crim Just) (IB 25 pts HL 15 pts)

Edge Hill – BBB–BBC 112–120 pts (Crimin)
Gloucestershire – BBC 112 pts (Crimin)
Glyndŵr – 112 pts (Crimin Crim Just)
Greenwich – 112 pts +interview (Crimin Crim Psy); BBC 112 pts (Crimin)
Huddersfield – BBC 112 pts (Crimin)
Hull – BBC 112 pts (Crimin) (IB 28 pts)
Kent – BBC (Crim Just Crimin; Soc Sci) (IB 34 pts HL 14 pts)
Kingston – 112 pts (Crimin courses; Hum Rts Soc Just)
Leeds Beckett – 112 pts (Crimin; Crimin Psy) (IB 24 pts)
Lincoln – BBC (Crimin) (IB 29 pts)
Liverpool Hope – BBC 112 pts (Crimin) (IB 28 pts)
Liverpool John Moores – BBC 112 pts (Crim Just; Crimin; Crimin Psy)
London (Birk) – ABB–BBC 112–128 pts (Soc Sci); BBB–BBC 112–120 pts (Crimin Crim Just)
London Met – BBC 112 pts (Crimin courses)
Manchester Met – 112 pts incl soc sci/hum (Crimin) (IB 26 pts)
Middlesex – 112 pts (Crimin (Crim Just); Crimin (Plcg); Crimin courses)
Nottingham Trent – BBC 112 pts (Crimin; Law Crimin)
Roehampton – 112 pts (Crimin)
Sheffield Hallam – BBC 112 pts (Crimin; Crimin Psy; Crimin Sociol)
Staffordshire – BBC 112 pts (Crimin; Plcg Crim Invstg; Psy Crimin)
Suffolk – BBC 112 pts (Soc Sci)
West London – BBC 112–120 pts (Crimin; Psy Crimin/Cnslg Theor)
Westminster – ABB–BBC 112–128 pts (Crimin) (IB 27 pts HL 4 Engl)
Worcester – 112 pts (Crimin Plcg)

104 pts **Abertay** – BCC (Crimin) (IB 29 pts)
Aberystwyth – ABB–BCC 104–128 pts (Hum Rts) (IB 30–28 pts)
Bangor – 104 pts (Crimin Crim Just)
Central Lancashire – 104–112 pts (Crimin courses); 104–120 pts (Plcg Crim Invstg)
Chester – BBC–BCC 104–112 pts (Crimin) (IB 26 pts)
Chichester – BBB–BCC incl sci/psy 104–120 pts (Crimin Foren Psy) (IB 28 pts HL 4 sci)
Coventry – BCC (Crimin) (IB 27 pts)
De Montfort – 104 pts (Crimin) (IB 24 pts)
Edinburgh Napier – BCC incl Engl (Plcg Crimin; Soc Sci) (IB 28 pts HL 654 incl 5 Engl); (Crimin) (IB 29 pts HL 655 incl Engl)
Glasgow Caledonian – BCC (Soc Sci) (IB 25 pts)
Greenwich – BCC incl chem 104 pts+interview (Foren Sci Crimin)
Leeds Trinity – 104 pts (Crimin Sociol)
Lincoln – BCC (Crimin Soc Plcy) (IB 28 pts)
Liverpool John Moores – BCC 104 pts (Crimin Sociol)
London South Bank – BCC (Crimin)
Northampton – BCC (Crimin)
Nottingham Trent – 104 pts (Comm Soty (Comb Hons) + Phil/Ling/Media)
Robert Gordon – BCC (App Soc Sci) (IB 28 pts)
Sheffield Hallam – BCC 104 pts (App Soc Sci)
Sunderland – 104 pts (Crimin)
West Scotland – BCC 104 pts (Crim Just) (IB 27 pts)

96 pts **Aberystwyth** – BBB–CCC 96–120 pts (Crimin) (IB 30–26 pts)
Anglia Ruskin – 96 pts (Crimin courses) (IB 24 pts)
Bishop Grosseteste – 96–112 pts (Ely Chld St courses)
Brighton – BBC–CCC 96–112 pts (Crimin Sociol; Psy Crimin; Soc Sci) (IB 26 pts); BCC–CCC 96–104 pts (Hum) (IB 26 pts)
Cumbria – 96–112 pts (Crimin; Crimin Law; Crimin Plcg Invstg)
Keele – CCC (Crimin; Crimin Comb Hons) (IB 28–26 pts)
Marjon – CCC 96 pts (Soc Sci)
Portsmouth – 96–120 pts (Crimin Crim Just; Crimin Cybercrim) (IB 29–27 pts HL 664–644)

Solent – 96–112 pts (Crim Invstg Foren Psy; Crimin)
Teesside – 96–112 pts (Crm Scn Sci)
Winchester – 96–112 pts (Crimin) (HL 44)
Wolverhampton – CCC/BCD 96 pts (Crimin Crim Just; Plcg Intel); CCC/BCD incl chem/biol 96 pts (Foren Sci Plcg)

88 pts   **Canterbury Christ Church** – C sci 88–112 pts (App Crimin)
Plymouth – 88–104 pts (Crimin Crim Just St) (IB 26–24 pts HL 4)
Teesside – 88–112 pts (Psy Crimin)

80 pts   **Bedfordshire** – 80 pts (Crimin); CC 80 pts (Soc St)
Bucks New – 80 pts (Crimin; Hlth Soc Sci)
South Wales – BCC–CDD 80–104 pts (Crimin Crim Just) (IB 29 pts)
Teesside – 80–104 pts (Crim Invstg; Crimin courses)

72 pts   **Farnborough (CT)** – 72 pts (Psy Crimin)
UHI – BC (Soc Sci)

64 pts   **London (Gold)** – CC +interview (App Soc Sci Commun Dev Yth Wk)

Open University – contact 0300 303 0073 or www.open.ac.uk/contact/new (Comb Soc Sci (Econ/Geog/Psy/Sociol); Crimin Psy)

Alternative offers
See **Chapter 6** and **Appendix 1** for grades/UCAS Tariff points information for other examinations.

DEGREE APPRENTICESHIPS
Chichester (Wkg Chld Yng Ppl Fmly).

EXAMPLES OF COLLEGES OFFERING COURSES IN THIS SUBJECT FIELD
Accrington and Rossendale (Coll); Blackburn (Coll); Blackpool and Fylde (Coll); Bolton (Coll); Cornwall (Coll); Coventry (Coll); Derby (Coll); Doncaster (Coll); Ealing, Hammersmith and West London (Coll); Exeter (Coll); Gloucestershire (Coll); Grŵp Llandrillo Menai; Lincoln (Coll); Middlesbrough (Coll); MidKent (Coll); North Lindsey (Coll); Norwich City (Coll); Peterborough (Coll); Richmond-upon-Thames (Coll); Sir Gâr (Coll); South Essex (Coll); Stamford New (Coll); Truro and Penwith (Coll); Warwickshire (Coll); West Anglia (Coll); Wirral Met (Coll); York (Coll).

CHOOSING YOUR COURSE (SEE ALSO CH.1)
Universities and colleges teaching quality See www.qaa.ac.uk; https://unistats.ac.uk.

Top research universities and colleges (REF 2014) See individual social science subjects.

Examples of sandwich degree courses Bangor; Bath; Coventry; Middlesex; Portsmouth; Surrey; Teesside.

ADMISSIONS INFORMATION
Number of applicants per place (approx) Abertay 4; Bangor 5; Bath 6; Bradford 15; Bristol (Chld St) 6; Cardiff 5; Cornwall (Coll) 2; Cumbria 4; De Montfort 1; Durham 6; East London 10; Edge Hill 5; Hull 5; Kingston 5; Leicester (Crimin) 5; Liverpool 10; London South Bank 3; Manchester Met 10; Middlesex 26; Northampton 5; Nottingham Trent 2; Roehampton 6; Sheffield Hallam 7; Staffordshire 2; Sunderland 11; West Scotland 5; Westminster 14; Winchester 5; York 5.

Advice to applicants and planning the UCAS personal statement The Social Sciences/Studies subject area covers several topics. Focus on these (or some of these) and state your main areas of interest, outlining your work experience, personal goals and motivation to follow the course. Show your interest in current affairs and especially in social issues and government policies.

Misconceptions about this course Cornwall (Coll) That students transfer to Plymouth at the end of Year 1: this is a three-year course in Cornwall.

Selection interviews Yes Anglia Ruskin; **Some** Bath, Cornwall (Coll), Kingston, Robert Gordon; **No** Bangor, Birmingham City, Coventry, Cumbria, Edge Hill, Essex, Glasgow Caledonian, Hull, Nottingham Trent, Roehampton, Staffordshire, Sunderland, West London, West Scotland, Westminster, Winchester.

Interview advice and questions Past questions have included: Define democracy. What is the role of the Church in nationalistic aspirations? Does today's government listen to its people? Questions on current affairs. How would you change the running of your school? What are the faults of the Labour Party/Conservative Party? Do you agree with the National Lottery? Is money from the National Lottery well spent? Give examples of how the social services have failed. What is your understanding of the social origins of problems? See also **Chapter 5**.

Reasons for rejection (non-academic) Stated preference for other institutions. Incompetence in answering questions.

AFTER-RESULTS ADVICE
Offers to applicants repeating A-levels Same Abertay; Anglia Ruskin; Bangor; Bradford; Chester; Cornwall (Coll); Coventry; Cumbria; Durham; Essex; Gloucestershire; Leeds; Liverpool; London Met; London South Bank; Manchester Met; Nottingham Trent; Roehampton; Sheffield Hallam; Staffordshire; Stirling; Winchester; Wolverhampton; **No** Glasgow.

GRADUATE DESTINATIONS AND EMPLOYMENT (2016/17 HESA)
Graduates surveyed See **Law**, **Politics** and **Psychology**.

Career note Graduates find careers in all aspects of social provision, for example health services, welfare agencies such as housing departments, the probation service, police forces, the prison service, personnel work and residential care and other careers not necessarily linked with their degree subjects.

OTHER DEGREE SUBJECTS FOR CONSIDERATION
Business Studies; Community Studies; Economics; Education; Geography; Government; Health Studies; Law; Politics; Psychology; Public Administration; Social Policy; Social Work; Sociology; Urban Studies.

SOCIAL WORK

(See also **Community Studies/Development, Social and Public Policy and Administration**)

Social Work courses (which lead to careers in social work) have similarities to those in Applied Social Studies, Social Policy and Administration, Community Studies and Health Studies. If you are offered a place on a Social Work course which leads to registration as a social worker, you must undergo the Disclosure and Barring Service (DBS) check. You will also have to provide health information and certification. Check for full details of training and careers in social work with the Health and Care Council (see **Appendix 3**). Students from England may be eligible for student bursaries from the NHS Business Services Authority.

Useful websites www.ageuk.org.uk; www.samaritans.org; https://socialcare.wales; www.sssc.uk.com; https://niscc.info; www.basw.co.uk

NB The points totals shown to the left of the institutions are for ease of reference only. It must not be assumed that Tariff points are always used by institutions or that they can be substituted for an offer in grades. The level of an offer is not necessarily indicative of the quality of a course.

COURSE OFFERS INFORMATION
Subject requirements/preferences GCSE English and mathematics usually required. **AL** No subjects specified. Other Disclosure and Barring Service (DBS) check and an occupational health check required. Check also with universities for applicant minimum age requirements.

Your target offers and examples of degree courses

128 pts **Bath** – ABB–BBB/BBC +aEPQ +interview (Soc Wk App Soc St) (IB 35 pts HL 655)
Birmingham – ABB +interview +test (Soc Wk) (IB 32 pts HL 655)
Edinburgh – ABB (Soc Wk) (IB 34 pts HL 655)
Leeds – ABB +interview +test (Soc Wk) (IB 34 pts HL 16 pts)
Nottingham – ABB +interview +test (Soc Wk) (IB 32 pts)
Queen's Belfast – ABB +interview (Soc Wk)

120 pts **Bournemouth** – 120–136 pts +interview (Soc Wk) (IB 33–31 pts)
Bradford – BBB 120 pts +interview (Soc Wk)
Coventry – BBB +interview (Soc Wk) (IB 30 pts HL 14 pts)
Derby – 120 pts +interview (App Soc Wk)
East Anglia – BBB +interview (Soc Wk) (IB 31 pts)
East London – 120 pts +interview +test (Soc Wk) (IB 33 pts)
Edge Hill – BBB 120 pts +interview +test (Soc Wk)
Essex – BBB +interview (Soc Wk) (IB 30 pts HL 555)
Greenwich – 120 pts +interview (Soc Wk)
Hertfordshire – BBB 120 pts +interview (Soc Wk)
Hull – BBB 120 pts +interview +test (Soc Wk) (IB 30 pts)
Kent – BBB +interview (Soc Wk) (IB 34 pts HL 15 pts)
Kingston – BBB 120 pts +interview +test (Soc Wk) (IB 27 pts)
Lancaster – BBB +interview +test (Soc Wk) (IB 30 pts HL 15 pts)
Leeds Beckett – 120 pts +interview (Soc Wk) (IB 26 pts)
Liverpool Hope – BBB 120 pts +interview (Soc Wk) (IB 28 pts)
London (Gold) – BBB +interview +test (Soc Wk) (IB 33 pts HL 655)
London Met – BBB 120 pts +interview +test (Soc Wk)
London South Bank – BBB +interview (Soc Wk)
Middlesex – 120 pts +interview +test (Soc Wk)
Northumbria – 120 pts +interview (Soc Wk)
Nottingham Trent – BBB 120 pts +interview (Soc Wk)
Salford – 120 pts +interview +test (Soc Wk)
Sheffield Hallam – BBB 120 pts +interview (Soc Wk)
Stirling – BBB +assessments (Soc Wk) (IB 32 pts)
Strathclyde – ABB–BBB +interview (Soc Wk)
Suffolk – BBB 120 pts +interview (Soc Wk)
Sunderland – 120 pts (Soc Wk)
Sussex – ABB–BBB +interview (Soc Wk) (IB 32–30 pts)
UWE Bristol – 120 pts +interview (Soc Wk)
York – BBB +interview (Soc Wk) (IB 31 pts)

112 pts **Anglia Ruskin** – 112 pts +interview (Soc Wk) (IB 26 pts)
Bedfordshire – 112 pts +interview (Soc Wk)
Birmingham (UC) – BBC 112 pts +interview (Soc Wk)
Birmingham City – 112 pts +interview +test (Soc Wk) (IB 28 pts)
Brighton – ABB–BBC 112–128 pts +interview (Soc Wk) (IB 27 pts)
Canterbury Christ Church – BBC +interview (Soc Wk)
Central Lancashire – 112 pts +interview +test (Soc Wk)
Chester – BBB–BBC 112–120 pts (Soc Wk) (IB 28 pts)
Glyndŵr – 112 pts +interview (Soc Wk)
Keele – BBB–BBC +interview +test (Soc Wk) (IB 30 pts)
Manchester Met – BBB–BBC 112–120 pts +interview (Soc Wk) (IB 29 pts)
Northampton – BBC (Soc Wk)
Portsmouth – 112 pts +interview (Soc Wk) (IB 25 pts)
South Wales – BBC +interview +test (Soc Wk) (IB 29 pts)
Staffordshire – BBC 112 pts (Soc Wk)
Teesside – 112–128 pts +interview (Soc Wk)

West London - BBC 112-120 pts +interview (Soc Wk)
Worcester - 112 pts +interview (Soc Wk)
104 pts **Cumbria** - 104-128 pts +interview +test (Soc Wk)
Gloucestershire - BCC 104 pts (Soc Wk)
Northampton - BCC (App Soc Cr Hlth St)
Oxford Brookes - BCC 104 pts +interview +test (Soc Wk) (IB 29 pts)
Plymouth - 104-120 pts (Soc Wk) (IB 28-27 pts)
Swansea - BCC (Soc Wk) (IB 34-33 pts)
Wolverhampton - BCC 104 pts +interview (Soc Wk)
96 pts **Birmingham (UC)** - CCC 96 pts (Hlth Soc Cr)
Bucks New - 96 pts +interview +test (Soc Wk)
Cardiff Met - 96 pts +interview (Hlth Soc Cr); 96 pts +interview +test (Soc Wk)
Chichester - BBC-CCC 96-112 pts +interview (Soc Wk) (IB 28 pts)
Glasgow Caledonian - CCC +interview (Soc Wk) (IB 24 pts)
HOW (Coll) - 96 pts (Soc Wk)
Robert Gordon - CCC +interview (Soc Wk) (IB 26 pts)
Solent - 96-112 pts +interview (Soc Wk)
West Scotland - CCC 96 pts (Soc Wk) (IB 24 pts)
Winchester - 96-112 pts +interview (Soc Wk) (HL 44)
88 pts **Dundee** - AB-CCC (Soc Wk) (IB 29 pts HL 554)
Winchester - 88-104 pts (Hlth Commun Soc Cr St)
80 pts **Bedfordshire** - CC 80 pts (Hlth Soc Cr)
64 pts **Colchester (UC)** - 64 pts +interview (Hlth Soc Cr)
London (Gold) - CC +interview (App Soc Sci Commun Dev Yth Wk)

Open University - contact 0300 303 0073 or www.open.ac.uk/contact/new (Soc Wk)

Alternative offers
See **Chapter 6** and **Appendix 1** for grades/UCAS Tariff points information for other examinations.

DEGREE APPRENTICESHIPS
Chester (Soc Sci Plc St); Chichester (Soc Wk).

EXAMPLES OF COLLEGES OFFERING COURSES IN THIS SUBJECT FIELD
Barnfield (Coll); Birmingham Met (Coll); Blackburn (Coll); Bradford College UC; Cornwall (Coll); Durham New (Coll); East Coast (Coll); Exeter (Coll); Furness (Coll); Gateshead (Coll); Grŵp Llandrillo Menai; Harrogate (Coll); Hartlepool (CFE); HOW (Coll); Hull (Coll); Leeds City (Coll); Liverpool City (Coll); MidKent (Coll); Newcastle (Coll); North Lindsey (Coll); Norwich City (Coll); Nottingham (Coll); Sir Gâr (Coll); South Cheshire (Coll); South City Birmingham (Coll); South Gloucestershire and Stroud (Coll); South Thames (Coll); Southport (Coll); Stockport (Coll); TEC Partnership; Truro and Penwith (Coll); Warrington and Vale Royal (Coll); Warwickshire (Coll); Wiltshire (Coll); Wirral Met (Coll).

CHOOSING YOUR COURSE (SEE ALSO CH.1)
Universities and colleges teaching quality See www.qaa.ac.uk; https://unistats.ac.uk.

Top research universities and colleges (REF 2014) (Social Work and Social Policy) London LSE; Glasgow; Edinburgh; Bath; Bristol; Oxford; East Anglia; Kent; Teesside; York; Leicester; London (UCL); Southampton.

ADMISSIONS INFORMATION
Number of applicants per place (approx) Bath 6; Birmingham 13; Bradford 10; Dundee 4; London Met 27; Northampton 7; Nottingham Trent 6; Sheffield Hallam 4; Staffordshire 3.

Advice to applicants and planning the UCAS personal statement The statement should show motivation for social work, relevant work experience, awareness of the demands of social work and give relevant personal information, for example disabilities. Awareness of the origins of personal and family difficulties, commitment to anti-discriminatory practice. Most applicants for these courses will have significant experience of a statutory care agency or voluntary/private organisation providing a social work or social care service. See also **Social and Public Policy and Administration** and **Appendix 4**.

Misconceptions about this course Winchester This is an intensive programme with professional placements and students have more contact hours than those on other courses.

Selection interviews
Yes Anglia Ruskin, Bath, Bedfordshire, Birmingham, Birmingham City, Bolton, Bournemouth, Bradford, Brighton, Canterbury Christ Church, Cardiff Met, Central Lancashire, Chichester, Coventry, Cumbria, East Anglia, Edge Hill, Glyndŵr, Greenwich, Hertfordshire, Huddersfield, Hull, Keele, Kent, Leeds Beckett, Liverpool Hope, London Met, Middlesex, Newman, Northumbria, Nottingham, Nottingham Trent, Plymouth, Portsmouth, Queen's Belfast, Robert Gordon, Sheffield Hallam, South Wales, Suffolk, Sussex, UWE Bristol, West London, Wolverhampton, Worcester, York; **Some** Winchester; **No** Chester, Dundee, Edinburgh, Gloucestershire, Lancaster, Liverpool John Moores, Staffordshire, Sunderland, Swansea, West Scotland.

Interview advice and questions What qualities are needed to be a social worker? What use do you think you will be to society as a social worker? Why should money be spent on prison offenders? Your younger brother is playing truant and mixing with bad company. Your parents don't know. What would you do? See also **Social and Public Policy and Administration** and **Chapter 5**.

Reasons for rejection (non-academic) Criminal convictions.

AFTER-RESULTS ADVICE
Offers to applicants repeating A-levels Same Lincoln; Liverpool Hope; Staffordshire; Suffolk; Wolverhampton.

GRADUATE DESTINATIONS AND EMPLOYMENT (2016/17 HESA)
Graduates surveyed 6,445 **Employed** 3,660 **In voluntary employment** 80 **In further study** 1,290 **Assumed unemployed** 245

Career note See **Social Sciences/Studies**.

OTHER DEGREE SUBJECTS FOR CONSIDERATION
Community Studies; Conductive Education; Criminology; Economics; Education; Health Studies; Law; Psychology; Public Sector Management and Administration; Social Policy; Sociology; Youth Studies.

SOCIOLOGY
(see also Anthropology, Social and Public Policy and Administration)

Sociology is the study of social organisation, social structures, systems, institutions and practices. Courses are likely to include the meaning and structure of, for example, race, ethnicity and gender, industrial behaviour, crime and deviance, health and illness. **NB** Sociology is not a training course for social workers, although some graduates take additional qualifications to qualify in social work.

Useful websites www.britsoc.co.uk; www.asanet.org; www.sociology.org.uk; www.sociology.org

NB The points totals shown to the left of the institutions are for ease of reference only. It must not be assumed that Tariff points are always used by institutions or that they can be substituted for an offer in grades. The level of an offer is not necessarily indicative of the quality of a course.

COURSE OFFERS INFORMATION
Subject requirements/preferences GCSE English and mathematics usually required. **AL** No subjects specified.

Your target offers and examples of degree courses

152 pts   **Cambridge** – A*AA +interview +HSPSAA (Hum Soc Pol Sci (Pol Sociol)) (IB 42–40 pts HL 776)

136 pts   **Bath** – AAB–ABB +aEPQ (Sociol) (IB 35 pts HL 665)

Bristol – AAB (Pol Sociol; Sociol; Sociol Phil) (IB 34 pts HL 17 pts)

Durham – AAB (Anth Sociol; Sociol) (IB 36 pts HL 665)

Exeter – AAB (Sociol) (IB 34 pts HL 665)

Glasgow – AAB (Sociol) (IB 36 pts HL 665 incl Engl+hum/lang)

London LSE – AAB (Sociol) (IB 37 pts HL 666)

Manchester – AAB (Econ Sociol) (IB 35 pts HL 665)

Warwick – AAB (Law Sociol) (IB 36 pts)

128 pts   **Bath** – ABB–BBB +aEPQ (Soc Sci) (IB 35 pts HL 655)

Birmingham – ABB (Educ Sociol) (IB 32 pts HL 655)

Bristol – ABB (Soc Plcy Sociol) (IB 32 pts HL 16 pts)

Cardiff – ABB (Jrnl Media Sociol; Sociol; Sociol Hist) (HL 17 pts)

City – ABB 128 pts (Sociol Psy) (IB 32 pts)

Edinburgh – ABB (Sociol) (IB 40–34 pts HL 766–655)

Lancaster – ABB (Crimin Sociol; Flm Sociol; Pol Sociol; Relig St Sociol; Sociol) (IB 32 pts HL 16 pts)

Leeds – ABB (Soc Pol Sociol; Sociol) (IB 34 pts HL 655)

Loughborough – ABB (Sociol) (IB 34 pts HL 655)

Manchester – ABB (Pol Sociol; Sociol) (IB 34 pts HL 655)

Newcastle – ABB (Sociol) (IB 32 pts)

Nottingham – ABB (Sociol; Sociol Soc Plcy) (IB 32 pts)

Sheffield – ABB (Engl Lang Sociol) (IB 33 pts); ABB–BBB+bEPQ (Pol Sociol) (IB 33 pts)

Southampton – AAB–ABB (Phil Sociol) (IB 34–32 pts HL 17–16 pts); ABB (Sociol) (IB 32 pts HL 16 pts)

Warwick – ABB (Sociol) (IB 34 pts)

York – ABB (Sociol; Sociol Educ; Sociol Soc Psy) (IB 34 pts)

120 pts   **Aberdeen** – BBB (Sociol) (IB 32 pts HL 555)

Aston – BBB (Psy Sociol) (IB 32 pts HL 655)

Brunel – BBB (Anth Sociol) (IB 30 pts)

Cardiff – BBB (Sociol Educ) (IB 32 pts HL 17–16 pts)

City – BBB 120 pts (Sociol) (IB 30 pts HL 555)

Essex – BBB (Sociol; Sociol Crimin; Sociol Hum Rts) (IB 30 pts HL 555)

Kent – BBB (Sociol) (IB 34 pts HL 15 pts)

Leicester – BBB–BBC+bEPQ (Sociol) (IB 28 pts)

Liverpool – BBB (Sociol) (IB 30 pts)

London (Gold) – BBB (Sociol) (IB 33 pts HL 655)

Northumbria – 120 pts (Sociol)

Queen's Belfast – BBB (Sociol courses) (IB 32 pts HL 655)

Sheffield – BBB (Sociol Soc Plcy) (IB 32 pts)

Stirling – BBB (Sociol Soc Plcy) (IB 32 pts)

Surrey – BBB (Sociol) (IB 32 pts)

Sussex – ABB–BBB (Sociol) (IB 32–30 pts)

112 pts   **Birmingham City** – BBC 112 pts (Sociol; Sociol Crimin) (IB 28 pts HL 14 pts)

Brunel – BBC (Sociol; Sociol (Media)) (IB 29 pts)

Coventry – BBC (Sociol; Sociol Crimin) (IB 29 pts)

Derby – 112 pts (Sociol; Sociol Comb Hons)

East London – 112 pts (Sociol) (IB 25 pts HL 15 pts)

Huddersfield – BBC 112 pts (Sociol)

Hull – BBC 112 pts (Crimin Sociol) (IB 28 pts)

Kingston – 112 pts (Sociol)

London Met – BBC 112 pts (Sociol)

Manchester Met – 112 pts (Crimin Sociol) (IB 26 pts); 112 pts incl soc sci/hum (Sociol) (IB 26 pts)

Nottingham Trent – BBC 112 pts (Sociol)
Plymouth – 112–120 pts (Psy Sociol) (IB 26 pts)
Roehampton – 112 pts (Sociol)
Salford – 112 pts (Sociol) (IB 31–30 pts)
Sheffield Hallam – BBC 112 pts (Sociol)
Suffolk – BBC 112 pts (Law Sociol; Psy Sociol)
UWE Bristol – 112 pts (Sociol)

104 pts **Abertay** – BCC (Sociol) (IB 29 pts)
Bournemouth – 104–120 pts (Sociol) (IB 31–28 pts)
Central Lancashire – 104 pts (Sociol)
Chester – BBC–BCC 104–112 pts (Sociol) (IB 26 pts)
Edge Hill – BBC–BCC 104–112 pts (Sociol)
Edinburgh Napier – BCC incl Engl (Psy Sociol) (IB 28 pts HL 654 incl 5 Engl)
Gloucestershire – BCC 104 pts (Sociol)
Greenwich – 104 pts (Sociol)
Leeds Beckett – 104 pts (Sociol) (IB 24 pts)
Liverpool John Moores – BCC 104 pts (Sociol) (IB -24 pts)
London South Bank – BCC (Sociol)
Northampton – BCC (Sociol; Sociol Crimin)
Oxford Brookes – BCC 104 pts (Sociol) (IB 29 pts)
Sunderland – 104 pts (Sociol)
Ulster – BCC (Sociol; Sociol Pol) (IB 24 pts HL 12 pts)
Winchester – 104–120 pts (Sociol) (HL 44)
Worcester – 104 pts (Sociol)

96 pts **Aberystwyth** – BBB–CCC incl hum 96–120 pts (Sociol) (IB 30–26 pts)
Anglia Ruskin – 96 pts (Sociol) (IB 24 pts)
Aston – BBC–CCC (Pol Sociol; Sociol courses) (IB 29 pts HL 554)
Bangor – 96 pts (Sociol; Sociol Comb Hons; Sociol Soc Pol)
Bath Spa – CCC (Sociol Comb Hons) (IB 26 pts)
Bishop Grosseteste – 96–112 pts (Sociol; Sociol Dr)
Bradford – CCC 96 pts (Sociol)
Brighton – BBC–CCC 96–112 pts (Crimin Sociol; Psy Sociol; Sociol courses) (IB 26 pts)
Keele – CCC (Sociol; Sociol Comb Hons) (IB 26 pts)
Middlesex – 96 pts (Sociol)
Portsmouth – 96–112 pts (Sociol; Sociol Psy) (IB 25 pts)
Westminster – BBB–CCC 96–120 pts (Sociol) (IB 27 pts)
Wolverhampton – CCC/BCD 96 pts (Phil Sociol; Relig St Sociol; Sociol; Sociol Pol)

88 pts **Canterbury Christ Church** – 88–112 pts (Sociol; Sociol Soc Plcy)
Plymouth – 88–104 pts (Sociol) (IB 26–24 pts HL 4)
Queen Margaret – CCD (Psy Sociol) (IB 26 pts)

80 pts **Bedfordshire** – 80 pts (Crimin Sociol)
South Wales – BCC–CDD 80–104 pts (Crimin Crim Just Sociol) (IB 29 pts)

72 pts **Teesside** – 72–96 pts (Sociol)

Alternative offers
See **Chapter 6** and **Appendix 1** for grades/UCAS Tariff points information for other examinations.

EXAMPLES OF COLLEGES OFFERING COURSES IN THIS SUBJECT FIELD
Blackburn (Coll); Bury (Coll); Cornwall (Coll); Farnborough (CT); Lincoln (Coll); Milton Keynes (Coll); Newham (CFE); Norwich City (Coll); Peterborough (Coll); Petroc; Richmond-upon-Thames (Coll); South Devon (Coll); Totton (Coll); West Anglia (Coll).

CHOOSING YOUR COURSE (SEE ALSO CH.1)
Universities and colleges teaching quality See www.qaa.ac.uk; https://unistats.ac.uk.

Examples of sandwich degree courses Aston; Bath; Brunel; Coventry; Middlesex; Plymouth; Surrey.

ADMISSIONS INFORMATION
Number of applicants per place (approx) Aston 8; Bangor 6; Bath 6; Birmingham 8; Birmingham City 12; Bristol 6; Cardiff 5; City 6; Durham 4; East London 8; Exeter 5; Gloucestershire 8; Greenwich 5; Hull 5; Kent 5; Kingston 9; Lancaster 6; Leeds 14; Leicester 4; Liverpool 10; Liverpool John Moores 10; London (Gold) 5; London LSE 8; London Met 3; Manchester 8; Northampton 3; Nottingham 5; Oxford Brookes 8; Plymouth 5; Roehampton 5; Sheffield Hallam 7; Southampton 4; Staffordshire 10; Sunderland 5; Warwick 20; Worcester 5; York 5.

Advice to applicants and planning the UCAS personal statement Show your ability to communicate and work as part of a group and your curiosity about issues such as social conflict and social change between social groups. Discuss your interests in sociology on the personal statement. Demonstrate an intellectual curiosity about sociology and social problems. See also **Social Sciences/Studies**. **Bristol** Deferred entry accepted.

Misconceptions about this course Birmingham Students with an interest in crime and deviance may be disappointed that we do not offer modules in this area. **London Met** That it is the stamping ground of student activists and has no relevance to the real world.

Selection interviews Yes Anglia Ruskin, Cambridge; **Some** Bath, Cardiff, Liverpool John Moores, London (Gold), Southampton, Warwick; **No** Aston, Birmingham, Birmingham City, Bristol, City, Derby, East London, Essex, Hull, Kent, Leeds, Leicester, Liverpool, Loughborough, Newcastle, Nottingham, Nottingham Trent, Portsmouth, Salford, Sheffield Hallam, St Mary's, Staffordshire, Surrey.

Interview advice and questions Past questions have included: Why do you want to study Sociology? What books have you read on the subject? How do you see the role of women changing in the next 20 years? See also **Chapter 5**.

Reasons for rejection (non-academic) Evidence of difficulty with written work. Non-attendance at Open Days (find out from your universities if your attendance will affect their offers). 'In the middle of an interview for Sociology, a student asked us if we could interview him for Sports Studies instead!' See also **Social and Public Policy and Administration**. **Durham** No evidence of awareness of what the course involves. **London Met** References which indicated that the individual would not be able to work effectively within a diverse student group; concern that the applicant had not put any serious thought into the choice of subject for study.

AFTER-RESULTS ADVICE
Offers to applicants repeating A-levels Higher East London; Newcastle; Nottingham Trent; Warwick; York; **Possibly higher** Leeds; Liverpool; **Same** Aston; Bangor; Bath; Birmingham; Birmingham City; Bristol; Brunel; Cardiff; Coventry; Derby; Durham; Essex; Gloucestershire; Hull; Kingston; Lancaster; Liverpool John Moores; London Met; Loughborough; Northumbria; Roehampton; Salford; Sheffield Hallam; Southampton; St Mary's; Staffordshire; **No** Cambridge; Glasgow.

GRADUATE DESTINATIONS AND EMPLOYMENT (2016/17 HESA)
Graduates surveyed 6,155 **Employed** 2,840 **In voluntary employment** 190 **In further study** 1,680 **Assumed unemployed** 340

Career note See **Social Sciences/Studies**.

OTHER DEGREE SUBJECTS FOR CONSIDERATION
Anthropology; Economic and Social History; Economics; Education; Geography; Government; Health Studies; History; Law; Politics; Psychology; Social Policy; Social Work.

SPANISH, PORTUGUESE AND LATIN AMERICAN STUDIES

(including **Hispanic Studies and Portuguese**; see also **Languages**)

Spanish, the world's second most spoken native language, can be studied with a vast array of other subjects. For those aspiring to gain an expertise in the Spanish-speaking world as well as the language, Latin American studies courses offer the opportunity to study the histories, ideologies, economics and politics of South and Central American states. Several courses offer the opportunity to study Portuguese.

Useful websites www.donquijote.co.uk; http://europa.eu; www.ciol.org.uk; www.bbc.co.uk/ languages; www.languageadvantage.com; www.languagematters.co.uk; http://studyspanish.com; www.spanishlanguageguide.com.

NB The points totals shown to the left of the institutions are for ease of reference only. It must not be assumed that Tariff points are always used by institutions or that they can be substituted for an offer in grades. The level of an offer is not necessarily indicative of the quality of a course.

COURSE OFFERS INFORMATION

Subject requirements/preferences GCSE English, mathematics or science and a foreign language.
AL Spanish required for most courses.

Your target offers and examples of degree courses

160 pts **St Andrews** – A*A*A incl maths (Maths Span) (IB 38 pts HL 666 incl maths)

152 pts **Cambridge** – A*AA incl lang +interview +MMLAA (Modn Mediev Langs) (IB 42–40 pts HL 776 incl lang)

Nottingham – A*AA (Econ Hisp St) (IB 38 pts)

144 pts **Imperial London** – AAA incl chem+maths +interview (Chem Fr/Ger/Span Sci) (IB 38 pts HL 6 chem+maths); AAA incl sci/maths (Biol Sci Span Sci) (IB 38 pts HL 66 incl biol+chem/ maths/phys)

Oxford – AAA +interview +MLAT (Port courses) (IB 38 pts HL 666); AAA incl Span +interview +MLAT (Modn Langs Span) (IB 38 pts HL 666 incl Span)

Southampton – AAA incl maths+Fr/Ger/Span (Maths Fr/Ger/Span) (IB 36 pts HL 18 pts incl 6 maths+Fr/Ger/Span)

136 pts **Bath** – AAB–ABB +aEPQ incl Span (Int Mgt Span) (IB 36 pts HL 665 incl 6 Span); AAB–ABB +aEPQ incl lang (Int Pol Modn Langs) (IB 35 pts HL 665 incl 7 lang)

Birmingham – AAB incl hist (Modn Langs Hist) (IB 32 pts HL 665)

Bristol – AAB incl Span (Hisp St; Span) (IB 34 pts HL 17 pts incl 5 Span)

Dundee – AAB incl Engl (Law Langs) (IB 36 pts HL 665 incl Engl)

Glasgow – AAB (Span) (IB 36 pts HL 665 incl eng/hum/lang)

Lancaster – AAB (Span St Geog) (IB 35 pts HL 16 pts incl 6 geog)

London (King's) – AAB (Euro St (Fr/Ger/Span) (Yr Abrd)) (IB 35 pts HL 665); AAB incl Fr/Span (Fr Span (Yr Abrd)) (IB 35 pts HL 665)

London (UCL) – AAB incl Span (Span Lat Am St) (IB 36 pts HL 17 pts incl 6 Span)

Southampton – AAB/ABB +aEPQ incl Engl+Fr/Ger/Span (Engl Fr/Ger/Span) (IB 34 pts HL 17 pts incl 65 Engl+Fr/Ger/Span); AAB incl Span +interview (Pol Span Lat Am St; Span (Lat Am St); Span courses) (IB 34 pts HL 17 pts incl 6 Span)

St Andrews – AAB (Span courses) (IB 36 pts HL 665)

York – AAB (Span courses) (IB 35 pts); AAB incl Fr (Fr Span Lang (Yr Abrd)) (IB 35 pts HL 6 Fr)

128 pts **Birmingham** – ABB (Modn Langs Span) (IB 32 pts HL 655); ABB incl lang (Modn Langs Hist Art) (IB 32 pts HL 655)

Edinburgh – AAA–ABB (Span courses) (IB 40–34 pts HL 766–655 incl 5 lang); AAB–ABB (Int Bus Fr/Ger/Span) (IB 40–34 pts HL 766–655)

Exeter – AAB–ABB incl Span (Span Arbc) (IB 34–32 pts HL 665–655)

Lancaster – ABB (Span St) (IB 32 pts HL 16 pts)

Leeds – ABB incl Span (Span; Span Port Lat Am St) (IB 34 pts HL 16 pts incl 6 Span)

Liverpool – ABB (Hisp St) (IB 33 pts)

London (QM) – ABB incl hum/soc sci (Hisp St courses) (IB 32 pts HL 655 incl hum/soc sci)

London (RH) – AAB–ABB (Euro Int St Fr/Ger/Ital/Span; Modn Lang Mus) (IB 32 pts HL 655); AAB–ABB incl lang (Modn Lang Dr) (IB 32 pts HL 655)

Manchester – ABB incl Span +interview (Span Port Lat Am St) (IB 34 pts HL 655 incl Span); ABB incl Span/Port (Span Port) (IB 34 pts HL 655 incl Span/Port); ABB incl lang (Span courses) (IB 34 pts HL 655 incl lang)

Northumbria – 128 pts (Int Bus Mgt Span)

Nottingham – ABB (Am St Lat Am St; Span Int Media Comms St) (IB 32 pts); ABB incl Engl (Engl Hisp St) (IB 32 pts HL 5 Engl); ABB incl Span (Hisp St) (IB 32 pts); ABB incl hist (Hisp St Hist) (IB 32 pts HL 5 hist)

Queen's Belfast – ABB (Span; Span Port St) (IB 33 pts HL 655 incl Span)

Sheffield – ABB (Modn Langs Cult) (IB 33 pts HL 5 lang)

Southampton – AAB–ABB incl Fr/Ger/Span (Flm Fr/Ger/Span) (IB 32 pts HL 6 Fr/Ger/Span)

Sussex – ABB 128 pts (Anth Lang) (32 pts)

Warwick – ABB incl lang (Hisp St courses) (IB 34 pts HL 5 lang)

120 pts   **Aberdeen** – BBB (Span Lat Am St) (IB 32 pts HL 555)

Aston – ABB–BBB (Int Bus Fr/Ger/Span) (IB 32 pts HL 665–655)

Cardiff – ABB–BBB (Span) (IB 32–30 pts HL 665–655)

Dundee – BBB (Span courses) (IB 30 pts HL 555)

Essex – BBB (Lat Am St Bus Mgt) (IB 30 pts); (Lat Am St courses; Span St Modn Langs) (IB 30 pts HL 555)

Heriot-Watt – BBB incl lang (App Langs Transl (Fr/Span)/(Ger/Span); Span App Lang St) (IB 30 pts HL 5 lang); BBB incl maths+Span (Maths Span) (IB 28 pts HL 5 maths+Span)

London (RH) – ABB–BBB (Modn Lang Lat; Modn Langs) (IB 32 pts HL 555)

Newcastle – ABB–BBB incl Span (Span Port Lat Am St) (IB 32 pts HL 6 Span)

Reading – BBB (Span) (IB 30 pts); BBB incl hist (Span Hist) (IB 30 pts HL 5 hist)

Stirling – BBB (Span Lat Am St) (IB 32 pts)

Strathclyde – ABB–BBB (Span courses) (IB 36 pts)

Surrey – BBB incl Span (Span courses) (IB 32 pts)

Swansea – BBB 120 pts (Span) (IB 32 pts)

112 pts   **Chester** – 112 pts incl Span (Span Port Lat Am St; Span courses) (IB 26 pts HL 5 Span)

Hull – BBC incl lang 112 pts (App Modn Lang (Fr/Ger/Span)) (IB 28 pts HL 5 lang)

London (Birk) – ABB–BBC 112–128 pts (Modn Langs (Fr/Ger/Ital/Jap/Port/Span))

104 pts   **Aberystwyth** – BBB–BCC 104–120 pts (Span Comb Hons; Span Lat Am St) (IB 30–28 pts HL 5 Span)

Central Lancashire – 104–112 pts (Int Bus Comm Modn For Lang); 104–112 pts incl Span/Russ (Span Russ); 104–112 pts incl lang (Modn Langs (2 Lang) (Fr/Ger/Span/Jap/Russ/Ital/Kor))

London (Birk) – ABB–BBC 104–128 pts (Span Port Lat Am St)

Manchester Met – BBC–BCC 104–112 pts (Ling Mand Chin/Fr/Ger/Ital/Span) (IB 26 pts); B Span 104–112 pts (Span St) (IB 26 pts)

Westminster – ABB–BCC incl Span (Transl (Span)) (IB 27 pts HL 4 Span)

96 pts   **Aston** – BBC–CCC (Span courses) (IB 29 pts HL 554)

Bangor – C Span 96 pts (Span courses) (HL 5 Span)

Portsmouth – 96–112 pts (Modn Langs) (IB 25 pts)

Alternative offers

See **Chapter 6** and **Appendix 1** for grades/UCAS Tariff points information for other examinations.

EXAMPLES OF COLLEGES OFFERING COURSES IN THIS SUBJECT FIELD

Richmond-upon-Thames (Coll).

CHOOSING YOUR COURSE (SEE ALSO CH.1)

Universities and colleges teaching quality See www.qaa.ac.uk; https://unistats.ac.uk.

Top research universities and colleges (REF 2014) See **Languages**.

Examples of sandwich degree courses Bangor.

ADMISSIONS INFORMATION

Number of applicants per place (approx) Birmingham 9; Bristol 4; Cardiff 3; Exeter 5; Hull 5; Leeds 10; Liverpool 6; London (King's) 6; London (QM) 5; London (UCL) 5; Middlesex 2; Nottingham 5; Southampton 8.

Advice to applicants and planning the UCAS personal statement Visits to Spanish-speaking countries should be discussed. Study the geography, culture, literature and politics of Spain, Portugal and/or Latin American nations and discuss your interests in full. Further information could be obtained from embassies in London. See also **Appendix 3** under **Languages**.

Selection interviews Yes Cambridge, Leeds, Oxford, Southampton; **Some** Cardiff, London (UCL); **No** Hull, London (QM), Nottingham, Swansea.

Interview advice and questions Candidates offering A-level Spanish are likely to be questioned on their A-level work, their reasons for wanting to take the subject and on their knowledge of Spain and Latin America and their peoples. Interest in these areas is important for all applicants. Student comment: 'Mostly questions about the literature I had read and I was given a poem and asked questions on it.' Questions were asked in the target language. 'There were two interviewers for the Spanish interview; they did their best to trip me up and to make me think under pressure by asking aggressive questions.' See **Chapter 5**.

AFTER-RESULTS ADVICE

Offers to applicants repeating A-levels Higher Leeds; **Same** Cardiff; Chester; Hull; Liverpool; Nottingham; Roehampton; Swansea; **No** Cambridge; Glasgow.

GRADUATE DESTINATIONS AND EMPLOYMENT (2016/17 HESA)

Spanish Studies graduates surveyed 865 **Employed** 460 **In voluntary employment** 30 **In further study** 205 **Assumed unemployed** 40

Career note See **Languages**.

OTHER DEGREE SUBJECTS FOR CONSIDERATION

International Business Studies; Latin American Studies; Linguistics; see other language tables.

SPEECH PATHOLOGY/SCIENCES/THERAPY

(including **Healthcare Science**; see also **Communication Studies/Communication, Health Sciences/Studies**)

Speech Pathology/Sciences/Therapy is the study of speech defects caused by accident, disease or psychological trauma. These can include failure to develop communication at the usual age, voice disorders, physical and learning disabilities and stammering. Courses lead to qualification as a speech therapist. This is one of many medical courses. See also **Medicine** and **Appendix 3**.

Useful websites www.rcslt.org; www.speechteach.co.uk; www.asha.org

NB The points totals shown to the left of the institutions are for ease of reference only. It must not be assumed that Tariff points are always used by institutions or that they can be substituted for an offer in grades. The level of an offer is not necessarily indicative of the quality of a course.

COURSE OFFERS INFORMATION

Subject requirements/preferences GCSE English language, a modern foreign language and biology/dual award science at grade B or above (5/6 or above). **AL** At least one science subject; biology may be stipulated, psychology and English language may be preferred. Other Disclosure and Barring Service (DBS) and occupational health checks essential for Speech Sciences/Speech Therapy applicants.

Your target offers and examples of degree courses

136 pts   **Manchester** – AAB +interview (Sp Lang Thera) (IB 35 pts HL 655)
            Newcastle – AAB incl sci (Sp Lang Thera) (IB 35 pts HL 555 incl sci)
            Queen Margaret – AAB incl sci/maths (Sp Lang Thera) (IB 32 pts)
            Reading – AAB (Sp Lang Thera) (IB 34 pts)

128 pts   **Canterbury Christ Church** – ABB +interview (Sp Lang Thera)
            Cardiff Met – ABB +interview (Sp Lang Thera)
            De Montfort – ABB +interview (Sp Lang Thera) (IB 30 pts)
            Leeds Beckett – ABB incl sci/psy/sociol/lang 128 pts +interview (Sp Lang Thera) (IB 27 pts)
            Reading – ABB (Psy Lang Sci) (IB 32 pts)
            Sheffield – ABB–BBB +bEPQ (Sp Lang Sci) (IB 33 pts)
            Strathclyde – AAB–ABB (Sp Lang Path) (IB 32 pts HL 6 Engl)

120 pts   **City** – BBB 120 pts +interview (Sp Lang Thera) (IB 33 pts)
            East Anglia – BBB/ABC +interview (Sp Lang Thera) (IB 31 pts)
            Essex – BBB +literacy +numeracy+ interview (Sp Lang Thera) (IB 30 pts HL 555)
            Marjon – BBB 120 pts +interview (Sp Lang Thera) (IB 30–28 pts)

112 pts   **Birmingham City** – BBB–BBC 112–120 pts+interview (Sp Lang Thera) (IB 30 pts)
            Derby – 112 pts +interview (Crea Expr Arts Hlth Wlbng (Dance/Dr/Mus/Art))
            Middlesex – C sci 112 pts +interview (Hlthcr Sci (Audiol))

Alternative offers
See **Chapter 6** and **Appendix 1** for grades/UCAS Tariff points information for other examinations.

CHOOSING YOUR COURSE (SEE ALSO CH.1)

Universities and colleges teaching quality See www.qaa.ac.uk; https://unistats.ac.uk.

Examples of sandwich degree courses Reading.

ADMISSIONS INFORMATION

Number of applicants per place (approx) Birmingham City 28; Cardiff Met 10; City 6; Manchester 13; Manchester Met 21; Newcastle 5.

Advice to applicants and planning the UCAS personal statement Contact with speech therapists and visits to their clinics are an essential part of the preparation for this career. Discuss your contacts in full, giving details of any work experience or work shadowing you have done and your interest in helping people to communicate, showing evidence of good 'people skills'. See also **Appendix 3** and **Chapter 5**. **Manchester** Selectors look for some practical experience with individuals who have communication or swallowing difficulties. (International students) Good English required because of placement periods.

Misconceptions about this course Cardiff Met Some are under the impression that good grades are not necessary, that it is an easy option and one has to speak with a standard pronunciation.

Selection interviews Yes Birmingham City, Cardiff Met, East Anglia, Leeds Beckett, Manchester Met, Marjon, Reading; **No** Sheffield.

Interview advice and questions Have you visited a speech and language therapy clinic? What did you see there? What made you want to become a speech therapist? What type of speech problems are there? What type of person would make a good speech therapist? Interviews often include an ear test (test of listening ability). See also **Chapter 5**. **Cardiff Met** Interviewees must demonstrate an insight into communication problems and explain how one speech sound is produced.

Reasons for rejection (non-academic) Insufficient knowledge of speech and language therapy. Lack of maturity. Poor communication skills. Written language problems.

AFTER-RESULTS ADVICE
Offers to applicants repeating A-levels Higher Birmingham City; Cardiff Met; **Possibly higher** Manchester Met; **Same** City; Newcastle.

GRADUATE DESTINATIONS AND EMPLOYMENT
Career note Speech therapists work mainly in NHS clinics, some work in hospitals and others in special schools or units for the mentally or physically handicapped. The demand for speech therapists is high.

OTHER DEGREE SUBJECTS FOR CONSIDERATION
Audiology; Communication Studies; Deaf Studies; Education; Health Studies; Linguistics; Psychology.

SPORTS SCIENCES/STUDIES

(see also **Leisure and Recreation Management/Studies, Physical Education**)

In addition to the theory and practice of many different sporting activities, Sports Sciences/Studies courses also cover the psychological aspects of sports and sports business administration. The geography, economics and sociology of recreation may also be included. The University Centres of Cricketing Excellence exist as part of a scheme introduced and funded by the England and Wales Cricket Board.

Useful websites www.uksport.gov.uk; www.laureus.com; www.wsff.org.uk; www.sta.co.uk; www.olympic.org; http://sportscotland.org.uk; www.thebapa.org.uk; www.planet-science.com; www.bases.org.uk; www.eis2win.co.uk

NB The points totals shown to the left of the institutions are for ease of reference only. It must not be assumed that Tariff points are always used by institutions or that they can be substituted for an offer in grades. The level of an offer is not necessarily indicative of the quality of a course.

COURSE OFFERS INFORMATION
Subject requirements/preferences GCSE English, mathematics and, often, a science subject. **AL** Science required for Sport Science courses. PE required for some Sport Studies courses. Other Disclosure and Barring Service (DBS) disclosure required for many courses. Evidence of commitment to sport.

Your target offers and examples of degree courses
144 pts **Bath** – AAA–AAB +aEPQ incl maths/sci (Spo Exer Sci) (IB 36 pts HL 666/765 incl 6 maths/sci)
136 pts **Bath** – AAB/A*AC/A*BB (Hlth Exer Sci) (IB 36 pts HL 665)
    Durham – AAB (Spo Exer Physl Actvt) (IB 36 pts HL 665)
    Glasgow – AAB incl biol/chem (Physiol Spo Sci) (IB 36 pts HL 665 incl sci)
    Loughborough – AAB (Geog Spo Sci; Spo Mgt) (IB 35 pts HL 665); AAB incl Engl (Engl Spo Sci) (IB 35 pts HL 665 incl Engl)
    Newcastle – AAA–AAB incl sci/maths (Spo Exer Sci) (IB 35–34 pts HL 5 sci)
    Ulster – AAB incl hum/soc sci/spo (Spo St); AAB incl sci/maths/spo (Spo Exer Sci)
128 pts **Bangor** – 128 pts (Spo Exer Psy)
    Birmingham – AAA–ABB incl sci/maths (Spo Exer Hlth Sci) (IB 32 pts HL 666–655 incl sci/maths); ABB (App Glf Mgt St) (IB 32 pts HL 655)
    Bournemouth – 128–144 pts incl biol/PE (Spo Thera) (IB 34–32 pts HL 5 biol/PE)
    Derby – 128 pts (Spo Thera Rehab); C biol/PE 128 pts (Spo Exer Sci)
    East Anglia – ABB–BBB +aEPQ (PE Spo Hlth) (IB 32 pts)

Edinburgh – ABB (Spo Recr Mgt) (IB 36–34 pts HL 666–655); ABB incl sci (App Spo Sci) (IB 37–34 pts HL 666–655 incl sci)

Exeter – AAA–ABB incl sci (Exer Spo Sci) (IB 36–32 pts HL 666–655 incl sci)

Leeds – AAA–ABB incl sci (Spo Exer Sci; Spo Sci Physiol) (IB 35–33 pts HL 18–17 pts incl 6 sci)

London (King's) – ABB incl sci/maths/PE (Spo Exer Med Sci) (IB 34 pts HL 655 incl sci/maths/PE)

Loughborough – AAA–ABB incl sci/maths (Spo Exer Sci) (IB 35–33 pts HL 18–17 pts incl 6 sci)

Northumbria – 128 pts (App Spo Exer Sci; Spo Mgt)

Nottingham Trent – ABB incl sci/PE 128 pts (Spo Exer Sci)

Portsmouth – 128 pts incl sci/PE (Spo Exer Sci) (IB 26 pts HL 5 sci/PE)

120 pts   **Aberdeen** – BBB incl maths/sci (Spo Exer Sci) (IB 32 pts HL 555 incl maths/sci)

Brunel – BBB (Psy (Spo Hlth Exer)) (IB 30 pts)

Cardiff Met – BB incl sci/maths/PE 120–128 pts (Spo Condit Rehab Msg; Spo Exer Sci)

Chester – 120 pts (Spo Exer Sci) (IB 28 pts)

Coventry – BBB (Spo Exer Psy) (IB 30 pts HL 15 pts)

Derby – 120 pts (Spo Exer St Comb Hons)

Essex – BBB incl sci/maths (Spo Exer Sci) (IB 30 pts HL 555)

Gloucestershire – BBB 120 pts (Spo Exer Sci)

Huddersfield – BBB incl sci/PE 120 pts (Spo Exer Sci)

Lincoln – BBB (Spo Exer Sci) (IB 30 pts)

Liverpool Hope – BBB 120 pts (Spo Exer Sci) (IB 28 pts)

Liverpool John Moores – BBB 120 pts (Spo Exer Sci) (IB 26 pts)

Manchester Met – BBB incl sci/PE 120 pts (Spo Exer Sci) (IB 26 pts HL 5 sci/PE)

Nottingham Trent – BBB incl sci/PE 120 pts (Spo Sci Mgt)

Stirling – BBB (Spo St) (IB 32 pts); BBB incl sci/maths (Spo Exer Sci) (IB 32 pts)

Strathclyde – ABB–BBB (Spo Physl Actvt) (IB 36 pts)

Surrey – BBB incl sci/PE (Spo Exer Sci) (IB 32 pts)

Swansea – AAB–BBB (Spo Exer Sci) (IB 32 pts)

UWE Bristol – C biol/PE 120 pts (Spo Rehab) (HL 5 biol/PE)

112 pts   **Bangor** – 112 pts (Spo Hlth Exer Sci; Spo Hlth PE; Spo Sci)

Bedfordshire – 112 pts (Spo Exer Sci)

Bolton – 112 pts incl spo/PE/sci +interview (Spo Rehab)

Bournemouth – 112–128 pts (Spo Exer Sci) (IB 32–30 pts)

Brighton – ABB–BBC 112–128 pts (Spo Exer Sci) (IB 27 pts)

Brunel – BBC incl maths/sci (Spo Hlth Exer Sci (Spo Dev)) (IB 29 pts HL 5 maths/sci); BBC incl sci/maths/PE (Spo Hlth Exer Sci; Spo Hlth Exer Sci (Coach); Spo Hlth Exer Sci (Hum Perf)) (IB 29 pts HL 5 sci/maths/PE)

Cardiff Met – 112–120 pts (Spo Coach; Spo PE St)

Central Lancashire – 112–128 pts incl biol/PE/spo sci (Spo Thera) (HL 5 biol/PE/spo sci)

Coventry – BBC (Spo Mgt) (IB 29 pts); BBC incl biol/PE (Spo Exer Thera) (IB 30 pts HL 5 biol)

Derby – 112 pts (Spo Educ)

East London – 112 pts (Spo Jrnl) (IB 25 pts HL 15 pts); 112 pts incl PE/spo/sci (Spo Exer Sci) (IB 25 pts HL 15 pts)

Edge Hill – BBC 112 pts (Spo Exer Sci; Spo Thera)

Gloucestershire – BBC 112 pts (Physl Educ; Spo Bus Coach; Spo Bus Mgt; Spo Thera)

Glyndŵr – 112 pts (Spo Coach Part Perf Dev; Spo Hlth Perf Sci)

Huddersfield – BBC 112 pts (Spo Jrnl)

Hull – BBC 112 pts (Spo Coach Perf Sci; Spo Exer Nutr; Spo Rehab) (IB 28 pts)

Leeds Beckett – 112 pts incl sci/PE (Physl Actvt Exer Hlth) (IB 25 pts)

Leeds Trinity – 112 pts (Spo Jrnl; Spo Psy)

Liverpool Hope – BBC 112 pts (Spo Psy) (IB 28 pts)

Liverpool John Moores – BBC 112 pts (Sci Ftbl) (IB -27 pts)

Marjon – BBC 112 pts (Spo Exer Sci; Spo Thera)

Middlesex – 112 pts incl sci (Spo Exer Rehab; Spo Exer Sci)

Newman – CC 112 pts (PE Spo; Spo Coach Perf)

Nottingham Trent – 112 pts incl maths (Spo Sci Maths); BBC incl sci/PE 112 pts (Coach Spo Sci)

Portsmouth – 112 pts (Spo Mgt Dev) (IB 25 pts)

Roehampton – 112 pts incl sci/PE (Spo Exer Sci)

Sheffield Hallam – BBC incl PE/soc sci/sci 112 pts (Spo Exer Sci); BBC incl PE/spo sci/sci 112 pts (Physl Actvt Spo Hlth; Spo Coach)

Staffordshire – BBC 112 pts (Spo Coach; Spo Exer Sci)

Sunderland – 112 pts (Spo Coach; Spo Exer Sci)

Ulster – BBC incl sci/maths/spo (Spo Physl Actvt Hlth) (IB 25 pts HL 12 pts)

Wolverhampton – BBC/CCA 112 pts (Spo Exer Sci)

Worcester – 112 pts (Spo Bus Mgt); 112 pts incl PE/hum biol +interview (Spo Thera)

104 pts **Abertay** – BCC incl sci/maths/PE (Spo Exer) (IB 29 pts)

Anglia Ruskin – 104 pts incl sci/PE (Spo Exer Sci) (IB 24 pts)

Birmingham (UC) – BCC 104 pts (Spo Thera)

Bournemouth – 104–120 pts (Spo Mgt) (IB 31–28 pts)

Central Lancashire – 104 pts +interview (Spo Jrnl); 104–112 pts (Out Advntr Ldrshp; Spo Exer Sci)

Edinburgh Napier – BCC incl sci/PE (Spo Exer Sci) (IB 28 pts HL 654 incl 5 sci)

Greenwich – 104 pts (PE Spo)

Hertfordshire – BCC incl sci 104 pts (Spo Exer Sci)

Kent – BCC (Spo Mgt) (IB 34 pts HL 15 pts); BCC incl sci/maths/PE (Spo Exer Hlth; Spo Exer Sci; Spo Thera Rehab) (IB 34 pts HL 15 pts)

Leeds Trinity – 104 pts (Exer Hlth Nutr; Spo Exer Sci; Spo Exer Sci (Spo Nutr))

Manchester Met – BBC–BCC 104–112 pts (Spo Bus Mgt; Spo Mark Mgt) (IB 26 pts)

Northampton – BCC incl sci/PE (Spo St courses)

Oxford Brookes – BCC incl sci/maths/PE 104 pts (Spo Exer Sci) (IB 29 pts)

Robert Gordon – BCC incl Engl+sci (App Spo Exer Sci) (IB 28 pts HL 555 incl Engl+sci)

Winchester – 104–120 pts (Spo Coach; Spo Mgt) (HL 44)

96 pts **Aberystwyth** – BBB–CCC 96–120 pts (Spo Exer Sci) (IB 30–26 pts)

Birmingham City – C sci/maths/PE 96–112 pts (Spo Exer Sci) (IB 28 pts HL4)

Bishop Grosseteste – 96–112 pts (Psy Spo)

Bolton – 96 pts+interview (Spo Dev Coach)

Brighton – BBC–CCC 96–112 pts (Spo Coach; Spo Jrnl) (IB 26 pts); BCC–CCC 96–104 pts (Spo St) (IB 26 pts)

Bucks New – CC 96 pts (Ftbl Bus Mark) (IB 28 pts)

Cardiff Met – BB 96–112 pts (Spo Physl Educ Hlth Dance) (IB 25 pts HL 13 pts)

Chester – BCC–CCC 96–104 pts (Spo Jrnl) (IB 26 pts)

Chichester – BBC–CCC 96–112 pts (Spo courses) (IB 28 pts)

Cumbria – 96–112 pts (Spo Rehab)

Greenwich – 96 pts incl sci (Spo Sci Coach)

Hertfordshire – CCC 96 pts (Spo St)

Kingston – C sci/PE 96 pts (Spo Sci; Spo Sci (Coach))

Marjon – CCC 96 pts (Spo Dev)

Sheffield Hallam – CCC 96 pts (Spo Bus Mgt; Spo Dev Coach)

Solent – 96–112 pts (App Spo Sci)

St Mary's – BBC–CCC 96–112 pts (Spo Coach Sci; Spo Exer Sci); BBC–CCC incl biol/PE+spo/sci 96–112 pts (Spo Rehab); BBC–CCC incl sci/spo 96–112 pts (Strg Condit Sci)

West Scotland – CCC incl sci 96 pts (Spo Exer Sci) (IB 27 pts)

York St John – 96 pts (PE Spo Coach; Spo Exer Thera)

88 pts **Canterbury Christ Church** – 88–112 pts (Spo Exer Sci courses)

London South Bank – CCD (Spo Exer Sci)

Teesside – 88–112 pts (Spo Exer Sci); 88–112 pts incl spo/sci/PE (Spo Thera Rehab)

Trinity Saint David – 88 pts+interview (Spo Mgt)

80 pts **Bedfordshire** – 80 pts (Ftbl St; Spo Sci Coach)

Bucks New – 80 pts (Spo Exer Sci)

London Met – BB incl biol/PE/spo sci 80 pts (Spo Exer Sci)

South Wales – BCC–CCD incl sci/PE 80–104 pts (Spo Exer Sci) (IB 29 pts HL 5 sci/maths/psy);
BCC–CDD 80–104 pts (Spo Exer Psy) (IB 29 pts); BCC–CDD incl sci/PE 80–104 pts (Ftbl
Coach Perf; Spo Coach Dev) (IB 29 pts HL 5 sci/maths/psy); BCC–CDD incl sci/maths/PE
80–104 pts (Rgby Coach Perf) (IB 29 pts HL 5 sci/maths/psy)

48 pts **Bolton** – 48 pts +interview +portfolio (Spo Rehab Fdn Yr)

Alternative offers

See **Chapter 6** and **Appendix 1** for grades/UCAS Tariff points information for other examinations.

EXAMPLES OF COLLEGES OFFERING COURSES IN THIS SUBJECT FIELD

Accrington and Rossendale (Coll); Askham Bryan (Coll); Bishop Burton (Coll); Blackpool and Fylde
(Coll); Bradford College UC; Colchester (UC); Easton Otley (Coll); Hartpury (Coll); Lakes (Coll); Leeds City
(Coll); Manchester (Coll); Myerscough (Coll); NCC Hackney; Newcastle (Coll); North Kent (Coll); North
Lindsey (Coll); Peterborough (Coll); Plumpton (Coll); Reaseheath (UC); Sir Gâr (Coll); South Devon
(Coll); South Essex (Coll); Stamford New (Coll); Tameside (Coll); Warwickshire (Coll); Westminster City
(Coll); Weston (Coll); York (Coll).

CHOOSING YOUR COURSE (SEE ALSO CH.1)

Universities and colleges teaching quality See www.qaa.ac.uk; https://unistats.ac.uk.

Top research universities and colleges (REF 2014) (Sports and Exercise Science, Leisure and
Tourism) Bristol, Liverpool John Moores, Leeds, Bath, Birmingham, Exeter, London (King's), Bangor,
Cardiff Met.

Examples of sandwich degree courses Bath; Bedfordshire; Bournemouth; Brighton; Brunel; Central
Lancashire; Coventry; Essex; Hertfordshire; Kingston; Leeds; Loughborough; Manchester Met;
Nottingham Trent; Portsmouth; Robert Gordon; Solent; Trinity Saint David; Ulster.

ADMISSIONS INFORMATION

Number of applicants per place (approx) Bangor 4; Bath 10; Birmingham 7; Cardiff Met 10; Cumbria
14, (Spo St) 6; Durham 6; Edinburgh 6; Exeter 23; Gloucestershire 8; Kingston 13; Leeds 25; Leeds
Trinity 6; Liverpool John Moores 4; Manchester Met 16; Northampton 4; Nottingham Trent 8; Oxford
Brookes 6; Roehampton 5; Sheffield Hallam 7; South Essex (Coll) 1; St Mary's 4; Staffordshire 12;
Stirling 8; Strathclyde 28; Sunderland 2; Swansea 6; Teesside 15; Winchester 5; Wolverhampton 4;
Worcester 10; York St John 4.

Advice to applicants and planning the UCAS personal statement See also **Physical Education**
and **Appendix 3**. **Cardiff Met** A strong personal statement required which clearly identifies current
performance profile and indicates a balanced lifestyle.

Misconceptions about this course Birmingham (App Glf Mgt St) Applicants do not appreciate the
academic depth required across key areas (it is, in a sense, a multiple Honours course covering
business management, sports science, coaching theory and materials science). **Swansea** (Spo Sci)
Applicants underestimate the quantity of maths on the course. Many applicants are uncertain about
the differences between Sports Studies and Sports Science.

Selection interviews Yes Bolton, Chichester, Robert Gordon, Stirling, Worcester; **Some** Bath, Leeds
Trinity; **No** Anglia Ruskin, Birmingham, Cardiff Met, Cumbria, Derby, Edinburgh, Essex, Leeds, Liverpool
John Moores, Nottingham Trent, Roehampton, Sheffield Hallam, St Mary's, Staffordshire, West
Scotland, Wolverhampton.

Interview advice and questions Applicants' interests in sport and their sporting activities are likely
to be discussed at length. Past questions include: How do you strike a balance between sport and
academic work? How many, and which, sports do you coach? For how long? Have you devised your
own coaching programme? What age range do you coach? Do you coach unsupervised? See also
Chapter 5. **Loughborough** A high level of sporting achievement is expected.

Reasons for rejection (non-academic) Not genuinely interested in outdoor activities. Poor sporting background or knowledge. Inability to apply their science to their specialist sport. Illiteracy. Using the course as a second option to Physiotherapy. Arrogance. Expectation that they will be playing sport all day. When the course is explained to them, some applicants realise that a more arts-based course would be more appropriate. **Ulster** Reasons relating to health and/or police checks.

AFTER-RESULTS ADVICE

Offers to applicants repeating A-levels Higher Swansea; **Same** Cardiff Met; Chichester; Derby; Lincoln; Liverpool John Moores; Loughborough; Roehampton; Sheffield Hallam; St Mary's; Staffordshire; Stirling; Sunderland; Winchester; Wolverhampton; York St John.

GRADUATE DESTINATIONS AND EMPLOYMENT (2016/17 HESA)

Graduates surveyed 8,860 **Employed** 3,755 **In voluntary employment** 250 **In further study** 2,810 **Assumed unemployed** 295

Career note Career options include sport development, coaching, teaching, outdoor centres, sports equipment development, sales, recreation management and professional sport.

OTHER DEGREE SUBJECTS FOR CONSIDERATION

Anatomy; Biology; Human Movement Studies; Leisure and Recreation Management; Nutrition; Physical Education; Physiology; Physiotherapy; Sports Equipment Product Design.

STATISTICS

(See also **Economics, Mathematics**)

Statistics has mathematical underpinnings but is primarily concerned with the collection, interpretation and analysis of data. Statistics are used to analyse and solve problems in a wide range of areas, particularly in the scientific, business, government and public services.

Useful websites www.rss.org.uk; www.gov.uk/government/statistics/announcements; www.ons.gov.uk

NB The points totals shown to the left of the institutions are for ease of reference only. It must not be assumed that Tariff points are always used by institutions or that they can be substituted for an offer in grades. The level of an offer is not necessarily indicative of the quality of a course.

COURSE OFFERS INFORMATION

Subject requirements/preferences GCSE English and mathematics. **AL** Mathematics required for all courses.

Your target offers and examples of degree courses

160 pts   **Imperial London** – A^*A^*A incl maths+fmaths +MAT/STEP (Maths Optim Stats; Maths Stats; Maths Stats Fin) (IB 39 pts HL 7 maths)

        Oxford – A^*A^*A incl maths +interview +MAT (Maths Stats) (IB 39 pts HL 766 incl 7 maths)

        St Andrews – A^*A^*A incl A^* maths (Stats) (IB 38 pts HL 666 incl maths)

152 pts   **Bath** – A^*AA incl maths+fmaths (Stats) (IB 36 pts HL 766/765 incl maths)

        Bristol – A^*A^*A–A^*AA incl maths+fmaths/sci/econ/comp (Maths Stats) (IB 40 pts HL 18 pts incl 7 maths 6 sci/econ/comp)

        London (UCL) – A^*AA incl maths (Stats; Stats Econ Fin; Stats Mgt Bus; Stats Sci (Int)) (IB 39 pts HL 19 pts incl 7 maths)

        London LSE – A^*AA incl maths (Fin Maths Stats) (IB 38 pts HL 766 incl 7 maths)

        Warwick – $A^*A^*A^*$–A^*AA incl maths (MORSE) (IB 38 pts HL 7 maths); A^*AA incl maths+fmaths (Maths Stats) (IB 38 pts HL7 maths)

144 pts   **Birmingham** – AAA incl maths (Mathem Econ Stats) (IB 32 pts HL 666)

        Glasgow – AAA/A^*AB incl maths (Fin Stats) (IB 38 pts HL 666 incl maths)

London LSE – AAA incl maths (Maths Stats Bus) (IB 38 pts HL 766 incl 7 maths)
Loughborough – AAA/A*AB incl maths (Maths Stats) (IB 37 pts HL 666 incl maths)
Manchester – A*AA–AAA incl maths +interview (Maths Stats) (IB 36 pts HL 666 incl maths)
Nottingham – A*AA–AAA incl maths (Stats) (IB 36 pts HL 6 maths)
Queen's Belfast – AAA/A*AB incl maths (Maths Stats OR (MSci)) (IB 36 pts HL 666 incl maths)
Southampton – AAA incl maths (Maths Stats) (IB 36 pts HL 18 pts incl 6 maths); AAA–AAB
+aEPQ incl maths (Maths OR Stats Econ (MORSE)) (IB 36 pts HL 18 pts incl 6 maths)
York – AAA incl maths (Maths Stats) (IB 36 pts HL 6 maths)

136 pts **Edinburgh** – A*AA–AAB incl maths (Maths Stats) (IB 37–32 pts HL 666–655 incl 6 maths)
Glasgow – AAB incl maths (Stats) (IB 36 pts HL 665 incl sci)
Heriot-Watt – AAB incl maths (Stats Data Sci) (IB 28 pts HL 6 maths)
Lancaster – AAA–AAB incl maths/fmaths (Maths Stats) (IB 36 pts HL 16 pts incl 6 maths)
Leeds – AAA/A*AB–AAB/A*BB incl maths (Maths Stats) (IB 35 pts HL 17 pts incl 6 maths)
London (QM) – AAB incl maths (Maths Stats) (IB 34 pts HL 665 incl maths)
Newcastle – AAB/A*BB incl maths (Maths Stats; Stats) (IB 34 pts HL 6 maths)
Queen's Belfast – AAB/A*BB incl maths (Maths Stats OR) (IB 34 pts HL 665 incl maths)

128 pts **Cardiff** – AAB–ABB incl maths (Maths OR Stats) (IB 36–34 pts HL 666–655 incl maths)
London (RH) – AAB–ABB incl maths (Maths Stats) (IB 32 pts HL 655 incl 6 maths)
Surrey – AAB–ABB incl maths (Maths Stats) (IB 34–32 pts HL 6 maths)

120 pts **Brunel** – BBB incl maths/fmaths (Maths Stats Mgt) (IB 30 pts HL 5 maths)
Heriot-Watt – BBB incl maths (Maths Stats) (IB 28 pts HL 5 maths)
Reading – ABC incl A maths (Maths Stats) (IB 30 pts HL C maths)
Strathclyde – ABB–BBB (Maths Stats Econ) (IB 32 pts HL 6 maths)

112 pts **Coventry** – BBB–BBC (Maths Stats) (IB 29 pts HL 5 maths)
London (Birk) – ABB–BBC incl B maths 112–128 pts (Maths Stats)
Plymouth – 112–128 pts incl maths (Maths Stats) (IB 30 pts HL 5 maths)
Portsmouth – 112–128 pts incl maths (Maths Stats) (IB 26–25 pts)
West London – BBC 112–120 pts (Maths Stats)

104 pts **Chichester** – BBC–BCC incl maths 104–112 pts (Maths Stats) (IB 28 pts HL 4 maths)
Greenwich – BCC incl maths 104 pts (Stats OR)

Alternative offers
See **Chapter 6** and **Appendix 1** for grades/UCAS Tariff points information for other examinations.

CHOOSING YOUR COURSE (SEE ALSO CH.1)

Universities and colleges teaching quality See www.qaa.ac.uk; https://unistats.ac.uk.

Top research universities and colleges (REF 2014) See **Mathematics**.

Examples of sandwich degree courses Bath; Brunel; Cardiff; Coventry; Greenwich; Kent; Kingston; Plymouth; Portsmouth; Reading; Surrey; UWE Bristol.

ADMISSIONS INFORMATION

Number of applicants per place (approx) Bath 7; Heriot-Watt 6; Lancaster 6; London (UCL) 9; London LSE 8; Southampton 10; York 5.

Advice to applicants and planning the UCAS personal statement Admissions tutors like to see applicants demonstrate a real passion for mathematics and desire to learn. If there are any branches of mathematics that particularly interest you, these should be mentioned on the statement. See also **Mathematics** and **Appendix 3**.

Selection interviews Some Bath, Greenwich, London (UCL); **No** Birmingham, East Anglia, Newcastle, Reading.

Interview advice and questions Questions could be asked on your A-level syllabus (particularly in mathematics). Applicants' knowledge of statistics and their interest in the subject are likely to be tested, together with their awareness of the application of statistics in commerce and industry. See also **Chapter 5**.

AFTER-RESULTS ADVICE
Offers to applicants repeating A-levels Higher Leeds; Newcastle; **Same** Birmingham.

GRADUATE DESTINATIONS AND EMPLOYMENT (2016/17 HESA)
Graduates surveyed 355 **Employed** 205 **In voluntary employment** 0 **In further study** 90 **Assumed unemployed** 15

Career note See **Mathematics**.

OTHER DEGREE SUBJECTS FOR CONSIDERATION
Accountancy; Actuarial Sciences; Business Information Technology; Business Studies; Computer Science; Economics; Financial Services; Mathematical Studies; Mathematics.

SURVEYING AND REAL ESTATE MANAGEMENT

(including Building Surveying, Quantity Surveying, Property Development and Rural Property Management. For Property, Finance and Investment see under Finance; see also Agricultural Sciences/Agriculture, Building And Construction, Housing, Town And Urban Planning)

Surveying covers a very diverse range of careers and courses and following a Royal Institution of Chartered Surveyors (RICS) accredited course is the accepted way to become a Chartered Surveyor. There are three main specialisms – the Built Environment (Building Surveying, Project Management and Quantity Surveying); Land Surveying (Rural, Planning, Environmental, Minerals and Waste Management); and Property Surveying (Commercial and Residential Property and Valuation, Facilities Management, Art and Antiques). Student membership of the RICS is possible. Not all the courses listed below receive RICS accreditation; check with the university or college prior to applying.

Useful websites www.rics.org/eu/surveying-profession/what-is-surveying/rics-students; www.cstt.org.uk

NB The points totals shown to the left of the institutions are for ease of reference only. It must not be assumed that Tariff points are always used by institutions or that they can be substituted for an offer in grades. The level of an offer is not necessarily indicative of the quality of a course.

COURSE OFFERS INFORMATION
Subject requirements/preferences GCSE English and mathematics grade A–C (7–4). **AL** No subjects specified; mathematics useful.

Your target offers and examples of degree courses
152 pts **Cambridge** – A*AA +interview +TSA (Lnd Econ) (IB 42–40 pts HL 776)
136 pts **London (UCL)** – AAB (Urb Plan Rl Est) (IB 36 pts HL 17 pts)
128 pts **Manchester** – ABB (Plan Rl Est) (IB 34 pts HL 655)
    Oxford Brookes – ABB 128 pts +interview (Rl Est) (IB 32 pts)
    Ulster – ABB incl maths/phys/chem/biol/eng/constr (Quant Surv Commer Mgt) (IB 27 pts HL 13 pts incl maths+sci)
120 pts **Aberdeen** – BBB (Rl Est Mgt) (IB 32 pts HL 555)
    London South Bank – BBB (Quant Surv)
    Loughborough – ABC/BBB 120 pts +interview (Commer Mgt Quant Surv) (IB 32 pts HL 555)
    Newcastle – ABB–BBB (Geosptl Surv Map) (IB 32 pts)
    Northumbria – 120 pts (Bld Surv; Quant Surv; Rl Est)
    Nottingham Trent – BBB 120 pts (Bld Surv; Rl Est)
    Reading – BBB (Bld Surv; Quant Surv) (IB 30 pts)
    UWE Bristol – 120 pts (Rl Est)
112 pts **Anglia Ruskin** – 112 pts (Bld Surv; Quant Surv) (IB 25 pts)
    Birmingham City – BBC 112 pts (Bld Surv; Quant Surv; Rl Est) (IB 28 pts HL 14 pts)

Coventry – BBB–BBC (Bld Surv; Quant Surv Commer Mgt) (IB 30 pts)
Derby – 112 pts (Prop Dev Comb Hons); BBC 112 pts (Constr Mgt Prop Dev)
Greenwich – BBC 112 pts (Quant Surv)
Kingston – 112 pts (Bld Surv; Rl Est Mgt Bus Expnc)
Leeds Beckett – 112 pts (Bld Surv; Quant Surv) (IB 25 pts)
Liverpool John Moores – BBC 112 pts (Bld Surv; Quant Surv; Rl Est) (IB 26 pts)
Nottingham Trent – BBC 112 pts (Quant Surv Commer Mgt)
Oxford Brookes – 112 pts (Quant Surv Commer Mgt) (IB 30 pts); BBC 112 pts (Plan Prop Dev) (IB 30 pts)
Portsmouth – 112–120 pts (Prop Dev) (IB -25 pts)
Sheffield Hallam – BBC 112 pts (Bld Surv; Quant Surv)
UWE Bristol – 112 pts (Bld Surv; Quant Surv Commer Mgt)
Ulster – BBC (Rl Est) (IB 25 pts HL 12 pts)
Westminster – ABB–BBC 112–128 pts (Bld Surv) (IB 27 pts HL 4 Engl); (Quant Surv Commer Mgt; Rl Est) (IB 27 pts HL 4 Engl lang)

104 pts   **Harper Adams** – 104 pts (Rl Est; Rur Prop Mgt) (IB 28 pts)
Plymouth – 104–112 pts (Bld Surv Env; Quant Surv) (IB 28 pts)
Royal Agricultural Univ – BCC 104 pts (Rl Est) (IB 26 pts)
Salford – 104 pts (Prop Rl Est) (IB 29 pts)
South Wales – BCC (Quant Surv Commer Mgt) (IB 29 pts)

96 pts   **Brighton** – BBC–CCC 96–112 pts (Bld Surv) (IB 26 pts)
Central Lancashire – 96 pts (Quant Surv)
East London – 96 pts (Surv Map Sci) (IB 24 pts HL 15 pts)
Glasgow Caledonian – CCC (Bld Surv; Quant Surv) (IB 24 pts)
London South Bank – CCC 96–112 pts (Commer Mgt (Quant Surv))
Robert Gordon – CCC (Surv) (IB 26 pts)
Trinity Saint David – 96 pts (Quant Surv)
UCEM – 96 pts (Bld Surv; Quant Surv; Rl Est Mgt)
Wolverhampton – CCC/BCD 96 pts (Bld Surv; Quant Surv)

80 pts   **South Wales** – BCC–CDD 80–104 pts (Bld Surv)

Alternative offers
See **Chapter 6** and **Appendix 1** for grades/UCAS Tariff points information for other examinations.

DEGREE APPRENTICESHIPS
Oxford Brookes (Chart Surv); Portsmouth (Bld Surv, Quant Surv, Rl Est); Reading (Quant Surv, Rl Est).

EXAMPLES OF COLLEGES OFFERING COURSES IN THIS SUBJECT FIELD
Blackburn (Coll); South Cheshire (Coll); UCEM.

CHOOSING YOUR COURSE (SEE ALSO CH.1)
Universities and colleges teaching quality See www.qaa.ac.uk; https://unistats.ac.uk. Check on RICS accreditation.

Examples of sandwich degree courses Anglia Ruskin; Birmingham City; Central Lancashire; Coventry; Glasgow Caledonian; Kingston; Leeds Beckett; Liverpool John Moores; London South Bank; Loughborough; Northumbria; Nottingham Trent; Oxford Brookes; Sheffield Hallam; Ulster; UWE Bristol; Wolverhampton.

ADMISSIONS INFORMATION
Number of applicants per place (approx) Anglia Ruskin 2; Birmingham City 4; Cambridge 4; Edinburgh Napier 7; Greenwich 8; Harper Adams 3; London South Bank 2; Nottingham Trent (Quant Surv) 10; Oxford Brookes 4; Robert Gordon 5; Royal Agricultural Univ 3; Sheffield Hallam (Quant Surv) 7; Westminster 10; Wolverhampton 6.

Admissions tutors' advice Nottingham Trent Candidates should demonstrate that they have researched the employment opportunities in the property and construction sectors.

Advice to applicants and planning the UCAS personal statement Surveyors work with architects and builders as well as in their own consultancies dealing with commercial and residential property. Work experience with various firms is strongly recommended depending on the type of surveying speciality preferred. Read surveying magazines. **Cambridge** Statements should be customised to the overall interests of students, not to the Land Economy Tripos specifically. **Oxford Brookes** Apply early. Applicants should be reflective. We are looking for at least 50%–60% of the personal statement to cover issues surrounding why they want to do the course, what motivates them about the subject, how they have developed their interest, how their A-levels have helped them and what they have gained from any work experience. Extracurricular activities are useful but should not dominate the statement.

Misconceptions about this course Royal Agricultural Univ The Rural Land Management course is not specifically about managing land, the course focuses on rural surveying.

Selection interviews Yes Birmingham City, Cambridge, Loughborough; **No** Anglia Ruskin, Glasgow Caledonian, Harper Adams, Kingston, Liverpool John Moores, Nottingham Trent, Oxford Brookes, Robert Gordon, Royal Agricultural Univ, Salford, Ulster.

Interview advice and questions What types of work are undertaken by surveyors? How do you qualify? What did you learn on your work experience? See also **Chapter 5**. **Cambridge** (Lnd Econ) Questions on subsidies and the euro and economics. Who owns London? How important is the modern day church in town planning? How important are natural resources to a country? Is it more important to focus on poverty at home or abroad? Is the environment a bigger crisis than poverty? Do you think that getting involved with poverty abroad is interfering with others 'freedoms'? (The questions were based on information given in the personal statement.) Students sit the TSA at interview.

Reasons for rejection (non-academic) Inability to communicate. Lack of motivation. Indecisiveness about reasons for choosing the course. **Loughborough** Applicants more suited to a practical type of course rather than an academic one. **Nottingham Trent** Incoherent and badly written application.

AFTER-RESULTS ADVICE
Offers to applicants repeating A-levels Higher Bolton; Nottingham Trent; **Same** Coventry; Edinburgh Napier; Liverpool John Moores; Oxford Brookes; Robert Gordon; Salford.

GRADUATE DESTINATIONS AND EMPLOYMENT
Career note See **Building and Construction**.

OTHER DEGREE SUBJECTS FOR CONSIDERATION
Architecture; Building and Construction; Civil Engineering; Estate Management; Town Planning; Urban Studies.

TEACHER TRAINING

(See also **Education Studies, Physical Education, Social Sciences/Studies**)

Abbreviations used in this table: ITE – Initial Teacher Education; ITT – Initial Teacher Training; P – Primary Teaching; QTS – Qualified Teacher Status; S – Secondary Teaching; STQ – Scottish Teaching Qualification.

Teacher training courses are offered in subject areas such as Art and Design (P); Biology (P S); Chemistry (S); Childhood (P); Computer Education (P); Creative and Performing Arts (P); Dance (P); Design and Technology (P S); Drama (P); English (P S); Environmental Science (P S); Environmental Studies (P); French (S); General Primary; Geography (P S); History (P S); Maths (P S); Music (P S); Physical Education/Movement Studies (P S); Religious Studies (P); Science (P S); Sociology (S); Textile

Design (S); Welsh (S). For further information on teaching as a career see websites below and **Appendix 3** for contact details. Over 50 taster courses are offered each year to those considering teaching as a career. Applicants aiming to quickly become qualified primary teachers in the United Kingdom should take care to apply for undergraduate courses which confer Qualified Teacher Status (QTS). Note that many institutions listed below also offer one-year Postgraduate Certificate in Education (PGCE) courses which qualify graduates to teach at primary and secondary level across a range of subjects. For UK secondary teachers, an undergraduate degree in a traditional academic subject followed by a PGCE is still the most common route to the classroom, although this is beginning to change with the growing popularity of new vocational routes. All institutions will require candidates to attend for interview, often with literacy and numeracy tests.

Useful websites www.gtcs.org.uk; www.ucas.com/teaching-in-the-uk; www.gov.uk/government/organisations/department-for-education

NB The points totals shown to the left of the institutions are for ease of reference only. It must not be assumed that Tariff points are always used by institutions or that they can be substituted for an offer in grades. The level of an offer is not necessarily indicative of the quality of a course.

COURSE OFFERS INFORMATION
Subject requirements/preferences See **Education Studies**.

Your target offers and examples of degree courses

152 pts **Cambridge** – A*AA +interview +EAA (Educ Engl Dr Arts; Educ Plcy Int Dev; Educ Psy Lrng) (IB 42–40 pts HL 776)

136 pts **Durham** – AAB (Educ St (Engl St/Geog/Hist/Phil/Psy/Sociol/Theol Relgn)) (IB 36 pts HL 665)
Glasgow – AAB incl Engl +interview (Educ P QTS) (IB 36 pts HL 665 incl Engl)
Stranmillis (UC) – AAB +interview (P Educ QTS)

128 pts **Durham** – ABB (P Educ) (IB 34 pts)
Edinburgh – ABB (P Educ Gael) (IB 34 pts HL 655 incl 5 Engl)
Strathclyde – AAB–ABB incl sci/maths (Chem Teach (MChem)) (IB 34 pts)

120 pts **Bangor** – 120 pts (P Educ QTS)
Brighton – BBB (P Educ) (IB 27 pts)
Chester – 120 pts +interview (P Educ QTS) (IB 28 pts)
Edge Hill – BBB 120 pts +interview (Ely Yrs Educ; P Educ QTS)
Liverpool Hope – BBB 120 pts (P Educ QTS) (IB 28 pts)
Nottingham Trent – BBB 120 pts +interview +test (P Educ QTS)
Reading – BBB incl Engl/hist/soc/phil/dr +interview (P Educ Engl Spec) (IB 30 pts HL 5 Engl/hist/soc/phil/dr); BBB incl art +interview (P Educ Art Spec) (IB 30 pts HL 5 art); BBB incl mus +gr 6 +interview (P Ed Mus Spec) (IB 30 pts HL 5 mus)
Stirling – BBB (Educ P; Educ S) (IB 32 pts); (Prof Educ P courses) (IB 32 pts HL 5 Engl)
Strathclyde – ABB–BBB (P Educ) (IB 36 pts)
Sunderland – BBB 120 pts +interview (P Educ)
West Scotland – BBB incl Engl 120 pts +interview (Educ) (IB 32 pts HL 444 incl Engl)
York St John – 120 pts +interview (P Educ)

112 pts **Bedfordshire** – 112 pts +interview (P Educ QTS)
Birmingham City – BBC 112 pts (P Educ QTS) (IB 28 pts)
Bishop Grosseteste – 112 pts (P Educ QTS)
Canterbury Christ Church – 112 pts +interview (P Educ)
Cardiff Met – BBC 112 pts +interview (P Educ QTS) (IB 24 pts)
Edge Hill – BBC incl Engl 112 pts +interview (S Educ QTS courses)
Gloucestershire – BBC 112 pts +interview (P Educ QTS)
Greenwich – 112 pts +interview (P Educ QTS)
Hertfordshire – BBC 112 pts +interview (P Educ QTS)
Huddersfield – BBC 112 pts (Ely Yrs)
Hull – BBC 112 pts +interview (P Teach) (IB 28 pts)
Kingston – 112 pts +interview +test (P Teach QTS) (IB 26 pts)

Leeds Beckett – 112 pts +interview (P Educ (QTS)) (IB 26 pts)
Leeds Trinity – 112 pts +interview (P Educ courses (QTS))
Manchester Met – BBC incl maths +interview +test (S Maths Educ QTS) (IB 25 pts)
Marjon – BBC 112 pts +interview (PE (S Educ QTS))
Middlesex – 112 pts +interview (P Educ QTS)
Plymouth – 112 pts +interview (P) (IB 28 pts)
Roehampton – 112 pts +interview (P Educ QTS)
Sheffield Hallam – BBC 112 pts +interview (P Educ QTS)
UWE Bristol – 112 pts +interview (P Educ ITE)
Winchester – 112–120 pts +interview (P Educ QTS)
Worcester – 112 pts +interview (P ITE)

104 pts   **Canterbury Christ Church** – 104–112 pts incl maths (Maths S Educ QTS)
Chichester – BCC 104 pts +interview (P Teach Ely Yrs QTS) (IB 30 pts); BCC incl maths 104 pts +interview (Maths Teach KS 2+3) (IB 28 pts HL 5 maths)
Cumbria – 104–128 pts +interview (P Educ QTS)
Gloucestershire – BCC 104 pts (Educ)
Kent – B maths 104–112 pts (Maths S Educ) (IB 24 pts)
Leeds Beckett – 104 pts (P Educ 2 Yr) (IB 24 pts)
Nottingham Trent – BCC 104 pts (Educ SEN Incln)
Oxford Brookes – BCC 104 pts +interview (P Teach Educ) (IB 29 pts)
Winchester – 104–120 pts (Educ St courses) (HL 44); (Educ St (Ely Chld)) (IB 44)

96 pts   **Bath Spa** – CCC (Educ P Ely Yrs) (IB 26 pts)
Bedfordshire – BBB–CCC 96–120 pts (Educ; Ely Chld Educ)
Birmingham City – 96 pts +interview (Cond Educ)
Marjon – CCC 96 pts (P Educ QTS)
Northampton – CCC (Chld Yth)
St Mary's – BCC–CCC 96–104 pts +interview (P Educ QTS)
Wolverhampton – CCC/BCD 96 pts +interview +test (P Educ)

Alternative offers
See **Chapter 6** and **Appendix 1** for grades/UCAS Tariff points information for other examinations.

EXAMPLES OF COLLEGES OFFERING COURSES IN THIS SUBJECT FIELD
Bedford (Coll); Bishop Burton (Coll); Bradford College UC; Carshalton (Coll); Cornwall (Coll); Grŵp Llandrillo Menai; Kensington Bus (Coll); Leeds City (Coll); Loughborough (Coll); Myerscough (Coll); Nottingham (Coll); Sir Gâr (Coll); South Cheshire (Coll); South Devon (Coll); South Essex (Coll); Wakefield (Coll); Warwickshire (Coll); Wigan and Leigh (Coll); Wiltshire (Coll); Yeovil (Coll).

CHOOSING YOUR COURSE (SEE ALSO CH.1)
Universities and colleges teaching quality See www.qaa.ac.uk; https://unistats.ac.uk.

Top research universities and colleges (REF 2014) See **Education Studies**.

Examples of sandwich degree courses Reading.

ADMISSIONS INFORMATION
Number of applicants per place (approx) Bangor 4; Bishop Grosseteste 12; Cardiff Met 3; Durham 3; Edge Hill 17; Gloucestershire 20; Greenwich 3; Hull 5; Kingston 9; Marjon 5; Middlesex 7; Northampton 7; Nottingham Trent 11; Oxford Brookes 6; Plymouth 26; Roehampton 6; Sheffield Hallam 7; St Mary's 19; Strathclyde 7; West Scotland 7; Winchester 5; Wolverhampton 4; Worcester 21.

Admissions tutors' advice Winchester Functional Skills Level 2 English is not accepted for Teaching courses.

Advice to applicants and planning the UCAS personal statement Too many candidates are applying without the required **GCSE** qualifications in place or pending (maths, English, science). Any application for teacher training courses requires candidates to have experience of observation in schools and with children relevant to the choice of age range. Describe what you have learned from this. Any work with young people should be described in detail, indicating any problems which you may have seen which children create for the teacher. Applicants are strongly advised to have had some teaching practice prior to interview and should give evidence of time spent in a primary or secondary school and an analysis of activity undertaken with children. Give details of music qualifications, if any. Admissions tutors look for precise, succinct, well-reasoned, well-written statements (no mistakes!). See also **Chapter 5**. **Chichester** Minimum of two weeks spent observing or helping out in a state school required. **West Scotland** Review the General Teaching Council for Scotland website for the latest news. It is important to know the current teaching policy and processes, the impact of technology, changes within the classroom and Curriculum for Excellence. Visit a school and ask about 'the day in the life of a teacher'.

Misconceptions about this course Winchester This is an intensive programme with professional placements and students have more contact hours than those on other courses.

Selection interviews Yes Brighton, Edge Hill, Edinburgh, Glasgow, Hertfordshire, Huddersfield, Hull, Leeds Trinity, Marjon, Middlesex, Oxford Brookes, Reading, Roehampton, South Wales, Sunderland, Sussex, UWE Bristol, Wolverhampton, York St John; **Some** Cumbria, Durham, Greenwich, Leeds Beckett, Winchester; **No** Birmingham City, Cardiff Met, Gloucestershire.

Interview advice and questions Questions invariably focus on why you want to teach and your experiences in the classroom. In some cases, you may be asked to write an essay on these topics. Questions in the past have included: What do you think are important issues in education at present? Discussion of coursework will take place for Art applicants.

Reasons for rejection (non-academic) Unable to meet the requirements of written standard English. Ungrammatical personal statements. Lack of research about teaching at primary or secondary levels. Lack of experience in schools. Insufficient experience of working with people.

AFTER-RESULTS ADVICE
Offers to applicants repeating A-levels Possibly higher Cumbria; **Same** Bangor; Bishop Grosseteste; Brighton; Canterbury Christ Church; Chester; Durham; Liverpool Hope; Marjon; Nottingham Trent; Oxford Brookes; Roehampton; St Mary's; Stirling; Sunderland; Winchester; Wolverhampton; Worcester; York St John; **No** Kingston.

GRADUATE DESTINATIONS AND EMPLOYMENT (2016/17 HESA)
Graduates surveyed 8,850 **Employed** 6,940 **In voluntary employment** 70 **In further study** 560 **Assumed unemployed** 155

Career note See **Education Studies**.

OTHER DEGREE SUBJECTS FOR CONSIDERATION
Education Studies; Psychology; Social Policy; Social Sciences; Social Work.

TOURISM AND TRAVEL

(see also **Business and Management Courses, Business and Management Courses (International and European), Business and Management Courses (Specialised), Hospitality and Event Management, Leisure and Recreation Management/Studies**)

Tourism and Travel courses are popular; some are combined with Hospitality Management which thus provides students with two possible career paths. Courses involve business studies and a detailed study of tourism and travel. Industrial placements are frequently involved and language options are often included. See also **Appendix 3**.

Useful websites www.wttc.org; www.abta.com; www.thebapa.org.uk; www.itt.co.uk; www.tmi.org.uk

NB The points totals shown to the left of the institutions are for ease of reference only. It must not be assumed that Tariff points are always used by institutions or that they can be substituted for an offer in grades. The level of an offer is not necessarily indicative of the quality of a course.

COURSE OFFERS INFORMATION

Subject requirements/preferences GCSE English and mathematics required. **AL** No subjects specified.

Your target offers and examples of degree courses

144 pts **Strathclyde** – AAA incl maths (Acc Hspty Tour Mgt) (IB 38 pts HL 6 maths)

120 pts **Northumbria** – 120 pts (Bus Tour Mgt; Tour Evnts Mgt)
Strathclyde – ABB–BBB (Hspty Tour Mgt) (IB 36 pts)
Surrey – BBB (Int Hspty Tour Mgt; Int Tour Mgt) (IB 32 pts); BBB 120 pts (Int Tour Mgt Trans) (IB 32 pts)

112 pts **Derby** – BBC 112 pts (Int Tour Mgt)
East London – 112 pts (Tour Mgt) (IB 25 pts HL 15 pts)
Greenwich – 112 pts (Tour Mgt)
Huddersfield – BBC 112 pts (Trav Tour Mgt)
Lincoln – BBC 112 pts (Int Tour Mgt) (IB 29 pts)
Liverpool Hope – BBC 112 pts (Tour Comb Hons; Tour Mgt) (IB 28 pts)
Suffolk – BBC 112 pts +interview (Evnt Tour Mgt; Tour Mgt)
Sunderland – 112 pts (Int Tour Hspty Mgt); BBC 112 pts (Tour Mgt)
West London – BBC 112 pts (Trav Tour Mgt)
Westminster – ABB–BBC 112–128 pts (Tour Bus; Tour Plan Mgt) (IB 27 pts)

104 pts **Anglia Ruskin** – BCC 104 pts (Bus Tour Mgt) (IB 24 pts)
Birmingham (UC) – BCC 104 pts (Int Tour Mgt)
Bournemouth – 104–120 pts (Tour Mgt) (IB 31–28 pts)
Coventry – 104 pts (Tour Hspty Mgt)
Gloucestershire – BCC 104 pts (Int Hsptlty Rsrt Tour Mgt)
London South Bank – BCC (Tour Hspty Mgt)
Manchester Met – BBC–BCC 104–112 pts (Int Tour Mgt) (IB 26 pts)
Northampton – BCC (Int Tour Mgt)
Queen Margaret – BCC (Int Hspty Tour Mgt) (IB 28 pts)

96 pts **Aberystwyth** – BBB–CCC 96–120 pts (Tour Mgt) (IB 30–26 pts)
Bath Spa – CCC (Bus Mgt (Tour Mgt)) (IB 26 pts)
Birmingham (UC) – CCC 96 pts (Int Tour Bus Mgt)
Brighton – BCC–CCC 96–104 pts (Int Tour Mgt) (IB 26 pts)
Cardiff Met – 96–112 pts (Int Tour Evnts Mgt)
Central Lancashire – 96–104 pts (Int Tour Mgt)
Edinburgh Napier – CCC (Int Tour Airln Mgt; Int Tour Mgt) (IB 27 pts HL 654)
Hertfordshire – CCC 96 pts (Int Tour Mgt; Tour Mgt)
Leeds Beckett – 96 pts (Int Tour Mgt)
London Met – CCC 96 pts (Tour Trav Mgt)
Middlesex – 96 pts (Int Tour Mgt)
Robert Gordon – CCC (Int Tour Mgt) (IB 26 pts)
Solent – 96–112 pts (Int Trav Tour Mgt)
Ulster – CCC (Int Trav Tour Mgt) (IB 26–24 pts HL 13–12 pts)
Wolverhampton – CCC/BCD 96 pts (Tour Mgt)
York St John – 96 pts (Tour Dest Mgt)

88 pts **Canterbury Christ Church** – 88–112 pts (Tour Mgt; Tour St courses)
Plymouth – 88–96 pts (Tour Mgt) (IB 26–24 pts); (Int Tour Mgt) (IB 26–24 pts HL 4); 88–96 pts+interview (Cru Mgt) (IB 26–24 pts HL 4)
Trinity Saint David – 88 pts+interview (Int Trav Tour Mgt)

80 pts **Bedfordshire** – 80 pts (Trav Avn Tour Mgt); 80–96 pts (Int Tour Mgt)
Bucks New – 80 pts (Int Tour Mgt Air Trav)
Trinity Saint David – 80 pts +interview (Tour Mgt)

64 pts   UHI – CC (Advntr Tour Mgt)

Alternative offers
See **Chapter 6** and **Appendix 1** for grades/UCAS Tariff points information for other examinations.

EXAMPLES OF COLLEGES OFFERING COURSES IN THIS SUBJECT FIELD

Barnet and Southgate (Coll); Barnsley (Coll); Basingstoke (CT); Bedford (Coll); Birmingham Met (Coll); Bishop Burton (Coll); Blackburn (Coll); Blackpool and Fylde (Coll); Bournemouth and Poole (Coll); Bournville (Coll); Bradford College UC; Bury (Coll); Central Bedfordshire (Coll); Chelmsford (Coll); Cornwall (Coll); Craven (Coll); Dearne Valley (Coll); Derby (Coll); Dudley (Coll); Durham New (Coll); East Surrey (Coll); Greater Brighton Met (Coll); Grŵp Llandrillo Menai; Guildford (Coll); Highbury Portsmouth (Coll); Hugh Baird (Coll); Hull (Coll); Kingston (Coll); Lancaster and Morecambe (Coll); Leeds City (Coll); Leicester (Coll); Liverpool City (Coll); London City (Coll); London UCK (Coll); Loughborough (Coll); Manchester (Coll); MidKent (Coll); Neath Port Talbot (Coll); Nescot; Newcastle (Coll); North Kent (Coll); North Notts (Coll); North Warwickshire and South Leicestershire (Coll); Northumberland (Coll); Norwich City (Coll); Nottingham (Coll); Redcar and Cleveland (Coll); South Cheshire (Coll); South Devon (Coll); Sunderland (Coll); TEC Partnership; Uxbridge (Coll); West Cheshire (Coll); West Herts (Coll); West Nottinghamshire (Coll); West Thames (Coll); Westminster City (Coll); Westminster Kingsway (Coll); Weston (Coll); Windsor Forest (Coll); Wirral Met (Coll).

CHOOSING YOUR COURSE (SEE ALSO CH.1)

Universities and colleges teaching quality See www.qaa.ac.uk; https://unistats.ac.uk.

Examples of sandwich degree courses Birmingham (UC); Bournemouth; Brighton; Chester; Chichester; Gloucestershire; Greenwich; Hertfordshire; Leeds Beckett; Lincoln; Liverpool John Moores; Manchester Met; Middlesex; Northumbria; Plymouth; Portsmouth; Solent; Stirling; Sunderland; Surrey; Trinity Saint David; Ulster; Wolverhampton.

ADMISSIONS INFORMATION

Number of applicants per place (approx) Birmingham (UC) 10; Derby 4; Sunderland 2.

Advice to applicants and planning the UCAS personal statement Work experience in the travel and tourism industry is important – in agencies, in the airline industry or hotels. This work should be described in detail. Any experience with people in sales work, dealing with the public – their problems and complaints – should also be included. Travel should be outlined, detailing places visited. Genuine interest in travel, diverse cultures and people. Good communication skills required. See also **Appendix 3**.

Misconceptions about this course Wolverhampton Some applicants are uncertain whether or not to take a Business Management course instead of Tourism Management. They should be aware that the latter will equip them with a tourism-specific knowledge of business.

Selection interviews Yes Plymouth; **No** Anglia Ruskin, Brighton, Derby, Sunderland, Surrey.

Interview advice and questions Past questions have included: What problems have you experienced when travelling? Questions on places visited. Experiences of air, rail and sea travel. What is marketing? What special qualities do you have that will be of use in the travel industry? See also **Chapter 5**.

Reasons for rejection (non-academic) Wolverhampton English language competence.

AFTER-RESULTS ADVICE

Offers to applicants repeating A-levels Same Anglia Ruskin; Birmingham (UC); Chester; Derby; Lincoln; Manchester Met; Northumbria; St Mary's; Wolverhampton.

GRADUATE DESTINATIONS AND EMPLOYMENT (2016/17 HESA)

Graduates surveyed See **Hospitality and Event Management**.

Career note See **Business and Management Courses**.

OTHER DEGREE SUBJECTS FOR CONSIDERATION

Airline and Airport Management; Business Studies; Events Management; Heritage Management; Hospitality Management; Leisure and Recreation Management; Travel Management.

TOWN AND URBAN PLANNING

(See also **Development Studies, Environmental Sciences, Housing, Surveying and Real Estate Management, Transport Management and Planning**)

Town and Urban Planning courses are very similar and some lead to qualification or part of a qualification as a member of the Royal Town Planning Institute (RTPI). Further information from the RTPI (see **Appendix 3**).

Useful websites www.rtpi.org.uk

NB The points totals shown to the left of the institutions are for ease of reference only. It must not be assumed that Tariff points are always used by institutions or that they can be substituted for an offer in grades. The level of an offer is not necessarily indicative of the quality of a course.

COURSE OFFERS INFORMATION

Subject requirements/preferences GCSE English and mathematics required. **AL** Geography may be specified. Note that a number of universities in the table below do not accept the UCAS tariff.

Your target offers and examples of degree courses

152 pts **Cambridge** – A*AA +interview +TSA (Lnd Econ) (IB 42–40 pts HL 776)
136 pts **London (UCL)** – AAB (Urb Plan Rl Est) (IB 36 pts HL 17 pts)
        London LSE – AAB (Env Dev) (IB 37 pts HL 666)
128 pts **Birmingham** – ABB (Geog Urb Reg Plan Comb Hons) (IB 32 pts HL 655)
        Liverpool – ABB (Twn Reg Plan) (IB 33 pts)
        London (UCL) – ABB (Urb St) (IB 34 pts HL 16 pts)
        Loughborough – ABB (Urb Plan) (IB 34 pts HL 655)
        Manchester – ABB (Env Mgt) (IB 34 pts HL 655)
        Queen's Belfast – ABB (Plan Env Dev) (IB 33 pts HL 655)
        Sheffield – ABB–BBB +bEPQ (Geog Plan) (IB 33 pts)
120 pts **Cardiff** – ABB–BBB (Hum Geog Plan) (HL 665)
        Dundee – BBB (Urb Plan) (IB 30 pts HL 555)
        Liverpool – BBB (Env Plan; Urb Plan) (IB 31 pts)
        Nottingham Trent – BBB 120 pts (Prop Dev Plan)
        Sheffield – BBB–BBC +bEPQ (Urb St; Urb St Plan) (IB 32 pts)
112 pts **Cardiff** – BBB–BBC (Urb Plan Dev) (HL 665–655)
        Derby – 112 pts (Log Sply Chn Mgt)
        Heriot-Watt – BBC (Urb Plan Prop Dev) (IB 29 pts)
        Leeds Beckett – 112 pts (Hum Geog Plan) (IB 25 pts)
        Newcastle – ABB–BBC (Urb Plan) (IB 32–28 pts)
        Oxford Brookes – BBC 112 pts (Plan Prop Dev; Urb Des Plan Dev) (IB 30 pts)
        Westminster – ABB–BBC 112–128 pts (Prop Plan) (IB 27 pts); ABB–BBC 112–128 pts +interview
           +portfolio (Des Cits Plan Archit) (IB 27 pts)
104 pts **London South Bank** – BCC (Urb Env Plan)
        UWE Bristol – 104 pts (Urb Plan)

Alternative offers
See **Chapter 6** and **Appendix 1** for grades/UCAS Tariff points information for other examinations.

CHOOSING YOUR COURSE (SEE ALSO CH.1)

Universities and colleges teaching quality See www.qaa.ac.uk; https://unistats.ac.uk.

Top research universities and colleges (REF 2014) See **Architecture**.

Examples of sandwich degree courses Cardiff; Nottingham Trent.

ADMISSIONS INFORMATION
Number of applicants per place (approx) Birmingham 2; Cardiff 6; Dundee 8; London (UCL) 6; London South Bank 3; Manchester 9; Newcastle 4; Oxford Brookes 4.

Advice to applicants and planning the UCAS personal statement Visit your local planning office and discuss the career with planners. Know plans and proposed developments in your area and any objections to them. Study the history of town planning worldwide and the development of new towns in the UK during the 20th century, for example Bournville, Milton Keynes, Port Sunlight, Welwyn Garden City, Cumbernauld, and the advantages and disadvantages which became apparent. See also **Appendix 3**. **Oxford Brookes** See **Surveying and Real Estate Management**.

Selection interviews Some Cardiff; **No** Dundee, Harper Adams, London (UCL), Newcastle, Oxford Brookes.

Interview advice and questions Since Town and Urban Planning courses are vocational, work experience in a planning office is relevant and questions are likely to be asked on the type of work done and the problems faced by planners. Questions in recent years have included: If you were re-planning your home county for the future, what points would you consider? How are statistics used in urban planning? How do you think the problem of inner cities can be solved? Have you visited your local planning office? See also **Chapter 5**.

Reasons for rejection (non-academic) Lack of commitment to study for a professional qualification in Town Planning.

AFTER-RESULTS ADVICE
Offers to applicants repeating A-levels Higher Newcastle; **Same** Cardiff; Dundee; London South Bank; Oxford Brookes.

GRADUATE DESTINATIONS AND EMPLOYMENT (2016/17 HESA)
Planning (urban, rural and regional) Graduates surveyed 485 **Employed** 300 **In voluntary employment** 0 **In further study** 115 **Assumed unemployed** 20

Career note Town Planning graduates have a choice of career options within local authority planning offices. In addition to working on individual projects on urban development, they will also be involved in advising, co-ordinating and adjudicating in disputes and appeals. Planners also work closely with economists, surveyors and sociologists and their skills open up a wide range of other careers.

OTHER DEGREE SUBJECTS FOR CONSIDERATION
Architecture; Countryside Management; Environmental Studies; Geography; Heritage Management; Housing; Land Economy; Property; Public Administration; Real Estate; Sociology; Surveying; Transport Management.

TRANSPORT MANAGEMENT AND PLANNING

(including **Aviation Management, Cruise Management and Transport Design;** see also **Engineering/Engineering Sciences, Town and Urban Planning**)

Transport Management and Planning is a specialised branch of business studies with many applications on land, sea and air. It is not as popular as the less specialised Business Studies courses but is just as relevant and will provide the student with an excellent introduction to management and its problems.

Useful websites www.nats.aero; www.ciltuk.org.uk

NB The points totals shown to the left of the institutions are for ease of reference only. It must not be assumed that Tariff points are always used by institutions or that they can be substituted for an offer in grades. The level of an offer is not necessarily indicative of the quality of a course.

COURSE OFFERS INFORMATION

Subject requirements/preferences GCSE English and mathematics required. **AL** No subjects specified.

Your target offers and examples of degree courses
136 pts   **Leeds** – AAB incl geog (Geog Trans St) (IB 35 pts HL 16 pts incl 5 geog)
128 pts   **Cardiff** – AAB–ABB (Bus Mgt (Log Ops)) (IB 34–32 pts HL 665–655)
120 pts   **Coventry** – ABB–BBB (Avn Mgt) (IB 31 pts)
         Huddersfield – BBB 120 pts (Air Trans Log Mgt)
         Northumbria – 120 pts (Bus Log Sply Chn Mgt)
         Surrey – BBB 120 pts (Int Tour Mgt Trans) (IB 32 pts)
112 pts   **Aston** – BBB–BBC (Trans Mgt) (IB 28 pts HL 544 incl sci/tech)
         Coventry – BBC incl art/des +interview +portfolio (Auto Trans Des) (IB 27 pts HL incl vis art/
           des tech)
         Derby – 112 pts (Log Sply Chn Mgt)
         Greenwich – 112 pts (Bus Log Trans Mgt)
         Huddersfield – BBC 112 pts (Trans Log Mgt)
         Staffordshire – BBC 112 pts (Ind Des Prod Trans)
         West London – BBC 112 pts (Airln Airpt Mgt; Strat Trans Mgt)
96 pts   **Birmingham (UC)** – CCC 96 pts (Avn Airpt Mgt)
        Bucks New – 96 pts (Air Trans Commer Plt Trg)
        London Met – CCC 96 pts (Airln Airpt Avn Mgt)
        Sheffield Hallam – CCC 96 pts (Airln Airpt Mgt)
        Solent – 96–112 pts (Int Airln Airpt Mgt)
88 pts   **Plymouth** – 88–96 pts +interview (Cru Mgt) (IB 26–24 pts HL 4)
80 pts   **Bucks New** – 80–96 pts (Airln Airpt Mgt)
72 pts   **West London** – BC/DDD 72 pts (Strat Trans Mgt Fdn Yr)
64 pts   **Newcastle (Coll)** – 64 pts (Airln Airpt Mgt)
48 pts   **Middlesbrough (Coll)** – 48 pts +interview (Airpt Airln Mgt)
32 pts   **Plymouth** – 32–80 pts (Marit Bus Log Fdn Yr) (IB 25–24 pts HL 4)

Alternative offers
See **Chapter 6** and **Appendix 1** for grades/UCAS Tariff points information for other examinations.

EXAMPLES OF COLLEGES OFFERING COURSES IN THIS SUBJECT FIELD

Bedford (Coll); Blackburn (Coll); Craven (Coll); MidKent (Coll); Myerscough (Coll); Newcastle (Coll); Norwich City (Coll); TEC Partnership; Wirral Met (Coll).

CHOOSING YOUR COURSE (SEE ALSO CH.1)

Universities and colleges teaching quality See www.qaa.ac.uk; https://unistats.ac.uk.

Examples of sandwich degree courses Aston; Coventry; Huddersfield; Liverpool John Moores; Loughborough.

ADMISSIONS INFORMATION

Number of applicants per place (approx) Aston 5; Huddersfield 3.

Advice to applicants and planning the UCAS personal statement Air, sea, road and rail transport are the main specialist areas. Contacts with those involved and work experience or work shadowing should be described in full. See also **Appendix 3**.

Selection interviews Yes Plymouth; **No** Aston, Bucks New, Huddersfield, Loughborough.

Interview advice and questions Some knowledge of the transport industry (land, sea and air) is likely to be important at interview. Reading around the subject is also important, as are any contacts with management staff in the industries. Past questions have included: What developments are taking place to reduce the number of cars on the roads? What transport problems are there in your own locality? How did you travel to your interview? What problems did you encounter? How could they have been overcome? See also **Chapter 5**.

AFTER-RESULTS ADVICE
Offers to applicants repeating A-levels Same Aston.

GRADUATE DESTINATIONS AND EMPLOYMENT
Career note Many graduates will aim for openings linked with specialisms in their degree courses. These could cover air, rail, sea, bus or freight transport in which they will be involved in the management and control of operations as well as marketing and financial operations.

OTHER DEGREE SUBJECTS FOR CONSIDERATION
Air Transport Engineering; Civil Engineering; Environmental Studies; Logistics; Marine Transport; Town and Country Planning; Urban Studies.

VETERINARY SCIENCE/MEDICINE

(including **Bioveterinary Sciences and Veterinary Nursing**; see also **Animal Sciences**)

Veterinary Medicine/Science degrees enable students to acquire the professional skills and experience to qualify as veterinary surgeons. Courses follow the same pattern, combining scientific training with practical experience. The demand for these courses is considerable (see below) and work experience is essential prior to application. For those with good degrees in specified subjects, graduate entry programmes can lead to veterinary qualification. See also **Appendix 3**.

Veterinary Nursing Honours degree courses combine both the academic learning and the nursing training required by the Royal College of Veterinary Surgeons, and can also include practice management. Foundation degrees in Veterinary Nursing are more widely available. Bioveterinary Sciences are usually three-year full-time BSc degree courses focusing on animal biology, management and disease, but do not qualify graduates to work as vets. For places in Veterinary Science/Medicine, applicants may select only four universities. Applicants to the University of Cambridge Veterinary School are required to sit the BioMedical Admissions Test (BMAT) (see **Chapter 5**).

Useful websites www.rcvs.org.uk; www.admissionstesting.org; www.bvna.org.uk; http://spvs.org.uk; www.bva.co.uk

NB The points totals shown to the left of the institutions are for ease of reference only. It must not be assumed that Tariff points are always used by institutions or that they can be substituted for an offer in grades. The level of an offer is not necessarily indicative of the quality of a course.

COURSE OFFERS INFORMATION
Subject requirements/preferences GCSE (Vet Sci/Med) Grade B (5/6) English, mathematics, physics, dual science if not at A-level. **AL** (Vet Sci/Med) See offers below. (Vet Nurs) Biology and another science may be required. Other Work experience essential for Veterinary Science/Medicine and Veterinary Nursing courses and preferred for other courses: check requirements. Health checks may be required. **Bristol** (Vet Sci) **GCSE** Grade A (7) in five subjects. Grade A (7) in mathematics if neither mathematics nor physics is offered at grade A at AS/A-level. **Glasgow** (Vet Med) **GCSE** Grade B (6) in English. **Liverpool** (Vet Sci) Minimum of seven GCSEs at grades AAABBBB (A/7 and B/6) or above, including English, mathematics and physics (either as a separate subject or as dual award science) are required. **London (RVC)** (Vet Med) **GCSE** Grade A (7) in five subjects. **Nottingham** (Vet Med) **GCSE** Grade A (7) in five subjects.

Your target offers and examples of degree courses

152 pts **Cambridge** – A*AA incl chem+sci/maths +interview +NSAA (Vet Med) (IB 42–40 pts HL 776 incl chem+sci/maths)

144 pts **Bristol** – AAA/A*AB incl chem+sci/maths +interview (Vet Sci) (IB 36 pts HL 18 pts incl 6 chem+sci/maths)

Edinburgh – AAA incl chem+biol +interview (Vet Med) (IB 38 pts HL 666 incl chem+biol)

Glasgow – AAA incl chem+biol +interview (Vet Med Srgy) (IB 38 pts HL 666 incl chem+biol)

Liverpool – AAA incl biol+chem (Vet Sci) (IB 36 pts HL 666 incl biol+chem)

London (RVC) – AAA incl chem+biol +interview (Vet Med) (IB 34 pts HL 766 incl chem+biol)

136 pts **Harper Keele Vet Sch** – AAB incl biol/chem+sci +interview (Vet Med Srgy) (IB 34 pts HL 666 incl biol/chem+sci)

Nottingham – AAB (Vet Med Srgy Prelim Yr) (IB 34 pts HL 665); AAB incl chem+biol (Vet Med Srgy) (IB 34 pts HL 665 incl biol+chem)

Surrey – AAB incl chem+biol +interview (Vet Med Sci) (IB 34 pts)

128 pts **Glasgow** – ABB incl chem+biol (Vet Biosci) (IB 36 pts HL 665)

Hartpury (Coll) – ABB incl biol (Biovet Sci)

Liverpool – ABB incl biol+sci (Biovet Sci) (IB 33 pts HL 6 biol)

120 pts **Lincoln** – BBB incl biol/chem 120 pts (Biovet Sci) (IB 30 pts HL 5 biol/chem)

London (RVC) – ABB–BBB incl chem/biol+sci/maths (Biovet Sci) (HL 655–555 incl chem/ biol+sci/maths)

Surrey – BBB incl biol+sci/maths (Vet Biosci) (IB 32 pts)

112 pts **Bristol** – BBC incl biol+chem (Vet Nurs Biovet Sci) (IB 29 pts HL 14 pts incl 5 biol+chem); BBC incl biol/chem +interview (Gateway Vet Sci) (IB 29 pts HL 5 biol/chem)

Nottingham – BBC incl biol+chem (Vet Med Gateway Yr) (IB 28 pts HL 554 incl 5 biol+chem)

104 pts **Aberystwyth** – ABB–BCC incl biol 104–128 pts (Eqn Vet Biosci; Vet Biosci) (IB 30–28 pts HL 5 biol)

Bishop Burton (Coll) – 104 pts (Biovet Sci)

Edinburgh Napier – BCC incl sci (Vet Nurs) (IB 28 pts HL 654 incl sci)

Harper Adams – 104–120 pts (Biovet Sci) (IB 28 pts HL 5)

London (RVC) – BCC incl biol +interview (Vet Nurs) (HL 544 incl 5 biol)

96 pts **Harper Adams** – C biol 96–112 pts +interview (Vet Nurs courses; Vet Physio) (IB 28 pts HL 6 biol)

London (RVC) – CCC incl chem+biol +interview (Vet Gateway) (HL 444 incl biol+chem)

Middlesex – CCC incl biol 96 pts +interview (Vet Nurs)

Writtle (UC) – C sci 96 pts (Biovet Sci) (IB 24 pts)

80 pts **Sparsholt (Coll)** – CCE incl lf sci (Vet Nurs (FdSc)) (IB 25 pts HL 4 biol)

64 pts **Nottingham Trent** – C sci 64 pts +interview (Vet Nurs)

48 pts **Cornwall (Coll)** – 48 pts +interview (Vet Nurs)

Glyndŵr – 48 pts +interview (Vet Nurs)

Alternative offers

See **Chapter 6** and **Appendix 1** for grades/UCAS Tariff points information for other examinations.

EXAMPLES OF COLLEGES OFFERING COURSES IN THIS SUBJECT FIELD

Askham Bryan (Coll); Bishop Burton (Coll); Canterbury (Coll); Chichester (Coll); Cornwall (Coll); Derby (Coll); Duchy Coll UC; Easton Otley (Coll); Hartpury (Coll); Kingston Maurward (Coll); Leeds City (Coll); Myerscough (Coll); Northumberland (Coll); Plumpton (Coll); Sheffield (Coll); Sir Gâr (Coll); Sparsholt (Coll); Warwickshire (Coll); West Anglia (Coll).

CHOOSING YOUR COURSE (SEE ALSO CH.1)

Universities and colleges teaching quality See www.qaa.ac.uk; https://unistats.ac.uk.

Top research universities and colleges (REF 2014) (Agriculture, Veterinary and Food Science) Warwick; Cambridge; Nottingham; Aberdeen; Glasgow; East Anglia; Bristol; Stirling; Queen's Belfast; Liverpool; Reading.

Examples of sandwich degree courses Harper Adams.

ADMISSIONS INFORMATION
Number of applicants per place (approx) Bristol (Vet Sci) 9, (Vet Nurs Biovet Sci) 12; Cambridge 4; Edinburgh 12; Glasgow 20; Liverpool 6; London (RVC) 5; Nottingham 10.

Advice to applicants and planning the UCAS personal statement Applicants for Veterinary Science must limit their choices to four universities and submit their applications by 15 October. They may add one alternative course. Work experience is almost always essential so discuss this in full, giving information about the size and type of practice and the type of work in which you were involved. As described below, there are several alternative options for work experience. These include work at a veterinary practice involving domestic animals, city and rural farms with dairy, beef cattle, sheep, pigs or poultry, kennels, catteries, laboratories, pet shops, wildlife parks, abattoirs and zoos. See also **Appendix 3**. **Bristol** Eight weeks of work experience, preferably including four weeks of veterinary experience in more than one practice and four weeks in a range of animal establishments. **Cambridge** Work experience expected. **Edinburgh** Competition for places is intense: 125 places are available for the 5-year programme and there are approximately 1,000 applicants each year. The strongest candidates are invited to an interview consisting of seven 10 minute stations that will focus on the applicants' work experience, awareness of animal welfare, career exploration, numeracy skills, data interpretation, ethical issues and a practical manual task. **Edinburgh Napier** For Vet Nursing, applicants must have 4 weeks' work experience in a veterinary practice and this must be stated in their personal statement. **Glasgow** A minimum of two weeks in a veterinary practice plus experience of work on a dairy farm, working at a stables, assisting at lambing, work at a cattery or kennels and if possible a visit to an abattoir. Additional experience at a zoo or wildlife park. **Liverpool** The selection process involves three areas: academic ability to cope with the course; knowledge of vocational aspects of veterinary science acquired through work experience in veterinary practice and 10 further weeks of experience working with animals; personal attributes that demonstrate responsibility and self motivation. **London (RVC)** (Vet Med) Hands-on experience needed: two weeks in a veterinary practice, and two weeks in another animal environment, such as a riding school, zoo or kennels. **Nottingham** Six weeks (minimum) of work experience required.

Misconceptions about this course Liverpool (Biovet Sci) Some applicants think that the course allows students to transfer to Veterinary Science: it does not.

Selection interviews Yes Cambridge, Edinburgh, Edinburgh Napier, Glasgow, Harper Adams, Liverpool (Interview advice can be found on http://www.liverpool.ac.uk/veterinary-science/undergraduate/prospective-applicants/), London (RVC), Nottingham, Surrey.

Interview advice and questions Past questions have included: Why do you want to be a vet? Have you visited a veterinary practice? What did you see? Do you think there should be a Vet National Health Service? What are your views on vivisection? What are your views on intensive factory farming? How can you justify thousands of pounds of taxpayers' money being spent on training you to be a vet when it could be used to train a civil engineer? When would you feel it your responsibility to tell battery hen farmers that they were being cruel to their livestock? What are your views on vegetarians? How does aspirin stop pain? Why does it only work for a certain length of time? Do you eat beef? Outline the bovine TB problem. Questions on A-level science syllabus. See also **Chapter 5**. **Glasgow** Applicants complete a questionnaire prior to interview. Questions cover experience with animals, reasons for choice of career, animal welfare, teamwork, work experience, stressful situations.

Reasons for rejection (non-academic) Failure to demonstrate motivation. Lack of basic knowledge or understanding of ethical and animal issues.

AFTER-RESULTS ADVICE
Offers to applicants repeating A-levels Higher Liverpool; **Same** London (RVC); **No** Cambridge; Edinburgh; Glasgow.

GRADUATE DESTINATIONS AND EMPLOYMENT (2016/17 HESA)
Graduates surveyed 645 **Employed** 590 **In voluntary employment** 15 **In further study** 15
Assumed unemployed 10

Career note Most veterinary surgeons work in private practice with the remainder involved in research in universities, government-financed research departments and in firms linked with farming, foodstuff manufacturers and pharmaceutical companies.

OTHER DEGREE SUBJECTS FOR CONSIDERATION
Agricultural Science; Agriculture; Animal Sciences; Biological Sciences; Biology; Dentistry; Equine Dental Science; Equine Management; Equine Studies; Medicine; Zoology.

ZOOLOGY

(including **Animal Biology**; see also **Agricultural Sciences/Agriculture, Animal Sciences, Biological Sciences, Biology**)

Zoology courses have a biological science foundation and could cover animal ecology, marine and fisheries biology, animal population, development and behaviour and, on some courses, wildlife management and fisheries.

Useful websites www.biaza.org.uk; www.zsl.org; www.abwak.org

NB The points totals shown to the left of the institutions are for ease of reference only. It must not be assumed that Tariff points are always used by institutions or that they can be substituted for an offer in grades. The level of an offer is not necessarily indicative of the quality of a course.

COURSE OFFERS INFORMATION
Subject requirements/preferences GCSE English and science/mathematics required or preferred. **AL** One or two sciences will be required.

Your target offers and examples of degree courses
160 pts Cambridge – A*A*A incl sci/maths +interview +NSAA (Nat Sci (Zool)) (IB 42–40 pts HL 776)
144 pts London (UCL) – AAA incl biol+sci/maths (Biol Sci (Zool)) (IB 38 pts HL 18 pts incl 6 biol+sci/maths)
     Sheffield – AAA incl biol+sci (Zool (MBiol)) (IB 36 pts HL 6 biol+sci)
136 pts Birmingham – AAB incl biol+sci (Biol Sci (Zool)) (IB 32 pts HL 665 incl biol+sci)
     Bristol – AAB incl sci/maths (Zool) (IB 34 pts HL 17 pts incl 6/5 sci/maths)
     Glasgow – AAB incl biol/chem (Zool) (IB 36 pts HL 665 incl sci)
     Lancaster – AAB incl sci/maths (Zool) (IB 35 pts HL 16 pts incl 6 sci)
     Leeds – AAA–AAB incl biol+sci (Zool) (IB 35–34 pts HL 18–17 pts incl 6 biol+sci)
     Nottingham – AAB incl biol+sci (Zool) (IB 34 pts HL 6/5 biol+sci)
     Sheffield – AAA–AAB incl biol+sci (Zool) (IB 36–34 pts HL 6 biol+sci)
     Southampton – AAB incl biol+sci/maths (Zool) (IB 34 pts HL 17 pts incl 6/5 biol+sci/maths)
     St Andrews – AAB incl biol+sci/maths (Zool) (IB 36 pts HL 665 incl 6 biol+sci/maths)
128 pts Cardiff – AAB–ABB incl biol/chem (Biol Sci (Zool)) (IB 34-32 pts HL 655 incl 6 biol/chem)
     Edinburgh – AAA–ABB incl biol+chem (Biol Sci (Zool)) (IB 37–32 pts HL 666–555 incl biol+chem)
     Exeter – AAB–ABB incl sci/maths (Zool (Cornwall)) (IB 34–32 pts HL 665–655 incl sci/maths)
     Leicester – ABB incl sci/maths (Biol Sci (Zool)) (IB 30 pts HL 6/5 sci/maths)
     Liverpool – ABB incl biol+sci (Zool) (IB 33 pts HL 6 biol)
     London (QM) – ABB incl biol (Zool) (IB 34 pts HL 655 incl biol)
     Manchester – AAA–ABB (Zool Modn Lang) (IB 36–33 pts HL 6–5 sci); AAA–ABB incl sci/maths +interview (Zool; Zool (Yr Ind)) (IB 36–33 pts HL 666–655 incl sci)
     Sussex – AAB–ABB (Zool) (IB 34–32 pts HL 5 sci)

120 pts   **Aberdeen** – BBB incl maths/sci (Zool) (IB 32 pts HL 555 incl maths/sci)
        Bangor – 120 pts incl biol (Mar Biol Zool); 120 pts incl biol+sci (Mar Vert Zool)
        Derby – C biol 120 pts (Zool)
        Hull – BBB 120 pts (Zool) (IB 30 pts HL 5 biol)
        Lincoln – BBB incl biol 120 pts (Zool) (IB 30 pts HL 5 biol)
        London (RH) – ABB–BBB incl biol (Zool) (IB 32 pts HL 555 incl biol)
        Newcastle – AAB–BBB incl biol+sci (Zool) (IB 34–32 pts HL 6 biol); ABB–BBB incl biol+sci
            (Mar Zool) (IB 32 pts)
        Queen's Belfast – BBB incl biol+sci/maths/geog (Zool) (IB 32 pts HL 655 incl sci/maths/geog)
        Reading – BBB incl biol+sci/maths (Zool) (IB 30 pts HL 5 biol+sci)
        Stirling – BBB incl biol+sci (Anim Biol) (IB 32 pts)
        Swansea – ABB–BBB incl biol (Zool) (IB 33–32 pts HL 5 biol)
112 pts   **Anglia Ruskin** – 112 pts incl biol (Zool) (IB 24 pts)
        Bangor – 112 pts incl biol (Zool Herp) (HL 5 biol); 112 pts incl biol+sci (Zool; Zool Cons; Zool
            Mar Zool) (HL 5 biol)
        Gloucestershire – BBC 112 pts (Anim Biol)
        Hartpury (Coll) – BBC incl biol (Zool)
        Liverpool John Moores – BBC incl biol 112 pts (Zool) (IB 26 pts)
        Nottingham Trent – BBC incl biol 112 pts (Zoo Biol)
        Roehampton – 112 pts incl biol/sci (Zool)
104 pts   **Aberystwyth** – BBB–BCC incl biol 104–120 pts (Anim Bhv; Zool) (IB 30–28 pts HL 5 biol)
        Chester – BBC–BCC incl biol/chem 104–112 pts (Zool) (IB 26 pts HL 5 biol); BBC–BCC incl biol
            104–112 pts (Anim Bhv Biol/Psy) (IB 26 pts HL 5 biol)
        Harper Adams – 104 pts (App Zool; Zool Entomol; Zool Env Mgt) (IB 28 pts)
        Manchester Met – BBC–BCC incl biol 104–112 pts (Anim Bhv; Wldlf Biol) (IB 26 pts HL 5 biol)
        Myerscough (Coll) – 104 pts +interview (Zool) (IB 24 pts)
        Oxford Brookes – BCC 104 pts (Anim Biol Cons) (IB 29 pts HL sci); BCC incl sci 104 pts (Biol
            Sci (Zool)) (IB 29 pts)
        Salford – 104–112 pts incl biol (Zool) (IB 30 pts HL 4 biol)
96 pts   **Cumbria** – BBC–CCC 96–112 pts +interview +portfolio (Wldlf Media)
        Worcester – 96–104 pts incl biol/sci (Anim Biol)
88 pts   **Reading** – BBB–CCD (Zool Fdn) (IB 30–24 pts)
        West Scotland – CCD incl biol 88–102 pts (App Biosci Zool) (IB 24 pts)
80 pts   **Cornwall (Coll)** – 80 pts (App Mar Zool)
        South Wales – BCC–CDD incl sci 80–112 pts (Nat Hist); BCC–CDD incl biol+sci 80–112 pts (Int
            Wldlf Biol)
64 pts   **Reaseheath (UC)** – 64 pts (Zoo Mgt)

Alternative offers
See **Chapter 6** and **Appendix 1** for grades/UCAS Tariff points information for other examinations.

EXAMPLES OF COLLEGES OFFERING COURSES IN THIS SUBJECT FIELD
Bishop Burton (Coll); Cornwall (Coll); Craven (Coll); Dudley (Coll); Easton Otley (Coll); Guildford (Coll); South Gloucestershire and Stroud (Coll); Sparsholt (Coll).

CHOOSING YOUR COURSE (SEE ALSO CH.1)
Universities and colleges teaching quality See www.qaa.ac.uk; https://unistats.ac.uk.

Examples of sandwich degree courses Cardiff; Leeds; Liverpool John Moores; Manchester; Nottingham Trent; Reading.

ADMISSIONS INFORMATION
Number of applicants per place (approx) Bangor 5; Bristol 6; Leeds 7; Liverpool John Moores 6; London (RH) 5; Newcastle 5; Nottingham 9; Southampton 7; Swansea 6.

Advice to applicants and planning the UCAS personal statement Interests in animals should be described, together with any first-hand experience gained. Visits to zoos, farms, fish farms, etc and field courses attended should be described, together with any special points of interest you noted.

Selection interviews Yes Manchester; **Some** Southampton; **No** Derby, Hull, Liverpool, London (RH), Newcastle, Roehampton, Swansea.

Interview advice and questions Past questions have included: Why do you want to study Zoology? What career do you hope to follow on graduation? Specimens may be given to identify. Questions usually asked on A-level subjects. See also **Chapter 5**.

AFTER-RESULTS ADVICE
Offers to applicants repeating A-levels Higher Bristol; Leeds; Swansea; **Same** Aberystwyth; Bangor; Derby; Hull; Liverpool; Liverpool John Moores; London (RH); Roehampton.

GRADUATE DESTINATIONS AND EMPLOYMENT (2016/17 HESA)
Graduates surveyed 1,140 **Employed** 435 **In voluntary employment** 70 **In further study** 350 **Assumed unemployed** 65

Career note See **Biology**.

OTHER DEGREE SUBJECTS FOR CONSIDERATION
Animal Ecology; Animal Sciences; Aquaculture; Biological Sciences; Biology; Ecology; Fisheries Management; Marine Biology; Parasitology; Veterinary Science; Wildlife Management.

INFORMATION FOR INTERNATIONAL STUDENTS

The choice of a subject to study (from over 50,000 degree courses) and of a university or college (from more than 150 institutions) is a major task for students living in the UK. For overseas and EU applicants it is even greater, and the decisions that have to be made need much careful planning, preferably beginning two years before the start of the course. **NB** Beware that there are some private institutions offering bogus degrees: check www.ucas.com to ensure your university and college choices are legitimate.

APPLICATIONS AND THE POINTS-BASED IMMIGRATION SYSTEM

In addition to submitting your application through UCAS (see **Chapter 4**) a Points-based Immigration System is in operation for overseas students. The main features of this system include:

- **Confirmation of Acceptance for Studies (CAS) number** When you accept an offer the institution will send you a CAS number which you will need to include on your visa application.
- **Maintenance** Students will need to show that they are able to pay for the first year's tuition fees, plus £1,265 per month for accommodation and living expenses if you are studying in London (which includes the University of London, institutions fully or partially in London, or in parts of Surrey, Hertfordshire and Essex), and £1,015 per month if you are studying in the rest of the UK. Additional funds and regulations apply for those bringing dependants into the UK.
- **Proof of qualifications** Your visa letter will list all the qualifications that you submitted to obtain your university place and original proof will be required of these qualifications when submitting your visa application. These documents will be checked by the Home Office. Any fraudulent documents will result in your visa application being rejected and a possible ban from entering the UK for 10 years.
- **Attendance** Once you have started your course, your attendance will be monitored. Non-attending students will be reported to the UK Border Agency.

Full details can be obtained from www.ukcisa.org.uk.

SELECTION, ADMISSION AND FINANCE

The first reason for making early contact with your preferred institution is to check their requirements for your chosen subject and their selection policies for overseas applicants. For example, for most Art and some Architecture courses you will have to present a portfolio of work or slides. For Music courses your application often will have to be accompanied by a recording you have made of your playing or singing and, in many cases, a personal audition will be necessary. Attendance at an interview in this country is compulsory for some universities and for some courses. At other institutions the interview may take place either via Skype or with a university or college representative in your own country.

The ability to speak and write good English is essential and many institutions require evidence of competence, for example scores from the International English Language Testing System (IELTS) or from the Trinity College London test (see www.ielts.org and www.trinitycollege.com/qualifications/SELT/UKVI). For some institutions, you may have to send examples of your written work. Each institution provides information about its English language entry requirements and a summary of this is given for each university listed below. International students should note that the recommended threshold for minimum English language requirements is IELTS 6.5–7.0 and an overall score of 5.5 (including 5.5 in each of the four skills) is a requirement for the visa application. Recent research indicates that students with a lower score may have difficulty in dealing with their course.

In the next chapter you will find a directory of universities and colleges in the UK, together with their contact details. Most universities and colleges in the UK have an overseas student adviser who can advise you on these and other points you need to consider, such as passports, visas, entry certificates, evidence of financial support, medical certificates, medical insurance, and the numbers of overseas students in the university from your own country. All these details are very important and need to be considered at the same time as choosing your course and institution.

The subject tables in **Chapter 7** provide a comprehensive picture of courses on offer and of comparative entry levels. However, before making an application, other factors should be considered, such as English language entry requirements (see above), the availability of English language teaching, living costs, tuition fees and any scholarships or other awards which might be offered. Detailed information about these can be obtained from the international offices in each university or college, British higher education fairs throughout the world and also the British Council (www.britishcouncil.org) offices abroad.

Below is a brief summary of the arrangements made by each university in the UK for international students aiming to take a full-time degree programme. The information is presented as follows:

- Institution.
- International student numbers.
- English language entry requirements for degree programmes, shown in IELTS scores. These vary between universities and courses, and can range from 7.5 to 5.5 and lower in some cases. See www.ielts.org. For full details, contact the university or college.
- Arrangements for English tuition courses.
- International Foundation courses.
- Annual tuition fees (approximate) for full-time undergraduate degree courses. Tuition fees also usually include fees for examinations and graduation. These figures are approximate and are subject to change each year. EU students currently pay 'home student' fees, except for those from the Channel Islands and the Isle of Man; students from an Overseas Territory may be eligible to pay home fees at universities and other institutions of higher education, provided that they meet any residence requirements. For a list of British and EU member states Overseas Territories, see page 484. More information for international students is available at the UK Council for International Student Affairs, www.ukcisa.org.uk. In the wake of the UK's withdrawal from the EU on 31 January 2020, EU students starting their course in September 2020 will pay 'home student' fees for the duration of their course. EU students starting their courses in September 2020 also remain eligible to apply for student funding under the current terms. Fees for EU students starting courses in the UK beyond 2020 are to be negotiated as part of the exit proceedings with the EU. Therefore, for the time being, until it is announced otherwise, EU students will continue to pay the same fees as home students.
- Annual living costs. These are also approximate and represent the costs for a single student over the year. The living costs shown cover university accommodation (usually guaranteed for the first year only), food, books, clothing and travel in the UK, but not travel to or from the UK. (Costs are likely to rise year by year in line with the rate of inflation in the UK.) Overseas students are normally permitted to take part-time work for a period of up to 20 hours per week if they are studying at degree level in the UK.
- Scholarships and awards for non-EU students (most universities offer awards for EU students).

UNIVERSITY INFORMATION AND FEES FOR UNDERGRADUATE INTERNATIONAL STUDENTS

Applicants should check university websites before applying. **The fees published below (unless otherwise stated) are those to be charged to students in 2020/21 (check websites for 2021/22 fees).**

Aberdeen Approximately 27% of students come from 120 nationalities. *English language entry requirement (or equivalent):* IELTS 6.0; Medicine 7.0. Academic English Preparation Programme, and five- and 10-week pre-sessional English courses available. *Fees:* £17,200–£19,700; Medicine £33,500. *Living costs:* £1,015 per month. International Student Scholarships available

Abertay International students are represented from over 60 countries around the world. International scholarships are available. *English language entry requirement (or equivalent):* IELTS 6.0 (no band less than 5.5). Pre-sessional English course available, also free English tuition throughout degree course. *Fees:* £13,800–£14,600. *Living costs:* £522–£642 per month.

Aberystwyth International students make up approximately 13% of the undergraduate student population. *English language entry requirement (or equivalent):* IELTS 6.0–7.0. Full-time tuition in English available. *Fees:* Arts and Social Science subjects £13,600; Science subjects £15,200. *Living costs:* £629 per month. International scholarships available.

AECC (UC) Over 50% of students are international. *English language entry requirement (or equivalent):* IELTS 6.0. *Fees:* £14,400–£16,500.

Anglia Ruskin Students from 177 countries. *English language entry requirement (or equivalent):* IELTS 6.0, with minimum of 5.5 in each element. A one-year International Foundation programme is available. *Fees:* £13,500. Scholarships available.

Arden This private university offers career-focused online distance learning courses worldwide, as well as blended learning study at their following UK study centres: Ealing, Tower Hill, Holborn, Birmingham and Manchester. *English language entry requirement (or equivalent):* IELTS 6.0, with minimum of 5.5 in each element. *Fees:* Contact the University.

Arts London A large number of international students from over 130 countries. *English language entry requirement (or equivalent):* IELTS 6.0 for practice-based courses, 6.5 for theory-based courses. Language Centre courses in academic English for four to 24 weeks. *Fees:* £22,920 per year. *Living costs:* £16,120–£18,200. Scholarships and bursaries available.

Aston International students from over 120 countries, with 3,000 of the total student population from overseas. *English language entry requirement (or equivalent):* IELTS 7.5–5.5. International Foundation programme offered as a bridge to the degree courses. Pre-sessional English classes also available for four, six, 12, 18 and 30 weeks. *Fees:* Languages and Social Science courses £14,300–£14,950; Engineering and Applied Science courses £16,000–£19,000; Life and Health Sciences £14,950–£17,550; Aston Business School £14,950. *Living costs:* £820 per month. Scholarships offered, including bursaries for Engineering and Science subjects.

Bangor Around 13% of the student population are international students. *English language entry requirement (or equivalent):* IELTS 6.0–7.0. Pre-sessional English courses available. *Fees:* Arts and Humanities £14,500–£15,300; Bangor Business School courses £14,500–£15,300; Education and Social Sciences £14,500; Engineering £16,800; Law £14,800; Sciences £15,800–£16,500. *Living costs:* £900–£1,100 per month. International entrance scholarships available.

Bath Over 1,500 international students from around 100 countries. *English language entry requirement (or equivalent):* IELTS 6.5–7.0. Pre-sessional programmes available. *Fees:* Humanities and Social Science £18,000; Management £20,000; Science and Engineering £22,300; MArch Yr 1 £14,250, Yr 2 £22,300. *Living costs:* £10,300. Scholarships, bursaries and awards available.

Bath Spa Staff and students from over 40 countries. *English language entry requirement (or equivalent):* IELTS 6.0 (minimum of 5.5 in all bands). Pre-sessional English courses for five or six weeks and 11 or 12 weeks. *Fees:* Classroom-based courses £13,300; laboratory/studio-based courses £14,300; Bath School of Art & Design £14,900. *Living costs:* £7,400–£9,840.

Bedfordshire Over 3,000 EU and international students. International scholarships are available. *English language entry requirement (or equivalent):* IELTS 6.0, with minimum of 5.5 in each band. Pre-sessional English course are available for two, four, eight, 12, 15 and 24 weeks. *Fees:* £12,650. *Living costs:* £6,500–£7,500.

Birmingham Over 6,500 international students from 150 countries. *English language entry requirement (or equivalent):* IELTS 6.0–7.0, depending on programme of study. Pre-sessional English language programmes last between six and 42 weeks depending on language proficiency (IELTS 4.0–7.0). *Fees:* Non-laboratory subjects £18,120–£21,180; Laboratory subjects £22,260–£24,660; Clinical courses £39,960. *Living costs:* £7,308–£8,820. Scholarships are offered by some subject departments including all Engineering subjects, Computer Science, Law, and Pharmacy.

Birmingham (UC) A quarter of the student population are from overseas and come from 65 countries. Specific entry requirements for each country are found on the College website. *English language entry requirement (or equivalent):* IELTS 6.0, with minimum of 5.5 in each band. Pre-sessional English programme for six or 10 weeks depending on language ability. *Fees:* £11,500. *Living costs:* £9,135.

Birmingham City Large number of international students from over 100 countries. *English language entry requirement (or equivalent):* IELTS 6.0, with minimum of 5.5 in each band. Pre-sessional language courses of six and 16 weeks. Orientation programme for all students. *Fees:* All undergraduate courses £12,800; Conservatoire/Acting courses £16,600. *Living costs:* £7,013.

Bishop Grosseteste *English language entry requirement (or equivalent):* IELTS 6.0, with minimum of 5.5 in each component. *Fees:* £11,820.

Bolton International students make up approximately 7% of the student population. *English language entry requirement (or equivalent):* IELTS 6.0. English pre-sessional programmes for five, nine, 13 and 27 weeks. Subject-specific Foundation programmes also available. *Fees:* £12,450. *Living costs:* £8,819.

Bournemouth A large number of international students. *English language entry requirement (or equivalent):* IELTS 6.0, with a minimum of 5.5 in each component. Pre-sessional English programmes from two to 39 weeks. *Fees:* £14,100–£15,000 *Living costs:* £7,000–£9,000 per year. Some subject awards available.

Bournemouth Arts *English language entry requirement (or equivalent):* IELTS: 6.0–6.5 overall, with a minimum of 5.5 in each band. English pre-sessional course available for five or 13 weeks depending on language ability. *Fees:* £16,950. *Living costs:* £6,500–£8,500.

BPP A private university dedicated to business and the professions with several study centres spread across England. Contact the University for information. *Fees:* Contact the University.

Bradford Over 150 countries represented (15%). *English language entry requirement (or equivalent):* IELTS 6.0, with minimum of 5.0 in each element. Pre-sessional English language courses for six, 10, 20 and 30 weeks. *Fees:* Lab-based courses £18,240; Classroom-based courses £15,320; Health Studies courses £15,324–£18,901. *Living costs:* £6,700–£11,495. Scholarships available.

Brighton Some 1,400 international students from over 100 countries. *English language entry requirement (or equivalent):* IELTS 6.0, with no less than 5.5 for each component. Pre-sessional English courses for four to 30 weeks. *Fees:* Classroom-based courses £13,384; Laboratory and workshop-based courses £14,460. *Living costs:* £800 per month. Merit-based scholarships available.

Brighton and Sussex (MS) *English language entry requirement (or equivalent):* IELTS 7.0, with no less than 7.0 in each section. *Fees:* £32,886. *Living costs:* £701–£1052 per month. Scholarships based on merit and financial need available.

Bristol Approximately 2,400 students from over 100 countries. *English language entry requirement (or equivalent):* IELTS 6.0–7.5 depending on programme of study. Pre-sessional language courses lasting six, 10 and 14 weeks and a year-long International Foundation programme. *Fees:* Arts and Social Sciences courses £19,500 (excluding Archaeology, Film, Theatre, Innovation and Liberal Arts, for which the Science course fees apply); Science and Engineering courses £24,000; Clinical courses £33,500. *Living costs:* £9,000–£14,500. Scholarships and bursaries available.

Brunel More than 3,100 international students from over 110 countries. *English language entry requirement (or equivalent):* IELTS 6.0–7.0. Pre-sessional English language courses available from six to 43 weeks. *Fees:* £15,400–£18,720. *Living costs:* £11,385. International, academic excellence and country-specific scholarships available.

Buckingham Over 100 nationalities represented at this small university. *English language entry requirement (or equivalent):* IELTS 6.5, with a minimum of 6.0 in each component. Foundation English courses offered. *Fees:* Eight-term degrees £17,400; nine-term degrees £15,822 for Years 1 and 2 and £3,955 for Year 3. *Living costs:* £8,200. International higher achiever scholarship and some bursaries available.

Bucks New Around 8% of the student population are international students, coming from over 50 countries. *English language entry requirement (or equivalent):* IELTS 6.0, with a minimum of 5.5 in each element. *Fees:* £12,000. *Living costs:* £6,000–£7,000. Academic achievement scholarships available.

Cambridge Over 800 international undergraduate students. *English language entry requirement (or equivalent):* IELTS 7.5 overall, with minimum of 7.0 in each element. Pre- and in-sessional English support is available. *Fees:* Tuition fees range between £21,168 and £55,272, depending on the course studied. College fees vary between £8,300 and £10,068 per year, depending on the college. *Living costs:* £9,160 Financial awards are offered to international students through the University of Cambridge and by some colleges. Scholarships for students from Canada and Hong Kong are also available.

Canterbury Christ Church International students from over 80 countries. *English language entry requirement (or equivalent):* IELTS 6.0, with a minimum of 5.5 in each section. Some non-standard programmes require IELTS 6.5 overall. *Fees:* £11,900. *Living costs:* £9,000. International student scholarship of £1,500 per year for up to three years of study.

Cardiff Over 7,500 international students from 100 countries. *English language entry requirement (or equivalent):* IELTS 6.5–7.0. Pre-sessional language courses from eight to 12 weeks. In-sessional support is also available. Induction course for all students. International Foundation courses for Business and Engineer *Fees:* Arts-based courses £15,950; Business School courses £16,950; science-based courses £19,950; clinical courses £38,059; healthcare sciences £24,938. *Living costs:* £6,756–£7,340. Scholarships available.

Cardiff Met The University has over 1,200 international students enrolled from more than 143 countries. *English language entry requirement (or equivalent):* IELTS 6.0, with a minimum of 5.5 in each section. International Foundation course and pre-sessional English courses available. *Fees:* £12,500. *Living costs:* £6,800–£7,600. Academic and sports scholarships available.

Central Lancashire Over 2,000 international students from over 100 countries. *English language entry requirement (or equivalent):* IELTS 6.0, with a minimum of 5.5 in each element. *Fees:* Non-laboratory courses £12,700; Laboratory courses £13,700. *Living costs:* £820 per month. Scholarships and bursaries available for international students. Scholarships for students from Indonesia and Palestine are also available.

Chester Over 20,000 students in total from over 130 countries globally. *English language entry requirement (or equivalent):* IELTS 6.0, with a minimum of 5.5 in each element. International Foundation programmes available in Business, Law and Social Sciences, Engineering and Computing, Life Sciences and Creative Arts. *Fees:* £12,450. *Living costs:* £8,268. International students are automatically considered for the University of Chester International Scholarship upon application.

Chichester International students from several countries. *English language entry requirement (or equivalent):* IELTS 6.0 or 5.5 if taking a joint degree with International English Studies. No component may be less than 5.5. Pre-sessional programme for five and 10 weeks available. *Fees:* £13,000. *Living costs:* £1,000 per month.

City A large international community with students from over 160 countries. *English language entry requirement (or equivalent):* IELTS 6.0 (6.5 for Law and Journalism). Pre-sessional English language courses are available as four-, eight- and 12-week programmes. International Foundation pathways in Actuarial Science and Business. *Fees:* £14,860. *Living costs:* £1,140 per month. Scholarships available.

Coventry About 2,500 international students. *English language entry requirement (or equivalent):* IELTS 6.0–7.0. International Foundation and pre-sessional English programmes available. *Fees:* £12,600–£14,850. *Living costs:* £6,000–£7,000. Scholarships available.

Cranfield Creative Arts *English language entry requirement (or equivalent):* IELTS 6.0 (no band less than 5.5). *Fees:* £16,250. *Living costs:* £5,000–£8,000. Undergraduate creative scholarships available.

Cumbria *English language entry requirement (or equivalent):* IELTS 6.0, with at least 5.5 in each component (7.0 for Nursing, Midwifery, Occupational Therapy and Social Work). International Foundation Programme and English language courses available. *Fees:* £10,500–£15,500. *Living costs:* £5,500. International scholarships available.

De Montfort Over 1,000 international students from more than 100 countries. *English language entry requirement (or equivalent):* IELTS 6.0–7.0. Pre-sessional English language courses and one-year International Foundation Certificate available. *Fees:* £13,250; Global Finance £15,500; Nursing £14,950. *Living costs:* £9,000–£11,000. Some scholarships for overseas students.

Derby Students from 100 countries. *English language entry requirement (or equivalent):* IELTS 6.0, with a minimum of 5.5 in all areas. Courses offered to those needing tuition in English language. International Foundation Programme and pre-sessional English courses available. *Fees:* £13,250; Occupational Therapy courses £14,250. *Living costs:* £208 per week. International scholarships available.

Dundee Students from approximately 83 countries. *English language entry requirement (or equivalent):* IELTS 6.0. Foundation programme pathways in Art and Design, Business, Physical Science and Engineering, Life and Biomedical Sciences, and Social Sciences available. *Fees:* £18,150 (non-laboratory); £21,950 (laboratory); £34,650 (Medicine). *Living costs:* £7,000–£8,000. International scholarships available.

Durham Over 4,500 international students from 156 countries. *English language entry requirement (or equivalent):* IELTS 6.5, with no component under 6.0. Pre- and in-sessional English language programmes available. *Fees:* £20,500 (Humanities)–£25,800 (Laboratory-based Sciences) *Living costs:* £5,000–£7,000. University-administered scholarships and bursaries as well as College and Departmental Prizes available.

Dyson Check the website for details: www.dysoninstitute.com/apply/.

East Anglia Over 4,000 international students from 120 countries. *English language entry requirement (or equivalent):* IELTS 6.0 (higher for some courses). International Foundation and pre-sessional programmes available. *Fees:* Classroom-based subjects £15,600; laboratory-based subjects £19,800; Medicine £30,600. *Living costs:* £7,200. International scholarships available.

East London International students from more than 120 countries. *English language entry requirement (or equivalent):* IELTS 5.5–6.0. Pre-sessional English courses of five, 10 and 15 weeks. *Fees:* £12,700. *Living costs:* £9,000. Range of international scholarships available.

Edge Hill There is a small number of international students. *English language entry requirement (or equivalent):* IELTS 6.0, with a minimum of 5.5 in each element. International Foundation Programme available. *Fees:* £12,250. *Living costs:* £7,000–£8,000. International students will automatically be considered for a scholarship upon application.

Edinburgh Some 4,000 international students from 120 countries. *English language entry requirement (or equivalent):* IELTS 7.0–7.5. English language courses offered throughout the year. *Fees:* £20,950–£27,550; Medicine £32,100–£49,900; Veterinary Medicine £32,850. *Living costs:* £695–£1,370 per month. International maths scholarship available.

Edinburgh Napier Approximately 4,000 international students. *English language entry requirement (or equivalent):* IELTS 6.0 overall with no component below 5.5. Pre- and in-sessional language support. *Fees:* Classroom-based and journalism courses £13,360; Laboratory-based courses £15,522. *Living costs:* £695–£1370 per month. Merit-based scholarships available as well as scholarships for students from Hong Kong and India.

Essex International students from over 135 countries. *English language entry requirement (or equivalent):* IELTS 6.0. Pre-sessional English language programmes from five to 25 weeks and academic English classes provided during the year. *Fees:* Computer Science and Electronic Engineering £18,730; Laboratory-based courses in Life Sciences and Psychology £18,170; Law, Economics, Government and Mathematical Sciences £16,860; History, Sociology, Language and Linguistics £16,050. *Living costs:* £5,700 to £7,500 per year. A comprehensive package of scholarships and bursaries is available. See www1.essex.ac.uk/fees-and-funding.

Exeter International students from over 140 countries. *English language entry requirement (or equivalent):* IELTS 6.5–7.5. International Foundation and Diploma programmes available as well as pre-sessional English language programmes of six and 10 weeks. *Fees:* Arts, Humanities and Social Sciences (including Business, Economics and Law) £18,500; Accounting and Finance, Business and Management and Economics £18,200; Biosciences, Mathematics, Geography, Psychology and Sports Sciences £20,500; Physics, Geology, Mining and Engineering £22,950; Combined Honours programmes that combine a science and a non-science subject £19,500; Medicine £35,750. *Living costs:* £9,500. A range of scholarships and awards are available. Further information is available at www.exeter.ac.uk/undergraduate/fees/scholarships.

Falmouth *English language entry requirement (or equivalent):* IELTS 6.0. Discipline-specific academic English courses available throughout the year. *Fees:* £16,000. *Living costs:* £320–£540 per week. International scholarships available.

Glasgow Over 2,000 international students. *English language entry requirement (or equivalent):* IELTS 6.5 (higher for some courses). Pre- and in-sessional English language courses available. *Fees:* Arts and Social Sciences programmes £18,370; Engineering, Science, College of Medical, Veterinary and Life Sciences programmes £21,920; Clinical courses £47,900; Veterinary Medicine and Surgery £30,500. *Living costs:* £12,100. Fee-waiver scholarships and automatic Fourth Year scholarships available (not for Dentistry, Medicine or Veterinary Science).

Glasgow Caledonian Students from more than 100 countries. *English language entry requirement (or equivalent):* IELTS 6.0, with minimum 5.5 in each element. English language programmes available. *Fees:* £12,250. *Living costs:* £1,015 per month. Merit-based scholarships as well as a guaranteed scholarship of £1,000 for full-time self-funded students.

Gloucestershire International students from more than 60 countries. *English language entry requirement (or equivalent):* IELTS 5.5. English language support and mentor scheme with other international students. *Fees:* £14,680. *Living costs:* £7,000–£9,135. International scholarships and bursaries available.

Glyndŵr The University welcomes students from Europe and worldwide. *English language entry requirement (or equivalent):* IELTS 6.0, with a minimum of 5.5 in each element. In-sessional and intensive English language courses available. *Fees:* £11,750. *Living costs:* £7,500. Scholarships available.

Greenwich 4,200 international students from over 140 countries. *English language entry requirement (or equivalent):* IELTS 6.0, with a minimum of 5.5 in each component. Pre-sessional English courses and International Foundation programmes available. *Fees:* £13,000. *Living costs:* £9,500–£10,500. Scholarships open to applicants from 25 countries.

Harper Adams Students from around 30 different countries. *English language entry requirement (or equivalent):* 6.0, with a minimum of 5.5 in each component. Pre-sessional English language programmes available from six weeks to six months. *Fees:* £10,600. *Living costs:* £6,955. Scholarships available.

Heriot-Watt One third of the student population are from outside of the UK. *English language entry requirement (or equivalent):* IELTS 6.0. Several English language courses are offered; these range in length depending on students' requirements. *Fees:* Laboratory-based Science and Engineering courses £19,400; Non-laboratory-based courses £15,080. *Living costs:* £695–£1,370 per month. Some international scholarships are available.

Hertfordshire More than 2,800 international students from over 100 countries are at present studying at the University. *English language entry requirement (or equivalent):* IELTS 6.0–7.0. English language tuition is offered in the one-year International Foundation course and in a pre-sessional intensive English course held during the summer months. *Fees:* £12,350. *Living costs:* £190–£240 per week. International scholarships available.

Huddersfield International students from over 80 countries. *English language entry requirement (or equivalent):* IELTS 6.0, with a minimum of 5.5 in each element. English language courses available and a one-year International Foundation course in English language with options in Business, Computing and Engineering *Fees:* Tuition fees range between £14,500 and £17,400. *Living costs:* £9,135. International students are automatically considered for a scholarship of up to £2,000 per year upon application.

Hull Ten per cent of students are from outside the EU. *English language entry requirement (or equivalent):* IELTS 6.0. English summer study programmes available. *Fees:* Non-science programmes £14,500; Science programmes £17,200. *Living costs:* £6,500–£8,500. Excellent overseas scholarship provisions depending on the chosen subject and the student's country of origin.

Hull York (MS) *English language entry requirement (or equivalent):* 7.5, with a minimum of 7.0 in each component. *Fees:* £33,700.

Imperial London International students from over 125 countries. *English language entry requirement (or equivalent):* IELTS 6.5–7.0. Pre-sessional English course available for three weeks. *Fees:* Engineering £31,750; Medicine £44,000; Medical Biosciences £31,000; Chemistry £33,000; Mathematics £30,000; Physics £33,000; Life Sciences £33,000. *Living costs:* £11,184–£14,496. Scholarships available.

Keele Large number of overseas students. *English language entry requirement (or equivalent):* IELTS 6.0–7.0. English language summer school before the start of degree course. International Foundation year degree programmes (entry IELTS 5.0). *Fees:* £13,505–£18,000; Medicine £32,000. *Living costs:* £7,300–£11,200. General, course-specific and country-specific scholarships available for international students. Bursaries also available.

Kent Over 150 different nationalities represented at the University. *English language entry requirement (or equivalent):* English language requirement (or equivalent): IELTS 6.5–7.0. Pre-sessional courses and International Foundation programme available. *Fees:* £16,200. *Living costs:* £7,000–£13,000. International scholarships worth £5,000 for each year of study available.

Kingston More than 2,000 international students. *English language entry requirement (or equivalent):* IELTS 6.0–7.0. Pre-sessional English language and subject-specific Foundation-level courses available. Free English support during degree studies. *Fees:* Classroom-based courses £13,100; Art and Design courses £15,600; Pharmacy and studio-based courses £15,000; Laboratory-based courses £14,600. *Living costs:* £6,500–£10,000. International scholarship worth £4,000 per year of study.

Lancaster Twenty-five per cent of student population from over 100 countries. *English language entry requirement (or equivalent):* IELTS 6.0–7.0. Pre-sessional and in-session English language courses cover reading, writing, listening and speaking skills. *Fees:* £18,700–£22,550; Medicine £34,700. *Living costs:* £7,840.

Leeds More than 6,000 students from outside the UK. *English language entry requirement (or equivalent):* IELTS 7.0–7.5, with a minimum of 5.5–6.5 in each component. *Fees:* £19,500–£23,750; Medicine £34,500. *Living costs:* £575–£760 per month. International subject-specific scholarships available.

Leeds Arts *English language entry requirement (or equivalent):* IELTS 5.5. *Fees:* BA degree courses £15,400; BMus £16,400.

Leeds Beckett Students from 125 countries and territories. *English language entry requirement (or equivalent):* IELTS 6.0 (IELTS 5.0 for the International Foundation programme, starting September or February). Also general English courses. *Fees:* £12,000. *Living costs:* £9,135. Scholarships available.

Leeds Trinity *English language entry requirement (or equivalent):* IELTS 6.0 overall, with a minimum of 5.5 in each component (may be higher for some courses). Pre-sessional English course available. *Fees:* £12,000. *Living costs:* £9,135. International scholarship worth £1,000 awarded based on academic and professional merit.

Leicester Over 4,000 international students from 110 countries. *English language entry requirement (or equivalent):* IELTS 6.5–7.5 (5.0 for the Foundation year). English language preparatory programmes and on-going support Foundation programme. *Fees:* Non-science degrees £17,450; science degrees £21,515; Medicine £23,000–£40,140. *Living costs:* £800 per month. International scholarships available.

Lincoln International students from over 100 countries. *English language entry requirement (or equivalent):* IELTS 6.0. Pre- and in-sessional English language courses available. *Fees:* £14,100 (Humanities)–£15,900 (Laboratory–based Sciences). *Living costs:* £800 per month. Scholarships for high-achieving international students. Engineering bursaries also available.

Liverpool Over 7,500 international students from more than 120 countries. *English language entry requirement (or equivalent):* Science and Engineering: IELTS 6.0 (minimum 5.5 in each component); Humanities and Social Sciences, Health and Life Sciences, Geography, Planning and Carmel College: IELTS 6.5. *Fees:* £17,050–£21,300; Dentistry, Medicine and Veterinary Science £36,300. *Living costs:* £440–£1,090 per month. Scholarships available, including special awards for students from Hong Kong.

Liverpool Hope Approximately 700 international students. *English language entry requirement (or equivalent):* IELTS 6.0. Language courses available. *Fees:* £11,400. *Living costs:* £7,380. International Excellence bursary and Music scholarship available.

Liverpool John Moores A large number of overseas students. *English language entry requirement (or equivalent):* IELTS 6.0. Pre-sessional and in-session English tuition available. *Fees:* Laboratory-based courses £16,100; Classroom-based courses £15,600. *Living costs:* £1,015 per month. International scholarships available.

London (Birk) Over 100,000 international students from more than 200 countries. *English language entry requirement (or equivalent):* IELTS 6.5. Pre-sessional English courses and free online study skills materials available. *Fees:* £14,000. *Living costs:* £13,675. Scholarships available.

London (Court) Students from around the world. *English language entry requirement (or equivalent):* IELTS 7.0. *Fees:* £19,871. *Living costs:* £1,500 per month. Scholarships available.

London (Gold) Students from more than 140 countries. *English language entry requirement (or equivalent):* IELTS 6.5. Pre-sessional programmes available. *Fees:* Art, Humanities and Social Sciences £16,390–£22,950; Psychology £17,400. *Living costs:* £640–£1,760 per month. Country-specific scholarships available.

London (Inst Paris) *English language entry requirement (or equivalent):* IELTS 6.5, with a minimum of 5.5 in each element. *Fees:* £18,000. *Living costs:* £296–£817 per month. Bursaries available.

London (Institute of Banking and Finance) The Institute offers a range of finance courses leading to professional qualifications. See the website for details: www.libf.ac.uk. Fees: £13,000

London (Interdisciplinary School) Information about this institution is still being confirmed. Please visit www.londoninterdisciplinaryschool.org for details.

London (King's) Thousands of international students from over 150 countries. *English language entry requirement (or equivalent):* IELTS 6.0–7.5. Pre-sessional summer courses and a one-year Foundation course available. *Fees:* Classroom-based £19,800; Laboratory-based £26,700; Pharmacy £24,650; Medicine £38,850. *Living costs:* £1,000–£1,200 per month. Awards available.

London (QM) Students from over 162 countries. *English language entry requirement (or equivalent):* IELTS 6.0–7.0. International Foundation course covering English language tuition and specialist courses in Business, Management, Economics, Mathematics, Spanish, Geography and European Studies. *Fees:* £18,000–£23,500; Dentistry and Medicine £38,000. *Living costs:* £1,050 per month. Subject-specific bursaries and scholarships available.

London (RH) Over 1,900 overseas students from nearly 100 countries. *English language entry requirement (or equivalent):* IELTS 6.5–7.0. Pre-sessional English course available. Ten-month Foundation course with studies in English language and introduction to specialist studies in a range of degree subjects. *Fees:* £17,300–£20,900. *Living costs:* £11,960–£12,129. Bursaries and scholarships available.

London (RVC) Many international students from countries all over the world. *English language entry requirement (or equivalent):* IELTS 6.5–7.0. *Fees:* £14,190–£36,060. *Living costs:* £13,388–£20,900. International scholarships available.

London (SOAS) Students from more than 133 countries. *English language entry requirement (or equivalent):* IELTS 7.0. A one-year Foundation programme and English language courses available with an entry requirement of IELTS 6.0–6.5 depending on the length. *Fees:* £18,630. *Living costs:* Over £1,000 per month.

London (St George's) There are a variety of courses that international and non-EU students can apply to. Full details on entry requirements for each individual course are available on the University website. *English language entry requirement (or equivalent):* a language level of at least CEFR B2. Pre-sessional English courses available. *Fees:* Physiotherapy £16,000; Biomedical Science £18,000; Diagnostic Radiography £16,000; Medicine £36,000. *Living costs:* £1,200 per month.

London (UCL) Overseas students make up 25% of the population. *English language entry requirement (or equivalent):* IELTS 6.5–7.5. *Fees:* £18,430–£34,660. *Living costs:* £15,103. Scholarships available.

London LSE International students represent 150 countries. *English language entry requirement (or equivalent):* IELTS 7.0. Academic English language courses available. *Fees:* £19,920. *Living costs:* £12,000. A limited number of international scholarships available.

London Met Students from 147 countries. *English language entry requirement (or equivalent):* IELTS 6.0. One-year International Foundation programme. Full range of English courses. *Fees:* £12,700. *Living costs:* £1,265 per month.

London Regent's Students from over 140 countries around the world. *English language entry requirement (or equivalent):* A range of English language qualifications accepted. *Fees:* £17,500. *Living costs:* £1,000–£1,200 per month. Scholarships available.

London South Bank Almost 2,000 international students from over 130 countries. *English language entry requirement (or equivalent):* IELTS 6.0. Pre-study English course and a University Foundation course for overseas students. *Fees:* From £13,780. *Living costs:* £820–£2,200 per month. Range of scholarships available.

Loughborough Some 1,000 undergraduate students from outside the UK. *English language entry requirement (or equivalent):* IELTS 6.5 with a minimum of 6.0 in all sub-tests. Special pre-sessional courses offered by the Student Support Centre. *Fees:* Classroom-based subjects and School of Business £18,650; Laboratory-based subjects £23,100. *Living costs:* £8,000. Self-funded international students are automatically considered for an international scholarship upon application.

Manchester A high proportion of international students from over 160 countries. *English language entry requirement (or equivalent):* IELTS 6.5–7.0. Foundation Year programme available as well as pre- and in-sessional English language courses. *Fees:* Non-laboratory £19,000; Laboratory £24,000; Clinical £44,000. *Living costs:* £9,445. Some scholarships and bursaries are available.

Manchester Met A large number of international students. *English language entry requirement (or equivalent):* IELTS 6.0, with a minimum of 5.5 in each component. General, academic and pre-sessional English language courses available. *Fees:* Classroom-based courses £15,000; Laboratory-based courses £16,500; Architecture £24,000. *Living costs:* £7,380. Variety of international scholarships and awards available.

Marjon *English language entry requirement (or equivalent):* IELTS 6.0. English Preparation Programme available. *Fees:* £12,000. *Living costs:* £1,000 per month.

Medway Sch Pharm Many students come from the EU and other parts of the world, including China, Canada, India, Iran and the USA. The Medway Students Association hosts numerous international societies for international students to socialise. *English language entry requirement (or equivalent):* IELTS 7.0. Cambridge English Advanced Certificate at grade B. *Fees:* £19,000 *Living costs:* £9,000

Middlesex Over 8,000 international students. *English language entry requirement (or equivalent):* IELTS 6.0, with a minimum of 5.5 in each component. Pre-sessional English course available. *Fees:* £13,400. *Living costs:* £950–£1,500 per month. Scholarships available.

NCH London Around 30% of the student population is made up of international students. *English language entry requirement (or equivalent):* IELTS 7.0, with a minimum of 6.5 in each component. *Fees:* £14,000. *Living costs:* £1,250 per month. International scholarship of £2,000 awarded based on academic ability.

Newcastle Over 2,500 students from outside the UK. *English language entry requirement (or equivalent):* IELTS 6.5. Pre- and in-sessional English language courses as well as an International Foundation programme. *Fees:* Non-science subjects £18,000; science subjects £22,800; Dentistry £36,400; Medicine £33,600. *Living costs:* £10,500–£11,500. International scholarships available.

Newman *English language entry requirement (or equivalent):* IELTS 6.0. *Fees:* £11,250. *Living costs:* £600–£1,015 per month. Scholarships available.

Northampton Over 1,000 international students from over 100 countries. *English language entry requirement (or equivalent):* IELTS 6.0, with a minimum of 5.5 in each component. English language courses available. *Fees:* £12,900 for all BA/BSc courses, except Podiatry and Occupational Therapy (£13,900). *Living costs:* £8,000–£10,000. Scholarships and bursaries available, see website for details.

Northumbria Students from over 100 countries. *English language entry requirement (or equivalent):* IELTS 5.5–7.0. English language and Foundation courses available. *Fees:* £15,500. *Living costs:* £1,015 per month. International scholarships available.

Norwich Arts Students from over 40 countries. *English language entry requirement (or equivalent):* IELTS 6.0 (with a minimum of 5.5 in all sections). *Fees:* £15,000.

Nottingham Students and staff from over 150 countries. *English language entry requirement (or equivalent):* IELTS 6.0–7.0 (7.5 for Medicine, Nursing and Midwifery, Physiotherapy and Sports Rehabilitation, and Veterinary Medicine and Science). Pre- and in-sessional English language courses available. *Fees:* £18,420–£23,760; Medicine £24,990. *Living costs:* £1,015 per month. International scholarships available.

Nottingham Trent Large number of overseas students. *English language entry requirement (or equivalent):* IELTS 6.0–7.0. English language courses (six to 20 weeks) available. *Fees:* £14,500. *Living costs:* £8,000. International scholarships available.

Open University Courses are open to students throughout the world with study online or with educational partners. Tutorial support is by telephone, fax, computer conferencing or email. *Fees:* Non-EU students' fees vary depending on type of course.

Oxford Students from 140 countries and territories. *English language entry requirement (or equivalent):* IELTS 7.0. English language courses available. *Fees:* Tuition fee £27,285–£36,065. *Living costs:* £1,014–£1,556 per month. University and college scholarships and awards are available.

Oxford Brookes Around 18% of the student population is made up of international students. *English language entry requirement (or equivalent):* IELTS 6.0–6.5. Large number of English language support courses offered. *Fees:* £13,900–£14,800. *Living costs:* £11,130. International scholarships available as well as family awards.

Plymouth Around 3,000 international students from over 100 countries. *English language entry requirement (or equivalent):* IELTS 6.0. Pre-sessional English courses available. *Fees:* £13,800. *Living costs:* £1,000 per month. International scholarships available.

Portsmouth Over 4,000 international students from 130 different countries. *English language entry requirement (or equivalent):* IELTS 6.0. Induction, academic skills and language courses available. *Fees:* Classroom-based courses £14,300; laboratory-based courses £16,400. *Living costs:* £7,000–£8,000. International scholarships available.

Queen Margaret Around 25% of students are international coming from over 70 countries. *English language entry requirement (or equivalent):* IELTS 6.5. English language support available. *Fees:* Classroom-based courses £13,000; Laboratory/studio-based courses £14,500. *Living costs:* £7,380. Scholarships for students from China, Canada, USA and India as well as other international scholarships.

Queen's Belfast International students from over 80 countries. *English language entry requirement (or equivalent):* IELTS 6.5–7.5. Special English language summer schools and pre-university language courses are provided, also weekly language courses. Orientation programme held before the start of the academic year. *Fees:* Classroom-based courses £16,900; Laboratory component courses £20,800; Pre-clinical/clinical courses £41,850. *Living costs:* £197 per week. International scholarships available.

Ravensbourne Univ There are over 94 nationalities represented at Ravensbourne. *English language entry requirement (or equivalent):* IELTS 5.0 for undergraduate, IELTS 5.5 for postgraduate. *Fees:* £14,500. *Living costs:* £11,385. Ravensbourne have a number of scholarships and awards available for Tier 4 International students.

Reading More than 5,000 students from over 140 countries. *English language entry requirement (or equivalent):* IELTS 6.5. International Foundation programme offering English language tuition and a choice of 15 specialist pathways. Other pre-sessional English courses offered. *Fees:* Non-laboratory courses £16,890; Laboratory courses £20,315. *Living costs:* £876–£1,116 per month. Some scholarships offered.

Richmond (Am Int Univ) *English language entry requirement (or equivalent):* IELTS 5.0 *Fees:* £14,750. *Living costs:* £11,385. Richmond University offers international scholarships of up to £4,500, depending on nationality.

Robert Gordon Over 1,000 international students from more than 65 countries. *English language entry requirement (or equivalent):* IELTS 6.0. Pre-sessional English programme available as well as language classes and one-to-one support during the year. *Fees:* £14,000–16,650. *Living costs:* £7,000–£9,000. Merit scholarships for specific subjects available.

Roehampton Students from more than 140 countries. *English language entry requirement (or equivalent):* IELTS 6.0, with a minimum of 5.5 in each component. International Foundation programme and pre-sessional English courses available. *Fees:* £13,145. *Living costs:* £7,500–£8,500. International scholarships available.

Royal Agricultural Univ International students from 45 different countries. *English language entry requirement (or equivalent):* IELTS 6.0. International Foundation Year and English language courses available. *Fees:* £10,200. *Living costs:* £8,000–£10,000. International scholarships available.

Salford More than 3,000 international students from over 100 countries. *English language entry requirement (or equivalent):* IELTS 6.0–7.0. English study programmes and a very comprehensive International Foundation year. *Fees:* £10,200–£13,300. *Living costs:* £7,624–£9,545. Scholarships and bursaries available.

Sheffield Over 6,500 international students from 150 countries. *English language entry requirement (or equivalent):* IELTS 7.0. Preparatory English courses and an international summer school with English classes. *Fees:* Arts, humanities, languages, law, management £17,600–£19,800; Architecture, Science and Engineering £22,600; Medicine £33,500; Dentistry £35,880. *Living costs:* £9,135. Faculty scholarships and international merit scholarships available.

Sheffield Hallam Over 100 countries represented by thousands of international students. *English language entry requirement (or equivalent):* IELTS 6.0–7.0. Pre-sessional and academic English language courses available. *Fees:* £13,650. *Living costs:* £800 per month. International scholarships available as well as country-specific scholarships for students from South Asia and South East Asia.

Solent Over 14% of the student population come from overseas, representing more than 100 different nationalities. *English language entry requirement (or equivalent):* IELTS 6.0. Induction programme and language tuition available. *Fees:* £12,500. *Living costs:* £8,000.

South Wales *English language entry requirement (or equivalent):* IELTS from 6.0. Pre-sessional course offered in English with course lengths of between five and 10 weeks depending on the applicant's proficiency. An International Foundation Programme is also offered. *Fees:* Aircraft Maintenance £19,500; other courses £13,200–£13,500. *Living costs:* £4,788–£8,820. International students automatically considered for a scholarship upon application.

Southampton Over 6,500 international students from more than 135 countries. *English language entry requirement (or equivalent):* IELTS 5.5–7.0. English courses offered and also an International Foundation course covering Arts, Humanities, Social Sciences and Law. *Fees:* £17,560–£21,580. *Living costs:* £7,200–£8,800. International Merit scholarship available.

St Andrews Over 1,500 international students from more than 120 different nationalities. *English language entry requirement (or equivalent):* IELTS 7.0–8.0. International Foundation programme available as well as pre- and in-sessional English language courses. *Fees:* £23,910; Medicine £31,950. *Living costs:* £14,000–£16,000. Scholarships available.

St Mary's Qualifications from any country will be considered and measured against British equivalents. Almost 10% of the student population are international. *English language entry requirement (or equivalent):* IELTS 6.0 (minimum 5.5 in each component); Nutrition BSc 6.5 (minimum 6.0 in each component). In-sessional English language programme available. *Fees:* £12,250. *Living costs:* £7,000–£8,000.

St Mary's (UC) Each year, St Mary's enrols over sixty international students through the Erasmus+ programme as well as the Irish American Scholars Programme. Enquiries should be addressed to the

International Secretary Briege Ellis. *Living costs:* £8,515. St Mary's applicants may be eligible for international scholarships offered through Queen's University Belfast.

Staffordshire Students from over 70 countries. *English language entry requirement (or equivalent):* IELTS 6.0. English tuition available. *Fees:* £14,000. *Living costs:* £7,000. International scholarships available.

Stirling Students from 120 nationalities. *English language entry requirement (or equivalent):* IELTS 6.0. English language tuition available as well as an International Foundation in Business, Finance, Economics and Marketing. *Fees:* £13,100–£15,600. *Living costs:* £6,470–£9,282. Some scholarships are available. Please see www.stir.ac.uk/scholarships.

Stranmillis (UC) *Fees:* £16,400. *Living costs:* £8,515. Stranmillis applicants may be eligible for international scholarships offered through Queen's University Belfast.

Strathclyde Students from 100 countries. *English language entry requirement (or equivalent):* IELTS 6.5. Pre-entry and pre-sessional English tuition available. *Fees:* £15,300–£21,500. *Living costs:* £8,000–£12,700.

Suffolk *Fees:* Classroom-based courses £11,790; Laboratory/studio/IT-based courses £13,000; MBA £16,380.

Sunderland International students come from over 100 countries. *English language entry requirement (or equivalent):* IELTS 6.0. English language tuition available. *Fees:* £12,000. *Living costs:* £485–£1,164 per month. International students are automatically considered for a £1,500 scholarship upon application.

Surrey Students from over 120 different countries. *English language entry requirement (or equivalent):* IELTS 6.5–7.5. English language courses and summer courses offered. *Fees:* £18,500–£21,700; Veterinary Medicine £33,400. *Living costs:* £6,884. Scholarships and bursaries offered, including awards for students on Civil Engineering courses.

Sussex More than 3,000 international students from over 140 countries. *English language entry requirement (or equivalent):* IELTS 6.5–7.0 (7.5 for Medicine). English language and study skills courses available. International Foundation courses offered, covering English language tuition and a choice of Humanities or Law. *Fees:* £18,500–£22,500. *Living costs:* £550–£1,120 per week. International scholarships available.

Swansea Students from over 100 countries. *English language entry requirement (or equivalent):* IELTS 6.0–6.5. Pre-sessional English language courses available and on-going support during degree courses. *Fees:* £15,900–£19,500. *Living costs:* £6,000–£9,000. Some overseas scholarships and prizes.

Teesside Students from over 100 countries. *English language entry requirement (or equivalent):* IELTS 5.5–7.0. Free English courses available throughout the year while following degree programmes. International summer school available. *Fees:* £13,000. *Living costs:* £1,015 per month. Scholarships available for self-funded students.

Trinity Saint David International students are well represented at the University. *English language entry requirement (or equivalent):* IELTS 6.5. International Foundation programme available. *Fees:* (2019/20) £11,500. *Living costs:* £6,500–£7,500. International scholarships available.

UCO Students from across the world including Australia, Brazil and Europe. *English language entry requirement (or equivalent):* IELTS 6.5 or above. *Fees:* £11,400.

UHI *English language entry requirement (or equivalent):* IELTS 6.0; minimum 5.5 in all four components. *Fees:* Art, Humanities, Social Science and Business courses £11,650; Science and Technology courses £12,800. *Living costs:* £610–£850 per month.

Ulster Students from over 100 countries. *English language entry requirement (or equivalent):* IELTS 6.0. Pre- and in-sessional English language courses available. *Fees:* (2019/20) £14,060. *Living costs:* £6,000–£7,000. International scholarships available.

Univ Law More than 1,200 students from over 100 countries. *English language entry requirement (or equivalent):* IELTS 7.0. *Fees:* £13,750–£16,400. *Living costs:* £6,000–£8,000. International scholarships available.

UWE Bristol More than 1,750 international students. *English language entry requirement (or equivalent):* IELTS 6.0, with a minimum of 5.5 in each component. Pre- and in-sessional English language courses offered. *Fees:* £13,500. *Living costs:* £1,015 per month. Scholarships based on academic, sports and entrepreneurial excellence available as well as country- and programme-specific scholarships.

Warwick Over 3,500 international students. *English language entry requirement (or equivalent):* IELTS 6.0 for Science courses, 6.5 for Arts courses, 6.5 for MORSE courses, and 7.0 for Social Studies and Business courses. English language support available. *Fees:* Classroom-based courses £20,210; Laboratory-based courses, plus Theatre and Performance Studies, Economics and Business courses (with a few exceptions) £25,770; Medicine £41,120. *Living costs:* £7,250–£12,040. More than 20 awards available for overseas students.

West London A large number of international students. *English language entry requirement (or equivalent):* IELTS 6.0. International Foundation programme and English language support available. *Fees:* £12,500. *Living costs:* £13,700. International scholarships available.

West Scotland Over 1,100 international students from around 70 countries. *English language entry requirement (or equivalent):* IELTS 6.0. English language Foundation course available. *Fees:* Classroom-based courses £12,000; laboratory-based courses £13,000. *Living costs:* £600 per month. International scholarships available.

Westminster Over 20,000 students from over 169 nations. *English language entry requirement (or equivalent):* IELTS 6.0. Pre- and in-sessional English courses available. *Fees:* £14,000. *Living costs:* £800 per month (minimum). International scholarships available.

Winchester Some 600 international students from over 60 countries. *English language entry requirement (or equivalent):* IELTS 6.0. Language courses available. *Fees:* £13,500. *Living costs:* £7,500–£8,500. International scholarships available.

Wolverhampton Over 2,500 international students from over 100 countries. *English language entry requirement (or equivalent):* IELTS 6.0. Four week English course available. International student programme. *Fees:* £12,250. *Living costs:* £7,200. Scholarships and bursaries available.

Worcester *English language entry requirement (or equivalent):* IELTS 6.0. English language support available. *Fees:* £12,700. *Living costs:* £6,000–£7,500. International scholarships of up to £3,000 available.

Writtle (UC) Students come from countries including China, Russia, Mexico, Ghana and Malaysia. *Fees:* £12,100.

York 15% of students from outside the UK. *English language entry requirement (or equivalent):* IELTS 6.0–7.0 (7.5 for Medicine). Pre-sessional English language courses. *Fees:* £17,890–£22,080. *Living costs:* £7,624–£9,665. Several scholarships for overseas students.

York St John *English language entry requirement (or equivalent):* IELTS 6.0. Pre-sessional courses and International Foundation Programme available. *Fees:* £12,750. *Living costs:* £1,015 per month.

BRITISH OVERSEAS TERRITORIES STUDENTS
Students from British Overseas Territories are treated as home students for fee purposes at universities and other institutions of higher education in England, Wales and Northern Ireland, provided they meet residency requirements. The territories to which this policy applies are:

British Overseas Territories Anguilla, Bermuda, British Antarctic Territory, British Indian Ocean Territory, British Virgin Islands, Cayman Islands, Falkland Islands, Montserrat, Pitcairn, Henderson, Ducie and Oeno Islands, South Georgia and the South Sandwich Islands, St Helena and Dependencies (Ascension Island and Tristan de Cunha), Turks and Caicos Islands.

Overseas Territories of EU member states Aruba, Faroe Islands, French Polynesia, French Southern and Antarctic Territories, Greenland, Bonaire, Curaçao, Saba, Sint Eustatius, Sint Maarten, the Territory of New Caledonia and Dependencies, St-Barthélemy (St Barth), St Pierre et Miquelon, Wallis and Futuna Islands.

DIRECTORY OF UNIVERSITIES AND OTHER INSTITUTIONS OFFERING HIGHER EDUCATION COURSES

SECTION 1: UNIVERSITIES AND UNIVERSITY COLLEGES

Listed below are universities and university colleges in the United Kingdom that offer degree and diploma courses at higher education level. Applications to these institutions are submitted through UCAS except for part-time courses, private universities and colleges, and further education courses. For current information refer to the websites shown and also to www.ucas.com for a comprehensive list of degree and diploma courses (see Appendix 4).

Aberdeen Tel 01224 272000; www.abdn.ac.uk
Abertay (Dundee) Tel 01382 308000; www.abertay.ac.uk
Aberystwyth Tel 01970 622021; www.aber.ac.uk
AECC (UC) (Bournemouth) Tel 01202 436 200; www.aecc.ac.uk
Anglia Ruskin (Cambridge) Tel 01245 686868; www.anglia.ac.uk
Arden (Coventry) Tel 0800 268 7737; www.arden.ac.uk
Arts London Tel 020 7514 6000; www.arts.ac.uk
Aston (Birmingham) Tel 0121 204 3000; www.aston.ac.uk
Bangor Tel 01248 383717; www.bangor.ac.uk
Bath Tel 01225 383019; www.bath.ac.uk
Bath Spa Tel 01225 875875; www.bathspa.ac.uk
Bedfordshire (Luton) Tel 01582 743500; www.beds.ac.uk
Birmingham Tel 0121 414 3344; www.birmingham.ac.uk
Birmingham (UC) Tel 0121 604 1040; www.ucb.ac.uk
Birmingham City Tel 01213 316295; www.bcu.ac.uk
Bishop Grosseteste (Lincoln) Tel 01522 527347; www.bishopg.ac.uk
Bolton Tel 01204 900600; www.bolton.ac.uk
Bournemouth (Poole) Tel 01202 961916; www1.bournemouth.ac.uk
Bournemouth Arts (Poole) Tel 01202 533011; www.aub.ac.uk
BPP (London) Tel 03300 603100; www.bpp.com
Bradford Tel 01274 232323; www.bradford.ac.uk
Brighton Tel 01273 644644; www.brighton.ac.uk
Brighton and Sussex (MS) Tel 01273 643528; www.bsms.ac.uk
Bristol Tel 0117 394 1649; www.bristol.ac.uk
Brunel (Uxbridge) Tel 01895 265265; www.brunel.ac.uk
Buckingham Tel 01280 820227; www.buckingham.ac.uk
Bucks New (High Wycombe) Tel 01494 522141; www.bucks.ac.uk
Cambridge Tel 01223 333308; www.cam.ac.uk
Canterbury Christ Church Tel 01227 928000; www.canterbury.ac.uk
Cardiff Tel 029 2087 9999; www.cardiff.ac.uk
Cardiff Met Tel 029 2041 6010; www.cardiffmet.ac.uk
Central Lancashire (Preston) Tel 01772 892444; www.uclan.ac.uk
Chester Tel 01244 511000; www.chester.ac.uk
Chichester Tel 01243 816000; www.chi.ac.uk
City (London) Tel 020 7040 5060; www.city.ac.uk
Coventry Tel 024 7765 7688; www.coventry.ac.uk

Cranfield Tel 01234 750111; www.cranfield.ac.uk/
Creative Arts (Farnham) Tel 01252 722441; www.uca.ac.uk
Cumbria Tel 0330 057 1675; www.cumbria.ac.uk
De Montfort (Leicester) Tel 0116 250 6070; www.dmu.ac.uk
Derby Tel 01332 591167; www.derby.ac.uk
Dundee Tel 01382 383838; www.dundee.ac.uk
Durham Tel 0191 334 6128; www.dur.ac.uk
Dyson (Malmesbury) Tel 01285 705228; www.dysoninstitute.com
East Anglia (Norwich) Tel 01603 591515; www.uea.ac.uk
East London Tel 020 8223 3333; www.uel.ac.uk
Edge Hill (Ormskirk) Tel 01695 650950; www.edgehill.ac.uk
Edinburgh Tel 0131 650 1000; www.ed.ac.uk
Edinburgh Napier Tel 0333 900 6040; www.napier.ac.uk
Essex (Colchester) Tel 01206 873666; www.essex.ac.uk
Exeter Tel 0300 555 6060; www.exeter.ac.uk
Falmouth Tel 01326 254350; www.falmouth.ac.uk
Glasgow Tel 0141 330 2000; www.gla.ac.uk
Glasgow Caledonian Tel 0141 331 8630; www.gcu.ac.uk
Gloucestershire (Cheltenham) Tel 03330 141414; www.glos.ac.uk
Glyndŵr (Wrexham) Tel 01978 293439; www.glyndwr.ac.uk
Greenwich (London) Tel 020 8331 9000; www.gre.ac.uk
Harper Adams (Newport) Tel 01952 815000; www.harper-adams.ac.uk
Heriot-Watt (Edinburgh) Tel 0131 449 5111; www.hw.ac.uk
Hertfordshire (Hatfield) Tel 01707 284800; www.herts.ac.uk
Huddersfield Tel 01484 472625; www.hud.ac.uk
Hull Tel 01482 346311; www.hull.ac.uk
Hull York (MS) Tel 01904 321690; www.hyms.ac.uk
Imperial London Tel 020 7589 5111; www.imperial.ac.uk
Keele Tel 01782 734010; www.keele.ac.uk
Kent (Canterbury) Tel 01227 768896; www.kent.ac.uk
Kingston (Kingston upon Thames) Tel 020 3308 9932; www.kingston.ac.uk
Lancaster Tel 01524 65201; www.lancaster.ac.uk
Leeds Tel 01133 432336; www.leeds.ac.uk
Leeds Arts Tel 0113 202 8039; www.leeds-art.ac.uk
Leeds Beckett Tel 0113 812 3113; www.leedsbeckett.ac.uk
Leeds Trinity Tel 0113 283 7123; www.leedstrinity.ac.uk
Leicester Tel 0116 252 2522; www.le.ac.uk
Lincoln Tel 01522 882000; www.lincoln.ac.uk
Liverpool Tel 01517 945927; www.liverpool.ac.uk
Liverpool Hope Tel 0151 291 3000; www.hope.ac.uk
Liverpool John Moores Tel 0151 231 5090; www.ljmu.ac.uk
London (Birk) Tel 020 7631 6000; www.bbk.ac.uk
London (Court) Tel 020 3947 7673; www.courtauld.ac.uk
London (Gold) Tel 020 7078 5300; www.gold.ac.uk
London (Inst Paris) Tel 01 44 11 73 83; www.ulip.london.ac.uk
London (Institute of Banking and Finance) Tel 020 7337 6293; www.libf.ac.uk
London (Institute of Cancer Research) Tel 020 7352 8133; www.icr.ac.uk
London (Interdisciplinary School) Tel 0203 409 1912;
London (King's) Tel 020 7836 5454; www.kcl.ac.uk

London (LSHTM) Tel 020 7636 8636; www.lshtm.ac.uk
London (QM) Tel 0800 376 1800; www.qmul.ac.uk
London (RH) (Egham) Tel 01784 414944; www.royalholloway.ac.uk
London (RVC) Tel 020 7468 5147; www.rvc.ac.uk
London (SOAS) Tel 020 7898 4700; www.soas.ac.uk
London (St George's) Tel 020 3897 2032; www.sgul.ac.uk
London (UCL) Tel 020 7679 2000; www.ucl.ac.uk
London LSE Tel 020 7405 7686; www.lse.ac.uk
London Met Tel 020 7423 0000; www.londonmet.ac.uk
London Regent's Tel 020 7487 7505; www.regents.ac.uk
London South Bank Tel 0800 923 8888; www.lsbu.ac.uk
Loughborough Tel 01509 274403; www.lboro.ac.uk
Manchester Tel 0161 275 2077; www.manchester.ac.uk
Manchester Met Tel 0161 247 6969; www.mmu.ac.uk
Marjon (Plymouth) Tel 01752 636890; www.marjon.ac.uk
Medway Sch Pharm (Chatham) Tel 01634 202935; www.msp.ac.uk
Middlesex (London) Tel 020 8411 5555; www.mdx.ac.uk
NCH London Tel 0207 637 4550; www.nchlondon.ac.uk
Newcastle (Newcastle-upon-Tyne) Tel 0191 208 6000; www.ncl.ac.uk
Newman (Birmingham) Tel 0121 476 1181; www.newman.ac.uk
Northampton Tel 0300 303 2772; www.northampton.ac.uk
Northumbria (Newcastle-upon-Tyne) Tel 0191 227 4646; www.northumbria.ac.uk
Norwich Arts Tel 01603 610561; www.nua.ac.uk
Nottingham Tel 0115 951 4749; www.nottingham.ac.uk
Nottingham Trent Tel 0115 848 4200; www.ntu.ac.uk
Open University (Milton Keynes) Tel 0300 303 5303; www.open.ac.uk
Oxford Tel 01865 270000; www.ox.ac.uk
Oxford Brookes Tel 01865 741111; www.brookes.ac.uk
Plymouth Tel 01752 585858; www.plymouth.ac.uk
Portsmouth Tel 023 9284 5566; www.port.ac.uk
Queen Margaret (Edinburgh) Tel 0131 474 0000; www.qmu.ac.uk
Queen's Belfast Tel 028 9024 5133; www.qub.ac.uk
Ravensbourne Univ (London) Tel 020 3040 3500; www.ravensbourne.ac.uk [C]
Reading Tel 0118 987 5123; www.reading.ac.uk
Richmond (Am Int Univ) (Richmond-upon-Thames) Tel 020 8332 8330; www.richmond.ac.uk
Robert Gordon (Aberdeen) Tel 01224 262728; www.rgu.ac.uk
Roehampton (London) Tel 020 8392 3232; www.roehampton.ac.uk
Royal Agricultural Univ (Cirencester) Tel 01285 889912; www.rau.ac.uk
Salford Tel 0161 295 4545; www.salford.ac.uk
Sheffield Tel 0114 222 8030; www.sheffield.ac.uk
Sheffield Hallam Tel 0114 225 5555; www.shu.ac.uk
Solent (Southampton) Tel 023 8201 5066; www.solent.ac.uk
South Wales (Pontypridd) Tel 03455 767778; www.southwales.ac.uk
Southampton Tel 023 8059 5000; www.southampton.ac.uk
St Andrews Tel 01334 466161; www.st-andrews.ac.uk
St Mary's (Twickenham) Tel 020 8240 2394; www.stmarys.ac.uk
St Mary's (UC) (Belfast) Tel 028 9032 7678; www.stmarys-belfast.ac.uk
Staffordshire (Stoke-on-Trent) Tel 01782 294400; www.staffs.ac.uk
Stirling Tel 01786 467044; www.stir.ac.uk

Stranmillis (UC) (Belfast) Tel 028 9038 1271; www.stran.ac.uk
Strathclyde (Glasgow) Tel 0141 552 4400; www.strath.ac.uk
Suffolk (Ipswich) Tel 01473 338833; www.uos.ac.uk
Sunderland Tel 0191 515 3000; www.sunderland.ac.uk
Surrey (Guildford) Tel 01483 682222; www.surrey.ac.uk
Sussex (Brighton) Tel 01273 606755; www.sussex.ac.uk
Swansea Tel 01792 205678; www.swansea.ac.uk
Teesside (Middlesbrough) Tel 01642 218121; www.tees.ac.uk
Trinity Saint David (Lampeter) Tel 0300 500 5054; www.uwtsd.ac.uk
UCO (London) Tel 020 7089 5316; www.uco.ac.uk
UHI (Inverness) Tel 01463 279190; www.uhi.ac.uk
Ulster (Belfast) Tel 028 7012 3456; www.ulster.ac.uk
Univ Law (Fitzrovia) Tel 01483 289997; www.law.ac.uk
UWE Bristol Tel 0117 328 3333; www.uwe.ac.uk
Warwick (Coventry) Tel 024 7652 3723; https://warwick.ac.uk
West London Tel 0800 036 8888; www.uwl.ac.uk
West Scotland (Paisley) Tel 0800 027 1000; www.uws.ac.uk
Westminster (London) Tel 020 7915 5511; www.westminster.ac.uk
Winchester Tel 01962 841515; www.winchester.ac.uk
Wolverhampton Tel 01902 323505; www.wlv.ac.uk
Worcester Tel 01905 855111; www.worc.ac.uk
Writtle (UC) (Chelmsford) Tel 01245 424200; www.writtle.ac.uk
York Tel 01904 320000; www.york.ac.uk
York St John Tel 01904 624624; www.yorksj.ac.uk

SECTION 2: SPECIALIST COLLEGES OF AGRICULTURE AND HORTICULTURE, ART, DANCE, DRAMA, FASHION, MUSIC, OSTEOPATHY AND SPEECH

Many colleges and institutes provide undergraduate and postgraduate courses in a wide range of subjects. While many universities and university colleges offer courses in art, design, music, drama, agriculture, horticulture and courses connected to the land-based industries, the specialist colleges listed below provide courses at many levels, often part-time, in these separate fields.

It is important that you read prospectuses and check websites carefully and go to Open Days to find out as much as you can about these colleges and about their courses which interest you. Applications for full-time courses at the institutions listed below are through UCAS.

Abbreviations used below A = Art and Design; **Ag** = Agriculture, Animals and Land-related courses; **C** = Communication; **D** = Drama, Performing and Theatre Arts; **Da** = Dance; **F** = Fashion; **H** = Horticulture and Landscape-related courses; **M** = Music; **T** = Technology and Engineering.

Academy of Live and Recorded Arts (ALRA) (London) Tel 020 8870 6475; https://alra.co.uk [**D**]
Architectural Association School of Architecture Tel 020 7887 4000; www.aaschool.ac.uk
Arts Educational Schools London (London) Tel 020 8987 6666; https://artsed.co.uk [**A**]
Ashridge Executive Education Tel 01442 902204; www.hult.edu/en/executive-education/
Askham Bryan College (York) Tel 01904 772277; www.askham-bryan.ac.uk [**Ag**]
Banbury and Bicester College Tel 0808 612 6008; www.activatelearning.ac.uk/banbury-bicester
Belfast Metropolitan College Tel 028 9026 5000; www.belfastmet.ac.uk
Berkshire College of Agriculture (Maidenhead) Tel 01628 827479; www.bca.ac.uk [**Ag**]
Bicton College (Budleigh Salterton) Tel 0330 123 2523; www.bicton.ac.uk [**Ag**]
Bishop Burton College Tel 01964 553000; www.bishopburton.ac.uk [**Ag**]
Bristol Old Vic Theatre School Tel 0117 973 3535; www.oldvic.ac.uk [**D**]
British College of Osteopathic Medicine (London) Tel 020 7435 6464; www.bcom.ac.uk

British Institute of Technology, England (London) Tel 020 8552 3071; www.bite.ac.uk

Brooksby Melton College (Melton Mowbray) Tel 01664 855444; www.brooksbymelton.ac.uk [**Ag**]

Camberwell College of Arts, University of the Arts London Tel 020 7514 6302; www.arts.ac.uk/colleges/camberwell-college-of-arts [**A**]

Capel Manor College (Enfield) Tel 0303 003 1234; www.capel.ac.uk [**H**]

Central Saint Martins College, University of the Arts London Tel 020 7514 7444; www.arts.ac.uk/csm [**A**]

Chelsea College of Arts, University of the Arts London Tel 020 7514 7751; www.arts.ac.uk/chelsea [**A**]

City and Guilds of London Art School Tel 020 7735 2306; www.cityandguildsartschool.ac.uk [**A**]

College of Agriculture, Food & Rural Enterprise (CAFRE) (Antrim) Tel 0800 028 4291; www.cafre.ac.uk [**Ag**]

Drama Centre London, University of the Arts London Tel 020 7514 2354; www.arts.ac.uk/csm/drama-centre-london [**D**]

Duchy College University Centre (Callington) Tel 0330 123 4784; www.duchy.ac.uk [**Ag**]

East 15 Acting School (Loughton) Tel 020 8418 7331; www.east15.ac.uk [**D**]

Easton and Otley College (Norwich) Tel 08000 224556; www.eastonotley.ac.uk [**Ag**]

European School of Osteopathy (Maidstone) Tel 01622 671558; www.eso.ac.uk

Fashion Retail Academy (London) Tel 0207 307 2345; www.fashionretailacademy.ac.uk [**F**]

Glasgow Clyde College Tel 0141 272 9000; www.glasgowclyde.ac.uk

Glasgow School of Art Tel 0141 353 4500; www.gsa.ac.uk [**A**]

Gray's School of Art, Robert Gordon University (Aberdeen) Tel 01224 262728; www.rgu.ac.uk/study/academic-schools/gray-s-school-of-art [**A**]

Guildford School of Acting, University of Surrey (Guildford) Tel 01483 682222; www.gsauk.org [**D**]

Guildhall School of Music and Drama (London) Tel 020 7628 2571; www.gsmd.ac.uk [**M**]

Hadlow University Centre (Tonbridge) Tel 01732 850551; www.hadlow.ac.uk [**Ag**]

Harper and Keele Veterinary School Tel Harper Adams 01952 820280; Keele 01782 732000; www.harperkeelevetschool.ac.uk

Hartpury College Tel 01452 702244; www.hartpury.ac.uk [**Ag**]

Heatherley School of Fine Art (London) Tel 020 7351 4190; www.heatherleys.org [**A**]

Hereford College of Arts Tel 01432 802878; www.hca.ac.uk [**A**]

Kent and Medway Medical School https://kmms.canterbury.ac.uk/kent-and-medway-medical-school.aspx

Kingston Maurward College (Dorchester) Tel 01305 215000; www.kmc.ac.uk [**Ag**]

Leeds College of Music Tel 0113 222 3488; www.lcm.ac.uk [**M**]

Liverpool Institute for Performing Arts Tel 0151 330 3000; www.lipa.ac.uk [**D**]

Liverpool School of Tropical Medicine Tel 0151 705 3100; www.lstmed.ac.uk

London Academy of Music and Dramatic Art (London) Tel 020 8834 0500; ww2.lamda.ac.uk [**M**]

London College of Communication, University of the Arts London Tel 020 7514 6599; www.arts.ac.uk/colleges/london-college-of-communication [**C**]

London College of Fashion, University of the Arts London Tel 020 7514 7400; www.arts.ac.uk/colleges/london-college-of-fashion [**F**]

Metanoia Institute (London) Tel 020 8579 2505; www.metanoia.ac.uk

Mont Rose College (London) Tel 020 8556 5009; https://mrcollege.ac.uk

Mountview Academy of Theatre Arts Tel 020 8881 2201; www.mountview.org.uk [**D**]

Myerscough College (Preston) Tel 01995 642222; www.myerscough.ac.uk [**Ag**]

Northern School of Contemporary Dance (Leeds) Tel 0113 219 3000; www.nscd.ac.uk [**Da**]

Plumpton College Tel 01273 890454; www.plumpton.ac.uk [**Ag**]

Plymouth College of Art Tel 01752 203434; www.plymouthart.ac.uk [**A**]

Rose Bruford College of Theatre and Performance (Sidcup) Tel 020 8308 2600; www.bruford.ac.uk [**D**]

Royal Academy of Dance (London) Tel 020 7326 8000; www.royalacademyofdance.org [**Da**]

Royal Academy of Dramatic Art (RADA) Tel 020 7636 7076; www.rada.ac.uk [**D**]

Royal Academy of Music, University of London Tel 020 7873 7373; www.ram.ac.uk [M]

Royal Central School of Speech and Drama, University of London Tel 020 7722 8183; www.cssd.ac.uk [D]

Royal College of Art Tel 020 7590 4444; www.rca.ac.uk [A]

Royal College of Music (London) Tel 020 7591 4300; www.rcm.ac.uk [M]

Royal Conservatoire of Scotland (Glasgow) Tel 0141 332 4101; www.rcs.ac.uk [M]

Royal Northern College of Music (Manchester) Tel 0161 907 5200; www.rncm.ac.uk [M]

Royal Welsh College of Music and Drama (Cardiff) Tel 029 2039 1361; www.rwcmd.ac.uk [M]

Ruskin School of Art, University of Oxford (Oxford) Tel 01865 276940; www.rsa.ox.ac.uk [A]

Scotland's Rural College (Edinburgh) Tel 0800 269 453; www.sruc.ac.uk [Ag]

Slade School of Fine Art, University College London Tel 020 7679 2313; www.ucl.ac.uk/slade [A]

Sparsholt College Hampshire (Winchester) Tel 01962 776441; www.sparsholt.ac.uk [H]

The National Film and Television School Tel 01494 671234; https://nfts.co.uk/

The Northern School of Art (Hartlepool) Tel 01429 422000; https://northernart.ac.uk [A]

Trinity Laban Conservatoire of Music and Dance (London) Tel 020 8305 4444; www.trinitylaban.ac.uk [M]

University Centre Reaseheath (Nantwich) Tel 01270 625131; www.reaseheath.ac.uk [Ag]

University College of Estate Management (Reading) Tel 0800 019 9697; www.ucem.ac.uk

Wimbledon College of Arts, University of the Arts London Tel 020 7514 9641; www.arts.ac.uk/wimbledon [A]

Winchester School of Art, University of Southampton Tel 023 8059 6900; www.southampton.ac.uk/wsa [A]

SECTION 3: FURTHER EDUCATION AND OTHER COLLEGES OFFERING HIGHER EDUCATION COURSES

Changes are taking place fast in this sector, with the merger of colleges and the introduction of University Centres. These are linked to further education colleges and to one or more universities, and provide Foundation and Honours degree courses (often part-time) and sometimes postgraduate qualifications.

The following institutions appear under various subject headings in the tables in **Chapter 7** and are in UCAS for some of their courses. See prospectuses and websites for application details.

Abingdon and Witney College Tel 01235 555585; www.abingdon-witney.ac.uk

Accrington and Rossendale College Tel 01254 389933; www.accross.ac.uk

Andover College Tel 01264 360000; www.andover.ac.uk

Argyll College, University of the Highlands and Islands (Dunoon) Tel 0345 230 9969; www.argyll.uhi.ac.uk

Ayrshire College Tel 0300 303 0303; www.ayrshire.ac.uk

Barking and Dagenham College (Romford) Tel 020 8090 3020; www.barkingdagenhamcollege.ac.uk

Barnet and Southgate College Tel 020 8266 4000; www.barnetsouthgate.ac.uk

Barnfield College (Luton) Tel 01582 569569; www.barnfield.ac.uk

Barnsley College Tel 01226 216123; www.barnsley.ac.uk

Basingstoke College of Technology Tel 01256 354141; www.bcot.ac.uk

Bath College Tel 01225 312191; www.bathcollege.ac.uk

Bedford College Tel 01234 291000; www.bedford.ac.uk

Birmingham Metropolitan College Tel 0121 4464545; www.bmet.ac.uk

Bishop Auckland College Tel 01388 443000; www.bacoll.ac.uk

Blackburn College Tel 01254 292929; www.blackburn.ac.uk

Blackpool and The Fylde College Tel 01253 504343; www.blackpool.ac.uk

Bolton College Tel 01204 482000; www.boltoncollege.ac.uk

Boston College Tel 01205 365701; www.boston.ac.uk

Bournemouth and Poole College Tel 01202 205205; www.thecollege.co.uk

Bournville College (Birmingham) Tel 0121 694 5000; www.sccb.ac.uk

Bracknell and Wokingham College Tel 0800 612 6008; www.activatelearning.ac.uk/bracknell-wokingham

Bradford College University Centre Tel 01274 088088; www.bradfordcollege.ac.uk

Bridgend College Tel 01656 302302; www1.bridgend.ac.uk

Bridgwater and Taunton College Tel 01278 455464; www.btc.ac.uk/

Brockenhurst College Tel 01590 625555; www.brock.ac.uk

Brooklands College (Weybridge) Tel 01932 797700; www.brooklands.ac.uk

Buckinghamshire College Group (Amersham; Aylesbury; High Wycombe) Tel 01494 585503; 01296 588595; 01494 585477; www.buckscollegegroup.ac.uk

Burnley College Tel 01282 733373; www.burnley.ac.uk

Burton and South Derbyshire College (Burton-upon-Trent) Tel 01283 494400; www.bsdc.ac.uk

Bury College Tel 0161 280 8280; www.burycollege.ac.uk

Buxton and Leek College Tel 0800 074 0099; www.blc.ac.uk

Calderdale College (Halifax) Tel 01422 399399; www.calderdale.ac.uk

Cambridge Regional College (Cambridge; Huntingdon) Tel 01223 418200; 01480 379100; www.camre.ac.uk

Canterbury College Tel 01227 811111; www.ekcgroup.ac.uk/colleges/canterbury-college

Carlisle College Tel 01228 822700; www.carlisle.ac.uk

Carmel College (St Helens) Tel 01744 452200; www.carmel.ac.uk

Carshalton College Tel 0208 544 4501; www.carshalton.ac.uk

CECOS London College Tel 020 7359 3316; www.cecos.ac.uk

Central Bedfordshire College (Dunstable) Tel 01582 477776; www.centralbeds.ac.uk

Central Campus, Sandwell College (West Bromwich) Tel 0800 622 006; www.sandwell.ac.uk

Central Film School London (London) Tel 0207 377 6060; www.centralfilmschool.com

Chelmsford College Tel 01245 293031; www.chelmsford.ac.uk

Chesterfield College Tel 01246 500500; www.chesterfield.ac.uk

Chichester College Tel 01243 786321; www.chichester.ac.uk

City and Islington College (London) Tel 020 7700 9200; www.candi.ac.uk

City College Norwich Tel 01603 773311; www.ccn.ac.uk

City College Plymouth Tel 01752 305300; www.cityplym.ac.uk

City of Bristol College Tel 0117 312 5000; www.cityofbristol.ac.uk

City of Liverpool College Tel 0151 252 3000; www.liv-coll.ac.uk

City of London College Tel 020 7247 2177; www.clc-london.ac.uk

City of Oxford College Tel 0800 612 6008; www.cityofoxford.ac.uk

City of Westminster College (London) Tel 020 7258 2721; www.cwc.ac.uk

City of Wolverhampton College Tel 01902 836000; www.wolvcoll.ac.uk

Cliff College (Derbyshire) Tel 01246 584202; www.cliffcollege.ac.uk

Coleg Sir Gâr (Pwll) Tel 01554 748000; www.colegsirgar.ac.uk

Coleg y Cymoedd (Aberdare) Tel 01685 887500; www.cymoedd.ac.uk

College of Haringey, Enfield and North East London Tel 020 8442 3055; www.conel.ac.uk

College of North West London Tel 020 8208 5000; www.cnwl.ac.uk

College of West Anglia (Norfolk) Tel 01553 761144; www.cwa.ac.uk

Cornwall College (Redruth) Tel 0330 123 2523; www.cornwall.ac.uk

Coventry College Tel 024 7693 2932; www.coventrycollege.ac.uk

Craven College (Skipton) Tel 01756 791411; www.craven-college.ac.uk

Darlington College Tel 01325 503030; www.darlington.ac.uk

Dearne Valley College (Rotherham) Tel 01709 513355; www.dearne-coll.ac.uk

Derby College Tel 01332 387473; www.derby-college.ac.uk

Derwentside College (Consett) Tel 01207 585900; www.derwentside.ac.uk

Doncaster College Tel 0800 358 7474; www.don.ac.uk

Dudley College Tel 01384 363000; www.dudleycol.ac.uk

Ealing, Hammersmith and West London College Tel 020 8741 1688; www.wlc.ac.uk

East Coast College (Great Yarmouth; Lowestoft) Tel 0800 854 695; www.eastcoast.ac.uk

East Durham College (Peterlee) Tel 0191 518 2000; www.eastdurham.ac.uk

East Kent College (Broadstairs) Tel 01843 605040; www.ekcgroup.ac.uk/

East Riding College (Beverley) Tel 0345 120 0044; www.eastridingcollege.ac.uk

East Surrey College (Redhill) Tel 01737 772611; www.esc.ac.uk

East Sussex College (Hastings) Tel 01424 442222; www.escg.ac.uk

Eastleigh College Tel 023 8091 1299; www.eastleigh.ac.uk

Edinburgh College Tel 0131 297 8300; www.edinburghcollege.ac.uk

European School of Economics (London) Tel 020 7935 3896; www.ese.ac.uk

Exeter College Tel 01392 400500; https://exe-coll.ac.uk

Fareham College Tel 01329 815200; www.fareham.ac.uk

Farnborough College of Technology Tel 01252 407040; www.farn-ct.ac.uk

Forth Valley College (Falkirk) Tel 01324 403000; www.forthvalley.ac.uk

Furness College (Barrow-in-Furness) Tel 01229 825017; www.furness.ac.uk

Gateshead College Tel 0191 490 2246; www.gateshead.ac.uk

Gloucestershire College Tel 0345 155 2020; www.gloscol.ac.uk

Gower College Swansea Tel 01792 284000; www.gcs.ac.uk

Grantham College Tel 0800 0521 577; www.grantham.ac.uk

Greater Brighton Metropolitan College Tel 01273 667759; www.gbmc.ac.uk

Grŵp Llandrillo Menai (Colwyn Bay) Tel 01492 542338 Coleg Llandrillo; 01341 422827 Coleg Meirion-Dwyfor.; www.gllm.ac.uk

Guildford College Tel 0800 612 6008; www.guildford.ac.uk

Halesowen College Tel 0121 602 7777; www.halesowen.ac.uk

Harlow College Tel 01279 868100; www.harlow-college.ac.uk

Harrogate College Tel 01423 879466; www.harrogate-college.ac.uk/

Harrow College Tel 020 8909 6000; www.harrow.ac.uk

Hartlepool College of Further Education Tel 01429 295000; www.hartlepoolfe.ac.uk

Havant and South Downs College (Waterlooville; Havant) Tel 023 9387 9999; www.hsdc.ac.uk

Havering College (Hornchurch) Tel 01708 455011; www.havering-college.ac.uk

Heart of Worcestershire College (Redditch) Tel 08448 802500; www.howcollege.ac.uk

Herefordshire and Ludlow College Tel 0800 032 1986; www.hlcollege.ac.uk

Hertford Regional College (Ware) Tel 01992 411400; www.hrc.ac.uk

Highbury College Portsmouth Tel 023 9238 3131; www.highbury.ac.uk

Highland Theological College, University of the Highlands and Islands (Dingwall) Tel 01349 780000; www.htc.uhi.ac.uk

Hopwood Hall College (Rochdale) Tel 01706 345346; www.hopwood.ac.uk

Hugh Baird College (Bootle) Tel 0151 353 4444; www.hughbaird.ac.uk

Hull College Tel 01482 329943; www.hull-college.ac.uk

Isle of Wight College Tel 01983 526631; www.iwcollege.ac.uk

Kendal College Tel 01539 814700; www.kendal.ac.uk

Kensington and Chelsea College (London) Tel 020 7573 3600; www.kcc.ac.uk

Kensington College of Business (London) Tel 020 7404 6330; www.kcb.ac.uk/

Kidderminster College Tel 01562 820811; www.kidderminster.ac.uk

Kingston College (Kingston upon Thames) Tel 020 8546 2151; www.kingston-college.ac.uk

Kirklees College (Huddersfield) Tel 01484 437070; www.kirkleescollege.ac.uk

Knowsley Community College (Huyton) Tel 0151 477 5850; www.knowsleycollege.ac.uk

Lakes College, West Cumbria (Workington) Tel 01946 839300; www.lcwc.ac.uk

Lambeth College (London) Tel 020 7501 5000; www.lambethcollege.ac.uk

Lancaster and Morecambe College Tel 01524 66215; 0800 306 306; www.lmc.ac.uk

Leeds City College Tel 0113 386 1997; www.leedscitycollege.ac.uk

Leeds College of Building Tel 0113 222 6000; www.lcb.ac.uk

Leicester College Tel 0116 224 2240; www.leicestercollege.ac.uk

Leo Baeck College (London) Tel 020 8349 5600; www.lbc.ac.uk

Lewisham Southwark College (London) Tel 020 3757 3000; www.lscollege.ac.uk

Lews Castle College, University of the Highlands and Islands (Isle of Lewis) Tel 01851 770000; www.lews.uhi.ac.uk

Lincoln College Tel General Enquiries 01522 876000; Course Enquiries 030 030 32435.; www.lincolncollege.ac.uk

London Business School Tel 020 7000 7000; www.london.edu

London School of Commerce Tel 020 7357 0077; www.lsclondon.co.uk

London School of Science and Technology (Wembley) Tel 020 8795 3863; www.lsst.ac

London South East Colleges (Bromley; Erith; Greenwich) Tel 020 3954 4000; www.lsec.ac.uk

Loughborough College Tel 01509 618375; www.loucoll.ac.uk

Macclesfield College of Further and Higher Education Tel 01625 410000; www.macclesfield.ac.uk

Middlesbrough College Tel 01642 333333; www.mbro.ac.uk

MidKent College (Gillingham) Tel 01634 402020; www.midkent.ac.uk

Milton Keynes College Tel 01908 684444; www.mkcollege.ac.uk

Moray College, University of the Highlands and Islands (Elgin) Tel 01343 576000; www.moray.uhi.ac.uk

Moulton College Tel 01604 491131; www.moulton.ac.uk

NAFC Marine Centre, University of the Highlands and Islands (Scalloway) Tel 01595 772001; www.nafc.uhi.ac.uk

Nazarene Theological College (Manchester) Tel 0161 445 3063; www.nazarene.ac.uk

Neath Port Talbot College Tel 01639 648000; www.nptcgroup.ac.uk

Nelson and Colne College Tel 01282 440200; www.nelson.ac.uk

Nescot, North East Surrey College of Technology (Epsom) Tel 020 8394 3038; www.nescot.ac.uk

New City College Hackney (London) Tel 020 7510 7777; www.hackney.ac.uk

New City College Redbridge (Romford) Tel 020 7510 7777; www.ncclondon.ac.uk/redbridge

New City College Tower Hamlets (London) Tel 020 7510 7510; www.ncclondon.ac.uk/tower-hamlets

New College Durham Tel 0191 375 4000; www.newcollegedurham.ac.uk

New College Stamford Tel 01780 484300; www.stamford.ac.uk

New College Swindon Tel 01793 611470; www.newcollege.ac.uk

Newbury College Tel 01635 845000; www.newbury-college.ac.uk

Newcastle College (Newcastle-upon-Tyne) Tel 0191 200 4000; www.ncl-coll.ac.uk

Newcastle-under-Lyme College Tel 01782 715111; https://nscg.ac.uk

Newham College (London) Tel 020 8257 4000; www.newham.ac.uk

Norland College (Bath) Tel 01225 904040; www.norland.ac.uk

North East Scotland College (Aberdeen) Tel 0300 330 5550; www.nescol.ac.uk

North Hertfordshire College (Stevenage) Tel 01462 424242; www.nhc.ac.uk

North Highland College, University of the Highlands and Islands (Thurso) Tel 01847 889250; www.northhighland.uhi.ac.uk

North Kent College (Dartford) Tel 01322 629400; www.northkent.ac.uk

North Lindsey College (Scunthorpe) Tel 01724 281111; www.northlindsey.ac.uk

North Notts College (Worksop) Tel 01909 504500; www.nnc.ac.uk

North Shropshire College (Oswestry) Tel 0800 440 2281; www.nsc.ac.uk

North Warwickshire and South Leicestershire College (Nuneaton) Tel 0330 058 3000; www.nwhc.ac.uk

Northampton College Tel 0300 123 2344; www.northamptoncollege.ac.uk

Northern Regional College (Ballymena) Tel 028 2563 6221; www.nrc.ac.uk

Northumberland College (Ashington) Tel 01670 841200; www.northumberland.ac.uk

Nottingham College Tel 01159 100100; www.nottinghamcollege.ac.uk

Oaklands College (St Albans) Tel 01727 737000; www.oaklands.ac.uk

Oldham College Tel 0161 785 4000; www.oldham.ac.uk

Orkney College, University of the Highlands and Islands (Kirkwall) Tel 01856 569000; www.orkney.uhi.ac.uk

Pearson College (London) Tel 0203 811 2307; www.pearsoncollegelondon.ac.uk

Pembrokeshire College (Haverfordwest) Tel 01437 753000; www.pembrokeshire.ac.uk

Perth College, University of the Highlands and Islands Tel 0345 270 1177; www.perth.uhi.ac.uk

Peter Symonds College (Winchester) Tel 01962 857500; www.psc.ac.uk

Peterborough Regional College Tel 0345 872 8722; www.peterborough.ac.uk

Petroc (Barnstaple) Tel 01271 345291; www.petroc.ac.uk

Portsmouth College Tel 023 9266 7521; www.portsmouth-college.ac.uk

Preston's College Tel 01772 225000; www.preston.ac.uk

Redcar and Cleveland College Tel 01642 473132; www.cleveland.ac.uk

Richmond and Hillcroft Adult Community College (RHACC) (Surbiton) Tel 020 8399 2688; www.hillcroft.ac.uk

Richmond-upon-Thames College (Twickenham) Tel 020 8607 8000; www.rutc.ac.uk

Riverside College (Widnes) Tel 0151 257 2800; www.riversidecollege.ac.uk

Rotherham College of Arts and Technology Tel 01709 362111; www.rotherham.ac.uk

Royal National College for the Blind (Hereford) Tel 01432 376621; www.rnc.ac.uk

Runshaw College (Chorley) Tel 01772 642040; www.runshaw.ac.uk

Ruskin College Tel 01865 759600; www.ruskin.ac.uk

Sabhal Mòr Ostaig, University of the Highlands and Islands (Sleat) Tel 01471 888304; www.smo.uhi.ac.uk

School of Advanced Study, University of London (London) Tel 020 7862 8653; www.sas.ac.uk

School of Audio Engineering Institute (Oxford) Tel 03330 112315; www.sae.edu

Scottish Association for Marine Science, University of the Highlands and Islands (Argyll) Tel 01631 559000; www.sams.ac.uk

Selby College Tel 01757 211000; www.selby.ac.uk

Sheffield College Tel 0114 260 2600; www.sheffcol.ac.uk

Shetland College, University of the Highlands and Islands (Lerwick) Tel 0845 272 3600; www.shetland.uhi.ac.uk

Shrewsbury College Tel 01743 342342; www.scg.ac.uk

Solihull College Tel 0121 678 7000; www.solihull.ac.uk

South and City College Birmingham (Digbeth) Tel 0121 694 5000; www.sccb.ac.uk

South Cheshire College (Crewe) Tel 01270 654654; www.ccsw.ac.uk

South Devon College (Paignton) Tel 08000 213181; www.southdevon.ac.uk

South Essex College Tel 0345 521 2345; www.southessex.ac.uk

South Gloucestershire and Stroud College Tel 01453 763424; www.sgscol.ac.uk

South Lanarkshire College (East Kilbride) Tel 01355 270750; www.south-lanarkshire-college.ac.uk

South Staffordshire College (Cannock) Tel 0300 456 2424; www.southstaffs.ac.uk

South Thames College (London) Tel 020 8918 7777; www.south-thames.ac.uk

Southampton City College Tel 023 8048 4848; www.southampton-city.ac.uk

Southern Regional College (Portadown) Tel 0300 123 1223; www.src.ac.uk

Southport College Tel 01704 392704; www.southport.ac.uk

St Helens College Tel 0800 996699; www.sthelens.ac.uk

Stafford College Tel 01785 223800; https://nscg.ac.uk

Stephenson College (Coalville) Tel 01530 836136; www.stephensoncoll.ac.uk

Stockport College Tel 0161 296 5000; www.stockport.ac.uk

Stockton Riverside College (Stockton-on-Tees) Tel 01642 865400; www.stockton.ac.uk

Stoke-on-Trent College Tel 01782 208208; www.stokecoll.ac.uk

Stratford-upon-Avon College Tel 01789 266245; www.stratford.ac.uk

Strode College (Street) Tel 01458 844400; www.strode-college.ac.uk

Strode's College (Egham) Tel 01784 437506; www.windsor-forest.ac.uk/strodes-college.html

Sunderland College Tel 0191 511 6000; https://sunderlandcollege.ac.uk

Tameside College (Ashton-under-Lyne) Tel 0161 908 6789; www.tameside.ac.uk

TEC Partnership (Grimsby) Tel 0800 315002; https://tecpartnership.com

Telford College Tel 01952 642200; www.telfordcollege.ac.uk

The Islamic College (London) Tel 020 8451 9993; www.islamic-college.ac.uk

The London College UCK Tel 020 7243 4000; www.lcuck.ac.uk

The Manchester College Tel 03333 222444; www.tmc.ac.uk

The Windsor Forest Colleges Group (Langley) Tel 01753 793288; www.windsor-forest.ac.uk

Tottenham Hotspur Foundation (London) Tel 020 8365 5138; www.tottenhamhotspur.com/foundation-test/about-us

Totton College (Southampton) Tel 02380 874874; www.totton.ac.uk

Trafford College (Altrincham) Tel 0161 886 7070; www.trafford.ac.uk

Tresham College of Further and Higher Education (Kettering) Tel 01536 413123; www.tresham.ac.uk

Truro and Penwith College Tel 01872 267061; www.truro-penwith.ac.uk

Tyne Coast College (South Shields; Wallsend) Tel 0191 427 3500; 0191 229 5000; www.tynecoast.ac.uk

University Campus Oldham Tel 0161 344 8800; www.uco.oldham.ac.uk

University Centre Colchester Tel 01206 712000; www.colchester.ac.uk

University Centre Croydon Tel 020 8760 5934; www.croydon.ac.uk

Uxbridge College Tel 01895 853333; www.uxbridge.ac.uk

Wakefield College Tel 01924 789111; www.wakefield.ac.uk

Walsall College Tel 01922 657000; www.walsallcollege.ac.uk

Waltham Forest College (London) Tel 020 8501 8501; www.waltham.ac.uk

Warrington and Vale Royal College (Warrington; Northwich) Tel 01925 494400; www.warrington.ac.uk

Warwickshire College (Leamington Spa) Tel 0300 456 0047; www.wcg.ac.uk

West Cheshire College (Ellesmere Port) Tel 01244 656555; www.ccsw.ac.uk

West Herts College (Watford) Tel 01923 812345; www.westherts.ac.uk

West Highland College, University of the Highlands and Islands (Fort William) Tel 01397 874000; www.whc.uhi.ac.uk

West Kent College (Tonbridge) Tel 01732 358101; www.westkent.ac.uk

West Nottinghamshire College (Mansfield) Tel 0808 100 3626; www.wnc.ac.uk

West Suffolk College (Bury St Edmunds) Tel 01284 701301; www.westsuffolkcollege.ac.uk

West Thames College (Isleworth) Tel 020 8326 2000; www.west-thames.ac.uk

Westminster Kingsway College (London) Tel 020 7963 4181; www.westking.ac.uk

Weston College (Weston-super-Mare) Tel 01934 411411; www.weston.ac.uk

Weymouth College Tel 01305 761100; www.weymouth.ac.uk

Wigan and Leigh College Tel 01942 761600; www.wigan-leigh.ac.uk

Wiltshire College (Chippenham) Tel 01225 350035; www.wiltshire.ac.uk

Wirral Metropolitan College (Birkenhead) Tel 0151 551 7777; www.wmc.ac.uk

Yeovil College Tel 01935 423921; www.yeovil.ac.uk

Yeovil College University Centre Tel 01935 845454; www.ycuc.ac.uk

York College Tel 01904 770100; www.yorkcollege.ac.uk

A-LEVELS AND AS • SCOTTISH HIGHERS/ADVANCED HIGHERS • ADVANCED WELSH BACCALAUREATE – SKILLS CHALLENGE CERTIFICATE • IB INTERNATIONAL BACCALAUREATE DIPLOMA (IB CERTIFICATE IN HIGHER LEVEL; IB CERTIFICATE IN STANDARD LEVEL; IB CERTIFICATE IN EXTENDED ESSAY; IB CERTIFICATE IN THEORY OF KNOWLEDGE) • BTEC LEVEL 3 NATIONAL EXTENDED DIPLOMA • EXTENDED PROJECT • MUSIC EXAMINATIONS • ART AND DESIGN FOUNDATION STUDIES

A-levels and AS

Grade					Tariff points
GCE & AVCE Double Award	A-level with additional AS	GCE A-level and AVCE	GCE AS Double Award	GCE AS & AS VCE	
A*A*					112
A*A					104
AA					96
AB					88
BB					80
	A*A				76
BC					72
	AA				68
CC	AB				64
CD	BB	A*			56
	BC				52
DD		A			48
	CC				44
	CD				42
DE		B	AA		40
			AB		36
	DD				34
EE		C	BB		32
	DE				30
			BC		28
		D	CC		24
	EE		CD		22
			DD	A	20
		E	DE	B	16
			EE	C	12
				D	10
				E	6

Scottish Highers/Advanced Highers

Grade	Higher	Advanced Higher
A	33	56
B	27	48
C	21	40
D	15	32

Advanced Welsh Baccalaureate – Skills Challenge Certificate

Grade	Tariff points
A*	56
A	48
B	40
C	32
D	24
E	16

IB International Baccalaureate Diploma

While the IB Diploma does not attract UCAS Tariff points, the constituent qualifications of the IB Diploma do, so the total Tariff points for an IB Diploma can be calculated by adding together each of the following four components:

IB Certificate in Higher Level

Grade	Tariff points
H7	56
H6	48
H5	32
H4	24
H3	12
H2	0
H1	0

Size band: 4
Grade bands: 3–14

IB Certificate in Standard Level

Grade	Tariff points
S7	28
S6	24
S5	16
S4	12
S3	6
S2	0
S1	0

Size band: 2
Grade bands: 3–14

IB Certificate in Extended Essay

Grade	Tariff points
A	12
B	10
C	8
D	6
E	4

Size band: 1
Grade bands 4–12

IB Certificate in Theory of Knowledge

Grade	Tariff points
A	12
B	10
C	8
D	6
E	4

Size band: 1
Grade bands: 4–12
Certificates in Extended Essay and Theory of Knowledge are awarded Tariff points when the certificates have been taken individually.

BTEC Level 3 National Extended Diploma

Grade	Tariff points
D*D*D*	168
D*D*D	160
D*DD	152
DDD	144
DDM	128
DMM	112
MMM	96
MMP	80
MPP	64
PPP	48

Size band: 4+4+4 = 12
Grade bands: 4–14

Extended Project - Stand alone

Grade	Tariff points
A*	28
A	24
B	20
C	16
D	12
E	8

Music examinations

Performance			Theory			Tariff points
Grade 8	Grade 7	Grade 6	Grade 8	Grade 7	Grade 6	
D						30
M						24
P						18
	D					16
	M	D				12
	P	M	D			10
		M				9
		P	D			8
			M			7
		P		P	D	6
					M	5
					P	4

Additional points will be awarded for music examinations from the Associated Board of the Royal Schools of Music (ABRSM), University of West London, Rockschool and Trinity Guildhall/Trinity College London (music examinations at grades 6, 7, 8 (D=Distinction; M=Merit; P=Pass)).

Art and Design Foundation Studies

Grade	Tariff points
D	112
M	96
P	80

Size band: 4+4 = 8
Grade bands: 10–14

NB Full acknowledgement is made to UCAS for this information. For further details of all qualifications awarded UCAS Tariff points see www.ucas.com/advisers/guides-and-resources/information-new-ucas-tariff-advisers. Note that the Tariff is constantly updated and new qualifications are introduced each year.

Universities in the UK accept a range of international qualifications and those which normally satisfy general entrance requirements are listed below. However, the specific levels of achievement or grades required for entry to degree courses with international qualifications will vary, depending on the popularity of the university or college and the chosen degree programme. The subject tables in **Chapter 7** provide a guide to the levels of entry to courses although direct comparisons between A-level grades and international qualifications are not always possible except for the three European examinations listed at the end of this Appendix. Students not holding the required qualifications should consider taking an International Foundation course.

International students whose mother tongue is not English and/or who have not studied for their secondary education in English will be required to pass a secure English language test (SELT) such as IELTS (International English Language Testing System) or the Trinity College London tests. Entry requirements vary between universities and courses. For the IELTS, scores can range from bands 1–9, but most universities' requirements range from 5.5 to 7.5.

Albania *Dëftesë Pjekurie* (Secondary School Leaving Certificate)/*Diplomë e Maturës Shtetërore* (Diploma of State Matura) plus International Foundation year
Algeria *Baccalauréat*
Argentina *Título de Bachiller* plus International Foundation year
Australia High School Certificate plus ATAR score of at least 80 or an Overall Position of 10 (Queensland)
Austria *Reifeprüfung/Matura* from *Allgemeinbildende Höhere Schulen* or *Reife und Diplomprüfung/ Matura* from *Berufsbildende Höhere Schulen* (BHS)
Bahrain Secondary School Leaving Certificate plus International Foundation year or equivalent
Bangladesh Higher Secondary Certificate (HSC)/Intermediate Certificate plus International Foundation year or equivalent
Belarus Certificate of General Secondary Education plus International Foundation year or equivalent
Belgium *Diploma van Secundair Onderwijs/Diploma van de Hogere Secundaire Technische School* or *Abschlusszeugnis der Oberstufe des Sekundarunterrichts* or *Diplôme d'Aptitude à Accéder à l'Enseignement Supérieur/Certificat d'Enseignement Secondaire Superieur*
Bermuda Associate Degree of Arts, Science or Applied Science
Bosnia-Herzegovina *Matura/Svjedodžba o Završenoj Srednjoj Skoli* (Secondary School Leaving Certificate)
Botswana Botswana General Certificate of Secondary Education Examination (BGCSE) plus International Foundation year
Brazil *Certificado de Conclusão de Ensino Médio/Certificado de Ensino Médio* or *Título de Técnico/Diploma de Tecnico de Nivel Medio* plus International Foundation year
Brunei Brunei GCE A-level
Bulgaria *Diploma za Zavarsheno Sredno (Spetsialno) Obrazovanie* (Diploma of Completed Secondary (Specialised) Education)
Burma Basic Education Standard X Examination/Matriculation Examination plus International Foundation year or equivalent
Cameroon General Certificate of Education Advanced Level plus International Foundation year or equivalent
Canada Ontario Secondary School Diploma with a minimum of 65–70% in six grade 12 U or M courses or Alberta/British Columbia/Nova Scotia High/Secondary School Graduation Diploma/Certificate with a minimum of 65–70% in at least five grade 12 courses or Manitoba High School Diploma with a minimum of 65–70% in at least five 300-level Grade 12 subjects

Chile Completion of two years of *Título de Bachiller/Bachillerato* or *Licencia de Educación Media* with International Foundation year

China National College Entrance Examination (NCEE/*Gaokao*) with a minimum score of 75% overall and 75% in any required subjects or Huikao (Senior Secondary School Certificate) with International Foundation year

Colombia *Bachillerato* plus International Foundation year

Croatia *Svjedodžba o Maturi* (Certificate of Maturity)

Cyprus *Apolytirion* or *Devlet Lise Diplomasi* (State High School Diploma) with International Foundation year

Czech Republic *Vysvedceni o Maturitni Zkousce/Maturita*

Denmark *Studentereksamen* or *Højere Forberedelseseksamen* (HF) or *Højere Handelseksamen* (HHX) or *Højere Teknisk Eksamen* (HTX)

Egypt Certificate of General Secondary Education plus International Foundation year

Estonia *Gümnaasiumi lõputunnistus* (Secondary School Certificate) at grade 12 together with an appropriate overall grade earned on the *Riigieksamid* (Upper Secondary School National Examination) or *Diplom* (from a *Kutsekõrgharidus*)

Finland *Ylioppilastutkinto/Studentexamen* (Matriculation certificate)

France *Baccalauréat* or *Option Internationale du Baccalauréat* (OIB)

Germany *Zeugnis der Allgemeinen Hochschulreife/Abitur* or *Fachgebundene Hochschulreife/Fachhochschulreife*

Greece *Apolytirio of Lykeio/Apolytirion* (minimum score 15) or appropriate scores in nationally examined Panhellenic Exams or appropriate scores in Network Foundation exams

Guyana Caribbean Advanced Proficiency Examination (CAPE) in three subjects

Hong Kong Hong Kong Diploma of Secondary Education (HKDSE) up to form 6 with score of 444

Hungary *Érettségi/Matura*

Iceland *Studentsprof*

India Higher Secondary School Certificate/Standard XII with an overall average of 60–65%

Indonesia *Ijazah–Sekolah Menengah Atas/Madrasah Aliyah* (SMA–MA) or *Surat Tanda Tamat Belajar Sekolah Menengah Umum Tingkat Atas* (STTB–SMA) (Certificate of Completion of Academic Secondary School) plus International Foundation year or equivalent

Iran *Peeshdaneshgahe* (pre-university certificate)

Iraq Certificate of Preparatory Education/Sixth Form Baccalauréat plus International Foundation year or equivalent

Ireland Irish Leaving Certificate Higher Level

Israel *Te'udat Bagrut/Bagrut* (Matriculation Certificate) with at least three subjects at levels 4 or 5

Italy *Esame di Stato* with good grades

Jamaica Caribbean Advanced Proficiency Examination (CAPE) in three subjects

Japan *Kotogakko Sotsugyo Shomeisho* (Upper Secondary School Leaving Certificate) plus International Foundation year or equivalent

Jordan *Tawjihi* (Secondary School Leaving Certificate) plus International Foundation year or equivalent

Kazakhstan Diploma of Completed Secondary Education plus International Foundation year or equivalent

Kenya Kenya Certificate of Secondary Education (KCSE) plus International Foundation year or equivalent

Kosovo *Diploma o Završenoj Srednjoj Skoli/Diplomë për Kryerjen e Shkollës së Mesme të Lartë/Matura* (High School Diploma)

Kuwait General Secondary Education Certificate plus International Foundation year or equivalent or Diploma/Certificate from PAAET Institute with an overall grade of Good (C or 2.0/4.0) or above

Latvia *Atestats par visparejo videjo izglitibu* (Attestation of General Secondary Education)

Lebanon *Baccalauréat General* or *Baccalauréat Technique* plus International Foundation year or equivalent

Libya Secondary Education Certificate plus International Foundation year or equivalent

Liechtenstein *Matura* (Type B or Type E)

Lithuania *Brandos Atestatas* (Certificate of Maturity)

Luxembourg *Diplôme de Fin d'Etudes Secondaires*

Macedonia Secondary School Leaving Diploma or Matura

Malawi Cambridge Overseas Higher School Certificate (COHSC) or a Malawi School Certificate of Education plus International Foundation year or equivalent

Malaysia *Sijil Tinggi Persekolahan Malaysia* (STPM, Malaysia Higher School Certificate) or Unified Examination Certificate (UEC) (Senior Middle Level) or *Sijil Pelajaran Malaysia* (SPM, Malaysia Certificate of Education) with grades of 1–6 plus International Foundation year or equivalent

Malta Advanced Matriculation (AM) or Matriculation Certificate Examination (University of Malta)

Mexico *Bachillerato* plus International Foundation year or equivalent

Moldova *Diploma de Bacalauréat* (Baccalaureate Diploma)

Montenegro *Maturski ispit/Diploma o završenoj srednjoj školi* (Secondary School Leaving Diploma)

Morocco *Diplôme du Baccalauréat* plus International Foundation year or equivalent

Netherlands *Diploma Voorbereidend Wetenschappelijk Onderwijs* (VWO)

Namibia Cambridge Overseas Higher School Certificate (COHSC)/GCE A level or a Namibia Senior Secondary Certificate (higher level) plus International Foundation year or equivalent

Nepal Higher Secondary Education Certificate plus International Foundation year or equivalent

Netherlands *Voorbereidend Wetenschappelijk Onderwijs* (VWO) with a grade of between 5.5–6.5

New Zealand University Entrance Certificate with National Certificates in Educational Achievement (NCEA) Level 3

Nigeria Senior Secondary School Certificate Education (SSCE)/West African Senior School Certificate (WASSC) plus International Foundation year or equivalent

Norway *Vitnemål for Videregående Opplæring* achieving *studiekompetanse* with a minimum grade of 3.5 overall

Oman General Secondary Education Certificate plus International Foundation year or equivalent

Pakistan Higher Secondary School Certificate plus International Foundation year or equivalent

Palestinian National Authority General Secondary Education Certificate plus International Foundation year or equivalent

Philippines High School Diploma plus International Foundation year or equivalent

Poland *Swiadectwo Dojrzałości/Matura*

Portugal *Certificado de fim de Estudos Secundários* or *Diploma Nível Secundário de Educação/Certificado Nível Secundário de Educação*

Qatar *Shahadat Al-Thanawaya Al-Aama* (General Secondary Education Certificate) or Qatar Senior School Certificate plus International Foundation year or equivalent

Russian Federation *Attestat o Srednem Obrzovanii* (Certificate of Secondary Education) plus International Foundation year or equivalent

Saudi Arabia *Thanawiya* (General Secondary Education Certificate) plus International Foundation year or equivalent

Serbia *Diploma o položenom završnom ispitu* (Diploma of Completed Final Examination) or *Diploma o položenom maturskom ispitu* (Secondary School Leaving Diploma) or *Diploma o stecenom srednem obrazovanju* (Diploma of Completed Secondary Education)

Sierra Leone West African Senior School Certificate (WASSC) plus International Foundation year or equivalent

Singapore Singapore/Cambridge GCE A-level

Slovakia *Maturitná skúška/Maturita* or *Vysvedcenie o Maturitnej Skúške* (School Leaving Certificate with Maturita from a SOU or SOŠ)

Slovenia *Matura*/Secondary School-Leaving Diploma/technical *Matura*

South Africa Senior Certificate (with matriculation endorsement) with minimum grades BBBCC or a National Senior Certificate with minimum grades of 66655

South Korea Korean High School Diploma plus International Foundation year or equivalent

Spain *Título de Bachillerato* or *Curso de Orientación Universitaria* (COU) (Pre-University course)

Sri Lanka Sri Lankan General Certificate of Education (Advanced level) qualifications

Sweden *Avgångsbetyg/Slutbetyg från Gymnasieskola*

Switzerland Federal Secondary School Leaving Certificate

Syria *Shahâda al-Thânawiyya al-camma* (Baccalauréat/General Secondary Certificate) plus International Foundation year or equivalent

Taiwan Senior High School Leaving Certificate plus International Foundation year or equivalent

Tanzania National Form VI Examination/Advanced Certificate of Secondary Education (ACSE) or Cambridge Overseas Higher School Certificate (COHSC)/East African Advanced Certificate of Education (EAACE)

Thailand Maw 6 (M6) with a score of 50% or above plus International Foundation year or equivalent
Tunisia *Baccalauréat* plus International Foundation year or equivalent
Turkey *Devlet Lise Diplomasi* (State High School Diploma) or *Lise Bitirme Diplomasi* (Private High School Diploma) plus International Foundation year or equivalent
Uganda Uganda Advanced Certificate of Education (UACE) or East African Advanced Certificate of Education or Cambridge Overseas Higher School Certificate (COHSC)
Ukraine Certificate of Complete General Secondary Education plus International Foundation year or equivalent
United Arab Emirates *Tawijihiyya* (Secondary Education Certificate) plus International Foundation year or equivalent
USA High School Graduation Diploma with a GPA of 3.0 overall plus good grades in SAT and/or APT/ACT
Uzbekistan *O'rta Ma'lumot To'g'risida Shahodatnoma* (Certificate of Completed Secondary Education) plus International Foundation year or equivalent
Venezuela *Título de Bachiller* plus International Foundation year or equivalent
Vietnam Upper Secondary School Graduation Diploma/National University Entrance Examination with a score of 5.0 or above plus International Foundation year or equivalent
Yemen *Shahadat Al-Thanawaya Al-Aama* (General Secondary Education Certificate) plus International Foundation year or equivalent
Zambia Zambia School Certificate plus International Foundation year or equivalent
Zimbabwe Cambridge Higher School Certificate or General Certificate of Education Advanced Level

COMPARISONS BETWEEN A LEVEL GRADES AND THE FOLLOWING EUROPEAN EXAMINATIONS

A-level grades	European Baccalaureate	French Baccalauréat	German Abitur
AAA	82–84%	14	1.2–1.3
AAB	79–81%	13.5	1.5
ABB	76–78%	13	1.8
BBB	74–75%	12.5	2.0
BBC	72–73%	12	2.2–2.3
BCC	70–71%	11.5	2.4

Professional associations vary in size and function and many offer examinations to provide members with vocational qualifications. However, many of the larger bodies do not conduct examinations but accept evidence provided by the satisfactory completion of appropriate degree and diploma courses. When applying for courses in vocational subjects, therefore, it is important to check whether your chosen course is accredited by a professional association, since membership of such bodies is usually necessary for progression in your chosen career after graduation.

Information about careers, which you can use as background information for your UCAS application, can be obtained from the organisations below listed under the subject table headings used in **Chapter 7**. Full details of professional associations, their examinations and the degree courses accredited by them are published in *British Qualifications* (see **Appendix 4**).

Some additional organisations that can provide useful careers-related information are listed below under the subject table headings and other sources of relevant information are indicated in the subject tables of **Chapter 7** and in **Appendix 4**.

Accountancy/Accounting
Accounting Technicians Ireland www.accountingtechniciansireland.ie
Association of Accounting Technicians www.aat.org.uk
Association of Chartered Certified Accountants www.accaglobal.com
Association of International Accountants www.aiaworldwide.com
Chartered Accountants Ireland www.charteredaccountants.ie
Chartered Institute of Internal Auditors www.iia.org.uk
Chartered Institute of Management Accountants www.cimaglobal.com
Chartered Institute of Public Finance and Accountancy www.cipfa.org
Chartered Institute of Taxation www.tax.org.uk
Institute of Chartered Accountants in England and Wales www.icaew.com
Institute of Chartered Accountants of Scotland www.icas.com
Institute of Financial Accountants www.ifa.org.uk

Actuarial Science/Studies
Institute and Faculty of Actuaries www.actuaries.org.uk

Agricultural Sciences/Agriculture
Innovation for Agriculture www.innovationforagriculture.org.uk
Institute of Chartered Foresters www.charteredforesters.org
Royal Forestry Society www.rfs.org.uk
Wood Technology Society www.iom3.org/wood-technology-society

Animal Sciences
British Horse Society www.bhs.org.uk
British Society of Animal Science www.bsas.org.uk

Anthropology
Association of Social Anthropologists of the UK and Commonwealth www.theasa.org
Royal Anthropological Institute www.therai.org.uk

Archaeology
Chartered Institute for Archaeologists www.archaeologists.net
Council for British Archaeology new.archaeologyuk.org

Architecture
Chartered Institute of Architectural Technologists www.ciat.org.uk
Royal Incorporation of Architects in Scotland www.rias.org.uk
Royal Institute of British Architects www.architecture.com

Art and Design
Arts Council England www.artscouncil.org.uk
Association of Illustrators www.theaoi.com
Association of Photographers www.the-aop.org
British Association of Art Therapists www.baat.org
British Association of Paintings Conservator-Restorers www.bapcr.org.uk
British Institute of Professional Photography www.bipp.com
Chartered Society of Designers www.csd.org.uk
Crafts Council www.craftscouncil.org.uk
Creative Scotland www.creativescotland.com
Design Council www.designcouncil.org.uk
Institute of Conservation www.icon.org.uk
Institute of Professional Goldsmiths www.ipgoldsmiths.com
National Society for Education in Art and Design www.nsead.org
Royal British Society of Sculptors www.rbs.org.uk
Textile Institute www.texi.org

Astronomy/Astrophysics
Royal Astronomical Society www.ras.org.uk

Biochemistry (see also Chemistry)
Association for Clinical Biochemistry and Laboratory Medicine www.acb.org.uk
Biochemical Society www.biochemistry.org
British Society for Immunology www.immunology.org

Biological Sciences/Biology
British Society for Genetic Medicine www.bsgm.org.uk
Genetics Society www.genetics.org.uk
Institute of Biomedical Science www.ibms.org
Royal Society of Biology www.rsb.org.uk

Building and Construction
Chartered Institute of Building www.ciob.org
Chartered Institution of Building Services Engineers www.cibse.org
Construction Industry Training Board www.citb.co.uk

Business and Management Courses
Chartered Institute of Personnel and Development www.cipd.co.uk
Chartered Institute of Public Relations www.cipr.co.uk
Chartered Management Institute www.managers.org.uk
Communications Advertising and Marketing Education Foundation
    www.camfoundation.com
Department for Business, Energy and Industrial Strategy www.gov.uk/government/organisations/
    department-for-business-energy-and-industrial-strategy
ICSA: The Governance Institute www.icsa.org.uk
Institute of Administrative Management www.instam.org
Institute of Consulting www.iconsulting.org.uk
Institute of Export & International Trade www.export.org.uk
Institute of Practitioners in Advertising www.ipa.co.uk
Institute of Sales Management www.ismprofessional.com
Skills CFA www.skillscfa.org

Chemistry
National Nanotechnology Initiative www.nano.gov
Royal Society of Chemistry www.rsc.org

Computer Science and Information Technology
BCS The Chartered Institute for IT www.bcs.org
Institution of Analysts and Programmers www.iap.org.uk
Learning and Performance Institute www.thelpi.org

Dance
Council for Dance Education and Training www.cdet.org.uk

Dentistry
British Association of Dental Nurses www.badn.org.uk
British Association of Dental Therapists www.badt.org.uk
British Dental Association www.bda.org
British Society of Dental Hygiene and Therapy www.bsdht.org.uk
Dental Laboratories Association www.dla.org.uk
Dental Technologists Association www.dta-uk.org
General Dental Council www.gdc-uk.org

Dietetics
British Dietetic Association www.bda.uk.com

Drama
Equity www.equity.org.uk
Society of British Theatre Designers www.theatredesign.org.uk

Economics
Royal Economic Society www.res.org.uk

Education and Teacher Training
Department for Education www.education.gov.uk
Education Workforce Council www.ewc.wales
General Teaching Council for Northern Ireland www.gtcni.org.uk
General Teaching Council for Scotland www.gtcs.org.uk

Engineering/Engineering Sciences
Energy Institute www.energyinst.org
Engineering Council UK www.engc.org.uk
Institute for Manufacturing www.ifm.eng.cam.ac.uk
Institute of Acoustics www.ioa.org.uk
Institute of Marine Engineering, Science and Technology www.imarest.org
Institution of Agricultural Engineers www.iagre.org
Institution of Civil Engineers www.ice.org.uk
Institution of Engineering Designers www.institution-engineering-designers.org.uk
Institution of Engineering and Technology www.theiet.org
Institution of Mechanical Engineers www.imeche.org
Nuclear Institute www.nuclearinst.com
Royal Aeronautical Society www.aerosociety.com

Environmental Science/Studies
Chartered Institute of Ecology and Environmental Management www.cieem.net
Chartered Institute of Environmental Health www.cieh.org
Chartered Institution of Wastes Management www.ciwm.co.uk
Chartered Institution of Water and Environmental Management www.ciwem.org

Environment Agency www.gov.uk/government/organisations/environment-agency
Institution of Environmental Sciences www.the-ies.org
Institution of Occupational Safety and Health www.iosh.co.uk
Royal Environmental Health Institute of Scotland www.rehis.com
Society for the Environment www.socenv.org.uk

Film, Radio, Video and TV Studies
British Film Institute www.bfi.org.uk
Creative Skillset (National Training Organisation for broadcast, film, video and multimedia) www.creative
  skillset.org

Finance (including Banking and Insurance)
Chartered Banker Institute www.charteredbanker.com
Chartered Institute of Loss Adjusters www.cila.co.uk
Chartered Insurance Institute www.cii.co.uk
Chartered Institute for Securities and Investment www.cisi.org
London Institute of Banking and Finance www.libf.ac.uk
Personal Finance Society www.thepfs.org

Food Science/Studies and Technology
Institute of Food Science and Technology www.ifst.org
Society of Food Hygiene and Technology www.sofht.co.uk

Forensic Science
Chartered Society of Forensic Sciences www.csofs.org

Geography
British Cartographic Society www.cartography.org.uk
Royal Geographical Society with IBG www.rgs.org
Royal Meteorological Society www.rmets.org

Geology/Geological Sciences
Geological Society www.geolsoc.org.uk

Health Sciences/Studies
British Academy of Audiology www.baaudiology.org
British and Irish Orthoptic Society www.orthoptics.org.uk
British Association of Prosthetists and Orthotists www.bapo.com
British Chiropractic Association https://chiropractic-uk.co.uk
British Occupational Hygiene Society www.bohs.org
General Osteopathic Council www.osteopathy.org.uk
Institute for Complementary and Natural Medicine www.icnm.org.uk
Institution of Occupational Safety and Health www.iosh.co.uk
Institute of Osteopathy www.osteopathy.org
Society of Homeopaths www.homeopathy-soh.org

History
Royal Historical Society www.royalhistsoc.org

Horticulture
Chartered Institute of Horticulture www.horticulture.org.uk

Hospitality and Event Management
Institute of Hospitality www.instituteofhospitality.org
People 1st www.people1st.co.uk

Housing
Chartered Institute of Housing www.cih.org

Human Resource Management
Chartered Institute of Personnel and Development www.cipd.co.uk

Information Management and Librarianship
Chartered Institute of Library and Information Professionals www.cilip.org.uk

Landscape Architecture
Landscape Institute www.landscapeinstitute.org

Languages
Chartered Institute of Linguists www.ciol.org.uk
Institute of Translation and Interpreting www.iti.org.uk

Law
Bar Council www.barcouncil.org.uk
Chartered Institute of Legal Executives www.cilex.org.uk
Faculty of Advocates www.advocates.org.uk
Law Society of England and Wales www.lawsociety.org.uk
Law Society of Northern Ireland www.lawsoc-ni.org
Law Society of Scotland www.lawscot.org.uk

Leisure and Recreation Management/Studies
Chartered Institute for the Management of Sport and Physical Activity www.cimspa.co.uk

Linguistics
British Association for Applied Linguistics www.baal.org.uk
Royal College of Speech and Language Therapists www.rcslt.org

Marine/Maritime Studies
Nautical Institute www.nautinst.org

Marketing (including Public Relations)
Chartered Institute of Marketing www.cim.co.uk
Chartered Institute of Public Relations www.cipr.co.uk
Institute of Sales Management www.ismprofessional.com

Materials Science/Metallurgy
Institute of Materials, Minerals and Mining www.iom3.org

Mathematics
Council for the Mathematical Sciences www.cms.ac.uk
Institute of Mathematics and its Applications www.ima.org.uk
London Mathematical Society www.lms.ac.uk
Mathematical Association www.m-a.org.uk

Media Studies
British Broadcasting Corporation www.bbc.co.uk/careers/home
National Council for the Training of Journalists www.nctj.com
Creative Skillset (National training organisation for broadcast, film, video and multimedia) www.creative
    skillset.org
Society for Editors and Proofreaders www.sfep.org.uk
Society of Authors www.societyofauthors.org

Medicine
British Medical Association www.bma.org.uk
General Medical Council www.gmc-uk.org
Institute for Complementary and Natural Medicine www.icnm.org.uk

Microbiology (see also **Biological Sciences/Biology**)
Microbiology Society www.microbiologysociety.org

Music
Incorporated Society of Musicians www.ism.org
Institute of Musical Instrument Technology www.imit.org.uk

Naval Architecture
Royal Institution of Naval Architects www.rina.org.uk

Neuroscience
InnerBody www.innerbody.com
Instant Anatomy www.instantanatomy.net

Nursing and Midwifery
Community Practitioners' and Health Visitors' Association www.unitetheunion.org/cphva
Health and Social Care in Northern Ireland http://online.hscni.net
Nursing and Midwifery Council www.nmc.org.uk
Royal College of Midwives www.rcm.org.uk
Royal College of Nursing www.rcn.org.uk

Nutrition (see **Dietetics**)

Occupational Therapy
British Association and College of Occupational Therapists www.cot.co.uk

Optometry
Association of British Dispensing Opticians www.abdo.org.uk
British and Irish Orthoptic Society www.orthoptics.org.uk
College of Optometrists www.college-optometrists.org
General Optical Council www.optical.org

Pharmacology
British Toxicology Society www.thebts.org

Pharmacy and Pharmaceutical Sciences
Royal Pharmaceutical Society of Great Britain www.rpharms.com

Photography
Association of Photographers www.the-aop.org
British Institute of Professional Photography www.bipp.com
Royal Photographic Society www.rps.org

Physical Education (see **Education and Teacher Training** and **Sports Sciences/Studies**)

Physics
Institute of Physics www.iop.org
Institute of Physics and Engineering in Medicine www.ipem.ac.uk

Physiotherapy
Association of Chartered Physiotherapists in Animal Therapy www.acpat.org
Chartered Society of Physiotherapy www.csp.org.uk

Plant Sciences (see **Biological Sciences/Biology**)

Podiatry (Chiropody)
Society of Chiropodists and Podiatrists and College of Podiatry www.scpod.org

Psychology
British Psychological Society www.bps.org.uk

Radiography
Society and College of Radiographers www.sor.org

Social Work
Health and Care Professions Council www.hcpc-uk.org
Northern Ireland Social Care Council www.niscc.info
Scottish Social Services Council www.sssc.uk.com
Social Care Wales www.socialcare.wales

Sociology
British Sociological Association www.britsoc.co.uk

Speech Pathology/Sciences/Therapy
Royal College of Speech and Language Therapists www.rcslt.org

Sports Sciences/Studies
British Association of Sport and Exercise Sciences www.bases.org.uk
Chartered Institute for the Management of Sport and Physical Activity www.cimspa.co.uk
English Institute of Sport www.eis2win.co.uk
Society of Sports Therapists www.society-of-sports-therapists.org
Sport England www.sportengland.org
Sportscotland www.sportscotland.org.uk
Sport Wales http://sport.wales
Sports Institute Northern Ireland www.sportni.net/performance/sports-institute-northern-ireland
UK Sport www.uksport.gov.uk

Statistics
Royal Statistical Society www.rss.org.uk

Surveying and Real Estate Management
Chartered Institute of Building www.ciob.org
Chartered Surveyors Training Trust www.cstt.org.uk
National Association of Estate Agents www.naea.co.uk
Royal Institution of Chartered Surveyors www.rics.org

Tourism and Travel
Institute of Travel and Tourism www.itt.co.uk

Town and Urban Planning
Royal Town Planning Institute www.rtpi.org.uk

Transport Management and Planning
Chartered Institute of Logistics and Transport www.ciltuk.org.uk

Veterinary Science/Medicine/Nursing
Association of Chartered Physiotherapists in Animal Therapy www.acpat.org
British Veterinary Nursing Association www.bvna.org.uk
Royal College of Veterinary Surgeons www.rcvs.org.uk
Royal Veterinary College www.rvc.ac.uk

Zoology
Royal Entomological Society www.royensoc.co.uk
Zoological Society of London www.zsl.org

Unless otherwise stated, the publications in this list are all available from Trotman Publishing.

STANDARD REFERENCE BOOKS
British Qualifications 2020, 50th edition, Kogan Page
British Vocational Qualifications, 12th edition, Kogan Page

OTHER BOOKS AND RESOURCES
Choosing Your Degree Course & University, 14th edition, Brian Heap
Destinations of Leavers from Higher Education 2016/17, Higher Education Statistics Agency Services (available from HESA)
Getting into course guides: Art & Design Courses, Business & Economics Courses, Dental School, Engineering Courses, Law, Medical School, Nursing & Midwifery, Oxford & Cambridge, Pharmacy and Pharmacology Courses, Physiotherapy Courses, Psychology Courses, Veterinary School
A Guide to Uni Life, Lucy Tobin
How to Complete Your UCAS Application: 2021 Entry, Ray Le Tarouilly
How to Write a Winning UCAS Personal Statement, 3rd edition, Ian Stannard
Studying Abroad, 3th edition
Studying and Learning at University, Alan Pritchard, SAGE Study Skills Series
The Times Good University Guide 2021, John O'Leary, Times Books

USEFUL WEBSITES
Education, course and applications information
www.disabilityrightsuk.org
www.erasmusplus.org.uk
www.gov.uk/browse/education
www.hesa.ac.uk (Higher Education Statistics Agency)
www.opendays.com (information on university and college Open Days)
www.ucas.com
https://unistats.ac.uk (official information from UK universities and colleges for comparing courses)

Careers information
www.army.mod.uk
www.aspire-igen.com/aspire-international
www.careerconnect.org.uk
www.healthcareers.nhs.uk
https://IndIgo.careers
www.insidecareers.co.uk
www.inspiringfutures.org.uk
www.milkround.com
www.prospects.ac.uk
www.socialworkandcarejobs.com
www.tomorrowsengineers.org.uk
www.trotman.co.uk

Gap years
www.etrust.org.uk/the-year-in-industry
www.gapyear.com
www.gap-year.com

Study overseas
www.acu.ac.uk (Association of Commonwealth Universities)
www.allaboutcollege.com
www.fulbright.org.uk (Fulbright Commission)
www.globalgraduates.com

COURSE INDEX

A

Accountancy/Accounting 93
Actuarial Science/Studies 97
Advertising 125, 165
African, Asian and Middle-
Eastern Studies 98
Agri-Business Management 165
Agricultural Sciences/
Agriculture 100
American Studies 103
Anatomical Science 383
Animal Biology 500
Animal Sciences 104
Animation 125
Anthropology 107
Arboriculture and Urban
Forestry 420
Archaeology 109
Architectural Engineering 111,
223
Architectural Technology 111
Architecture 111
Art and Design (3D design)
133
Art and Design (Fashion and
Textiles) 119
Art and Design (Fine Art) 122
Art and Design (General) 115
Art and Design (Graphic
Design) 125
Art and Design (Interior,
Product and Industrial
Design) 129
Artificial Intelligence 184
Asia-Pacific Studies 97
Astronomy and Astrophysics
134
Audio Engineering 215
Autism Studies 427
Automotive Engineering 238
Aviation Management 478

B

Biblical Studies 438
Biochemistry 137
Biological Sciences 140
Biology 147
Biomedical Engineering 243

Biomedical Materials Science
140
Biomedical Science 140
Biotechnology 150
Bioveterinary Sciences 480
Brewing and Distilling 140
British Sign Language 324
Broadcast Media Technologies
358
Building and Construction 151
Building Services Engineering
151
Building Surveying 469
Business and Management
Courses 154
Business and Management
Courses (International and
European) 162
Business and Management
Courses (Specialised) 165
Business Information Systems
184, 226
Business Management with a
European Language 162
Business, Marketing and
Consumer Behaviour 165

C

Celtic and Linguistics 168
Celtic, Irish, Scottish and
Welsh Studies 168
Ceramics 133
Chemistry 169
Chinese 173
Chiropractic 417
Civil and Coastal Engineering
223
Civil and Environmental
Engineering 223
Civil and Transportation
Engineering 223
Classics and Classical Studies/
Civilisation 175
Climate Change 251
Cognitive Science 427
Combined and Liberal Arts
Courses 177
Combined Social Sciences 446

Communication and Media 179
Communication Studies/
Communication 179
Community Studies/
Development 181
Computer Games
Development 183
Computer Networks 184
Computer Science 184
Computer Science and
Information Technology 184
Computing 184
Construction and Project
Management 151
Counselling Psychology 427
Counter Terrorism 433
Creative Writing 245
Criminal Justice 446
Criminology 342, 446
Cruise Management 478

D

Dance/Dance Studies 190
Deaf Studies 283
Dental Hygiene and Dental
Therapy 193
Dentistry 193
Design 125
Design Crafts 133
Development Studies 196
Dietetics 197
Divinity 438
Drama 199
Drawing 115

E

Earth Sciences 277
East Asian Studies 97
Ecology 251
Economics 204
Education Studies 208
Engineering (Acoustics and
Sound) 215
Engineering (Aeronautical
and Aerospace) 217
Engineering (Chemical) 220
Engineering (Civil) 223
Engineering
(Communications) 226

Engineering (Computer, Control, Software and Systems) 228
Engineering Design 212
Engineering (Electrical and Electronic) 231
Engineering (Manufacturing and Production) 236
Engineering (Mechanical) 238
Engineering (Medical) 243
Engineering/Engineering Sciences 212
English 245
Environmental Hazards 251
Environmental Health 251
Environmental Management 251, 476
Environmental Sciences 251
Equine Science 104
European Politics 423
European Studies 255, 324
Events Management 302

F

Film, Radio, Video and TV Studies 256
Finance 260
Finance and Investment Banking 260
Financial Services 260
Fire Engineering 220
Food Science with Business 165
Food Science/Studies and Technology 264
Footwear Design 129
Forensic Psychology 427
Forensic Science 140
Forestry 100
French 266
Furniture Design 129

G

Gaelic Studies 168
Games Technology 184
Garden Design 301, 321
General Engineering 212
Genetics 270
Geography 271
Geology/Geological Sciences 277
Geophysics 277
Geoscience 277
German 280
Glass and Ceramics 133
Government 423
Graphic Communication 125
Greek 282

H

Health Sciences/Studies 283
Healthcare Science 460
Hebrew 438
Herbal Medicine 398
Heritage Studies 288
Hispanic Studies 457
History 288
History (Ancient) 296
History and East European Cultural Studies 441
History (Economic and Social) 297
History of Art 298
Horticulture 301
Hospitality and Event Management 302
Housing 304
Human Resource Management 306
Human Rights 446
Human Sciences/Human Biosciences 308

I

Illustration 125
Immunology 140
Informatics 309
Information Management and Librarianship 309
Information Systems 184
Integrated Engineering 212
Interior Design 129
International Development 311
International Relations 311
Islamic Studies 438
Italian 313

J

Japanese 315
Jewellery and Metalwork 133
Journalism 317

K

Korean 173

L

Landscape Architecture 321
Languages 324
Latin 327
Law 328
Leisure and Recreation Management/Studies 338
Linguistics 339
Literature 341

M

Marine Biology 147, 344
Marine Geography 344
Marine/Maritime Studies 344
Marine Technology with Offshore Engineering 223
Marketing 346
Marketing Communication Management 179
Materials Science/Metallurgy 350
Mathematical Sciences 352
Mathematics 352
Mechanical and Medical Engineering 243
Mechatronics 238
Media Studies 358
Medical Imaging 436
Medical Physics 243
Medical Science 140
Medical Sciences 361
Medicine 361
Medieval Studies 288
Meteorology and Climate Science 251
Microbiology 374
Midwifery 384
Modelmaking 133
Modern Languages 324
Motorsport Engineering 238
Music 376
Music Technology 376

N

Natural Sciences 381
Neuroscience 383
Nuclear Engineering 220
Nursing and Midwifery 384
Nutrition 390
Nutrition and Public Health 283

O

Occupational Therapy 393
Oceanography 344
Operating Department Practice 385
Ophthalmic Dispensing 395
Optometry (Ophthalmic Optics) 395
Oral Health Science 193
Orthoptics 283, 395
Osteopathy 283

P

Painting 115
Painting and Printmaking 122
Paramedic Science 283

Peace Studies and International Relations 311
Performing Arts/Studies 199
Petrol Engineering 220
Pharmacology 396
Pharmacy and Pharmaceutical Sciences 398
Philosophy 401
Philosophy, Politics and Economics (PPE) 204, 404, 423
Photography 406
Physical Education 408
Physics 410
Physiology 416
Physiology and Pharmacology 396
Physiotherapy 417
Planetary Science with Astronomy 134
Plant Sciences 420
Podiatry (Chiropody) 421
Politics 423
Portuguese 457
Printed Textiles and Surface Pattern Design 119
Product Design 129, 212
Product Design Technology 129
Professional Policing 416
Property Development 469
Property, Finance and Investment 260
Prosthetics and Orthotics 150, 283
Psychology 427

Public Health 283
Public Relations 165, 179, 360
Publishing 165

Q
Quantity Surveying 469

R
Radiography 436
Religious Studies 438
Retail Management 440
Rural Property Management 469
Russian and Arabic 441
Russian and East European Studies 441
Russian and History 441

S
Scandinavian Studies 443
Sculpture and Environmental Art 122
Silversmithing and Jewellery 133
Social and Public Policy and Administration 444
Social Anthropology 107
Social Sciences/Studies 446
Social Work 450
Sociology 453
Sound Technology 215
South Asian Studies 97
Space Science and Robotics 134
Spanish, Portuguese and Latin American Studies 457
Speech Pathology/Sciences/ Therapy 460

Sports Sciences/Studies 461
Sports Therapy 417
Statistics 467

Surveying and Real Estate Management 469

T
Teacher Training 471
Theatre Arts 199
Theatre Design 129, 199
Theatre Studies 199
Theology 438
Tourism and Travel 474
Town and Urban Planning 476
Translation Studies 324
Transport Design 129, 478
Transport Management and Planning 478

V
Veterinary Nursing 480
Veterinary Physiotherapy 417
Veterinary Science/Medicine 480
Virology and Immunology 140
Visual Communication 125

W
War Studies 311
Web Design and Development 184

Z
Zoology 482

INDEX OF ADVERTISERS

The University of Law 325–7
University of Law: Business School 156, 163, 261, 341

Mander Portman Woodward inside front cover, outside back cover, 119, 155, 355
The University of Sheffield 272–3, 316–17

NOTES